THE LOST PARDON OF BILLY THE KID

AN ANALYSIS FACTORING IN THE SANTA FE RING, GOVERNOR LEW WALLACE'S DILEMMA, AND A TERRITORY IN REBELLION

BY
GALE COOPER

GELCOUR
BOOKS

OTHER BILLY THE KID BOOKS BY GALE COOPER:

BILLY AND PAULITA: THE SAGA OF BILLY THE KID, PAULITA MAXWELL, AND THE SANTA FE RING

BILLY THE KID'S WRITINGS, WORDS, AND WIT

THE SANTA FE RING VERSUS BILLY THE KID: THE MAKING OF AN AMERICAN MONSTER

BILLY THE KID'S PRETENDERS BRUSHY BILL & JOHN MILLER

CRACKING THE BILLY THE KID CASE HOAX: THE STRANGE PLOT TO EXHUME BILLY THE KID, CONVICT SHERIFF PAT GARRETT OF MURDER, AND BECOME PRESIDENT OF THE UNITED STATES

BLANDINA SEGALE, THE NUN WHO RODE ON BILLY THE KID: SLEUTHING A FOISTED FRONTIER FABLE

THE COLD CASE BILLY THE KID MEGAHOAX: A RASCALLY REPLAY OF BILLY THE KID CASE'S FORENSIC FLIMFLAM AND BRUSHY BILL'S BILLY THE KID BAMBOOZLE

**For Billy Bonney, who fought for justice,
and who deserved justice**

"Considering the active part Governor Wallace took on our side and the friendly relations that existed between him and me, and the promise he made me, I think he ought to pardon me ... I think it hard that I should be the only one to suffer the extreme penalty of the law."

Interview with Billy Bonney,
April 16, 1881, *Mesilla News*

COPYRIGHT © 2018 Gale Cooper
SECOND EDITION

ALL RIGHTS RESERVED
*Reproductions, excerpts, or transmittals
of the author's original cover art or text in this book
are prohibited in any form without written permission of the author.
Infringers will be prosecuted to the fullest extent of the law.*

ISBN: 978-1-949626-02-5 HARDCOVER
ISBN: 978-1-949626-03-2 PAPERBACK
Library of Congress Control Number: 2018954302

FIRST EDITION © 2017 Gale Cooper

GELCOUR BOOKS
2270D Wyoming Boulevard NE, Suite 217
Albuquerque, NM 87112

WEBSITE:
GaleCooperBillyTheKidBooks.com

YOUTUBE:
Gale Cooper's Real Billy The Kid

ORDERING THIS BOOK:
Amazon.com, BarnesandNoble.com, bookstores

Printed in the United States of America
on acid free paper

CONTENTS

PREFACE xiii
AUTHOR'S FOREWORD xv
ACKNOWLEDGMENTS xvii
METHODOLOGY xvii

CHAPTER 1: PARDON PERSPECTIVE

OVERVIEW 3
HISTORY OF BILLY BONNEY 8
BILLY BONNEY'S ADVOCATES 28
A TERRITORY IN REBELLION 36

CHAPTER 2: THE SANTA FE RING

SANTA FE RING ROOTS 43
TERRITORIAL SANTA FE RING BOSS
    THOMAS BENTON CATRON 48
CO-FOUNDING SANTA FE RING BOSS
    STEPHEN BENTON ELKINS 107
THE SANTA FE RING'S FORMULA 114
ANTI-RING REVOLTS 114

CHAPTER 3: LEGISLATURE REVOLT AGAINST THE SANTA FE RING: 1872

THE SANTA FE RING EXTENDS ITS POWER 117
THE 1872 LEGISLATURE REVOLT 118
AFTERMATH OF LEGISLATURE REVOLT 123
RING CREATION OF THE OUTLAW MYTH 130
DEAD GOVERNOR MARSH GIDDINGS REPLACED
    BY SAMUEL BEACH AXTELL 136

CHAPTER 4: GRANT COUNTY REBELLION AGAINST THE SANTA FE RING: 1876

THE GRANT COUNTY REBELLION: 1876 139
SECESSION AND ANNEXATION 140
GRANT COUNTY DECLARATION OF INDEPENDENCE 141
DEFLATED REBELLION 144

CHAPTER 5: COLFAX COUNTY WAR AGAINST THE SANTA FE RING: 1877

- COLFAX COUNTY WAR OVERVIEW 149
- THE BEAUBIEN-MIRANDA AND MAXWELL LAND GRANT: 1841-1870 150
- MAXWELL LAND GRANT COMPANY CONFLICT: 1870-1887 152
- RING MURDER OF FRANKLIN J. TOLBY: 1875 155
- REVEREND OSCAR P. McMAINS'S PURSUIT OF TOLBY'S RING KILLERS: 1875 157
- RING RETALIATIONS, CITIZENS' EXPOSÉS, AND TERROR: 1875-1876 160
- ANTI-RING ACTIVIST VOICE: MARY TIBBLES MCPHERSON 182
- CAPITULATION OF FRANK SPRINGER 223
- OUTCOME OF THE COLFAX COUNTY WAR 237
- RETURN OF THE SANTA FE RING TO COLFAX COUNTY 237

CHAPTER 6: LINCOLN COUNTY'S SANTA FE RING "TROUBLES": 1878

- A MAGNIFICENT FIGHT FOR FREEDOM 241
- HERO IN WAITING: BILLY BONNEY 243
- LINCOLN COUNTY SANTA FE RING BOSSES 244
- ABOUT JOHN HENRY TUNSTALL 245
- RING HARASSMENT TO ENABLE MURDER 251
- RESPONSE FROM COLFAX COUNTY 260

CHAPTER 7: LINCOLN COUNTY GALVANIZES AGAINST THE SANTA FE RING: 1878

- CHOOSING REVOLUTION 265
- HISTORY OF THE REGULATORS 265
- POLITICIZING OF BILLY BONNEY 268
- LEGAL PURSUIT OF TUNSTALL'S KILLERS 273
- RING RESPONSES 274
- CITIZENS RESIST THE RING: MARCH-APRIL, 1878 277
- LINCOLN COUNTY GRAND JURY: APRIL, 1878 283
- HOPE IN LINCOLN COUNTY 286
- RING OBSTRUCTION OF JUSTICE 288
- ENTER FORT STANTON COMMANDER NATHAN AUGUSTUS MONROE DUDLEY 289

CHAPTER 8: LINCOLN COUNTY WAR AGAINST THE SANTA FE RING: FEBRUARY 18, 1878 - JULY 19, 1878

THE UNSUNG FREEDOM FIGHT 297
THE RING'S MURDEROUS RESPONSES................................. 298
INVESTIGATOR FRANK WARNER ANGEL
   BRINGS HOPE: MAY 4, 1878.. 299
CATRON'S FEDERAL INDICTMENT PLOT:
   JUNE 21, 1878... 324
CITIZENS REQUEST PRESIDENTIAL AID............................. 328
RING MASSACRE AT SAN PATRICIO:
   JULY 3, 1878 334
THE "REGULATOR MANIFESTO": JULY 13, 1878................. 335
LOST BATTLE OF THE LINCOLN COUNTY WAR:
   JULY 14-19, 1878 337

CHAPTER 9: LINCOLN COUNTY WAR AFTERMATH: JULY 26, 1878 - OCTOBER 24, 1878

AFTERMATH OF BATTLE: JULY 20,1878.............................. 343
OTHERS SEEKING JUSTICE 343
BRAVE WIDOW SUSAN McSWEEN 351
FIRST FAME OF BILLY BONNEY 351

CHAPTER 10: INVESTIGATOR ANGEL'S CAPITULATION: OCTOBER, 1878

FRANK WARNER ANGEL'S RING COVER-UP 355
REPORT ON TUNSTALL'S MURDER....................................... 356
REPORT ON LINCOLN COUNTY TROUBLES........................ 358
PRESSURE REGARDING AXTELL.. 360
REPORT ON S.B. AXTELL 363
REPORT ON T.B. CATRON 372
RAYMOND MORLEY'S RESPONSE TO ANGEL'S
   REPORTS: AUGUST 15, 1878 379
AFTERMATH OF THE ANGEL REPORTS 380

CHAPTER 11: ENTER LEW WALLACE: 1878

ABOUT LEW WALLACE AND SHILOH 383
LEW WALLACE'S BIOGRAPHY 403

CHAPTER 12: LEW WALLACE ARRIVES IN NEW MEXICO TERRITORY: OCTOBER 1, 1878

LEW WALLACE, RELUCTANT GOVERNOR 423
WALLACE ARRIVES IN SANTA FE: OCTOBER 1, 1878 425
WALLACE GETS SECRET ANGEL NOTEBOOK 428
OUTLAW MYTH PROPAGANDA 432
WALLACE SEEKS MARTIAL LAW: OCTOBER 4, 1878 436
A PRESIDENTIAL PROCLAMATION: OCTOBER 7, 1878 442
WALLACE SEEKS APPROVAL 443
WALLACE'S "PACIFICATION PLAN" FOR
    LINCOLN COUNTY: OCTOBER 26, 1878 445
WALLACE AS DECORATOR: OCTOBER 23, 1878 447
WALLACE'S FIRST GUBERNATORIAL PARDON:
    OCTOBER 24, 1878 449
HUSTON CHAPMAN WRITES TO WALLACE:
    OCTOBER 24, 1878 450
WALLACE'S AMNESTY PROCLAMATION:
    NOVEMBER 13, 1878 451
FAILED APPOINTMENT OF ATTORNEY IRA LEONARD:
    NOVEMBER 13, 1878 454
WALLACE'S WAR DEPARTMENT FRUSTRATION 455
BOASTING TO SCHURZ: NOVEMBER 13, 1878 456
WALLACE'S SECRET SANTA FE RING LETTER TO
    ABSALOM MARKLAND: NOVEMBER 14, 1878 457
ATTEMPTING TO ESCAPE: NOVEMBER 18, 1878 459
RING REMOVAL RUMORS: DECEMBER 9, 1878 460

CHAPTER 13: LEW WALLACE'S DUDLEY-CHAPMAN CRISIS: OCTOBER, 1878 -FEBRUARY 18, 1879

THE DUDLEY PROBLEM 463
HUSTON CHAPMAN'S ONSLAUGHT:
    NOVEMBER 25th AND 29th, 1878 467
WALLACE AND DUDLEY CLASH... 471
THE RING RESPONDS TO CHAPMAN 482
MORE VOICES JOIN CHAPMAN'S 483
FIDDLING AS ROME BURNS 487
RING ASSASSINATION OF HUSTON CHAPMAN.................. 490
AFTERMATH OF CHAPMAN'S MURDER: WALLACE'S
    PURSUIT OF MYTHICAL OUTLAWS....................... 491
GRANT COUNTY CONDEMNS WALLACE:
    MARCH 1, 1879 497

PLANNING A LINCOLN COUNTY VISIT:
    MARCH 1, 1879 499
ENTER ATTORNEY IRA LEONARD 499
LETTER FROM HUSTON CHAPMAN'S FATHER:
    MARCH 20, 1879 504

CHAPTER 14: LEW WALLACE IN LINCOLN PURSUING OUTLAWS: MARCH 5, 1879 - MAY 15, 1879

COMING OF A "SAVIOR 509
IRA LEONARD FILES CHARGES AGAINST
    COMMANDER N.A.M. DUDLEY: MARCH 4, 1879 510
REMOVING DUDLEY: MARCH 8, 1879 518
WALLACE MEDDLES WITH FORT STANTON 523
ARRESTING CHAPMAN'S MURDERERS 525
ESCAPE OF THE PRISONERS: MARCH 18, 1879 532
PURSUIT OF MYTHICAL OUTLAWS 535
WALLACE FEIGNS FACT-FINDING 548
DUDLEY REQUESTS A COURT OF INQUIRY 552

CHAPTER 15: BILLY BONNEY'S PARDON BARGAIN WITH LEW WALLACE: MARCH 13-20, 1879

LIFE TRAJECTORIES INTERSECT 555
THE PARDON SCHEME 556
PARDON BARGAIN IN THE FIRST LETTER
    TO LEW WALLACE: MARCH 13, 1879 558
WALLACE'S RESPONSE: MARCH 15, 1879 560
MEETING OF WALLACE AND "THE KID"
    MARCH 17, 1879 563
HECTIC LETTER DAY OF MARCH 20, 1879 564
WALLACE'S REVEALING PROGRESS REPORT
    TO CARL SCHURZ: MARCH 21, 1879 567
WALLACE'S BILLY BONNEY INTERVIEW:
    MARCH 23, 1879 572
THE "BILLIE" LETTER: MARCH 24, 1879 575
FORESHADOWING WALLACE'S PARDON
    BARGAIN BETRAYAL 583
WALLACE USES IRA LEONARD FOR
    GRAND JURY PROSECUTIONS: APRIL 6, 1879 588
MORE RINGITE PRISONERS ESCAPE JUSTICE:
    APRIL 13, 1879 590

WALLACE REPORTS PROGRESS TO SCHURZ:
    APRIL 18, 1879 593

CHAPTER 16: PARDON BARGAIN FULFILLED BY BILLY BONNEY AND AFTERMATH: APRIL, 1879 - MAY 8, 1879

BILLY TESTIFIES FOR THE PARDON BARGAIN 597
VENUE CHANGE FOR BILLY BONNEY:
    APRIL 21, 1879 601
ATTEMPTED ASSASSINATION OF IRA LEONARD:
    APRIL 25, 1879 603
GRAND JURY INDICTMENTS AND PARDONS 606
WALLACE BLAMES "OUTLAWS" 611
CHAPMAN'S FAMILY AWAITS JUSTICE 613

CHAPTER 17: THE DUDLEY COURT OF INQUIRY: MAY - JULY, 1979

THE RING'S LAST LIABILITY 617
LEW WALLACE TESTIFIES: MAY 12-15, 1879 620
IRA LEONARD'S COURT UPDATES AND SANTA FE
    RING EXPOSÉ: MAY 20 AND 23, 1879 634
SUSAN McSWEEN TESTIFIES: MAY 23-24, 26, 1879 645
BILLY BONNEY TESTIFIES: MAY 28-29, 1879 657
DUDLEY'S CAVALRYMEN TESTIFY: MAY 30, 31 1879 663
IRA LEONARD'S RAGE AND DESPAIR: JUNE 6, 1879 665
WALLACE WOOS CARL SCHURZ WITH
    PARDONS AND OUTLAWS: JUNE 11, 1879 666
IRA LEONARD'S "OLD SCOUNDREL" LETTER:
    JUNE 13, 1879 671
BILLY DEPARTS JAIL: JUNE 17, 1879 674
N.A.M. DUDLEY TESTIFIES: JUNE 28-30, 1878 674
WALLACE TO SCHURZ: JULY 3, 1879 680
HENRY WALDO'S CLOSING ARGUMENT:
    JULY 5, 1879 681
PROSECUTOR'S CLOSING ARGUMENT: JULY 5, 1879 688
THE COURT'S JUDGMENT: JULY 5, 187 690
WALLACE'S DAMAGE CONTROL AFTER THE
    COURT OF INQUIRY: JULY-SEPTEMBER, 1879 693
IRA LEONARD PERSISTS WITH CIVIL SUIT:
    JULY 14, 1879 697

CHAPTER 18: HUNTING THE IMAGINARY KID GANG: 1880

THE GATHERING STORM 701
ENTER SECRET SERVICE SPECIAL OPERATIVE
    AZARIAH WILD: SEPTEMBER 7, 1880 708
ENTER PAT GARRETT 730
THE WITCH-HUNT AGAINST BILLY 732
AFTERMATH OF AZARIAH WILD 738
WALLACE PLANS ESCAPE 745
BILLY GETS MORE LURID PRESS 747

CHAPTER 19: BILLY BONNEY CAPTURED AND JAILED: DECEMBER, 1880

CAPTURE AT STINKING SPRINGS: DECEMBER 21, 1880 755
TRANSPORT TO THE SANTA FE JAIL 756
KILLING ANOTHER REBEL: MIMBRES APACHE
    CHIEF VICTORIO: OCTOBER 14, 1880 760
BILLY'S FOUR LAST AND UNANSWERED
    PARDON PLEA LETTERS TO LEW WALLACE:
    JANUARY 1, 1881 - MARCH 27, 1881 764

CHAPTER 20: BILLY BONNEY'S TRIALS BY THE SANTA FE RING: MARCH-APRIL, 1881

HANGING TRIALS IN MESILLA 773
BILLY'S RESPONSE TO SENTENCING: APRIL 15, 1881 784
SECRET TRANSPORT FROM MESILLA 786
LEW WALLACE'S BRIGHT FUTURE 787

CHAPTER 21: BILLY BONNEY'S GREAT ESCAPE AND KILLING APRIL 28 - JULY 14, 1881

BREAKING JAIL: APRIL 28, 1881 791
BILLY ON THE RUN 792
WALLACE FINALLY OVERTLY REJECTS PARDON:
    APRIL 28, 1881 792
PRESS FAME OF THE GREAT ESCAPE 795
WALLACE'S FIRST BILLY THE KID OUTLAW
    MYTH ARTICLE: MAY 16, 1881 795
LEW WALLACE EXITS: MAY 28, 1881 799
NEXT BILLY THE KID ARTICLE: JUNE 18, 1881 801
KILLING BILLY IN FORT SUMNER: JULY 14, 1881 806

CHAPTER 22: THE SANTA FE RING REGROUPS

THE SANTA FE RING UNCHECKED 811
LEW WALLACE ON CATRON AND THE RING:
    NOVEMBER 6, 1897 816
SANTA FE RING FIGHTER IN THE 20th CENTURY 817

CHAPTER 23: LEW WALLACE'S LITERARY CREATION OF THE OUTLAW MYTH OF BILLY THE KID

LEW WALLACE'S PARDON PROMISE OBSESSION 821
"LEW WALLACE'S FOE" ARTICLE: DECEMBER 10, 1893..... 822
"STREET PICKINGS" ARTICLE: JANUARY 6, 1894 826
PARALLEL SHILOH AND PARDON OBSESSIONS................ 828
BILLY THE KID AS A CHARACTER FOR A NOVEL 828
"GEN. WALLACE'S FEUD WITH BILLY THE KID"
    ARTICLE: JUNE 23, 1900 831
"GEN. LEW WALLACE WRITES A ROMANCE OF
    BILLY THE KID" ARTICLE: JUNE 8, 1902 838
LEW WALLACE'S PARTING WORDS: JANUARY 6, 1905...... 845

CHAPTER 24: SUMMARIZED ANALYSIS AND CONCLUSION

LEGACY OF THE LOST PARDON OF BILLY THE KID 849
HOW BILLY THE KID'S PARDON WAS LOST 850
WAS BILLY THE KID'S PARDON JUSTIFIED 854
CONCLUSION 856

SOURCES AND INDEX

ANNOTATED BIBLIOGRAPHY
    General References 859
    Legal References for Pardon and Criminal Cases............ 859
    Historical Organizations (Period) 859
    New Mexico Territory Rebellions Against
        the Santa Fe Ring...870
    Historical Figures (Period) 876
INDEX 953

PREFACE

This here author's kept me jawing for every one of her books on Billy Bonney - Billy the Kid's actual name. Course, with me being a fictional New Mexican old-timer, I can say whatever the hell I want - excuse the French - cause ain't nothing nobody can do to a fella that don't exist. So I do.

But I tell you what, this here author's courting trouble by setting the record straight on Billy, who was a freedom fighter with a wild streak, and a way with a gun or a gal. That's advertising a show-down with some mighty bad fellas needing Billy to be some low down outlaw to hide their dirt that's been piling up since 1866 hereabouts. And that stuff from a bull's rear - if you get my drift - goes back to when Billy could read it hisself.

Anyways, this here book is big enough in importance to shade an elephant. It solves the biggest mystery in Billy's life: How come he never got him his pardon? Billy supposably made him a pardon deal with New Mexico Territory's Governor Lew Wallace to wipe out his murder indictments for three fellas killed in the Lincoln County War. Billy kept his end. Wallace acted like the deal never happened. So Billy got him no pardon - even when looking into the eyeballs of his other option: hanging by his neck as a ticket to the pearly gates.

The how come as to why Lew Wallace didn't give Billy no pardon - with Billy pleading for it like his life depended on it, cause it did - is more twisted then a snake heading through a cactus patch. Course, Billy's main pardon problem was his enemies: the Santa Fe Ring - New Mexico Territory politicians, judges, lawmen, lawyers, reporters, and moneybags in cahoots to line their pockets - same as them running New Mexico today.

After the original Santa Fe Ring won the Lincoln County War against Billy's side's freedom fight to stop them - and after them not killed on Billy's side hightailed it out of the Territory - those sonsobitches Ringmen - excuse the French - commenced calling him "the outlaw Billy the Kid" to put him six feet under, cause he kept on fighting them by hisself, and was young enough to keep going for years. So the last thing them crooks - who was near enough to Hell to smell smoke - wanted was him being pardoned and proving they deserved a mid-air ballet from a cottonwood or a new abode in the hoosegow.

Another pardon problem of Billy's was that high-class new Governor, Lew Wallace, thought the sun rose just to hear him crow. And getting into bed - so to speak - with that teenager with a family tree no better then a shrub, and a wardrobe looking like the homeless person he was - was as appealing to ol' famous General Lew as siding with a wet dog at a parlor social. Also, Wallace was a best-seller book writer, so he could tell where a story was heading: namely his own happy ending would end if he butted heads with the Ring and pardoned their enemy, the Kid.

Anyways, if Billy got that governor's pardon from Lew Wallace, we'da never have heard of him, cause Sheriff Pat Garrett woulda had no legal way to track him down; the Ring's hanging judge woulda had no murder cases for trials; the Kid's great escape from the Lincoln County courthouse jail and from hanging woulda never happened; and, course, Garrett wouldn'ta killed him in Pete Maxwell's bedroom on July 14, 1881. In other words, Billy woulda become some regular, boring, unknown old-timer - like me.

So, rightly, one could say the Old West woulda missed one of its best chunks of history if Lew Wallace had pardoned Billy Bonney - though Billy probly woulda settled for that trade-off.

Also, this here book proves that the author still has a head of steam for setting things right for Billy. I'd conclude that - even though a pardon after you're dead is useful as a milk bucket under a bull - Billy probly woulda been appreciative of her working so damn hard - excuse the French - to prove he deserved it. Fighting for justice was right up his alley.

        Vern Blanton Johnson, Jr.
        Lincoln, Lincoln County, New Mexico
        March 30, 2017

AUTHOR'S FOREWORD

It took me almost 20 years of researching and writing about Billy the Kid to feel ready to tackle his lost pardon. But it was not just my knowledge or amassed library of over 40,000 pages of archival documents and books that made me ready. It was not my being a Harvard Medical School educated M.D. psychiatrist, with forensic specialty in murder consultation, that made me ready. It was my fateful confrontation, from 2003 to the present, with the current incarnation of Territorial New Mexico's political cabal - known then as the Santa Fe Ring - that forced me to come face to face with terrifying, vindictive, pervasive corruption, impervious to prosecution.

I fought and exposed that modern corruption in my books, and, as my own attorney, in the state legal system up to the Supreme Court. The inconceivable coincidence was that my fight was to save the history of Billy the Kid from the modern Ring's profiteering hijacking hoax. And the old Ring's profiteering machinations had spawned the outlaw myth of "Billy the Kid." So, by coincidence, I have lived for almost a decade and a half within the same, nightmarish, criminal matrix in which had unfolded the drama of the lost pardon of Billy the Kid. That was why I was ready to write this book. I was toughened by familiarity, injustice, and outrage.

So I can write with empathy and insight about the many freedom fights against the Santa Fe Ring which wracked New Mexico Territory in the 1870's, as citizens suffered - without any legal recourse - land grabs, disenfranchisements, malicious prosecutions, and assassinations; all culminating in the law enforcement and military atrocities that crushed the Lincoln County War rebellion, and yielded teenaged Billy Bonney as hero, gadfly, and martyr.

Into that Territory of New Mexico dominated by the Santa Fe Ring - and labeled, by a descendant of its northern freedom fighters, "Satan's Paradise," for its beauty and evil - had come interim Governor Lew Wallace. He would face a dilemma: granting of his promised pardon to Billy Bonney was equivalent to exposing and condemning the Santa Fe Ring. For Wallace, the pressures were personal, as he was forced to relive his Civil War failure at the Battle of Shiloh, while his future political goals were threatened. His had to choose between sacrificing the boy or himself. His choice, yielding the lost pardon, guaranteed survival of the Ring to the present.

The continuing Santa Fe Ring force field has also warped modern Billy the Kid historical writings into timid conservatism of recitation of names, dates, and events, stripped of their anti-Ring motive and their context in the progression of Territorial anti-Ring uprisings. Worse, it has yielded pandering historical writers willfully concealing the old Santa Fe Ring and the fight against it, while fabricating the freedom fighters as outlaws.

The failure of historical authorities has played into the core goal of the old and new Santa Fe Ring: keeping its existence secret. It was, and is, a unique form of organized crime. Its illegal collusions have never been touched by the full light of exposure; and its participants have never been touched by the full weight of the law. Unlike the similar American Mafia that has been prosecuted by adversarial public entities, the Ring *is* the public entities! There was in the days of Billy the Kid, and there is now, nowhere to turn for justice in New Mexico.

And because I want my readers not only to understand intellectually the circumstances and events, but also to feel the Ring's rapacious and murderous might, and the desperate fervor of the anti-Ring uprisings, I have included the relevant contemporary documents - many from Billy Bonney himself - so participants can be heard and judged directly. As I had a character in my 2012 docufiction novel, *Billy and Paulita*, say to Lincoln County newcomer, Billy: "Lincoln County is a moral proving ground. Evil here's so powerful it breaks people where they're weakest." The lost pardon of Billy the Kid reveals that "moral proving ground," as each person in its drama chooses their actions.

In the center of those tumultuous times was young Billy Bonney himself, branded "Billy the Kid" by his enemies, and transformed in the crucible of revolution from a violent, homeless, juvenile delinquent to a charismatic hero embodying the people's fight against the Santa Fe Ring. Because he was unforgettable, history can now pass judgment on those who judged him. The secrecy is ended. And justice is, at last, possible.

Gale Cooper, M.D.
Sandia Park, New Mexico
April 9, 2017

ACKNOWLEDGMENTS

Overriding is my debt to Billy Bonney, whose cause, courage, intelligence, and joie de vivre are my inspiration.

Historical bedrock is from books by Frederick Nolan on Billy the Kid, the Lincoln County War, and John Henry Tunstall. As valuable is Leon Metz's Pat Garrett biography and Jerry Weddle's book on Billy Bonney's adolescence. Period military consultation was by Steven Alley, curator at the Kansas Fort Leavenworth Army Museum; historians Jim Minor and Tim Smith at the Shiloh National Military Park; and Bill Gwaltney, a General Miles Marching and Chowder Society re-enactor.

National Archive specialists were Clarence Lyons, Wayne DeCesar, and Fred Romanski at the Civilian Records Branch; Dr. Milt Gustafson at the Civilian Records Branch Classification; Janice Wiggins at the Justice Department; Joseph Schwarz at the Department of Interior; Michael Sampson at the Secret Service Library Counterfeit Division; and Mike Meir at the Department of War, Old Military and Civil Branch.

Collections used were at the Las Cruces, New Mexico State University Library's Rio Grande Historical Collections' Herman B. Weisner Papers, ca. 1957-1992; the Albuquerque, University of New Mexico Center for Southwest Studies, University Library, Thomas B. Catron Papers; the Roswell, Chavez County Historical Center for Southeast New Mexico; the State of New Mexico Office of Cultural Affairs Historic Preservation Division; the Office of the New Mexico State Historian; the Silver City Museum and Library; the Midland, Texas Nita Stewart and J. Evetts Haley Memorial Library and Historical Center; the Canyon, Texas Panhandle-Plains Historical Museum; the Austin, Texas, University of Texas Center for American History's Earle Vandale Collection, 1813-946; the Morgantown, West Virginia & Regional History Center at West Virginia University Library, Stephen B. Elkins Papers; and the Freemont, Ohio, President Rutherford B. Hayes's Memorial Library papers of Rutherford B. Hayes.

Collections used for William Bonney's and Lew Wallace's documents were the Santa Fe, New Mexico, Fray Angélico Chávez Historical Library; and the Indianapolis, Indiana Historical Society's Lew and Wallace Collection. Lew Wallace's literary writings were at the Lilly Library of the Bloomington campus of Indiana State University.

New Mexico Territory newspapers were obtained from New Mexico Highland University for the Las Vegas *Daily Optic* and Las Vegas *Gazette*; the Rio Grande Historical Collections at the New Mexico State University Library at Las Cruces; the Center For Southwestern Research at the University of New Mexico Library in Albuquerque; and private collectors.

METHODOLOGY

PRIMARY DOCUMENTS: To make more vivid the world of the lost pardon, primary documents are presented in full, in italics for handwriting, in two column newsprint for articles, and in distinctive font for published books. Retained are approximate layouts of original documents, along with their misspellings, punctuation errors (usually no periods at end of sentences, with run-ins lacking capitalization of the first word of the next sentence; or with unmarked contractions like "dont"). And in 19th century writing, the word "country" is often used to mean local area, not America.

COMMENTARY: For elucidation, highlighted "Analysis" summaries are provided, boldface is added to accentuate archival texts, bracketed "Author's Notes" are inserted, and the "Bibliography" is annotated.

Missing names, corrections, or added information in primary documents is given in brackets. And the original author's cross-outs are retained.

For certain book or thesis citations, their page numbers are provided in the text.

FACILITATIONS: "Santa Fe Ring" is often shortened to "Ring" and its members are often identified by their contemporary appellation of "Ringite." Bibliography entries are arranged chronologically. Repetitions of historical facts are used to build the reader's working awareness of the complex information involved. For navigation within the book, internal page references are provided.

CHAPTER 1
PARDON PERSPECTIVE

OVERVIEW

ANALYSIS: Determining why Billy the Kid did not get the pardon he believed was promised him by New Mexico Territory Governor Lew Wallace requires perspective from political to psychological, and yields revisionist reformulation of the history within the matrix of Territorial control by the Santa Fe Ring.

A complex question in Old West history is why William Henry "Billy" Bonney aka Billy the Kid was not issued the pardon for his three Lincoln County War murder indictments, which he believed New Mexico Territorial Governor Lew Wallace had promised. The results of that lost pardon were tragic: his hanging trial, jailbreak murder of two deputy guards, and killing by Sheriff Pat Garrett.

Implicit are related questions. Had the pardon promise been real, or merely Governor Wallace's trick of wording? Or had Wallace reneged? Or had Wallace yielded to corrupt pressures? Was a pardon deserved? Did Wallace have power to grant that pardon? Did Billy fulfill his side of the pardon bargain? Why did Billy's lawyer never make a formal petition for pardon to Wallace? Who were the pardon's opponents? Were others pardoned by Wallace for their Lincoln County War indictments? Could the Secret Service also have pardoned Billy? Why did Billy risk a pardon rejection, when simply leaving the Territory would have ensured safety? Were others secretly involved in seeking Billy's pardon? Why did Billy testify in a Court of Inquiry against a military commander, separate from the pardon bargain? Why has it taken so long to sort the facts? Should there be a posthumous pardon for Billy the Kid?

Available for analyzing the lost pardon mystery is a mountain of contemporary evidence. Its decade of the 1870's was a time of populist upheaval in New Mexico Territory. Generated were petitions, letters both personal and official, exposés, transcripts of civilian and military court trials, affidavits and depositions, arrest warrants, federal and territorial indictments, official pardons, account books, Secret Service records, investigative reports for the

U.S. Departments of Justice and the Interior, a death warrant, Coroner's Jury reports, and newspaper articles. The year after killing Billy, Pat Garrett, with a ghostwriter, published a dime novel-style book about Billy the Kid. In the twentieth century, old-timers published autobiographical versions about that period and about knowing Billy.

Billy Bonney himself left a profusion of his own words in an affidavit, a deposition to a presidential investigator, a possible Lincoln County War manifesto, pardon pleas and other letters to Governor Lew Wallace, an interview recorded by Wallace, testimony to a military Court of Inquiry, a letter to an attorney about his hanging trial, and newspaper interviews.

Ironically, most of Billy Bonney's writings are known only because Lew Wallace saved them. Departing the Territory in 1881, Wallace took them along with his official gubernatorial documents. Subsequently, his descendants donated them to historical societies. And, late in life, Wallace published newspaper articles, which he saved, about Billy the Kid and the pardon.

Pardon drama participants were thrust together during New Mexico Territory's freedom fights of the 1870's against the burgeoning, corrupt, political cabal called the Santa Fe Ring. Popular uprisings against it occurred in 1872 with the Legislature Revolt, in 1876 with the Grant County Rebellion, in 1877 with the Colfax County War, and in 1878 with the Lincoln County War. All were crushed by the Ring. In that brutal decade, the Ring robbed Hispanic citizens of land grants, Homestead Act farmers were bled by Ring-backed mercantile monopolies, and cattle rustling met the Ring's military and Indian reservation beef contracts. Legislators, governors, judges, lawmen, and the soldiers became Ringites. Ring assassins eliminated opponents. The backdrop was genocidal subjugation of native Americans, as America lurched toward rapaciously accumulated wealth by an unchecked few. Jeopardized were the Revolutionary War's democratic intent, and the Civil War's promise of freedom for all. But inspiration from those earlier revolutions still vitalized Americans; especially within the western Frontier's enduring illusion of freedom, which fueled New Mexico Territory's idealistic uprisings.

The Santa Fe Ring started in 1866 as a land-grab scheme of Thomas Benton Catron and Stephen Benton Elkins: avaricious, politically conniving, lawyer friends, newly arrived from Missouri. They defrauded Hispanic grant holders of millions of acres, while shielding their crimes by complicit public official cronies. By the 1870's, these robber barons extended their political power nationally, with Territorial Delegate to Congress Elkins in Washington, D.C., and U.S. Attorney Catron as "boss" of the Territorial Ring. As the Ring enhanced its compatriots' powers politically and economically, it destroyed opponents by malicious prosecution, obstruction of justice, and assassination. Key to its criminal survival was maintaining a secret existence.

Culminating grass-roots anti-Ring responses was Lincoln County's Regulator movement, harking back to 1771's North Carolina Regulators, whose uprisings foreshadowed the 1776 Revolutionary War against British oppression. During the 1878 Lincoln County War, teenaged Billy Bonney participated in all Regulator anti-Ring encounters. The three murders, for which he was indicted and requested pardon, occurred during them.

The Regulator victims were Lincoln County lawmen - Sheriff William Brady, his Deputy George Hindman, and his posseman Andrew "Buckshot" Roberts - all Ringite assassins of Ring opponent, John Henry Tunstall, using T.B. Catron's preferred killing with guise of law. Tunstall, an honest, wealthy British merchant and cattle ranching investor, was Billy's boss and citizens' hope. But Catron had identical economic goals in Lincoln County, and orchestrated Tunstall's elimination by malicious prosecution of Tunstall's friend, Attorney Alexander McSween, to enable Tunstall's murder by Brady. Backed by Ringite Territorial Governor Samuel Beach Axtell, Brady then obstructed arrest of Tunstall's killers.

Opposition to the Ring's crime came from Lincoln County Justice of the Peace John "Squire" Wilson's deputizing of citizens - including Billy - to arrest Tunstall's killers. And when Governor Axtell illegally outlawed them, self-named Regulators were organized, with McSween as leader. Protecting McSween from certain assassination, Regulators ambushed Brady and Hindman; later killing Roberts, resisting arrest for Tunstall's murder.

The Ring countered by attacking Regulators, with Catron, as U.S. Attorney, filing a federal murder case against them. Unprecedented Ring atrocities followed, first by massacre of Hispanic Regulator loyalists on July 3, 1878 in San Patricio, then in the Lincoln County War's final battle of July 14th to 19th, 1878, under puppet sheriff, George Peppin, using rustler gangs and troops under local Commander N.A.M. Dudley. McSween was murdered, his home set on fire, and Tunstall's store looted. As an escaping defender from that burning house, Billy became a local hero, having already possibly crafted the pre-battle Regulator Manifesto. And Billy had cemented his activism by giving an affidavit for Tunstall's Coroner's Jury against the murderers.

After death, McSween scored a victory: his reporting of Tunstall's murder to the British ambassador triggered a presidential investigation into culpability of U.S. officials. But unbeknownst to McSween, President Rutherford B. Hayes knew about the Ring from Colfax County's exposés during their earlier War. So Hayes's investigator, Frank Warner Angel, merely implemented cover-up, adding token removal of Governor Axtell. But again Billy proved anti-Ring commitment by giving Angel his deposition naming Ringites involved in Tunstall's killing.

Axtell's replacement, in 1878, was past Civil War General, attorney, and best-selling novelist, Lew Wallace. Citizens believed Wallace would end Ring oppression. In 1879, in that context, Billy proposed his pardon bargain following another Ring assassination: of Huston Chapman, McSween's wife's lawyer. The bargain Billy offered, and believed accepted, was giving eye-witness Grand Jury testimony against Chapman's murderers in exchange for annulment of his three murder indictments. Billy gave the testimony, got indictments, but Wallace issued no pardon.

Wallace, the first non-Ring governor since 1869, came to the Territory secretly briefed on the Ring, but self-protectively immediately issued an Amnesty Proclamation shielding Ringites for Lincoln County War crimes. But, by chance, Wallace's charade and Ring exposure were threatened by Billy's pardon request, as tied to Regulator killings of Tunstall's assassins. Furthermore, the British Ambassador already knew from Alexander McSween about public officials' involvement in Tunstall's murder. And President Hayes would likely abandon Ringites if they jeopardized his administration's undeservedly clean reputation (unlike past president Ulysses S. Grant's ring-ridden one).

So the Ring responded with fierce desperation. Wallace was defamed; his political future imperiled. Billy, and all Regulators, were vilified by T.B. Catron's outlaw myth naming them criminals and rustlers causing Lincoln County's "troubles."

Risk to the Ring next came from McSween's widow, who got a new lawyer to prosecute Dudley. Catron, who had represented Dudley for two past court martials, assigned a law firm member for Dudley's defense in his military Court of Inquiry. There, though not part of his pardon bargain, Billy continued his anti-Ring mission by giving eye-witness testimony that Dudley's officers fired treasonously at him and other civilians escaping the burning McSween house. Wallace also testified against Dudley. But to the Ring-biased judges, Catron's lawyer denigrated Billy as a murdering outlaw, and humiliated Wallace as an incompetent. And the corrupt court exonerated Dudley.

So the pressure switched to Wallace to prove his assigned pacification of Lincoln County to his superiors in Washington, D.C. His own psychological issues and future ambitions gained precedence. And knowing that Billy was on the Ring's outlaw list, made granting his pardon Wallace's personal risk. So Wallace procrastinated, and focused on writing his novel, *Ben-Hur*.

Regaining its foothold, the Ring continued its extermination policy, bringing in the Secret Service to commit arguably its first political murders by killing remaining Regulators - with gadfly Billy in particular - by fabricating them as a major counterfeiting and rustling gang in the Territory. But Billy offered to testify against real counterfeiters in exchange for a Secret Service-orchestrated pardon. So the Ring changed strategy, focusing solely on Billy as "gang leader," while ensuring election of a Ring-compliant sheriff, Pat Garrett, to kill him.

Billy's 1880 near killing by Garrett at Stinking Springs, and 1881 hanging trial resulted. This time, Wallace, confident in his future with success of *Ben-Hur* and with a promised ambassadorship to Turkey, announced pardon refusal. Billy's jailbreak just before hanging was soon followed by Garrett's successful killing of him. Wallace, meanwhile, had departed his interim governorship before Billy's death.

Wallace's life of success was marred, however, by obsession with Billy and the pardon, which he reworked in literary scenarios. And the never-exposed Santa Fe Ring flourished, with Catron becoming one of the two first Senators at New Mexico's statehood. As Wallace and the Ring had known, the pardon of Billy the Kid could have changed history's outcome.

But unforeseen by Lew Wallace and Thomas Benton Catron, was that killing Billy Bonney would not end justice. Billy's posthumous fame brought ensuing generations' curiosity, scrutiny, and judgment, as the massive paper trail remained waiting as evidence echoing truth.

HISTORY OF BILLY BONNEY

ANALYSIS: Billy Bonney's hardscrabble, mostly homeless, life of 21 years is the arena of his lost pardon. It was just one of his many traumatic losses, which included his illegitimate birth-father's abandonment; the tuberculosis death of his mother in his early adolescence; theft of his inheritance by his stepfather; Ring murders of his father-figure bosses John Tunstall, Dick Brewer, and Alexander McSween; Ring assassination of another paternal substitute, Attorney Huston Chapman; loss of his Tunstall-promised ranch after Tunstall's murder; betrayal by his last sought father-figure, Governor Lew Wallace; and resignation of his long-term attorney, Ira Leonard, at his hanging trial. By 17½, Billy had surmounted his juvenile criminality, reinventing himself as a Tunstall anti-Ring freedom fighter; and persisted as such before and after the lost Lincoln County War by being a Deputy Constable and posseman to apprehend Tunstall's killers, giving a deposition on Tunstall's murder to a presidential investigator, protecting Alexander McSween in that War, testifying in courts about Chapman's murder and Commander N.A.M. Dudley's treasonously shooting soldiers, attempting to bring Wallace to the anti-Ring side, almost testifying for the Secret Service about counterfeiters and rustlers; and doing retaliatory guerrilla rustling on Ringmen. In all, Billy was involved in nine killings, three of which occurred in Lincoln County War Regulator groups and were at issue in his pardon bargain with Governor Lew Wallace.

In a hot, full-mooned, New Mexico Territory night as bright as day, the 21 year old, homeless youth, Billy Bonney, with trusting stockinged feet, approached the porticoed, two story, Fort Sumner mansion of the Maxwell family, at about a quarter to mid-night.

That day, July 14, 1881, was the third anniversary of the Lincoln County War's start, which had left him branded as the outlaw, "Billy the Kid;" though, to himself, he was a freedom fighter: the last Regulator and that War's only participant to be convicted and sentenced. His April 13, 1881, first degree murder sentence was death by hanging.

That July night, Billy intended to cut a dinner steak from the side of beef hanging - at the patrón's generosity - on the mansion's north porch. But first he would check in, as requested, with that patrón and town owner, Peter Maxwell, at the man's south porch's corner bedroom.

Asleep in that mansion was Billy's secret lover, Maxwell's sister, Paulita, seventeen, and just pregnant with Billy's child. Also there, lived a never-emancipated Navajo slave, Deluvina; purchased, as a child, by Peter's and Paulita's fabulously wealthy, deceased father, Lucien Bonaparte Maxwell. Then, the family lived in Cimarron, a New Mexico Territory town in Colfax County, which Lucien had created on his and his wife's almost two million acre land grant, later named after himself.

That was before Lucien was cheated in the sale of that Maxwell Land Grant by lawyers, Thomas Benton Catron and Stephen Benton Elkins, who used their profits to propel their Santa Fe Ring. As Billy knew, that corrupt collusion of politicians, attorneys, lawmen, judges, and big money still held New Mexico Territory in a stranglehold. As a hero in the failed Lincoln County War of 1878, Billy had fought that Ring. The year before, had been the anti-Ring Colfax County War on that Maxwell Grant land. The year before that, Grant County's citizens had threatened secession to Arizona Territory to escape Ring clutches. If Billy was thinking about his mortal danger, he knew its source was the Ring. If he thought about injustice, its focus would have been his pardon withheld by departed Territorial Governor Lew Wallace.

That July of 1881 day was 2½ months since Billy's jailbreak escape from his scheduled hanging on May 13th. He knew that Lincoln County Sheriff Pat Garrett would be in pursuit. Garrett had captured him on December 22, 1880 at Stinking Springs for his hanging trial. And in Billy's April 28, 1881 escape from Garrett's Lincoln jail, he had shot dead his deputy guards: James Bell and Robert Olinger. Garrett would kill him on sight.

When first tracking Billy in late 1880, Garrett had killed Billy's friends, Tom O'Folliard and Charlie Bowdre - missing Billy only by accident in two consecutive ambushes: at Fort Sumner and Stinking Springs. In fact, at the Stinking Springs capture of Billy and his companions, Garrett killed Bowdre by mistaking him for Billy: the prize for which the Ring had made Garrett a Sheriff.

Billy, to be near Paulita, had recklessly chosen return to Fort Sumner, instead of fleeing to Old Mexico, the natural choice given his bi-culturalism. But he relied on the Maxwell family's protection, as well the affection of the townspeople, who had known him since late 1877. And optimism and uncanny ability to escape danger characterized him. It would take unfathomable betrayal to bring his death.

Billy's entire life had been traumatic. Illegitimate, he was a second son, born on November 23, 1859, in New York City, as William Henry McCarty. Raised in Indiana with his older brother, Josie, by his mother, Catherine, he became "Henry Antrim" after she married an Indiana man, William Henry Harrison Antrim, in 1873, after the family relocated to New Mexico Territory. Antrim became a miner; and the family lived in Silver City. Antrim was a rejecting father, evicting Billy at 14½ to homelessness when Catherine died of tuberculosis in 1874. By 1879, Billy wrote coldly to Lew Wallace: *"Antrim is my stepfather's name."* But Billy's longing for a father remained. He even sometimes used the painful name "Antrim" for himself.

In Silver City's school, Billy likely learned Spencerian cursive script, which he later used for his pardon request. He also became fluent in Spanish; and, atypically, was equally comfortable in Anglo and Hispanic sub-cultures in those racist times.

By 1975, 15½ year old Billy spent his last year in Silver City doing petty thievery, and butcher shop and hotel work; while altercations with local boys revealed his violent temperament. By September, Silver City Sheriff, Harvey Whitehill arrested him for burglary, and laundry and revolver robbery; his adult accomplice having escaped. Facing ten years hard labor - the Territory's statutes making no provision for juveniles - he achieved his first dramatic escape: through the jail's chimney. He fled across the border to Arizona Territory's little town of Bonita.

In Arizona, as Henry Antrim, Billy again combined work - as a cook at a small hotel - with crime: stealing military blankets, saddles, and horses; while ominously developing shootist skills. In 1876, incarcerated at local Fort Grant's guardhouse with his older accomplice, John Mackie, he escaped through a roof ventilation space. But he stayed defiantly in Bonita, relying on his rustling charges being dropped on a technicality, and first demonstrating risky behavior for his unconscious wish to have a "home."

On August 17, 1877, Billy's life again changed horrifically. His argument at Bonita's Atkins Cantina with a bullying blacksmith, Frank "Windy" Cahill, escalated to Billy's fatally shooting that unknowably unarmed man. Billy escaped on a stolen horse. The Coroner's Jury declared him - as Henry Antrim - guilty of homicide, though in absentia; ignoring self-defense. So at 17½, Billy was almost hanged for murder. Billy fled back to New Mexico Territory with an alias: William Henry Bonney - Billy Bonney. "Bonney" was likely his mother's maiden name.

In New Mexico Territory, by the next month of September, 1877, Billy attached himself to familiar sociopaths in Jessie Evans's murderous and rustling Santa Fe Ring-affiliated gang. And since Ringites ended up immune to prosecution and profited financially, intelligent and energetic Billy, unknown to history, would have likely had a wealthy and long life.

But Billy had a conversion. He met kind, wealthy Englishman John Henry Tunstall, a Ring competitor. By the next month, October of 1877, Billy left Jessie Evans's gang to become a Tunstall ranch hand. Soon Tunstall's men affectionately nicknamed him "Kid." Tunstall was the lost father found; even gifting him, under the Homestead Act, a ranch on the Peñasco River in partnership with another employee, half-Chickasaw Fred Waite. That was likely Billy's proudest and most optimistic moment.

Billy had stumbled into a noble cause: ending Ring oppression. His gunman skill now elevated him as a protector of the good. His hair-trigger temper became vehemence for justice. And the town of Lincoln, as well as Tunstall's ranch on the Feliz River, became home. But Billy's tragic destiny was unrelenting. After only 4½ months, this idyllic time ended with Tunstall's Ring murder.

Lincoln, site of the future Lincoln County War, had already sustained Ring abuses through mercantile monopoly of "the House": a huge, two-story adobe, general store run by its local Ring bosses, Emil Fritz, Lawrence Murphy, James Dolan, and John Riley for secret partner Thomas Benton Catron. They bled cash-poor Mexicans and Anglo homesteaders with usurious credit. Redress was impossible, since law enforcement and courts were Ring-controlled. Terror reigned. In 1875, when rancher, Robert Casey, defeated Murphy in a Lincoln election, he was assassinated the same day. Three weeks later, Lincoln's anti-Ring, Mexican community leader, Juan Patrón, was shot by Riley; though accidentally surviving as a limping cripple.

Hope for change began in late 1876 with arrival in Lincoln of English merchant, John Henry Tunstall; persuaded to settle there by a resident attorney, Alexander McSween; a Ring opponent, but once legal counsel to "the House." Tunstall and McSween planned to defeat the Ring by fair mercantile and ranching competition.

By 1877, Tunstall had built - just a quarter mile northeast of "the House" - his own general store and bank. And he started two cattle ranches to wrest from "the House" its beef and flour traderships to local Fort Stanton and the nearby Mescalero Indian

Reservation. He even ran a press exposé of Lincoln County Sheriff William Brady's abuse of taxpayer money to pay for Ring cattle. So Tunstall and McSween were slated for the Ring's hit list.

Ringmen preferred to kill with guise of legality. So they entangled Tunstall in fabricated criminality, starting with false prosecution of McSween, who was then attorney for the estate of the House's founding partner, Emil Fritz, who died intestate in 1874, but left two local siblings and a life insurance policy.

The Ring seized on that life insurance policy. In 1877, McSween had successfully litigated to get its $10,000 proceeds from its withholding New York City insurance company, minus $3,000 to the collections firm - leaving $7,000. Knowing that the House faced bankruptcy from Tunstall's competition, and would extort that sum from Fritz's local heirs, McSween retained it while seeking possible heirs in Germany. He underestimated Ring evil.

In December of 1877, McSween left on business to St. Louis with his wife and with Tunstall's business associate, the cattle king, John Chisum, then also president of the bank in Tunstall's store. The Ring pounced, declaring McSween an absconding embezzler of the Fritz insurance money. Ring boss Catron, then U.S. Attorney, issued his arrest warrant for capture. Chisum was also jailed in retaliation for backing Tunstall. On February 4, 1878, McSween had his hearing in Mesilla under Ringite District Judge Warren Bristol (later Billy's hanging judge), who indicted McSween for embezzling, intending his incarceration and killing in Lincoln by its Ringite Sheriff, William Brady. McSween was saved by the honest Deputy Sheriff, Adolph Barrier, from his Las Vegas, New Mexico, arrest site, who kept him in personal custody.

But Judge Bristol had set the Ring's desired traps to enable assassination of McSween and Tunstall. When he indicted McSween, he did two things. First, he set the bail at $8,000, with approval only by Ringite District Attorney William Rynerson; who refused all bondsmen to leave McSween open to Sheriff Brady's fatal custody at any time.

Bristol's second stipulation was Tunstall's trap. Bristol attached McSween's property to the sum of $10,000 - falsely deemed the embezzled total - to satisfy any judgment against him at that April's Grand Jury. Then he declared falsely that Tunstall was in business partnership with McSween, so as to also attach Tunstall's property. And Bristol empowered Sheriff Brady and his deputies to do attachment inventories at both men's properties. That harassment was to provoke Tunstall and his men to violence to justify his killing. But Tunstall merely said that any man's life was worth more than all he owned. Billy, with Tunstall three months, must have been overwhelmed by this surprising idealism.

But Tunstall sought to transfer his fine horses, which were immune to the attachment, from his Feliz River Ranch. On February 18, 1878, Brady used that stock movement back toward Lincoln to assassinate Tunstall. He sent his large posse (including Jessie Evans and his boys) in pursuit of Tunstall and his men, including Billy, for alleged theft of attached property. Tunstall, becoming isolated, was murdered, his horse slain; with both corpses mutilated. This martyrdom, coupled with more Ring outrages, triggered the Lincoln County War.

Lincoln County Justice of the Peace John "Squire" Wilson issued murder warrants for James Dolan, Jessie Evans, and other possemen. For service, Wilson appointed, as Deputy Constables under Town Constable Atanacio Martinez, Billy and Fred Waite. And Billy had already given an affidavit for the Coroner's jury as to first-hand knowledge of the murderers.

But Brady shielded the killers by brief illegal incarceration of Billy, Waite, and Martinez in Lincoln's pit jail. And he confiscated Billy's Winchester '73 carbine - likely a gift from Tunstall.

Next, "Squire" Wilson defied the Ring by deputizing Tunstall's foreman, Dick Brewer; who, in turn, made Tunstall's men, including now-released Billy, his possemen to serve those murder warrants. Billy, then 18, was still a lawman.

Meanwhile, Attorney Alexander McSween, certain of risk from Brady, went into hiding with Deputy Sheriff Barrier; mostly in the nearby Hispanic town of San Patricio.

By March of 1878, Dick Brewer's posse had captured Tunstall murder possemen, William "Buck" Morton and Frank Baker, who were shot attempting escape. Billy was in the firing group.

At that point, including "Windy" Cahill, Billy Bonney was now involved in three killings.

The Ring retaliated. Ringite Governor Samuel Beach Axtell, by illegal proclamation, removed Wilson's Justice of the Peace powers to retroactively outlaw Brewer's posse; then declared Sheriff Brady to be Lincoln County's only law enforcer.

Enraged, Tunstall's men named themselves "Regulators" after pre-Revolutionary War freedom fighters. Included were Tunstall men - Billy; Fred Waite; John Middleton; Jim "Frenchie" French;

farmer cousins, George and Frank Coe; and homesteader, Charlie Bowdre - and a John Chisum cattle detective, Frank MacNab. Dick Brewer was chosen as leader. Only one month after Tunstall died, Billy was being schooled in politics of revolution.

The Ring's next chance to assassinate McSween was April 1, 1878, when he returned to Lincoln for his Grand Jury embezzlement trial. That morning, to save him, Regulators with carbines, and Billy with only a revolver, ambushed Brady and his three deputies from behind an adobe corral wall at Tunstall's store. Brady and his Deputy, George Hindman, died. Recklessly, Billy, with Jim French, ran out to retrieve his confiscated, Winchester '73 carbine from Brady's body. Both got leg wounds from firing surviving deputy, Jacob Basil "Billy" Matthews. But Billy regained his symbol of father-figure Tunstall. (It is likely the carbine held in Billy's tintype two years hence.)

Three days later, on April 4, 1878, Deputy Dick Brewer, seeking stolen Tunstall horses, led Billy, John Middleton, Fred Waite, Frank Coe, George Coe, and Charlie Bowdre to Blazer's Mill - a privately owned, way station and grist mill within the Mescalero Indian Reservation. There, they encountered bounty-hunter and Tunstall murder posseman, Andrew "Buckshot" Roberts, for whom they had a warrant. With Roberts firing his Winchester carbine, Bowdre shot him in the belly. Roberts's bullet hit Bowdre's belt buckle, ricocheted, and wrenched George Coe's revolver, mutilating his trigger finger. Another Roberts shot hit Middleton's chest, though Middleton survived. Then Roberts killed Brewer, later dying himself from Bowdre's wound. Billy had not fired a shot. Roberts had demonstrably resisted arrest murderously, while necessitating self defense. But Catron, as U.S. Attorney, seized on this killing to file his federal indictment against the Regulators, including Billy, claiming the murder site was the Mescalero Reservation, under federal control.

Billy's murder involvement now totaled six men; though only "Windy" Cahill was demonstrably by his hand.

At the April, 1878, Lincoln Grand Jury, McSween was declared innocent of embezzling. He continued his anti-Ring fight backed by the Regulators, though they had never been paid; John Chisum having dishonestly reneged. Revolutionary fervor sufficed. And Billy, their hot-headed fearless zealot, was becoming an inspiration - with McSween as his new father substitute.

McSween's tactic was seeking high-level intervention. Knowing that murder of a foreign citizen could elicit a Washington D.C. investigation, he filed a complaint to the British ambassador and to President Rutherford B. Hayes, accusing U.S. officials of murdering Tunstall. In response, investigating attorney, Frank Warner Angel, was sent by the Departments of the Interior and Justice. Arriving May 4, 1878, Angel took over a hundred depositions. Billy, volunteering for one, entered the national stage.

Public optimism of Ring defeat further grew when the Lincoln County Commissioners' appointed neutral John Copeland, as Sheriff replacing Brady. And "Squire" Wilson, ignoring Axtell's proclamation, continued to function as Justice of the Peace.

Optimism was short-lived. New Regulator leader, Frank MacNab, was killed in ambush on April 28th by Ringite Seven Rivers cattle rustlers. By May 28th, because new Sheriff Copeland forgot to post his tax collecting bond, Governor Axtell, by another proclamation, removed him and appointed as Sheriff, Ringite George Peppin, Brady's deputy, present at Brady's killing.

War fervor built, with furious Regulators and Mexicans calling themselves "McSweens." Billy's affiliation with local, firebrand youth, Yginio Salazar, and Billy's closeness to Hispanic residents of nearby San Patricio and Picacho, had arguably brought them into the McSween alliance. By April 30, 1878, McSweens were skirmishing with Ring partisans, known as "Murphy-Dolans;" though Lawrence Murphy was then dying of alcoholism. And Catron took over his ranch. McSween again hid, often in San Patricio. In revenge, Sheriff George Peppin, with John Kinney's Ring-rustler gang from Mesilla, on July 3rd massacred residents and destroyed property there. On July 13th, the defiant "Regulator Manifesto" was sent to Catron's brother-in-law, then managing Catron's ranch, threatening retaliation against Catron himself. Signed only "Regulator," it was likely by Billy.

The Lincoln County War's culminating battle began the next day: July 14, 1878. McSween, with 60 men - Regulators and Hispanic residents of San Patricio and Picacho - occupied Lincoln. Reflecting McSween's intended peaceful victory was that his wife, Susan, and her sister with five children remained in his double-winged house; along with the sister's attorney husband's law intern, Harvey Morris.

McSween's men took strategic positions in houses throughout the mile-long town, most of whose inhabitants had fled. When

Seven Rivers and John Kinney outlaws joined James Dolan and Sheriff George Peppin, Billy; his friends, Yginio Salazar and Tom O'Folliard; and San Patricio men - José Chávez y Chávez, Ignacio Gonzales, Florencio Chávez, Francisco Zamora, and Vincente Romero - rushed to McSween's house, joining guard, Jim French.

Though Murphy-Dolan men occupied foothills south of Lincoln, they were held at bay for five days by shooting McSweens. Regulators were about to win. But McSween did not realize that Fort Stanton's new commander, Lieutenant Colonel N.A.M. Dudley, was beholden to the Ring. McSween was also reassured by the Posse Comitatus Act, passed the month before in Washington D.C., baring military intervention in civilian disputes.

On July 16th, Dudley began his invention by sending to Lincoln, for "fact-finding," 9th Cavalry Private Berry Robinson, who was almost hit in the mutual gunfire. Next, on July 18th, James Dolan documented for Dudley that women and children were at risk at the Lincoln home of Ring-loyalist, Saturnino Baca.

The next day, July 19th, violating the Posse Comitatus Act, Dudley marched on Lincoln with 39 troops - white infantry, black 9th Cavalry, and white officers - two ambulances; a mountain howitzer cannon; and a Gatling machine-gun, that period's most awesome weapon of war. Panicked McSweens - except for those in his besieged house - fled north across the nearby Bonito River. Dudley himself threatened McSween that if any soldier was shot, he would raze his house. He then left three soldiers on McSween's property to inhibit shooting, and left three more to shield Sheriff Peppin. Next, by death threats, Dudley forced Justice of the Peace Wilson to write arrest warrants for McSween and his men as attempted murderers of Private Robinson. Next, feigning non-intervention, Dudley encamped with the rest of his troops at the east side of Lincoln.

Backed by military presence, Sheriff Peppin's outlaw posseman surrounded McSween's house and set fire to its west wing. Eventually evacuated were McSween's family, after Dudley had refused Susan McSween's personal plea for him to save her husband. The obvious intent was to kill McSween and his men.

By nightfall, the McSween house conflagration - worsened by an exploding keg of gunpowder for bullet-making - left all trapped in the east wing. At about 9 p.m., escape was attempted into fire-lit shooting Ringites. With Billy was law intern, Harvey Morris, whom he saw fatally shot. And before Billy escaped across the Bonito River at the property's rear - to rescue by fellow

Regulators - he witnessed Dudley's treasonous crime: three of his white soldiers, imbedded with the assailants, fired a volley at those escaping. Arguably, they had killed Harvey Morris.

The Murphy-Dolans shot dead McSween, Francisco Zamora, and Vincente Romero. Yginio Salazar survived with two bullets in his back. The Ring won. Symbolizing horror, McSween's starving, yard chickens ate the eyeballs of his corpse. Again was Ring murder and mutilation in Lincoln County.

No one had realized that Ring influence extended to Washington, D.C. Investigator Frank Warner Angel, after documenting crimes of Governor Axtell, U.S. Attorney Catron, and Sheriff Brady's posse, nevertheless concluded in his report - likely under duress - that no U.S. officials were involved in Tunstall's murder. In the cover-up, Catron resigned as U.S. Attorney. And President Hayes removed expendable Governor Axtell, replacing him with Civil War General Lew Wallace. So, by the end of 1878, citizens again had hope, though Lincoln men like Juan Patrón and Justice of the Peace "Squire" Wilson were left at risk after demonstrating Regulator sympathies. But Frank Warner Angel secretly tried to help - again implying his forced cover-up reports - by writing for Lew Wallace a notebook listing Ringites, and sending him an exposé on the Santa Fe Ring printed in 1877.

Though most Regulators fled the Territory, Billy stayed and engaged in the Regulator Manifesto's guerrilla stock rustling with Tom O'Folliard and Charlie Bowdre - who had relocated to Fort Sumner with his wife Manuela. For his stolen stock, Billy used non-Ring outlets: Pat Coghlan in the western part of the Territory; and Dan Dedrick. Dedrick was a counterfeiter and rustler owner of Bosque Grande, a ranch 12 miles south of Fort Sumner, who, with his two brothers, also owned a livery stable in White Oaks, a town about 45 miles northwest of Lincoln. Those brothers were another stock outlet for Billy. Billy also sold rustled horses in Tascosa, Texas; where he wrote a subsequently famous, bill of sale to a friendly doctor, Henry Hoyt, for an expensive sorrel horse - a likely gift to a father-figure, since it had been Sheriff Brady's. Billy bolstered this petty rustling with gambling. He was again a homeless drifter. That would now be permanent.

Amidst public hope, on October 1, 1878, new Governor, Lew Wallace took office. A high-achieving elitist, he was the son of an

Indiana governor; a Civil War Major General; an Abraham Lincoln murder trial prosecutor; author of best-selling novel, *The Fair God*; and was writing *Ben-Hur A Tale of the Christ*. He had sought exotic ambassadorship, like to Turkey, not governorship of backwater New Mexico Territory. So, to dispatch quickly with Lincoln County "troubles" without confronting the Santa Fe Ring, he issued, a month after arriving, an Amnesty Proclamation; though excluding those already indicted. Billy had been indicted for the Brady, Hindman, and Roberts murders.

There were more sources of hope. The new Sheriff, George Kimbrell - having been appointed to replace Sheriff George Peppin who resigned - was anti-Ring. And McSween's intrepid widow, Susan, had brought to Lincoln an attorney, Huston Chapman, to charge Commander N.A.M. Dudley with the Lincoln County War battle's murder of her husband and the arson of her home.

In that atmosphere of legal scrutiny and Ring caution, James Dolan made peace overtures, first to Susan McSween, then to Billy - a proof of that teenager's Ring threat. Bi-lingual Billy's bond to Hispanic people had arguably contributed to their joining the War; and could yield another uprising - as Catron's feared.

The Billy-Dolan peace meeting was fatefully scheduled on the February 18, 1879 anniversary of Tunstall's murder. It ended in calamity. As James Dolan; Billy; Jessie Evans and Jessie's new gang member, Billy Campbell; and Billy's Regulator friends, Tom O'Folliard and Josiah "Doc" Scurlock, walked Lincoln's dark street after the meeting, they encountered Chapman. Dolan and Campbell fired at point-blank range, killing him, then ignited his clothing. Billy was again an eye-witness. And again there was murder and mutilation in Lincoln County.

Huston Chapman's murder forced Governor Wallace to go to Lincoln - a task he had delayed for five months after arriving. Once there, however, he still avoided Ring confrontation, presenting instead a quixotic plan to eliminate vague "outlaws and rustlers." The Ring had already identified Regulators as "outlaws;" with Billy on their list as "the Kid."

Focus on Billy - likely through Dolan - made Wallace put the astronomical reward of $1,000 on his head. Billy responded with his pardon plea, writing on March 13, 1879, to offer Wallace his eye-witness testimony against Chapman's murderers in exchange for annulling his Lincoln County War indictments. It was Billy's bold and calculated risk to negate Ring power over himself.

Billy's articulate letter, in fine Spencerian handwriting, led to his March 17, 1879, nighttime meeting with Wallace in Justice of the Peace "Squire" Wilson's Lincoln house. Evidence indicates, furthermore, that Wilson covertly backed Billy's plea. There, Billy believed Wallace agreed to his pardon bargain. And Billy subsequently clung to it, and to Wallace, with tragic results.

To prevent Ring assassination before testifying, Billy requested, in writing, from Wallace a sham arrest. (He had already lived through Ring assassinations of John Tunstall, Alexander McSween, Harvey Morris, Francisco Zamora, Vincente Romero, and Huston Chapman.) Billy was kept in the home of his Lincoln friend and Regulator partisan, Juan Patrón, the town Jailer; where Wallace, housed next door, interviewed him and received an additional letter from Billy about Lincoln County War issues.

Billy fulfilled his pardon bargain the next month by testifying in the April Lincoln County Grand jury. He achieved indictment of Chapman's killers, with James Dolan and Billy Campbell for first degree murder, and Jessie Evans as accessory. But with his being in custody, Ringite District Attorney William Rynerson, in collusion with District Judge Warren Bristol, had his trial venue for his indictments switched from Lincoln to Doña Ana County to guarantee a hanging sentence. Still Wallace issued no pardon.

By that April of 1879, Alexander McSween's widow, Susan, retained Attorney Ira Leonard, dead Attorney Huston Chapman's office-mate from Las Vegas, to prosecute Dudley. In response, under advisement of Catron's law firm, where Catron himself had defended him for two prior court martials, Dudley got defamatory affidavits about her from Ring partisans to diminish her credibility; and requested a military Court of Inquiry, where judges would be biased, and where he would be defended by Catron's law firm member, Henry Waldo. Furthermore, on April 25th, Ira Leonard's assassination was attempted.

Wallace had already removed Dudley. He testified against him in the Court of Inquiry, and was viciously and humiliatingly attacked by Waldo. Though testifying against Dudley was not part of Billy's own pardon bargain, he testified with his own anti-Ring agenda on May 28th and 29th of 1879, devastatingly reporting the three white soldiers firing a volley at him and others - meaning officers; meaning under Dudley's orders; meaning violating the Posse Comitatus Act and justifying court martial and hanging. Billy's courage made Attorney Leonard take him as client.

By July of 1879, the biased Court of Inquiry exonerated Dudley. And Billy, with no pardon and imminent transport to Mesilla for a hanging trial, exited his bogus jailing.

The Ring recouped. By October of 1879, Susan McSween lost her civil trial against Dudley in Mesilla - to which her venue had been changed by Judge Warren Bristol. That month, Judge Bristol also voided James Dolan's Chapman murder indictment based on no witnesses daring to appear for a trial. Dolan, certain of immunity, had even purchased Tunstall's store, while Catron had taken over "the House;" thus continuing the local Ring monopoly. Tunstall's ranch property was seized illegally; and Billy's Peñasco River ranch was gifted to Jacob Basil "Billy" Matthews, head posseman for Tunstall's murder. And there was a more subtle Ring victory: Lew Wallace's humiliation in the Court of Inquiry made him shun Lincoln County "troubles" and Billy's pardon.

Billy's future killer, Patrick "Pat" Floyd Garrett, had arrived in New Mexico Territory's Fort Sumner the year before. Born to an Alabama plantation family, relocated to Claiborne Parrish, Louisiana, when 9½ - and Billy was just born - young Garrett had even been willed a slave. After his family lost everything in the Civil War, he drifted westward to Texas, where he possibly murdered a black man, before becoming a buffalo hunter from 1876 to 1878 with two partners and a kid named Joe Briscoe. Garrett murdered Briscoe, but claimed self-defense. He never met fellow buffalo hunter, John William Poe; but later, his, Poe's, and Billy's histories would merge on the night of July 14, 1881.

In Fort Sumner, tall Garrett met transient kid, Billy Bonney, gambling at Hargrove's or Beaver Smith's Saloons. They were given townspeople's nicknames, "Big Casino" and "Little Casino," for their poker playing and height discrepancies.

The original Fort Sumner was built in 1865 by the U.S. government on desert flatlands east of the Pecos River for soldiers guarding Bosque Redondo: a concentration camp for 3,500 Navajos and 400 Apaches, until their scandalous starvation caused release of the Navajos to their homeland in 1868; the Apaches having already escaped. In 1870, Fort Sumner was purchased by Lucien Bonaparte Maxwell, one of New Mexico Territory's richest men. Converting it into a town around its parade ground, and using the surrounding thousands of acres for sheep raising, he settled there with his wife, Luz Beaubien; daughters, including Paulita; and only son, Peter. Retained was the military cemetery for his family. Eventually it received Billy's body, to lie beside Pat Garrett's earlier shooting victims: Billy's Regulator pals, Tom O'Folliard and Charlie Bowdre. Maxwell died in 1875, leaving the town to his wife and son, Peter; who became the family's ruin through mismanagement. But when Pat Garrett and Billy Bonney gambled there, Fort Sumner was still thriving.

Before buying Fort Sumner, Lucien Maxwell's wealth came from his marriage to Luz Beaubien, an heiress of the almost two million acre Beaubien-Miranda Land Grant, followed by his purchase of the Grant's shares from her siblings. He then sold it as the Maxwell Land Grant. But he was cheated by his robber baron attorneys and politicians, Thomas Benton Catron and Steven Benton Elkins, who resold it for double the money. Their profit and land grab scheme fortified their Santa Fe Ring, whose monopolistic goals and crimes were abetted by other public officials, lawmen, and the military. Catron and Elkins profited immensely in land, railroads, banks, and mines. Catron eventually owned six million acres - more than anyone in U.S. history. And in the Lincoln County War period, Catron held the Territory's highest legal position: U.S. Attorney. By 1912's New Mexico statehood, he became one of the two first senators.

By 1878, before the Lincoln County War, Pat Garrett and Billy Bonney led separate lives, though connected by Fort Sumner's Gutierrez sisters: Juanita, Apolinaria, and Celsa. Billy befriended Celsa, married to her cousin, Saval Gutierrez, a Maxwell sheep herder. Billy's July 14, 1881 death walk would start at their house. Garrett married Juanita, who died soon after of a possible miscarriage. Two years later, in 1880, Garrett married Apolinaria, with whom he would father eight children. It was a double marriage with his Fort Sumner, best friend, Maxwell's foreman, Barney Mason, later a spy assisting Garrett's capture of Billy.

In 1878, Pat Garrett had been desperate for employment. At Fort Sumner, he drove a wagon for Peter Maxwell; helped a local hog raiser, Thomas "Kip" McKinney; and bartended at Hargrove's Saloon. He would have had no exposure to Lincoln County War issues. Then came 1880 and the opportunity of his life. Lincoln County - the largest county in America; almost a quarter of New Mexico Territory, and big enough to fit Massachusetts, Connecticut, Vermont, Rhode Island, and Delaware - needed a new sheriff for its November election, one compatible with Santa Fe Ring interests. To qualify, Garrett moved with his wife,

Apolinaria, to that county's town of Roswell; adding, as a boarder, an unemployed journalist named Ashmun "Ash" Upson. In 1882, Upson would ghostwrite Garrett's book about killing Billy the Kid.

By 1880, the Ring's outlaw myth propaganda had advertised Billy's gunman reputation. That almost succeeded in his killing on January 3, 1880 at Fort Sumner's Hargrove's Saloon. A Texan bounty hunter named Joe Grant tried to shoot him in the back. Saved by Grant's gun's misfiring, Billy retaliated fatally. Obvious self-defense, that killing was not legally pursued.

Billy was now linked to murders of seven men: Frank "Windy" Cahill, William Brady, George Hindman, Andrew "Buckshot" Roberts, William "Buck" Morton, Frank Baker, and Joe Grant.

That 1880, when his now-famous tintype photograph was taken, Billy may have heard first mythological whispers of his having killed a man for each year of his life. The Ring was setting its legal trap for capturing and killing him. In addition to murderer and rustler, he would be declared a counterfeiter to bring in the Secret Service, a branch of the U.S. Treasury Department with funding to track him down. Catron's Lincoln County agent, James Dolan, initiated it by reporting receipt of a counterfeit $100 bill in his Lincoln store. And Catron or Elkins were the likely contact to Secret Service Chief, James Brooks.

By September 11, 1880, Secret Service Special Operative Azariah Wild was sent to Lincoln. Dolan's counterfeit bill, falsely linked to Billy, actually came from two youths, Billy Wilson and Tom Cooper, employed by the real counterfeiter, Dan Dedrick. But they occasionally rustled with Billy and his regulars: Tom O'Folliard, Charlie Bowdre, and a "Dirty Dave" Rudabaugh. Billy himself used Dedrick as an outlet for rustled stock, along with Dedrick's brothers at their White Oaks livery.

Gullible Operative Azariah Wild was led to believe by James Dolan and Catron's brother-in-law, Edgar Walz - then managing Catron's Lincoln County cattle ranch - that Billy was in the country's largest counterfeiting and rustling gang. In December of 1880, the *New York Sun* featured Billy in "Outlaws of New Mexico. The Exploits of a band headed by a New York Youth, War Against a Gang of Cattle Thieves, Murderers, and Counterfeiters." Billy was alias "the Kid." The Ring launched his national fame.

The Ring's plot almost backfired when Azariah Wild was told by Attorney Ira Leonard that his client, Billy Bonney, would testify against the counterfeiters. On October 8, 1880, Wild wrote in his daily report to Chief James Brooks that he himself would arrange a pardon for Billy in exchange for that testimony. But Wild confided that pardon plan to his Ringite informers, who convinced him that Billy, staying in Fort Sumner, was the gang's leader! In his report for October 11, 1880, Wild wrote that he intended to arrest those Fort Sumner desperados in Fort Sumner. By then, Billy was cautious. He held up the stagecoach with Operative Wild's mail, read that report, and avoided apprehension by avoiding the meeting with Leonard and Wild. But another pardon was lost.

The Ring still needed to eliminate Billy. The next option was getting a Lincoln County Sheriff willing do it. The current Sheriff, George Kimbrell, who had assisted in Billy's sham arrest, was a McSween-side sympathizer. The Ring chose Pat Garrett. Secretly, Wild worked with Garrett to form a dragnet to capture Billy and his "rustler-counterfeiter gang;" while, for the upcoming sheriff's election, Garrett was advertised as a law-and-order man to new gold-rush settlers in White Oaks, unaware of Lincoln County War issues, but a third of Lincoln County's voters.

In the November 2, 1880 sheriff's election, Pat Garrett got 358 votes to George Kimbrell's 141. Azariah Wild, convinced by his Ringite contacts that Kimbrell protected the "Kid gang," also gave Garrett immediate Territorial power for capture by appointing him Deputy U.S. Marshall before he became Sheriff in January of 1881. Unaware, Billy would have wrongly thought that Garret's lawman authority was limited to Lincoln County, not Fort Sumner's San Miguel County where he stayed.

Also, unaware of his locally publicized "outlawry," Billy still brought stolen horses to the Dedrick's White Oaks livery. On November 22, 1880, a White Oaks posse ambushed him, Tom O'Folliard, Billy Wilson, Tom Pickett, and "Dirty" Dave Rudabaugh at nearby Coyote Spring, shooting two of their horses before Billy's group escaped. Six days later, that posse attacked them again at the way station ranch of "Whiskey" Jim Greathouse, 45 miles northeast of White Oaks; accidentally killing one of their own men, Jim Carlyle, but blaming Billy.

That accusation prompted Billy's only letter of 1880 to Governor Lew Wallace. On December 12th, he wrote, denying his outlawry and murdering of Jim Carlyle. He even described his

Robin Hood role of seeking justice for the downtrodden. Wallace never answered. Instead, on December 22nd, Wallace placed a Las Vegas *Daily Gazette* notice: "Billy the Kid: $500 Reward." He would repeat that reward notice in the *Daily New Mexican* on May 3, 1881, after Billy's jailbreak. Wallace's betrayal of the supposed pardon bargain was complete.

By December of 1880, dreadful days began for Billy. U.S. Marshall, Pat Garrett, coordinating with Azariah Wild, had assembled posses to ride after Billy; using Texans, since New Mexicans, to whom Billy was a freedom fighting hero, refused. Garrett's first ambush was on December 19, 1880, when Billy, Tom O'Folliard, Charlie Bowdre, Billy Wilson, Tom Pickett, and Dave Rudabaugh rode into Fort Sumner in a snowstorm. O'Folliard was shot dead by Garrett. The rest escaped.

Billy's group tried to flee the Territory in another snowstorm; but stopped, about 16 miles from Fort Sumner, on December 21, 1880, at a rock-walled, windowless, shepherds' line cabin at Stinking Springs. There Garrett ambushed them the next morning, killing Charlie Bowdre, whom he mistook for Billy, his intended victim. The rest surrendered. It would be seven months before Garrett succeeded in his mission to kill Billy.

Garrett transported his prisoners by train, via Las Vegas, New Mexico, to the Santa Fe jail. Billy remained in jail from December 27, 1880 to March 28, 1881, because the Ring awaited completion of the railroad to Mesilla to impede any rescue. But Billy almost escaped by tunneling out with fellow prisoners.

From his cell, Billy wrote four unanswered letters to Wallace, in 1881, pleading for his pardon: writing on March 4th: "*I have done everything that I promised you I would, and you have done nothing that you promised me.*" On March 2nd, he threatened: "*I have some letters which date back two years and there are Parties who are very anxious to get them but I will not dispose of them until I see you.*" Wallace never got over that audacity or his own guilt, reworking the pardon obsessively till the end of his life in vindictive fictionalized writings on the outlaw "Billy the Kid."

Billy's Mesilla murder trial, under Judge Warren Bristol, began on March 30, 1881, with jurors unaware of Lincoln County War's issues, and without any Lincolnites daring to be witnesses for his defense. Attorney Ira Leonard represented Billy for past U.S. Attorney Catron's 1878 federal indictment, Case Number 411, the United States versus Charles Bowdre, Josiah Scurlock, Henry Brown, William Bonney alias Henry Antrim alias the Kid, John Middleton, Frederick Waite, Jim French, and George Coe for the murder of Andrew "Buckshot" Roberts. Surprising everyone, Leonard got it quashed as invalid, since the federal government had no jurisdiction over Blazer's Mill, the murder site; since private property, like it, was under Territorial jurisdiction. Its being surrounded by the federally-controlled Mescalero Reservation was irrelevant.

Remaining were only the Brady and Hindman Territorial indictments; and, though Billy been firing the a group of Regulators, he had only a revolver lacking accurate range. But, suddenly, Leonard withdrew, likely after a Ring threat. That was disastrous for Billy. He got Ring-biased, court appointed attorney, Albert Jennings Fountain, who considered him an outlaw.

On April 8th and 9th of 1881, was Billy's Brady murder trial. His Spanish-speaking jury, given no translator, heard only prosecution witnesses - including James Dolan. After Judge Bristol's biased instructions (with translator) made Billy's mere presence equivalent to firing the fatal shot, the jury found Billy guilty of first degree murder; its sole punishment being hanging. On April 13th, Judge Bristol set Billy's hanging date for May 13th, insuring insufficient time for appeal. Billy was to be hanged in Lincoln by its Sheriff, Pat Garrett.

From the Mesilla jail, Billy wrote to Attorney Edgar Caypless - conducting his replevin case against Stinking Springs posseman, Frank Stewart - hoping to get money from sale of his stolen bay mare to pay for an appeal. Billy did not plead again with Wallace for the pardon. Unbeknownst to him, Lew Wallace had even taken the precaution of writing his death warrant for Pat Garrett.

Ironically, the new Lincoln jail, where Billy was incarcerated to await hanging, was in the past "House," which Catron had taken over by mortgaging, and then sold to Lincoln County for conversion to its courthouse with second floor jail.

On April 21, 1881, Billy arrived to Sheriff Garrett's custody. For his 24 hour guard, Garrett deputized a White Oaks man, James Bell, and a Seven Rivers man Bob Olinger. Garrett's further precaution was shackling Billy at wrists and ankles, with securing to a floor ring - all to guarantee Billy's hanging death.

But on April 28th, with Garrett away collecting White Oaks's taxes, Billy escaped using a revolver left in the outhouse by an accomplice, or by wresting away Deputy James Bell's revolver. For providing an outhouse gun, the likely person was the building's caretaker, Gottfried Gauss, Tunstall's past cook, who had been at the ranch on Tunstall's murder day, and present during the Ring's Lincoln County War outrages. With the revolver, Billy shot Bell dead as the man fled down the jail's stairway to sound alarm.

Deputy Bob Olinger, across the street at the Wortley Hotel at lunch with jail prisoners, either heard the shot or was directed to the ambush. Billy waited at the second-floor window, and killed him with his own Whitney double-barrel shotgun.

Billy then spent hours using a miner's pick, supplied by Gauss, to break his leg chain to enable riding; while gathered Lincoln townspeople, in passive resistance, did nothing to stop him. He finally rode away on a pony supplied by Gauss.

As of that April 28, 1881 escape, Billy was involved in the murder of nine men; James Bell and Robert Olinger adding to Frank "Windy" Cahill and Joe Grant as Billy's only provable killings.

Of the dead, Billy would have said that that Cahill's and Grant's killings were in self-defense; that he was a legal posseman at the group shooting of escaping arrested Tunstall murderers, William "Buck" Morton and Frank Baker; that his gun lacked range to hit Sheriff William Brady or Deputy George Hindman, and their killings by the Regulators were to save Alexander McSween from them; that he had not shot Andrew "Buckshot" Roberts, a Tunstall murderer and murderer of Dick Brewer firing at his group, and killed solely by Charlie Bowdre in self defense; and that Deputy James Bell, after refusing to be tied, had tried to run for help, so was killed to save himself from unjust hanging (and Bell had been in the White Oaks posse which killed Jim Carlyle and falsely accused him).

Only Seven Rivers rustler, Bob Olinger, would have been admittedly hated as being in each Lincoln County War period crime - Tunstall's murder, Frank MacNab's ambush murder, and the War's skirmishes and battle. Billy's rage was so great, that he smashed apart Olinger's shotgun to throw it on his corpse, delaying his own escape.

That count of nine killed men - with only four certain - remained as Billy's final true tally.

Billy's escape route was across the Capitan Mountains to the Las Tablas home of his friend, Yginio Salazar; then to Fort Sumner and Paulita, where he hid in the Maxwell's sheep camps, confident of protection by the Maxwells and townspeople. He was unaware that Pat Garrett was paying Maxwell foreman, Barney Mason, through Secret Service Agent Azariah Wild, as a spy.

Garrett's two deputies for the pursuit of Billy to Fort Sumner - John William Poe and Thomas "Kip" McKinney - did not know Billy. Poe, a buffalo hunter, past Deputy U.S. Marshall in Texas, cattle detective, and recent White Oaks settler, had met Garrett during the Wild-assisted tracking of the "Kid gang." McKinney knew Garrett from their 1878, hog farming days.

Once in Fort Sumner, Garrett, doubting Billy's presence, was urged by Poe to stay. On July 14, 1881, Poe searched the town and also checked with Sunnyside postmaster, Milnor Rudulph, seven miles to its north. That night, convinced Billy was nearby, he, Garrett, and McKinney planned an ambush in Peter Maxwell's bedroom, with Maxwell as traitor. Unknown accomplices likely directed Billy to Maxwell's bedroom, where Garrett waited, with Poe and McKinney outside to kill Billy if he escaped.

Near midnight, Billy proceeded from the converted barracks house of Celsa and Saval Gutierrez, carrying their butcher knife across the parade ground to cut a dinner steak in light of the almost-full huge moon. He first went toward Maxwell's bedroom; but seeing Poe, asked in Spanish who he was, then entered. Inside, to Maxwell in bed as decoy, Billy asked again in Spanish who was there, possibly sensing Garrett in the darkness.

Garrett then shot Billy. Poe, McKinney, and townspeople heard the shot. Next, Garrett fired wild. Billy was already dead.

The townspeople held a night vigil for Billy in their carpenter's shop. The Coroner's Jury, the next day on July 15, 1881, had as President, Ringite Postmaster Milnor Rudulph. The terrified juryman had no alternative but to sign his concluding statement:

> [O]ur verdict is that the deed of said Garrett was justifiable homicide and we are unanimous in the opinion that the gratitude of all the community is due to the said Garrett for his deed and is worthy of being rewarded.

Ring terrorism was now complete. A generation of silence ensued before any dared contradict the Santa Fe Ring's outlaw mythology of Billy the Kid.

BILLY BONNEY'S ADVOCATES

ANALYSIS: Contradicting Billy Bonney's Santa Fe Ring outlaw mythology began in the 20th century, when his aging contemporaries felt safe enough to praise him in autobiographies riding on coattails of his growing posthumous fame.

Compared to Billy Bonney's recorded, 19th century, Santa Fe Ring outlaw mythology in his lifetime, exacerbated by Pat Garrett's outlaw myth book, *Authentic Life of Billy the Kid*, issued the year after he killed him, Billy's contemporary advocates and fellow freedom fighters were self-protectively silent. The few who wrote, waited till old age. And they recorded his charismatic, bi-cultural, brilliance. But none dared mention the Santa Fe Ring.

FRANK AND GEORGE COE

John Tunstall's employees, local Homestead Act farmers, like cousins Frank and George Coe, affectionately nick-named new ranch hand, teenaged Billy Bonney, as "Kid." Frank and George were 26 and 21 respectively when Billy met them in late 1877, when he was 17. By 1878, after Tunstall's murder, the Coes became his fellow Regulators. After the lost Lincoln County War, the Coes fled to northwest New Mexico Territory, near Farmington, not returning to Lincoln County until 1884.

In 1878, George Coe was federally indicted by U.S. Attorney Thomas Benton Catron, along with Billy and other Regulators, for the April 4, 1878 murder of Andrew "Buckshot" Roberts at Blazer's Mill. Frank and George were both indicted Territorially in 1878 by the Lincoln County Grand Jury for the murders of William Brady and George Hindman. They were never prosecuted.

FRANK COE

As an old-timer, Frank Coe wrote about Billy in an unpublished letter to a William Steele Dean, dated August 3, 1926. He emphasized Billy's multiculturalism, and above-average height (5'6" was average), belying his mythologized "shortness":

[He was] 5ft 8in, weight 138 lb stood straight as an Indian, fine looking a lad as I ever met. He was a lady's man, the Mex girls were all crazy about him. He spoke their language well. He was a fine dancer, could go all their gaits and was one of them. **He was a wonder, you would have been proud to know him.**

On September 16, 1923, Frank Coe - like Billy, considering himself a Regulator soldier - gave a quote to the *El Paso Times*:

> [Billy] was brave and reliable, one of the best soldiers we had. He never pushed his advice or opinions, but he had a wonderful presence of mind; the tighter the place the more he showed his cool nerve and quick brain.

Frank Coe also related Billy's shootist preoccupation:

> He never seemed to care for money, except to buy cartridges with; then he would much prefer to gamble for them straight. Cartridges were scarce, and he always used about 10 times as many as any one else.

GEORGE COE

In 1934, George Coe published *Frontier Fighter: The Autobiography of George Coe Who Fought and Rode With Billy the Kid*. He confirmed Sheriff William Brady as dangerously brutal - even before John Tunstall's arrival - abusing him and fellow farmer and future Regulator, Josiah "Doc" Scurlock, by false arrest. And he described Tunstall's paternal affection for Billy:

> Tunstall seemed really devoted to the Kid. One day I was in Lincoln and I asked him about Billy.
> "George, that's the finest lad I ever met," he said. "He's a revelation to me every day and would do anything to please me. I'm going to make a man out of that boy yet. He has it in him."

George Coe also emphasized Billy's charisma:

Billy came down to the Dick Brewer Ranch on the Ruidoso. He was the center of interest everywhere he went, and though heavily armed, he seemed as gentlemanly as a college-bred youth. He quickly became acquainted with everybody, and because of his humorous and pleasing personality grew to be a community favorite. In fact, Billy was so popular there wasn't enough of him to go around. He had a beautiful voice and sang like a bird. One of our special amusements was to get together every few nights and have singing. The thrill of those happy evenings still lingers – a pleasant memory – and tonight I would give a lot to live through one again. Frank Coe and I played the fiddles, and all of us danced, and here Billy, too, was in demand.

About Lincoln County War fighting, George Coe quoted Billy to show the boy's militant fervor in the Lincoln County War:

"As for ... giving up to that outfit, we'll die first."

Billy himself exhibited that same brave bellicosity in his March 20, 1879 pardon bargain letter to Governor Lew Wallace:

"I am not afraid to die like a man fighting but I would not like to be killed like a dog unarmed."

George Coe gave a telling anecdote about Billy's teasing bravado which occurred around April 3, 1878 in the lead-up to the Lincoln County War. It shows how this teenager inspired grown men, and foreshadowed Billy's undaunted and ironic press interviews after his capture and after his hanging trial:

We made a big bonfire, and sat around swapping lies and bragging ... Then we talked about riding into Lincoln and setting in short order all the difficulties that were troubling the people there. We were a brave band as we told it.

Our guns, which formed the most important part of our possessions, had been placed carelessly around against nearby trees. **Billy sized up the situation and,** looking for a little fun and excitement with an inexperienced bunch of greenhorns, he slipped about five or six cartridges out of his belt and tossed them into the fire. In less than a minute they began to go off, and such a mad dash for tall timber you have never seen ... I looked back as I ran, and there stood the Kid with his arms folded, perfectly unconcerned ...

"Well, you're a damn fine bunch of soldiers. Run like a bunch of coyotes and forget to take your guns. I just wanted to break you in a little before we met the enemy, and, boys, I'm sure proud of your nerve."

GOTTFRIED GAUSS

German-born Gottfried Gauss, 56 at Billy's great escape from Lincoln's courthouse jail, was part of Billy's Lincoln County history from that teenager's October of 1877 arrival as a John Tunstall ranch hand - when Gauss was Tunstall's cook - through the Lincoln County War period, and to Billy's 1881 jailbreak, when Gauss was the Lincoln courthouse jail's caretaker and likely supplier of Billy's escape revolver. Gauss's anti-Ring stance went back to 1876 when he was employed in "the House's" L.G. Murphy and Company incarnation, and was cheated out of his wages and profits from its brewery, which he ran.

Billy himself mentioned Gauss in his June 8, 1878 deposition to Presidential Investigator Frank Warner Angel as being at Tunstall's Feliz River ranch before Tunstall's ambush-murder, as well as during the earlier intimidation of its ranch hands by Sheriff William Brady's possemen. Billy's transcriptionist wrote: *"The persons at the ranch were R. M. Brewer, John Middleton, G. Gauss, M. Martz, R.A. Widenmann, Henry Brown, F.T. Waite, W<u>m</u> McClosky and this deponent."* The night before Tunstall made his fatal return ride with his men and horses to Lincoln from that ranch, he assigned Gauss to stay. Thus, Gauss witnessed Brady's arriving murder posse. Billy's transcriptionist quoted him:

Deponent further says that on the night of the 17th of February A.D. 1878 J.H. Tunstall arrived at the ranch and informed all persons there that reliable information had reached him that J.B. Matthews [Sheriff Brady's Chief Deputy] was gathering a large party of outlaws and desperados as a posse and the said posse was coming to the ranch, the Mexicans in the party to gather up the cattle and the balance of the party to kill the persons at the ranch. It was thereupon decided that all persons at the ranch excepting G. Gauss, were to leave ...

On March 1, 1890, in an interview with the *Lincoln County Leader* about Billy's jailbreak, Gauss implied enabling by non-intervening Lincolnites, as well as his own sympathy for Billy. Gauss may have directed Deputy Bob Olinger to the courthouse's east side, where Billy shot him. Gauss stated:

I was crossing the yard behind the courthouse, when I heard a shot fired then a tussle upstairs in the courthouse, somebody hurrying downstairs, and deputy sheriff Bell emerging from the door running toward me. He ran right into my arms, expired the same moment, and I laid him down, dead. That I was in a hurry to secure assistance, or perhaps to save myself, everybody will believe.

When I arrived at the garden gate leading to the street, in front of the courthouse, I saw the other deputy sheriff Olinger, coming out of the hotel opposite, with the four or five other county prisoners, where they had taken their dinner. I called to him to come quick. He did so, leaving his prisoners in front of the hotel. When he had come up close to me, and while I was standing not a yard apart, I told him that

I was just after laying Bell dead on the ground in the yard behind. Before he could reply, he was struck by a well-directed shot fired from a window above us, and fell dead at my feet. I ran for my life to reach my room and safety, when Billy the Kid called to me: "Don't run, I wouldn't hurt you – I am alone, and master not only of the courthouse, but also of the town, for I will allow nobody to come near us." "You go," he said, "and saddle one of Judge (Ira) Leonard's horses, and I will clear out as soon as I have the shackles loosened from my legs." With a little prospecting pick I had thrown to him through the window he was working for at least an hour, and could not accomplish more than to free one leg. He came to the conclusion to wait a better chance, tie one shackle to his waistbelt, and start out. Meanwhile

I had saddled a small skittish pony belonging to Billy Burt (the county clerk), as there was no other horse available, and had also, by Billy's command, tied a pair of red blankets behind the saddle ...

When Billy went down the stairs at last, on passing the body of Bell he said, "I'm sorry I had to kill him but I couldn't help it."

On passing the body of Olinger he gave him a tip with his boot, saying, "You are not going to round me up again." And so Billy the Kid started out that evening, after he had shaken hands with everybody around and after having a little difficulty in mounting on account of the shackle on his leg, he went on his way rejoicing.

IRA LEONARD

Billy's best friend in a high place, New York-born Attorney Ira Leonard, bravely took Susan McSween's case against Commander N.A.M. Dudley right after the Ring murdered his office-mate predecessor: Attorney Huston Chapman. Leonard was 46 when he met Billy in Lincoln in 1879, when the boy was risking his life to testify against Chapman's killers in Lincoln County's April Grand Jury; followed by the boy's assisting the prosecution by testifying in Dudley's Court of Inquiry the next month. As will be seen, Leonard was also fully aware of the Santa Fe Ring.

Leonard appears to have known about Lew Wallace's pardon bargain with Billy from its making, since he kept Wallace informed about Billy's Grand Jury testimony: that bargain's crux. In an April 20, 1879 letter to Wallace, Leonard wrote sympathetically about Billy's courtroom pressure:

I will tell you Gov. that the prosecuting officer of this Dist. [William Rynerson] is no friend to the enforcement of the law. He is bent on going for the Kid & ... is proposed to destroy his testimony & influence. He is bent on pushing him to the wall. He is a Dolan man and is defending him by his conduct all he can.

Surely sealing Ira Leonard's anti-Ring fears was its assassination attempt on himself on April 25, 1879 in Lincoln. It mimicked the nighttime shooting of Huston Chapman, 67 days earlier; and arguably was also done by local Ringite, James Dolan.

On May 20, 1879 (See my pp. 634-642 for full letter), Leonard described its lead-up threat to Governor Lew Wallace, writing:

> *[Ringite District Attorney William Rynerson] aroused among the friends of the outlaws here a feeling of antagonism against me that resulted in their posting on a tree to which I had my horse hitched addressed to me informing me that if I did not leave the country "they would take my scalp and send me to hell."*

Another similar threat in April of 1881, likely led to Leonard's abrupt abandoning of his successful defense of Billy in Mesilla. Leonard had no known later writings about Billy.

HENRY HOYT

Henry Hoyt was a 24 year old medical doctor, working as a mail rider, when he met Billy Bonney in Tascosa, Texas, three months after the lost Lincoln County War. Billy and fellow Regulators, Charlie Bowdre and Tom O'Folliard, were selling horses, rustled in retaliation from Ringmen, as forewarned in Billy's "Regulator Manifesto" letter of July 13, 1878 to Catron's Carrizozo cattle ranch manager and brother-in-law, Edgar Walz.

Billy became attached to intellectual Hoyt as another father-figure, and gifted him with a sorrel horse. Apparently, to avoid suspicion - and with likelihood that the horse, Dandy Dick, had belonged to killed Sheriff William Brady, and may have been stolen from Ringmen, Charles Fritz or Edgar Walz - Billy created an elaborate bill of sale for Hoyt.

Dated October 24, 1878, written in Spencerian penmanship, it used correct legalese and was properly signed by witnesses. Teenaged Billy, then 18, impressed Hoyt enough to save it.

Henry Hoyt, like the Coe cousins, Frank and George, admired Billy's intelligence and bi-culturalism. In his autobiographical, 1829 book, *A Frontier Doctor*, Hoyt wrote about Billy:

> After learning his history directly from himself and recognizing his many superior natural qualifications, I often urged him, while he was free and the going was good, to leave the country, settle in Mexico or South America, and begin all over again. He spoke Spanish like a

native and although only a beardless boy was nevertheless a natural leader of men. With his poise, iron nerve, and all-around efficiency properly applied, he could have made a success anywhere.

JOHN P. MEADOWS

A cattle rancher living in New Mexico from early 1880, John P. Meadows, when an old-timer, gave interviews to historians about having known Billy, and performed about it in an historical pageant called "Days of Billy the Kid in Story, Song and Dance" on February 26, 1931 in Roswell, New Mexico. Subsequently, Meadows used his "Days of Billy the Kid" act for serialized newspaper accounts in the *Roswell Daily Record* on March 2nd, 3rd, and 4th of 1931. That year, Meadows also typed a 78 page manuscript with information about Billy. And from August 8, 1935 to June 25, 1936, the *Alamogordo News* printed almost forty reminiscence articles by him. These recollections are collected in a 2004 book titled *Pat Garrett and Billy the Kid as I Knew Them: Reminiscences of John P. Meadows*. *Reminiscences* gives insight into how Billy inspired the older men. Meadows stated:

> When he was rough, he was as rough as men ever get to be, yet he had a good streak in him.

Reminiscences also intriguingly refers to Billy's having a letter, now lost, from Wallace about the pardon promise. Though Meadows garbles the bargain as based on "standing trial," instead of "testifying in a trial," the letter's existence repeats Billy's own claim to Wallace written from the Santa Fe jail. Meadows wrote:

> He had a letter which he showed me from the governor, Lew. Wallace, which said that if he came in and stood his trial and was convicted, the governor would pardon him.

Billy's March 2, 1881 jail letter to Wallace had stated:

> *"I have some letters which date back two years and there are Parties who are very anxious to get them but*

I will not dispose of them until I see you. that is if you come immediately."

E.C. "TEDDY BLUE" ABBOTT

E.C. "Teddy Blue" Abbott, a cowboy about Billy's age, roving through New Mexico Territory in 1878, and having merely heard of him, recorded Billy's atypical multiculturalism.

That implied Billy could instigate a Hispanic revolt against the land-grabbing, Anglo, Ring minority. As will be seen, by March 26, 1873, Ringite Governor Marsh Giddings warned the Secretary of the Interior by letter about a dangerous *"revolution of the legislature's Democrats"* and *"vilest of the vile [Mexicans],"* when *"[n]early all the people of the Territory are Mexican 86,000 out of 93,000."* Thomas Benton Catron himself confirmed that fear of uprisings in his February 10, 1913 *Washington Times* article stating, "Mexicans ... were perfectly equal to starting five new revolutions in five days." As will be seen, Catron's anxiety connects to the lost pardon and to the Ring's mission to eliminate Billy by fabrication of his outlaw myth.

In 1955, as an old-timer, "Teddy Blue" Abbott published *We Pointed Them North: Recollections of a Cowpuncher*. Open about his own racism, Abbott reported, as common knowledge, the existence of two sides, with Billy as the Mexican's hero, writing:

> The Lincoln County troubles was still going on, and you had to be either for Billy the Kid or against him. It wasn't my fight ... it was the Mexicans that made a hero of him.

A TERRITORY IN REBELLION

ANALYSIS: In the 1870's, there was a cataclysmic clash when the rapidly and rapaciously rising despotic Santa Fe Ring encountered citizens' democratic idealism engendered by the Revolutionary and Civil Wars, and the frontier's promise of freedom. Popular uprisings were triggered; 1878's Lincoln County War being the culmination with the Ring retaliations having progressed from malicious prosecutions to terrorist atrocities and military treason. And the Ring's victory in that War's battle achieved a frightened silence that concealed the freedom fights and its own existence.

REVOLUTIONARY SPIRIT

The United States was born in revolution and declaration of independence on July 4, 1776. And that new nation, still fettered by slavery, was further liberated by revolution in its Civil War almost a hundred years later.

Thomas Jefferson, as an author of the "Declaration of Independence" had opined in a January 30, 1787 letter to fellow freedom fighter, James Madison, that a revolution "*at least once every 20 years [is] a medicine necessary for the sound health of government.*" And Jefferson's words of rebellion in that first "Declaration" had led British citizens of the 13 colonies into war fervor and victory. Jefferson wrote:

We hold these truths to be self-evident, that all men are created equal, that they are endowed by their Creator with certain unalienable rights ... That whenever any form of government becomes destructive of these ends, it is the right of the people to alter or abolish it.

In his "Emancipation Proclamation," President Abraham Lincoln had completed that declaration for all, declaring:

That on the first day of January, in the year of our Lord one thousand eight hundred and sixty-three, all persons held as slaves within any State ... shall be then, thenceforward, and forever free.

A hundred years after America's first victorious uprising, and slightly over a decade after defeat of slavery, that revolutionary spirit seized New Mexico Territory. Then the oppressor of democratic rights was the Santa Fe Ring. Thomas Jefferson, in his January 30, 1787 letter to James Madison had anticipated such a threat by contending that societies exist under three forms:

[The first is without government; the second, is like the United States] wherein the will of every one has a just influence, [and the third is] governments of force: as is the case in all other monarchies and in most of the other republics ... It is a government of wolves over sheep.

By the 1870's the wolves of force were unchecked and marauding in Mexico Territory as the rapacious, despotic, and murderous Santa Fe Ring.

The 1870's were also a time when freedom and liberty were still enlivened by recent memory. To common people, democracy held the vigor of its revolutionary victory of 1776, with 50,000 dead and wounded, and then at about its centenary. And the Civil War, spilling blood of over 646,000 dead and wounded to make all people free, had touched the lives of most people then living.

Proof of liberation's fervor and optimism were New Mexico Territory's uprisings of 1872, 1876, 1877, and 1878 against Santa Fe Ring tyranny. And when Billy's group chose its name for its 1878 escalation to war, it was the "Regulators." That harked back to the first Regulators of 1771: pre-Revolutionary War, North Carolina farmers who opposed and died fighting corrupt and colluding Crown sheriffs and governors in haunting replication of Lincoln County's identically titled oppressors.

And the western frontier, the vast continental expanse symbolizing never-ending resources and resourcefulness was still America's reality; then birthing anti-Ring opponents as varied as Cimarron grandmother, Mary McPherson; Lincoln community leader, Juan Patrón; British merchant and rancher, John Tunstall; Attorney and Presbyterian zealot Alexander McSween; Lincoln County War widow and litigant, Susan McSween; teenaged ranch hand, Billy Bonney; and many others.

But dark clouds of despair were massing. All Ring opposition would eventually be crushed by failed checks and balances of executive, legislative, and judicial branches; and by a reign of terror. Territorial military might backed the Ring against citizens. Judges merely advanced the Ring's malicious prosecutions and obstructions of justice. Politicians gained power by elections rigged by the Ring. Outlaw thugs assassinated Ring opponents. And the administration of President Rutherford B. Hayes was complicit. Not one Ringite ever suffered legal penalty. And not one Ringite ever broke ranks to expose the Ring.

The aftermath was the victorious Ring's re-writing of history and concealing or expurgating evidence to achieve the ultimate goal of organized crime: invisibility. And there came no pardon for the last freedom fighter and political gadfly of the 1870's: Billy Bonney. That time was the making of American monsters. A monster was the Santa Fe Ring itself. A monster was its Territorial boss and tyrannical originator, Thomas Benton Catron.

And a "monster" was their creation, "Billy the Kid": the mythological outlaw, rustler, counterfeiter, gang leader and senseless serial killer of a man for each of his twenty-one years.

The Ring's achievement was the great American secret: that democracy had sustained a terrible wound. Comprehending Billy the Kid's lost pardon is one beginning of its healing.

CHAPTER 2

THE SANTA FE RING

SANTA FE RING ROOTS

ANALYSIS: The Santa Fe Ring is a little studied, and never fully exposed, form of organized crime by malignant cronyism; unique in that it infiltrated New Mexico Territory's executive, judicial, legislative, and law enforcement entities, subverting democracy. Its self-serving goals were financial gain, power, and secrecy of its existence. Opponents were defeated by rigged elections, malicious prosecution, military interventions, and assassination. But it was nearly destroyed by one teenager: Billy Bonney, whom it outlawed for hanging as "Billy the Kid."

THE RING ENTITY

Rings, as a secret, corrupt, self-serving entity comprising colluding profiteering individuals, formed in 19th century America, and relied on informal associations and layered responsibility to deny legal culpability by duplicitous evasions.

It was not until 1970, and to address the American Mafia, that this form of organized crime was made easier to prosecute by the Racketeer Influenced and Corrupt Organizations Act (RICO); broadened in 1997 to include conspiracy for the same criminal objective, stating: "If conspirators have a plan which calls for some conspirators to commit the crime and others to provide support, the supporters are as guilty as the perpetrators."

In the days of the Santa Fe Ring, that racketeering was called "friendship." And, unlike the American Mafia, it has never been fully exposed or ever prosecuted.

BACKGROUND

The Santa Fe Ring originated in 1866 as a land-grab scheme of Missourians, Stephen Benton Elkins and Thomas Benton Catron, past college friends and attorneys, seeking wealth after the Civil War by exploiting a legal loophole in New Mexico Territory's Spanish and Mexican land grants following the Mexican War's

1848 Treaty of Guadalupe Hidalgo: Hispanic grant holders were allowed to retain their land; but had to prove ownership. Titles were reviewed by a Surveyor General, then approval by Congress. So Catron and Elkins could represent naïve grant holders, acquire their land far below value; then survey it with accomplices for maximal boundaries to keep or to sell to "friends."

A compliant political and judicial system was needed to shield that corrupt scheme involving millions of acres. So both men assumed legislative and judicial positions and networked with powerful "friends;" first Territorial, then national. Their almost immediate vast profits yielded diversification into banks, loans, railroads, mining, mercantile enterprises, and ranching. And their core strategies of unwavering loyalty to all "friends," impenetrable secrecy about their Ring, and brutal elimination of opponents never changed. It resulted in unspeakable atrocities committed in their monopolistic thrust, and utter immunity to prosecution, since all forms of legal redress were blocked by compatriots.

To comprehend Billy Bonney's history and that of the Lincoln County War uprising, the Santa Fe Ring must be factored in. Reasons for Billy's lost pardon and necessary killing can be sought in the struggle against Ring dominance - from the local level of Lincoln County, and throughout the Territory. Billy's life intersected the Ring's rapid and violent growth in the 1870's, when its Territorial control was still jeopardized both by its Anglo opponents and its Hispanic victims. The Ring's response was subjugation of the populace by a reign of terror; and elimination of adversaries by intimidation, malicious prosecution and murder. And for overt rebellions, the military acted as its enforcing arm.

The Ring's first major growth occurred by defrauding the Maxwell Land Grant's owner of his two million acres. Billy Bonney's history was entwined with that Maxwell family and would parallel them in tragedy. By the time Billy re-entered New Mexico Territory from Arizona Territory in 1877, the Ring had already crushed an 1872 revolt of the legislature, and grass-roots rebellions in 1876 and 1877. By the following year, Billy himself would be fighting that Ring in the Lincoln County War. And a year later, in 1879, new Governor Lew Wallace would face a dilemma of Billy's pardon being linked to defying the Ring.

Historian, D.W. Meinig, in his 1998 book, *The Shaping of America, A Geographical Perspective on 500 Years of History, Volume. 3, Transcontinental America 1850 - 1915* considered the Santa Fe Ring an economic phenomenon imperiling democracy:

In the 1870's anticipation of railroad connections to the East began to alter the prospects [in New Mexico] for profits and position. Slowly forming over the years, the "Santa Fe Ring" now emerged into full notoriety: "it was essentially a set of lawyers, politicians, and businessmen who united to run the territory and to make money off this particular region. Although located on the frontier, the ring reflected the corporative, monopolistic, and multiple enterprise tendencies of all American business after the Civil War. Its uniqueness lay in the fact that, rather than dealing with some manufactured item, they regarded land as their first medium of currency." "Land" meant litigation, and "down the trail from the states came ... an amazing number of lawyers" who, "still stumbling over their Spanish, would build their own political and economic empire out of the tangled heritage of land grants." And so ... "eventually over 80 per cent of the Spanish grants went to American lawyers and settlers." Important differences were the presence in New Mexico of a much greater number of Hispanic peasants and communities well rooted on the land, the considerable resistance and violence generated by this American assault, and the sullen resentment created in an increasingly constricted and impoverished people who felt they had been cheated out of much of their lands. In contrast to common representations it was not a case of vigorous, expanding society moving upon "a static culture," for "the Hispanos were still settling and conquering New Mexico, ever-extending their control" when the Anglos arrived. Here ... the conflict arose not just out of simple imperial position and crass chicanery but out of the clash of two fundamentally different sets of values, perceptions, and motivations. For ordinary Hispanos land was simply basic ... "to help one live as one ought to live" - including the continuity of such life generation after generation ... To the Anglos land was a commodity to buy and sell, to exploit as quickly as possible, a means of profit and propellant of one's personal progress. Furthermore, "American land policy featured precise measurement and documentation, assumed individual ownership, and came out of a tradition that expected western land to be open for settlement." And it came out of eastern lands - out of the humid woodlands of Europe and America - and its assumptions about settlement and family farms, its rigid uniform rectangular survey system, its laws relating to water, cultivation, and seasonal use were incongruous with the needs and practices of Hispano farming and stock raising in the arid southwest ... This process of Anglo encroachment went through several phases over several decades but reached an important victory in an early court approval of the Maxwell Grant, an infamous case wherein the original 97,000 acres was inflated to nearly 2 million covering a huge county-sized area of prime piedmont lands. Well before the owner had certain title to this baronial tract he sold it to London speculators, and ... the invasion of New Mexico had taken on a new momentum.

By 1873, Ring-founding Catron and Elkins made a crucial step: division of roles, with Catron as Territorial boss, and Elkins as nationally and politically based in Washington, D.C. to shield their corruption. By the time of Billy the Kid, President Rutherford B. Hayes covered-up the Ring so successfully that his, and his complicit cabinetmen's, reputations were unscathed.

But it was Catron's meganomaniacal, conscienceless, and vindictive nature which created Santa Fe Ring style. Like other tyrants, his domination relied on extermination. And in 1912, with New Mexico's statehood, he brought his Ring's corruption into the 20th century by spending a million dollars in apparent bribes to legislators for his appointment as one the state's first two senators. But Catron's greatest accomplishment was creating a criminal organization with no member ever prosecuted and maintaining its invisibility to the present.

That contrasted the parallel criminal career of William Magear "Boss" Tweed, head of New York City's Democratic party machine, Tammany Hall. Tweed's Tammany Hall Ring was exposed, and he died in prison, the subject of Thomas Nast's devastating political cartoons. Before "Boss" Tweed got convicted in the 1870's for pocketing up to $200 million taxpayer dollars, he had growled: "Stop them damned pictures." Loss of secrecy ruined Tweed.

Catron's and Elkins's Santa Fe Ring ultimately yielded an oligarchy controlling New Mexico Territory by fear and favor. It marked the division into two Americas, with a ruling elite and the ruled. And it was the Ring's destruction of opposition in the days of Billy the Kid that gave it the victor's option of writing the history, vilifying adversaries, and destroying incriminatory evidence. It was so successful, that the pre-Lincoln County War uprisings against it are largely unknown; the Lincoln County War is unrecognized as a freedom fight; and Billy Bonney is mythologized as an outlaw and serial murderer instead of the Ring's most dangerous, freedom fighting opponent.

Conrad Keeler Naegle, historian of 1976's anti-Ring Grant County Rebellion, stated in a 1968 *Arizona and the West* article:

> Catron, [the Ring's] long-term leader, probably wielded more power in New Mexico, for almost half a century, than any other single individual. The Ring was composed of a majority of the legal profession, a number of probate and supreme court judges, governors, and other prominent men in the Territory. Although basically Anglo-Republican, it also included a few Spanish-Americans and Democrats among its adherents. (pp. 226-227)

Naegle, in his *The History of Silver City, New Mexico 1870-1886* doctoral thesis, concluded that the Ring had "retarded progress in New Mexico." It had purged New Mexico's valuable and honorable citizens by murder and forced flight, and had drained public resources for private gain. The pall that settled after the Ring crushed the Lincoln County War and killed Billy Bonney never lifted. But there was an unexpected vulnerability: Billy's fame could bring the Ring into modern scrutiny.

Catron's hagiographer, Victor Westphall, in his 1973 *Thomas Benton Catron and His Era*, like Catron, makes light of the Ring. He quotes an 1899 *Los Angeles Times* article:

> A political contest in New Mexico that does not ... result in the assassination of a few prominent citizens is a popular failure. (p. 285)

TERRITORIAL SANTA FE RING BOSS
THOMAS BENTON CATRON

ANALYSIS: Thomas Benton Catron was a robber baron, who, with his fellow lawyer and politician, Stephen Benton Elkins, founded New Mexico Territory's secretive Santa Fe Ring. Catron, as Territorial boss, and Elkins in Washington, D.C., linked profiteering public officials. Catron crushed opponents by malicious prosecution, obstruction of justice, and assassination; becoming America's largest landowner and a New Mexico senator.

Thomas Benton Catron, a gluttonously bloated facsimile of robber baron cartoons by 19th century artist Thomas Nast, in 1866 co-founded the Santa Fe Ring and set New Mexico's pattern of malignant cronyism infiltrating government and law enforcement. In his deadly force field, lives were warped by fear or favor, and opponents murdered. His fulfilled hope, like any criminal's, was hiding his crimes till death gave him immunity.

Catron's whitewashing biographer, Victor Westphall, repeats his cover-ups and gives accidental incriminations, thereby demonstrating Catron's role in the lost pardon of Billy the Kid.

EXISTENCE OF THE SANTA FE RING

Victor Westphall's mission - like Catron's - was denial of Santa Fe Ring existence. Westphall omits contemporary exposés and anti-Ring Territorial uprisings in the 1870's; calling the Ring "romantic imagination [of] ... a sinister organization with members dedicated to unqualified promotion of their own selfish interests ... accompanied by connotations of violence, deception, deceit, fraud, and other nefarious implications." (pp. 98-99) For that, Westphall blames Democrats and fate:

> Thomas Benton Catron was present when the Republican party in New Mexico was organized in the winter of 1867 and when the epithet "Santa Fe Ring" was applied to its leaders. It was Catron's fate to become the acknowledged head of both party and ring ... (p. 97) While Catron was often assailed as leader of the Ring, he held that position by virtue of ability as a common spokesman for others interested in common goals. (p. 201)

But Westphall reveals public awareness, quoting October 27, 1880's Las Cruces *Thirty-Four Newspaper's* urging voters who desire "an honest administration of public affairs in this Territory [to] assist to overthrow the Santa Fe Ring by depositing his ballot against its [Catron-backed] candidate [Tranquilino Luna for Delegate to Congress]." It stated:

> The Santa Fe Ring is the most corrupt combination that ever cursed any country or community. It has controlled the machinery of the Republican party in the Territory for the past twelve years. It has vilified, oppressed or otherwise sought to ruin every man who had the independence and hardihood to oppose its corrupt schemes. It has grown fat upon the prostitution of the party it controls. It has used its power in the courts to defend its criminal tools from merited punishment. It has retained its power by wholesale bribery and intimidation of voters. It has threatened innocent men with prosecution in the courts, should they dare to oppose it. It has promised indicted criminals immunity from punishment if they would assist it to retain its power. The people of this county and every county will be benefitted by its overthrow. (p. 186)

Luna won as Delegate. Westphall calls voting for him "three or four times," a "zeal for his candidacy" (p. 188), rather than election fraud. But Luna's opponent, Miguel Otero, wrote: "[Luna] was well groomed by the 'Santa Fe Ring,' the real machine controlling the political situation in New Mexico." (p. 188)

In the 1880's, with the Ring securely in power, newspapers futilely reported controlled juries, fraudulent votes, and bribed legislators. (p. 192) The March 4, 1884's *Albuquerque Daily Democrat* declared:

> The Ring must soon discover that the time has passed in New Mexico when men can be herded like so many sheep and be made to move at the wave of the hand in violation of law, and every precedent known to the laws governing free people. (p. 191)

That 1884, Reverend Oscar P. McMains (unidentified by Westphall as the Colfax County War's anti-Ring successor to Ring-murdered Franklin Tolby), introduced a later defeated, legislative memorial censuring Catron and Elkins for their land grant thefts. The March 15, 1884 *Albuquerque Daily Democrat* reported:

> [McMains's] reference to Tom Catron and the territorial courts, which aided and abetted the land steals that have been going on the last twenty years, was received with deafening applause and showed ... that the house is becoming deeply interested in putting a stop to the disgraceful and dishonest work of the ring. (p. 193)

Also in 1884, when anti-Ring Edmund G. Ross was appointed Governor by President Grover Cleveland, "he learned that important people within his own party were tainted with what he considered the stigma of Ring association." (p. 199) The bar association of 1886 then blocked Ross by its approval power over the legislature's bills; which Westphall admits "meant that the bar association - which was essentially the Santa Fe Ring - effectively controlled the legislature ... Ross learned that economic factors frequently outweighed political implications in the thinking of Ring members." (p. 201) Westphall concedes:

> This dual [party] relationship more than anything else explains the enigma of the Santa Fe Ring. It was groupings in constant flux of persons whose common interests brought them together for mutual action on specific problems that arose from time to time. Thoroughly democratic in its way, it was a devilish thing to fight for those who wanted to lash out at something they could get hold of. (p. 202)

Ring accusations against Catron continued into the 20th century as shown by December 11, 1911 letter of a Bronson Cutting to a James Roger Addison:

> Catron was the boss of the Territory from 1865 [sic - 1866] to 1900 and is probably still the most

unscrupulous man in the Southwest. His methods of wholesale assassination and blackmail are [notorious]. [H]e still runs the gang in this country. (p. 98)

Westphall uses the Ring's cover-up that it was not a formal organization: "There was no network of control in an organized sense; there was mutual cooperation ... for particular events or projects" (p. 99); and it was a "nebulous entity." (p. 199) Such evaded culpability was satirized by cartoonist, Thomas Nast, who drew "Boss" Tweed's Tammany Hall Ring as a circle of men, each pointing to the other, saying, " 'Twas Him." Westphall ignores that by 1970, that form of organized crime by colluding members was defined for prosecution as racketeering.

EARLY YEARS

Thomas Benton Catron, born on October 6, 1840, was 26 at the 1866 start of his Santa Fe Ring. He was fourth of nine children in a Lexington, Missouri, farm family with German original surname "Kettenring" - not Hispanic "Catrón," still heard in New Mexico. His "Thomas Benton" honored Missouri Senator Thomas Hart Benton, coiner of racist "manifest destiny." In 1857, at Lexington's Masonic College, he met Stephen Benton Elkins, a year younger. In 1859, they roomed together at the University of Missouri. In the Civil War, Catron, then a Democrat, was a Confederate Second Lieutenant in the Missouri State Guard. Ironically, he arrived near Pittsburgh Landing on April 11, 1862, five days after Union-side Major General Lew Wallace had his personal debacle there at the Battle of Shiloh. Catron served till May 10, 1865.

In 1863, Elkins set their direction after his brief Civil War Union service, when he settled in New Mexico Territory that November. In 1864, he was admitted to the law bar, set up his practice in Doña Ana County's Mesilla, and was elected to the Territorial legislature's House of Representatives; moving in 1865 to its Santa Fe location.

In 1866, Elkins convinced Catron, who had studied law for the past year, to practice in New Mexico Territory. Elkins joined him in his cross-country trip as both schemed. Westphall states: "Oral tradition indicates that on their journey Catron and Elkins mutually resolved to seek a seat in the United States Senate [and to create] economic empires." (pp. 21, 25) Elkins also encouraged Catron to learn Spanish, like himself. (p. 22) That implied the fully-formed scheme of land grab from Hispanic land grant owners while acting as attorneys for their title approvals.

Catron arrived in Santa Fe on July 27, 1866. In 12 years his Ring would achieve complete Territorial control. In Santa Fe, as a legal assistant and scrivener, he opportunistically switched parties, making as a friend Attorney William Breeden, the Territory's Republican party founder. With Breeden's backing, five months after arriving, in December of 1866, with Governor Robert B. Mitchell touring till 1867, Catron was appointed District Attorney for the 3rd Judicial District by Acting Governor W.F.M. Arney. Arney also appointed Elkins as Attorney General. Catron's appointment was protested by the Territorial legislature's Council; but returned Governor Mitchell merely upheld Catron's appointment; and, furthermore, promoted Elkins to Territorial U.S. Attorney. (p. 28) Catron began law practice in Mesilla, and was admitted to the bar on June 15, 1867. So by 1867, the year after Catron arrived, the infant Ring thrived.

In late 1868, Catron was elected to the Territorial House of Representatives. In 1869, Governor Robert Mitchell, on Elkins's recommendation, appointed Catron Attorney General, as well as District Attorney for the 1st Judicial District. So Catron moved his law practice to Santa Fe. As Attorney General, Catron was Territorial prosecuting attorney in counties of Santa Fe, San Miguel, Santa Aña, Mora, Taos, Rio Arriba, and Colfax; and advised legislators and the Governor. And as District Attorney of the 1st Judicial District, Catron was Chief Justice of the Supreme Court. As U.S. Attorney, Elkins was chief federal prosecutor. So potential malicious prosecution of opponents was in place.

In 1870, William A. Pile, the first clearly Ring-beholden Governor, took office. He retained Catron as Attorney General on recommendations of Elkins and Ring-loyalist Chief Justice Joseph G. Palen. In Governor Pile's scandal-filled administration, he and Catron were accused of destroying archives and conspiring to split state offices with Democrats. (pp. 31-32)

In March of 1872, President Ulysses S. Grant promoted Catron from Attorney General to Territorial U.S. Attorney. Catron held that office until his forced resignation in 1878.

In 1873, President Grant appointed another Ringite Governor, Marsh Giddings. That year, Elkins was elected Delegate to Congress, extending Ring influence to Washington, D.C. His election was accused of bribery and vote-fixing by Catron:

Following the 1873 election, charges were also leveled at Catron. It was alleged that many persons in San Miguel and Mora Counties were arrested and accused [indicted by Catron] of illegal trading with Comanche Indians and were placed under bond and forced to appear for trial in Santa Fe. Upon payment of fees to United States Attorney Catron, and agreement on their part to vote for Elkins, they were released. Again, it was claimed that 600 suits were brought by Catron against persons living in Taos County for living on Indian lands. All but two of the suits were dismissed. It was charged that the suits were brought for the twofold purpose of getting fees for the prosecution and whipping in votes for Elkins. (pp. 113-114; 132)

In 1875, Elkins was again elected Territorial Delegate to Congress, again with claims of fraudulent vote counts (p. 113); and with Colfax County citizens' accusations of the Ring's assassination of their anti-Ring leader, Reverend Franklin Tolby.

That year, Governor Marsh Giddings died in office, and President Ulysses S. Grant appointed Utah Territory Governor Samuel Beach Axtell. Axtell became a major Ring agent, and a crucial figure in the Lincoln County War history of Billy Bonney and the Regulator movement.

EARLY ENTREPRENEURIAL ENDEAVORS

On arrival in 1866, Catron began his quest for wealth. "While [Catron and Elkins] enjoyed politics, the political career of each was motivated ... by the part that politics could play in developing their respective economic empires." (p. 25) That translated into "friends" profiting by cash or kind.

LAND GRANTS

By early 1869, Catron and Elkins "turned their attention to acquiring large amounts of land in New Mexico by dealing in land grants." (p. 34) Catron ultimately owned "at least thirty four [land grants, as well as] property in Mexico, California, Oregon, Colorado, Arizona, Kansas and Missouri;" though it may have been more, since his records were "fragmentary." (pp. 71-72)

This "empire building ... witnessed Catron's ultimate ownership of nearly as much land as the states of Delaware and Rhode Island combined;" (p. 33) making him "the largest individual landowner in the history of the United States" (p. ix), with up to six million acres.

Westphall, omitting Catron, confines grant frauds to nameless "speculators":

> [Speculators] coveted the large grants made by former Spanish and Mexican governments. New arrivals saw an opportunity for rapid gains, and life in the Territory became centered around traffic in these grants. (p. 35)

Westphall also blames, as "Yankee newcomers," attorneys exaggerating complexity of confirming title, then taking land in payment from grant holders (pp. 35-36) - the Ring's own ploy.

As to Catron, Westphall states: "[He] has been accused of immoral, if not illegal, practices in connection with land grants he acquired" (p. 41). Westphall denies proof; omitting Catron's expurgations and an 1888 office fire. "Another claim is that Catron took advantage of the ignorance of grantees in negotiating purchases and paid only a fraction of what land was worth." (p. 42) Westphall rationalizes that land was cheap, for example: "[I]n 1871, Jesus Lujan sold the Eaton grant of 81,032.67 acres to Nicholas Pino for eighteen dollars cash." (p. 42) In fact, that merely demonstrates how the land grant scam worked.

Catron himself revealed his land speculation scheme in a July 30, 1896 letter to a Don Matais Contreras, stating that he rarely purchased grant land outright, but received a percentage of the land in lieu of his cash fee as a grant holder's attorney. And Westphall reveals that Catron kept his shares in the Mora Grant under Elkins's name (p. 40); gave a fifth of the shares to Surveyor General T. Rush Spencer in return for trying to sell the grant; got the grant holders to deed the land to him in exchange for his doing the partitioning; and, in 1909, gave the grant to his son. (pp. 40-45) Westphall also describes how, in 1885, Catron's Tierra Amarilla Grant, surveyed by Catron's business partner, Surveyor General Henry M. Atkinson, was found to have exaggerated extent (p. 51); and later admits Atkinson's "outright malfeasance in office." (p. 151)

Omitted in Westphall's fraud discussion is the 1870 grant sale that arguably fueled the new Ring: the Maxwell Land Grant: acquired by Catron and Elkins by cheating its owner, Lucien Maxwell; then immediately reselling it to speculators for double the money. And omitted is their 1876, fraudulent, 500,000 acre Uña de Gato Grant sale to an Arkansas Senator, Stephen Wallace Dorsey, transacted by Ringite Governor Samuel Beach Axtell.

Furthermore, concealed by Westphall is that the cause of the Colfax County War was brutal evicting of the Maxwell Land Grant's settlers by Elkins with Catron by malicious prosecutions and troops. Instead, Westphall fabricates Catron's benevolence:

> [Catron] was also accused of driving people from their homes who had settled on land he had acquired ... In fact, there are numerous instances in which he arranged for squatters ... to retain the land on which they lived. (p. 71)

RAILROADS, MINING, BANKING, MONEY-LENDING, AND RANCHING

Catron had railroad connections; serving as attorney for the Atchison, Topeka, and Santa Fe railroad through the Maxwell Land Grant; as well as for the Southern Pacific; El Paso and South Western; and Denver and Rio Grande Railroads.

Catron's mining investments involved "friends" as partners; including Elkins, Lehman Spiegelberg (Santa Fe mercantile supplier to "the House"), Charles B. Thayer, and William A. Pile (the Governor, who in 1870 made Catron Attorney General). Omitted by Westphall is that the Aztec gold mine - merely listed among Catron's mines (p. 66) - was kept by Catron from the Maxwell Land Grant' sale, and was the world's largest.

Westphall states: "Another facet of Catron's varied career in New Mexico was that of a banker. He participated in the sale of the First National Bank in Santa Fe from Lucien B. Maxwell." (p. 67) Omitted is that the First National Bank of Santa Fe was founded by Catron's and Elkins's tricking of Maxwell to invest from his $650,000 land grant sale to become its president. They then founded the competing National Bank of New Mexico to force Maxwell out, taking control themselves with Elkins as president. Catron remained a major First National Bank of Santa Fe stockholder from 1871 to his 1907 stock sale to his son, Charles.

Westphall admits that Catron's extensive money-lending yielded "tradition that he habitually placed persons politically in his debt by loaning them money and making no effort to collect." (p. 267) Catron began money-lending at his 1866 arrival; and it led to regional Ring infiltrations. Given cattle as collateral, Catron first sold them as beef to Fort Bayard, near Grant County's Silver City. (p. 33) By 1868, receipts show Catron was in a relationship with Lincoln County sutler's store partner, Lawrence Murphy (p. 74), who held the Fort Stanton beef contract; later becoming one of Catron's agents for his Lincoln County mercantile monopoly: "the House." Loans functioned as bribes, as with new Governor, Samuel Beach Axtell, getting a $1,800 loan in 1876, and becoming a major Ring agent. Catron's loans yielded services. One recipient was Pat Garrett, Billy's killer. (p. 388) And Ralph Emerson Twitchell's 1901 loan involved Catron's covering money that Twitchell had embezzled as District Attorney. (p. 390) Omitted is that Twitchell's loan resembled Catron's 1878 cover-up "loan" to Sheriff William Brady, who had used Lincoln County tax money to pay for Ring cattle - which Catron reimbursed after John Tunstall exposed that crime. Omitted also is that when Twitchell wrote his 1912, two volume, *The Leading Facts of New Mexico History*, he denied Santa Fe Ring existence.

Catron's cattle ranching included the early 1870's Pecos River cow camp, fronted by "the House" in Lincoln; and the Carrizozo Land and Cattle Company ranch from 1878 to 1882, run by Catron's brother-in-law, Edgar Walz. Omitted by Westphall is that the latter ranch was a motive for assassinating competitor, John Tunstall, and involved supplying beef to Fort Stanton and the Mescalero Indian Reservation. In 1878, Catron was also supplying beef to a William Rosenthal for a San Carlos Indian Reservation beef contract. (p. 132) For his 1882 incorporated Boston and New Mexico Cattle Company, Catron partnered with Ring "friend" and land grant acreage inflator, Surveyor General Henry M. Atkinson. Catron's 1885 Tularosa Land and Cattle Company rewarded with partnership his murderous Lincoln County War period "friends": past "House" partner John H. Riley and past District Attorney William L. Rynerson. It controlled water rights, and charged their rental, along vast lands on both sides of the Tularosa River, and from the Mescalero Indian Reservation to 10 miles west of the town of Tularosa. (p. 69) Omitted by Westphall is that, in 1880, Catron eliminated future competition for that Tularosa Cattle Company by attacking rancher, Pat Coghlan, in Tularosa valley's Three Rivers, by accusing him to the Secret Service of being a member of the fabricated Billy the Kid gang. In 1886, Catron started the American Valley Company cattle ranch, also with Henry Atkinson, which involved murder of its two original land owners; with Catron suspected but not prosecuted. (pp. 163, 324-325)

INITIAL ANTI-RING UPRISINGS

Westphall hides escalating pre-Lincoln County War anti-Ring uprisings by omitting cause; by non-chronological placement after the later 1878 Lincoln County War; by leaving out the 1876 Grant County Rebellion; and by excluding these revolts' exposés of Catron, Elkins, Axtell, Bristol, and the Santa Fe Ring. Westphall thereby conceals the Ring's opposed Territorial take-overs.

But below are summarized these rebellions with Westphall's inadvertent reveals.

THE LEGISLATURE REVOLT: 1872

The first overt anti-Ring rebellion began in December of 1871 in the legislature in Santa Fe, in what Westphall obscures as "an event [in] a struggle for political power, involving Catron and his bid to be named United States attorney." (p. 103) He reduces the revolt to one bill on December 30, 1871, which transferred Ringite Judge Joseph Palen to the 3rd Judicial District, from the 1st in Santa Fe; where Palen was accused of issuing biased decisions for Catron and Elkins in exchange for "sharing plunder." (p. 105)

In fact, there were multiple anti-Ring bills passed in that legislative session. So in January of 1872, Ringite Governor Marsh Giddings vetoed them all. An anti-Ring revolt of legislators resulted in take-over of the House of Representatives from its Ringite Speaker, Milnor Rudulph (the 1881 President of Billy's Coroner's Jury praising Pat Garrett for the killing), in what Westphall calls "lawless and revolutionary maneuvers [of the] legislative mob." (pp. 104-105) Rudulph and two other legislators were arrested, giving Catron, as Attorney General, the chance to involve the Supreme Court by filing the men's writs of *habeas corpus* to demand swift trial. Governor Giddings then brought into the legislative hall Santa Fe County's Sheriff and troops. Then the Supreme Court decided - as intended by Catron - not just to grant *habeas corpus*, but to void all anti-Ring acts of that session.

And in February of 1872, in failed attempt to oppose Catron's appointment by President Ulysses S. Grant as U.S. Attorney, an August Kirchner sent his affidavit to Chairman of the Judiciary Committee, Senator Lyman Trumball, stating that Catron and Elkins had bribed him to buy legislators' votes to shield Judge Joseph Palen. But Governor Giddings countered by telegramming Attorney General George H. Williams in Washington, D.C. to call Kirchner's affidavit "grossly false." (p. 107)

Within a month of becoming U.S. Attorney, Catron indicted the legislators of the anti-Palen bill (p. 108), beginning the malicious prosecutions for which he used his office as a weapon against opponents till his forced resignation in 1878.

The Legislature revolt was remembered. Westphall cites an article in the *Las Vegas Independent Democrat* - written in 1895 during an attempt to disbar Catron - and citing a September 2, 1884 *Las Vegas Optic* article. It stated that "'Catron was called a corrupt partner of a venal judge [Palen]," which Westphall says Catron denied. (p. 105) The article stated:

> T.B. Catron's reputation now being "smirched" by evidence that he was a briber and too dishonest even to practice law in New Mexico, was made more than twenty-five years ago, and in 1872 it was so bad that United States troops were called in at Santa Fe to prevent the outraged people of the town from hanging him. At that time ... the Santa Fe Ring was in its prime. Thomas B. Catron was Attorney General, James [sic -Joseph] Palen was United States Judge [Chief Justice], and Steve Elkins was general manager of the deviltry.
>
> [Westphall continues with admitted paraphrasing.]
>
> This corrupt combination exasperated the people, who presented petitions for Palen's removal. These petitions were headed off by Elkins, so the legislature passed a bill assigning Palen to another district. The Ring's governor [Marsh Giddings] vetoed the bill, so a popular movement was organized to pass it over the veto. Catron and Elkins bought off a number of legislators including August Kirchner. Elkins promised him a favorable decision in a certain suit should Palen not be removed. [A sworn affidavit of February 1, 1872 sent by Kirchner to U.S.

Senator Lyman Trumbull stated that Catron and Elkins tried to get him to buy legislators' votes.] Elkins also promised to cancel a $780 mortgage on the property of Pascual Baca for his vote. At the hour of the gathering of the assembly the town was wild with excitement, so the sheriff called upon General Gorden Granger for troops to prevent the people from assassinating Catron, Elkins, Palen, and Breeden on the spot. Elkins was afraid to let the matter come to a vote, so instructed his tool, Speaker Milnor Rudulph, to adjourn the House before a quorum was present. Rudulph did so, then wandered off outside the town threatening to kill whoever pursued him. The sheriff swore in old Jesus Baca ... as deputy, and instructed him to bring Ruculph back. He found the speaker and ... led him back to the legislative chamber. (p. 106)

To excuse Catron, Westphall cites Governor Giddings's 1872 cover-up telegram to Attorney General Williams, stating that Catron was backed "by the better classes of citizens,' and the Territory saved from "anarchy [when] a minority had attempted to take over the legislature." (p. 108) In fact, the suppressed revolt marked Catron's expanding of individual malicious prosecutions to his outlaw myth for legal or physical destruction all opponents. That ploy would impact the lost pardon of Billy the Kid.

THE COLFAX COUNTY WAR: 1877

Westphall obscures the 1877 Colfax County War, stemming from the Ring's 1870 sale of the Maxwell Land Grant, by omitting its existence, presenting only riots of its settlers opposing eviction, placing it non-chronologically after the 1878 Lincoln County War which it heralded by Ring outrages, and labeling it meaninglessly in a garbled chapter called "Partisan Repercussions."

As to the Grant, Lucien Maxwell's receiving only $650,000 in the sale by Catron and Elkins is omitted; though implied is that Maxwell was given a minimized acreage tally of 97,000 from a December of 1869 Secretary of the Interior ruling (p. 100), likely to trick him into a smaller sale price. In fact, the resale price was $1,350,000, paid the same year by speculators: Colorado Senator, Gerome Bunty Chaffee, a Colorado mine owner; Colorado congressman, George Chilcott; Cimarron lawyer and mine investor, Charles Holly; and entrepreneur, Wilson Waddingham; with Elkins as lawyer. (p. 100) Waddingham became Catron's friend and business associate. (pp. 60, 136) That syndicate resurveyed in January of 1870 to yield about 2 million acres. This was unsurprisingly approved by "friend" and Surveyor General T. Rush Spencer, a member of their company. (p. 100)

The Chaffe syndicate then negotiated the grant's sale to British investors, headed by a John Collinson, who, as foreigners, could not own New Mexico Territory land. Catron and Elkins likely enlisted three New Mexicans to front them for filing as the Maxwell Land Grant and Railway Company: Ringite Governor William Pile; Territorial Surveyor General T. Rush Spencer - syndicate member and approver of the inflated survey - and past Territorial Chief Justice John S. Watts. (p. 101)

That year Governor Pile also reappointed Catron as Attorney General, and engaged with him in destroying archives and splitting state offices with Democrats. (pp. 31-31) John Watts resurfaced for filing U.S. Attorney Catron's June 21, 1878 federal indictment Number 411 against Billy Bonney and other Regulators in "Buckshot" Roberts's killing. (As will be seen, that indictment left Catron in control of Regulators' fates to block any Territorial pardons.)

Ownership of the Maxwell Land Grant was assumed by the British Collinson syndicate in April of 1870, with intent to subdivide it for sale to new settlers. Elkins had been made President of their Board of Directors. And William R. Morley, a railroad engineer, was Vice-President and Executive Officer. Other Directors were H.M. Porter, J.B. Maingay, Probate Judge Melvin W. Mills, and Dr. R.H. Longwill. (Longwill and Mills later became Catron's and Elkins's accomplices to Ring assassination in Colfax County of anti-Ring Reverend Franklin Tolby.)

Because settlers on the grant, since Lucien Maxwell's day, believed they owned their land, Elkins and Catron sought to eliminate them; first by Elkins's evictions as syndicate attorney. Catron could also prosecute them as both as Territorial Attorney General (p. 102) and as District Attorney of the 1st Judicial District, including Colfax County. And by October 27, 1870, with defiant settlers rioting in the Grant's Elizabethtown, Elkins had Governor William Pile send in troops for suppression.

On September 17, 1870, Elkins also tried to increase Catron's power by resigning as U.S. Attorney and recommending him. That was blocked by "protesting" (p. 102); though Elkins got him the appointment in March of 1872 with President Grant.

In 1873, Grant settler evictions were again attempted; though Westphall blames resulting uprisings on instigation by Director Raymond Morley and his lawyer friend, Frank Springer. Westphall implies that Elkins's Grant connection ended by his relocating, that year, to Washington, D.C. as Territorial Delegate to Congress; omitting that the Ring's connection was retained, since "Catron was made a director of the company so he could serve as their attorney." (p. 109) Also, Elkins then promoted Grant interests with Congressional bills. (p. 113) Westphall adds disingenuously: "As United States attorney [Catron] had no contact with eviction of settlers which was a district court matter involving the territorial attorney general: William Breeden" (p. 109) - omitting Breeden's Ring tie. And in 1874, Elkins became Catron's law partner (p. 110), continuing till 1895.

By 1874, the mismanaged Maxwell Land Grant and Railway Company was bankrupt; and by 1876 the Grant was auctioned for back taxes. Unsurprisingly, it ended up - with collusion of Director Melvin Mills - directly in Catron's possession for a mere $20,000!

> [T]he property was auctioned on December 16 [1876] to Melvin W. Mills for $16,479.46. The money for purchase of the tax deed was raised by a Santa Fe group headed by Catron. On July 19, 1877, Mills deeded the property to Catron for $20,000 ... There seems little doubt ... that this was a maneuver by Catron to acquire the property for himself and his group. (p. 110)

But the stockholders redeemed the Grant (p. 110), presumably paying Catron. By then, Morley and Springer opposed as Ringites Catron, Elkins, and Directors Longwill, and Mills. That resulted in Catron's failed "Dear Ben plot" of 1876 to use Ringite Governor Samuel Beach Axtell to assassinate them; which Westphall rationalizes as misunderstanding of Axtell's intent. (p. 127)

In March 3, 1877, Ringite Surveyor General Henry M. Atkinson awarded the Maxwell Land Grant's surveying contract to Elkins's brother, John T. Elkins. In an implausibly brief 21 days, John Elkins reported it as having 1,714,764.94 acres. (p. 111) On June 5, 1878, Catron's law partner, William T. Thornton acted as its receiver when its patent was issued by

Secretary of the Interior Carl Schurz (who also participated that year in covering up the Ring's involvement in Tunstall's assassination in the Angel reports). Catron remained as the Maxwell Land Grant Company's lawyer into the 1900's.

Westphall omits the Colfax County War and its Ring exposés, claiming only: "Catron acquired the role of villain in oral tradition surrounding Colfax County troubles." (p. 115) In fact, exposés were printed by Raymond Morley and Frank Springer in their *Cimarron News and Press*; and Mary McPherson wrote to Washington D.C. Westphall calls the articles a "feud [with Catron about] little things." (pp. 114-115) And he attacks McPherson, Catron's most hated adversary there, stating:

> While Catron's contretemps in Colfax County - and they were fundamental to his public career - started in disagreements with Morley and Springer, their culmination can be attributed to one person more than any other: Mary E. McPherson, mother-in-law of William R. Morley, and mother of Morley's wife, Ada. (p. 116)

To terrorize McPherson and Morley into silence or relocation, Catron, in 1875, attacked Morley's wife, Ada (McPherson's daughter), by malicious prosecution after Ada fearfully removed one of her mother's Ring exposé letters from Cimarron's post office's box. The Ringite Postmaster, John B. McCullich, reported it to Catron, who, as U.S. Attorney federally indicted Ada and issued her arrest warrant for mail theft. Westphall claims by 1876 "Catron dropped the case." (pp. 117) But it was never dropped, as her family attested to, along with the concomitant fear that caused her husband to flee the Territory with her and their children.

Also omitted by Westphall, is Catron's more dramatic 1875 crime: accomplice to murder. His Ringite Maxwell Land Grant Company Directors, Longwill and Mills, using local thugs, assassinated Colfax County's vocal anti-Ring, anti-Grant, pro-settler, article writing, Reverend Franklin Tolby. Then, to shield those murderers from prosecution, Governor S.B. Axtell removed Colfax County courts, transferring all cases to distant Taos County for hearing. Also omitted is that the next year, 1876, Axtell did the "Dear Ben plot" in attempted assassination of Morley and Springer with legal guise of their "resisting arrest."

Ring lethality did not faze Mary McPherson. In 1877, she mailed voluminous exposés of the Santa Fe Ring, Catron, Elkins, and other Ringites, to President Rutherford B. Hayes and Secretary of the Interior Carl Schurz. But Westphall scoffs at her complaints:

> [McPherson] lamented that [Catron] used his official position to oppress the innocent instead of punishing the guilty; that he shook indictments over the heads of the people until they promised to vote for Elkins; that court was adjourned while he pursued this method of electioneering; and that one could avoid indictment by feeing Catron ... She then implied that Catron was, in some way, responsible for ... the punitive removal of courts from Colfax County to Taos County; the assassination of Rev. Thomas [sic – Franklin] J. Tolby; the freeing from jail of all those supposed to be implicated in the murder; the indictment of those searching out the assassins; and the leaguing together of all U.S. officials to oppress the people. (p. 118)

Westphall trivializes McPherson's complaining as pique about Catron's arguing with her daughter about use of the Maxwell Land Grant Company's buggy! And he misrepresents her complaints as a single 1877 letter to Attorney General Alphonso Taft. (See my pp. 184-186 for full letter) Westphall then states that Catron denied all the complaints, and blamed trouble-making "mobs." (pp. 119-120) In fact, Catron used his outlaw myth to vilify as "mobs" citizens attempting to arrest Tolby's murders, and to justify removal of Colfax County courts to Taos County. (See my pp. 187-190 for full letter)

Westphall conceals that the Ring's Colfax County crimes were replicated the next year, in 1878, by Tunstall's assassination, by blocking arrest of his murderers, and by outlawing arresting deputies as outlaws (including Billy Bonney). And he conceals the big picture: "To do all these things would have required more official power on the part of Catron than he possibly could have possessed." (p. 118) In truth, the Santa Fe Ring, in control by 1877, did have this horrific power.

CATRON'S LINCOLN COUNTY INVOLVEMENT

Victor Westphall omits that the Lincoln County War period marked the burgeoning Santa Fe Ring's most uninhibited atrocities of murder, massacre, and military treason; while risking exposure by assassinating a British citizen, John Tunstall, and facing defeat by mass uprising in that War's final battle. And that battle's antecedent "Regulator Manifesto" and consequent Dudley Court of Inquiry, and Frank Warner Angel investigations almost undid cover-ups. Westphall's response is garbling and minimizing:

> It has been an historical supposition that the Lincoln County troubles were abetted by the Republican Santa Fe Ring through persecution of McSween and his adherents, and for championing the Murphy-Dolan cause ... yet McSween was evidently a Republican while Murphy was certainly a Democrat ... Economic considerations seem to have been the determining factor in the factional alignments. (p. 78)

But Westphall inadvertently incriminates by giving Catron's economic links, which gave his monopolistic motive to eliminate Tunstall for mercantile and ranching goals. As discussed, Catron early on had military beef contracts. Westphall dates Catron's Lincoln County involvement to at least 1868 by receipts he had signed by Lawrence Murphy for merchandise from C. Brown & Co. of Santa Fe (p. 74), where Catron had just relocated; and which survived Catron's 1888 expurgating office fire. That implied Catron's Fort Stanton beef supplying via Emil Fritz and Lawrence Murphy, then at its sutler's store as L.G. Murphy and Company. At the Fort were other future Ringites: store employee and future partner, James Dolan, and then-Captain and future Lincoln County Sheriff, William Brady.

Catron's part is also likely in "the House's" 1873 founding, when Murphy and Dolan were expelled from the Fort after Dolan shot a soldier; Fritz then being in Germany, where he died in 1874. These mere shop owners then implausibly built the county's largest adobe structure as their two-story general store and post office in Lincoln, nick-named "the House;" making Catron a likely silent partner for its funding. And the enriched builder was future Ringite Lincoln County War Sheriff, George Peppin.

Westphall cites Catron's loans to "the House" as of November of 1876: "Catron loaned money to the Murphy firm and to Lawrence G. Murphy personally." (p. 79) That year, John Riley became Dolan's partner and "cattle dealer" in "the House" - then called J.J. Dolan Co. (p. 76) Riley later became Catron's ranching partner in his Tularosa Land and Cattle Company. And Westphall reveals Catron as "the House's" silent partner at Dolan's Pecos River Cow Camp (p. 87), holding John Chisum's rustled cattle.

By 1877 and 1878, Alexander McSween and John Tunstall were impacting Catron by exposing "the House's" illegalities in military and Mescalero Indian Reservation contracts by selling rustled cattle and mealy flour. In 1878, McSween's complaint caused Department of Interior Investigator E.C. Watkins's investigation, which concluded that Indian Agent Frederick Godfroy gave Mescalero Reservation supplies, like blankets, to "the House;" and cattle came from Mesilla rustler John Kinney. And Agent Godfroy billed the government for rations for 1,500 hundred Apaches, with only a few hundred resident. Crucially, Westphall reveals that Indian Agent Frederick Godfroy was Catron's agent.

That Godfroy connection to Catron was through Blazer's Mill-based Justice of the Peace, David Easton, "Catron's agent, representing him in business interests in the area;" according to a complaint cited by Fort Stanton's Commander, N.A.M. Dudley, about Catron's and Easton's inferior supplies to Fort Stanton. (p. 94) That proves Dudley knew Catron was behind "the House's" Fort Stanton supply contract - via David Easton as his agent in Blazer's Mill, within the Mescalero Indian Reservation perimeter.

David Easton was also agent for another of Catron's Lincoln County "business interests": "a brewery located at Fort Stanton." (p. 94) That "the House's" founders began that brewery when at their sutler's store, shows Catron's early connection. Intriguingly, the sutler partners also ran a counterfeiting press in a nearby cave; making counterfeiting another possible Catron business, and a possible inspiration for accusing Billy to the Secret Service in 1880 as the Territory's main counterfeiter!

And Easton being Catron's agent, explains Easton's Ringite motive, when, as a Justice of the Peace, he wrote false warrants outlawing McSweens to be used for Catron's malicious prosecutions in the Lincoln County War. His warrants followed an April 29, 1878 skirmish in which Seven Rivers Ring-rustlers murder-ambushed new Regulator leader Frank MacNab (replacing "Buckshot Roberts's murder victim, Dick Brewer). The next day, April 30th, Seven Rivers rustlers entered Lincoln to kill Alexander McSween and the Regulators; but, in the ensuing gunfight, some of them were killed. McSween obtained murder warrants against MacNab's killers from San Patricio Justice of the Peace Gregorio Trujillo for service by Sheriff John Copeland. But on May 30th, Easton wrote his warrants using affidavits by Ringites James Dolan, George Peppin, and Jacob Basil "Billy" Matthews naming McSween, William Bonney alias Kid, and others unknown, with murder and assault with the intent to kill the four dead and one injured Seven Rivers men. But Easton then quit, fearing reprisals. That undid Catron's intended malicious prosecution, since it voided Easton's warrants. That is why Commander Dudley, 80 days later, on July 19th, after marching with his infantry and cavalry on Lincoln, and learning that there were no valid warrants against McSweens to feign a reason for his backing Sheriff George Peppin, had to force Justice of the Peace "Squire" Wilson into writing warrants against McSween and Regulators for alleged shooting at Dudley's fact-finder, 9th Cavalryman, Private Berry Robinson on July 16th.

Westphall tops off Catron's Lincoln County interests by stating that, besides David Easton, Catron's brother-in-law, Edgar Walz, was his agent there. Walz ran Catron's 12,800 acre Carrizozo Land and Cattle Company ranch, which, Westphall relates, was gotten from dying Lawrence Murphy to settle his debt to Catron. "When Murphy died, Catron took possession of the ranch." (p. 81) This implies Catron's massive money-lending to "the House," since the ranch was 20 square miles. And Westphall also states that the Pecos River Cow Camp, fronted by "the House," also held Catron's cattle. (p. 87)

By 1878, Catron finally emerged from his shadowy relationship with "the House," then facing bankrupting from Tunstall's competition. Westphall states:

"On January 12, 1878, James J. Dolan and John H. Riley executed a mortgage deed conveying to Catron forty acres of land in Lincoln together with their house, store [collectively "the House"], and all personal property, including a herd of about 2,000 cattle at Seven Rivers. The loan from Catron had been needed to pay Spiegelberg brothers [supplier merchants] in Santa Fe." (p. 81)

That transaction was done in Lincoln by Catron's law partner, William T. Thornton. (p. 82) Catron then put his brother-in-law, Edgar Walz in charge of "the House." (p. 81) So when Tunstall was assassinated on February 18, 1878, "the House" was Catron's. And it was Catron who sold it to Lincoln County in January of 1881. (It became the courthouse-jail for Billy awaiting hanging.)

Westphall adds that when Commander Dudley filed his complaint about Catron's inferior supplies to Fort Stanton, Dudley was considered "obnoxious to certain prominent parties connected with the Santa Fe Ring, among them a swarm of sore-headed contractors." (p. 94-95) So revealed is a veritable Ringite mercantile "swarm" supplying Lincoln County!

To protect his Lincoln County interests, Catron needed a Ring-beholden Territorial Governor. Westphall cites Governor S.B. Axtell's May of 1878 loan of $1,8000 as from John Riley (p. 78); omitting that as a "House" partner Riley was Catron's agent, and that the favor yielded Axtell's illegal proclamations shielding Tunstall's Ringite murderers from prosecution

But Westphall, having inadvertently given Catron's Lincoln County holdings, agents, and motives, concludes unconvincingly:

> If one examines the record of [Catron's] affairs in that time and place objectively, it can be seen that he does not fit well the role of conniving manipulator that tradition has assessed to him. Furthermore, there is little reasonable basis for claiming in the pages of history that he supported partisan intervention in the quarrel. He owned property there and wanted it protected. (p. 96)

LINCOLN COUNTY WAR

The 1878 Lincoln County War represented Catron's and his Ring's greatest risk of exposure and defeat. From the 1875 assassination of Lincoln County's Ring-opponent rancher, Robert Casey, Catron had been solidifying his Ring investments with "the House's" mercantile monopoly. Catron's success depended on eliminating John Tunstall - followed by Alexander McSween and the Regulators - since Tunstall was a major competitor with ready money, a general store, and two cattle ranches controlling thousands of acres of water rights along the Feliz and Peñasco Rivers - consequently controlling grazing land to the Pecos River.

But Ring-denying Westphall parrots Ring cover-up of the Lincoln County War as local mercantile conflict, and adds his spin of competition between Democrats and Republicans:

> It has been an historical supposition that the Lincoln County troubles were abetted by the Republican Santa Fe Ring through persecution of McSween and his adherents, and for championing the Murphy-Dolan cause ... yet McSween was evidently a Republican while Murphy was certainly a Democrat ... Economic considerations seem to have been the determining factor in the factional alignments." (p. 78)

In truth, Catron had to end Tunstall's competition to ensure Ring survival. The key problem for Ring expansion in 1877, when Tunstall established his store, bank, and ranches, was that the Territory was cash poor. The original Elkins-Catron scheme defrauded grant holders of vast amounts of land. But land's value was in use. Catron chose cattle and railroad routes. But his tenuous grip was shown; since, in just one year, by 1878, Tunstall's business bankrupted "the House." Tunstall was one of the few people in the Territory with comparatively limitless cash through his wealthy British father's investment plan; so he could compete aggressively. And, by chance, his businesses overlapped Catron's. In a fair market, Tunstall would have won. Magnifying risk to the Ring was Attorney Alexander McSween, with anti-Ring fervor of the Colfax County War's Reverend Franklin Tolby, and with aggressive exposés like Mary McPherson's. So Tunstall's and McSween's risk of assassination by Catron was maximal.

There was further reason for Tunstall's and McSween's danger. From 1866 to 1877, the Ring concealed its existence while infiltrating public offices and attacking opponents. By the end of 1877, after Mary McPherson ended that secrecy by Ring exposés to the Hayes administration, and Hayes took no action, Catron was emboldened, and was progressing from eliminating political opponents to eliminating economic competitors. Repeated would be his usual malicious prosecutions, murders, and obstruction of justice; but with new confidence in immunity that yielded terrorist atrocities by his complicit lawmen, attorneys, judges, and soldiers.

But more threats to Ring power arose with 1878's Regulator movement following Tunstall's assassination, with mobilizing of aggrieved Hispanic people, with passage of the Posse Comitatus Act blocking military intervention in civilian disturbances, and with rise of Billy Bonney as boy hero of the anti-Ring freedom fight. Catron and his minions responded with make-or-break crimes: Governor S.B. Axtell issued illegal proclamations to block arrest of Tunstall's murderers, and the military intervened with weapons of war to murder citizens - even women and children.

Westphall's mission was to hide these terrible truths. So the horrific War and its terminal battle becomes an "imbroglio" - meaning "quarrel" - while Catron's role is hidden by calling it "shrouded with mystery" (p. 74); and claiming a spurious alibi that "at no time was he personally in the region" (p. 78) - ignoring Catron's Ring boss role and local agents.

Westphall's ploy, besides trivializing the War to local mercantile competition, repeats Catron's own: vilifying of opponents as outlaws. Westphall writes: "Far removed from more settled sections of the Territory, law here became largely what the residents made it." (p. 75)

So Attorney Alexander McSween is maligned as "ambitious and aggressive;" and his 1876 quitting as "the House's" attorney to reject its corruption, is called "conflict with Murphy." (p. 77) McSween is also fabricated as owning Tustall's store and bank:

> But [McSween] was not content merely to practice law ... He started a bank and opened a store to challenge Murphy's trade monopoly. Chisum probably supplied the financial backing for the store. McSween was jealous of Murphy's economic and political power and sought to replace him as a leader in the community. His methods were contentious. (p. 77)

Westphall's outlaw fabrication calls John Chisum - Tunstall's ally and president of his bank - an "outlaw," because Catron, as U.S. Attorney, had prosecuted Chisum since 1875. (p. 77) Omitted is its being malicious prosecution; with Chisum falsely arrested in 1877, with McSween, and imprisoned in the Las Vegas jail.

Westphall fabricates Tunstall as an "outlaw" in dishonest business partnership with McSween. That maligning repeats Catron's plot: using District Judge Warren Bristol and District Attorney William Rynerson to falsely accuse Tunstall of being in partnership with McSween to entangle him with McSween's equally fabricated Fritz life insurance embezzlement case. This plot was intended to harass Tunstall by attaching his property to provoke his violence toward Lincoln lawmen, Sheriff William Brady and his deputies, to justify his killing as self-defense (like Catron's 1876 Colfax County "Dear Ben plot" to assassinate Raymond Morley and Frank Springer.) So Westphall lies:

> [T]unstall had earlier met Alexander A. McSween in Santa Fe, and they now became closely allied in business. Tunstall furnished financial backing that enabled McSween to make more extensive inroads in the financial monopoly that had been enjoyed by L.G. Murphy & Co. Tunstall ... did not scruple at sharp business practices along the way ... [He] was a foreigner who even wrote home about his machinations. (p. 79)

As to the Emil Fritz life insurance policy case, Westphall inadvertently removes Catron's frontmen, Rynerson and Bristol, to reveal him as its prime mover. Though the historical issue was Fritz's heirs seeking payment of the $10,000 insurance policy of Fritz - dead in 1874, and collected, in part, by McSween - Westphall invents instead that the heirs contacted Lawrence Murphy complaining about McSween's high fees to them; and that:

> Murphy retained Catron and William L. Rynerson to recover the money. These attorneys obtained a judgment against McSween ... McSween refused to pay the judgment, and his property was attached. Tunstall's holdings were also attached on the representation that he had an interest in McSween's affairs. (p. 80)

Added to Westphall's Lincoln County "outlaw" list, is "Billy the Kid," fabricated as leader of the "forces." Westphall writes:

> McSween, when the indictment for embezzlement was returned against him, hired gunmen to protect himself from arrest. Among those was Billy the Kid, who became the leader of the McSween forces. (p. 80)

In Westphall's fiction, Lincoln County divided along partisan lines with Chisum joining villain McSween, and good-hearted Murphy-Dolans using "smaller sheep and cattle growers to whom they had been generous in extending credit" (p. 80); omitting that those "growers" were Catron's murderous rustlers.

Westphall addresses a real precipitant of Tunstall's murder: his exposé of tax money abuse in his January 18, 1878 *Mesilla Independent* article, "A Tax-Payer's Complaint;" which stated:

Major Brady ... collected over twenty-five hundred dollars, Territorial funds ... Said cheque was presented for payment by John H. Riley, Esq, of the firm of J.J. Dolan & Co. This last amount was paid by the last named gentleman to Underwood and Nash for cattle.

Westphall supplies James Dolan's cover-up response that illness in Brady's family had prevented his turning over the tax money, while making Catron the major player: "Catron had paid the money on behalf of Brady with proceeds of Indian Department vouchers made out to John H. Riley and forwarded to the First National Bank in Santa Fe for deposit." (p. 82) For someone not 'personally in the region," Catron was hands on!

Westphall also reveals Catron as directly involved in the McSween-Tunstall malicious prosecution by expanding it from District Attorney Rynerson's refusing McSween's bondsmen in his embezzlement case, to Catron's personal intimidation of a bondsman. Westphall's states Lincoln's Jose Montaño 'informed McSween of a threat made by Dolan - that, if Montano became surety for McSween's bond, he would have him persecuted by United States Attorney Catron for cutting timber on public land." (p. 83) Westphall calls prosecution Catron's duty, omitting that Catron's obstruction of McSween's bail posting was intended to leave McSween in Sheriff Brady's murderous hands if incarcerated in Lincoln's pit jail.

Westfall fabricates circumstances of Tunstall's February 18, 1878 murder as Sheriff Brady's sending one deputy, William Morton; omitting that Morton was Catron's Pecos River Cow Camp foreman, omitting that illegal attachment of Tunstall's property caused that posse, and omitting that Brady's posse was huge, consisting of his deputies, and Seven Rivers and Jessie Evans's rustlers. But Westphall admits that Catron was accused:

It was a cowardly murder probably planned by no one in advance, but it gave rise to much speculation, then and since, of a sinister plot involving not only Dolan and Riley, but also Sheriff Brady, United States Attorney Catron, and District Attorney Rynerson. (p. 83)

Westphall then inadvertently clarifies a post-murder incident in which John Riley, fearing retribution, went to McSween's house and accidentally dropped his codebook holding a February 14, 1878 letter from Rynerson to Dolan and Riley planning Tunstall's murder (which Westphall opines was a forgery). The codebook is quoted by Westphall (omitting "Alexander McSween .... 'Diablo.' "):

"T.B. Catron ..... " Grapes;" L.G. Murphy .... " Box;" F. Godfroy [Mescalero Indian Agent] .... "Hampton;" Indians .... "Tree;". W.L. Rynerson ...."Oyster;" First National Bank of Santa Fe .... "Terror;" Second National Bank of Santa Fe .... "Fearful"(p. 84)

Westfall says "codes were used in communications intended to be private ... [and used by Catron] on numerous occasions." (p. 84); but omits that the list was all Ring-related. And the example Westphall gives reveals Catron's transaction with Wilson Waddingham, a Maxwell Land Grant purchaser front-man:

Claudicant Dame Saveloy Frache Fiveate Dollars Drawcansir Gravey and Fowling Drawcansir himself Dame Walloon Gravey Wareful Warily peeress Fowling capitulary Bacchanal Your Niece Acerous.

[Translated as] I have telegraphic communication with Dame in which he says one thousand four hundred dollars is due Gravey and five hundred dollars is due himself Dame will wait as long as possible Gravey in want of money Wants you if possible to pay five hundred dollars cash balance Your note will be accepted. (p. 84)

Westphall also tries to legitimize Ringites' illegal obstruction of the arrest of Tunstall's murderers. He admits that Brady immediately involved Catron as U.S. Attorney, and that Catron used Governor Axtell to request President Hayes's authorizing of troops - Catron's obvious plan to crush remaining Lincoln County opposition. As to Axtell's illegal blocking of Justice of the Peace John Wilson's arrest warrants for Tunstall's murderers and outlawing his legally deputized warrant servers (an illegality that later got Axtell removed as Governor), Westphall lies:

> From a standpoint of establishing jurisdiction, there was some logic in [Axtell's] proclamation of March 9 [1878] that only District Judge Warren H. Bristol and Sheriff Brady had the right to enforce law in Lincoln County. (p. 85)

Westphall then blames Axtell's and Brady's victims for seeking justice; particularly McSween and Billy the Kid:

> The thwarted [by Axtell's outlawing proclamation] McSween adherents now went outside the law as decreed by Governor Axtell, in the guise of "Regulators." Two of the murderers of Tunstall were captured and shot down. On April 1 [1878] Sheriff Brady and a deputy, George Hindman, were shot from ambush ... Billy the Kid led the attack aided, it was charged, by McSween partisans. Open warfare followed. (p. 86)

Westphall then, to obfuscate the July 13, 1878 Regulator Manifesto - the declaration of Ring opposition issued the day before the Lincoln County War battle began - accidently exposes Catron. Westphall ante-dates it three months to a fabricated threat against the Catron-Dolan Pecos River Cow Camp: "That same day [May 1], men in charge of Catron's cattle on the Pecos were warned by Regulators that unless they left the ranch and cattle they would be killed." (p. 87) This references an outlaw myth vilifying Regulators in John Riley's May 19, 1878 letter to Commander Dudley fabricating that they had stolen 2,000 of Catron's Pecos cattle and had murdered a Catron man (p. 87); which Westphall, hiding all Lincoln County War issues, says was "to hamper Riley in fulfilling his contract with Godfroy." (p. 88) But all that confirms Catron as their silent partner. Westphall completes the Catron link by claiming that Catron's "recovered" cattle were brought to his Carrizozo Land and Cattle

Company ranch. (p. 88) And he quotes the whole Manifesto to show threat to Catron's property, but misses that it implicates Catron, Thornton, Kinney, Walz, and Murphys; and proves the anti-Ring thrust of the next day's Lincoln County War battle by stating: "[W]e are all aware that your brother-in-law, T.B. Catron sustains the Murphy Kinney party" ... etc. (p. 91)

Westphall even reveals Catron as authoring that Pecos Cow Camp outlaw myth by quoting his May 30, 1878 letter to Axtell:

> I also learn that all the stockmen on the lower Pecos living near my cattle have been compelled to abandon their stock and go to the mountains where they are awaiting an attack. There seems to be no authority in the county of Lincoln to compel people to keep the peace or obey the law, and there seems to be an utter disregard of all law in the county as well as life and private rights. I would most respectfully request that some steps be taken to disarm all parties carrying arms, and that the military be instructed to see that they all keep the peace.
>
> I am informed that the sheriff [John Copeland] keeps with his deputies large posses armed who are one of the factions only and who take occasion at all time to kill persons and take the property of the other faction whenever they get an opportunity. There is no power from what I can learn that can keep the peace in that county, except the military. (pp. 89-90)

Governor Axtell's next illegal proclamation, on May 28, 1878, which removed Lincoln County Commissioners appointed Sheriff, John Copeland as replacing dead Brady, is reworked by Westphall to fabricate that Copeland - a local rancher - was an "outlaw" in the also fabricated cow camp cattle theft. But Westphall admits that Axtell's replacement for him, George Peppin, was "a Dolan-Riley partisan." (p. 90)

Catron's outlaw myth - to justify exterminating McSween and the Regulators - is presented by Westphall as Sheriff Peppin's having "had no more success in controlling lawlessness than had his predecessor." (p. 90) In truth, the only lawlessness in predecessor Sheriff John Copeland's one month tenure was attacks on McSween and Regulators by Seven Rivers rustlers.

Westphall claims the Ring's use of the Mesilla rustler gang of John Kinney was "legend ... that Catron was responsible for Kinney's participation in Lincoln County troubles." (p. 90). That conceals rustler Kinney as a Ring cattle supplier, and that he was needed as a Ring fighter because locals were anti-Ring. But Westphall helpfully links Catron to Kinney through Catron's law partner, William Thornton, as defending Kinney for cattle rustling; and further links Catron through Rynerson: "If any Territorial official is to be charged with recruitment of the outlaw element, it must be District Attorney Rynerson." (p. 90) Adding to this failing white-wash, Westphall acknowledges that Sheriff Peppin used Kinney's men for his own posse - but omits that the "use" was the Ring's July 3, 1878 San Patricio retaliatory massacre for its residents' shielding McSween. Westphall further implicates by stating: "There were those in Lincoln who thought - or at least pretended to think - that Catron supported Kinney ... and this writer cannot claim of certain knowledge that he did not."

The Lincoln County War six day battle occurs in a vacuum, since Westphall conceals earlier anti-Ring revolts and its own anti-Ring freedom fight to portray it as local conflict. He reduces it to one day, called an "affray" from "violent emotions": "These emotions would soon result in the famous affray in Lincoln on July 19, 1878, when the McSween house was burned and several persons killed." (p. 126) Then he avoids its telling: "The oft-told account of the battle of Lincoln, culminating with the burning of the McSween house and the slaying of Alexander A. McSween and others on July 19, need not be told here." (p. 92) But it did need to be told to show Ring atrocities of burning down a house around men, women, and children; murdering Alexander McSween, Harvey Morris, Francisco Zamora, and Vincente Romero; and inciting military treason.

But Westphall does reveal Catron's role in that battle's decisive military intervention by Commander N.A.M. Dudley. Catron set the stage for Dudley by informing District Commander Edward Hatch about need for troops, which Hatch relayed on April 23, 1878 to army headquarters at Fort Leavenworth. (p. 86) Westphall confirms that Dudley was beholden to Catron for defending him in his court martials of 1871 and 1877: "[I]t has been conjectured that Dudley was grateful for this ... [and] followed Catron's advice on how to proceed with his new command at Fort Stanton." (p. 94) Indeed, Dudley risked another court martial, and even hanging for treason, by violating the Posse Comitatus Act to march on Lincoln on July 19, 1878. Dudley's justifiable trepidation explains his death threat that day to coerce Justice of the Peace Wilson into writing false arrest warrants for McSween and others to give color of rightness to his intervention. Westphall covers up that fiasco: "Dudley's staff officers persuaded a reluctant justice of the peace." (p. 93) Westphall calls Dudley's Posse Comitatus Act violation a need to protect women and children; ignoring that Dudley enabled arson of McSween's house around its trapped women and children.

As to the immediate post-war looting of Tunstall's store made possible by Dudley, Westphall uses fabrications of Catron's brother-in-law agent, Edgar Walz, in town on July 21st (a day after the looting), who blames "Mexicans" and Susan McSween. (p. 93) Westphall then cites Dudley's defamatory affidavits from Catron's law firm against widow Susan McSween's chastity to state snidely that she was not grieving that much after the War, since she was having sex with Jim French, a Regulator.

DUDLEY COURT OF INQUIRY

Westphall belittles Susan McSween's military court charges against Commander Dudley as to get money for her burned-down house and for defamation (p. 94); omitting her charge of murdering her husband. Westfall admits that Dudley's defense by Henry Waldo yielded "accusations of acting in concert with the Santa Fe Ring." (p. 126) In fact, Waldo was Catron's and Elkins's fellow Missourian, added to the firm in 1874. At stake, if Dudley lost, was exposing the Ring and its crimes. So Westphall minimizes the Court to investigating Dudley's conduct as commander; but does add that Catron's law partner participated:

> Catron's law partner [William T.] Thornton had assisted Henry L. Waldo in April 1879 [sic – May to July 1879] to successfully defend Dudley before a board [sic – military court] of inquiry which had investigated his conduct as commanding officer at Fort Stanton. (p. 95)

Westphall then misstates Susan McSween's civil case against Dudley, omitting that Judge Warren Bristol had changed its venue from knowledgeable Lincoln County to Doña Ana County's Mesilla, that her attendance was blocked by Ring death threats, and that Dudley's exoneration in the military court (thanks to Catron) swayed that civil court. But Westphall reveals another Ring lawyer, Sidney Barnes, as defending Dudley in Mesilla.

> On December 6, 1879, Susan McSween's case charging Dudley with arson and libel [by defamatory affidavits] was tried in Mesilla. United States Attorney Sidney M. Barnes was assigned to defend Dudley, while Ira E. Leonard presented the case for the prosecution. Catron, despite Dudley's earlier intimation, had no part in the trial during which Susan McSween, the leading prosecution witness, failed to appear. Dudley was acquitted by a jury that deliberated only a few minutes. (p. 95)

THE FRANK WARNER ANGEL CATRON REPORT

Westphall's responses to Frank Warner Angel's investigative report on Catron for the Department of Justice hides its likely linking of Catron in his official capacity as Territorial U.S. Attorney to Tunstall's murder, and to the report's causing Catron's October 10, 1878 resignation as U.S. Attorney. Instead, Westphall distracts with the outlaw myth:

> Conditions of crime and lawlessness prompting the investigation by Frank Warner Angel and his report on conduct of officials in New Mexico had their genesis in the years following the Civil war. The situation had become serious by the time Samuel B. Axtell became governor of New Mexico on July 30, 1375. (p. 122)

Westphall obscures Catron's resignation. He blames Mary McPherson's "letter" [to Attorney General Alphonso Taft] as "the beginning of circumstances eventually resulting in Catron's resignation as United States attorney." (p. 121) He blames Democrats' anti-Santa Fe Ring press making Catron want "to be free of public office to more effectively combat their attacks."

(p. 125) He blames "Boss" Tweed's April 1878 death - seven months earlier - as reminding people about "ringleaders." (p. 126) He blames Republicans' political power causing their blame for "chaotic conditions" in Colfax and Lincoln Counties. (p. 126) He blames "national and international repercussions" of Tunstall's murder, called a "Territorial matter," not federal (p. 125); omitting that murder of a foreign citizen precipitated federal investigations. He blames Governor Axtell: "His approach, weak and vacillating, was not adequate; law and order gave way to open rebellion against authority." (p. 124) In fact, Axtell was an aggressive Ring instrument, who removed Colfax County's courts by proclamation to obstruct prosecution of Franklin Tolby's murderers; fronted the Ring's fraudulent sale of the Uña de Gato Land Grant; used the "Dear Ben plot" to attempt killing of Raymond Morley, Frank Springer, and others; shielded Tunstall's murderers by proclamations to outlaw arresting lawmen; and appointed Ringite Lincoln County Sheriff George Peppin after unjust removal of Sheriff John Copeland.

Westphall admits that the "attorney general" [Charles Devens] ordered Catron, as U.S. Attorney, to investigate if U.S. officials caused Tunstall's murder; but Catron had not, as Angel complained to Washington, D.C. Westphall finesses: "No record has been found that Catron immediately replied." (p. 125)

Westphall does reveal that Catron pressured Dudley to give perjured affidavits for that Angel report. Dudley refused:

> [Dudley] said he had refused to comply with Catron's insulting written demand at the time Catron's official conduct [as U.S. Attorney connected to the Tunstall murder] was being investigated by Frank Warner Angel, that he go blind and certify to the United States attorney general [Charles Devens] that certain parties who had made affidavits against Catron were unreliable and unprincipled men ... Dudley characterized Catron as an all-powerful unscrupulous lawyer. (p. 95)

Omitted is Catron's desperation. His October, 1878 Angel report forced him resign to stop his and the Ring's exposure. Westphall even cites Elkins's incriminatory August 15, 1879 letter to Catron about his intervening with the Hayes administration to save him from indictment or dismissal (See my pp. 374-378), but minimizes it as just nastiness in business conflicts. (p. 133)

Westphall adds that Catron was replaced as U.S. Attorney by Sidney Barnes. (p. 134) Omitted is that Ringite Barnes defended Dudley in 1879 in Susan McSween's civil trial; in 1880, helped Secret Service Agent Azariah Wild track down Billy; and, in 1881, was a prosecutor in Billy's hanging trials. The Ring was unbroken.

Westphall concludes with Angel's arguably coerced conclusion that U.S. officials were not involved in Tunstall's killing (p. 127) - which was contradicted by Angel's own evidence.

Then Westphall addresses the Catron report by repeating Catron's excuses of not responding because of pressures from work and Democrats (p. 129); and paraphrases Catron's global denials to Angel's Ring-focused interrogatories. (pp. 131-133)

Westphall concludes that Angel's report did not exist:

> One of the unanswered, and apparently unanswerable, questions of history is whether Angel ever made a formal report of charges against Catron. A careful search of the National Archives discloses no report. Likewise, there is no record of the affidavits submitted to Catron for answer, nor of those in his defense. The interrogatories, though, are at hand. (p. 130)

In contradiction, Westphall admits that thirteen years later, in 1892, Catron ordered Elkins to destroy the report as damaging:

> In 1892, Catron was running for delegate to the United States Congress. Word came to him that his political opponents intended to secure a copy of Angel's report on charges against him to use for political mudslinging. Catron wrote to S.B. Elkins, then secretary of war, requesting him to see that the attorney general did not issue a copy of the report to anyone ... Elkins assured Catron that the attorney general would comply with the wish. The following year Catron requested that Elkins secure the report and destroy it. Elkins replied that he had caused diligent search to be made in the attorney general's department for Angel's report but that it could not be found. (p. 130)

More likely Elkins's sly stating "it could not be found," tacitly confirmed its destruction - instead of confessing in writing.

CATRON'S LIFE AFTER KILLING BILLY BONNEY

By the 1881 killing of Billy Bonney, the Ring had eliminated the last person likely to inspire anti-Ring revolt. It had murdered, terrified, forced flight, paid-off, or politically engulfed all involved; and was immune to exposés. Ringite Governor Lionel Sheldon - Governor Lew Wallace's 1881 replacement - wrote complacently: "The desperado and thieving element has substantially disappeared, and nothing more is heard of vigilantes or lynch law." (p. 184) And in 1888, Catron's office fire conveniently destroyed evidence of the Ring's criminal ascendancy. So smugness left Westphall less cautious in using post-1870's documentation by press, adversaries, and Catron's own words.

So the remainder of Westphall's biography inadvertently documents Catron's sociopathic pattern of vindictive brutality, malicious harassment, attempted murders, and murders. And Catron's being Ring "boss" becomes a common accusation. Indeed, Westphall, blaming Democrats, states that by 1880 "Catron came to be singled out as the leader of [the Santa Fe Ring]." (p. 185)

AMERICAN VALLEY COMPANY COMPETITOR MURDERS

In 1886, Catron returned to the cattle business, partnering in the American Valley Company with past Surveyor General Henry M. Atkinson (who helped inflate the Maxwell Land Grant, and was Catron's partner in another cattle company: the 1882 Boston and New Mexico Cattle Company). Through water rights, it controlled three million acres of grazing land, which Catron and Elkins had assisted in legally confirming in 1882. (pp. 151-152)

But it added more opportunistic murders to Catron's score. In 1883, when an Alexis Grossetete and his partner Robert Elsinger claimed that the forming American Valley Company's land belonged to them, they were murdered on May 6th by "employees" of that company. Two of the killer "employees" were professional gunmen hired days earlier (pp. 154-155, 163) (reminiscent of the assassins of Franklin Tolby, and of Jessie Evans and his boys being on Sheriff Brady's Tunstall murder posse). Another of the "employees" was the brother of a one-third share owner, John P.

Casey. Catron was entangled as being the company's attorney since 1882 (p. 153); and, after the murders, buying company cattle from one of the alleged killers, and loaning Casey $6,000. (p. 156)

Though the alleged killers were not convicted, Westphall admits that Catron was suspected: "A whispering campaign started by John P. Casey ... insinuating that Catron was implicated in the murders was an important factor in Catron's defeat in the ... election [of 1892 for Delegate to Congress] ... Innuendo continues to the present." (p. 163)

Casey subsequently mortgaged his company interest to Henry Atkinson in May of 1883 (p. 157); and in April of 1885 Catron bought Casey's interest, becoming Atkinson's partner at the company's 1886 incorporation. (p. 159) Atkinson died that year, so Catron took over thanks to dead Grossetete and Elsinger.

POLITICAL ADVANCEMENT, ANTI-RING WHITE CAPS REVOLT, AND A FAILED ASSASSINATION ATTEMPT

Catron had a long political career in the Territorial legislature. In 1868, he was elected to its House of Representatives; and in 1884, 1888, and 1890, to its Council. His defeat in 1880 for backing 1878's removed Governor S.B. Axtell for Chief Justice of the Territorial Supreme Court, got him "characterized as leader of the 'thirty-third degree ringsters.' "(p. 189)

And Catron's 1884 election to the Council was unsuccessfully contested as voter fraud, causing legislature take-over by his opponents as a "Rump Council," with his group being called the "Catron Council" and linked to the Santa Fe Ring. (pp. 190-191). During the turmoil, the March 13, 1884 *Santa Fe Weekly New Mexican Review* accused him and his Ring of controlling grand juries and attempting to bribe the Clerk of the Rump Council. And Colfax County War hero, Oscar McMains, introduced his subsequently defeated memorial accusing him of land grant "steals." (pp. 193) Westphall glosses over that revolt as "enmities that had been building for years came to fruition." (p. 207) This climate of mounting accusations may have precipitated Catron's precautionary, evidence destroying, office fire by 1888.

In 1891, an ambiguous assassination attempt occurred, though mimicking Catron's usual pattern of killing opponents with guise of law. But Westphall likens it to "political intrigues ... that threatened the life of ... Catron." (p. 208) The opponents were leaders of a group called White Caps. Westphall, applying the outlawing myth, calls them "as tough a bunch of badmen as could likely be found outside a penitentiary." (p. 209)

Omitted is that these Mexican-American Las Gorras Blancas, or White Caps (using the French Revolution's Phrygian liberty cap), were ranchers who fought Ring land grabs. Westphall confirms that the *Las Vegas Optic* backed them "calling Catron a land grabber." (p. 211) In fact, their movement resembled the Lincoln County Regulators. March 12, 1880's *Las Vegas Optic* published their "Proclamation" - like 1878's "Regulator Manifesto - stating:

> Our purpose is to protect the rights and interests of the people in general; especially those of the helpless classes ... We want no "land grabbers" or obstructionists to interfere. We will watch them ... There is a wide difference between New Mexico's "law" and "justice." And justice is God's law, and that we must have at all hazards ... The People are suffering from the effects of partisan "bossism" and these bosses had better quietly hold their peace. The people have been persecuted and hacked about in every which way to satisfy their caprice. If they persist in their usual methods retribution will be their reward.

So Catron may have tried to frame their leaders. On February 5, 1891, after shots were fired into a Council meeting, Catron accused them of attempting to kill him. (p. 213) But Westphall admits a counter-claim that intended victims were legislators voting "against the Santa Fe Ring" (p. 215) But Catron failed to get the leaders indicted. (p. 215)

BORREGO MURDER TRIAL
FOR THE MURDER OF FRANCISCO CHAVEZ

In 1894, Catron ran for Territorial Delegate to Congress amid opponents' accusations of his being complicit to the 1883 American Valley Company murders of Alexis Grossetete and Robert Elsinger. They also sought Frank Warner Angel's Catron report; causing Catron to use Elkins for its destruction. (pp. 324-325)

Nevertheless, Catron won, serving from March 4, 1895 to March 4, 1897. But his 1896 run for a second term was complicated by another murder, and by its resulting famous Borrego murder trial and dramatic aftermath.

It was Catron's next close call with criminal exposure - earlier ones being in the Colfax and Lincoln County Wars - and arose from the May 29, 1892 murder of Democrat Santa Fe Sheriff and Catron's opponent, Francisco Chavez. And Chavez had told people he feared assassination. So Catron was accused. Westphall blames "political intrigues" (pp. 208), which he blames on the unrelated White Cap movement for "malignant influence on receptive element in Santa Fe" (pp. 212) - presumably on victim, Chavez; whom Westphall opines could have been the February 5, 1891 Council chamber shooter. (p. 213) And Westphall claims the subsequent murder trial - where Catron was defense lawyer for the other accused killers - attempted to implicate Catron:

> More effort was being spent by the prosecution, including the entire Democratic party in the Territory, in trying to link him to the murder than in attempting to convict the defendants. (p. 242)

Westphall uses Catron's alibi of not being in town (the same one Westphall used to excuse him from Lincoln County War responsibility); and calls his accusers outlaws. Quoted is Catron's August 24, 1895 letter to Elkins in Washington, D.C: "[Prosecution witnesses are] penitentiary convicts ... and disreputable characters, unworthy of credit or belief." (p. 242)

But Westphall discloses Catron's connection to the killers through a secret Republican organization called the Knights of Liberty to which he belonged with one of his law partners, Charles A. Spiess, along with the future killers: Francisco Gonzales y Borrego; his brother, Antonio Gonzales y Borrego; Laurencio Alarid; and Patricio Valencia. That organization's violence - reflecting Catron's usual *modus operandi* - is blamed by Westphall on members "of limited privilege in social attainments." Francisco Gonzales y Borrego had murdered before, being twice successfully defended by Catron as self-defense killings. (pp. 209, 225) Westphall also states that the killers "had worked actively with [Catron] in ... recruitment for loyal Republicans." (pp. 267) As example, Westphall gives a July 23, 1890 letter of Francisco Gonzales y Borrego to Catron - two years before Chavez's killing - to show Catron's loyalty to "friends"- meaning Catron's later Borrego trial representation of him. (p. 268) In fact, it reveals how Catron achieved vote-buying through an agent. Borrego wrote:

Honorable T.B. Catron

dear Sir I have the honor to report to you that I have two men that they have agreed to come to the Republican party but know that they always want some money they want $10.00 each ... I will tell you that each of them is worth two votes.

Yours
Francisco Gonzales y Borrego

Westphall also blames Catron's past law partner, Democrat William T. Thornton, for accusing Catron and publicizing Chavez's killing. As background, in April of 1893, Thornton was appointed Territorial Governor; so Westphall accuses him of persecuting Catron in "a no-holds-barred political fight" (p. 221) - omitting Thornton's insider knowledge of Catron's chronic criminality. When, in June of 1893, Democrat Jacob H. Crist, was appointed District Attorney of the 1st Judicial District in Santa Fe, Thornton's syndicate bought the *Santa Fe New Mexican* and joined with Crist's *Santa Fe Weekly Sun* as the *Santa Fe Weekly New Mexican*. Westphall blames that newspaper's exposés on Democrats accusing Catron. (pp. 220-221) In fact, it was like the anti-Ring Colfax County War's *Cimarron News and Press*. Additionally, Governor Thornton removed Ringite Sheriff Charles M. Conklin for embezzling public funds (like Sheriff Brady's embezzling tax money), replacing him with a William P. Cunningham. (p. 219)

On January 10, 1894, Sheriff Cunningham arrested Francisco Gonzales y Borrego; his brother, Antonio Gonzales y Borrego; Laurencio Alarid; and Patricio Valencia for Sheriff Chavez's murder. (p. 222)

Pre-trial hearings began on January 14, 1894, with added assistant prosecutor Napoleon B. Laughlin, for what became the publicized Borrego murder case. Westphall, claiming Democrats' bias, quotes headlines like: "Ex-Sheriff Chavez Assassinated Because of his Political Influence." (p. 224)

And Westphall discount's the *Santa Fe Weekly New Mexican*'s reporting that a prosecution witness, Juan Gallegos, had been told by one of the five accused murderers - who was killed at capture of the other four - that Catron had offered him $700 to kill Francisco Chavez, with legal defense included. (p. 225) (Omitted is that, in 1875, Clay Allison of Colfax County also claimed Catron offered him $700 to kill anti-Ring Franklin Tolby.) The judge did not charge Catron, but sent the other four to trial.

Westphall quotes Francisco Chavez's mother, who blamed Catron in her letter, reprinted in March 8, 1894's *Santa Fe Weekly New Mexican* - which Westphall calls a forgery. She stated:

> Mr. Catron, you are not above suspicion of knowing more about the assassination of my son than you have found it convenient to reveal, this suspicion is a natural one, the murderers as far as discovered are political partisans of yours, they frequented your office, were members of the same society, sworn with you to mutually protect each other, you have always defended them in their commissions of crimes, you have gone on their bail bonds and thus turned them loose on the community to commit other murders, and now in order to justify your conduct and the assassinations, you attempt to slander the memory of my dead son. (p. 226)

The 37 day trial of Chavez's murderers began on April 28, 1895; with Catron already elected as Territorial Delegate to Congress. It had Catron's usual defamatory outlawing. He attacked arresting Sheriff William Cunningham with a May 14, 1895 letter from a Richard Hudson accusing Cunningham and his deputies of a plot to kill the defendants if acquitted. (p. 227) Hudson reappears again in 1897 helping Catron to influence President William McKinley against appointing Catron's enemy, Miguel Ortega, as governor. (p. 273)

On May 29, 1895, the four defendants were convicted of first degree murder and sentenced to hang. So Catron got defamatory affidavits - here from jurors - to claim prosecution violations; but the judge rejected them. And in July of 1895, the defendants confessed to murdering Chavez in plea bargaining. (p. 229)

Catron's law partner, Charles A. Spiess, requested a subsequently denied appeal based on another defamatory affidavit, here by a juryman alleging Sheriff William Cunningham tampered with the jurymen. (pp. 228-229)

But Catron, the likely accomplice, emerged untouched. And that 1895, Elkins became a U.S. Senator from West Virginia, holding office, and Ring influence there, until 1911, when he died.

DISBARMENT PROCEEDINGS

On August 20, 1895, as Borrego trial fall-out, its prosecutor, District Attorney Jacob H. Crist, initiated disbarment proceedings against Catron in the Territorial Supreme Court. The charges, and Catron's responses, expose his criminality, vindictiveness, and Ring invulnerability. But it was arguably Catron's moment of greatest risk of Ring exposure. As Westphall admits:

> [Catron] secretly feared that it was the purpose of his antagonists to conduct a protracted investigation that would keep his name constantly in the public attention and thus hamper his effectiveness as a public leader. (p. 248)

Westphall, as usual, demonizes opponents and blames vague "enmities and intrigues." He "outlaws" Crist, a Democrat, by accusing him of an 1884 murder - for which he was not charged - at a mining company Catron owned, and at which he was Superintendant. (p. 230) Westphall vilifies Catron's Supreme Court Judge, Napoleon Bonaparte Laughlin, who supported disbarment; calling him a Democrat business partner of Crist, whom Catron considered "controlled by the smallest kind of men [who administered] law according to favor and the desires of friends [and] committed deliberate perjury." (p. 239)

District Attorney Jacob H. Crist's obstruction of justice charges for the Borregos' trial were summarized by Westphall from Catron's August 24, 1895 letter to Elkins in Washington, D.C.: 1) witness influence; 2) affidavit claiming Catron offered a man a bribe of $175 to rob information from Crist's office about how Crist intended to prevent Catron getting a retrial for one of the murderers; 3) claim that Catron went to Fort Wingate to induce a witness to change his testimony; 4) was bribing a mother to make her two sons testify on behalf of the murderers instead of the prosecution; and 5) Catron's own bribery attempt on one of those two sons to get defense testimony. (pp. 240-242)

Crist also charged Catron's law partner, Charles A. Spiess, of attempted bribery: 1) of a woman to deny Francisco Gonzales y Borrego's murder confession to her; and 2) of a man to make him state that Governor William Thornton had tried to bribe him to testify for the prosecution. (pp. 242-243)

Catron himself shamelessly pressured the five Supreme Court judges: Chief Justice Smith, Needham Collier, Gideon B. Bantz, Humphrey B. Hamilton, and Napoleon B. Laughlin. Westphall provides Catron's October 25, 1895 letter to his friend, *Socorro Chieftain* publisher W.S. Williams, to coerce his judges. Ignoring that it alone merited disbarment and proved Ring obstruction of justice, Westphall presents the outrageous missive:

> Catron requested that Williams confer with Judge Humphrey B. Hamilton ... and see that, if [Judge] Laughlin filed a dissenting opinion, the court prepare a finding absolutely vindicating himself and Spiess ... He wished Hamilton to prepare a ... positive opinion in the case that would take the guts out of anything that Laughlin wrote. [He stated,] "Hamilton should ... see that the decision is an absolute, complete, unconditional vindication. This is what I ask him. He can afford to give it." (pp. 253-254)

On September 9, 1897, S.B. Elkins assisted long-distance by influencing his wife's cousin, Justice Gideon Bantz, writing in his letter:

> *Mr. Catron's prominence in the capital territory and his leadership together with his positive character has aroused not only opposition, but antagonism from certain quarters, and no doubt there are many people in the capital territory who would like to break him down, and this may cut some figure in the proceedings to disbar him.*

For opponents, Catron unleashed his rabid fury, revealing how he must have ordered his atrocities of the 1870's. He used the press as a weapon; with Westphall citing Catron's letter of October 25, 1895 to his newspaperman friend, W.S. Williams: "Catron believed that newspapers from one end of the country to the other should 'open up like a line of sharp-shooters against Smith, Crist, and Thornton.' " (p. 251)

For Supreme Court Chief Justice Thomas J. Smith, above manipulation, Catron devised a smear campaign of fabricated letters to destroy him personally and professionally; since, as Westphall states, Catron knew Smith "was very tender in regard to newspaper articles." (p. 249) So on October 9, 1895, Catron gave complicit editor, Thomas Hughes, an anonymous letter, written by himself, defaming Smith under the title "Is It Honesty or Partisanship?" Westphall, not providing the letter-article, misleadingly paraphrases it as: "Smith had cast himself in the role of prosecutor and, therefore, disqualified himself from judging the case [and] was also accused of selecting members of the investigating committee ... hostile to Catron." (p. 246)

In fact, Catron's published anonymous letter is an excellent demonstration of his conscienceless sociopathy and Machiavellian evil, as he defames honest judge Smith by fabricated events, manipulates the Bar Association into an adversarial relationship with the Supreme Court, promotes himself as victim of "partisan effort to ruin the character of an attorney [himself] whose only crime is that he was, at the last election, selected by a majority of about 3,000 votes to represent New Mexico in congress," and portrays himself as an attacked champion of the common man by Smith's "zeal to cripple the influence of Catron [himself] to aid New Mexico and her people." And in just 16 days, this outrageous ploy was rewarded, not excoriated. As "Anonymous," Catron wrote:

IS IT HONESTY OR PARTISANSHIP?

Last Sunday evening Chief Justice Smith, of the supreme court of this territory, wired W.B. Childers that he intended to spend the night with him in this city.

It has been reliably ascertained that the object of this visit to Albuquerque, outside of his own district, and away from Santa Fe, the seat of the supreme court, was to consult with Childers, one of the attorneys designated to "formulate" charges against T.B. Catron, based on information in the nature of affidavits and copies of a part of the evidence in the First Judicial District Court in the case for murder of Chavez, presented by J.H. Crist. Judge Smith notwithstanding the fact that he is a member of the supreme court, and as such one of the judges to hear and try such charges, has contrary to all precedent, delicacy and the ethics pertaining to the judicial action, descended from the high position which he should have commanded, so as to appear in the **partisan effort to ruin the character of an attorney whose only crime is that he was, at the last election, selected by a majority of about 3,000 votes to represent New Mexico in congress. In his zeal to cripple the influence of Catron to aid New Mexico and her people**, Judge Smith has made this visit to

Albuquerque, and at the residence of Childers took up nearly the whole night in delivering the case and its merits. It is well understood that prior to any action taken in the supreme court in this matter Judge Smith also met and had a full consultation with Childers, Crist and other attorneys who were at enmity with Catron, in regard to the propriety and feasibility of pushing the cause against Catron; that it was there determined that it was necessary to push them for political and personal reasons; that Judge Smith would see that they were referred to a special committee of the bar, composed of a majority who would be hostile to Catron either politically or personally or both, but that it should be so done that it should be made to appear to the other members of the supreme court that it was intended to be non-partisan.

They should formulate the charges with the affidavits and parts of the evidence of persons who were ex-penitentiary convicts and jail birds, confessed prostitutes, and vagrants. It seems that this information was given out before any announcement came from the court as to what would be done.

At least one of the attorneys so consulted by Judge Smith let out enough to show that a consultation had been had and partly what had been agreed upon.

We are happy to say that we have no information that more than one member of the court participated in this conference nor do we believe the others would have done so, if requested even by the chief justice.

It is worthy of notice that the committee appointed was made up of three democrats, two of them were hostile to Catron, one of them W.H. Childers, and the only republican lawyer in New Mexico who is at enmity with Catron, that he, F.A. Fiske, stated his enmity in the court and asked to be excused from sitting on the committee, but the request was promptly denied by Judge Smith, acting apparently for the court, but without any consultation with any of the members thereof.

The court, however, a day or two afterwards, when Judge Smith had attended the meeting and gone away on one of his periodical absences as a non-resident judge, being composed of the remaining four members, still in session and attending to their duties, unanimously excused Fiske from sitting on the committee on the ground that he was an improper person and appointed B.S. Rodney in his stead.

We do not desire or intend to reflect on the supreme court or any member of it, only to state the facts as we have heard them, for the information of the public. We do think, however, that the meeting of Judge Smith was most reprehensible. He had no more occasion to consult with a member of that committee in advance than he had to become the prosecutor in that or any other cause which might come before him in the supreme court or the district court. He sits as a juror, having taken an active part in advising in regard to the cause, having manifested his prejudice, if we are correctly informed, he is no longer qualified in that case. Yet if appearance and reports are true, he has not dignified himself as a fair, upright and manly judge should have done. No judge having any regard for his office or for the esteem of his fellows since the time of Bacon and Jeffreys has ever allowed himself to be consulted or to take part in advising the course to be pursued in a given case. The management of causes and the propriety of the course to be pursued and the accusation to be presented in any case should be left to the legal profession and in a case like this to the Bar Association of New Mexico, to which Catron and Spiess are both members, and where such matters properly belong.

It cannot scarcely be considered that Judge Smith has acted fairly and impartially in this cause if the facts as we learned them be true. The other members of that court should see that the judicial ermine is not dragged in the mud of politics and of personal enmity and should properly check any partisan zeal or political hostility which may be manifested in that cause if there be any display thereof. The cutting off of a member of the bar from practice of his profession is the destruction of property; it cuts off his income and materially injures his character and standing with his constituents. **Mr. Catron, as we learn, has for more than twenty-eight years practiced his profession in the courts of this territory. His character as an attorney has never before been assailed. He stands as an honest, upright and pure attorney.** Such record cannot be brushed aside or wiped out by such testimony as is sought to be presented against him. Catron and Spiess are both members of the Bar Association of New Mexico, which has been in existence for the last ten years. All of the most energetic, able and upright members of the bar belong to it. Since its organization, no charges have ever been entertained by any court against a member of that association, unless it first came from the association or the grievance committee thereof, or was referred by the court to the same for its consideration or action. In this way the best results have been reached. Why should a different course be pursued now? **Is it because there is a want of confidence in the Bar Association that the supreme court cannot trust three-fourths of the members of the association?**

Is it not pretended that a single act enlarged against Catron or Spiess occurred before the supreme court or in connection with the business before the supreme court. On the contrary it appears that if such acts occurred at all they occurred in the district court on a trial before Judge Hamilton. The Bar Association is amply capable to assume control in this matter and to inquire into the correctness and probable truth of the charges. In this way an attorney's character, business and standing would not be jeopardized or injured by an untrue consideration of facts and of their character.

Why does the supreme court assume to take control and ignore the Bar Association of which each member of the court is a member? Why is the grievance committee of that association, composed of such men as N.B. Field, George W. Knaebel, S.B. Newcomb, Frank Springer and A.A. Jones, ignored? Are not these men capable of locking into the truth and reasonableness of the charges? These are men whose integrity, ability and fairness cannot be questioned, unless it be by those who seek to perpetrate a wrong. It is no partisan committee. Three of its members are democrats, and two republicans. Two of them, Newcomb and Jones, have been placed on the committee to formulate these charges, but Field, Knaebel and Springer have been shoved aside, Field being chairman. Instead of three such men as Field, Knaebel and Springer, Victory, Childers and Fiske, persons either politically or personally hostile to T.B. Catron were placed with the committee. Why was this? Was it fair, or was it that they did not believe in the honesty, integrity and fairness of Springer and Knaebel and Field? Or was it possibly in order that the advocates of certain peculiar ideas should go upon the committee to besmirch the character of other members of the bar? We hope the latter is not the case. We believe it is not; but if it is such, then to what a low, contemptible, degraded and insignificant place can the judiciary descend?

It is said that after the conference between Smith and Childers on Sunday night, which lasted until 5 o'clock next morning, the conclusion reached was that the charges must be prosecuted most rigorously, that the Democrat, a newspaper under the control and management of Childers, should be brought to their aid; therefore an article either written or inspired by Childers was published influencing the public of the fact that although Crist, the district attorney of Santa Fe and the man who preferred the charges against Catron and Spiess had been detected in unprofessional conduct, yet the same could not be considered in connection with the charges against Catron. We never understood or thought they should, and we understand that Catron objects to the same also. That article says, in substance, that the full bench, after considering the charges, determined them of sufficient gravity to be examined into and had appointed a committee to consider them and present charges if found sufficient, and that the committee had so found them and presented the charges, and then draws the conclusion therefrom that the charges should be considered well founded and proper.

The individual who penned or inspired that article, or both, and everyone else who knows anything, knows that the members of the supreme court individually never read over the alleged charges and annexed papers, presented by Crist, nor have they heard them read over, but without reading or hearing them read referred them on the representation of someone to the committee with instructions simply to formulate charges based thereon; but not to examine into the truth of the facts or the probability of their correctness. It is further well known that Catron's attorneys applied to the court on motion and asked to have the charges investigated by the committee and their powers enlarged for that purpose, so that they might determine whether there was any reasonable foundation for preferring charges. The supreme court refused to accede to this motion; that thereafter the committee itself applied to the court and requested to be informed as to their duties, and most if not all the committee stated that if they were required to examine the facts of the charges or do anything except to act ministerially in formulating charges upon the supposed facts before them, that they declined to act upon the committee; they were therefore informed by the court that they were to formulate charges based upon the matters presented to them and stand between the court and wrong. What that meant does not seem very clear.

These facts, although done in private with closed doors, none present but four members of the court and the committee, have reached the light of day.

How can it be said that the court or any committee has any manner passed upon the correctness of the charges or the possibility of sustaining them. No investigation had been made by either.

Why were not these charges preferred in the district court, where the facts complained of are said to have happened, if at all? And that also before Judge Hamilton?

They were in fact, as we learn, presented to Judge Hamilton, in fact he was present and heard the testimony of each of the witnesses, also the cross-examination and other evidence contradictory and explanatory thereof, and in impeachment thereof, which cross-examination and other evidence contradictory and explanatory, has not yet been presented to the supreme court. Yet, in view of all the facts, which were virtually known to Judge Hamilton, he declined to entertain the charges. So they are taken to another court whose dignity or character was not in any manner trenched upon, if the charges be true and are even sustainable. None of the cross-examination, none of the contradictory evidence, none of the explanatory evidence or impeaching is brought before the supreme court, although Judge Hamilton had it all.

The facts before the supreme court are simply garbled. None of the testimony showing the character of the witnesses by whom it is sought to establish the charges is presented to the supreme court, so that they could pass upon the reliability of the proposed evidence. Why has that been omitted? Why has that not been called to the attention of the supreme court? Why has the committee not been allowed to look into these facts? We do not believe the supreme court desires to do wrong, but we think it should be more careful and cautious in attacking the reputation of a lawyer of more than a quarter century's standing, of the chosen representative of the people, of one against whom there has never been a scintilla proven regarding his integrity or standing. All the facts, at least those which have been made public, pro and con, touching upon them, should have been testified to, and the character of the witnesses should have been looked into, either by the supreme court or the committee, before they undertook to plaster the character of anyone with stigma, as is now sought to be done.

We believe that in the view of the fact that the testimony produced by the prosecution from penitentiary convicts, incumbents of the jails, notorious and confessed prostitutes, thieves and vagrants as they all are, the good standing of Mr. Catron as manifested by the confidence of three-fourths of the members of the Bar Association, men who have associated with him for years, who have enjoyed his hospitality, have been favored by him with every courtesy and every kindness, who have always been treated with the greatest of consideration and who esteemed him sufficiently to make him the representative of their numbers at the head of that association, which they have formed for their individual guide and government, should have some weight. The judge or the juror who would refuse to give such endorsement weight and take that of a penitentiary convict, of a public prostitute or of a petty thief instead, can hardly expect to go down to future generations possessing a reputation for the greatest amount of integrity and wisdom.

We do not write these facts to influence the supreme court, we expect it to be guided wisely and entirely by the merits of the case; we do demand, however, that the case shall be tried according to law, that a proper weight be given in view of all the facts and surroundings to the testimony of each witness; we do demand that politics shall be eliminated, that personal hostility and enmity shall be set aside and nothing but the strictest kind of justice and honesty shall prevail.

The next day, October 10, 1895, conscienceless Catron responded as himself to complicit *Albuquerque Daily Citizen's* editor Thomas Hughes, who printed it with perjured commentary:

> Editor of the Citizen:
> I have noticed an article in the Citizen of the 9th inst., which seems to reflect on Chief Justice Smith, and have learned that it is claimed by some of my political and personal enemies that I inspired the article or wrote it. As you are aware I had nothing to do with it. I cannot believe that a gentleman occupying the high and responsible position of Chief justice of this Territory has been guilty of the great impropriety of counseling in regard to the conduct or merit of any cause to come before him. I suggest that you make this communication public, as an attempt is being made, as I understand, to prejudice me in the case pending against me in the supreme court.
>
> We publish the foregoing as requested and state that our information came from other sources than that of Mr. Catron. He is not in any manner responsible for that article and we gladly print what Mr. Catron says, so as to put him right, as also the Chief Justice, to whom we desire to do no wrong ... [It] was published on what we deemed reliable authority gathered from various sources. (p. 248)

Westphall also quotes Catron's October 10, 1895, secret plot letter to editor, Thomas Hughes. It reveal's Catron's psychopathic use of a "friend" accomplice, bribery, and intended destruction of evidence by destroying that letter. (pp. 247-248) Catron wrote:

> Dear Hughes,
> The editorial in your paper came to hand today and the democrats and members of the supreme court are very indignant. I have just wired you that I would meet you at your office, but on reflection ... I have requested Mr. Fort to go down. It may be the fiery and untamed chief justice [Smith] may wish to take out a writ of contempt against you ... and should they get a contempt on you, you must

absolutely stand pat and not give away any information that will injure me. If you should have to undergo any punishment I will undertake to make up the difference in any event. What I was thinking was that it might be well, if you do not desire to be brought up for contempt, for you to take a short trip to Arizona on some business ... as they may issue their warrant secretly. However, if you are willing to stand the proceeding, it might be a good thing as it will advertise your paper all over the territory ... I wish you would not however in any manner connect me with the article [in their plot]. Simply say that it was based on information gathered by you from various sources in the public ... A little thing which they could connect me with now might turn the entire court against me and cause them to believe thieves, whores and convicts ...

This will be handed to you by Mr. Fort; do not let it get into anyone else's hands. Better destroy it at once.

Very truly yours,
T.B. Catron

Though Westphall dismisses this Catron press plot as a "fit of uncontrollable pique," he admits that Thomas Hughes was fined and jailed for 60 days for perjury and contempt. (pp. 254-255) Westphall, ignoring Catron's complicitness, used the bizarre saga merely to demonstrate Catron's loyalty:

Tom Catron did not forget his promise to "make up the difference" for Thomas Hughes forbearance in accepting quietly the jail sentence on behalf of Catron and the Republican Party in New Mexico ... Catron responded with financial aid. (p. 260)

Catron next tried "to embarrass Judge Thomas J. Smith at every turn." (p. 250) He got his usual defamatory affidavits to claim Smith had accepted bribes to reverse another judge's decision. (p. 252) He then sent for publication a raving letter of October 25, 1895 to his friend, W.S. Williams, publisher of the *Socorro Chieftain*. It unmasks Catron as an obscene, slandering, jeering, degenerate monster. Catron wrote:

Tom Smith, son of "Extra Billy" Smith, brother of ... the embezzler, who fled from justice in Arizona, and brother of the other Smith who took a prominent part in the murder of Dave Broderick ... says he washes his hands of the Catron & Spiess case. If he does he ought to do so near the Rio Grande, as the filth he has personally injected into it from his own hands would pollute the waters of that stream to such an extent that it would cause an epidemic along the whole course of that river ...

Who is Tom Smith anyhow ? ... Is he the same Tom Smith who has frequently been found drunk in Las Vegas and after having befouled himself been carried home by his companions to avoid scandal? Is he the same doubting Thomas, who was drunk on the bench at Vegas and was kindly advised to adjourn court because he was sick ...

The [Albuquerque Daily] Citizen article surely had some effect. It knocked the saw-dust out of Smith five times in five minutes and then gave him a congestive chill, by which he was confined to bed ... Thomas, keep cool, or you will lose all your saw-dust and have another chill.

Some hard things are said about Tom Smith, and his moral character, but it is whispered that his physical manhood is even more a myth than his morality, for instance ... he smothers his poor rotting physique with musk and perfume. Is it true that in reality the chief justice is physically that which his lady-like manners indicate. We might cite his "domestic bliss" as another proof, but that isn't necessary.

The chief justice of New Mexico wears a cape overcoat. The cape has a delicate white silk lining. No matter whether the wind blows ... this "man" keeps his pretty little silk cape folded neatly back, so as to expose the captivating lining. How proud we ought to be of our lady-like chief justice? Everyone will anxiously await the appearance of the "manly" creature with his new spring bonnet next Easter. (pp. 251-253)

Catron's deranged sadism continued. In a November 11, 1895 letter to a T.W. Collier, he sneered about Chief Justice Smith's sensitivity to the bad press he himself was generating:

His skin is so thin that the slightest attack punctures him. I think the papers should now puncture him so much that his skin will be too open for a first class sieve. (p. 249)

Catron's criminality prevailed. In the Supreme Court's October 25, 1895 decision vindicating him and law partner, Charles A. Spiess, traumatized Chief Justice Thomas J. Smith was absent, claiming illness. With his own *Albuquerque Daily Citizen* plot not yet revealed, Catron gloated with mad pseudo-religiosity in a October 29, 1895 letter to a Walter C. Hadley:

[Smith], thank heaven, took the diarrhoea from the article published in the "Citizen" and was soon after thrown into a congestive chill, from which doubtless under the interposition of divine providence he was not allowed to recover in time to take part in the nefarious transaction. (p. 259)

Justice Hamilton wrote the majority opinion in favor of Catron, essentially quoting the Catron-Hughes plot's "Anonymous" letter, stating that "the low moral character and poor reputation for veracity of the prosecution witnesses rendered their testimony beyond belief." (p. 257) The one dissenting Justice, Napoleon B. Laughlin, objected to total elimination of prosecution witnesses' testimony by alleging they lacked moral character. (Omitted by Westphall is that Catron's firm's comparable defaming of Susan McSween's moral character had been used to destroy her credibility for her litigation against Ringite Commander N.A.M. Dudley.)

But Catron's vengeful fury continued. He still wanted to literally destroy his opponents: Prosecutor District Attorney Jacob H. Crist and dissenting Justice Napoleon Bonaparte Laughlin. And if Catron's close-call as murder suspect for Francisco Chavez had not been so recent, Crist would have likely joined Catron's long assassination list. But Catron nevertheless spewed retaliation. Westphall states:

By October 25 [1895] the Supreme Court had rendered a verdict in favor of Catron. The protective motive in securing Crist's arrest was removed, and punitive impulse was the remaining factor. By this time the desire to punish Crist was sufficiently strong for Catron to press for capture of his tormentor." (p. 240)

For his usual malicious prosecution, Catron had hired investigators to seek past Crist indictments, getting copies of his over decade old, petty Colorado indictment for "larceny of household furniture." (p. 233) Catron paid $100 in costs to guarantee Crist's arrest. (pp. 234-235) Then, knowing of Crist's traveling, Catron arranged his arrest through a U.S. Marshal in Winslow, Arizona. (This repeated Catron's 1877 malicious arrest of Alexander McSween in Las Vegas on his fake embezzling charge, and his 1880 presentation to the Secret Service of Billy Bonney's 1877 Arizona murder indictment for "Windy Cahill.)

For dissenting Judge Napoleon Bonaparte Laughlin, Catron's revenge was to destroy his reputation in Washington, D.C. by sending a defamatory letter on July 18, 1896 to politically powerful William J. Mills (later New Mexico Territorial Chief Justice and last Territorial governor). Catron wrote:

> This man Laughlin is trying to hamstring all of us here. He tried to disbar me and when he could not do it he wrote a filthy, dirty, dissenting opinion, had it published and caused his clerk to send a copy to every member of Congress and every head of Department in Washington, with the idea of breaking down my influence. (p. 258)

The outrageous outcome of Catron's disbarment case was his immediate election as President of the New Mexico Bar Association, which he had cleverly flattered in his *Albuquerque Daily Citizen a*nonymous letter plot! He served from 1895 to 1896.

Westphall concludes that Catron was a martyr: "[T]he tribulations he encountered brought him the fame that helped overcome adversities. (p. 268) In truth, Catron's immunity to murder indictment in the Francisco Chavez case, followed by defeat of his justified disbarment, marked his and the Santa Fe Ring's unassailable ascendancy.

FAILED REELECTION AS TERRITORIAL DELEGATE AND COMPLETED BORREGO CASE HANGINGS

In 1896, Catron ran for a second term as Delegate to Congress. About his first term, the *Las Vegas Daily Optic* of September 30, 1896 wrote: "Mr. Catron has shown his incompetency to serve."

Catron tried to throw the election. His contact was Richard C. Kerens, a Republican operative instrumental in Benjamin Harrison's election as President, and doing railroad investing with Elkins (p. 55). Catron wrote on August 31, 1896 requesting Kerens to implement vote-fixing by moving miners hostile to him to another locality before the election, so they would lose residency qualification to vote. (Sluga thesis, p. 19)

Meanwhile, Catron attacked Governor William T. Thornton for supporting hanging of the Borrego case murderers by shamelessly repeating his *Albuquerque Daily Citizen* press plot with another anonymous defamatory letter on September 11, 1896. It stated:

> "Poker Bill" is now engaged in playing a game in which the lives of four men are at stake ... [But] he will see that [two] are sentenced [instead] to the penitentiary for life, provided they will make a confession that will hurt Hon. T.B. Catron in the campaign. (p. 262)

But Thornton, rough as Catron, retaliated in September 11, 1896's *Santa Fe Daily New Mexican*, calling him a "poltroon" - or "dastardly coward" - and exposing his writing the "Poker Bill" letter and authoring the Hughes press plot too. Thornton wrote:

> This communication to the *Citizen* was prepared in your office, and at your dictation. In keeping with your well known character, you were too much of a poltroon to assume the responsibility thereof by affixing your name thereto ... Your accusations against me are on the par with the slanderous charges which you prepared and caused to be published against the Chief Justice of this Territory last year, when you permitted the Editor of the *Albuquerque Citizen*, in whose paper you had it published, to go to prison and suffer your act. Then, as now, you sent out your slanderous shaft under a nom de plum. [sic] Now, as

then, you will show yourself to be too much of a poltroon and coward to assume personal responsibility for a communication which you know, and knew when you sent it, to be false and slanderous, but will attempt to throw the responsibility upon some of your willing tools that you keep around you. (pp. 262-263)

Westphall states, "Thornton's letter provoked Catron mightily; in fact, it appears to have been one of the few times in his political life that he considered using bodily violence." (p. 263) In fact, this omits Catron's 20 years of assassinating opponents - including Franklin Tolby, Robert Casey, John Tunstall, Alexander McSween, Francisco Zamora, Harvey Morris, Vincente Romero, Billy Bonney; and likely murders of Alexis Grossetete, Robert Elsinger, and Francisco Chavez - and attempted assassinations of Raymond Morley, Frank Springer, Oscar P. McMains, and Ira Leonard.

Catron's private and threatening September 16, 1896 response letter to his past law partner, Thornton, reveals Catron's insane criminal mind as his paranoia projects onto Thornton his own malignant and murderous wishes. Catron wrote:

[Your letter] has the appearance of being designed to provoke me to some act of violence, which might give your adherents an opportunity to injure me physically... I prefer to consider your act that of one smarting under some fancied injury, to such a degree as to render you temporarily insane." (p. 263)

Catron also sought revenge of removing Thornton as Governor. On September 16, 1896, he contacted President Grover Cleveland with his well-worn accusation of outlawry; here accusing Thornton of inciting "blood-shed." It is terrifying ranting of madman Catron, frothing with his blood-thirsty urges:

The letter of Gov. Thornton [in the September 11, 1896 of the *Santa Fe Daily New Mexican* and exposing his "Poker Bill" defamation plot] is regarded here by all good citizens as being ... calculated to bring about a state of unrest and possible blood-shed. It is calculated to lower the character of our territory ... He is insane in his desire to hold office and exercise power ... I have no doubt that Thornton's letter to me was written with the design of getting me into some kind of broil and having me killed. (pp. 269-270)

It should be remembered that 27 years earlier, if Governor Lew Wallace had pardoned Ring enemy, Billy the Kid, he would have faced the same viciously insane Catron assault - and he knew it. And it repeats press onslaught and Secret Service action used by Catron to destroy his outlaw creation: "Billy the Kid."

The same letter demonstrated Catron's loyalty to "friends." To Cleveland, he recommended one of Billy Bonney's killers, Pat Garrett's Deputy, John William Poe, to replace Thornton (p. 270); though Westphall omits that connection. Catron also used Elkins in Washington, D.C. to influence Cleveland for Thornton's removal, but failed. (p. 270) And Thornton himself stopped short of becoming the only Ring-insider informer.

As to the impending Borrego case hangings, Catron resorted to claiming trial witnesses had lied; and trying to manipulate President Cleveland and his wife (showing his own Washington influence.) The executions took place on April 2, 1897.

And responding to truthful press exposures, voters did not reelect Catron as Territorial Delegate to Congress.

ATTACKING POLITICAL OPPONENT, MIGUEL A. OTERO

Having failed to remove opponent Governor William Thornton, Catron tried to control the next appointment. Westphall states that on May 2, 1897, among others, Attorney Henry Waldo (Catron's law firm member and Dudley's defense lawyer) and John Riley (past partner in "the House" and Catron's business partner) met with new president, William McKinley, to block Catron's adversary Miguel A. Otero. (p. 273) But McKinley appointed Otero, who was confirmed on June 2, 1897. Of Catron, Otero wrote: "It was inevitable that we should conflict. He was dictatorial and absolutely ruthless in his methods." (p. 276) "[He used] his brains and energy to crushing opposition to himself with no thought of public welfare." (p. 283)

During Otero's governorship, with Senator Elkins's assistance, Catron sought reappointment as U.S. Attorney. (His resignation had been forced in 1878 after his Angel report). On December 16, 1897, Catron, referencing past briberies to get Ring-style pay-back, wrote to a Joshua S. Raynolds of Albuquerque about that reappointment: *"I am entitled to same from a political standpoint ... having made the race paying all the expenses of the territorial committee and the general campaign expenses."*

Opposition to Catron's appointment came from past Governor Lew Wallace, then safely out of New Mexico Territory's Ring clutches, and aware of Catron's Santa Fe Ring abuse of power during his own administration. On August 4, 1897, Catron wrote with understatement to Elkins about Wallace's intervention: *"He and I were not on friendly terms while he was governor."* Westphall's spin is that the rejected appointment was "prejudiced by his enemies in Washington." (p. 281)

Catron then unleashed his usual vengeance. He filed charges against Governor Otero to President William McKinley and Vice-president Theodore Roosevelt to block Otero's reappointment at his term's end on June 7, 1901. On April 4, 1901, Catron sent his Otero accusations to ally, Richard C. Kerens. Catron's accusations are a bizarre projection of himself, and repeat his perverted sexual slanders as reflected in the 1878 Susan McSween affidavits and his October 25, 1895 *Socorro Chieftain* homophobic rant about Judge Thomas Smith. Catron wrote:

> *His administration has been guilty of the most wholesale plunder of the resources of this territory ... This man is vicious and venal to the core ... A few years ago he ... lived with a Public Prostitute ... Otero has surrounded himself generally with the most disreputable class of men ... We wish to help New Mexico, to protect us from outrage, wrong, robbery and plunder.*

But Otero was reappointed in June of 1901. After President William McKinley's September 14, 1901 assassination, Catron again enlisted Elkins on November 11, 1901, writing:

> *You must see that Otero is not reappointed – that some other name is sent to the senate, and if his name should be sent to the senate, you must fight him and reject it.*

Humorless Catron even accused Otero to new President Theodore Roosevelt as having a "ring!" Westphall quoted him:

> This appointment [of Governor Otero for a second term] ... is going to injure the Territory very much and hold it down. If the ring rule which now prevails here is to continue, I am of the opinion that many of our best people will pull out. (p. 288)

Catron next attacked an Otero backer, past Rough Rider, W.H. Llewellyn, by resurrecting Llewellyn's attempted murder case, dismissed in his boyhood as self-defense. Catron's plot failed with Rough Rider loyalist Roosevelt.

Catron then tried for a third time to have Otero removed, in what Westphall calls a "fight for control of the Republican party in New Mexico." (p. 290). Omitted, however, is that Catron's accusations continued weirdly to mirror his own dirty dealings. In his September 20, 1902 letter to a Dave Winters, Catron wrote:

> [Otero backers] have made a very villainous, mean ugly fight against me ... by means of lying, by the expenditure of money, by threatening individuals ... [by] threatening to prosecute ... they have worked a great many people to change them over. (p. 291)

Failing removal, Catron tried for a third time to block Otero's reappointment. As Westphall wrote, sweetening Catron's insane vindictiveness: "[Catron's] lifelong habit of persistent attention to detail finally paid off. He had been quietly adding details to a considerable body of charges against the governor." (p. 293) Catron claimed that Otero was involved in theft of military equipment. He went personally to meet secretly with President Roosevelt on June 14, 1905, and did end Otero's tenure (though Otero claimed he refused reappointment) (pp. 295-296)

Catron next succeeded in getting Herbert J. Hagerman appointed Governor. He then contacted his father, James J. Hagerman - involved in "investigating" Otero - to make his son appoint him Attorney General. Catron shamelessly argued for need to prosecute *"plunderers of the Public Funds;"* but secretly sought his usual *"immediate control of all prosecutions and investigations"* - as he had used as Attorney General and U.S. Attorney for malicious prosecutions of opponents since the days of Judge Joseph Palen and the Legislature Revolt. On November 22, 1905, Catron wrote to James Hagerman:

> *[If your son] is to be appointed, I shall be very pleased ... if he will take immediate steps to have the "Augean stables" cleaned ... as Hercules was required to clean the ancient ones; to do this he should appoint a new Attorney General, a new District Attorney at this place and new Territorial officials ... Criminal prosecution should be vigorously carried out against these plunderers of the Public Funds; I know upon investigation, that the grossest rottenness will be found everywhere. What I wish ... is to be appointed Attorney General ... I will want, if I am appointed Attorney General, a new District Attorney at Santa Fe; one with whom I Could work in absolute harmony; he would have immediate control of all prosecutions and investigations, which should be pushed through rapidly and with energy ...*
>
> *I write you this letter in confidence, except so far as I request to act in the matter, I would ask in that case that it go no further than what I have indicated.* (Sluga, pp. 87-88)

Catron was not appointed. Governor Herbert Hagerman's administration was so corrupt anyway that President Roosevelt removed him the next year, on April 20, 1907; replacing him with George Curry, a Catron "friend." So Catron did prevail.

In 1906, Catron was elected as Mayor of Santa Fe on April 6, 1906, serving till 1908. In 1908, he had Elkins successfully influence the U.S. Senate for Curry's reconfirmation. (p. 303) When Curry resigned on February 25, 1909, he was replaced as governor with another Catron "friend," William J. Mills.

STATEHOOD

Westphall dates Catron's goal of being New Mexico's first senator to his original cross-country trip with Elkins:

> [A]nother factor in his desire for statehood ... is hope that he would one day become a United States senator from the new state. This consideration is so extensively indicated in his correspondence as to give credence to the tradition that he and Elkins first mutually agreed to aspire to this lofty station when traveling to New Mexico ... in 1866. (p. 311)

Westphall adds monetary motive from Catron's February 3, 1894 letter to friend, Richard C. Kerens: "If I can get New Mexico a state ... my property will be doubled in value." (p. 312)

Elkins died on January 4, 1911, missing the statehood resolution signed by President Taft on August 21, 1911. New Mexico was admitted as the 47th state on January 6, 1912.

U.S. SENATOR: MARCH 27, 1912 to MARCH 4, 1917

When Catron ran for senator, past Reverend Tolby murder accomplice, Melvin Mills, Catron's "confidant in crucial political matters" (p 349), wrote to him on September 12, 1911:

> There are a few men who are candidates that I guess have some money ... some of this filthy stuff to scatter about. If so, they will likely be able to work up a combination that will lay us one side; not withstanding all our service in behalf of New Mexico. (p. 350)

Westphall ignores Mills's competitive bribery hint and denies contemporary newspaper accounts that Catron did bribe legislators to get their votes for him as senator. (p. 354) But Westphall quotes Catron's son, Charles C. Catron, implying bribery of legislators. On June 3, 1921, Charles wrote to a Major Harry F. Cameron after his father's death:

> My father probably spent over a million dollars in following up his hobby [of politics]. I in turn have learned to detest it ... and have conducted all of my father's business in [law]. (p. 387)

On April 2, 1912, Catron, then almost 72, was sworn in as New Mexico's Senator, along with Albert Fall. Catron held office from March 27, 1912 to March 4, 1917.

As Senator, Catron's attitude about the Spanish-American War is revealing. Westphall paraphrases a *Washington Times* article of February 10, 1913 to present Catron's fear" about Mexican uprisings. Catron believed that:

"Mexicans ... were perfectly equal to starting five new revolutions in five days ... He was convinced that intervention was inevitable and should have been carried out earlier." (p. 375)

And on May 28, 1911, Catron had written to his son Thom:

"[I]t is the disposition of most all of the Spanish-American people to indulge in revolutions." (Hefferan, thesis p. 111)

This Catron fear of Hispanic "revolutions" dovetails as motive for his massive military intervention in the 1878 Lincoln County War battle - with Fort Stanton Commander N.A.M. Dudley bringing in a Gatling machine gun and howitzer cannon capable of leveling Lincoln - where opponents were primarily Hispanic; and for comparable overkill in 1880 by using the Secret Service to eliminate possible future instigator of another Hispanic revolt: Billy Bonney.

DEATH AND LEGACY

Catron, when 80, died in bed on May 15, 1921, 79 days after still-existing Catron County was carved out in New Mexico on February 25, 1921. A George W. Pritchard, for his eulogy, effused: "Hypocrisy was never laid at his door ... No man had a bigger kinder heart than he ... The last half-century of the state would be incomplete with the work of his life left out." (pp. 393-394) An E. Dana Johnson of the *Santa Fe New Mexican* skirted truth: "He was frankly a 'practical politician;' the appellation 'boss' complimented instead of offending him." (p. 395) And Victor Westphall flattered: "As Confederate, as Unionist, and as an American, he had faith in the land and its people and gave unstintingly of his time, his fortune, and his energy in a personal demonstration of that faith." (p. 383)

Omitted by all were Thomas Benton Catron's real achievements: he was a murdering criminal who never got caught; and he invented a form of organized crime in which conspiring public official compatriots created a fiefdom, and insulated themselves from exposure or prosecution.

CO-FOUNDING SANTA FE RING BOSS STEPHEN BENTON ELKINS

ANALYSIS: Stephen Benton Elkins, an attorney and politician, was Thomas Benton Catron's co-founder of the Santa Fe Ring. Coming first to New Mexico Territory, he brought in Catron, before leaving in 1873 to a political career exerting Ring influence in Washington, D.C. Like Catron, he was never prosecuted for crimes which left him rich and powerful as a New Mexico legislator, Attorney General, U.S. Attorney, and Delegate to Congress; then U.S. Senator from West Virginia and Secretary of War.

Like Thomas Benton Catron, Stephen Benton Elkins had a loyalist biographer, Oscar Doane Lambert, author of the 1955 *Stephen Benton Elkins: American Foursquare*. As Lambert gushed: "Nature had endowed him with those rare qualities which prepare one for unusual service ... which humanity receives from its greatest souls." (p. 26) And the "Santa Fe Ring" never appears. Nevertheless, as with Catron's hagiographer, Victor Westphall, the devil emerges in details from Lambert's use of Elkins's Papers of 1870 to 1911 in West Virginia University.

Elkins, named, like Catron, after Missouri's "manifest destiny" Senator, Thomas Benton, was born near New Lexington, Ohio, on September 26, 1841 to a slave-trader father, and moved at age three to Westport, Missouri. At the Masonic School in Lexington, Missouri, he met Catron; and both attended the University of Missouri together. In the Civil War, Elkins was a Union captain in the 77th Missouri Infantry, mustering out in 1863.

That 1863, he met a Henry Connelly, a Santa Fe Trail trader appointed governor of Arizona Territory by President Lincoln; and a Richard C. McCormick, appointed its Secretary. Elkins joined a Connelly wagon train to New Mexico Territory, studying Spanish on the trip, and settled in Doña Ana County's Mesilla. There he read law with another new friend, Chief Justice Kirby Benedict, who recommended him to the law bar that year. Elkins was appointed District Attorney of the 3rd Judicial District.

In 1864 Elkins was elected to the Territorial legislature for Doña Ana County, serving until 1865, when he moved his law practice to Santa Fe, working on land grant titles and apparently conceiving the land grab scheme which began the Santa Fe Ring.

In June of 1866, Elkins returned to Missouri to marry a Sarah Jacobs, and traveled back with her and Catron by wagon train. (p. 32) Lambert addressed the men's planned scheme with racism likely shared by Elkins, whom he calls "all in all, Anglo-Saxon." (p. 55) "Spaniards and Mexicans had millions of acres ... but little interest in retaining it. They were too indolent to cultivate the soil and gave no attention to speculating it." (p. 36) Lambert emphasizes Elkins's grant lands focus: "[He] possessed a keen insight into the enormous possibilities of timber, minerals, coal and the fertile lands that remained hidden in the region." (p. 49)

Lambert is unashamed by the speculation, stating:

> A number of speculators, among whom [Elkins] was the master spirit, resolved to acquire legal titles to some of the old Spanish grants that showed prospects of becoming valuable property ... In order to clear these cases he set to work in the office of the Surveyor General of the Territory whose duties came under the supervision of the Department of the Interior of the United States. As he cleared case after case, Elkins would buy the title from alleged Mexican owners, have surveys made, pay off the delinquent claims and taxes and have the titles confirmed by the Commissioner of the General Land Office in Washington. The Surveyor General of the Territory made the surveys and filed his reports in the office of the Secretary of the Interior. In this manner Elkins and his coworkers validated their [own] claims. (p. 34)

Lambert confirms that speculation was how Elkins acquired about 2 million acres; becoming, like Catron, one of America's largest land holders. (pp. 34, 50) As to their decisive land grant client, Lambert states that Lucien Maxwell hired Elkins to secure the title to his land grant, paying him the huge retainer of $7,000. (p. 31) Though omitting Elkins's and Catron's initial 1870 purchase from Maxwell, Lambert confirms Elkins as negotiating the subsequent 1870 sale with Colorado Senator Jerome Bunty Chaffe to a Dutch syndicate for about $1,400,000, of which Chaffe received $500,000. (p. 31) Omitted is the additional manipulation of Lucien Maxwell into founding the First National Bank of Santa Fe; then Elkins's replacing him as its president, and serving till

1883. Lambert confirms Elkins's intended use of the Maxwell Land Grant for railroad development, and using his 1873 election to the U.S. Congress as Territorial Delegate to implement confirmation of the Maxwell Land Grant's title. (p. 35)

Santa Fe Ring-exposing author, Norman Cleaveland, in his 1871 book *The Morleys: Young Upstarts on the Southwest Frontier*, quotes a September 14, 1892 speech by a past New Mexico Territorial Surveyor General about Elkins and his abuse of land grants:

> Elkins dealings were mainly in Spanish grants, which he bought for a very small price. Elkins became a member of the land ring of the Territory, and largely through his influence the survey of these grants was made to contain hundreds of thousands of acres that did not belong to them. He thus became a great land holder, for through the manipulation of committees in Congress, grants thus illegally surveyed were confirmed with their factitious boundaries. (Cleaveland, p. 74)

Elkins was appointed as Territorial Attorney General in 1867. Omitted is that the appointment was by Ringite Governor Marsh Giddings. Lambert notes that Elkins, under U.S. Attorney General William M. Evetts, made "a lifelong friendship" with him. (p. 39) Omitted is that Evetts, as Secretary of State, became a valuable Ring loyalist in President Rutherford B. Hayes's cabinet during the Lincoln County War period's Ring cover-ups.

From 1867 to 1870, Elkins was appointed U.S. Attorney, first by President Andrew Johnson, then by President Ulysses S. Grant. In 1873, he was elected Territorial Delegate to Congress, and re-elected in 1875. He, thereby, exerted crucial Ring influence in Washington, D.C. Both elections were contested as fraudulent. Norman Cleaveland stated in *The Morleys*:

> Elkins ... received a certificate of election, though he actually had not received a majority of votes. He was counted in ... by the leaders of the Republican Party ... This is a rather graphic example of how the Santa Fe Ring controlled the election machinery as well as the agencies of government in New Mexico. (Cleaveland, p. 77)

In U.S. Congress, Elkins added powerful friends: Speaker of the House James Gillespie Blaine, whom he backed in Blaine's failed bids for president; President Ulysses S. Grant; and future President, James Abram Garfield. And after his wife died, Elkins married, on April 14, 1875, a Hallie Davis, daughter of wealthy and powerful West Virginia Senator H.G. Davis. Davis owned West Virginia land rich in timber and minerals - especially coal for railroads - and made Elkins his business partner. (p. 53)

Elkins's 1876 backing of Rutherford B. Hayes for president became key to Ring crime cover-up in its rapacious 1870's growth. Lambert states that Hayes "manifested considerable reliance" on Elkins's counsel. (p. 132)

When Elkins's second term as Delegate to Congress expired in 1877, he opened a Washington, D.C. "lucrative [law] practice ... buying and selling land in New Mexico ... [and] shares in his mining stock." (pp. 53-54) In 1878, Elkins moved his law practice to New York. (pp. 53-54, 88) Omitted is that Catron was then running their Ring in New Mexico Territory. But Lambert writes: "Atchison, Chaffee, Catron and others had become railroad architects of the Southwest, all of whom were now on intimate business terms with Stephen B. Elkins." (p. 57)

By 1880, " Elkins ... gave his attention to selling land in New Mexico, buying coal and timber in West Virginia, and operating silver mines in Colorado." (p. 88) Elkins also backed Garfield's presidential run, and was considered for Secretary of the Interior; as recommended by fellow Missourian, Ringite Henry L. Waldo, then Chief Justice of New Mexico Territory's Supreme Court (p. 89) and past Catron law firm member who represented Dudley.

Well-positioned Elkins profited by insider trading. For example, on February 28, 1881, in New York, he received a tip from Washington, D.C.: "Funding Bill will not pass Congress ... If it is not, there will be a drop in prices tomorrow ... Read, ponder, digest and act ... There can be no doubt that Elkins was buying and selling on the stock exchange." (p. 91)

By 1884, again backing James Gillespie Blaine for President, Elkins united with Illinois Senator John A. Logan, who went to Santa Fe to see Elkins's lands and visit ex-Senator Gerome B. Chaffee in Colorado. (p. 93) Lambert writes: "[T]he young vigorous leader [Elkins] was building a political machine." (p. 94) Lambert does note that the Massachusetts Reform Club, which included William Evetts and past Hayes administration Secretary of the Interior Carl Schurz, "denounced Blaine and Logan as corrupt men dealing in corrupt practices," and favored Democrat Grover Cleveland. (p. 99) Blaine was accused of dealing in fraudulent railroad stock. (p. 100) So Elkins, using usual Ring-style defamatory affidavits, accused Cleveland of "being a grossly dissipated man who indulged in debauchery." (p. 100) And when Cleveland won, Elkins claimed vote miscount. (p. 102)

Lambert states: "[I]n a great measure Stephen B. Elkins named the President of the United States from 1889 to 1893." (p. 119) In 1888, James Blaine, not running, schemed with Elkins in a March 1, 1888 letter to elect Benjamin Harrison, writing:

> Sherman ought not to be nominated ... [H]e is not in sympathy with our friends ... The one ... who in my judgment can make the best run is Ben Harrison ... Keep this letter sacredly-private. (p. 120)

By 1889, Elkins was very rich, living in his Deer Park, Maryland, Halliehurst mansion - named after his wife - with "the general appearance of a medieval castle" adjacent to his father-in-law's mansion (p. 72), owning 100,000 acres with coal and timber rights, and was building railroads. In 1890, Elkins organized and became president of the Elk Garden Coal Company along with the Davis Coal and Coke Company. By 1906 it got a charter as the West Virginia Coal Company, with stock of $6,000,000. (p. 75)

As to Elkins's ongoing business interest New Mexico Territory, by 1884, he owned gold and coal-rich 26 026 acres in Santa Fe County, organized as the Carillos Coal and Iron Company; which he sold for $1,000,000, in 1891, to the Atchison, Topeka and Santa Fe Railway Company.

Lambert wrote about a land deal of Elkins with Catron:

> Thomas B. Catron, Elkins' friend of long standing ... bought and sold land, took part in mining adventures and railroad building [in New Mexico Territory]. On June 20, 1902, Catron offered to Elkins a half-interest in the Tierra Amarilla Land Grant, containing about 500,000 acres, and located in New Mexico and Colorado ... Catron added,

"I also authorize you to sell all my interest in said tract of land on such terms as to you may appear best." (pp. 77-78)

Lambert states that President Benjamin Harrison used Elkins as "one of his confidential advisors," writing jokingly, for example, to Elkins on February 22, 1889, after putting James G. Blaine on his cabinet: "I cannot put all your friends on the Cabinet, for they are more than eight." (pp. 130)

Likewise Elkins recommended Ringite, ousted Governor Samuel Beach Axtell for New Mexico Territory Chief Justice. Harrison refused on June 30, 1891, writing: "I found that he would be attacked in the committee of the judiciary." (p. 133)

Lambert states that Elkins was lending money to Russell B. Harrison, President Harrison's son, who provided Elkins with insider information on August 15, 1891 that the Cabinet position of Secretary of War would be available. (p. 135) By December of 1891, President Harrison appointed Elkins.

Analyzing Elkins's power, Democratic West Virginia Senator C.J. Faulkner was quoted by Lambert from the December 17, 1891 Baltimore, Maryland, *The Sun*:

I will tell you the secret of Elkins' political as well as business success. He is the staunchest friend I ever saw, and a man must be true to his friends, if he succeeds in anything. (p. 141)

Elkins was even rumored to be Harrison's Vice-President pick if Harrison ran again in 1892. (p. 141) But the next President was Grover Cleveland. Elkins resigned as Secretary of War in 1893, returning to business of "the largest [coal] mines and the nearest deposits of steam-making coal to the Atlantic coast." (p. 160)

In 1894, Elkins was elected U.S. Senator from West Virginia under President Grover Cleveland, serving till his death.

As Senator, Elkins influenced President William McKinley, stating: "I have introduced a thousand men to President McKinley." (p. 225) During McKinley's administration, a scandal revealed Elkins's protected status. On June 8, 1897, Elkins's tax evasion was reported by the Cincinnati *Commercial Tribune*. Lambert paraphrased:

It seems that Senator Elkins was one of the five stockholders in the North American Commercial Company that had leased from the United States the sea Islands of Alaska. While carrying on the business of taking seals and selling the pelts, the company had failed to pay the legal taxes or rentals. In view of this default, the Government instituted a suit against the North American Commercial Company and secured a judgment of $1,188,000. The defendants appealed. While the case was pending in the courts, the Company continued to slaughter seals. Consequently, if the case could be held in the courts several years for final adjudication, the Company could have time to complete the destruction of the herds, give up its contracts and forfeit its bond guarantee of $500,000 to the Government. (pp. 224-225)

During the government's token responses (like suggesting branding seals), Elkins got West Virginian George M. Bowers appointed U.S. Fish Commissioner in 1898. Bowers took control of the Bering Sea fisheries, and left Elkins unimpeded and unprosecuted. (p. 225)

By 1900, with McKinley's Vice-President dead, Elkins lost in a bid for Vice-President to McKinley's pick of Theodore Roosevelt. McKinley died in 1901, making Roosevelt President. By 1904, for Roosevelt's re-election, Elkins was a possible Vice-President. (p. 252) Despite his seal killing tax problems, he was made Chairman of the Interstate Commerce committee. (p. 285) In 1908, Elkins was a possible presidential candidate, but Roosevelt backed William H. Taft. (p. 295)

By mid-1910, Elkins was ill. Brutish Catron wrote him on December 21, 1910: "I hear you are suffering from cancer of the stomach ... and you are starving to death." (p. 327) On November 8, 1910, for the Congressional session in December of 1910, Elkins rode his private railway car on the Baltimore and Ohio Railroad to Washington, D.C. He died on January 5, 1911.

Oscar Doane Lambert eulogized: "Big ideas [like his] ... compose the substance that made America great." (p. 78) In truth, Elkins's backing shielded and nurtured the Santa Fe Ring.

THE SANTA FE RING'S FORMULA

Thomas Nast's famous cartoon circle of ringmen each pointing blame the other as " 'Twas him" to deny guilt, was bested by the Santa Fe Ring formula. Members concealed each other and the Ring's existence by outlawing their victims as " 'Twas him." Tweed was convicted. No Ringites ever were. Their formula for perfect crime - intrinsic to analysis of the lost pardon of Billy the Kid - is as follows:

- having silent complicit "friends;"
- conducting crimes for personal profit - like land grabs, usurious loans, mercantile monopolies, cattle rustling to supply beef for military and Indian Reservations;
- diversifying from land-grab, to banking, loans, railroads, mining, and ranching, while blocking competition;
- offering unwavering loyalty to members high and low;
- infiltrating by bribery, intimidation, and election rigging all public power sites: executive, legislative, judicial, and law enforcement;
- extending reach to Washington, D.C.;
- concealing activities by denying Ring existence and expurgating incriminatory evidence;
- controlling the press;
- destroying opponents by malicious prosecution, forced flight, and assassination;
- using beholden military, lawmen, and outlaw thugs as enforcers;
- blocking legal redress against guilty members by removing courts or adversarial public officials, and by generating defamatory affidavits against credibility; and
- creating the outlaw myth against opponents to write self-serving cover-up history.

ANTI-RING REVOLTS

Missing from Victor Westphall's and Oscar Doane Lambert's books is that there occurred major uprisings against the Santa Fe Ring from 1872 to 1878, three of which were defeated by military intervention. The last to be crushed was the Lincoln County War, which sealed Billy Bonney's fate.

CHAPTER 3

LEGISLATURE REVOLT AGAINST THE SANTA FE RING: 1872

THE SANTA FE RING EXTENDS ITS POWER

ANALYSIS: Soon after arriving in New Mexico Territory in 1866, Thomas Benton Catron, with Stephen Benton Elkin's backing, was appointed Territorial Attorney General; as both added governors, judges, and legislators to their Santa Fe Ring.

TERRITORIAL GOVERNORS ROBERT MITCHELL, WILLIAM PILE, AND MARSH GIDDINGS; 1866-1875

In December of 1866, Thomas Benton Catron, only five months after his Territorial arrival, was backed by Republican Party head William Breeden to be District Attorney for the 3rd Judicial District (though Catron was not admitted to the bar until the following year). That appointment was irregular, being done by Acting Governor W.F.M. Arney instead of Democrat Territorial Governor Robert Byington Mitchell, appointed in June of 1866, but frequently traveling. Arney also appointed Stephen Benton Elkins as Attorney General. Catron's appointment was unsuccessfully contested by the Territorial legislature's upper House, the Council, based on his service as a Confederate officer. (Westphall, p. 27) And returned Governor Mitchell merely promoted Elkins to Territorial U.S. Attorney. So by 1867, the year after Catron arrived, the Ring had attained judicial power.

On August 16, 1869, President Ulysses S. Grant appointed Republican William Anderson Pile from St. Louis, Missouri, as the next Governor of New Mexico Territory. Pile retained Catron as Attorney General based on recommendations by Elkins and Territorial Chief Justice Joseph G. Palen - whose Ringite corruption would lead, in part, to the 1872 Legislature Revolt. In Governor Pile's scandal-filled administration, he and Catron were accused - without consequences - of selling and destroying Territorial archives. Popularly called "The Battle of the Archives," it was anti-Ring to the extent that Catron precipitated it by taking the archive room as his own office and disposing of its records with Pile's permission. Pile was further accused of improperly retaining

Catron as Attorney General. Both Pile and Catron were accused of conspiring to split state offices with Democrats if statehood occurred. (Westphall, pp. 31-32) Pile also suppressed Maxwell Land Grant's settlers' anti-Ring Elizabethtown riot by Proclamation of April 17, 1871 to assist Elkins's evictions of them. Those riots became the 1877 Colfax County War.

On August 4, 1871, President Grant appointed as next Governor, Marsh Giddings of Michigan. Giddings's actions in the 1871-1872 legislature's Santa Fe session further empowered the Ring and precipitated the uprising I named the 1872 Legislature Revolt: the first anti-Ring uprising. Giddings died in office in June 3, 1875; but in his three years he advanced the Ring, used troops against its adversaries, applied Ring-style patronage for political appointments, and taxed land grants to facilitate Ring take-overs from impecunious owners. With Catron, Giddings also began the Ring pattern of vilifying opponents as "outlaws."

THE 1872 LEGISLATURE REVOLT

ANALYSIS: *In the January 1872 Legislature Revolt - the first New Mexico Territory uprising against the Santa Fe Ring - Democratic legislators in the 1871 to 1872 session passed acts to block Ring control. In response, Ringite Governor Marsh Giddings brought in troops and the U.S. Marshal; Ringites took over the legislature; and the anti-Ring legislation was vetoed by Giddings and nullified in an emergency Supreme Court session. Giddings, in February of 1872, blocked future opposition by a Proclamation reapportioning the legislature to halve representation of anti-Ring Grant, Doña Ana, and Lincoln Counties.*

Ironically, the first anti-Santa Fe Ring revolt was precipitated, in part, by thwarted interests of Grant County's Silver City; where Billy Bonney spent early adolescence from 1873 to 1875, and may have heard residents' angry talk about Ring oppression.

The uprising was by Democratic legislators in the 1871 to 1872 session of the Territorial legislature in Santa Fe, and named by me "the 1872 Legislature Revolt." Ringites, including Governor Marsh Giddings, recognized the threat to their control of Territorial politics, as evidenced by Giddings's writing, the next year, to the Department of Interior, calling that revolt *"that terrible war"* and *"one of the most reckless revolutionary efforts made any where."* And the Ring's successful suppression of the 1872 Legislature Revolt set its future patterns of bribery; abuse of executive, legislative and judicial power; and engaging troops for suppression - ultimately for arson and murder.

The 1872 Legislature Revolt is obscured by Ring-denier historians, like Victor Westphall and William Keleher in their respective 1973, *Thomas Benton Catron and His Era,* and 1957, *Violence in Lincoln County.* Exposing the Revolt as anti-Ring was Conrad Keeler Naegle, historian of the Grant County Rebellion (as fueled by the earlier Legislature Revolt) in his 1943 doctoral thesis and in his 1968 article in *Arizona and the West* journal. Naegle used the legislature's own published transcripts: *Diario del Consejo* and *Journal of the House of Representatives*.

Precipitant to the 1872 Legislature Revolt was Democratic legislators' passing of legislation to limit the then largely Republican Ring's abuses. At the session's start, on December 7, 1871, Democrats controlled the Council and seemed likely to gain the House of Representatives. Ultimately, to defeat those legislators, federal troops were used. Naegle, in his *Arizona and the West* article, quoted contemporary reporting:

> In January 1872, the Denver *Rocky Mountain News* described a recent event in Santa Fe, New Mexico, which it called "unparalled in the history of western politics." Federal troops had been stationed in the halls of the Territorial legislature to assure control by the Santa Fe Ring, a political and economic clique. (Naegle, p. 225)

Naegle, in his thesis, quoted outraged President of the Council Don Diego Archuleta, who proclaimed:

> "Before we submit to such despotic action on the part of the Executive, the Mexican people had better be placed upon reservations as the Indians are now. We had better resign our seats than to beg our rights of the newly fledged governor who seeks to overawe us, and force us to obedience to his despotic will by the presence of U.S. bayonets." (Naegle, p. 37)

The legislation passed by the House was for Silver City's incorporation and Grant County's establishing a public school system. Then on December 30, 1871, the Council and House passed by large majorities a direct attack on the Ring by redistricting Ring-biased judges. The main goal was to transfer Ringite Chief Justice and Supreme Court Justice Joseph G. Palen from Santa Fe's 1st Judicial District Court to remote 3rd Judicial District Court in Mesilla, to the southwest. (Naegle, thesis, p. 32)

Victor Westphall feigned the revolt as "attempt to humiliate" Palen (Westphall, p. 107). But Westphall confirms Palen's clique:

> [Palen] became a particular friend of [Republican Party head] William Breeden, and the two, along with Elkins and Catron, were repeatedly and vehemently accused by enemy newspapers of largely controlling the Territorial courts. (Westphall, p. 103)

Westphall rationalized that Catron's opponents, Alexander P. Sullivan, editor of the *Santa Fe Post*, and Territorial Secretary Henry Wetter, wanted Palen removed to prevent their own indictment for business dealings; and "Attorney General Catron was in a position to bring indictments and Judge Palen to sit in judgment." (Westphall, p. 104) Omitted is the Ring's pattern of malicious prosecution - with Attorney General Catron indicting and a Ringite judge convicting - which caused the Palen transfer. Westphall also reveals that legislator August Kirchner, on February 1, 1872, sent an affidavit to U.S. Senator Lyman Trunbull, Chairman of the Judiciary Committee, swearing "Catron and Elkins had approached him ... to buy legislative votes in an effort to leave Palen undisturbed." (Westphall, p. 107)

On January 4, 1872, Governor Marsh Giddings vetoed the Palen reassignment bill. "Journal of the House of Representatives" of that session, states: "Governor [Giddings] vetoed the act on the grounds that the assembly ... had no power to make changes without first gaining the consent of Congress." But Naegle states that this violated "U.S. Statutes at Large" adopted by New Mexico on September 9, 1850, which stated: "The legislative assemblies of New Mexico ... may assign the judges ... in such manner as deems proper and convenient." (Naegle, thesis, p. 32)

On January 5th, to block Democratic vote over-riding Governor Giddings's Palen veto, Ringites added names of four absent Taos legislators for a Republican majority. (Naegle, thesis, p. 34) Then, on January 9th, the Ring tried to end the proceedings as null and void. (Naegle, thesis, p. 33)

On January 10th, the four Taos men arrived. But rather than vote, Ringite Speaker Milnor Rudulph (who was later President of Billy Bonney's Coroner's Jury, making a report praising Pat Garrett for killing him) illegally halted the legislature. After objection by the Democratic majority, Rudulph declared the House adjourned and left, taking ten legislators with him.

The Legislature Revolt began that January 10th of 1872. Remaining legislators refused Ring steamrolling; declared that no legal adjournment by vote had occurred; and stated that, with Speaker Rudulph gone, there was a vacancy. So they elected as new Speaker Silver City mine developer, John R. Johnson. (Naegle, thesis, p. 34) They then directed the Sergeant-at-Arms to get Santa Fe County Sheriff Carlos M. Conklin to arrest and bring back exited legislators for a quorum. Returned were arrested Milnor Rudulph and two others. (Naegle, thesis, p. 37)

Ringites retaliated. On January 11th, Governor Giddings and Milnor Rudulph, calling himself "Speaker," declared "anarchy and rebellion" to enable General Gordon Granger, Commanding the U.S. military district for New Mexico, to send a squad from Fort Marcy into the legislature. (Keleher, p. 12) Chief Justice Palen called in Santa Fe's U.S. Marshal John Pratt with deputies. Catron, as Attorney General, filed writs of *habeas corpus* in the Supreme Court to free Rudulph and the two other legislators as illegally detained and to enable calling an emergency Supreme Court session to decide on that *habeas corpus*. (Westphall, p. 105)

So on January 11th, with Rudulph calling himself "Speaker," there were two competing Houses of Representatives; though the majority supported Speaker John R. Johnson. Johnson introduced a bill for Grant County's taxing to create a public school system. (Naegle thesis, p. 37) But Catron and Elkins allegedly then bribed Johnson's Councilmen - including a Candelario Garcia and original protester, Don Diego Archuleta - to vote for Rudulph's House. (Naegle, thesis, p. 37) A September 2, 1884 *Las Vegas Optic* article referenced that bribery in the 1895 disbarment attempt against Catron, stating:

> Catron and Elkins bought off a number of legislators including August Kirchner [to make him retract his affidavit to Trumbull about Catron trying to use him to bribe legislators to protect Palen] Elkins promised [Kirchner] a favorable decision in a certain suit should Palen not be removed. Elkins also promised to cancel a $780 mortgage on the property of Pascual Baca for his vote.

On January 12th, Speaker John R. Johnson was seized by Fort Marcy troops, and U.S. Marshal Pratt's lawmen escorted Milnor Rudulph to the Speaker's chair. Rudulph then suspended the legislature pending the Supreme Court's meeting. (Keleher, p. 12) But the Johnson House defiantly tried to have Silver City's incorporation - already passed by the House in December - also passed by the Council. (Naegle, thesis, p. 28)

On January 22nd, to crush the Revolt, the Supreme Court, under Judge Hezekiah S. Johnson, - with troops and lawmen present for intimidation - wrongly exceeded the *habeas corpus* issue to declare null and void all passed Democratic legislation. The Democrats accused Judge Hezekiah Johnson of being "but a puppet of Judge Palen." (Keleher, p. 12) Westphall stated:

> [The Supreme Court] ruled that the attempt to take over the House of Representatives was illegal and void. Forces of the United States marshal's office, reinforced by United States soldiers, stood by to see that there was no further interference. The Republican majority passed a resolution expunging from the record and nullifying all proceedings of the revolutionary Democratic minority. (Westphall, p. 105)

Thus, legislative acts beneficial to Grant County and Silver City were voided, and corrupt Ringite judges stayed put. The 1872 Legislature Revolt ended with Ring victory and consolidation of power, and a successfully tested technique for tyrannical suppression using complicit lawmen and troops.

Then the Ring, ever cognizant of its incriminating paper trails, expurgated the records of the 1872 Legislature Revolt. Naegle, in his *Arizona and the West* article, wrote:

> [A] report titled *Diario del Consejo Legislativo del Territorio de Nuevo Mejico, Session de 1871-1872*, was made by a special committee of the Council concerning the stationing of federal troops in the legislative halls. The *Diario* is a scarce item, for **an attempt apparently was made to destroy or steal all copies.** A copy was found by this writer in 1942 in the basement of the old Supreme Court building [in Santa Fe]. (Naegle, p. 227)

AFTERMATH OF LEGISLATURE REVOLT

After January's 1872 Legislature Revolt, the Ring's stranglehold tightened. First, Governor Marsh Giddings issued a gerrymandering Proclamation on February 28, 1872, denying equal representation to Democratic counties by redistricting legislative representation by combining Grant, Doña Ana, and Lincoln Counties, while halving their legislative representatives to two with just one senator. (Similarly, next Ringite governor, S.B. Axtell, blocked prosecutions of Ringite murderers in 1876 in Colfax County by removing its courts; and in 1878 by removing Lincoln County's Justice of the Peace. The Colfax and Lincoln County Wars resulted.) Naegle wrote:

> This [denial of equal representation to Democratic Counties] marked the beginning of gerrymandering in New Mexico and was the second factor [after illegal disposal of the Johnson House's legislation for Grant County] that served to crystallize the desire of the people of Silver City to be free from the domination of the Santa Fe "ring." (pp. 38-39)

By the next year, 1873, Governor Giddings used Ring-style patronage to appoint officials without proper legislative approval; even making his own son Adjutant General. Resulting charges against Giddings to the Department of the Interior led to his son's withdrawal. But Giddings was not censured, and was backed by Catron, William Breeden, and even Judge Joseph Palen.

Those charges against Giddings revealed growing class struggle against the Ring. An example is Delegate to Congress José Gallegos's protest to President Ulysses S. Grant:

Washington March 13th 1873
To the President of the United States:
Sir.
My people are extremely anxious to have Governor Giddings removed as Governor; he are officious, meddling, disagreeable man to my peoples.
I will not ask the appoint of any particular man, but the names of W<u>m</u> L. McKnight of Ill, and that of Col Isaac S. Stewart late Paymaster in the Army have been presented for my

considerations by their friends. The appointment of either of these gentlemen would be accepted by my people with great satisfaction and gratitude.

Very Truly Yours.
Jose M. Gallegos

Giddings first responded to his charges on March 26, 1873 to the Secretary of the Interior by merely denying them as relayed by *"my friend Hon. Thos. W. Ferry U.S. Senator."*

Giddings's next response to the charges, on April 3, 1873, was a scrawled, agitated, rambling, 27 page letter, blaming his charges on the *"revolution"* of the legislature's Democrats, past corrupt officials, and *"vilest of the vile" Mexicans from "slums of vice"* in Santa Fe. With Ringite racism, Giddings complained: *"Nearly all the people of the Territory are Mexican 86,000 out of 93,000."* In fact, Giddings was initiating the Ring's outlaw myth, writing:

Santa Fe New Mexico
April 3, 1873
To His
Hon the Sec of the Interior
Washington D.C.
Sir – A transfer of Territorial officers from the State Dept. to the Dept of the interior of which I was just advised by the Secretary of State, and a renewal of charges heretofore made against me, to the Secretary of State, with some little additions thereto, force me to make a statement to your Dept. of my conduct ... I have not the charges, but an outline of them from Senator Ferry ...

The legislature convened about the first of December [1871] and everything looked well. It looked as if the recommendations of my message would be headed, and legislation made to correspond. But after a little time and before legislation had proceeded much there arose trouble. Party spirit came up. The democrats feared the republican party would gain something if the recommendations of the governor were carried out. Aside from this arose another serious difficulty. A most shameful and causeless attack was made upon Chief Justice Palen ...

[Palen's enemies] all combined to disgrace, and get rid of Chief Justice Palen ... [T]hese men conspiring together with the worst democrats, secured passage of a bill ... by the most wicked falsehood, whereby Chief Justice Palen was thrown out of the Santa Fe District ... so as to disgrace him & prevent his presiding

in certain cases of interest to the parties who had joined the conspiracy ...

[AUTHOR'S NOTE: Giddings conceals that the opposition was to Ring control, and omits Palen's biased decisions.]

[AUTHOR'S NOTE: Giddings next describes the 1872 Legislature Revolt to justify its crushing.]

This brought a terrible war. The republican members saw they had been misled, and stood by the executive ... The democrats were determined to prevent a vote that would sustain me ...
Upon my vetoing this measure to displace Judge Palen the House broke up and divided into two parts ... Two days before the close of the session, we succeeded in effecting a compromise ...
Thos B. Catron now U.S. Attorney & then my Territorial Attorney learning that the Sec. of the Territory, as a part of this progression to break up my legislature, who refusing and neglecting to pay the members their per diem allowance, himself actually paid the republican members who could not remain without pay and with other friends provided for expenses of various kinds to hold the legislature together until we could defeat the revolution and secure needed laws. He has not yet been reimbursed.

[AUTHOR'S NOTE: This hides Catron's bribery of legislators. Years later, Catron's son Charles related that Catron spent $1 million for politicing. Here, the "needed laws" were to advance the Ring; and impecunious opponents were being forced to leave for lack of salaries. Catron's bribes in other situations were "loans," like the $1,800 paid to the next Governor, S.B. Axtell. And by that 1872, Catron and Elkins were rich, having sold the Maxwell Land Grant and established the First National Bank of Santa Fe. The defeat of the 1872 Legislature Revolt shows how their money and influence was expanding Santa Fe Ring stranglehold on the Territory.]

But the best evidence that my course was satisfactory is shown in the fact that all the public offices and the best citizens of the Territory stood by me with their money and their influence. And though this extraordinary aid ... we were enabled to keep the legislature together, and to pass more really valuable laws within the last two days of the session than had been secured before by many years of legislation.

The greatest excitement prevailed when the House divided & it continued for weeks. The Speaker was obliged for some days to call in the military to his aid.

[AUTHOR'S NOTE: This covers up that "The Speaker" was Ringite Milnor Rudolph, not the elected Speaker, John Johnson; and covers up that Giddings himself called in the soldiers.]

Outsiders were set on to crowd into the House, make noise & disturbance & bring on a riot ...

[AUTHOR'S NOTE: This begins the Ring's outlaw myth demonizing opponents. The "riot" was legislators' response to Ringites illegal take-over of the legislature.]

For many days a fight seemed inevitable. Riot & bloodshed were imminent ... [E]very member was armed and at any moment a fight might occur. At last, I went into the House, took a seat by the side of the Speaker and remained there for hours for the passions to cool, and until the adjournment of the House for the day.

After all we secured the passage of some excellent measures, and it is universally conceded now by the best men here, that we have made more real progress within the last year and a half than has ever been accomplished within any six years prior to my coming ...

[AUTHOR'S NOTE: Giddings omits that "the Speaker" whom he backed was Ringite Milnor Rudolph, whose House was legitimized by Catron's bribing to get legislators' votes; and that troops were stationed right there for intimidation as Ringite legislation by "the best men" passed.]

[AUTHOR'S NOTE: Giddings next addressed appointing his son as Adjutant General, by calling accusers bad people or enemies of Palen and himself; and that the two Special Agents sent to investigate him were wrong to support accusations. He adds that Catron, as U.S. Attorney (since that February), filed charges against one of those Agents (this being the malicious prosecution that became Catron's hallmark).]

[AUTHOR'S NOTE: Next Giddings covers up his Ringite appointments without legislative approval by blaming the 1872 Legislature Revolt, omitting that they would have been blocked if subjected to approval.]

*The legislature was in a state of revolution and until within two days before the close of the session, we could do nothing, and therefore the whole legislature for two years had to be done. Appointments were not thought of - nor were they of any consequence compared to the passage of more important laws for taxation to run the Territorial government & other grave matters. And these matters occupied the entire & every moments attention of the legislature during these two days. Even the appointment of senators & representatives had to be neglected & **I was driven to make this appointment to stand for ten years in consequence of the neglect of the legislature.***

And worse than all during the last five days of the session, exhausted by the constant night and day effort to prevent riot revolution & bloodshed for so many weeks I was broken down by sickness so that my family nearly despaired of my recovery, and I had to trust nearly everything for a time to my Territorial Attorney [Catron] for examination of acts to be approved or otherwise.

[AUTHOR'S NOTE: Giddings let that Catron took over the legislature to run the government! The correct substitute for a Governor was the Territorial Secretary. And the claimed delay in appointment of officials was Catron's subversive filibuster to insure appointment of Ringites – as did occur.]

On the last day of the session & just before its close & between eleven and twelve oclock noon the hour of closing, a democratic member of the council who had fought me all winter arose & introduced a resolution requiring the governor to send to the council the names of his appointees. Every member of that body knew my situation [having left as sick], and although it was a democratic trick & the resolution passed, yet no member ... or other person was authorized to notify me, as appears by the record, but from some source [likely Catron] I was informed of what had been done, and knowing it was a trick I endeavored to get up & go to my table & send in names at the same time remarking to those present that it was a trick & that the council should have advised me in time if any desired to bring up that business, but before I could get to my room and write a line the legislature had adjourned.

After the legislature had adjourned I had to apportion the Territory and to appoint the Attorney General, Auditor of Public Documents, Treasurer. Quartermaster General, Adjutant General [his son, William], Librarian, and attorneys for the several Judicial Districts & perhaps others.

All these appointments were made upon the recommendations of the best citizens of the Territory including generally the Federal officers [like Catron as U.S. Attorney] & a large portion of the republican members of the legislature ...

As to putting off nominations for fear they would not be confirmed, how senseless, and what if the council did not confirm ... & less than two days the council must by law adjourn & the same result would have been secured. This charge is rather thin ...

[AUTHOR'S NOTE: Giddings omits that his "best men" were Ringites; and that he was avoiding legislative approval.]

The men who are making & pushing charges against me are not the friends of Gen. Grant's Administration ... [and I assisted] in nominating president Lincoln and Grant ... **[A]fter having broken down here the most wicked revolution against the government and this administration & maintained as by a miracle the perfect administration of that part of the public affairs entrusted to me,** *and brought great credit here upon Gen Grant & his administration as it is understood I carry out his views ... I say I can not but feel that I am entitled from my experience to exercise somewhat my own discretion in the appointment of the little offices relating to Territorial affairs, and* <u>entitled to be believed</u> *after more than* <u>thirty years</u> *of public life, in which my statements have never before been called into question ...*

[AUTHOR'S NOTE: Giddings plays his political card, omitting that it does not make illegal appointments legal. But the real issue is the rise of rings which contaminated the Grant administration with corruption - and left later administrations of Hayes and Garfield beholden to the Santa Fe Ring itself.]

I seek to do the will of the government but first of all to do right.

If I am in accord with the government I want to know it. If I am not I desire to know above all things wherein I am not.
     Very respectfully
      Your obt servt
       Marsh Giddings

Governor Giddings enclosed the following letter of support for himself, outrageously signed by Catron and other Ringites:

Cimarron New Mexico
March 26 1873

Hon Thomas W. Ferry
U.S. Senate

Sir — *We have just learned that the character of the Adjutant General of New Mexico has been attacked at Washington with the view evidently, not so much as to effect him as to injure his father the Governor [Marsh Giddings].*

Therefore we desire today, to you and to all whom it may concern, that we have known William M. Giddings for more than a year last past, and are acquainted with his character - And we desire to say that he is a gentleman in his bearing and demeanor - that he is a man of good moral character - that he is competent to fill the office he occupies, and we have heard no complaint that his duties of said office were not satisfactorily performed.

He was appointed to the place upon recommendation of nearly all the Federal and Territorial Officers in the Territory, as also of a large portion of the members of the legislature.

Very Respectfully

T.B. Catron Attorney of U.S. for New Mexico
M.A. Breeden Clerk 1st Jud. Dist Court N.M.
Wm Breeden Attorney at Law
José D. Sena Attorney at Law
J.G. Palen Chief Justice Sup. Court N.M.
T.F. Conway Atty. Gen. New Mexico

On April 20, 1873, Giddings followed up by letter to the Department of the Interior, promoting his legislation on land grant surveying for taxation, and omitting its enabling of the Ring's land-grab. It was the Ring's manifesto of power. He wrote:

By the enactment of these laws in the last two days of the session our securities doubled in value within six months, and our debt of 75,000 or 80,000 will be paid off within three years if the property is properly assessed & tax collected. We have now highway laws, railroad laws & the whole face of things material is changed and set ahead nearly a quarter of a century ...

In accomplishing these great results I have been sustained by **Chief Justice Palen and the other Judges. The U.S. Attorney Catron, the Attorney General Conway, Col. Wm Breeden former Clerk Sup Court here, S.B. Elkins Prest First Nt Bk Santa Fe** *& his cashiers & Directors and in fact all the Federal &*

Territorial Officers ... & every prominent republican with some of the best democrats in the Territory.

I should not have mentioned these things now lest in the course of events these facts so few as they were communicated went to the Sec. of State & I desired therefore to give just an out live view of the unexpected success we had met here in this apparently dead country & community, against **one of the most reckless revolutionary efforts made any where** *...*

The administration will never have a nobler set of men to aid it, then those who surrounded me [by protection] in our Territorial rebellion, and these men today stand as firm by me as stand the hills & mountains around us.

RING CREATION OF THE OUTLAW MYTH

The Ring learned from the 1872 Legislature Revolt. By 1873, Ringites would never again legitimize opposition as "revolution" or "rebellion." Only "outlaw" would label their adversaries for malicious prosecution and assassination as their Territorial take-over progressed through complicit governors, lawyers, judges, lawmen, and military officers deploying federal troops.

By 1874, Catron and the Ring had sights on one of the next counties for take-over: Lincoln. To set the stage for its military suppression, on January 10, 1874, Judge Warren Bristol wrote to Governor Giddings. Four years later, the Ring would murder John Tunstall and Alexander McSween there, and the military would, indeed, intervene. Importantly, by 1874, Bristol created the foundation "outlaw" myth to justify Ring aggression. Bristol wrote:

Santa Fe N.M.
January 10, 1874

To the Governor
 Sir
  From sources of information that I deem perfectly reliable I am satisfied that there are public disorders in Lincoln County that call for an extraordinary and vigorous remedy

Since the beginning of last month these disturbances have culminated in a regular guerrilla warfare between the Mexicans and Texans and is being carried on very much in the same spirit that activates hostile Indian tribes. Hundreds are already implicated in an open breach of the laws

Hundred parties are frequently meeting and firing upon each other at sight

These disorders are so wide spread and the people of the County so generally implicated either openly or through sympathy that I deem it out of the question to obtain juries in that county who will find indictments or verdicts impartially and justly

In fact all along at the several terms of the District Court that I have held in that county I have been exceedingly embarrassed for the want of reliable juries. The gravest crimes have been too often passed over unnoticed

Previous to my advent to the Judicial District of which Lincoln county is a part little or no effort had been made to sustain the courts in that county - it being occupied mainly by Mexicans

Within the last two or three years the eastern and central portions of the county have been settled to a considerable extent by cattle dealers - herders and ranchmen mostly from the border of Texas including a number of what are commonly known as "Cowboys"

This population made up of these mixed elements has had but little or no schooling in the duties and responsibilities of self-government and are prone upon very slight or no provocation to use their weapons

Our judicial system - as you are aware - applicable to that as well as every county in this Territory is precisely the same as that in the most civilized and orderly communities throughout the land. Under this judicial system the <u>people</u> through their juries perform an important part in the administration of the criminal laws. If through terror or sympathy or any other cause they fail to perform their duties as jurors faithfully and promptly under the instructions of the Court - then it follows that the Court to that extent must necessarily fail in the maintenance of public order

Complaints growing out of these present disturbances in some instances I understand have been made to the local Magistrate and warrants issued but that no arrests have been made

Complaint has also been made to me since my arrival in Santa Fe in regard to one of these shooting forays in which four men were killed and three individuals wounded. Upon this complaint I have issued a warrant ... But ... from what I learn of the situation of affairs in that county **I have every reason to believe that the Sheriff will not and cannot make the arrests with any force in his command.**

The next term of the District Court for that county will not be held until the middle of April next - In the mean time prompt and vigorous measures ought to be adopted to quell the disturbances and disarm the contending parties - **At present I see no way whereby this can be done effectively except by a sufficient military force**

I deem it my duty to lay this matter before you hoping that through your instrumentality the required aid may be obtained
I have the honor to be
Very respectfully
Warren Bristol
Associate Justice

Two days later, on January 12, 1874, Governor Giddings passed this fabrication to Secretary of the Interior as: "In relation to disturbances in Lincoln County New Mexico." It was forwarded to the Secretary of War on January 28, 1874, stating:

Territory of New Mexico
Executive Office
Santa Fe January 12 1874

Hon. C. Delano
Secretary of the Interior
Sir

I have the honor to inform you that for a number of weeks just past there have been disturbances between the Mexicans and Texans living in the extreme southern part of New Mexico in Lincoln County. Sometime in December the military commandant here at Santa Fe was so kind as to furnish me copies of some letters he had received from that vicinity showing a bad state of feelings in that quarter, and especially a communication from Major John S. Mason which is herewith enclosed.

At the time I received it, Hon John D Bail our Territorial Attorney for the 3ᵈ Judicial District was here in Santa Fe as a member of the council in the Legislative Assembly, and upon conferring with him in regard to the affairs in Lincoln County which is a part of his District and where he has been many years acquainted, he was confident that Mason was laboring under some mistakes, that he had probably obtained his information from unreliable sources, and that the information given to the military officers more generally came from the Texans who could converse more readily than the Mexicans who speak only the Spanish language, & Bail believed that there was a strong prejudice existing against the Mexicans as well with the military as with the American people, chiefly from Texas who are constantly having troubles with the Mexicans who are looked upon by the Texans as an inferior race & whom they continue to call peons while very many of these Mexicans are as highly educated & as law abiding and intelligent men as the large portion of the border Texans.

And the Spanish speaking Mexican is quite as proud of his origin as can the Texan be of his own. And there have several times come to me evidences of a strong prejudice in the part of the soldiers against the Mexicans, who are generally a pastoral people inclined to peace, quiet & indolence ... **Still I think the officers generally seek to do right, and there is great need of the military if we can use them in aid of the civil authorities**. The difficulties & disorders in that county have been continually increasing until there is now a guerrilla war being carried on among the inhabitants of the county and no one however law abiding now feels safe. The Texan owners & herders of Stock Ranch men and "Cowboys" are generally well armed with the best of fire arms, while the Mexicans are generally but poorly armed. The Mexicans I learn remain on their grounds while the Texans it is said upon the least provocation make use of their weapons and if pursued, make for Texas and out of reach.

That there is wrong on both sides there can be no doubt but wholesale butchery of men women & children should be prevented if possible. **We have no Territorial military force nor can we organize one.** The legislature a few days since gave the executive power to offer a small reward in such cases and messengers from that county having been sent here for some aid, I made a proclamation offering a reward of $500 for the apprehension of certain criminals there, and at the same time Judge Bristol issued his warrant for the apprehension of the same parties.

The most deplorable state of things exists there now as will be seen upon examining the statement of Judge Bristol & others herewith enclosed.

Upon examining the papers and advising with Judge Bristol, and the Attorney of that District as well as the Attorney of the 2ᵈ District all of them well acquainted with the people and the causes of the trouble, **all concur that it was my duty in order to prevent any further murders to ask the aid of the military forces nearby in keeping the peace, and to aid if necessary** the civil authorities in the execution of civil process until we could receive instructions from the general government.

And I therefore made a statement today of the facts substantially as given by Judge Bristol and others, to Col. John J Gregg commanding the military forces here, and appended thereto a request that he "would furnish such military force as the exigencies of the case may require to <u>aid the civil</u> authorities in executing the lawful processes of the civil courts and authorities, and to aid the officers and authorities in the arrest of criminal violators of the laws, and to aid in keeping the peace among and between people of said county of Lincoln until order shall be restored to the inhabitants of said county or until some further order or direction can be obtained from the general government."

I could make no <u>order</u> on such military officer, but it seemed to me that right & humanity dictated that I should make such <u>request</u> on him, and let him do so much, and as the law should direct under the circumstances. **Last year I made a request for some military aid in the case of disturbances in Cimarron in the northern part of the Territory and was telegraphed I think by Gen Sheridan that a small force had been ordered to that point to aid the civil authorities.**

In this deplorable state of affairs and on the border where are more or less likely to have constant repetitions of like occurrences it becomes, it seems to me, an absolute necessity that we should have some instructions or directions of some kind for guidance in such emergencies. **The civil authorities are powerless to do anything in these remote parts - No Territorial military power in existence, and no power to create a military force, we are driven to the terrible necessity of seeing these murders committed where these border feuds exist unless we can have the aid of their military forces of the United States stationed in the Territory.** And if we can have such aid we need instructions as to what necessities shall arise before the aid can be called for.

Every military officer with whom I have been able to communicate in this Territory on the subject has seemed to be wholly in doubt as to what emergencies would constitute a sufficient cause for the use of the military to aid the civil authorities.

I have therefore laid the whole matter before you as far as I can learn the facts and shall be glad to carry out any directions or suggestions from your Department, in regard to this and like cases.

I have the honor to be
Very Respectfully
Your obt servt
Marsh Giddings
Gov. New Mexico

Since writing the foregoing I have received some additional information. I learn from Judge Bristol and others that there are really no civil authorities by way of courts through whom any demand can be made on the military for aid. - That the Justices of the peace, and they are not numerous, are themselves implicated in the disorders or if not [,] dare not issue papers for arrests - that the Judge of Probate having resigned and the Sheriff having put himself away from the scene of the disturbances, there are no civil authorities seeking to quiet the disorders by calling for military aid or otherwise. The District Judge 300 miles from the place & now in Santa Fe may issue his warrant but he is too far away from parties and witnesses to be of much service. The military authorities would undoubtedly go to the aid of the civil if there was any active civil authority in the county. There being none - what should be done. Judge Bristol is exceedingly anxious on the subject, not only for this occasion but for future occurrences.

On the other hand, from a letter just received from Lincoln County I learn that they are holding Peace meetings with good prospect of preventing further bloodshed for the present.

We are so differently situated from the people of the States away in the borders of a remote Territory that it seems improbable to keep order under the same rules & regulations <u>only</u>, which are sufficient for a well settled state. And the judge so desires me to seek some direction for the future.

Truly yours Giddings

DEAD GOVERNOR MARSH GIDDINGS REPLACED BY SAMUEL BEACH AXTELL

After Marsh Giddings died in office on June 5, 1875, President Ulysses S. Grant appointed Governor of Utah, Samuel Beach Axtell, to his position. Axtell's Governor's "Message" to the legislature's 22nd Session, gave pro-Ring property assessment:

> You can in no better way equalize taxation and prevent the crime of false assessments than by assessing the property of the Territory yourselves. Determine the rate per hundred dollars all property shall pay other than the property you especially specify; determine how much per head horses, cattle, sheep and other animals should pay; grading them; and land per acre; grading this also as improved, unimproved etc, *exempt nothing, and permit no deduction for debt.* You will thus render it impossible for fraud and cunning to escape the just and honorable burden of taxation ... and fix a penalty for false returns. In this way you can reach equal taxation; unjust and unequal taxation, like unjust weights and measures, is an abomination to both God and man.

So by 1875, the Santa Fe Ring fox was in charge of the Territorial hen coop. Land grant holders could now be taxed out of ownership as they turned futilely to attorneys like Thomas Benton Catron for protection.

By 1876, Axtell was the Ring's front for attempted murder and murder of its Colfax County opponents, while he facilitated land grant sales there and caused the 1877 Colfax County War by removing their courts. The next year he backed the Ring's reign of terror, murders, and blockade of justice in the Lincoln County War. But first came the Grant County Rebellion in 1876.

CHAPTER 4

GRANT COUNTY REBELLION AGAINST THE SANTA FE RING: 1876

THE GRANT COUNTY REBELLION: 1876

ANALYSIS: *Grant County citizens never forgot Ring injustices that both caused and followed the 1872 Legislature Revolt. By 1876, they rebelled, intending to secede from New Mexico Territory, and published a "Declaration of Independence" for annexation to Arizona Territory. This second anti-Ring uprising also failed; this time by intervention in Washington, D.C. as well as lack of leadership. So Grant County was spared the Ring's violence which came next in Colfax and Lincoln Counties.*

SPIRIT OF THE 1872 LEGISLATURE REVOLT

Grant County, site of the second anti-Santa Fe Ring rebellion, was named after Ulysses S. Grant and was formed in 1868 by the Territorial legislature by division from Doña Ana County. It occupied the southwestern corner of New Mexico Territory, and bordered Arizona Territory on its west. That boundary was set in 1863 when the federal government divided western New Mexico Territory into Arizona Territory. Only 50 miles from that border was Silver City, its mining-rich county seat, founded in 1870.

As mentioned, the historian for the 1876 Grant County Rebellion is Conrad Keeler Naegle, with his 1943 doctoral thesis titled *The History of Silver City, New Mexico 1870-1886*; and an article in *Arizona and the West: A Quarterly Journal of History* titled "The Rebellion of Grant County, New Mexico in 1876." Naegle noted that the Ring was involved from Grant County's inception, with its first district court in 1868 having Thomas Benton Catron himself as District Attorney. (Naegle thesis, p. 3)

Naegle wrote that the Grant County Rebellion grew from the 1872 Legislature Revolt, which he called an "unsuccessful attempt to oust the 'ring' from its control over the Territorial legislature in order to prevent it from obstructing further the will of the people." He noted that Grant County residents, especially in Silver City, were "well educated and of means"

(Naegle thesis, p. 29), and by 1871 wanted to escape Ring clutches. Naegle quoted from the March 23, 1871 Las Cruces *Borderer*:

> As early as 1871 these liberty-loving Americans had voiced their desire for annexation to Arizona, in order that they might be freed from domination by the Santa Fe "ring" that had "so faithfully and ably misrepresented" them. (Naegle thesis, p. 31)

Grant County's "liberty-loving" had contributed to the 1872 Legislature Revolt as its attempt to legislate increased self-government through bills for incorporation of Silver City and for the right of taxation to create a public school system had resulted in Ring backlash. Naegle wrote:

> These high-handed measures of the "ring," coupled with the forestalling of the incorporation of Silver City and the substitution of an inadequate school law ... were almost more than the people of Silver City and southwestern New Mexico could endure. On the other hand they had come so near to upsetting the "apple-cart" [by the 1872 Legislature Revolt] that the "ring" took steps to curb the rising power of ... those of southern New Mexico who had proved such virile opposition. (Naegle thesis, pp. 37-38)

SECESSION AND ANNEXATION

By August 8, 1875, the Grant County *Herald* reported that Grant County's citizens sought secession from the Territory to escape the Ring's "political vassalage." (Naegle thesis, p. 39)

The Grant County Rebellion intentionally coincided with the American Revolution's centennial. On September 16, 1876, the Grant County *Herald* published "A Contemplated Political Change." Announced was a citizens' meeting to discuss annexation of Grant County to Arizona Territory to leave behind the "dictatorial and corrupt spirit" of men in Santa Fe. (Naegle thesis, p. 40) Three causes were listed:

> First: legislation by "Americans" would be more liberal and better suited to the progress of the county, for the primary interest of both Grant County and Arizona was mining.
> Second: Grant County has been denied equal representation in the legislative assembly of the Territory ...
> Third: that after attempts to procure remedial legislation they have been denied redress, and held in a state of vassalage without hope of relief.

Naegle noted: "[T]he people of Grant County seemed to be unanimously in favor of the measure." (Naegle thesis, p. 41) And the September 23, 1876 Tucson *Arizona Citizen* urged Grant County not to "sort o' wait and hear from Santa Fe ... before taking action [to join their Arizona Territory]."

On September 30, 1876, the *Herald* announced that the "Annexation Meeting" would be in Silver City on October 4th at 2 o'clock p.m. in Burns Hall. Sixty-two citizens, mostly from Silver City, had pledged to approve secession. (Naegle thesis, p. 41)

GRANT COUNTY DECLARATION OF INDEPENDENCE

At the October 4, 1876 Grant County Annexation Meeting, legislator John M. Ginn was elected Presiding Officer, and James Corbin as Secretary. A committee of five was elected to write resolutions: James Mullen, Peter Graves, William H. Eckles, Robert Metcalf, and D.B. Rhea as chairman. That day, they authored the "Grant County Declaration of Independence." The independence sought was from the Santa Fe Ring, called a "selfish oligarchy" functioning for "selfish interest." A committee of eight was chosen to write for Congress the memorial for annexation.

On Saturday, October 7, 1876, the Grant County *Herald* printed in full the "Grant County Declaration of Independence":

> Pursuant to call, a meeting of the citizens of Grant county, New Mexico, was held at Burns Hall, in Silver City, October 4, 1876, for the purpose of considering the propriety of severing our connections with New Mexico and annexing to the Territory of Arizona.
> On motion, J.M. Ginn was called to the chair who explained the object of the meeting and for-

cibly set forth the advantages to be derived from such a union.

On motion of I. N. Stevens Jas. Corbin was elected Secretary. After which James Mullen was loudly called for who responded and gave most satisfactory reasons why Grant County should ally her destinies with Arizona.

Upon motion of D. B. Rea it was moved and carried that a committee of five be appointed on resolutions. whereupon the Chair assigned as committeemen: D.B. Rea, CHAIRMAN, James Mullen, Peter Graves, W.H. Eckles, and Robert Metcalf.

During the absence of the committee, Colonel Ledbetter was called upon and entertained the meeting with some happy remarks, setting forth advantages of becoming a part of a progressive people, which were well timed and well received.

Mr. Rea, Chairman of the Committee on Resolutions, reported the following, which were read and unanimously adopted:

Whereas: Pursuant to a call published in the Grant County HERALD, signed by many prominent citizens of the said county, to make such steps as may be deemed necessary to sever our relations as a county from the Territory of New Mexico and annex to the Territory of Arizona; and we the citizens of Grant County here assembled, having met pursuant to said call, do hereby declare it is our earnest wish to join our political destinies with the neighboring Territory of Arizona and cease our political connection with the Territory of New Mexico, of which our county forms a part and for taking this important step we assign the following as some of the principal reasons for the desired change:

1. That we are geographically nearer the center of population and capital of said Territory of Arizona than that of the present Territory.

2. That we have a near community of interest with the said Territory of Arizona, in that our leading pursuit, which is mining, is identical with theirs.

3. That the laws enacted by our Territory are unsuited to our wants, and we consider those which govern our neighboring Territory better adapted to the exigencies of a mining community.

4. That we, as a community, are denied legal representation with the other counties of the Territory, and have little

or no voice in the enactment of laws which are necessary to our welfare which we believe would be remedied by the liberal-minded people of Arizona.

5. That we consider the Territory of New Mexico badly governed owing to the fact that the chief power in the Territorial legislation rests in the hands of a selfish oligarchy, who designedly wield the same in their own selfish interest, and owing to the prevailing temper and habits of her people we see no hope for relief in the near future.

6. That our geographical situation in relation to the Southern Pacific Railroad is such as induces us to believe that material interests will be greatly advanced by joining on to Arizona.

7. That this portion of our Territory is subject to Indian depredations from the same Apache bands who have their homes in Southern Arizona, and consequently a means of common defense in the way of a militia system could be better integrated and carried out by a political union with said Territory, whose interests in that respect is identical with ours; therefore be it

Resolved: That it is the wish of the people of Grant County, as expressed through the persons here assembled, that the necessary steps to be taken at once to further that view herein expressed.

Resolved: That the Governor and all other officials of the Territory of Arizona and also all her influential citizens be requested to co-operate with us in this movement.

Upon motion of W.H. Eckles, annexation be voted upon at our county election in November next was carried.

Mr. Rea moved that a committee of correspondence consisting of eight persons be appointed by the Chair. Carried ...

Mr. Lucas moved that the proceedings of this meeting be published in the Grant County HERALD and copies of same be forwarded to the Arizona papers and publication requested. Carried.

Mr. Wilson moved that the Chairman authorize a sufficient number of extra copies of the proceedings of this meeting to be published by the HERALD and forwarded by the committee to each member of the U.S. Senate and House of Representatves. Carried

DEFLATED REBELLION

On November 7, 1876, Grant County citizens voted almost unanimously for annexation to Arizona Territory. On January 3, 1877, Arizona Territory's Governor A.P.K. Safford seconded Grant County's annexation. (Naegle thesis, pp. 45-46)

Then national politics collided. November 1876's national election yielded Democratic control of the House. But anti-corruption Presidential candidate, Democrat Samuel J. Tilden, who had brought down William "Boss" Tweed's Tammany Hall Ring, lost by one electoral vote to Republican, Rutherford B. Hayes. Tilden claimed voter fraud in Florida, possibly engineered by voting overseer, Civil War Major General Lew Wallace (whom Hayes appointed by 1878 as New Mexico Territory's Governor). So Republican victor, Hayes, opposed Democratic Arizona's benefiting by inclusion of mine-rich Grant County.

Into that hostile political climate, on October 29, 1877, Arizona representative R.S. Stevens introduced to Congress House Resolution 795 for Grant County's annexation. It was referred to the committee on Territories, where it was killed. No one realized that President Hayes was entangled with the Santa Fe Ring. And Grant County's escape from that Ring was blocked.

Historian Naegle saw the positive:

> The Silver City [and Grant County] "rebels" had failed in their attempted "secession," but they reaped a victory in defeat. The specter of House Resolution 794 hovered over that "selfish oligarchy" ... and thus enabled the citizens of Silver City to have enacted almost any legislation they desired, for those "political parasites" feared that the attempt might be repeated. They had no desire to lose New Mexico's richest county as a source of revenue." (Naegle thesis, pp. 48-49)

Omitted is that the Grant County Rebellion ended with a whimper of accepting Ring concessions. Silver City was incorporated in 1878, enabling electing of their own public officials and assessing and collecting of their own taxes to create public schools. But there was no restoration of equal legislative representation, lost to Governor Marsh Giddings's 1872 gerrymandering. The rebellion of Grant County had deflated, lacking leadership and spirit for further fighting. Instead, Grant County retreated into silence and non-intervention as the Ring's rampages escalated in other parts of the Territory.

By the October 7, 1876 "Grant County Declaration of Independence," New Mexico Territory's Governor was Ringite Samuel Beach Axtell, who had been in office since the year before. He was gaining an education on how to crush anti-Ring uprisings. In the future, concessions would be replaced by brutality.

And in Arizona Territory, a 16 year old using the name Henry Antrim, having escaped Silver City's jail on September 23, 1775 for his burglary and robbery charges, and having fled New Mexico Territory in his own bid for freedom, was supporting himself as a cook at a small hotel; and as a thief of military horses, saddles, and blankets. And he was likely perfecting his hobby: gunmanship. But there was still no need for inventing his new name: William Henry "Billy" Bonney.

CHAPTER 5

COLFAX COUNTY WAR AGAINST THE SANTA FE RING: 1877

COLFAX COUNTY WAR OVERVIEW

ANALYSIS: *Peaking in 1877 with anti-Ring exposés, the Colfax County War pitted original Maxwell Land Grant settlers against the Santa Fe Ring-backed Maxwell Land Grant and Railway Company attempting their eviction after purchasing the Grant. The Ring, escalating its violence after the 1872 Legislature Revolt and 1876 Grant County Rebellion, resorted to murder and illegal removal of courts to block redress. Ultimately, 200 people died in uprisings from 1873 to 1887; with the 1875 Ring murder of anti-Ring leader, Reverend Franklin Tolby, being its lightning rod.*

COLFAX COUNTY WAR SOURCES

The Colfax County War - actually warring, since its anti-Ring uprisings spanned 1873 to 1887 without a central battle - peaked in 1877 with anti-Ring exposés in press and in complaints to the Hayes administration. No historian has yet documented its specific uprisings, its 200 victims, or noted its place in the Territory's escalating, anti-Ring, freedom fights.

Books do feature its major figures: Ring-murdered Revered Franklin J. Tolby, Ring-prosecuted Reverend Oscar P. McMains, anti-Ring gunslinger Clay Allison, railroadman Raymond Morley, and Attorney Frank Springer. Used here are: Norman Cleaveland's 1971 *The Morleys: Young Upstarts on the Southwest Frontier*; Morris F. Taylor's 1979 *O.P. McMains and the Maxwell Land Grant Conflict*; Agnes Morley Cleaveland's 1941 *No Life for a Lady* and 1952 *Satan's Paradise: From Lucien Maxwell to Fred Lambert*; and Jim Berry Pearson's 1961 *The Maxwell Land Grant*. Replicating Ring cover-ups, are Victor Westphall's 1973 *Thomas Benton Catron and His Era* and William Keleher's 1964 *The Maxwell Land Grant: A New Mexico Item*. The War is mentioned in David L. Caffey's 2007 *Frank Springer & New Mexico: From the Colfax County War to the Emergence of Modern Santa Fe*.

The Colfax County War did generate a treasure-trove of contemporary sources documenting the Santa Fe Ring's existence, its members and crimes, and citizens' attempts to end Ring tyranny. The *Cimarron News and Press*, under editors Raymond Morley and Attorney Frank Springer, published anti-Ring articles. Morley's mother-in-law, Mary Tibbles McPherson, became an anti-Ring fighter, who, in 1877, wrote extensive exposés for Washington, D.C. officials; and foreshadowed the Lincoln County War the next year by detailing crimes of T.B. Catron, S.B. Elkins, Governor S.B Axtell, Chief Justice Henry Waldo, and 3rd Judicial District Judge Warren Bristol. And Mary McPherson's daughter, Ada Morley, wife of Raymond Morley, wrote letters revealing citizens' terror at Ring retributions.

COLFAX COUNTY WAR AND BILLY BONNEY

Billy Bonney was connected to the Colfax County War through love and death, because it involved the almost two million acre Maxwell Land Grant. Profit from its 1870 sale, arranged by T.B. Catron and S.B. Benton Elkins, rocketed their Ring to power. The Grant's owner, Lucien Bonaparte Maxwell, then purchased eastern New Mexico Territory's demilitarized Fort Sumner, to relocate his family and make a town of that name. There, Maxwell's teenaged daughter, Paulita, became Billy's secret lover. Maxwell's widow, Luz Beaubien Maxwell, protected Billy after his 1881 jailbreak. And in the Maxwell's Fort Sumner mansion, occurred Billy's fatal ambush by Pat Garrett.

THE BEAUBIEN-MIRANDA AND MAXWELL LAND GRANT: 1841-1870

The anti-Ring fight in Colfax County is rooted in the history of the Maxwell Land Grant and its settlers. The land was originally part of Mexico, occupying what would become northern New Mexico and southern Colorado Territories. It was given by the last Mexican Governor, Manuel Armijo, in 1841, to Charles Hipolite Trotier de Beaubien, a French Canadian relocated to Taos, who, in 1823, had married Spanish heiress, María Paula Lovato, two years after Mexico won independence from Spain. Calling himself Don Carlos Beaubien, he was in partnership with a Guadalupe Miranda, Armijo's secretary. Armijo approved their land grant on January 8, 1841 as the Beaubien-Miranda, continuing the 2½ century policy to encourage settlement. By 1841, it had just seven more years until Mexico lost the Mexican-American War.

The year of establishing the Beaubien-Miranda Land Grant brought to Taos Lucien Bonaparte Maxwell, a son of the wealthy, politically active, Illinois, Menard family, along with his frontiersman friend, Kit Carson. Maxwell married Don Carlos Beaubien's daughter, Luz Trotier de Beaubien. Among their children were Paulita, who became Billy Bonney's sweetheart; and Peter, who betrayed Billy to Pat Garrett's ambush.

In 1848, the Beaubien-Miranda Land Grant was impacted by the Treaty of Guadalupe Hidalgo, which ended the Mexican-American War and ceded Mexico's huge northern half to the United States. It permitted Spanish and Mexican grant holders to retain ownership after Congressional approval of the titles and boundaries. Approval required submission of grant documents to the Surveyor General for recommendation to the Commissioner of the General Land Grant Office. If that Commissioner accepted the surveyed boundaries, the grant was submitted to Congress for confirmation and issuance of a patent to the claimants. The Santa Fe Ring was founded to exploit that approval process.

The Beaubien-Miranda Grant's heir, Carlos Beaubien's only son, Narcisc, was killed on January 18, 1847 in the Taos Rebellion during the Spanish-American War. Beaubien then made Lucien Maxwell his heir. When Beaubien died in 1864, Maxwell bought all Grant shares from his wife's sisters and from Beaubien's original partner, Guadalupe Miranda, making it the Maxwell Land Grant.

Lucien Maxwell was larger than life, lavishly generous, and frivolously grandiose. On the Grant, he ranched sheep; encouraged settlement; and founded Rayado, Elizabethtown, and Cimarron, where he built his gigantic mansion, a store, and a three story gristmill. But his beneficent control faltered as squatters flooded in after the 1866 discovery of gold near Mount Baldy. But Maxwell got his Aztec gold mine, the world's richest.

By 1867 Elizabethtown had 7,000 settlers. Ignoring Maxwell, they petitioned the Territorial Legislature to rename the Grant's land as Colfax County, after President Ulysses S. Grant's Vice-President, Schyler Colfax. Approved in January of 1869, Elizabethtown was its county seat and its settlers were legally empowered. Also in 1869, Maxwell, trying to establish the Grant's boundaries, was limited to 97,000 acres by Secretary of the Interior Jacob D. Cox.

In 1870, seeking escape from the Grant's complexities, naïve Lucien Maxwell became prey to land grant attorneys, T.B. Catron and S.B. Elkins, selling it to them for $650,000. Catron and Elkins quickly resold it at double the price to speculators, with its size inflated to about 2 million acres with complicit surveyors.

Maxwell continued his bad choices by moving his family from the magnificent Grant to the bleak flatlands of demilitarized Fort Sumner, situated in Bosque Redondo, an abandoned Navajo and Apache concentration camp, which he bought for $5,000. There he ranched sheep, planted corn and peaches, and refurbished its buildings skirting a parade ground, making the officers' quarters his mansion - and the future site of Billy Bonney's killing.

Equally misguided were Maxwell's investments advised by Elkins and Catron. By September of 1870, he invested $150,000 from his sale to found the First National Bank of Santa Fe and become President. The next year, Elkins and Catron founded the competing National Bank of New Mexico to force his sale to them. Elkins became president, and the First National Bank of Santa Fe became central to Santa Fe Ring finances. With Elkins's and Catron's advice, Maxwell also invested $150,000 into the Kansas Pacific Railroad; but quickly lost the money when it reorganized. A broken man, Maxwell died on July 25, 1875. His inadvertent revenge was the Colfax County War.

From the time of Maxwell's 1870 sale, the Grant's owners and officers were linked in settlers' minds with the Santa Fe Ring.

MAXWELL LAND GRANT COMPANY CONFLICT: 1870-1887

After Lucien Maxwell's 1870 sale of his Grant, Elkins, Catron and American speculators sold it to British, then Dutch, buyers; followed by an audacious, brief, take-over by Catron himself.

In 1871, the American speculators - Colorado Senator Gerome B. Chaffee; Colorado congressman, George M. Chilcott; Cimarron lawyer and mining investor, Charles F. Holly; and entrepreneur, Wilson Waddington, with Elkins as their lawyer, sold it to a British syndicate, under John Collinson of London, for $1,350,000: yielding profit fueling the Santa Fe Ring. Another attorney in the transaction was William Evetts, a past U.S. Attorney General and future Secretary of State under President Rutherford B. Hayes. The British syndicate resurveyed to achieve about two million acres, which was approved by Surveyor General T. Rush Spencer, a member of their company - as was Elkins.

In 1872, the British syndicate sold the Grant to Dutch investors for $5,000,000. The Dutch investors incorporated as the Maxwell Land Grant and Railway Company with Elkins as president of their board of directors and Catron as their attorney (as he remained into the 1900's). According to Norman Cleaveland, Elkins was also an owner. (Cleaveland, p. 75) The Company's intent was sale of mining claims, timber tracts, coal tracts, agricultural land, grazing land, and railroad passageway over its Raton Pass. In 1877, President Hayes's Secretary of the Interior, Carl Schurz, required resurvey of the Grant for final Congressional confirmation. Ring-beholden Surveyor General Henry M. Atkinson (Catron's later cattle ranching partner in the American Valley Company) awarded the surveying contract to Elkins's brother, John T. Elkins, who, in an implausible 21 days, alleged 1,714,764.94 acres. On June 5, 1878, the Grant's patent was issued by Secretary of the Interior Carl Schurz (who that year also helped cover up the Ring's killing of John Tunstall).

Norman Cleaveland, in his 1971 book *The Morleys*, indicates the Grant's fraud by quoting a September 14, 1892 speech by past New Mexico Territorial Surveyor General about Elkins and his corrupt practice of buying grant lands, then resurveying for inflated size. Cleaveland wrote:

> [Elkins] made himself particularly conspicuous as the hero of the famous Maxwell Grant, which as Secretary [of the Interior Jacob D.] Cox decided in 1869, contained only about 96,000 acres, but which under the manipulation of Elkins, was surveyed and patented for 1,714,764 acres, of nearly 2,680 square miles. (Cleaveland, p. 74)

The Maxwell Land Grant Company from the start considered the settlers "squatters" to be eliminated. In 1872, when Elkins failed to remove them by notices, Catron, as Territorial Attorney General, evicted them. But instead of leaving, Elizabethtown's residents rioted in protest to keep their properties. The Colfax County War had begun.

In response, Ringite Governor Marsh Giddings, after petition by Elkins, sent in local Fort Union troops; just as he had used Fort Marcy troops to suppress the Legislature Revolt earlier that year. (Noteworthy is that that Fort Union's future commander, Nathan Augustus Monroe Dudley, in 1878, would, with his new command at Fort Stanton, likewise use troops for Ring-partisan crushing of the Lincoln County War's freedom fighters.) To further curtail Elizabethtown's settlers' power, Giddings, in a disempowering move, like he had used after the 1872 Legislature Revolt, moved Colfax County's seat from Elizabethtown to Cimarron, where the Maxwell Land Grant Company was headquartered in Maxwell's past mansion. Again eviction notices were sent and ignored.

In 1873, The Land Grant Company hired 26 year old William Raymond Morley from Iowa as Chief Construction Engineer of the Atchison Topeka and Santa Fe Railroad. He was then made their vice-president under President Elkins; a strategic strengthening of their railroad connection, since their Company owned a route over the Raton Pass. As Catron and Elkins had known, a key value to the Grant was that the old Santa Fe Trail's pass through the mountains at the Colorado border was ideal for track extension into New Mexico Territory. Morley brought to Cimarron his wife, Ada McPherson Morley. They were given use of the Maxwell mansion as their home. Morley also became editor of the *Cimarron Press*, founded by the Grant Company. But he quickly became anti-Ring, bringing to Cimarron his Iowa attorney friend, Frank Springer, to negotiate with the settlers in place of Catron.

In 1874, the Ring made its next move with Elkins as Territorial Delegate to U.S. Congress exerting Washington, D.C. Ring influence. The Department of the Interior, ignoring the 1860 Congressional act, declared the Grant public domain. Then, with Catron replacing Elkins as president of the Grant Company's board of directors (Westphall, p. 109), it defaulted on its property tax bond. As Norman Cleaveland stated: "Morley blamed Elkins and Catron ... and felt the Santa Fe Ring was attempting to gain control of the Grant as they controlled almost everything else in New Mexico." (Cleaveland, p. 87)

To that end, Colfax County Ringite attorney and frontman, Melvin W. Mills, purchased the entire Grant at public auction for its back taxes of $16,479! Catron was poised to buy it from Mills for $20,000 - one cent per acre! This plot was halted by the Dutch owners redeeming the property. But Catron's machination was publicly exposed.

That 1874, the beleaguered settlers got a voice. Raymond Morley added Frank Springer as co-editor to *Cimarron News*, making it anti-Ring. That year, they opposed Elkins's re-election as Delegate to Congress, and consolidated with unsuspected Ringite, Will Dawson's, Elizabethtown *Press and Telegraph* as the

Cimarron News and Press. Cleaveland wrote: "[Morley and Springer] undoubtedly considered a newspaper a necessity in any effective opposition to the Santa Fe Ring which controlled most of the other newspapers in the Territory." (Cleaveland, p. 84)

By 1875, settlers' anti-Ring fervor increased. In that summer's elections, local Ringites, Attorney Melvin W. Mills and Land Grant Company stockholder, Dr. Robert Longwill, were elected respectively representative to the legislature and as Probate Judge. Once elected, Mills and Longwill shielded a local Ringite, Francisco "Pancho" Griego, from being charged for murdering two soldiers in a gambling quarrel in Cimarron's St. James Hotel. Norman Cleaveland confirms that Raymond Morley and Ring opponent, Methodist Minister Franklin J. Tolby, were, at the time, anonymously writing exposé articles for the *New York Sun* about the Ring's "stranglehold." (Cleaveland, p. 87).

The Ring retaliated, murdering Tolby on September of 1875. Likely instigators of his thug killers were Mills and Longwill. That marked Catron's new Ring strategy: terrorism. The stratagem would be replicated in three years in Lincoln County with Ringites James Dolan, John Riley, and Sheriff William Brady using outlaw Jessie Evans and his gang to murder John Tunstall.

RING MURDER OF FRANKLIN J. TOLBY: 1875

The Maxwell Land Grant Company, under Ringite guidance, used hired gunslingers to halt opposition and force the settlers off their land. The resisting fighters of Colfax County War would lack a central battle, but had a martyr: Methodist Reverend Franklin J. Tolby, a missionary circuit-rider to Colfax County's Cimarron and Elizabethtown. He had become an anti-Ring, anti-Land Grant Company, pro-settler activist. From Indiana, Tolby arrived at Cimarron on January 1, 1874. By July of 1875, an unsigned letter printed in the *New York Sun*, and believed to be by him, accused Catron, Elkins, and Chief Justice and 1st Judicial District Court Judge, Joseph P. Palen, of being Ring leaders. Palen had kept his judgeship after the defeated 1872 Legislature Revolt.

By early September of 1875, Reverend Tolby and Judge Palen were witnessed in public altercation in Cimarron. Tolby accused Palen of bias in shielding Ringite Francisco "Pancho" Griego after his murder of the two soldiers at the St. James Hotel that May. It was known that Griego helped elect Ringites Melvin Mills and Dr. Robert Longwill to the legislature in 1872, and that Griego was protected from indictment by Catron as U.S. Attorney and by Attorney William Breeden. Palen attacked Tolby for criticizing his court. Defiantly, Tolby stated - according to Frank Springer's August 9, 1978 deposition to Presidential Investigator Frank Warner Angel - that he would "write up [Palen] so that 200,000 readers should see the record." This threat appeared to confirm also that Tolby was authoring the anonymous *New York Sun* letters exposing Palen, Catron, Elkins and their Ring. (Cleaveland, pp. 97-98) Tolby had also opposed Ring-backed S.B. Axtell as Governor. (Taylor, p. 39)

On September 14, 1875, Franklin Tolby, alone on horseback, was assassinated when returning on a remote canyon road to Cimarron after preaching at Elizabethtown. He was 33, and married with three children. His concealed corpse had two bullets in its back, his horse was tethered, and there was no sign of robbery. Tolby's believed Ring assassination added fuel to the Colfax County War's fighting.

Tolby's martyrdom switched Ring-backer, prior Confederate soldier, Clay Allison, to anti-Ring. He was a Grant settler since 1866, cattle rancher, racist, drunk, and trigger-happy gunslinger. That summer, he had backed Elkins for Delegate to Congress, Longwill for Territorial Representative to the legislature, and Mills for Colfax County's Probate Judge. Allison was also rumored to have refused $700 to kill Tolby himself. He ended up Colfax County's less charismatic - and, at 35, a much older - version of Billy the Kid; dying at 47 by a drunken fall from a wagon. But later, Allison's boorish aggression blurred into Ring mythologists' fabricated "outlaw Billy the Kid." Norman Cleaveland's quote of Cimarron businessman Henry M. Porter about Clay Allison foreshadows the Ring's future defamation of Billy:

> The younger set ... would frequently come to Cimarron, get full, and as they called it shoot up the town; that is shoot at men, chickens, dogs, pigs, and at the pictures on the walls of the bar rooms, make men they did not fancy dance at the point of their guns ... for their amusement. During these escapades the stores and houses would be closed and the streets deserted. (Cleaveland, pp. 79-80)

Clay Allison, for accusing Tolby's Ringite killers, earned Ring retaliation of malicious prosecution murder indictments under a Ring-controlled court in Taos County. And there also emerged a new anti-Ring leader: Reverend Oscar P. McMains.

REVEREND OSCAR P. McMAINS'S PURSUIT OF TOLBY'S RING KILLERS: 1875

From murdered Reverend Franklin J. Tolby's blood, sprang Reverend Oscar P. McMains, a more aggressive Ring opponent. A high-minded, hot-tempered, circuit riding Methodist missionary, he came to Cimarron from Colorado in June of 1875, becoming Tolby's assistant, while working as a printer for the *Cimarron News and Press*.

After Tolby's September 14, 1875 murder, Oscar McMains took over Tolby's missionary circuit as well as assuming leadership of pro-settler opposition to the Maxwell Land Grant Company and the Santa Fe Ring. Importantly, he sought justice for Tolby.

Since the Ringite Colfax County Sheriff did nothing, McMains organized what he called the "Colfax County Ring" to arrest Tolby's Santa Fe Ring murderers (as the Lincoln County Regulators would attempt arrest of John Tunstall's Ringite murderers). McMains soon ferreted out the killers; thus, becoming himself the Ring's likely next victim.

He exposed Ringite mail contractor, Florencio Donoghue, who admitted to hiring a new Cimarron Constable, Cruz Vega, to deliver mail for just the murder day along the murder site canyon. But the Sheriff refused to arrest Vega, a nephew of Ringite Francisco "Pancho" Griego. (In 1878, Ringite Lincoln County Sheriff William Brady would identically block arrest of John Tunstall's Ringite murderers.)

So Oscar McMains and his men took it upon themselves to question Cruz Vega at the ranch where he worked. Vega's recalcitrance led to a feigned hanging and his confession of his witnessing the murder, which he stated was actually done by a Manuel Cardenas. Vega added that Cardenas had been hired by Florencio Donoghue to kill Tolby. When the vigilantes threatened more violence, McMains left. Among those remaining was Clay Allison. Though all were masked, Allison was believed to have completed Cruz Vega's lynching.

As to Clay Allison, on November 1, 1875, Cruz Vega's uncle, Francisco "Pancho" Griego, drunkenly accosted him at the Saint

James Hotel, across the street from the Maxwell mansion. Allison killed him with three shots, claiming self defense.

As to Manuel Cardenas, an arrest warrant was issued based on Cruz Vega's accusation. Cardenas was arrested in Elizabethtown and questioned by its Justice of the Peace on November 6th. Cardenas accused Vega of the murder, but admitted that he and Vega had been hired for $500 by Ringites Florencio Donoghue, Attorney Melvin Mills, Dr. Robert Longwill, and now-dead Francisco "Pancho" Griego, to do the killing.

Cimarron was in an uproar. Ada Morley, in her diary, as quoted by her grandson, Norman Cleaveland, called it "The Week of the Reign of Terror." (Cleaveland, p. 122) Clay Allison failed to catch Longwill, who escaped to Fort Union after Cardenas's accusation, then to Catron's protection in Santa Fe. Donoghue, Mills, and Cardenas were arrested. For intimidation, on November 8, 1875, Governor Axtell sent Fort Union's 9th Cavalry to Cimarron. Norman Cleaveland wrote that fearing his murder by the troops, his grandfather, Raymond Morley, fled town:

> [I]n Colfax County the U.S. Army from Fort Union was at the service of the Santa Fe Ring. Grandfather knew the leaders of the Ring well enough to be convinced that they would not hesitate to use the Army to advance their political and financial interests. (Cleaveland, p. 102)

As terrified Ada Morley wrote to her hiding husband that November 8, 1875 day, *"The revolution has begun in earnest."* Meanwhile, her firebrand visiting mother, Mary McPherson, was busy writing all the "news" to send to him. (Cleaveland, p. 102)

On November 11, 1875, Manuel Cardenas, Melvin Mills, and Florencio Donoghue had a preliminary hearing in Cimarron under Justice of the Peace Trauer. To represent these defendants, Catron sent his law firm member and fellow Missourian, Henry Waldo. (Four years later, in 1879, Waldo would defend Ringite Commander N.A.M. Dudley for his Lincoln County War atrocities.) At the hearing, Oscar McMains questioned the witnesses. Cardenas withdrew his confession and Mills denied involvement; but Donoghue's murder threat against Tolby had been witnessed. Only Mills was released for lack of evidence.

On November 11th, the Ring murdered again. The victim was stool pigeon Manuel Cardenas. When he was being led back to jail after the hearing, masked men shot him in the head.

Oscar McMains then organized and co-chaired a citizens' committee. Frank Springer was Secretary. It met on November 10, 1875, as reported in the *Cimarron News and Press*, to determine the Ring's role in Tolby's "murderous assassination." Already subjected to the Ring's public "outlawing," they countered that they "represent all portions of the county and all citizens ... We are not a mob of lawless men as has been reported abroad, bent upon violence and defiance of law, but on the contrary have assembled legally and quietly for the purpose of the doing of justice and securing the punishment of crime." Mary McPherson enclosed that article in her complaint to Washington, D.C. It established murderers Cruz Vega and Manuel Cardinas as "the tools of other parties;" and that troops were illegally used obstruct justice. It stated:

Whereas; On the 14th day of September, A.D. 1875, the Rev F.J. Tolby, a minister of the gospel resident among us, and a man who for sterling qualities, both as a minister and a citizen, commanded the highest respect and esteem among all the people of this county, was foully assassinated, while traveling upon the public highway, and, Whereas the report of this murder ... has created an impression that the lives of peaceable citizens are not safe here, and has thereby worked a great detriment and injury to our county, deterring many persons from settling and making their homes here ...

That the facts disclosed revealed **deliberately planned assassination, in which the men Cruz Vega and Manuel Cardinas were the tools of other parties**, who from some motive, aside from plunder, planned the murder and procured the two men above named to perform the cowardly act.

That we regard those who procured the commission of the murder as far more guilty if possible, than the duped and hired tools, and that if satisfactory evidence is found to discover and identify any such party or parties there should not be permitted to them any loophole to escape the extreme penalty of the law ...

That we regard the action of the United States authorities at Fort Union in concealing R. [Robert] H. Longwill [Ringman who hired Cruz Vega and Manuel Cardinas], and shielding him from arrest by properly authorized officers of the county, with warrants legally issued, and thereby enabling him to escape, and avoid an examination here, upon charges made against him, as **an unwarrantable obstruction of justice and an arbitrary and illegal use of power of the army** of the United States, and it deserves reprehension and condemnation of all citizens.

By 1878, Tolby's murder was replicated in John Tunstall's killing by Ringites' hired thugs, followed by blocked prosecutions. Thus, Tolby's killers, Florencio Donoghue, Robert Longwill and Melvin Mills - like Tunstall's killers - got no penalty. But McMains, Morley, and Springer were in line for assassination; while McMains was charged with Cruz Vega's murder.

RING RETALIATIONS, CITIZENS' EXPOSÉS, AND TERROR: 1875-1876

RING DECLARES COLFAX COUNTY IN ANARCHY

The Ring's naming of opponents as outlaws for malicious prosecution - begun in 1872 by Governor Marsh Giddings and U.S. Attorney Catron for the Legislature Revolt - was used to accuse Colfax County settlers of "lawlessness" for attempting arrest of Melvin Mills and Robert Longwill for Tolby's murder. On November 16, 1875, Ring mouthpiece, *Santa Fe Weekly New Mexican*, in "Anarchy in Cimarron," reported:

The situation in Cimarron remains in many respects about as reported in our issue of yesterday. There seems to be an armed band of men in and about town bent on violence, lawlessness and ruling to suit themselves; they declare they are assisting civil authorities, but from all we can learn compel them to do as they see fit. The citizens are terrified and many of them have left to save their lives. **Mr. Mills and Donoghue who have been charged with complicity in the murder of Tolby (which we believe to be entirely unfounded) are in the hands of the mob**, and it is said they declare their intention not to surrender [to] them even on writ of habeas corpus. **U.S. troops are on the ground and they will prevent violence and bloodshed if they have notice in time**; but even their presence has not had the effect to disperse the mob who seem to have control of the prisoners and the administration of affairs.

By December 21, 1875, Ringite Will Dawson, who, in 1874, had merged his *Elizabeth City Railway Press and Telegraph* to Morley's and Springer's *Cimarron News* as the *Cimarron News and Press*, published, on his own, a pro-Ring obituary of hated 1st Judicial District Judge Joseph Palen - whose judgeship position was assumed by Catron's law firm member, Henry Waldo.

"THE TERRITORY OF ELKINS" RING EXPOSÉ

On December 22, 1875, the *New York Sun* published an anti-Ring article about Tolby's murder: "The Territory of Elkins.' Assassination of Supposed Sun Correspondent. The Murder of the Rev. F.J. Tolby in New Mexico. A Probate Judge Accused of Complicity in the Crime. Indignation Meeting." Norman Cleaveland confirmed that his mother, Agnes Morley Cleaveland, Ada and Raymond's child, knew Raymond was authoring *Sun* articles as well as Tolby. Agnes confirmed it in her 1941 book *No Life for A Lady*. (Agnes Cleaveland, p. 7) And Mary McPherson included "The Territory of Elkins" in her 1877 anti-Ring complaint to Washington, D.C. It stated:

"THE TERRITORY OF ELKINS."
Assassination of Supposed Sun Correspondent. The Murder of the Rev. F.J. Tolby in New Mexico. A Probate Judge Accused of Complicity in the Crime. Indignation Meeting.

"Santa Fe, N.M., Nov. 26. - **The political revolution which has taken place and is still in progress in this Territory is mainly attributed to the exposures of the Santa Fé Ring which have appeared in the Sun, and which have created great consternation among our corrupt officials, the Sun having a wide circulation in this region.** By means of libel suits, and still more effectual measures, **the Ring** has succeeded in intimidating the local press, with one or two exceptions; **and so long as the courts are constituted as they are at present, it is absolutely unsafe for any man to actively oppose the corrupt scheme of the Ring.** The nature of the means taken to harass those who show rebellious spirit has already been described in this correspondence, and events of recent occurrence, which will form the subject of this letter, will give the reader an idea of the difficulties which are encountered by those who are striving to effect a reform in the administration in our territorial affairs.

"On the 14th of September last, the Rev. F.J. Tolby, a minister of the gospel, generally respected and beloved, was brutally murdered on the highway while passing through a lonely canyon. The murder was involved in mystery for a time. Mr. Tolby was an active, bold, and outspoken man, who took much interest in public affairs, and did not hesitate to express his opinion. **He was not known to have an enemy in the world, save members of the Ring whom he had vigorously and publicly** denounced for their offence against society.

It is said that a few days before his death Mr. Tolby had a warm discussion with Judge Palen of the first Judicial District, one of the chiefs of the Ring, who tried to intimidate him without effect, for the preacher boldly announced his intention of writing of the Ring rascalities for the eastern press, and up to the time of his murder he exerted all his influence against the rogues in office.

"It was known that Mr. Tolby had threatened to make exposures through the press, and in some quarters he was suspected of having written the letter to the Sun which excited such commotion in the Federal Ring. These, and other circumstances, excited suspicion from the first that he had fallen a victim to the malevolence of the Ring, or of some of its members, but for a long time no direct proof of it could be obtained. At last, however, the actual murderers were hunted down, and when it was found that they implicated the principal members of the Colfax county branch of the Ring as the instigators of the crime, the indignation of the people knew no bounds. At one time it was feared that every one of the politicians named in the connection with the murder would be strung up by the neck without the intervention of judge or jury; but calmer counsel prevailed, and acting upon information gained from the murderers and other sources, warrants were issued for the arrest of the accused parties.

"The persons charged by the murderers as the planners and accessories to the murder are the recognized strikers of the Ring in Colfax county. Some of them were lately elected to office through the influence of the Ring. Their names are R. [Robert] H. Longwill, Probate Judge; M. [Melvin] W. Mills, member of the Legislature; F. [Florencio] Donoghue and F. [Francisco] Griego. Longwill fled to this city [Santa Fe] where he still remains, protected by his Ring friends from arrest. Mills was discharged for want of evidence. Donoghue is in jail awaiting trial in default of $20,000 bail, and Griego is dead ... Although there was no legal evidence to prove that the recognized leaders of the Ring either had any connection with the assassination of Mr. Tolby, or knew that such an atrocious crime was in contemplation, yet it is impossible to make the majority of the people of Cimarron and vicinity believe that they are altogether guiltless, and the feeling against all persons who are supposed to be connected in any way to the operation of Elkins & Co. is bitter in the extreme ...

"On the 10th of November [1876] a mass meeting of the citizens of Colfax county was held in the court house in

Cimarron, which was largely attended by the leading men from all parts of the county. **The Rev. O.P. McMains presided, and resolutions were adopted that the killing of Mr. Tolby was a deliberately planned assassination, in which the actual murderers were the tools of other parties, who aside from plunder, planned the murder; and those who procured the murder are far more guilty, if possible, than the duped and hired tools**, and that, if satisfactory evidence is found to discover and identify any such party or parties, there should not be permitted to them any loophole to escape the extreme penalty of the law.

"**If a new election for Delegate to Congress could be held for tomorrow, Elkins would be defeated by such a tremendous majority that not even the tools of the Santa Fé Ring would dare attempt the job of counting him in.**

On December 31, 1875, Will Dawson, with Morley and Springer out of town, again enraged settlers by his *Cimarron News and Press* editorial attack on that *Sun* article. He wrote:

We find another one of those lying, brutal letters in the New York Weekly Sun of the 22d inst., without signature, and purporting to come out of Santa Fe. The writer, whoever he may be, will be looked upon as a coward, a disturber of the peace, as well as a slanderer upon the good name and fair fame of this portion of New Mexico ... There can be none but the worst imaginable motive in any one who will persist in keeping alive the bad condition of feeling in this county which has grown out of distressing crimes, ending in blood and death.

Over 150 Colfax County settlers, including Raymond Morley and Frank Springer, published a signed response letter to Dawson. And Morley and Springer withdrew as *Cimarron News and Press* editors. Mary McPherson used that response letter, titled by her "What the People of Colfax Say," as part of her personally published, August of 1877 booklet sent to the Departments of Interior and Justice as: "In the Matter of the Charges vs. Gov. S.B. Axtell and Other New Mexico Officials." Its salient point - prophetic for Lincoln County - was: "[T]he history of the past few years has shown that through the regular legal actions of the authorities in power, such cruel and bloodthirsty deeds [as Tolby's murder] are not likely to be punished." The response letter stated:

Will. D. Dawson, Publisher News and Press:

"Sir, - In your issue of Dec. 31st, you take the occasion to depart from the former [Anti-Ring] course of your paper and to condemn in the strongest terms a certain article in the New York Sun, which gives an account of the recent troubles in Colfax County, growing out of the murder of Rev. F.J. Tolby.

"We the citizens of Colfax County, have read the account in the *Sun*, and notwithstanding your severe denunciation of it, declare that it is in substance true, and that your comments are unjust in the extreme, not only as regards the article in question, but also as regards to further articles in the *Sun* which have opened the eyes of the world to the corruptions which have and do exist in New Mexico politics, and we hope and trust that the *Sun* and the newspaper press generally will continue their efforts until a thorough investigation, from proper sources, is made, which will bring about a better state of things. Further than this, we consider, notwithstanding your insinuations to the contrary, that the action of the people in investigating the Tolby murderers and punishing such of them as were caught, was a public necessity, and for the public good, inasmuch as **the history of the past few years has shown that through the regular legal actions of the authorities in power, such cruel and bloodthirsty deeds are not likely to be punished.** We hereby request you to publish with this the *Sun* article referred to, with your criticism on the same, that all may see and know where the right is.

[153 signatures follow, including Raymond Morley's, Frank Springer's, Oscar McMains's, and Clay Allison's]

Mary McPherson then added in her "In the Matter of the Charges vs. Gov. S.B. Axtell and Other New Mexico Officials," the Ring's malicious prosecution, as well as Catron's lying, stating:

> An attempt to indict all the signers of the petition was made, but was abandoned from motives of policy, and indictments for other alleged offences instead, were secured against upward of fifty persons. Catron, in his "defense," (Feb. 24 last,) [Catron's February 24, 1877 response letter to McPherson] at the Department of Justice, admits: "I was not a member of the Legislature, and had no official connection except as an attorney. Disorders prevailed, and W.R. Morley encouraged the lawlessness and murder by his newspaper."

On January 19, 1876, Clay Allison took his own action. With others, he nocturnally raided the *Cimarron News and Press* office and typeset a red headline: "CLAY ALLISON'S EDITION." Then he threw the printing machinery into the Cimarron River. The next day, sobered-up, he reimbursed Morley's wife, Ada, for new equipment. Then Morley and Springer resumed editorships of the *Cimarron News and Press* without Dawson.

RING REMOVAL OF COLFAX COUNTY COURTS

With Colfax County not backing down, the Ring chose suppression. On January 14, 1876, the Maxwell Land Grant Company, with Governor Axtell's backing, petitioned the courts to force settlers to buy or rent their land, with eviction for refusal.

The same day, without notification or debate, Axtell removed Colfax County's courts by backing a bill in the legislature to attach Colfax to distant Taos County for judicial purposes. This replicated Governor Marsh Giddings's 1872 disempowerment of Grant, Doña Ana, and Lincoln Counties by removing their legislative representatives. Furthermore, Colfax County residents were barred from Taos juries; and any Colfax County witness in litigation had to travel a 55 mile, sometimes impassable, road over a mountain range to Taos. When Axtell was telegraphed to withhold his signature until meeting with a Cimarron delegation, he responded. "Bill Signed. S.B. Axtell."

The immediate motive was to block trials of Tolby's murderers, and to convict indicted Oscar McMains as Cruz Vega's killer. The long-range plan was to snuff out the Colfax County War.

On January 19 1876, Raymond Morley, local merchant Henry M. Porter, and Sheriff William Cunningham sent telegrams to Governor Axtell to plead for restoration of their courts. Axtell's answer was snide Ring totalitarianism, using the outlaw myth:

> "*Law requires two terms be held in Taos. Should it appear that its objects have been accomplished, the Governor is authorized to restore courts to Colfax ... I see two sides. Broken laws, property wantonly destroyed and murdered men are on one side. I have no compromise to make.*" (Cleaveland, p. 113)

Springer, Morley, Porter, and Allison then asked Axtell to meet them in Cimarron. Their signatures became a Ring hit list.

Then Springer went to Santa Fe to meet with Axtell about the removed courts. In his deposition of August 9, 1978 to Frank Warner Angel, Springer stated:

[Axtell] spoke with extreme bitterness about the people of Colfax county, and informed me that he had visited every other county in the Territory, and had intended to visit Colfax in its turn, but now he should not do so. I asked and urged him to go to Cimarron and see the people and learn the facts for himself, but he positively refused, and said that he was fully informed about matters in that county and didn't need further information. **He said there were bad men there and that he intended to have them punished or compelled to leave the county, if it took all the troops in New Mexico.** *He spoke particularly and repeatedly of one [Clay] Allison and seemed very bitter towards him and mentioned him especially as one whom he intended to have indicted and punished, or compelled to leave the county.*

RING PLOT TO ASSASSINATE MORLEY, SPRINGER, ALLISON, AND PORTER: MARCH, 1876

The Ring knew its main Colfax County opponents. The next step was killing them. By then, using troops for citizens' suppression included Governor Marsh Giddings's bringing Fort Marcy soldiers to the 1872 Legislature Revolt; Giddings's stationing of troops in its Catron and Palen instigated Supreme Court session to nullify that legislature's acts; Giddings's 1872 setting of Fort Union troops against Elizabethtown settlers fighting evictions; and Governor S.B. Axtell's employing Fort Union troops in November of 1875 to block arrests of Franklin Tolby's killers. And Fort Union troops would be used later in 1876 to prevent dissent during the Taos County Grand Jury's unjust murder trials clearing Tolby's killers; and, by 1878, Fort Stanton soldiers under Commander N.A.M. Dudley would enable murder and arson to stop Regulators' certain victory in the Lincoln County War. So it was natural that, in 1876, Governor Axtell employed Fort Union troops to carry out assassination of Colfax County's anti-Ring leaders under guise of law.

Axtell's plan became known as the "Dear Ben plot." In March of 1876, Ringite 2nd Judicial District Judge Benjamin Stevens arrived in Cimarron in the middle of a week bringing a telegram as a lure from Axtell, while also having a secret telegraphed letter from Axtell. Arriving also, at Stevens's request, were Fort Union 9th Cavalry under a Captain F. Moore. Stevens, knowing Morley, invited him to his hotel room across the street in the St. James, and gave him the lure telegram stating Axtell was coming by Saturday's coach for a secret meeting with Morley, Springer, Allison, and Porter, as they had requested. In fact, they were to be met by the black 9th Cavalrymen; the twisted logic being that racist Allison would react violently and justify killing all four men.

Morley was warned of the plot, possibly by the telegraph operator giving him Axtell's secret telegraphed letter to Benjamin Stevens as *"Dear Ben."* It said: *"Do not hesitate at extreme measures. Your honor is at stake now and failure is fatal."* Axtell later denied authorship, but Captain F. Moore of that 9th Cavalry division confirmed the plot. The telegram stated:

Dear Ben – The second telegram delivered to you at Fort Union, directed to Cimarron, was intended to leak, but the operator here says he cannot raise the Cimarron office. If I was expected, our friends would probably be on hand, as the guard is only a Government escort. I do not think your definite business is suspected. Wade [James F. Wade, Commander Fort Union] informed Hatch [General Edward S. Hatch, Commander, District of New Mexico] that he had been ready all the time to assist you, but could not find that you wanted to do it. Hatch says that their opinion is that you weakened and do not want to arrest the man. **Have your men placed to arrest him and to kill all the men who resist you or stand with those who do resist you. Our man signed the invitation with others who were at that meeting for me to visit Colfax – Porter, Morley, Springer, et. al.** *Now, if they expect me Saturday, they will be on hand.* **Send me letters by messenger, and do not hesitate at extreme measures. Your honor is at stake now, and a failure is fatal.** *If others resist or attempt murder, bring them also. Hatch is excited, and wishes, of course, to put all the blame on the civil officers. I am more anxious on your account than for any other reason. I clearly see that we have no friends in Colfax, and I have suspected all along that some of our pretended friends were traitors. Yours &c., S.B. Axtell*

To ensure success, Axtell had already removed Colfax County's elected Sheriff, O.K. Chittenden, by claiming he had not filed his tax bond. (As Axtell repeated on May 28, 1878 to remove anti-Ring Lincoln County Sheriff John Copeland.) Axtell then appointed a Ringite and complicit sheriff named Rinehart.

Morley warned the others. So the plot failed when none were present when the fatal Saturday coach arrived.

But the Fort Union troops stayed in Cimarron for a week, even accompanying Ringite Sheriff Rinehart to Clay Allison's ranch to arrest him for murders of Griego, Vega, and even for killing Cardenas - apparently still trying to make him react violently to justify his killing. (Inciting of violence to justify murder was done twice in Lincoln County in 1878 by Sheriff William Brady: first to harass John Tunstall and Alexander McSween by property attachments during the Ring's malicious harassment embezzlement case; then using troops against McSween at John Chisum's ranch before the Lincoln County War.)

One year later, in 1877, Morley and Springer published that secret "Dear Ben plot" telegram in their *Cimarron News and Press*. Mary McPherson added it to her complaint to the Departments of Justice and the Interior about Axtell and other Ringites; and Frank Springer gave it in his August 9, 1878 deposition to Investigator Frank Warner Angel to justify removing Axtell as Governor.

ADA MORLEY'S MALICIOUS PROSECUTION BY U.S. ATTORNEY THOMAS BENTON CATRON: 1875

Catron's malicious prosecution of Raymond Morley's wife, Ada, laid bare his megalomaniacal and despotic madness, full-blown by 1875. To avenge himself on her anti-Ring husband, Catron, as U.S. Attorney, tortured her legally; intending also to intimidate her visiting and outspoken mother, Mary Tibbles McPherson.

The triggering incident involved McPherson, inspired by Reverend Franklin J. Tolby before his murder. She mailed an anti-Ring letter to Washington, D.C. at the Cimarron post office. Ada, frightened by its ramifications to her family, retrieved it from the postal box. Ada's grandson, Norman Cleaveland, recounted: "The postmaster, being a political appointee - which in New Mexico meant an appointee of the Santa Fe Ring - would have to follow the party line regarding the Morleys ... It was a made-to-order situation for the Santa Fe Ring." (Cleaveland, p. 91)

As discussed above, Victor Westphall falsely claimed that Ada and Catron merely argued about use of the Land Grant Company buggy, and that she was not indicted. But Norman Cleaveland published the truth of U.S. Attorney Catron's indictment of her for mail theft in his 1871 book, *The Morleys*. Cleaveland wrote:

That [buggy taking] injury to his ego apparently was serious enough in Catron's eyes to justify his indictment of Granny for the very serious charge of robbing the United States post office. And with practically all the courts and law enforcement agencies, including the U.S. Army, under his control, the Morleys and Mother McPherson had real cause for concern ... (pp. 94-95)

Ada's daughter, Agnes Morley Cleaveland, described her mother's ongoing terror in her 1941 book, *No Life for a Lady*: "When my mother told me this story in 1884, the statute of limitations had not yet taken effect. 'I'm still under indictment,' she said." (Agnes Cleaveland, p. 9)

Norman Cleaveland stated that Attorney Frank Springer tried to intervene with local Ringite Probate Judge Robert H. Longwill (later Tolby's unpunished killer) to prevent Ada's indictment. But Longwill tried to extort Springer into silencing his press. Springer then turned to Attorney Melvin W. Mills (later also Tolby's unpunished killer), who litigated for the Ring in Colfax County; and learned that Ada would certainly be indicted by Catron. Springer then acquired a secret sadistic letter written by Mills to Longwill, which Springer presented in his deposition to investigator Frank Warner Angel on August 9, 1878. It stated:

Santa Fe, N.M.

July 18 [1875]

Dear Doctor.

We are having great times here - the delegation from Cimarron is here and I think we have the best of everything. Springer gets a dam cold reception from every body. Mrs M- [Morley] will be indicted without fail ... the mission of S- [Springer] to keep Mrs M- from being indicted is a total failure.

Yours very truly
Mills

This arrogant and mocking voice of organized crime should be remembered. Its smug immunity is heard again in the Lincoln County War period's unguarded communications of Ringites James Dolan and District Attorney William Rynerson, and in the defense arguments of Attorney Henry Waldo in the military Court of Inquiry for Lieutenant Colonel N.A.M Dudley.

It is also important to remember that this Mills-Longwill letter was written as these men were arranging the murder of Franklin Tolby, two months away, on September 14, 1875.

Their criminal collusion is also illustrated in their December 5, 1873 letter provided as "Exhibit A" by Attorney Frank Springer in his August 9, 1878 deposition to Presidential Investigator Frank Warner Angel. It stated:

"Santa Fe, N.M.
Dec 5th 1873
Dear Doctor [Robert H. Longwill].
Thought I would write you how things are running. C. [Catron] is in good humor and said that your money had come, or rather that $18,000 would be paid in Smith & Humphreys judgment ...

The legislature is doing well and we will pass more laws than there was ever passed before ... If you should think best to have it [the fence law] passed let me know ... **I can pass any law I want to in spite of anybody that is not here or most anybody that might come here.** *I gave your compliments to Ben Stevens [accomplice in Governor Axtell's "Dear Ben plot" to kill Frank Springer, Raymond Morley, and Clay Allison] and he said that he owed you a very great obligation for treating him.* **I believe – I have got in with the big side by a little sharp figuring.**

Destroy. <u>Strictly private</u>
Mills

By the time Ada Morley was indicted by the Ring-controlled Taos Grand Jury in 1875, Catron had already murdered Tolby through his agents Longwill and Mills, and had attempted murder of Springer, Morley, Porter, and Allison. In two more years, Catron's despotic and unrelenting fury would be unleashed against John Tunstall, Alexander McSween, the Regulators, residents of San Patricio, and, finally, Billy Bonney himself.

Catron's viciousness against Ada Morley is further shown in the buggy incident as presented in a March 31, 1876 deposition by an Asa F. Middaugh, partner in the banking firm of Porter and Middaugh. (Henry Porter was one intended "Dear Ben plot" victim.) Ada's grandson, Norman Cleaveland, in his book, *The Morleys*, felt the buggy incident showed Catron's power struggle. He was in Cimarron as the Grant Company attorney, and wanted to use its buggy. But since her husband, Raymond Morley was the company's manager, she expressed anti-Ring spite by taking it herself. That made Catron furious. The Middaugh deposition about the incident was "Exhibit B" in Frank Springer's August 9, 1878 deposition to Frank Warner Angel. Middaugh stated:

Territory of Colorado)
County of Rio Grande)

Asa F. Middaugh, being duly sworn, on his oath deponent says, that on or about the fifth day of April AD 1875, at the town of Cimarron New Mexico, he had a conversation with Thomas B. Catron in reference to certain charges which had been or were being made against Mrs Ada M. Morley, wife of W.R. Morley, of taking a letter out of the Cimarron Post Office. That during said conversation Catron declared that Mrs Morley had insulted him by taking away a certain buggy at a time when said Catron wanted to use it, and that said Morley [W.R. Morley in his Cimarron News and Press] had been throwing mud at him, **and that he - said Catron - had a chance to get even now, and he would be a fool if he did not take advantage of it. Said conversation being with reference to possible criminal proceedings against said Mrs Morley in the United States District Court, and said Catron being then the United States District Attorney.** *It was deponent's understanding from the language of said Catron that he, said Catron, meant that he had a chance to have said Ada M. Morley indicted and prosecuted for taking a letter out of the Post Office, and that he would be a fool not to do it in order to avenge himself for the real or fancied insult which had been offered him by said Ada M. Morley.*

Asa F. Middaugh

Subscribed and sworn to before me
this 31st day of March AD 1876

Thomas W. Smith
Notary Public

ADA MORLEY'S MARCH 7, 1877 TERRIFIED LETTER

Oddly present in Mary McPherson's official file in the Department of the Interior's National Archives is a private letter to her from her frightened daughter, Ada Morley, dated March 7, 1877. It would have been mailed to Washington, D.C. while Mary was there vainly trying to meet with President Hayes and other officials about the Ring. It creates the question as to whether her mail was intercepted and if she ever received it. Notwithstanding, it is the best contemporary rendition of terror and hopelessness of citizens living under Catron's lethal and despotic Ring regime. Ada Morley wrote:

Cimarron New Mexico March 7th 1877
My dear Mother
Yes, we [with her husband, Raymond Morley] have received all your letters at Vermejo and here, but we have hesitated about replying for many reasons. I have little hope of your being able to cause any removals [of Governor Axtell, Judges Henry Waldo and Warren Bristol, and Thomas Benton Catron] for you know the Republicans have gained the day and our <u>ex-Rebels</u> here are the finest Republicans in New Mexico. Only this - Hayes and his friends will have friends to put in office and in the confusion and change we might get a new set of Officials. I am really afraid to write on these matters. Elkins of course is there trying to keep his friends in their present positions and as I said I have little hope or faith that you can succeed. You ask <u>what</u> we want. You ought to know. You have been here and know how we are oppressed and persecuted - You know too how ~~you~~ the Court has been robbed from Colfax Co. This last is the worst. Had we our court we would be comparatively safe. The Citizens signed a petition to the Gov. asking him to give us back our court but he refused saying "it had been taken away for the purpose of accomplishing certain objects and that the objects <u>had not</u> yet been accomplished." You know what they have done and that McMains is to be tried in three weeks [another Ring malicious prosecution] and <u>I'm sure</u> they will convict him though he is innocent as Agnes [her little daughter] of murder. I am half crazy too because Raym [her husband, Raymond] must go to be tried - it will cost a hundred dollars then he will likely be indicted again for something - and I often think they will manage to kill him in some way or other. If they do I'd be a second Mrs Tolby. They'd hear from me ...

[AUTHOR'S NOTE: Ada is aware of the Ring's malicious prosecution with murderous intent. Soon Susan McSween would join the growing ranks of Ring widows after 1878's Lincoln County War murder of her husband, Alexander.]

Every body here is discouraged and disheartened. All that I see you can do is to have an Agent sent but a secret one. He could see & hear and learn all – and such bloody work as has been done here is dreadful. Well, could we have our court back – and the Gov now has the power to annul the law we would be happy. Grant County by desperately fighting the Santa Fe Ring will probably join Arizona. That move will help us <u>for it will</u> cause an investigation and the public attention turned this way.

[AUTHOR'S NOTE: Ada Morley is aware of the anti-Ring 1876 Grant County Rebellion.]

Mother one thing worries me. You have not the means to carry you through and we have not money enough to pay <u>our</u> debts. O! and should you fail in this the Official here will torture Raym to death. He will have to take the blows here for your mistakes. I often wish you <u>had done</u> as you promised gone to <u>Iowa</u> and settled down quietly. Should you succeed what a glorious and great blessing it would be for this Godforsaken country. But I dont see how you can. People wont put in black & white what <u>they know</u>.

[AUTHOR'S NOTE: Ada is right about the silence. Hers is a rare document putting in writing the horror of Ring injustices.]

An Agent sent will be the only thing possible of good you can do. You spread your strength too much. Let Postmasters alone.
Get an investigation or an Agent or something to turn attention this way. That's all we need.

[AUTHOR'S NOTE: The tragedy of this statement will be apparent by the end of 1878, when Investigator Frank Warner Angel merely submitted Ring cover-up reports for the Hayes administration.]

Who is ===/===? Maybe he is anything but what he pretends. We are afraid and cautious. Does he intend interesting himself in the Maxwell [Land Grant]? Fortunes have been made out of it and many more can be made. But tell me what is his object ...

[AUTHOR'S NOTE: Concealed is W.B. Matchett, Mary's attorney co-filer, as required in Washington, D.C. for a layman's filing.]

I am so afraid for McMains. This term of court it makes me sick. If only we had a new Judge [replacing Henry Waldo] here or Governor or something. Well I get like everybody else when I commence writing and feel like giving up entirely. But Hayes may make changes if he will and when he learns these men have been rebels and are turncoat Republicans [Catron] he may in mercy do something, but had Tilden been elected we would have been sure of new officials ...

Later ~

Who is ===/===? Be careful lest hes some rogue. We are all afraid till we know more. I do pray you may succeed but I don't see how you can. I have no faith, none at all. I'm worried most about money matters. You'll spend all your money and to whom can you look for aid. If you can get a place in Washington to make a cent you better do it. Get a position of some kind. Indeed mother I fear you'll see the day you'll curse your present work and time you stay in Washington. Then I fear Raym and I will have all the blame here to bear. Had we known of your intention to go to Washington we would have opposed it to the bitter end. How will you ever get out of Washington ...

Rayms health is only fair. He has quit smoking. I think he is less nervous now. He has changed so much in some ways. Willie [older son, William Raymond Jr.] loves him and he can do as much with Agnes [their daughter] as I. Is in every way good and devoted to his family. I wish you could see him. We are a loving and happy family – All well.

Write often to your daughter   Ada

THE MORLEY'S FORCED FLIGHT

By 1879, Raymond and Ada Morley, like most victims of Ring persecution, fled the Territory according to their daughter, Agnes, in her 1941 book *No Life for a Lady*. They went to Old Mexico, where Raymond worked in railroad construction until 1882 when he was killed by an alleged accidental rifle discharge. (Agnes Cleaveland, pp. 14-16)

In her other book, *Satan's Paradise*, Agnes is poignantly accurate about the Ring's traumatic legacy: [T]he Santa Fé Ring was a closely knit political organization exerting a powerful influence ... which left its impress upon its descendants even unto the third and fourth generation, and to which much of the turmoil that enveloped the Maxwell Grant was traceable." As outspoken as her grandmother, Mary McPherson and mother Ada Morley, Agnes condemns the Ring's "hell broth, which became known as the Colfax County War." (Agnes Cleaveland, p. 65) More poignantly, in that book, Agnes exhibits post traumatic stress disorder echoing through her family as the horror "that [Tolby's] murderer made a mistake: that the bullet was intended for [my father] Superintendant Morley ... Morley was a man marked by the corrupt [Ring] politicians who struggled to control New Mexico ... In his editorial capacity [of the *Cimarron News and Press*], he incurred the wrath of the Santa Fé Ring. (Agnes Cleaveland, pp. 73-74)

RING-CONTROLLED TAOS GRAND JURY OF 1875

After Governor S.B. Axtell's transfer of Colfax County's courts, the July 1875 Grand Jury met in Taos County. Everything was in place for obstruction of justice without recourse.

According to Norman Cleaveland, Ada Morley was indicted for mail theft at a United States post office. He added: "And with practically all courts and law enforcement agencies, including the U.S. Army, under [Catron's] control, the Morleys and Mother McPherson had real reason for concern." (Cleaveland, p. 94) But Ringite Francisco "Pancho" Griego was not indicted for murdering two soldiers at the St. James Hotel that May. As Norman Cleaveland wrote: "As a prominent citizen of the Spanish-American community, he [Griego] would be very useful to the Santa Fe Ring. Such was the power of the Ring in manipulating 'justice.'" (Cleaveland, p. 97)

RING-CONTROLLED TAOS GRAND JURY OF 1876

The April 1876 Grand Jury also met in Taos County. Fort Union troops were present for intimidation. The presiding judge was Ringite Chief Justice and 1st Judicial District Judge Henry Waldo, in Catron's law firm and replacing deceased Judge Joseph Palen in 1875. Ringite Attorney General William Breeden (past head of the Territorial Republican Party and Catron's original 1866 backer) was assigned to "assist" the jury with investigations.

For the trial of Franklin Tolby's killers, Melvin Mills was represented by unfortunately self-serving, Frank Springer. McMains was the star witness, but refused to name Tolby's murderers with certainty because Judge Waldo outrageously instructed the jurymen to charge him with libel if he did.

Judge Waldo gave the following prejudicial instructions to the jurymen as reported in the *Daily New Mexican* of May 1, 1876 and quoted in the Pueblo, Colorado *Chieftain*, May 25, 1876:

"Your jurisdiction is extended over a district of county to whose inhabitants no doubt such annexation was and is somewhat obnoxious, and who may be disposed to resent such legislation, as a reproach to them as a community." In the same statement he explained that the districts had been combined because Cimarron's reputation was notorious and the three killings [Tolby, Vega, and Cardenas] were only the more spectacular examples of lawlessness. Instructing the jurors to identify and indict the killers, he also directed them, **in the Tolby case, to return indictments for libel if certain men had been maliciously and falsely implicated**. (Taylor, p. 49)

Judge Waldo's decision was quoted by Norman Cleaveland:

The fullest investigation which the grand jury could make was given to the charges against Mills, Longwill and Donoghue; and all persons who were supposed to have any knowledge of the facts as far as the Grand Jury could learn, were brought before it and thoroughly examined, being permitted to tell what they knew. The Grand Jury was unable to discover the least evidence which implicated either of the persons above named in the assassination, the charges brought against them, as far as the jury could ascertain, being based solely on rumors and suspicion.

From the evidence placed before the Grand Jury it appears that the only persons that is responsible to suppose had knowledge of the assassination were themselves murdered [Vega and Cardenas] while in the custody of persons ostensibly engaged in an investigation to discover the facts about Mr. Tolby's murder [McMains and others]. (Cleaveland, p. 124)

So Ringite Melvin Mills was acquitted.

Then the Ring's opponents were attacked. Clay Allison was indicted for three murders: Francisco "Pancho" Griego, Cruz Vega, and Manuel Cardenas; and of libel for accusing Melvin Mills, Robert Longwill, and Florencio Donoghue of murdering Franklin Tolby. Oscar P. McMains was indicted for the lynch murder of Cruz Vega. He was jailed in Cimarron, at the impossibly high bail of $20,000 set by Judge Waldo, to await trial (or assassination). (This scenario, would be repeated with Alexander McSween in Lincoln County, by his fake embezzlement case arrest, then by Judge Warren Bristol setting an impossible-to-fulfill bond plus harassing property attachments to give opportunity for his assassination.) The Pueblo, *Colorado Chieftain*, whose staff knew Oscar McMains, on May 25, 1876, denounced his indictment as Santa Fe Ring scapegoating.

McMains himself tried intervention by his politically powerful, Republican brother-in-law in Indiana, Attorney William Fishback, who got President Hayes to refer the case to Attorney General Charles Devens. Devens ordered New Mexico's Attorney General William Breeden, a Ringman, to suspend McMains's case. Instead, Ring paper, the *Santa Fe Daily New Mexican* got a leak of those secret negotiations and accused Devens of meddling. The leaker was obvious: Catron. According to Victor Westphall in his *Thomas Benton Catron and His Era*, U.S. Attorney Catron notified Devens that jurisdiction was solely his. (Westphall, p. 125) Devens then telegraphed Governor Axtell to request suspension of McMains's case, but was, of course, refused by that Ringite. (Taylor, p. 53) So Oscar McMains remained in Ring clutches, defended by fence-riding Attorney Frank Springer and a W.D Lee.

RING-CONTROLLED TAOS TRIALS OF 1877 IN THE EYES OF THE MORLEYS AND MARY McPHERSON

Mary McPherson's son-in-law, Raymond Morley, wrote to her on March 6, 1877, in the midst of his own crisis of Catron's malicious prosecution of Ada, and his fears of vindictive repercussions of Mary's exposés in Washington, D.C. McPherson enclosed his letter in her addendum to her May 1877 anti-Ring complaint to President Hayes and the Department of the Interior. He wrote:

Cimarron, March 6th 1877
.... I was astonished beyond measure at your proceedings, and have fears as to the result: at the same time I will not throw a straw in your way, but will do what I can to help matters..

Efforts have been made to get the Court back here, but failed. **The Ring will not permit it, and say that the objects for which the Court was taken away have not been accomplished: Now you know what the objects were - to defeat the Tolby investigation, and to punish Colfax County for presuming to interfere in such matters.** *I have to go to court the last of the month - and you know what a Taos court is.* **The election of Hayes leads many to think that the old regime will hold over [the ring corruption of President Grant], and that other Tolby affairs will happen.**

[AUTHOR'S NOTE: This is prophetic. The next year were Ring murders of John Tunstall, Alexander McSween, and their followers; and the start of Ring revenge against the Regulators and Billy Bonney.]

The people are badly discouraged, and many talk of leaving the county, as their only protection against the machinations of their enemies in power. **New Mexico today is ruled by five of the Ring, supported as they have been by Federal authority; and the use of troops.**

[AUTHOR'S NOTE: This is prophetic. Troops under Commander Dudley would defeat Regulator freedom fighters the next year in the Lincoln County War. Also, Raymond Morley is alone in understanding Ring extension to the federal government.]

If you can affect any removals, you will certainly do good.

[AUTHOR'S NOTE: Morley seems unaware that President Hayes and Secretary of the Interior Schurz helped Ring cover-up.]

Four or five men run this Territory, and run it with unparalled desperation ... The removal of one or two, even, of these officials would remedy the great evil; provided men were in their places who could not be controlled by the Ring. *If the office of Chief Justice alone could be filled by a new man with good motives and principles, a short time would defeat the rest.*

[AUTHOR'S NOTE: The Chief Justice was Ringite Henry Waldo, whom Billy Bonney himself would face as the defense attorney in the corrupt Dudley Court of Inquiry in May of 1879, which covered-up the Ring murder of Alexander McSween.]

The Governor [Axtell], Chief Justice [Waldo], and U.S. Attorney [Catron] control New Mexico ... If you could remove any of these men, do so by all means. But to get evidence of the facts, which you and all of us are convinced, can only be done in one way, viz: If a secret agent were to come here <u>duly authorized</u> , he could get them – get evidence to astonish the world!

[AUTHOR'S NOTE: Morley is prophetic about Frank Warner Angel sent the next year by the Departments of Justice and the Interior to investigate; but cannot foresee Ring obstruction of his investigation on the Washington, D.C. level resulting only in cover-up.]

But people are afraid to tell what they know in affidavits until they feel sure it will not pass into the hands of the enemy to be used against themselves ... But secrecy is all important - <u>publicity is dangerous in the extreme</u>. You must be cautious also what you do, or it will react on us here ...

[AUTHOR'S NOTE: By the 1890's Morley was shot dead; the cause given as an accidental firing of a rifle.]

Remember that Elkins [sic - Union], Catron, and Waldo were all in the Rebel cause from and about Westport, Missouri, and all red hot Democrats up to their appointment for office, since when, they were radical of radicals ... I would urge that if you can effect any removal do so before the Taos court; or if a secret agent could be sent, let him get here to witness the performance.

As a specimen of the way New Mexico is governed, see in solicitor's Office, Treasury Dep't, in 1872, just prior to Elkins election – six hundred suits [in Taos County] brought by the U.S. Attorney [Catron setting up Elkin's election of Delegate to Congress] ... and only two or three tried – the rest dismissed. It is charged that this was for the double purpose of whipping in voters, and getting fees for prosecution [and Elkins won, becoming Delegate to Congress] ...

Effect one removal, - the Governor or Chief Justice, and if a Governor could be appointed who knew the circumstances here, it would be best, - <u>any good, square man would do</u>. A removal or two *would restore confidence, so that evidence and petitions could be gotten ... but as it is now people are disheartened.*

[AUTHOR'S NOTE: Morley is prophetic, and may have added weight to Lew Wallace's eventual appointment as governor.]

Grant, the other American County [meaning Anglo like Colfax County], is likely to secede and join Arizona, to get away from the Ring.

[AUTHOR'S NOTE: Like his wife, Ada, Morley is aware of the Grant County Rebellion.]

> W.R. Morley
> Vice Prest & Executive Officer
> Max. [Maxwell] Land Grant & R'wy Co.

MARY McPHERSON INTERVENES FOR McMAINS

Mary McPherson's hand-written complaint to President Hayes, filed May 1, 1877 as "W.B. Matchett and Mary E. McPherson 'Make certain charges against the U.S. Officials in the Territory of New Mexico,' " tried to help Oscar McMains. It enclosed April 21, 1877 Pueblo, Colorado, *Enterprise and Chronicle* article, "At It Again," by a J.J. Lambert. She wrote:

McMains:

Upon the murder of Tolby, Mr. McMains, a printer by profession, and also a [Methodist] missionary, took an active part in ferreting out the perpetrators [Cruz Vega, Manuel Cardinas, Robert H. Longwill, M. [Melvin] W. Mills, and Florencio Donoghue], and drew upon him the wrath of the powers in Santa Fe, and from that period until the present, they have pursued him with a foolish persistency that is too apparent to be misinterpreted. He has ever been a true and unwavering friend of the [settlers of Land] Grants.

The manner in which the Court at Taos has recently treated this subject upon argument before it, will not relieve it from an inexplicable suspicion.

[ENCLOSED ARTICLE]:

At It Again

The latest advices from New Mexico are to the effect that the "ring" are at their old tricks ...

One of our correspondents says: "People here are in constant fear and nobody dares to raise his voice against the terrible anarchy we are undergoing in this country. These gentlemen and their organ at Santa Fe, (The *New Mexican*) seem to have an absolute power in everything in New Mexico. They run our legislature and make this ignorant people pass such laws as will gratify their rapacious ambition. They control the courts to such an extent that respectable citizens regard them as a public calamity. They have juries appointed, who, instead of bringing peace to the community, will cause but alarm to the people. As a general thing thieves and murderers are turned loose."

The lawyers of New Mexico, with the exception of a very few honorable exceptions, are members of this corrupt ring ... **A defendant who has been prosecuted by the ringites has but little chance of being defended, and even if he does succeed in obtaining the services of an attorney, the rulings of the courts are always against him.**

In August of 1877, jailed Reverend Oscar McMains was tried before a Taos County Grand Jury for Catron's federal charge of the Cruz Vega killing; but, defended by Attorney Frank Springer and W.D. Lee, had his indictment quashed. So he was immediately re-indicted in "Territory vs. O.P. McMains" for that killing. But Springer and Lee got a venue change to Mora County.

MCMAINS'S TERRITORIAL MURDER TRIALS: 1877 AND 1878

Reverend Oscar McMains's Mora County trial for the killing of Cruz Vega was held on August 22nd and 23rd, 1877, still under Ringite Judge Henry Waldo, and with Ringite Attorney General William Breeden as prosecutor.

Attorneys Frank Springer and W.D. Lee argued his innocence, since McMains had left before Cruz Vega's lynching. The unprejudiced jurymen ruled murder in the "fifth degree," with sole penalty of a $300 fine. The Ring was foiled, though Waldo's instructions had urged first degree to allow hanging by lying that the Taos jury had already found McMains guilty.

But Oscar McMains refused to accept guilt or pay the fine. Springer and Lee got a new trial over Judge Waldo's objection. It was in Colfax County, which had regained its courts by January of 1878. In that trial, McMains's Cruz Vega murder indictment was thrown out by Judge L. Bradford Prince based on lack of evidence.

But the Ring still won. After three years of McMains's malicious prosecution, no one dared accuse Tolby's murderers: Ringmen, Florencio Donoghue, Robert Mills, and Melvin Longwill. For the rest of his life, McMains continued his opposition to Ring control of the Maxwell Land Grant and Railway Company, as well as the Ring's fraudulent, 500,000 acre Uña de Gato Land Grant, sold through Governor S.B. Axtell as Ring frontmen to an Arkansas Senator, Stephen Wallace Dorsey.

McMains died of natural causes on April 15, 1899. His anti-Grant colleague, F.B. Chaplin eulogized in his obituary his fighting "crime and corruption, ever pleading for right in defense of the poor." But the *Raton Range* of April 20, 1899 did Ringite outlaw myth crowing: "O.P. McMains, the agitator, is dead."

ANTI-RING ACTIVIST VOICE: MARY TIBBLES MCPHERSON

ANALYSIS: From Iowa, Mary Tibbles McPherson became an unsung Colfax County War heroine when, visiting her daughter, Ada Morley, and son-in-law Raymond Morley, in Cimarron from early 1875 to the end of 1876, she was inspired by Reverend Franklin Tolby, then by his murder and efforts of Reverend Oscar McMains. So in 1877 she exposed the Santa Fe Ring to Washington, D.C., leaving no doubt that President Rutherford B. Hayes and Secretary of the Interior Carl Schurz were fully aware of it before the next anti-Ring uprising - the Lincoln County War - and investigator Frank Warner Angel's 1878 reports. She was even undaunted by Catron's malicious prosecution of her daughter, Ada; or by the Ring's "Dear Ben plot" to murder her son-in-law Raymond Morley. Later, the Morley's daughter, Agnes Morley Cleaveland, and Agnes's son, Norman Cleaveland, continued the family's Santa Fe Ring condemnation into the 20th century.

At the peak of the Colfax County War, in 1877, Mary Tibbles McPherson presented her unflinching documentation of Ringites and their crimes against the backdrop of Grant settlers' uprisings, Ringite sheriffs served eviction notices, pastures set afire, cattle stolen, homes and ranches raided, and 200 killed.

She was born to a freedom fighting family. Her brother, Thomas Henry Tibbles, was an abolitionist follower of John Brown; fighter for Native American rights; Methodist missionary; editor of the Omaha, Nebraska, *Daily Herald*; and eventual 1904 Populist Party vice-president nominee advocating for Native Americans and Blacks, and for income and inheritance taxation. According to Tibbles, in his 1905 biography, *Buckskin and Blanket Days,* Mary was born in Ohio and raised in frontier Illinois in the 1840's; before their family, with nine children, moved to frontier Iowa. There, the children were almost killed by a wolf pack, and saved by the family dog and their shot-gun wielding mother. Tibbles wrote as to their descent from six generations of pioneers: "[N]o government official interfered with their business or pleasure. They were free men." (p. 22)

Mary, after marriage to Iowa politician and judge, Marcus McPherson would fight another "wolf pack": the Santa Fe Ring. And the Ring's attack on "free men" elicited her fight to prevent democracy's "tragedy written in the future."

As explained by her great-grandson, Norman Cleaveland in his 1971 book, *The Morleys: Young Upstarts of the* Southwest, she arrived from Iowa in the spring of 1875 to visit her daughter, Ada, and son-in-law, Raymond Morley - both relocated from Iowa - to meet her year old granddaughter, Agnes (his mother). McPherson was inspired by the anti-Ring mission of Reverend Franklin Tolby; then by his murder. Immediately, she placed in Cimarron's post office mailbox her first letter of anti-Ring complaint to Washington D.C. Frightened of repercussions, Ada retrieved it; giving Catron, as described above, the opportunity for revenge on her family by malicious prosecution of Ada for mail theft.

By 1877, having collected enough incriminatory evidence, and having experienced Ring terrorism directly in Reverend Tolby's murder and attack on her own family in Cimarron, Mary McPherson's solution was straight-forward: move to Washington, D.C. for direct access to President Rutherford B. Hayes and members of his administration, present legal arguments to get Ringites removed from public office, and expose their illegal land grab schemes and political crimes. She was a fearless, angry, articulate, unrelenting, and unflinching chronicler of the Santa Fe Ring; with focus on Colfax County's oppression by Governor Samuel Beach Axtell as a Ring frontman for land grabs, Judge Warren Bristol as a Ringite shield, and T.B. Catron and S.B. Elkins as the Ring's heads.

MARY McPHERSON'S SANTA FE RING EXPOSÉS: 1877

Mary McPherson's 1877 anti-Ring exposés - to Colfax County locals, to the Department of Interior's Secretary Carl Schurz, to Department of Justice's Attorney General Charles Devens, and to President Rutherford B. Hayes himself - belie all cover-ups of the Ring's existence, and incriminate its colluding officials. Land-grabbing, voter bribery and intimidation, punitive disenfranchisement of Colfax County, malicious prosecution, attempted murder and murder, were her litany; becoming the Ring's blueprints in 1878 for subjugating Lincoln County War.

Her indirect homage was fear and cover-up of Ring-denying Catron biographer, Victor Westphall in his 1973 *Thomas Benton Catron and His Era*. Though her exposés are in the National Archives, he pretends her complaint was a single letter to Attorney General Alphonso Taft on February 7, 1877, which he shrinks to Ada's tiff with Catron about the company buggy.

Her actual anti-Ring complaints, from February to August of 1877, are 141 pages of letters; affidavits; petitions; newspaper articles; charges against Ringites for removal; recording of troops intimidating civilians; and documentation of Franklin Tolby's murder. She accused main Ringites: U.S. Attorney T.B. Catron, Congressional Delegate S.B. Elkins, Chief Justices Joseph Palen and Henry Waldo, and Judge Warren Bristol. Appropriately and bravely, she first attacked Catron himself.

"CHARGES AGAINST THOMAS B. CATRON, U.S. ATTORNEY, AND OTHERS": FEBRUARY 7, 1877

On February 7, 1877, Mary McPherson, relocated to Washington, D.C., began her crusade against the Santa Fe Ring with Attorney General Alphonso Taft (about to be replaced by Charles Devens in the Hayes administration). She mailed him her handwritten "Charges against Thomas B. Catron, U.S. Attorney, and Others," which was filed in Washington, D.C. on February 14, 1877. Her first complaint said it all: "*I wish to bring to your attention the sufferings of the people of New Mexico ... In searching out the assassins, the evidence pointed strongly to U.S. officials ... all US officers out there are in league together, and the people are the sufferers.*" The next year, 1878, it would be Investigator Frank Warner Angel's Washington, D.C. task to cover up her damning facts. She wrote:

Washington Feb 7th 1877

Atty Gen Taft
     Sir.
          I wish to bring to your attention the sufferings of the people of New Mexico, and especially of Colfax Co, where I ~~have~~ *resided from Feb 1975 until Oct 1976. I would ask you to investigate the situation of the people in that Territory and prove the truth and falsity of my statements.*

The county of Colfax is now "attached to Taos, for judicial purposes" that the U.S. officials may punish persons through the courts, who have boldly taken stand for their inalienable rights, that of life and liberty and the pursuit of their respective callings.

I think I shall be able to bring facts to establish the opinion freely spoken, that Thomas B Catron uses his official position to oppose the innocent instead of punishing the guilty *- "That court was dismissed" in Cimarron Colfax Co. in Aug '75 for several days and that Thomas B Catron took individuals in his pockets and went to districts which were for Valdez" and as the phrase there is "shook them over the heads of the parties wishing to vote thus, until they promised and did vote for Elkins" - that it was said "the court adjourned to go electioneering."*

It is always said that "feeing [paying off] Catron one will not be indicted" *- That this Catron was a member of the Maxwell Land Grant Co, whose Executive officer was WR Morley. This Co gave Morley use of a buggy and tram, aside from Co business. Court was in session. This buggy was taken to bring Catron and others to Cimarron. But during the court, the wife of WR Morley took this buggy, to which she had a right, and fulfilled a previous engagement. This was, when Mr Catron wished the buggy, in preference to "staging" [going by stagecoach]. Within a year, report said an indictment was found in Santa Fe against Mrs W.R. Morley for robbing the mails When it was found there was one, Catron was reported to have said, "Yes there <u>is</u> one, <u>that woman insulted me</u> and I intend to punish or repay her." He referred to her using her own buggy, given in her husbands salary and gave this as reason for bringing out this indictment. This indictment was seen by her husband WR Morley in the hands of U.S. Marshall John Pratt.* **This is only a case in point one out of a number occurring constantly.**

I was only visiting my daughter but remained to protect her. I was told two years before leaving that I was to be indicted for libel, said to her founded on my writing the state of affairs to the Board of Missions of M E Church in N.Y. City. Indictment never served if procured.

Forty men in Colfax Co have been dragged to court for near or quite two years, "to intimidate them," it is said and still their trial is postponed.

Rev F.J. Tolby remarked "that the Courts of N.M. were now for political purposes" and in a short time was assassinated, *when returning from an appointment to preach. He said he was going to inform parties at Washington.*

In searching out the assassins, the evidence pointed strongly to U.S. officials, *this was the impression of every good citizen ... The evidence pointed to the Rep. of the county [Melvin W. Mills]. He went to Santa Fe and had law enacted attaching Colfax to Taos Co.* **At this [Taos] court all suppond [sic - subpoenaed] to be implicated in the plot [to kill Tolby] were <u>set free</u> and all parties in Colfax searching out assassins were found [issued] <u>murder indictments</u>; until it was said "to be indicted was a work of respectability" – which it really was.** *Twenty five or more were to be arrested for murder, all living in Colfax. Two only were arrested, one of those the successor of Rev F.J. Tolby [Oscar P. McMains] who was instrumental in searching for the assassins.*

Indeed it is a matter patent to all good persons that they should fear the courts and all criminals feel safe to prosecute their wickedness, as not one has ever received their rewards [recompense]. They all escape justice.

It is said Thomas B Catron and his associates the present Judge,   his name has escaped me [Henry Waldo], are pitted against Colfax Co and especially against those searching out the assassins of Rev FJ Tolby.

I do not know myself but it is prevalent among the people that **all US officers out there are in league together, and the people are the sufferers.**

                        Very Respectfully
                        Mrs Mary E. McPherson
                        1127 Thirteenth St

T.B. Catron responded to the true and devastating charges to the Attorney General Alphonso Taft on February 24, 1877 - and filed there on March 6, 1877 - as "Answering Charges of Mary E. McPherson." It was the first test of how far Washington D.C. and the new administration of Rutherford B. Hayes would go to cover-up the Ring, and of the power of S.B. Elkins to call in favors for its shielding. The result was that no investigation followed.

With smug sociopathic complacency, Catron denied everything, and called McPherson insane: *"such an idea could only emanate in the brain of a crazy person."* He used his time-tested outlawing and defaming of adversaries. He gave Ring mantras: *"[L]awlessness seemed to prevail in the county of Colfax ... It is absolutely false, that I have in any maneuver or at any time used my official position to oppress any one instead of punishing the guilty ... I simply know that the Courts of New Mexico are as free from politics as any Courts in the United States."* And about the Ring, he, as its head, hissed: *"It is utterly false that the U.S. officials in this Territory are in any manner engaged together so that the people are sufferers, or that there is any combination among them for any purpose whatever."* Catron wrote:

Office of
T.B. Catron,
Attorney at Law
& U.S. Attorney
Santa Fé, N.M. Feb 24 1877

Alfonso Taft –
Attorney General
Washington D.C.
Sir: I am just in possession of your communication of the 14th inst. enclosing the communication of Mrs Mary E McPherson, which I herewith return as requested. I will notice the charges made by Mrs McPherson in detail –
The county of Colfax is "attached to the county of Taos for Judicial Purposes," this was done by the last Legislature, for the reason that **lawlessness seemed to prevail in the county of Colfax at the time; several men had been taken and hung or shot, by armed bands of men, one from the hands of the authorities, and no effort was made to stop it by the people of Colfax, but in the contrary the same was encouraged** *by W.R. Morley the*

son-in-law of Mrs McPherson who, at the time, was editor of the news-paper in said county of Colfax. As I am informed it was believed that no grand-jury could be found to indict for these outrages, or petit jury to convict them, in Colfax Co. I was not a member of that Legislature nor had I any connection with it. The courts of both Taos & Colfax counties are courts in which no United States business was transacted, they were courts established by the Legislature under Section 1874 of the Revised Statutes of the United States, and I had no official connection with the same, except as <u>an</u> <u>Attorney</u> who practiced therein, all my official business as U.S. Attorney being at the time confined to the U.S. Branch of the court in said District held at Santa Fe. The Attorney General of the Territory William Breeden being the person who had charge of the prosecutions in those counties.

It is absolutely false, that I have in any maneuver or at any time used my official position to oppress any one instead of punishing the guilty. It is absolutely untrue that Court was dismissed in Aug. 75 for several days or that I took any indictment or indictments and went to any district with them or took any indictments over the heads of any one whatsoever until they promised to vote for Elkins or any thing else to that effect, or that said court adjourned to go electioneering. As before stated I have nothing whatever to do with the indictments in said Court, they being all for the offenses against the laws of the Territory and not the United States. I may have been employed to defend some of the accused.

It is absolutely untrue and false that any one can or ever has feed me to present an indictment and I deny that there is any suspicion that I ever received a fee to prevent an indictment, **such an idea could only emanate in the brain of a crazy person**.

Mrs. W.R. Morley was not indicted by the U.S. jury in Santa Fe for stealing a letter from the U.S. mail, the circumstances are as follows as detailed before the Grand Jury by the Post-master and his deputy; viz

The sister [sic - mother-in-law, Mary McPherson] of W.R. Morley went to the post-office and dropped a letter in the box, the deputy Miss Bishop was standing by the box and noticed the letter and address, in a few minutes Mrs Morley her sister-in-law [sic – daughter] went to the post office very hurriedly and said she Mrs Morley had made a mistake and dropped in the wrong letter, and without waiting she ran to the box picked up the letters selected one and left the office. Mrs Bishop then stepped to the box *and examined and found the letter put in by Morley's sister [sic – mother-in-law] gone. She informed the Post-master Mr John B McCullich, who immediately called in Mrs Morley and accused her of taking the letter, she first admitted it then denied it. Some little talk was had about the matter when Mr Morley threatened to prosecute McCullich for neglect of his duties in reference to the letter. Mr McCullich then wrote to me at Santa Fe informing me of the facts and requested that he and his deputy Miss Bishop be summoned before the Grand Jury of the U.S. at Santa Fe which I caused to be done, and* **on their testimony an indictment was presented.** *It is absolutely false that I ever said that Mrs. Morley had insulted me or that I intended to punish her, or that I refused to her use, of the buggy, referred to, or that I gave that as a reason for prosecuting the indictment. Some time before the indictment was framed I was approached by a friend of Mr Morley [Attorney Frank Springer] and requested to prevent an indictment where I answered that, that was a matter for Mr McCullich and the Grand Jury, that if Mr McCullich did not ask the matter to be pushed, that I would be governed by his wishes, that he had requested to be summoned before the jury and I had done so. And that in that matter neither Mr Morley nor his wife had the right to ask any favors of me, which is about all I ever said about the matter. It is absolutely untrue that Marshal Pratt ever had the indictment in his hands he had a warrant for the arrest of Mrs Morley, but I requested him not to serve it, as I had learned Mrs Morley was in a state of pregnancy, and arresting her might result to her seriously; before the next term of Court Mrs Morley and her husband left the Territory and as Mr McCullich did not wish to follow the matter up any further, at his insistence, I discontinued the case. As to any indictment against Mrs McPherson for libel, I could have nothing to do with it, that being a Territorial offense, but I will say this is the first time I have heard of it. As Mrs McPherson has referred to the board of Missions of M.E. Church in New York City - I would refer you to the correspondence of Rev Thomas Warwood of that church, with said board of missions, to which she had preferred charges against him, they can probably tell who or what Mrs McPherson is.*

If any men had been dragged or taken to Court to intimidate them it has not been the United States side of the Court. Yet from my knowledge of the facts I pronounce Mrs McPhersons letter on that point, as to any court in this Territory untrue. Some 30 or 40 persons who committed the outrages which induced the Legislature to attach Colfax to Taos Co. for judicial purposes, have been indicted in Taos Co, some have been tried and convicted others have not been arrested others who have been arrested have applied for continuances which at their own insistence have been granted. I do not think a single trial has been delayed by the Territory.

I know nothing about what Mr Tolby said or thought, **I simply know that the Courts of New Mexico are as free from politics as any Courts in the United States. I have never before heard it intimated that any U.S. official was under the least suspicion of being implicated in the murder of Tolby**, the matter has been twice very thoroughly investigated and there was not a scintilla of evidence against a single U.S. official ... There was not a particle of evidence against the Representative of Colfax Co [Melvin Mills] with reference to the murder of Tolby, that representative instead of getting the law passed attaching Colfax to Taos Co. did, as I am informed, oppose the enactment of the law, very vigorously.

Several persons were arrested who were indicted for murders. Others are at large who are indicted as I am informed, but whom the officers have so far been unable to arrest others have left the country. **Mr FJ Tolbys successor is indicted for murder in being instrumental in lynching a man I am told the proofs are positive, given by a man whom he induced to entice the victim out into the hands of the mob who both hung and shot him.** The successor of Mr Tolby Mr McMains was present and assisted as I am told.

It is utterly false that either I or the present Judge [Henry] Waldo are in any manner pitted against Colfax Co or those searching out the assassins of Tolby but I assert on the contrary that we have both used our utmost endeavors to find the guilty parties and have them punished ...

It is utterly false that the U.S. officials in this Territory are in any manner leagued together so that the people are sufferers, or that there is any combination among them for any purpose whatever –

Thanking you for referring this communication of Mrs McPherson to me and giving me the opportunity to contradict the charges made.

        I am very respectfully,
                Thomas B. Catron
                U.S. Atty

"CHARGES AGAINST NEW MEXICAN OFFICIALS, TOGETHER WITH CORROBORATION OF EVIDENCE": MARCH, 1877 AND APRIL, 1877 (FILED IN WASHINGTON, D.C. MAY 1, 1877)

For her next hand-written complaint, Mary McPherson added the Washington lawyer, W.B. Matchett, about whom her daughter, Ada Morley, had questioned in her March 7, 1877 letter. Apparently Secretary of the Interior Carl Schurz demanded a lawyer for her complaints to be read. Matchett's added legalese improves her layman effort of her February 4, 1877 complaint against Catron. On May 1, 1877, McPherson and Matchett filed their charges of March and April 1877 in Washington, D.C. as "Charges Against New Mexican Officials, Together With Corroboration Evidence," which included "Petition to Remove Judge Bristol" and two lists of "Charges Against S.B. Axtell, Governor of New Mexico." Its format was a cover letter to President Hayes, with insertions of evidence and lists of charges.

The Ring's organized crime was spelled out: *"[The named public officials] conspired together to corrupt and defraud justice and defeat the ends thereof, both by fraudulent and illegal practices in their respective Districts and offices; and by procuring the passage of insidious legislative enactments tending to dismemberment, confusion, and centralization of power and designed to protect infamy, legalize crime, deprive its citizens of personal liberty, and the right of trial by jury; compass the revenues of the Territory and the property of its citizens for purposes of private gain ... It is in evidence that for several years these parties have been in collusion in a general plan having for its aim the centralizing of power, the reduction of large and valuable private Grants of land within the Territory to their personal use and benefit, by corrupt Territorial and Congressional enactments, and by passage of bills of attainment & de facto laws depriving the citizens of due process of law ... To accomplish these purposes this Ring so formed appears to have paused at nothing however difficult or questionable."*

McPherson's and Matchett's goal was explicit: *"[T]hey therefore respectfully request their removal from office."* Named was the Santa Fe Ring and its members: U.S. Attorney Thomas Benton Catron and Delegate to Congress Stephen Benton Elkins, Governor Samuel Beach Axtell, Chief Justice Henry Waldo, and District Judge Warren Bristol. They wrote:

To the President:

The undersigned in behalf of the people of the Territory of New Mexico herewith present the following <u>*charges*</u> *with evidence in support thereof against the persons named herein and ask your early consideration of the same:*

They charge the United States District Attorney, Thomas B. Catron; Associate Justice Warren Bristol; Henry L. Waldo, Chief Justice; Samuel B. Axtell, Governor, and others of the said Territory, to them unknown, as having conspired together to corrupt and defraud justice and defeat the ends thereof, both by fraudulent and illegal practices in their respective Districts and offices; and by procuring the passage of insidious legislative enactments tending to dismemberment, confusion, and centralization of power and designed to protect infamy, legalize crime, deprive its citizens of personal liberty, and the right of trial by jury; compass the revenues of the Territory and the property of its citizens for purposes of private gain ... And they therefore respectfully request their removal from office:

It is in evidence that for several years these parties have been in collusion in a general plan having for its aim the centralizing of power, the reduction of large and valuable private Grants of land within the Territory to their personal use and benefit, by corrupt Territorial and Congressional enactments, and by passage of bills of attainment & de facto laws depriving the citizens of due process of law, legalizing crime and then punishing the criminal, and thereby making the Court a vehicle to compass their covert and vindictive designs, thus rendering its edicts a farce and bringing its judicial character into distrust and contempt.

To accomplish these purposes this Ring so formed appears to have paused at nothing however difficult or questionable. This course has kept back the prosperity of the Territory and its people in a continued state of disquiet and insecurity both of persons and property – An inside view of this matter may be better obtained by a glance at its origin:

Among the possessions acquired by the Treaty of 1848 with Mexico, were large private Grants of land, both to individuals and corporations – (about 150 in number) – which excited at once the cupidity and avarice of the of the unscrupulous adventurer and the wily politician.

The failure of the U.S. Government to afford the relief guaranteed by the Treaty and by the Confirmatory Act of 1860, June the 21st, left matters in an unsettled state as to titles, which fact was soon taken advantage of by the settlers and caused difficulties to arise between them and the holders of the Grants. Upon the influence of population these difficulties were increased and under the constant pressure they were compelled to take sides against the Grants.

The Ring perceiving their opportunity, forced themselves into power, and began a system of corrupt and compulsory legislation, oppressive in its exactions upon the grantees and those who sided with them, to worry them into submission, or by fraudulently depreciating their titles, compel them either to abandon their grants entirely, or sell at a sacrifice and quit the Territory. Many did this, - some did not. Under this compulsion the Ring or their friends became the purchasers ...

[INSERT] *"The Real Purpose of the New Mexico State Bill"*

[AUTHOR'S NOTE: Omitted is McPherson's speculation that the Ring's land grab was for Mormon colonization.]

It is essential for them [the Ring] to get possession of most of the valuable land in the Territory; and for this purpose the situation is particularly favorable, since nearly all the good land is included in the old Spanish and Mexican Grants of which there are upwards of 150, ranging in size from a few thousands to one or more millions of acres.

At present these lands are chiefly owned by natives, who own little else, and with title as yet imperfected by the Federal Government ... In most cases however the grants are owned jointly by a number of people, the descendants of the original grantees, and agents have been at work and bought one or more interests on many of the grants.

The Legislature of New Mexico under the dictation of the Ring of speculators [Catron and Elkins], recently passed a law, by which the district court can order the whole of a grant, to be sold at public auction, upon such notice as it sees fit, upon the demand of any one of the parties in interest, no matter how small that interest may be. By this means all these grants are to be forced to sale, for cash, and as the titles are in an unsettled state, and most of the papers and records are in the hands of the Ring, there can be little petition in bidding, and the lands will be obtained at nominal figures ...

To make forced sale of these lands, as is contemplated, would not be easily accomplished without some show of force, as the owners, who have lived on them all their lives, and whose ancestors for generations occupied, cultivated, and defended them would rebel ... [But] supported by the whole power of the [Ulysses S.] Grant administration, the natives will have little chance for a successful resistance to the atrocious.

[INSERT] *"Legislative Action on Land Partition"*

[AUTHOR'S NOTE: Attacked is the act partitioning land by court-appointed commissioners empowered to divide it as they saw fit to establish taxes. It enabled Ring take-over by crippling owners with taxes.]

[A] delinquent tax payer became not only liable to a civil suit for unpaid taxes [and] to have his property sold summarily by the sheriff, but also to be arrested, convicted, and punished as a criminal ... Now, as taxation is a new thing to the Mexicans - the Territorial Government having been supported by licenses and special taxes prior to the accession of the Ring to power ... thousands became delinquent, and at present the courts are busy with indictments for their offence which will be held over the head of the unfortunates until after election when they will be dismissed with costs and attorney's fees ...

[AUTHOR'S NOTE: This describes Ring method for controlling elections by forced voting.]

This law ... is peculiarly adapted to some of the larger Spanish grants consisting of hundreds of thousands of acres ... No one but a capitalist has the means to purchase the whole ... In brief they [grant holders] will be compelled to sell their home for a song, and be turned loose upon the face of the earth, all for the benefit of a few scheming speculators, who will then perfect the title with the general government and have a clear title to the property ...

[AUTHOR'S NOTE: This was the Catron and Elkins land grab formula used for getting the Maxwell Land Grant from Lucien Maxwell and arguably yielding the foundation profit for their Santa Fe Ring.]

[LETTER TO PRESIDENT HAYES CONTINUES]

It will be seen that immediately upon the passage of this law, a move was made at both ends of the line – the Delegate in Congress [Elkins] arose in his place and presented a bill providing for the confirmation of a large number of private claims in New Mexico ... and the U.S. District Attorney, Catron, of New Mexico (becoming solicitor for private parties in their prosecution) filed bills under the "Partition" Act versus the Maxwell Land Grant and Railway Company ...

Another convenient system of iniquity is that relating to Indictments: They are obtained with the greatest possible ease imaginable – and in any numbers required for the emergency – and for the same offence – in some cases several indictments for the same offence.

[AUTHOR'S NOTE: McPherson understood how Catron and Elkins worked the Ring from Territorial to federal levels, for their land grants scheme or for malicious prosecutions.]

That Colfax County made the most diligent opposition to the attempts of the Ring to deprive them of their rights and subject them to their schemes. (In fact this is the only county that saved itself from their rapacity.)

Failing in this, the pretext soon came, upon the assassination of a Methodist Missionary, named Tolby, - a worthy man, - who at the first sympathized with the Ring, but, upon maturer reflection, abandoned them, when they hired two assassins to deliberately murder him, after they (the Ring) had publicly warned him to leave the country, - which he failed to do ...

[INSERTS] Tolby's Coroner's Jury Report and of newspaper articles about his September 14, 1875 murder, exposure of Ring complicity, and Governor Axtell's transfer, by Legislative act, of Colfax County's courts to Taos County to shield from Tolby's Ringite murderers Melvin Mills and Robert Longwill, and to harass by malicious prosecution Colfax County citizens for their Ring opposition.]

[INSERT] November 10, 1875 *Cimarron News and Press* article about Colfax County citizens meeting on Tolby's murder. (See my p. 159)

[INSERT] December 22, 1875 *New York Sun* article, *"The Territory of Elkins. Assassination of Supposed Sun Correspondent. The Murder of the Rev. F.J. Tolby in New Mexico. A Probate Judge Accused of Complicity in the Crime. Indignation Meeting,"* about Ring complicity in Tolby's murder. (See my pp. 161-163)

[INSERT] *"Petition and Charges to Remove Judge Bristol"* Copy of a February 18, 1876 Grant County petition to President Rutherford B. Hayes to remove Judge Warren Bristol, and reprinted in the *Cimarron News and Press* in 1877 from the *Grant County Herald*. McPherson and Matchett added that in a later Grant County citizens' meeting "a long letter was read from U.S. Attorney T.B. Catron in which he denies the charges ... against Bristol."]

[AUTHOR'S NOTE: The charges constituted Bristol's using his court to benefit the Ring and punish its opponents. By 1878, Bristol's role in the Ring's malicious prosecution of Alexander McSween and John Tunstall led to their murders and the Lincoln County War. Bristol was also Billy Bonney's hanging judge in Mesilla in March and April of 1881.]

We the undersigned citizens of the Third Judicial District of the Territory of New Mexico, without regard to party, would respectfully request and petition for the removal of Judge Warren Bristol from the office of Judge of the District and Territory aforesaid, <u>for the following special and general reasons</u>.

1st. *We charge that Warren Bristol has been guilty of secretly making known his opinions to attorneys engaged on the side of a cause pending before him, and informing them as to the nature and character of his decisions, several days before delivering them judicially from the bench.*

2nd. *We charge that in consequence of his secretly making known his opinions that great advantage thereby resulted to the parties employing said attorneys, and great loss and injury to the opposite party.*

3rd. *We charge that Warren Bristol in an important mining suit, in which A.W. Bremen and Silas Tidwell were plaintiff, and Robert B. Wilson made defendant, secretly advised with an attorney of said plaintiffs, and informed and advised him as to the proper steps he should pursue in conducting the cause during the very time that the subject matter of his secret advice was under consideration by said Warren Bristol, as judge.*

4th. *We charge Warren Bristol with writing out a full and complete form for relocating a mine for one of the plaintiffs aforesaid, while the title to said mine was then a matter before his court for adjudication.*

5th. *We charge that Judge Bristol imprisoned an honorable and worthy citizen of Grant County for contempt ... for no other reason than that he availed himself of information communicated to him by his counsel, which had been prematurely and secretly revealed by the said Judge Bristol.*

6th. *We charge that Judge Bristol during the July term of court 1875, held in Grant County, did in open court publicly confer that he had been guilty of revealing a secret opinion to one of the attorneys employed by said Bremen and Tidwell, but rendered no valid excuse for such injudicial conduct.*

7th. *We charge Judge Bristol with granting a writ of restitution to the plaintiff in a suit of ejectment after an appeal had been allowed and perfected to the Supreme Court, in the absence of any statutory provision authorizing such to issue.*

8th. *We charge that Judge Bristol acting as Judge aforesaid, actually refused in an important murder trial, after the prisoners arraignment at the first term to grant continuance, although proper affidavits were filed according to law, for the procurement of absent material witnesses, and forced the prisoner to trial which resulted in his conviction and execution.*

[AUTHOR'S NOTE: Bristol's improper rush to conviction and execution was repeated in his hanging trial of Billy Bonney on April 8-9, 1881, with sentencing on April 13, 1881 and hanging date set for May 13, 1881, to hinder appeal.]

9th. *We charge that Judge Bristol in another important murder trial absolutely refused to the prisoner the right of compulsory process to procure witnesses in his behalf.*

10th. *We charge that Judge Bristol as Judge aforesaid, willfully refused in two other important murder trials to allow the defendants to exercise their right to the full number of peremptory challenges to jurors, given by the statute in such cases although his attention was repeatedly called to the statutory provision allowing the defendant the right to ten preemptory charges.*

11th. We charge that the said Judge Bristol made a false accusation from the bench against the grand jurymen of Grant County, N.M. and that they, in proper justification of themselves, were forced to state publicly and in print that such accusation was false, and furthermore, that said public statement of the grand jurymen aforesaid has not, and cannot be denied by the said Judge Bristol.

12th. **We charge that Judge Bristol is guilty of manifest partiality, while acting in the trial of causes.**

13th. And generally we charge that Judge Bristol, as judge aforesaid, frequently consults and advises with attorneys about causes coming and pending before his court for adjudication, who are interested in the results of the suits as feed attorneys.

14th. We charge that Judge Bristol frequently makes rulings in important causes involving large amounts of property and the liberty of citizens, without proper thought and investigation, and that consequent to this, he constantly changes his rulings during the progress of important trials, and orders his clerk to expunge the record, in order to hide his indolence and ignorance, and thus deprives parties litigante of the proper recorded history of the causes.

15th. We charge that Judge Bristol is ignorant of the fundamental rules and principles of law with which every tyro should be conversant, and that he is indolent and not disposed to study, thus causing a universal feeling among the people of insecurity to life, liberty and property.

16th. We charge that Judge Bristol appointed a man clerk of his court, whom he knew all the time to be lewdly and publicly living with a kept mistress, and notwithstanding he is still so living, continues to retain him as clerk of his court.

17th. We aver that all of the foregoing statements and specifications can be substantiated on oath, by good, respectable citizens of this Territory irrespective of party predilection.

There follows about 250 signatures among which are many of the most influential men in that section of the territory.

[INSERT] April 21, 1877 *Enterprise and Chronicle* article from Pueblo, Colorado, by a J.J. Lambert titled "At It Again," about Oscar McMains's pursuit of Franklin Tolby's killers, and his consequent Ring harassment. (See my p. 181)

[INSERT] Affidavits [here excerpted] on Ring corruption.

[On August 6, 1877] I, John L. Taylor, a resident of San Miguel Co., N.M. do voluntarily make the following statements.

*I have resided in said Territory and in said County for the past twenty-two (22) years – Am well informed as to the political history of the Territory. I have been credibly informed by various persons, all well known to me, **that during the first candicacy of Stephen B. Elkins for Representative in the U.S. Congress from this Territory, many persons in San Miguel and Moro Counties were arrested, charged with illegal trading with the Comanche Tribe of Indians ... They were placed under bonds, and when they appeared for trial at Santa Fe, they were released** – as I am informed by them and verily believe – **upon the payment of fees to prosecuting Attorney, and the agreement upon their part to cast their Ballots for said S.B. Elkins.** The above-mentioned transactions took place about four years ago [in 1873].*

John L. Taylor

[AUTHOR'S NOTE: This documents the Ring's vote fixing.]

****

*[On August 30, 1877] Frank Springer [Colfax County resident], being duly sworn says ... upon information and local newspaper reports of the time, that said Axtell has made visits to every other county in the Territory [except Colfax] ... much of the time in company with Wilson Waddingham, Esq. a well-known speculator in land grants ... **and when he passed through [Colfax County], in company with Senator S. [Stephen] W. Dorsey, [it was] for the purposes as was generally understood, of selling to him the Una de Gato grant** in the eastern part of Colfax County; and, to facilitate that sale, among other corrupt motives, the courts had been moved by Axtell from Colfax to Taos County.*

[AUTHOR'S NOTE: This documents Axtell as a Ring frontman in grant fraud. In 1878, Investigator Angel confirmed the Uña de Gato Land Grant used forged documents for boundary inflation, to the detriment of its Colfax County settlers/landowners.]

****

[On July 1, 1877] a Louis Kingman of Santa Fe gave his deposition and stated,] The new facts [of forged Uña de Gato Grant papers] combined with the statements of reputable citizens of Santa Fe lead me to the belief that the Une de Gato grant is fraudulent and I am informed by persons who are familiar with the Mexicans of Santa Fe Co. that the Mexicans who were brought before James K. Proudfit Surveyor of N.M. to prove up the title to the said Une de Gato grant bear a bad reputation and ... that for the sum of one dollar these particular witnesses would swear to anything that might be required of them –

Thomas B. Catron the United States District Attorney for New Mexico is generally understood to represent and to be interested in this grant.

[LETTER TO PRESIDENT HAYES CONCLUDES]

[AUTHOR'S NOTE: Not realizing that the Ring extended to Washington, D.C., they appeal to Hayes for investigation.]

It is requested that there be a thorough and rigid investigation of the matters herein charged, that crime shall not run riot, nor its perpetrators go unpunished; and, that the laws of the land be administered in such a manner as to command the respect and cheerful obedience of the people.

Respectfully
W.B. Matchett
Mary E. McPherson
In behalf of the people of New Mexico

<u>Washington, April, 1877</u>

[INSERT] "CHARGES AGAINST S.B. AXTELL" (March 1877)

<u>Charges</u>, against
S.B. Axtell, Governor of New Mexico:

<u>First</u>. *– His connection with a corrupt combination of men in procuring the enactment of laws inimical to the interests of the people of the Territory, and especially of Colfax County, having for their object the removal of their Courts ... thus depriving them of the right to a speedy and impartial trial by jury of their own countrymen in the district where the crimes charged were alleged to have been committed ...*

Through the operations of this combination, the Legislature of the Territory enacted a law authorizing the Governor ... to remove the Court from its proper locality, to any distant point. And in pursuance of this law, he did so cause the removal of the said Court from Cimarron, Colfax County, on or about March, 1876, to Taos, Taos County, a distance of about fifty-five miles [and over a mountain range], for the purpose of punishing the people of Colfax County for attempting to ferret out the perpetrators of a cold blooded murder of a Methodist preacher named Tolby, which the officers of the law had failed or declined to do. This removal of the Court compelled all persons charged with crime or as witnesses to leave their avocations and travel, some of them fifty to one hundred fifty miles over and beyond a range of mountains ten thousand feet in height and now covered with snow, encamping enroute to attend said court upon fine or imprisonment for refusal under this oppressive law.

It will be seen, by the following item clipped from the Santa Fe paper, that the Governor had been petitioned [by Colfax County citizens] on the subject of the return of the Court, but denied the petition, alleging that the "objects for which it had been removed had not yet been accomplished" – the real "purpose" being to drive the people from the country, or worry them into submission ...

Thus the designs of these men are apparent: The County of Colfax, the most covered by large private grants, being the most persistent in their opposition, are to be gotten rid of ...

They allege,

2<u>dly</u> - His (the Governor's) collusion with said combination having for their ultimate object the reduction of large private grants of land to public domain, with a view to private gain ...

To show somewhat the "objects" of these men, which they affirm "had not yet been accomplished," it will be necessary to look a moment at the question of the system of "Grants," which affects the Territory of New Mexico, more than any other, and probably the <u>County of Colfax</u>, more than any other. Taking one, for instance, for example, the "<u>Maxwell and Beaubier</u>" Land Grant: under the laws of New Mexico, this grant was confirmed by "<u>natural</u>" metes and bounds, as "<u>rivers</u> and <u>mountains</u>" &c. Quite early, a party arose, who contested the validity of the claim so made, and contended that only about a <u>tenth</u> or <u>twentieth</u> of that amount of land was conveyed by Mexican Law, and further confirmed by the Treaty of Guadalupe Hidalgo, and by the law of the U.S. Congress of 1860. To this end, they [Ringites] have kept up a "running fire" *against the [land] holders, and they have been in a constant state of unrest and insecurity ...*

With this explanation, it is clear to see what the "object" is ... to pass laws prescribing the "Grants," – "<u>run</u>" all people from the Territory who differ with them, <u>or who have differed</u> with them, in the past - either by frightening them off by "indictments," or, impoverishing them by oppressive enactments ...

It is clear therefore from the foregoing statement of facts, that ... Governor S.B. Axtell [is] unfit to represent the people ... and we therefore ask for his removal.

Accompanying are letters and papers from citizens of the Territory, which we put in evidence, and request in behalf of the people of the Territory the earliest attention of the government to the matter.

Very respectfully
Your obdt serts.
W.B. Matchett
M.E. McPherson

Washington, March, 1877

[INSERT] "Charges, against S.B. Axtel, Governor of New Mexico"

[AUTHOR'S NOTE: This is another list of Axtell charges.]

<u>Charges</u>, against
S.B. Axtel, Governor of New Mexico:

<u>First</u>. – His refusal to execute properly the laws of the Territory by removing their Courts, and refusing to return the same upon petition.

<u>Second</u>. – His neglect to listen to the petitions of the people of the Territory, to either visit them or interest himself in, or redress their grievances.

<u>Third</u>. – His denial of justice in his refusal to give them a speedy trial by a jury of their peers, and within the District where the pretended crimes with which they stand charged were alleged to have been committed.

[AUTHOR'S NOTE: This Ring ploy of venue change to get an ignorant or Ring-compliant jury would be used in 1881 against Billy Bonney to get a hanging jury in Doña Ana County.]

Fourth. His collusion with the "Rings," having for their direct object the reduction of the private Grants to public domain by a class legislation, with a view not only to enhance himself, but ... the driving out of all good citizens from the Territory.

ADDENDUM TO COMPLAINT: MAY 3, 1877

On May 3, 1877, McPherson and Matchett sent, via President Hayes, an addendum to their March, April, 1877 complaint. It was Raymond Morley's March 6, 1877 letter to be forwarded to Secretary of the Interior Carl Schurz. It stated:

To The President

Please make the enclosed a part of the evidence in the case of "Charges against New Mexican Officials" together with the corroboration evidence filed at the Department of Interior.

Yours respectfully
Mary E. McPherson

****

Washington D.C.
May 3, A.D. 1877

Washington, May 5th '77

To the Honor
The Secretary of the Interior,

Sir – Accompanying please find <u>copy</u> of charges, &c., against S.B. Axtell, Governor, and other New Mexican Officials, filed with the President in April last, which, together with the papers in evidence, we desire made a part thereof, in the proceedings now instituted in your Department against the said Governor James B. Axtell.

Very respectfully
Your obedient sevts,
W.B. Matchett
M.E. McPherson
In behalf of the citizens of New Mexico

[ENCLOSURE] "*Extracts*," March 6, 1877 letter from Raymond Morley, about unjust Taos courts and Catron's malicious harassment. (See my pp. 178-180 for full letter)

PUBLIC RECORDS REQUEST TO SECRETARY OF INTERIOR CARL SCHURZ: JULY 26, 1877

Mary McPherson then encountered corruptions' basic response: stonewalling. On July 26, 1877, she and W.B. Matchett made an ignored public records request to Secretary of the Interior Carl Schurz about the Ring, writing:

Washington, July 26th, 1877
To the Hon.
    The Secretary of the Interior -
        We have respectfully to request that the following named records, documents, papers, communications and correspondence be supplied in the case now pending before The Interior Department in the "Charges vs. Governor S.B. Axtell in connection with the Santa Fe Ring" of New Mexico; the same to be made a part thereof:
    First: The correspondence between Solicitor General Phillips, or, of the Department of Justice, with the Federal Judiciary of New Mexico concerning the Taos Court and its rulings.
    Second: All papers, evidence, Petitions etc, in relation to the charges filed at same Department (and all such filed during a period of four years last past - especially the answer of U.S. Attorney Thomas B. Catron in answer to M.E. McPherson of New Mexico.
    Third: All recent correspondence by and between S.B. Elkins, Ex-Delegate, and the other New Mexican Officials charged, in relation to the charges, and how they should be met.
    Fourth: Gov. Axtell's application for the Office of Governor, and the letters and endorsements in support of the same.
    Fifth Gov. Wm A. Pile's Public Proclamation in relation to New Mexico troubles, while Governor of said Territory.
    Sixth: Dates of appointments and periods of service of S.B. Elkins, and Thomas B. Catron, as U.S. Attorneys of New Mexico, with their endorsements for same.
    Seventh: Any letters, Statements, and evidence in the possession of the President, which he may see fit to communicate, not incompatible with the public interest.
    Very respy your obdt. serv'ts.
    W.B. Matchett
    & M.E. McPherson, For New Mexico

CHARGES PLACED WITH ATTORNEY GENERAL CHARLES DEVENS: AUGUST 23, 1877

With no answer from the Secretary of the Interior, on August 23, 1877, Mary McPherson tried to contact Attorney General Charles Devens. She was again stonewalled. She wrote:

Washington D.C.
Aug 23 1877

To the President
Please place before the Attorney General for immediate action "The Charges vs. New Mexican Officials" now on file, as evidence in the case of Gov Axtell of New Mexico.
Respectfully
Mary E. McPherson

McPHERSON REQUESTS TO BE HEARD IN PERSON: SEPTEMBER 30, 1877

By September 30, 1877, Mary McPherson sought audience with Secretary of the Interior Carl Schurz, and was stonewalled. She wrote:

Sep 30th 1877.

Hon Carl Schurz.
  Sir.
    I desire to know when I can be heard through the Attys employed in the case of the Charges vs Governor Axtell.
During the progress of the case you refused to hear us "as it was ex parte," but at the same time Solicitor, to whom you referred us promised to sit at the time for us to be heard, and we left the case open, for introduction of final evidence.
This has not been complied with.
Please send a reply. I read the note in the "Nation and Star" that the case was decided.
I shall not accept newspaper reports as a decision in a case of the Interior.
Most Respectfully
M.E. McPherson

AXTELL IN THE LOOP: JUNE 23, 1877

Mary McPherson's charges were too dangerous to merely stonewall. So Secretary of the Interior Carl Schurz gave them to Governor S.B. Axtell, who, "immediately wired back that to couple his name with 'land rings was libel and slander' and he requested an investigation." On June 23, 1877, Axtell wrote to Schurz "denying all allegations and citing lawlessness as the reason for relocating courts to Taos for sole purpose of bringing justice to certain parties who seemed to overawe the juries in [Colfax] county." (Cleaveland, pp. 135-136)

While Axtell was bluffing, the Ring was in full swing. Elkins was planning resurvey of the Maxwell Land Grant that September under his brother, John, to confirm an almost two million acres.

And that same fall of 1877, Axtell himself was fronting for the Ring for the fraudulent 500,000 acre Uña de Gato Land Grant sale in eastern Colfax County to Arkansas Senator Stephen Wallace Dorsey. According to Norman Cleaveland, that fraud was revealed to Raymond Morley by past New Mexico Surveyor Lewis Kingman who had surveyed that Grant's area. Kingman stated:

The tract was generally known and believed to be public lands until the spring of 1874 when papers purporting to be the original papers of the Grant were brought to the county clerk's office of Colfax County ... to be recorded - and contrary to the usual custom were recorded by someone other than the county clerk. Lewis Kingman, suspecting forgery, went to the Surveyor General's office in Santa Fe and examined the original papers, and found erasures and alterations that confirmed fraud. Frank Springer signed Kingman's affidavit, and confirmed that Axtell had passed through Cimarron with Senator Dorsey for the purpose as was generally understood of selling him the Una de Gato grant. (Cleaveland, pp. 142-143)

That Ring sale, exposed as fraudulent by Frank Warner Angel, led to a July, 1887 *North American Review* article titled "Land Stealing in New Mexico" by Surveyor General George W. Julian. His summary confirmed, a decade later, Mary McPherson's Ring charges. Julian wrote:

[T]he wholesale plunder of the public domain was carried on ... through extravagant and fraudulent surveys ... The influence of these claimants over the fortunes of New Mexico is perfectly notorious. They have hovered over the Territory like a pestilence. To a fearful extent they have dominated governors, judges, District Attorneys, Legislatures, surveyors general and their deputies, marshals, treasurers, county commissioners and the controlling business interests of the people. They have confounded political historians and subordinated everything to the greed for land. (Cleaveland, p. 143)

MCPHERSON'S PRINTED BOOKLET: "IN THE MATTER OF CHARGES VS. GOV. S.B. AXTELL AND OTHER NEW MEXICO OFFICIALS; SUBMITTED TO THE DEPARTMENTS OF THE INTERIOR AND JUSTICE, AUGUST, 1877"

ANALYSIS: In August of 1877, Mary McPherson wrote the best contemporary documentation of the Ring, titled: "In the Matter of Charges vs. Gov. S.B. Axtell and Other New Mexico Officials; Submitted to the Departments of the Interior and Justice, August, 1877," it likely added impetus to the Frank Warner Angel investigation, and could have prevented the Lincoln County War.

Mary McPherson's 31 page, typeset booklet titled "In the Matter of Charges vs. Gov. S.B. Axtell and Other New Mexico Officials; Submitted to the Departments of the Interior and Justice, August, 1877" fully exposed the Santa Fe Ring. Intriguingly, future New Mexico Territorial Governor Lew Wallace owned it (now in his collected papers in the Indiana Historical Society). Possibly Investigator Frank Warner Angel gave it to him after his thwarted reports. It could have prevented the Lincoln County War; and it heralded its atrocities.

For it, McPherson distilled her past complaints, articles, and petitions, with her sights set on exposing the Santa Fe Ring, its fraudulent land grant grabs, its murder of opponent Franklin Tolby, its false indictments of the next opponent, Oscar McMains, and its suppression of Colfax County settlers by removing their courts to block their legal redress against land grabs. And she dispensed with lawyer, W.B. Matchett. McPherson wrote:

IN THE MATTER OF THE CHARGES VS. GOV. S.B. AXTELL AND OTHER NEW MEXICO OFFICIALS; SUBMITTED TO THE DEPARTMENTS OF THE INTERIOR AND OF JUSTICE, AUGUST, 1877.

ARGUMENT:

In the matter of the Charges against Governor Samuel B. Axtell, of New Mexico, (in connection with other Federal Officials of said Territory,) we respectfully submit:

That it is clearly proven that he is a member of, and in full sympathy with, a **corrupt ring, at Santa Fé**; and that in collusion with them he has aided and abetted the consummation of Legislative, Congressional, and other acts, intended and designed for personal aggrandizement and the oppression of the people, and should therefore be removed from office.

WHAT ARE THE FACTS?

That there has existed in Santa Fé for several years past, a Ring, is now beyond question. That this Ring has, by its power and influence, controlled all the offices, revenues, and Courts of the Territory, - and that they have used this power to oppress, intimidate and plunder the people, cannot now be denied. And just what period it formed, it is not now possible to know; but it grew, and grew quietly. It existed when **Axtell** became Governor, they securing his appointment. It has even grown to such proportions that it has defied the power of the General Government, and has treated its mandates with contempt, - justifying its course, perhaps, by presuming on the slender tenure by which it is supposed to hold its own office; as well as taking advantage of the general upheavals threatening the nation ... - all tending and designed to render themselves secure from the national interference ...

THE LAND-GRANT INTEREST.

The private grants of the Territory, number among the hundreds, dating back, some of them, nearly 200 years; - some of them inchoate, and others with imperfect titles, and some of them with no titles at all. Here was the field of the **Ring's** speculations. Their object seems to have been in some cases to resuscitate old, dead claims; in others, to depreciate sound titles, buy in, or get in, and then procure territorial and congressional action rendering the titles valid! In this branch of the business, they also had the assistance and connivance of the Courts. **S.B. Elkins**, who appears to have emigrated thither the earliest of the party, occupied all the Federal offices in succession up to delegate in Congress; and during this *heigira*, seemed to have opened his "mine" in Grants, and became interested himself very largely, and interested others, placing that interest in hands that would be most effective. For, as early as June, 1872, he appears, together with the present U.S. Attorney, **Thos. B. Catron**, (what their offices were at that period, will appear,) as the managing firm of the "Sierra Mosca Grant," No. 75 – (date of Grant, 1846.) In 1873, he appears in the Martinez and Padilla Grant, No. 74, (date 1742.) And in the Bernalillo Grant, No. 83, the present Chief Justice, **H.L. Waldo**, appears, Feby. 20th, 1874, as he does also in the Angostura Grant, No. 94, Feby. 28, 1874.

Thos. B. Catron, also, is interested in the Ojo Caliente Grant, (Hot Springs,) No. 77; while the Governor of the Territory, **Samuel B. Axtell,** is, at this time, upon one of the Grants of his interest, the Una de Gata, No. 94, in Colfax Co., bargaining its sale to **U.S. Senator [Stephen W.] Dorsey** of Arkansas. How many more of these large grants these parties are interested in, may appear more fully below.

On the 28th of January, 1874, **Elkins** wrote the Com'r of the General Land Office, to "proceed with the surveys" of another Grant, the Maxwell, in Colfax Co., for the purpose of having the Government survey it into "sections" at its own expense, for their benefit.

On the 17th of December, 1875, however, **Mr. Elkins** arose in his place in the House of Representatives, (44th Cong., 1st Sess.,) and presented House Bill, No. 344, entitled "A Bill to confirm private land-claims in the Territory of New Mexico." This bill embraced claims numbered from "49" to "104," inclusive. In the latter clause of the 1st section, a provision inserted as follows viz: "*Provided*, that such confirmation shall only be construed as a quit-claim, or relinquishment, of all title or claim on the part of the United States to any of the lands embraced in either of the said claims, and shall not affect the adverse rights of any person or persons, to the same or any part thereof." And, in the last clause of the 3d section, it is provided still further, "That no grant bearing date since the 18th day of August, 1824, shall be confirmed or patent issue for mere [more] than eleven leagues of land for each original claimant or grantee under said Mexican Government."

Now, the meaning is simply this: Take, for example, claim No. 75, the Sierra Mosca Grant, (one of the claims in which **"Elkins, Catron & Co."** are interested;[)] the "original claimant" may be one person: the first part of the bill provides that the Government shall divest itself of all claims on about 200,000 acres of land. While the last clause gives to this "one" "original claimant" about 49,000 acres only." What is to be done with the balance? Why, that belongs to **Elkins and Co.**! But suppose the Grant embraces less than "eleven square leagues?" Why, the Government would have to make up the balance from other lands.

This is but a sample of the half a hundred claims sought to be confirmed by this bill. How many others they have an interest in is left for future development at the Land Office. That many of these claims were dead, and were only "revived" by this **Ring** is fully shown. And this Bill, No. 344, was reported back to the House without amendment, with a substantial report by the Committee favoring it.

Now for the sequel: When the Bill came up for debate, it was probed and killed ... [based on the argument that the grants were confirmed by the Treaty of Guadalupe Hidalgo, so it was superfluous to confirm them again.]

On January 12, '76, **Elkins** introduced another bill, entitled, "A Bill to enable claimants to lands within the limits of the Territories of New Mexico, Arizona and Colorado to institute proceedings to try the validity of their claims ... [The bill died in the House.] [I]t was to follow as a counterpart an act passed by the other end of the line in Santa Fé, entitled, "An act relating to partition of real estate and for other purposes," (passed about

January 16, 1876,) and means one and the same thing, viz: **to go into the Courts of New Mexico, manipulated by the Ring, and get just such decisions as they wanted to complete this general land steal or "partition" of other men's property among themselves!**

Elkins, the Delegate, failed in his three Bills, but **Catron & Co.** at Santa Fé succeeded in theirs, and **Gov. S.B. Axtell** was a party to it and gave his signature. Immediately, **Catron & Co.** acted upon the Territorial "Partition Act," and filed Bills *vs.* The Maxwell Land Grant and other grants ... [the issue being an attempt to seize the land of Grant settlers – the cause of the Colfax County War.]

[T]he interest of these men in these grants is unaffected; it is still intact, and, in many instances, this interest is the result of the improper resuscitation of old claims that have been dead hundreds of years! It is held to be against the interests of public policy, if not improper, for persons holding official relations with the Government or Congress, to legislate or become interested in or prosecute claims to money or lands, when the Government is the most remotely interested ...

THE OFFICIAL "SLATE."

Now let us see how these men manage to get into office, and then help their friends in, in order to carry out their schemes: Elkins held the office of U.S. Attorney for a long time previous to 1872; at that time he gave place to his friend and partner, Catron, while he ran for Delegate to Congress. The record which he gives of himself is found in the Congressional Directory, 44th Congress, 1876. "Member of the Legislature, 1864-1865: Territorial, District, and then Attorney General and U.S. Attorney: was elected to 43d Congress and was re-elected to 44th, as a Republican, by 1580 majority over Pedro Valdez, Dem." **For the correctness of this latter statement we refer to the record**; it is shown that in three precincts of Valencia county alone they report for Elkins in 1,500 majority, when there were but between 600 and 700 inhabitants, and Rio Arriba county gave Elkins a larger majority than there were votes cast, while Sweetwater precinct, Mora county, cast 13 votes, 10 of which were for Valdez, and when the ballot box arrived at Mora it was found to contain a majority of 80 votes for Elkins and none for Valdez! ...

HOW IT WAS BROUGHT ABOUT.

In 1873 when Elkins ran for Congress, this Ring had about 600 persons indicted for living on Indian lands, and these indictments were hung over their heads until they voted for him – when they were all dismissed. **They were defended by the Ring counsel Elkins & Co.; Catron and he arranging it between them.** The fees and expenses in each case could not have cost the Government less than $20. If any one should speak out against their way of doing things, they would at once disbar them: such was the case with Judge Benedict, ex-Chief Justice of the Territory, and several others of almost equal note, among them the present editor of the Grant County *Herald* ...

The **Ring** had **Axtell** appointed Governor in 1875, and, when **[Henry] Waldo** (Chief Justice) was up for confirmation, he came near defeat by the opposition from the Territory. **(The Ring secured Waldo's appointment on the death of Palen, Chief Justice, in '75.)**

In February, 1876, a petition was signed by 250 well known citizens of New Mexico for the removal of **Judge [Warren] Bristol** (associate Justice,) and **sent to Washington. They filed charges with affidavits, in support. So strong was the Ring influence, that no attention was paid to it.**

PETITION TO REMOVE JUDGE BRISTOL, (Feb. 18, '76.)

We the undersigned citizens of the Third Judicial District of the Territory of New Mexico, without regard to party, would respectfully request and petition for the removal of **Judge Warren Bristol** from the office of Judge of the District and Territory aforesaid, for the following special and general reasons.

1st. We charge that Warren Bristol has been guilty of secretly making known his opinions to attorneys engaged on the side of a cause pending before him, and informing them as to the nature and character of his decisions, several days before delivering them judicially from the bench.

2nd. We charge that in consequence of his secretly making known his opinions that great advantage thereby resulted to the parties employing said attorneys, and great loss and injury to the opposite party.

3d. We charge that Warren Bristol in an important mining suit, in which Martin W. Bremen and Silas Tidwell were plaintiffs, and Robert B. Wilson made defendant, secretly advised with an attorney of said plaintiffs, and informed and advised him as to the proper steps he should pursue in conducting the cause during the very time that the subject matter of his secret advice was under consideration by said Warren Bristol, as Judge.

4th. We charge Warren Bristol with writing out a full and complete form for re-locating a mine for one of the plaintiffs aforesaid, while the title to said mine was then a matter before his court for adjudication.

5th. We charge that Judge Bristol imprisoned an honorable and worthy citizen of Grant County, for contempt, during the pleasure of the court, for no other reason than that he availed himself of information communicated to him by his counsel, which had been prematurely and secretly revealed by the said Judge Bristol.

6th. We charge that Judge Bristol, during the July term of court 1875, held in Grant county, did in open court publicly confess that he had been guilty of revealing a secret opinion to one of the attorneys employed by said Bremen and Tidwell, but rendered no valid excuse for such injudicial conduct.

7th. We charge Judge Bristol with granting a writ of restitution to the plaintiff in a suit of ejectment after an appeal had been allowed and perfected to the Supreme Court, in the absence of any statutory provision authorizing such to issue.

8th. **We charge that Judge Bristol, acting as Judge aforesaid, actually refused in an important murder trial, after the prisoners arraignment at the first term, to grant continuance, although proper affidavits were filed according to law, for the procurement of absent material witnesses, and forced the prisoner to trial which resulted in his conviction and execution.**

9th. We charge that Judge Bristol in another important murder trial absolutely refused to the prisoner the right of compulsory process to procure witnesses in his behalf.

10th. We charge that Judge Bristol, as Judge aforesaid, willfully refused in two other important murder trials, to allow the defendants to exercise their right to the full number of peremptory challenges to jurors, given by the statutes in such cases, although his attention was repeatedly called to the statutory provision allowing the defendant the right to ten preemptory charges.

11th. We charge that the said Judge Bristol made a false accusation from the bench against the grand jurymen of Grant County, N.M. and that they, in proper justification of themselves, were forced to state publicly and in print that such accusation was false; and furthermore, that said public statement of the grand jurymen aforesaid has not, and cannot be denied by the said Judge Bristol.

12th. **We charge that Judge Bristol is guilty of manifest partiality, while acting in the trial of causes.**

13th. And generally we charge that Judge Bristol, as judge aforesaid, frequently consults and advises with attorneys about causes coming and pending before his court for adjudication, who are interested in the results of the suits as feed attorneys.

14th. We charge that Judge Bristol frequently makes rulings in important causes involving large amounts of property and the liberty of citizens, without proper thought and investigation; and that, in consequence of this, he constantly changes his rulings during the progress of important trials, and orders his clerk to expunge the records, in order to hide his indolence and ignorance, and thus deprives parties litigante of the proper recorded history of the causes.

15th. We charge that Judge Bristol is ignorant of the fundamental rules and principles of law with which every tyro should be conversant, and that he is indolent and not disposed to study, thus causing a universal feeling among the people of insecurity to life, liberty and property.

16th. We charge that Judge Bristol appointed a man clerk of his court, whom he knew all the time to be lewdly and publicly living with a kept mistress; and notwithstanding he is still so living, continues to retain him as clerk of his court.

17th. We aver that all of the foregoing statements and specifications can be substantiated on oath, by good, respectable citizens of this Territory irrespective of party predilections.

Here follows about 250 signatures among which are many of the most influential men in that section of the Territory.

THE REMOVAL OF THE COURTS.

We come now to the more serious part of this business. What the Ring failed to do in manipulating the Courts in *one* place, they assayed to do by removing them in another. **In January, 1876, they pushed through the Territorial Legislature an act to "annex the county of Colfax to that of Taos," the object of which was to punish the citizens of that county [Colfax] for charging the "Ring" with the assassination of Rev. F.J. Tolby.** Now, let us see what reason they had for this charge: Tolby was an outspoken man, became offensive to the **Ring**, and must be "got rid of." In going from Elizabethtown to Cimarron, his home, after filling an appointment, he was assassinated while passing through a lone canyon. Suspicion fell on a Mexican named Cruz Vega, who had been employed by one **Donoghue (of the Ring)** to carry the mail for two trips only, as the **Court Judge J.G. Palen, (also of the Ring,)** had taken possession of the stage, to carry itself around to his appointments. Tolby had had a disagreement with Palen on account of some evidence he, Tolby, had volunteered before the Grand Jury in Colfax against a Mexican named **Fran. Griego alias Pancho**, for the killing of three U.S. soldiers. **Pancho was a Ring man** and a deputy sheriff; the **Ring cleared him**. The office of Governor also being vacant [with the death of Governor Marsh Giddings], Tolby was working for Brooks of Arkansas for the appointment, while the Ring wanted Axtell. Tolby died, and the Ring elected their man.

THEIR GUILT.

Vegas [Vega] being questioned closely, admitted knowledge of the murder and finally his guilt was beyond question ... This man, in his confession, implicated one Cardenas, a worthless fellow; **stated that Cardenas did it for the sum of $500 paid him by the allies of this Ring**. Soon after, Cardenas was arrested and corroborated the story of Vega, in that Vegas [Vega] did it for $500; that the money was paid by [M.W.] Mills, R.H. Longwill, Francisco Griego, (Pancho,) and F. Donoghue, and before he knew of Vegas' confession ...

The following is in the record:

"City and county:

"In accordance with the confession of Manuel Cardenas, Justice Trauer issued warrants for the arrest of **R.H. Longwill, M.W. Mills, and F. Donoghue, - Pancho Griego** having been killed in attempting to assassinate Capt. R.C. Allison.

"Captain R.C. Allison, Jas. Allison and P. Burleson, were sent after **Longwill**, who had fled.

"**Cardenas** brought from Elizabethtown and lodged in jail at Cimarron, for protection, (as he had turned State's evidence.)

"Lieut. Cornish and 17 men [soldiers] arrived at Cimarron to do guard duty.

[AUTHOR'S NOTE: Use of troops for citizens' suppression.]

"R.C. Allison was examined for the shooting of Francisco Griego, and cleared on the ground of justifiable homicide ...

"United States vs. Mills, Donoghue, and Cardenas for the murder of Tolby." ...

DECISION.

"Nov. 11, '75. We find that Manuel Cardenas is guilty of murder of Rev. F.J. Tolby, and Florence Donoghue is guilty as accessory thereto, and it is ordered that they be committed to jail to await the action of the grand jury ... There is not sufficient evidence vs. M.N. Mills to bind him over: it is ordered that he be discharged. R.H. Longwill not having been arrested, [fleeing to Santa Fe] no decision is given as to him.

SAM'L S. Trauer, *Justice of the Peace*

MASS MEETING.

At a mass meeting it was resolved "That we regard those who procured the commission of murder as far more guilty, if possible, than the duped and hired tools, and that if satisfactory evidence is found to discover and identify such party or parties there should not be permitted to them any loop-hole to escape the extreme penalty of the law ...

The following also from the leading editorial of the Ring organ, the Santa Fé New Mexican ... speaks for itself, ([Judge Henry] Waldo was there defending the Ring's allies ...)

[AUTHOR'S NOTE: Below is typical Ring-biased press, and duplicitous use of one Ringite to vouch for others.]

"We had the pleasure of meeting Mr. Waldo on his return from Cimarron. There have been so many conflicting reports of the condition of affairs in the county of Colfax and so much uncertainty in regard thereto, that it is a relief to learn the particulars definitely. One thing we are very glad to learn, and of which we are assured by **Mr. Waldo**, and that is the quiet and order which he found existing among the people on his arrival there ... interrupted only by the unfortunate taking off of the man Cardenas. This occurrence we extremely regret, for whatever may have been his crimes, and there seems to have been little doubt that he was either the murderer or one of the murderers of Mr. Tolby – still it is far better for the cause of justice that the penalty of the law should be inflicted upon the violators thereof by the law. We gather from Mr. Waldo that the proceedings before the magistrates were of such a character that ... a full and thorough investigation of all the facts and circumstances that might be thought in any way connected with the killing of Mr. Tolby.

THE RING'S DEFENSE.

The Defense of the Ring and of Axtell, is managed by Catron and Waldo. They prepare his papers and swear each other through! The defense of Catron and Waldo in the Department of Justice, is the same in language, direction, and in some cases, the same handwriting of Axtell's defense, in the Interior Department! Axtell's statement is sworn to be before Waldo! ...

[AUTHOR'S NOTE: An omitted section has concern that Axtell's land-grab agenda was pro-Mormon settlement.]

THE "OTHER" LAW: COLFAX UNITED TO TAOS.

This law passed Febru'y, 1876, was gotten through the Legislature to "punish the people of Colfax county." It provided that the Court should be removed from Cimarron, Colfax county, to Taos, in Taos county, a distance of 55 miles, over a mountain range 10,000 feet high, at times impassable; that after two terms the Governor might at his option return it, which he has not yet done. This act was a trick to **repay the Colfax people for meddling [accusing the Ring] in the trial of the murderers of Tolby**, and demanding their arrest and punishment. The main provision was: "The Grand Jury empanelled in the district court of the county of Taos, shall be sworn and charged to inquire as to offences and other matters in said county of Colfax." The "other matters" may possibly have reference to the manly, intelligent and effective manner in which **the Colfax people opposed the aggression of what is known there as the "Santa Fe Ring" upon the system of Land Grants, the private property of persons who had received them from Mexico under the Treaty of Guadalupe Hidalgo.**

The Gov. says: "I deny being in a combination of men" to pass laws inimical, &c. The law annexing the County of Colfax to the county of Taos for judicial purposes, is the only one to which the people of Colfax county particularly objected, so far as I know; that law was passed with the concurrence of at least two-thirds of the members of the Legislature. **I understand that the course of the Legislature in that respect was approved by the Chief Justice" and "the U.S. Attorney,."** Of course the Chief Justice and the U.S. Attorney approved of it , for they drew it; had it presented and pressed to its passage! It was a Ring measure and intended for "Ring purposes" ...

The Gov. further says: "I had no objection to the 'measure' or part in its passage, except that I signed and approved the law" ...

And the refreshing part of all this is, the Gov. says, that **"the course of the Legislature in that respect was approved by the Chief Justice (Waldo) and the U.S. Attorney" (Catron!) both Ring managers!**

[AUTHOR'S NOTE: Next McPherson angrily exposes the Ring murder of Tolby and framing of Oscar McMains for Manuel Cardenas's murder to get him hanged by the Taos court.]

The Gov. says: "I transmit herewith a copy of the charge of the **Chief Justice (Waldo!)** to the Grand Jury at the Taos Court, on the facts which included the action of the Legislature," &c. Now what is this "charge" but a covert attempt to hide the true "cause" of the Colfax troubles and strike at somebody else over the corpse of the murdered Tolby? **It is a plain, transparent ruse to direct attention from the subject of the murder of Tolby to the lynching of his murderers** [only Cruz Vega was lynched, Manuel Cardenas was shot] **after the authorities had utterly failed or willfully neglected to do their duty, and arrest and bring to trial and punishment men** [Donoghue, Mills, and Longwill] **plainly implicated in the murder of Tolby!** They had "got rid" of one preacher [Tolby]; they wanted to get rid of another [O.P. McMains]! besides others who were distasteful to them, and they supposed "two terms" would be sufficient. "All was quiet and orderly in Cimarron!"

But, the Governor says: "I am informed that the grand-jury; and the **'Attorney General,' (Breeden!)** – made the most careful and thorough investigation, but we were unable to discover any evidence as to the murder of Mr. Tolby."

And immediately thereafter he adds: "Some of the persons engaged in the killing of the man Vega, are now under indictment (!) for that offence, amongst others, Rev. Oscar P. McMains, who is alleged to have been the leading spirit in the affair!" Here is a case of special pleading for you! **The "dead" Tolby is of no account. The "living" McMains is, – and the Ring wants him, dead or alive!** ...

It will be noticed that the troubles arose with the Ring in Santa Fé and were bruited about the country long before McMains arose, and it is straining a very nice point for these gentlemen to try to saddle their Colfax county indiscretions on him.

The Governor adds: "It is true that I refused to restore the District Court to Colfax County, and in this I am sustained by all the **Territorial and Federal officers here, 'including' the Chief**

Justice and Attorney General Breeden!" (Certainly!) "That the 'time' has nor yet come for the return of the Court, is approved by 'its' officers!" (of course, the same men, all through – the Chief Justice, the U.S. Attorney [Catron] and Attorney General [Breeden]! ... Colfax has been "quiet" since Waldo spoke there! but the "Rev. Oscar P. McMains" – the opposer of the "Ring" – is not yet tried, or made to "leave" the county, although he has had hanging over his head for two years "several indictments" which the Ring organ in Santa Fé says, "can be secured at Taos, and are bad things to have lying around loose!" And although his counsel has repeatedly asked an appeal to the Supreme Court of the U.S., the Ring-Court have as often quashed the indictment to defeat the appeal, and then had him re-indicted again and imprisoned ...

[AUTHOR'S NOTE: This is the Ring pattern of malicious prosecution of opponents, to be repeated in Lincoln County.]

The following editorial from the *News and Press*, the organ of Colfax Co., Feb. 11, 1876, edited by W.R. Morley, Esq., is pertinent here:

"TAOS COUNTY', Nee COLFAX – A COUNTY THAT WAS, BUT IS NO MORE.

... "Now it is a notable fact, that no notice was taken by the powers that be, of any crime or disorder in the county, until the indignant populace got after the Tolby assassins ... and some of Elkins party charged in connection with the Tolby murder, it was discovered at Santa Fé that this county was in a state of rebellion, etc. In one sense they were right. It is a state of rebellion against Elkins and his combination, which no legislative act can subdue.

"As soon as the period of retribution in the Tolby case begun, sensational reports were spread abroad ... and the impression was sought to be created that the people of the county were in a state of anarchy and lawlessness, and that the lives of innocent persons were in jeopardy here. Every little scrap of the frontier history of the county was raked up and thrown into the scale to make the case, and every sort of false and ridiculous argument used to induce the legislature to pass the annexation [to Taos County] bill. Many of these charges are utterly false, and the argument deduced without an iota of truth ..."

[AUTHOR'S NOTE: This is the Ring pattern of vilifying opponents by the outlaw myth, to be used in Lincoln County.]

The following are the articles referred to in the above:

[INSERT] December 22, 1875 *New York Weekly Sun* article about that paper's commentator - likely Franklin Tolby - having been murdered for anti-Ring accusations.

[INSERT] August 2, 1877 *Cimarron News and Press's* brief notice titled "U.S. Attorney Catron and the Maxwell," stating: "Mr. M.W. Mills has conveyed his tax title to the Maxwell grant to Thomas B. Catron, of Santa Fé."

[INSERTS] Letters from S.B. Elkins and other Ring backers to President Hayes and to the Department of the Interior backing Governor S.B. Axtell.

REVIEW.

TOLBY opposed the Ring's schemes of plunder and violations of law, and Tolby must fall!

ALLISON stood, with an iron hand, between their rapacity and the people of Colfax, and they struck at him with would-be assassins, - not daring to do it themselves!

MORLEY fought the battle of the Grants, and failing to reach him by their "system" [scheme] of "indictments" - they touch his family with the tongue of slander. [Catron's malicious prosecution of Ada Morley for mail theft.]

McMAINS - the successor of Tolby - would not bow to the "Ring," and, determining to ferret out the murderers of his brother [missionary], found them too near their doors, and he too must fall under their proscription.

Let these Ring managers - Axtell, Catron, Waldo, Breeden, Elkins & Co., - not imagine for a moment that they can "divert" the attention from their own crimes and thereby thwart justice, by attempting to hide behind the blood of the guilty Vega, while that of the murdered Tolby cries out from the canyon: There is "another" account to settle first! They know who were the lynchers of Vega, - why do they not tackle them? Because they do not dare do it, for they are in possession of their secrets, and they do not care to face them. Let these gentlemen understand that they have

"Sown the wind,
"And have reaped the whirlwind!"

And they must not "wince" if they rest under the suspicion of "judicial murder!"

THE RESPONSIBILITY.

Now, what we say is that the Governor, S.B. Axtell, is responsible for all this. He should have "controlled" this Ring while it was his power to do it, and not let the Ring control him! He should be impeached.

And if the [federal] Government allow them [Ringites] to retain their place and power, in the face of this showing; it deserves to have its authority defied; and no one will wonder at the slow decay that will follow in the wake of the administration, and render the Republic itself unstable!

Respectfully submitted, M.E. McPherson,
In behalf of the Citizens of Colfax Co., New Mexico.
WASHINGTON, August, 1877.

RING COLLUSION WITH PRESIDENT HAYES: JUNE 11, 1877

Unlike Mary McPherson, the Ring had easy access to complicit President Rutherford B. Hayes, and colluded with him to ignore and to cover-up Colfax County's anti-Ring charges and exposés. Elkins, ending his second term as Territorial Delegate to Congress, and progressively gaining the immense, corrupt political power he would exert throughout his career, wrote to Hayes backing Governor S.B. Axtell. Noteworthy is that Elkins argued in favor of Axtell by using the Ring's outlawing of opponents, calling Axtell's critics *"irresponsible parties ... [and] a few bad people to whom ... the Governor gave offence in attempting to repress violence and murder."* Elkins wrote:

June 11, 1877

To the President:
I trouble you to say a word in behalf of Gov. Axtell of New Mexico whose removal I am informed is now under consideration.
During Gov. Axtell's administration in New Mexico he has given general satisfaction, and the bonafide citizens, property holders & good people without distinction of party heartily indorse him, and believe him to be a worthy and efficient officer.
The charges filed against him in the Interior Department are for the most part vague & indefinite and as far as certain are absolutely false. ***They are profered by irresponsible parties now residents who have no interest in the Territory & to satisfy a few bad people to whom I am informed the Governor gave offence in attempting to repress violence and murder.***
If the Administration should <u>remove Go. Axtell</u> *on the charges profered it will join hands with irresponsible parties who have no interest in New Mexico in doing a gross injustice to a good man a worthy officer and a republican.*
<u>*Against such action*</u> *as a citizen of New Mexico deeply interested in her welfare and as a friend of your administration I beg to record my* <u>*protest*</u>*.*

Very respectfully
S.B. Elkins
Ex <u>*Delegate*</u> *New Mexico*

CAPITULATION OF FRANK SPRINGER

ANALYSIS: *Besides Mary McPherson, Attorney Frank Springer could have broken the Santa Fe Ring. But he was an opportunist, vacillating between anti-Ring exposés in his Cimarron News and Press, and legal defense of Ringites. By the time of his August 9, 1878 deposition to Frank Warner Angel, though providing evidence of Ring crimes, he concluded with the lie that U.S. officials were not behind the "troubles" in Colfax and Lincoln Counties.*

Author David L. Caffey is Frank Springer's uncritical biographer in his 2007 *Frank Springer & New Mexico: From the Colfax County War to the Emergence of Modern Santa Fe.*

Frank Springer was born 1848. As a 24 year old, financially ambitious Iowa attorney, he arrived in Cimarron in 1873 on invitation of his past Iowa classmate, William Raymond Morley, then vice president of the Maxwell Land Grant and Railway Company, to assist with Company conflicts with Grant settlers. The Company's main attorney was then Thomas Benton Catron. So Springer arrived in the early days of the Colfax County War.

Though Springer became co-editor with Raymond Morley of the *Cimarron News and Press*, wealth was his lure. Caffey quotes him: "When I have made my fortune, perhaps I may come back to Iowa to live. I would much prefer it, were money made as easily as here." (Caffee, p. 21)

As corrupting for Frank Springer were his political ambitions. In 1875, two years after arriving, he ran for Colfax County Representative to the legislature. He lost to Ringite Attorney Melvin Mills - just before Mills implemented the murder of Reverend Franklin J. Tolby, and Governor Samuel Beach Axtell removed Colfax County's courts to Taos County to prevent prosecution of Tolby's Ringite murderers.

The following year, 1876, Springer was an intended victim of the Ring's "Dear Ben plot" to murder him, Raymond Morley, Henry Porter, and Clay Allison. Nevertheless, he later defended Tolby's killer, Melvin Mills, at the Taos Grand Jury, getting Mills's acquittal.

But Springer hedged his bets by also defending Colfax County's anti-Ring crusader, Oscar P. McMains. And he certainly knew anti-Ring fighter Mary Tibbles McPherson.

By April of 1878, with the death of Ringite District Attorney Ben Stevens - arranger with Governor S.B. Axtell of the "Dear Ben plot" - Springer chose a self-serving option of scapegoating Axtell, instead of exposing the Ring. So on June 10, 1878, he wrote a cover letter to Secretary of the Interior Carl Schurz accompanying a Colfax County petition to President Hayes charging Axtell with crimes. It was returned to him by direction of President Hayes on July 12, 1878, and may have contributed to the adminstration's decision after the final Lincoln County War battle, and via the investigation by Frank Warner Angel, to take the same pro-Ring cover-up strategy of merely scapegoating Axtell by removal to feign action. Springer wrote:

FRANK SPRINGER,
ATTORNEY AND COUNSELOR AT LAW,

Cimarron, New Mexico, June 10, 1878

Hon Carl Schurz,
   Secretary of the Interior
      Sir:

I endorse herewith, directed to the President charges against S.B. Axtell, Governor of New Mexico, supported by affidavits verifying the facts stated.

As one whose life was jeopardized by the action of Mr. Axtell, whether through malevolence, stupidity, or blind partisanship matters little. I submit the facts and request you to present them to the President.
            Very respectfully
               Frank Springer

[ENCLOSED: THE COMPLAINT]

To His Excellency, the President of the United States:
            The undersigned, a citizen of the County of Colfax, Territory of New Mexico, begs to call your attention to the official conduct of Samuel B. Axtell, Governor of New Mexico, which show that said Axtell has by false pretense and representation procured the use of United States troops, and employed them in the County of Colfax in a manner directly calculated to produce confusion and bloodshed, and to create disturbance of the public peace in a time of quiet.

That under pretence of a desire to arrest a certain person for some pretended offence, not disclosed, said Axtell planned and conspired by falsehood and treachery to induce a number of peaceable citizens to assemble in a place and under circumstances where under the instructions given by said Axtell for the occasion it was almost certain that most of them would be killed. That had not the plot of said Axtell been discovered in time, it is very probable that it would have resulted in the death of the undersigned, and several other law abiding citizens assembled for a peaceful purpose upon the strength of an invitation to meet the governor. And it is the belief of the undersigned that it was expected by said Axtell that such would be the result of the sending of U.S. troops to said Colfax County.

That the real object of said Axtell was not merely the arrest of a certain person is indicated by the fact that when afterwards *arrested by the military this person was at once released and that said Axtell – while Governor of New Mexico – afterwards made an appointment with the person and traveled with him in a friendly way in the stage coach.*

The undersigned respectfully submits that whether through ignorance or corrupt motive, the action of said Axtell is to keep many parts of the territory in a state of turmoil and confusion when intelligent and non partisan action on the part of the executive might end much of the difficulty. His use of the military force of the United States has been partisan in every instance and the undersigned submits that no person capable of forming such a letter of instructions as the one set forth in the accompanying affidavit is fit to be entrusted with any power whatever, and respectfully asks that he be removed from his position.
Very respectfully
Your obedient Servant, Frank Springer

DEPOSITION OF FRANK SPRINGER: AUGUST 9, 1878

On August 9, 1878, a month after the Lincoln County War's bloody final battle, and aware of Mary McPherson's exposés the year before, Frank Springer gave a deposition to the Departments of Justice and the Interior's Investigator of the Lincoln County and Territorial "troubles," Frank Warner Angel. Of all Angel's deponents, Springer was arguably the only one with enough power and prestige to end cover-up of the Santa Fe Ring's crimes and force federal retribution. But Springer showed only self-serving opportunism by presenting the Ring, and crimes by Catron, Elkins, Axtell, and other Ringites; but then denying knowledge of involvement of U.S. officials in *"any mismanagement, corruption, fraud, or improper action"* causing the Territorial "troubles." So his deposition documents specifics of the Colfax County War's struggles, while being a testament to the Ring's suppression by fear of whistleblowing's consequences. Springer stated:

Deposition of Frank Springer, of Cimarron, New Mexico, given at the request of Frank Warner Angel Esq. upon interrogatories propounded by him.

Int 1. What is your name and occupation?
    A. My name is Frank Springer and I am by profession an attorney of law.

Int 2. What do you know about troubles in Colfax County. When and how did they originate, and what was their character ...

A. I came to Colfax County in February 1873, and have no personal knowledge of affairs in New Mexico previous to that time. There had been some troubles in Colfax County before that, I learned, coming out of controversies between the Maxwell Land Grant and Railway Company and settlers in regard to title and possessions of portions of a large Mexican grant, claimed by the company. **I heard a great deal of talk at that time and afterwards about a so called "Ring" which it was alleged controlled to a large extent the courts in New Mexico. The names of Judge Palen, Mr. Elkins, Mr. Catron were mentioned most frequently in this connection** and in regard to Colfax County the name of Dr. R. [Robert] H. Longwill was often spoken of as being connected with ... the so-called "Ring." He was probate judge in the county when I came here ... It was a frequent subject of comment that through the persons above mentioned the power of the courts were unfairly used to advance the interests of the said Maxwell Land Grant and Railway Company ...

Int 3. You have spoken of a "Ring." What do you know of its existence?

A. The facts upon which its existence was predicated were not generally within my personal knowledge except as to the facts connected with subsequent troubles in Colfax County which impressed me with the belief that a few men had almost absolute control of affairs in the territory. In 1873, Mr. M. [Melvin] W. Mills who had been a prominent opponent of the Maxwell Company and of the men who controlled it, was elected a member of the territorial legislature. Very soon after this he became very intimate with Dr. Longwill, whom he had before strongly opposed. And after he went to Santa Fe to attend the session of the legislature, he wrote to Longwill, in which he informed him that **"by a little sharp figuring" he had got "in with the big side": a copy of the letter is hereto attached as "Exhibit A." From that time on [Melvin] Mills became and continued very intimate with [Robert] Longwill as well as with Messrs Elkins and Catron, and represented their business and political matters in the county to a very large extent** ... And in 1875, when Mills was again a candidate for the legislature and Longwill for Probate Judge all their powers were exerted to promote his election. A circumstance came under my observation during that election campaign which impressed this *strongly in my mind. In June 1875, a man by the name of Francisco Griego murdered two soldiers in Cimarron in a gaming table quarrel, shooting and stabbing them in the back. He fled and was a fugitive for sometime. When at last he came in and gave himself up, he was at once taken before the Justice of the Peace who was a clerk in [Melvin] Mills office and examined and bound over to await the action of the Grand Jury, in $1,000- bail, this action of the Justice being taken after an hour recess and a consultation with Longwill and Mills ... The political campaign was then opening and some weeks afterward I had a conversation with one C. Lara, an especial friend of Griego, who was then actively working in the interest of the Longwill and Mills ticket, as was also Griego himself. Lara had previously been on the other side, and in my asking him the reason of his change of attitude he told me that his friend was in danger of prosecution for the killing of the soldiers and that he -* **Lara − had been to Santa Fe and had talked with the gentlemen, and that they promised him that if he and Griego would use all their influence with the Mexicans in favor of the ticket of Elkins [running as Delegate to the U.S. Senate] and   [blacked out] his friend Griego should not suffer, and that for this reason he was obliged to work on such that he had always before opposed. Upon my asking him who the gentlemen were who had promised him, he mentioned with much reluctance Messrs Breeden and Catron** ... *[Francisco] Griego was discharged without being indicted for anything, nor were any further proceedings taken against him in the matter.*

[AUTHOR'S NOTE: Killer thug Griego's Ring immunity was repeated in 1878 by Jessie Evans's and John Kinney's gangs.]

Int 4. What was the cause of the troubles in Colfax County since you lived there?
    A. The assassination of Rev. F.J. Tolby in September, 1875.
Int 5. State the circumstances connected with the death of Tolby, and what followed ...
    A. F.J. Tolby was a minister of the Methodist church who had been stationed in Cimarron and had been doing missionary work in the county for nearly a year. He was a man of ability and rather free in talking about men and their acts. During the first weekend in September 1875, while the court was in session in Cimarron Judge Palen and Tolby had a rather spirited altercation,

*the judge denouncing him for some remarks he heard made about the court and its actions. Tolby immediately declared he would **"write up that judge so that 200,000 readers should see his record,"** which led some to suppose that he might have been the author of some letters which had appeared in the eastern press reflecting on Palen, Elkins and others.*

On the 16th of Sept, 1875, just after the election and the adjournment of District Court, Tolby was found murdered in the canyon between Cimarron and Elizabethtown. He had started from the latter place two days before, and had been dead two days apparently. He was shot from behind with two bullets and his watch and money were not taken. Mystery surrounded the affair for a time. When at last circumstantial evidence fixed the guilt upon two Mexicans, one of whom had been employed for that day only by [Florencio] Donoghue, the mail contractor, to carry the mail on horseback along that road.

[AUTHOR'S NOTE: This scenario was replicated in 1878's Lincoln County murder of John Tunstall using Jessie Evans and his boys in concert with Sheriff William Brady's posse.]

*The county was intensely excited over the murder, and the people generally were fiercely indignant, and determined to punish the guilty if they could find them. The two Mexicans were arrested separately. one of them – [Cruz] Vega - after having a rope put around his neck and strung up a few seconds, made a statement to the effect that Tolby had been killed by the other Mexican – [Manuel] Cardenas – that he saw him do it, and **that they had been hired by [Francisco] Griego and [Florencio] Donoghue to do it**. The other one – Cardenas – without any violence being used, stated that Vega had killed Tolby, that he saw him do it, and that they had been hired to do it by Longwill, Mills, Donoghue and Griego. Vega was taken by a mob and hanged. Griego was killed by R.C. [Clay] Allison in self defense, [Francisco] Griego trying to kill him. As soon as Longwill was informed of the statement Cardenas had made, he left the town and relocated to Santa Fe, after eluding a vigorous pursuit. Mills and Donoghue were arrested, and an examination had before magistrate, which resulted in the discharge of Mr. Mills for want of evidence, and the commitment of Donoghue and Cardenas. Previous to the examination Cardenas was visited in jail by three prominent friends of the parties accused ... **The examination before the magistrate was concluded about ten o'clock at night and while Cardenas*** *was being taken from the court room to the jail under a guard, a man sprang from behind a corner and shot Cardenas dead, and escaped out of sight ... This act always remained a mystery. It cannot be reasonably charged to the friends of Tolby, for it was clearly to their interest to keep him. During the pendency of these proceedings a detachment of U.S. troops arrived from Fort Union being sent in ... at the request of Gov. Axtell, it being declared that the town was in a state of riot and anarchy, and life and property in danger from a mob.*

[AUTHOR'S NOTE: This suppression of civilians in service of the Ring by using the military would be repeated in the Lincoln County War to achieve murder and arson.]

The troops remained several days & found nothing to do – found the people quiet and peaceable and the law taking its course, but very bitter and excited feeling among them on account of the murder of Tolby. Some minutes afterward [Florencio] Donoghue was taken to Santa Fe on a writ of <u>Habeas Corpus</u> and released on $1000 bail. He and [Robert] Longwill have ever since remained there.

[AUTHOR'S NOTE: The Ring's freeing of members was repeated after the 1879 Lincoln County murder of Attorney Huston Chapman, after Governor Lew Wallace arrested James Dolan, Billy Matthews, and Seven Rivers boys, imprisoning them in Fort Stanton. They were released by Ring attorneys using *habeas corpus* and never prosecuted.]

At a term of court subsequently, in Taos, the Grand Jury ignored the charges against them ...

[AUTHOR'S NOTE: Axtell had moved courts from Colfax to Taos County, where the juries could be controlled by the Ring.]

Int 6. What action did the governor take to prevent the troubles in Colfax County?
    A. He took no action in regard to the county until after the passage of the act [of January 14, 1876 attaching Colfax County to Taos County so as to move the courts from Colfax County to Taos County] except to send troops during ... the examination of the parties charged with complicity in the Tolby murder ...
Int 7. Was it necessary to attach Colfax to Taos Co. for judicial purposes?

A. No, not for any legitimate end.
Int 8. What was the object of attaching Colfax County to Taos?
   A. The alleged reason was that lawlessness persisted in Colfax and the laws could not be enforced, but it was not true ... In my opinion, judging by what occurred subsequently, as well as at the time, the real object of annexation of Colfax Co to Taos was to so intimidate and punish by means of indictments found by juries of Mexicans full of ignorance & prejudice [about Colfax County], the people who had taken an active part in the search for the Tolby murderers, and who had been strongly hostile to the suspected parties [Catron and Elkins and local Ring members], and thus enable these parties to regain control in the County which through these events they had lost ...

[AUTHOR'S NOTE: This tactic was repeated by the Ring in Lincoln County following Tunstall's murder by Axtell's March 6, 1878 proclamation removing Justice of the Peace John Wilson so as to shield the Ringite murderers, then by District Attorney Rynerson's and Judge Warren Bristol's venue change transfer to Mesilla their cases, to get jurors ignorant of the issues and guarantee acquittals. The same may be said of the 1879 transfer of Billy Bonney's case to Doña Ana County to avoid Lincoln County jurors aware of the War issues, and who might have freed him or refused a first degree murder verdict.]

Int 9. Could the laws at this time be enforced honestly and impartially in Colfax County?
   A. ... So far as the people of the county were concerned, yes.
Int 10. Did the people take any action to prevent the change of the courts?
   A. There was no time for any. The bill was introduced the day before the close of the session of the legislature ... Several gentlemen telegraphed Axtell requesting him to withhold his signature ... He telegraphed in reply "Bill signed. S.B. Axtell."

[AUTHOR'S NOTE: This was repeated by Governor Axtell by his illegal Lincoln County Proclamation invalidating Justice of the Peace Wilson's deputy appointments - including Billy Bonney.]

Int 11. What action did the Governor take to enforce the bill?
   A. ... He said there were bad men there and that he intended to have them punished if or compelled to leave the county if it took all the troops in New Mexico ...

[AUTHOR'S NOTE: This is the Ring's outlaw myth tactic, later repeated in Lincoln County and against Billy Bonney.]

Int 12. Was there any resistance to the court [transfer] offered or threatened?
A. Not to my knowledge ...
Int 13. Was it a benefit or not to attach Colfax County to Taos? ...
A. ... It was a gross injury and injustice to the people of Colfax County ...
Int 14. Could the troubles in Colfax County have been quieted in any other way? ...
A. As I stated, there were no troubles calling for any outsider influence ...
Int 15. What was done, if anything, by the Governor, in regard to Colfax County after the passage of the act?

[AUTHOR'S NOTE: Springer gives the "Dear Ben plot." Its tactic was repeated in Lincoln County in 1878 by property attachments by Ringite Sheriff William Brady to induce violence to justify murdering Tunstall and McSween in "self defense."]

A. In the meantime Axtell had removed the Sheriff of Colfax County, who had been elected, and appointed in his place one of the strong partisans of Elkins, [Robert] Longwill et. al. [the Santa Fe Ring]... [District Attorney of the Second Judicial District Benjamin Stevens] went to Cimarron ... telling the people that he was going to try to induce the Governor to visit the county. Instead of going to Santa Fe, he went to Fort Union. Whence he returned to Cimarron in a few days, and followed by a company of U.S. soldiers of the 9th cavalry (colored) ... He exhibited a telegram from the Governor, which read as follows: "Do not let it be known that I will be in Cimarron in Saturday's coach. Body guard all right." Stevens ... said it now proved his efforts with the Governor had been successful and that the Governor was coming to visit the county and would expect to meet those who had signed the invitation to him, and that they must be on hand at the arrival of the coach on the following Saturday to meet with him. He especially mentioned [Clay] Allison, as one that ought to be on hand. He also urged on Mr Morley with whom he had been talking, to keep the matter quiet as the governor did not want a crowd, but only wanted to meet those who had invited him. The Governor did not intend to be present or to visit Colfax at the time, and did not in fact arrive on Saturdays coach, but the telegram and the action of Stevens made in furtherance of a plot which the details are set forth in a letter which the Governor wrote to Ben Stevens at the time of sending the telegram, and of which the following is a correct copy:

[INSERT] 1876 "Dear Ben plot" letter, published in 1877 in the *Cimarron News and Press*. (See my p. 167)

The plot disclosed in the foregoing letter was discovered, and none of the parties mentioned were on hand, so the scheme ended in failure. The Mr Porter mentioned in the forgoing letter was the leading banker and merchant in the county who possessed large influence and was a strong opponent of the party which had been controlling the county [the Santa Fe Ring]. Mr Morley and myself had actively opposed them politically, and were at the time owners and controllers of the newspaper in Cimarron which was vigorously attacking all parties concerned with removal of the courts, and exposing the violations thereof. The person referred to as "our man" was ... Mr R.C. [Clay] Allison ... He occupied a prominent place in the eyes of the public on account of his well known desperate courage and resolute character. He had never refused to face the legal consequences of his acts. He was ... a man of strong impulses and quick temper, prompt to react to any injury or to resist an indignity. His character was well known, and he was recognized as a leader among the cattle men of the county. **He had been on most friendly terms with [Robert] Longwill and his associates, and had, together with his friends, vigorously supported them during the election of Sept, 1875.** He had When Tolby was murdered he had greatly invested himself in trying to discover the murderer, and took a leading part in the arrest and examination of those charged with complicity therein and had led a hot pursuit of Longwill on that occasion ... But whether there was or not [any grounds to arrest him], it is almost certain, that if when he had come to the coach upon the invitation of the Governor to meet and pay respect to him as the Executive of the Territory, he had found himself beset with negro soldiers seeking to arrest him [as a known racist], his first motion would have been resistance, and in that case, according to the instructions of Gov Axtell not only he, but those who stood with him, were to be killed, and among those ... were named "Porter, Morley, Springer."

The character of Allison was well known to the Governor ... and it was well known to everybody that he would not quietly submit in the manner described and planned ... It is my belief that it was expected that Allison would resist, and that the soldiers would then fire on the party indiscriminately, in which the chances were that most of us would be killed. The result of which would have been 1st the parties named would have been out of the way & 2nd the people of the county would have been driven to desperation, and an excuse afforded for keeping troops in the county, and through these means it may have been hoped that control of the county could be regained by Axtell and the party in whose favor he has become partizan [the Ring] ...
Int 16, 17, 18, 19, are answered in my last answer.
Int 20. Was there any law as to restoring the courts to Colfax County?
    A. Yes ... [T]he Governor might restore the courts to Colfax County by proclamation.
Int 21. Did the people try to induce the Governor to restore the courts?
    A. Yes. After two terms had been held in Taos, petitions were signed by many citizens, and presented to the Governor by Hon. W.L. South, member elect, of the Territorial House of Representatives of Colfax County. Mr South reported that the Governor promised to do so after certain objects had been accomplished, but he never did it.

[AUTHOR'S NOTE: What follows gives the Ring's land-grab scheme connected to Colfax County court's removal: make a new county for the Uña de Gato Land Grant there. This tactic was replicated after the lost Lincoln County War when the Ring grabbed murdered Tunstall's Lincoln store and his 3,000 acres of ranchland along the Feliz and Peñasco Rivers.]

In the summer of 1877, Gov Axtell came to Colfax County in company with Senator S.W. Dorsey to examine a tract of land in the eastern part of the county called the "Uña de Gato Grant' ... He met many citizens in the eastern part of the county, to whom he said that the courts would never be restored to the county at Cimarron ... but told them that they ought to cut loose from the Cimarron crowd and have a new county for themselves ...
Int 22. Have the courts been restored? ...

A. Yes, by act of the legislature – January 1878.
Int 23. Had the Governor any reason for refusing the request of the people to have the courts restored to Colfax County?
A. No legitimate reason ... A large number of indictments were formed against parties in Colfax County for crimes alleged to have been committed there, and with the exception of pleas of guilty to minor offences ... there have been but very few convictions ...
Int 24. Do you know anything about the indictment of Mrs W.R. Morley"

[AUTHOR'S NOTE: Springer next presents U.S. Attorney Catron's malicious prosecution of Ada Morley, clearly attributing it to attacking her Ring opponent, husband, Raymond Morley: "it was an unworthy way to fight a man by attacking his family." Catron's vicious sadism with its entanglement with the buggy incident with Ada should not be missed.]

*A. In July 1875, I learned that there was to be a prosecution commenced in the U.S. Dist Court in Santa Fe against Mrs Morley, the wife of W.R. Morley, on a charge of abstracting a letter from the Post Office at Cimarron [which she claimed was from a family member, her mother, Mary McPherson] ... I wrote to Dr [Robert] Longwill [a subsequent Tolby murderer] and appealed to him to use his influence to stop it as **it was an unworthy way to fight a man by attacking his family. He promised to do so, but said to me that "Morley ought to stop attacking Elkins through the newspaper." Mr Morley was then opposing the party of Elkins and his friends politically.** I went to Santa Fe ... and found that it was determined that Mrs Morley should be indicted, and my opinion was confirmed by a letter written by Mr [Melvin] Mills to Dr Longwill ... of which the following is a copy [below]. As bearing on the subject of the proceedings, I refer to the affidavit of A. [Asa] F. Middaugh of a conversation between him and Mr Catron of which I attach hereto as Exhibit B as a true copy [below].*

In August following I was present at a conversation between W.R. Morley and John Pratt, U.S. Marshall for New Mexico at Clifton in Colfax County ... Morley said to him to tell Mr Catron to crack ahead with it [serve arrest warrant on his wife], that what he had already done would cost Elkins 500 votes [for Delegate to the U.S. Senate] ... Nothing was ever done in the case. Mrs Morley was never arrested.

Int 25. Do you know of any mismanagement, corruption, fraud, or improper action by any U.S. official in his official capacity or of any fact or facts which would render him an improper person to be such official, which the Departments of Justice and Interior should be informed of? If so state names or facts in detail!

[AUTHOR'S NOTE: This is the key question. Next Springer folds and shields the Ring – to save his life and future. He obviously knew Angel's report could not be kept from Elkins in Washington, D.C., and doubletalks evasively, ending: *"I have no personal knowledge further that I recall."* And, equally self-serving Angel likely bet that Springer would balk, allowing Angel to save himself by demonstrating that a knowledgeable deponent swore under oath that *"no U.S. officials were involved in Territorial mismanagement, corruption, fraud, or improper action."*]

A. I know of a case in which four indictments were found in the U.S. Court against Dr Wm N. Michaels of this place, two in charges of selling liquor & two tobacco, without the U.S. license ... Whether any official is responsible for them I do not know ... I have no personal knowledge further that I recall.

[AUTHOR'S NOTE: Springer's fearful folding heralded the generation of silence following the Ring's July 14, 1881 killing of the last remaining Regulator: Billy Bonney.]

Frank Springer

Subscribed and sworn to before me by Frank Springer on the ninth day of August AD, 1878.

Henry Wigham
Notary Public

[EXHIBIT A] The December 5, 1873 letter of Attorney Melvin W. Mills to Dr. Robert H. Longwill gloating about Catron's indictment of Ada Morley for mail theft. (See my p. 170)

[EXHIBIT B] March 31, 1876 Deposition of Asa F. Middaugh about Catron's vindictive motive in prosecuting Ada Morley. (See my p. 171)

OUTCOME OF THE COLFAX COUNTY WAR

ANALYSIS: Though settler skirmishes continued in Colfax County till the late 1880's, focused Ring opposition ended with Mary McPherson's stonewalling, with relentless prosecution of Oscar McMains, with Frank Springer's betrayal in his deposition, and with Raymond and Ada Morley's fleeing the Territory. But Colfax County settlers probably considered as victories regaining their courts and seeing Ringite Governor Axtell removed in 1878.

REMOVAL OF GOVERNOR AXTELL

The Hayes administration scapegoated Governor S.B. Axtell to hide the Santa Fe Ring. Axtell was even informally suspended on September 4, 1878, before Angel even submitted his October 3, 1879 report against him with the Department of the Interior.

But Colfax County citizens likely felt victory, especially in light of avoiding the horrific bloodshed of the lost Lincoln County War 210 miles to the south and two months earlier.

On September 6, 1878, Raymond Morley's and Frank Springer's *Cimarron News and Press*, celebrated with headlines: "Rejoicing at Cimarron," "Axtell's Head Falls at Last," and "General Lew. Wallace Appointed Governor." They jibed at Ringite presses: "It will now be in order for the [*Santa Fe Weekly*] *New Mexican* and *Las Vegas Gazette* to wear the usual badge of mourning for 30 days."

But those two papers, unruffled, merely praised Axtell on September 21st and October 19th, 1878.

RETURN OF THE SANTA FE RING TO COLFAX COUNTY

Colfax County's rejoicing was naïve. The frightened voice of Mary McPherson's daughter, Ada Morley, had reflected true Ring threat, herself victim of Catron's malicious prosecution, and her husband victim of intended murder in the "Dear Ben plot." On March 7, 1877, she had written to her mother in Washington, D.C.: *"I am really afraid to write on these matters. Elkins of course is trying to keep his friends in their present positions and as I said I have little hope or faith that you can succeed."*

By 1878, the land-grab vision of Catron and Elkins was realized. The Raton Pass of the Maxwell Land Grant along the old

Santa Fe Trail was purchased as an ideal railroad route by the Atchison, Topeka, and Santa Fe to run its tracks southward from Colorado into New Mexico Territory. Sale go-between was engineer, Raymond Morley, then back in that railroad's employment. Frank Springer had a life of political dabbling, business diversity, and financial success. By 1882, Colfax County's seat was relocated from Cimarron to Springer, named after him by the Atchison, Topeka, and Santa Fe. And it took until an April 18, 1887 Federal Supreme Court decree for the Ring to achieve eviction of all Maxwell Land Grant settlers.

Extending those Atchison, Topeka, and Santa Fe Railroad tracks intersected Billy Bonney's fate. He would languish in the Santa Fe jail from January 1st to March 28th, 1881, still pleading with Governor Lew Wallace for his pardon, but awaiting completion of those tracks for transport southward, since the Ring feared his partisan rescue from a stagecoach before his inevitable hanging sentence by Ringite Judge Warren Bristol in Mesilla.

The real Colfax County War achievement was finalizing the Ring's blueprint for unbeatable organized crime: control the governor, legislature, courts, law enforcement, and press; conduct malicious prosecution; use the outlaw myth against adversaries; remove legal redress to give members immunity from prosecution; rely on troops for intimidation and killing; enlist henchmen for assassination to conceal higher echelons from complicity; and expurgate incriminating documents. The Lincoln County War period would prove effectiveness of that strategy with tragic results for democracy.

But there was a fatal flaw in Catron's and Elkins's plan. The Ring needed secrecy. Lacking charisma, those at the Colfax County War's anti-Ring forefront sank into historical oblivion lasting to this day. But the Ring was about to encounter a teenager, just renamed by himself as "Billy Bonney," whom the world would never forget. He would thrust on them the glare of insatiable curiosity illuminating his life and death, until their atrocities were inescapably known. And on August 17, 1877, his trajectory was a mad dash from Arizona Territory to New Mexico Territory on a stolen racehorse to escape hanging for killing in self-defense Frank "Windy" Cahill. He may have heard of Jessie Evans and his boys: rustlers and killers for the Santa Fe Ring. By that September, he would be riding for them and the Ring as just another gunman.

CHAPTER 6
LINCOLN COUNTY'S SANTA FE RING "TROUBLES": 1878

A MAGNIFICENT FIGHT FOR FREEDOM

ANALYSIS: The Lincoln County War was the Santa Fe Ring's greatest triumph not only by removing mercantile, banking, and ranching competition; not only by crushing opposition; but by using the outlaw myth to conceal it as a freedom fight against tyranny. The War was also the Ring's long-term historical undoing by creating and publicizing larger-than-life "Billy the Kid."

There existed no Lincoln County "troubles," if that meant generalized outlawry. True troubles were years of citizens' desperate responses to Santa Fe Ring incursions and escalating crimes, until 1878's culminating Lincoln County War battle.

Thomas Benton Catron wanted to control Lincoln County, then the largest county in the United States and its Territories; constituting the southeast quarter of New Mexico Territory, and the size of combined Massachusetts, Connecticut, Vermont, Rhode Island, and Delaware. And his Ring was maturing from land-grab to land use for cattle ranching, and to mercantile endeavors.

Catron had invested in "the House," a mercantile monopoly on 40 acres in Lincoln, making its respective partners - Emil Fritz, Lawrence Murphy, James Dolan, and John Riley - his local Ring bosses. They sold goods and supplies on usurious credit to local cash-strapped townspeople and homesteaders. In addition, "the House" held traderships to the local Mescalero Indian Reservation and the local fort, Stanton, for beef and flour. "The House's" supplying of mealy flour and rustled cattle for beef were ignored by Ring-biased Fort Stanton's commander, George Purington, and by complicit Indian Reservation Agent, Frederick Godfroy.

Catron also took possession, in 1878, of deceased and indebted Lawrence Murphy's ranch, putting it under management of his brother-in-law, Edgar Walz, as the Carrizozo Land and Cattle Company; with likely goal of expanding to control of Lincoln County's three east-to-west rivers - the Hondo, Feliz, and Peñasco - thereby actually controlling water for cattle ranges over thousands of acres eastward to the north-to-south Pecos River.

Catron's problem was that opponents and competitors were already present, and needed elimination. In 1875, Robert Casey, cattle ranching on the Hondo, was murdered by Ring thug Willie Wilson in Lincoln immediately after Casey won an election against Lawrence Murphy. And Juan Patrón, Lincoln's anti-Ring Hispanic leader, was crippled in an assassination attempt by John Riley. Recent British settler, John Henry Tunstall, by 1877, had built his own large Lincoln general store with a bank, whose fair dealings threatened to bankrupt the House. In addition, Tunstall used his ranch hands, like Billy Bonney, to homestead land on the Peñasco River for ranching, and purchased another ranch from Ringite Jacob Basil "Billy" Matthews on the Feliz River.

So by 1878, it was Tunstall who already controlled the vast range to the Pecos River. And there was John Chisum, the cattle king, with his herd of 80,000 head along the Pecos, in alliance with Tunstall, and president of his bank. And there was high-minded Attorney Alexander McSween, who knew the Ring's dark secrets after working from 1875 to 1876 for "the House;" and now inspiring anti-Ring fervor in Tunstall, while legally representing aggrieved Hispanic clients. And there were the anti-Ring Lincolnites, embittered by Ring violence and mercantile usury.

The magnitude of threat to Catron's empire building was far greater than Grant County's 1876 succession plan, or Colfax County's exposés and riots. These adversaries would not change sides like Attorney Frank Springer, or retreat like Raymond Morley. And their zeal would convert teenaged delinquent Billy Bonney to their cause, and accidentally create the sole opponent able to achieving the Ring's downfall - in life, or after his killing.

The Ring's economic oppression was exacerbated by malicious prosecutions by Lincoln County Sheriff, William Brady, 3rd Judicial District Judge Warren Bristol, and District Attorney William L. Rynerson. Thug enforcers were Ring rustlers like Jessie Evans and his boys; John Kinney's Mesilla gang; and Seven Rivers rustler-ranchers, like the Olinger and Jones brothers.

But a critical factor was Lincoln County citizens' isolation. They knew about Catron's Ring, but not its power by 1877, or the past uprisings against it. They wrongly believed justice could come from President Hayes, unaware of his Ring bias and S.B. Elkins's Washington, D.C. influence. They never suspected local military alliance with the Ring. And Lincoln County lacked educated and wealthy citizens or a newspaper to give a voice to rebellion like the Grant County *Herald* or Colfax County *Cimarron News and Press*.

But there were unique strengths, unanticipated by the Ring. In Lincoln County, citizens were willing to take up arms against oppression. So the Ring would face its first Hispanic uprising, with men of San Patricio and Picacho constituting the majority of Lincoln County War fighters. And if momentum could have continued, that ethnicity constituted a Territorial majority that could have defeated the Ring by voters or combat (as Governor Marsh Giddings prophetically warned in 1872).

HERO IN WAITING: BILLY BONNEY

By chance, almost 18 year old Billy Bonney probably exceeded his Lincoln County compatriots in appraising their enemy, since in the two months prior to his being hired as a ranch hand by John Tunstall, he had developed friendships with Ringite Seven Rivers men, had ridden with Ring outlaw Jessie Evans and his gang, and had likely met James Dolan: all to be his Lincoln County War adversaries.

There was more. By late 1877 or early 1878, Billy became acquainted with the Maxwell family in Fort Sumner; and the teenaged daughter of Lucien and Luz Maxwell, Paulita, became his secret sweetheart. So he must have heard first-hand from the Maxwells about Catron's and Elkins's *de facto* theft of their Land Grant, their exile to desolate Fort Sumner, and Lucien's early death in 1875 after trauma from his losses.

So by 18, Billy would have had a measure of Ring crimes exceeding other Lincoln County fighters. And, but for a quirk of fate - his meeting kind and honest John Tunstall - he would have fought for the Ring side in the ensuing conflict.

In fact, Billy was so charismatic and competent that the Ring was loath to let him go. James Dolan, following the Lincoln County War, and a year after Tunstall's murder for which he was indicted, courted Billy in a "peace meeting" in Lincoln. It unexpectedly ended in Dolan's, Jessie Evans's and Billy Campbell's murder of anti-Ring Attorney Huston Chapman - with Billy as witness. So even after the War, Billy could have returned to the Ring's criminal fold where the realistic prospects - as had tempted the fall of Attorney Frank Springer - were prosperity and safety. But Billy again rejected the Ring.

Instead he would request a pardon from new Governor Lew Wallace to remove the Ring's prosecutory power over himself, and free himself to continue his anti-Ring fight.

LINCOLN COUNTY SANTA FE RING BOSSES

The local Ring mercantile monopoly emanated from "the House," the biggest building in Lincoln County. That enterprise began as a Fort Stanton sutler's store run by Emil Fritz and Lawrence Murphy, with younger James Dolan as clerk. As discussed, Catron himself had financial interest from the group's start. Always rooted in corruption, the group operated an illegal whiskey still and a counterfeit money printing press in a nearby cave. In 1873, violent-tempered Dolan, attempted to kill black 9th Cavalry Captain James F. Randlett. Dolan and Murphy were arrested. But intervention by U.S. Attorney Catron was likely, since their charges were dropped, and Randlett was charged instead! Randlett filed a complaint to the Adjutant General on July 22, 1873, as quoted by historian Frederick Nolan in his *Life and Death of John Henry Tunstall*. Randlett wrote:

[T]heir prices for goods sold to enlisted men [are] extortionate almost to robbery. [They] have been engaged in supplying the Indians supposed to be on this reservation; I soon became convinced they were swindling the Government ... outrageously ... one officer of the Army told me that Murphy has said he would kill me, and that so mighty was the power of the firm that they could get false testimony enough to deprive me of my Commission as an officer. Murphy I am told ... has said that if he could not have his way in feeding the Indians [the beef, flour, and hay contract to Fort Stanton] he would put them on the Warpath [likely because Murphy was also supplying illegal whiskey to them]. (Nolan, p. 186)

To escape exposure of Ring entanglement, the merchants were likely relocated to Lincoln, nine miles away. With money likely Catron's, they hired Lincoln builder, George Peppin, to create their grand two-story adobe "House" at the one mile long town's southwest terminus. Catron emerged publicly as financial backer in 1878 when he mortgaged "the House" at their bankruptcy.

And with the Ring's loyalty to "friends," the sutler store period had yielded connection to Fort Stanton soldier, William Brady, who became Lincoln County Sheriff. And builder George Peppin became Brady's Deputy; and later, the illegally Ring-appointed Sheriff of Lincoln County for the Lincoln County War.

ABOUT JOHN HENRY TUNSTALL

ANALYSIS: British John Henry Tunstall became a new type of Ring opponent: an economic competitor with the rare commodity of cash for investments in stores and ranches. Tunstall also changed Billy Bonney's life with his goodness and generosity, becoming, in the 4½ months Billy knew him as his ranch hand, a father figure who converted him from a delinquent to a rebel with a cause. Tunstall's sweetness and humor appear in letters to his beloved family in London. And Tunstall's Ring murder martyrdom would galvanize the Lincoln County War and Billy's anti-Ring mission.

AN INNOCENT ARRIVES IN SATAN'S PARADISE

In the fall of 1876, Lincoln attorney, Alexander McSween, convinced wealthy young Englishman, John Henry Tunstall, to locate to Lincoln County to expand his family's mercantile empire. McSween had his own agenda. Almost a Presbyterian minister, he had moved from St. Louis to Lincoln in 1875 and worked as "the House's" attorney until quitting in 1876, repelled by their corruption. He continued private legal practice, and owned land in Lincoln. Like Colfax County's Reverend Franklin Tolby, he became a Ring opponent. Bringing rich Tunstall to cash-poor Lincoln, where even "the House" struggled financially, could break the Ring's monopoly.

By 1877, John Tunstall had built, on the northeast side of Lincoln's only street, a large single-story building housing his store, bank, and personal apartment, just a quarter mile from "the House." For bank president, he chose cattle king, John Chisum. Under the Desert Land Act, Tunstall also acquired almost four thousand acres of ranchland along Lincoln County's more southern rivers, the Feliz and the Peñasco; thus controlling miles of grazing land by having its only water. And McSween built a large house: a two-wing structure for himself and his wife, Susan, on one side; and the other side for his brother-in-law and law partner, David Shield, husband of Susan's sister, Elizabeth, with their five children. In that building McSween and Shield also had their law office, with Shield's law student, Harvey Morris.

Tunstall joined McSween's anti-Ring campaign, and planned to wrest from "the House" its beef and flour traderships; while, at the same time, waging a newspaper campaign starting with exposé of Lincoln County Sheriff William Brady's use of tax money to buy cattle for the Ring. Thus, the Ring faced an alliance of rich Tunstall, anti-Ring McSween, and cattle king Chisum.

Historian Frederick Nolan's 1965 biography, *The Life and Death of John Henry Tunstall*, reprints the affectionate letters by Tunstall to his London family. With a love-saturated life opposite to that of adversity-hardened Billy Bonney, Tunstall lacked cynicism to recognize the lethal evil in "Satan's Paradise."

Born March 6, 1853 in England to John Partridge Tunstall and Emily Ramie Tunstall, John adored his three sisters, Emily Frances, Lilian, and Mabel, whom he nicknamed his "Trinity": "Minnie," "Jack," and "Punch." And he addressed his father with whimsical humor as "Beloved Governor." The family home was at prosperous 7 Belsize Terrace in London; and they owned the mercantile business Turner, Beeton and Tunstall in Victoria, British Columbia.

Though Tunstall never mentioned Billy in his letters home in the 4 ½ months he knew the boy, Tunstall, poignantly blind in his right eye, must have offered to that rough teenager a revelation of gentle and vulnerable goodness, becoming a father-figure and inspiration. One can experience Tunstall from his letters.

On June 12, 1876, Tunstall, seeking business opportunities, wrote home from California:

My desire is for wealth, that I may have the means of smoothing the path of life for Old Min & our two pets, & in fact of doing for them, as you, my much Beloved Governor, would have them done by ... I look ahead & anticipate the hardships (as they are called) somewhat as a sailor does, but I have no fear, but that the ship will stand it alright; & I have great faith in the captain. (Nolan, p. 133)

By June 17, 1876, Tunstall wrote from the San Louis Obispo, California, ranch of a Robert Flint, who pointed him toward New Mexico, but warned about dangers of "the ring":

The climate of New Mexico is he says cold in winter, he said it would be very cold for stock ...
He says the American population is very small, that the people are very poor ... **He says the politics are in the hands of a ring who control things as they like.** *According to his account, there are very few sheep & cattle there. He says that as soon as I go there, everyone will know my business, that it is*

"a rare field full of razors" ... *He ... advised me to get posted on cattle.* (Nolan, pp. 137-138)

On August 15, 1876, confident of family backing, Tunstall arrived in Santa Fe, and wrote home to "Much Beloved Governor" about planning to invest seven thousand pounds of family money to be paid back from future earnings. He clearly misconstrued the "ring" as just political, and not also an economic monopoly. And threat of "smelling powder" was as unreal and amusing to him as if in a dime novel. Tunstall wrote:

This is the first place I have been in which everyone goes armed, all the men have a great "six shooter" slung on their hip, & a knife on the other as counterpoise ... [But he did not see himself as having to use a gun.] That sort of experience & adventure depends somewhat upon a man's disposition & habits & the places he frequents; a man who gambles & drinks is very apt to be "that, or thar abouts" when any shooting takes place, as he belongs to the shooting crowd & will be with his crowd; **but a man who attends to his own business only & above everything else does not figure in politics may live in this country a great while without smelling powder.** (Nolan, p. 155)

By October 28, 1876, to "Much Beloved Governor," Tunstall described his first meeting with Attorney Alexander McSween:

There is a very nice young fellow here just now from Lincoln County, a lawyer by profession, who has the outward appearance of an honest man, (Herlow [owner of the Santa Fe hotel where Tunstall was staying in his New Mexico visit] speaks highly of him) he has been trying to persuade me to go into stock & not buy land but I have seen too much of California to do so unless I am obliged. But I must say his plan has a great deal to recommend it. (Nolan, p. 180)

NEW RESIDENT OF LINCOLN COUNTY

John Henry Tunstall had stumbled not only into Lincoln County business competition with the Ring, but into becoming the first obstacle to aggressively monopolistic plans of Catron - via local Ringites - as he expanded his Ring from land grabs to business and cattle ranching.

At stake were deeper specifics. The Ring, through "the House," granted usurious credit to the locals. Tunstall could beat that. The Ring, through "the House," was meeting contracts to Fort Stanton and the Mescalero Indian Reservation with inferior flour and with beef from rustled cattle. Tunstall, backed by cattle king, John Chisum, and local homesteaders, was a better supplier. Catron was establishing a 12,800 acre cattle ranch in nearby Carrizozo. Tunstall, by purchase and Homestead Act, controlled thousands of miles of grazing land along the Feliz and Peñasco Rivers south of Lincoln all the way to the Pecos River.

Though it did not occur to Tunstall that the Ring tolerated no opposition, his family were more realistic. On March 9, 1877, to "Much Beloved Father," he responded to their concerns.

As regards my getting shot, I don't expect it. There are two very prolific causes for shooting in this country, viz., drink and jealousy. I don't frequent the locality of the former ... & I don't make myself an object for the excitement of the latter ... I have a presentment that I shall not get killed but that I shall live to accomplish my schemes & will give those three Pets such a time as will make their heads swim (as we say on the frontier).

[AUTHOR'S NOTE: Tunstall next blithely refers to the Ring, thinking their shenanigans mere humorous caricatures.]

The whole of this country (New Mexico) is under the control of a ring composed of two or three lawyers ... & their practices & power throughout New Mexico are quite astonishing *... I will give you just an instance; they passed a law, in the legislature, allowing a man to defend himself in court through an attorney without appearing in person. At the sitting then, of all the courts, men who had been in the graves a dozen years or more were indicted, summoned for various causes, one of the ring defended the case, & another, who was the public prosecutor, received $20 for his services to the Territory, which of course, belonged to the ring. This is ... but a sample of their most innocent means of making money.* (Nolan, pp. 200-201)

Unaware of sealing his own death warrant, on March 23, 1877, Tunstall wrote to "Much Beloved Governor" about investing thousands of dollars for his plans. He even directed the money to be sent to the Ring's First National Bank at Santa Fe, making T.B. Catron privy to his plans and resources:

I shall acquire property, which in the event of my death you could recover every cent of ...

[And] groceries in this country, realize a profit of 50 percent on the return & they are a cash item ... In the third place, the Mexican is a "borrowing" animal ... but unlike most borrowers, he will pay willingly as soon as it is in his power ...

Now ... what scheme, if practicable, would catch the ready money of the Indian department & the Army, & avoid the dangers of too many debtors ...

The first part of the question is simple to answer; by having hay, beef, corn or flour raised within the district, Uncle Sam is compelled to patronize you ...

All the fixtures necessary to run my store will be a desk, a scale, & a safe, & I should need all of these if I had nothing but a cattle ranch. (Nolan, pp. 205-207)

Tunstall's 24th birthday was on March 6, 1877; he would not make his 25th. On April 27, 1877, to "Much Beloved Father," he prattled about "rings." As self-styled "Adventurer," he foolishly thinks a "ring" is a way to do business, so presents his own plan:

[Y]ou would very likely think that I must be crazy to talk about making money in this country at all; Everything in New Mexico, that pays at all (you may say) is worked by a "ring," there is the "Indian ring," the "army ring," "the political ring," the "legal ring," the "Roman Catholic ring," the "cattle ring," the "horsethieves ring," the "land ring," and half a dozen other rings; **now to make things stick "to do any good," it is necessary to either get into a ring or to make one out for yourself. I am at work at present making a ring & have succeeded admirably so far;** *you see, an adventurer like myself does not present a very formidable aspect when "in the ring," but anyone as well posted as myself can very nearly break up an incipient ring single-handed, by skirmishing on the outskirts ...*

I propose to confine my operations to Lincoln County, but I intend to handle it in such a way as to get the half of every dollar that is made in the county by anyone; & with our means we could get things in that shape in three years if we only used two thirds of our capital in the undertaking. (Nolan, p. 213)

So Tunstall would build a big store only a quarter mile from "the House," hire ranch hands for whom he would use the Desert

Land Act to secure his controlling 640 acre parcels along the Feliz and Peñasco Rivers, since, as a foreigner, he was ineligible. (Billy Bonney would, thus, get a Peñasco River ranch.). True to British proclivities as a landed gentleman, Tunstall also bought fine horses, and became emotionally attached to them. That last idiosyncrasy would be the immediate cause of his death.

THE RING STRIKES BACK

With its established method of escalating harassment to force flight, the Ring used Jessie Evans's gang to steal Tunstall's horses and mules. Tunstall describes that crime in his letters home of November 29, 1877 and January 9, 1878, which go back to September 29, 1877. (Nolan, pp. 243-249) Tunstall, amused by Jessie Evans's tag for him - "The Englishman" - refers to "the House;" but is unaware of danger from either; though he realizes the gang was *"incited [by] some people we know very well ... & whose business I have very nearly taken away"*: i.e., the Ring. He tells of his men's post-theft capture of Jessie Evans and his gang; and that *"Jesse Evans says he can't tell how he failed to hit Dick [Brewer, Tunstall's foreman] as he had three fair, square shots at him & he was saving his shots for him alone."* As blithely, Tunstall quotes Lincoln County's Justice of the Peace John "Squire" Wilson: *"Well, Englishman, they seem bound to drive you out of the country."* Tunstall had a about a month to live. He had written:

My horses, 2 of them, & a pair of magnificent mules that I own had been stolen by some desperados named Jesse Evans & Frank Baker who belong to & are at the head of a very numerous band (100 men in all) that raid on stock in this country ... They had, it appears, threatened to kill McSween & Brewer & "That Englishman" on sight, **they were incited to make these threats by some people we know very well, against whom McS[ween] is bringing a lawsuit** *[part of the Emil Fritz estate resolution],* **with whom Brewer has had difficulty about a ranch** *[Murphy and Dolan sold him his ranch without having its title, and McSween told Brewer],* **& whose business I have very nearly taken away.** (Nolan, p. 243)

[AUTHOR'S NOTE: Tunstall next describes giving his men carbines, one likely the Winchester '73 carbine which Billy cherished, and later retrieved from Brady's body, after Brady's confiscation on February 20, 1878 and after Tunstall's murder.]

> *I had a case of carbines in just before they left [Brewer and his men, including Billy] & they each carried one of them, they are the finest weapon manufactured & you bet there was no discount on the way those boys could handle them.* (Nolan, p. 249)

By November 7, 1877, Tunstall faced another Ring tactic: obstruction of justice to shield members. Thus, Jessie Evans and his gang, arrested for his horse and mule theft and held in Lincoln's pit jail, were abetted in escape by Sheriff Brady. And Brady tried a "Dear Ben-style plot" to incite violence to justify self-defense killing, here by accusing Tunstall of aiding the Evans gang's escape - as told by Alexander McSween in his June 6, 1878 deposition to Investigator Frank Warner Angel (with McSween then having only 44 days before his own Ring murder), as follows:

> *A few days afterward [following the Evans gang's escape] Sheriff Brady came to Tunstalls store in a half intoxicated condition and indirectly accused Mr Tunstall of giving the credit of the arrest of said outlaws to R.M. Brewer (now deceased) and ... accused Mr Tunstall of having tried to aid Baker, Evans, Hill & Davis to escape. Mr. Tunstall told him you know their shackles are filed, & there are holes cut in the logs and take no pains to secure them, and do you dare to accuse me who have aided in the arrest of these persons, who have threatened my life, with assisting them to escape. Sheriff Brady thereupon put his hand on his revolver as though he was going to draw it and I stepped between them and placing my hand on his shoulder said it ill becomes you as a peace officer to violate the law by shooting.* **Brady replied I won't shoot you now, you haven't long to run** *... and then left the store.*

RING HARASSMENT TO ENABLE MURDER

By late 1877, Catron ramped up his attack to malicious prosecution. His diabolically convoluted plot used as its hook Tunstall's friend, Alexander McSween, as the attorney attempting collection of a $10,000 life insurance policy of "House" partner, Emil Fritz, who died intestate in Germany in 1874. McSween represented the heirs, including German non-English-speaking Charles Fritz and Emilie Scholand. McSween knew that "House" partners, James Dolan and John Riley, wanted that money to stave off bankruptcy. Because the New York policy holder withheld payment, necessitating litigation in New York, McSween ultimately collected only $7,000, after subtracting his own legal fees. But complying with a probate case's due diligence, he delayed payment until seeking additional heirs in Germany. Also, he awaited Territorial Probate Court's decision on Dolan's fraudulent claim that Fritz's estate owed "the House" over $76,000. But McSween was unaware that Charles Fritz was under Ring control by mortgage of his ranch near Lincoln; or that Catron, Dolan, District Attorney Rynerson, and Judge Bristol were poised to attack. Charles's sister, Emilie Scholand, was manipulated by Dolan and Rynerson into filing an embezzlement complaint with Bristol on December 21, 1877 claiming he stole their policy money.

On December 25, 1877, as U.S. Attorney, Catron acted. Knowing that McSween and his wife, Susan - along with Tunstall's ranching associate and bank president, John Chisum - were leaving to St. Louis for business, Catron alleged they were absconding with the money, and used Bristol's warrant to arrest McSween for embezzlement, and one for Chisum as reneging on loans. Both were terrifyingly seized in Las Vegas, New Mexico, by the San Miguel Sheriff. And McSween's arrest warrant gave the inflated allegedly embezzled sum as $10,000, stating:

Territory of New Mexico)
Third Judicial District)
 The Territory of New Mexico to the Sheriff or any constable of the County of San Miguel in said Territory.
 Whereas Emily Scholand has made complaint to me on oath that she is informed and verily believes that Alexander McSween has committed the crime of embezzlement by **embezzling and comuting to his own use the sum of ten thousand dollars** *belonging to the estate of Emil Fritz deceased at the County of Lincoln in said Territory on the tenth day of December in the year A.D. 1877. Now therefore you are hereby commanded to arrest the said Alexander McSween forthwith and bring him before me in the Third Judicial District of said Territory together with this writ that he may be dealt with according to law.*
   Given under my hand at
   Mesilla County of Dona Ana
   Territory of New Mexico this 21st day of
   December A.D. 1877.
    Warren Bristol
    District Judge

McSween and Chisum were jailed in Las Vegas. McSween was then transported to Lincoln by Deputy Sheriff Adolph Barrier, who, knowing his Ring risk kept him in personal custody instead of yielding him to murderous Sheriff Brady. But crafty Chisum stayed in the remote jail to wait out the Ring's inevitable violence.

TUNSTALL EXPOSES THE RING: JANUARY 18, 1878

On January 18, 1878, John Tunstall dutifully joined the fray as a "taxpayer's" "duty" by publicly attacking the Ring by an editorial titled "A Tax-Payer's Complaint" in the Mesilla *Independent*, and quoting Governor S.B. Axtell's report to the legislature. Tunstall stated:

**From Lincoln County:
A Tax-Payer's Complaint**

Office of John H. Tunstall
Lincoln, Lincoln Co. N.M.,
January 18, 1878

"THE PRESENT SHERIFF OF LINCOLN COUNTY HAS PAID NOTHING DURING HIS TERM OF OFFICE"
Governor's Message for 1878

Editor of the Independent:

The above extract is a sad and unanswerable comment on the efficiency of Sheriff Brady, and cannot be charged upon "croakers." Major Brady, as the records of this County show, collected over twenty-five hundred dollars, Territorial funds. Of this sum Alex. A. McSween Esq, of this place, paid him over fifteen hundred dollars by cheque on the First National Bank of Santa Fe, August 23, 1877.

Said cheque was presented for payment by John H. Riley, Esq, of the firm of J.J. Dolan & Co. This last amount was paid by the last named gentleman to Underwood and Nash for cattle. Thus passed away over fifteen hundred dollars belonging to the Territory of New Mexico.

With the exception of thirty-nine dollars, all the taxes for Lincoln County for 1877 were promptly paid as due.

Let not Lincoln County suffer the delinquency of one, two or three men.

By the exercise of proper vigilance the tax-payer can readily ascertain what has become of that he has paid for the implied protection of the commonwealth. It is not only his privilege but his duty. A delinquent tax-payer is bad; a delinquent tax collector is worse. J.H.T.

On January 29, 1878, James Dolan, omitting Catron's payoff of the debt, responded for the Ring in the Mesilla *Independent*.

Answer to a Tax-payer's Complaint.
Las Cruces, N.M.,
January 29, 1878
To the Editor of the Independent:

Dear Sir – In answer to a communication in reference to taxpayers of Lincoln County published in your issue of the 26th inst. and signed J.H.T., I wish to state that every thing contained therein is false. In reference to Sheriff Brady, I will state that he deposited with our house Territorial funds amounting to nearly $2,000 subject to his order and payable on demand. Owing to sickness in the family of Sheriff Brady he was unable to be in Santa Fe in time to settle his account with the Territory. This I hope will explain satisfactorily how the Gov. in his Message had our County (Lincoln) delinquent. If Mr. J.H.T. was recognized as a gentleman, and could be admitted into respectable circles in our community, he might be better posted on public affairs. For my part, I can't see the object of Mr. J.H.T.'s letter, unless it is to have the public believe that A.A. McSween is one of the largest taxpayers in our County, when in fact he is one of the smallest. Sheriff Brady is ready and willing at any time to show uneasy taxpayers what disposition he has made of the money paid by them; he can also show clean receipts from the Territorial treasurer of his account.

Respectfully,
J.J. Dolan.

Tunstall saw his "fight" merely as a bracing endurance game, missing its danger; and continued to write home optimistically. On January 20, 1878, he asked for more money, stating:

I have secured a beautiful cattle range & have it working on a most economical basis ... I have about 300 head [of cattle] & ought to get to work getting the rest as soon as possible, these would if bought right at cost about $12.00 per head, this foots up to $8,400.00. There are some lands yet that I want to buy & that we ought to have, as there is a fortune in them if secured in connection with what I have already got my claws into, that will cost something like 1500 (pounds) ... The longer I live & the more I see, the more I get confirmed in my land views. That I can make a fortune here I feel convinced if I only have strength enough to play the cards ... I won't give up or back down, as long as I can give another kick. (Nolan, p. 263)

On January 30th and 31st, 1878, Tunstall wrote his last letter to "Much Beloved Governor." He had 18 days to live; having faced continuous Ring harassment, including spying on his mail by Dolan as Lincoln's Postmaster (with post office in "the House"). Tunstall was then about to travel to Mesilla for a hearing under Judge Warren Bristol on McSween's embezzlement indictment; not realizing it was a premeditated entrapment of himself. But his tender preoccupation was with a new blind horse, and his increasing mastery of Spanish. Tunstall wrote:

[Blind] Colonel, is, as I told you, a splendid saddle horse, I have got very much attached to him ... He will come when I call him, & follow me around as if he could see ...

I am about to secure a property ... that in the course of ten years will be a splendid fortune in itself. My letters are apt to be tampered with in the mail, so I won't do more than tell you what I think about it, without telling you what it is ...

I have of course by this time got well established, the Mexicans think that "El Englais" does not dress & put on quite as much style as they would do if they "Vale tanto" (were worth as much as he) "Perro es muy buen hombre, muy rico" (but he is a first rate man & very rich.) (Nolan, pp. 264-266)

MALICIOUS PROSECUTION OF TUNSTALL

Unaware of exposés a year earlier by Mary McPherson and others in Cimarron about Ring corruption of 3rd Judicial District Judge Warren Bristol, on February 4, 1878, Alexander McSween, with Deputy Adolph Barrier and law partner, David Shield, went for his embezzlement hearing with Bristol in Mesilla. Tunstall and Justice of the Peace John "Squire" Wilson came for support. At the hearing, Bristol set the Ring's traps to enable assassination of McSween and Tunstall. To leave McSween vulnerable to Sheriff William Brady, Bristol ordered bail of $8,000 to be approved solely by District Attorney Rynerson; who would refuse all payments so Brady could take custody. To ensnare Tunstall, Bristol falsely declared him McSween's business partner, and, thus, also responsible for the debt; and ordered property attachment of both to the allegedly embezzled sum of $10,000. Brady was ordered to do those attachments - again repeating a "Dear Ben-style plot" to incite violence by these men or Tunstall's employees (like hot-headed Billy Bonney) to justify murder.

On February 8, 1878, Brady began attachments by ransacking McSween's Lincoln house. Tunstall's store, bank, apartment, and ranches were likewise invaded, though Brady's inventory sum far exceeded the required $10,000. In the February 11, 1878 inventory at Tunstall's store, furious Billy Bonney almost tipped the balance to violence; though he was restrained by Tunstall employee, Fred Waite, his partner in the Peñasco River ranch.

McSween, to prove Rynerson's obstruction of his bondsmen, in his June 6, 1878 deposition to Frank Warner Angel, gave as Exhibit 15, Rynerson's rejection of a $35,500 bond for his $8,000 bail - Tunstall by then having been assassinated. McSween stated:

Territory of New Mexico)
County of Lincoln   )

Before me the undersigned authority personally came and appeared on this the 9th day of February AD 1878 J.H. Tunstall, James West, John N. Copeland, Isaac Ellis, Francisco Romero y Valencia & Jose Montena [Montaño] whose names are signed to the above instrument of writing, who each having first by me duly sworn according to law upon his oath says that he is worth the amount set opposite to his name below in property situated within the Territory of New Mexico, over and above all his just debts and liabilities and property exempt by law from execution and forced sale.

J.H. Tunstall	*$2000^{00}*
James West	*$4000^{00}*
John N. Copeland	*$3000^{00}*
Isaac Ellis	*$4000^{00}*
Francisco Romero y Valencia	*$2000^{00}*
Jose Montena [Montaño]	*$1500^{00}*

Attest
Isaac Ellis
John B. Wilson

Sworn to and subscribed before me by [repeat of above names and sums].
Witness my hand and Notarial Seal
D.P. Shield
Notary Public

Endorsed

The within Bond is not approved for reasons as follows. Before approving the within Bond the surities must justify before the undersigned as I have reason to doubt that the surities for the most part are worth the amount set opposite their names ... Furthermore the death of one of the surities [Tunstall] who is a partner (said to be) of the principal somewhat complicates the matter.

W.L. Rynerson
Dist. Attny

McSWEEN'S CONTINUED ANTI-RING CRUSADE: FEBRUARY 11, 1878

McSween continued his anti-Ring crusade; and, knowing his innocence, assumed he would prevail. So on February 11, 1878, seven days before Tunstall's assassination, he exposed "the House's" contracts to Secretary of the Interior Carl Schurz about Mescalero Indian Agent Frederick Godfroy's beef and flour frauds; thereby inadvertently exposing Catron, since Godfroy was his agent through David Easton, as discussed above. McSween wrote:

It looks as though the agent were the property of J.J. Dolan & J.H. Riley, known here as Dolan & Co. For the past two years these men have had the flour & beef contracts (as subcontractors I think) ... and have delivered articles unfit for use. Sprouted half rotten wheat has been mashed and turned in as first rate flour ... These fellows are also Indian traders. At their store they receive "surplus" by an underground railway process [selling the Indians' supplies in their store as received from Agent Godfroy].

The beef they furnish is of poorest quality ... They never kill the number reported nor do they feed the number of Indians they report ... I suggest you send a detective here who will ferret this matter; he'll find things as I have stated them. (Nolan, p. 266)

DISTRICT ATTORNEY RYNERSON'S "FRIENDS RILEY AND DOLAN" MURDER LETTER: FEBRUARY 14, 1878

Having failed to incite violence, the Ring resorted to ambush murder. The plot is given in District Attorney William Rynerson's secret, February 14, 1878 letter to James Dolan, four days before Tunstall's murder; and was found in John Riley's accidentally dropped code-book, as discussed above. Rynerson wrote:

LAW OFFICE OF
WILLIAM L. RYNERSON
District Attorney 3ᵈ Judicial District, New Mexico

Las Cruces, N.M. Feby 14th 1878

Friends Riley & Dolan,
    Lincoln N.M.
    I have just received letters from you mailed 10th inst. Glad to know that you (Dolan) got home OK and that business was going on OK. If Mr Weidman [Tunstall employee] interfered with or resisted the Sheriff in Discharge of his duty Brady did right in arresting him, And any one else who does so must receive the same attention. Brady goes into the store in McS' place and takes his interest. Tunstall will have same right there he had heretofore but he neither must not obstruct the sheriff or resist him in the discharge of his duties. If he tries to make trouble the Sheriff must meet the occasion <u>firmly</u> and legally. I believe Tunstall is in with the swindlers with the rogue McSween. They have the money belonging to the Fritz estate and they know it. It must be made hot for them all the hotter the better. Especially is this necessary now that it has been discovered that there is no hell.
    It may be that the villain <u>Green</u> "Juan Baptista" Wilson will play into their hands as Alcade. If so, he should be moved around a little. Shake that McSween outfit up till it shells out and squares up, and then shake it out of Lincoln. I will aid to punish the scoundrels all I can. Get the people with you. Control Juan Patron if possible. You know how to do it. Have good men about to aid Sheriff Brady, and be assured that I shall help you all I can, for I believe there was never found a more scoundrely set than that outfit.
                        Yours &c
                        W L Rynerson

ASSASSINATION SOLUTION

Only 56 days after Catron began malicious prosecution of McSween and Tunstall on December 25, 1877, he achieved Tunstall's murder by Sheriff Brady and his posse, including the Jessie Evans gang, by false claim that Tunstall was evading attachment by herding his actually exempt horses to Lincoln from his Feliz River Ranch; though Tunstall was doing it simply to protect his beloved horses. Ring urgency to kill likely resulted from the April 1878 convening of the Lincoln County Grand jury, with likelihood of McSween's exoneration from embezzlement; thus, freeing Tunstall of legal harassments from the concocted "partnership." And it was obvious that intimidation had failed to force flight of both men.

Separated from his fleeing men by Brady's attackers, Tunstall died alone on February 18, 1878, replicating the Ring's assassination of Franklin Tolby three years earlier. It was an intentionally terrifying execution, with coupe de grâce exploding Tunstall's skull with a circumferential fracture. In perverted mockery, his hat was placed on his likewise murdered horse's head. Rumor later had the horse's severed tail rammed in Tunstall's mouth; though, more likely, it was genital mutilation with the horse penis as desecration. And, like Tolby's corpse, Tunstall's was hidden to delay pursuit of his killers.

The trauma to 18 year old Billy Bonney was unimaginable. Collapsed after only 4½ months was his newfound "family" with its marvelous father figure and a future as a rancher on the Peñasco River. Ended was a life of normalcy.

Tunstall's Coroner's Jury Report was done on February 19, 1878. Since Billy Bonney gave an eye-witness affidavit that day, he likely gave evidence at the inquest also. Named as Tunstall's murders were Jessie Evans, Frank Baker, Thomas Hill, Deputy George Hindman, J.J. Dolan, William Morton, and others not identified. From that list, Lincoln County Justice of the Peace John "Squire" Wilson generated arrest warrants.

But the Ring was poised to repeat the 1875 obstruction of justice used in Franklin Tolby's murder to shield its hitmen, Cruz Vega and Manuel Cardenas, and frontmen, Robert Longwill and Melvin Mills. In Lincoln County, the frontmen were James Dolan, Sheriff William Brady, and Chief Deputy Billy Matthews.

For the usual Ring cover-up, Fort Stanton surgeon, Dr. Daniel Appel, wrote a fraudulent autopsy report attributing the circumferential split in Tunstall's skull to thinning by venereal disease, which Appel fabricated as cause for Tunstall's insane shooting first at the posseman. That sham scenario required Appel's reversing the bullet's entry wound to the front of the head. But McSween countered the fakery by a legitimate autopsy by Lincoln's Dr. Taylor Ealy. The Coroner's Jury declared:

Territory of New Mexico)
County of Lincoln   )

We the undersigned Justice of the Peace and Coroners Jury who sat upon the inquest held this 19<u>th</u> day of February 1878 on the body of John H. Tunstall here found in precinct N<u>o</u> 1 of the County of Lincoln, Territory of New Mexico find that the deceased came to his death on or about the 18<u>th</u> day of Feb'y 1878 by means of divers bullets shot and sent forth out of and from deadly weapons and upon the head and body of said John H. Tunstall which said deadly weapons were there and then held by one or more of the persons who are herewith written, to wit, Jessie Evans, Frank Baker, Thomas Hill, George Hindman, J.J. Dolan, William Morton, and others not identified before the Coroners Jury.

We the undersigned to the best of our knowledge & belief, from the evidence of the Coroners inquest believe the above statement to be a true and impartial verdict.

GeoB Barker
R.M. Gilbert
John Newcomb
Samuel Smith
Benj'n Ellis
John B. Wilson
            Justice of the Peace in and for precinct N<u>o</u> 1,
            Lincoln County, Territory of New Mexico

RESPONSE FROM COLFAX COUNTY

The Ring was poised to commit further terrorist atrocities on the isolated Lincoln populace. Within a mere six years, had been the 1872 Legislature Revolt, Grant County Rebellion, and the Colfax County War. And there was just one man who could have united the counties and exposed the Ring in his newspaper: Attorney Frank Springer. But it risked the death he had narrowly missed in 1876's "Dear Ben plot." To Springer's credit, he tried a secret intervention by using a contact connected to a new Lincoln resident.

Presbyterian missionary and doctor, Taylor Ealy, a nephew of Senator Rush Clark and likely attracted by Alexander McSween's plans to build a church and school of that denomination in Lincoln, did the second autopsy on Tunstall and later settled his family into dead Tunstall's apartment in the store. So Frank Springer chose as his confidential contact Senator Rush Clark.

Springer's warning letter, written 51 days after Tunstall's homicide, is prophetic. He describes immanent danger of *"the whole power of the Territorial government, strengthened by the active aid of the U.S. military forces,"* as he had himself experienced with the Ring's use of Fort Union troops in his own murder attempt. And Springer does not hesitate to call Tunstall's murder *"a deliberately planned assassination."*

Sadly, by August 9, 1878, then aware of the horrors wreaked by the Ring in the intervening Lincoln County War battle, Springer took no more risks; and denied to Investigator Frank Warner Angel knowledge of guilt of United States officials; thus, concealing his own statement in that Rush Clark letter: *"The republican party & a republican administration owes it to itself to see that such abuses are not perpetrated under its name."* And a mystery remains: From whom was Frank Springer receiving his referenced *"mass of private information?"* Who had vainly sought his aid? Springer wrote:

<u>Confidential</u>   *Cimarron, N.M.*
Apr 9, 1878

Hon Rush Clark.
    My dear Sir:
        I hope you have received a full account of the Troubles in Lincoln County from your nephew [Taylor Ealy], whose statements, as a disinterested party, would be entitled to great weight. **There is no doubt, in my mind, from a mass of private information I have received, that the whole power of the Territorial government, strengthened by the active aid of the U.S. military forces, has been either ignorantly or intentionally used to protect and assist a small combination of corrupt men – speculators in military and Indian contracts – against the best men in the county.** *That the men thus protected & aided by the govt. had in their employ members of a band of desperados, cattle thieves, highwaymen & murderers, who have infested that region for a long time to the terror of good citizens, and that J.H. Tunstall an estimable man, connected with a wealthy family in England, who has invested $15000 in business & proposed to invest $100,000 – was murdered by some of these very outlaws who were serving in the sheriffs*

posse, attempting to seize Tunstall's private property for another man's debt. There is no doubt that the U.S. troops have been employed in a most illegal manner, to search private houses & arrest peaceable citizens without warrant. **No effort has been made by the Territorial Governor, or the U.S. troops to arrest the murderers of Tunstall, but the governor by the President's authority, called upon the troops practically to protect them from arrest. Nobody doubts that his murder was a deliberately planned assassination.** The people seem to be driven to desperation by these acts and scenes of violence have been enacted. I have no interest in the matter & no acquaintance with the principal actors, but I would like to see an end to wholesale crime in the Territory & would like to see the power of the U.S. Govt employed to punish & not to aid in protecting criminals. I believe the people there have done some wrong, but they have been crazed to see the murderers of Tunstall running at liberty under the protection of the authorities. I have sent you newspapers with reports of all the late doings there & most of it I believe to be reliable. **The republican party & a republican administration owes it to itself to see that such abuses are not perpetrated under its name** ...

> Yours very truly
> *Frank Springer*

CHAPTER 7

LINCOLN COUNTY GALVANIZES AGAINST THE SANTA FE RING: 1878

CHOOSING REVOLUTION

ANALYSIS: Thomas Benton Catron seemingly believed Lincoln County would succumb to his Colfax County tactics of malicious prosecution and murder. The reverse happened, with rise of the Regulator movement joined by the outraged Hispanic populace. Unexpected also was emergence of its charismatic symbol of militant zeal: Billy Bonney was entering the world stage.

T.B. Catron underestimated Lincoln County's citizens and democracy's power when he had John Tunstall murdered, and shielded the killers with lawmen and troops. Citizens apparently recalled July 4, 1776's "Declaration of Independence": *"[W]hen a long train of abuses and usurpations, pursuing invariably the same Object evinces a design to reduce them under absolute Despotism, it is their right, it is their duty, to throw off such Government, and provide new Guards for their future security."*

So Tunstall's employees united for justice, calling themselves "Regulators." The long exploited Hispanic population identified with their cause. And they had a leader: Alexander McSween.

Zealot Billy Bonney may have suggested the name from Edward L. Wheeler's dime novel "The Deadwood Dick Library, A Tale of the Regulators and Road-Agents of the Black Hills, The Double Daggers; or, Deadwood Dick's Defiance," published by *Beadles Half Dime Library* in 1877. It proclaimed that "Regulators strike blows in defense of justice." It would be fitting if Billy got that slim booklet from Tunstall's store in the 4½ months he worked for and idolized that man.

HISTORY OF THE REGULATORS

The original Regulators were 18th century American colonial, pre-Revolutionary War freedom fighters, extolled in song and dime novels. The Regulator movement began in North Carolina in 1771, five years before the "Declaration of Independence." Their fight, like Lincoln County's, was against corrupt public officials and lawmen.

The colonial Regulator movement's main historian is Marjoline Kars in her 2002's *Breaking Loose Together: The Regulator Rebellion in Pre-Revolutionary North Carolina*. There, public official elites conducted land grabs. Poor homesteaders, working to purchase their land, relied on credit and payment by harvests, but were subjected to stolen titles and usurious interest. Pious pacifist activists first wrote the 1766 Sandy Creek Manifesto. By 1768, arose militant "Regulators," inspired by 1765's Stamp Act protestors, the "Sons of Liberty," who opposed British taxation of stamped paper, including newspapers and legal documents.

North Carolina's version of 1870's Ringite governors was Governor William Tryon, who dissolved the legislature's Assembly to block its delegates from attending New York City's Stamp Act Congress, which achieved the Act's repeal in 1766. Kars quotes Pauline Maier's 1991 book *From Resistance to Revolution*:

> [There is] a particular strand of Anglo-American political thought which legitimated resistance by making it, like obedience, a cornerstone of the social contract. This contract rested on the notion that people could protect their liberties by transferring part of their power and sovereignty to government and abiding by that same government's just laws. When the authorities abused this trust and evaded the laws or passed oppressive ones, people were obliged to obtain relief by legal and peaceful means, such as petitions and elections. But when such attempts were ignored, did not produce results, or were subverted by corrupt authorities, forceful popular resistance was deemed a civic duty crucial to the preservation of the public good. (Kars, p. 134)

Implicit in that democratic consciousness, was oppressed citizens' "expectation of freedom" (Kars, p. 120): seeing themselves as "Regulators ... not as enemies of government but as its true defenders." (Kars, p. 131) The Regulators' head was Herman Husband, who wrote: "All we want is to be Governed by law, and not by the Will of officers, which to us is perfectly despotick and arbitrary." He added that such was merely "the iron hand of tyranny." (Kars, pp. 135, 152)

But North Carolina injustice continued with tax collecting sheriffs repossessing property for resale at personal profit, with elections to the legislative Assembly corruptly controlled, and by courts threatening prosecution of contempt against protesters. And the despotic Assembly of 1768 appropriated 15,000 pounds to build a "palace" for Governor Tryon with poll and liquor taxes.

So, in 1768, the Regulators printed a public announcement that they would put their officials under "honester Regulation than they have been for some time past." (Kars, pp. 137-138)

Suppression by troops resulted. Colonel Edmund Fanning called Regulators outlaws in "defiance of law and contempt of authority." (Kars, p. 139) Governor Tryon wrote that the Regulators were "destroying the Peace of this Government, and the Security of its inhabitants" (Kars, p. 154), and briefly jailed Herman Husband. In trials, Fanning himself was convicted of extortion, but fined just one penny for each offense. (Kars, p. 159). And taxation to build Tryon's palace was approved.

In September, 1770, failure of peaceful redress yielded a Regulator skirmish in Hallborough. In response, Herman Husband was barred from the Assembly on fabricated libel charges. And the December 15, 1770 Johnston Riot Act was passed to allow military intervention if ten or more men refused to disperse in an hour after being ordered, making them chargeable as felons, with two charges punishable by execution. Herman Husband was imprisoned under that Riot Act and the libel charge, but was freed on February 7, 1771 by a grand jury.

The final fight was the May 16, 1771 Battle of Alamance where 2,000 leaderless Regulators, lacking ammunition, met 1,100 British troops with six swivel guns and two brass cannons. Three Regulators, sent to negotiate peace, were taken prisoner by Governor Tryon, who shot one in sight of the Regulators. Then Tryon's army rampaged, destroying farms and crops of Regulator leaders. Six prisoners were hanged at Hillsborough on June 19, 1771. A bounty was placed on Husband, dead or alive. And Governor Tryon foreshadowed an Amnesty Proclamation over a century later by post-Lincoln County War Governor, Lew Wallace. It declared:

> While the Piedmont population was thus intimidated and terrorized, Tryon issued a proclamation promising to pardon all Regulators who would ... promise to pay their taxes and obey all laws. He excluded outlawed Regulators and prisoners. (Kars, p. 204)

Some call the Battle of Alamance the American Revolution's first battle. Kars states: "Regulators envisioned a world ... in which morality and economics would not be separate." (Kars, p. 215)

Lincoln County Regulators may have heard the North Carolina Regulators' freedom song, eventually collected in 1947 in Arthur Palmer Hudson's "Songs of the Carolina Regulators":

> From Hillsborough town the first of May
> March'd those murdering traitors.
> They went to oppose the honest men
> That were called the Regulators. (Hudson, p. 146)

POLITICIZING OF BILLY BONNEY

After his mother's tuberculosis death in 1874, Billy Bonney had helplessly endured injustice of his stepfather's stealing their house and possessions, leaving him homeless at 14½. His rage manifested in a year of delinquency in Silver City, before he escaped jailing for robbery and burglary to flee to Arizona Territory. There he escalated to stealing military horses and blankets; then to killing a man, likely in self defense, in a cantina altercation, resulting in his flight back to New Mexico Territory.

But John Tunstall's Ring murder crystallized a new identity for that teenager. Not only did he join the anti-Ring cause, but from the day after Tunstall's killing, he began risking his life to legally testify against Ringites; becoming the Ring's main gadfly, as epitomized in his pardon bargain with Lew Wallace *"as a witness against those that murdered Mr. Chapman."* By then, Billy could have galvanized another anti-Ring war.

FIRST LEGAL TESTIMONY: FEBRUARY 19,1878

The day after Tunstall's February 18, 1878 murder, Billy's voice is first heard publicly. On February 19th, he gave an eye-witness affidavit to Justice of the Peace John "Squire" Wilson, along with Tunstall's foreman, Richard "Dick" Brewer, naming the killers as Sheriff Brady's possemen: *"James J. Dolan, Frank Baker, Jessie Evans, George Davis, A.H. Mills, W.S. Morton, [omitted first name, William] Moore, George Hindman, [Frank] Rivers, Pantaleon Gallegos, divers other persons unknown."* It yielded Wilson's legal arrest warrants, stating:

Territory of New Mexico)
County of Lincoln)

    Be it remembered that before the undersigned Justice of the Peace in and for the County and Territory aforesaid, personally came R.M. Brewer & **W. Bonney** *who being duly sworn according to law deposeth & saith that at the County and Territory aforesaid on the 18th day of February 1878 in and upon the [presence] of J.H. Tunstall, Robt A. Widenman[n], R.M. Brewer,* **William Boney** *[sic] & John Middleton, then and there in the Peace of the Territory an assault was made with divers deadly weapons to wit with Winchester Guns and Colts Revolvers, and divers other deadly weapons by James J. Dolan, Frank Baker, Jessie Evans, George Davis, A.H. Mills, W.S. Morton, [omitted first name] Moore, George Hindman, [Frank] Rivers, Pantaleon Gallegos, divers other persons unknown and did then and there as affiant believes wounded & killed J.H. Tunstall contrary to the statute in such case made and provided against the Peace & dignity of the Territory.*

                                                                R.M. Brewer
                                                               William Bonney.

Sworn to & subscribed before me this 19th day of February 1878.
                                                                John B. Wilson
                                                           Justice of the Peace

DEPOSITION ON TUNSTALL'S MURDER: JUNE 8, 1878

    On June 8, 1878, Billy next gave his articulate deposition on Tunstall's murder to Investigator Frank Warner Angel, and risked his life by coming to Lincoln after Governor Axtell's outlawing of the Regulators; and after his own April Grand Jury indictments for the Brady, Hindman, and Roberts killings. Billy stated:

Territory of New Mexico)
County of Lincoln)
)

    William H. Bonney was duly sworn, deposand says that he is a resident of said county, that on the 11th day of February A.D. 1878 he in company with Robt. A. Widenmann and Fred T. Waite went to the ranch of J. H. Tunstall on the Rio Feliz, that **he and said Fred T. Waite at the time intended to go to the Rio Peñasco to take up a ranch** *for the purpose of farming. That the cattle on the ranch of said J. H. Tunstall were throughout* the County of Lincoln, known to be the property of said Tunstall; that on the 13th of February A.D. 1878 one J.B. Matthews claiming to be a Deputy Sheriff came to the ranch of said J.H. Tunstall in company with Jesse Evans, Frank Baker, Tom Hill and [Frank] Rivers, known outlaws who had been confined to the Lincoln County jail and had succeeded in making their escape, John Hurley, George Hindman, [Andrew] Roberts and an Indian aka Poncearo the latter said to be the murderer of Benaito Cruz, for the arrest of murderers of whom (Benaito Cruz) the Governor of this Territory offers a reward of $500. Before the arrival of said J.B. Matthews, deputy Sheriff, and his posse, having been informed that said deputy sheriff and posse were going to round up all the cattle and drive them off and kill the persons at the ranch, the persons at the ranch cut portholes into the walls of the house and filled sacks with earth, so that they, the persons at the ranch, should they be attacked or murder attempted, could defend themselves, this course being thought necessary **as the sheriffs posse was composed of murderers, outlaws, and desperate characters none of whom has any interest at stake in the County, nor being residents of said County**. That said Matthews when within about 50 yards of the house was called to stop and advance alone and state his business, that said Matthews after arriving at the ranch said that he had come to attach the cattle and property of A.A McSween, that **said Matthews was informed that A.A. McSween had no cattle or property there**, but that if he had he, said Matthews could take it. That said Matthews said that he thought some of the cattle belonging to R. M. Brewer whose cattle were also at the ranch of J.H. Tunstall, belonged to A.A. McSween, that said Matthews was told by said Brewer that he Matthews could round up the cattle and that he, Brewer, would help him. That said Matthews said that he would go back to Lincoln to get new instructions and if he came back to the ranch he would come back with one man. That said Matthews and his posse were then invited by R. M. Brewer to come to the house to get something to eat.

Deponent further states that Robert A. Widenmann told R.M. Brewer and the others at the ranch, that he was going to arrest Frank Baker, Jesse Evans and Tom Hill said Widenmann having warrants for them. That said Widenmann was told by Brewer and the others at the ranch that the arrest could not be made because if it was made they, all the persons at the ranch would be killed and murdered by J.J. Dolan and their party. That said Evans *advanced upon said Widenmann, said Evans swinging his gun and catching it cocked and pointed directly at said Widenmann. That said Jesse Evans asked said Widenmann whether he Widenmann, was hunting for him, Evans, to which Widenmann answered that if he was looking for him, he, Evans, would find it out. Evans also asked Widenmann whether he had a warrant for him; Widenmann answered that it was his (Widenmann's) business. Evans told Wedinmann, that if he ever came to arrest him (Evans) he, Evans would pick Widenmann as the first man to shoot at, to which Widenmann answered that that was all right, that two could play at that game. That during the talking Frank Baker stood near said Widenmann, swinging his pistol on his finger, catching it full cocked pointed at said Widenmann.*

The persons at the ranch were R. M. Brewer, John Middleton, G. Gayss [Gauss], M. Martz, R.A. Widenmann, Henry Brown, F.T. Waite, Wm McClosky and this deponent. J.B. Matthews after eating started for Lincoln with John Hurley and Ponceano the rest of the party or posse saying they were going to the Rio Peñasco. Deponent started to Lincoln with Robert A. Widenmann and F.T. Waite and arrived at Lincoln the same evening and again left Lincoln on the next day, February the 14th in company with the above named persons, having heard that said Matthews was going back to the ranch of said J.H. Tunstall with a large party of men to take the cattle and deponent and Widenmann and Waite arrived at said ranch the same day.

Deponent states that on the road to Lincoln he heard said Matthews ask said Widenmann whether any resistance would be offered if he Matthews returned to take the cattle, to which said Widenmann answered that no resistance would be offered if the cattle were left at the ranch but if an attempt was made to drive the cattle to the Indian Agency and kill them for beef as he, said Matthews had been heard to say would be done, he, said Widenmann, would do all in his power to prevent this.

Deponent further says that on the night of the 17th of February A.D. 1878 J.H. Tunstall arrived at the ranch and informed all persons there that reliable information had reached him that J.B. Matthews was gathering a large party of outlaws and desperados as a posse and the said posse was coming to the ranch, the Mexicans in the party to gather up the cattle and the balance of the party to kill the persons at the ranch. It was thereupon decided that all persons at the ranch excepting G. Gauss, were to leave and Wm McClosky was that night sent to the Rio Peñasco to inform the posse who were camped there, that they could come over and round up the cattle, count them and leave a man there to take care of them and that Mr. Tunstall would also leave a man there to help round up and count the cattle and help take care of them, and said McClosky was also ordered to go to Martin Martz, who had left Tunstalls ranch when deponent, Widenmann and Waite returned to the town of Lincoln on the 13th of February and asked him said Martz to come to the ranch of said Tunstall and aid the sheriffs posse in rounding up and counting the cattle and to stay at the ranch and take care of the cattle.

Deponent left the ranch of said Tunstall in company with J.H. Tunstall, R.A. Widenmann, R.M. Brewer, John Middleton, F.T. Waite, said Tunstall, Widenmann, Brewer, Middleton and deponent driving the loose horses, Waite driving the wagon. Said Waite took the road for Lincoln with the wagon, the rest of the party taking the trail with the horses. **Deponent says that all the horses which he and the party were driving, excepting 3 had been released by sheriff Brady at Lincoln that one of these 3 horses belonged to R.M. Brewer, and the other was traded by Brewer to Tunstall for one of the released horses.**

Deponent further says, that when he and the party has traveled to within about 3 miles from the Rio Ruidoso he and John Middleton were in drag in the rear of the balance of the party as just upon reaching the brow of a hill they saw a large party of men coming towards them from the rear at full speed and that he and Middleton at once rode forward to inform the balance of the party of the fact. Deponent had not more than barely reached Brewer and Widenmann who were some 200 or 300 yards to the left of the trail when the attacking party cleared the brow of the hill and commenced firing at him, Widenmann and Brewer. Deponent, Widenmann and Brewer rode over a hill towards another which was covered with large rocks and trees in order to defend themselves and make a stand. But the attacking party, undoubtedly seeing Tunstall, left off pursuing deponent and the two with him and turned back at the caño in which the trail was. Shortly afterwards we heard two or three separate and distinct shots and the remark was then made by Middleton that they, the attacking party must have killed Tunstall. Middleton had in the meantime joined deponent and Widenmann and Brewer. Deponent then made the rest of his way to Lincoln in company with Robt. A. Widenmann, Brewer, Waite and Middleton stopping on the Rio Ruidoso in order to get men to look for the body of J.H. Tunstall.

Deponent further says that neither he nor any of the party fired off either rifle or pistol and that neither he nor the parties with him fired a shot.
William H. Bonney

Sworn and subscribed before me this eighth day of June A.D. 1878.
John B. Wilson
Justice of the Peace

LEGAL PURSUIT OF TUNSTALL'S KILLERS

DEPUTIZING OF TUNSTALL'S MEN

Using Billy's and Dick Brewer's affidavit, on February 20, 1878, Justice of the Peace "Squire" Wilson generated arrest warrants. After Sheriff Brady refused to serve them, Wilson concluded that *"there being then and there no officers to serve such warrant the undersigned as directed by law, in such cases specially empowered Richard H. Brewer to serve the same endorsing such deputation on said last mentioned warrant."* Wilson wrote:

The Territory of New Mexico)
County of Lincoln   )

I, John B. Wilson justice of the Peace in and for precinct № 1 Lincoln County, New Mexico, do hereby certify that on or about the 19th day of February 1878 **W. Boney** *[sic] and R.M. Brewer filed in my office affidavits charging John [James] J. Dolan, J. Conovair, Frank Baker, Jessie Evans, Tom Hill, George Davis, A.L. Roberts, P. [Panteleon] Gallegos, T. Green, J. Awly, A.H. Mills, "Dutch Charley" proper name unknown, R.W. Beckwith, William Morton, George Hindman, J.B. Matthews and others with having murdered and killed one John H. Tunstall at the said County of Lincoln on or about the 18th day of February 1878, that on or about the 20th day of Feby 1878, I secured warrants on said affidavits for the arrest of the parties above named and directed the same to the Constable of for precinct № one in said County to wit: Antonacio Martines [Martinez].*

That on or about the 20th day of Feby 1878 said warrant was returned "not served" that on or about the said last mentioned day the undersigned issued an alias warrant for the apprehension of the above named persons, and there being then and there no officers to serve such warrant the undersigned as directed by law, in such cases specially empowered Richard H. Brewer to serve the same endorsing such deputation on said last mentioned warrant.

In testimony whereof I have hereinto set my hand at Lincoln Precinct № 1 Lincoln County, N. Mexico this 31ˢᵗ day of August 1878.

John Wilson
Justice of the Peace

This document allowed Special Constable Dick Brewer to deputize Billy and Fred Waite as Deputy Constables under Lincoln Town Constable Atanacio Martinez to serve the arrest warrants.

COMPLAINT TO THE BRITISH AMBASSADOR

On February 23, 1878, after determining that murder of a British subject, like Tunstall, triggered federal investigation, Alexander McSween wrote a complaint to British Ambassador Sir Edward Thornton. And for the remainder of McSween's life - a mere 146 days before his own Ring assassination - he never lost his faith that legal justice would prevail.

KILLING OF MORTON AND BAKER: MARCH 9, 1878

With Wilson's arrest warrants, Special Constable Brewer, with Tunstall's men - including Billy - as his posse, on March 6, 1878 apprehended Catron-Dolan Cow Camp foreman, William "Buck" Morton, and Jessie Evans's gang member, Frank Baker. On March 9ᵗʰ, these men were fatally shot attempting escape en route to Lincoln for incarceration and trial. Billy likely fired at them with the others. All claimed self defense, since Morton grabbed a pistol from posseman, William McClosky, killing him.

RING RESPONSES

MILITARY INTERVENTION: FEBRUARY 19, 1878

Unaware that Sheriff William Brady was already colluding with Commander George Purington and Governor S.B. Axtell to get troops approved by New Mexico's District Commander,

General Edward Hatch, to suppress Lincolnites, Alexander McSween requested soldiers from Purington on February 19, 1878, the day after Tunstall's killing. So Purington sent to Lincoln First Lieutenant Cyrus Delaney and a 9th Cavalry squad to "the House," enabling the murderers' escape. Brady even led cavalrymen to Tunstall's store to get hay for their horses. So McSween had Justice of the Peace Wilson issue an arrest warrant for hay theft against Brady, with a $200 bond. McSween and Wilson still believed there was legal recourse against the Ring.

OBSTRUCTING WARRANTS: FEBRUARY 20, 1878

On February 20, 1878, when Town Constable Atanacio Martinez and Deputy Constables, Billy Bonney and Fred Waite, accompanied by a citizens' committee led by Hispanic leader and Lincoln County jailor, Juan Patrón, went to "the House" to serve Wilson's alias warrants for Tunstall's murderers, Sheriff Brady arrested Martinez, Bonney, and Waite. Lacking legal basis, with Ring bravado, Brady's boasted he simply had the power to do so. He also confiscated Billy's Winchester '73 carbine – Billy's prized possession - and marched his captives in intimidating display through Lincoln to the pit jail. They were illegally held until February 22nd, demonstrating likely motive of restraining them until the completion of Tunstall burial to the east of his store that day. And Brady did not return Billy's carbine.

GOVERNOR'S PROCLAMATION: MARCH 9, 1878

On March 9, 1878, with a Fort Stanton military escort including Commander George Purington, Governor S.B. Axtell arrived in Lincoln, where residents thought he was coming to hear their Citizens' Committee's grievances against Sheriff Brady. Instead, Ringite Axtell was intervening to obstruct their justice - just as he had done in Colfax County in 1875 by removing its courts to thwart conviction of Franklin Tolby's Ringite killers.

That day, Axtell issued an illegal Proclamation removing Justice of the Peace "Squire" Wilson, so as to declare his deputizings illegal, and to make Sheriff William Brady Lincoln County's only law enforcer. Since Tunstall's deputized men, including Billy, had already killed Morton and Baker that same day, that called them murderers, not lawmen. Axtell wrote:

Proclamation

To the Citizens of Lincoln County.

The disturbed condition of affairs at the County seat brings me to Lincoln County at this time; my only object is to assist good citizens to uphold the laws and to keep the peace, to enable that all act intelligently, it is important that the following facts should be clearly understood.

1st

John B. Wilson's appointment by the County Commissioners as a Justice of the Peace was illegal and void, and all processes issued by him were void, and said Wilson has no authority whatsoever to act as Justice of the Peace.

2nd

The appointment of Robt Wiedeman as U.S. Marshall has been revoked and said Wiedeman is not now a peace officer nor has he any power or authority whatever to act as such.

3rd

The President of the United States upon an application made by me as Governor has directed the Post Commander Col. George A. Purington to assist Territorial civil officers in maintaining order and enforcing local process. It follows from the above statement that there is no legal processes in this case to be enforced except the writs and processes issued out of the Third Judicial District Court by Judge Bristol and there are no Territorial Officers here to enforce them except Sheriff Brady and his Deputies.

Nor therefore in consideration of the premises I do hereby command all persons to disarm and return to their homes and usual occupations, under penalty of being arrested and confined in jail as disturbers of the Public peace.

S.B. Axtell
Governor of N.M.
Lincoln, March 9, 1878

AXTELL SEEKS TROOPS: MARCH AND JULY, 1878

On March 3, 1878[7], Governor S.B. Axtell wrote to President Rutherford B. Hayes, using the Ring's outlawing of opponents to justify using troops.

He repeated his request on July 17, 1878, for military intervention in the Lincoln County War's battle. Then, avoiding personal risk, he temporarily left the Territory. Axtell wrote:

Copy [of telegram]
Executive Office
Santa Fe, N.M.
Mch. 3, 1878

To the President.
Washington, D.C.
I am unable to enforce the law and to protect life and property in this Territory, and request assistance from the President.

S.B. Axtell
Governor

****

Executive Office
Santa Fe, N.M.
July 17th 1878

His Excellency Mr President
Sir:
I respectfully request leave of absence for ninety days to visit my family in Ohio. Hon. W.G. Ritch Secy. Of the Ty. will remain in Santa Fe during my absence.
Respectfully
Your Obt. Servt.
S.B. Axtell
Governor N.M.

CITIZENS RESIST THE RING: MARCH-APRIL, 1878

LETTER TO DEPARTMENT OF INTERIOR BY MONTEGUE LEVERSON: MARCH 16, 1878

Montegue Leverson, a politically connected, Colorado friend of John Chisum's, hoping for a New Mexico Territory governorship, went to Lincoln to intervene. On March 16, 1878, on Juan Patrón's crossed-out letterhead, he wrote to Secretary of the Interior Carl Schurz, enclosing a letter to President Hayes blaming the Ring; unaware that both men were already informed the year before about those U.S. officials' corruption and murdering by Mary McPherson, whom they had stonewalled. Leverson wrote:

LINCOLN, LINCOLN CO. N.M.   *16 March*   *1878*

Hon Carl Schurz
    Secy of the Interior
Dear Sir.
    I earnestly entreat you to read the enclosed letter and to hand it to the president and beg his earnest attention to its contents. I refer you also to my former letters on the subject of the state of affairs here, sent by me to the president from Santa Fe ...
I expect to be back in Santa Fe in 10 or 12 days, and shall be ready to give my aid in any manner that may be desired for the purpose of putting an end to the <u>organized anarchy</u> prevailing in this Territory and to bring justice to the evil doers.
                        Respectfully
                        Montegue Leverson

[ENCLOSED LETTER]:
                    Lincoln, Lincoln Co. New Mexico
                          March 16<u>th</u> 1878.
His Excellency Rutherford B. Hayes
    President of the United States.
Excellency!
    Since my last letter to your Excellency on the state of affairs in this Territory, I have come here to select, in this garden of New Mexico, a suitable location for a colony from Old and New England. Whether such colony will be formed, will depend on the restoration of peace, and life and property being made secure in this distracted country; **the insecurity of life and property and the <u>disturbed condition</u> of affairs <u>being caused by the United States officials</u>!**
    I have made careful inquiry <u>from both sides</u> into the base and brutal murder of Mr. Tunstall ... and I solemnly assure you that a <u>real</u> investigation will prove conclusively that the murder was plotted and contrived by the District Attorney of the Third Judicial District [William Rynerson] by whom the District Judge [Warren Bristol] is used as a tool!
    I deeply regret to add that the Governor [S.B. Axtell] has <u>illegally</u> and <u>despotically</u> exerted his favor to screen the murderers, as the document herewith will prove ...
    When Mr. Tunstall was murdered ... sworn informations were presented to Mr. Wilson [Justice of the Peace], on which he issued <u>warrants for arrest of the actual murderers</u>.

"Paper C" [attached Axtell proclamation] will show your Excellency the conduct of the Governor thereupon, <u>for the purpose of screening the murderers from arrest</u>. Even if Mr. Wilson's appointment had been illegal (which it was not) I need not remind your Excellency that he (the Governor) had neither right nor power to pass upon it ...

But illegal as was the Governor's conduct, it has been none the less disastrous having served to discourage and demoralize the honest portion of the community ...

The assassins assert that Mr. Tunstall was killed while in the act of resisting the Sheriff's posse. The statement is <u>wholly false, and will be proved to be so on the first inquiry.</u> [H]is murders were men who had escaped jail [Jessie Evans and his boys], but had been joined to the Sheriff's posse for the express purpose of the murder. <u>All this can be proved by irreproachable testimony</u>, Your Excellency! Mr. Tunstall was a British subject, and *it is not likely that the British Government will allow the murder of one of its subjects <u>by United States officials and their appointees</u>, to pass without a rigorous investigation, and a demand of indemnity for the family of the murdered man.*

[AUTHOR'S NOTE: This is the red flag that necessitated President Hayes's Frank Warner Angel cover-up investigation.]

For the honor of the United States I entreat your Excellency to anticipate the action of the British Government by yourself causing an investigation to be made, not only into this matter but into the general state of affairs in New Mexico. Your Excellency will then find that the U.S. Attorney [Thomas Benton Catron] and the Surveyor General have been plundering and defrauding the United States, that the former has been in the habit of forging indictments which were never found by any grand jury, of purchasing testimony, and of other malfeasance too numerous to be here mentioned.

[AUTHOR'S NOTE: Condemnation of Catron and his Ring.]

But to render life and property even temporarily secure pending such investigation, <u>as well as to prevent the destruction of evidences</u> of crime, I respectfully suggest that the following measures should be taken immediately and by telegraph:

1<u>st</u> The suspension of the Governor [Axtell].

2ᵈ *The suspension of the U.S. Attorney [Catron], and* <u>immediate</u> *appointment of some one to take possession of the books and papers of the office.*

[AUTHOR'S NOTE: By 1888, Catron had a expurgating fire in his law office, destroying incriminatory documents.]

3ᵈ *Orders to the person to be appointed (pro tem) to act as Governor to remove the District Attorney of the 3ᵈ Judicial District [Rynerson], and by telegraph to appoint some person in his place to take possession of books and papers before they can be destroyed ...*

Charges against the Judge of the 3ᵈ Judicial District were (I am informed) presented about two years since [Grant County petition], and are now on file in the Attorney General's office. Of these charges, if their nature be as stated to me, some are of a very serious nature, <u>**but have never been investigated,**</u> *owing, it is alleged, to the influences brought ... by the United States District Attorney for New Mexico [Catron], thro Mr. Elkins.*

[AUTHOR'S NOTE: Leverson may also be aware of Mary McPherson's exposés - possibly through Cimarron's Frank Springer - and knows how the Ring has Catron working New Mexico Territory and Elkins working Washington, D.C.]

<u>*Fresh and still more serious charges*</u> *are ready to be presented the moment it is seen that there would be any hope of an impartial investigation.*

I have the honor to be your Excellency's most obedient servant.

Montegue R. Leverson.

REGULATOR AMBUSH OF WILLIAM BRADY AND GEORGE HINDMAN: APRIL 1, 1878

Sheriff William Brady was the Ringite directly responsible for Tunstall's murder. His Deputy, George Hindman, was named in the Brewer-Bonney affidavit of February 19, 1878 as in the murder posse. After Governor S.B. Axtell's illegal, February 9, 1878 Proclamation giving sole legal power to Brady, it was obvious that the Ring was setting up McSween's murder by Brady.

The Regulators knew that McSween, with his wife, had been hiding-out at John Chisum's Pecos River area South Spring River Ranch. On March 28, 1878, Sheriff Brady had already brought

Fort Stanton troops there as his posse to arrest McSween for not filing his bail-bond (maliciously blocked by District Attorney William Rynerson) and likely to murder him once in custody. But Chisum had concealed McSween.

Brady's next chance to murder was at McSween's return to Lincoln for his Grand Jury embezzlement trial. McSween had even naively tried to arrange a safe escort by Fort Stanton soldiers; thus, revealing his day of return as April 1, 1878. The troops never arrived, leaving him unprotected. Chisum, more canny than McSween, apparently told the Regulators to be in Lincoln to protect McSween, since Deputy Sheriff Adolph Barrier had finally returned to Las Vegas. As further precaution, Chisum himself, along with Montegue Leverson, accompanied McSween and his wife, Susan, in their buggy to Lincoln.

So on April 1, 1878, the Regulators, including Billy, were secretly in Lincoln, concealed in Tunstall's corral behind the long building of his combined store, bank, and personal apartment. They observed Brady, brandishing Billy's confiscated Winchester '73 carbine, with Deputies George Hindman, Jacob Basil "Billy" Matthews, George Peppin, and Jack Long, walking the single street to the east where McSween would arrive.

At 9:00 a.m., the Regulators acted, firing from behind the corral's adobe wall, and at the difficult angle created by the obscuring east side with Tunstall's apartment. Matthews, Peppin, and Long escaped. Brady and Hindman did not. In the firing group, only Billy would have lacked a carbine, likely using a Colt .44 revolver, lacking range for the necessary 60 yards. But after Brady's killing, Billy ran out, with Jim "Frenchie" French for cover, to retrieve his precious carbine from Brady's corpse. He and French were wounded by shooting Billy Matthews. The Regulators then fled the town, having ensured McSween's safe arrival.

On April 3, 1878, Ringite George Peppin arrested Alexander McSween and his brother-in-law Attorney David Shield for the Brady-Hindman killings, ignoring McSween's stating their innocence and that Peppin was no longer a Deputy after Brady was dead. Nevertheless, Peppin used Commander George Purington first to illegally search McSween's house and Tunstall's store, then to incarcerate both men at Fort Stanton (with Susan McSween insisting on staying there too with her husband). Montegue Leverson, still in Lincoln, confronted Purington for Constitutional violations, and got Purington's thuggish Ringite curse: "Damn the Constitution and you for an ass." Leverson then wrote his documenting complaint to President Rutherford B. Hayes, unaware that Hayes was shielding the Ring. But Leverson may have saved incarcerated McSween from murder at Fort Stanton by making intent too obvious.

REGULATORS' ATTEMPTED ARREST AND KILLING OF "BUCKSHOT" ROBERTS: APRIL 4, 1878

The Regulators ignored Governor Axtell's March 9, 1878 Proclamation, and continued to serve Wilson's warrants. Regulator leader Dick Brewer had one for Andrew "Buckshot" Roberts, a murder posseman then planning to flee the Territory. The Regulators, seeking Tunstall's cattle stolen by the Ring after his murder, chanced to meet Roberts, on April 4, 1878, at Blazer's Mill, the private way station, post office, and grist mill of Dr. Joseph Blazer within the Mescalero Indian Reservation.

Roberts refused arrest and opened fire with his carbine, a bullet entering John Middleton's chest; and one striking Charlie Bowdre's belt buckle and ricocheting to wrench the revolver from George Coe's hand, mutilating his trigger finger. Bowdre, in justifiable self defense, shot Roberts in the abdomen. After seeking shelter in Dr. Blazer's office, Roberts, still shooting, fatally hit Dick Brewer. So Roberts, an accomplice to Tunstall's murder, had now murdered another innocent man and injured others. Billy had not fired a shot. By the next day, Roberts died of his single wound.

And, with Dick Brewer's death, Billy lost another father figure. Billy would have read the newspaper article, later given by Alexander McSween as "Exhibit 17" in his June 6, 1878 deposition to Investigator Frank Warner Angel. It stated:

The following for the death of Brewer has been sent us for publication:

"We the undersigned residents of Lincoln county, in the Territory of New Mexico, deeply deplore the loss our county sustains by the death of Richard M. Brewer, a young man of irreproachable character, who commanded the respect and admiration of all who knew him ... He was a hard working, generous, sober, upright and noble minded young man. Cattle thieves and murderers and their "kid-gloved" friends ["The House"] hated him, and promised him a violent death years ago.

In good faith he went as special constable to arrest the murders of John H. Tunstall, by virtue of a warrant issued by John B. Wilson, a Justice of the peace in the town of Lincoln. Before he could make his return thereon, Governor Axtell issued a proclamation to the effect that Wilson as not a legal J.P., although the act of our legislature, by virtue of which said Wilson was appointed justice, was approved by his Excellency. Mr. Wilson had acted as such justice for over a year without having his authority questioned. Immediately after the issue of that proclamation, our late sheriff and those who were interested in screening the murderers, obtained warrants against Mr. Brewer and posse for having made an effort to execute the warrant issued by Wilson. Brewer and his posse knew well that if the late sheriff arrested them they would be murdered, so they took to the mountains.

We tender our heartfelt sympathy to the aged parents of the deceased Richard M. Brewer, and other relatives in Wisconsin, and we beg to assure them that whilst they have lost a good son and relative, we feel that our county has lost one of her best citizens.

(Signed) John S. Chisum. J. Ellis & Sons, Merchants. G.B. Barber, Surveyor and Civil Engineer. J.B. Patron, Speaker of the House of Representatives. Jose Montana, Merchant. McSween & Shield, Attorneys, J.N. Copeland, Sheriff, J. Newcomb, T.F. Ealy, M.D. Dow Brothers, Merchants; R.M. Gilbert, A. Wilson, W. Fields, C. Sampson, and ONE HUNDRED AND FIFTY OTHERS.

APPOINTMENT OF ANTI-RING SHERIFF, JOHN COPELAND: APRIL 9, 1878

By April 9, 1878, citizens had reason for hope. Their County Commissioners appointed popular local rancher, John Copeland, as Sheriff to replace dead William Brady.

LINCOLN COUNTY GRAND JURY: APRIL, 1878

The April 1878 Lincoln County Grand Jury exonerated McSween of embezzling. It indicted Tunstall's murderers, and also indicted Billy and other Regulators for the murders of Brady, Hindman, and Roberts. Presence of Fort Stanton Soldiers - like suppressive troops used in the 1872 Legislature Revolt and in the Colfax County War and "Dear Ben plot" - was misconstrued by citizens as protection.

With his usual faith in the law, McSween had provided his accounting for the Fritz insurance policy case to disprove embezzlement (and later gave it to Frank Warner Angel as Exhibit 7 in his deposition of June 6, 1878). It stated:

Donnell Lawson & Co.   *92 Broadway*
    Bankers   *New York.*
                                   July 19 – 1877

Alexander A. McSween
         Lincoln N.M.
Dear Sir
       We credit you $7,148.49 proceeds, Life Ins Policy Emil Fritz after deducting our com's [commissions] as per agreement with you which we mention here, that the parties for whom you are acting may see it was the best could be done under the circumstances & has resulted greatly to the interest of all concerned.

       The settlement offered you was $6500 less 700\underline{00}$ charges, reducing the amount to 5800\underline{00}$.

       Out proposition to you was $6500 less the 700\underline{00}$ charges, reducing the amount to 5800\underline{00}$.

       Our proposition to you was to advance this the 700\underline{00}$ & and get possession of the policy & proof & guarantee you the 5800\underline{00}$ ourselves & prosecute the case in the courts.

       In consideration of this advance & <u>guarantee</u> we were to receive one half the surplus after paying over to you the 5800\underline{00}$ & remembering ourselves for the outlay of 700\underline{00}$ attorneys fees, &c. Under the old arrangement 5800\underline{00}$ is all you could have obtained, whereas now you get $7,148$\underline{49}$.

       The following statement shows the whole transaction.
Received from our lawyers
     From this deduct
         Advance $700.
Lawyers fees and telegrams   803.03
Out ½ net profit   <u>*1348.51*</u>
       To your Cr [credit]
Thus   *10,000.*
Less advance 700
Fees & Tel   *803.03*   <u>*1, 503.03*</u>
                           $8,496.97
Am't Guaranteed   *5800.00*
½ of this net profit   *½ 2,696.97*
     To us   _____   *1,348.48   ½*
       The other ½ 1348, added to $5800 + 7,148.49.

       This we think must surely give great satisfaction to you & more especially to the parties you represent.

Lincolnites had that Grand Jury's outcome published:

NEW MEXICO.

Report of the Grand Jury of Lincoln County.

Through the courtesy of Harry Wigham, editor of the Cimarron News and Press, we are enabled to give the following document to our readers at this date:

To the Hon. Warren Bristol, Associate Judge of the Supreme Court of the Territory of New Mexico, and Presiding Judge of the 3d Judicial District thereof:

The grand jury of the April, 1878, term of the District Court for the County of Lincoln, deeply deplore the present insecurity of life and property, though the revival and continuance of the troubles of past years.

The murder of John H. Tunstall, for brutality and malice, is without a parallel and without a shadow of justification. By this inhuman act our county has lost one of our BEST and most useful men, - one who brought intelligence, industry, and capital to the development of Lincoln county. We equally condemn the most brutal murder of our late sheriff, William Brady, and George Hindman. In each of the cases, where the evidence would warrant it, we have made presentments.

Had his Excellency, S.B. Axtell, when here, ascertained from the people the cause of our troubles, as he was requested, valuable lives would have been spared our community; especially do we condemn that portion of his proclamation relating to J.B. Wilson as J.P. Mr. Wilson acted in good faith as J.P. over a year. Mr. Brewer, deceased, arrested, as we are informed, some of the alleged murderers of Mr. Tunstall by virtue of warrants issued by Mr. Wilson. The part of the proclamation referred to virtually outlawed Mr. Brewer and posse. In fact, they were hunted to the mountains by our late sheriff with U.S. soldiers. We believe that had the governor done his duty whilst here, these unfortunate occurrences would have been spared us.

Under the impression that stealing the property of the United States was a crime against our territory, we heard evidence in regard to the administration of affairs at the Mescalaro Apache Indian agency in the county; but we are now informed by the District Attorney [William Rynerson] that crimes of the character thus investigated by us are not indictable in this court. We have, however, ascertained by evidence that the Indians are systematically robbed by their agent [Frederick Godfroy] of a large and varied assortment of supplies. We mention this here for the reason that it will explain why the Indians are migrating mauraders and steal from and murder our citizens. The witnesses by whom these facts can be proven are

residents of this town and neighborhood, and a list of them has been furnished by us to the United States District clerk.
Signed J.H. BLAZER. Foreman.

HOPE IN LINCOLN COUNTY

CITIZENS PETITION HAYES: APRIL 26, 1878

After his exoneration, Alexander McSween returned to anti-Ring campaigning focused on Tunstall's murder, being joined by other Lincolnites; all underestimating Ring risk. They wrote:

LAW OFFICE
OF
McSWEEN & SHIELD
Lincoln County Bank Building

𝕷𝖎𝖓𝖈𝖔𝖑𝖓, 𝕹𝖊𝖜 𝕸𝖊𝖝𝖎𝖈𝖔, *April 26, 1878*

To his Excellency Rutherford B. Hayes, President of the United States of America:

Excellency! The undersigned have the Honor of transmitting you, as requested, a copy of the proceedings of a meeting held by the citizens of Lincoln County N.M., relative to the late troubles
Respectfully
A.A. McSween
B.H. Ellis
Secretaries

The attached transcript was later published in the *Mesilla Independent* and the *Cimarron News and Press*. It stated:

Pursuant to an hours notice, after the adjournment of the District Court April 24th 1878, the citizens of Lincoln County, from every section thereof, assembled at the Court House to express their sentiments relative to the present troubles. The room was crowded.

The Hon. J.B. Patron called the meeting to order, and nominated the Hon. Florencio Gonzales, Probate Judge, for President, and Capt. Saturnino Baca and Jose Montaño, County Treasurer, for Vice Presidents, with Alex. A. McSween and B.H. Ellis as secretaries.

Judge Gonzales stated the object of the meeting to be the consideration of our present troubles. His speech was vociferously cheered, and interrupted by frequent applause.

Speeches were also made by Hon. J.B. Patron, Jose Montano and Mr. Herford. The latter gentleman closed with these significant remarks: "I trust that the pledges of friendship and good feeling made this evening in so solemn and appropriate a manner, may never be marred or broken."

The Chair appointed Hon. J.B. Patron, Messrs. John S. Chisum, and Avery M. Clenny a committee to draft and submit Resolutions. In due time they submitted the following, which were unanimously adopted:

Be it Resolved: That it is the sense of this meeting that our present troubles are only a continuance of old feuds dating back five or six years that will now cease as the cause has been removed.

Be it Resolved: That thanks of the people of Lincoln County are due, and are hereby tendered to Lieut. Col. Dudley U.S.A. Commanding Fort Stanton N.M. for his conduct as an officer and Gentleman. That we do and will consider the day he took command at Fort Stanton an important era in the history of our county. That we assure him of our appreciation of the intelligent, cautious and earnest manner in which he has applied himself in ferreting out the cause of our troubles. That his non-partisan conduct and frankness towards the people on the one hand and the men on the other, is a guarantee that he <u>alone</u> is the Commanding Officer at Fort Stanton, and that therefore we tender him our heartfelt thanks in recognition of our appreciation of a man who discharges his duty <u>fully</u>.

[AUTHOR'S NOTE: Dudley was made Fort Stanton Commander on April 5, 1878, so his Ringite loyalty was still unknown.]

That we condemn without qualification, the conduct of the Governor, S.B. Axtell, while here in March last. That his refusal to investigate our troubles stamps him as a little, one-sided partisan. That his conduct and proclamation of March 9, 1878, are unworthy of an officer filling his exalted station. That as a result of that proclamation, he is responsible for the loss of life that has occurred in this County since his visit.

Be it Resolved: That we recognize with inexpressible pleasure the good and united feeling that binds all our people, Mexicans and Americans, together! That we recognize our mutual dependence upon each other, and that we pledge our lives and our property to the protection of each other, and the maintenance of the laws.

Be it Resolved: That a vote of thanks be tendered the United States Soldiers, Non-commissioned Officers and Privates for their commendable conduct while here during Court.

Be it Resolved: That we tender our thanks to John N. Copeland for having accepted the office of Sheriff and for his important and efficient discharge of duty as such since he took charge.

Signed Florencio Gonzales President
Alex. A. McSween
B.H. Ellis   Secretaries

RING OBSTRUCTION OF JUSTICE

RYNERSON'S REFUSAL TO ARREST TUNSTALL'S INDICTED MURDERERS: MAY 2, 1878

After the April 1878 Grand Jury indicted Tunstall's killers, Ringite District Attorney William Rynerson refused to issue their arrest warrants. McSween intervened, and got Rynerson's mocking letter of May 2, 1878, which McSween presented to Investigator Frank Warner Angel as Exhibit 20 in his deposition of June 6, 1878. Rynerson's sneering - mimicking Catron's, with whom he was later a business partner - mirrors his own being the unpunished murderer of Territorial Chief Justice John P. Slough in 1867 - defended in court by Elkins himself. So Rynerson flaunted Ringite immunity, knowing McSween was a dead man walking. But he did issue arrest warrants for Regulators indicted for killings of Brady, Hindman, and Roberts. For those indictments, Billy would request the pardon. Rynerson wrote:

Las Cruces N.M.
May 2d 1878

A.A. McSween Esq
    Law office of McSween & Shield
            Lincoln N.M.
Dear Sir: I am just in receipt of yours of the date of 2 of st ulto, directed to me in which you say "If parties have been indicted by the last Grand Jury for the murder of J.H. Tunstall, I wish to ask you to place warrants in the hands of our Sheriff for their arrest please reply." In reply I have to say that I shall discharge my duty, without let or hindrance from anyone, and when warrants are

necessary in every case they will be issued and placed in the hands of the proper officer. Just whom you mean by "our Sheriff" is not clear to me, as in the past few months it is said you had some interest in more than one sheriff. You may mean Martines, you may mean Barrier, or you may mean someone else whom I do not know that you have reduced to possession and are pleased to designate as our (your) Sheriff and since you have undertaken the task of directing me in my duties I may be permitted to suggest that you seem to have forgotten to dictate or direct as to what should be done as to the warrants. "If parties have been indicted by the last Grand Jury for the murder of" Sheriff Brady, George Hindman, A.L. Roberts, and others in Lincoln County.

Passing strange
Very Respt'y
W.L. Rynerson
Dist. Atty

ENTER FORT STANTON COMMANDER NATHAN AUGUSTUS MONROE DUDLEY

ANALYSIS: *On April 5, 1878, Fort Union's Commander Nathan Augustus Monroe Dudley replaced Fort Stanton's unpopular Commander George Purington. Ring-beholden Dudley was an uncouth, alcoholic, career soldier, and already twice court martialed. His illegal intervention in the upcoming Lincoln County War would ensure Ring victory. But naïve Lincoln County citizens, including Alexander McSween, believed he was their protector - until it was too late.*

By April 5, 1878, unbeknownst to Lincoln County citizens, the fate of their anti-Ring struggle for justice against John Henry Tunstall's murderers was sealed. And more horrors awaited them. In the guise of conciliation, Fort Stanton's Commander, Lieutenant George Purington - whose Ring affiliation had been too obvious by his shielding of the murderers in "the House" on the night of Tunstall's killing - was replaced by Fort Union's Commander, Nathan Augustus Monroe Dudley. Ominously, but unknown by Lincolnites, it was from Fort Union that troops had been drawn by the Ring to suppress the Cimarron populace after Franklin Tolby's murder, as well as for intended murder of Ring opponents in the "Dear Ben plot." And Dudley's troops would soon commit far worse crimes in 3½ months in Lincoln County.

BIOGRAPHY

Nathan Augustus Monroe Dudley is best known for his intervention in the Lincoln County War battle on July 19, 1878, a year after the second of his two court martials for drunkenness and brutality to a fellow soldier. Dudley's Lincoln County War intervention was treasonous under the Posse Comitatus Act, passed on June 18, 1878, a month before he violated it. The Act barred military intervention in civilian conflicts. Dudley's intervention caused then-prevailing McSween's side to lose the war, as well as enabling Ringite Sheriff George Peppin's posse to murder Alexander McSween, Harvey Morris, Francisco Zamora, and Vincente Romero; to endanger women and children in McSween's family in his besieged house; and to destroy that house by arson. When taking legal action following the war's atrocities, it was on Dudley that McSween's widow, Susan, focused her blame and legal actions.

Dudley's apologist, though revealing, biographer is E. Donald Kaye, in his 1997 *Nathan Augustus Monroe Dudley, 1825-1910: Rogue, Hero, or Both?* Kaye also quotes from Leo E. Oliva's 1993, *Fort Union and the Frontier Army in the Southwest.* There is no mention of the Santa Fe Ring.

Nathan Augustus Monroe Dudley was born on August 20, 1825 in Lexington, Massachusetts. At 15, he began his lifelong military career by enlisting in peacetime Massachusetts militia.

In 1855, he was made a First Lieutenant in Company E, 10th U.S. Infantry, and was involved in a massacre of Sioux in Nebraska, where their village was plundered for artifacts for the Smithsonian Museum. In 1866, he fought Cheyenne and Sioux. In 1857 to 1858, as acting Commander of Company E, he fought in the Mormon War in Utah against Brigham Young. There, a Captain Tracey wrote that Dudley was an "ass." And a Captain Jesse A. Grove wrote: "Dudley is a noisy, boisterous fellow ... As a soldier he is not considered equal to most of the others." In 1861, Dudley was promoted to Captain of Company E, and had his first court martial trial for unbecoming conduct of lying to another officer. He was found not guilty.

In March of 1862, he was made a Colonel, but was never promoted above brevet brigadier general of volunteers in the Civil War; during which he was in no major battles, but became known as "Gold Lace Dudley" for bombastically embellishing his uniform.

In June of 1862, with his 30th Massachusetts Infantry regiment, he burned down the plantation of a suspected Rebel fighter, George Keller, around the absent man's wife, her parents, her daughter and two other women - in eerie foreshadowing of his atrocity to the besieged McSween home and family 16 years later.

After the Civil War, he was transferred to the 3rd U.S. Cavalry, where he faced two more court martials. In 1871, he was found guilty of drunkenness on duty at Arizona Territory's Camp McDowell, and was punished by a two month stay in that Territory's Camp Bowie. And General Edward Hatch tried to remove him from service because of his alcoholism.

In 1877, he was court martialed again. Having been made Lieutenant Colonel of the 9th Cavalry on July 1, 1876, and Commander of Fort Union in 1877, his behavior caused his arrest by Hatch. He was charged with drunkenness on duty, disrespect to his superior officer, and an improper intervention in a civilian matter by trying to force a marriage between the raped post chaplain's daughter and her rapist. For his trial, he was represented by T.B. Catron and his law partner, William T. Thornton. His resulting few months of pay reduction was even remitted. Dudley's Ringite loyalty was the result.

That Dudley was also likely bribed by his Fort Stanton days can be surmised by the extreme risk he took by violating the Posse Comitatus Act. And after his death, his wife willed expensive jewelry - beyond Dudley's means - to her grandson.

The year after his second lost court martial, on April 5, 1878, Dudley was transferred to the Ring's next site of action: Lincoln County's Fort Stanton, nine miles from Lincoln, where the intent was to drive out or murder merchant John Henry Tunstall and anti-Ring lawyer, Alexander McSween. Ringite previous Commander, George Purington, had became too noxious to Lincolnites by partisan interventions, but was kept at Fort Stanton nevertheless as a liaison with "the House's" local Ring bosses, James Dolan and John Riley, with their beef and flour contract to Fort Stanton.

Dudley rapidly proved his Ring value, assisting Sheriff George Peppin in a June 28, 1878 raid on San Patricio in failed attempt to capture or murder Alexander McSween.

Then, on the Lincoln County War's fifth day of July 18, 1878, Dudley planned his attack with James Dolan at Fort Stanton. The next day he marched on Lincoln with cavalry, infantry, a Gatling gun and a howitzer cannon. He personally threatened Alexander

McSween with razing of his house if a shot was fired against his soldiers, thus obstruction action by McSween's defenders. His intimidating troops and weaponry also caused flight of the rest of McSween's men throughout the town. He later enabled arson of McSween's besieged house around its fighters - including Billy Bonney - and McSween's wife and her sister with five children. And when Susan McSween went to his camp in town to plead for her husband's life, with typical Ringite mockery, Dudley insulted and defamed her while refusing aid. On the Lincoln County War battle's sixth day, Dudley effected defeat of the winning McSween side, just 3 months and 15 days after his posting.

In October of 1878, Susan McSween hired Las Vegas attorney, Huston Chapman, to seek physical protection from Dudley, as well as to prosecute him in military and civil courts for murder of her husband and arson of her house. Dudley responded by sending soldiers to threaten her and Chapman. Chapman was then murdered by Dolan and compatriots on February 18, 1879 in apparent attempt to stop Dudley's legal prosecution.

On March 7, 1879, new Territorial Governor, Lew Wallace, requested that General Hatch remove Dudley as Fort Stanton's Commander because of Lincolnites fear of him. Dudley, confident of Ring protection and biased judges, requested a military Court of Inquiry into his conduct. And with Catron's law partner, Henry Waldo, he obtained defamatory affidavits from Ringites against Susan McSween to discredit her testimony.

From May 2, 1879 to July 8, 1879, Dudley faced the Fort Stanton Court of Inquiry as to court martial. An outcome of court martial and hanging for treason would have been justified. Represented atypically by a civilian, not military, lawyer, Henry Waldo, Dudley's Chief Judge of the three appointed was his best friend from Fort Union, Colonel Galusha Pennypacker. In the Court of Inquiry, Dudley's own 9th cavalrymen bravely testified that they heard him colluding with Sheriff Peppin, and confirmed his knowing the arson plan and intent to kill Alexander McSween. Billy Bonney testified from May 28th to 29th that he saw three white soldiers firing a volley at those escaping the blazing house: meaning officers and under Dudley's orders; and that they possibly murdered escaping law student, Harvey Morris, in Billy's group. Lew Wallace also testified against Dudley from May 12th to May 15th, and was humiliated by Henry Waldo. Wallace's embarrassment had dire implications for Lincoln County and Billy Bonney's pardon. And Dudley was exonerated by the Court.

Commander of the Department of Missouri, Major General John Pope, disagreeing with Dudley's biased Court of Inquiry judgment, objected to Washington, D.C., but the decision was backed by General of the Army, W.T. Sherman.

In November of 1879, swayed by Dudley's military court vindication, a civilian court in Mesilla, under Judge Warren Bristol, cleared him of Susan McSween's charges. And she had been obstructed from attending to give testimony by Ring death threats.

Dudley was transferred back to Command at Fort Union on January 14, 1880. That year, he was in Colonel George Buell's campaign against Mimbres Apache Chief Victorio, which drove Victorio with his immediate tribe to Mexico where they were massacred. In 1887, transferred to the Midwest as a 1st Cavalry Colonel, Dudley fought in Montana's Crow War. In that timeframe, an officer named Amos Kimball wrote: "I guess you heard that Dudley made Colonel. The army bureaucracy is like a giant cesspool, where the biggest chunks rise to the top."

In 1889, Dudley retired at required 64. In 1904, he received honorary promotion - as did all officers on the retired list - his was to Brigadier General in the regular army.

Dudley died on April 29, 1910, and was buried in Arlington National Cemetery; his treasonous murders in Lincoln and his genocide of Native Americans without retribution.

CHAPTER 8

LINCOLN COUNTY WAR AGAINST THE SANTA FE RING: FEBRUARY 18, 1878 - JULY 19, 1878

THE UNSUNG FREEDOM FIGHT

ANALYSIS: After exhausting all legal attempts to arrest John Tunstall's murderers; after Governor S.B. Axtell's Petitions illegally removing their Justice of the Peace, outlawing of his appointed lawmen, and replacing their newly appointed Sheriff; after futilely petitioning President Hayes; and after witnessing escalating attempts to murder Alexander McSween, Lincoln County citizens took up arms against the Ring.

When did the Lincoln County War begin? Billy Bonney must have reflected contemporary consensus in his March 13, 1879 letter to new Governor, Lew Wallace, when he began his pardon request. He wrote: "*I have indictments against me for things that happened in the late Lincoln County War and am afraid to give up because my Enimies would Kill me.*"

The indictments Billy cites date to April of 1878's Regulator killings of Tunstall's murderers: William Brady, George Hindman, and Andrew "Buckshot" Roberts. So Billy called those actions part of *"the late Lincoln County War."* And he would likely have included the Regulators' self-defense killings, the month before, yielding no indictments, of Tunstall's murderers: Frank Baker and William "Buck" Morton. So the War began with Tunstall's murder.

As to their adversaries, Billy cites the Ring in his July 13, 1878 "Regulator Manifesto," stating: *"Mr. Walz. Sir: - We are all aware that your brother-in-law, T.B. Catron sustains the Murphy-Kinney party."* That "party" headed by T.B. Catron, included Lincoln County Sheriff George Peppin and his Deputies; and the criminal rustler gangs of Jessie Evans, John Kinney, and Seven Rivers boys. It would take until July 19th to realize that Commander N.A.M. Dudley was included. But Billy then testified, on May 28, 1879, against him in the military Court of Inquiry.

Everyone would have dated the War's end to the battle of July 14th to 19th of 1878, ending with the Regulators' defeat.

As to total deaths in the Lincoln County War, Billy gave a cheeky response for an April 3, 1881 Santa Fe *Daily New Mexican* article titled "Something About the Kid." Aware of his outlaw myth press, he was in custody awaiting his Mesilla hanging trial. He stated: "At least two hundred men have been killed in Lincoln County during the past three years, but I did not kill all of them."

THE RING'S MURDEROUS RESPONSES

USE OF TROOPS AGAINST McSWEEN

After John Tunstall's killing, Ringite use of troops became increasingly obvious, until citizens' resentment resulted in replacement of Commander George Purington with N.A.M. Dudley on April 5, 1878. But Dudley continued pro-Ring troop interventions, culminating in his July 19, 1878 action in the Lincoln County War battle.

FIRST MAJOR SKIRMISHES: APRIL 29-30, 1878

On April 29, 1878, Seven Rivers rancher-rustlers and John Kinney's gang from Mesilla, calling themselves a posse to arrest murderers of Brady, Hindman, and Roberts, rode toward Lincoln, where Regulators were stationed in Isaac Ellis's house. Frank MacNab, replacing murdered Dick Brewer as their leader, left with Frank Coe to do recognizance. Near Charles Fritz's ranch, they were ambushed by the Ringite "posse." MacNab was killed. Coe was taken captive.

On April 30, 1878, first facing organized attackers, Regulators in the Ellis house fought over 30 invaders from Seven Rivers. George Coe wounded "Dutch" Charlie Kruling; and four other assailants were killed. By afternoon, Dudley, at overwhelmed Sheriff Copeland's request, sent Second Lieutenant George Smith with a squad of 19 to Lincoln. Twenty-seven Seven Rivers men were taken to Fort Stanton. And prisoner Frank Coe was released.

McSween then resumed hiding, largely in San Patricio, where the Ring would soon revenge itself by massacre.

WARRANTS FOR McSWEEN AND "THE KID": APRIL 30, 1878

Ringites' murder of Frank MacNab was reported by Alexander McSween to San Patricio Justice of the Peace Gregorio Trujillo to obtain arrest warrants against the Seven Rivers men. And James Dolan rode to Blazer's Mill to get warrants from Catron's agent, Justice of the Peace David Easton, against McSween, William Bonney alias Henry Antrim alias Kid, and others unknown, for murder and assault with the intent to kill. The victims were the four dead Seven Rivers men and one injured "Dutch" Charlie Kruling. Demonstrated was the Ring now considered Billy enough risk to single him out.

As discussed above, Easton then quit, invalidating his warrants, as Commander Dudley would realize in horror on the day of the Lincoln County War's final battle.

DUDLEY INTERVENES: MAY 4, 1878

Though Commander Dudley had been optimistically welcomed by Lincolnites on April 5, 1878, by May 4th, he showed his Ring allegiance. That day, Sheriff George Copeland gave him the arrest warrants for MacNab's Seven Rivers murderers being held at Fort Stanton. Their hearing date was for May 6th.

Instead, Dudley presented to Copeland Easton's arrest warrants for McSween and "the Kid," then forced him by "military escort" to go to San Patricio to arrest McSween and Billy. But they were not found.

Dudley then released the Seven Rivers men. None ever stood trial. They were free to kill again - and would be part of Sheriff George Peppin's murderous posse by that July's battle.

AXTELL'S SECOND PROCLAMATION: MAY 28, 1878

On May 28, 1878, Governor S.B. Axtell, by Proclamation, removed Sheriff John Copeland - in office only 49 days - giving cause as Copeland's not having posted his tax collector bond in his first month in office. Axtell replaced him with Ringite George Peppin, Brady's deputy and Tunstall murder posseman.

INVESTIGATOR FRANK WARNER ANGEL BRINGS HOPE: MAY 4, 1878

Unlike their 1877 Colfax County War predecessors, Lincolnites could force their grievances on President Rutherford B. Hayes and his cabinetmen because of the potential for international incident with British Ambassador Edward Thornton demanding investigation of John Tunstall's murder.

So on May 4, 1878, by presidential order, Attorney Frank Warner Angel, an investigator reporting to the Departments of Justice and Interior, was sent to New Mexico Territory to conduct multiple investigations, which included the Lincoln County "troubles," the murder of John Tunstall, corruption in the Mescalero Indian Reservation's Agency, and land grant frauds. The immediate cause had been Alexander McSween's complaints, but the mission assigned to Angel to determine involvement of U.S. officials, more closely matched Mary McPherson's exposés of the year before. By the next month, on June 8, 1878, Billy would risk his life by coming to Lincoln to give Angel his own deposition on Tunstall's murder.

DEPOSITION OF ALEXANDER McSWEEN: JUNE 6, 1878

On June 6, 1878, Alexander McSween gave his deposition to Attorney Frank Warner Angel, 43 days before the Ring killed him. Though Angel took 39 depositions, McSween's is the most complete, contemporary rendition of Lincoln County's "troubles" and War. And it belies Angel's future, likely coerced, conclusion that U.S. officials were not involved in John Tunstall's murder.

McSween's 69 page deposition, with 21 exhibits totaling 111 pages, was by far Angel's longest. It meticulously detailed the bogus embezzlement case against McSween to achieve Tunstall's murder by its false property attachments; and documents murder attempts on McSween. McSween recounts partisanship of Lincoln County Sheriffs William Brady and George Peppin and their deputies; of District Attorney William Rynerson; and of Mescalero Indian Reservation Agent Frederick Godfroy. He documents the arrogance of power of "the House's" Lawrence Murphy, James Dolan, and John Riley; along with their use of outlaws, Jessie Evans and his gang, as enforcers and rustlers. He makes clear partisan interventions of Governor S.B. Axtell, of Fort Stanton soldiers under Commander George Purington, and of U.S. Attorney Catron, who, by then, had mortgaged "the House" from Dolan and Riley.

McSween knows that "the House" partners claimed they were backed by *"all the power in Santa Fe,"* but seems unaware of Colfax County War exposés. And unimaginable to him was that Commander Dudley would be the Ring's weapon against himself.

After Tunstall's death, McSween was Billy's next father figure; and Billy's subsequent acts and writings show his inspiration by both men. One can visualize Billy hearing McSween's renditions of Ring injustice and his risk of murder as given in his deposition. McSween stated:

Territory of New Mexico)
County of Lincoln   )
    Alexander A. McSween being duly sworn says. I have resided in Lincoln County since the 3ᵈ day of March 1875 and since that time am conversant with the state of affairs that has existed in that County and I am acquainted with the People of that County. I am a lawyer by profession and have been and now am engaged in the practice of my profession.
    I have given the subject of what has caused the trouble in Lincoln County considerable attention and study, and have inquired and talked with a great number of persons as to the causes which has produced the state of affairs which has resulted in the death of John H. Tunstall and as to the general lawlessness that exists in said County.
    From this examination and inquiry of the matter I am informed that Lawrence G. Murphy and Emil Fritz doing business under the style of L.G. Murphy & Co had the monopoly for sale of merchandise in this County, and used their power to oppress and grind out all they could from the farmers and force those who were opposed to them to leave the County. For instance the farmers would buy merchandise of them at exorbitant prices, and were compelled to turn in their produce in payment thereof that suited L.G. Murphy & Co, and if the farmers refused so to do, they were subjected to litigation and the whole judicial machinery was used ... to accomplish that object the result of these proceedings were that L.G. Murphy & Co were absolute monarchs of Lincoln County and ruled their subjects (the farmers and others) with oppressive iron heel. This state of affairs has existed for some time, at least ten years, and was carried out either by L.G. Murphy & Co or their successors.
    The said L.G. Murphy & Co in carrying out their schemes would drive out a settler who had opposed them ... and without a particle of right title or claim take possession of such persons real estate and claim that it belonged to them, and then rent it to some other person who was led to believe that it belonged to them – and if such person should afterwards find out that they had no right

title or interest in the property, and refused to pay them for the rental thereof, a system of persecution would be instituted which resulted in either the opposing party giving in or leaving the County. This rule of Murphy & Co and their successors continued until the matter was precipitated by the event of the killing of John. H. Tunstall – and that in order to support this monarchy it is reported that L.G. Murphy & Co and their successors have latterly surrounded themselves, and were employing the most desperate characters in the County. And affairs were carried by such a high hand after deponent came to this County and Murphy desiring to regain lost power and obtain control over the people desired ... to organize a vigilance committee ostensibly to put down horse stealing but really as after facts show to kill persons who were opposed to him, and among other persons to be disposed of he named to me that he was going to have this vigilance committee kill Hon. J.B. Patron, Stephen Stanley and Richard M. Brewer since deceased and he informed me that in as much as I appeared to support them I would have to leave the County – **Deponent further says that he discountenanced in every way this measure and used his influence to prevent that state of affairs, wishing rather that the people would stand by and see the laws enforced, these facts and the further fact that the people were determined to throw off the burden of Murphy & Co found that the power to influence courts, juries, and even to kill persons was being lost ... compelled them to resort to more desperate measures which culminated in the death of John H. Tunstall.**

Deponent has heard L.G. Murphy assert that he controlled not only the courts and juries, but that he could cause the death of any person who opposed him ...

The foregoing facts I believe are the formative cause of the troubles in Lincoln County at the present time. The direct and immediate cause ... was the death of John H. Tunstall which occurred as herein stated.

In November of 1876 John H. Tunstall came to this County for the purpose as he said of going into the stock raising business, & took steps to secure four thousand acres of land for that purpose and invested about $2500 in his business of stock raising and in merchandise for a store which he opened in Lincoln. At this time the firm of J.J. Dolan and John H. Riley seemed to be friends of his, and knowing that he had considerable money to invest, they tried to have him as far away from Lincoln as they could and also to get his money away so that he would be financially crippled and for that purpose tried to have him purchase L.G. Murphy's ranch at Fairview about 35 miles from Lincoln and knowing that I was a friend of Tunstall, they tried to induce me to use my influence with Tunstall to have him buy it and promised me if I would induce Tunstall to buy it, that they would give me $5000. I informed Tunstall of this offer and told him that they had no good title to the land and Tunstall refused to buy – this was the beginning of the enmity of Murphy, Dolan, & Riley against Tunstall.

During the month of August 1877 horses were stolen from Tunstall and myself by Jessie Evans and Tom Hill ... They were afterwards arrested at Beckwiths on the Seven Rivers by Sheriff Brady and lodged in [the pit] jail at Lincoln under an indictment for stealing said horses. That on or about the [blank] day of November 1877 I was informed by J.B. Patron that Evans, Baker, Hill, and Davis had filed off their shackles and cut the logs in their cell and were ready to make their escape. I told him to inform Sherriff Brady ... whereupon Brady, Patron, & Shields went and examined the said prisoners and the jail and found the statement to be true and correct. The Sheriff however took no precautionary steps to better secure their confinement.

A few days afterward Sheriff Brady came to Tunstalls store in a half intoxicated condition and indirectly accused Mr Tunstall of giving the credit of the arrest of said outlaws to R.M. Brewer (now deceased) and ... accused Mr Tunstall of having tried to aid Baker, Evans, Hill & Davis to escape. Mr. Tunstall told him you know their shackles are filed, & there are holes cut in the logs and take no pains to secure them, and do you dare to accuse me who have aided in the arrest of these persons, who have threatened my life, with assisting them to escape. Sheriff Brady thereupon put his hand on his revolver as though he was going to draw it and I stepped between them and placing my hand on his shoulder said it ill becomes you as a peace officer to violate the law by shooting. **Brady replied I won't shoot you now, you haven't long to run** ... and then left the store ...

A day or so after the prisoners referred above made their escape during the night ... Upon further investigation I found that no one had been left in charge of the jail that night, and that the doors [to the guardhouse above the pit, with its trap door opening up to the guardhouse] had not even been locked ... I am informed and verily believe that the augers and files ... [used to break the shackles] were packed in goods bought in the store of J.J. Dolan &

Co where Murphy resided, and by one of their employees (Pantaleon Gallegos) delivered to the said prisoners ... I went to Sheriff Brady and offered to raise twenty men to go and recapture the escaped prisoners. Brady replied I arrested them once and I will be d – if I am going to do it again ... Subsequently some of the escaped prisoners ... were seen at the store of J.J. Dolan ...

About this time it was reported that J.J. Dolan and Co were using the Territorial Tax money which Sheriff Brady had collected and not paid over to the Treasurer. In order to ... see if they were endeavoring to run the County in their own interests ... I enquired of them ... why they did not get the tax money from Brady, and Dolan said that Riley had already got it – [but Riley used that money to buy cattle for "The House"].

About June 24, 1874 Emil Fritz died in Germany, at this time his partner L.G. Murphy was Probate Judge. No steps were taken to administer on the estate of Fritz until about April 20, 1875 when one William Brady the late Sheriff of Lincoln Co. was appointed Administrator by said Murphy. At that time Dolan who had been clerk for L.G. Murphy & Co and afterwards partner of L.G. Murphy, and the said L.G. Murphy admitted to me that according to the books of the firm the said Emil Fritz had an interest in the business at the time of his death to the amount of about $48000 ... and that they desired that Charles Fritz and Emilie Scholand, brother and sister of the deceased, should have whatever interest Emil Fritz had in the business.

About that time I was employed by Brady administrator to make collections for the estate, and instructed by him that Dolan & Murphy should receive all money collected, *among the assets of the estate was a life insurance policy on the life of Fritz in the Merchants Life Insurance Company of New York City for $10000. Mr Brady, administrator, informed deponent that this policy had been placed in the hands of Levi Spiegelberg of New York City a member of the firm of Spiegelberg Brothers of Santa Fe New Mexico, by Mr L.G. Murphy without consulting him. (Brady)*

About the month of February 1876 I went in company with Mr Brady to Santa Fe, during our journey we became quite confidential with each other. Brady told me among other things that he was in the power of L.G. Murphy. After we got to Santa Fe he informed me that J.J. Dolan the junior partner of said Murphy had compelled him to give an order on Levi Spiegelberg, to place the money received on the Fritz policy to the credit of L.G. Murphy & Co with Spiegelberg & Bros of Santa Fe New Mexico, with whom at that time said L.G. Murphy & Co were greatly indebted for goods and merchandise.

In October 1876 Brady resigned his adminintratorship of the Fritz estate, and Emilie Scholand and Charles Fritz were appointed administratrix and administrator ... I was then employed by them on behalf of the estate [T]his policy among other things was placed in my hands to be attended to.

On that behalf I proceeded to St. Louis and consulted with parties as to the best course to be pursued in collecting the money, and also to obtain letters to some responsible part[ies] in New York City in order to collect the money on said policy. I received a letter of introduction to Donnell Lawson & Co Bankers of New York City. I proceeded to New York City – and after considerable trouble with Levi Spiegelberg ... who refused to deliver the papers in his possession belonging to the said estate, claiming among other things that he had an order from Brady the late adm. to pay the money to his firm Spiegelberg Bros of Santa Fe after several consultations with lawyers and said Levi Spiegelberg I obtained the papers. I thereupon entered into an agreement with Donnell Lawson & Co under and in pursuance of a power of attorney ...

On my return to Lincoln I found J.H. Riley was exceedingly angry and was trying to create trouble, during my absence he had broken into my office and destroyed some of my furniture grossly insulted my wife and vowed that he would run me out of the County.

About December 21, 1876 I caused notice to be served on the administratrix and administrator of the Fritz estate, and such proceedings were thereupon had that my accounts were approved by the Probate Judge ...

During the month of May 1877 L.G. Murphy of the late firm of L.G. Murphy & Co petitioned the Probate Court that a commission be appointed to examine the books of said firm in order to find out if ... the said [Fritz] estate was indebted to him ...

By this report it will appear that L.G. Murphy was indebted to said estate in the sum of $23376.10.

On or about the 1st day of August 1877 I received a letter from Donnell Lawson & Co Dated 19 July 1877, [and] a bill from Stam & Ruggles attorneys ...

That thereupon and on or about the 1st day of August 1877 I sent a letter to Mrs Emilie Scholan[d] and Charles Fritz administratrix and administrator of said Fritz estate informing them of the fact that the policy of insurance on the life of Fritz had been collected ... which letter was subsequently acknowledged by them to have been received in Aug aforesaid.

Deponent further says that on the same day ... he sent a copy of the same to L.G. Murphy out of courtesy [H]e [deponent] claims about this time for the first time to have some claim against the estate.

That hereafter and on or about the month of November 1877 I was requested to go to St. Louis on professional business, making no secret of my proposed journey. I even wrote friendly letters to my friends, among others Judge Bristol Judge Newcomb, A.J. Fountain and J.D. Bail informing them in connection with other business of my proposed trip and of the length of time I expected to be absent which was not to exceed six months.

Deponent further says that on or about the 15th of December 1877 Charles Fritz ... was in the office of deponent, then well knowing that deponent intended to go to St. Louis as aforesaid, that deponent informed said Fritz then and there **that as soon as he or any other person was authorized by Emilie Scholand to receive and receipt deponent for the money [from the Fritz estate], the money would be paid.** *Deponent further informed said Fritz of the nature of his business to St. Louis, how long he expected to be absent and who would attend to his business during his absence. That said Fritz therefore expressed himself as satisfied with deponents statement of the affairs of the estate ... D.P. Shield [McSween's law partner and brother-in-law] was present during said interview.*

Deponent further says that he has always been ready and now is, to pay over to the administrator and the administratrix of said estate the amount of money in his hands over and above the allowances made him by the Probate Court ... and his commission per agreement.

During January (1878) term of the Probate Court in and for said Lincoln County, said L.G. Murphy filed a claim against said estate of Fritz deceased to the amount of $76000 every dollar of which was disapproved by said Court and from which decision there has been no appeal the proof being that said Murphy owed the said estate about $30000 [$23,376.10]. **That deponent knows of his own knowledge that should he turn all the moneys in his hands over to said administrator and administratrix, without deducting his fees therefrom, he would never get a cent for his professional services to** *said estate ... the administrator and administratrix aforesaid being completely in the power of Murphy Dolan and Riley aforesaid, that said Fritz as deponent has been informed and believes has been threatened with summary vengeance by said Murphy Dolan & Riley if he and the administratrix should settle with deponent upon any other terms than receiving all the money in my hands collected for the aforesaid estate without the deduction of my account ... they threatening him [Charles Fritz] with ruin on the ground that he is heavily indebted to them. In this matter they (Murphy Dolan & Riley) have threatened to run him out of the County without a shirt unless he does as they desire him to do.*

I left Lincoln on the 18th of December 1877 in company with my wife and John S. Chisum my client and whose business I was then going to St. Louis to attend to.

On the 23rd of December 1877 we arrived at Las Vegas New Mexico. On the morning of the 24th I went to the office of Louis Salebasher a brother attorney. **He informed me that he had a telegram from T.B. Catron U.S. District Attorney inquiring if I was in Las Vegas.** *I told him to telegraph Mr Catron that I was, and then I determined and did wait to see what he wanted of me. [O]n the night of the 24 of December 1877 the Sheriff of San Miguel County called on my room at the hotel in Las Vegas and said he had a telegram from W.L. Rynerson Territorial District Attorney for the 3d Judicial District requesting him to arrest me for the crime of embezzlement and that the warrant would be sent on. The Sheriff left me at the hotel on my own parole and I waited until the warrant arrived, whereupon I & Mr Chisum were lodged in jail. I requested the Sheriff to take me before Judge Bristol for examination. [H]e refused. Whereupon I sent word to J.B. Patron to tell Sheriff Brady of Lincoln County who were both then in Santa Fe that I was a prisoner in jail and that I wanted him to take me down before Judge Bristol.*

Not hearing from Sheriff Brady and the Sheriff of San Miguel County refusing to take me before Judge Bristol I offered the said Sheriff of San Miguel County to give bonds in the quantity of $20000 to be approved by him for my appearance before Judge Bristol within ten days, at my own expense **to answer for the charge of embezzlement of $10000 realized from the aforementioned policy of insurance.** *He thereupon ... telegraphed to Santa Fe for instructions [from Catron] and refused* to accept the said offer made by me. He subsequently in conformity to the instructions received by telegraph from W.L. Rynerson proposed to me a compromise and let me go on my journey. This I refused absolutely to do preferring to return and face my accusers and stand trial.

On the 4<u>th</u> of January 1878 having been confined all this time in jail I proceeded to Mesilla by way of Lincoln in charge of Deputy Sheriff A.P. Barrier. I arrived at Mesilla on or about the 1<u>st</u> of February and thereafter I had an examination before Judge Bristol and after the evidence against me had been introduced, and it appeared that the testimony of Hon J.B. Patron who was in attendance at the session of the Legislature Hon Florencio Gonzales Probate Judge of Lincoln County and certain papers and files in his office were necessary for my case and on the suggestion of Judge Bristol and the Territorial District Attorney [Rynerson] I consented to a continuance until the meeting of the Grand Jury at Lincoln County April term of the District Court of said County whereupon bail was fixed by Judge Bristol at $8000 to be approved by the Territorial District Attorney and I was delivered to the charge of Deputy Sheriff Barrier aforesaid to be taken to Lincoln County and delivered to and held by Sheriff Brady of said County until I should give the aforesaid bail.

On or about the 5th day of February 1878 I started for Lincoln in charge of Deputy Sheriff Barrier and in the company with D.P. Shield J.B. Wilson and J.H. Tunstall. On the evening of the same day we camped at St Augustine [Shedd's Ranch], and shortly after going into camp Jessie Evans, Frank Baker, Long alias "[Frank] Rivers" notorious outlaws came into our camp and inquired as if we had passed J.J. Dolan on the road, whereupon D.P. Shields [Shield] replied that we had not that he understood that Mr Dolan would not leave till tomorrow morning (the 6<u>th</u>) Baker said that they had found Jimmie meaning (J.J. Dolan) very punctual in their arrangements with them and that Dolan had made an appointment with them to meet them here and that they believed he would come.

Deponent further says that it was a notorious fact that this Evans, Baker, Rivers and others had determined to take J.H. Tunstalls and my life owing to our activity in having them previously arrested for horse stealing.

Deponent further says that about one or two o'clock of the morning of the 6th of February 1878 said J.J. Dolan reached San Augustine aforesaid.

About 8 or 9 oclock of the said day whilst Tunstall, D.P. Shield, J.B. Wilson and this deponent were eating breakfast at their camping place at the east end of San Augustine corral, deponent saw J.J. Dolan with gun in hand and another man descending a house occupied by Mr. Shedd, said house being situated about 70 or 80 yards due south of where deponent, Tunstall, Wilson Shield and Barrier were camped said J.J. Dolan and the person accompanying him appeared to be going in a westerly direction thus hiding themselves from us by the southeast corner of said corral.

In a few minutes said J.J. Dolan and Jessie Evans came around the southeast corner of said corral. Mr. Dolan drew his Winchester carbine on Mr Tunstall and asked him if he was ready to fight and settle their difficulties. Mr Tunstall asked him if he asked him to fight a duel. Mr. Dolan replied "You d – d coward. I want you to fight and settle our difficulties." Dolan drew his gun cocked, on Mr Tunstall three times. Mr Barrier placed himself between or in line with Dolan & Evans and saved as I believe the lives of Tunstall and myself. When Mr Dolan was leaving he used these words "you won't fight this morning, you d – d coward but I'll get you soon." *[A]fter he had gone off about 20 yards he turned around and said to Tunstall "When you write to the "Independent" again say that I am with "The Boys." The term "The Boys" being used in Lincoln and neighborhood to denote notorious thieves and murderers such as Evans, Baker, Hill, and Davis – and the reason that he mentioned the "Independent" was because Tunstall had written said newspaper published at Mesilla New Mexico a letter dated January 18, 1878 which letter was published ... in its issue of the 26$^{\underline{th}}$ January 1878 charging W$^{\underline{m}}$ Brady Sheriff as aforesaid with having allowed said J.J. Dolan& Co to use the Territorial funds collected by said Brady as Ex officio collector of said Lincoln County and the Governor of said Territory in his message to the Legislature having reported that said Brady was in default in payment of the money collected by him (said Brady) ...*

Deponent further says that said letter elicited a reply from said J.J. Dolan, which was published in said Independent on or about the 2^d of February 1878 ...

Deponent further says that after the occurrence of the attempted killing of Tunstall and myself related above we started for Lincoln, after traveling about 20 miles we were passed on the road by said J.J. Dolan, Evans, Baker, Hill and Long alias "Rivers". Evans and

Baker rode with Mr Dolan in his ambulance [military conveyance]. It was known to Mr Dolan at the time that all these men were highwaymen and escaped prisoners.

On or about the 7th we saw Baker Hill and Long alias "Rivers" at the Mescalero Indian Agency – at this place they appeared to be quite familiar with Maj. Godfroy the agent ...

Deponent further says that when he arrived at the town of Lincoln he was informed that a courier had proceeded me from Mesilla with a writ of attachment. That Riley, Dolan and Murphy and Sheriff Brady were in ecstasy over deponents prospective confinement in the County [pit] jail and I was informed that Sheriff Brady was making the occasion a subject of merriment by making contracts to grind corn in the mexican mills to make gruel for my maintenance that said Riley had swept out the jail in order that he might in future have it to say that he swept out the room in which I was incarcerated. [T]hat said Brady expressed himself in the presence of E.A. Dow and others to the effect that Tunstall and I had reported that he (Brady) was a defaulter to the Territory, but that he meant to show us that he would not make a default in confining this deponent in jail and taking the spirit out of him – that he may have allowed Baker Evans and Hill to escape but that he would not allow deponent to do so.

Deponent further says that he found a writ of attachment had been issued out of the Third Judicial District Court in which said Emilie Scholand and Charles Fritz were plaintiffs – that it was dated the 7th of February 1878 and that **the Sheriff commenced to attach thereunder on the 8th it having been sent a distance of about 154 miles in almost unprecedented short time for this Territory – that he [Brady] not only attached my personal property but also my real, together with the property of J.H. Tunstall ... He (the Sheriff) was commanded to attach and safely keep so much property as would secure the sum of $8000 but he attached property both real and personal worth over $40000. At this time I was not Mr Tunstalls partner though I was to become such by articles of agreement in May 1878.** I was his attorney and took an active part in the management of his business ... No resistance of any kind or character was offered by deponent to the Sheriff Brady in the execution of said writ of attachment ...

Deponent further says that on or about the 14th of February 1878 Mr Tunstall was informed that one J.B. Matthews (who was in the employ of Murphy and attended to any thing that Dolan and

Riley desired done) was at his (Tunstalls) Ranch with said Baker Evans Hill and Davis as Sheriffs posse to attach Tunstalls cattle and horses as the property of this deponent. That said J.B. Matthews as Sheriff Bradys Deputy was informed that deponent had neither cattle or horses there but that he could "round up" and if he found any he could take them, that he could not take Tunstalls property ... That said J.B. Matthews stated that he would return to Lincoln and report to Brady - that he would return in a day or so probably but that he would bring only one man with him.

R.M. Brewer who was Tunstalls foreman told him [Matthews] that when he came he would "round up" the cattle & horses & he could see if there were any of McSweens horses or cattle there. On or about the 14th of February 1878 Robert Widenman[n] came in from Tunstalls cattle ranch and informed Tunstall in my hearing ... that he was satisfied that Matthews intended to raise a large posse and take the cattle by force, that for that purpose said Baker had gone down to Dolan & Companys cow camp on the Pecos with instructions to Wm Morton their foreman to raise all the men he could and meet Matthews with his posse at Turkey Springs a few miles from Tunstalls cattle ranch on the evening of the 16th February 1878. **Mr Tunstall was informed in my hearing by George Washington [a Lincoln resident] that Murphy, Riley & Dolan had helped Matthews to raise a force to the number of 43 men, that said Riley informed him (Washington) that there was no use in McSweens and Tunstalls trying to get away from them this time as they had them completely in their power that they could not possibly be beat as they had the District Attorney (meaning Rynerson) the Court and all the power in Santa Fe [Catron] to back them, that their plan was to take the cattle from Tunstalls ranch ... so as to draw the men in Tunstalls house out of it, then the balance of the posse were to take possession of the house and "get" Tunstalls men.** *[U]pon this information Mr Tunstall canceled to go to the ranch and induced his men to leave and allow Matthews and posse to take the property and seek his remedy in the courts, for the purpose as he informed me he left Lincoln on the night of the 16th. This was the last time I saw Tunstall alive.*

I have been informed by R.M. Brewer (deceased) John Middleton, **W Bonney***, R.A. Widenmann, F.T. Waite and Henry Brown that as Tunstall reached his cattle ranch on the night of the*

17th and commanded them all to leave the ranch and come to Lincoln which they did McCloskey (deceased) informed me that Mr Tunstall [told him] to get one Martin ["Dutch" Martin Martz] who was a good cattle man to come to the ranch and turn the cattle over to Deputy Sheriff J.B. Matthews ... **that he would not sacrifice the life of one of his men for all the cattle for they would all be killed if they remained at the ranch.** *Said McCloskey informed me further that he not only delivered that verbal message to said Martin but told the same to said J.B. Matthews and informed him that Mr Tunstall would offer no resistance to the taking of the property, though none of it belonged to this deponent.*

Deponent further says that on the night of the 18th February 1878 he was informed by R.M. Brewer, **W. Bonney***, J. Middleton and R.A. Widenmann that said J.H. Tunstall was murdered on the road to Lincoln about 30 miles from his cattle ranch by Jessie Evans, Frank Baker, J.J. Dolan, W. Morton, T. Cocoran, P. Gallegos, A.L. Roberts, Tom Hill, George Davis, Robert W. Beckwith, Tom Green, George Hindman, J. Hurley and others to the number of 18 men ... I am informed that Tom Green who was present when the murder was committed that Morton who was acting as Deputy under orders from said Deputy Matthews called out to Tunstall to stop that he wanted to see him and that they did not want to hurt him, and that thereupon Mr Tunstall dismounted and walked towards Morton and delivered him a Colts pistol carried by him (Tunstall) and that a few minutes thereafter Jessie Evans aforesaid took aim at Mr Tunstall and shot him the ball taking effect in his breast and that as he (Tunstall) fell on his face, said Morton fired another shot at Mr Tunstall out of Tunstalls revolver the ball entering the back of his head and coming out in the forehead and that* **thereafter Morton walked to Tunstalls horse and shot another shot out of Tunstalls pistol at said horse whereupon the horse dropped dead and that the murderers carried the corpse of said Tunstall and laid him close to the said horse putting his hat under the dead horse's head.**

On the night last above this deponent wrote a note to John Newcomb requesting him to go to where Tunstalls corpse was and bring it into Lincoln that it might have a decent burial. That on the night of the 19th February 1878 said John Newcomb with others brought into Lincoln the lifeless body of said Tunstall. Said Newcomb informed me then and there that ... when he found the body it was lying close by the side of the dead horse ... and that Tunstalls hat was lying under the head of said dead horse. That on the night of the day last mentioned a coroners inquest was held on the body of said Tunstall ... **That on or about the 20th I carried the body of said Tunstall to be embalmed and a post mortem examination made by Drs Ealy and Appel, that not only was the body shot as already stated but the skull was broken into pieces by a blow from some instrument after being shot as aforesaid,** *that on the 19th day of February 1878 I caused affidavits to be filed before J.B. Wilson Justice of the Peace within the said town of Lincoln charging the murder of Mr Tunstall on the parties named upon which affidavits a warrant of arrest for such parties was duly issued and said affidavits placed in the hands of Atonacio Martinez constable in and for said town of Lincoln for execution ...*

That upon the 20th day of February 1878 said constable Martinez called upon W. Bonney and F.T. Waite to help him serve said warrant. *That it was well known that ten or twelve of the murderers of Mr Tunstall were then and there in the house ["The House"] of L.G. Murphy Dolan and Riley aforesaid – That as this deponent is informed by said constable said constable proceeded to said house ... to make arrests ...* **[H]e met the said Sheriff Brady who without any warrant or authority of law took the said Bonney and Waite [and Constable Martinez] prisoners and refused to aid or allow them to arrest though the majority of said murderers were then and there with said Sheriff. [T]hat on the evening of the day last mentioned said Constable was released and Bonney and Waite retained for two days more.**

That after the burial of Mr Tunstall on the 22nd of February 1878 a meeting of the citizens of Lincoln County was held to prevent further bloodshed if possible – that at such meeting Hon Florencio Gonzales Probate Judge of said County, Isaac Ellis, merchant, Jose Montaño, merchant, and John Newcomb farmer were appointed a committee to wait for said Sheriff Brady to ascertain why he prevented the said constable from executing said warrant and making arrests as therein directed and took said constable and posse as aforesaid prisoners and still **held Bonney and Waite as such. [T]hey informed me on their return that Sheriff Brady said he held both the constable and posse prisoners because he had the power,** *they further informed me that ... he would not take a* bond of any kind from the deponent for said property [in the embezzlement case].

Deponent further says that five or six deputies were put by said Brady in charge of the store of J.H. Tunstall, decd. with its stock of general merchandise attached as the property of deponent ... [T]hat on or about the 18th day of February 1878 said Sheriff Brady had a detachment of United States soldiers from Fort Stanton stationed at the house of Murphy, Dolan & Riley aforesaid and that he caused to be issued for the horses belonging to such detachment the hay belonging to Mr Tunstall in his lifetime without authority or permission ... [T]hat on the 19th day of February 1878 an affidavit was filed with said J.B. Wilson Justice of the Peace charging said Deputy Brady deputies as aforesaid with appropriation of goods [the hay] ... and that as a result ... Brady was held to await the action of the Lincoln County Grand Jury for April 1878 ...

Deponent further says that on the 11th day of February 1878 he made and executed an appearance bond as required by Judge Bristol and sent the same by Registered Letter to W.L. Rynerson District Attorney ... Said bond was refused ... Jose Montaño merchant in said town of Lincoln volunteered to become one of my bondsmen ... Subsequently he [Montaño] informed deponent that he was threatened with ruin by J.J. Dolan & Co if he became one of my bondsmen. The said Sheriff as said Montaño informed the deponent, used all his influence with said Montaño to prevent his becoming one of my surities ... so as to prevent me from giving bonds and to oblige me to go to jail. Joseph H. Blazer informed me that J.J. Dolan & Co had also threatened that if he became one of my bondsmen they would have him prosecuted for cutting timber in the Public Lands ... in the U.S. Courts by T.B. Catron U.S. District Attorney in Santa Fe.

A few days after the execution of said Bond said Sheriff Brady called upon said Jose Montaño as the latter informed me, with a letter purporting to be from said W.L. Rynerson to the effect that though a friend to said Montaño he could not accept him a bond of this amount and requesting that he draw his name from said bond. After such representations and coaxing by said Sheriff, said Montaño signed a letter complying with said request of withdrawal, written by said Brady. The surities on said bond *justified in different sums amounting to the aggregate sum of $34500.* **Deponent was informed by G. Washington that he heard Brady and Riley aforesaid say that there was no use in deponent trying to give bonds as W.L. Rynerson aforesaid would not approve of any that he (deponent) would give & that he would have to go to jail.**

Deponent now learnt that J.J. Dolan went to Mesilla to get an alias warrant for this deponent [Alias warrants are issued when a person fails to respond to a citation; here posting bond in lieu of going to jail. If there has been no final judgment - here by the Grand Jury - bond can be posted to lift that warrant; but here all bonds have been purposefully refused to justify Brady's jailing McSween], said **Deputy Sheriff Barrier having failed to deliver me to said Brady he having been induced to that course by the representations of the best citizens in said County that if he delivered this deponent to said Brady deponent would thereby lose his life** – [T]hat this deponent informed the said Deputy Sheriff from Las Vegas that as a matter of law he would be guilty of contempt of court by failing to comply with his warrant, but that from that species of offences he could purge himself but at no time did I ask or request said Barrier not to comply with his warrant though **I believed then as I do now that had I been delivered to Brady aforesaid I would have been murdered ...**

Deponent further says that a day or so after the death of Tunstall Col. Purington, Lieutenant Goodwin, Delaney, Payne, and Humphrey U.S. A. Fort Stanton N.M. called at the residence of deponent (where a large number of men all farmers or stockmen had congregated of their own free will and arrived as they expressed it to protect the life of the deponent) in order to ascertain in a friendly unofficial way the state of affairs ... **Said Col. Purington then and there in a private interview informed me that he was satisfied that Tunstall was brutally murdered at the instigation of "The House" a term used here to mean Murphy, Dolan & Riley aforesaid that it was a fact that could not be disputed that they supported thieves and murderers by buying stolen cattle from them (the thieves) and that it was no doubt but that they brought Evans Baker, Hill and Davis aforesaid into the County this time for a bad purpose – that there was no doubt in his mind that if said Barrier would turn me over to Brady aforesaid I would be killed.**

Deponent further says that on or about the 24th of February 1878 he was informed that said J.J. Dolan went to Mesilla to see W.L. Rynerson aforesaid for the purpose of obtaining an alias warrant for my arrest and another for the arrest of said Barrier and that though I was entreated by the citizens both American and Mexican to quit the town of Lincoln at once for a while, that I done so first remaining at one farm house and then another. That on or about the 9th day of March I returned to the town of Lincoln with the determination to remain there and submit to any order said Brady might get against me even if I lost my life. [U]pon my arrival at Lincoln about 2 pm of the day last mentioned I learnt that his Excellency S.B. Axtell Governor of New Mexico had been to Lincoln and had left a short time before my arrival and that he had removed J.B. Wilson Justice of the Peace aforesaid.

Everybody with whom I conversed appeared to be very much disheartened owing to the refusal of the Governor to hear them in relation to the troubles and in removing Wilson claiming that the Governor had espoused the cause of Murphy Dolan & Riley aforesaid and cited the fact ... that he had procured troops for said Brady by order of the President. *D.P. Shield, I. Ellis and R.A. Widenmann informed me that the Governor positively refused to hear anything from the people about the troubles ...*

Hon F. Gonsales [Gonzales, San Patricio Probate Judge], I. Ellis, J. Montaño and J. Newcomb aforesaid and many others insisted that I absent myself under the circumstances as hereinbefore stated until the meeting of the District Court to which I reluctantly consented.

On or about the [blank] day of [blank] 1878 R.M. Brewer was deputized by J.B. Wilson Justice of the Peace to serve a warrant for the arrest of W. Morton and Frank Baker two of the alleged murderers of Tunstall ...

That said Morton and Baker were then at the cow camp of J.J. Dolan & Co aforesaid on the Pecos River a distance of at least 150 miles. That on or about the night of the 10th of March 1878 R.M. Brewer came to see me before I should leave the town of Lincoln that then and there he informed me that he and posse arrested said Morton & Baker and that within 30 miles of Lincoln, W Morton snatched the pistol of one W McCloskey ... now one of Brewers posse and shot said McCloskey in the head and then put to the mountains ... that *thereupon the posse chased and killed said Morton & Baker. Said Brewer after relating the death of said three persons ... requested me to advise him as to how to make his return. Deponent then informed Mr Brewer of the Governors visit, his removal of J.B. Wilson, his forbading said Wilson in person not to exercise the functions of such Justice of the Peace any longer and that he was about to issue a proclamation ... I further informed Brewer that I understood that Murphy Dolan and Riley had taken steps to have him and posse arrested for undertaking to arrest Morton & Baker by virtue of warrants issued by said J.B. Wilson. I advised Mr Brewer to keep away from Lincoln and out of the way of Murphy, Dolan & Riley until the District Court convened when I was satisfied we would get justice. I parted with Brewer on the night last aforesaid and have not seen him since and am credibly informed that he is dead. I knew Mr Brewer since I came to the County of Lincoln. He was a man who never drank any kind of liquor nor quarreled with anyone and was thoroughly honest. He was a hardworking farmer and stockman. Our people ... considered him one of our best & most peaceful citizens. He was not on good terms with Murphy Dolan & Riley, he often expressed himself to the effect that he knew they wanted to kill him. He strongly opposed the organization of the Vigilance Committee referred to elsewhere in this statement. I know of my own knowledge that he paid them in two years $1000 rental for a piece of unsurveyed public lands and when he refused to continue to pay they wanted him killed or out of the way.*

Deponent further says that from the time he returned from Mesilla until he left Lincoln ... nearly every person who came to see him urged him to leave the town until Court met stating that unless deponent done so he would lose his life. [T]hat on or about 10 of March 1878 deponent left the town of Lincoln in company with G. Washington, G. Robinson and Deputy Sheriff A. P. Barrier aforesaid for [John Chisum's] South Spring River Ranch in said County of Lincoln a distance of 70 miles from said town of Lincoln where I remained until on or about the 29 of March 1878 when I left in company with J. Chisum, R.M. Gilbert Dr M.R. Leverson ... and my wife for the town of Lincoln to attend court.

On the 28th day of March 1878 said Sheriff Brady with a posse of soldiers went to South Spring River Ranch to summons jurors, John S. Chisum informed me that Brady then and there assured him that he did not want to arrest me ... as he knew

I would be at court. By a clerical mistake the venire was made returnable on the 1ˢᵗ Monday of April whereas the term set by law for the holding of the District Court of said County of Lincoln is the second Monday of April ...

But for the fact that the Sheriff stated as I am informed that court was to have begun on the 1ˢᵗ Monday I should not have left South Spring River Ranch for another week, having no faith in the guarantees of Brady that he would not arrest me ... **On the 1ˢᵗ day of April 1878 in company with the aforementioned persons I went to the town of Lincoln and then and there learnt for the first time that said Brady and Geo Hindman had been killed on said day.** *On said day in the evening at Lincoln one George W. Peppin, a tool of Murphy Dolan & Riley, with Lieut Smith and a few soldiers from the fort arrested me on the alias warrant already referred to said G.W. Peppin claiming to be acting as the Deputy of the dead Sheriff Brady.*

Seeing that Peppin aforesaid, J.B. Matthews aforesaid and three of Tunstalls alleged murderers were endorsed in all they done by Col George Purington with U.S. soldiers I appealed to Col Purington for protection. He acknowledged that if he left me in custody of said Peppin Matthews et al, he believed that I would be killed by them, but he claimed that he had no place for me at the fort. My friends insisted that W. Dowling Post Trader at Fort Stanton had a room that I could secure ... After much entreaty he consented to take me up to the fort where subsequently he came near preventing me from securing a room aforesaid.

He appeared to be anxious to leave me in custody of Peppin aforesaid ...

Deponent further says that G.W. Peppin went to said Col Purington and asked him (Purington) if he would allow him (Peppin) to search the house of deponent for arms. Purington replied in the affirmative. Peppin and posse then went to the house to search, deponent forbade them to enter unless they had a warrant. I used these words on that occasion "Peppin you know that you are not an officer, but were you you can't search without a warrant for that purpose" whereupon Matthews aforesaid replied "We can't aye we'll show you what we can do" ... During all this Dr Leverson [McSween's houseguest] said to Purington that the constitution of the U.S. guaranteed a man immunity from search seizure &c whereupon Col Purington used these words "Damn the constitution and you for a fool" ...

Deponent further says that D.P. Shield G. Washington, Geo Robinson, and R.A. Widenmann were arrested by said G.W. Peppin & posse without warrant charging them with being implicated in the murder of Brady and Hindman. That Col Purington was appealed to by said persons for protection and that he consented to take them to the fort with the deponent ... Purington placed a guard at each door [of the custody rooms] ... with orders to shoot any or all of us who left the rooms without permission ...

[AUTHOR'S NOTE: N.A.M. Dudley assumed Fort Stanton's Command on April 5, 1878, and granted them "the liberty of the Post until the District Court convened." So McSween wrongly thought that Dudley, unlike Purington, was unbiased.]

The District Court convened April 8, 1978 ...
Deponent further says that the Grand Jury for the April (1878) term of said District Court for the County of Lincoln examined the charges of embezzlement against this deponent and their findings [were that deponent was innocent of embezzling] ...
That on or about the 18th day of February 1878 JH Riley aforesaid came to the residence of the deponent in a drunken condition, that at this time Mr Riley was anxious to show that he had no weapons about his person and to convince persons in the room [gathered after Tunstall's murder] of that fact turned out his pockets, that in doing so he threw out a memorandum book and after asking the men in the house ... if they wanted to kill him and receiving a reply in the negative took his departure leaving said memorandum book on the table at the residence of the deponent.
Deponent says that he examined said book with great care, that he found a letter in it in the handwriting of said W.L. Rynerson addressed to Dolan & Riley [the February 14, 1878 Friends Dolan and Riley letter anticipating Tunstall's murder] ... there was also a memorandum of cattle received by said Dolan & Riley from notorious cattle thieves whose names were given. ***That it also contained a list of names of persons well known in this county for their friendship for or opposition to said Dolan & Riley opposite each name was a nome de plume.***
Catron being "Grapes" Godfroy "Hampton" Burnstein (Indian agent clerk) "soapweed" Indians "Tree" Delaney

(soldier at Fort Stanton) *"Warwick"* Murphy aforesaid *"Box"* Rynerson (District Attorney aforesaid) *"Oyster"* Dowling (Post Trader at Fort Stanton) *"Pimp"* and McSween (the deponent) *"Diablo"* – Devil &c &c

Deponent further says that he has often expressed himself to the effect that he was determined to use all lawful means to bring the murderers of Tunstall to justice if it cost him every dollar he possessed or could earn. That after the adjournment of the April 1878 term of the said District Court for Lincoln County deponent learnt from the Sheriff of said County [John Copeland] that the **Prosecuting Attorney said W.L. Rynerson had failed and refused to place warrants in his hands for the arrest of parties indicted for the murder of Tunstall [Dolan, Evans, and Seven Rivers boys], but had placed warrants in the Sheriff's hands for the arrest of all indicted persons supposed to sympathize with feeling against Murphy, Dolan and Riley**

[AUTHOR'S NOTE: These are the indictments of Billy Bonney and others for the murders of Brady, Hindman, and Roberts that would be the basis of Billy's pardon appeal in 1879.]

that thereupon and on or about the 27th day of April 1878 deponent addressed and sent a letter to W.L. Rynerson asking him to place warrants in the hands of said Sheriff for the arrest of all persons indicted by said Grand Jury for the murder of said Tunstall ... that afterwards to wit on or about the 4th day of May 1878 deponent received from said W.L. Rynerson and answer to said letter dated April 27 1878.

Deponent further says that from all he can gather the recent troubles in Lincoln County are owing to the determination of Murphy Dolan and Riley to prevent opposition to their business and that nothing else is the cause of Tunstalls death

[AUTHOR'S NOTE: McSween never fully conceptualized the Santa Fe Ring's motive in the conflict, though he was aware of "the House's" connection to T.B. Catron.]

that the deponent has been satisfied that the parties named (Murphy Dolan and Riley) have been working to take the life of this deponent for the last two years, and that to do that said Dolan offered one Stephen Stanley (as deponent is informed and believes)

$1000. This deponent declares in the most solemn manner that he knows of no reason for the hatred of Murphy Dolan and Riley towards him other than deponent has professionally and as a neighbor helped people to throw off the yoke of said Murphy, Dolan & Riley, informing parties of their rights when requested so to do, and by encouraging emigration [like Tunstall's] and helping those who were in the County to remain whether acceptable to Murphy Dolan & Riley or not. That I have done all in my power, a man and a citizen, to stimulate our people to energy and independence of action and character and that this course caused Murphy, Dolan & Riley together with their way of dealing with the people to lose their power, their loss of power having finally culminated in the death of Tunstall. That a petition ... was signed by every resident of Lincoln County to whom it was presented asking them to leave the County and giving as a reason that our people might have permanent peace.

Deponent further says that on or about the 4<u>th</u> day of April 1878 Richard M. Brewer aforesaid and A.L. Roberts one of the alleged murderers of Tunstall was killed at Mescalero Apache Indian Agency in this county under the following circumstances as was related to me by one who was present and saw the shooting from beginning to end (Frank Coe) ... Brewer Coe and others went to the Agency – some to look for stolen stock – some for business – all to talk to the Indian Agent for harboring alleged murderers and thieves who were helping Murphy, Dolan & Riley against the people, there they met A.L. Roberts one of Tunstalls alleged murderers who drew his gun on Chas Bowdre and fired as he [Bowdre] approached said Roberts, the bullet grazing Bowdres abdomen, whereupon Bowdre fired at Roberts, the bullet entering the stomach of Roberts. Roberts now shot Middleton & Coe not fatally, and killed Brewer aforesaid.

That on or about the 1<u>st</u> day of May I was informed by Saturnino Baca that five men had wanted to enter his house & secrete themselves for the purpose of killing me and others – that they said they had killed a man or two [killed Frank MacNab] a few miles below belonging to the "Regulators." **We now received tidings to the effect that ten or twelve men were stationed at the house ["the House"] west of my house formerly occupied by Murphy, Dolan & Riley but now controlled by T.B. Catron U.S. District Attorney Santa Fe – being represented by his**

brother in law E.A. Walz *... [and] that there were 20 more well armed men on the East of my residence – [U]pon this information the sheriff (Copeland) placed 4 or 5 men on my house for the protection of my life and property and done the same as he and others informed me in the centre and at the east end of the town. Learning that these men numbered 30 or more men said Copeland as I am informed sent for a detachment of soldiers to aid him in resisting said bands of men. From Frank Coe I learned that when on his way home from said Lincoln to wit on or about the 11th day of May 1878 [sic – April 29, 1878] in company with Frank McNab [MacNab] and James Sanders they were fired at by different parties of men in ambush in different directions, killed McNab [MacNab] and dangerously if not fatally wounded Sanders ... and holding said [Frank] Coe until next day as hostage – that the party after that came to the town of Lincoln and divided as already stated. [J]ust about noon of said day firing was commenced by the Sheriffs party or by the murderers ... About 3 o'clock in the afternoon of the same day Lieut Smith and a number of soldiers with Sheriff Copeland took about 22 men prisoners. Deponent has been informed that said 22 men after killing McNab [MacNab] and wounding Sanders as aforesaid desired to attack the store of I. Ellis but that after going near the building about daylight next day said posse found the doors and windows of said house were kept closed for the purpose they supposed of concealing armed men [Regulators] from their view and so abandoned the purpose.*

That on or about the 3rd day of May 1878 an affidavit was filed with J.G. Trujillo Justice of the Peace of Precinct No 2 in said Lincoln County charging R.W. Beckwith, Johnson and 20 others with the murder of McNab [MacNab] and wounding of Sanders aforesaid – that a warrant was issued on said affidavit and was placed in the hands of Sheriff Copeland for execution. That on or about the 4th day of May 1878 this deponent with several others went to Precinct No 2 for the purpose of testifying against the 22 men aforesaid.

That on or about the 6th day of May 1878 Lieuts. Goodwin and Smith with about 25 soldiers in charge of the said Sheriff came to said Precinct No 2 with warrants for the arrest of all witnesses against said 22 men – that the warrant on which affidavit and others were sought to be arrested was issued by D. Easton Justice of the Peace for Precinct No 3 and that the offence charged was assault with intent to kill based upon an affidavit before some military officer in Fort Stanton by said G.W. Peppin and

J.B. Matthews - That this deponent was grossly insulted by Lieut Goodwin - That said Goodwin refused to obey the Sheriff and informed the Sheriff then and there that he would not allow any one to be arrested unless the Sheriff turned the deponent over to him (Goodwin) to be taken to Fort Stanton - That said Goodwin positively refused to obey the Sheriffs orders – That Goodwin by his words and acts showed himself to be a bitter partisan – That after reaching Fort Stanton this deponent with I. Ellis & Sons and others were put in the guardhouse in Fort Stanton – that we were kept in confinement for two days – that we were taken from the guard house to have an examination by a justice of the peace – that the 22 men referred to as I am informed were turned loose and failed to be taken or go before a Justice of the Peace so the charge of murder still remains against them without examination.

Deponent has been informed that said Johnson with the balance of the 22 men as posse, was acting as the Deputy of Sheriff Brady who had been dead at that time about two months a fact known to said Johnson & his party [thus, not a legal deputy].

Deponent has been informed that said 22 men started from the Pecos [the Seven Rivers boys] for Lincoln for the purpose of killing I. Ellis, Sheriff Copeland and this deponent.

Deponent further says that nearly all of said 22 men were the persons and tools of said Murphy Dolan & Riley deriving their support chiefly from said Murphy Dolan & Riley ...

Deponent further says that Tunstall was one of the quietest and most inoffensive men he has ever seen, a man who neither offended by word or deed – he was industrious and thoroughly honest and truthful.

Deponent further says he has given a concrete statement of the troubles in said Lincoln Co that culminated in the death of Tunstall and of the discord and violence that has followed so far as the knowledge and information of the deponent extends – that he has given a true statement of events without regard as to the light in which the same may place him.

A.A. McSween

Read subscribed and sworn to before me this 6<u>th</u> day of June 1878 –
Rafael Sutienes
Probate Clerk
By Juan B. Patron
Deputy [Clerk]

CATRON'S FEDERAL INDICTMENT PLOT: JUNE 21, 1878

With his opponents unexpectedly fighting back without sign of retreat, and a presidential investigation ongoing into the role of U.S. officials - like himself - in John Tunstall's murder and Lincoln County "troubles," Thomas Benton Catron intervened personally to bolster his standard Ring outlaw myth. Among his scapegoats would be Billy as "the Kid;" a local nickname Catron likely learned from James Dolan.

The Brady and Hindman killings came under Territorial law, not Catron's federal jurisdiction. So Catron alleged that the Blazer's Mill killing of Andrew "Buckshot" Roberts was on federal land of the Mescalero Indian Reservation, so that he, as U.S. Attorney, could file federal Case 411 against the Regulators as: "United States vs. Charles Bowdry [Bowdre], Doc Scurlock, Henry Brown, Henry Antrim - alias Kid - John Middleton, Stephen Stevens, John Scroggins, George Coe and Frederick Waite."

The implication of this crafty maneuver went unrecognized until 1881. And unbeknownst to Billy, his pardon from Governor Lew Wallace would depended on it. Catron wrote:

The United States of America)
Territory of New Mexico   )
Third Judicial District   )

In the United States District Court for the Third Judicial District of the June Term of 1878.
The Grand Jury of the United States of America from the body of the good and lawful men of the Third Judicial District aforesaid – duly empanneled sworn and charged to the Term of aforesaid to inquire in and for the body of the Third Judicial District aforesaid upon their oaths do present that Charles Bowdry [Bowdre], Doc Scurlock, Henry Brown, **Henry Antrim – alias Kid** *– John Middleton, Stephen Stevens, John Scroggins, George Coe and Frederick Waite, late of the Third Judicial District in the Territory of New Mexico on the fifth [sic - fourth] day of April in the year of our Lord Eighteen hundred and Seventy-eight* **at and in this reservation of the Mescalero Apache Indians in the Said Third Judicial District, Said Reservation then and there being a part of the Indian country,** *with force*

and armed in and upon one Andrew Roberts then and there being in the Said Reservation feloniously, willfully, unlawfully of this malice aforethought and from a premeditated design to effect the death of the Said Andrew Roberts, did make an assault, and that the Said Charles Bowdry [Bowdre], Doc Scurlock, Henry Brown, **Henry Antrim – alias Kid** – John Middleton, Stephen Stevens, John Scroggins, George Coe and Frederick Waite certain guns then and there loaded and charged with gunpowder and divers leaden bullets, which said guns the Said Charles Bowdry [Bowdre], Doc Scurlock, Henry Brown, **Henry Antrim (alias Kid)** John Middleton, Stephen Stevens, John Scroggins, George Coe and Frederick Waite in their hands then and there had and held to, against and upon the Said Andrew Roberts there and then within the Said Reservation feloniously, willfully, unlawfully of this malice aforethought and from a premeditated design to effect the death of the Said Andrew Roberts – did shoot and discharge, and that the Said Charles Bowdry [Bowdre], Doc Scurlock, Henry Brown, **Henry Antrim – alias Kid** – John Middleton, Stephen Stevens, John Scroggins, George Coe and Frederick Waite, with the leaden Bullets aforesaid, out of the guns aforesaid, then and there by force of the gunpowder that discharged and sent forth as aforesaid and on Roberts in and upon the right side of the belly of him the Said Andrew Roberts then and there within the Said Reservation feloniously, willfully, unlawfully of this malice aforethought and from a premeditated design to effect the death of the Said Andrew Roberts, did strike, penetrate and wound, giving to the said Andrew Roberts then and there and within the said Reservation and with the leaden Bullets aforesaid, that discharged and sent forth out of the guns aforesaid by the said Andrew [Charles] Bowdry [Bowdre], Doc Scurlock, Henry Brown, **Henry Antrim – alias Kid** – John Middleton, Stephen Stevens, John Scroggins, George Coe and Frederick Waite in and upon the right side of the belly of him the said Andrew Roberts one mortal wound of the depth of ten inches and of breadth of one half of an inch of which said mortal wound the Said Andrew Roberts then and there at the said Reservation instantly died and so the Jury aforesaid upon their oaths as aforesaid do say that the Said Charles Bowdry [Bowdre], Doc Scurlock, Henry Brown, **Henry Antrim – alias Kid** – John Middleton, Stephen Stevens, John Scroggins, George Coe and Frederick Waite the Said Andrew Roberts in manner and form aforesaid feloniously, *willfully, unlawfully of this malice aforethought and from a premeditated design to effect the death of the Said Andrew Roberts, did kill and murder against the form of the Statute in such case made and provided against the Peace & dignity of the United States. And the Jurors aforesaid upon their oaths aforesaid do further present that Charles Bowdry [Bowdre] late of the Third Judicial District in the Territory of New Mexico on the fifth day of April in the year AD Eighteen hundred and Seventy-eight at and within the Reservation of the Mescalero Apache Indians said Reservation being then and there situate in the Third Judicial District aforesaid and then and there being Indian Country in and upon Andrew Roberts then and there being in the Said Reservation in the Said District, feloniously, willfully, unlawfully of his malice aforethought and from a premeditated design to effect the death of the Said Andrew Roberts did make an assault and that the Said Charles Bowdry a certain gun then and there loaded and charged with gunpowder and one leaden Bullet which gun he the Said Charles Bowdry [Bowdre] in his right hand then and there had and held to at against and upon the Said Andrew Roberts then and there within the Said Reservation feloniously, willfully, unlawfully of his malice aforethought and from a premeditated design to effect the death of the Said Andrew Roberts, did shoot and discharge and that the Said Charles Bowdry [Bowdre] with the leaden Bullet aforesaid out of the gun aforesaid then and there by force of the gunpowder aforesaid shot and sent forth as aforesaid the Said Andrew Roberts in and from the right side of the belly of him the Said Andrew Roberts then and there and in the Said Reservation feloniously, willfully, unlawfully of his malice aforethought and from a premeditated design to effect the death of the Said Andrew Roberts, did strike, penetrate and wound, giving to the Said Andrew Roberts then and there with the leaden Bullet aforesaid so as aforesaid that discharged and sent forth out of the gun aforesaid by the Said Charles in and upon the right side of the belly of the Said Andrew Roberts one mortal wound of ten inches and of breadth of one half of an inch of which said mortal wound the Said Andrew Roberts then and there at the said Reservation instantly died and the Jury aforesaid upon their oaths aforesaid do further present that Doc Scurlock, Henry Brown,* **Henry Antrim – alias Kid** *– John Middleton, Stephen Stevens, John Scroggins, George Coe and Frederick Waite* of the Third Judicial District aforesaid and on the day and year aforesaid with force and arms at the Said Reservation in the Said District aforesaid feloniously was present aiding and abetting and assisting the [Said] Charles Bowdry [Bowdre] the felony and murder aforesaid to do and commit against the form of the Statute in such case made and provided against the Peace & dignity of the United States and the Jurors aforesaid upon their oaths aforesaid do say that the Said Charles Bowdry Doc Scurlock, Henry Brown, **Henry Antrim – alias Kid** – John Middleton, Stephen Stevens, John Scroggins, George Coe and Frederick Waite in manner and form aforesaid feloniously, willfully, unlawfully of his malice aforethought and from a premeditated design to effect the death of him the Said Andrew Roberts, him the Said Roberts did kill and murder against the form of the Statute in such case made and provided and against the peace and dignity of the United States.

      Thomas B. Catron
      United States Attorney
      for New Mexico

411

The United States
vs)
)
Charles Bowdry [Bowdre], Doc Scurlock, Henry Brown, **Henry Antrim alias "Kid,"** John Middleton, Stephen Stevens, John Scroggins, George Coe and Frederick Waite

A true bill
 C.P. Crawford
 Foreman of the Grand Jury

Witnesses

Aurelius Wilson, John Palen, John Watts, J.H. Blazer, Sam F. Mills, [missing first name] Howe, William Gentry

Filed in my Office
the 21 day of June 1878
 John S. Crouch, Clerk

CITIZENS REQUEST PRESIDENTIAL AID

LETTER OF GEORGE COE: JUNE 22, 1878

The voice of the Regulators can be heard in the June 22, 1878 letter of J. Isaacs and George Coe to President Rutherford B. Hayes against Territorial U.S. officials. Like Billy and Alexander McSween, they believed he would help. They received no answer. They wrote:

Coes Ranch, Chicora Park,
Colfax Co. New Mexico
22 June, 1878.
To His Excellency R.B. Hayes President of the United States
Excellency

We are two residents of Lincoln Co., who after incurring the greatest peril to life and property at the hands of thieves and murderers whom the Governor and U.S. troops aid and abet in their crimes, have succeeded in bringing whole skins to this section where the brother of one of us possesses this ranch.

We respectfully desire to call to your attention the necessity of removing the present Governor of New Mexico, unless in your excellencys opinion the people of the territory are to be regarded as his charges.

Enough has already been laid before your Excellency with regard to Mr. Axtell's conduct to render it highly indecorous that he should be longer retained in office as Governor. **His proclamation in Lincoln Co. which he has never attempted to deny, was so palpable a usurpation and so evidently issued to secure the escape of Mr. Tunstall's murderers that nothing else should have been needed for his removal;** *but an act which he has recently committed; which in fact induced us to quit the County, and is rapidly depopulating it is, if possible, still worse.*

On the death of Sheriff Brady the county commissioners appointed Mr. John Copeland, a gentleman respected by all the honest men of Lincoln Co. to be sheriff in his place, the power of appointment to vacancies in county offices being by law vested in them. Mr. Axtell set aside this appointment and appointed in his place one G.W. Peppin, a man not only totally unable to furnish the bonds required by law, but against whom <u>three warrants for three several murders committed by him, were in the hands</u> of the officers of the law, at the very time the Governor appointed him.

Further – Mr. Catron the U.S. District Attorney having transferred to him the property of the Murphy Dolan & Reilly gang has got the U.S. troops to be sent to round up and collect, not really <u>his</u> cattle but the cattle stolen from Mr. Hunter by the man employed for that purpose by Murphy Dolan and Reilly and the U.S. troops are now being used for that purpose.

All who have seen Mr. Angel feel great confidence in his skill and integrity, but we feel assured of this, that if the U.S. officials who are the head and front of all these thieves fail in the efforts they will make to <u>buy up</u> Mr. Angel, they will proceed to steal his papers, and if necessary for that purpose will <u>murder</u> him.

Thus it is due to the safety of the commissioner your Excellency has appointed <u>as a security for his life</u> that Axtell be immediately removed. By the constitution of the United States – (which when brought to the notice of Col. Purington as forbidding his illegal acts, <u>was publicly damned by him.</u>) – the right to bear arms is secured to the citizens, **the U.S. troops in pursuance of orders from the Governor and Gen. Hatch are violently disarming all the honest citizens, leaving the thieves armed.**

We are informed that the mainstay and support of Mr. Axtell is General Garfield.

[AUTHOR'S NOTE: Republican James Abram Garfield became President after Hayes, and backed the Ring.]

Having every confidence in Gen. Garfields integrity, we presume his mind has been abused. We would therefore suggest that your Excellency cause to be laid before him all the papers the administration has received on the subject.

We believe he will be likely to place confidence in the statement by Dr. M. N. Leverson of Douglas Co. Colorado whom he will remember from several of his publications, and particularly on "the uses and functions of money" published in 1867.

Yours Respectfully
J Isaacs
G.N. Co?

MONTEGUE LEVERSON INTERVENES: JUNE 28, 1878

Montegue Leverson's June 28, 1878 letter to President Hayes and Secretary of the Interior Carl Schurz, titled "Affairs of New Mexico," was returned to him *"by direction of the President"* without action on July 12, 1878, two days before the Lincoln County War battle's start. Leverson's accusations of Catron, Elkins, and the Santa Fe Ring were ignored by those Ring-complicit politicians, but show that before Angel's reports they knew U.S. officials were involved in Tunstall's murder and Lincoln County "troubles." Furthermore, Leverson saw through the Angel investigation, stating concern *"that the present investigation is meant to be a whitewashing one."* Leverson wrote:

Post Office   Leverson Ranch.
Larkspur   Douglas Co., Colorado

28 June 1878

Dear Sir:

It is with the greatest reluctance that I yield to the solicitations which have reached me in great number by every main since my return, to address you once more upon the affairs of New Mexico. I have been the more reluctant again to intrude myself upon your notice because Mr. Angel, the gentleman charged to investigate & report to the administration has impressed me most favorably, and inspired me with great confidence both in his ability and integrity.

The unfortunate citizens of New Mexico – clinging to any hope of relief from the <u>very slavery in which they are held</u> – seem to attach a weight to such poor representations as I may make to the administration, which <u>unfortunately</u> for them I know too well they do not possess. I do honestly aver that I believe my representations <u>ought</u> to have the weight these citizens seem to think they do possess and that by reason of my services to the Union during the war (declared by the Hon C.F. Adams to have been "worth an army corps") & by my services to the Republican party since I have lived in this country: but I have no "political influence" being a single citizen whose only desire is <u>to see the right prevail</u>.

But I can no longer refuse the aid of my humble efforts to the heartrending entreaties made to me; and I write to point out to you the terrible wrong which is being daily done to the citizens of New Mexico by the president allowing that man Axtel [Axtell throughout] to remain governor of the Territory.

Surely the administration <u>must</u> feel that a governor should exist for the good of the people, <u>not</u> the people for the governor's benefit – Yet is the conduct of the administration such as would be rational, only on the contrary supposition!

During the whole time Mr. Axtel has been governor, robbery and murder and the blackmailing of respectable citizens by the law officers of the U.S. have been rife & common throughout the Territory, the governor has thus failed in his first duty of maintaining peace and order & seeing that the laws are executed, & surely whether his failure be owing to incompetency or to guilt, ought on <u>this account alone</u> to be removed.

His appointment of Rynerson, the murderer of C.J. Slough to be District Attorney in the 3rd Judicial Dist – is another sufficient reason for his removal.

His infamous proclamation made so evidently to ensure the escape of the murderers of Mr. Tunstall, is yet another, <u>even tho' he were innocent of that motive</u>; because of the <u>Usurpation</u> of <u>Judicial</u> authority palpable on the face of it needing no evidence but the document itself, which even the governor's effrontery has not attempted to deny.

But <u>worse, if that be possible</u>, has since happened

On the death of Sheriff Brady, the County Commissioners appointed a Mr. Copeland, a gentleman who had the confidence of all the good citizens of Lincoln Co, to be sheriff; the governor has set aside this appointment and appointed one G. <u>Peppin</u> to be sheriff of Lincoln Co; although <u>at the very time of that appointment 3 warrants for 3 several murders committed by Peppin</u> were in the hands of the proper law officers for his arrest!

Since then, by the desire of the Gov, and in <u>express violation of the constitution of the United States</u>, the military authorities have issued orders to the U.S. troops, <u>which these troops are carrying out</u>, to disarm all persons carrying arms except the Sheriff (!) & his posse; in other words, they disarm the honest men, leaving their arms to the thieves and murderers!

It is impossible for me to express to you in a letter, the mistrust & fear evinced by the people of the Territory, even in the bona fides of the present administration, and I must in all honesty acknowledge that the past and present course even of the present administration affords but too much ground for such mistrust; nothing indeed but the strong faith I have in <u>you</u> personally, in President Hayes and the very favorable impression produced upon me by Mr. Angel would have overcome like mistrust even in my part.

I will presently name to you some of the reasons which cause this mistrust on the part of the citizens, **meanwhile permit me to call attention to the consequences of it; viz: that much most important testimony will not be forthcoming because of the terror dominating those who should give it.**

[AUTHOR'S NOTE: In this atmosphere, Billy would also give his deposition to Investigator Angel on June 8, 1878.]

*The investigation on which Mr. Angel is embarked will necessarily occupy several months, **meanwhile the <u>governed</u> are subjected to all the oppression of [Santa Fe] Ring misrule, a misrule which that of the Tweed in New York was justice and truth in comparison!***

There is not one of the citizens but feels convinced that if the investigation is meant in real earnest, **and the Santa Fe ring fails to "buy up" Mr. Angel** – *which it is my belief registered through the past.*

Now as to some of the causes of the prevailing mistrust of the bona fides of even the present investigation.

1. The most weighty and alarming is the continuance of Mr. Axtel in office in the teeth of his usurpation (by the proclamation before mentioned) and of his appointment of the murderer Peppin to be sheriff, and after his own letter to "Ben Stevens" plotting the murder of the best citizens of Colfax Co: has been made public and brought to the notice of the administration.

*2. **The continued employment of U.S. troops in the aid of unlawful and <u>criminal</u> acts of the "Santa Fe ring"** and their continued and open violation of the Constitution of the U.S. as by disarming citizens & searching houses and making arrests without color of warrant or lawful authority.*

3. The total disregard by the administration of the charges proferred against Axtel in 1877; charges supported upon oath.

*4. **The <u>betrayal</u>, aye the <u>immediate</u> betrayal of those affidavits to Hon S.B. Elkins, the brains of the 'Santa Fe ring" altho these affidavits had been obtained under pledge of confidence,** until a public investigation should be had, made or at least authorized by yourself!*

*5. **The immediate communication to Catron of the times appointed by Mr. Axtel for his departure from Santa Fe for***

Lincoln Co, and of the postponements made by him from time to time for the <u>express</u> purpose of avoiding the company of W. Thornton (Catron's law firm partner) who nevertheless, through the information promised him by the military at Santa Fe, actually traveled down to Ft. Stanton in Mr. Angel's company!

*6. The permission given by Lieut. Loud of Santa Fe to a man stated to be a noted cattle thief **and <u>known to be employed by Catron</u>** (one McCabe) to ride down to <u>Stanton in the U.S. ambulance with Angel!</u>*

The foregoing are a few of the reasons which, not unreasonably, <u>you must admit</u>, have excited suspicion in the minds of the citizens that the present investigation is meant to be <u>a whitewashing one</u>, and I respectfully urge that some <u>proof</u> should be published to the people that it is meant in all honesty.

I do assure you, and Mr. Angel will bear witness to the fact that I have expended great efforts to conquer this suspicion, and to give all who put any confidence in me, confidence in the bona fides of the investigation; and I am in the daily receipt of letters tending to show that my efforts have had some success among parties who, but for my urgency and professions of belief, would have held aloof & even fled the county. And yet, it is my faith as I have before said in <u>you personally</u>, in President Hayes and in Mr. Angel which alone enable me to continue trustful, notwithstanding the evidence <u>apparently furnished</u> to the contrary by the facts and circumstances above detailed (1-6 pp 7-8)

I have, since I commenced this letter, received a letter from a Mr. Coe informing me of more citizen's on Lincoln Co. who have abandoned their all (himself being one) rather than continue subject to the oppression and the peril which daily beset them and their families while in Lincoln Co.

He also asks me in his own name and in that of a number of friends to proceed to Washington to lay before the President a fuller statement than can be made in writing of the oppression under which the honest and downtrodden citizens of New Mexico are laboring, offering that he and his friends would pay my expenses and liberal fee.

If I thought I could do good by going to Washington I would do so, (altho' just now, it would greatly derange my own affairs,) <u>without any fee</u>; but I feel that even my necessary expenses of transportation and subsistence (if worthy of being incurred at all,) *should be defrayed by the U.S. and not by the victims of U.S. misrule, but I feel also that there would be nothing to be gained by my presence in Washington, unless I were there in consequence of the desire of the president to obtain a more accurate knowledge of the state of affairs in New Mex than could be obtained from written communications. Only then, on the invitation of the administration would I care to make the sacrifice of my private affairs which my going to Washington would entail, because only in the event of such invitation should I hope for any beneficial result.*

Apologizing for this lengthy intrusion which I hope may be the last. I have the honor to be
  Your obedient
    Montegue Leverson

RING MASSACRE AT SAN PATRICIO: JULY 3, 1878

Racism was key to the Santa Fe Ring's premeditated take-over of New Mexico Territory. The native Hispanic population, considered defenseless by Catron and Elkins in their original land-grab formulation, bore the brunt of the Ring's plunder, terrorist intimidation, and manipulation. The words of Governor Marsh Giddings in his April 3, 1873 letter to the Department of Interior addressing the accusations against him for suppressing the 1872 Legislature Revolt say it all: calling Mexicans *"vilest of the vile"* from *"slums of vice"* in Santa Fe. He complained: *"Nearly all the people of the Territory are Mexican 86,000 out of 93,000."* They were the Ring's intended victims.

Fusing of Ring racism and rage at opposition yielded the July 3, 1878 massacre at San Patricio, 12 miles east of Lincoln. Its citizens, likely inspired by bi-cultural Billy Bonney who often stayed with them, had protected McSween and Regulators during Catron's embezzling case before and after Tunstall's murder; and they hid McSween after his Grand Jury exoneration, which resulted in more blatant Ring attempts to kill him.

Earlier, on June 28, 1878, Sheriff George Peppin had used Fort Stanton's new Commander, N.A.M. Dudley with troops, in violation of the Posse Comitatus Act passed 10 days before, to invade San Patricio in a failed raid to catch or kill McSween and Regulators.

The Ring's retaliatory massacre at San Patricio for its loyalty to McSween and Regulators occurred five days after that Peppin-Dudley raid, and 11 days before the Lincoln County War battle began. The attackers were Sheriff George Peppin, bringing Mesilla's John Kinney and his rustlers as his "posse." Men, women, children, and farm animals were slaughtered; property was destroyed. Its result was that most of McSween's 60 fighters were men from San Patricio and Picacho, making the Lincoln County War's battle the Territory's biggest Hispanic anti-Ring uprising. But no one was ever prosecuted for the massacre. And the fury at the atrocity remains to today in descendants.

THE "REGULATOR MANIFESTO": JULY 13, 1878

What I have named the "Regulator Manifesto" - the grand anti-Ring declaration of the Lincoln County War - is a letter likely written in response to the San Patricio massacre. Dated July 13, 1878 - 10 days after the terrorist act, and one day before the Lincoln County War battle began - it is signed only "*Regulator.*"

It exists as a copy. It was attributed to Charles Bowdre by early historian, Maurice Garland Fulton, who claimed that its recipient, T.B. Catron's brother-in-law, Edgar Walz, identified Bowdre's handwriting. The copy is in the Washington, D.C., National Archives Records of the Adjutant General's Office.

But I believe it is Billy Bonney's first anti-Ring production, either dictated to Bowdre, or in his own hand, and misconstrued by Walz. It has Billy's zealot's bellicosity, bi-cultural loyalties, and articulateness. Noteworthy is that it is on behalf of even "*the poorest Mexican.*" It correctly calls the Ring a "*murderous band,*" including T.B. Catron; Catron's law firm partner, William Thornton; Catron's brother-in-law, Edgar Walz; "the House" as the "*Murphy party;*" and John Kinney's outlaw gang.

It expresses Billy's hot-tempered retribution with awareness that the Regulators were marching on Lincoln the next day, July 14, 1878: "*[T]he man who plans destruction shall have destruction measured on him.*" It matches Billy's literary skill as evident the next year, on March 20, 1879, in one of his pardon bargain letters to Governor Lew Wallace, stating: "*I am not afraid to die like a man fighting but I would not like to be killed like a dog unarmed.*" And Edgar Walz, by late 1878 and through 1880, became one target of Billy's retaliative guerrilla rustling - just what the Regulator Manifesto threatened.

Walz, as managing Catron's Carrizozo cattle ranch, found the Manifesto either sufficiently alarming or incriminating to give it to Fort Stanton's Post Adjutant: Ringite Second Lieutenant 9th Cavalry Millard Fillmore Goodwin. Goodwin, in turn, made its *"true copy"* - pointing to future incriminatory intent. He had it certified by Ringite David M. Easton, concealing the fact that he was no longer a Justice of the Peace, having resigned after the "Buckshot" Roberts killing on April 4, 1878. Easton stated:

I certify that the above is a true copy of a letter received by Edgar A. Walz on July 14" 1878.

D.W. Easton

Below Easton's certification, the apparent copyist, Thomas Blair, Captain 15th Infantry, signed and wrote: *"A true copy."* Then Post Adjutant Goodwin signed it as *"a true copy."*

The "Regulator Manifesto" states:

In Camp, July 13, 1878.

Mr. Walz. Sir: - We are all aware that your brother-in-law, T.B. Catron sustains the Murphy-Kinney party, and take this method of informing you that if any property belonging to the residents of this county is stolen or destroyed, Mr. Catron's property will be dealt with as nearly as can be in the way in which the party he sustains deals with the property stolen or destroyed by them.

We returned Mr. Thornton the horses we took for the purpose of keeping the Murphy crowd from pursuing us with the promise that these horses should not again be used for that purpose. Now we know that the Tunstall estate cattle are pledged to Kinney and party. If they are taken, a similar number will be taken from your brother [in-law, Catron]. It is our object and efforts to protect property, but the man who plans destruction shall have destruction measured on him. Steal from the poorest or richest American or Mexican, and the full measure of the injury you do, shall be visited upon the property of Mr. Catron. This murderous band is harbored by you as your guest, and with the consent of Catron occupies your property.

Regulator

LOST BATTLE OF THE LINCOLN COUNTY WAR: JULY 14-19, 1878

On the July 13, 1878 day of the "Regulator Manifesto, Investigator Frank Warner Angel was in Las Vegas, New Mexico, taking the deposition of honorable Deputy Sheriff Adolph Barrier, who had risked his life to save McSween from the Ring because, as he told Angel: *"justice should be meted out to everyone without fear or favor."* Alexander McSween, the Regulators, and men of San Patricio and Picacho were about to take a stand for that democratic ideal in a six day battle.

DAY 1: JULY 14, 1878

Eminent battle was no secret. Most townspeople fled Lincoln, leaving in town Sheriff George Peppin, Deputies Billy Mathews and Jack Long, James Dolan, and Ring-biased Saturnino Baca and his family. John Riley was in Santa Fe plotting with Catron about evasion of the month-old Posse Comitatus Act, which blocked military intervention in civilian conflicts. Heading to Lincoln were an outlaw hoard of about 60 - Seven Rivers rustler-ranchers and Mesilla's John Kinney and his gang - to become Peppin's "posse." And outlaw, Jessie Evans, was likely with Dolan.

Reflecting McSween's optimism for peaceable victory, his family remained. In his house were his wife, Susan; her sister, Elizabeth Shield, with her five young children; and David Shield's law intern, Harvey Morris; Shield being away - more evidence that all were sure of an innocuous confrontation In the Tunstall store's apartment were Dr. Taylor Ealy, his wife, and two children. Justice of the Peace "Squire" Wilson stayed defiantly in his house, having ignored Governor Axtell's Proclamation removing his title.

After leaving the safe haven of John Chisum's South Spring River Ranch, McSween arrived in Lincoln with his men, including Billy, and homesteader Josiah "Doc" Scurlock as new Regulator head, replacing murdered Frank MacNab.

McSween's men took strategic positions along Lincoln's single street to hold the town: occupying Tunstall's store, and houses of Jose Montaño, Juan Patrón, and Isaac Ellis. At the western terminus were only "the House" and Ring haven, Wortley Hotel.

McSween's men, not sharing his optimism, had well provisioned his house, including a keg of gunpowder for reloading ammunition. But initially McSween apparently only permitted

Jim "Frenchie" French into his house as a guard. But arrival of shooting Seven Rivers and Kinney men, convinced him to add, from the Montaño house, Billy, Yginio Salazar, Tom O'Folliard, Jose Chávez y Chávez, Francisco Zamora, and Vincente Romero from San Patricio; and Ignacio Gonzales and Florencio Chávez from Picacho. The terrain of Lincoln was ideal for McSween's intended defense. To the south were nearby, sparsely vegetated, high foothills, which would leave assailants exposed to gunfire. To the north, immediately behind McSween's house, was the Bonito River, blocking positioning of adversaries.

DAY 2: JULY 15, 1878

In McSween's house, his men blockaded windows and cut portholes in its adobe bricks to shoot through. McSween, with his usual punctilious legality, sent by messenger an eviction letter to Saturnino Baca, his tenant in a house east of Tunstall's store, with grounds of Baca's giving aid to men threatening his life. Baca, a Ring stooge, relayed the letter to James Dolan at "the House" to claim that his wife and children were in danger from McSween to justify military intervention.

But that day, the only aggression was Deputy Jack Long's attempt to serve the invalid David Easton warrants on McSween and "the Kid" for the April 30, 1878 killings and wounding of the Seven Rivers attackers. But Long retreated at warning shots from inside. And McSween apparently remained confident.

DAY 3: JULY 16, 1878

Stymied Ringites took action to get military aid by using the outlaw myth. Sheriff George Peppin sent a letter to Fort Stanton Commander N.A.M. Dudley stating: *"Sir. If you could loan me a howitzer, I am sure that parties for whom I have warrants would surrender. We are being attacked by a lawless mob."* That enabled Dudley to send to Lincoln a courier, 9th Cavalry Private Berry Robinson, for "fact finding." A staged shot at Berry, likely from "the House," caused his horse to throw him. Uninjured and remounted, he escaped back to the Fort. But McSween was now set up for another malicious prosecution: attempted murder of a soldier, as the Ring attempted to maneuver around the Posse Comitatus Act's mine field of restrictions on intervention.

DAY 4: JULY 17, 1878

With Private Berry Robinson "attacked," Commander Dudley took action. By Fort Stanton's telegraph, he was likely receiving instructions from Catron on evading the Posse Comitatus Act. So, that day, Fort Stanton Post Surgeon Daniel Appel, writer of Tunstall's fraudulent autopsy report; Ringite Captain George Purington, still at the Fort; and five soldiers went to Lincoln. There they questioned McSween about the Private Robinson shooting, and ignored his denial. Peppin used the cease-fire of troops' presence to position men on the south foothills.

That day had first casualties. From the Montaño house, Fernando Herrera, Charlie Bowdre's brother-in-law, fatally shot, with his Sharps Big Fifty buffalo rifle, Seven Rivers posseman, Charlie Crawford, 915 yards away on the south foothills. And Isaac Ellis's son, Ben, was wounded by Peppin's men shooting down from those foothills. From then on, carnage would be solely by the Ring.

DAY 5: JULY 18, 1878

Since the south foothills were easily defended, McSween began to anticipate a near-bloodless victory. And charismatic Billy inspired all, with Susan McSween later describing him as "lively."

DAY 6: JULY 19, 1878

On July 19, 1878, Commander N.A.M. Dudley marched on Lincoln, treasonously violating the June 18, 1878 Posse Comitatus Act. With terrorist intent, he brought into the tiny town a howitzer cannon, Gatling machine-gun, and infantry and cavalry; all sufficient to level it and kill everyone. And he personally threatened McSween with annihilation. He was intervening as a partisan in a civilian conflict and endangering women and children in the McSween and Ealy houses.

After learning that Easton's warrants were invalid, in likely panic, Dudley forced refusing Justice of the Peace Wilson by death threat to write false arrest warrants for McSween and "the Kid," using the Private Berry Robinson shooting. Dudley then became an accomplice to possemen's arson of McSween's house by positioning his soldiers on the property to block defensive firing. He further had soldiers accompany Peppin as a guard.

When the McSween house inmates, including Billy, attempted nighttime escape from the burning building, Dudley ordered and positioned three officers to fire on them, becoming accomplice to Sheriff Peppin's posse's murdering Alexander McSween, Harvey Morris, Francisco Zamora; and Vincente Romero; or possibly even committing the murder of Morris themselves. Escaping Yginio Salazar was left with bullets in his back for life. McSween's house was destroyed.

McSween's side injured no one that day. But Seven Rivers posseman, Robert Beckwith, was killed by friendly fire.

And that night, during Billy's escape with others, he witnessed the three white soldiers fire a volley at them. His cool-headed moment amidst catastrophe and lurid firelight illumination would impact his pardon bargain when he later decided to take his own action against Commander Dudley by testifying against him in that soldier's military Court of Inquiry.

With the decisive, horrific, and illegal crushing of the Lincoln County War freedom fight by the Ring, the sole hope of the people in Lincoln, Colfax, and Grant Counties would rest with a new governor: Lew Wallace. And unlike most of the Regulators, Billy Bonney had no plans to move from New Mexico Territory, his home.

CHAPTER 9

LINCOLN COUNTY WAR AFTERMATH: JULY 20, 1878 - OCTOBER 24, 1878

AFTERMATH OF BATTLE: JULY 20, 1878

On July 20, 1878, the day after the Lincoln County War battle, McSween's bullet-riddled corpse was found in his rear yard with its eyeballs eaten by his starving chickens. Next door, Sheriff George Peppin's outlaw possemen, with complicit presence of Commander N.A.M. Dudley, looted Tunstall's store.

Opposition to the Ring had been crushed. The immediate response was the exodus from the Territory by most of the Regulators; and frightened silence of Lincoln County's population.

But there would be a final surge for freedom. Its leader would be teenaged Billy Bonney, aided covertly by a few Lincolnites. And Alexander McSween's brave widow, Susan, would seek justice against the criminal most obvious to her: N.A.M. Dudley.

OTHERS SEEKING JUSTICE

John Tunstall's father, John Partridge Tunstall, from London, pursued reparations of $200,000 for his son's murder and theft of his property. He filed charges with Foreign Secretary Lord Salisbury and Prime Minister William Gladstone. But the elder Tunstall's linking of United States officials, likely caused the Santa Fe Ring's self-protective blockade through then-Senator S.B. Elkins; until the father's death in the late 1880's ended the pursuit. But the trauma echoed through generations. When a descendant of Tunstall's sister Minnie came with his family to America in 2010 for a Billy the Kid convention, he needed assurance that they would not risk death like John Tunstall.

There is no historian who has documented the unhealable traumas to the children of David and Elizabeth Shield from the six day battle; or to their helpless violated parents themselves. But David Shield, relocating his family and law practice back to Las Vegas, New Mexico, and taking his agonized and now impoverished sister-in-law, Susan, to live temporarily with them, did attempt to seek justice on his own. And joining in from the safe distance of Colorado was Montegue Leverson.

LETTER FROM ATTORNEY DAVID SHIELD TO MONTEGUE LEVERSON: JULY 26, 1878

David Shield - presumably suffering from survivor's guilt and trepidation about harboring the next likely Ring victim: his sister-in-law, Susan McSween - on July 26, 1878 wrote to Montegue Leverson about the murder of Alexander McSween, seven days before. It demonstrates Shield's knowledge of Ring power: *"they control everything here."* It is noteworthy that this was the only way for Leverson to get the news. The huge battle was missing from all newspapers. Shield wrote:

ALEX A. McSWEEN
DAVID P. SHIELD

LAW OFFICE
-OF-
MCSWEEN & SHIELD,
Lincoln County Bank Building,
Las Vegas

Lincoln, New Mexico, _____July 26_____ 1878___

Dr. M.R. Leverson.
Dear Sir
Your letter *of the 23rd inst is at hand and content noted. The same will receive proper attention. I had read a letter about 2 hours previous hereto announcing the murder of A A McSween in his own house and the burning of his ~~his~~ & the house in which my family resides together with the contents thereof on the 20th [19th] inst. My family I learn are at Fort Stanton & will come here the first opportunity. The destitute condition in which they are in I trust will be sufficient apology to you for my asking of you a loan of One Hundred Dollars for ninety days ... The full particulars I have not received but expect to in a short time when recd I will communicate with you.* **The ring element here ... are jubilant over the news but their joy will be turned to grief. I would not have asked you for the loan but I do not wish to place myself under any obligations to the ring or their clique & they control everything here ...**

Yours Truly
DP Shield

LETTER FROM MONTEGUE LEVERSON TO PRESIDENT HAYES: JULY 30, 1878

Montegue Leverson, addressing David Shield's news, wrote on July 30, 1878 to President Hayes about the murders of Alexander McSween and Frank MacNab; with a copy to Secretary of the Interior Carl Schurz. Though unaware that their loyalties were to the Ring, he stated correctly: "*your Excellency's administration is accountable before God and man.*" Leverson wrote:

Post Office   Leverson Ranch.
Larkspur   Douglas Co., Colorado

28 June [sic- July] 1878

His Excellency Rutherford B Hayes
    President of the U.S.
Excellency
    I enclose a letter I have just received [July 26, 1878 letter from David Shield] advising me of the murder of another admirable gentleman A.A. McSween. For this murder – as also for that of McNab [Frank MacNab] committed some weeks ago your Excellency's administration is accountable before God and man.
    You have now known long enough the character of the wretches appointed to office [Catron as U.S. Attorney] by your predecessor [President Ulysses S. Grant]. Your Excellency was warned that this would be the result of continuing them in office *and all you have done has been to send down an able and upright gentleman to <u>investigate!!</u> Meanwhile men equal to yourself in every quality of heart and mind are being daily murdered by procurement of the villains your predecessor appointed to office and you maintain there!*
    Excellency I have no way sought the office – dangerous indeed for a man who does his duty of governor of New Mexico, but I know my name has been mentioned in that connection to the administration.
    Tho' it would entail heavy pecuniary sacrifices on my part I would accept the office & pledge myself to restore peace and order to New Mexico within 60 days of my installation or perish in the attempt.

                                        Respectfully
                                       Montegue Leverson

LETTER OF MONTEGUE LEVERSON TO SECRETARY OF THE INTERIOR CARL SCHURZ: JULY 28(?), 1878

Montegue Leverson's letter of July 28(?) 1878 to Secretary of the Interior Carl Schurz confirms common knowledge of the Ring, Catron, and assassinations. Leverson even hints at the link of the Hayes administration to the Ring. Leverson wrote:

Post Office　　　　　　　　Leverson Ranch.
Larkspur　　　　　　　　　Douglas Co., Colorado

[28] June [sic- July] 1878

Hon Carl Schurz
　　Secy of the Interior
　D Sir.
　　*I send you herewith copy of a letter I have published & I send it to you for several reasons. First to show you **how the possession of power has corrupted the Republican leaders [Catron and the Ring] in this State,** as indeed might well have been judged by you by their endorsement of the execrable mal-administration of President Grant during his 2ⁿᵈ term & sneering condemnation of every good thing done by President Hayes; **and secondly to suggest to the administration the impolicy and <u>positive wickedness</u> of submitting to the dictation or influence of the old and proved-to-be corrupt republican politicians [Catron and the Ring], which I greatly fear the president has lately shown signs of doing in various instances, of which his <u>non action</u> in New Mex ie his abstaining from affording the oppressed people of that Territory the relief they need, seems to me a very grave indication.***

　　My letter, of which the [newspaper published] copy is sent you, has led to my being requested to stump this State for the Democratic party this fall.

　　*Altho' that party is by no means so purified by adversity as to command my hearty adherence, **the Republican leaders, <u>here and in New Mexico,</u> are so bad, that I shall probably comply with the request ... <u>if the administration should not anticipate my efforts by affording</u> the needed relief.***

　　In this connection I will add some remarks somewhat personal on a matter lately ... brought under my notice but <u>before</u> I published the enclosed letter.

I am told that my name has been urged on the administration as a fitting person to be appointed governor of New Mex <u>for the benefit of the people.</u>

I <u>do not seek, I have not sought, I do not desire</u> the appointment: not because I dread the danger (as you will presently observe) although strongly persuaded I should not live 3 months in New Mexico for even now, further plots have been laid for my life by the ruffians now holding power one of which lately failed signally. They have laid their plans – of course neither Axtel [Axtell] nor Catron has appeared openly in the matter, to get hold of some 5 or 6000$\underline{00}$ worth of my property expecting I should go down in person to save it. The coach was stopped the day they expected me by two masked & armed ruffians who demanded the way bill & who cursed & swore when they found <u>I</u> was <u>not</u> in the coach but allowed it to proceed without robbing it!

[AUTHOR'S NOTE: This little-known Ringite attempted assassination of Leverson, repeats Governor Axtell's "Dear Ben plot" in Colfax County to murder Ring adversaries Raymond Morley, Frank Springer, Henry Porter, and Clay Allison; and the Ring's later malicious prosecution of Alexander McSween and John Tunstall in the fake Fritz life insurance embezzlement case to set up their murders.]

Nevertheless I <u>would cheerfully sacrifice my own private business & peril my life</u>, to furnish security for the lives and property of the citizens; the only purpose for which government should be tolerated at all!

Were I appointed governor my first act would be to request that the U.S. troops be ordered to confine their activities to protecting the citizens from the Indians & to aid the U.S. Marshall, instead of as heretofore, aiding the thieves and murderers to rob and murder, making searches and arrests without warrant, depriving the good citizens of their arms (all in violation of the constitution) & helping the U.S. Attorney of New Mex to steal J.H. Tunstalls cattle!

[AUTHOR'S NOTE: Leverson knows the Ring misused troops in Cimarron, against McSween (as he confronted), and in the Lincoln County War battle. So he opposes it. Noteworthy, by October of 1878, would be Governor Lew Wallace's almost immediate and horrifying plan to get martial law and soldiers intervention to "end" Lincoln County "troubles."]

> *Without the use of the U.S. army an efficient and <u>upright</u> governor would restore peace to New Mexico within 60 days relying on the people only to aid him.*
>
> I do not doubt that the [published] letter, a copy of which I enclose, will utterly extinguish such poor chance, if ever there were one, of my being chosen by the president for ~~the~~ governor of New Mex, tho it might be otherwise if appointment to office were determined only by the fitness of the appointee to benefit the people. In such case that letter would neither forward nor obstruct. Unhappily things are in such a state that sometimes I begin to almost "despair of the Republic."
>
> Very respectfully
Montegue R. Leverson

[ENCLOSURE] Undated newspaper article.

INDIGNANT

A genuine Republican at the Lack of Truth in His Party Press

To the Editor of the Democrat ... And because in this state that [Republican] party has become the [party of fraud, the party of illegality and usurpation, I now fall into line with the opponents of that party ... In order that the assault attempted upon constitutional liberty may be defeated and the breach effectively repaired, every honest citizen of this state, every lover of its liberties, whether he call himself democrat or republican, should, in the absence of a people's ticket, vote for the nominees of the democratic party to both branches of our state legislature. He who does otherwise will thereby prove that he cares more for party than for freedom.

LETTER OF CITIZEN JOHN G. HUBBARD TO PRESIDENT HAYES: AUGUST 1, 1878

There were also New Mexico Territory citizens brave enough to complain to President Hayes, as shown by this August 1, 1878 letter from a John G. Hubbard focused on Axtell's "Dear Ben plot." Hubbard correctly identifies the Ring, and links its use of the military to suppress or to murder citizens in both Colfax and Lincoln Counties. He wrote:

N.M. Aug 1 of 1878

To The Prest U.S.
    My Dear Sir:

        *Herewith I hand you an extract from one of our N.M. papers relative to Gov Axtell of New Mexico to which I would draw your Especial attention, this man Axtell is a very dangerous one & calculated to do <u>any administration a great deal of harm</u>, & who certainly is void of moral honesty & steeped deeply in crime as well and has appeared by strict investigation of **the poor suffering New Mexicans, who from pure loyalty to the Govmt and an indisposition to create trouble, have quietly acquiesed to the Ring &c.***
With marked esteem   Yours truly
                John G. Hubbard

[ENCLOSURE] Newspaper article dated July 31, 1878.

WHY AXTELL WANTED TROOPS

SANTA FE, July 31. The popular demand for a reduction of the regular army finds support in the history of its doings in New Mexico for the past few years. **The fact is, the United States troops, like everything else official and public in New Mexico, have been chiefly used to advance the interests of the Santa Fe Ring, headed by Elkins, Catron, Axtell, and the rest;** and the district commander, Col. Hatch of the Ninth Cavalry seems to be so entirely wrapped up in these men, and has employed his soldiers in such complete subservience to their wishes that the sinuous folds of the **Ring** have enveloped him also.

It is now something more than two years since Colfax county had an experience with these fellows not unlike that which Lincoln county has more recently gone through. The facts are worth recalling. The Rev. F.J. Tolby, a man respected and loved by the community, was murdered on the highway. His watch and money were not taken. It was clear that the motive of the murder was not robbery. He had made himself obnoxious to **the Ring** by bold public denunciations of its members and tools. Some of the latter prudently fled the county. One man who did not get away soon enough was hanged by the people, and others would have been if the people could have laid hands on them.

Gov. Axtell came to the rescue as usual. He removed the Sheriff whom the people has elected, and put in his place a man whom they detested, and who managed in the brief time he remained in office to steal $1000 of school money. He wrote on to Washington for authority to send troops into the county. He sent District Attorney Ben Stevens to superintend the military operations. A company of forty-five soldiers, under the command of Capt. F. Moore, marched into Colfax. Some twelve – or fifteen – leading citizens wrote to the governor asking him to visit the county and see for himself whether the alleged lawlessness really existed.

The troops remained two or three weeks, arrested one man [Clay Allison], immediately turned him loose, and finally marched back to Fort Union, having found no disorders to suppress, and no shadow of excuse for further stay.

The true design of this foray has lately been exposed in the Cimarron *News and Press* which publishes a telegram and letter sent at the time by Axtell to his agent, District Attorney Stevens. The plan was to create a disturbance, and kill off some persons who were in the way of **the Ring**. I give the documents; they are interesting reading coming from the Governor of a Territory. The telegram was sent to Stevens at Fort Union, and runs as follows:

Do not let it be known that I will be in Cimarron on Saturday's coach. Body guard all right.   S.B. Axtell

The letter was as follows:

DEAR BEN: The second telegram delivered to you at Fort Union, directed to Cimarron, was intended to leak, but the operator here says he cannot raise the Cimarron office. If I was expected our friends would probably be on hand, as the guard is only a Government escort. I do not think your definite business is suspected. Wade informed Hatch that he had been ready all the time to assist you, but could not find that you wanted to do it. Hatch says their opinion is that you weakened and do not want to arrest the man. *Have your men placed to arrest him and to kill all the men who resist you, or stand with those who do resist you.* Our man signed the invitation with others who were at that meeting for me to visit Colfax – Porter, Morley, Springer, et al. Now, if they expect me Saturday, they will be on hand. Send me letters by messenger; and do not hesitate at extreme measures. Your honor is at stake now, and a failure is fatal. If others resist, or attempt murder, bring them also. Hatch is excited, and writes, of course, to put all the blame on the civil officers. I am more anxious on your account than for any other reason. I clearly see that we have no friends in Colfax, and I have suspected all along that some of our pretended friends were traitors.
Yours &c.   S. B. Axtell

The Porter, Morley, and Springer here mentioned were among the leading citizens of the county, and strong opponents of **the Ring** and its defunct Colfax county branch ... That the troops were sent on an infamous bushwacking expedition nobody here doubts.

BRAVE WIDOW SUSAN MCSWEEN

Susan McSween, like Mary McPherson before her, took courageous action. Not only did she return to Lincoln the day after her husband's murder and her home's arson, but she tried to stop looting of Tunstall's store. Then, moving to Las Vegas to live with the Shield family, she hired an attorney there named Huston Chapman, presumably after refusal by David Shield. One-armed from a childhood shotgun accident, Chapman compensated by doughtiness. His father had founded Portland, Oregon's first newspaper: the *Oregonian*. He and Susan would have known that their plan to prosecute Commander N.A.M. Dudley for murder and arson risked their lives. And she would also have met Chapman's office-mate: Attorney Ira Leonard. Both men became intrinsic to the fate of Billy Bonney and his pardon.

FIRST FAME OF BILLY BONNEY

By July 19, 1878's conclusion to the Lincoln County War, Billy Bonney, 18 years 7 months and 27 days old, was locally famous. His youth, gunmanship, and fierceness against Ringites had earned affection and respect. As John P. Meadows, who knew him, had summed it up in his 1931 talks and newspaper articles about the "Days of Billy the Kid": "When he was rough, he was as rough as men ever get to be, yet he had a good streak in him." And Billy's bi-culturalism appealed to the majority of Lincoln County citizens, who were Hispanic. But what was to seal Billy's fame was his brilliance, literacy, and audacious self-confidence; fueled by America's promise that he was the equal of any man. In 7 months and 22 days he would write his first letter to the highest official in the Territory, Governor Lew Wallace. And he would ensure that future Lincoln County War history condemned the Ring.

But by October 24, he was in his new role as warned in his Regulator Manifesto: he was revenge-rustling from Ringites. He sold that stock to a Dan Dedrick with a ranch on the Pecos River, and with a livery in Lincoln County's White Oaks; and to a Pat Coghlan at Three Rivers, in the western part of the Territory.

Billy was also selling horses himself in Tascosa, Texas. There on October 24, 1878, he sold to a Dr. Henry Hoyt a sorrel horse likely once Sheriff Brady's and likely stolen by Billy from the Catron-Walz ranch in Carrizozo. Billy put a high value on the horse when he wrote out Hoyt's bill of sale, which demonstrated another transformation: Billy had acquired legalese, possibly from Alexander McSween. It would be used in 132 days to write a pardon plea letter to Governor Lew Wallace. To Hoyt, Billy wrote:

> *Tascoso Texas*
> *Thursday Oct 24th*
> *1878*
>
> *Know all persons by these presents that I do hereby Sell and deliver to Henry F. Hoyt one Sorrel Horse Branded BB on left hip and other indistinct Branded on Shoulders for the sum of Seventyfive $ dollars in hand received*
> *W HBonney*

Henry Hoyt, befriended by Billy as another father-figure, admired his intelligence and bi-culturalism. In his 1929 autobiography, *A Frontier Doctor*, Hoyt wrote that Billy was a "natural leader of men" and could "settle in Mexico or South America, and begin all over again." Hoyt was likely unaware that by then teenaged Billy was hardened by more traumas than most endure in a lifetime; and he had no intention of leaving his New Mexico home. Billy had become the Ring's greatest nightmare: the person who could defeat them.

But that same October 24, 1878, Susan McSween's attorney, Huston Chapman, in Las Vegas, New Mexico, was writing a letter to new Governor Lew Wallace that would seal his, Wallace's, and Billy's fate.

CHAPTER 10
INVESTIGATOR ANGEL'S CAPITULATION: OCTOBER, 1878

FRANK WARNER ANGEL'S RING COVER-UP

ANALYSIS: *The fate of New Mexico Territory, Lincoln County, and the Santa Fe Ring rested with Attorney Frank Warner Angel's October, 1878 reports on his massive, five month investigation as to murder and fraud by U.S. officials. Angel had collected the damning evidence, but he knew his own fate depended on what he concluded about the Santa Fe Ring, so he became a reluctant actor in its cover-up.*

HISTORY PENNED BY VICTORS

Investigator for the Departments of Justice and the Interior Frank Warner Angel could have destroyed the Santa Fe Ring. But that would have destroyed himself. So, like Colfax County's Attorney Frank Springer, he capitulated. But Angel had generated profuse proof of Ring illegalities in his depositions with attendant exhibits. So, in likely moral outrage, he presented that raw evidence to his superiors, while writing contradictory concluding reports absolving U.S. officials - thus, enabling someone in the future to break the Ring.

Angel's appointment was likely a mistake. President Rutherford B. Hayes and Secretary of the Interior Carl Schurz needed a simple cover-up for British Ambassador Sir Edward Thornton about U.S. officials' role in John Tunstall's murder. Instead, by assigning brilliant lawyer and investigator Angel, they almost exposed the Ring. Angel had also been mistaken. He likely thought he was assigned a legitimate investigation until his contradictory conclusion was forced on him by Hayes.

The outcome was Angel's contrived reports of October 1878. Worse, to shield the Ring, he blamed fictional outlaws for Lincoln County's "troubles," conforming to the Ring's strategy going back to the 1872 Legislature Revolt. And to feign action, he then scapegoated Governor S.B. Axtell. Angel's reward, the month after submitting his reports, was promotion to Assistant District Attorney of Eastern District of New York State.

But Angel's conscience yielded his covert anti-Ring action. Knowing Civil War Major General Lew Wallace was replacing Axtell, he secretly wrote for him a small red notebook naming Ringites. It was enough for Wallace to break the Ring himself.

REPORT ON TUNSTALL'S MURDER

Before he prepared the October 4, 1878 primary report of his New Mexico Territory assignment - "In the Matter of the Cause and Circumstances of the Death of John H. Tunstall, A British Subject - Frank Warner Angel had taken 39 depositions, including ones from Alexander McSween, Deputy Sheriff Adolph Barrier, Frank Springer, and Billy Bonney. Since he also traveled throughout the Territory investigating land grant fraud and Indian Agency violations, he was exposed to additional facts about Ring members and crimes. His reports demonstrate his truncating of truth. For Tunstall's murder, he reported to the Justice Department's Attorney General Charles Devens, writing:

<u>Department of Justice</u>.

| In the Matter
~ of the ~
cause and circumstances of the death
~ of ~
John H. Tunstall,
a British Subject. | <u>To the Honorable</u>
<u>Charles Devens</u>,
<u>Attorney General</u> |

In compliance with your instructions to make careful inquiry into the cause and circumstances of the death of John H. Tunstall, a British subject, and whether the death of said Tunstall was brought about through the lawless and corrupt conduct of United States officials in the Territory of New Mexico, and to report thereon.

I have the honor to submit the following report in relation to the premises.
<u>*First:*</u> *- As to the cause of the death of John H. Tunstall.*
John H. Tunstall by his straight-forward and honest business transactions with the people of Lincoln County, New Mexico ... had

been instrumental in the arrest of certain notorious horse thieves ... He had exposed embezzlement of Territorial officers ... He had incurred the anger of persons who had control of the County, and who used that control for private gain .. He had introduced honesty and square dealings in his business ... and to the enmity of those persons, can be attributed the only cause of his death ...

Second: - *As to the circumstances of his death.*

An attachment had been obtained against the property of one Alexander A. McSween ...

It was claimed that said Tunstall was McSween's partner ...

The Sheriff in order to attach certain property, viz; stock and horses, alleged to belong to McSween and Tunstall sent his deputy to Tunstall's ranch to attach the same ... - when said deputy visited said ranch and was informed that he could attach the stock and leave a person with it until the Courts could adjudicate to whom the stock belonged ... - he left without attaching said property, and immediately assembles a large posse among ... whom were the most desperate out-laws of the Territory ... They again started for Tunstall's ranch, in the mean-time Mr. Tunstall had been informed of the action of the Sheriff, and believing that the real purpose was to murder and not attach ... left his ranch, taking with him all the horses and started for Lincoln, the County seat ...

Directly after Tunstall had left his ranch, The Deputy Sheriff and said posse arrived there, and finding that Tunstall had left with the horses, deputized W. Morton ... who selected eighteen men and started out ostensibly to capture the horses. After riding about thirty miles, they came up to Tunstall and his party with the horses, and commenced firing on them ... - Immediately Tunstall and his party left the horses and attempted to escape ... were pursued and Tunstall was killed some hundred yards or more from the horses ...

Who shot Tunstall will never be known. But there is no doubt that W<u>m</u> S. Morton, Jesse [Jessie] Evans and [Tom] Hill were the only persons present and saw the shooting, and that two of those persons murdered him ... For Tunstall was shot in two places – in the head and breast ... Of these persons Morton and Hill were afterwards killed, and the only survivor is Jesse [Jessie] Evans a notorious out-law, murderer and horse-thief. Of these persons Evans and Hill had been arrested at the instigation of Tunstall.

They were at enmity with Tunstall, and enmity with them meant murder ...

There was no object for following after Tunstall – except to murder him, for they had the horses ... which they desired to attach before they commenced to pursue him and his party. These facts, together with the bitter feeling existing against Tunstall, by certain persons to whom he had become obnoxious ... and the deputy allowing those notorious out-laws to accompany him ... lead me to the conclusion that John H. Tunstall was murdered in cold blood ... and was not shot in attempting to resist an officer of the law ...

<u>Third:</u> *- Was the death of John H. Tunstall brought about by the lawless and corrupt action of United States officials –*

After diligent enquiry and examination of a great number of witnesses, I report that the death of John H. Tunstall was not brought about through the lawless and corrupt action of United States officials in the Territory of New Mexico.

All of which is respectfully submitted
                            Frank Warner Angel
                                  Special Agent.

REPORT ON LINCOLN COUNTY TROUBLES

Key to concealing the Ring's crimes and opponents, was Angel's using "troubles" instead of "rebellions" in his October 4, 1878 report: "In the Matter of the Lincoln County Troubles." He used vague lawlessness and the outlaw myth to cover-up the Lincoln County War freedom fight. This was his capitulation:

<u>Department of Justice</u>.

In the Matter ~ of the ~ Lincoln County Troubles.	<u>To the Honorable</u> <u>Charles Devens</u>, <u>Attorney</u> General

                            The history of Lincoln County has been one of blood shed from the day of its organization.

These troubles have existed for years with occasional break-outs, each one being more severe than the other.

L.G. Murphy & Co. had the monopoly of all business in the County, controlled governmental contracts, and used their power to oppress and grind out all they could from the farmers, and force those who were opposed to them to leave the County.

This has resulted in the formation of two parties, one led by Murphy & Co., and the other by McSween (now dead). Both have done many things contrary to the law, both violated the law. McSween, I firmly believe acted conscientiously - Murphy & Co. for private gain and revenge.

Bands of desperate characters who are ever found on the frontier, particularly along the Texas border, who have no interest in Lincoln County, men who live by plunder, and who only flourish where they can evade the law, have naturally gravitated to one or the other of these parties, and are now in their pay, being hired for so much a day to fight their battles.

Gov. Axtell appoints Peppin a leader of the Murphy & Co. faction, as Sheriff, he comes to Lincoln accompanied by John Kinney and his notorious band of out-laws and murderers as a body guard to assist him in upholding law and order. McSween then collects around himself an equally distinguished body. The County becomes the Elysium for out-laws and murderers.

A battle is fought – for five days it rages – more desperate action than was seen in these unfortunate days, by both sides, is rarely witnessed. Both parties desire revenge and they are now reorganizing and collecting more desperate characters (if that were possible), than they previously had. Before I left Santa Fe, it was reported that there were two hundred armed men in the field.

Men are shot down "on sight" because they belong to one or the other party, and the residents of the County have been forced to take one side or the other from inclination or necessity. One day Murphy & Co. and his party of out-laws control the County – the next day McSween and his "out-fit" would be the masters.

When these men were not engaged in battle, and when the County seemingly was at peace, they were employed to steal cattle, either from the farmers or the Indians – a ready market and no questions asked, was found in the persons who held government contracts. If the people protested, they were persecuted and driven out the County.

This state of affairs would be carried to such an extent, that it would end in a fight or a war similar to the one now being waged in the County.

During these years the law-abiding citizens, or those who would be if they could, have been reduced to poverty by professional thieves, who have made the County their camping ground without the least fear of molestation.

The laws cannot be enforced, for the reason that if the Murphy party are in power then the law is all Murphy – and if the McSween party are in power then the law is all McSween.

The leaders of these parties have created a storm that they cannot control, and it has reached such proportions that the whole Territory cannot put it down. Lands go uncultivated; ranches are abandoned; merchants have closed their stores; citizens have left the homes they have occupied for years; business has ceased, and lawlessness and murder are the order of the day.

These out-laws who prowl the County with the avowed purpose of murder, who have no interests in the County or wrongs of their own to redress, no matter on which side they belong, should be hunted down, and made to answer for their crimes.

The Territory has no militia, and the County being in the hands of those armed out-laws, the laws and mandates of the Courts cannot be enforced or respected, nor lives or property protected. It is impossible for even the Courts to be held.

I would respectfully refer to my report to the Interior Department on the charges against Governor Axtell as to the additional causes for the existing troubles in Lincoln County.

I would most respectfully recommend that such assistance be given the Governor of New Mexico that the laws may be enforced and respected, and life and property protected.

<u>Washington, October 4th 1878.</u>

Frank Warner Angel
Special Agent.

PRESSURE REGARDING AXTELL

That Ringites pressured Frank Warner Angel for cover-ups during his preparation of his reports is documented angrily by him from his New York City office in letters to his superiors, leaving the possibility that he was initially unaware that his conclusions had been pre-determined by the Hayes administration, or that it was Ring-biased.

On August 24, 1878, Angel complained to Secretary of the Interior Carl Schurz - to whom he was also reporting - about Governor Axtell's obstruction of his investigation. Angel wrote:

>>>No 62 Liberty Street
>>>New York City Aug 24 1878

The Honorable
C. Schurz
Secretary of the Interior
Sir:

I enclose copies of a letter received by me from Gov Axtell (marked A) and my reply thereto (marked B) – by which you will see that we did not part the best of friends on his part.

I have given him thirty days to reply subject to <u>your approval</u>.

He claims that the Interior Departments have no control over him – and that he will not be investi<u>gated by me.</u>

I have returned to N.Y. and with the counsel of the Honorable Attorney General [Charles Devens] I am to remain here until I index, & arrange my testimony & prepare my reports.

I have had a very difficult and dangerous mission, **and every obstacle thrown in my way by officials in New Mexico** *– and yet notwithstanding this I have accomplished a great deal.*

As soon as I receive the Governors reply, unless ordered sooner by you, will prepare and forward my reports –

>>>*Very respectfully*
>>>*Your obedient Servant*
>>>*Frank Warner Angel*
>>>*Special Agt.*

[ENCLOSED]

[On August 12, 1878, Axtell had written]:

A. "*Your communication of 11th Inst (Sunday) was duly received. You furnish me with a list of 31 interrogations which imply about as many charges of corrupt misconduct in office and ask that I should reply to them in 24 hours. Do you think this is reasonable?*"

[On August 13, 1878, Angel responded]:

B. "*I have found certain parts of this Territory in a terrible and deplorable state – some one is responsible for the same – and with a view to try and discover if you were responsible for the same I prepared and forwarded the interrogations to you ...You desire to know if I had given you a reasonable time to reply to said interrogations. I can only say that if I was the accused party I should not want desire or wish twenty four hours to answer same.*

By September 6,1878, Angel wrote again to Carl Schurz to complain not only that District Attorney William Rynerson was pressuring him about Axtell, but also that Rynerson himself was a biased Axtell appointee and *"open to censure"* for oppressive and unjust *"exercise of the functions of his office."* This angrily approached condemning the Ring. Angel wrote:

                    No 62 Liberty St
                    New York Sept 6 1878

The Hon C. Schurz
    Secretary of the Interior
    Sir:

  I have just been favored by a call from W.L. Rynerson <u>Territorial</u> Dist. Attorney 3^d District New Mexico – in the interest of Gov. Axtel. I presume that he will pay you a visit.

  He desired to know on what grounds I reported in favor of the removal of Gov Axtel. I declined to answer without the permission of the Department –

  He is an appointee of Gov Axtel – a strong partisan – and his conduct in the Lincoln County troubles is open to censure – He has not used his office for the punishment of all parties alike – He has been oppressive in the exercise of the functions of his office and due allowance must be taken of what he says – I do not believe he will willfully tell an untruth – but his interests are with the officials who have suffered the existing troubles to continue in New Mexico –

[AUTHOR'S NOTE: So, on September 6, 1878, Angel clearly blames New Mexico officials for the "troubles." By his October, 1878 reports, he will hide that conclusion to shield the Santa Fe Ring.]

                Your obedient servant
                  Frank Warner Angel
                  Special Apt- [Appointee]

REPORT ON S.B. AXTELL

It appears that by late September, Angel retreated from Ring accusations to scapegoat Governor S.B. Axtell for all accusations. Thus, Angel's report "In the Matter of Investigation of the Charges Against S.B. Axtell Governor of New Mexico" gave the excuse to remove him as a sham intervention. Noteworthy is that Angel apparently used Mary McPherson's complaints to Hayes and Schurz, while dishonestly hiding her accusations of the Ring, Catron, Elkins, Bristol, and murdering of opponents. Angel wrote:

Interior Department.

> *In the Matter of the*
> *investigation of the*
> *charges _____*
> *_____ against _____*
> *S.B. Axtel*
> *Governor of New Mexico*

To the Honorable
C. Schurz,
Secretary of the Interior

In compliance with your request made at the time I made my first report herein I herewith make my supplemental and final report as to the charges against said S.B. Axtel [Axtell throughout]. Since making said report I have found no reason for changing the same – but on the contrary believe as I did then that the best interests of New Mexico demanded the removal of S.B. Axtel as Governor.

A brief resuma of the facts laid before you at the time will be necessary to make this report complete.

Under your instructions I visited New Mexico for the purpose of ascertaining if there was any truth to the repeated complaints made to the Department as to fraud incompetency and corruption of United States officials. *I determined to see with my own eyes and hear with my own ears. I traveled over most of the Territory. I visited almost every important town and talked with the principal citizens thereof.*

I was met by every opposition possible by the United States civil officials and every obstacle thrown in my way by them to prevent a full and complete examination - with one exception and that of the surveyor general who not only sought but insisted on a full and thorough examination as will more fully appear in my report submitted as to his office.

I found universal complaint against the administration of affairs in the Territory and from facts coming under my observation and affidavits of the people the following charges in substance were made against the Governor of said Territory.

First

<u>That</u> the Governor had taken strictly partizan [partisan throughout] action as to the troubles in Lincoln County.

Second

<u>That</u> he refused to listen to the complaints of the people in that County.

Third

<u>That</u> he had been paid the sum of two thousand dollars to influence his action.

Fourth

<u>That</u> he arbitrarily removed Territorial officers thereby outlawing citizens, and usurping the functions of the Judiciary.

Fifth

<u>That</u> he removed officials and in their place appointed strong partizans.

Sixth

<u>That</u> all action taken by him has increased rather than quieted the troubles in Lincoln County.

Seventh

<u>That</u> he appointed officials to office and kept them there who were supported by the worst out-laws and murderers that the Territory could produce.

Eighth

<u>That</u> he knowingly appointed bad men to office.

Ninth

<u>That</u> he was a tool of designing men weak and arbitrary in exercising the functions of his office.

Tenth

<u>That</u> *he was a mormon and desired to turn the Territory into a mormon settlement.*

Eleventh

<u>That</u> *he conspired to murder innocent and law abiding citizens because they opposed his wishes and were exerting their influence against him.*

Twelfth

<u>That</u> *he arbitrarily refused to restore the Courts to Colfax County and refused to listen to the petitions of the people of that County for the restoration thereof.*

<u>The Governor</u> *at first refused to be investigated preferring to ignore the complaints against him on the grounds that the Department of the Interior had no power to investigate him ... He has not even answered the charges by a sworn statement. I received just before making my first report a news paper article which was not even signed by him to reply to the charges against him.*

<u>By</u> *much care and patience I have investigated the above charges impartially, seeking to obtain the truth and punish the guilty.*

<u>Many things</u> *came to my notice and observation of which no affidavits could be obtained. Many suspicious circumstances existed which convinced me beyond a peradventure that Gov Axtel was an improper person for the place. He is a man of strong prejudices, impulsive, conceited and easily flattered – all these make a man easily influenced –* **a complete tool in the hands of designing men.**

[AUTHOR'S NOTE: As if wanting to tell the truth, Angel hints throughout about Ring control of Axtell, and Ring crimes.]

<u>As to the charges one and two I found</u> *Lincoln County convulsed by an internal war. I enquired the cause. Some one was responsible for the blood shed in that County. I found two parties in the field one headed by Murphy Dolan and Riley – the other lead [led] by McSween – both had done many things contrary to the law – both were violating the law – McSween I firmly believe acted conscientious – Murphy Dolan & Riley for revenge and personal gain. The Governor came, heard the Murphy Dolan and Riley side, refused to hear the people who were with McSween or the residents of the County and acted strictly in advancing the Murphy Dolan and Riley party – Murder and unlawful acts followed instead of*

*peace and quiet which could have been accomplished if the Governor had acted as he should have done and listened patiently to both sides. The opportunity presented itself to him to have quieted and stopped the trouble in Lincoln Co – by his partizan action he allowed it to pass and the continuations of **the troubles that exist today in Lincoln County are chargeable to him**. He was a partizan either through corruption or weakness and charges first and second have been sustained.*

Charge Third – The facts are that in May 1876 Gov Axtel borrowed of Mr Riley $1800 and it is alleged that the same was paid in November ... I do not believe that Gov. Axtel received this money to directly influence his action. It was some time before the troubles actually commenced in Lincoln Co. – although they were brewing at the time.

[AUTHOR'S NOTE: Robert Casey was killed in 1875 the Ring.]

The only influence this transaction could have on the action of Gov. Axtell was in as much as Riley had befriended him to return the compliment, and certainly his official action lays him open to serious suspicion that his friendship for Murphy Dolan and Riley was stronger than his duty to the people and the government he represented.

Charge Fourth – I find that this charge has been fully sustained.

By his proclamation of March 9, 1878 ... he usurped the functions of the Judiciary and in fact removed J.B. Wilson a Justice of the Peace , and thereby made certain persons who were in good faith enforcing the warrants issued by said Wilson out laws ...

[AUTHOR'S NOTE: This confirms legality of deputizings of Billy and Fred Waite under Town Constable Atanacio Martinez.]

What right had he to do this? He did not veto the bill under which Wilson was appointed – and suffered him to act some months before he arbitrarily removed him.

Charge Fifth – John Copeland after the murder of Sheriff Brady was appointed Sheriff. He was an honest conscientious man, perhaps he was not the strongest man in character that ever existed – but I am yet to hear of any arbitrary act on his part any murder, robbery, arson in which he had been a party or of his being supported while in office by a band of notorious out laws and non residents. He was on the contrary surrounded by and had the confidence of a majority of the residents of the County – one of the County Commissioners was his bonds-man. By the laws of the Territory the Sheriff is ex-officio tax collector. The bonds as collector have to be fixed by the County Commissioners after they have ascertained the amount of taxes to be collected. Copeland had nothing to do with this – and owing to the troubled states of affairs in the county the County Commissioners could not find the amount of taxes to be collected.

The Governor immediately seizes the opportunity to aid Murphy Dolan & Riley. He this time acts strictly within the letter of the law, and would that I could say the interest of the law and non-partizan. He removes Copeland and appoints G.W. Peppin, one of the leaders of the Murphy Dolan and Riley party – who comes from Mesilla accompanied by his murderous out fit of out laws, as a body guard to assist him in enforcing law and order. Again we have an unusual number of murders, robbery and accompanied with arson, and after Kinney and his party have accomplished their mission of murdering McSween and robbing and stealing all they can

[AUTHOR'S NOTE: Here is Angel's reprehensible cover-up of the Lincoln County War battle, its military involvement, and the Ring murder of Alexander McSween. His dishonesty was to avoid blaming U.S. officials - instead blaming Peppin and Kinney! And hidden is that the "*stealing*" was looting of Tunstall's store.]

they retire on their laurels and return from whence they came, and Sheriff Peppin without the confidence in himself retreats to Fort Stanton at which place he is under the case and protection of the soldiers.
I find that Gov Axtel acted in the interests of the Murphy Dolan & Riley party and was strictly partisan and that the charge is sustained.

<u>Charge Sixth</u> – *I report that this charge has been sustained as already set forth.*

<u>Charge Seventh</u> – *I report that this charge has been sustained as appears by facts set forth under Charge Fifth.*
<u>Charge Eighth</u> – *Under this charge is the appointment of Col Chaves and Peppin. It was rumored that Col Chaves had falsified the election returns as a reward he was nominated and appointed Territorial District Attorney. There is however no*

evidence of this fact and I accordingly report that as to this part of the charge the same is not sustained, But that as to Peppin the charge is sustained.

The Governor replies that he appointed Peppin under recommendation of W.L. Rynerson ... Rynerson is undoubtedly a good lawyer but he is nevertheless a strong partisan and his record in the Lincoln County troubles show that he has used his office for oppressive purposes. The Governor must have known this, therefore with knowledge of Peppin's character he acted again strictly partizan and appointed an improper man.

[AUTHOR'S NOTE: Angel fabricated Axtell's bias as from a Riley loan, but exposes collusion with Rynerson, and almost the Ring.]

Charge Ninth: I find has been sustained as appears from the facts set forth herein.

Charge Tenth As to this charge there are no substantiated facts to show that he is a mormon. I therefore report that the same is not sustained.

Charge Eleventh – On considering this charge we must go back in the Unwritten History of New Mexico to the time when Colfax County **by the arbitrary and unlawful acts of certain officials***, became too hot for them, and they had to leave the County for the Countys good.*

[AUTHOR'S NOTE: This is another secret swipe at the Ring]

The plan was devised and carried out to join Colfax County & Taos County for judicial purposes and a bill was rushed through the Legislature and signed at once accomplishing this design. Immediately the people at Cimarron telegraphed Gov Axtell <u>"Requesting him to withhold his signature until a delegation from Colfax could wait upon him."</u> *The reply came back* <u>"Bill signed S.B. Axtell."</u> *If there was trouble in Colfax County which could not be quieted – then there was a justification in having this bill. It would then have been an excellent measure.*

But the facts show that when this bill was passed the troubles in Colfax Co had been quieted and stopped and that there was more lawlessness in other parts of the Territory than in Colfax ...

No benefit resulted from their change – but on the contrary it was a gross injury and injustice to the people of Colfax County. The two counties are separated by a range of high mountains, the lowest pass 9000 feet in altitude, which when the Court is in session are difficult and dangerous to cross. It required a journey over three mountains of 54 miles to reach Court. The juries were entirely taken from Taos County, manipulated by **Pedro Sanches** *a ringite, and prejudiced by outside influence.*

[AUTHOR'S NOTE: Accidentally, Angel slips up and reveals the Santa Fe Ring: "*ringite*" and "*outside influence!*"]

There never could be a fair trial in criminal proceedings and all most all civil business was suspended ... - it was a great expense to Colfax Co for witnesses and fees.

Is it surprising that opposition to the arbitrary Governor arose – and with opposition came murderousness and revenge on the part of the opposed.[?]

[AUTHOR'S NOTE: This double-talk obfuscates the Ring murder of Franklin Tolby and Colfax County Ring exposés.]

The Governor was visited at Santa Fe said he was hartily [heartily] in favor of the bill and spoke with extreme bitterness about the people of Colfax County – and refused to go to Colfax Co and investigate the facts for himself saying "He was fully advised about matters in their County and didn't need further information"...

After this at a public meeting at Cimarron an invitation in courteous language was addressed to the Governor inviting him to visit Colfax County and make a thorough investigation and learn the facts for himself. This invitation was signed by ten or twelve prominent citizens. To this the Governor makes no reply or acknowledgment ...

At this stage Ben Stevens Territorial District Attorney, an appointee of the Governor appears.

He circulates the report that he is going to try and have the Governor visit Colfax, leaves Cimarron goes to Fort Union, and returns in a few days with a company of soldiers (colored), and exhibits a telegram from the Governor which reads as follows "Do not let it be known that I will be in Cimarron on Saturdays coach. Body guard all right" and said it was proof that the Governor is coming to visit the County and would expect to meet those who had signed the invitation and that they must be on hand on the arrival of the coach to meet him. He requested that the matter be kept quiet as the Governor did not want a crowd but only wanted to meet those who had invited him ...

The facts subsequently show that the Governor did not intend to visit Colfax Co. and that the action of Stevens was in furtherance of a plot as will appear by the following [pasted on] letter [as reprinted in the Cimarron News and Press] –

Dear Ben – The second telegram delivered to you at Fort Union directed to Cimarron, was intended to leak, but the operator here says he cannot raise the Cimarron office. If I was expected our friends would probably be on hand, as the guard is only a Government escort. I do not think your definite business is suspected. Wade informed Hatch that he had been ready all the time to assist you, but could not find that you wanted to do it. Hatch says that their opinion is that you weakened and do not want to arrest the man. *Have your men placed to arrest him and to kill all the men who resist you or stand with those who do resist you.* Our man signed the invitation with others who were at that meeting for me to visit Colfax – Porter, Morley, Springer, et. al. Now, if they expect me Saturday, they will be on hand. Send me letters by messenger, and do not hesitate at extreme measures. Your honor is at stake now, and a failure is fatal. If others resist or attempt murder, bring them also. Hatch is excited, and wishes, of course, to put all the blame on the civil officers. I am more anxious on your account than for any other reason. I clearly see that we have no friends in Colfax, and I have suspected all along that some of our pretended friends were traitors.

Yours &c.,   S.B. Axtell

– *was there ever a cooler devised plot with a Governor as sponsor?*

The Governor admits the letter in toto … "That it sounds like me." and then subsequently attempts to explain away part of its terrible features …

He makes no attempt as to the telegram. Nor why he wished it to "leak." But by a down right falsehood he attempts to assemble certain persons who are obnoxious to him so that in the event of resistance, to be arrested, of a person by the name of [Clay] Allison an excuse would be offered "to kill all the men who resist or stand with those who resist you." He does not explain this. He cannot.

Stevens and the soldiers were sent by Governor Axtel ostensibly to arrest a person by the name of [Clay] Allison – but reading the foregoing telegram and letter I do not believe that it was the real object, for Allison was afterwards arrested and at once set at liberty … and Governor Axtel subsequently made an appointment and traveled with said Allison in a friendly way in the stage coach …

Any man capable of framing and trying to enforce such a letter of instructions as the one set forth in this report is not fit to be entrusted with any power whatever – I therefore report that this charge has been sustained.

[AUTHOR'S NOTE: Angel's outrage at the "Dear Ben plot" is hypocritically disingenuous, since he is covering it up as a Ring tactic also used for murdering Tunstall and McSween.]

<u>Charge Twelfth</u> : *On February 1876 a bill was passed through the Legislature providing that the Courts should be removed from Cimarron Colfax County to Taos, Taos County and that after two terms the Governor might at his option restore the Courts to Colfax County. For the reasons set forth under Charge Eleventh I find that this charge is sustained.*

<u>In conclusion</u> *I respectfully submit that whether through ignorance or corrupt motives the action of said Axtel has been to keep many parts of the Territory of New Mexico in a state of turmoil and confusion, when intelligent and non-partizan action on his part might have avoided much of the difficulty, and that the removal of Governor Axtell viewed with the evidence and his reply received before my first report, was an absolute necessity, and it becomes more evident that such was the right course on receiving his subsequent replies.*

It is seldom that history states more corruption, fraud, mismanagement, plots and murders, than New Mexico, has been the theatre under the administration of Governor Axtel –

[AUTHOR'S NOTE: Angel lists the Ring's "*corruption, fraud, mismanagement, plots and murders,*" but capitulates by blaming it all on Axtell.]

I transmit herewith the testimony herein –
All of which is respectfully submitted -
<u>Dated Washington, October 3 1878.</u>

Frank Warner Angel
Special Agent
Department Interior.

REPORT ON T.B. CATRON

Frank Warner Angel actually needed only a single report to reveal the motive and murderer of John Tunstall: one on Thomas Benton Catron. Of course, Catron knew this. So he obstructed Angel by refusing to provide requested documents for his report, then giving blanket denial in interrogatory questions provided by Angel. Furthermore, S.B. Elkins intervened personally to shield Catron. But a report on Catron was apparently presented to the Department of Justice. And it resulted in Catron's resignation as U.S. Attorney on October 10, 1878 - to take effect November 10, 1878 - to avert official removal, ramifications of Ring exposure, and destruction of Catron's Territorial influence and ambitions.

As discussed, Catron rightly feared that report, and had Elkins expurgate it by 1892. By then, Catron also staged the 1888 fire in his law office to destroy other incriminating records of his Ring crimes and cronies.

A LETTER TO PRESIDENT HAYES ABOUT ANGEL'S CATRON INVESTIGATION: AUGUST 29, 1878

A major clue about the Catron report's existence is an August 29, 1878 letter to President Hayes by a John C. Routt, a possible Catron frontman. It inadvertently confirmed that Angel's initial investigation was into *"supposed misconduct of Gov Axtell and [U.S.] District Attorney Catron"* in *"effort being made to remove the said officers."* That meant by August of 1878, the Ring knew that Catron, as well as Axtell, were marked for removal! That meant U.S. officials were being accused! The letter may have been by Catron himself – like his 1890's "anonymous" letters to the press - since it uses his outlaw myth to call accusations not from *"the best people in and around Santa Fe,"* and it threatens that the removals would encourage *"the lawless conduct that has caused so much trouble in the Territory."* Routt wrote:

Santa Fe. New Mexico.
Aug 29ᵗʰ 1878

President Hayes.

Dear Sir.
I am here on a visit to my daughter and have more by accident than otherwise heard statements pro and con in relation to the causes of the recent troubles in this Territory ***and also***

in relation to the supposed misconduct of Gov Axtell and [U.S.] District Attorney Catron. I also learned that there is an effort being made to remove the said officers, and from all I can learn, in my judgment the charges against those officials have been made without good cause, and [without] the best people in and around Santa Fe. I think it would be against the interest of the Territory to remove the said [without] the best people in and around Santa Fe. I think it would be against the interest of the Territory to remove the said officials or either of them ... It seems to me that this removal would have much influence to encourage the lawless conduct that has caused so much trouble in the Territory ... It would also encourage the unlawful conduct of persons who are responsible for the murder and killing that has recently taken place in this Territory ... This statement is also made at my own suggestion ...
John C. Routt

LEW WALLACE CONFIRMS THE CATRON REPORT: FEBRUARY 16, 1880

Unaware that Catron was pretending his Angel Report did not exist, Lew Wallace referenced it (implying he may have read it himself) to Secretary of the Interior Carl Schurz in a letter draft of February 16, 1880, though he apparently crossed it out for his mailed version. (See my pp. 701-703 for full letter) Wallace wrote:

> *Mr. Catron is not unknown to fame in your department ... He also figures largely, I am told in the report of Mr. Angel, in which, as late U.S. District Attorney, he was admitted to a kind of head-centership of the famous old Santa Fe ring.*

ELKINS LETTER TO ATTORNEY GENERAL CHARLES DEVENS BACKING CATRON: SEPTEMBER 24, 1878

It took a crisis for Catron and Elkins to do their own dirty work directly. But Angel's report on Catron risked removal of the Ring's Territorial head and exposure of its crimes. So Elkins acted on September 24, 1878, from his mansion in Deer Park, Maryland, with the report's potential recipient: Attorney General Charles Devens, who apparently had no Ring affiliation. But Deven's fellow Cabinet member, Secretary of State William

Evetts, was a Ringite who had assisted Catron and Elkins as an attorney for finalizing their purchase of the Maxwell Land Grant to cheat Lucien Maxwell. Of course, Secretary of the Interior Carl Schurz, recipient of Mary McPherson's exposés, was involved in Ring cover-up. And it all came down to President Hayes's Ring shielding. So it seems that Evart's and Schurz's input to Devens, plus Elkins's coming to Washington, D.C. for secret lobbying, resulted in two outcomes: 1) secret pressuring of Angel to remove all mention of his mission to investigate *"supposed misconduct of ... [U.S.] District Attorney Catron ... [and the] effort being made to remove [him];"* and 2) secret negotiating of Catron's resignation. Elkins wrote:

Deer Park Md.
Sept. 24 1878

Hon Chas Devens,
Attorney General
Sir:
I have just received from Mr. Catron a telegraphic message informing me that his testimony & answer was delayed in being forwarded until the 19th inst. & requested me to ask that no action be taken until they should be received. I think they will reach the Department by the 26th – unless there is some unusual delay & I hope you will grant his request in this respect –
Very Respectfully
S.B. Elkins

N.B.
I will be in Washington on Monday next, & if it would be agreeable to you to hear me, I would like to make a statement in Mr. Catrons behalf. With the testimony & his answer & the facts I know I think it can be clearly established that only bitter political & personal enemies have assailed him & the charges are unfounded. I have written the president today & hope the letter will be refer to you as in it I   [missing line]   the present term.
If you desire him to appear a telegraph to him at Mesilla New Mexico will reach him in time – if not & you will kindly notify me. I will telegraph him.
Very Respectfully
S.B. Elkins

ELKINS'S SECRET COVER-UP LETTER TO CATRON: AUGUST 15, 1879

A behind-the-scenes glimpse of the political maneuvering around Angel's reports, comes from Senator Elkins. He was less scrupulous than Catron in his expurgations; so his revealing typed copy of his August 15, 1879 letter to Catron still exists in his collected papers donated to the University of West Virginia's History Center.

Known as "smooth Steve" to his political enemies, Elkins preferred honeyed persuasion to Catron's brutish threats. In this dramatically important letter - discussed above as defensively minimized by Catron's historian, Victor Westphall - Elkins checkmates Catron in a dispute about their entangled business dealings (with some of Catron's holdings hidden under Elkins's name), by high-pressure reminder that in 1878 he saved Catron from the Hayes administration's ordered dismissal or indictment - following Angel's investigation and report. Of course, that confirms the report's existence. But it also shows how close Catron's unrestrained crimes - including malicious prosecution and murder - had brought him and the Ring to destruction.

Elkins stated in the typed retained copy: "About 1 year ago when your enemies were fighting you both in New Mexico and Washington and your dismissal as U.S. Attorney was ordered and an indictment talked of strongly, I let every other matter drop and devoted myself to your defense. I never exerted myself more in my life, and I have been assured by the authorities that but for me and the fight I made you would have been dismissed."

Elkins also reminded Catron how he manipulated Washington officials for the Ring, stating: "As to my going to Washington for you I have made a great many journeys there for you." The letter also shows power struggle by these two moral monstrosities over their Ring spoils, and their matched power of evil, as Elkins purrs: "I don't think yet you would do me an injury and unless you compel me to open hostility I will always be ready to do you a kindness." Elkins wrote:

Halliehurst,
Elkins, West Virginia

118 Broadway,
New York City.
Aug. 15, 1879

My dear Tom,

I have waited some time to reply to your lengthy letter of the 1st. inst. ...

About 1 year ago when your enemies were fighting you both in New Mexico and Washington and your dismissal as U.S. Attorney was ordered and an indictment talked of strongly, I let every other matter drop and devoted myself to your defense.

I never exerted myself more in my life, and I have been assured by the authorities that but for me and the fight I made you would have been dismissed.

In this defense I incurred obligations that to this day I am discharging. I am glad I succeeded because it gave me pleasure to serve you. I will not refer to any other matter or thing between us but ask you to measure back any twelve or thirteen years. You don't forget easily.

If I had never known you before the contest I made for you and your honor I thought that of it self was sufficient to bind you to me forever and that nothing I might do could invoke your enmity, - but how deceived I have been when I read your letter before me I can but ask is there any one in whom one can trust, how weak is human friendship.

We have had out differences, - all men have, - but I never thought you would try to force my resignation as President [of the First National Bank of Santa Fe] and added to this you criticize my charge of $100 for going to sell the Steven's property.

Ingratitude is a sin. I am not going to try and answer your letter in detail. I have fully written you about the bank and I will say now that I never wrote the officers anything but asking kindness and indulgence to you. I have repeatedly asked them so far as the interests of the Bank would permit it to help you and lend you all the money they could. <u>I stand squarely upon this</u>

record. **If I had wanted to injure you I need not have hunted for ways and means.** I also call your attention to the fact that I told you if you would send your note, here, I would endorse it and get you the money to the extent of $10 or $20,000.

Now as to the presidency of the bank, I don't care to hold the place a moment and particularly with even one stockholder opposed. I have told you repeatedly I wanted to resign, - and this is my purpose but I won't do it nor think of it if you undertake to compel me to do so. The Bank has never done me a service, I have never borrowed a dollar from it and hope I never may. If in my administration I have made mistakes, they have been in the interests of the Bank.

You call at once for deeds to all of your property in my name. You don't offer to make any deeds to me but I am willing to make a full settlement with you and interchange deeds. I made you a statement long ago about the interests I have in my name belonging to me and you have always been protected on my books, but for two years or more I have been urging and you have been promising to make me a statement of land you hold for me in your name.

Why don't you send me a statement? You always said I had an interest in the lands you own on the Puerco River and some grants near Santa Fe, also that I was interested with you in a fifth of the Aztec mine [world's richest gold mine].

You did not pay for coal lands on the Galisteo not did I pay for Aztec and several other matters.

Now make me a statement and let us have a settlement. I may go out this Fall, hope to do so. If not Waddingham tells me you are coming on for Julia [Catron's wife], why couldn't we then arrange our matters. I[t] will be difficult unless we are together. As to the Mora grant, I don't think I can make deeds to the parties. I am the trustee and you know there are disputes whether there are four or five owners but if you are in pressing need I can make a deed to the coal lands and to the Ortiz Grant, but I don't know the description of the coal lands. If you will look over the patents in my safe or the vault and make a deed to the Coal Lands and Ortiz Grant I will gladly sign it.

As to the Merita Juana Lopez [grant], why do you call for the deed there? Why don't you send me a deed to my four ninths. I don't remember anything about the Bernardo Martin [grant]. Will do anything you say is right, - indeed as badly as I think you have treated me I will do everything I can to help you and put our matters in shape.

Did you ever get the Booth voucher paid? Probably I can sell some of your interests in the East. I think the time is near at hand when we can sell some of our property to advantage and I have been preparing for this. If you think however you can do better with your property otherwise I have no objections.

As to my going to Washington for you I have made a great many journeys there for you and I should go now but I don't believe I could do anything with the Commissioner. Am afraid not but if you think you want me to do so I will try.

After reading this I wish you could get your consent to withdraw your letter before me. It may not do you any material service - but it is best to be friends when it is so easy. I am not angry at your action, I am only sorry and disappointed. **I don't think yet you would do me an injury and unless you compel me to open hostility I will always be ready to do you a kindness.**

If I were in New Mexico these differences and misunderstandings would not be, they ought not to be and if they continue the fault will not be mine.

Send the agreement Collinson sent me about the Bosque del Apache Grant.

Very truly,
signed S.B. Elkins

RAYMOND MORLEY'S RESPONSE TO ANGEL'S REPORTS: AUGUST 15, 1878

Historian Norman Cleaveland, in his book *The Morleys: Young Upstarts in the Southwest*, provides the perspective of his grandfather, Raymond Morley, to Frank Warner Angel's investigation from Morley's August 15, 1878 letter to his wife, Ada. (Cleaveland, pp. 152-155) And about the Lincoln County War, Morley knows Murphy-Dolans fight for the Ring, stating: *"In the meantime the Ring seems more and more desperate. If I am a good guesser, the War in Lincoln is far from over. The Murphy party say they mean to kill or drive every McSween man from Lincoln. The latter will probably fight or if from being overpowered they leave now, it will be with a burning desire for vengeance and they will retaliate when opportunity offers."* Billy's pardon quest would be part of that creative retaliation. Morley wrote:

Silver City
August 15, 1878

My Darling –
    Your letter of the 7*th* came last night and it was a good long newsy letter cheerful letter – such a one as I like ... I am a little uneasy about matters in Colfax for there seems to be danger that the Ring may try to stir up a war over Grant matters. What I look for is an effort to divide the people by getting some to lease all the ranges at a nominal price and try to drive the others off by that means and thus get up a feud among the people, but I hope the people will see this in time and prevent it ... It may be that [W.T.] Thornton's action [Catron's law partner, and court-appointed receiver in June of 1878 during a conflicted Maxwell Land Grant Company reorganization] will only solidify the people but self-interest may be played upon to make trouble ...
    About Angel, I don't know what to think. I feel a good deal as you do. He may do right and he may not. The feeling seems to be general on the part of both parties that he will or has reported serious charges vs. Axtell and Catron, but this may be a blind. In the meantime the Ring seems more and more desperate. If I am a good guesser, the War in Lincoln is far from over. I expect every day to hear of more bloodshed. The Murphy party say they mean to kill or drive every McSween man from Lincoln. The latter will probably fight or if from being overpowered they leave now, it will be

*with a burning desire for vengeance and they will retaliate when opportunity offers. Compromise seems impossible ... Both parties have practically hoisted the black flag [displayed by Santa Ana at the Alamo, meaning no surrender, only death]. On the other hand, **if the Ring party succeeds** the leaders who have employed their men will have on their hands a bunch of men of whom it will be hard to rid themselves and who are liable when the time comes when they want to get rid of them will turn upon them as was the case in Colfax County in 1871. The whole structure is built on sand and climb and claw as they will, it will not stand.*

*Politically, I am not wholly idle ... **There is some talk of Waldo [for political office], but the Democrats do not forget that he was a schoolmate of Elkins and Catron. They brought him here. He worked with them [as a lawyer in Catron's firm]. They appointed him Judge and Axtell made him Attorney General** ...*

*So far as the past has shown ... we had better stick to railroading and that so long as we do we will succeed, at least in designating routes if not in building them afterwards. **I feel so strong on that score now that I have little fear of the Ring being able to influence the R.R. people to oust me** ...*

Kiss the babies many times for papa and believe me
    Yours lovingly and faithfully,
        Raymond

AFTERMATH OF THE ANGEL REPORTS

Unscathed by the compromised reports of Frank Warner Angel, the Santa Fe Ring was unleashed by late 1878 in full viciousness to exterminate their last adversaries. There would be one potential obstacle: uncertain loyalties of Lew Wallace, the new Territorial Governor replacing Samuel Beach Axtell. It must have confused one-dimensional Ringites, whose only gluttonous goals were money and power, to contemplate the romantic complexity of Lew Wallace: Civil War Major General; graphic artist; best-selling author of an historical novel, *The Fair God*, about conquistador Hernando Cortez; famous prosecuting attorney who hanged Abraham Lincoln's murderers; and, at the time, writing a novel called *Ben-Hur* about the coming of Jesus Christ.

CHAPTER 11
ENTER LEW WALLACE: 1878

ABOUT LEW WALLACE AND SHILOH

ANALYSIS: In 1879, Lew Wallace was 52 when he first met 19 year old Billy Bonney seeking a pardon. By then, Wallace had been seeking his own pardon obsessively for 17 years. It was for his failure as a General in the first day of the Civil War battle of Shiloh. It was refused by that battle's General - then President - Ulysses S. Grant. By Billy's killing two years later because of Wallace's withheld pardon to him, Wallace had already fled his brief, New Mexico Territory governorship for ambassadorship to Turkey. His novel, Ben-Hur: A Tale of the Christ, completed in Santa Fe, was a best-seller. But Wallace was not at peace. He added another obsession to Shiloh. It was Billy the Kid. He kept all his written communications with Billy. And, for the rest of his life, in literary reworkings published in newspapers, he obsessively reworked the pardon, its bargain, and his role. His own pardon lost, and Billy's pardon ungranted, were his unhealable wounds.

SHILOH: WALLACE'S UNHEALABLE ACHILLES' HEEL

Lew Wallace, a handsome, eccentric, narcissistic, multi-talented, elitist authoritarian, was more dreamer than soldier. His Civil War service in the 1862 Battle of Shiloh gave him a psychic wound that skewed his life, and helps to explain Billy Bonney's lost pardon. Wallace's personality and Shiloh are dramatized in the following excerpts from my 2012 novel, *Billy and Paulita*.

AUGUST 31, 1878   1:10 PM   SATURDAY

With his Cabinetmen reassembled, Hayes began by asking what they knew about Lew Wallace, his prospective pick for governor.

Secretary of War George McCrary said, "Ulysses S. Grant detested him after Shiloh. And in July of sixty-four, Lew Wallace initiated the battle at Monocacy Junction without orders. Later, he claimed it saved President Lincoln from kidnapping. He once said to me, 'Washington lay exposed in its nakedness.' "

Carl Schurz joked: "The poet who was a general. Or the general who was a poet."

"Gentlemen," chuckled the president, "let's go over the specifics and make our decision. Troops won't kidnap me, but my wife will - for dinner." They laughed.

Schurz said, "I have taken a special interest in Lew Wallace. Do not forget that I rescued my old professor from Spandau prison. I have a weakness for intellectuals." He adjusted his pince-nez and straightened his notes. "My assignment was to interview him. This is what I learned.

"Louis Wallace - who renamed himself 'Lew' because he thought it sounded better - was born in Brookville, Indiana, on April tenth of eighteen twenty-seven. His father was the Governor of Indiana in thirty-seven. Lew became an attorney. For a wife he picked a very rich girl. In the War - probably because of his father - Governor Oliver Morton of Indiana made him Indiana's Adjutant General with the responsibility to raise troops. Then Lew was made Colonel of the Eleventh Regiment of Indiana Volunteers.

"It was for this regiment that this poetic romantic - so dashing that the paintings of him imply broken hearts - designed the Zouave costume. With the red pantaloons, tight green jackets, and little caps, to me the pictures look like organ grinder monkeys."

Hayes smiled. "It wasn't as bad as that, Carl. But they did stand out in parades."

"That I can imagine. And we will see how eccentric is this Lew. We come to the battle of Shiloh in Tennessee. Do not forget - because we have seen such horrors later - Shiloh, in sixty-two, was the biggest battle ever fought on American soil. Twenty-three thousand seven hundred forty-six casualties; more than the total casualties of your Revolutionary War, War of Eighteen Twelve, and the Mexican War combined.

"Originally it was called the battle of Pittsburgh Landing. Wallace was positioned at Crump's Landing six miles north of Pittsburgh Landing, near the north to south Tennessee River.

"In my mind, the key to Shiloh is not often mentioned, which is that, through his own spies, Lew Wallace learned that the Confederate army under General Albert Sidney Johnston was approaching. Did he inform General Grant? No. Why? He has said he assumed Grant would know something that big. Well, he didn't. And, the month before, Wallace had again been promoted - this time to Major General: the highest rank a man could reach at the time.

"Back to Shiloh. Two main routes went to Pittsburgh Landing: one direct - the River Road - one indirect, the Shunpike Road. With the terrain, the River Road went a bit east before going south. The Shunpike went quite west before looping back.

"Then came April fourth. Wallace's scout, Bell, reported to him that the rebel army was heading from Corinth to Pittsburgh Landing.

"So Wallace wrote a note - probably poetic - and gave it to his orderly Simpson to inform Grant. But - as revealed in the intense controversy that followed - Wallace told Simpson if he couldn't deliver it directly to Grant, he should *mail it*. Gentlemen, Simpson mailed it!

"Ulysses Grant said he never got the letter, which can be believed since - as you say in this country - 'all hell broke loose' two days later on April sixth, when everyone was asleep, except for the Confederate army. Wallace was awakened by his sentinel, who told him he heard guns from the south. So Wallace did the natural thing: went for breakfast on a steamboat on the Tennessee River.

"At eight-thirty, Grant's boat, the Tigress, passed his. Grant asked Wallace if he had heard gunfire. Wallace answered *only* that he had. So Grant told him to hold in readiness.

"At eleven-thirty, Grant sent Captain Baxter, his Chief Quartermaster, to tell Wallace to come to Pittsburgh Landing for a battle. Poor Baxter wrote those orders from Grant on a paper picked up in the Tigress's ladies' room. History has not told us what he was doing there. The note - whose penmanship Wallace criticized - Wallace later said he had lost. More unfortunate was what came next.

"Wallace had those two roads to get to the battle. Guess what he did?" The men were smiling. Schurz was their eccentric. "He had lunch. After that, he took the longer Shunpike, having decided that, by then, Grant must have the enemy retreating westward - which was where that road would first put him. In reality, a Confederate artillery of sixty-two cannon were firing on desperate Union men trapped at Pittsburgh Landing.

"Soon, Wallace was met by a messenger from Grant saying, 'Hurry up;' and, strangely - to Wallace - departing eastward.

"Nevertheless, Lew Wallace blithely proceeded west until met by another Grant messenger. When that one also left in the 'wrong direction,' it occurred to Wallace that *he* had made a mistake. So what did he do? Stopped to wait for his stragglers.

"Then came two more couriers who reported that they were losing at Pittsburgh Landing, and pleaded with him to release troops. He refused. He felt it would make a bad impression if they did not arrive as a unit. But he did proceed southeast.

"That left Wallace with Snake Creek to cross. It was a bog. So he and his men descended waist deep. He later revealed that he decided not to worry about their uniforms. That is fortunate or this might still be a slave owning country - though poor Abe Lincoln might still be alive.

"At that point, Lew Wallace was only a half mile from the battle. Since he was not Alexander the Great, famous for his lightning marches, he chose to bed down in that bog. He leaned on a tree. Sleep was further interrupted by mournful cries of the wounded at the adjacent battlefield.

"Wallace did arrive the next morning. Union General Buell had already crossed the Tennessee River with eighteen thousand more troops for Grant. As you know, that day, Grant won.

"Then, not surprisingly, Grant removed Wallace from any future command of troops. Maybe he hoped to humiliate Wallace into leaving the army; but it only stimulated his flurry of writing, in which he denied wrongdoing, but concluded that the war was young and they were all still learning.

"But Lew was bored. So, in August of sixty-two, when his friend Governor Oliver Morton summoned him to assist in organizing the defense of Cincinnati, Ohio, he went - obviously alone.

By coincidence, heading in that same direction were Confederate troops under General Kirby Smith.

"When Wallace found out, he took over Cincinnati without asking anyone, declared martial law, and composed a literary piece of sorts: a proclamation demanding that all inhabitants defend their city.

"Unable to get rid of him, the army next tried sending him to miserable Camp Chase, which held five thousand, renegade Union soldiers. His assignment was to prepare these derelicts to fight Indians in Minnesota. To everyone's surprise but his own, he did shape up and send off this criminal crew. I do not know, however, if they merely deserted again.

"Then came Lincoln's reelection. Wallace was sent to Baltimore, Maryland, to protect poling places. He got carried away, as usual, and was about to hang four men - declaring, without proof, that they were Confederate spies - when Lincoln leashed him.

"Then April fourteenth of sixty-five passed at Ford's Theater. Because he was an accomplished lawyer and a loyal Republican, Wallace was appointed by President Andrew Johnson as judge in the Lincoln assassins' military trial.

"But it has been the conclusion of our less hysterical times that Wallace bullied and hampered their lawyers. And making the eight defendants wear bizarre pointed caps covering their heads, does smack of his costuming dramas. As you all know, the hanging of the defendants, David Herald, George Atzarodt, and Lewis Payne, has left people uneasy because their fellow gallows victim, Mary Surratt - John Wilkes Booth's landlady - was considered innocent. The so-called accomplices, Doctor Samuel Mudd, who set Booth's broken leg; Edward Spangler; Samuel Arnold; and Michael O'Laughlin were also sentenced - again at Wallace's adamancy - to life in prison on the Dry Tortugas in Florida. President Johnson pardoned them later; though, by then, O'Laughlin had died of yellow fever.

"But this courtroom experience prepared Lew Wallace for his next assignment: heading the Andersonville War Crimes trial against Confederate prison keeper, Captain Henry Wirz, in August of sixty-five. Wirz too was hanged, though without public regret.

"And Wallace continued to wax poetic. On July fourth of sixty-six, he presented his old friend Governor Oliver Morton with the battle flags of the Indiana regiments and said ..." Schurz took up a paper: " *'In the armies of Persia was a chosen band called the Immortals bearing spears pointed with pomegranates of silver and gold. We, too, have our Immortals! And instead of a king to serve they have for leader that man of God and the people, Lincoln the Martyr.'*

" This writing makes me miss Abe even more. Gentleman, how do you point a spear with a pomegranate?" Several laughed.

"Then comes Mexico. Wallace had earlier convinced Lincoln and Grant that the Texan Confederates planned to join French Imperialists under Napoleon the Third's puppet king, Archduke Maximillian of Austria.

"So, in late sixty-five, Lew did an arms running scheme for anti-imperialist Mexicans. They graciously took the arms and ungraciously never paid him.

"It is true that Lew Wallace has never shown venality. He has barely shown practicality.

"In sixty-six, he made an even stranger Mexican plan: offering their then president, Benito Juárez, to import American colonists to defend their border from Indians in exchange for free land. Can you imagine Juárez wanting to give up more land to Americans?

"But Wallace happily declared that the experience helped him finish his novel on Mexico, *The Fair God* - which has gotten so much literary acclaim.

"In seventy, Wallace ran for the House of Representatives from Indiana. The Democrats made much of Shiloh and the hanging of Missus Surratt. He lost, but blamed election fraud.

"Since seventy-four, he has engaged in private law practice back in Crawfordsville, Indiana, and is working on a book on Jewish history called *Ben-Hur*.

"And, as you all know, he campaigned loyally in Florida for Rutherford's presidential bid."

Suave William Evetts said, "He almost got hisereward this year. He was offered the ambassadorship of Bolivia, but refused. Probably the low salary."

Schurz laughed. "Not the five thousand dollars. He didn't like the landscape."

"So he might accept the Governorship of New Mexico Territory, which pays only two thousand six hundred dollars a year?" asked John Sherman.

"Apparently, yes. He thinks New Mexico Territory will look like Jerusalem and assist in completing his new book."

"Thank you, Carl," said Hayes, smiling. "Informative and amusing. Is Lew Wallace right as its next governor?"

"I will be a more serious," said Schurz, adjusting his pince-nez and reverting to token idealist. "This Lew Wallace, as I said, reminds me of my old professor. Then I risked my life to rescue him. Now I would let him stay. Intellectuals ruined our revolution. They were all mind and no heart. They cared only to act clever - not to act. I left the country in disgust.

"And, with Lew Wallace, possessing a mind able to be a lawyer, a general, and a writer, only gave him vanity to override orders with his own incorrect decisions, and to become despotic with horrible consequences like Missus Surrat. Does this bother him? Not at all. Because he feels nothing. We would send into this faraway battleground the opposite of our Angel. Please excuse my pun."

"Carl," smiled Hayes, "I'll continue that pun. We don't want an avenging Angel sent. This war needs to stay in darkness. I'm confident that Lew Wallace won't embarrass the Republican Party."

"And how many more will die?" asked Carl Schurz, exaggerating melancholy resignation.

"As many as have died likewise through history," said Hayes. "And now it's time for dinner."

SEPTEMBER 13, 1878   5:58 AM   FRIDAY

[I]n his Patent Office Building professional quarters, Carl Schurz was sitting with Lew Wallace. Schurz asked him whether - after reading the Angel reports - he still wanted to be governor of New Mexico Territory.

The long-limbed graceful man, with military erectness, nodded grandly. His gray-woven black hair still had the profuse forelock of his youth; and his united mustache and long rectangular beard, in imagined style of an Abyssinian king, had likewise been sported for thirty years. Schurz complimented his book, *The Fair God*. Wallace added that it was being called the great American novel. His next, set in ancient Jerusalem, was the telling of Christ's coming.

"And the governorship would not interfere with that coming?" red-headed Schurz smiled.

"Indeed, not," said Wallace. "And I would step into paternal gubernatorial footprints, confirming, at fifty-one, that I am at last a man. Well I know the yoke of parental authority. My father - as Indiana Governor only about a decade after Tippecanoe and the killing of that fanatical Tecumseh - was well-respected, and, at home, a taskmaster. Even my blessed mother - who died when I was but five - had her stern ways. As to punishments, she was as creative as I was incorrigible. She would tie me to a bedpost or dress me in a girl's frock. She was as determined to make a man of me as was he."

"And you served your country well. President Hayes wants to remove any last obstacles to your reward."

"Shiloh," Wallace answered bitterly. Drawn heavy brows accentuated his indignant brown eyes. "Someone had to bear blame for that first day. It enables me to write from experience about Jesus - the greatest martyr of all - having myself also tasted the gall and vinegar of injustice."

Carl Schurz asked, given that perspective, what had been his impression of the Angel reports. Without telling Hayes, he had rebelliously provided Wallace with copies of them all.

Wallace said, "Voluminous but fascinating. Change names and weaponry, and one would have ancient combatants with pagan gods appeased by blood sacrifice. My own Mexico experiences revealed to me the primitive Christianity left by Hernándo Cortés - my 'fair God'- after he defeated Aztec Emperor Montezuma. And recall: the Christ casted out demons. Now I too shall have the opportunity to dwell in a land where the Devil still walks the streets." He chuckled. "A privilege few authors of biblical tales receive."

Schurz asked if his wife would mind living in that backward place. Wallace said, "Susan loves adventure - as I do - but not privation. It may be of historical fascination to reside in the Palace of the Governors - which I read was built at the start of the seventeenth century by Don Pedro de Peralta, Spain's first governor. But then it really was a palace. Now it would be rather like taking her to live in the ruins of the Coliseum. Pre-wife repairs will be paramount.

"As to my own pilgrimage to that unholy land: if I have not brought peace to Lincoln County in the sixty days following my October first swearing in, I shall be ashamed of myself. After all, I shall be residing in Santa Fe, in the valley of a mountain range known as Sangre de Cristo: 'Blood of Christ.' What better place to both write about, as well as bring forth, a tale of redemption and salvation."

MORE ON ULYSSES S. GRANT AND SHILOH

Geoffrey Perret, in his insightful biography, *Ulysses S. Grant: Soldier & President*, summarizes General Lew Wallace's failure in the battle of Pittsburgh Landing - which was later named 'Shiloh" after the small Shiloh Methodist Church left standing in that blood-soaked battlefield.

Perret considered Wallace a military incompetent with a "novelist's mind, not a soldier's." He further blamed Wallace's Shiloh debacle to his competitively seeking his own fame. Perret, as a military strategist, described the enraged frustration that Grant himself must have felt that April 6, 1862. Perret wrote:

What [Grant] was counting on [on April 6, 1862] even more than [General Don Carlos] Buell [arriving the next day with 18,000 troops] was for Lew Wallace to appear over on the right about noon. Something strange happened to his order, however. It had been lost ...

Even so, there was a well-known rule for what to do in case of doubt – march to the sound of the drums. Wallace did not do that. He marched instead to the sound of his own drummer. Wallace argued for years afterward that had he had done as Grant wanted he would have found himself on his own, confronting half the rebel army, because Sherman's troops had fallen back toward the river. **A competent commander, however, would have sent scouts forward to inspect the roads leading south and staff officers to confer with Sherman and coordinate the link up of the two divisions.**

Wallace had been a speaker of the Indiana State legislature and came from an important political family. He also had military experience, having commanded a company of volunteers during the Mexican War. After Mexico, he pursued his military interests through involvement in the Indiana militia ... For all his keen interest in military service, however, **Wallace lacked the temperament for combat command. What he possessed was the base metal – a romantic attachment to military glory.** He was a talented young man, with a brilliant imagination and an artistic temperament. **Wallace had a novelist's mind, not a soldier's. And now his vivid imagination detected an opportunity for fame.**

Instead of advancing straight toward Sherman as Grant directed, he would swing far to the west, pass around Sherman and enter the battle poised to make an attack of his own. With any luck he might fall on the unsuspecting [Confederate General Albert Sidney] Johnston's open left flank and save the day. It might have worked too, under someone who knew the local road net or could at least read a map. Trouble was, Wallace got hopelessly lost. He spent the entire day leading his seven thousand desperately needed men up one country lane, then down another ...

Grant sent an aide ... in a frantic search for Wallace, but it did no good. Once Wallace got lost, he stayed lost ...

Pittsburg Landing [battle of Shiloh] was not the South's lost opportunity but the North's. By noon [on April 6th], Grant's actions had a clear pattern: He was trying to deploy his army to bring off one of the greatest battles of annihilation in the history of war. If Wallace advanced as ordered on the right and [Brigadier General, and past navy-man William T.] Nelson advanced as ordered on the left, the [Union] Army of the Tennessee would be poised to launch a double envelopment, much as Hannibal had done in Cannae ...

The war in the West could have been won in a day had it not depended on a fictioneer advancing on one flank and a strange sailor on the other. They moved slowly, haltingly, like men lost in the fog, unable to comprehend simple orders or to grasp a simple idea ...

[T]hey not only robbed Grant of his Cannae but ruined even the hope of seizing the initiative. All he could do was fight the kind of battle he liked least, a defensive one. And he would have to do it with what he already had on the field – five infantry divisions, around twelve hundred cavalry, a hundred cannon, and himself ...

Shooting had become sporadic as Lew Wallace finally arrived ... He entered the battlefield roughly three miles from where he started, but had marched his men at least fifteen miles to reach it, resting from time to time ...

By afternoon [of the second day of battle], every foot of ground the Federals had lost had been recaptured ...

Grant's losses came to thirteen thousand killed, wounded and missing; the Confederates had lost close to twelve thousand ... (Perret, pp. 191-199)

[In July of 1862], Grant managed to do something he had been longing to do for three months [since Shiloh]: He got Lew Wallace out of the Army. He sent Wallace back to Indiana on leave, where Wallace got involved in recruiting new regiments. When Wallace grew bored with recruiting and let it be known that he was ready to return, Grant informed the War Department that there was no assignment in his department that Wallace might fill. **This was the payback for Wallace's hopeless combat performance. Getting rid of Lew Wallace was Grant's farewell to the battle of Shiloh.** (Perret, pp. 214-215)

WALLACE'S PARDON OBSESSION ABOUT SHILOH

Until Ulysses S. Grant's July 23, 1885 death, Lew Wallace pleaded with him, like with a rejecting father, to revise his Shiloh judgment. Illustrative is Wallace's 1868 long letter to Grant: nine, closely written, legal-sized pages. It is Wallace's own request for pardon; or as he called it: *"a note of acquittal from blame"* and *"an exoneration"* - one he never got from Grant.

The letter, undimmed in urgency six years after Shiloh, still denies responsibility; and even insolently accuses Grant of blaming him to cover up his own bad orders (on the unsigned note to Wallace lost by Wallace's Adjutant General), and then lying about those orders in his subsequent complaint about Wallace. Then Wallace alternatively blames Grant's messenger for writing out a wrong order himself. Finally, Wallace claims he assumed Grant wanted him to show up for battle the next day - so he took his time: *"making but five miles in seven hours."* But Wallace omits that his own intelligence revealed before the battle that Grant would face Confederate General Johnson's entire army, that Grant's messengers were sent to get him for battle that first day, and that he sent no scouts of his own to sort out uncertainty.

The big picture is that Wallace was in agony, but had no idea what he did wrong militarily, merely feeling martyred by Grant (a possible scenario that later gave rise to Wallace's novel's hero, Judah Ben-Hur, plus the plot for *Ben-Hur: A Tale of the Christ*).

And Wallace's blinding selfishness left him oblivious to the carnage he had caused, feeling solely his personal pain: *"The many misconceptions which have been attached to my movements on that bloody Sunday, have, it must be confessed, made me extremely sensitive upon the subject; you can imagine, therefore, with what anxiety your reply will be waited."* In his draft, Wallace wrote:

<u>Gen. Wallace to Gen. Grant</u>.
Washington City. Feb. 28. 1868.
General.
About a year after the battle of Pittsburgh Landing, it came to my knowledge that I was suffering, in your opinion, from erroneous information upon the subject of my conduct and movements, as commander of the 3rd Division of your army, during the first day of the battle named. To place myself right in your estimation, and in that of the army generally, I asked a Court of Inquiry, by letter to the Sec. of War (Mr. Stanton,) July 17, 1863.

After several months, during which the application received no attention from the Secretary, I withdrew it by advice of friends, Gen. Sherman, amongst others. The course I then resolved upon, that counseled by Gen. Sherman, was to carry my explanation directly to you; and such continued my intention until the battle of Monocacy; after which your treatment of me became so uniformly kind and considerate, that I was led to believe the disagreements connected with Pittsburgh Landing forgotten; a result to which I tacitly assented notwithstanding the record of that battle as you had made it, in the form of an endorsement on my official report, was grievously against me.

A recent circumstance, however, has made it essential to my good name, which I cannot bring myself to believe you wish to see destroyed, ~~has made it essential~~ *to go back to my former purpose; in pursuance of which, the object of this letter is simply to introduce certain statements of gentlemen lately in the army, your friends as well as mine, in hopes that the explanations to be found therein* **will be sufficient to authorize you to give me a note of acquittal from blame**, *plain enough to allay the suspicion and charges to which I have been so painfully subjugated. The statements are in the form of extracts, pertinent to the subject, from letters now in my possession, from Gen. James R. Ross, Gen. Dan Macabley, Capt. A.D. Ware, Gen. Silas A Strickland, and Gen. Ino. M. Thayer, now U.S. Senator from Nebraska – all of my command on the day in question, present with me, well known to you, and of unimpeachable honor. I could have obtained many more letters of like purport, but selected these because their authors had peculiar opportunities for information upon points considered of chief importance. It is possible that my explanation of the matter would be sufficient for the object in view; however that may be, it is my judgment now, that* **the charges against me have gone so far, and been put in such grave form, that public opinion may require an exoneration**, *though it come from your hand, to be based upon the testimony of others.*

Permit me to say further, that as to the order you started to me by Capt. Baxter, I do not understand there is any question of veracity between us. You tell me that, from the battlefield, you dispatched a verbal order, by the officer named, to be delivered to me at Crump's Landing, directing me to march my division to <u>Pittsburgh Landing by the road parallel with the river;</u> *and supposing, as you did, that the order would reach me by 11 o'clock, A.M., you reasonably calculated that my command* would be on the field by 1 o'clock, P.M. Now, in all candor, if you have been, as I have been informed, of opinion that I received that order as it was given, and at the time stated, (11 o'clock, A.M.,) and that for any reason such as personal feeling against you, or that I lost my way, or took the wrong road, or lingered on the march, **making but five miles in seven hours**, it must be admitted that you were justified in any, even the most extreme, judgment against me; and I must myself confess that your moderation was greater than mine would likely have been had our positions been reversed. I do not flinch from that conclusion at all; but what I do say, in defense, is that the opinion, and the conclusion, which is its corollary, are both wrong, because the order admitted to have been dispatched was <u>not delivered to me in form or substance as dispatched</u>; on the contrary, the order I received from your messenger was in writing, unsigned, and contained substantially the following instructions _____

"You will leave a force at Crump's Landing sufficient to guard the public property there; then march the rest of your division, and effect a junction with the right of the army; after which you will form your line of battle at right angle with the river; and act as circumstances dictate."

This order was read by Col. Ross under circumstances well calculated to impress it upon his memory. It was given also, to Col. Knefler, my Adj. Gen., and by him read and unfortunately lost. Finally, its support as stated by the above, is vouched for by Capt. Ware, at the time my A.D.C. To refuse credit to my version of its contents will be very hard indeed, corroborated as it is by so many gentlemen of unquestionable veracity, and such an excellent opportunity for information of the point.

I think myself warranted now in asserting upon the credit of the three officers just named, as well as my own, that the terms of the order as it was delivered to me, the objective of my march was not Pittsburgh Landing, as you intended, but the right of the army, resting when the battle opened in the morning, at a point quite three miles out from that Landing on the road to Purdy.

As a general principle, it must be admitted that when you entrusted the order to a proper messenger for delivery to me, your responsibility ceased; but I turn, and ask you, appealing to your experience and justice, how am I to be held responsible for the execution of the order, if it never reached me? Or if it reached me conveying an idea radically different from that originally given?

Of necessity, I was accountable for the execution of the order <u>as it was received</u>; and if it was not received in a form to convey your design, but was promptly executed, neither of us is responsible for the result – it was not your mistake, nor was it mine.

Having established the purport, at least, of the order as it came to my hand, the next inquiry is Did I proceed to execute it? And how?

On these heads all the letters filed are applicable; they show, as I think, that I took measures anticipatory of the order you gave me personally on your passage up the river to the battlefield; viz., to hold myself in readiness for order to march in any direction; that my brigades were ordered to concentrate at the place most proper and convenient for a prompt execution of the orders whatever they might be, because it was at the junction of two roads, the one leading to Pittsburgh Landing, the other to the right of the army, to one of which points, it may be added, I was sure of being ultimately sent, if the exigencies of the battle should require the presence of my command; that after you parted from me going up the river, I took measures to forward your messenger to me instantly upon his arrival, (see Col. Ross' letter,) then rode to the place of concentration, and waited impatiently and anxiously the expected instructions; that they came to hand about 12 o'clock, (my own remembrance is 11:30 A.M.); and that the officer who brought them also brought news that you were driving the enemy all along the line. (See letters of Gen. Knefler and Col. Ross.) Up to that time, therefore, I certainly was blameless. But let me ask you to stop here, and consider the effect upon my mind and subsequent movements of the information, thus reliably obtained, that **the battle was won**. *What inducement could I have had to march away from, or linger on the road to, a victory? Upon the hypothesis that the good news was true, how could I have imagined, had there been so much as a doubt as to the intent of the order received, a necessity for my command at Pittsburgh Landing?*

But proceeding – The letters further establish that, immediately upon receiving the order, I put my column <u>en route</u> to execute it.

Now come the questions. Did I take the right road to effect the junction with the right of the army? Or one leading to Purdy, away from the battle? Pertinent to these enquiries, Gen. Knefler says that the road chosen for the movement had been patrolled and pignetted by my cavalry; by their reports, if nothing else, I must have been posted as to its terminus; in corroboration of this *assertion, please notice that Gen. Macauley, Gen. Strickland, Gen. Thayer, and Gen. Knefler all allude to the fact that the head of the column was approaching, nor going away from, the firing, when the countermarch took place. Consider further that the most imperative necessities of my situation, isolated as it had been from the main army, were to know all the communications with that army, and to keep them clear, and in order for rapid movement. Not only did I know the road, but every step my division took from the initial point of the march up to the moment of the change of direction, was, as is well known to every intelligent soldier in the column, a step nearer the firing, and therefore a step ~~nearer~~ toward the battle. While on this inquiry, let me add, that the report of my being set right, after marching upon the wrong road, has in it this much truth, and no more – When about a mile from the position which had been occupied by the right of the army, (Gen. Sherman's division,) Capt. Rowley overtook me, and told me that you had sent him to hurry me up, and that our lines had been carried by the enemy, and the army driven back almost to the river – a very different story from that brought me by Capt. Baxter! Capt. Rowley set me right as <u>to the condition of the battle</u>, not as to <u>the road I was following</u>. Col. McPherson and Maj. Rawlins, the other officers of your staff mentioned as having been sent to me, met me after the countermarch, when my command was on the river road, moving to Pittsburgh Landing.*

Concerning the countermarch, I would remark that the condition of the battle, as reported by Capt. Rowley, made it prudent, if not necessary. My column was only five thousand men of all arms. **Reflecting upon it now, I am still of opinion that it did better service next day in your new line of battle, than it could have done operating alone and unsupported in the rear of the whole rebel army, where I was certainly taking it when "set right," by the Captain.**

Instead of making the change of direction, when it was resolved upon, by a countermarch, the result proved that it should have been effected by a general right about. The former maneuver was chosen, however, because I was confident of finding a crossroad to the river road long before the head of the column double upon its front (See Col. Ross' statement of the effort made to accomplish this idea.)

One of the results I confidently anticipate is that you will be satisfied of the wrong done me (unintentionally, I believe) by Col. Badeau, when, in his book, he describes me as consuming seven hours in marching five miles in the direction of the battle. The march actually performed in that time was not less than fifteen miles over an execrable dirt road.

Your opinion, as addressed in your letter to the War Office, July 13, 1863, that Gen. Morgan L. Smith, had he been put in command, could have had the division in the battle by 1 o'clock P.M., is, in direct terms, based upon the condition that Gen. S. [Smith] received your orders as you supposed them communicated to me. But suppose he had not received the orders as originally given; suppose, on the contrary, the orders actually received by him had the effect to send him in another direction than Pittsburgh Landing; and suppose that, on approaching his objective, he had found himself in the rear of the whole rebel army, and in his judgment compelled, by that circumstance, together with the bad fortune of our own army, to a further movement of quite ten miles, - all which were terrible realities in my case, - I am sure you are too just a man to have held him accountable for the hours, however precious, thus necessarily lost.

With these remarks I place the letters of the officers named in your hands. They will satisfy you, I think, that **the exoneration I seek will be an act of simple justice. The many misconceptions which have been attached to my movements on that bloody Sunday, have, it must be confessed, made me extremely sensitive upon the subject; you can imagine, therefore, with what anxiety your reply will be waited.**

Very respectfully,
Your friend,
Lew. Wallace

Three years later, in 1871, Wallace turned his Shiloh pardon obsession into grist for a verse drama like Shakespeare's, titled *Commodus: An Historical Play*. Wallace wrote:

I also know the sickness called remorse.
I know its signs and gestures, look and voice -
I know that pardon is its only cure,
And well I know for that the tortured soul
Would barter all it has or hopes to have.

About twenty years later, Wallace was still obsessed with pardon for Shiloh, and was still creating different self-serving versions of the events. On January 16, 1886, he gave an interview to the Crawfordsville *Saturday Evening Journal* titled "Gen. Lew Wallace. Visit to His Pleasant Home in the Athens of Indiana. Reminiscences of the Great Rebellion - Cause of General Grant's Prejudice Against Him." In this version, his publicized mistake becomes an artifact of Grant's bad memory and of an unnamed, malingering enemy of Wallace's at Grant's headquarters. This version denies getting orders to march on the day he missed the battle; and considers the outcome a novice error. And Wallace fabricates that his removal from command in the western army was not because of his ineptitude. Such recurring fictionalizing to suit himself would be evident in his lifelong reworkings of the pardon bargain with "Billy the Kid." The unnamed reporter wrote:

The war of the Rebellion in which he bore a part, was touched upon, and necessarily the battle of Shiloh and his connection therewith ... I asked what he supposed was the cause of General Grant's reflections on him in the *Century* article. "Grant," said he, "was a wonderful man. He wrote that article without notes or other data except his own recollection of the affair, and as my part in that battle had been the occasion of a heated controversy, in all of the forepart of which his impression of my conduct had been very strongly prejudicial to me, it had been so fixed in his mind that he had forgotten his later and more candid examination of the matter and his change of mind on the subject, and wrote of the battle according to his first impressions. It is proper to say that Gen. Grant did not get those impressions of my conduct from himself, but they were originated, fostered, and fed by an unrelenting enemy I had in headquarters [a staff officer, Captain Hillyer] ... "It was not until more than a year after the battle, General Grant neither verbally nor in writing had ever intimated to me that any blame was attached to me, and as all the disasters which happened to our force on that fatal Sunday occurred before I received my order to march, I never could see how I was to blame for any of them. But one day, more than a year after the battle, I was in Washington City, in the War Department, when one of the clerks threw over to me a package of official papers ... I found that it was an endorsement by General Grant upon my official report [of the battle] discrediting the report itself. This was the first I ever heard or knew of fault being found with me ... but I think the fine Italian hand of Hillyer is to be seen in the endorsement on the report and its concealment from me."

"Your being relieved from command in the western army was not, then, in consequence of anything done or omitted at Shiloh?"

"No, indeed!" said the General ...

"What efforts did you make to disabuse the mind of General Grant in regard to the Shiloh matter?"

"About the fore part of 1868 my friends urged that I should make some publication showing that I had not lost my way, taking the wrong road, or been dilatory in marching to the field of battle, so I addressed a letter to my staff officers, and brigade commanders, requesting a statement from them as to the occurrences on Sunday ... I submitted them to Grant ... By the way, we can always fight a battle better when it is over ... General Grant, in his *Century* article, says I would not have made the same mistake later in the war."

On September 13, 1893, Lew Wallace, still seeking pardon for Shiloh, gave the *Indianapolis News* his "Lew Wallace at Shiloh. What the General Has to Say Further on This Question - Buell's Army." Its gist is that 31 years later, Wallace was still trying to blame Grant, not himself, for Shiloh. One should note, however, Wallace's narcissistic blind spot: that Grant, in despair for the previous day's debacle, was not in a mood for "glorious" conversation. It was uncertain whether they could prevail on Shiloh's desperate second day. The article stated:

When asked if he [Wallace] saw General Grant on Sunday night after his arrival at Pittsburgh Landing, he replied: "No; I had my orders to take my position on the right of his army and did so. The following morning General Grant rode out to my division, and I asked him if he had any special orders to give me as to the manner in which I should open the fight, and he said only to 'move out in that direction,' moving his hand toward the rebels, and to use my own judgment after that."

"Did he tell you [Union General Carlos] Buell's army had arrived and was on the field?"

"No; I did not know that Buell had arrived until after dinner ... I have always wondered why General Grant did not tell me that morning that Buell's army had arrived and was on the field. It would have been glorious news to all of us and would have inspired everybody with confidence ...

On a lecture tour, Wallace gave an October 11, 1894 interview to the Spokane, Washington, *Weekly Review* titled "Lew Wallace at Shiloh. Through an Orderly's Error He Took the Wrong Road." Here he blamed the orderly and Grant. The article stated:

> During an informal reception to General Lew Wallace by about 35 G.A.R. comrades at the Hotel Spokane yesterday he related the story of the part he took in the Battle of Shiloh, which differs materially from the accounts given in the books. He was guarding the stores below Pittsburgh Landing when Grant passed up on a steamer and ordered him to hold himself in readiness. Firing could be distinctly heard and the men were chafing to participate. He had corduroyed the upper road, to facilitate the transportation of the artillery. An orderly came from Grant with instructions to move immediately. The order had been given verbally and the orderly had written it, but omitted to insert the words 'by the lower road," when Rawlins dashed up with a supplemental order from Grant to hurry and informed him that the original order was to move by the lower road. He retraced his course and had to drag the wagons and artillery through mud up to the axels. It was after dusk when he took his position as directed.

Seven years later, Wallace visited the Shiloh historic monument. On December 6, 1901, he gave an interview to the Weekly *Crawfordsville Journal* as "Home from Shiloh. Gen. Wallace and Capt. Geo. R. Brown Pleased With Work of the Commission." Wallace still hoped for pardon, stating:

> "Since I was there last the place has been changed from what was a dreary and desolate wilderness to what one can readily see will soon be one of the most beautiful parks in the whole country ... The monuments for the Indiana, Ohio, Iowa and Pennsylvania positions will soon be placed, and then one will easily be enabled, with the aid of a guide book to trace the action."

On January 24, 1902, Wallace was interviewed in the Weekly *Crawfordsville Journal* in "Hotel Lobby Gleanings. Gen. Wallace's Royalties from 'Ben-Hur' Are Satisfactory. He is Now Absorbed in Writing His Autobiography." The reporter quoted Wallace:

> "I have to-day been in the midst of the battle of Donnelson..." He expects next to take up the Battle of Shiloh."

LEW WALLACE'S BIOGRAPHY

ANALYSIS: *Lew Wallace's psyche was surprisingly similar to Billy Bonney's, having been formed by traumas of early parental death and unusual talents; even though, from birth, Wallace and Billy were at opposite ends of America's class system. Their lives became a compulsive search for a father-figure and for love. Both never healed. Both held resulting rage that could erupt as killing. Billy's victims were shot with debatable legality. Wallace killed by sentenced hangings, though not necessarily justly, as in the case of John Wilkes Booth's innocent, boarding house landlady, Mary Surratt. But Wallace's sadistic toying with Billy by withholding a life-saving pardon epitomized Wallace's flawed character. And he remained obsessed with Billy and the lost pardon for the rest of his life, as if dead Billy unconsciously became his own damaged self.*

Lew Wallace's affectionate biographers are Robert and Katherine Morsberger in 1980's *Lew Wallace: Militant Romantic*. And his own autobiography in progress was edited and published posthumously by his wife, Susan, in 1906, a year after his death.

Louis Wallace was born in Brookville, Indiana on April 10, 1827 - 54 years plus one day to when Billy the Kid would be convicted of first degree murder for lack of Wallace's pardon. From birth, Wallace's opportunity for future success was predictable. The irony would be that his eventual fame was eclipsed by his penniless and homeless victim: Billy Bonney.

At Wallace's birth, his West Point educated, lawyer father, David, had been married four years to his mother, Ester (later Judah Ben-Hur's mother's name). Their first son, William, was then two. Two more brothers followed by 1831. By that year, when Louis was five, David Wallace was elected as Indiana's Lieutenant Governor, the third son died of scarlet fever and the family moved to Covington, Indiana.

Louis, a book-loving dreamer and hyperkinetic forest wanderer, remembered his father's punishments of birch whippings and his mother's punishments of roping him to a bedframe and dressing him in her garments. When 69, he called such punishers an "offender in far greater degree than his victim." But their sadism's power became his own.

He was eight years old when his mother died of tuberculosis, as would Billy's mother die prematurely when he only 13½. And, like for Billy, the mother's death caused loss of home, since Louis's father, like Billy's stepfather, abandoned him - in Louis's case, to live with a neighbor. When nine, Louis pathetically followed his older college-bound brother to Crawfordsville, Indiana, where his father paid his board until he himself moved to there with a new wife. She was a sister-in-law of Dr. Richard Gatling, inventor of the Gatling machine-gun.

In an interview for the *Crawfordsville Journal* of March 20, 1901, titled "An Incident. Gen. Wallace Tells of His First Meeting With His Stepmother in Crawfordsville," Wallace, then almost 74, recalled trauma of that re-marriage; but, more importantly, his father's implied selfish callousness. Wallace was quoted:

> "I remember distinctly how astonished we all were when the stage from Indianapolis drove up one day and my father alighted with our new mother. We had known nothing of his intentions, and when we were summoned to the tavern kept by Maj. Ristine, a famous resort in that part of the country, I, at least, was inclined to be rebellious, and have nothing to do with this mother that our father had given us."

Solidified at a young age was Lewis's defensive rebelliousness against authority figures (which would yield disaster at Shiloh), coupled with his identification with his sadistic aggressor parents (a cruel trait of which Billy Bonney would be a victim).

By 1837, when Lewis was 10, David Wallace became Indiana's Governor; and Lewis was moved again, now to Indianapolis. By then, his talent in illustrating was scorned as effete by his father. Lewis sought solace in books, as Billy would with dime novels. By the next year, 1838, Lewis's father, as Governor, was involved in massacring 150 Potawatomis Indians, who were refusing illegal relocation. By the 1840's, David Wallace returned to private law practice, though he abandoned Lewis again that year, sending him for a 12 month stay with an aunt in Centerville, Indiana.

By 15, Louis showed literary flair, writing his first novel, *The Man at Arms: A Tale of the Tenth Century*, a Romeo and Juliet-style fiction set in the Crusades and in Jerusalem. His young hero, after travails and wartime heroism, is accepted by his "Juliet's" father. Louis's unconscious quest for paternal acceptance had crystallized as creativity - mingled with lure of the Holy Land. Narcissistic grandiosity and elitist self-love became Lewis's compensation for feeling unlovable. Wallace would always be the "man at arms," fighting for "the father's" acceptance.

At 16, Louis ran away with a friend to join a real war: Texas's War of Independence. Apprehended, he faced his angry father, who abandoned him again; saying cruelly, as Lew quoted in his late-life *Autobiography*: "I am resolved that from today you must go out and earn your own livelihood." Lewis was abruptly homeless. In a Weekly *Crawfordsville Journal* article of February 7, 1902, titled "Lew Wallace's Grit. How the General Fought Adversity in His Youth - His Father's Admonition." Wallace gave an optimistically reworked rendition of his abandonment:

I shall never forget what my father did when I returned home [six weeks after leaving college]. He called me into his office and took from a pigeon-hole in his desk a package of papers neatly folded and tied with red tape. He was a very systematic man, because perhaps of his West Point training. The papers proved to be receipts for my tuition, which he had carefully preserved. He called off the items and asked me to add them. The total, I confess, staggered me.

"That sum, my son," he said, with a tone of regret in his voice, represents what I have expended to provide you with a good education.

"After mature reflection I have come to the conclusion that I have done for you, in that direction, all that can be reasonably expected of any parent, and I have therefore, called you in to tell you that you have now reached an age when you must take up the lines yourself ... I shall not upbraid you for your neglect, but rather pity you for the indifference you have shown for the golden opportunities you have been enabled to enjoy through my indulgence" ... It set me thinking. The next day I set out with a determination to accomplish something for myself.

Likewise, young teenaged Billy Bonney was cast from his Silver City house by his avaricious unloving step-father right after his mother's death. Paternal abandonment and the quest for a father's love shaped them both. Wallace would spend the rest of his life trying to get Ulysses S. Grant's forgiveness for Shiloh; and would write *Ben-Hur*, a story of sudden betrayal of the hero by a powerful official, and of redemption by a better man: Christ himself. But facing brilliant Billy, needing a pardon's redemption in 1879, Wallace would revert to his own sadistic father, David, torturing the boy for almost three years while condemning him to death. And Billy, having clung successively to father-figures John Tunstall, then Alexander McSween, would refuse to leave the Territory and abandon hope that Wallace would finally rescue him.

On his own, teenaged Wallace lived by odd jobs, while educating himself, in eerie facsimile of the later abandoned Billy Bonney. In this period, Wallace became fascinated with the Mexico of Conquistador Hernando Cortez. He learned Spanish - as would Billy. Thirty years later, Wallace's romance of Mexico would become his first best-selling novel: *The Fair Prince*. But, in his imagination he was already a "prince," as was Billy in his own way: At 16, Billy had discovered princely power of the revolver.

By 17, Louis apprenticed himself to become a lawyer. But in two years, Mexican-American War fervor seized him, and he raised a company. As he left for Mexico, his father's farewell was: "Come back a man." Louis cried as if that was redemption.

In Mexico, 19 year old Wallace saw privation and death, and revealed his elitist prejudices, writing to his brother, William, on March 26, 1846:

The Spaniards are the only educated class ... The native Mexican in his ignorance and mental imbecility bears the same relation to them as the imported African to us ... Their minds like the Indian's are entirely composed of cunning, low-trickery, and inclinations to deceit and treachery; while in disposition their loves are passionate, friendships deep, and hatreds wild ... and only to be eradicated by blood.

In 33 years, almost to the day, in Lincoln, New Mexico Territory, that elitist eye would judge a scruffy, 19 year old, reputed outlaw called "the Kid," who had come believing they were negotiating a pardon; while Wallace seethed with his own secret *"hatreds wild"* that could only *"be eradicated by blood."*

By 1847, Wallace was back in Indiana, his enlistment expired without his seeing battle. The War was won by the United States the following year. At the end of his life, in his *Autobiography*, Wallace wrote: "[N]either have I at any time been troubled with a qualm about the propriety even to righteousness of the war." In fact, by 19, his defenses were so ossified into an aggressor role, that he would feel no future qualms about anything except a thwarting of his own ambitions. Unhealable, he was already a narcissistic monster. In his *Autobiography*, he wrote: "My nobelist dream of life has been one of fame."

By 1848, Wallace met young and wealthy Susan Arnold Elston from Crawfordsville, Indiana, who became his wife and life-long love; and whose adulation for him matched his own. By 1849, he got his law license, and they married in 1852; with their only child, Henry, being born the next year. In 1859, his father died aged 60; thus, missing the profuse later achievements his son amassed for him as their unconscious recipient. "Come back a man" was never forgotten. But how could it now be proved? At least his wife bolstered him. In Wallace's later, unpublished and undated biography of her, he wrote: "Probably no man, in his efforts to achieve renown, was ever better seconded by his wife." And Crawfordsville, Indiana, represented their happy haven.

The 1850's marked the establishment of the Republican Party, with slavery as its issue; and with Wallace sympathizing with rights of ownership, harkening back to his father's racist stance against the Potawatomis Indians. But he backed the Union side. In 1856, he organized a militia of Crawfordsville men as the Montgomery Guards; whom he whimsically outfitted in red, blue, and gray pantalooned uniforms patterned on pictures he found in a magazine article about French-Algerian Zouaves. In 1856, he was elected state senator. By 1859, destiny carried him to a debate between Stephen A. Douglas and Abraham Lincoln, who repeated his "House divided against itself cannot stand speech." Wallace, inspired, would eventually court Lincoln as a new father-figure, and as a Republican himself.

But Wallace's earlier father substitute was Indiana's governor, Oliver P. Morton. When, on April 13, 1861, Fort Sumter was attacked, Morton made him an Adjutant General in charge of raising troops. Wallace chose command as a Colonel of the 11th Regiment of Indiana Volunteers, which he drilled as Zouaves. And he made up a new name for himself: "Lew" - as would Billy, becoming "Bonney." By June, Wallace's regiment had a successful skirmish which he initiated without orders in Romney, West Virginia; for which he got praised, not blamed, by President Lincoln. Soon after, some of his troops drew their first Confederate blood near Romney, with 28 dead Rebels and loss of just one of their men. Wallace was congratulated by General George B. McClellan for "heroic courage" of his regiment. Fatherly praise was accumulating. But the enlistment period ended.

By August of 1861, Wallace had mustered a new regiment, and was to report to austere, Brigadier General Charles F. Smith, two decades his senior and another father figure. Soon Wallace was complaining privately and competitively about Smith's inadequacy. At 34, Wallace was made a Brigadier General of volunteers, getting a brigade command on September 3, 1861; and getting paternal encouragement from Smith, who then died abruptly on April 25, 1862, from an accidental fall when visiting Wallace prior to the Battle of Shiloh: an "abandonment" like Wallace's own father's premature death. And Smith's command was assumed by Ulysses S. Grant for the fateful battle.

By 1862, Wallace had been made Commander of Fort Henry. Brigadier General Ulysses S. Grant, however, left him there while the February siege of Fort Donelson began. Without orders from Grant, and ignoring Grant's order to avoid general engagement, Wallace joined the battle. He sent a brigade to reinforce Brigadier General George B. McClellan's division, thus, maintaining the Union line, followed by regaining lost ground. The next month he was promoted to Major General of volunteers - his insubordination rewarded, not reprimanded.

Then came the Battle of Shiloh, Tennessee, starting on April 6, 1862, and resulting in Wallace's unhealable trauma. As dramatized above, on the first day of fighting, Wallace never arrived with his 7,500 troops, when Grant and Sherman were under fierce attack by Confederate General Albert Sidney Johnston. Grant had ordered Wallace to march to Pittsburgh Landing to reinforce Brigadier General William Tecumseh Sherman. Wallace decided on his own to take the upper, longer, swampy Shunpike road, further delaying to unite his separated troops. Grant had actually ordered him to take the shorter, lower road to Pittsburgh Landing. Wallace's absence on the first day of Shiloh caused extreme Union casualties and the Union's near defeat. The next day, Wallace, finally at the battle, assisted Union victory. But the final tally of Union casualties was 13,047 - with 1,754 killed, 8,408 wounded, and 2,885 missing. Confederate casualties were 10,699 - 1,728 killed, 8,012 wounded, and 959 missing or captured. That horrific total of 23,746 casualties exceeded combined casualties of the Revolutionary War, the War of 1812, and the Mexican-American War.

Public outrage from the North resulted in Grant's public blaming of Wallace and removing him from his command in June of 1862. Wallace returned to Crawfordsville with humiliation, rage at perceived unjust blame, and rejection by this father substitute; who would become the General-in-Chief of the Union armies and a U.S. President - and inadvertently mirrored Wallace's high-achieving abandoning father, David. The result of Shiloh was a post-traumatic stress disorder that would color the rest of

Wallace's life - and be a crucial variable in his actions in the Billy Bonney pardon period beginning in 17 years.

In August of 1862, sympathetic intervention of his backer, Indiana Governor Morton, got Wallace sent alone to Cincinnati, Ohio. Heading there also were Confederate troops under General Kirby Smith. When Wallace found out, he decided to draft a proclamation forcing the 200,000 inhabitants to defend their city. That worked; but it did not eradicate the curse of Shiloh.

Through 1863, Wallace was given no major command, and his attempt to have General Sherman intervene with Grant failed. On July 18th, as stated in his *Autobiography*, he even requested a court of inquiry on his Shiloh conduct. The request was rejected by then General-in-Chief Henry W. Halleck, who wrote on it: *"I do not think that Genl. Wallace is worth the trouble & expense of either court of inquiry or court martial."* This was salt of scorn in his Shiloh wound. How could he ever be "a man?" Wallace wrote pathetically to Secretary of War Edwin M. Stanton, pleading unsuccessfully for active duty: *"The armies are moving, battles are being fought. I am ashamed to be made to stay at home."* Stanton recommended Wallace's removal from service to President Lincoln, who refused with wished-for paternal protection.

For Lincoln's 1864 reelection, loyalist Wallace was sent by the President to Baltimore, Maryland, to "protect" poling places - or to influence their result by his military presence. But, as mentioned, he hysterically decided to hang four, possibly innocent, men whom he called Confederate spies; though Lincoln stopped him.

In July of 1864, in Maryland, occurred the Battle of Monocacy, where Wallace was the only Union officer available for command. His outnumbered force was defeated by Jubal A. Early; but he delayed Early's advance to Washington, D.C. long enough for the city to organize and repel that Confederate army. Wallace sung his own praises as the President's protector; but they could not heal the wound of Shiloh.

In 1864, Wallace directed secret governmental aid to Mexico to aid President Benito Juárez in expelling French colonizing forces under Napoleon III, who had imposed a puppet emperor; Archduke Maximilian of Austria and his wife, Carlotta. Wallace, on his own, as usual, fantasized that Texan Confederates would join Maximillion to make an independent empire. By then, the Confederacy was failing, and Wallace hoped to bring the trans-Mississippi states and territories back into the Union. So he drew up an Amnesty Proclamation for soldiers and civilians - just as he would do later in 1878 New Mexico Territory. He envisioned a bloodless coup that would reunite more of America than achieved by Grant's battles. But Wallace's plan was rejected by Confederate General John G. Walker, who called it an attempt to induce "blackest treason" and wrote to Wallace, as quoted in his *Autobiography*, about the secret plotting: "Whenever you are willing ... to treat equal with equal, an officer of your high rank and character, clothed with the proper authority from your government, will not be reduced to the necessity of seeking an obscure corner of the Confederacy to inaugurate negotiations." Walker must have known about Shiloh. He used it spitefully. But Wallace's failure was mitigated by the May 26, 1864 surrender of the Confederate Trans-Mississippi Department.

Then, on April 15, 1865, President Abraham Lincoln was assassinated at Ford's Theater. Wallace, as an accomplished lawyer and loyal Republican, was appointed by new President Andrew Johnson to the military commission convened for the conspirators' trial - the actual assassin, John Wilkes Booth having already been killed. Subconsciously for Wallace, the assassination must have repeated sadness at his father's premature death, and deeper grief at losing this more forgiving and protective father figure.

Wallace's response was sadistic revenge. In the trial, prosecutor Wallace was accused of "intolerance" by a *New York World* reporter; and accused of suppressing defense evidence, permitting perjury, and misusing the concept of conspiracy to attain the July 7, 1865 hangings of Lewis Powell, David Herold, George Atzerodt, and probably innocent Mary Surratt - the first woman hanged by the federal government. And before her hanging, there had been a pardon petition for Mary Surratt. Wallace had refused to sign it, and never professed to feeling guilty. All this hard-hearted behavior would be familiar 14 years later during his tenure as Governor in New Mexico Territory.

In 1865, Wallace was President of the military commission for Court Martial of Andersonville prison camp's Captain Henry Wirz, which succeeded in his hanging. There, Wallace also harassed the defense, tampered evidence, admitted hearsay evidence, and attempted and failed to get Confederate President Jefferson Davis implicated and tried also, as having given Wirz orders.

Then, on November 30, 1865, Wallace left the army. To his killed wartime battle adversaries, Wallace had added five hangings, while failing to hang even more in Cincinnati. So in the

War and its aftermath, Lew Wallace was connected to the deaths of thousands. Sadistic power balanced Shiloh's failure.

Wallace, continuing to seek grand vindication, turned to Mexico, still trying to liberate itself from the French to install Benito Juárez. Wallace's quixotic plans to supply arms to Juárez for military intervention - and get a reward of $100,000 - failed. But Emperor Maximillion was executed on June 10, 1867 and Juárez became President. Wallace was left festering at injustice to himself and loss of imaginary riches. So Shiloh recycled.

Wallace returned to Crawfordsville with limited finances and fear of failure at 40. Shiloh had ended hope of a military career. That his immediate family now called him "the General" was no solace. His rich brother-in-law, Isaac Elston, Jr., owner of the Elston Bank in Crawfordsville, scorned him. And Wallace had to return to law practice and work in Elston's bank. His 16 year old asthmatic son, Henry, was entering Crawfordsville's Wabash College. A hoped-for tour lecturing about Mexico got no backing.

In 1868, Wallace tried politics; losing a seat in Congress amidst press reviling his hanging of innocent Mary Surratt. And his enemy Grant was by then President. In 1870, Wallace tried again for a seat in Congress, losing to attacks about Shiloh and Surratt. He compensated by buying a bigger house on what had been the pasture of his wife's father.

In 1872, Wallace campaigned for Grant's re-election; though Grant ignored his continuing pleas for a Shiloh vindication. Grant also refused his request for an ambassadorship.

Wallace found an outlet in writing literary fantasy, completing two plays: *The Blue and the Gray* or *Conciliated* about the Civil War; and *Commodus: An Historical Play*, in 1871. With the latter, set in ancient Rome, he hoped to rival verse plays of Shakespeare. Pardon was *Commodus's* theme - as it had been his own obsession since Shiloh. But it was rejected by publishers.

In 1873, his failed plays led him to complete his 30 year old manuscript, *The Fair God: A Tale of the Conquest of Mexico*. It became a best-seller. Ever seeking fatherly approval, he sent Grant a copy. Grant did not respond. Shiloh's stain was indelible.

In 1876, came Wallace's campaigning for Republican presidential hopeful, Rutherford B. Hayes, who would defeat Democrat Samuel Tilden in a tainted election. Tilden, famous as the Ring-breaker of New York's Tammany Hall under William "Boss" Tweed, attained a popular vote victory. Hayes won by one electoral vote. Democrats claimed voter fraud. Wallace had been present as a legal counsel for the canvassing board for the Florida recount, where Tilden led by 45 votes. The canvassing board threw out Tilden's votes to declare Hayes the winner. But Democrats still claimed Tilden won. Canny lawyer Wallace argued that the Democrats had empowered the canvassing board. So Hayes prevailed; and Wallace was the one who telegraphed him on January 2, 1877 to confirm his victory. At last, Wallace had a beholden father-figure in power. But Hayes's victory was called "The Crime of '76." And Wallace was its implementer. But as with the hangings in Abraham Lincoln's alleged murderers' trial, Wallace had no guilt. And, probably for the first time since 1862, he must have thought that his Shiloh nightmare was over. He could "come home." But he was now a heartless fragile shell.

On December 16, 1876 he gave an interview to the Crawfordsville, Indiana, *Saturday Evening Journal* about fraud in Florida's election results.

> GEN. LEW WALLACE reached home last Saturday night from Florida where he has been, with others, for the past month endeavoring to see a fair count ... They [two other men accompanied him] found, upon reaching there, that there were no Republican lawyers in Florida ... [Wallace says there was] tampering with returns and ballots after election, or grossly irregular and illegal voting. The canvassing board consisted of two Republicans and one Democrat. The Democrat voted with the Republicans in throwing out enough votes to increase Hayes' majority from 40, what the face of the returns showed, to 506. After he [the Democrat] had done it ... he came back and wanted to reconsider his action. He had been "bulldozed" by his Democratic friends. Gen. Wallace says that Florida is as truly and honestly a Hayes state as Iowa or Ohio ... Gen. Wallace gives it as his opinion that Hayes will be inaugurated ...

Thus, Wallace indirectly and unintentionally helped Hayes continue cronyism corruption from the Grant administration. The main benefactor would be the Santa Fe Ring, which Wallace would face himself in two years in New Mexico Territory.

On March 9, 1877, right after Hayes's inauguration, Wallace requested an exotic ambassadorship to Italy, Brazil, Spain, or Mexico. While waiting in Crawfordsville, he continued work on his psychologically cathartic *Ben-Hur* novel, with its hero struggling for pardon from unjust accusation and enslavement by a high Roman official. Shiloh was being reworked into a tale of salvation.

In August of 1878, President Hayes offered Wallace a Bolivian ambassadorship, which he superciliously refused.

That month, as reported in an August 27, 1877 edition of the *Indianapolis Journal* as "Fighting the Indians. Sketches of General Lew Wallace's Plan for Conducting the Frontier Warfare," he had met in Washington, D.C. with Secretary of War George McCrary to present his plan for exterminating Native Americans. It was reminiscent of his father's massacre of Potawatomis Indians in 1838, and reflected his own early prejudices of Mexicans having "*mental imbicility*" like "*the imported African;*" and Native Americans having "*cunning low-trickery, and ... treachery, with "hatreds wild*" that could only "*be eradicated by blood.*" Wallace was quoted in that newspaper:

"The plan I had to suggest to the Secretary," said the General, "was this: The formation of a corps that shall be devoted to work on the plains ... and by experience become acquainted with the same mode of warfare that is practiced by the native inhabitant ... [T]he Russians, on their vast frontier, they keep their unruly subjects under control by the native methods of fighting ... I contended that the pony was there for the white man as well as the Indian ... [T]he scouts are the fear and dread of the Indians. They surpass the redskins in cunning, in endurance ... and the corps I propose would grow more and more like the scouts every day – more and more valuable for the preservation of the lives of the settlers and the protection of their property.

Possibly this cruel zeal was relayed to Hayes, since he offered the Governorship of Territorial New Mexico the same month. Wallace accepted. He had attained his own father's level of public office. And he merged his florid fantasies of Old Mexico with the western frontier. The citizenry's desperate hope would soon become merely fodder for his continuing saga of his own life.

Wallace was briefed in Washington on September 13, 1878 by Secretary of the Interior Carl Schurz, who became his next recipient of father transference, along with President Hayes himself. Wallace was given enough facts to comprehend the Territorial crises: the removal of corrupt Governor S.B. Axtell, a post-war turmoil of fighting factions, and ongoing Indian Wars. And Frank Warner Angel, still harboring an unrequited anti-Ring agenda, secretly sent him a notebook he prepared on the Santa Fe Ring, and possibly also gave Mary McPherson's printed booklet of

August, 1877: "In the Matter of the Charges vs. Gov. S. B. Axtell and Other New Mexico Officials; Submitted to the Departments of the Interior and of Justice." (Both were in Wallace's papers as donated to the Indianapolis, Indiana Historical Society in 1940).

Wallace's subsequent communications and acts prove that he had no interest in laboring for justice. His intent was rapid quieting of the Territory; keeping his wife, Susan, amused in boring Santa Fe; finishing *Ben-Hur*; making some mining investments; and leaving quickly to a fancy ambassadorship.

Wallace arrived in Santa Fe on September 30, 1878, and was sworn in as the Territory's 11th governor on October 1st. Immediately, he tried to get Hayes to declare martial law so he could summarily hang troublemakers; as he had attempted during the Civil War with fantasized "Confederate spies" in 1864 in Baltimore, Maryland, and in 1862 in Cincinnati, Ohio. On October 7, 1877, Hayes merely issued a Proclamation admonishing citizens to be law-abiding. But Wallace persisted with his attempt to make "*war against the murderous bands*," as he wrote on October 14, 1877, already carried away by his bloody fantasies of frontier outlaws and red Indians.

By October 23rd, flighty Wallace had turned his focus to renovation of the Palace of the Governors. And he created a writing schedule for his *Ben-Hur: A Tale of the Christ*.

On November 13, 1878, still attempting a rapid solution in Lincoln County, he issued a blanket Amnesty Proclamation for civilians and soldiers, as he had done in 1864 while in Mexico to induce adjacent Confederate states to abandon their war.

As to comprehending Territorial issues, he apparently sought out his own "upper class." He consulted with Thomas Benton Catron himself, whose law office occupied the east side of the plaza - with Wallace's Palace of the Governors on the north. From Ringite U.S. Marshal John Sherman, by October 6th, he received a list of "outlaws" - mostly Regulators, including Billy Bonney as "the Kid." And he wrote profusely to father-figure men he sought to impress: Secretary of the Interior Carl Schurz and President Hayes. Wallace gave himself 60 days to quiet the Territory. He had no inkling that in six months fate would place his reputation and his future in the hands of that outlaw called "the Kid."

But he had a warning sign of brewing trouble. At his October arrival, he was contacted by an Attorney Huston Chapman, representing a widow named Susan McSween for possible litigation against Fort Stanton's Commander N.A.M. Dudley for arson and murder, and as threatening her current safety. Wallace refused to take action - given his knee-jerk elitism and military bias. By January of 1879, his wife, Susan, and son, Henry, joined him in Santa Fe. Susan hated Santa Fe.

Wallace's Lincoln County shunning came to a forced ending with the February 18, 1879, Lincoln, Ring murder of Huston Chapman - to which Billy Bonney was eye-witness. By March, Wallace arrived there, soon requesting removal of Commander Dudley as another fast-fix to silence Lincolnites. But that incurred dreaded wrath of a military officer: now Dudley. Dudley was no Grant, but to vulnerable Wallace Shiloh's specter loomed again, with added anxiety about failure in the eyes of Hayes and Schurz. He was on the verge of a relapsing post-traumatic stress disorder.

Right then, he heard from "the Kid," already moderately famous through local hero-worship and Ring transmogrification; and cocky enough to propose a pardon deal, as part of his own tragic and parallel compulsive quest for a father and forgiveness. Billy began his plea with a March 13, 1879 letter to Wallace, bargaining audaciously to give eye-witness testimony against Chapman's murderers in exchange for a pardon for his Lincoln County War indictments for the Brady, Hindman, and Roberts killings. Wallace should have seen it as the godsend he needed to quickly quell the population agitated by Chapman's murder. And he was freely granting pardons anyway to indicted others like past Sheriff Brady's Deputy Jacob "Billy" Matthews, a Tunstall murder posseman.

The unforeseen complication would be personalities and politics, as he and Billy arranged a meeting four days later in the home of Justice of the Peace John "Squire" Wilson. Billy apparently thought things went well, because he immediately planned a sham arrest so he could be safe in Lincoln's pit jail while awaiting the April Grand Jury for his testimony. Billy was wrong. In that meeting, Wallace had encountered the inconceivable: a boy of such starting brilliance, charisma, and confidence that he violated Wallace's class boundaries. "The General's" pompous grandiosity did not intimidate that boy. Wallace must have experienced the power shift of the abused child who, as an adult, identifies with his past aggressor. He now had the power. Billy's life depended on him. Wallace had already responded two days earlier by letter that: *"I have the authority to exempt you from prosecution."* Would he now be tempted use that ambiguous wording - promising nothing - as a lawyer's trick?

While Billy was incarcerated in the home of Lincoln Jailer, Juan Patrón, who saved him from the pit jail, Wallace, staying next door, interviewed him on March 23, 1879. In the six days since their first meeting, Wallace seems to have hardened, and was barely listening as he took notes on actual outlaws, killings, and rustling. But Billy, now trying to impress his best father-figure yet, was describing Lincoln County War Ringites, thinking that he was recruiting a powerful ally. The pardon was becoming secondary to winning against the Ring. By the next day, Billy sent a letter to Wallace with more war-period circumstances, and signed with a child-like intimate "Billie."

Not to be underestimated is that Wallace had a real son: Henry, then 26, subservient and in awe of him; who would spend his entire life serving "the General" as business agent, and becoming his archivist. But Billy was as brash and grandiose as Wallace himself. He was no "Henry."

If Wallace was psychologically ambivalent about pardoning Billy, the next chance event tipped the balance. On May 2, 1879, began the Court of Inquiry for possible court martial of Fort Stanton's Commander Nathan Augustus Monroe Dudley. And Susan McSween's new lawyer, Ira Leonard, replacing murdered Huston Chapman, was assisting the military prosecutor and working with Wallace, who was to testify against Dudley.

Besides the fact that Attorney Leonard became Billy's advocate, Wallace should have been moved by that boy's testifying against Dudley irrespective of his pardon bargain. But Wallace was humiliated by his own weak testifying under Dudley's brutal disrespectful lawyer, Henry Waldo, from Catron's law firm. Wallace's debacle there became second only to Shiloh itself. Almost immediately after his five days of grilling, he retreated to Santa Fe. His flaring sadism, a defense against Waldo's emasculation, congealed against Billy over whom he did hold power. That was the psychological side of Wallace's pardon issues.

There was a political side too. Wallace was fully aware of the Santa Fe Ring and its role in the Lincoln County War and Territorial corruption. But that stimulated not an urge to help oppressed citizenry, but to save himself from its retribution. To pardon Billy - branded an outlaw by Ring propaganda, and the Ring's major enemy - would destroy his own political future.

By June of 1879, the Court of Inquiry's corrupt exoneration of Dudley, reflecting its scorn of powerless Wallace, left Wallace wanting Billy dead.

By 1880, Wallace knew about the Ring-instigated Secret Service tracking of Billy by Special Agent Azariah Wild from that September to December. So Wallace issued his first reward notice on December 22, 1880, with $500 of his own money for capturing "Billy the Kid."

After Billy's pursuit and capture by then Lincoln County Deputy Sheriff Pat Garrett, Wallace both ignored and retained all Billy's letters to himself - including the 1879 pardon bargain ones, that of December 12, 1880 denying the murder of Jim Carlyle; and four March 1881 letters from the Santa Fe jail pleading for the pardon.

In January of 1880, Wallace announced to the legislature that he had restored peace in Lincoln County; indifferent to the fact that its abused and ignored citizens had retreated into hopeless silence that would last for generations, as the Ring flourished unchecked. And in September of 1880, Wallace took a two month leave to campaign for James Garfield's presidential bid.

But Wallace had another freedom fighter to contend with brutally: Mimbres Apache Chief Victorio, who, like Wallace's father's massacred Potawatomis Indians, fought back after illegal seizure of his tribe's land. As usual, Wallace requested military intervention. To Wallace's relief, Victorio and his tribe were massacred in Mexico on October 28, 1880. And when Wallace returned to the subdued Territory in November of 1880, he occupied himself with mining investments.

In 1880, Wallace also completed *Ben-Hur: A Tale of the Christ*; which was published on November 12, 1880. It was an immediate best-seller, which he sent in his unremitting quest for fatherly approval to both President Hayes and then President-elect Garfield.

It was Garfield who offered Wallace the Ambassadorship to Turkey. In the Territory, planning his early departure from his interim governorship, Wallace still had to deal with Billy - now sentenced to hang - and the pardon. So on April 13, 1881 he issued his own gubernatorial death sentence for Sheriff Pat Garrett. On April 28, 1881, he also gave a newspaper interview about refusing the pardon as being undeserved. Coincidentally, Billy escaped jail that day, resulting in Wallace's second newspaper reward offer on May 3, 1881. Then Wallace left the Territory forever on May 28, 1881. By the end of June of 1881, he and his wife were on a boat en route to Constantinople. And Billy had two weeks left to live.

From 1881 to 1885, Wallace was Ambassador to Turkey, now in a real palace on the Bosphorus River; and befriending the head of the Ottoman empire, Sultan Abdul Hamid. He toured Jerusalem, Cairo, and Rome. He had entered his own romantic tales; and acclaim became real.

Garfield was assassinated on September 19, 1881. In 1884, Wallace, with Susan, took a leave from Constantinople to campaign for Republican James Blaine for president. Then the ghost of Shiloh rose again. That year, *Century* magazine began first-person articles which became a book titled *Battles and Leaders of the Civil War*. Ulysses S. Grant would write about Shiloh. Wallace again pleaded with Grant for its pardon. But Grant, dying of throat cancer, damned him with the same quote in *Century* magazine's *Battles* book in his *Personal Memoirs*, writing:

> Wallace did not arrive in time to take part in the first day's fight. General Wallace has since claimed that the order delivered to him by Captain Baxter was simply to join the right of the army, and the road over which he marched would have taken him to the road from Pittsburgh to Purdy where it crosses Owl Creek on the right of Sherman; but this is not where I ordered him nor where I wanted him to go. I never could see and do not know why any order was necessary further than to direct him to come to Pittsburgh Landing.
> (Grant, *Battles and Leaders of the Civil War*, p. 468)

Then Wallace spent one more happy year in Constantinople. After return to Crawfordsville, he toured the country giving romanticized lectures on his adventures. In 1893, drawing on his Turkey experience, he published another successful historical novel: *The Prince of India: Or Why Constantinople Fell*.

In 1893, Shiloh rose again, this time by Wallace's own attendance at its veterans' reunion, where he compulsively argued on his own behalf. In 1898, as if still trying to exorcise Shiloh, at 71, he offered to create a division of troops for the Spanish American War; but was denied. He even masochistically tried to enlist as a private, but was rejected based on age. He could not stop. In 1901, he went to Shiloh's battlefield, trying unsuccessfully to persuade the Shiloh Military Park Commission to present his version of the first day. Nevertheless, he returned in 1903 for the 41st anniversary of the battle and gave a speech with his version.

And his obsession with Billy Bonney and the pardon likewise continued. By 1900 and 1902 he wrote long articles about the "Romance of Billy the Kid." Billy also appeared in his late-life *Autobiography*. And if death had not cut Wallace short in 1905, Billy would have probably become an incorrigible outlaw and wanton serial killer in an historical novel on the West, where Wallace himself was the hero and object of Billy's murderous obsession. And the pardon was reworked as definitely promised - as if at the end of life Wallace was confessing as penance. But even that was undone by falsely blaming Billy for ruining the bargain by not keeping his side by continuing outlawry.

In the summer of 1904, Wallace was declining with stomach cancer. But he opposed a senate bill combining New Mexico and Arizona Territories, announcing hypocritically: "I love the people of New Mexico. I lived with them for two and a half years as their Governor, and I know their condition and their needs."

Wallace died on February 15, 1905 at 77. His self-aggrandizing *Lew Wallace: An Autobiography*, was completed in 1906 by his wife, Susan, who died in 1907.

Susan, Henry, and Henry's son, Lew Wallace Jr., preserved all Lew's papers - including all those of Billy the Kid. And when donating the Lew Wallace collection to the Indiana Historical Society and the Bloomington, Indiana Lilly Library (including the original manuscript of *Ben-Hur*), Lew Wallace Jr. saved for the family two items from the thousands of pages: Billy Bonney's first pardon plea letter of 1879, and Billy's Santa Fe jail letter of 1881 implying that he possessed Wallace's letters (now unknown) proving the pardon promise. "The General" must have let it be known to his kin that there was something special about them. William N. Wallace, Lew Wallace's great-grandson and Lew Wallace Jr.'s son, sold those two letters to New Mexico's Historical Museum in Santa Fe.

That same William N. Wallace, in 2010, still calling his ancestor "the General," helped me to stop a modern Santa Fe Ring Governor's plot of a hoaxed publicity-stunt pardon for Billy the Kid to be granted to an old-timer, dead, Texan pretender named Oliver "Brushy Bill" Roberts; and thereby helped me save Billy Bonney's history.

CHAPTER 12

LEW WALLACE ARRIVES IN NEW MEXICO TERRITORY: OCTOBER 1, 1878

LEW WALLACE, RELUCTANT GOVERNOR

ANALYSIS: After the Civil War, Lew Wallace sought positions and ambassadorships that stimulated his love of the exotic and need for grand titles. But he ended up, in October of 1878, with a Governorship in backwater New Mexico Territory to complete the 2½ years of removed S.B. Axtell's term, and left before it was over. During his unappealing tenure, he fatefully bargained with Billy Bonney about the pardon which could have changed history.

DESIRED APPOINTMENTS

In favor by possible vote-fixing to give Rutherford B. Hayes his electoral vote to win the presidency, Lew Wallace was positioned to request exotic ambassadorships. So he wrote to Hayes:

> Washington, March 9, 1877
> His Excellency, President Hayes.
> Dear Sir:
> I avail myself of your request this morning. It is hardly necessary to give reasons for the preference of the Italian mission over all others of the second class.
> The Brazilian embassy would be my next preference. Our manufactured products ought to command the markets of that country. A generous transmission of comparative details, reaching everybody through the State Department, would go far to achieve the object by inducing enterprises.
> The Spanish mission is very attractive – only I am afraid of the possible complications to which we are momentarily liable in that quarter.
> Mexico would be my last choice. At the same time my knowledge of the country and people might make me more serviceable there than elsewhere.
> It is for you to say.
> Very Truly, your friend,
> Lew. Wallace

GOVERNORSHIP APPOINTMENT: SEPTEMBER 4th 1878

By September of 1878, removal of Governor Samuel Beach Axtell was planned by President Hayes. Wallace's offer of that governorship came from Secretary of the Interior Carl Schurz on September 4th. So Wallace followed his deceased father's footsteps as a governor; albeit in a dreary trouble-ridden setting. Schurz informed Wallace by letter, writing:

Department of the Interior
Washington September 4th *1878.*

Gen'l. Lewis Wallace,
   Crawfordsville,
      Indiana,
Sir:
   I transmit herewith an order from the President for the suspension of Mr. Samuel B. Axtell from his office as Governor of the Territory of New Mexico, together with a designation for yourself, to perform the duties of said suspended officer, subject to all the provisions of law applicable thereto.
   You will deliver said order of suspension to Governor Axtell upon your arrival at the capital of New Mexico, and when you enter upon the duties of your office you will at once report the fact to this Department.
   The enclosed oaths of office you will take and subscribe on the day when you relieve Mr. Axtell, one of which oaths you will cause to be filed in the office of the Secretary of New Mexico, and the other you will duly forward executed to this Department, without delay.
                         Very respectfully, &c.
                         C. Schurz
                         Secretary

Secretary of War George McCrary relayed Wallace's appointment to General Edward Hatch, Commanding Officer of the Southwest District, and a Civil War veteran who detested Wallace for Shiloh. McCrary wrote:

War Department
Washington City,
Sept. 18th 1878.

General Edward Hatch
　Commanding District of New Mexico,
　　Santa Fe, N.M.
　General:
　　　This will be presented to you by Gen. Lew Wallace, the newly appointed Governor of New Mexico, who leaves here today for his post of duty. In view of recent serious disturbances in various portions of the Territory, Governor Wallace will in accordance with the desire of this Department, as well as his own inclination, shortly make a tour of the Territory and especially the disturbed regions.

As his mission will be in the interest of peace and order, and to carry out measures in which the Army and Government are interested, I desire to furnish him with Transportation and such Escort as may be deemed necessary and proper. Please consider yourself authorized and instructed to furnish Governor Wallace such aid in this direction as may be practicable.
　　　I have the honor to be
　　　　　Very respectfully
　　　　　　Your obdt. Servant
　　　　　　　Geo. W. McCrary
　　　　　　　Secy. of War.

WALLACE ARRIVES IN SANTA FE: OCTOBER 1, 1878

Ever-energetic, Lew Wallace hit the ground running at his October 1, 1878 Santa Fe arrival. He was sworn in that day:

October 1st 1878

And now comes Louis Wallace, and files his commission and official oath and enters upon the duties of his office as Governor of New Mexico.

Oath

I Lewis Wallace, do solemnly swear that I have never borne arms against the United States since I have been a citizen thereof; that I have voluntarily given no aid, countinence, counsel, or encouragement, to persons engaged in armed hostility thereto; that I have neither sought nor accepted, not attempted to exercise the functions of any office whatever, under any authority or pretended authority, in hostility to the United States; that I have not yielded to a voluntary support to any pretended Government, authority, power or constitution within the United States, hostile or inimical. And I do further swear, that to the best of my knowledge and ability, I will support and defend the Constitution of the United States, against all enemies foreign and domestic; and that I will bear true faith and allegiance to the laws, that I take this obligation freely without any mental reservation or purpose of evasion; and that I will well and faithfully discharge the duties of the office on which I am about to enter. So help me God.

Lew Wallace

That October 1, 1878, Wallace also wrote to Secretary of the Interior Carl Schurz - from whom he would constantly seek approval - to update him on his swearing in and confronting *"the disorders"* by *"extreme measures."* Always authoritarian, he wanted martial law. And he avoided Lincoln County, despite promising to *"go see the people immediately."* Only Huston Chapman's murder, 4 months and 18 days later, on February 18, 1879, would force contact with its riff-raff. Wallace wrote:

Santa Fe, Oct. 1, 1878
Hon. C. Schurz,
Sec. Dept. Interior.
Sir.
I have the honor to inform you that in compliance with your instructions, dated September 4th, 1878, I qualified as Governor of New Mexico yesterday at 3:10 o'clock, P.M. Please find the oath enclosed.

This morning I addressed a note to Gov. S.B. Axtell, informing him that I had qualified, and delivering him the order of suspension directed to him by the President.

On my way from Trinidad [Colorado], I stopped a day and a night in Cimarron, Colfax County [New Mexico], one of the localities about which a great deal has been said in connection with disorders. Without reference to the past, there certainly appears to be a good feeling on the part of the citizens there, and a decided disposition to keep the law.

As to Lincoln County, I shall go see the people immediately. *Whatever the result may be, I shall be careful that my action shall serve the President as a full justification should extreme measures become necessary.*

I shall take great pleasure in keeping you informed of the situation in the Territory.

Very respectfully,
Your friend & s'v't,
Lew Wallace

Wallace's Territorial arrival was reported on October 5, 1878 in the *Albuquerque Review*. Demonstrated was that Wallace had been met by the toxic embrace of the Santa Fe Ring. Passing southward through Colfax County's Cimarron to Santa Fe, he was with Catron's law firm member, Henry Waldo and Ringite U.S. Marshal John E. Sherman. Then it was Judge Warren Bristol who swore him in as Governor. The unnamed reporter wrote:

Quite a number of those who had vainly hoped that the removal of the late Governor Axtell, would not be consummated by the arrival of Gen. Lew Wallace until after the convening of the next Congress, were not only disappointed but quite surprised when the wires gave information on Saturday that he was in Cimarron and that he would come on at once to Santa Fe.

He did come, and the removal of Axtell is now an accomplished fact. Gen. Wallace arrived here on Saturday night, and on Monday accompanied by U.S. Marshal John E. Sherman and Judge Henry L. Waldo called at the gubernatorial residence ... and informed Axtell of the object of his visit to New Mexico ... [New] Governor [Wallace] said he came to New Mexico as a representative of no particular act of men or party, but as governor of the whole people: that he had not been here long enough to become effectively well posted to say what would be done, but that his intention was to do just what he believed right when the facts were known to him.

The next day, October 6, 1878, U.S. Marshal John Sherman gave Wallace a list of the "outlaws" allegedly causing the Territory's problems - most were past Regulators. William Bonny "the Kid" was number 14. The Ring worked fast.

WALLACE GETS SECRET ANGEL NOTEBOOK

As discussed, at arrival on October 1, 1878, Lew Wallace was prepared for the Santa Fe Ring because Frank Warner Angel counteracted his reports' cover-ups by secretly giving him a handwritten notebook listing Ringites and others so he could attack it himself. Dangerous Catron had no entry, but is referenced seven times, with others called his partner or his *"tools."* Now in Lew Wallace's collected papers in the Indiana Historical Society on microfilm - with the original possibly expurgated. Its cover reads: "Gov. Lew. Wallace / Santa Fe, N.M."

Also in the Collected Papers, and presumably also provided by Angel, is Mary McPherson's type-set booklet of August, 1877 titled: "In the Matter of Charges vs. Gov. S.B. Axtell and Other New Mexico Officials." (See my pp. 208-222) The notebook stated:

Newspapers

Albuquerque Review, Independent
News & Press, Cimarron Ind – not a very high toned paper – It is agst. the gov.
Las Vegas Gazette, Republican – Favors the ring –
Santa Fe New Mexican, Ring paper, Republican
The Sentinal Santa Fe, Independent
Santa Fe News, Democratic
The Independent, Mesilla Independent, Mesilla News, Ring papers

---

Andrews Enos Santa Fe, reliable
Ayers John, Honest – Liquor his worst enemy
Axtel S.B. Santa Fe, conceited – egotistical, easily flattered, Tool unwittingly of the ring – goes off" half cocked"
Arney W.F.M. Santa Fe, The great American liar - Look out for him – No power or influence – Runs the Palace for Axtel
Atkinson Wm. Santa Fe, Surveyor Gen – Honest and very reliable, only official who courted investigation
Boyle Andrew, at present at Mesilla, Outlaw murderer
Blazer, Jos. H. Lincoln Co., Reliable – Knows a great deal – Will not tell what he knows -
Bartlett Chas H. Lincoln County, honest -
Barrier Adolph P. - Las Vegas, Dept. Sheriff – Favors McSween party – Has acted for the right so far –

Beardsley Ezra I Cimarron, not reliable – Ex Post Master ofc not correct – since been made all O.K.

Berillia Sheriff at Mesilla, Not reliable - Ring tool

Breeden M.A. Santa Fe, post master, weak ring man, can be lead with a string

Bruden Col Santa Fe, I do not think he is reliable

Bristol W. Mesilla, Ast. Justice – Honest and reliable outside of Lincoln troubles

Beckwiths [blank] Pecos, Look out for the old man, The boys are honest & reliable outside of Lincoln Co troubles –

Bail [blank] [John] Mesilla, reliable and square man

Carroll Henry Capt – Hatch man, Fort Stanton, Reliable outside of Hatch matters

Coghlan Pat, Honest great friend of Murphy party, Godfroy & that crowd – resides at Tulerosa

Cline – [blank] Lincoln, reliable – I do not think he is mixed up in the Lincoln troubles -

Copeland John M Sheriff, removed by Gov – Lincoln, McSween party, I think is reliable

Chaves A. Albuquerque, Territorial Dist. Atty, Strong ring man – Has reputation of altering election returns 1875

Crouch Jno [John] A. Mesilla U.S. Clerk – Editor Mesilla Independent Trickish not reliable in every respect

Conway Thos Santa Fe, Lawyer some ability – I think reliable

Coe boys Lincoln, I think are reliable especially Frank

Chisum John S. Pecos, Backbone of McSween party – Sharp be careful with him

D'Sena Jose D – Santa Fe, Politician considerable influence – not entirely reliable

Davis Geo Lincoln, outlaw murderer

Dorsey W. near Cimarron, Senator – be careful with him

Dolan J.J. Lincoln Leader in Lincoln Co, trouble, Murphy party, Brave sharp - determined fellow – Badly mixed up with ring &c

Dudley, N.A.M. Fort Stanton Post Commander – Honest mortal enemy of Hatch, Talks too much, rely on him rather than Hatch

Dowlin Will Post Trader, Fort Stanton, Honest reliable – is Co Commissioner

Delgado F. Santa Fe, I think reliable, great church man

Evans Jesse Lincoln Co – outlaw – murderer –

Ellis [Isaac and Ben] Lincoln – There are two of these persons – McSween men but I think they are good citizens and reliable -

***Elkins S.B.** "Silver tongued" further comment unnecessary -*
***Elkins John** brother of S.B. Honest but dependent upon brother – strong ring man -*
Eley Rev at Las Vegas, weak, not reliable, McSween man
Ellison Sam – Santa Fe, weak tool, of Catron
Fields Westley – Lincoln Co, I think is reliable
Farmer Jos H. Lincoln Co, honest -
Fiske E.A. Santa Fe, Lawyer – Shrewd – honest reliable – can be of great service to you. He controls the U.S. Marshal Has been of great service to me - Well posted as to the people and frauds in the Territory
Fisher   Santa Fe, of Fisher and Lucas, reliable -
Gallegos Panteleon, Not reliable in employ of Dolan – a tool -
Godfrey C.F. Indian Agent near Ft. Stanton, Badly mixed up
Gonsoles [Gonsolez] F Probate Judge, Lincoln, reliable
Grace Fred Santa Fe Politician
Griffin W.W. Santa Fe, reliable & honest, in 1st Nat Bank & is influenced by Elkins
Howe Albert H. Lincoln Co, I think is reliable
Hurley John Lincoln – Easily influenced – Murphy party
Hubbel Judge Las Vegas, I think reliable, likes his toddy
Hill John Albuquerque, Under ring influence
Hatch E. Santa Dist Commander, Dudleys mortal enemy - Rumors- of his fraud and corruption To be handled with gloves
Hockradle Jerrie, Murphy man but honest & I think reliable
Jones   Mesilla, Catrons tool – not reliable
Kriling Chas Pecos, Honest but not reliable
Leverson M.R. Now on his ranch Larkspur Col – knows 6 times more than he can prove & 6 times more than anyone else – He can be of service to you <u>use him</u> Don't commit yourself – <u>Strong McSween man The Great American letters newspaper &c writer"</u>
Lee Wm D Cimarron, reliable but weak, under influence of Springer
Loud Lieut. Santa Fe, officious – Works for the ring – not reliable
Longwill Dr Santa Fe, Good Dr – but mixed up in Colfax Co trouble, Axtel man, ring man, do not rely on him -
Lucas   Santa Fe, of Fisher & Lucas – very reliable and a square man
Laudon "Judge" Santa Fe, reliable – but I think a democrat
Matthews J.B. Dept Sheriff Lincoln – Partisan Murphy party

Montaño Jose Lincoln, I think reliable –

Mattherson M. Socorro, Minister, Has done good work in Socorro & I think reliable

McPherson Mrs M.E. Washington D.C. Not reliable – Is interested or mixed up in Colfax Co troubles

McDaniels Jim Lincoln, desperado

Murphy L.G. Santa Fe, Mixed up in Lincoln Co – now a drunkard, no reliability He believes himself a martyr & McSween the devil – Handle him with gloves –

McMullen Wm Santa Fe, not reliable

McSween Mrs – Lincoln now at Las Vegas – Sharp woman now that her husband is dead, a tiger <u>use her however ("molasses catches more flies than vinegar")</u>

McCandleis Chas Santa Fe, Sup. Judge <u>very</u> reliable, good man to work with

Michaels Dr Cimarron, Sharp fellow, Axtel man –

Newcomb John Lincoln, Honest, McSween party, I think reliable -

Patron J.B. – Lincoln, Has considerable influence with Mexicans – not entirely reliable

Perry S.R. Pecos – I think reliable – But of no standing

Probst   Santa Fe, Honest – reliable – but shallow -

Purington G.A. Fort Stanton Captain - Honest but is a Hatch man

Peppin G.W. Present Sheriff Lincoln Co – Weak Murphy man – Partisan, not reliable -

Romero J. Delegate, influenced by Elkins

Romero R. La Cueva, Smart young man, I think reliable –

"Roxey" Lincoln, Outlaw

Riley J.H. Las Cruces – Sharp cunning fellow also leader of Murphy party Lincoln – Very disapated, not reliable – interested with Catron in Gov Contracts

Ritch W.G. Santa Fe Sec Territory, Axtel man, otherwise reliable

Rynerson W.L. Territorial Dist Atty Mesilla – Strong partisan, Axtel man – Murphy man – has used his office oppressively – not reliable

Stanley Steph Lincoln D.B. dishonest drunkard

Sherman John Jr – U.S. Marshal Santa Fe (Bro of Secy) means to tell all he knows – reliable – but not much back bone unless "braced up" Use him through Fiske E.A.

Springer F. Cimarron, Reliable, educated – runs Cimarron – very hostile to Gov Axtel –

Shields D.P. Las Vegas, Brother in law McSween, I believe reliable

Smith G.A. Santa Fe U.S. Collector – Old foggy used by Catron, makes good returns to Government not reliable
Spiegelberg Bros Santa Fe, Not reliable, use them agst Z Staub Bros & visa versa
Staab Z & Bro Santa Fe Axes to grind not reliable, use them agst Speigelberg Bros & vice versa
Smith G. G. Santa Fe, Pastor Presp. Church, I do not believe he is reliable –
Strachan W.J. Santa Fe , A democrat but I think reliable, **Catrons enemy** *–*
Tompkins R.H. Santa Fe, honest - & I think reliable – Old age against him –
Thornton W.T. Santa Fe, Catrons partner
Thayer Chas Santa Fe, Gambler – honest & I think reliable
Upson M.A. Roswell, Smart but dishonest, not reliable –
Wilson Andrew Lincoln Co, Reliable
Wakefiels E.H. Las Cruces, has mail contract from there to Ft Stanton, easily influenced, Murphy party – I think he means to be honest
Widenmann R.A. Now at Mesilla, Great friend of McSween – given to boasting, veracity doubtful when he speaks of himself, well connected in the east & well educated
Whigham Henry Cimarron, Editor Cimarron News & Press – Not very reliable unless backed by Frank Springer, McSween man
Waldo H Santa Fe, Present Atty. Gen Honest good lawyer and reliable but great friend of Axtel
Wilson J.B. Lincoln Justice of Peace, "Old fox" and very <u>weak</u> – easily influenced On the fence
West Jos Lincoln, honest & I believe reliable
Watts J.H. Santa Fe, I think he is reliable
Walz E.A. Lincoln – a tool of Catron – a boy – not reliable

OUTLAW MYTH PROPAGANDA

ANALYSIS: *Rather than confronting Lincoln County War issues, or the cover-up of the Ring's role, or Lincoln County citizens' hope for justice, Lew Wallace chose to use the Ring's outlaw myth to feign action by show of force, then to depart himself as soon as possible for greener pastures. So he used U.S. Marshal John Sherman's "outlaw" list in hopes of capturing its accused men for jailing or hanging by use of troops under martial law.*

The Lincoln County troubles did involve "outlaws." Besides Territorial Ringite public officials, they were local bosses James Dolan and John Riley; Jessie Evans and his gang; Seven Rivers and John Kinney rustler-killers; and treasonous Fort Stanton Commander N.A.M Dudley. But Lew Wallace preferred Ring propaganda which fabricated the "troubles" and Lincoln County War as random rustling and murdering by vague "outlaws." His simple solution was eliminating them. He reverted to his authoritarian penchant for hangings and martial law. For Billy Bonney, the writing was on the wall.

DUDLEY DISTRACTS FROM HIS CRIMINALITY

Fort Stanton Commander N.A.M. Dudley, besides having Ring loyalty, wanted to distract Governor Wallace from his own Lincoln County War crimes. So Dudley joined the "outlaw" chorus in a likely prompted letter of September 29, 1878 to his central command. Noteworthy is that his messenger was James Dolan.

Dudley's concocted *"gang of sixty to eighty strong"* would become the outlaw myth's statistic to exterminate the last Regulator resistance. And, by the following year, the figure would be falsely attached to Billy Bonney to justify his lethal pursuit by the Secret Service as that gang's leader. Dudley wrote:

Head Quarters, Fort Stanton, N.M.
Sept. 29th 1878
3 o'clock, P.M.

To the Asst. Adjt. General,
District of New Mexico.
Sir:
I avail myself of the opportunity to send this in advance of the next mail by Mr. Dolan, who leaves here tonight for Santa Fe, N.M.

The party of men styling themselves the **"Wrestlers"** *["Rustlers"] made up of renegades from Texas especially, some of whom have been partisans with both of the leading factions here, since I assumed command, have renewed their raiding with almost unparalled vigor.*

[AUTHOR'S NOTE: Amusingly muddling his apparent "rustlers" prompt as "wrestlers," Dudley presented the Ring's propaganda of the Lincoln County War as: 1) outlaws were the troublemakers; 2) the McSween side was outlaws; and 3) Dudley's duty had been to fight outlaw McSweens.]

Yesterday they attacked a party of laborers cutting hay near the Ranch of Jose Chaves, five miles below Fritz's Farm, and without the least provocation killed three of the party, two of the sons of Chaves ...

I have reliable information that the gang of which these men are a part, are from sixty to eighty strong, *and are en route from Seven Rivers, and south of there.*

*I respectfully and earnestly ask in the name of God and humanity, that **I may be allowed t o use the Forces of my army command, to drive these murderers, horse-thieves, and escaped convicts out of the county. The wives and daughters of quiet and good citizens are being daily sullied by these desperados, driven into the mountains, hiding to save their lives.** This too, almost in sight of the Garrison.*

[AUTHOR'S NOTE: Dudley sets up a future defense for his Posse Comitatus Act violation in the Lincoln County War, by asking now to be permitted intervention by the Act's loophole excuse of justified intervention for protecting women and children.]

I am, Sir, in every opportunity,
Your obedient servant,
N.A.M. Dudley,
Lieut. Col. 9th Cav.
Commanding Post.

BRISTOL BLOCKS LINCOLN COUNTY'S OCTOBER 1878 GRAND JURY SESSION: OCTOBER 4, 1878

Without reliably corrupt Governor S.B. Axtell, the Ring resorted to 3rd Judicial District Judge Warren Bristol for dirty-work. On October 4, 1878, in Lew Wallace's fourth day as Governor, the Ring sought to replicate Axtell's Colfax County removal of courts to block prosecution of murderers of Franklin Tolby, and Axtell's Lincoln County removal of Justice of the Peace "Squire" Wilson to block prosecution of John Tunstall's murderers.

So Bristol telegrammed U.S. Marshal John Sherman to complain that he could not hold court in Lincoln County because a jury was impossible for lack of *"the better class of the population,"* and as *"tainted"* by *"gross partisanship."* That translated into blocking the fall Grand Jury which would have indicted that July's San Patricio massacre perpetrators and Lincoln County

War battle Ringite arsonists and murderers of McSween, Harvey Morris, Francisco Zamora, and Vincente Romero. So Dudley and Peppin were not indicted until 1879. Bristol wrote:

> *My reasons for not holding October term of Court in Lincoln County, based on best information I can obtain are as follows: First, the Sheriff [Peppin] has either abandoned or been driven from his Office or duty, and taken refuge at Fort Stanton for protection. He refuses to go out. Second: The Prosecuting Attorney is absent from the Territory. Third: a large part of the better class of the population, from which Jurors should be drawn, have fled the County. Fourth: The County is completely demoralized. The troubles have arisen from the contending parties, both, in my opinion, equally bad, each having in its employ professional assassins, whose crimes it seems to shield and if necessary defend. Fifth: to accomplish these ends witnesses are intimidated, killed or driven from the County. Sixth: It is impossible at present to obtain fair juries, whose findings and verdicts will not be tainted with gross partisanship. Seventh: the Court can only act through such subordinate officials as are furnished by election or appointment & juries taken directly from the people. When these from any cause, utterly fail in their duties, the holding of Court for the time being, would be but a mockery.*

[AUTHOR'S NOTE: Ringite Bristol is blocking legal redress.]

Eighth: It is believed by those well informed, as to the affairs of that County, that during the present state of public feeling and animosity, the assemblage of a body of men, by attempting to hold Court, unrestrained by the military or any adequate force, as they would be, would be more likely to result in serious disturbances than otherwise and do more harm than good.

[AUTHOR'S NOTE: Sought is Ring suppression by use of troops, as in the 1872 Legislature Revolt, Colfax County War, and Lincoln County War.]

Ninth: There seems to be lacking that degree of force, which is necessary to render the execution of the mandates of the Court at all possible.

Bristol
Judge.

WALLACE SEEKS MARTIAL LAW: OCTOBER 4, 1878

On October 4, 1878, Lew Wallace, always "the General" in glorious battle in his over-heated fantasy life, and a seemingly dream-come-true Ring dupe, on his fourth day in office, and in receipt of Judge Bristol's telegram via U.S. Marshal John Sherman, requested from Secretary of the Interior Carl Schurz arms and martial law to hunt down "outlaws." And in two days, on October 6th, Wallace would be helpfully sent U.S. Marshall Sherman's outlaw list having Regulators. Wallace wrote:

Executive Office, Santa Fe, N.M.
October 4, 1878.
Hon. C. Schurz,
   Sec. Interior. Washington City, D.C.
Dear Sir: I have the honor to enclose herewith a requisition upon the Honorable Sec. of War for the full quota of arms, equipments, ammunition &c. due the Territory of New Mexico. Let me hope you will approve it, and forward to the Secretary of War, with request that the requisition be filled with the latest and most approved breech-loading rifles, and shipped at the earliest moment possible.
   I have the honor to be,
      Your friend & s'v't,
         Lew Wallace
         Gov. New Mexico.

Peripatetic Wallace, that same day, wrote the same request to Secretary of War John McCrary to fight imaginary outlaws having imaginary *"latest and most improved firearms."* Wallace wrote:

Executive Office, Santa Fe, Oct. 4, 1878.
   Hon. Geo. W. McCrary,
      Sec. of War
      Washington City, D.C.
   Sir:
      By the statute now in force, I understand the Territory of New Mexico is entitled, without reference to former account, to two thousand stand of arms; and I hereby make requisition in its behalf for the quota in full, including equipment, ammunition &c.

I beg to urge prompt attention to this matter, and add an entreaty that my requisition may not be filled with obsolete or condemned arms. The present great necessities of the Territory demand the latest and most approved model of breech-loading rifles, muskets, and carbines. **Against Indians in out midst, and bands of outlaws on the borders, our people, as now provided, cannot make a show of resistance. To add to the hardship, those from whom attack may be looked for, are armed with the latest and most improved firearms;** *wherefore to be successful in organizing the militia, and make them in the least effective, I am sure you will agree with me that it is of the first importance to be able to send them to the field, when occasion arises, upon an equality with the enemy as respects armament. Wherefore I beg you to give my requisition in this regard special favor, as well as speedy attention.*

As I have made arrangement with a Maj. Belcher Quartermaster of the post here for their storage temporarily I suggest that the packages be consigned to him originally, to be receipted for by me upon their arrival ...

In conclusion, to help my requests as above, I beg leave to point to the condition of the Territory at this moment of writing.

Very respectfully
Lew Wallace

WALLACE'S OUTLAW FOCUS: OCTOBER 5, 1878

By the next day, October 5, 1878, Wallace had worked himself into the foggy-headed hysteria that made him a liability at Shiloh. He deluged Secretary of the Interior Carl Schurz with documentation for his intended military campaign against "outlaws" with "*insurrection in the county of Lincoln.*" He wrote:

Santa Fe, New Mexico. Oct. 5. 1878.
Hon. C. Schurz, Secretary Interior Department.
Washington City, D.C.
As to the basis of the request which I have to prefer relative to affairs in the county of Lincoln in this Territory, I beg attention to the following reports.
(No. 1 – Dudley's to Hatch, Sept. 29, 1878.
No. 2 – Sherman's, Oct. 4, 1878.

No. 3. Bristol's, Oct. 4, 1878.)

These papers are all official, and disclose plainly the condition of the county. With no organized militia in the Territory or arms belonging to it, with the court closed, the sheriff shut up in the fort, the Marshal unable to make arrests, the good people unable to protect themselves, the regulars fixed to their posts by orders necessitated by Act of Congress, June 18, 1878 [Posse Comitatus Act], I am powerless to maintain the peace or remedy the unhappy state of affairs in this section referred to. ***In my judgment nothing remains for me to do except to call upon the President to exercise his constitutional authority, and declare the existence of insurrection in the county of Lincoln, place the county without loss of time under martial law, suspend the writ of habeas corpus therein, and appoint a military commission to come and hold sessions there for the trial and punishment of offenders.*** *In no other way can citizens be made safe in person and property. The Legislature of the Territory is not assembled, nor can it be in time to accomplish any quick result; no doubt it would unite with me in this request. I am loath to put such a mortification upon a high spirited people; at the same time I do not hesitate to charge the necessity for it to the aforesaid law, by which the regulars in the Territory are forbidden as* posse comitati.

The proclamation of the President should be limited to a time when the militia of the Territory can be organized and armed. By mail today I send requisitions for the quota of arms due.

[AUTHOR'S NOTE: Wallace has fabricated a desperate situation, but the horrific outrage of his request for martial law, arrests without time limit of *habeas corpus*, and military trial against the captured must be viewed in light of the Lincoln County War's military atrocities just three months earlier.]

I suggest obtaining the active co-operation of the Texas rangers on their side of the line. Doubtless the Texas State authorities will be glad to join the movement. Their combination with the regulars on this side will bring permanency of peace, by ***stamping out the robber element and breaking up their corrals and depots of plunder. The great need is for a few rugged examples.***

I send this by telegraph, because the wait on the mails will but give further time for outrage and murder.

Lew. Wallace
Governor of New Mexico

SHERMAN'S OUTLAW LIST: OCTOBER 6, 1878

On October 6, 1878, Ringite U.S. Marshal John Sherman manipulatively sent Wallace an outlaw myth list of the Territory's *"worst outlaws."* By March 11, 1879, Wallace recopied it for new Fort Stanton Commander Captain Henry Carroll to carry out their capture. William Bonney, as "The Kid," is number 14. It stated:

1 John Slaughter	*(Murder)*
2 Andrew Boyle	*(Horse stealing)*
3 John Selman	*(Murder)*
4 _____ Selman, alias "Tom Cat."	*(Murder)*
5 Gus Gildey	"
6 _____ Irvin	"
7 Reese Gobles	*(Murder)*
8 "Rustling Bob"	*(Murder)*
9 Robert Speakes	"
10 "The Pilgrim"	"
11 John Beckwith	*(Horse stealing)*
Hugh M. Beckwith	*(Murder)*
12 Jim French	"
13 Joe [Josiah "Doc"] Scurlock	"
14 "The Kid" William Bonney	"
15 Tom Folliard [O'Folliard]	"
16 Charles Bowdrey [Bowdre]	"
17 Henry Brown	"
18 John Middleton	"
19 Fred Weight [Waite]	"
20 Jacob B. Matthews	"
21 Jesse [Jessie] Evans	"
22 James J. Dolan	"
23 George Davis, alias "Tom Jones"	"
24 _____ [Frank] Rivers	"
25 Injenio [Ygenio] Salazar	"
26 John Jones	"
27 William Jones	"
28 ~~William~~ James [Jim] Jones	"
29 Marion Turner	"
30 Caleb Hall (Collins)	"
31 Haskell [Heiskell] Jones	"
32 Joseph Hill, alias Olney	"

33 Buck Powell "
34 James Hyson "
35 Jake Owens "
36 Frank Wheeler "

WALLACE ACCUSES "WRESTLERS": OCTOBER 7, 1878

With the Ring's rapid telegraph communication, it may be guessed that these usually humorless men rolled with laughter at Lew Wallace's gullibility. On October 7, 1878, Wallace was relaying to Secretary of the Interior Carl Schurz Commander N.A.M. Dudley's crazy and sordid rape story about "Wrestlers" from that soldier's apparently muddled Ring prompt for "rustlers." Wallace wrote:

> Executive Office, Santa Fe, N.M.
> Oct. 7, 1878.
>
> Hon. C. Schurz.
> Secretary Interior Department.
> Washington, D.C.
>
> In further exemplification of affairs in Lincoln county accept extract received today from Dudley, commanding Fort Stanton. "On Saturday night a party of "Wrestlers" visited the Ranch of a peaceable citizen by the name of Bartlett. He had two employees who are married, living a short distance from his house. The Wrestlers took the wives of these two men, and forced them into the bush, stripped them naked and used them at their pleasure." Same report (Dudley's) says the people are flying in search of protection.
>
> If I seem to hurry you, your great heart will excuse me.
>
> Lew Wallace.
> Gov. New Mexico

WALLACE ACCUSES BRISTOL'S AND DUDLEY'S FABRICATED OUTLAW HORDE: OCTOBER 14, 1878

Seven days later, on October 14, 1878, Wallace telegraphed Carl Schurz, about *"outlaws"* according to Dudley and Bristol. Their number had swelled to *"80 to 150" "Texans"* and *"Buffalo hunters"* in Wallace's wild west hyperbole his for desired *"war."* Other than relief that Wallace was not fighting the Ring, Schurz and Hayes must have wondered how out-of-control Wallace would become in his manic jousting of windmills. Wallace wrote:

I received last night a petition signed by the Probate Judge, two county commissioners, four justices of the peace in Lincoln county, representing the county infested by bands of non-residents who rob and kill at pleasure; that enforcement of law is not possible, because of inferiority of civil power. Petitioners pray protection as guaranteed by treaty Guadalupe-Hidalgo, for themselves and people of the county. Date October 8th.

Also letter from Col. Dudley, Fort Stanton, October 10th, saying, "Affairs at the present writing here are in a more deplorable condition than they have ever been before. Ten murders have been reported within the last fifteen days. No man, woman or child is safe in the county outside of the shadow of the military." Dudley also reports to Gen. Hatch, 10th instant, two men were shot and one hung near old Fort Sumner, three others killed at Puerta de Luna. All these since his last report.

Also yesterday (13th) I received reliable intelligence that a party of outlaws were organizing in north-eastern part of New Mexico to go to Lincoln county: that they had purchased arms and seven thousand rounds of ammunition, their object being to run off cattle and horses, and fight if attacked. Copies of these reports I will forward by mail.

The better opinion here is that present trouble is from Texans and Buffalo hunters, who, thinking the regulars tied up in law, believe it a good time to rape, steal, burn and kill. They number now 80 to 150, and are fast increasing.

My judgment is that to refer the matter to the civil authorities is childish. Read again what Judge Bristol said about juries in Lincoln county; observe the petition of the officers of the county given above. So the putting of the military ay my command or that of Sheriff is but a half way measure. We cannot act without process; while courts must sit surrounded by bayonets, and juries deliberate in dread of assassination.

In fact, there is nothing to be done but make war upon murderous bands. When prisoners are taken, let them be sent before a military commission, appointed to sit continuously at Fort Stanton. In other words, martial law for the counties of Lincoln and Doña Ana. The proclamation in quickest time possible.

Lew. Wallace.
Gov. New Mexico

A PRESIDENTIAL PROCLAMATION: OCTOBER 7, 1878

Wallace's headlong rush was stopped. President Hayes refused martial law - and his own obvious involvement - and merely issued a Proclamation admonishing people to go home and stop making trouble. It ran only from October 7th to 13th of 1878, written in Spanish and English. It stated:

BY THE PRESIDENT OF THE UNITED STATES OF AMERICA:

A PROCLAMATION.

WHEREAS, it is provided in the laws of the United States, that whenever by reason of unlawful obstructions, combinations or assemblages of persons, or rebellion against the authority of the government of the United States, it shall become impracticable in the judgment of the President to enforce by the ordinary course of judicial proceedings, the laws of the United States within any state or locality, it shall be lawful for the President to call forth the militia of any or all of the states, and to employ such parts of the land and naval forces of the United States as he may deem necessary to enforce the faithful execution of the laws of the United States, or to suppress such rebellion in whatever state or territory thereof the laws of the United States may be forcibly opposed or execution thereof forcibly obstructed; and

WHEREAS it has been made to appear to me, that by reason of unlawful combinations and assemblages of persons in arms, it has become impracticable to enforce by the ordinary course of judicial proceedings, the laws of the United States within the Territory of New Mexico, and especially within Lincoln County thereof, and that the laws of the United States have been forcibly opposed, and the execution thereof forcibly resisted; and

WHEREAS, the laws of the United States require that whenever it may be necessary in the judgment of the President to use the military force for the purpose of enforcing the faithful execution of the laws of the United States he shall forthwith by proclamation command such insurgents to disperse and retire peacefully to their respective abodes within a limited time. Now therefore, I RUTHERFORD B. HAYES, President of the United States, do hereby admonish all good citizens of the United States, and especially of the Territory of New Mexico, against aiding, countenancing, abetting or taking part in such unlawful proceedings, and I do hereby warn all persons engaged in or connected with said obstruction of the laws to disperse and return peaceably to their respective abodes on or before noon of the thirteenth day of October instant.

IN WITNESS whereof I have hereto set my hand and caused the Seal of the United States to be affixed. Done in the City of Washington this seventh day of October the year of our Lord eighteen hundred seventy-eight, and of the Independence of the United States the one hundred and third.

RUTHERFORD B. HAYES.

By the President:
F.W. SEWARD, Acting Secretary of State.

WALLACE SEEKS APPROVAL

WALLACE TO EVETTS: OCTOBER 9, 1878

Wallace's boundless energy was fueled by desperate desire to be appreciated. On October 9, 1878, the next father figure he courted was Secretary of State William Evetts, actually a Ringite. Wallace even fabricated that he was going to Lincoln County - and *"immediately."* He wrote:

Executive Office, Santa Fe. N.M.
October 9, 1878

Hon. W.M. Evetts
Secretary of State,
Washington D.C.
Sir:
I have the honor to acknowledge receipt by telegram of the President's Proclamation, addressed to the People of New Mexico, and dated October 7th inst.

The time (the 13th prox.) being so short, to have the Proclamation posted in Lincoln County speedily as possible, I had it telegraphed from this city the day of its receipt to Judge Bristol, with request that he would have it printed in Messilla [Mesilla], and dispatched thence by courier to the counties Lincoln and Doña Ana for posting. Distribution to the other counties was effected from Santa Fe.

I shall go down to Lincoln county immediately the better to report the effect of the Proclamation, and the manner in which it was observed.

Very respectfully, Your friend & s'v't,
Lew Wallace, Gov. New Mexico.

WALLACE TO HATCH: OCTOBER 20, 1878

Wallace, undaunted by Hayes's insipid response, used his Presidential Proclamation to keep rallying his imaginary troops for his desired war on imaginary "outlawry." On October 20, 1878, he decided to put General Edward Hatch in the loop. But he omitted his promise to Secretary of State William Evetts about actually going to Lincoln - presumably crawling with the great unwashed of infiltrating buffalo hunters, wrestlers, rustlers, rapists, murderers, and drunken vagrants - not just local, but drawn magnetically from adjoining Texas. Wallace wrote:

Executive Office, Santa Fe. N.M.
October 20, 1878

Col. Edward Hatch,
Com. of Dist. New Mexico.
Sir:
You will oblige me very much by informing me if you have advices from the commanding officer in Fort Stanton of a later date than the 13th inst., touching the President's Proclamation to the people of this Territory dated 7th, October. My particular point of inquiry is as to the manner in which the President's directions in that paper have been observed in Lincoln County.
Very respectfully,
Your friend, & s'v't,
Lew Wallace,
Gov. New Mexico.

WALLACE TO SCHURZ: OCTOBER 22, 1878

By October 22, Wallace reported again to father-figure Schurz that he was already a success thanks to father-figure Hayes, since there had been *"no report of violence or wrong."* Wallace wrote:

Executive Office, Santa Fe. N.M.
October 22, 1878
Hon. C. Schurz, Sec. Int. Dept. Washington D.C.
Sir:
I have the honor to inform you that since the posting of the President's Proclamation of the 7th inst. In Lincoln and Doña Ana counties there has been no report of violence or wrong in those localities. For this time at least the order has had sufficient effect ...

The better people everywhere have heartily approved the measure. The result will doubtless be gratifying to the President and all his advisors. It certainly is to me.

You may rest assured that I shall not use the military unless it be absolutely necessary; then, however, I shall ask and use the full measure of martial law, with a commission for the trial and punishment of offenders. As such a resort is naturally distasteful, I hope it may be avoided.

Having the honor to be,
Very respectfully,
Your friend & s'v't,
Lew. Wallace,
Gov. New Mexico

WALLACE'S "PACIFICATION PLAN" FOR LINCOLN COUNTY: OCTOBER 26, 1878

WALLACE MAKES A PLAN FOR QUICK SUCCESS

In less than a month after assuming office, Lew Wallace's outlaw fantasy had inflated to quick *"pacification"* of Lincoln County. With his narcissistic insensitivity, he wanted troops sent to Lincoln, forgetting it was just three months since Commander N.A.M. Dudley's military terrorism there. Refusing to visit Lincoln himself, he imagined its citizens fearing outlaws and entangled in *"feuds, fights or factions."* On October 26, 1878, he mailed his plan to General Edward Hatch, stating:

Executive Office, Santa Fe. N.M.
October 26, 1878

Gen. Edward Hatch,
Com'g, Dist. New Mexico.
Sir:
I think all that is needed now for the thorough pacification of Lincoln County is –
1. The dispatch of your available forces to Fort Stanton, and their distribution in Territory camps, as your good judgment will suggest, in both Lincoln and Doña Ana counties.

2. An immediate thorough scouring of those counties in search of and to break up camps and corrals of such outlaws as may be remaining there; the scouting to be done by several parties in different directions, say from El Paso and Fort Stanton simultaneously.

3. Orders to arrest all persons or bands of persons found in such camps and corrals or on the highways in possession of stolen property and who cannot give a satisfactory account of themselves or of the manner in which they came into the possession of the property found with them at the time ...

4. As to prisoners taken under the foregoing orders, they should be held securely until the proper court of the county ... can be held for finding indictments, issue of warrants, and trial ...

5. Property taken from persons arrested or bands dispersed, should be ... held for identification and reclamation by owners.

6. Officers charged with the foregoing orders should be allowed, in their discretion, to release parties arrested when satisfied of mistake ...

Pardon me if I presume to suggest great care on your part in the selection of the officers chargeable with these duties, which should be understood as having connection exclusively with the present situation in the counties named, disassociated with any past feuds, fights or factions; for which reason, as well as to make the duties more acceptable to the good citizens and actual residents, I think it would be advisable to select ... officers who are not accused of connection with such feuds or supposed to have had any part in them ... Your good judgment I have no doubt will improve upon the suggestion.

Very respectfully, sir,
Your friend & s'v't,
Lew. Wallace,
Governor of New Mexico

The next day, on October 27, 1878, Wallace's desire for soldiers was flattered. Army Headquarters in Santa Fe informed Commander N.A.M. Dudley by 1st Lieutenant and Adjutant of the 9th Cavalry John S. Loud (identified as *"Works for the ring"* in Angel's secret notebook) to grant Wallace troops. Ignored was Wallace's recommendation for sending only officers unconnected to feuds and fighting - meaning the Lincoln County War.

WALLACE AS DECORATOR: OCTOBER 23, 1878

Presumably back to writing *Ben-Hur: A Tale of the Christ* in its violet ink, Wallace seems to have finally paused to take a breath and look around. So he realized his Palace of the Governors looked and smelled terrible. Something needed to be done before his wife, Susan, arrived. So he apparently turned his literary skill from creating Lincoln County's fantasy outlaws to creating imaginary and nameless "doctors" who wrote a letter (in his handwriting) on October 23, 1878 to Secretary of the Interior Carl Schurz advising urgent need for redecorating. The "doctors" wrote:

Santa Fe, New Mexico
October 23ᵈ, 1878.

Hon. Carl Schurz.
Sir:
Yesterday, at the request of Governor Wallace the undersigned, physicians resident in this city, went through the building known as the "Palace," and carefully inspected it with reference to its present sanitary condition, the especial object being to inquire into its fitness as an abode for a family and for offices.

We found the east end of the structure set apart for legislative purposes, and the west occupied by the United States Marshal, leaving the central part for assignment to the Governor. Speaking generally, the only portions habitable are the Marshal's quarters, and suite of rooms in possession of Messrs Breeden and Waldo, lawyers; and these have been recently made so by the gentlemen occupying them.

The legislative halls are simply man traps. It is no exaggeration to say, one would not stable our horses in them.

The quarters immemorially assigned to the Governors of this Territory are somewhat better, because more roomy; judged, however, by the laws of modern hygiene, they are as unfit for human habitation as the legislative halls would be for horse-stabling.

The whole house is of <u>adobe</u>, or sun-dried mud in blocks made coherent by straw; and while we do not condemn the material, which has been the resort here from the beginning, it is nevertheless a fact well understood that after a long period of constant use houses so constructed become untenable, and have to be torn away and rebuilt or abandoned. The pertinency of the remark will be understood when we inform that the date of the building this "palace" is lost even to tradition. The one fact certainly known about it is that it has been in constant use over two hundred years.

But going to particulars, and confining ourselves to the Governor's quarters, both the outer and interior walls are from 4 to 8 feet thick. The roof is of mud two feet thick, tamped upon boards supported by unhewn logs. The entire front (south side) is curtained by a portico, the effect of which, sanitarily viewed, is to utterly exclude the sunlight from the interior.

Passing into the interior, we find rooms from 20 to 24 feet square, all pervaded by a damp, earthy odor, mixed not a little with the scent of vermin. The causes of the trouble are easily found: The floors are of boards laid on the ground; the ceilings of flimsy cotton goods, tacked to the logs which stay the mud roof; the doors are without transoms; a few of the rooms have fire places, while with exception of the kitchen, they are each provided with but a small window which will not admit of lowering from the top and do not extend to the floor. The best apartments in the quarter, consequently, are in fact no better than so many division cells of a cave, subject, as respects human habitation, to all the ills of a cave. But for the dryness and wonderful purity of the Santa Fe climate, it would not be possible for men of the strongest constitution to live in them healthfully. As it is, their tenants are subject to neurologic afflictions, and catarrhs, and diseases of every kind incident to damp, unlighted, unventilated chambers – this notwithstanding the building is situated in the most healthy portion of the city, itself, in our opinion, the most healthy in the United States.

The result of our investigation is, that in its present condition the whole structure, with exception possibly of the west end rooms occupied by the Marshal, is highly dangerous to life, and we urge the total abandonment of the premises as a dwelling.

It may be re-arranged and repaired, however, so as to be made serviceable for public offices a number of years longer – possibly until the Territory becomes a State. With this idea, we venture to recommend as follows:

1. Raise the floors quite three feet, leaving air space beneath, provided with ventilating apertures on the north and south sides.

2. Make corresponding increases in the height of ceiling.

3. Increase the number of windows in the several rooms, bringing the sills to a level with the floor.

4. Construct the roof with reference to attic space for ventilation, covering it with tin, and inserting ample skylighting.
5. Plaster and hand finish the walls and ceilings.

We may observe, in explanation, that the necessity for raising the floor is referable to the fact, that for a very considerable space the ground in the back yard, sloping but slightly from the wall of the building, is from 2 to 3 feet higher than the floor.

Very respectfully, Sir,
Your friends and servants,
[no signatures present]

WALLACE'S FIRST GUBERNATORIAL PARDON: OCTOBER 24, 1878

Twenty-three days after assuming the governorship, Lew Wallace exercised another of his past pacifying tricks: pardoning. The recipient was an Ursula Montoya for saying "*injurious words.*" Wallace wrote her a legal affidavit of pardon:

Santa Fe,
Executive Office, New Mexico,
October 24, 1878.

To whom it may concern:
Whereas, it has been made known to the undersigned that Ursula Montoya, of Placer, in the county of Santa Fe, in said Territory, was, on the 7th day of October, 1878, convicted by Agapito Sena, a Justice of the Peace in and for the said county, of speaking injurious words to an Ignacia Gonzales, and fined $25, and costs.

Now this is to certify that upon petition of Antonio Ortiz y Salazar and others, reciting the facts and circumstances of the offense and trial, by virtue of the power in me vested by law, the undersigned does hereby grant the said Ursula full pardon for the said offense, together with remission of said fine. And it is decided that she be discharged from custody.

Witness my hand to the seal of the Territory, this 24th day of October, 1878.

That same October 24th day, Billy Bonney, in Tascosa, Texas, wrote out in Spencerian script and correct legalese, the bill of sale to Dr. Henry Hoyt for dead Sheriff Brady's rustled horse. In 4 months and 17 days, Billy would apply these skills and that audacity to write to Governor Lew Wallace for his pardon.

HUSTON CHAPMAN WRITES TO WALLACE: OCTOBER 24, 1878

That same October 24th as Wallace wrote his decorating plan to Carl Schurz, reality intruded. Susan McSween's attorney, Huston Chapman, sent him a letter. It is unlikely that Wallace remembered Frank Warner Angel's entry in the secret notebook: "*McSween Mrs – Lincoln now at Las Vegas – Sharp woman now that her husband is dead, a tiger <u>use her however ("molasses catches more flies than vinegar")</u>.*" That "tiger," like Mary McPherson before her, wanted justice. She wanted to prosecute the man responsible for the murder of her husband and arson of her home: Commander N.A.M. Dudley. Apparently her traumatized and unwilling brother-in-law, Attorney David Shield, referred her to fellow Las Vegas, attorney, Huston I. Chapman; sharing an office with an Attorney Ira Leonard.

So Susan McSween started the chain reaction with Dudley and the Ring that would lead to Chapman's assassination; Billy's pardon plea and his getting Ira Leonard as an attorney; Wallace's reliving his Shiloh humiliation; and, ultimately, to Billy's killing.

So on October 24, 1878, with 3 months and 25 days to his Ring murder, Chapman mailed his complaint about Dudley, unaware that Dudley was a lynchpin in Wallace's military fantasies for suppressing Lincoln County, and unaware that conflict with an officer was Wallace's Achilles heel. Chapman wrote:

Las Vegas, New Mexico
October 24th, 1878.

Gov Lew Wallace,
Santa Fe, N.M.
My Dear Sir -
You will please pardon me for presuming so much upon your kindness, but knowing your earnest desire to protect the interest of any citizen of this Territory, and to see justice done all, I have made it my warrant for writing you in regard to affairs in Lincoln County.

From advices received this morning from Lincoln, affairs there seem as unsettled as ever and the people are expecting, really wishing for, martial law to be proclaimed by you. As such an event is very probably in the next few days, I desire to call your attention to one person whose actions have been offensive in the extreme to a large number of the best citizens of that County, and that man is Col. Dudley. I am in possession of facts which make Col Dudley criminally responsible for the killing of McSween and he has threatened that in case martial law was declared that he would arrest Mrs. McSween and her friends immediately. Through fear of his threat Mrs. McSween left Lincoln and is now visiting here, until such time as she may with safety return home. She has fears of harm only from Col Dudley and in case he has the power he will do all in his power to annoy and arrest her. Mrs. McSween has some interests in Lincoln County which really demands her presence there at the meeting of the Probate Court next month, but in view of the threats made by Col Dudley she is afraid to return there. As the attorney of Mrs. McSween I ask that should martial law be proclaimed in Lincoln County you will prevent Col. Dudley from exercising any authority that would enable him in any way to interfere with Mrs. McSween, or her affairs. Believe me that I do not wish to influence you in any action in regard to the affairs in that county and am sorry to be forced to lay these complaints before you, but owing to the very prominent and partisan manner in which Col Dudley has acted I think you will agree with me that he is not a fit man to act in so delicate and complicated a matter.

There seems to be but one opinion entertained by the people and that is that you are determined to see that ample justice is had in Lincoln County.

Hoping that you will pardon any liberty I have assumed in making these suggestions, I am

Yours very truly
H.I. Chapman

WALLACE'S AMNESTY PROCLAMATION: NOVEMBER 13, 1878

Real outrages in Lincoln County, as documented in Attorney Huston Chapman's October 24, 1878 letter, apparently forced Lew Wallace to go farther than his outlaw elimination plan to distract citizens so he could continue his writing, decorating, and progress reports. As a lawyer, he would must have checked a volume of *Compiled Laws of New Mexico in Accordance With an Act of the Legislature* in the Palace of the Governors. As to pardoning, Section 3457 stated:

> Any person against whom prosecution shall have been commenced under the laws of this territory for an offence against the law, any such person may be surrendered *or* not surrendered, at the discretion of the governor, before he shall have been tried or set at liberty, or if he shall be sentenced or punished for the same.

Pardon was at "the discretion of the governor." And a general pardon is an Amnesty Proclamation. Wallace had already unsuccessfully floated one in 1864 for civilians and soldiers in Confederate trans-Mississippi states and territories to lure them into rejoining the Union. So he tried it again, now including soldiers with civilians to dispose of all possible complainers in one fell swoop. It would backfire badly. He wrote:

Proclamation by the Governor.

For information of the people of the United States, and of the citizens of the Territory of New Mexico in especial, the undersigned announces that the disorders lately prevalent in Lincoln County in said Territory, have been happily brought to an end. Persons having business and property interests therein, and who are themselves peaceably disposed, may go to and from the County without hindrance or molestation. Individuals resident there, but who have been driven away, or who, from choice, sought safety elsewhere, are invited to return, under assurance that ample measures have been taken and are now and will be continued in force, to make them secure in person and property. And that the people of Lincoln County may be helped more speedily to the management of their civil affairs, as contemplated by law, and to induce them to lay aside forever the divisions and feuds which, by national notoriety, have been so prejudicial to their locality and the whole Territory, the undersigned, by virtue of authority in him vested, further proclaims a general pardon for misdemeanors and offences committed in the said County of Lincoln against the laws of the said Territory in connection with the aforesaid disorders, between the first day of February, 1878, and the date of this proclamation.

And it is expressly understood that the foregoing pardon is upon the conditions and limitations following:

It shall not apply except to officers of the United States Army stationed in the said County during the said disorders, and to persons who, at the time of the commission of the offence or misdemeanor of which they may be accused were, with good intent, residents citizens of the said Territory, and who shall have hereafter kept the peace, and conducted themselves in all respects as becomes good citizens.

Neither shall it be pleaded by any person in bar of conviction under indictment now found and returned for any such crimes and misdemeanors, nor operate the release of any party undergoing pains and penalties consequent upon sentence heretofore had for any crime or misdemeanor.

In witness whereof I have hereunto set my hand and caused the seal of the Territory of New Mexico to be affixed.

{SEAL} Done at the city of Santa Fé, this 13th day of November, A.D. 1878
LEWIS WALLACE,
By the Governor,
W.G. Ritch, Secretary

PRESIDENTIAL APPROVAL: NOVEMBER 23, 1878

At last, Wallace got what he wanted: approval from Schurz and Hayes. It was for his "Amnesty Proclamation," with its fake *"announcing the termination of the disturbances."* Schurz wrote:

Department of the Interior

Washington November 23rd, 1878,

General Lewis Wallace
Governor of the Territory of New Mexico.
Sir:
I acknowledge the receipt of your letter of the 13th instant giving an account of your proceedings to suppress the disorders lately prevalent in Lincoln County in the Territory of New Mexico, accompanied, among the other papers, by the proclamation issued by you on the 13th of November 1878, announcing the termination of the disturbances and offering, under certain limitations and

conditions Amnesty to a portion of those who participated in the disturbances. In reply I have to state that your action in this matter has the approval of the President.
>Very respectfully
>C. Schurz
>Secretary

FAILED APPOINTMENT OF ATTORNEY IRA LEONARD: NOVEMBER 13, 1878

On the same day as writing his Amnesty Proclamation, on November 13, 1878, Wallace did something that could have actually benefited Lincoln County's and Territorial anti-Ring struggles. He recommended to Secretary of Interior Carl Schurz Las Vegas attorney, Ira Leonard, for a judgeship in the 1st Judicial District in Santa Fe. Leonard, of course, did not get it - it was the epicenter of Ringite judicial control. Wallace was likely also unaware that Leonard was the office-mate of anti-Dudley Attorney Huston Chapman.

On November 15th, Carl Schurz forwarded Wallace's letter to Attorney General Charles Devens. Wallace had written:

>Executive Office, Nov. 13. 1878

>Hon. Carl Schurz,
>Sec. Dept. Interior
>Washington City.

>Sir.
>I enclose a paper, signed by all the leading attorneys of this city, praying speedy action in the matter of Judge of the 1st Judicial District in this Territory, and requesting the appointment of Hon. Ira E. Leonard, to be Judge.
>There is no question of great necessity for speedy action in the matter; and if no appointment has been made when this reaches you, I unite with the signatories in their request in behalf of Judge Leonard.
>>Very respectfully
>>Lew. Wallace,
>>Gov. New Mexico

WALLACE'S WAR DEPARTMENT FRUSTRATION: NOVEMBER 23, 1878

On November 23, 1878, Wallace's plan for independent military companies - like his Civil War Zouaves - to *"defend themselves"* in his "war" against "outlaws" was rejected by Secretary of War George McCrary. McCrary even wanted Wallace to post personal bond for arms. McCrary, aware of Shiloh, wrote:

November 23rd, 1878.

Sir:
I have the honor to acknowledge the receipt of your letter of the 4th ultimo, making special requisition, without reference to former accounts, for two thousand stands of arms, equipments, ammunition &c., and in reply, beg to invite your attention to the views of the Judge Advocate General of the Army touching these issues submitted in his report dated 9th instant, which is approved, and a copy of which hereto subjoined. "The Act of July 3, 1876, authorizing the Secretary of War to issue arms in cases like the within, provides that issues shall be made "<u>only</u>" upon certain "conditions" – one of which is that the requisition shall show "that militia companies are regularly organized and under control of the Governor." In this case it is not shown that the militia of the Territory is, in any degree, organized: indeed the inference from the Governor's communications would be that it had not yet been organized.

"A second condition prescribed in the Act is that the Governor "shall give a good and sufficient bond for the return of said arms or payment for the same at such time as the Secretary of War may designate."

"It is not specified that the bond shall be an official bond, nor indicated what shall be the security given. In the absence of such indication, a personal bond with surities in the usual form would, it is believed, be equally with an official bond, a substantial compliance with the law.

"In this case, however, an official bond has been tendered, in which the Territory is undertaken to be bound. But in the recent case of a similar bond by the Governor of West Virginia, reported

upon to the Secretary of War on September last, it was held by the Judge Advocate General that such bond could not bind the State unless, by some constitutional or statutory provision, the Governor was expressly authorized to bind it – which did not appear."

"Similarly, in the present case, unless it should be shown that the Governor of New Mexico was authorized by the laws of the Territory to bind it to the penalty of the within bond, the same would not be held to be "good and sufficient" under the Act.

"It may be added that the within bond, though purporting, in the body, to be "sealed", bears no seal, either official or personal."

The bond is herewith returned.
> Very respectfully,
> Your obedient servant,
> Geo. W. McCrary
> Secretary of War

The Governor
Of the Territory of New Mexico

BOASTING TO SCHURZ: NOVEMBER 13, 1878

That busy November 13th still left Wallace energy to write a glowing progress report about himself to Carl Schurz - even pretending that he had achieved a *"great point gained to drive the outlaws of the Territory without bloodshed ... The trouble is ended now."* In a confidential letter the next day, he would be more honest about his future and true Territorial adversaries. Wallace wrote to Schurz:

> Executive Office, Santa Fe, N.M.
> November 13. 1878

Hon. C. Schurz,
Sec. Dept. Interior
Washington, D.C.
Sir.

I have the honor to forward you the following report.

The opinion expressed in a former communication was well founded. Thirty days have elapsed since publication of the President's proclamation, requiring the disturbers of peace in Lincoln County to disperse and, as shown by dispatches of Col. Dudley Commanding at Fort Stanton, there has been no instance of violence in that time.

I was a great point gained to drive the outlaws of the Territory without bloodshed; the next was to prevent their return. For that purpose, availing myself of the order of the Hon. Secretary of War and Gen. Sherman (to whom my hearty acknowledgments are due), issued in connection with the President's proclamation, I addressed a request to Gen. Hatch, Commanding the District of New Mexico, to the effect that he send all his available force to Lincoln and Doña counties, under certain orders. Herewith, marked No. 1.

Gen. Hatch placed me under great obligation by complying promptly. A copy of his orders is also forwarded you marked No. 2.

The troops being distributed in the counties, as much for the moral effect of their presence as from any expectation that there would be a reason for their use, I waited expiration of thirty days; then, there being no repeat of disturbance or outrage, I concluded the people might be in a state affirmed to avail themselves of amnesty for the past, and begin anew. It is easy to see how, without something of the kind, the vendetta-spirit which has marked the outbreak might go on indefinitely. Accordingly I have this day issued a proclamation, announcing the end of the disturbances, inviting peaceably disposed citizens who have been driven away to return to their homes, and offering a general pardon, the latter carefully guarded in expression and limitation, as you will perceive by reference to the copy enclosed, marked No. 3.

It is my opinion that the present status continuing thirty days, or sixty, at the furtherest, affairs in Lincoln county will settle down and go on in peace. The trouble is ended now, and I have only to prevent its renewal, and help the people back to quiet control.

> *Very respectfully*
> *Your friend & s'v't,*
> *Lew. Wallace,*
> *Gov. New Mexico*

WALLACE'S SECRET SANTA FE RING LETTER TO ABSALOM MARKLAND: NOVEMBER 14, 1878

Lew Wallace's secret letter November 14, 1878, the day after his Amnesty Proclamation, to his trusted Civil War friend, Absalom Markland, ends any question of Wallace's awareness of the Santa Fe Ring. He frankly admits its pressure, and that the Ring wants to remove him!

Colonel Absalom Hanks Markland (1825-1888) was a life-long friend and confidant of Ulysses S. Grant; a major figure in the development of the U.S. Postal Service; and, according to Grant's biographer Geoffrey Perret, was very smart. Grant assigned Markland to his Civil War headquarters, made him a Washington postal agent and U.S. Special Mail Agent for the Union Army, and gifted him with the historic saddle he used throughout the Civil War. Abraham Lincoln was also Markland's friend. And Markland may have assisted Wallace with his pleas for a Shiloh pardon. To this trusted friend, Wallace could write rare truth:

Santa Fe, N.M.
Nov. 14, 1878.

Col. A.H. Markland,
My dear Colonel:
Our mutual friend, Mr. Hinds, who will hand you this, goes to Washington tomorrow; and I write late at night.

Enclosed find a paper with markings which may interest you and Mrs. M., to whom please give my regards. They will tell you with what success I operate to finish the outlawry in this Territory, and how it was done.

After you have read them, a word as to my confirmation.

I came here, and found a "Ring" with a hand on the throat of the Territory. I refused to join them, and now they are proposing to fight me in the Senate. Ex Delegate Elkins is head-center in Washington. *He is the fellow who got the* <u>Washington Sunday Herald</u> *to publish the lie which the paper enclosed contradicts. The paper, by the way, is the Democratic organ of the Territory.*

Elkins will rely on Orth, in the House, and Davis, of Virginia, and Dorsey, of Arkansas ... Davis is Elkins' father-in-law. ***Dorsey was an associate of the ring in land-grant speculation****, which came to grief in New Mexico a few weeks ago. The paper upon which the grant was based was a forgery – and Dorsey knew the fact before he went into it – that is, before he went before the Surveyor General.*

[AUTHOR'S NOTE: This is the Uña de Gato Land Grant fraud exposed by an Angel report, as well as by Mary McPherson and Frank Springer. Past Governor Axtell was Ring agent to buyer Senator Stephen W. Dorsey. Angel's Wallace notebook stated: "Dorsey W. near Cimarron, Senator – be careful with him."]

Now can't you turn out and help me in the business? You know everybody, and just who to see, and how to get at them. Give me a little of your old time energy, and do me a little of the old style fighting. And write to me when you have looked the ground over.

Say to Mrs. Markland that this is singular country. Six sevenths of the population are Mexican, and so is society and the customs generally. I would like it, but I shrink from bringing my wife. After the Senate has pronounced on me, if unfavorably, of course I will go home – if yea, it is probable I'll go back any hour for my wife's sake.

Write me,

Truly, your friend,
Lew. Wallace.

ATTEMPTING TO ESCAPE: NOVEMBER 18, 1878

By November 18, 1878, Wallace wanted to escape his job, which was proving more horrible than anticipated. On November 18, 1878 he floated, to no avail, a proposal to Secretary of State William Evetts hinting that he was *"entitled to promotion"* of an ambassadorship since he had already solved the Territory's problems! Wallace wrote:

Executive Office, Santa Fe, N.M.

November 18, 1878.

Hon. Will. Evetts
Sec' of State
Washington, D.C.
Dear Sir:

I take the liberty of sending you a copy of the Democratic organ of New Mexico, containing some <u>markings</u>, which will show the progress made in suppressing the insurrectionary troubles in Lincoln county.

That task would seem to have been my special mission here; and as it is accomplished, do you not think me entitled to promotion? As the field in which your hand has to appear is a very wide one, with much to be done in it, I would be particularly happy if you would entrust me with some fitting part of the work.

The speech you were going to make in New York, and did make, has not yet come to hand.

Very respectfully, your friend,
Lew. Wallace.

RING REMOVAL RUMORS: DECEMBER 9, 1878

The Ring matched Lew Wallace's wish that he was out of the Territory. Wallace had sought reassurance from Carl Schurz about the rumored Ring attempts to remove him as he had described in the November 14, 1878 letter to Absalom Markland. Though Schurz was supportive, it was now clear that Wallace was factoring in Ring retaliation to protect his future appointments after his Territorial governorship. And the pressure on Wallace would become greatest when it came to pardoning Billy the Kid. Schurz answered Wallace on December 9, 1878, writing:

DEPARTMENT OF THE INTERIOR
WASHINGTON.

December 9, 1878.

Dear Governor:
I have received your letter of Nov. 28th. So far I have not heard of any intention on the part of anybody in the Senate to defeat your confirmation. If inquiry should be made of this Department you may be assured that the removal of Governor Axtell and your appointment will be put in the true light.
Truly yours,
C. Schurz

CHAPTER 13

LEW WALLACE'S DUDLEY-CHAPMAN CRISIS: OCTOBER, 1878 - FEBRUARY 18, 1879

THE DUDLEY PROBLEM

ANALYSIS: *Commander Dudley, twice court martialed drunkard and treasonous criminal of the Lincoln County War battle, became the Ring's reason to commit its next assassination. And Dudley became Lew Wallace's nightmare of legal and military entanglements, with Wallace blamed and shamed by the Ring.*

WALLACE FACES DUDLEY: OCTOBER 28, 1878

Lew Wallace's response to Huston Chapman's October 24, 1878 complaint about N.A.M. Dudley was attempted placation of both. He would include Dudley in his Amnesty Proclamation. And he would try to address Chapman's grievances by removing Dudley as Commander based on his being a local irritant. That way he could blame Lincolnites for the accusations. The last thing Wallace wanted - as the Civil War's most humiliated General - was to incur military wrath. And he wanted Dudley's help for his outlaw scapegoating plan. Events were getting perilously close to striking his old Shiloh wound.

On October 28, 1878, four days after getting Chapman's letter, Wallace wrote to General Edward Hatch, New Mexico Territory's Commander, calling *"incredible"* Chapman's *"accusations;"* but also granting Chapman's request for Susan McSween's safe-guard. Adding to the awkwardness, was Hatch's involvement in Shiloh; but Hatch disliked Dudley also. And Hatch knew that if Dudley was found guilty of Posse Comitatus Act violation, he himself would be blameworthy as his superior. Wallace wrote:

Executive Office, Santa Fe, N.M.
October 28, 1878.

Gen. Edward Hatch,
Comg. Dist. New Mexico.
Sir:
I enclose you a copy of a letter received from Las Vegas, which will explain itself.

>   *Confidentially speaking, the accusations therein against Col. Dudley strike me as incredible; at the same time, it is apparent that Mrs. McSween, whether with or without cause, is alarmed; wherefore, as it appears she has business in Lincoln county requiring her personal attention, with a view wholly to put her at rest, I respectfully request a special safeguard for her, which, if forwarded to me, I will cause to be duly transmitted.*
>
>   *You will further oblige me by calling Col. Dudley's attention to the matter. As he will be directly in charge of the troops to be moved into Lincoln and Doña Ana counties, the charges preferred by Mr. Chapman seriously affect his fitness for the delicate duty.*
>
>
>
> *Very respectfully*
> *Your friend & s'v't,*
> *Lew. Wallace, Gov. New Mexico.*
>
>

Hatch stonewalled Wallace. On November 9, 1878, Wallace tried again; his nervous draft having more cross-outs than any other retained copy in his collected papers. Wallace wrote:

>
>
> *Executive Office, Santa Fe, N.M.*
> *Nov. 9. 1878*
>
>
>
> *Gen. Edward Hatch,*
> *Comg. District New Mexico.*
> *Sir:*
>
>   *In a communication, dated October 28. inst., I requested, for reasons stated, a safe-guard for Mrs. McSween, now at Las Vegas, stating that, if it were sent to me, I would attend to its transmittal.*
>
>   *I accompanied the communication with a letter from Mr. Chapman, Las Vegas, containing certain charges against Col. Dudley, commanding at Fort Stanton,* ~~which I thought of a serious character~~ *and while I expressed* ~~my disbelief of them~~ *the opinion that the Colonel could not have been guilty of them, I also requested* ~~that~~ *you to be good enough to* ~~have them~~ *submit the letter to him, my object being to give him an opportunity to be heard upon the subject.*
>
>   ~~Nearly two weeks have passed, and~~ *As yet* ~~the~~ *I have not had so much as an acknowledgment of the receipt of the communication. I hope the failure has arisen from oversight or press of* ~~duty~~ *other matters.*

465

Permit me to repeat my request for the safe-guard of the lady, and ~~also~~ ask if Col. Dudley's attention has been called to Mr. Chapman's charges, and if there has been reply from him.
Very Respectfully,
Your friend & s'v't,
Lew. Wallace,
Gov. New Mexico.

DUDLEY'S RESPONSE: NOVEMBER 9, 1878

After Hatch's apparent order by telegraph, Dudley responded the same November 9th to Wallace with bombastic snideness reeking of Ring protection and dictation by Catron or Henry Waldo. Enclosed were usual defamatory affidavits by Ringites - here against Susan McSween's chastity - to devalue her credibility for court testimony. Implied ominously was Ringite gearing up for murders of Susan McSween and Huston Chapmen. Dudley wrote:

Headquarters.
Fort Stanton, N.M.
Nov. 9' 1878

To his Excellency,
Lew. Wallace.
Governor Territory of New Mexico
    Sir:
        I am in receipt of a copy of letter written by one H.I. Chapman, calling himself the Attorney of Mrs. A.A. McSween, widow of the late McSween, lawyer at Lincoln N.M., also your letter addressed to the District Commander, both having been referred to me for remark.
    I have no comments to make upon either, except to respectfully invite your attention to the seven affidavits and one certificate sent to District Headquarters, from parties here, who know the facts in the case, and the woman equally as well, who asks for a safeguard.
    I have requested that they be laid before you at once, for the reason that I believe you should know the character of some of your informants, regarding matters upon which you are to act.
    If these papers do not satisfy you, any number of a similar kind can be forwarded. *I am prepared to defend myself from any and all attacks, coming from whatever source they may, and shall require no time to do it, and shall not need the services of an attorney either.*

[AUTHOR'S NOTE: These are the affidavits against Susan McSween, made by Ringmen accusing her of sexual misconduct. Key, however, is the wording: "*If these papers do not satisfy you.*" Wallace would answer on November 14th that Dudley's <u>response</u> was "*satisfactory.*" But Dudley and his lawyers would twist that to mean that Wallace was <u>satisfied as to his innocence</u>, since the accusing woman was unreliable.]

I have complete reports of every detachment, guard, posse and escort that has left this post, since I assumed command, at 12 PM, April 5th 1878.

Not an officer or soldier of my command has ever left the reservation on any duty appertaining to Lincoln County affairs, even as a simple courier, unless he went under carefully written orders, and a full report was required of the result of the tour, and which I have now in my possession, all of which are matters of record.

I am not here, quietly to submit, and allow such allegations against myself, as your Excellency has seen proper to forward to District Headquarters, without making an unqualified denial, and I defy proof to the contrary.

Very Respectfully,
Your Obt. Servant
N.A.M. Dudley
Lieut Col 9' Cavalry
Comdg Post.

Wallace's November 13, 1878 "Amnesty Proclamation" was, in part, his assurance to Dudley that he would be pardoned - no matter what crimes he committed in the Lincoln County War. Wallace apparently missed its implication that Dudley needed pardoning. Dudley - and the Ring waiting to pounce - did not.

And in Wallace's November 14, 1878 response back to Hatch about Dudley's reply - a day after issuing the Amnesty Proclamation - he blundered again by an unctuous attempt to placate Dudley as a military authority-figure entangled with transference to unforgiving Grant and to his own cruel father. So Wallace told Hatch that Dudley's response to Huston Chapman's charges was "*perfectly satisfactory.*" That obsequious phrasing merely meant that Dudley had finally responded to him as requested; not that Dudley's actions, or the enclosed defamatory affidavits about Susan McSween, were acceptable. But of all the words that Lew Wallace would ever write, those two would haunt him by the time that letter was presented back to him as an Exhibit in May of 1879 in Dudley's military Court of Inquiry with Henry Waldo's biting accusation that he had already excnerated Dudley. And in that placating November 14, 1878 letter to Hatch, Wallace even backed down on his requested "*safeguard*" for Susan McSween. When push came to shove, Wallace favored safeguard for Lew Wallace. Wallace wrote in his agitated crossed-out draft:

Executive Office, Santa Fe, N.M.
November 14, 1878

Col. Edward Hatch,
Com'g. Dist. New Mexico.
Sir:
In am in receipt of Col. Dudley's reply to the charges against him respecting Mrs. McSween contained in a letter to me from H.I. Chapman, Esq., of Las Vegas.
Be good enough to say to Col. Dudley that the reply is perfectly satisfactory, and that he did not need to go to so much trouble *to me. And as to the request for a "safeguard" please consider it withdrawn.*

Very Respectfully,
Lew. Wallace,
Gov. New Mexico.

HUSTON CHAPMAN'S ONSLAUGHT: NOVEMBER 25th AND 29th, 1878

By late November, aggressive Attorney Huston Chapman was directly insulting Wallace as well as Dudley. By his November 25, 1878 letter, he blamed Wallace more than Dudley. Chapman, appearing ready to complain to President Hayes, snarled:

You attach much importance to the awe-inspiring influence of the military, but it would pain you to see in what contempt they are held by the people whose confidence they have so shamefully abused. These depraved specimens of humanity who disgrace the name of soldier by the debauchery and immoral conduct are little to be relied upon in any matter where they are interested.
It is a matter of surprise to me that a man like Col. Dudley, who is a whiskey barrel in the morning and a barrel of whiskey at

night, is entrusted with so important a position, or even retained in the army where his debaucheries must work such a damaging influence upon younger and better officers, and thus destroy their usefulness.

Col. Dudley is continually under the influence of liquor and has used his position as commandant of Ft. Stanton to insult and abuse offending citizens until his conduct has become a reproach to the military service of the country and an insult to every officer who tries to maintain the dignity of his position. I desire particularly to call your attention to the conduct of this man Dudley to the end that in the future we may know upon whom to place the responsibility for his wrongdoings. (Nolan, *The Lincoln County War: A Documentary History*, p. 359)

Then on November 29, 1878, five days after Wallace secretly confided to Absalom Markland about his knowledge of the Santa Fe Ring, Chapman sent Wallace another letter which ruined Wallace's ongoing subterfuge of the outlaw myth. Chapman blamed that Ring for Lincoln County's crisis.

One can surmise that since Chapman accompanied Susan McSween back to Lincoln that month from Las Vegas, he likely met Billy Bonney, still a Regulator, presenting himself secretly as eager to protect her. And Chapman's bellicose approach, his anti-Ring stance, his accusing of Dudley, and his confrontation of the Governor could have contributed to the cocky tone of Billy's pardon plea to Wallace four months hence.

Chapman's correct analysis in his November 29, 1878 letter to Wallace is that his Amnesty Proclamation had wrongly shielded Sheriff George Peppin and Commander N.A.M. Dudley from deserved murder indictments. Inadvertently, Chapman also hit Wallace's other painful spot besides Shiloh - fear of failure - by threatening to publish a newspaper article accusing Wallace of failing in his duty by not coming to Lincoln County. Crushed also was Wallace's self-delusion that he was being seen as the people's "savior," like the Christ he was creating in *Ben-Hur*. Threatened was his hope to steer between the "Devil" of the Santa Fe Ring and the "deep blue sea" of citizens' needs. But Wallace, with his severe character flaws, was only able to respond self-protectively: seeking favor from superiors, and continuing his "war" on "outlaws." Thus, he would indirectly work to destroy the Ring's last Regulator opponents. Chapman wrote:

Lincoln, Lincoln Co., N.M.
November 29 1878.

Governor Lew. Wallace,
    Santa Fe, New Mexico.
        Dear Governor.
                You must pardon me for so often presuming upon your kindness, but I write this letter to inform you of the true status of affairs in Lincoln County. To-day this town was thrown into a panic by two hundred deputy sheriffs charging into town on their horses with their guns cocked and directed at the house of Mrs. McSween. A few minutes afterwards a posse of soldiers under the command of one Lieut Goodwin came riding into town with three horse-thieves who had formerly been of Sheriff Peppin's posse, and were brought in for examination before the Justice of the Peace. What I have to complain of is the riotous manner in which the military, Sheriff and deputies charge about over the county giving unnecessary alarm and anxiety to peaceably disposed citizens. The Sheriff's deputies who were with the military were drunk and had with them a flask of whiskey from which they were continually drinking and their conduct was anything but that of a peace officer. One of the deputies, who accompanied the military, fired his gun into the street to the great danger of peaceable citizens, and in fact there was no disturbance except that made by the military and drunken deputies. I will tell you candidly that the people have more fear of outrages from the military and the quasi sheriff who is harbored and protected at Ft. Stanton than from any other source. The people have too painful a remembrance of the murder of McSween by order of that "<u>brave and accomplished</u>" soldier Col. Dudley, to rest quietly while he is permitted to continue his acts of rapine and murder ... Your own proclamation that peace had been restored in Lincoln County supersedes the necessity of further aid from the Government and prevents the use of the military to aid the civil authorities in Lincoln County, and I have advised the citizens here to shoot any officer who shall in any manner attempt their arrest, or interfere with their rights. I have counseled the people to observe your proclamation and will continue to do so as long as the military and Sheriff Peppin and his outlaws observe it, but while I counsel its observance I question your authority to grant amnesty before conviction in trial for offences against the laws. The McSween men are willing to stand their trial in the proper courts of the territory,

or to observe your proclamation, **<u>provided</u>, the other side or "ring" observe it,** but they will never allow themselves to be arrested by murderers like Col. Dudley and Sheriff Peppin, but will peaceably surrender to any decent man who may be sent with a warrant for their arrest. When the courts are held in this county Dudley and Peppin will be arrested and tried for the murder of McSween and others and the legality of your amnesty proclamation will then be tested. I cannot but think that if you had visited Lincoln County, as you should have done, that you would have acted differently, and not have pardoned notorious outlaws and murderers. You have been grossly imposed upon by the military who have lied to you in order to shield themselves from the outrages they have committed in this county. There is not an honest man in Lincoln who would believe Col. Dudley on oath, yet you rely on him for all your information, and have pardoned him for the murder of an innocent man. I can assure you that the people take no stock in your amnesty proclamation and they think you have been derelict in your sworn duty as Governor in not visiting Lincoln County and acquainting yourself with the true state of affairs.

The people of Lincoln County are disgusted and tired of the neglect and indifference shown them by you, and next week they intend holding a mass-meeting to give expression to their sentiment, and unless you come here before that time you may expect to be severely denounced in language more forcible than polite.

To show you in what contempt and distrust the military are held by the people I will cite one instance: When your proclamation was received by at Ft. Stanton by Col. Dudley, he at once sent for the leading citizens of Lincoln to come to the Fort and with him, but not <u>one</u> man responded to his invitation. They had been treacherously betrayed once before, and they refused to be duped again. Yet this is your confidential advisor as to affairs in Lincoln County.

I have written this letter at the earnest solicitation of many prominent citizens in hopes that you might be induced to come to Lincoln County and inform yourself as to the affairs here. And I can assure you that I have written this letter with the best of motivation and the kindest wishes for your success as chief executive of the Territory; and in my feeble way I have tried to assure the people that you would yet come to Lincoln County and personally hear their grievance.

I am now preparing a statement of facts for publication, which, I am sorry to say will reflect upon you for not coming here in person, for no one can get a correct idea of the outrages that have been committed here by quietly sitting in Santa Fe and depending on drunken officers for information. A decent respect for the people of this county would have caused you to have come here in person and ascertained who was responsible for all the trouble, and then you should have seen that the guilty were punished. I am no believer in making the laws a convenience or prostituting them for the sake of peace, and the people of this county will not submit to it quietly.

Fort Stanton is to-day and has been during all the troubles, the rendezvous of the worst outlaws that have infested Lincoln County, and to-day the disreputable class who are harbored there is a disgrace to the Government. The horse and cattle thieves who are, and have been, depredating throughout the county [Seven Rivers and John Kinney's men] were deputies under that notorious murder[er] the <u>quasi</u> Sheriff, Peppin, and they have always been favored associates of the officers at the Fort.

I desire to retain your friendship but I owe a duty to the people of this county, and will discharge it to the very best of my ability, and without fear or favor. I earnestly desire to see your administration as chief executive of the territory made as popular as possible, but I believe that it can only be done by firmly upholding the supremacy of the law and punishing wrong-doing.

Hoping that upon receipt of this you may find it convenient to visit Lincoln County and confer with the people.
I remain as ever,

Yours very truly
H.I. Chapman.

WALLACE AND DUDLEY CLASH

ATTEMPTING DUDLEY'S PLACATION: NOVEMBER 30, 1878

On November 30, 1878, Wallace's response the day after Huston Chapman's last letter, was a nervous attempt to placate Dudley by letter, even offering to pay out of his own pocket for Dudley's messenger who had posted President Hayes's October 7, 1878 Proclamation in Lincoln. In Wallace's letter, one can see the Wallace who failed at Shiloh: vacillating and weak. Lost in psychological conflicts, Wallace again cannot show up for the real battle: against Dudley and the Ring. Unbeknownst to Wallace, he could do no right against the Ring's onslaught: a variation of its unrelenting harassment of opponents. Wallace even obsequiously omitted "Governor of New Mexico" in signing. He wrote:

*Executive Office, Santa Fe, N.M.
November 30, 1878*

Dear Sir:
Your favor containing the duplicate accounts of the messenger who posted the President's Proclamation was duly received and forwarded, with the accounts, to the Sec. of the Dept. Interior ...
If the claimant is pressing, I will anticipate the action of government, and send you the money for him ...
Enclosed find a half-sheet of the <u>Rocky Mountain Sentinel</u> in which you will doubtless be interested. Your reports furnished me a perfect answer to the gentlemen in the Territory who are fighting my confirmation on the ground that my proclamation is false and Lincoln county not pacified.
Amongst others whom my action has much outraged is the virtuous editor of the <u>Mesilla News</u> [Albert Jennings Fountain]. Have you seen his last issue. He goes for me in good style because I presumed to include officers of the army in the terms of my amnesty. I have a good reason for that, by the way, which I will explain when I see you.
Very truly,
Your friend,
Lew. Wallace

ATTEMPTING DUDLEY'S REMOVAL: DECEMBER 7, 1878

Lew Wallace could create fictional people, but could not read real ones. By December 7, 1878, he apparently thought he had adequately paved the way to remove "local irritant" Dudley to pacify Lincolnites. But removal was even more of an accusation of wrongdoing than pardoning Dudley in the Amnesty Proclamation. Wallace was heading for an unwanted show-down with soldiers. Nevertheless, still placatingly praising Dudley, he wrote:

Santa Fe, New Mexico,
Executive Office, Dec. 7th, 1878.

Col. Edward Hatch,
Comd'g Dist. of New Mexico
Sir:
    I am constrained to request that Lieut Col. N.A.M. Dudley, commanding at Fort Stanton be relieved, and an officer of equal rank ability and firmness be ordered to his place.
    In doing this I mean no disparagement of Col. Dudley. Not once in a life time, probably, is an officer engaged with duties more dismal and difficult than have fallen to him of late, and that he has maintained himself so long is the highest and best proof of qualities of exceeding value to the country and the Service. It is, however, apparent, that he has excited the animosity of parties in Lincoln County to such degree as to embarrass the administration of affairs in that locality. The same result may happen to any other gentleman whom you may assign to succeed him, yet, in view of the important part the military are called upon to perform in keeping the status there as at present, I think it better that you send to that command a stranger to the people - at least one that has had no connection whatever to the feuds that have divided them.
                              Very respectfully
                                Your friend,
                                Lew Wallace
                                Gov. New Mexico

DUDLEY'S "OPEN LETTER" TO WALLACE: DECEMBER 14, 1878

    It appears that from Lew Wallace's October 1, 1878 arrival, U.S. Attorney T.B. Catron had strategized Dudley's protection from litigation which risked exposing the Ring. By Saturday, December 14, 1878, that trap was sprung: preempt Dudley's accusations by blaming Wallace as a bad governor; garble events of the Lincoln County War; then blame "outlaws."
    That day, the Ringite Santa Fe *Weekly New Mexican*, under the headline "An Open Letter, By Lieut. Col. N.A.M. Dudley, 9th Cavalry, to His Excellency Governor Lew Wallace" - and reprinted in the *Mesilla News* of December 21, 1878 - made their conflict public. This published letter has usual Ringite word twisting, denying guilt, and lying; coupled with defaming

opponent Wallace as a hypocrite, incompetent, and a liar. Attached was a signed letter of support from Fort Stanton officers (who were participants in the Lincoln County War Battle). The Ring was testing Wallace's mettle.

Wallace folded. He did not expose real Lincoln County War issues, and did not accuse Dudley of murder and treason. He refused to ruin his own future ambitions. He would next learn how rough Ringites played. The hook would be his Hatch letter's *"perfectly satisfactory"* to begin a web of lies. Wallace's humiliation began. Shiloh's specter was rising. And attached to Dudley's indignant missive, was a signed letter of support from Fort Stanton officers who were in the Lincoln County War battle - three of whom shot at escaping McSweens. That would make eye-witness Billy Bonney, in eight months, the person who could break the Ring. The Santa Fe *Weekly New Mexican* printed:

AN OPEN LETTER
By Lieut. Col. N.A.M. Dudley, 9th Cavalry, to his Excellency Governor Lew Wallace.

Fort Stanton, New Mexico,
Nov. 30, 1878
To His Excellency,
Lewis Wallace,
Governor of the Territory of New Mexico

Sir: I have the honor to acknowledge the receipt of your communication of the 16th inst., wherein you state that my letter to District Headquarters and the several affidavits accompanying it, relating to the charges laid before you by H.I. Chapman of Las Vegas based upon representations of one Mrs. A.A. McSween, had been submitted to you by Act. Assist. Adjutant General of the District, and that you made the answer, that **the matter was "perfectly satisfactory."**

You further state: "I also requested that the application (which you had made) for a safe guard for Mrs. McSween be recalled."

You also stated: "The indignation (meaning the writer) showed was not at all displeasing to me, the same charge preferred against me, if untrue, would have certainly moved me the same way."

In the same letter you further state, referring to myself: "If you will examine the files at Headquarters here, you will find a communication over my hand, addressed to General Hatch, and of a date prior to the receipt of either of your replies, in which I stated explicitly, that I do not believe the charges against you." These statements are made three days after the date of your Proclamation.

Having permitted yourself to be the medium of forwarding to my senior such false, grave and slanderous charges, founded, as I have reason to believe, on the representations of a notoriously bad woman, it would, it seems to me, under the circumstances have been only justice, to have furnished myself, also, with a copy of your letter, setting forth your disbelief of the charges in question; but, instead, your Excellency promulgated an official Proclamation dated the 13th inst., granting a general pardon among others, to "officers of the United States Army stationed in the County of Lincoln, Territory of New Mexico, during the late disorders" for misdemeanors and offences committed in said County of Lincoln against the laws of said Territory, in connection with the aforesaid disorder, between the 1st day of February, 1878, and the 13th day of November, same year.

Not having any leniency for myself and well knowing that no officer serving in the country has, and as your Excellency cannot very consistently grant a pardon to an individual, or to a class or body of men who have not committed a crime, I am with other officers of my command, at a loss to correctly interpret this part of the Proclamation.

I am not aware of having done a single illegal act, one that be construed into a violation of law and order, neither do I know of any officer in the Army serving in Lincoln County, having done so since I assumed command at Fort Stanton, on the 5th day of April last.

Not an officer or soldier of my command, has ever left the Military reservation, on any duty appertaining to Lincoln County affairs, even as a simple courier, unless he went under carefully written orders, and a full written report required, of the result of the tour performed, all of which orders and reports are matters of official record, and in my personal possession at the present time.

I unqualifiedly assert, that neither your Excellency, or any official can find the first objectionable act of myself, or any member of my command, or one that can be construed, in any possible way, into a misdemeanor, offence, or violation of any single Territorial law of New Mexico, in any of these orders or reports.

On the contrary, if your Excellency had taken the trouble, as I respectfully invited you to do, when you first arrived in the Territory, and examined the official weekly reports, made by myself to the Headquarters of the District, you would have learned what kind of duty had been required of the officers and men serving here and how that duty has been performed.

It certainly is very singular, that neither Major General Pope, Commanding the Department of Missouri, or General Hatch, Commanding the District of New Mexico, should have not discovered that the officers of the Army, serving in the County of Lincoln, were guilty of misdemeanors, and violation of Territorial laws, for they both have complete and full reports, on every movement made by the command, weekly, and neither of these officers has personally deemed it necessary to visit this region ever to send an officer to investigate the conduct of either myself or the officers serving under my command.

Your Excellency alone, without an investigation, except an exparte one without having given one of the parties thus accused, an opportunity to explain their position, are charged with acts seriously affecting their honor, and pardoned for the same in one document just promulgated by your Excellency.

The Proclamation in question grants a pardon to officers who have on repeated occasions risked their lives, under fire at times, to aid and protect the women and children of Lincoln County against the outrages of armed organized bands of murderers, horse thieves, and convicted as well as unconvicted felons ...

[AUTHOR'S NOTE: This is the Ring's outlaw myth: soldiers were protecting citizens against outlaws. And Wallace also used it as path of least resistance.]

There can be but one construction placed upon the language of the Proclamation. It virtually charges myself and officers of the Army who have been on duty here since the 1st of February last, with having violated the laws of the Territory, and then proceed to pardon us; classing one and all of us, with the murderers, cattle thieves, and outlaws who killed Sheriff Brady, Roberts, Bernstein, Beckwith, Tunstall, and a score of other citizens of the county.

[AUTHOR'S NOTE: Billy will need the Wallace pardon for the Brady, Hindman, and Roberts killings; but they are being advertised by the Ring as acts of outlawry alone. And do not miss that Ring-murdered Tunstall is slipped in as killed by vague "outlaws" too.]

I earnestly submit, that to warrant giving publicity to such defamatory charges in a public proclamation, against a body of officers of long service and good repute, it was but just to have allowed them a hearing first; not to come to a hasty conclusion, based on evidence on a solely exparte character not even submitting to them a synopsis of the charges for which they are pardoned.

I respectfully request to be informed of what offence I am charged, and who my accusers are. I shall have no trouble in exhibiting their characters in a similar light, that you have had of the woman who solicited and obtained a safe guard for herself [Susan McSween]. It is my right to be so informed, and until I am found guilty of any violations of the laws of the Territory, I respectfully decline accepting a pardon at the hands of your Excellency.

If this pardon is only to prevent further annoyance to myself and the officers of my command, in the nature of vexations, suits of the law, at the hands of evil disposed persons, then, in that case, I for myself and them sincerely thank you for the intervention.

From the extraordinary wording of your Excellency's Proclamation, its readers, scattered all over the country, will wonder what crimes the officers of the Army stationed in Lincoln County, N.M., have committed against the laws of the Territory they were employed to guard, protect and aid in executing, which brought forth a general pardon from the governor.

We, one and all, feel most painfully, to be published to the country in this manner, you Excellency have been a soldier, cannot on reflection blame those who are now, for most earnestly placing on record this solemn, but respectful protest against such allegations.

Without any intention of criticizing the official course of your Excellency, permit me to state that you have now been more than eight weeks in the Territory, and have never been during this period, within nearly 200 miles of the scene of the terrible death struggles, that have been enacted in this county, during this time.

Five innocent persons, natives, and residents of the County of Lincoln, have been inhumanely murdered in about the same number of hours, all within a few miles of each other, and without the slightest provocation. Women have been dragged from their private conveyances, from off the public mail highways and treated in a manner too disgusting to be related here. Whole bands of horses have been stolen and driven off, in the presence of their honest owners in broad daylight. Herds of cattle containing hundreds of head, have been taken in the same manner, their herders killed, and not a single arrest has ever been made by the civil authorities since I have been in the county.

[AUTHOR'S NOTE: Irrelevant description of crimes following anarchy after the War is used here to distract from Dudley's own crimes committed during the War. In fact, he is arguably responsible for anarchy. As to arrests since Dudley arrived in April of 1878, that was when Governor Axtell and Sheriff Brady blocked arresting Tunstall's killers.]

Many of the facts have been laid before your Excellency, immediately after their occurring, and until the President's Proclamation dated on the 7th October, what steps, I ask have been taken by the Territorial officers to put a stop to such unlawful conduct? I answer None!

The occasional passing of troops over the public roads have had the effect to give the poor frightened settlers an opportunity of a few hours of seeming security. Where ever the colored cavalry have made their appearance, doors that have been for weeks or months barred, and barricaded windows, have been opened for a few hours. Husbands and sons have enjoyed the luxury of a night's rest at their homes when ever the troops have camped a single night near their ranches.

For weeks and months, they have been compelled to seek safety in the caverns, and mountain fastness against the very class of men included with the officers of the United States Army, in the pardon of your Excellency.

In coming to the Territory your Excellency passed through a section of the country, which has been the retreat and asylum for many of the class, who have raided and assisted in every way possible to bring upon Lincoln County the long train of crimes and disaster, which have almost depopulated it.

[AUTHOR'S NOTE: This may refer to Wallace's Cimarron meeting with Frank Springer, learned by Catron; adding credence to him as authoring this "Open Letter" to advance his outlaw myth to conceal the Ring's War crimes.]

Pardon me for saying, it is not to be wondered at, that you have received erroneous views of the exact state of affairs here. I most respectfully ask you to come to Lincoln County, and see and judge for yourself, from personal observation, of the facts.

I am aware that it is not within the province of an officer of the Army, to make such suggestions to a civil functionary, occupying the high position of yourself, much less criticize his official course; but when false and unjust accusations are made, against either myself, or the gallant officers of my command, it becomes my duty to demand for them and myself a hearing and not allow a general pardon to be promulgated for them or myself, for offences we know not of, and of which we feel wholly guiltless.

I am Sir, respectfully
Your obdt. Servant
N.A.M. Dudley
Lieut. Col. 9th Cavalry

Fort Stanton, New Mexico
November 30, 1878

General N.A.M. Dudley
Fort Stanton, New Mexico

Dear General – We, the undersigned officers of the U.S. Army, stationed at this Post during the recent troubles in Lincoln County, have heard and read an open letter addressed by you to His Excellency the Governor of New Mexico and desire to say that the said letter expresses most fully and explicitly our feelings upon the subject, in this publicly declining to accept for us the pardon rendered by His Excellency.

D.M. Appel, Asst. Surgeon, U.S.A. Post Surgeon; G.W. Smith, 2nd Lt. 9th Cav. Post

Adjutant; M.F. Goodwin, 2nd Lt. 9th Cavalry; Sam S. Pague, 2nd Lt. 15th Inf. And A.A.Q.M. and A.C.S.; J.H. French, 2nd Lt. 9th Cav. Comdg. Co. M.

[AUTHOR'S NOTE: Dudley's supporters are Ringites. Appel was the son-in-law of Mescalaro Indian Reservation Agent Frederick Godfroy, exposed by McSween and Angel; and the officers had marched on Lincoln with Dudley, and three of them had fired at escaping McSweens. Goodwin was present when Susan McSween made her plea for protection at Dudley's camp, and was ridiculed by obscenities.]

WALLACE ON THE DEFENSIVE: DECEMBER 16, 1878

The Ring's "Open Letter" put Wallace on the defensive. On December 16, 1878, he responded to the "Open Letter" article's "Lt. Col. N.A.M. Dudley, Ast. Surg. D.M. Appel, Lieut. S.W. Smith, Lieut. M.F. Goodwin, Lieut. S.S. Pagen, Lieut. J.H. French" by treating these Lincoln County's terrorists with deference. Wallace was failing - just as at Shiloh. Wallace wrote:

EXECUTIVE OFFICE,
Territory of New Mexico.
Santa Fe, New Mexico, Dec. 16, 1878.

Gentlemen.

The public interests with which I am officially charged make it in my judgment, exceedingly improper for me to answer publicly your letters in the <u>New Mexican</u> on the 14th instant.

If, however, you will any of you call at my office, I will take pleasure in showing you that the insertion in the Proclamation of the clause of which you complain was even more than a kindness to such of you that were on duty in Lincoln county during the disorders there. Or if you cannot accept my invitation in person, I will make the same showing to any gentleman whom [you] may appoint to receive it.

Very respectfully
Your friend,
Lew Wallace,
Gov. New Mexico

TURNING TO SCHURZ: DECEMBER 21, 1878

With risk of Huston Chapman complaining to Washington, D.C. himself, and with his relationship with N.A.M. Dudley in ruins, Lew Wallace took action on December 21, 1878: writing to Secretary of the Interior Schurz. In his first battle facing a Ring stand-off, Wallace failed morally: discrediting Chapman and revealing that he would betray to save himself. In three months, Billy's pardon would depend on this flawed man. Wallace wrote:

Executive Office
Territory of New Mexico
Santa Fe, New Mexico, Dec. 21 1878

Hon. C. Schurz,
 Sec. Interior Dept.
  Sir:
   I have the honor to report that affairs of this Territory are moving on quietly, and offering nothing worthy extended notice.
   In Lincoln County the peaceable status continues.
   The commandant at Fort Stanton (Lt. Col. Dudley) grew indignant about the clause in my amnesty proclamation which extended its privileges to the officers of the army, and he rushed into print to his own detriment. I have requested the military authorities to relieve him. I send you the <u>New Mexican</u>, containing his paper, and the <u>Sentinel</u>, with an answer to it, though not from me.
   An individual by the name of Chapman went to the plaza (town of Lincoln) and tried to get up a disturbance, but failed. The burden of his plaint was that I had not visited the town to get the truth there instead of the Fort. On the other hand Dudley's grief is that I did not come to the Fort to get the truth there. Now as the two places, town and Fort were centers of the two factions, it was not possible for me to go to either without provoking jealousy and bad feeling: so I stayed away from both, and am well satisfied that I did so.
   To-day I am going down the country to be gone a few days.
    I have the honor to be,
     Very Respectfully,
      Your friend & Sv't.
       Lew Wallace,
        Gov. New Mexico

SECRETARY OF WAR BACKS DUDLEY: DECEMBER 31, 1878

By December 31, 1878, Wallace was in trouble with soldiers - up to the Secretary of War himself. By requesting Dudley's removal, he had carelessly blamed Dudley's superiors: General Edward Hatch, Commanding District New Mexico; and above him Major General John Pope, Commanding the Department of Missouri. And the silly reason Wallace had given for insulting them all was Dudley's being irritating. And a removal request by a civilian was frowned-upon. So it passed, in accumulating refusals, from Hatch, to Washington D.C.'s General W.T. Sherman, to Secretary of War George McCrary. McCrary wrote:

Headquarters of the Army
Washington, D.C. December 31, 1878

Respectfully forwarded to the Honorable Secretary of War.
I disapprove of this for the reason that it is unjust. In politics charges are made to resolve conflicts of opinion, but in military government such action implies censure.
To relieve Lieutenant Colonel Dudley now would leave him without recourse.
There is no military reason why he should be displaced of his command at Fort Stanton. He is not required to report to, or explain his public acts, to the Governor of New Mexico. But will promptly do so to his superiors, including the Secretary of War, and the President of the United States, when called upon.
If Governor Wallace will prefer charges against Lieut. Col. Dudley, they can now be thoroughly examined and tried by the laws of the land, but if the mere request of a Governor of a Territory is to damage an officer of the army in his reputation and good name; then there is an end to a system which now enables the Executive of the nation to interpose the disinterested and impartial action of the Army and conflicting factions.
There is a principal involved in this case. Lt. Col. Dudley, by no action of his own, has been placed between two factions of desperate men on the frontier. These spare no efforts, and resort to any falsehood to remove an obstacle. This obstacle now seems to be Lt. Col. Dudley, U.S. Army, an officer of high repute, sustained in his immediate action by Generals Hatch, Pope and Sheridan. I add

my own, asking specific military reasons for the Governor of New Mexico, that the questions involved may be settled now on this spot.

W.T. Sherman General

The Secretary of War concurs with the views of General Sherman, and declines to relieve Colonel Dudley

THE RING RESPONDS TO CHAPMAN

DOLAN THREATENS CHAPMAN: DECEMBER 31, 1878

From late October of 1878, the Ring had faced Huston Chapman and Susan McSween: both more threatening than John Tunstall and Alexander McSween, since they had monstrous crimes to prosecute. So James Dolan was enlisted to send Lew Wallace his own version of Axtell's Cimarron "Dear Ben plot" letter or of Rynerson's February 14, 1878 "Friends Riley and Dolan" for killing Tunstall. Dolan stated: *"I and many of our Citizens feel Confident that if this man was silenced, the troubles would End."* Unfortunately, Lew Wallace agreed, and did nothing. Dolan wrote:

<u>Confidential</u>   Lincoln, N.M.
    Dec 31st 1878
Governor Lew Wallace
    Santa Fe, N.M.
My Dear Governor –
    On my arrival at Fort Stanton, I reported Your Explanation to the Comdg Officer (Gen'l Dudley) – he seemed too much pleased, and said that if it was possible that You and him "Could meet and talk matters over with Each other for an hour" he was "satisfied that You would be fast friends." I also explained matters to Sheriff Peppin and many of our citizens all of whom were pleased. I am Convinced that the Explanation has Caused a very different feeling from that in Existence before I came down. Mr. Delany has also interested himself in giving Your Explanation both to the officers and citizens. Your [informant Chapman] appears to be the only man in this County who is trying to Continue the old feelings. **I and many of our Citizens feel Confident that if this man was silenced, the troubles would End.** I presume ere this you have heard of the trouble which

Lieut French got into with Chapman and Mrs. McSween – from what I can learn about the affair it originated from an attempt to make arrests of men for whom the Deputy U.S. Marshal had warrants – It may be that Mr. French was over zealous in the attempt. Still I consider this all, Can be said against him. I have learned enough since I returned here that should I remain in this County, my fate will be that of Major Brady and others. I only intend remaining until such time as I Can straighten up my business to the interests of the Creditors, and as per agreement with them. It makes me and my friends mighty sore, that we are compelled to leave our homes and businesses, which we are Compelled to do, or put ourselves on Equal footing with the outlaw and assassin. Hoping, Governor, that you wont Consider this letter presuming on Your Kindness, and with Kind regards I remain
Yours Respectfully
Jas J. Dolan
P.S.
Should it ever be in my power to do anything in this section that would be of interest to you always Command me.
Dolan

MORE VOICES JOIN CHAPMAN'S

ANALYSIS: As Huston Chapman's tragedy loomed, unaware citizens still saw new Governor Lew Wallace as their savior, and pleaded for his help.

JUSTICE OF THE PEACE WILSON TRIES TO PROTECT LINCOLN FROM DUDLEY

Unaware that Lew Wallace was floundering in Santa Fe Ring mire, Lincoln County Justice of the Peace John "Squire" Wilson bravely stepped forward once again to help his oppressed fellow citizens despite his traumatic Lincoln County War experiences. Brave Wilson had already defied Sheriff William Brady's protecting of Tunstall's killers by himself appointing Billy Bonney and Fred Waite as Deputy Constables to serve arrest warrants. Wilson had ignored Governor S.B. Axtell's illegal Proclamation removing him. And Wilson only wrote false arrest warrants for Alexander McSween and Billy Bonney for attempted murder of Private Berry Robinson after Dudley's death threat. And soon Wilson would secretly attempt to get Billy a pardon.

So on January 11, 1879, Wilson wrote to Wallace, trying to avoid martial law and more military terrorism. Later, that letter would be used by Dudley's defense in his military Court of Inquiry, to claim Wilson backed Dudley as keeping peace. Wallace answered with elitist condescension on January 18, 1879, writing:

> *Executive Office*
> *Territory of New Mexico*
> *Santa Fe, New Mexico*
> *Jany 18th 1879.*

John B. Wilson
  Lincoln New Mexico
       Dear Sir.

I hasten to acknowledge receipt of your favor of the 11th Jan. ult., and admit the pleasure and satisfaction it gave me.

The assurance from so responsible a source that the spirit heretofore existing in the county to kill and carry on a revolution has certainly eased, and the further assurance that all the good citizens are using all the means in their power to maintain the laws, and forget and forgive the past, and that they are all determined to use patience and discretion in all things heretofore, strengthen my hope that your dark days are over, and I shall continue in that faith until I know the contrary.

The tenor of your whole letter is of a sensible man, desirous of peace and all it brings to individuals as well as communities. Two things I desire you to understand: <u>first</u>, evils such as have afflicted your county always bring consequences which live after them, not to be cured in a week or a year, not to be cured at all except by exercise of greatest patience and moderation on the part of the people; <u>secondly</u>, to help restore order by all the means in my power consistent with the law is and shall be both my duty and pleasure. ***And I beg you to do enough justice to my intelligence to believe that I well understand there will be greater credit to me if perfect pacification is effected without resort to martial law than with it. With that idea I have acted heretofore. In that spirit I promise you not to resort to it except as a dire necessity.*** *I have put it off, and will as long as the people manifest their action and conduct that they have the aims and purposes of which you speak so earnestly.*

My greatest desire now in connection with your county is to see the administration of civil affairs more in the hands of genuine citizens, and going on regularly as in well ordered localities elsewhere, wholly independent of the military. If the present status continues, there is no reason why such should not be.

If you think me controlled by gentlemen at the Fort, and that all my information is derived from that source, suppose you take it upon yourself to keep me posted. I write you to do so. Only write me facts as they transpire, without abusing anybody and trusting some little to my judgment. Avoid personalities and give me plain facts having due reference in time, place and persons. Your communications shall in all cases be confidential where you intimate a wish to have that effect.

I have arranged with Judge Bristol to accompany him to Lincoln in the next session of your county court, provided the situation continues such as to make the holding a session justifiable and possible. Meantime I trust you will exercise your influence to establish order and refer all disputes to the courts, which are better arbitrators than the pistol.

Renewing my thanks for your favor, I beg you to believe me
Most sincerely
Your friend
Lew Wallace

On February 6, 1879, Wallace answered another Wilson letter, this time about preventing U.S. Marshal John Sherman's appointing of a deputy sheriff there. Uncaring, Wallace did not ask the obvious: Why? It would have anticipated another Ring take-over event in 12 days: Huston Chapman's assassination. Wallace wrote:

EXECUTIVE OFFICE,

Territory of New Mexico.

Santa Fe, New Mexico, Feb. 6   1879.

John B. Wilson, Esq
Lincoln, New Mexico
Dear Sir.
Your favors are both to hand, and place me under renewed obligations.

I have seen Marshall Sherman as you requested, and he replied that he would not now appoint a deputy in Lincoln County. As the matter is his exclusively, one will have to wait his pleasure.

I suppose you saw the Mesilla Independent containing your letter in full, also the <u>Sentinel</u> (Santa Fe) with the extracts from your favor to me. The comments of both papers were in the right direction, and particularly gratifying.

By the way, be good enough to send me certified copies of the affidavits lodged in your office against Col. Dudley and Lt. French, with the warrants issued upon them. Also furnish me a certified statement of the proceedings to date against those officers. The use I have for them I will explain when I see you.

Very respectfully
Your friend
Lew. Wallace

DAVID SHIELD TRIES TO PROTECT SUSAN McSWEEN: FEBRUARY 11, 1879

Apparently Lew Wallace's savior aura drew out timid and traumatized Attorney David Shield, in attempt to help his sister-in-law, Susan McSween. His February 11, 1879 letter requested copies of Dudley's affidavits against her, implying that he was secretly assisting Chapman for her future litigation. Shield wrote:

Santa Fe N.M. Feb 11th 1879

To his Excellency
   Lewis Wallace
      Gov of New Mexico

Dear Sir

It is rumored that "Eight long affidavits" are in your possession or under your control which were forwarded by the officer in command at Fort Stanton NM. that said affidavits contain grave and serious charges against the character and reputation of Mrs McSween (the widow of the late AA McSween who was murdered at Lincoln NM the 19th day of July last) If the rumors of the contents of said affidavits are correct I have no hesitation in pronouncing them false and untrue and I state it as my deliberate opinion that said affidavits were made and furnished for the express purpose of preventing a full and impartial investigation of the murder of said McSween and of bringing to justice the parties guilty of said crime I deem it my duty and therefore respectfully ask that you furnish me copies of the same in order that I may be able to present to the Masonic

Order the matter in a correct light for investigation as the said AA McSween decd was a Master Mason and I am informed that said Officer is also a member of said order

Trusting that the request thus made will be granted
I remain
Very Truly
Your obt Servt
D.P. Shield

Wallace responded the same day by refusing to provide the affidavits. As usual, his elitist bias favored those in power. But in seven days, he would be forced to reach out to "plebeians" to save himself from Lincoln County's next assassination crisis. He wrote:

Executive Office, Santa Fe, N.M.
February 11, 1879.

D.P. Shield, Esq.
Dear Sir.

I am in receipt of your letter, of this date, requesting inspection and copies of certain affidavits rumored to be in my possession, and forwarded to me by the officer in command at Fort Stanton, N.M., and said to contain grave and serious charges against the character and reputation of Mrs. McSween.

You must permit me to decline acceding to your request. The relations I hold to the officer mentioned, being official and intimately connected with public duties of a serious ~~nature~~ character make it improper for me even indirectly to be concerned in any prosecution of any kind against him.

Very respectfully,
Your friend,
Lew. Wallace.

FIDDLING AS ROME BURNS

ENTERTAINING FAMILY AND DECORATING

As Lew Wallace was grandly answering Wilson and Shield, he was distracted, having traveled to Colorado to meet his arriving wife, Susan. He had also resumed decorating the Palace of the Governors, updating Schurz on February 5, 1879:

EXECUTIVE OFFICE,
Territory of New Mexico.

Santa Fe, New Mexico, February 5, 1879.

Hon. C. Schurz,
Sec. Dept. Interior.
Sir.

I have just returned from Trinidad, Col. where I went to bring my family to this city. Going for such a purpose, I did not think it necessary to bother you with a request for permission in the first instance. I hope you will approve this absence.

Among your favors awaiting me here, I find one notifying me that you had approved the request to Secretary Sherman touching on the use of the portions of the "Palace" shortly to be vacated by the U.S. Marshal Sherman. Also another relative to the archives of the Territory, which are at least in part in a most woeful condition. Permit me to ask if I am to consider myself authorized to employ a competent person to do the overhauling and arrangement of the papers. It is not everybody who is fit for the work. A good English and Spanish scholar will be required, and he will of course have to be paid as an expert. And besides six weeks or two months may be necessary to do the task thoroughly. Quite a large number of portfolios of several sizes will also be needed as they are nearly all in M.S. From this you will understand why I prefer a clear authorization. In making it, I further suggest that you empower me to make demand for papers, books, memoranda &c. properly of the "archives," and receive them from all persons having them or any of them in possession.

The next point will be where to store them, and their custody. The only place fit I know is the fire-proof vault, formerly part of the Depository and now in the office of Marshal Sherman ...

In the connection I beg to add that I am informed a number of persons are applying for the Marshal's quarters. General Smith, I am told, wants it for his land office. So with the signal corps stationed here. Now, if there is any rivalry about the matter, I suggest the decision be held over until Marshal Sherman arrives in Washington, which will be immediately that his court, now in session, shall adjourn.

      Very respectfully
      Your friend and servant,
      Lew. Wallace
      Gov. New Mexico

On February 12, 1879, Wallace again urged building repairs to Schurz. That day, Chapman had six days to live. Wallace wrote:

Executive Office, Santa Fe, New Mexico.
February 12. 1879.

Hon. C. Schurz,
Sec. Interior Dept
Sir:

I beg leave to call your attention to the condition of the house called the "Palace," and advise you that unless it is repaired in an early day a great portion of it is likely to become uninhabitable ruin.

For your more thorough understanding, I called upon three of the first medical gentlemen of the city to make examination and report upon the building, and I enclose result of their inquest marked Enclosure No. 1 and Enclosure No. 2.

The property is of great value to the Government, and if attended to in time can be made serviceable for many years to come.

I do not know that you have jurisdiction over the matter: in the event you have not, however, I imagine you will take interest in it and refer its consideration to the proper official, and in that event it will give me pleasure to furnish him with all essential information.

Very respectfully
Your friend and servant,
Lew. Wallace
Gov. New Mexico

WALLACE CONSIDERS A LINCOLN COUNTY VISIT: FEBRUARY 11, 1878

Lew Wallace believed the Ring's outlaw propaganda enough to desire a military escort should he visit Lincoln. So on February 11, 1879, Wallace made his escort request to Mexico's Chief Quartermaster General J.J. Dana, though still procrastinating by stating it was *"impossible to say exactly when I will start."* And by informing soldiers of his possible visit, he may have inadvertently sealed Huston Chapman's fate for elimination in seven days to prevent litigation against Dudley with his backing. Wallace wrote:

> *Executive Office, Santa Fe, New Mexico.*
> *February 11, 1879.*
>
> Gen. J.J. Dana.
> Chief Quart. District of New Mexico.
> Dear Sir.
> *It will be necessary for me shortly to go to various parts of the Territory, beginning with Mesilla and Lincoln, at which latter I will probably be detained a month or six weeks.*
>
> *As it is impossible to say exactly when I will start, and as it may happen that when the time does come your vehicles will be engaged or in use, I have thought it better to ask in advance if it will be in your power to arrange for placing an ambulance at my disposal.*
>
> *If the idea meets your approval, and this request is within your authority, permit me to suggest that it might be well enough at the same time to make provision for furnishing me an outfit for a reasonable escort. However I dislike to travel with such an appendage, it may nevertheless become necessary.*
>
> *I have the honor to be,*
> *Very respectfully,*
> *Your friend & servant,*
> *Lew. Wallace,*
> *Governor New Mexico*

Wallace delayed going to Lincoln County till March 1, 1879, 20 days after Chapman's murder, about which he learned from Territorial Secretary William Ritch. To avoid Lincoln itself, he planned to reside nine miles away at Fort Stanton; forgetting its officers were enraged at his having Dudley removed, and that Ringite prior Commander, George Purington, had been reinstated as Commander. Wallace was as befuddled as on his opposite-direction way to do battle at Shiloh.

RING ASSASSINATION OF HUSTON CHAPMAN

On the night of February 18, 1879 - the first anniversary of Tunstall's murder - one armed Attorney Huston Chapman joined the growing list of exterminated Ring opponents: Franklin Tolby, John Tunstall, Alexander McSween, Harvey Morris, Francisco Romero, Vincente Zamora, and San Patricio's massacre victims. Though Chapman's Ring murder was inevitable, it occurred that day by coincidences of his having accompanied his client, Susan

McSween, back to Lincoln from Las Vegas; and of, earlier that evening, James Dolan and T.B. Catron's brother-in-law, Edgar Walz, having had a "peace meeting" with Billy Bonney in town. Present also had been their hitman thugs, Jessie Evans and gang member, Billy Campbell, as likely protection. That conciliatory meeting was a measure of Billy's growing local fame and power.

On about 8 p.m. that dark night, on Lincoln's single street, Chapman accidentally encountered the wandering "peace" group, after it exited Juan Patrón's house, where Campbell had drunkenly threatened Patrón. Recognizing Chapman, Dolan shot him point-blank, followed by Billy Campbell, shouting revealingly that he did it for God and Colonel Dudley. Evans was their back-up, as Walz watched. Dolan then doused Chapman's corpse with liquor from his pocket flask, and ignited it. Billy was eye-witness. Susan McSween, in town, and equally marked for death, would have heard the shots, eight months after her husband's murder.

And Billy would again convert his traumatic loss to action. This time, he would bargain for a pardon based on having personal incriminating evidence against Ringites. He would never again try to make peace with the Ring.

AFTERMATH OF CHAPMAN'S MURDER: WALLACE'S PURSUIT OF MYTHICAL OUTLAWS

ANALYSIS: Lew Wallace's response to humiliation of Huston Chapman's murder was to apply his novelist skills to the Ring's outlaw fiction to safeguard his own future. His sources were the October 6, 1878 "outlaw" list with Regulators from U.S. Marshal John Sherman, and input from James Dolan. Wallace was directed to "outlaws" William Bonney "the Kid," and Yginio Salazar. He had no idea of what he was doing, but the Ring did: both teenagers were primed for more anti-Ring rebellion, therefore qualifying for the next round of extermination. Wallace, with his usual impulsive hyperbole, put the astronomical award of $1,000 on "the Kid" - presumably dead or alive."

SHERIFF GEORGE KIMBRELL PURSUES BONNEY AND SALAZAR: FEBRUARY 20, 1879

After Huston Chapman's murder, Lew Wallace had a high priority: avoid going to Lincoln with its angry rabble. So he used the outlaw myth to force new Lincoln County Sheriff George

Kimbrell to catch his chosen scapegoats: William Bonney "the Kid" and Yginio Salazar. With his usual insensitivity, it did not occur to Wallace that Kimbrell and Lincolnites considered them heroes. And Wallace neither knew - nor would have cared - that Billy's best friend, Yginio was second generation anti-Ring: his father having been a Lincoln County Constable murdered in 1873. Wallace apparently picked Yginio for Mexican flavor, as he likely chose "the Kid" for his catchy moniker and local fame.

To Ringites, Wallace was a dream come true. Under smoke-screen of his hair-brained war on outlaws, they could finish eliminating enemies. Then Wallace went further. He directed Kimbrell to use Fort Stanton troops for hunting and killing - the same troops that had terrorized Lincoln seven months earlier.

George Kimbrell had replaced Ringite Sheriff George Peppin, who had quit after the Lincoln County War. Kimbrell was a popular non-Ringite. Married to a Picacho townswoman, and living there, he obviously knew about the massacre at San Patricio, but kept his feelings private. There were other ways he could, and would, aid "the Kid" and Yginio.

So Kimbrell's forced tracking began with a letter to Fort Stanton Second Lieutenant Millard Filmore Goodwin - likely one of Dudley's three white officers who shot at escaping McSweens. Kimbrell's letter, as copied by Goodwin for a likely Ringite paper trail against Wallace - as using, not criticizing, troops - stated:

Lincoln, N.M.

February 20, 1879.

Lieut M.F. Goodwin
Comand'g Troops at
Lincoln, N.M.

Sir: -

I have the honor to request that you will furnish me a posse of six soldiers, to enable me to make the arrest of William Bonney, charged with murder, and a Mexican named Salazar.

I am unable to obtain a civil posse.

Respectfully
Your Obd't Servant
George Kimball [Kimbrell]
Sheriff Lincoln, Co. N.M.

SOLDIERS RAID SAN PATRICIO AGAIN: FEBRUARY 23, 1879

Lew Wallace's troops request through Sheriff George Kimbrell, as copied by Second Lieutenant Millard Filmore Goodwin, was fodder for a Ring claim that Wallace regarded soldiers as citizens' protectors - a key defense if Dudley faced court martial for his Lincoln County War intervention. So on February 23, 1878, Goodwin wrote to his Post Adjutant, quoting an undated letter from Kimbrell, which stated:

In my opinion, - although I can not say that troops are really necessary - I think if a detachment was retained there for a short time, it would enable the citizens of the town to organize some means of their own protection.
I am, Sir,
Very Respectfully,
Your Obedient Servant,
George Kimball [Kimbrell]

In fact, Wallace had forced Kimbrell to use troops to again to raid San Patricio, this time in failed capture of "the Kid" and Yginio Salazar. To residents, it would have been a horrible flashback to Sheriff George Peppin's using the same soldiers on June 28, 1878 to pursue Alexander McSween and the Regulators; and to the July 3, 1878 massacre there by Peppin and John Kinney's gang. It was obvious Ring intimidation. Goodwin wrote:

Fort Stanton, N.M.
February 23, 1879.

Post Adjutant,
Fort Stanton, N.M.
Sir: -
I have the honor to submit the following report regarding my duties performed in compliance with S.O. No. 26. Adj. Fort Stanton, N.M., February 19, 1879.
I arrived at Lincoln, N.M. at 9 A.M., February 19, 1879, and immediately reported to the Sheriff of the County, George Kimball [Kimbrell], and informed him that I had orders to assist him in preserving peace and order, and in making arrests when he was unable to do so without the assistance of the military.

>   *I found the people in the Plaza considerably frightened; they all informed me the cause was due to the meeting of the two opposite parties in their town, on which occasion a man had been killed, and they were unable to keep peace without the help of the military. I was told by several of the citizens that they had been laboring under the mistaken idea regarding the things they had been told 'they were only partisans,' and they were, in fact, afraid to come to Fort Stanton, but having found out they were mistaken, they had arrived at the conclusion that they were now needing the protection of the military, and they could not get along without it, and asked me if I would notify the Commanding Officer of the Post [Dudley] of their change in feeling and sentiment, and request him to come to the Plaza, and allow them an opportunity to explain the situation, and state their case to him in person. I notified the Commanding Officer of this.*
>
>   **On the written application of the Sheriff (enclosed marked No. 1) I sent six (6) men to San Patricio to endeavor to arrest "Kid" and a Mexican. The party was unsuccessful. The whereabouts of the two men is not known; supposed, however, to be near the above mentioned place.**
>
>   M.F. Goodwin,
2nd Lieut 9" Cav.
late Comd'g detachment

DUDLEY PURSUES "THE KID": FEBRUARY 24, 1879

N.A.M. Dudley, the real outlaw, gleefully joined the "outlaw" pursuit himself, writing on February 24, 1878 to headquarters about "*Bonney alias 'Kid.'* " Dudley stated:

>   Hdgr's Fort Stanton, N.M.
>
>   February 24, 1879.
>
>   Acting Asst. Adjutant General,
>   District of New Mexico,
>   Santa Fe, N.M.
>   Sir: -
>   *I enclose herewith report of 2^d Lieut. M.F. Goodwin, 9" Cavalry, of his tour of duty performed while carrying out the instructions contained in par. 1 S.O. No. 26, C.S. Post, marked No. 1. also* **copy of Sheriff's requisition for detachment to aid in the arrest of Bonny, alias "Kid," marked as No. 2.**

As will be seen by par. 4 S.O. No. 26, C.S. Post Hdqr's, an officer with a detachment of Cavalry and Infantry are stationed at the County seat. There seems to be considerable fright, which is gradually falling into simple anxiety as to what is the result of the leaders of the two factions combining. I predict a more quiet state of affairs until the courts meet in April, than has been for a long time. When the courts meet, I would not be surprised if an attempt was made to put out of the way and "bull-doze" important witnesses in criminal cases.

Very Respectfully,
Your Obedient Servant,
N.A.M. Dudley
Lieut. Colonel 9" Cavalry
Commanding

WALLACE REPORTS HUSTON CHAPMAN'S MURDER TO CARL SCHURZ: FEBRUARY 27, 1879

Frenetically implementing his "outlaw" excuse, Lew Wallace procrastinated nine days to report Huston Chapman's murder to Carl Schurz, and to reveal his failed "pacification." On February 27, 1879, he wrote a draft which reveals the real Lew Wallace: an incompetent leader who lied to hide his mistakes. For Shiloh, the lie involved "orders." The lie now, concealing the Ring, was that Chapman's murder was by an *"alliance"* of *"notorious characters"* and *"outlaws"* who *"run to the mountains."* And Wallace wanted soldiers to pursue them.

One should remember that Schurz and Hayes knew the Ring was systematically murdering opponents. They knew Colfax County's charges about Franklin Tolby's murder, and Axtell's "Dear Ben plot" to kill more adversaries. They had just covered up Angel's reports almost exposing Ringite U.S. officials who killed John Tunstall. And they had just negotiated with S.B. Elkins to finesse T.B. Catron's cover-up as a criminal U.S. Attorney by permitting his resignation in lieu of indicting or dismissing him. So Wallace and Washington were merely conducting a charade to keep secret the Ring. And scapegoated for the public would be "outlaws;" until only one was left to kill: Billy the Kid.

So Wallace now floated to Schurz his plan of going to Lincoln County on his mission to rid it of the "outlaws" causing "the troubles." Wallace wrote:

Executive Office,
Santa Fe, N.M.
February 27, 1879.

Hon. C. Schurz,
Sec'y Interior Dept.
Sir:

One H.I. Chapman, lawyer, was assassinated in front of the Court House in Lincoln the night of the 18th ult., producing a sensation amounting to panic in the town. A request was sent to Col. Dudley, at Fort Stanton, for troops to protect the lives and property. The affair seems to have stopped with the murder of Chapman; yet Col. Dudley went over in person, carrying with him the equivalent of two companies. He also took a Gatling gun. Upon his own showing, a sergeant with a patrol would have been sufficient. The effect of his ridiculous action will be, I fear, to throw the people into a state of unnecessary alarm.

I have further information that certain notorious characters, who have long been under indictment, but by skillful dodging, have managed to escape arrest, have formed an alliance which looks like preparation for raids when the spring opens. If so, their seizure will now put a quietus upon them. With that idea, I proposed a plan of campaign – the word may be excused - against them. To prevent interference by justices of the peace, who are for the most part terrorized past recollection of duty to the public, the intention is to make use of the warrants issued from the U.S. Court for offenses against the United States, thus removing the old obstacle found in preliminary examinations by justices ~~of the peace~~.

[AUTHOR'S NOTE: Wallace is repeating the spirit of Governor Axtell's Proclamation which removed Justice of the Peace Wilson's power. And he is doing worse: using past U.S. Attorney Catron's federal indictment to single out and attack the last remaining Regulators: Billy Bonney, "Doc" Scurlock, Charlie Bowdre, and Tom O'Folliard.]

The outlaws have always run to the mountains, in my judgment the only way to get them was by untiring use of the troops and Indian scouts. The plan was submitted to General Hatch, commanding the District of New Mexico, and he has approved and entered heartedly into it. He will go with me and in person direct the movements of the troops. I ~~will~~ rely greatly upon his judgment and energy.

Accordingly I will leave for Lincoln tomorrow; and it is uncertain how long I will be gone. I thought it best to inform you of my intention and departure, and request official communications to be addressed to me at ~~Lincoln~~, Fort Stanton, Lincoln County, N.M., care of Commandant of Post, until notice of my return to Santa Fe.

[AUTHOR'S NOTE: In his draft, Wallace first wrote Lincoln, but changed it to Fort Stanton – so repugnant was it for him to deal directly with the riff-raff and the truth.]

The disposition of the resident citizens there continues excellent. If they can be protected for a season against raiders from abroad, the <u>morale</u> of the community will restore itself. So it is important that we take the initiative, and make this country too hot for harborage of their enemies.

I have the honor to be,
Very respectfully,
Your friend & s'v't,
Lew. Wallace,
Gov. New Mexico.

[Added along the side of the draft is a postscript]:

Sometime ago I requested that Col. Dudley might be relieved from the command of Fort Stanton. My application was curtly refused by General Sherman, and it was demanded of me that I should make military charges against Col. Dudley. It will be developed why I made the request.

Very resp.
Your friend & s'vt,
Lew. Wallace

GRANT COUNTY CONDEMNS WALLACE: MARCH 1, 1879

Lew Wallace was fooling himself while placating Ringites; but he did not fool rebellion-tempered Grant County citizens. On March 1, 1879, Silver City's Grant County *Herald* published "Wallace and Lincoln County." Chapman's killing had started Wallace's rising crescendo of humiliation. It stated:

A few weeks since, while Governor Wallace was at Trinidad, Col., he was interviewed by a reporter of the Denver *Tribune* and ... gave some very remarkable information in regard to the condition of affairs in this Territory – particularly those portions of it which he has never visited. Among other things, the Governor assured the reporter that, upon reaching his post of duty, "he found the Territory in a state of anarchy and confusion," that "by systematic management," etc. "he had brought about a state of prolonged peace," and furthermore that "lawless men" who previous to his advent, had "infested," "carried terror" and all that sort of thing, "have a wholesome fear of the present authorities."

Had the story which Wallace told the single merit of truthfulness, it would still be open to criticism, because of the narrator's evident anxiety to secure to himself all credit for what had been accomplished; but unfortunately the entire statement is false: Governor Wallace did not find the Territory in a state of anarchy and confusion. Previous to his arrival, our most sparsely populated county had been the scene of bitter and deadly strife between contending factions, but throughout the rest of the Territory order prevailed ... Moreover, Governor Wallace, with all his "systematic management," has not "brought about a state of prolonged peace," even in the single county where disturbances had occurred; and it is unfortunately true that the "lawless men" of Lincoln are not imbued with a "wholesome fear of the present authorities."

The Governor found the County of Lincoln in a greatly disturbed condition. Numerous murders had been committed ... At the time of his arrival the bloodiest part of the struggle was over, but lawless acts still frequent. He issued a proclamation. After the lapse of several weeks, we were granted with a companion document ... But ... the condition of affairs in Lincoln county was substantially the same, at the time of the second proclamation, announcing the restoration of order and proffering amnesty alike to innocent and guilty, was issued, as it had been weeks before when the Governor threatened a declaration of martial law.

In our telegraphic columns today, we publish an account of another murder [Huston Chapman's] committed upon the principal street of the town of Lincoln. The admirers of the Governor will doubtless receive the news with mingled feelings of surprise and chagrin ... **It is charitable to think that Governor Wallace himself supposed a good deal to have been accomplished ... but upon its face, the whole affair looks very much as though he had tried to manufacture capital from misrepresentation**.

PLANNING A LINCOLN COUNTY VISIT: MARCH 1, 1879

Wallace still delayed going to Lincoln, as shown by his March 1, 1878 letter announcing departure to Territorial Secretary William Ritch, his Santa Fe proxy. His crossed-out February 27th became March 1st. He did not want to go. He wrote:

> Executive Office,
> Santa Fe, N.M.
> ~~February 27,~~ March 1, 1879.
>
> Hon. W.G. Ritch
> Sec. New Mexico
> Sir:
> I will leave this afternoon for Lincoln county. As it is uncertain how long I will be gone, should anything requesting my official action come to you, be good enough to forward it to me at Fort Stanton, care of Commandant at the Post.
>
> Very respectfully,
> Your friend & servant,
> Lew. Wallace

ENTER ATTORNEY IRA LEONARD

ANALYSIS: Just when Lew Wallace was feigning action in Huston Chapman's murder with his outlaw myth, reality struck again with Susan McSween's hiring of Attorney Ira Leonard to continue her litigation against N.A.M. Dudley. Wallace knew Leonard, having recommended him on November 13, 1878 for a judgeship. Brave Leonard, by taking the McSween case, must have known his risk from the Ring. And soon he also became Billy Bonney's pardon advocate and Lew Wallace's voice of conscience. His uncompromising morality and idealism would mark him life-long for the Ring's vindictive revenge.

LEW WALLACE'S VOICE OF CONSCIENCE

Ira E. Leonard - almost 47 when he met Billy Bonney - was born on March 15, 1832 in Genesee County, New York. In his youth in Batavia, New York, and in Boston, his profession was printer; first at the Batavia *Republican Advocate*. Compatible with his later idealism, in 1852 Leonard worked to set type for the first edition of Harriett Beecher Stowe's *Uncle Tom's Cabin*. In the 1850's, he also studied law in Batavia with a Judge Moses Taggart, and attended Albany Law School, graduating in 1855. That year he married, and they had a daughter in 1857.

By 1859, Leonard moved his family to Watertown, Wisconsin, to join a law practice; and had three more children. In 1865, he moved his family to Jefferson County, Missouri, where he practiced law, and had a fifth child and namesake in 1867. That year he was appointed Circuit Prosecuting Attorney of the 18th Judicial District, keeping that position till 1870.

For his candidacy for state Supreme Court Judge, the *St. Louis Globe* of September 7, 1872 stated: "[He] attracted special commendation by his fearless action in the suppression of disorder and mob law in those districts where ... incompetency ... has allowed the existing ruffianism to become a disgrace to the state." And September 7, 1872's *St. Louis Democrat* stated: "[He] won golden opinions as to being a fearless Circuit Judge in a district infested by desperate law-breakers." By 1874, Leonard's asthma necessitated his relocation with his family to Boulder, Colorado. There, he failed in his 1875 request to Attorney General Charles Devens for a federal judgeship for lack of an available vacancy.

In 1878, again for his debilitating asthma, Leonard moved with his family to Las Vegas, New Mexico. There he befriended Attorneys David Shield, Susan McSween's brother-in-law, and new arrival, Huston Chapman, who became Leonard's office-mate.

Lew Wallace may have met Leonard in September of 1878 in Las Vegas, as he journeyed southward to begin his governorship in Santa Fe, and following his meeting with Attorney Frank Springer in Cimarron. That both Springer and Leonard were anti-Ring makes possible Wallace's having an early notion of confronting that political machine. Further confirmation may have been Wallace's almost immediate recommendation of Leonard, on November 13, 1878 - the same day as his Amnesty Proclamation - to judgeship of the 1st Judicial District of Santa Fe County - a usurpation of its Ring control - or of the 3rd Judicial District to replace Ringite Warren Bristol. The judgeships were refused by Secretary of the Interior Carl Schurz and Attorney General Charles Devens; though Leonard got a lesser judgeship.

After Chapman's February 18, 1879 murder, Leonard wrote to Wallace on February 24, 1879. Still seeing Wallace as a savior, Leonard urged him to go to Lincoln as he himself intended. Leonard also proposed a newspaper in Lincoln County for an anti-Ring voice. It never materialized. Leonard was the last thing Wallace wanted: a conscience. Leonard wrote:

Las Vegas, N.M.
Febry 24 th 1879

Gov Wallace
　Santa Fe

Dear Gov. You have undoubtedly learned ere this of the assassination of H.I. Chapman at Lincoln on the night of Febry 18th – He left here for Lincoln Wednesday Febry 12th at about noon, and from a letter I received from Sidney Wilson an Attorney at that place it seems Chapman had just arrived in town when he was assassinated. he could have been there but a few minutes when the act occurred. **The morning Chapman left here I had a long talk with him concerning his course down there, and advised him to be careful and more discreet in his conduct, if not he might have trouble. he said he had no reason to apprehend trouble from any other source than through Col Dudley and Lt. French from what he then revealed to me I came to the conclusion that he had undoubtedly good reasons to fear from that source, and I cannot shake the conviction from my mind that if the truth could be reached about this dastardly assassination that it could be traced close to the door of those two officers – When I see you I can give you some circumstances that fasten that conviction on my mind, and constitute to me "proof as strong as holy writ" of their implication in it.**

I hope Gov you will go down to Lincoln when the Court ~~sets~~ convenes there. I intend to go -

I have a favor to ask of you I want to get the laws of the Territory from 1865 down to the present time. and if it would not be asking too much I wish you would procure the same from [Territorial] Secretary [William Ritch] or have him send the same to me. I understand that some sessions are hard to be obtained but as a favor they can all be procured. General Bower procured a set for Mr. Mills a few days ago. Do not do this Gov if it will cause you any trouble. I desired these laws to take down to Lincoln with me as I understand they have not a complete set there and I wanted to use them before Probate Court –

[AUTHOR'S NOTE: Leonard had also taken over Chapman's probate cases for Susan McSween regarding her deceased husband's and Tunstall's estates.]

Let me hear from you and if I can be of any service to you command me. Col. Webb will go to Lincoln with me. **We have in view the establishment of ~~of~~ a paper there, notwithstanding the uncertainty ~~of~~ & insecurity at present afforded to life & property A newspaper will revolutionize that country and bring order out of chaos.**

Yours truly

Ira E. Leonard

It appears that Wallace initially confided in Leonard about the Ring, as he did with Absalom Markland. But by February of 1879, three months after Leonard's failed judgeship appointments, Wallace was in secret retreat from it. While Leonard had become its open adversary by replacing Chapman as Susan McSween's *pro bono* lawyer against Dudley.

In a May 20, 1879 letter to Wallace (See my pp. 634-642 for full letter), Leonard referenced their relationship and his own April 1, 1879 arrival in Lincoln, still believing Wallace was pursuing Ring criminals. This misapprehension had also made Leonard think the March, 1879 pardon bargain with Billy Bonney had been sincere. Leonard wrote:

[A]s you will remember when I came here [to Lincoln] from Las Vegas about the 1st of April last with the intention of remaining if I considered it safe to do so, I had a conference with you, and you stated to me the situation in which you were placed in coming into this distracted county where lawlessness and disorder was the rule instead of the exception, you stated to me also that you had no one with whom to advise, and had no authority to employ counsel but desired me to assist in prosecuting, and bringing to justice the outlaws then under arrest [Chapman's murders and Seven Rivers rustlers] and who might be arrested. I promised to give you my best endeavors in that direction whether I was ever compensated for it or not.

By that May 20th, Wallace was back in Santa Fe, but he had been in Lincoln with Leonard (and Billy) for April's Grand Jury and the later Dudley Court of Inquiry. Wallace would be in a bind. The outlaw myth could not indefinitely fool Leonard, who, in addition, was trying to aid Billy's pardon bargain fulfillment.

Ultimately, Leonard's legal representing of Susan McSween and Billy Bonney - with consequent Ring blockade of his career, coupled with traumatic Ring near-assassinations in 1879 and 1881 - would ultimately impoverish him; as he would write to Lew Wallace on November 26, 1888.

But in 1880, Leonard lived in Lincoln and White Oaks, where he next tried unsuccessfully to get Billy a pardon through Secret Service Operative Azariah Wild. After Billy's capture by Pat Garrett on March 22, 1881, Leonard protectively traveled with him by train and coach to Mesilla. He was Billy's defense attorney on March 30, 1881 for the "Buckshot" Roberts federal indictment, arguing its invalidity since the killing occurred on Territorial land of Blazers Mill, not on federal land of the Mescalero Indian Reservation. On April 6, 1881, Judge Bristol was forced to quash that indictment. But a likely Ring death threat forced him to withdraw, leaving Billy to the destructive representation of court-appointed Attorneys Albert Jennings Fountain and John D. Bail, with resultant hanging sentence for William Brady's killing.

It is not known if Leonard was in Lincoln at Billy's jailbreak on April 28, 1881; though he then boarded in Isaac Ellis's house. Leonard's reaction to Billy's killing on July 14, 1881 is unknown.

Leonard continued as Susan McSween's lawyer after she remarried and added surname Barber, still settling the estates of John Tunstall and Alexander McSween. With sad irony, he was paid by land, which he sold to successful James Dolan by 1883.

But by 1882, he was postmaster at Socorro, New Mexico. Likely because of his ill health, his ventures in owning the *Socorro Sun*, in a law partnership, in a ranch, and in mining investments were all unsuccessful. In 1888, he moved to San Bernadino, California, with his son, Ira, but his asthma worsened. On November 26, 1888, he contacted Lew Wallace for help in getting the 2nd Judicial District Judgeship; writing pathetically: *"I need the position because I am unable to engage in active practice and am very poor and the salary would enable me to live and support my family and save something."* Wallace apparently recommended him to Attorney General W.H. Miller, but that failed because of Ring-style affidavits discrediting his health and accusing him of being a mining fraudster and unethical lawyer. As discussed, Catron never relented in revenge.

Leonard died on July 6, 1889, another unsung and heroic Lincoln County freedom fighter; with his Las Cruces *Rio Grande Republican* obituary merely stating: "[He] had been ailing for some time and his death was not unexpected." He was buried by his son William in Boulder, Colorado.

LETTER FROM HUSTON CHAPMAN'S FATHER: MARCH 20, 1879

On March 20, 1879, Ira Leonard got a heartbreaking letter from W.W. Chapman, Huston Chapman's father. He forwarded it to Lew Wallace. If Wallace's sole focus was not himself, he might have been moved to nobility by W.W. Chapman's ideals. That founder of the *Oregonian* newspaper had written: "*It is through the Executive and Judiciary that men are made to respect the laws. It is upon this theory that our institutions regard the Military subject to the civil powers, and is upon this theory alone that peace can be restored to your distracted Territory. Men must understand that the poorest and most humble citizen may seek with perfect safety through the judiciary a relief of grievances, and that the highest and most exalted must submit to judicial examination when charged with crimes or misdemeanors.*" But W.W. Chapman was unaware that democracy's intended checks and balances were destroyed under Ringite legislative and judicial control; and that Wallace had abnegated his executive power. Chapman wrote:

Portland Oregon
March 20th 1879

Hon Ira Leonard
 Dear Sir:
   Yours of the 1st inst. came to hand in due course of mail together with the accompanying papers.

 After the receipt of yours of the 23rd February I felt very anxious to learn more of the particulars of my sons assassination. Yours of 1st inst., the extract from the Governor's letter to you, and the printed communication published in the Gazette - I have no doubt convey a correct out line of the circumstances under which this atrocious murder was committed. We deeply mourn the loss of our son. On account of having by accident in his early youth lost one arm he was always an object of our more anxious solicitude, and we preferred that he should remain near home, but his energy and enterprise knew no bounds, and he spurned the idea that he could not accomplish with one hand anything that others could with two. And though he had but one arm I am persuaded that the assassin gave him no chance for his life. I have carefully considered your letters and the documents you have favored me with and I fail to find anything implicating him in wrongdoing; or that honorable men should deem cause for a personal assault.

I have not yet seen any report of the Coroners Inquest. Whether it will throw any light upon the immediate circumstances attending the murder is doubtful. It may not be permitted to make an impartial examination. Nothing that can now be done, can recall my son to life, or compensate his relatives and friends for his loss. The whole question is merged in a vindication of the law, and the protection of the lives and property of your citizens. This cannot be done by military rule. It can only be accomplished by upholding the civil powers in enforcing the laws through which individuals are held responsible for their violation.

So far as I have information I commend the course of Governor Wallace, and it was a great mistake that his recommendation that for a change of commandants at Fort Stanton was not carried out. In restoring peace and quiet it was essential that there should have been a cordial support by the Military Commandant of Fort Staunton [Stanton] to the Governor who is by law entrusted with the enforcement of the law, and the preservation of the public peace. Whether there was any just grounds to suppose Col. Dudley not suitable for this purpose, if the Governor believed him to be unsuitable, other commandants should have supplied his place. **It is through the Executive and Judiciary that men are made to respect the laws. It is upon this theory that our institutions regard the Military subject to the civil powers, and is upon this theory alone that peace can be restored to your distracted Territory. Men must understand that the poorest and most humble citizen may seek with perfect safety through the judiciary a relief of grievances, and that the highest and most exalted must submit to judicial examination when charged with crimes or misdemeanors.**

The course of Gov Wallace in promptly repairing to Lincoln entitles him to the respect of all law abiding citizens, and I predict that if a suitable commandant is at Fort Staunton [Stanton] he will restore peace to your Territory and cause the civil Government to be respected.

Its not in my powers at present to go to Washington, but I have written to the Secretary of War whom I believe to be a just man and will no doubt do what is right if properly informed.

It is suggested that this assassin was so close as to set my sons clothing on fire. If Huston had, or was supposed to have documents or evidence against any one, is it not as likely that the possession or destruction of those papers was as important to the assassins as putting him out of the way of using them, and that his clothes were fired to either destroy them or obliterate the loss of them by robbery –

I shall be glad to learn that his remains were properly cared for. Its possible he had a trunk and papers which you will oblige me by preserving

I am under great obligations to you for the interest you have taken on behalf of my son, and in communicating with me and I hope you will continue to write me from time to time of the state of affairs.

Very truly
Your obt servt
W.W. Chapman

CHAPTER 14

LEW WALLACE IN LINCOLN PURSUING OUTLAWS: MARCH 5, 1879 - MAY 15, 1879

COMING OF A "SAVIOR"

ANALYSIS: Having been forced to go to Lincoln after Huston Chapman's murder, Lew Wallace intended to feign action and avoid Ring confrontation by focus on the outlaw myth. But Susan McSween's and Ira Leonard's beginning litigation against Commander N.A.M. Dudley made Wallace remove him. In the muddle, Wallace convinced himself and the Lincolnites that he was their savior; as he would soon convince Billy Bonney.

With what must have been a tangled tizzy of anger at Huston Chapman's embarrassing murder, fear of Ring confrontation, and pressure to demonstrate action, Lew Wallace left Santa Fe with District Commander General Edward Hatch on March 1, 1879 for Fort Stanton. Hatch stayed there. Wallace delayed going to Lincoln till March 5th. To desperate Lincolnites, a savior had come. But the salvation Wallace sought was resurrection of his own foundering reputation. And the only demons he hoped to exorcise were mythical outlaws, not hellish Ringites.

As usual, Wallace's solace was literary fantasy, now put into his progressing *Ben-Hur: A Tale of the Christ* where his own youthful handsomeness was added to his own bearing his "cross" of injustices - all imposed on a real Savior. He wrote:

> The features [of the Christ], it should be further said, were ruled by a certain expression which, as the viewer chose, might with equal correctness have been called the effect of intelligence, love, pity, or sorrow; though, in better speech, it was a blending of them all - a look easy to fancy as a mark of a sinless soul doomed to the sight and understanding of the utter sinfulness of those among whom it was passing; yet withal no one could have observed the face with a thought of weakness in the man; so, at least, would not they who know that the qualities mentioned - love, sorrow, pity - are the results of a

consciousness of strength to bear suffering oftener than strength to do; such has been the might of martyrs and devotees and the myriads written down in the saintly calendars. And such, indeed, was the air of this one.

IRA LEONARD FILES CHARGES AGAINST COMMANDER N.A.M. DUDLEY: MARCH 4, 1879

Even before Lew Wallace arrived in Lincoln to conduct what he must have considered his sly strategy - pursuit of mythical outlaws - reality struck again. On March 4, 1879, Ira Leonard and Susan McSween continued Huston Chapman's litigation against N.A.M. Dudley. They were risking their lives. Buried to the east of Susan's burned-down house and looted Tunstall store were now John Tunstall, Frank MacNab, Alexander McSween, Harvey Morris, and Huston Chapman. And to Dudley's Lincoln County War crimes, they had now added Chapman's murder. The charges were for the next month's April Lincoln County Grand Jury, where Susan might also testify against Sheriff George Peppin as a murderer and arsonist accomplice of Dudley.

Leonard had already made the charges public in a March 1, 1879 *Las Vegas Gazette* article linking Dudley to Huston Chapman's assassination. Leonard had written:

Charges and specifications against Lieutenant Colonel N.A.M. Dudley, Commander at Fort Stanton, New Mexico.

That Lieutenant Colonel Dudley, Commander at Fort Stanton, New Mexico, on the 19th day of July A.D. 1878 without authority of law, or by any right vested in him so to be, did take a squad of armed soldiers, numbering around 60, also one cannon and one Gatling gun, and went to the town of Lincoln, and assigned and gave aid to an armed band of outlaws, and by reason of the aid furnished by said Dudley, and the soldiers under his command and direction, aided in killing one A.A. McSween, a citizen of said county; that at the same time and place the said Dudley aided in the crime of arson, by causing the house of said McSween to be set on fire, the lives of the inmates therein put in jeopardy, that at the same time the said Dudley caused said building to be fired, there were in the house two defenseless females, and five infant children; that his conduct on that occasion was most brutal and inhuman, and unbecoming a soldier and officer.

2nd

That at the same time and place as last above stated the said Lieutenant Colonel N.A.M. Dudley, did maliciously, and willfully, and corruptly for the purpose of giving a color of right to his wicked and unlawful action, compel one John B. Wilson, a Justice of the Peace of said town of Lincoln aforesaid and by threat of ironing and imprisonment, said John B. Wilson, if he refused to issue a warrant for the arrest of said A.A. McSween, and other citizens of said county, and that by reason of said threat and the fear of violence and imprisonment from said Dudley, the said John B. Wilson did issue the warrants demanded by the said Lieutenant Colonel N.A.M. Dudley for the apprehension of said A.A. McSween and others.

3rd

That on the 20th day of July A.A. 1878 at the town of Lincoln, in the County of Lincoln, in said Territory of New Mexico, the said Lieutenant Colonel N.A.M. Dudley, with his soldiers entered the store belonging to the estate of John H. Tunstall and plundered upwards of six thousand dollars worth of goods, and when the said Dudley was appealed to, to prevent the same, he aided the plunderers to consummate their objective.

4th

That sometime during the month of November or December A.D. 1878 the said Lieutenant Colonel N.A.M. Dudley, at the county of Lincoln aforesaid did procure base and wicked men to make false and slanderous charges and statements against the character and virtue of Mrs. S.E. McSween, the widow of said A.A. McSween murdered as aforesaid, and did cause the same to be filed in the military department of the government for the purpose of ruining her reputation, and destroying her influence in seeking redress for Lieutenant Colonel N.A.M. Dudley's gross outrages perpetrated by the said Dudley against her.

5th

That during the fall of 1878, one Easton (whose given name is unknown to me) had a contract for delivering corn at Fort Stanton aforesaid and that Lieutenant Colonel N.A.M. Dudley demanded of him an affidavit, testifying against the character of S.E. McSween for truth and chastity, and upon the refusal of said Easton to swear to the statements demanded, he ordered that no more corn should be received from him.

6th

That during the month of November or December A.D. 1878 the said Lieutenant Colonel N.A.M. Dudley, Commander of the post at Fort Stanton as aforesaid, in order to subvert the ends of justice, and to prevent Governor Lew Wallace from restoring peace in said county did maliciously and falsely publish an open letter, in the New Mexican, a newspaper published at Santa Fe, New Mexico, which letter was calculated and intended to foment the disturbances then rife in said county, and that he did in that open letter make false and malicious charges against the character of Mrs. S.E. McSween, and called attention to certain false and wicked affidavits which he had forwarded to District Headquarters concerning her.

7th

That on or about the 12th day of December A.D. 1878, Lieutenant Colonel N.A.M. Dudley, Commander of Fort Stanton as aforesaid, detailed a squad of soldiers under the command of Lieutenant J.H. French, one of the officers at said post, to go to the town of Lincoln to aid and assist the sheriff of said county in discharge of his duties at a Probate Court to be held in said county, that while the said French was at Lincoln as aforesaid, he became intoxicated, and while in a drunken debauch went with certain of the soldiers under his command to the house of a Mexican by the name of Maximo (surname unknown) and without any right or authority to interfere with said citizen, broke into his house and abused him in a shameful manner, and threatened to kill him, and on the same occasion, the said Lieutenant J.H. French as aforesaid did break and violently enter the house of one John Copeland, of Lincoln, Lincoln County aforesaid, and then and there use abusive, threatening, and insulting language to the wife of said Copeland, and that the said French had no authority or power to enter the house, but the same was a willful assault by him upon innocent an unoffending citizens, and that the said Lieutenant French at the same time and place without right or authority violently and being in a drunken and debauched condition entered the private dwelling of Mrs. S.E. McSween, with two or more armed soldiers, and did then and there, use towards the said Mrs. McSween, abusive and insulting language, did without any right place her under arrest, and treat her with violence, and he did then and there without authority, arrest one H.I. Chapmen who was endeavoring to protect the said Mrs. McSween from the violence and insult of said Lieutenant French, and he threatened the life of said Chapman, if he interfered to protect the said Mrs. McSween, that notwithstanding, the said Lieutenant Colonel N.A.M. Dudley was fully advised of the conduct of said Lieutenant French, on said occasion, and knew, and was fully cognizant of his violation of duty as a soldier, and of his drunken and disorderly conduct, took no measures to have the said French punished or brought to an account for the same, but on the contrary, when the said H.I. Chapman complained before J.B. Wilson, a Justice of the Peace of the town of Lincoln, against said French, he was held to bail by the said Justice to answer to the charge before the Grand Jury of the said county. For his said conduct as aforesaid, the said Lieutenant Colonel N.A.M. Dudley, in an act of retaliation against Chapman, corruptly, willfully, and maliciously caused the said Chapman to be classified as one of the outlaws, and breakers of the peace of Lincoln County and denied him the privilege of the post, and promulgated a military order to that effect.

Lincoln, New Mexico
March 4th 1879
　　I, the undersigned certify that I believe the above charges and specifications to be true, and that the same are not made through malice or ill will towards the said Lieutenant Colonel N.A.M. Dudley, French, or either of them, but for the purpose of having a full and fair investigation of the same, and if substantiated to have the officers named herein punished.
Ira E. Leonard

That same March 4, 1878, Ira Leonard also raised possibility of a military court of inquiry for Dudley's potential court martial - and even hanging for treason - by contacting Secretary of War George McCrary. Leonard wrote:

Las Vegas, New Mexico
March 4, 1879

To Honorable Secretary of War
Washington, D.C.
Sir:
　　You are perhaps fully aware of the outrages that have been perpetrated in Lincoln County, New Mexico, during the past year, and to the extent to which they have been carried, and are still progressing.

The proclamation of the President and the action of the local authorities have been so far inadequate to stop them. I enclose you an article of the latest acts of violence and murder in said county, that of H. I. Chapman.

I also enclose charges and specifications against Lieutenant Colonel N.A.M. Dudley and Lieutenant French.

I do not know that this is the proper mode of reaching the matter, but if not, I desire to be advised as I believe the charges are substantially true and justice demands an impartial investigation of them.

Yours, etc.,
Ira E. Leonard

[ARTICLE ENCLOSED] *Las Vegas Gazette, March 1, 1879*

DEATH OF CHAPMAN.

The people of Las Vegas were greatly shocked on Sunday last to hear of the cold blooded murder, in Lincoln County: on the 18th of February of H.I. Chapman, Esq.

Mr. Chapman was a young lawyer from Portland, Oregon, and the son of the Honorable W.W. Chapman of that place. Immediately prior to his coming to Las Vegas, he was engaged as one of the civil engineers at the A.T.&S.F.R.R., and had charge of bridge construction.

In September last, he came to Las Vegas to commence the practice of his profession and remained here about two months, when he was employed by Mrs. McSween to go to Lincoln County, and assist her in the settlement of her husband's estate.

The citizens of this territory are pretty familiar with the lawlessness, and wholesale murders, and outrages that have perpetrated in that county within the last year. They have been carried on to such an extent that the President of the United States in September last, issued a proclamation directed to the insurgents and bandits, to disperse, and following the proclamation of the President was one of amnesty by Governor Lew Wallace, forgiving past offences and inviting the people to quiet and peace. Troops have been distributed in different parts of the country to maintain and prevent lawlessness.

When Mr. Chapman went to Lincoln it was supposed that life was reasonably secure, and that citizens could pursue their ordinary avocations without fear of assassination.

Those who are familiar with the disturbances that have left the county in a state of revolution and disorder for so long a time, knew that A.A. McSween, the husband of Mrs. McSween, was shot and killed on the 19th of July last, under circumstances that led her and his friends to believe that the murder of McSween was brought about, and in fact directly aided by Lieutenant Colonel Dudley, of the 9th U.S. Cavalry, and commander of the military post at Fort Stanton, in that county, and that a bitter feeling has existed and shown itself on the part of Col. Dudley towards Mrs. McSween since then, which was practically demonstrated in Col. Dudley's open letter published a few weeks hence in the Santa Fe papers and addressed to Governor Wallace, in which he characterizes Mrs. McSween as being everything except a good woman.

It had even extended so far that when the Probate Court was held in Lincoln County in December last, and a posse of soldiers had been detailed from the fort to aid the sheriff in performing his duties, which soldiers were in charge of Lieut. French, an officer under Col. Dudley: that French took a squad of soldiers at night and went to the house of Mrs. McSween and there greatly insulted her, made threats of violence, and directed the soldiers to arrest Mr. Chapman, and threatened to blow his brains out if he resisted. For this outrage a complaint was made before a Justice of the Peace in Lincoln by Mr. Chapman, and Lt. French was held to bail to await the action of the Grand Jury of that county, and as a matter of retaliation Mr. Chapman was, by order of the post commander, excluded from the privilege of the post and denounced as one of the outlaws of Lincoln County.

When the military become the perpetrators of outrages, when the houses of private citizens, in pursuit of their vocation, were invaded and lawlessly broken into by military officers and their squads of soldiers, and violence inflicted upon them, Mr. Chapman thought it was time to take steps to see if citizens had any rights that the military were bound to respect, and he left Lincoln about 20th January to go to Santa Fe to see what could be done towards protecting and securing the people against these continued outrages.

The following article which appeared in this paper Feb. 8th 1879 shows the results of Mr. Chapman's visit to Santa Fe.

Mr. H. I. Chapman has just returned from Santa Fe, where he went for the purpose of securing arrest of Col. Dudley who is charged with the murder of A.A. McSween, on the 19th day of July, 1878. Mr. Chapman was informed by the military at Santa Fe that he could not see any of the reports, orders, or affidavits that had been received from Col. Dudley except upon the express order of the Secretary of War, whereupon Mr. Chapman concluded that it was useless to attempt to do anything more here but will lay the whole matter before the Secretary of War, and ask an investigation of the charges against Col. Dudley.

The military are in possession of most of the testimony against Dudley and will do nothing to further it unless ordered by the Secretary of War.

Mr. Chapman will go to Lincoln to gather evidence to lay before the government, both as to the murder of McSween and Tunstall.

On the 12th of February Mr. Chapman left here to return to Lincoln and had been there but a very short time when he was assassinated, as will appear from the following article copied from the News and Press of Cimarron.

A gentleman in Lincoln County writes us this week the particulars of another atrocious deed in the blood stained town of Lincoln. The victim this time was H.I. Chapman, who but a short time since, was in the employ of the A.T.&SF Railway company as a civil engineer. He left the road and located in Las Vegas to practice law. Here he was employed by Mrs. A.A. McSween to settle up the estate of her late husband, and attend to other legal business in which she was interested.

These required his presence in Lincoln. He had been there but a very short time when he came in collision with Col. Dudley, the commander at Fort Stanton, who, throughout the troubles in that county, has shown a bitter partisan spirit against the McSween faction.

On the 18th inst. Mr. Chapman and Hon. Juan Patron had just arrived from Las Vegas and discovered that Dolan, Capt. Jesse Evans and others of that party were in town apparently bent on mischief, and in a short time they were called upon by some of the men, who were with some difficulty prevented from taking the life of Mr. Patron. A little later Mr. Chapman was walking down to his office when he was fired on by some of the Evans gang, who were running the town, and instantly killed, two balls striking him in the breast.

Not satisfied with killing this poor one armed man, they set fire to his clothing and left him to burn in the street. At the time of writing our correspondent says Sheriff Kimball [Kimbrell] and twenty four soldiers were in the town of Lincoln, but that no arrest had yet been made. The Coroner's inquest was to be held that day.

This comes from letting notorious desperados run at large. We shall expect to see Governor Wallace use all the power he may possess to hunt these infamous assassins down, and if there is any virtue in the laws, they should be disposed of so that it would be impossible for them again stealthily and in cold blood to take the life of a law abiding citizen.

The honor of the territory demands that such cowardly scoundrels should not be permitted to run at large no matter what it may cost to arrest them. But unless there is a change made in the Commanding Officer at Fort Stanton we shall have little faith in the Governor receiving any substantial aid from the military.

The Dolan faction will be spared as much as possible by the present commandant of the post.

With General Pope rest the responsibility of continuing Col. Dudley in command, but rather making a change which the bitter feeling in that county engendered by the part he played in the McSween massacre alone, would permit the feud to continue, and the lives of good men to be sacrificed to his caprice. It will be almost impossible for the executive to restore order in Lincoln County until a change is made in some of the officers at Fort Stanton.

A more cold blooded and dastardly outrage could hardly be conceived of. If the policy of Governor Wallace had been carried out when he came to this territory and assumed the duties of his office, this gross murder would never have occurred. He saw the situation of matters in Lincoln County and that Col. Dudley was implicated in them, and was believed by one faction to be giving aid and assistance to the other, and in fact to have been instrumental in causing the death of A.A. McSween.

When the Governor issued the Proclamation of Amnesty and Pardon, he desired to have all the influence which could impair or retard speedy restoration, peace and order, thoroughly removed. Knowing this feeling against Dudley, he desired that a change in the post commanders should be made, but General Pope, Commander of this Military District, would not act, and treated his request with indifference, or paid no regard to it.

When Col. Dudley saw his advantage he became more overbearing and insolent, he paraded himself before the public in a bombastic letter addressed to the Governor attacking the Governor and his motives, and formuated a beastly tirade against Mrs. McSween, attacking her private character, and charging her with being a woman of bad reputation.

It may be from a military stand point regarded brave for a military officer shielded behind government barracks to attack a defenseless woman whose husband has been murdered in cold blood by aid and assistance furnished a lawless band of desperados by that officer, but to the outside world it looks like an act fit only to emanate from a cowardly poltroon.

Mr. Chapman determined to see justice done to the victims of Dudley's and French's caprice, they were in a fair way of having their conduct exposed and being brought to justice for their crimes, and it was essential that he should be disposed of to prevent their exposure and punishment. The act was accomplished, perhaps not by these men, but very evidently by those who had been shielded and protected at the government post and who had been mentioned in the outrages perpetrated in the county.

On the morning Mr. Chapman left here, the 12th of February, the writer had a long talk with him concerning the situation, and the danger his life was exposed to in consequence of the active part he took against Dudley and French. He frankly stated he did fear violence incited by them, but from no other source: he said that notwithstanding the danger that surrounded him, he should try and have them brought to justice.

We who knew Chapman in this county, know he was an earnest upright man, and that he met his death through his earnest and strong adherence to his friends, at the hands of as base a set of cowards and murderers as ever infested a civilized country.

The question now rears how long the people of this territory have got to submit to this state of things, and there is no adequate mode of reaching and punishing these assassins who render life and property so insecure in our territory.

We do hope that the government will be aroused to take such active measures as will afford protection and security to the lives of its citizens.

E.

[ENCLOSED: The Charges Against Dudley]

REMOVING DUDLEY: MARCH 8, 1879

At his March 5, 1879 Lincoln arrival, Wallace was diverted from pursuing his outlaw myth by locals' angry clamor about dead Chapman and dangerous Dudley, coupled with Ira Leonard's charges. So on March 7, 1879, Wallace again requested General Hatch to remove Dudley from command. He likely hoped Dudley would quietly depart. But with his usual strategic disconnect, Wallace was passing the blame to Hatch, who must have been as furious as had been Ulysses S. Grant at Shiloh. Wallace wrote:

Lincoln, N.M., March 7, 1879.

General Edward Hatch,
Comdg. Dist. N.M.
Sir:
I have the honor to repeat the request made on a former occasion, that Lieut. Col. N.A.M. Dudley be relieved of command at Fort Stanton.
This is done upon conviction that he is so compromised by connection with the troubles in this county

that his usefulness in the effort now making to restore order is utterly gone. The intimidation under which really well disposed people are suffering, and which prevents my securing affidavits as the foundation of legal proceedings against parties already in arrest, results in great part from dread of misdirection of authority by him.

It is with the greatest possible regret I add, if I am to believe the information which has come to me, the dread referred to is not irrational. In justice to Col. Dudley, and that he may take such course as he deems best to have an investigation ~~of his conduct~~ with a view to his exoneration, and also that you may take such action as your sense of duty may suggest under the circumstances, **I will ~~also add~~ state in general terms that it is charged here that Lieut. Col. Dudley is responsible for the killing of McSween and the men who were shot with that person; that he was an influential participant in that affair, and yet is an active partisan. I have ~~also~~ information also connecting him with the more recent murder of H.I. Chapman: to the effect that he knew the man would be killed, and announced it the day of the night of the killing, and that one of the murderers stated publicly that he had promised Colonel Dudley to do the deed.** I am further informed that another man was driven in fear of his life from Lincoln to Fort Stanton [Juan Patrón]: that a band of armed men followed him there, and hunted for him about the Trader's Store, avowing a purpose to kill him; that the party pursued appealed to Col. Dudley for protection, but was turned away, and escaped with difficulty; that there was no investigation of this affair by Col. Dudley, and that the would-be murderers were not interrupted in their hunt, which was repeated through two days, but were permitted to leave at their leisure, and within a night or two after, engaged in the killing of Chapman in the town of Lincoln.

I beg to say distinctly that I make you these statements as information came to me in a manner to make the giving the statement and the request which precedes it matters of official duty. You will greatly ~~oblige~~ favor me by furnishing Lt. Col. Dudley a copy of this communication.

I have the honor to be,
Very respectfully
Your friend and servant.
Lew Wallace.
Gov. New Mexico.

HATCH REMOVES DUDLEY: MARCH 8, 1879

General Edward Hatch, at Fort Stanton, removed Dudley from his command there the next day, March 8, 1879. He had no choice. Dudley's part in yet another Lincoln murder was too risky for another cover-up. Hatch wrote:

> *Headquarters District of New Mexico*
> In the Field Fort Stanton, N.M.
>   March 8th   1879
>
> SPECIAL FIELD ORDERS,
>   No. 2
>   Lieutenant Colonel N.A.M. Dudley 9th, U.S. Cavalry, is hereby relieved from command and duty at Fort Stanton New Mexico; he will proceed to Fort Union N.M. reporting his arrival to the A.A.A. Genl. Dist. of New Mexico, to await such action as the Dept. Commander may take upon the allegations preferred by his Excellency the Governor of New Mexico. Lt. Col. Dudley is authorized to take quarters of Fort Union.
>   Edward Hatch
>   *Colonel 9th Cavalry, Commanding.*

Headquarters District of New Mexico
In the field Fort Stanton, N.M.
March 8, 1879

To the Assistant Adjutant General
Fort Leavenworth, Kansas
Sir:
I have the honor to enclose allegations of His Excellency, the Governor of New Mexico against Lieut. Col. N.A.M. Dudley, and Special Field Order No. 2, District of New Mexico, ordering Col. Dudley to Fort Union to await your action.

The allegations made by the Governor are of such a serious nature, and the condition of affairs are such I have deemed it for the best interest of the service to relieve Col. Dudley from command at Fort Stanton and remove him from the neighborhood, neither did I consider it advisable to place him in command of Fort Union, until the General Commanding has taken action in the matter.

The Governor is confident that he has ample proof to establish all he has alleged, and in justice to Col. Dudley a thorough investigation should be made.

From the evidence now in possession of the Governor, he seems warranted in making these serious charges The Governor intends to remain in Lincoln until affairs are brought to a more peaceable condition and he depends entirely on the aid from the military granted him by the Secretary of War, to secure this desirable end.

I consider it of the upmost importance that he should be on satisfactory terms with the commander at Fort Stanton, now rendered impossible by the request of the Governor, that he be relieved of duty founded upon such serious accusations.

I consider it therefore imperative to comply with the instructions to furnish such aid as the Governor requires, from the Secretary of war that the change should be made, and have acted accordingly.

Very respectfully,
Your obedient servant,
Edward Hatch
Colonel 9th Cavalry
Comg. Dist. Of N.M.

DUDLEY'S RESPONSE TO HATCH: MARCH 9, 1879

Twice court martialed N.A.M. Dudley was no virgin to accusations; but Attorney Ira Leonard's were the worst. In 1871, at Camp McDowell, Dudley's offences had included drunkenness. In 1877, he temporarily lost command at Fort Union for drunkenness and behavior unbecoming an officer.

But Dudley was confident of Catron's repeated protection. His favor to the Ring had been successful murders of two major opponents: Alexander McSween and Huston Chapman. And his defamatory affidavits against Susan McSween were ready for discrediting her court testimony.

So, under likely advisement from Catron, or his firm member, Henry Waldo, Dudley responded by denials to Hatch on March 9, 1879, in attempt to ferret out Lew Wallace's evidence; the most serious accusation being McSween's murder, which he replied hopefully was *"based upon rumor solely."* Unbeknownst to his Ring handlers, in four days, Billy Bonney would present himself to Wallace for a pardon. And he was an eye-witness not only to Chapman's murder, but also to Dudley's guilt of his troops firing on escaping McSweens. The Ring was in trouble. Dudley wrote:

Colonel E. Hatch
9th Cavalry
Commanding New Mexico

Sir:

I respectfully request that I be furnished without delay an official copy of all charges, giving the specific dates, and with a list of the witnesses to the same which Governor Wallace, Territory of New Mexico, has made against me.

The communication purporting to be a copy of the Governor's charge against me furnished by the District Commander first charges that the intimidation used by myself prevents parties from making affidavits against parties already in arrest, and a misdirection of authority by myself.

The records of the Adjutant's office at this post will annihilate this charge. If not, I will produce before sundown twenty witnesses, an equal proportion from each faction to sustain my assertion.

The 2nd charge of my being responsible for the murder of McSween is based upon rumor solely. The Governor states that it is charged here.

If so grave a charge as the one proferred by Governor Wallace in this paper is to be used by the District Commander in disgracing an officer of my service and record, I am entitled to know who the witnesses to this charge are and what of their characters.

The 3rd charge of connecting me with the murder of Chapman is simply absurd and can be proven at any hour the Governor may appoint. This charge is based, so stated, upon information which can be furnished by the Governor.

The charge of driving a single man or woman, by the writer, away from the post who has ever asked protection of me is simply a lie, and I will defy the slightest proof of it.

His Excellency the Governor in the last paragraph of his letter states that these charges are made on information or hearsay which in my opinion is not sufficient to justify the prompt action taken on them by the Governor or the District Commander, carrying with it as it does the disgrace of an officer of my rank or even any other grade, this to the face of my repeated assertion that I am able to prove the utter falsity of every charge or intimation against me.

Respectfully,
N.A.M. Dudley
Lieut. Col. 9th Cavalry

HATCH ELABORATES TO WALLACE: MARCH 11, 1879

Back in his Santa Fe headquarters, General Edward Hatch responded on March 11, 1879 to Lew Wallace, whose post traumatic stress disorder from Shiloh was acting up as anxiety: worry that Dudley could override the removal. But Hatch's letter only worsened anxiety by proving that Wallace's feared scenario was happening: he was pitted against an officer, and even had to prepare a witness list against Dudley. And all that should be telegraphed to Hayes. He was trapped in reality. Hatch wrote:

Headquarters District of New Mexico
Santa Fe, N.M., ____March 11____ 1879

His Excellency
The Governor New Mexico
Dr Governor
Col Dudley has received his order and disobeys the order at this peril.
In due time it will be known whether he has sent such a telegram.
You need not be in any manner worried about the matter. he has no command and should he not obey the order will surely be tried. It is doubtful whether he would send a telegram over my head to Washington he wished Capt. Carroll to do so who declined. all that is necessary for you to do is to prepare a list of witnesses to who sustain the allegations.

Very respectfully
Yours
Edward Hatch
B Maj Genl

If you think it necessary send telegram the President

WALLACE MEDDLES WITH FORT STANTON

Lew Wallace never remained long in reality's grip. Rationalizing Dudley's removal as his own success, he segued into second-guessing the military (like in the Battle of Shiloh's first day when he ignored orders to go directly to Pittsburgh Landing, but headed to where he decided General Grant's forces would end up as the enemy retreated - except they did not retreat).

So on March 9, 1879, two days after having Dudley removed, Wallace started to reorganize Fort Stanton. Writing to General Hatch, he requested that acting Commander Captain Carroll be made permanent commander; and that past Commander George Purington, now acting Commander, not be considered because of his past partisanship. So, in his new flurry, Wallace made another enemy at the fort: Purington. Since its guard house was the only viable local jail, it would soon become a sieve to any Ringside prisoners Wallace might put there. Wallace wrote:

Lincoln, N.M., March 9, 1879.

General Edward Hatch,
Comd'g. Dist. N.M.

Sir:
I beg leave to request that you allow Captain Carroll to remain, for a time at least, in command of Fort Stanton. His action of late has commended him so greatly that he appears to be the man for the place. Besides, I have made it a point today to sound the people here, there being a number of refuges amongst them, and find that Col. Purington may prove objectionable because of a prevailing belief that he was committed to one of the old factions. It will be understood of course that I have ~~personally~~ no objection to Col. Purington, personally, whose reputation is that of a good soldier, but the immediate object of attainment being just now the ~~restoration~~ revival of public confidence, I respectfully submit it as a point of ~~first~~ importance that the command of the Fort, upon which everything depends, should, as a matter of policy and for a time at least, be given to the officer who was least connected with the past troubles. ~~and is most generally acceptable to the people.~~

In the same connection, and for the same reasons, I have also to request that you select for the permanent command some officer who has had no connection whatever with the affairs of the county in the past.

I have the honor to be,
Very truly, your friend and servant,
Lew Wallace,
Gov. New Mexico.

ARRESTING CHAPMAN'S MURDERERS

On his March 5, 1879 arrival in Lincoln, Wallace's pursuit of mythical outlaws had been intercepted by the reality that Huston Chapman had been murdered only 15 days earlier, almost in front of the house in which he was now staying; and the locals were fuming. So he had to pursue real outlaws: Chapman's murderers, James Dolan, Billy Campbell, Jessie Evans, and Billy Matthews. The primary killer, Dolan, was on Wallace's October of 1878 Sherman "outlaw" list. Wallace later reported to Carl Schurz on March 21, 1879 (See my pp. 567-571 for full letter) that he had to apprehend Chapman's killers without warrants because Lincolnites were afraid to give affidavits (though he omitted that the fear was of joining the Ringites' hit list).

It should be recognized that without prosecution witnesses willing to testify in court, Dolan, Campbell, Evans, and Matthews could not have been convicted. Ringite Judge Warren Bristol would have quashed their indictments for lack of evidence - as he did in October of 1878 for Dolan's indictment for Tunstall's murder. But, in just eight days, to Ringite horror, an unexpected eye-witness would volunteer for the prosecution: Billy Bonney.

About James Dolan, Wallace had a bizarrely quixotic fantasy, revealed in his March 21, 1879 letter to Carl Schurz. Knowing that Dolan had "*larger money interests in the county*," he planned to make him "*pliant as a witness!*" Lethal local Ring boss Dolan, certain of Ringite immunity, must have considered Wallace an idiotic twit. But Dolan may have played along to feed Wallace the Regulators' names and locations for Wallace's pursuits of "outlaws" - like Bonney, Salazar, Scurlock, and Bowdre.

INVOLVING GENERAL HATCH: MARCH 5, 1879

On March 5, 1879, having just left General Edward Hatch at Fort Stanton, but now in frenetically productive mode in Lincoln, Wallace wrote back to him wanting his authorization to incarcerate Chapman's not-yet-captured killers in Fort Stanton; forgetting Ringite loyalty of its officers, who detested him. And he was likely unaware that, on May 4, 1878, Dudley had freed the 27 Seven Rivers murderers of Regulator Frank MacNab to thwart then Sheriff John Copeland's arrest of them. More dramatically, as Wallace writes, Dolan and his fellow killers were then in the smug safety of Catron's Carrizozo ranch. Wallace wrote:

> *Lincoln. Lincoln County. N.M.*
> *March 5, 1879.*
>
> Col. Edward Hatch
> Com'g Dist. New Mexico.
> Sir:
> I have information that William Campbell, J.B. Matthews and Jesse Evans were of the party engaged in the killing of H.I. Chapman, in this place, the night of the 18 February ult., **and that they are now with J.J. Dolan at Curisoso [Carrizozo] Ranch.** You will please send a sufficient force to arrest them; and when arrested, have them brought to Fort Stanton, and held securely until their cases can be investigated by the grand jury at the coming session of the Lincoln county court next month. I suggest the detachment be started immediately.
> I have the honor to be,
> Very respectfully,
> Your friend & servant,
> Lew. Wallace,
> Gov. New Mexico

The next day, March 6, 1879, Hatch put a stick in the wheel, wanting arrest warrants, and Sheriff George Kimbrell apprehending the killers. Wallace was forced to beg and to take personal responsibility. But as a lawyer, he should have anticipated future release of his prisoners by *habeas corpus*. Catron would not miss that option - one he had already used to suppress the 1872 Legislature Revolt. Wallace wrote:

> *Lincoln, N.M., March 6, 1879.*
>
> Gen. Edward Hatch,
> Com'g Dist. New Mexico.
> Sir:
> In your communication today, speaking of the arrest of Campbell and others, you desire the Sheriff to be at the Fort with warrants when the prisoners arrive. The truth is that the people here are so intimidated that some days will have to [pass] before they can be screwed up to the point of making the necessary affidavits. It follows that I must take the responsibility of requesting you to keep the arrested parties until their cases can be investigated by a grand jury. And that I have done. See my letter of

yesterday. **Hold them, I beg of you. To let them go now is to lose everything at the beginning of the struggle.**

When Capt. Carroll can conveniently come over, I will esteem it a favor if he will do so.

Very respectfully,
Your friend & servant
Lew. Wallace,
Gov. New Mexico.

INVOLVING JUSTICE OF THE PEACE WILSON: MARCH 8, 1879

By March 8, 1879, Evans, Campbell, and Matthews were caught; and worked-up Wallace wrote from Fort Stanton to Justice of the Peace "Squire" Wilson in Lincoln. In his fevered imagination, Wallace was leading a charge with "trooper" Wilson: *"Stand firm now, and we will win!"* It is unclear what Wallace wanted to "win." He certainly was not fighting the Ring. But Wilson must have assumed he was; especially after Wallace's removal of Dudley. And, as will be seen, Wallace's progress was being communicated to Billy Bonney as his pardon plan was being hatched by Wilson and Juan Patrón, to be delivered in five days.

In his dizzy tizzy, Wallace wanted Wilson to honor affidavits presented by District Attorney William Rynerson and Attorney Henry Waldo - forgetting they were Ringites. And in his wartime fantasy, he calls Rynerson Colonel. Wallace wrote:

Fort Stanton, March 8, 1879
J. B. Wilson, Eq.
Dear Sir.

I understand that affidavits will be filed against the prisoners now in military custody here, the object being to force a trial. If such a step should be taken by any person not representing the Territory *as its lawful attorney, you may be sure it is taken in the interest of the prisoners, not the Territory. The prisoners, you will see at a glance, cannot prosecute themselves; nor can their attorney prosecute them; he can only defend when a prosecution is duly begun.*

I have therefore to request that you will *decline to entertain any affidavit not presented to you by an attorney representing the Territory – and such will be either Col. Rynerson, or Atty. Gen. Waldo, or some person appointed in writing by me as Governor.*

I take the liberty also of cautioning you that a Justice of the Peace is not authorized by law to issue writs of habeas corpus. Possibly you may be applied to for such a writ. Don't entertain the application.

I will be over this evening.

Col. Dudley has been relieved of the command of Fort Stanton, and ordered to Fort Union to await the order of General Pope.

Stand firm now, and we will win!

Truly, your friend,
Lew. Wallace,
Governor New Mexico

INVOLVING COMMANDER HENRY CARROLL

Peripatetically, on March 10, 1879, Lew Wallace wrote two letters to Captain Henry Carroll. The first held his realization that Fort Stanton was not secure for his prisoners. He wrote grandly to Carroll (though they were both at the Fort) about transferring them to Fort Union; apparently forgetting that it was Dudley's past posting as Commander, and site of his stationing after removal; and forgetting that the accused were Dudley's accomplices in Chapman's murder! But the transfer was ignored. To military men, Wallace was a joke. Wallace wrote:

Fort Stanton, N.M., March 10, 1879.
Capt. H. Carroll
Com'g Fort Stanton,
Sir:
Under the circumstances, particularly in the absence of suitable cells for the safekeeping of Jesse Evans, Jacob B. Matthews and William Campbell, charged with the murder of H.I. Chapman, I have to request you to be good enough to send them, securely guarded and with the usual precautions against escape, to Fort Union, and there turn them over to the commanding officer. Enclosed find a request to that officer. The sooner they are gone the better.

Very respectfully,
Your friend & servant,
Lew Wallace,
Gov. New Mexico.

That same March 10th, rushing back to Lincoln, Wallace saw James Dolan, and excitedly wrote his second letter to Captain Carroll to arrange Dolan's apprehension for Chapman's murder. Likely informed, Dolan simply went to Fort Stanton and surrendered, though given free run there. Wallace had written:

Lincoln, N.M., March 10, 1879.
Capt. H. Carroll
Com'g Fort Stanton,
Sir:
J.J. Dolan was down here tonight. Arrest him upon his return to the Fort, and put him in close confinement for the murder of H.I. Chapman. *Respectfully*
Your friend & servant,
Lew Wallace,
Gov. New Mexico.

Though Wallace would boast to Carl Schurz in a March 21, 1879 letter (See my pp. 567-571 for full letter) that his capture of Chapman's killers had a *"moral effect;"* the day before, he had been less sanguine, writing a nervously changed plan on March 11th to beleaguered Captain Carroll not to transfer Evans, Campbell, Matthews, and Dolan to Fort Union. He wrote:

Lincoln, N.M., March 11, 1879.
Capt. Henry Carroll, Com'g Fort Stanton,
Sir: Upon reflection, I am of the opinion that if Col. Dudley is really going to Fort Union, the four prisoners – Evans, Campbell, Matthews and Dolan - had better be kept in close confinement in Fort Stanton. First. They will be less likely to bother us with habeas corpus; Second. The escorts will weaken your detachments for the other proposed duties.
So hold on till you see what the Colonel [Dudley] does – or at least I can see you.
Respectfully,
Your friend,
Lew Wallace,
Gov. New Mexico.

DOLAN MAKES THREATS: MARCH 14th AND 29th, 1879

Though James Dolan was his prisoner for committing murder, with his usual fuzzy thinking, Lew Wallace decided to use him as an informer, as he wrote to Secretary of the Interior Carl Schurz on March 21, 1879: *"Of the same gang is J.J. Dolan; but ... I had hopes that his larger money interests in the county, amounting to $70,000 or $80,000, would make him pliant for use as a witness."* As to being a "pliant," local, vicious, Ring boss Dolan, saw Wallace as the "pliant" dupe. From his Fort Stanton "imprisonment," Dolan manipulated Wallace by letters, mockingly calling him *"Lewis"* and *"friend;"* and indicating chillingly that he was aware of Wallace's day old secret negotiation with Billy - with whom Dolan had himself been negotiating for peace 24 days earlier - thus implying the messengers for letters were spies.

On March 14, 1879, Dolan wrote to Wallace in his big lurid script, based on *"reliable authority."* He was trying to scare snooping Wallace out of Lincoln and away from the Dudley investigation by alluding to a possible attack on the ambulance transporting Wallace from Fort Stanton to Lincoln. But any likely "killers" would be "Dear Ben-style plot" Ringites. Dolan wrote:

Fort Stanton N M
Mc'h 14 1879

Governor Lewis Wallace
    Lincoln, N.M.
Governor: -
    I hear from reliable authority that it has been reported to you that I was one of a party who stopped Your Ambulance the other evening while en route to the plaza [of Lincoln]. Such report is basely false, and I feel confident that it is a ruse resorted to by my treacherous enemies with a view of prejudicing You against me. I Sincerely regret my action, which gave my Enemies the opportunity for the charge, and which they, so promptly, availed themselves of. If You can afford me an opportunity of seeing You, You will please do so, as I am anxious to give You an explanation. This news causes me much uneasiness, and I ask that You give the matter a thorough investigation at Your earliest Convenience. Hoping that you will pardon me for the liberty I take in writing to You, and that I can still look to you as a friend. I remain
        Your humble servant
        Jas. J. Dolan

By March 29, 1879, Dolan mailed a more direct death threat. In fact, by April 25, 1879, in 31 days, Dolan would attempt assassination of Susan McSween's new lawyer, Ira Leonard, in Lincoln - only 66 days after Dolan's point blank shot murdered her past lawyer, Huston Chapman. Now Dolan was trying to make Wallace retreat; while also flattering his ludicrous vanity. As will later be seen from Wallace's late life writings about Billy the Kid, he would rework these Dolan "murder plot" letters - which he kept - as fodder to fabricate the outlaw Billy the Kid's obsession with killing him. Dolan wrote:

Fort Stanton N M
Mc'h 29' 1879

My Dear Governor: -
Attorney [Ringite Sidney] Wilson told me yesterday that Your "life was threatened," and told it in such a manner that I was Compelled to believe that You Considered me the author; and that in Case it should happen, my "life would be taken in one hour after" &c. Governor, I cant believe for a moment that You would do me such an injustice, as to think that I was connected in any way with such threat – And won't, until I see, or hear from You – Still, this news, with my present Condition, and the many rumors about the underhanded work which is going on against me, makes me feel anything but happy.

I don't doubt in the least but what there are bad men roaming over this County that would kill any man, friend or Enemy, should Either be in their way, therefore, You can't be <u>too Careful</u>.

I have good reasons for believing that there are now men in the Plaza, who would kill You in a moment, providing they were certain they Could get away with it, and that I would suffer thereby.

I wish that I could be close to you when those making the threat intended carrying it out, I would try to Convince You that such was not my nature. I sincerely hope that the report will prove without foundation. I don't write this to you as Governor of New Mexico, or with the expectation of its influencing Your Official action toward me in any Manner, whatever. It is simply, because You have Commanded my respect, from the first time we met, that I look upon You as a friend. And it grieves me to think You would give such a report credence.

I learned Yesterday that my Pony had been stolen from the Carriso [Carrizozo] Ranch by the two men who Escaped from here. The Pony is known all through Southern New Mexico as being mine, and when seen with those men [Jessie Evans and Billy Campbell], another report will be circulated that I am aiding them. wishing You success in Your arduous undertaking, I remain
Yours Respectfully
Jas. J. <u>Dolan</u>

ESCAPE OF THE PRISONERS: MARCH 18, 1879

By March 18, 1878, likely surprising no one but Lew Wallace, Jessie Evans and Billy Campbell had "escaped" with help of a Fort Stanton soldier, "Texas Jack," who then deserted. Other likely helpers had real names: "Purington, "Goodwin," "Smith," and "Appel." Dolan had stayed, likely to keep Catron informed by Fort Stanton's telegraph. Wallace missed the omen, but escape of real outlaws boded no justice. Wallace was likely unaware, but since the Ring's 1866 birth, no Ringite had ever been convicted.

On March 19, 1879, Wallace offered a reward of $1,000 for the capture of Evans and Campbell - just like he had with Billy Bonney that February. Tellingly, by 1880, when Pat Garrett tried to collect another Wallace award of $500 for actually capturing Billy, it emerged that they were Wallace's "personal" rewards, and he had no intention of paying. As usual, he was writing fiction.

INVOLVING JAILOR JUAN PATRÓN: MARCH 19, 1879

On March 19th, Wallace sought help from Lincoln Jailor and its Hispanic community leader, Juan Patrón. Wallace wrote:

Lincoln, N.M., March 19, 1879.
Dr.[Dear] Juan Patron.
Sir:
Be good enough to send word to all your men to turn out soon as possible to join in the hunt for Jesse Evans and William [Campbell], who escaped from Fort Stanton last night.
Say to your men that, as Governor of New Mexico, I offer a reward of $1000 for Evans and Campbell.
Lew Wallace.
Gov. New Mexico.

INVOLVING CAPTAIN CARROLL: MARCH 19, 1879

That March 19, 1879, Wallace also wrote again to Captain Henry Carroll, telling him how to use his troops to apprehend escapees Evans and Campbell! Though Wallace had no idea where they were, he had, on his own, sent some cavalrymen - presumably taken from their Lincoln positions - to search along the Ruidoso River. Wallace had retained those troops in Lincoln as part of his "war" on "outlaws." Wallace wrote:

Fort Stanton, N.M., March 19, 1879.
Captain H. Carroll.
Sir:
With Evans and Campbell at large, I suggest it would be advisable to take the infantry detachment from Lincoln. The six cavalry men I sent up the Riodoso [Ruidoso River] in search of the fugitives. Some force should remain in the town.
Respectfully
Your friend & s'v't,
Lew. Wallace,
Gov. New Mexico.

INVOLVING IRA LEONARD: APRIL 9, 1879

By April 9, 1879, Ira Leonard wrote an idealistic letter to Wallace as "savior" to provide information. Leonard wrote:

Lincoln, New Mexico April 9, 1879
Dear Gov.
One Wm Wilson, a saloon keeper & gambler here, furnished a horse for Campbell & Evans and that horse is the one at the Fort that me and the party of soldiers brought in from Evans camp. I ordered or rather advised the Sheriff to arrest Wilson and take him to the Fort as being accessory after the fact to the murder and aiding in the escape of the murderers. I hope it will meet your concurrence as we have got to strike terror into the hearts of these desperados. Have him kept there until the action of the Grand Jury.
I want to see you very much and have a talk about the matters. I have a firm belief that if we had a half dozen good men we

could with the aid they would require drive these fellows all out of the country, in thirty days. I have no faith in the Military too slow and too much red tape. These scoundrels sit on the hills and laugh at them. Dangerous diseases requite heroic treatment that's what is needed now.

Yours &c
Ira E. Leonard

That April 9th, Wallace answered Leonard in a cloud of fantasy, converting the loss of Campbell and Evans into literary drama; and converting Leonard into the disciple of his savior-like martyrdom, stating: "*You have no idea how pleasant it is to have one hearty assistant and sympathizer ... To work trying to do a little good, but with all the world against you, requires the will of a martyr.*" Wallace wrote:

Fort Stanton, April 9, 1879
Hon. I.E. Leonard
Dear Sir:
Your favors both received. The arrest of Wilson was a blow at the right time and in the right direction. There are two other individuals in the Plaza who need close watching. Dr. Guerney and Ballard.

You are right in your heroic treatment of this case. Keep up the application – let us give the fellows no rest.

I felt so sorry for old man Howells that I came near spoiling the cattle broth. I'll set my teeth now.

You have no idea how pleasant it is to have one hearty assistant and sympathizer with my work. To work trying to do a little good, but with all the world against you, requires the will of a martyr.

I have detachments out following Campbell and Evans. Mc[Daniels ?] I feel sure is with them.
Yours truly, Lew. Wallace.

That day, April 9th, Leonard responded he would come to Fort Stanton to meet with Wallace the next day, April 10th, "*if the wind does not blow so I can't.*" Leonard was impeded not only by Wallace, but by his asthma.

PURSUIT OF MYTHICAL OUTLAWS

Though diverted by realities of removing N.A.M. Dudley from Fort Stanton's command, and catching and losing Chapman's killers, Wallace began his war on mythical outlaws on arrival in Lincoln on March 5, 1879. He replaced his first dime novel border-Texan-buffalo-hunting-desperado-rapist-rustler-wrestlers invading the Territory, with Regulators on U.S. Marshall Sherman's October 6, 1878 outlaw list. He left unexplained those men's connection to real Lincoln County War crimes: murdering John Tunstall, Alexander McSween, Harvey Morris, Francisco Zamora, and Vincente Romero; and massacring at San Patricio.

For his ploy, Wallace mimicked his showy, bizarre Zouave costuming for his Civil War troops by decking out his mobilized toy soldier Lincolnites against "outlaws" with flamboyant titles: like: "Cattle Keeper of the County" and "Captain of the Rangers."

He apparently did not realize that his "outlaw" concoction included real Ring rustler-murderers: Seven Rivers boys and John Kinney's gang. But 18 days after Wallace initiated his March 5, 1879 pursuit of fake outlaws in Lincoln County, on March 24, 1878, teenaged Billy Bonney, putting faith in that hypocrite, would, as a favor in an interview, set him straight.

SOLDIERS AGAINST OUTLAWS

GENERAL HATCH AGAINST "OUTLAWS": MARCH 6-7, 1879

Lew Wallace had started pursuing "outlaws" in late February of 1879 from Santa Fe to sham action after Huston Chapman's murder. Then his scapegoats were Billy Bonney "the Kid" and Yginio Salazar. His offered reward was a gigantic $1,000.

On his second day in Lincoln, March 6, 1878, Wallace renewed that chase in a letter to General Edward Hatch. Wallace's chilling callousness is revealed by its stationery. Since his Lincoln abode in José Montaño's house put him across the street from Tunstall's store, he took that dead man's letterhead to write about capturing the men who fought to get justice for his murder.

The letter implies that he used a Ringite spy - likely James Dolan - who disclosed that Billy was with Tom O'Folliard at Yginio Salazar's Las Tablas home. But saying Billy was leaving the Territory was likely Wallace's embellishment to add urgency.

Most important, however, is Wallace's stated reason for their apprehension: as accessories to Chapman's murder! It was Wallace's clever fictional solution to sparing Ringites, and updating his war on outlaws. Wallace wrote:

OFFICE OF
JOHN H. TUNSTALL ,
Lincoln, Lincoln County, New Mexico.

Lincoln, N.M., _____ *187__*

Lincoln, N.M., March 6, 1879.
Gen. Edward Hatch.
Com'g Dist New Mexico.
Sir:
I have just ascertained that "The Kid" is at a place called Las Tablas, a plazita up near Capitan's ranch. He has with him Thomas Folliard [O'Folliard] ~~He was~~ and was going out of the Territory, but stopped there to rest his horses, saying he might stay a few days. He was at the house of one Higinio [Yginio] Salazar.

You will oblige me by sending a detachment after the two men; and if they are caught, securing them in Fort Stanton, for trial as accessories to the murder of Chapman.

If the men are found to have left Las Pablas [Tablas], I beg they may be pursued until caught. The details are commanded to your fort.

I have the honor to be
Your friend and servant
Lew Wallace,
Gov. New Mexico.

That same March 6th, Wallace wrote a second letter to General Hatch about pursuing Regulators Josiah "Doc" Scurlock and Charlie Bowdre. It contains a clue impacting Wallace's pardon bargain with Billy Bonney, 11 days hence. Though still chasing Regulators from his October 6, 1878 Sherman "outlaw" list, he obviously was using a new Ringite source, since he now was able to correct Sherman's misspelling of "Bowdrey" to "Bowdre," as well as knowing about past U.S. Attorney T.B. Catron's federal indictment No. 411 for Andrew "Buckshot" Roberts's killing. That meant that before savvy lawyer Wallace heard from Billy on

March 13, 1879, he knew that Billy's Lincoln County War indictment was immune to gubernatorial pardon! As Wallace made sure to inform Hatch: Scurlock's and Bowdre's arrest warrant was issued from *"the U.S. Court;"* meaning it was a federal case by Catron as U.S. Attorney, not a Territorial one. Pardon could come only from President Hayes. That fact aids analysis as to whether Wallace, from the start, merely played a lawyer's game with Billy by lure of a pardon which he could not grant on a technicality. Wallace wrote:

Lincoln, N.M., March 6, 1879.
Gen. Edward Hatch,
Com'g Dist. New Mexico.

Sir:
I have reliable information that J.G. Scurlock and Charles Bowdre are now at a ranch called Taiban, about twelve miles east of Fort Sumner. **They are parties included in the writ issued by Judge Bristol out of the U.S. Court upon indictment for the murder of Andrew L. Roberts in April 1878.** *Up to this time it has seemed impossible to secure their arrest. But Sheriff Kimbrell having been appointed Deputy U.S. Marshal, and qualified as such, and being now in possession of the writ, and willing to attempt the arrest, I have to request you will send me a detachment (under energetic officer) to accompany him or his deputy in the effort to secure these men. I would suggest that you select a good trailer – an Indian, if possible – and provide the detachment suitably for a long chase. If the officer can come over with his men tonight, I will bring him in communication with a party here who knows the best route to the point indicated.*

I have the honor to be,
Very respectfully,
Your friend & servant
Lew. Wallace,
Gov. New Mexico.

Bemused Hatch, merely tried to switch the quixotic search to Fort Union, and wrote:

Headquarters District of New Mexico

Ft Stanton   Santa Fe N.M. Feby [March?] 7, 1879
Gov Lew Wallace
Lincoln.
Dr Sir
   Mathews has just been sent in. The men Scurlock & Bowdrey at Sumner or reputed there and are probably north of that point, at least 175 miles from here will require more than ordinary preparation for send[ing] should prefer sending troops from Union they would be much more likely to succeed than if sent from here.
   Yours Truly
   Edward Hatch
Mr Watts sends box of cigars and note. E.H.

COMMANDER CARROLL AGAINST "OUTLAWS": MARCH 11, 1879

Undaunted by General Edward Hatch's lack of enthusiasm, Wallace turned to Fort Stanton Commander Henry Carroll, whom he had backed over Captain George Purington to replace Dudley, removed four days earlier. To Carroll, Wallace sent a copy of the October 1878 U.S. Marshal John Sherman "outlaw" list. It should be noted that Wallace's last batch of captives - Evans, Campbell, Matthews and Dolan - were then still at Fort Stanton, where Wallace now wanted to add these men.

Wallace was back to manic fantasizing, including *"Indian trailers"* and outlaws as *"Black Knights."* Wallace wrote:

Lincoln. N.M. March 11, 1879.
   Capt. Henry Carroll,
   Com'g Fort Stanton.
   Sir:
   I beg to submit to you a list of persons whom it is necessary, in my judgment, to arrest speedily as possible, and, until further directions, hold securely in Fort Stanton.
   Your good judgment will inform you how to proceed in the matter. I only suggest great care in the management, as it is more desirable to get the parties named than to run them off.
   The following is the list [Sherman's "outlaw list followed] ...

The accusations against these parties are murder and grand larceny – mostly murder.

I send you a party who knows where most of them can be found, and who will serve you as guide.

Please outfit your detachments for continuous and vigorous work. If you have, or can employ Indian trailers, it will be better.

Push the "Black Knights" and their confederates without rest, and regardless of boundary lines.

I have the honor to be,
Very respectfully,
Your friend,
Lew. Wallace,
Gov. New Mexico"

By the next day, March 12, 1879, Wallace, in full charge at windmills, and his prisoners still held, added to Captain Henry Carroll's work-list rounding up rustlers' rustled cattle. At his most fanciful, Wallace wanted all suspiciously branded or unbranded cattle to be removed from *"camps"* and *"nests"* of *"outlaws"* and somehow all held by homesteader farmer John Newcomb (one of the trackers who found Tunstall's body), to whom Wallace gave the title of "Cattle Keeper of the County." Owners could then claim them. But Wallace was babbling absurdities. Rustled cattle came primarily from John Chisum's herd of 80,000, stretched along the Pecos River, over a hundred miles from Lincoln. When stolen, primarily by the Seven Rivers boys, they were kept at Catron's Pecos River Cow Camp, Catron's Carrizozo Ranch, and Shedds Ranch; or rapidly processed at the slaughterhouse of John Kinney's gang. So Wallace's rustlers accidentally were Ringites. And of the "camps" he wanted searched, the chief repositories were Catron's. Unwitting Wallace wrote:

Lincoln, N.M. March 12. '79.

Capt. Henry Carroll
Com'g Fort Stanton
Sir:

I send you herewith a complete copy of the cattle brands regularly recorded in the Clerk's office of Lincoln county.

The object is to furnish your chiefs of detachments a key in aid of performance of the following instructions, which you will oblige me by giving them, with such other orders in the connection as your experience and judgment will suggest.

Please instruct them:

I. To visit and thoroughly overhaul every cattle-camp, corral and herding place they may hear of in the county of Lincoln.

II. If, at any such camp &c., or elsewhere they find cattle, horses or mules <u>without brands</u>, they will cut all such out, drive them to Lincoln, turn them over to Florencio Gonzales, probate judge of Lincoln county, to be by him turned over to John Newcomb, cattle keeper of the county.

III. If, at any such camp &c., they find any <u>branded cattle</u> &c., they will examine the brands by comparison with the copy of the recorded brands herewith enclosed, to ascertain if the person in whose possession the cattle &c. are found, is the owner of the brand: if, by such comparison, it should appear that any of the brands on the cattle &c. are not his, said person will be required to produce for inspection a certificate of sale, in accordance with the law of the Territory, of which law a copy is also enclosed herewith; if the person cannot produce such bill of sale for the cattle with brands not his own, he will be arrested, brought to Fort Stanton, and there held for trial, and the cattle &c. will be taken, driven to Lincoln, turned over to the Probate judge, to be by him turned over to the Keeper of Cattle for the county.

IV. If they find cattle, horses or mules in possession of any person, the original brand on which has been disfigured, altered or erased, or shall appear to have been so disfigured, altered or erased, the animals will be taken and driven to the Probate judge [at San Patricio Florencio] (Gonzales) to be by him turned over to Keeper Newcomb; and the persons found in possession of such animals will be arrested, carried to Fort Stanton, and there be held for trial.

It is hoped, Captain, by a vigorous execution of the foregoing instructions, all of which are based on the laws of the Territory, to break up the many camps in the county known to be but nests for outlaws and depots of stolen property. The duty will be disagreeable and unusual, but I trust your officers will see both the purpose and the necessity, and enter heartily into the work.

I have the honor to be,
Very respectfully,
Your friend,
Lew. Wallace,
Gov. New Mexico

CITIZENS AGAINST "OUTLAWS

With outrageously narcissistic oblivion, Lew Wallace made Lincoln officials - Justice of the Peace "Squire Wilson, Jailer Juan Patrón, and Sheriff George Kimbrell - pursue Regulators. The first two men were themselves victims of Ring murder attempts. Kimbrell was married to a woman in Picacho, from which some of McSween's fighters came. All considered Regulators as heroes. Wallace's acts may have motivated these men's covert effort, discussed in the next chapter, to save Billy Bonney by a pardon.

JAILOR JUAN PATRÓN AND SHERIFF GEORGE KIMBRELL AGAINST OUTLAWS

Immediately on arriving in Lincoln on March 5, 1879, Lew Wallace hectically handed out his preposterous titles and assignments. Jailor Juan Patrón became "Captain of the Rangers" to capture Regulators. In fact, Patrón had likely survived the Lincoln County War period only because of them. John Riley had already tried to kill him in 1876, soon after the murder of "the House's" other opponent Robert Casey; leaving Patrón a limping cripple. In the Lincoln County War, Patrón had fled to Fort Stanton to avoid being killed, but Commander Dudley almost killed him there. And on the February 18, 1879 night of Huston Chapman's murder, Billy Campbell initially tried to kill Patrón.

All that made horrific Wallace's March 5, 1879 assignment for Patrón to capture last Regulator leader: "Doc" Scurlock; and Charlie Bowdre, a past farmer neighbor of the Coes, and John Tunstall's past employee. Unlike Regulators John Middleton, Jim "Frenchie" French, Fred Waite, and Henry Brown, these men had refused to flee the Territory. Noteworthy is that Wallace staying next door to Patrón in Jose Montaño's house, pompously used a messenger to take his letter from door to door. Wallace wrote:

> Lincoln, N.M., March 5, 1879.
> Captain Juan Patron.
> Sir:
> Please select ten of your Rangers, make the necessary preparation, and set out quickly as possible to arrest Scurlock and Bowdrey [Bowdre], who are thought to be at a ranch 10 or 12 miles east of old Fort Sumner. Use your best endeavor to accomplish the purpose.

> *Take the old dry trail north of the plaza, travel in the night time, lying over in cover during the day. Avoid persons and houses on the way. Strike the Pecos at some point north of Sumner and approach the ranch from that direction.*
>
> > *Respectfully*
> > *Your friend,*
> > *Lew. Wallace,*
> > *Gov. New Mexico.*

That March 5th, Wallace sent a second letter to Patrón about using Sheriff George Kimbrell, Sheriff George Peppin's replacement, on the same hated mission. Wallace wrote:

> *Lincoln, N.M., March 5, 1879.*
> *Captain Juan Patron.*
> *Sir:*
> *Please report to Sheriff Kimbrell, who has instructions relative to the use of your Company, which will be under his direction during my absence.*
> *Read his instructions that you may understand them thoroughly.*
>
> > *Respectfully*
> > *Your friend,*
> > *Lew. Wallace,*
> > *Gov. New Mexico.*

Patrón kept his feelings to himself, but, as will be seen in the next chapter, he was by then plotting with Justice of the Peace "Squire" Wilson the pardon plan for Billy Bonney. As Wallace's "Captain of the Rangers," Patrón feigned compliance.

By March 29, 1879, Patrón had already taken Billy into his home for the pardon bargain's sham arrest. On that day, Patrón wrote Wallace two letters. As will be seen in the next chapter, he was sharing their fancy embossed stationery with Billy to write one of his own pardon letters to Wallace!

It must have been obvious to anyone in Lincoln that Patrón would capture no Regulator "outlaws;" though he did try to apprehend Evans and Campbell after their "escape." Patrón wrote:

Lincoln, N.M.
March 29, 1879

His Exc. Gov. Lew Wallace,
Fort Stanton, N. Mex.
Sir:
Lieutenant Martin Sanches arrived this afternoon, and could not find the parties he was after. The "parties" suspected were peaceful miners.

Our horses are in very poor condition, hardly able to walk. We have no new information of the whereabouts of the outlaws.
Expecting your orders, I remain
Very respectfully,
Juan B. Patron

****

Lincoln, N.M.
March 29, 1879

His Exc. Lew Wallace,
Governor of New Mexico
Dear Sir: I am in receipt of yours of this date.
I will immediately send a party of men as you direct.
Sanches came in this afternoon and was unsuccessful in his expedition.
We have no clue as to the whereabouts of Evans or Campbell.
Everything is quiet down here.
Truly Yours,
Juan B. Patron

JUSTICE OF THE PEACE WILSON AGAINST OUTLAWS

As insensitive as involving Juan Patrón, was Wallace's assignment of "outlaw" apprehension to equally traumatized Justice of the Peace "Squire" Wilson. The year before, Wilson had been removed from office by then Governor S.B. Axtell to shield Tunstall's Ring killers from his warrants. If Wallace had paused to think, that was Axtell's illegal act which led to his removal and to his own governorship appointment! Wilson had also gotten a death threat from Commander Dudley on the last day of the Lincoln County War battle to force his writing illegal warrants against Alexander McSween and Billy Bonney.

Wilson wrote an undated page for Wallace about cattle holdings and outlawry. Wallace wrote on its bottom: *"Paper from Sqr. Wilson."* Wilson, not the most literate man, wrote:

Nash has about 120 head in with Paxton and Pearce dont know his Brand Buck Powel & Raynor also has about 300 head in the herd of Paxton & Pearce Brand Figure 9 probably on Left side & hip that is all in the teritory Just over the line in texas Beckwith creling & olinger have about 1400 Head all together Beckwiths Brand RB connected on Left hip creling & olinger AHB connected on Left side the Jones Boys have some cattle on the west side of the River about Popes crossing dont know many some Branded [gives drawn symbols] Speaks & others Have some of tunstalls cattle

[On the reverse side, Wilson wrote]:

Chisums herd about 1200 Head Range from 12 mile Bend to Good Bend distance about 50 miles Roil & others But Roil principal Business in charge of Herd
Vonsuikel Herd camp at Bosque Grandy about 350 head Brand V on shoulder it on side N̶ N on hip known as the copelarys cattle __ Thomas Gardners Herd Seven Rivers about 140 Head Y Believe on side & hip ___ Paxton & Pierces Herd about 900 Brand P on side & hip _____

Probable fighting men John Jones Jim Jones Bil Jones George Davis Mron Turner Bob Speaks Gunter John Smith or Silton & tom cat or Silvan & that is all I know about Seven Rivers that are Desperate men

On April 8, 1879, Wilson initialed a one-page letter warning to Wallace about assassination rumors. In fact, the intended next victim was Ira Leonard. Wilson wrote:

Lincoln april 8th 79
Dear Governer Wallace
<u>it is said that G Pepin told a mexican that the</u> ~~of a~~ <u>pimping</u> *Governer thought Himself safe at town. But the first thing He knew He would Be killed & then the other officers of such as sheriff & probate & Justices could easily Be Done away With So you can se what they are after Be very careful about yourself*

also said you Would not Be attacked on the Road when you had an escort But in town   *confidential*
Yours in truth
JBW

DEPUTY SHERIFF ROBERT GILBERT AGAINST OUTLAWS

Sheriff George Kimbrell's deputy, Robert M. Gilbert, also got Wallace's "outlaw" assignment. Gilbert had been on John Tunstall's coroner's jury, so he knew Ring terrorism from the start. In his June 1, 1879 letter to Wallace, he was less diplomatic than Juan Patrón, making clear that Ringites blocked him from arresting Lincoln County War criminals. This was a reality that Wallace did not want to hear. It was ignored. Gilbert wrote:

Lincoln N.M
June 1st 1879

Hon Lew Wallice: got
Sante Fea N.M
        Dear sir I drop you a few lines relative to some matters in our county affairs I was call on by Kimbrell the sheriff to go up to Fort Stanton and make arrest on Mailon Pierce Joseph Nash Wallice Olinger Robert Olinger Marion Turner and Andrew Boyle [Seven Rivers boys] and on arriving att *at the commanders quarters was informed by the commanders wife that he was very sick suffering with* nucla *neralga I said that I wanted to see him that I was Deputy Sheriff Gilbert she then said that she would see him and I remained on side of the house for some time and then she came out and asked me what I wanted I said to her I wanted a posse of 5 or 6 men to arrest some men in the post for whome I had warrants for and I wanted the men quick and if the commander pleased to attend to my wants soon so in a few minutes the commander Capt Purington came out and asked me who I had warrants for in the Post I said the warrants were issued from the district court he then asked me to let him see the warrants I says as you are commander of the post I have no objection and handed the warrants to him and he remarked that Judge Warren Bristol promised that these warrants should not be sent here and asked how I got them I said they were put in my hands by Sheriff Kimbrell then he stated that I would have to wait untill the court of enquiry broke up so that he could see Judge Waldo. so in a*

course of time Waldo came and in a few minutes he said make out the requisition and mention the names of all that you want to arrest I said is that really necessary and he said yes that he would not give a posse to arrest himself then I said I would make it out and did giving the above names and gave it to him and seeing Turners name said why did you not showe me the warrant for Turner before I said I did not think of it or did not think it any use he then asked me for the warrant and I said to him that it was isued from Justice court he then remarke that I could have men to arrest under Justices warrant then I said give me the posse and I will leave Turner out he then sent for the posse after nearly 2 hours delay and when the posse came he instructed them not to assist in arresting Mr Turner but assist in arresting the others so I went in search for the men found Mr Pierce and arrested such and no persons els for a while finally Turner came out cursing me and saying that I had no posse to arrest him and d-d your old soul you cant arrest me I then threw my gun on him and said I will show you and did and conducted him and Pierce to the guard house and released the possee the commander said to me that some person *had come up from Lincoln and had* told the bo*ys that there was warrants out for them I supposed it was the account of not more than two being found and my previously wanting to be in a hurry to make the arrest and stating that the parties may leave which he said they would not! so I went back up to the Settlers store and found Andrew boil [Boyle] and started to make an arrest on him and he said that he protested the arrest as he had a summons from the United States I said that did not make any difference do you resist the arrest and at the time Judge Waldo stepted up to me and said do you not know how to arrest a man and slaped me on the shoulder and said that is way which I did the same to Boile [Boyle] and said go with me at which time boile [Boyle] rose and started along with me when Waldo remarked to me that he would have me punished for contempt of court I remarked that I cannot help it I had already made the arrest and walked on with the prisner down to the commanding quarters and delivered Mr Boil [Boyle] at this time waldo came and said that he was attorney gen of the Ter and why did I not ask him for advise I said that I did not even know that you were attorney gen of the Ter then some one present said why did you not see a lawyer concerning the arresting these men and I stated that I counseled with lawyers and Dondly remarked that Judge Leonard was no lawyer I mentioned no names of lawyers of any person* **Judge Waldo read some law stating very**

clearly that no arrest could be made on witnesses during their attendance on courts to and from and that I had better releace the prisners that I had arrested belonging to the court of enquiry and stated that he would releace them the next day before the court though he would not advise me to releace them in any way that their being confined in prison some person would suffer for it so then I wrote out a releace and let them loos I think that this militia in this county ought to be stronger and more active the long expected escort came in today for the scout down the river and has capt carrol orders not to assist in rounding up cattle nor holding them nor to make any arrest were there is no sheriff only to guard prisners very scrct orders Capt Carrol seems to in good spirits do all you can for this part of the county and as speedy as possible   R.M. Gibert
Deputy Sheriff
Lincoln county. N M

INDIANS AGAINST "OUTLAWS": MARCH 12, 1879

By March 12, 1879, Lew Wallace's "outlaw" solution inflated to using Native Americans as trackers, as in the Indian Wars. So he turned astoundingly to Mescalero Indian Reservation Agent Frederick Godfroy, who, as Investigator Frank Warner Angel, in his October 2, 1878 "Examination of charges against F.C. Godfroy, Indian Agent, Mescalero, N.M." had already reported, was guilty of defrauding the U.S. government in collusion with "the House" by providing the Reservation with mealy flour and stolen cattle for beef. Godfroy, a cog in Catron's intended cattle monopoly in Lincoln County, must have been amused by Wallace's absurdity of stating to him: "*I recognize, of course, that you are officially interested in putting a stop quickly as possible to the lawlessness now prevalent.*" Wallace wrote:

Lincoln, March 12, 1879,
Major F.C. Godfroy,
Agt. Mescalero Apaches.
Dear Sir:
You can be of the greatest possible help to me in the effort now making to catch the thieves and murderers in this part of the Territory, by allowing the military through whom I [am] trying to operate, the assistance of some of your Indians as guides to detachments – say ten men in all.

I respectfully request your friendly co-operation in that way and to that extent.

If the proposal is agreeable, please direct Romain Chiquit, the sub-chief, to report with guides to Capt. Carroll, at the Fort, ready to set out immediately.

I recognize, of course, that you are officially interested in putting a stop quickly as possible to the lawlessness now prevalent.

Very respectfully,
Your friend,
Lew. Wallace,

WALLACE FEIGNS FACT-FINDING

Lew Wallace further misled Lincolnites as to action by fact-finding interviews. Billy Bonney himself would volunteer for one on March 23, 1879, and add to it by a letter the next day.

"DEPOSITION" OF JUSTICE OF THE PEACE WILSON

"Squire" Wilson must have believed he finally got a hearing for his Lincoln County War liturgy of crimes and traumas in what Wallace represented to him as a deposition; though, in fact, it was not signed, dated, or notarized. And when Wallace was questioned in the Dudley Court of Inquiry, he had no memory of specifics from these interviews, which had likely bored him by being too close to the realities he was trying to avoid. It stated:

> *Territory of New Mexico*
> *County of Lincoln*
> *Before me the undersigned authority personally came and appeared John Wilson who after being duly sworn according to law deposeth and saith*
> *That he is a duly elected Justice of the Peace in Precinct No. 1 in Lincoln County New Mexico and that he was ordered by Col Dudley Commanding Fort Stanton in New Mexico on or about the 19th of July 1878 to take the affidavits of Col Purington, Capt Blair and Dr Appel accusing A.A. McSween and others that was in his house on July 16th 1878 of having committed an assault on the person of one Berry Robinson a Soldier of Fort Stanton by having*

shot 4 or more shots at him with intent to kill as they had been informed and believed.

I told Col Dudley that I was not certain whether it was lawful for me to issue such an order or not and I thought it was the duty of a United States commissioner to issue it as there was a Soldier concerned in it and he got very angry at me for refusing to issue it on that ground and told me if I did not take the affidavits and issue the warrant forthwith that he would put me in double irons and would report me to the Governor and he called me a coward and said many other bad words to me

I then went to my office and took the affidavits of the above named Officers as aforesaid and after they signed and swore to it I issued the warrant to the Sheriff of Lincoln County for the arrest of A.A. McSween and others that was in the house on the 16th of July 1878 as per affidavit and gave it to George W. Peppin to serve returnable forthwith and said warrant has not been returned to my office up to this date by Peppin or any other person for him **I did not issue said warrant by my own will but by the preemptory order of Col Dudley** he Dudley coming in person to my office before I had it ready and told me I was not trying to issue the warrant in a hurry as it was my duty to do Col Dudley was the only person that appeared to be so much interested in the issue of the warrant I was not ordered or solicited by any other person but by Col Dudley to issue the warrant above mentioned for the arrest of McSween and others **to the best of my knowledge Col Dudley was sure desirous to have McSween and parties arrested than all the others.** Parties that was in Lincoln at the time not even the Sheriff asked me to issue the warrant I give it to the Sheriff without him asking me for it I further state that Col Dudley camped ~~his~~ with his command about 30 yds north east of the house of Jose Montaño in Lincoln and planted a cannon about 15 yds from the front and pointing towards said house and **told a woman that understood English to tell the people in the house that if there was a shot fired out of the house over his Soldiers that he would fire on the house with the cannon which was pointed at the house at the time**

Col Dudley stopped in Lincoln with his command until after McSween's house was burnt and McSween and others killed then left with his command for Fort Stanton leaving 3 soldiers at [Saturnino] Baca's house [Ringite resident in Lincoln] to protect Baca's family.

"DEPOSITION" OF ISAAC ELLIS

Minor merchant Isaac Ellis and his family lived at the far northeast side of Lincoln. In the Lincoln County War's battle, McSweens were stationed there, but fled when Dudley arrived. Ellis's "deposition" described specific war horrors: Dudley entering with artillery; his intervening for the Peppin side; his threatening Ellis with the destruction of his house - even with its women and children inside; Peppin's possemen stealing coal oil kerosene from him to burn down McSween's house around its trapped people; and the ensuing slaughter of those fleeing. It stated:

Territory of New Mexico
  County of Lincoln
  Before me the undersigned authority personally came and appeared Isaac Ellis personally known to me as such. Who being duly sworn according to law deposeth and saith to wit,
  That the deponent is a Merchant of the Town of Lincoln County of Lincoln Territory of New Mexico. That on or about the 17th of July 1878 Sheriff Peppins and Posse attacked the Town of Lincoln, and kept up firing from the neighboring hills until the morning of the 19th when Lieut Col N.A.M. Dudley with Capt George Purington Capt Blair Lieut Goodwin and Dr Appell [Appel] of Fort Stanton with a company of Soldiers and 2 pieces of Artillery [howitzer cannon and Gatling gun] arrived here, and went into camp about the center of Town, and sent for the deponent me, and when I arrived at his camp he seemed to be greatly excited.
  *When I was informed by said Col Dudley that **if a gun was fired out of mine or any house in Town he would immediately tear it to the ground regardless of women and children** and while [I was] at the camp of Col N.A.M. Dudley the socalled Sheriff George W. Peppin came riding into camp with 3 Soldiers and I think Peppin was riding a Government Horse and after talking a short time with said Dudley, Dudley order[ed] the Soldiers to go back with sheriff Peppin. I then returned to my house. the said Dudley set one piece of artillery about 200 feet from and pointing towards my house **in a short time the Said Peppin together with about nine men came from the direction of the camp of said Dudley and came in my house and ordered me to give them coal oil [kerosene] for which they stated they intended to use in setting fire to the house of A.A. McSween. they further stated that they had him in the house and*

intended to burn him out They took the coal oil with them and went back, when opposite the camp Dudley came out and they Dudley and Peppin talked for some time. they went on towards the house of A.A. McSween and in a little while firing commenced around McSweens and we soon saw smoke arise and firing was kept up until about nine oclock at night

the following morning McSween with three others [Harvey Morris, Francisco Zamora, Vincente Romero] was found dead in the yard riddled with bullets and said house and contents totally destroyed by fire

and the same morning the store of John H. Tunstall decd was broke open and robed of about Six Thousand Dollars worth of Goods. after the Store was rob, Col Dudley broke up camp and returned to Fort Stanton

"DEPOSITION" OF SAM CORBET

Sam Corbet had been John Tunstall's shopkeeper. He would have experienced the illegal, brutal property attachment there by Sheriff Brady as prelude to Tunstall's murder. In the Lincoln County War's battle, a few McSweens occupied the store, with Dr. Taylor Ealy and his family being in Tunstall's apartment. Corbet describes the next day's looting of the store, enabled by Sheriff Peppin and Commander Dudley. Corbet stated:

Territory of New Mexico
County of Lincoln
Before me the undersigned authority personally came and appeared Samuel R. Corbet well known to me to be such. That the deponent was clerking in the Store belonging to the Estate of John H. Tunstall until it was broken open and robbed of its entire contents, and since that time has been clerking for Isaac Ellis & Sons Merchants of the Town of Lincoln County of Lincoln Territory of New Mexico ... about 9 oclock in the morning [of July 20th, after the killing of McSween and others the day before] I went to the Store and found Sheriff Peppin and about eight of his posse in the Store. I spoke to Sheriff Peppin and asked him if he could not stop the men from taking the Goods out of the Store, and he told me that he was not responsible for nothing and went out. Col Dudley was in the store and saw men carrying out goods he walk out with Peppin and they talked a while in the street. the same day Col Dudley with his command went back to Ft Stanton.

DUDLEY REQUESTS A COURT OF INQUIRY

On March 13, 1879 - the same day Billy Bonney sent his pardon plea letter - a new crisis of reality ensued for Lew Wallace. It began by removed Commander N.A.M. Dudley requesting the Adjutant General in Washington, D.C. to grant him a military court of inquiry *"to clear his name"* from its besmirching by the Governor. Wallace would be forced to testify against Dudley to justify himself. The worst scenario that Wallace could conceive had come to pass. And unbeknownst to him, that Court would be intentionally delayed till May to ensure availability of its chief judge: Colonel Galusha Pennypacker from Fort Union, Dudley's best friend from his service there. Dudley wrote:

Fort Stanton, New Mexico
March 10th via Mesilla
March 13, 1879

To Adjutant General – Army
Washington, D.C.

Notwithstanding decision of the Honorable Secretary of war Colonel Hatch has relieved me of command – Fort Stanton, ordered me to Fort Union to await orders , on request of Governor Wallace, accompanied by statement charging me with complicity of murder of McSween and others.
I have offered to refute at once every one of the allegations, but have been positively refused the opportunity to do so. Neither of these parties have given me the slightest chance to explain my act. I am disgraced without a hearing and deprived of even preparing a defense.
General Hatch states to an officer before leaving post today, he did not believe Governor Wallace could sustain his allegations against me. I respectfully ask Court of Inquiry to meet without delay at Stanton to thoroughly investigate my conduct, also for authority to remain here until Court meets.
I believe my defense would be seriously prejudiced by my going to Union.
Answer by telegraph to Mesilla, N.M.
                                    Dudley

CHAPTER 15

BILLY BONNEY'S PARDON BARGAIN WITH LEW WALLACE: MARCH 13-20, 1879

LIFE TRAJECTORIES INTERSECT

ANALYSIS: The outcome of Billy Bonney's pardon bargain to Governor Lew Wallace depended on political and psychological factors beyond their control, and would alter both their lives: yielding Billy's death and Wallace's guilt-ridden obsession.

When the lives of Billy Bonney and Lew Wallace first crossed on March 13, 1879, Billy was recently 19, and Wallace almost 52. Each was in desperate crisis. Billy, in little over a year, had lost a law-abiding life as a ranch owner and protégé of John Tunstall to become a hunted outcast. Wallace, intending fleeting sojourn in a backwater governorship, was mired in a military crisis that risked his future and flashed back to his Shiloh debacle. Each saw the other as famous, and needed the other. Risking hanging, Billy needed a pardon to free himself from Ring prosecution. Wallace needed to prove pacification of the Territory to escape its political quagmire into reward of an exotic ambassadorship.

From opposite ends of the social spectrum, they were surprisingly similar. Both longed for unattained fatherly love, both had lost young mothers to T.B., both were cast out too early and too harshly from home. Billy, though born in New York City, had an Indiana childhood as did Wallace. Both felt wrongly outlawed, Billy by the Ring for rebelling, Wallace by General Grant for Shiloh. Both had survived life's adversities by boundless energy, intellectual brilliance, multiple talents, tenacity, and bravado. Both were, at that moment, the most charismatic and unusual people in the Territory. Their relationship would be a failure. Its result would have surprised them both: Billy's long-range fame would far eclipse Wallace's; and, after elapse of generations, Billy would become the person who could finally break the Santa Fe Ring.

By offering his pardon bargain to Lew Wallace, Billy did not know that he was heading into true tragedy - where the only possible outcome is personal disaster, because all avenues of success were politically and psychologically blocked.

THE PARDON SCHEME

ANALYSIS: *My authentication of the "Billie" letter fragment as being authored by Billy Bonney, proved that his pardon request to Governor Lew Wallace was backed as an anti-Ring endeavor by Justice of the Peace "Squire" Wilson, Jailor Juan Patrón, and Sheriff George Kimbrell. Evidence also points to Wallace making an ambiguous bargain to get Billy's testimony against Huston Chapman's killers, while delaying action to assess his personal risk from pardoning a Ring enemy. Wallace's decision was crystallized by coincidence: the outcome of the Dudley Court of Inquiry as being a Ring victory.*

The pardon bargain was simple: Billy Bonney approached Governor Lew Wallace; an apparent savior, then in Lincoln, hearing hopeful citizens' Lincoln County War grievances. Billy offered to trade his eye-witness testimony in 1879's April Grand Jury against Huston Chapman's murderers for a gubernatorial pardon for his Lincoln County War indictments for Regulator killings of Sheriff William Brady; Deputy Sheriff George Hindman; and murder posseman, Andrew "Buckshot" Roberts.

In my 2011 book, *Billy the Kid's Writings, Words, and Wit*, I added a new perspective to that pardon bargain, which Billy first presented Wallace by a letter on about March 13, 1879. In the past, the pardon request was seen as solely Billy's. But my authentication of a new Billy the Kid letter for that book justified a new hypothesis. That new letter, likely written on March 24, 1879, was on expensive stationery, uniquely embossed with a Lady Liberty symbol. Billy would have had no access to it. But in Lincoln at that time, his freedom fighting, public official partisans, Justice of the Peace "Squire" Wilson and jailor Juan Patrón, were using it for their own letters to Wallace. My conclusion was that they gave it to their homeless hero of the Lincoln County War to make the best possible presentation to the Governor.

Going further, I asserted that Wilson, Patrón, and Sheriff Kimbrell were secretly assisting Billy with the pardon plan itself. As discussed in the past chapter, all had personally experienced Ring oppression and horrors of the Lincoln County War. Moreover, unlike most Regulators, Billy had refused to leave the Territory. If they could free him from his Lincoln County War indictments, he was a potential leader in their ongoing Anglo-Hispanic struggle against the Santa Fe Ring.

Furthermore, Billy had already courageously proved his anti-Ring commitment in presence of Wilson and Patrón. On February 19, 1878, he had given an eye-witness affidavit to Justice of the Peace Wilson about John Tunstall's murder; as a Deputy Town Constable, he had tried to serve the Tunstall murder warrants in company of Patrón and a citizens' committee, and had been illegally arrested by Sheriff Brady; he was on Dick Brewer's posse to apprehend Tunstall's killers; he had risked his life on June 6, 1878 by coming to Lincoln after Governor Axtell's Regulator outlawing to give Investigator Frank Warner Angel a deposition about Tunstall's murder; and he had participated in all Regulator skirmishes. In the Lincoln County War, he had defended McSween. Now he had eye-witness evidence against Huston Chapman's assassins: James Dolan, Billy Campbell, and Jessie Evans. And in the April 1879 Lincoln Grand Jury he intended to testify also against N.A.M. Dudley and George Peppin for the Lincoln County War battle's murders and arson; as he would testify the next month in Fort Stanton's Court of Inquiry against Dudley. And Wilson, Patrón, and Kimbrell knew that Billy was no "outlaw" matching Wallace's mythology.

Furthermore, Regulator victims were all Ringites; hated by Wilson, Patrón, and Kimbrell for their crimes. And the Ring's murder victims had gotten no justice: John Tunstall, Dick Brewer, Frank MacNab, Alexander McSween, Harvey Morris, Vincente Romero, Francisco Zamora, and those massacred in San Patricio. There was no doubt to men like Wilson, Patrón, and Kimbrell that freedom fighting Billy deserved a pardon.

The actions of Wilson, Patrón, and Kimbrell bear out their active and protective intent. Besides supplying stationery and likely encouragement, Wilson hosted the secret nighttime meeting of Billy and Wallace on March 17, 1879 in his Lincoln house, and would have witnessed the pardon bargain. Though Wallace denied for decades making the bargain, in a 1902 newspaper article he reversed, stating in that meeting he had promised Billy "a pardon in his pocket" for testifying. And, with Wilson as go-between, Billy next planned a sham arrest with Wallace, Kimbrell, and Patrón to avoid being killed by the Ring as a witness-in-waiting. Then, Sheriff Kimbrell personally accompanied Billy from "arrest" in San Patricio to Lincoln. But being jailed there meant being held in its dreaded pit jail - so vulnerable to assassinations that Deputy Sheriff Adolph Barrier had kept Alexander McSween in personal custody, rather than let him be put there. So Patrón, as Jailor, protected Billy by offering his own home as "jail." And he housed Billy there like a family member for three months.

All that only magnifies the tragedy to come for Billy Bonney. There is no indication that Wallace was committed to the pardon. He had U.S. Attorney Catron's federal indictment for the Andrew "Buckshot" Roberts killing, requiring presidential pardon; unlike the Territorial indictments for the Brady and Hindman killings. And it appears that Billy's cocky attitude of being an equal to any man stimulated competitive and sadistic feelings in Wallace, who required adulation - even from his wife and son. But most of all, the Ring could not tolerate a pardon of their last remaining adversary, who could renew the anti-Ring rebellion.

But in March of 1879, amidst public excitement of Wallace's glamorous prancing about town and making show of seeking justice, there was no way for Billy or his backers to anticipate being duped. But once that became obvious, months hence, Billy's backers would retreat for the rest of their lives into silence. Billy would ultimately face the Ring unpardoned and alone, but defiant.

PARDON BARGAIN IN THE FIRST LETTER TO LEW WALLACE: MARCH 13, 1879

There was reason for Billy Bonney to trust Lew Wallace. Wallace represented the Regulator's only Lincoln County War victory: removal of Ringite Governor Samuel Beach Axtell. It was reasonable to assume that Wallace was sympathetic to, and versed in, the issues that had made him a mid-term replacement.

Since Billy's prior indictments for Brady, Hindman, and Roberts excluded him from Wallace's Amnesty Proclamation, he sought their pardon. Just 23 days after Huston Chapman's killing, on about March 13, 1879, he wrote to Wallace proposing his testifying as an eye-witness against the murderers in exchange for an annulling of his Lincoln County War indictments. Noteworthy is that Billy wrote *"annuly"* - to mean annul. That was technically correct legally; a pardon being granted after a sentencing, not before. That may represent Justice of the Peace Wilson's input.

Billy's letter was breathtakingly audacious and egalitarian. Undeniably, he felt Wallace's equal. Even Wallace's son Henry, then 26, did not feel that! As to Wallace's huge reward of $1,000 - presumably dead or alive - Billy airily dismissed it as negotiable; rewording it as, *"which as I can understand it means alive as a witness,"* to segue into his bargain's terms: exchanging his testimony for the annulling! And Billy's brilliance was obvious. He was no ordinary "outlaw." His fine Spencerian penmanship, and correct spelling of even *"indictments"* must have surprised Wallace. But unspoken were Billy's optimism that Wallace was a gateway to Regulator victory; and Billy's courage in facing betrayal, arrest, and hanging instead of just fleeing the Territory.

A subtlety is Billy's possible reference to his anti-Ring helpers. He writes: *"[A]s to my Character I refer to any of the Citizens, for the majority of them are my Friends and have been helping me all they could."* More poignant is his tentative reaching out to another father-figure after his loss of Tunstall, McSween, and Chapman: *"I am called Kid Antrim but Antrim is my stepfathers name."* He was available for adoption as "Bonney!"

And Wallace, wallowing in eight days of Lincolnites' dreary plebian complaining; and pressured by six days of fall-out from removing Dudley, was suddenly offered a solution to his Chapman crisis wrapped in romance of an outlaw boy of the wild frontier. And the accused murderers were already held at Fort Stanton.

So Wallace must have checked around little Lincoln about this W.H. Bonney. Assumedly, the traumatized citizens - having three murdered mutilated bodies in a year (Tunstall, McSween, and Chapman) and a battle with terrorist military intervention - were reticent. More talkative would have been smug Ring-partisans like Saturnino Baca and Edgar Walz to whom "the Kid" was indeed their "outlaw." And those sly Ringites would not hesitate to accuse Billy, not the accused, of Chapman's murder! Wallace would need to sort it all out, the exact task he had hoped to avoid in his assigned Territorial pacification mission.

Billy wrote, without dating, on about March 13, 1879:

> *To his Excellency the Governor.*
> *General Lew. Wallace*
> *Dear Sir I have heard that You will give one thousand $ dollars for my body which as I can understand it means alive as a witness. I know it is as a witness against those that murdered Mr. Chapman. if it was so as that I could appear at Court, I could give the desired information. but I have indictments against me for things that happened in the late Lincoln County War and am afraid to give up because my Enimies would Kill me. the day Mr. Chapman was murderded I was in Lincoln, at the*

request of good citizens to meet Mr. J. J. Dolan to meet as Friends. So as to be able to lay aside our arms and go to Work. I was present when Mr. Chapman was murderded and know who did it and if it were not for these indictments I would have made it clear before now. if it is in your power to Annully those indictments I hope you will do so so as to give me a chance to explain. please send me an annser telling me what you can do. You can send annser by bearer.

I have no wish to fight any more indeed I have not raised an arm since Your proclamation. as to my Character I refer to any of the Citizens, for the majority of them are my Friends and have been helping me all they could. I am called Kid Antrim but Antrim is my stepfathers name.
Waiting for an annser I remain
Your Obedient Servant
W.H. Bonney

WALLACE'S RESPONSE: MARCH 15, 1879

On March 15, 1879, Lew Wallace, in full authoritarian stance, responded to Billy as the wily attorney who had succeeded in hanging John Wilkes Booth's innocent landlady, Mrs. Surratt. Wallace was leaving open getting the boy's testimony, then hanging him as a trophy in his war against "outlaws." Pompously, Wallace even gave Billy directions around Lincoln: the town Billy obviously knew well, having been a Tunstall employee there and fighting in its War's battle eight months earlier. And Wallace insultingly linked him to outlaw Jessie Evans, one of Tunstall's and Chapman's killers.

Much more ominous was Wallace's lawyer's trick: feigning a pardon bargain by saying: *"I have the authority to exempt you from prosecution, if you will testify to what you say you know."* Wallace may *"have the authority,"* but he is not saying he will use it to pardon Billy! It should also be recalled, that Wallace was a professional writer, able to state clearly his intent. Further pointing to willful deceit, is Wallace's knowledge, as discussed above, of U.S. Attorney Catron's federal warrant for the Roberts killing. It meant that, as a Territorial official, Wallace *did not* have authority to pardon Billy. Only President Hayes could pardon a federal offence.

I take this as proof that Wallace, even at the start, had minimal intent to pardon Billy; and was merely setting a trap to capture him, and later decide his fate; while he awaited further development of Ring successes or defeats. Wallace wrote:

Lincoln, March 15, 1879.
W.W. Bonney.
   Come to the house of Old Squire Wilson (not the lawyer [Sidney Wilson]) at nine (9) o'clock next Monday night alone. I don't mean his office, but his residence. Follow along the foot of the mountain south of the town, come in at that side, and knock on the east door. ***I have the authority to exempt you from prosecution, if you will testify to what you say you know.***
   The object of the meeting at Squire Wilson's is to arrange the matter in a way to make your life safe. To do that the utmost secrecy is to be used. So come alone. Don't tell anybody - not a living soul - where you are coming or the object. If you could trust Jesse Evans, you can trust me.
Lew Wallace

LEGAL IMPLICATIONS OF THE BARGAIN

With their letters of March 13(?)th and 15th, Billy and Wallace had put the pardon bargain in writing, formalizing it legally. The question is: Did Wallace have legal justification to deviate after accepting the linking of exemption from prosecution to fulfilling its one condition: "*if you will testify to what you say you know.*"

Firstly, Wallace told the truth about his Territorial "authority" to pardon, as stated in 1897's *Compiled Laws of New Mexico*. That Wallace used their earlier version as a reference is shown in his March 21, 1879 letter to Carl Schurz, stating: "*To reach them ... I based a plan upon the law of the Territory regulating brands for animals. You will find the Acts in the Compiled Laws page 52.*" As to pardon, Section 3457 of the *Compiled Laws* stated:

> Any person **against whom prosecution shall have been commenced** under the laws of this territory for an offence against the law, **any such person may be surrendered or not surrendered, at the discretion of the governor**, before he shall have been tried or set at liberty, or if he shall be sentenced or punished for the same.

Wallace lacked legal justification to escape his agreement, despite his manipulatively ambiguous wording; because it was validated by accepted intent, and tit-for-tat expectation. The 1999 edition of *Black's Law Dictionary* states as to "agreement":

> **agreement.** 1. A mutual understanding between two or more persons about their relative rights and duties regarding past or future performances; a manifestation of mutual assent by two or more persons. 2. The parties' actual bargain as found in their language or by implication from other circumstances, including course of ... performance. (p. 67)

As to a "bargain," *Black's Law Dictionary* states:

> **bargain,** *n.* An agreement between parties for the exchange of promises or performances. (p. 143)

Also, layman Billy would have seen Wallace's March 15th letter as a "promise." In his March 4, 1881 letter to Wallace from the Santa Fe jail, Billy wrote: *"I have done everything that I promised you I would, and You have done nothing that You promised me."* As to a "promise," *Black's Law Dictionary* states:

> **promise,** *n.* 1. The manifestation of an intention to act ... in a specified manner, conveyed in such a way that another is justified in understanding that a commitment has been made; a person's assurance that the person will ... do something. (p. 1229)

That concept of "promise" was strengthened by its intertwined mutuality: i.e.; if I do this, you will do that. *Black's Law Dictionary* states:

> **mutual promises.** Promises given simultaneously by two parties, each promise serving as consideration for the other (p. 1230); [with "consideration" being] "an act ... or a return promise .. received by a promisor from a promise." (p. 300)

So if Wallace reneged on annulling the indictments after Billy testified, or later refused to pardon him after his 1881 sentencing, Wallace would betray not only Billy, but his own integrity. And since Wallace was not a sociopath like T.B. Catron or James Dolan, his conscience would torment him for the rest of his life.

There was more. In Billy's desperate March 2, 1881 letter from the Santa Fe jail (which particularly upset Wallace), he wrote:

I have some letters which date back two years and there are Parties who are very anxious to get them but I will not dispose of them until I see you. that is if you come immediately.

Dating back two years, puts the letters in this 1879 pardon bargain period, implying Wallace had also put the promise in writing. If so, Wallace, who kept copies of his correspondence with Billy, expurgated this evidence. And Billy's originals are lost.

So by March 15, 1879, Billy was legally correct to assume that he was given a pardon bargain. For him, the issue was how to fulfill his side by giving testimony without being eliminated by the Ring; or as he had written: *"my Enimies would Kill me."* So Billy put his faith in Wallace once the bargain was accepted. And he did not think it peculiar that Wallace wanted secrecy: *"Don't tell anybody - not a living soul - where you are coming or the object ... you can trust me."*

MEETING OF WALLACE AND "THE KID": MARCH 17, 1879

For the supposedly secret meeting of Lew Wallace and Billy Bonney on March 17, 1879 at 9 PM, Justice of the Peace "Squire" Wilson was present, since it occurred in his little house on Lincoln's single street's south side. With his friend Wilson as witness, Billy must have been certain of his pardon bargain; especially if Wallace said, "Testify ... before the Grand Jury and the trial court and convict the murderer of Chapman and I will let you go scot-free with a pardon in your pocket for all your misdeeds;" as Wallace claimed in a newspaper interview 23 years later for *New York World Magazine* of June 8, 1902, titled: "General Lew Wallace Writes a Romance of 'Billy the Kid.' " Specifics of this meeting are unknown, but Wallace remained obsessed with it and the pardon promise, guiltily reworking it for the rest of his life.

HECTIC LETTER DAY OF MARCH 20, 1879

The March 18, 1879 "escape" from Fort Stanton of Billy Campbell and Jessie Evans impacted the pardon bargain by loss of defendants against whom Billy could testify. Also "held" at the Fort by Wallace - besides James Dolan and Billy Matthews - were 20 Seven Rivers boys. All had free run of the premises.

A flurry of letters on March 20th between Billy and Lew Wallace ensued, with Wilson as go-between. Once reassured by a letter from Wallace, delivered by an unknown messenger, Billy next wanted arrangements for the sham arrest he had devised.

Noteworthy is propinquity of the letter-writers. Wallace was at José Montaño's house, close to Wilson's. San Patricio, the address on Billy's letters, was 12 miles away. But with a $1,000 bounty on his head, Billy likely used - as he would say - "a blind." He might very well have been hiding in Lincoln under Wilson's protection.

BILLY'S LETTER TO "FRIEND" WILSON

Billy began March 20th's letters by writing to Wilson to check on the feigned arrest plan with Wallace. It must have been delivered early, because time remained for others. But once Wilson got it, he could walk to José Montaño's house to pick up Wallace's response. Billy wrote:

>   *San Patricio*
>   *Thursday 20th*
>   *1879*
>   *Friend Wilson.*
>   *Please   tell   You   know*
>   *who that I do not know what to do, now*
>   *as those Prisoners have escaped. So send word*
>   *by bearer. a note through You it may be he has made*
>   *different arrangements if not and he still wants it the same*
>   *to Send :William Hudgins [Hudgens]: as Deputy, to the*
>   *Junction tomorrow at three Oclock with some men you know*
>   *to be all right. Send a note telling me what to do*
>   *WHBonney*
>   *P.S. do not send Soldiers*

WALLACE'S LETTER TO WILSON

Wallace's letter to Wilson demonstrates that he was taking precautions to protect his valuable witness, Billy, since he wanted Wilson to vouch for Kimbrell. Wallace wrote:

> *Fort Stanton. March 20, 1879*
> *Squire Wilson*
> *I enclose a note for Bonney. Read it, and forward at once. I presume the messenger is waiting.*
> *If you know why Kimbrell should not go rather than Hudgens, hold on till I get over this evening.*
> *Yours, Lew Wallace.*

WALLACE'S ENCLOSED LETTER TO BILLY

The "*note for Bonney*" enclosed with Wallace's letter to Wilson exists as Wallace's draft. It further implies a pardon trick, since Wallace, with his lawyer's sensitivity to wording, even crossed out the bargain's references: "*I will comply with my part if you will with yours*" and substituted "*arrangement*" for "*understanding;*" as if avoiding to imply promise or pardon in writing. Wallace wrote:

> *The escape makes no difference in arrangements.* ~~*I will comply with my part if you will with yours*~~.
> *To remove all suspicions of* ~~*arrangement*~~ *understanding, I think it better to put the arresting party in charge of Sheriff Kimball [Kimbrell], who will be instructed to see that no violence is used.*
> *This will go to you tonight.* ~~*If you still insist upon Hudgens, let me know*~~. *If I don't* ~~*get*~~ *receive other word from you the party (all citizens) will be at the junction by three o'clock* ~~*tomorrow*~~.

BILLY'S SECOND LETTER TO WALLACE

Billy's second letter that day must have gone out almost immediately upon receiving Wallace's response to his "Friend Wilson" letter. The sham arrest, which Billy devised himself, would put him into dreaded custody for Ring-style killing. Billy even identified for Wallace as a risk to him Second Lieutenant Millard Filmore Goodwin; one of the three officers whom Billy likely saw shooting at his group when escaping the burning McSween house. Billy was trying to maximize his survival odds. Evident also is Billy's grand awareness of his hero role: "*I am not afraid to die like a man fighting but I would not like to be killed like a dog unarmed.*" And even at this dangerous moment, Billy was also trying to enlist Wallace in a mutual fight for justice; including giving that past General advice on how to capture escapees: "*it is not my place to advise you, but I am anxious to have them caught.*" Billy's overwrought excitement at this superlative father-figure was evident even to him, since he apologized for "*having so much to say.*" And Billy permitted the sham arrest the next day: March 21, 1879. Billy wrote:

San Pa<u>tricio</u>

Lincoln <u>County</u>
<u>Thursday</u> 20th <u>1879</u>
General. Lew. Wallace:

Sir. I will keep the appointment I made. but be Sure and have men come that You can depend on I am not afraid to die like a man fighting but I would not like to be killed like a dog unarmed. tell Kimbal [Kimbrell] to let his men be placed around the house and for him to come in alone: and he can arrest us. all I am afraid of is that in the Fort we might be poisoned or killed through a window at night. but You can arrange that all right. tell the Commanding Officer to watch)Let Goodwin(he would not hesitate to do anything there Will be danger on the road of Somebody Waylaying us to kill us on the road to the Fort. You will never catch those fellows on the road Watch Fritzes. Captain Bacas ranch and the Brewery they Will either go to Seven Rivers or to Jicarillo Mountains they will stay around close untill the scouting parties come in. give a spy a pair of glasses and let him get on the mountain back of Fritzes and watch and if they are there there will be provisions carried to them. it is not my place to advise you, but I am anxious to have them caught, and perhaps know how men hide from Soldiers, better than you. please excuse me for having so much to say

and I still remain Yours Truly
W H. Bonney

P.S.
I have changed my mind Send Kimbal [Kinbrell] to Gutieres just below San Patricio one mile, because Sanger and Ballard are or were great friends of Camels [Billy Campbell's] Ballard told me ~~today~~ *yesterday to leave for you were doing everything to catch me. it was a blind to get me to leave tell Kimbal [Kimbrell] not to come before 3 oclock for I may not be there before*

WALLACE'S REVEALING PROGRESS REPORT TO CARL SCHURZ: MARCH 21, 1879

Lew Wallace's long progress report letter to Secretary of the interior Carl Schurz was written on March 21, 1879, the day of Billy's sham arrest. With legal storm clouds on his horizon, Wallace was advertising sunny success, along with enclosing copies of his letters to General Edward Hatch. Ominously for Billy - and likely reflecting Wallace's ambivalence for pardoning or for handing him over to the Ring - is that Wallace mentions affidavits about Chapman's murder, but omits that he has an eye-witness to testify against the killers. Instead, he promotes his "outlaw" campaign as *"taking the head off the evil."* And he even encloses his March 11, 1879 letter to Captain Henry Carroll with U.S. Marshal John Sherman's outlaw list, which included *" 'The Kid' William Bonney."* Wallace wrote:

Lincoln, March 21, 1879.
Hon. C. Schurz,
Sec'y Dept. Interior.
Sir:
 My time has been so constantly occupied in getting my work into operation and hearing people who have grievances and information, that I have had no opportunity to write you ~~in full~~ *as might be desired. At last, however,* ~~I can do so,~~ *everything being in progress, I can send you a sufficient outline.*
 General Hatch and I left Santa Fe the 1st of March. In the afternoon of the 5th, within a few miles of Fort Stanton we separated, he going to the Fort, I coming to Lincoln, the county seat ...
 A short interview with the leading citizens satisfied me that it would not be possible in the beginning to obtain affidavits against parties well known to be guilty of crimes; this on account of the terrorism so general after the brutal assassination of

H.I. Chapman, the night of the 18th ~~March~~ February. ~~Affidavits were very desirable as the basis of formal criminal proceedings.~~ Accepting the necessity of the ~~case~~ situation, I decided to proceed immediately without warrants. After the criminals were in custody, the popular fear would be removed, and, with the toning up of confidence, testimony came in abundance – such was my hope. Accordingly the same evening ~~I sent~~ the following request was sent to the Fort, which is ten miles away.

[ENCLOSURE] Copy March 5, 1879 letter to Hatch telling him how to capture Chapman's killers (See my p. 526)

[AUTHOR'S NOTE: For his outlaw myth, Wallace blurs Chapman's killers with irrelevant others, omits that Ringite Dolan was Chapman's primary killer, and focuses on Evans who was merely present. And Wallace concludes with his other focus of concern: Commander Dudley.]

General Hatch promptly complied, and next day the three – Campbell, Evans, and Matthews – were secured, and in due time lodged in the Fort. These men, you should understand, were all principals in the Chapman murder. Two of them are the most desperate of the outlaws. Evans ~~was~~ is one of the murderers of Tunstall. He and Campbell have to answer for several other lives feloniously taken. Of the same gang is J.J. Dolan; but as I had hopes that his larger money interests in the county, amounting to $70,000 or $80,000, would make him pliant for use as a witness, he was not included in the order of arrest. Two days afterwards he came and voluntarily surrendered himself to me; whereupon, with the same object in view, I took his parole & confining him to the limits of the Fort. ~~Within two days~~ Subsequently, he violated his parole, and by my order was put in close confinement. Dolan, it should be observed, is ~~also~~ under heavy bond for his appearance at Court to answer ~~a char~~ an indictment for the murder of Tunstill [Tunstall]. ~~It should~~ I set much store upon the moral effect of the prompt seizure of these men.

In course of my interviews with the people, both Mexican and American, of the town and county, it became apparent that ~~all~~ attempts to restore confidence would be ~~long defeated delayed~~ delayed if not wholly fruitless, while Lt. Col. N.A.M. Dudley, 9th Cavalry, was in command of Fort Stanton. I addressed the following communication to General Hatch:

[ENCLOSURE] Copy Match 7, 1879 letter to Hatch telling him to remove N.A.M. Dudley from Fort Stanton command. Wallace claims Dudley's culpability in killing of McSween and others with him, as well as in the killing of Huston Chapman and the attempted killing of Juan Patrón. But, avoiding Ring reference, Wallace omits the Lincoln County War as the context for Dudley's killing of McSween and Chapmen. (See my pp. 518-519)

[AUTHOR'S NOTE: Next Wallace credits himself for Hatch's removal of Dudley, unaware that Schurz and the President did not want Dudley charged to reopen the can of worms that Angel had just closed the past October. The last thing they wanted was *"an astonishing showing of other incidental misconduct and abuse of authority"* **by public officials. But Wallace reassuringly ends with his "outlaw" solution.]**

It is almost needless to say General Hatch relieved Col. Dudley upon the request as presented, and ordered him to Fort Union to await orders. **It is my belief that the charges can be sustained; and that, in the* ~~same~~ *connection, there will be an astonishing showing of other incidental misconduct and abuse of authority, all tending to establish that the Colonel was a* ~~promoter of disorder and the hand~~ *most mischievous partisan if not actually a promoter of disorder.*

Captain Henry Carroll was the successor in command of the Fort.

I next busied myself making a list of outlaws to proceed against. On the 11th March, I was able to send ~~Ca~~ *the following communication.*

[AUTHOR'S NOTE: Next Wallace gives his "outlaw" solution.]

[ENCLOSURE] Wallace's March 11, 1879 letter to Captain Henry Carrol with recopied Sherman outlaw list, and calling outlaws "Black Knights" (See my pp. 538-539)

[AUTHOR'S NOTE: Wallace's following outlaw fabrications are despicable in light of his having spent the past month talking to Lincolnites, and Billy himself. He well knows the difference between the random killers he describes, and the Lincoln County War freedom fighters. But he makes clear his *"war"* **is against those on Sherman's outlaw list. Remember this is the period in which Billy believed he had a real pardon bargain.]**

The list, I stop to remark, is by no means perfect; yet it was enough to begin with. Some of those named are guilty of double murders; some of triple. A party of them halted in front of a Mexican house, and called for watermelons, and shot the boy who was helping them dead. The same party killed three men at work in a hay field, and complemented the deed by shooting a crazy boy. Another party murdered an entire family of Mexicans – men, women, and children – nine in all. The other day Capt. Carroll passed by the place of the butchery, and found the skeleton of a boy in a sitting posture leaning against a tree. The head had rolled off the shoulders, and lay upon the ground <u>with a cigar in its mouth</u>. **These ~~samples~~ illustrations will furnish an idea of the nature of the men against whom I find it necessary to proceed ~~against~~ in a kind of war.** *I cannot hope to get them all on account of the country, which for brigands is better ~~formed~~ even than northern Italy: yet there will be enough for wholesome examples. At this writing there are four detachments of troops executing the orders for the arrest of the outlaws promptly given by Capt. Carroll ~~at my~~ upon receipt of my request.*

If, however, I should be fortunate enough to get all ~~that~~ the list, it would be no more than **taking the head off the evil.** ~~*leaving it To accomplish end it permanent cure, it is necessary to get down to the paps the roots and dig them up.*~~ **To dig up the roots, it is necessary to ~~break up~~ crush the number of cattle camps** *– such as Slaughter's, Beckwith's, Shedds, and thoroughly cleanse the region about the Seven Rivers. These are the places ~~to~~ from which the thieves and murderers ~~issued f~~ issue to do their work, and to which, when the work is done, they retire for rest, safety, and to ~~trade off~~ unload their plunder ~~sheep, horses, cattle,~~ of whatever kind. ~~and boast their~~*

To reach them I based a plan upon the law of the Territory regulating brands for animals. You will find the Acts in the Compiled Laws page 52. My scheme is disclosed in the following letter.

[ENCLOSURE] Wallace's March 12, 1879 letter to Captain Carroll with his campaign against rustling - and inadvertent revealing of some Ring locales for holding rustled cattle, and with preposterous scenarios for collecting all rustled cattle on property of homestead farmer, John Newcomb, as "Cattle Keeper of the County." (See my pp. 539-540)

[AUTHOR'S NOTE: Next Wallace continued his absurd rustling solution for Schurz with his fantasy of at least 1,000 reclaimed cattle milling about tiny Lincoln so the "*owners*" could reclaim them. Then he slips in that his *only* setback was escape of Chapman killers, Evans and Campbell – real outlaws!]

Besides overhauling and breaking up the camps and depots alluded to, I hope, by bringing stolen cattle &c. to the county seat, to furnish every honest citizen an opportunity to reclaim his lost property; **something he has not dared attempt while it was in possession of the outlaws or their receivers.** *And more still, it is my expectation to put the cattle business, which is the most exclusive industry of this portion of the Territory, in course of transaction regardful of the law. Several herds are now on the way here. To* show the extent *give you an idea of the extent of the illicit business, a herd of over a thousand head, belonging to Slaughter, whose name heads the list of murderers, is coming.*

The only set back in my operation yet sustained was the escape a few nights ago of two of my prisoners, Campbell and Evans. They were helped out of the guard-house at the Fort by a faithless sentinel, who deserted with them. I have offered $1000 for their return, and hope to recapture them yet.

> I hope the honor to be,
> Very respectfully,
> Your friend & servant,
> Lew. Wallace,
> Gov. New Mexico.

Having thus set my measures afoot, I am waiting here for Judge Ira Leonard; when he comes, I shall employ him as an attorney in behalf of the Territory in connection with this business; then I shall go to Mesilla, over in Doña Ana county, to concert action with the commandant of Fort Bliss, looking to thorough cleansing of that county. In probability the purification will take the whole summer.

With a hope that my action will meet your approval and that of the President, I am, most respectfully,

Your friend & servant,
Lew. Wallace,
Gov. New Mexico.

WALLACE'S BILLY BONNEY INTERVIEW: MARCH 23, 1879

In Lincoln, Lew Wallace and Billy were housed next door to each other; with Billy in Juan Patrón's house, and Wallace at José Montaño's. After Billy was there for two days, on March 23, 1879, Wallace interviewed him for the "outlaw" campaign. He recorded it on legal-length paper, asking nothing about the Lincoln County War. But missed by Wallace were Billy's dating by Lincoln County War events: the *"Rustlers"* gang that *"had been with Peppin's posse,"* the Owens gang *"organized before the burning of McSween's house,"* men going *"thence to the Feliz where they took the Tunstall cattle,"* a certain man *"had no cattle when the War started."* And Billy's ironic aside on a Regulator-shot Tunstall murderer was: *"Frank Baker (killed)."*

But Billy demonstrated a breath-taking fund of knowledge of individuals and Territorial geography, implying justification for the Ring's fear of him as a future rebel leader. And Billy was apparently delighted with his new father-figure; and helpfully followed up with additional information by letter the next day.

Wallace's writings about Billy in the 1900's make clear that they had more conversation than the interview notes indicate, or that they had other meetings. For example, Wallace knew Billy was born in New York City and lived in Terre Haute, Indiana, as a child, before moving to New Mexico. Billy must have poured out his life story. And a described incident of Wallace asking Billy for a shooting demonstration could realistically have happened in the back of Juan Patrón's house facing the south hills. But for Billy's March 23, 1879 interview, Wallace recorded:

William Bonney ("Kid")
relative to arrangement
with him.

Notes:

3-23-1879

Statements by Kid, made Sunday night March 23, 1879

1. There is a cattle trail beginning about 5 miles above Yellow Lake in a cañon, running a little west of north to Cisneza del Matcho (Mule Spring) and continuing around the point of the

Capitan Mountains down toward Carrizozo in the direction of the Rio Grande. Frank Wheeler, Jake Owens and Dutch Chris are supposed to have used this trail taking a bunch of cattle over. Vansickle told K. so. They stopped and killed two beavers for Sam Corbet – hush money to Vansickle to whom they gave the beavers. Vansickle also said the Owens-Wheeler outfit mentioning "Chris" Ladbessor using this trail for about a year, but that lately their horses had given out, and of 140 head which they started to work they had only got through with 40. That now they were going to the Reservation to make a raid on the Indian horses to work on.

The Rustlers.

The "Rustlers," Kid says: were organized in Fort Stanton. Before they organized as "Rustlers" they had been with Peppin's posse. They came from Texas. Owens was conspicuous amongst them. **They were organized before the burning of McSween's house**, and after that they went on their first trip down the county as far as the Coe's ranch and **thence to the Feliz where they took the Tunstall cattle.** From the Feliz they went to the Pecos, where some of them deserted, Owens amongst them. (Martin, known to Sam Corbet) was in charge of the Tunstall cattle, and was taken prisoner, and saw them kill one of their own party. On the same trip they burnt Lola Wise's house, and took some horses. Coe at the time was ranching at the house. On this trip they moved behind a body of soldiers, one company, and a company of Navajo Scouts. They moved in sight of the soldiers, taking horses, insulting women. Lorenzo Trujillo (Jus. Peder) Juan Trujillo, Jose M. Gutierres, Pancho Sanchez, Santos Tafoya, are witnesses against them. They stopped on Pecos at Seven Rivers. Collins, now at Silver City, was one of the outfit – nick-named the Prowler by the cowboys. At Seven Rivers. There joined them Gus Gildey (wanted at San Antonio for killing Mexicans) Gildey is carrying the mail now from Stockton to Seven Rivers – James Irvin and Reese Gobles, (rumored that their bodies were found in a drift down the Pecos) – Rustling Bob (found dead in the Pecos, killed by his own party) – John Selman (whereabouts unknown) came to Roswell while [Captain] Carroll was there –

The R's [Rustlers] stayed at Seven Rivers; which they left on their second trip via the Berenda for Fort Stanton. On their return back they killed Chavez boys and the crazy boy, Lorenzo – and the Sanchez boy, 14 years old. They also committed many robberies.

They broke up after reaching the Pecos, promising to return when some more horses got fat.

Shedd's Ranch

The trail used going from Seven Rivers to Shedd's was round the S.W. part of the Guadalupe Mts. by a tank on the right hand of trail: from Shedd's the drives would be over to Las Cruces Jesse Evans, Frank Baker (killed) Jim McDaniels (at Cruces, ranging between Cruces and El Paso) Reed at Shedd's bought cattle from them – also sold cattle to E.C. Priest, butcher in Cruces. "Big Mose" (at Cruces last heard from) and [blank], deserter from cavalry – (went to Arizona)

Mimbres

Used to be called Mormon City – situated 30 miles on the road to Cruces from Silver City south. A great many of what are known as "West Harden gang" are there. Among them Joe Olney, known in Mimbres as Joe Hill; he has a ranch in old Mexico somewheres near Coralitos. He makes trips up in this country: was at Penasco not long ago.

San Nicholas Spring

Is about 18 miles from Shedd's Ranch on the road to Tularosa, left hand road. There's a house at the spring and about 4 or 5 miles from it N.W. is another corral of brush and a spring, situated in a cañon. There Jim McDaniels used to keep stolen Indian horses. McD. one of the Rio Grande posse. Kid says the latter is still used.

The Jones Family

Came from Texas. Used to keep saloon at Fort Griffin. The family consists of the father, Jim Jones, John Jones, boy about 10 years old, a girl about 13, and the mother. Marion Turner lives with the family, and he killed a Mexican man at Blazers Mill "just to see him kick." He had no cattle **when the War started**. *The Jones, John and Jim, killed a man named Riley, a partner of theirs, on the Penasco 3 or 4 years ago.*

THE "BILLIE" LETTER: MARCH 24, 1879

ANALYSIS: The letter fragment signed "Billie," which I authenticated as by Billy Bonney and dated to March 24, 1879, reveals his trust in Lew Wallace and their pardon bargain, and his fantasy of assisting Wallace in pursuing justice for Lincoln County War issues. And its fancy hand-made stationery with pulp pattern "finger print" and unique Lady Liberty head embossure enabled my connecting it to the men then using it themselves and providing it to Billy, and likely secretly assisting his pardon quest: Justice of the Peace "Squire Wilson" and his jailor, Juan Patrón.

The two-sided signed "Billie" letter fragment is in the Indiana Historical Society's Lew Wallace collection, having been in Wallace's personal possession with his other Billy the Kid letters. I authenticated it in my book *Billy the Kid's Writings, Words, and Wit* by Billy Bonney's uniquely modified Spencerian handwriting; his idiosyncratic punctuation, grammar, and misspellings; and content known only to him. It was logically dated to March 24, 1879, as a follow-up to his March 23, 1879 Wallace "Interview," since Billy refers to Jesse Evans's gang and certain places as having already been "*mentioned*" by him to Wallace.

One can imagine Billy, excited after his second night-time interview with Wallace in seven days, continuing his informing once back in Juan Patrón's house-jail next door. And the fancy embossed stationery Billy used on was then being used by Jailor Patrón and Justice of the Peace Wilson to write to Wallace themselves; and named by me "Lady Liberty stationery." It was likely obtained by those officials from Tunstall's store, since shopkeepers had hand-embossing presses to customize paper.

That Billy was being provided with the best paper in Lincoln, made me surmise that Wilson and Patrón, considering Billy their Lincoln County War hero, were secretly assisting him with his pardon plea. And they would have favored his giving eye-witness testimony to convict Huston Chapman's hated killers.

Billy's first letter offering the pardon bargain to Wallace on March 13(?), 1879, had been on different fancy stationery, embossed with the U.S. Capitol building; and was then being used by McSween loyalist, Probate Judge Florencio Gonzales in Regulator haven, San Patricio. And in that letter Billy referred to "*Friends ... helping me all they could.*" He also gave San Patricio as his address in his March 20, 1879 letter to Wallace.

This scenario of Billy's partisans opens the possibility that earlier in March of 1879, Wilson and Patrón were hiding Billy in Lincoln, or its vicinity, after Wallace offered his $1000 reward; thus, making Billy's inside address as "San Patricio" in his letter of March 20, 1879 purposefully misleading.

Furthermore, Billy's having loyalists is historically known. By 1880, Sheriff Pat Garrett had to use Texan possemen to hunt him, because New Mexicans refused. And in 1881, the Ring feared Billy's partisans enough to hold him three extra months in the Santa Fe jail to await railroad completion for transport to his Mesilla trial to avoid his rescue from a stagecoach. Billy described backers himself. In his March 4, 1881 letter from the Santa Fe jail, he threatened Wallace with a rescue: *"I guess they mean to Send me up without giving me any Show but they will have a nice time doing it. I am not entirely without friends."* And when Billy made his courthouse-jail escape on April 28, 1881, the Lincolnites - including Wilson and Patrón - did nothing to stop him. There were different ways to win the Lincoln County War: one was passive resistance.

PARDON SCENARIO USING THE "LADY LIBERTY" STATIONERY TRAIL

So one can postulate that in March of 1879 Billy had Lincoln area backers wanting his indictments voided. Probate Judge Florencio Gonzales and Justice of the Peace "Squire" Wilson could have devised the clemency plan with Billy to present to the new governor, already housed in Lincoln. Those officials were angry men. Gonzales remembered Sheriff Peppin's July 3, 1878 massacre at his town. Wilson had been victimized both by Governor Axtell and Commander Dudley.

Evidence of their collusion may be in Billy's first letter to Wallace, of March 13th. It has his own wit and bravado, but also has technical legalese, implying assistance: using the correct word "annul" (his *"annuly"*) for eliminating his indictments, instead of "pardon" (which is after conviction). That it was written in San Patricio at Probate Judge Florencio Gonzales's office can be guessed from its stationery embossed with the national capital, since four months earlier, Gonzalez himself had used it to write a letter to newly arrived Governor Wallace about local problems.

The plot of partisans may have thickened when Lew Wallace decided to question a logical person - Justice of the Peace Wilson -

about Billy's March 13th letter's bargain; never imagining that Wilson's offer of his own house for a personal meeting with the boy on the 17th coincided with a larger coordination.

The next steps - planning the sham arrest and incarceration, which were likely Billy's survivalist idea - involved more friends: Deputy Sheriff Robert Gilbert and jailor Juan Patrón, in addition to "Squire" Wilson; all had "Lady Liberty" stationery to give Billy; who, on March 20th, wrote to Wilson on it, while, I would guess, hiding in Lincoln, but bluffing Wallace that same day by using "*San Patricio*" for his writing location.

After "arrest" by Sheriff George Kimbrell, "jailed" Billy had access to Juan Patrón's dwindling "Lady Liberty" paper; possibly being shared with "Squire" Wilson up the street, and with Attorney Ira Leonard's assistant, George Taylor - both men being in town for the April Grand Jury and Dudley Court of Inquiry.

The aid to Billy may have increased as these public officials realized Wallace was nonsensically focused on mythical outlawry. Wilson or Patrón could have encouraged Wallace to interview Billy for real issues. Wallace did, on March 23rd.

The next day, the 24th, Billy apparently asked Patrón for stationery for a follow-up to Wallace. So Patrón gave him his best: "Lady Liberty" stationery, the last page of which is now the fragment signed "Billie."

As to deeper meaning, that signature said it all: "*Billie.*" Within 11 days of contacting Lew Wallace, Billy had abandoned his first letter's formal "*W.H. Bonney.*" "*Billie*" was used trustingly within three days of their meeting at "Squire" Wilson's house, where Wallace, marveling at the remote night-time romance of a frontier town and bloodthirsty bandit king, must have misleadingly appeared to Billy as enthralled by his unexpected cleverness, knowledge, and firearms (he brought along his precious Tunstall Winchester '73 carbine).

So the name "*Billie*" tumbled out after merely the second meeting at the Sunday March 23rd interview, evidencing trust and hope never to be experienced again by Billy. "*Billie*" was his most intimate name: the name a loving father could use; the name so boyish as to engender protectiveness, while the information he gave was calculated to engender paternal respect to forge an alliance for anti-Ring justice.

Anticipating clemency, anticipating a life in which his intelligence allowed any profession - even becoming an attorney like Lew Wallace - Billy struggled to enter that new world.

And Billy, given amnesty, could have married Paulita Maxwell, and stayed in New Mexico Territory, the only place that felt like home, after experiencing Tunstall, McSween, Chapman, Wilson, Patrón, and his friends in San Patricio. Writing *"Billie"* was probably his most vulnerable moment: dropping his rough façade to be the child he never was.

And, acquisitive Wallace, living out of his suitcase in Lincoln, saved all the letters on "Lady Liberty" stationery; though losing, in jumbled papers then, or after his death two decades later, the front pages of that March 24th "Lady Liberty" letter signed "Billie" - as possibly never read, and certainly never appreciated - but as a valued souvenir of his adventure with "the Kid."

THE "BILLIE" LETTER: MARCH 24, 1879

The "Billie" letter fragment of March 24, 1879 is the only known document by Billy Bonney describing Lincoln County War events (besides his affidavit and deposition on Tunstall's murder). It continued his March 23, 1879 "Interview" with Lew Wallace by specifics, as well as clarifying his wartime murder indictments: the essence of their pardon bargain. Billy wrote:

... on the Pecos. All that I can remember are the So Called Dolan Outfit but they are all up here now. and on the Rio <u>Grande</u> this man Cris Moten I believe his name is he drove a herd of 80 head one Year ago last December in Company with Frank Wheeler Frank <u>Baker</u> deceased Jesse Evans George Davis alias Tom Jones. Tom Hill, his name in Texas being Tom Chelson also deceased, they drove the cattle to the Indian Reservation and sold them to John Riley and JJ Dolan. and the cattle were turned in for Beef for the Indians the Beckwith family made their boasts that they came to Seven Rivers a little over four years ago with one Milch Cow borrowed from John Chisum they had when I was there Year ago one thousand six hundred head of cattle. the male members of the family are Henry beckwith and John Beckwith Robert <u>Beckwith</u> was killed the time McSween's house was burned. Charles [blank] Robert Olinger and Wallace Olinger are of the same gang. their cattle ranch is Situated at Rock Corral twelve miles below Seven Rivers on the Pecos. Paxton and Pierce are Still below them forty miles from Seven Rivers there are four of them Paxton: Pierce: Jim Raymers, and Buck Powel. they had when I seen them last about one thousand head of cattle: at Rocky Arroyo

there is another Ranch belonging to [blank] Smith who Operated on the Penasco last year with the Jesse Evans gang those and the places I mentioned are all I know of this man Chris Moten at the time they stole those Cattle was in the employ of <u>Dolan</u> and <u>Co.</u> I afterwards Seen Some of the cattle at the Rinconada Bonita on the reservation those were the men we were in search of when we went to the Agency. the Beckwith family were attending to their own Business when this War started but G.W. Peppin told them that this was John Chisums War. and so they took a hand thinking they would lose their Cattle in case that he Chisum won the fight. this is all the information I can give you on this point
Yours Respectfully Billie

"BILLIE" LETTER COMMENTARY

The "Billie" letter has Lincoln County War issues, and implies Billy's hope to enlist Wallace in the anti-Ring crusade. And his comments on the "Buckshot" Roberts killing pertained to the pardon bargain, though he was unaware of its federal implication. Commentary is as follows:

on the Pecos.

[AUTHOR'S NOTE: The fragment starts with a sentence ending. But "on the Pecos" were Lincoln County War participants. On the Pecos was cattle king, John Chisum, who betrayed Tunstall and McSween, and reneged on his promise to pay Regulators' wages. Billy possibly shared his anger at Chisum in the missing page(s) here or in his Interview, and did blame Chisum in his December 12, 1880 letter to Wallace. Wallace later used it in his Billy the Kid fictions as Billy's "outlaw" revenge motive to hide his anti-Ring cause. On the Pecos were Seven Rivers Ringite rustlers who murdered Regulator leader, Frank MacNab, and participated in the Lincoln County War battle's killings. And on the Pecos was the Catron-Dolan cow-camp south of Seven Rivers, holding rustled stock for the Ring's military and Indian reservation contracts. Its foreman, William "Buck" Morton, was killed by the Regulators as a Tunstall murderer.]

all that I can remember are the So Called <u>Dolan</u> Outfit but they are all up here now:

[AUTHOR'S NOTE: This is special information that Billy would know: that by 1879 Dolan no longer had the Pecos cow-camp

after he went bankrupt in 1878 from mercantile competition with Tunstall. Intriguingly, Dolan's name is underlined for emphasis; and Dolan certainly was the Ring's boss in Lincoln County, and was probably was key to calling in Commander N.A.M. Dudley during the Lincoln County War battle when Dolan realized the McSween side was winning.]

and on the Rio G<u>rande</u> this man Cris Moten I believe his name is he drove a herd of)80(head one Year ago last December in Company with Frank Wheeler Frank <u>Baker</u> deceased Jesse Evans George Davis alias Tom Jones. Tom Hill, his name in Texas being Tom Chelson also deceased.

[AUTHOR'S NOTE: Billy lists outlaw Jessie Evans's men: Frank Baker, George Davis, and Tom Hill - names left out by Wallace in his "Interview." Billy knew them, and rode with them in September of 1877. They were involved in killing Tunstall. And Evans was at Chapman's killing. And Billy snidely calls Frank Baker "*deceased*." Tunstall murderer Baker, was a Regulator victim on March 9, 1878. Billy was likely one of his killers.]

[AUTHOR'S NOTE: As intimate, is Billy's knowledge of the death of Evans's gang member, Tom Hill, as well as his alias and place of origin. Though Billy again only says "*deceased*," it was an obscure killing; implying that Billy kept track of erstwhile associates. During an Evan's gang robbery, Hill was shot by a Cherokee partner of a German sheep herder named John Wagner near Shedd's Ranch: a Ring outlet for rustled stock, and a safe haven for Jessie and his boys. In that shooting, Jessie was hit in the right wrist.]

they drove the cattle to the Indian Reservation and sold them to John Riley and JJ Dolan. and the cattle were turned in for Beef for the Indians

[AUTHOR'S NOTE: This amazing statement shows Billy's insider's knowledge of Ring dynamics that led to Tunstall's murder and the Lincoln County War. It is also the key point which Wallace avoided in his "Interview": <u>that rustling was a Ring endeavor to meet beef contracts for the Mescalaro Indian Reservation and for Fort Stanton.</u> Tunstall was working to supplant the Ring with his own contracts to both entities with his cattle ranches on the Feliz and Peñasco Rivers, where Billy and Fred Waite were Homestead Act owners. That Ring competition was why Tunstall had to die. So, here Billy is giving Wallace the dynamics he needed to really end the Lincoln County "troubles" - dynamics which Wallace had concealed.]

the Beckwith family made their boasts that they came to Seven Rivers a little over four years ago with one Milch Cow borrowed from John Chisum they had when I was there Year ago one thousand six hundred head of cattle.

[AUTHOR'S NOTE: This is Billy's wry sense of humor, about the Beckwith family "borrowing" a cow from Chisum; but in four years acquiring almost 2000 head. This was the description of Seven Rivers rustling for the Ring. And it is insider information. In September of 1877, when Billy first returned to New Mexico Territory from Arizona Territory, he stayed with the Jones family at Seven Rivers, and got to know the Beckwiths. John and Robert Beckwith eventually fought for the Ring in the Lincoln County War (and Robert was killed by friendly fire).]

the male members of the family are Henry beckwith and John Beckwith Robert <u>Beckwith</u> was killed the time McSween's house was burned.

[AUTHOR'S NOTE: Billy not only elaborates on the Beckwith family members, but connects Robert Beckwith's death to the most dramatic event of the Lincoln County War battle: the murder of Alexander McSween during attempted escape. Billy's reference to "*the time McSween's house was burned*" implies his assumption that Wallace knows he is referring to that arson. And they may have discussed it at the "Squire" Wilson house meeting on March 17th. Billy states that Bob Beckwith "*was killed*," omitting here that it occurred when he was serving arrest warrants on McSween and was caught in friendly fire during McSween's murder by Peppin's posse.]

Charles [blank] Robert Olinger and Wallace Olinger are of the same gang. their cattle ranch is situated at Rock Corral twelve miles below Seven Rivers on the Pecos.

[AUTHOR'S NOTE: Billy is clear on the Olinger brothers, Robert and Wallace as being in "*the same gang*," meaning the Seven Rivers boys. Robert, as most hated Ringite, was Billy's murder victim in jailbreak of April 28, 1881. The ranch Billy locates has the brothers' stock rustled from John Chisum.].

Paxton and Pierce are Still below them forty miles from Seven Rivers there are four of them Paxton: Pierce: Jim Raymen, and Buck Powel. they had when I seen them last about one thousand head of cattle: at Rocky Arroya there is another Ranch belonging to Smith who Operated on the Penasco last year with the Jesse Evans gang

[AUTHOR'S NOTE: Billy is listing more associates of Ring rustler Jessie Evans.]

those and the places I mentioned

[AUTHOR'S NOTE: Stating *"and the places I mentioned"* implies his Wallace "Interview," now with follow-up specifics.]

are all I know of this man Chris Moten at the time they stole those Cattle was in the employ of J.J. <u>Dolan</u> and <u>Co.</u>

[AUTHOR'S NOTE: Since the fragment began with Dolan's outfit and with Jessie Evans gang rustlers' named along with Cris Moten, Billy may be linking Moten for Wallace to Ring rustling.]

I afterwards Seen Some of the cattle at the Rinconada Bonita on the reservation those were the men we were in search of when we went to the Agency.

[AUTHOR'S NOTE: This refers to "Buckshot" Roberts's Regulator killing on April 4, 1878 at Blazer's Mill in the Mescalaro Indian Reservation. Billy calls it the *"Agency"* because Indian Agent, Frederick Godfroy, lived in its way station. Billy may be following up his "Interview" statement to Wallace as to *"those were the men we were in search of when we went to the Agency."* That pertains to the pardon bargain, since Roberts's killing there was one of Billy's indictments.]

the Beckwith family were attending to their own Business when this War started but G.W. Peppin told them that this was John Chisums War and so they took a hand thinking they would loose their Cattle in case that he Chisum won the fight.

[AUTHOR'S NOTE: Billy is giving insider information about why the Seven Rivers men fought on the Ring side in the Lincoln County War: that Chisum had sided with Tunstall and McSween, and they were Murphy-Dolan Ringites.]

this is all the information I can give you on this point

Yours Respectfully Billie

FORESHADOWING WALLACE'S PARDON BARGAIN BETRAYAL

ANALYSIS: By March of 1879's end, it was clear that the pardon bargain would have a tragic outcome, since Billy relied on Wallace's integrity, while Wallace expressed only scorn of him to President Hayes and Secretary of the Interior Schurz.

WALLACE TO THE PRESIDENT: MARCH 31, 1879

On March 31, 1879, Wallace sent Secretary of the interior Carl Schurz a letter to forward to President Hayes, asking again for martial law to cover-up his slipping control. Wallace wrote:

President R.B. Hayes.
*The feuds recently in Lincoln county, New Mexico, left a large many thieves and murderers, who, with others of like class since added to their number, are now confederated for plunder. The laws of the Territory contain no provision availing against such federation, and the legislature is not in session. On account of intimidation of good people, brought about by murder and assassinations, there is little hope that jurors will act with freedom, and it is certain that witnesses residing in exposed situations dare not testify what they know of offences committed. A number of prisoners are in custody for high crimes who must in ordinary course go free, and speedily because persons having knowledge of their guilt are afraid to make affidavits for the issuance of warrants. Wherefore, as against evil-doers, the courts are useless, and procedures under civil law of no effect except acquittal; making the condition such that **it is my duty to request you to proceed under your October proclamation, and place the counties of Lincoln and Doña Ana in said Territory under martial law**, the latter because it offers a convenient refuge for criminals flying from the former. By such means only, in my judgment, can the lives of good citizens be made safe and permanent peace eventually attained. Speedy action is desirable, since resort is being already had to the habeas corpus act.*
Very respectfully,
Lewis Wallace
Governor of New Mexico.

"PRECIOUS SPECIMEN" LETTER TO CARL SCHURZ: MARCH 31, 1879

Eighteen days after his first contact with Billy Bonney, and having read the boy's articulate letters and shared two face-to-face meetings, Lew Wallace was as unmovable and sadistic as his own father when having power over a vulnerable youth.

Wallace's letter of March 31, 1879 to Secretary of the Interior Carl Schurz is the writing on the wall for honoring any pardon bargain. Wallace snidely calls Billy a *"precious specimen nick-named "The Kid,"* portrays him as an incarcerated outlaw *"whom the Sheriff is holding here in the Plaza,"* omits that his imprisonment was voluntary as a star witness against Chapman's murderers, hides the pardon bargain, and cites him only in service of his outlaw myth ploy: *"The desperadoes include some of the most noted of their class in the United States."* Wallace clearly had made his pardon decision. Unbeknownst to Billy, there was no hope for him. Wallace wrote:

> *Lincoln, N.M., March 31, 1879*
> *Hon. Carl Schurz*
> *Sec'y Dept Interior.*
> *Sir:*
> *Today I forward a telegram to you, with another to the President, requesting him to proceed under his October proclamation and place this county and Doña Ana under martial law.*
> *The step is induced by several reasons; chiefly, first, because it is apparent to me that the military do not enter heartily into the work requested of them. The work itself is ~~no doubt~~ evidently distasteful, and they are really acting under direction of civilians.*

[AUTHOR'S NOTE: This failure was likely soldiers' passive resistance to Wallace's preposterous time-wasting demands.]

> *In the next place, my expectation of revival of courage and confidence on the part of the better people of the county is far from realized. The escape of Campbell and Evans shook their faith in the soldiers. As jurors and witnesses they are singularly unreliable on account of their fear of retaliation, if those whom they may be called upon to try ~~and~~ or against whom they may testify should go free – and that, they say, is the assured event*

of trial in court. To add to their difficulties, no one of them seems to know who the other is serving. There is no such thing amongst them as real confidence in each other. Should the county court open next Monday week in ~~the~~ regular session, the liberation of the ~~nine~~ twelve prisoners now in custody, ~~would~~ six for murder, six for horse and cattle stealing – would, in my opinion, be assured. And what that would end in you can readily perceive.

To still further weaken my confidence in juries as instruments of the law in this county, I have been forced to take account of the fact that everybody of any force or character has in some way been committed to one side or the other in the **recent war,** *and is yet all alive with prejudices and partialities.*

[AUTHOR'S NOTE: This is the only time that Wallace correctly calls the conflict a war, but he conceals particulars.]

A precious specimen nick-named "The Kid," whom the Sheriff is holding here in the Plaza, as it is called, is an object of tender regard. I heard singing and music the other night; going to the door, I found the minstrels of the village actually serenading the fellow in his prison.

[AUTHOR'S NOTE: Every part is a lie: 1) implying real incarceration, 2) implying that Billy was reprehensible, 3) implying that citizens' affection was inexplicable. This despicable betrayal by Wallace is the turning point for Billy. Wallace, derisively blaming everyone but himself, cannot admit this one brave ally, pouring his heart out, risking his life, and trusting in his justice. Wallace was as irredeemable a moral monstrosity as was T.B. Catron himself.]

So speaking generally, the prisoners are good brave boys according to the side on which they have been fighting ~~and killing if their fighting and killing had been on the side of the persons with whom I talk~~. These prejudices and partialities are as certain to follow jurors into the box the day of the empannelling as that the day will come. **Either the verdict will be acquittals or there will be no verdicts.**

There is no penitentiary in the Territory, if peradventure a ~~sentence~~ verdict of hard labor should be obtained; neither is there any law authorizing me or any other official to contract elsewhere for the keeping a convict. So, too, there is but one lawyer in the county. I offered him an employment in behalf of the Territory. ~~Either~~ He did not dare accept the offer. As attorney for the prisoners he is moving in the matter of habeas corpus writs, and will succeed in setting at liberty seven of my most important prisoners, unless I decline to obey the order of the court – the seven are in arrest without warrants. Only a military commission can bring them to punishment.

[AUTHOR'S NOTE: The Attorney is Sidney Barnes, beholden to the Ring against Wallace to free the prisoners.]

Enough is disclosed to put you in possession of the reasons underlying my clear conviction that coming session of the court will in the present situation be useful only to the wrong-doers; leaving, as I see now after nearly one months study and patient exertion upon the very ground, nothing to be hoped except from martial law.

[AUTHOR'S NOTE: Wallace is lying. Lincoln County's jurors knew the issues; and would correctly indict Ringites.]

The desperadoes include some of the most noted of their class in the United States, and they cannot be made to quit except by actual war – by guns and pistols, not with writs or lectures, and then only by co-operative action between the military of New Mexico, Texas, and Arizona.

[AUTHOR'S NOTE: This is the outlaw myth, with Wallace's murderous intent, which would leave Billy its scapegoat.]

Please give one glance at the ~~region afflicted by them~~ country of Lincoln as it is defined on the map, note its extent and local advantages for operations like theirs, and you will see the force of these latter words.

I hope the President will act upon my request. The expeditions to which I have alluded have not been entirely barren of good results; one is certain, the enemy have been driven to their hiding places, and will not re-appear before the preliminary measures essential to the proposed new regime can be taken.

I have the honor to be,
Very respectfully,
Your friend & servant,
Lew. Wallace,
Gov. New Mexico.

Judge Bristol has been notified of my opinion as to the advisability of holding his court, and my intention to ask a declaration of martial law. His views coincide with mine.

To enable the inhabitants of the town to defend themselves and property, of which latter they have very little left, on the former not any chance to put in their crops, I authorized a military organization of thirty two men – all who had arms and horses.

The instructions given the regular troops, copies of which were furnished you in my last letter, are continuous in their operation and will be carried out as the officers are more or less zealous not being able to do more. I will return to Santa Fe the last of this week or the first of next.

[AUTHOR'S NOTE: Billy would never hear from Wallace again.]

PARDON SADISM YIELDS LITERARY INSPIRATION

As revealing of perfidy was Wallace's March 31, 1879 Carl Schurz letter, was his unconscious translation of it into his historical novel, *Ben-Hur*, which he was then writing. Its sadistic theme of tortured, enslaved hero Judah Ben-Hur has a pardon theme, likely fed by Wallace's power over "the Kid." As will be seen, Wallace continued obsessive literary reworking of Billy's pardon bargain almost up to his death 26 years later. His *Ben-Hur* pardon fantasy is on page 152 of the 1880 first edition:

"Go now," [Arrius the slave master] said, "and do not build upon what has passed between us. Perhaps I do but play with thee ..."

A short while after Ben-Hur was upon his bench again.

A man's task is always light if his heart is light. Handling the oar did not seem so toilsome to Judah. A hope had come to him, like a singing bird. He could hardly see the visitor or hear its song; that it was there, though, he knew; his feelings told him so. The caution of the tribune – "Perhaps I do but play with thee" – was dismissed often as it recurred to his mind. That he had been called by the great man and asked his story was bread upon which he fed his hungry spirit. Surely something good would come of it. The light about his bench was clear and bright with promises.

WALLACE USES IRA LEONARD FOR GRAND JURY PROSECUTIONS: APRIL 6, 1879

Ira Leonard arrived in Lincoln on April 1, 1879 for the Lincoln County Grand Jury. He had already planned with Lew Wallace to consult informally in prosecutions, as he alluded to later in a May 20, 1879 letter to Wallace. (See my pp. 634-642 for full letter) The plan in that letter of anti-Ring Leonard assisting Ringite District Attorney William Rynerson, smacks of another of Wallace's callous and careless concoctions. And Rynerson's response of being *"highly gratified"* smacks of that man's sardonic humor. It should be noted that Leonard knew Wallace's secret: that Billy would be testifying against Chapman's murderers - and would be the prosecution witness the Ring feared most. Leonard wrote:

When Judge Bristol arrived here to hold Court, accompanied by Col. W.L. Rynerson the prosecuting Atty. of this District, about the middle of April, you, Col. Rynerson and I had a conference together in which you stated to him that ***you had made arrangements with me to assist him in the prosecution of the persons under arrest****, and also to assist in the prosecution of those who would likely be indicted at the then approaching term on the Court, and as I understood him* ***he seemed highly gratified*** *at the arrangement and so expressed himself to you and myself at the time.*

Leonard complained later in that May 20, 1879 letter to Wallace about his frustration with Rynerson, stating:

Now Governor, I want to state to you the conduct of the District Attorney which I consider contemptible, notwithstanding the understanding we had together, and his apparent gratification that I was to assist him. You had scarcely gone before he commenced as I afterwards learned to vilify you for procuring aid for him, and commenced shirking the entire responsibility of the prosecution unto me. He told the people, prisoners, and all with whom he confessed that he was simply the official figure head, and that I was the governor's prosecutor, that I was the man the Governor had selected to see them punished. He was to my own knowledge in secret and open conference with Dolan the murderer of Chapman, and intends to defend him at Socorro, the place to which the venue is changed, it being out of his District and he connived to procure the change of venue from the District for that purpose.

He aroused among the friends of the outlaws [Ringite rustlers and murderers] here a feeing of antagonism against me.

Lew Wallace had a Pinochio-Jiminy Cricket relationship with Attorney Ira Leonard: being the liar to Leonard's voice of conscience. By the April Grand Jury, Wallace, needing indictments to prove his own effectiveness, assumed his officious persona of "The General" on April 6, 1879. Noteworthy is that Wallace never mentioned Billy as his star witness. Wallace wrote:

> *Lincoln Fort Stanton, April 6, 1879*
> *Judge I.E. Leonard*
> *Dear Sir:*
> *It is important to take steps now to protect the coming court. The question is how to do it best.*
> *For this I wish to station outposts of soldiers half a mile outside the town, to take off the arms of all persons coming in not authorized to carry arms. If there was some one to declare an ordinance or town regulation covering this point, one would be fixed beautifully.*
> *Can't the Probate Judge (Gonzales) or Squire Wilson or Alcade make the ordinance? I have a copy of the Territorial laws. Be good enough to look into the matter, and if such authorized person can be had, draft the ordinance, and let it be published and printed immediately.*
> *They managed the making of the town laws in Las Vegas before – How was it done? Answer by this courier.*
> *Truly, yours,*
> *Lew Wallace*
> *Gov. New Mexico*

Leonard was in Lincoln; and, like everyone else Wallace had roped in, also had to report on mythical outlaws. On borrowed letterhead, on April 8. 1879, he wrote, interjecting Ring realities of the ongoing *"cruel war"* and Huston Chapman's bereaved father, encouraging Wallace: "*I wish you would write him it would be a consolation to him.*" Leonard wrote:

𝕷incoln, 𝕹ew 𝕸exico, <u>April 8<u>th</u> 187<u>9</u></u>

Gov Lew Wallace
    Fort Stanton N.M.

My dear Gov. You may have learned the result of the cattle examination the Probate Judge deciding to hold them for claimants. I was pretty well convinced ~~that~~ *in the case of Howell that he was the rightful owner, but having failed to comply with the law in having them branded the court decided to hold them. It may be hard on the old man but it is necessary to learn stock owners that they must comply with the laws if they desire the protection which it affords.*

I enclose a letter I received from Chapman's father yesterday, his views are sound & I wish you would write him it would be a consolation to him to receive a letter from you –

I wrote you yesterday about the session acts. I need them very much, they are not here or but few of them I should very much regret being mistaken in any advice I might give the Sheriff [George Kimbrell] on account of any changes which may have been made in the laws. I know they are difficult to obtain but they can be had from the Sec. [William Ritch] and I wish you would have him send them to me – **and I will return them if necessary when the cruel "war is over" – Matters appear to be quiet but there is no telling when the elements may break loose***.*

I am quite convinced that the philosophical remark of the Dutchman, "that the longer a man lives the more he finds out," is true, and that it is not safe for one to trust his grandfather in this country ...

Yours truly
Ira E. Leonard

MORE RINGITE PRISONERS ESCAPE JUSTICE: APRIL 13, 1879

As Wallace played sado-masochistic games with captive Billy, reality struck him once again. On April 13, 1879, the Ring acted to protect their own. Wallace had even bemoaned the possibility to Carl Schurz in his letter of March 31, 1879, knowing his hands were legally tied. Wallace had written:

[There is no] law authorizing me or any other official to contract elsewhere for the keeping a convict. So, too, there is but one lawyer in the county [Ringite Sidney Wilson in Lincoln]. I offered him an employment in behalf of the Territory ... He did not dare accept the offer. **As attorney for the prisoners he is moving in the matter of habeas corpus writs, and will succeed in setting at liberty seven of my most important prisoners,** *unless I decline to obey the order of the court - the seven are in arrest without warrants. Only a military commission can bring them to punishment.*

To Fort Stanton, the Ring now sent heavy-hitting attorneys - Simon Newcomb (who would be one of Billy's prosecuting attorneys in his Mesilla hanging trial), Sidney Wilson, and Albert Jennings Fountain (who would be one of Billy's court-appointed attorneys in his Mesilla hanging trial) - along with Judge Warren Bristol, to free Wallace's remaining prisoners: James Dolan and the 20 Seven Rivers men. They filed writs of *habeas corpus* - claiming no legal justification existed to hold them longer before the Grand Jury that month. Bristol rubber-stamped that.

In his later letter of May 20, 1879 to Wallace (See my pp. 634-642 for full letter), Ira Leonard bemoaned the outcome as based on *"flimsy technicalities upon which many of the desperate men were released."* Leonard then revealed the intellectual and strategic mediocrity which continuously blunted his noble efforts. Though he was communicating about the Santa Fe Ring in this letter and its cover letter of May 23rd, he overlooked Judge Bristol's role, stating: *"It seemed to me ... that Judge Bristol had the timidity of a child and stood in fear of the desperate characters that curse this country instead of the boldness and determination to bring them to justice."* Such non-astute analysis would be to Billy's detriment when Leonard became his lawyer, but neglected to file a necessary Petition for Pardon. As to Bristol, Leonard was clearly unaware of Mary McPherson's 1877 exposés on him - and Wallace, secretly betraying the anti-Ring cause, stayed silent about possessing her typeset publication. The upshot was that Billy was now the sole "outlaw" in Lew Wallace's "captivity."

That day, Billy's risk went up tremendously with his *"enimies"* on the lose. District Attorney Rynerson could simply walk him the short distance from Juan Partón's house-jail to Lincoln's courthouse, where Judge Bristol could act on Billy's 1878 murder indictments by declaring Lincoln County too partisan for a "fair" trial, change his venue to Doña Ana County, and send him immediately for a hanging trial to Mesilla. Only Wallace's annulling of Billy's indictments could prevent all that.

So Billy awaited the Grand Jury, believing his testimony would free him. And Wallace, chasing mythical outlaws while preparing for his Dudley Court of Inquiry testimony the following month, day-dreamed that Dudley's certain conviction would end Lincoln County's "troubles." Realistic was only was Billy's growing friendship with Ira Leonard.

Earlier in that day of April 13th, Wallace wrote to Leonard a muddled mix about the upcoming freeing and his outlaw chase:

> *Lincoln Fort Stanton, April 13, 1879*
> *Judge I.E. Leonard*
>
> *Dear Judge:*
> *Your favor with the prisoners, received.*
> *Capt. Carroll will make the affidavit, upon which warrants will be immediately issued ...*
> *There are now here attorneys Thornton [law partner of T.B. Catron], Newcomb, Fountain and another whom I don't know. They all seem to have been engaged for all the prisoners, though Sidney Wilson is ahead of them in the matter of fees. He has skimmed the pail and got the cream off the milk.*
> *The Judge (Bristol) is to let me know this evening whether he will proceed with the criminal side of his court and what he will do generally. Meantime there is much writing going on. Sunday might it be, and I hear the work is devoted to petitions for habeas corpus writs. When the writs are issued and heard, I will send my ambulance [military transport vehicle from the Fort] to bring you here; for they will be heard in chamber by the Judge at the post.*
> *Dudley came in today, and is at Purington's quarters.*
> *Take in the other "buffalos" and insist upon Kimbrell's getting their arms in his possession. He left Monk's at the hotel.*
>
> *Yours truly,*
> *Lew Wallace*

Leonard responded that day: *"I will have vagrant act enforced also any violation of law carrying arms,"* unaware that the Ring was mobilizing at Fort Stanton and Lincoln.

WALLACE REPORTS PROGRESS TO SCHURZ: APRIL 18, 1879

Wallace's ability to write fiction was useful on April 18, 1879. In the midst of Ring fires lit all around him, he proclaimed "progress" to Secretary of the Interior Carl Schurz in the form of the Lincoln County Grand Jury's commencement. Wallace wrote:

Fort Stanton, April 18. 1879.
Hon. C. Schurz
Sec'y Dept. Interior.
Dear Sir:
I have the honor to inform you that affairs in Lincoln county are progressing favorably as could be expected.

Court opened at the county seat Monday morning, having eighteen prisoners charged with murder and grand larcenies to occupy its time and attention. How successful the session will be I am not yet able to say. The juries are selected and sworn and hopes are indulged that they will come up to the necessities of the situation and do their duty.

This morning I start for Santa Fe to make some preparation for Col. Dudley's court of inquiry, which begins on the 25 proximo. I am sorry it was not postponed until after the county court is through.

Very respectfully,
Your friend,
Lew. Wallace

CHAPTER 16

PARDON BARGAIN FULFILLED BY BILLY BONNEY AND AFTERMATH: APRIL, 1879 - MAY 8, 1879

BILLY TESTIFIES FOR THE PARDON BARGAIN

ANALYSIS: Billy Bonney fulfilled his side of the pardon bargain by testifying in the April 1879 Lincoln County Grand Jury against Huston Chapman's murderers. And he achieved indictments of James Dolan and Billy Campbell for first degree murder, and of Jessie Evans as accessory to that murder.

BILLY'S GRAND JURY TESTIMONY: APRIL, 1879

The transcript of the April, 1879 Lincoln County Grand Jury under District Judge Warren Bristol likely fell victim to the Ring's usual expurgation of incriminating records. But Billy's testifying can be confirmed by contemporary records.

Attorney Ira Leonard, knowing about Billy's pardon bargain, dutifully confirmed his testifying to Lew Wallace on April 20, 1879. He described Ring pressure, writing: *"[Rynerson] is bent on going for the Kid ... to destroy his testimony & influence he is bent on pushing him to the wall. He is a Dolan man and is defending him by his conduct all he can."* Billy's unflappable testimony likely engendered Leonard's admiration and loyalty. Leonard wrote:

Sunday eve April 20th 1879
Lincoln Plaza
Dear Gov. The air is filled tonight with "rumors of wars" or rumors that the military force is to be immediately withdrawn from here. Lee Keyser came from the Fort this evening and brought the intelligence, and one of Col. Dudleys particular friends is offering to bet five to one that he will be commissioned out at the Post in twenty days I have suspicion that there may be something of the kind up, that is the withdrawal of the troops – The soldier you ordered to report to me and remain with me had orders last night to leave and report to the Fort so after one days duty he took his leave under orders –

[AUTHOR'S NOTE: Guard removal may have been preparation for Leonard's planned Ring assassination in two days.]

I had made an arrangement with the Sheriff to take those Hudgens boys and Henry to Fort Stockton and deliver them over to the authorities there with their stolen plunder. It would be the best thing that could be done if they could be sent through the country where the outlaws congregate under a strong Military guard with their stolen property & returned to the field where they perpetrated their crimes. That would be a sort of comity worth something because we could then establish relations with Texas which would induce them to pick up thieves who plunder from here and bring them to us and vice versa and a very short time would induce these fiends to leave this field for one more healthy to operate in. My plan was to have him write to the officers at the Fort Stockton telling them that he would have these thieves at El Paso at a certain time and to be there ready to move property & secure them. I tell you Gov they shall not get away We have got to use extraordinary measures and I think my plan a good one to break up this plundering. What do you think of it. If the people have got to depend on themselves without aid a short course can be made of it. The only remains left is to take these parties by force & ask surrender to the authorities where they can be punished & have them bring our outlaws back to us and my word for it will be but a short time before they will skin out of this country –

Court is moving on have tried no more habeas corpus cases I stave them off – **I tell you Gov that the prosecuting officer of this Dist [William Rynerson] is no friend to the enforcement of the law. He is bent on going for the Kid & notwithstanding he knows how it is proposed to destroy his testimony & influence he is bent on pushing him to the wall He is a Dolan man and is defending him by his conduct all he can**

I am going to have the Sheriff demand a Military escort & then shove these prisoners into Texas – It may be he can't get it but we will try for it –

Be sure & send me Session laws if you have to borrow them of Judge Waldo for awhile –

Write me & keep me posted

Yours &c
Ira Leonard

BILLY ACHIEVES INDICTMENTS: APRIL 28, 1879

District Attorney William L. Rynerson's filing on April 28, 1879 verified the Chapman case's indictments: James Dolan and Billy Campbell, for murder; and Jessie Evans as accessory to murder. It should be noted that Rynerson was required merely to record the Grand Jury's indictments; but not required to issue arrest warrants. Evans and Campbell had already escaped. And Dolan was never arrested or tried - a repeat of Dolan's shielding from his murder of Tunstall. Rynerson wrote:

The Territory of New Mexico
County of Lincoln
In the District Court of the County of
Lincoln at the April A.D. 1879 Term Thereof
The Grand Jurors for the Territory of New Mexico taken from the body of the good and lawful men of the County of Lincoln in the Territory of New Mexico, duly elected, empanelled, sworn and charged at the term aforesaid, to inquiry in and for the body of the County of Lincoln aforesaid, upon the oaths do present that **James J. Dolan and William Campbell** *late of the County of Lincoln in the Territory aforesaid on the nineteenth [eighteenth] day of February in the year of our Lord one thousand eight hundred and seventy nine at the County and Territory aforesaid with force and arms in and upon one Huston I. Chapman then and there being of their malice aforethought, unlawfully, feloniously, willfully, and from a premeditated design to effect the death of him the said Huston I. Chapman did make an assault. And that the said James J. Dolan and the said William Campbell certain pistols then and there loaded and charged with gunpowder and divers leaden bullets,* **(which pistols they the said James J. Dolan and the said William Campbell in their right hands then and there had and held) to against and upon the said Huston I. Chapman then and there of their malice aforethought unlawfully, feloniously, willfully and from a premeditated design to effect the death of the said Huston I. Chapman did shoot and discharge.** *And that they the said James J. Dolan and the said William Campbell with the leaden bullets aforesaid out of the pistols aforesaid then and there by force of the gunpowder shot and sent forth as aforesaid the said Huston I. Chapman in and upon the left breast of him the said Huston I.*

Chapman **then and there of their malice aforethought, unlawfully, feloniously, willfully, and from a premeditated design to effect the death of him the said Huston I. Chapman did strike, penetrate and wound, giving the said Huston I. Chapman then and there with leaden bullets aforesaid so as aforesaid shot discharged and sent forth out of the pistols aforesaid by the said James J. Dolan and the said William Campbell in and upon the left breast of him the said Huston I. Chapman one mortal wound the said Huston I. Chapman then and there instantly died.** *And so the jurors aforesaid upon their oaths aforesaid do say that the said James J. Dolan and the said William Campbell the said Huston I. Chapman in manner and form aforesaid and by the means aforesaid of their malice aforethought* **unlawfully, feloniously, willfully, and from a premeditated design to effect the death of him the said Huston I. Chapman did kill and murder.**

And the jurors aforesaid upon their oaths aforesaid do further present that **Jessie Evans** *late of the County and territory aforesaid before the said Huston I. Chapman was killed and murdered as aforesaid in form as aforesaid to wit on the nineteenth [eighteenth] day of February in the year aforesaid at the County aforesaid* **did feloniously and maliciously unlawfully and from a premeditated design to effect the death of him the said Huston I. Chapman, incite move procure and counsel, hire and command the said James J. Dolan and the said William Campbell the said felony, to wit the murder of the said Huston I. Chapman as aforesaid** *in manner and form aforesaid to do and commit against the form of the statute in such case made and provided against the peace and dignity of the Territory of New Mexico.*

W.L. Rynerson
District Attorney
3rd Jud Dist N.M.

GRANT COUNTY HERALD REPORTS: MAY 10, 1879

Billy Bonney's Grand Jury testimony was also confirmed in May 10, 1879's Grant County *Herald,* as reprinted from the Mesilla *Thirty Four.* It also reported that Rynerson kept Billy in custody. Noteworthy were many granted pardons using the Amnesty Proclamation, and Billy's early publicity. It stated:

At the recent term of court in Lincoln, about 200 indictments were found. Among them, Col. Dudley and George W. Peppin for burning McSween's house, **Dolan and Campbell for the Chapman murder, in which the Kid is the principal witness**; about 25 persons for the murder of MacNab; Tom O'Folliard for stealing Fritz's horses. But two criminal cases were tried - that of Lucas Gallagos for the murder of his nephew. He was found guilty and sentenced to one year; and a case of assault in which the accused was acquitted. No civil case was tried. In nearly all of them, one or the other party was dead. O'Folliard, Jack Long, Marion Turner, and others, plead the governors [Amnesty] pardon and were discharged. Peppin, Dolan and Matthews took a change of venue to Socorro, and Dudley took a change of verue to Dona Ana county. **The District Attorney would not consent to the release of the Kid for turning State's evidence. His case comes to Dona Ana county**. The greater portion of persons indicted will probably come forward and plead the governor's [Amnesty] pardon. Dolan and Matthews, indicted in the last term for the Tunstall murder, also go to Socorro on change of venue. Opinion is divided as to what the result will be. Some think a fresh outbreak is imminent, and others that the trouble is over. The two opposing factions have about exhausted themselves and future troubles will only arise from bands passing through and pluncering. Jesse Evans and Campbell have not been rearrested.

VENUE CHANGE FOR BILLY BONNEY: APRIL 21, 1879

Billy Bonney had predicted his mortal danger in his first letter on March 13(?), 1879 to Lew Wallace: "*I have indictments against me for things that happened in the late Lincoln County War and am afraid to give up because my Enimies would Kill me.*" The measure of Wallace's callousness was on April 21, 1879, when he did not grant Billy's pardon after the Ring implemented its preferred style of killing: under guise of law. Judge Warren Bristol changed Billy's trial venue for his three indictments to Doña Ana County's Mesilla court to guarantee hanging by a jury ignorant of Lincoln County War issues - repeating the 1876 tactic of Governor S.B. Axtell removing Colfax County courts so Franklin Tolby's Ringite murderers would face a naïve Taos County jury. Though on the indictment also, John Middleton and Henry Brown, had long escaped from the Territory. District Attorney William Rynerson filed the order on April 21, 1879. And Ringites, John Long and Marion Turner, witnessed it. Rynerson wrote:

Territory of New Mexico
District Court 3d Judicial
District County of Lincoln
April Term A.D. 1881

In the Third Judicial
District Court April Term / 1879

Territory of New Mexico)
vs)
) *Murder*
John Middleton & Henry Brown)
William Bonney alias Kid)
Alias William Antrim)

Now comes the said Territory by her attorney W.L. Rynerson District attorney of the said Third Judicial District and moves the Court for a change of venue from said County of Lincoln in above titled cause as to the said defendant William Bonney alias "Kid" alias William Antrim for reasons set forth in the affidavit following and annexed.
W.L. Rynerson
Dist. Atty –

Territory of New Mexico) *SS.*
County of Lincoln)

W.L. Rynerson District Attorney of the Third Judicial District of the said Territory of New Mexico being first duly sworn deposes and says that justice cannot be done the said Territory on the trial of the said defendant William Bonney alias Kid alias William Antrim in the said County of Lincoln for the reason that jurors in attendance and all those liable to be summoned for the trial of said defendant, by reason of

partisanship in the late and existing troubles and lawlessness in said County have so prejudiced the said jurors that they cannot fairly and impartially try the said defendant; and for the further reason that said jurors and the witnesses in said cause are so intimidated by lawless men in said Lincoln County by fear of violence and lawlessness against their persons and property on the part of said lawless men that the said jurors and witnesses cannot fearlessly and justly perform their respective duties at said trial in said Lincoln County.
W.L. Rynerson

Sworn & subscribed before me in open court April 21, 1879.
Louis H. Baldy, Clerk

Territory of New Mexico   )
County of Lincoln   )

Marion Turner and John Long being each duly sworn depose and say severally that they have heard the Foregoing affidavit read and know the contents thereof and that the matters and things as therein stated are true.
John Long
Marian Turner

ATTEMPTED ASSASSINATION OF IRA LEONARD: APRIL 25, 1879

After Huston Chapman's assassination just a month earlier, Ira Leonard was naturally anxious during the Grand Jury. From Lincoln, he wrote to Lew Wallace on April 12, 1879 about rough characters coming to town, apparently Ringites. Leonard wrote:

𝕷incoln, 𝕹ew 𝕸exico, *April 12th 1879*

Gov Lew Wallace
    Fort Stanton N.M.   Dear Gov.
                    I was disappointed in not seeing you when I went to the Fort. I hope you will be down while the court is in session.
    There are some suspicious circumstances as that require vigilance to ascertain whether there is any meaning attached to

them or not, for the last two or three days there have straggled in here from four to six hard looking characters a day, cowboys from Texas and Buffalo hunters. One gives this reason or another that for coming here but **I have an idea that the object is to rescue their friends if brought here for trial, they are all camping about or near the town so I am informed.**

I am satisfied that old Dr Gurnsey is in the camp with Campbell & Evans. He left here three days ago on a pretended prospecting tour this morning ... If I had known it at the time I should have put some one on his trail – Ballard is also gone it is said to his store but I don't believe it.

       Yours truly
         Ira E. Leonard

The next day, April 13th, Wallace's remaining Fort Stanton prisoners were freed.

So it was likely James Dolan, who, on April 25, 1879, tried to kill Ira Leonard; though he was never charged. That day, Leonard's legal assistant, George Taylor, informed Wallace, who added a misdated note to the letter: "*May 21st, 79, From Geo. Taylor. Esq - giving act of the shooting into Judge Leonard's house.*" Taylor also obsequiously flattered by adding Wallace's interests: outlawry and mining opportunities. Taylor wrote:

Lincoln New Mexico April 25th-79

  Governor Lew Wallace
    My dear Governor
      I thought I would give you a little sketch of matters here as some things that have happened since you left may be interesting to you.

  Last night two of those outlawed scoundrels who are so numerous around here made a dash through town horseback and fired into our building.

  *Judge Leonard had changed the place of his bed and they seemed to be aware of the fact for the bullets were directed where he lay, fortunately the side of the house was struck and no damage done but had they not been going so rapidly **when they fired they may have accomplished their purpose which was evidently to kill or injure the Judge so he cannot prosecute them**.*

  Col Rynerson the prosecuting attorney for the territory is either afraid or anxious to screen these villains you have arrested;

he is entering into his work with no spirit and leaves all the work for the Judge only interfering to raise obstacles in the way of bringing the rascals to justice.

I have no confidence in him he has been engaged in murderous scrapes himself and can't help but have a fellow feeling for men who are in the same trouble he has been in himself.

[Attorney Sidney] Wilson is in great trouble, the men who employed him are now trying to get back their horses and arms from him; he is denouncing them as a set of ___ cutthroats and murderers and swearing he will never defend another one of them, he told me he had heard them make desperate threats against parties who have been prominent in arresting them, and particularly against Judge Leonard against whom they are very hostile. singulously they have no feeling against Rynerson but all their animosity is directed against the Judge.

You should have laughed had you seen us rushing around for our weapons when we were fired into last night, it was a complete surprise to as we had not anticipated anything of the kind. I thought when you were here you took most too many precautions I see now I was mistaken there is no telling when the scoundrels will make a break on us, they are thirsting for revenge and plunder and the instant the military are withdrawn from here we will have the same bloody contests over again that have taken place here before.

We are now well armed and ready to give the outlaws a good reception when they come as they surely will if that military scoundrel Col Dudley is exonerated from his crimes and again placed in command. it is a mystery to me how that man can be permitted to disgrace the army as he does, using it to persecute and murder the honest people of this county and aid and protect the most desperate thieves and outlaws in the United States in their crimes.

The mining interests are looking better every day. I believe we will soon have some good developments made.

I will write you the news as they occur, I hope you will soon return as these outlaws stand in great dread of you and your presence here gives us all a greater sense of security than even the military as they could not prevent the outrage of last night.

Respectfully
George Taylor
Lincoln New Mexico

GRAND JURY INDICTMENTS AND PARDONS

As Fort Stanton's Captain George Purington reported bitterly on May 3, 1879 to Headquarters, the April, 1879 Lincoln County Grand Jury made *"two hundred indictments against one of the factions [Murphy-Dolans], and none against the other [McSweens]."* Indicted by the knowledgeable jurymen were N.A.M. Dudley, past Sheriff George Peppin, and James Dolan, confirming the jurors' ability to convict Ringites for their Lincoln County War crimes. But of the indicted, none would ever be prosecuted. And Lew Wallace himself would indirectly pardon some of them. After these latest obstructions of justice, Lincolnites would withdraw permanently into learned helplessness. Purington wrote:

Headquarters, Fort Stanton, N.M.
May 3ᵈ 1879.

To the A.A.A. General
Dist. N.M.

Sir. –

The District Court adjourned on Thursday the 1ˢᵗ inst. ***The Grand Jury returned nearly two hundred indictments against one of the factions [Murphy-Dolans], and none against the other [McSweens].*** *Lieut. Col. N.A.M. Dudley, U.S.A., was indicted for arson. He appeared in Court and took a change of venue to Doña Ana County, to appear on the 16ᵗʰ of June. He was held on his own recognizance, in two thousand dollars ($2000⁰⁰) to so appear.* ***Most of the citizen prisoners who were indicted by the Grand Jury were arraigned and pleaded the Governor's pardon. The Court held that the Governor's proclamation was a general amnesty for all offences coming within its provisions.*** *The prisoners were discharged.* ***Doc. Scurlock and the "Kid," the two most notorious murderers of the County, have been in custody of the Sheriff at Lincoln. The Grand Jury did not indict them.*** *The Sheriff [George Kimbrell] who is Deputy U.S. Marshal released them although he knew that there were indictments against them for murder in the U.S. Court [past U.S. Attorney T.B. Catron's federal indictment No. 411 done in 1878], and the warrants for their arrest said to be in his hands.*

[AUTHOR'S NOTE: Billy stayed in jail after testifying to testify against Dudley in the Court of Inquiry. "Doc" Scurlock eventually left the Territory. Ringite Purlington's calling them the most "notorious murderers," of course omitted that Dolan was involved in murdering Tunstall, McSween, and Chapman. But it was in keeping with the Ring's cover-up outlaw myth.]

Mr. Dolan, and Ex-Sheriff Peppin did not avail themselves of the Governor's proclamation. They changed their venue to Socorro County. Mr. Dolan is still in confinement at the Post. Mr. Peppin is under bonds ...

Peace and quiet reign and I can see no reason for further disturbance. The militia company organized by the Governor is quite sufficient to preserve the peace ...

Between fifty (50) and seventy five (75) subpoenas have been received by the Judge Advocate of the Court of Inquiry in Lieut Colonel Dudley's case, most of which have been served.

The Judge Advocate [Galusha Pennypacker] arrived on April 24th, '79 and Major Osborn and Captain Brinkerhoff [the two other Judges] of the Court [of Inquiry] arrived on the 1st instant.

I am, Sir,
Very respectfully
Your obedient servant,
Geo. C. Purington
Capt. 9th Cavalry
Comadg

WALLACE'S INDIRECT PARDONING OF RINGITES: MAY 1, 1879

The heinousness of Lew Wallace's betrayal of his pardon bargain with Billy Bonney is shown by his laxity in pardoning anyone except Billy. He condoned the April of 1879's Lincoln Grand Jury's pardon through Judge Warren Bristol of any indicted Ringites who ignored his November 13, 1878 Amnesty Proclamation's clause excluding the indicted and plead amnesty in bar of their future prosecution. For Wallace, that was another way to avoid Ring confrontation by permitting the Ring to shield its members from penalties. And Wallace later blithely rationalized that Amnesty Proclamation violation, in a June 11, 1879 letter to Carl Schurz, as avoiding future costly trials. (See my pp. 666-670 for full letter) Wallace wrote to Schurz:

[M]y amnesty proclamation has had exactly the effect intended; which was to shear the past off, and make present and future all questions which might require official action ... To illustrate, the grand jury empanelled for the recent county court was, with one or two exceptions, composed of men accounted of the McSween or anti-Dolan party, for it is undeniable that nearly all citizens eligible as grand-jurors are ~~inimical to the latter~~ of that persuasion. They found nearly 200 indictments, the whole, with a few exceptions, against the Dolan people. Nearly 200 indictments in a county of a voting population of 150 ~~in all~~ total! You cannot fail to see what would have come of trial of the accused - how long they would have lasted - the expenses to a county which has nothing in its treasury ... **As it was most of the indicted appeared in court and plead the amnesty in bar [of further prosecution].** <u>Hereafter the labors of grand juries will be confined strictly to offences subsequent to my proclamation</u>.

It should be recalled that Wallace had already essentially pardoned all non-indicted Ringites in that Amnesty Proclamation. And indicted James Dolan, George Peppin, and N.A.M. Dudley were shielded by Bristol in that 1879 Grand Jury by change of trial venues out of knowledgeable Lincoln County, where he later dismissed Dolan's and Peppin's cases based on no prosecution witnesses from Lincoln County daring to come to a trial. And Dudley was cleared by arguing his exoneration in his military Court of Inquiry. Ultimately only Billy was left without a pardon and with a hanging sentence. That is why he told a *Mesilla News* reporter on April 15, 1881, after his hanging trial: "I think it hard that I should be the only one to suffer the extreme penalty of the law."

For the Ringmen's District Court pardons, on May 1, 1879, T.B. Catron; his law partner, William Thornton; and Ringite Attorneys Sidney Wilson and Simon B. Newcomb (in 1881, one of Billy's prosecuting attorneys in his Mesilla hanging trial) had brazenly quoted in their Pardon Petition the Proclamation's exclusionary clause: *"And it is expressly understood that the foregoing pardon is upon the conditions and limitations following: ... Neither shall it be pleaded by any person in bar of conviction under indictment now found."* Then they ignored it. They had filed for, and gotten, pardons for Jacob Basil "Billy" Matthews, William Powell, John Long, and John Hurlie. For their Pardon Petition to Judge Bristol, Catron and the others wrote:

Territory of New Mexico
County of Lincoln

In the Third Judicial
District Court April Term / 1879

Territory of New Mexico
vs

Jacob B. Matthews)
William B. Powell)
John Long and)
John Hurlie et al Defets)
)

Now at this day comes the above named defendants Jacob B. Matthews, William B. Powell, John Long, and John Hurlie into Court and for plea to the said supposed crime charged in the indictment in the cause say that not confessing the alleged crime and allegations denying the commission thereof that they ought not to be persecuted for said supposed crime for that they have been fully pardoned and granted an amnesty by his excellency Governor Lew Wallace Governor of the Territory of New Mexico, which said pardon, so far as it relates to these defendants is in words and figures as follows:

For information of the people of the United States, and of the citizens of the Territory of New Mexico in especial, the undersigned announces that the disorders lately prevalent in Lincoln County in said Territory, have been happily brought to an end. Persons having business and property interests therein, and who are themselves peaceably disposed, may go to and from the County without hindrance or molestation. Individuals resident there, but who have been driven away, or who from choice sought safety elsewhere, are invited to return, under assurance that ample measures have been taken and are now and will be continued in force, to make them secure in person and property. And that the people of Lincoln County may be helped more speedily to the management of their civil affairs, as contemplated by law, and to induce them to lay aside forever the divisions and feuds which, by national notoriety have been so prejudicial to their locality and the whole Territory, the undersigned, by virtue of authority in him vested, further proclaims a general pardon for misdemeanors and offences committed in the said County of Lincoln against the laws of the said Territory in connection with the aforesaid disorders, between the first day of February, 1878, and the date of this proclamation.

And it is expressly understood that the foregoing pardon is upon the conditions and limitations following:

It shall not apply to officers of the United States Army stationed in the said County during the said disorders and to persons who, at the time of the commission of the offence or misdemeanor of which they may have been accused were with good intent, residents citizens of the said Territory, and who shall have hereafter kept the peace, and conducted themselves in all respects as becomes good citizens.

Neither shall it be pleaded by any person in bar of conviction under indictment now found and returned for any such crimes and misdemeanors, nor operate the release of any party undergoing pains and penalties consequent upon sentence heretofore had for any crime or misdemeanor. In witness whereof I have set my hand and caused the seal of the Territory of N.M. to be official: Dated 13th day of Nov 1878 Lew Wallace.

That said alleged crime grew out of and was connected with the Disorders in Lincoln County mentioned in said pardon after the 1st day of February 1878 and before the issuing thereof, that said defendants were at the time they are accused with the commission of said crime, with good intent resident citizens of said Territory, and that they have ever since the issuing of said pardon kept the peace and conducted themselves in all respects as becomes good citizens, and that they were not at the time indicted for said alleged crime.

S.B. Newcomb
Sidney Wilson &
Catron and Thornton
Attorneys for Defts

MYSTERY OF IRA LEONARD'S PARDON INACTION

One can question why Attorney Ira Leonard, present to aid the prosecution in that 1879 Grand Jury, had not himself file a Petition for Billy's pardon citing either amnesty in bar of prosecution used by Carton and associates, or citing Billy's own bargain. By 1880, Leonard certainly did try to arrange a different pardon for Billy through Secret Service Operative Azariah Wild.

One can postulate that Leonard was too traumatized to function properly after just surviving his own Ring assassination attempt on April 25, 1879 - a month after Huston Chapman's actual murder. And Leonard also backed away in 1881 after representing Billy at his Mesilla trial and getting the "Buckshot" Roberts indictment quashed; but then suddenly withdrawing from Billy's defense after another likely Ring death threat.

One can also postulate that Leonard lacked legal sophistication of Ringite attorneys to file for a Pardon Petition. As evidence, is his lackluster consulting with the prosecuting officer in the Dudley Court of Inquiry. Though nothing could have altered the corrupt outcome there, Leonard's tendency to rely on sincerity instead of aggressive and sterling legal arguing was evident.

Most likely, however, Leonard was paralyzed by the futility of fighting the Ring. Indicted Ringites could plead for amnesty and get pardoned. But if Billy had done that through Leonard, Judge Bristol would simply have rejected the Petition. Even more difficult, would have been formulating that Petition's argument, since it needed anti-Ring contentions linking the killings of Roberts, Brady, and Hindman to mitigation of Billy's deputizing and the Lincoln County War freedom fight. That would have risked Leonard's life, as well as being rejected by Bristol.

And yet more difficult, would have been revealing Wallace's bargain with Billy to argue pardon based on it. That would have ended for Leonard any friendly relationship with Wallace, who had kept it secret. And the pardon bargain was so anti-Ring that it would have been rejected by Bristol; and it would have tempted the Ring's murder of Leonard and Billy, and political revenge on Wallace. Only Billy, committed to the freedom fight against the Ring, had the stomach for such risk-taking.

But the outcome was clear: the only real chance Billy then had with Wallace was Leonard's appealing to Wallace's conscience, coupled with filing a Pardon Petition to pressure Wallace's action.

WALLACE BLAMES "OUTLAWS"

Having gone through the charade of the 1879 Lincoln County Grand Jury which yielded indictments without consequences and Ringite pardons, Lew Wallace returned to his outlaw myth.

On May 5, 1879, Wallace - omitting reducing Lincoln County citizenry to legal impotence - fictionalized the outcome for Secretary of the Interior Carl Schurz as: *"Lincoln county is enjoying a term of peace."* Feigning action, he expanded his outlaw myth. The letter's content makes clear that only 49 days from the March 17, 1879 pardon bargain meeting with Billy, and less than one month after Billy's Chapman testimony fulfilling that bargain, Wallace had no intention to honor it. Wallace also knew, things were about to get worse. The Dudley Court of Inquiry was starting. So Wallace stuck to the outlaw myth, stating:

EXECUTIVE OFFICE,
Territory of New Mexico.
𝒮𝒶𝓃𝓉𝒶 𝐹𝑒, 𝒩𝑒𝓌 𝑀𝑒𝓍𝒾𝒸𝑜, May 5, 1879.

Hon. C. Schurz
Sec. Dept. Interior.
Sir:
I have the honor to inform you that all the recent reports, military and otherwise, justify me in saying Lincoln county is enjoying a term of peace. It is to be hoped the interval will continue. That it is due to the active measures taken against the outlaws the last month or two cannot be doubted.

The report I sent you descriptive of affairs in <u>Lincoln County</u> seems to have fallen into the hands of reporters who did not hesitate to speak of it as applicable to <u>the whole Territory</u>. As their statement was extensively copied, my enemies here and elsewhere took it up to my injury. I am sure you did not so intend; and if you will cause a correction to be published, the favor will be appreciated.

You may have probably observed the newspaper references to recent mineral discoveries in a district called <u>Los Cerillos</u> about 20 miles from this city. I have been to that locality twice, and made careful inspection of the discoveries. It is hardly impossible to exaggerate their extent and richness. I shall be greatly deceived if we have not here a greater than Leadville.

I leave this afternoon to be present as a witness in the Court appointed for Lt. Col. N.A.M. Dudley, and as I cannot say when I will return to Santa Fe, official communications will reach me at Fort Stanton.

I have the honor to be,
Very truly, your friend,
Lew. Wallace,
Gov. New Mexico.

By May 7, 1879, Wallace's communication to Carl Schurz from Lincoln was leaked - likely by him - to the *Chicago Times*; leading to his Santa Fe *Sentinel* interview quoted that day in the Denver *Daily Tribune*. Wallace made Lincoln County an epicenter of outlawry; its freedom fight concealed. Soon he would single out one outlaw for literary impact: Billy the Kid. Wallace was quoted:

"The article represents me describing the Territory of New Mexico as overrun by a hoard of thieves, murderers and banditti ... The letter in question had relation to the situation in Lincoln county exclusively, and was in no wise applicable to any other portion of the Territory. It gives me great pleasure to say that outside of that one county life and property are as safe as in any State in this Union."

CHAPMAN'S FAMILY AWAITS JUSTICE

On May 8, 1879, Huston Chapman's father, W.W. Chapman, unaware of Ring machinations, contacted Ira Leonard about the progress of justice for his son. He wrote:

Portland Oregon

May 8th 1879

Hon Ira E Leonard
Las Vegas N.M.

My dear friend
Since receiving yours of the 1st March I received a letter from a gentleman in Lincoln giving me some more of the particulars of my sons death, of the arrest and escape of the assassins, also of the arrest of Dudley. But nothing further. I have anxiously hoped to receive something further from you as to the results. The indications of the Governors letters of which you favored me with a copy were that he would discharge his duty in enforcing the law and bringing the offenders to justice. And from what I learn he has met the expectations of his friends and the public, generally. Everything which has transpired since proves the correctness of the recommendations made by the Governor in respect to removing Dudley from the command at Fort Stanton.

I have written to the Secretary of War soon after receiving your letters. I have reason to think the Secretary has or will supersede him at Fort Stanton.

I shall be thankful to you for information from time to time of the progress of investigations. Whether the offenders have been recaptured and tried and what has been done with Dudley with such other additional information upon the subject as you have. Thanking you again for kindness
I am yours truly
WW Chapman

CHAPTER 17

THE DUDLEY COURT OF INQUIRY: MAY - JULY, 1979

THE RING'S LAST LIABILITY

> *ANALYSIS: Right after the 1879 Lincoln County Grand Jury, Billy Bonney still trusted Lew Wallace. With his sham jailing as cover, he volunteered to testify in the Dudley Court of Inquiry as eye-witness to soldiers firing on civilians in the Lincoln County War's battle. That proved his anti-Ring commitment, since it was unrelated to his pardon bargain. But for Wallace, that military court would repeat Shiloh's humiliation, making him retreat even more from Lincoln County and from his pardon promise to Billy. And for the Santa Fe Ring, that Court of Inquiry was a test of its ability to maintain cover-up of its War crimes.*

WALLACE WRITES TO SCHURZ: APRIL 4, 1879

By the time Lew Wallace wrote, on April 4, 1879, to Secretary of the Interior Carl Schurz, he and Schurz knew about the March 4, 1879 charges filed by Attorney Ira Leonard and Susan McSween with Secretary of War George McCrary against past Fort Stanton Commander N.A.M. Dudley, which likely incorporated legal work of Huston Chapman before his murder. So Wallace cautiously updated Schurz by minimizing the upcoming military court as an *"unfortunate"* intrusion on his attention for the April Grand Jury to start in 10 days. In fact, he was doing little preparation for either unpleasant confrontation. He wrote:

> Lincoln, April 4, 1879.
> Hon. C. Schurz,
> Sec. Dept. Interior
> Sir:
> I have official information that a court of inquiry for Col. Dudley has been ordered to assemble at Fort Stanton April 16th instant. The time is very unfortunate so far as I am concerned in that affair inasmuch as the District Court for this county begins on the 14th April, and will require all my attention without any extraneous distraction. It would be a great relief to me

if the session of the Inquiry could be postponed to a later period. Please submit the matter to the President and Honorable Secretary of War.

My work goes forward somewhat slowly but well enough to keep me in hope. The third detachment of which I spoke in my last is returned, and there are now fifteen prisoners in custody, some of them very desperate characters. Henceforward everything depends on the conduct of jurors and witnesses. I confess much doubt on the subject.

[AUTHOR'S NOTE: Wallace's nervous comment of "doubt" about the Grand Jury's outcome puts in perspective how Billy Bonney's pardon bargain's testimony saved the day for Wallace. But Wallace would ignore that.]

Still it is my opinion that the experiment should be tried; if there is failure, if, on account of intimidation, partiality, prejudice or corruption, there be acquittals grossly wrong, then the last civil resort will have been spent, leaving only martial law. And then the President will be amply justified in taking that last step; but until then I do not wish to give up my present effort or relax it in the least. The political situation in Washington, as I see it from this distance, requires so much on the President's behalf.

One further point. It was understood between General Hatch and I, when we came down from Santa Fe, that more troops were to be sent to this county; and after he left for Fort Bliss, I specially requested three companies be ordered to Fort Stanton. I suppose the General has forgotten all about it. Not a man has come. Lt. Bullis casually on a scout here, was ordered to remain at Stanton, but having started on his return to Texas, it is more than probable the order did not reach him in time. His command is composed of Seminole Indians, and his outfit is the most perfect ever devised for just such operations as are required for the work in hand. Do me the favor to see if he cannot be sent to the commanding officer at Stanton. If he cannot, please see the Secretary of War and urge him to dispatch thither at least three companies more of cavalry.

With great respect,
Your friend & servant,
Lew. Wallace,
Gov. New Mexico.

LEONARD PREPARES FOR THE COURT OF INQUIRY

Attorney Ira Leonard, apparently never aware of Lew Wallace's cover-ups for the Ring, had formulated his March 4, 1879 charges against N.A.M. Dudley to expose the Ring's role in the Lincoln County War conflict and its military intervention. (See my pp. 510-515 for the full charges). And given Leonard's long March 1, 1879 *Las Vegas Gazette* article on the charges and Huston Chapman's murder, the public also knew the trial's treasonous implications. Dudley's summarized charges were:

(1) did take into Lincoln on July 19, 1878 a squad of about 60 soldiers with *"one cannon and one Gatling gun" "without authority of law ... [to give] aid to an armed band of outlaws, and ... aided in killing one A.A. McSween ... [and] aided in the crime of arson, by causing the house of said McSween to be set on fire, the lives of the inmates therein put in jeopardy ... [including] two defenseless females, and five infant children; that his conduct on that occasion was most brutal and inhuman, and unbecoming a soldier and officer;"*

(2) did corruptly and willfully to give *"color of right to his wicked and unlawful action'* compel Justice of the Peace John Wilson *"by threat of ironing and imprisonment"* to *"issue a warrant for the arrest of said A.A. McSween, and other citizens of said county;"*

(3) did, on July 20, 1878, with soldiers and others, plunder the Tunstall store of *"upwards of six thousand dollars worth of goods;"*

(4) did *"procure base and wicked men to make false and slanderous charges and statements against the character and virtue of Mrs. S.E. McSween, the widow of said A.A. McSween ... for the purpose of ruining her reputation, and destroying her influence in seeking redress for ... Dudley's gross outrages perpetrated ... against her;"*

(5) did cancel a contract for corn delivery from [no first name] Easton when he refused to give *"him an affidavit, testifying against the character of S.E. McSween for truth and chastity;"*

(6) did try to subvert justice and *"prevent Governor Lew Wallace from restoring peace"* in *"November or December A.D. 1878"* [December 14, 1878] by publishing an open letter *"in the New Mexican ... calculated and intended to foment the disturbances then rife in said county, and ... [to] make false and malicious charges against the character of Mrs. S.E. McSween;"*

(7) did on about December 12, 1878 send a *"squad of soldiers under the command of Lieutenant J.H. French, one of the officers at said post, to go to the town of Lincoln ... [and] in a drunken debauch ... [he] entered the private dwelling of Mrs. S.E. McSween, with two or more armed soldiers, and [used abusive language to Mrs. McSween and] did without any right place her under arrest, and treat her with violence, and he did then and there without authority, arrest one H.I. Chapmen who was endeavoring to protect the said Mrs. McSween ... and he threatened the life of said Chapman ...[and Dudley] took no measures to have the said French punished .... [and] in an act of retaliation against Chapman .. classified [him] as one of the outlaws [in] Lincoln County."*

LEW WALLACE TESTIFIES: MAY 12-15, 1879

Lew Wallace faced a dilemma. His request for Dudley's removal from Fort Stanton's command, allied him to the Court of Inquiry's prosecution. And that left him attacking not just a military officer, but the Santa Fe Ring itself. It must have been the lowest point in his life other than Shiloh. And his compatriots would be a mediocre military prosecutor - Recorder/Judge Advocate Captain Henry H. Humphreys, 15th Infantry at Fort Bliss - assisted by equally lackluster Ira Leonard.

LETTER TO JUDGE ADVOCATE HUMPHREYS: MAY 10, 1879

When Wallace wrote on May 10, 1879 to Judge Advocate Captain Henry Humphreys, with the Court of Inquiry in progress for just eight days, he may have hoped that his subpoenaed hearing could be behind closed doors. But he was forced to testify in open court before the three military judges. And he would be cross-examined by defense attorney, Henry Waldo, a past Chief Justice, reputed the best trial lawyer in the Territory, and a Ringite in Catron's law firm. Wallace wrote:

Fort Stanton, May 10, 1879
Capt. H. Humphreys
Judge Advocate
Sir.
Since requesting March 7, 1879 that Lt. Col. N.A.M. Dudley be relieved from command of Fort Stanton, I have heard that formal charges and specifications were preferred against him by Hon. I. E. Leonard. Having still later, been served with subpoena to appear before the court of inquiry appointed for Lt. Col. Dudley, I beg to be now officially informed whether my appearance in the court is to be that of accuser or witness; and if the former, when, upon what form of papers, and in what order of proceeding, separate or conjoint with Judge Leonard's charges, my hearing is to be had.

Very respectfully
Your friend & obt svt.
Lew Wallace
Gov. New Mexico

WALLACE'S TERRIBLE TESTIMONY

When Lew Wallace was a prosecutor in the Abraham Lincoln murder trial, he was criticized as sly and brutal. He would now be on the receiving end from Attorney Henry Waldo. And he would show the psychological failing that made him retreat to fantasy instead of action at Shiloh. He had wasted his time in Lincoln forcing tales for his outlaw myth, and had gathered no evidence of Dudley's crimes. He had not even bothered to speak to the victim, Susan McSween. He was further hamstrung by his dishonest self-protective agenda of hiding Lincoln County War issues and the Ring, instead using the outlaw myth to demonize the McSween side. In fact, while testifying for the prosecution, he was placatingly trying to shield Dudley. His humiliating, five day testimony, in which he seemed incompetent, was from May 12th to May 15th, 1879. Note that the "Recorder" is prosecutor, Henry Humphreys, with Ira Leonard. The transcript follows:

Court of Inquiry Rooms
Fort Stanton, N.M.
May 12, 1879
4th Day [of the Court of Inquiry]
10 A.M.

Present:
Col. G. Pennypacker 16th Infantry
Major N.W. Osborne 15th Infantry
Captain H.R. Brinkerhoff 15th Infantry
Captain H.H. Humphreys 15th Infantry, Recorder
Lieut. Col. Dudley, and his Counsel, and Mr. Ira E. Leonard

HIS EXCELLENCY GOVERNOR LEW WALLACE ...

Q. by Recorder. Please state your name and place of residence, and position you occupy.
Answer. My name is Lewis Wallace, am Governor of the Territory of New Mexico, resident of Santa Fe.
Q. by Recorder. Please state ... what this instrument is.
Answer. This is a letter of request from me officially to Colonel Edward Hatch, Commanding District of New Mexico, asking that Lieutenant Colonel Dudley be relieved of Command of Fort Stanton, for the reasons therein given. It is dated Lincoln, N.M. March 7, 1879.
Q. by Recorder. In this letter you use the expression, "and yet is an active partisan." Please state to the Court on what facts you have made such an allegation.
Answer. I beg to call your attention to the language of the letter, which is as follows: "I would state in general terms, it is charged here (meaning in Lincoln), that he, Lieutenant Colonel Dudley, is responsible for the killing of McSween."

Objected to by Lieutenant Colonel Dudley, through Counsel. The witness is asked a pointed and direct question, and it is asked that he give a pointed and categorical answer ...
Court cleared and closed.
Court opened and its decision announced. Lieutenant Colonel Dudley and Counsel and Ira E. Leonard being present.
Objection sustained. The witness will confine himself to explicit and direct answer to the question ...

Q. by Recorder. It is charged here in your letter "and yet is an active partisan." On what do you base such an allegation?
Answer. The charge is based upon the conclusion drawn from a number of official dispatches from Colonel Dudley, to the Commander of the District, Colonel Hatch: from reports of different sources of the relation between Colonel Dudley and others of the so

called leaders, or influential and active men, of that one of the parties disturbing the country: also upon certain acts of Colonel Dudley towards certain individuals, or supposed members of the so called party, or the party rather, known as the McSween party.

[AUTHOR'S NOTE: This vague response was from Wallace's lack of preparation and fear of antagonizing the Ring. It would characterize and render meaningless his entire testimony.]

Objection was here made by Lieutenant Colonel Dudley to the answer of the witness being received in evidence: except that portion which reads as follows: also upon certain acts of Colonel Dudley towards certain individuals, or supposed members of the so called party known as the McSween party. upon the ground that this is an investigation of elicit facts, and not to collect the conclusions of the witness, on the reports that may have reached him, the dispatches to themselves being the best evidence ... and move to strike the same from the record.

The Recorder replied, that the testimony was original. As to the facts, whether true or false; that is a matter for the Court to decide when all the testimony is completed, the Court will reject the same.

Court cleared and closed.
Court opened and the decision of the Court announced ...
Objection not sustained.

The Recorder then asked Lieutenant Colonel Dudley if he admitted to the open letter as printed in the New Mexican, which had been read in Court. Lieutenant Colonel Dudley admitted same.

Q. by Recorder. On what day did you assume the duties of your office?
Answer. First of October last.
Q. by Recorder. Please state to the Court what is this communication?
Answer. This is a letter from me dated Santa Fe, New Mexico, November 16, 1878, addressed to Lieutenant Colonel Dudley at Fort Stanton, New Mexico, it is the first draft of the copy of a letter sent by me to Lieutenant Colonel Dudley of that date. (Recorder then read to the Court this letter and proclamation.)
Q. by Recorder. What caused you to write this letter of 16th November, 1878, referred to in Lieutenant Colonel Dudley's open letter of November 30th, 1878?

Answer. A Gentleman named H.I. Chapmen, at the time practicing law in Las Vegas, had written a letter to me: (Lieutenant Colonel Dudley then produced the letter.)

Q. by Recorder. Is this the letter referred to by you, in your answer to the question?

Answer. It is a copy of one of the letters, it is the letter referred to in part of the unfinished answer.

Recorder then stated that the evidence is explanatory, and a part of the history of the transaction and not submitted as evidence against Lieutenant Colonel Dudley in the investigation now pending ...

Q. by Recorder. What do you mean by "perfectly satisfactory" in the letter that you wrote in answer to the letter of Colonel Dudley of November 9, 1878?

Objection was here made by Lieutenant Colonel Dudley ...
Court cleared and closed.
Court opened and its decision announced ...
Objection not sustained. Witness will answer the question.

(Witness resuming) The words "perfectly satisfactory" have reference to Colonel Dudley's letter of November 9th which I had interpreted as a denial of the charges contained in the letter of Mr. Chapman, which at my instance had been referred to Colonel Hatch for remarks.

Q. by Recorder. Had it any reference to the enclosure contained in that letter embracing the affidavits?

Objected to, because the answer involves an explanation of the intention of the writer, when the letter its self, the best evidence of such intention, is before the Court. The letter is written by a public officer in regard to public affairs of the greatest moment. It is presumed that he used the most careful, accurate and pregnant language to express his meaning. It was a solemn an act as the making of a contract ...

Recorder replied as follows: This letter embraced more than the letters that were accompanying it. Several affidavits, all of which were enclosed in the letter. And the Court should be advised as to what the Governor intended to receive as satisfying in reply, whether the letter its self or all of its accompaniments, including the affidavits. If a contract is uncertain or indefinite, evidence may always be given to explain the contract and its meaning.

Court cleared and closed.
Court opened and its decision announced ...
Objection not sustained.

(Witness resuming.) I did not understand enclosures to be more than referred to by letter. The enclosures were not within the meaning of the words "perfectly satisfactory" ... The affidavits or enclosures are alluded to elsewhere in my letter ... I did not mean to say that I was satisfied that Mrs. McSween was a woman of bad repute.

Court adjourned.

May 13, 1879
5th *Day [of the Court of Inquiry]...*

... Q. by Recorder. What information did you receive, if any, that induced you to issue the Proclamation of Pardon, and from whom did you receive it?
Answer. I received information from Colonel Dudley through official dispatches from that officer forwarded by that officer, to District Headquarters ... which led me to believe that peace and quiet had been prevailing in Lincoln County for a number of weeks, and such being the condition of affairs in that country, I hoped the Proclamation to make the condition perpetual.
Q. by Recorder. Did the reports from Colonel Dudley, upon which you based your Proclamation of Pardon, correspond with the declaration in his open letter of the outrages narrated in said letter, if not, where did they differ ...
Answer. I was very much surprised when the open letter, as printed in the New Mexican was laid upon my table. The paragraphs which occasioned my surprise were the three beginning with the sentence "without any intention" [and continuing] ... of codifying the official course of your Excellency, permit me to say that you have now been more than eight weeks in the territory, and have never been during this period, within nearly 200 miles of the scene of the terrible death struggles that have been enacted in this county during that time. Five innocent persons, natives and residents of the county of Lincoln have been inhumanely murdered ... Herds of cattle ... have been taken ... and not a single arrest has ever been made by the civil authorities, since I have been in the county. Many of these facts have been laid before your Excellency ...

what steps, I ask, have been taken by the territorial officers to put a stop to such unlawful conduct? I answer none ... I must respectfully ask you to come to Lincoln County, and see and judge for yourself from personal observation of the facts" ... *[This] narration of outrages committed in that period of time, was inconsistent with the statements forwarded by him [Dudley] to Headquarters ...*

Q. by Recorder. State what facts, if any, occurred growing out of the open letter of Colonel Dudley's that embarrassed your efforts to restore peace in Lincoln County, and in what manner they promoted the disturbances then rife in the county? ...

Answer. Shortly after publication of the open letter, I was awaited upon at my office in Santa Fe, by two gentlemen who demanded of me inspection of the affidavits referred to in the open letter. Being refused inspection of the letter and affidavits, one of them, Mr. Chapmen, returned to Lincoln, where at the house he resided, in a high state of indignation and wrath against Colonel Dudley, and the military, and about that time he commenced some criminal proceedings against Colonel Dudley.

[AUTHOR'S NOTE: Betraying Wallace is blaming Chapman and Shield for seeking the Susan McSween affidavits, instead of blaming Dudley - and getting into evidence - his War crimes. So Wallace implies that trouble-making Chapman and Shield made spiteful litigation against Dudley to stir up the locals.]

Lieutenant Colonel Dudley, by his counsel, objects to the admission of any testimony as to the commencement of criminal proceedings ...
Objection is sustained.

Q. by Recorder. What effect had the open letter of Colonel Dudley's in re-opening the difficulties in Lincoln County, if any?
Answer. ... After the publication of the open letter the indignation of Mrs. McSween's friends proceeded to action against Colonel Dudley, and went on until the affair finally culminated in the murder of Mr. Chapman in the streets of the town of Lincoln.

[AUTHOR'S NOTE: Wallace is lying. The litigation was about Dudley's Lincoln County War crimes. Chapman's murder was to stop that litigation. The open letter was irrelevant. Do not miss that Wallace is betraying the prosecution for which he is supposedly testifying on Susan McSween's behalf!]

Court adjourned.

May 14, 1879
6th Day [of Court of Inquiry] ...

... Q. by Recorder. State what facts came to your knowledge, concerning the acts of the military which led you to include them in the Proclamation of Pardon?
Answer. **It came to my knowledge, that it was the intention of certain parties living in Lincoln, who I had reason to believe were endeavoring to revive the McSween faction, intending commencement of prosecution of a criminal nature against Colonel Dudley.** Mr. Chapman waited upon me in my office at Santa Fe stated to me that he, amongst others intended such a course, for which purpose it was his design to resort to the Grand Jury of the next Court. I remonstrated against such a course, but without effect. **I then resolved that such should not be done if I could help it, or at least could furnish Colonel Dudley with a plea in case of such prosecution, if he chose in the event of his indictment to plead it.**

[AUTHOR'S NOTE: Wallace is still siding with Dudley, while testifying against him! He blames "*the McSween faction*" instead of Dudley's War crimes. This is the same lying outlawing ruse he would use against Billy to deny the pardon.]

I did not stop to consider whether Colonel Dudley was guilty or not guilty in connection with the McSween killing affair. I foresaw if he were indicted, he would be put at great cost, vexation and harassment, I foresaw he might be confronted by a partisan jury.
The proclamation at the time of Chapman's visit was in the rough, and under consideration. The sentence applying to officers of the army was then not in it.
Immediately after the departure of Mr. Chapman with the intention stated and never dreaming that it would be construed as an insult I drew out a rough draft of the Proclamation, and inserted the sentence.
I used the word officers, plural, to avoid mentioning specially and singly, Lieutenant Colonel Dudley's name, for that I thought would be offensive to him; further I thought it justice, as I was proposing amnesty to civilians, it should also be extended to military officers, whose duties, without choice on their part, might have thrown them into the troubles then prevalent and made them special marks for enmity.

Prosecution was subsequently begun by Mr. Chapman against Colonel Dudley.

Colonel Dudley, by his Counsel, objects to the admission of any testimony as to the prosecution by Chapman ... against Colonel Dudley ...
Objection sustained.

[AUTHOR'S NOTE: Here begins Henry Waldo's objections to keep out damning evidence - like the reasons Chapman was litigating which justified Dudley's court martial. And the corrupt Court would uphold those objections.]

... Q. by Recorder. State all that you know concerning the charges you made against Colonel Dudley in your letter to General Hatch, of March 7, 1879, asking his removal as Commandant of Fort Stanton?
Answer. The conviction which is in the statement ... which read as follows: "that he, Colonel Dudley, is so compromised by connection with the troubles in the county, that his usefulness in the effort now making to restore order, is utterly gone," was founded upon information which had in part come to me by conversations and writing, received by me from persons living in the county of Lincoln, but chiefly from information derived from citizens living in the town of Lincoln, and others living in the vicinity. Upon my coming down on the commencement of March last, a consequence of the investigation I then instituted relating to the situation of affairs in the county, was the conclusion that a considerable portion of the people resident in Lincoln and that neighborhood ... upon whom I might reasonably rely for support in the effort I proposed making against disturbers of the peace, and persons charged with high crimes, were suffering from intimidation to such an extent as to seriously embarrass the efforts proposed, and that the intimidation was a consequence of the dread which such people have come to entertain against Colonel Dudley as Commandant at Fort Stanton.
Upon hearing recitals of Colonel Dudley's actions in course of his connection with civil affairs in the county, and particularly his dealing with individuals, and his conduct on the day of the burning of the McSween house, I further concluded that dread on the part of the people spoken was not irrational.
That Colonel Dudley might be put in possession of the nature of some of the charges ... and also that the Commandant of the

District [Edward Hatch] might from their statement form a judgment of the proper course to be pursued ... I put in the letter of request some of the charges ... It was not then pretended that the charges were anything more than hearsay accusations ...

Lieutenant Colonel Dudley, by his counsel, objected and moves the Court to disregard as evidence all that portion of the witnesses answers commencing with the reading of the extract from his letter of March 7, 1879 ... If Colonel Dudley has been guilty of misconduct it is ... capable of being established by the witnesses personally cognizant of it, and not by ... reports of third parties ... Objection sustained.
The Recorder announced that he had finished with the witness.

[AUTHOR'S NOTE: The Court sustained blocking of Wallace's accusations, since he himself called them hearsay.]

Witness cross examined.

[AUTHOR'S NOTE: Below is the embarrassing testimony on Wallace's "perfectly satisfactory" comment on Dudley's letter.]

Q. by Lieut. Col. Dudley. Did not the affidavit referred to in your letter of Nov. 16, 1878 as well as the letter enclosing them form a part of the reply of Colonel Dudley submitted to you for consideration?
Answer. I did not so consider, I understood Colonel Dudley's letter to refer me to the affidavits which were merely enclosures accompanying the letter .. I read them at the time of receiving the letter.
Q. by Lieut. Col. Dudley. In your letter of Nov. 16th 1878 you used the words "Your former letter upon the same subject with the several affidavits accompanying it were submitted to me, etc." Why did you allude to the affidavits at all, if you did not intend to include them under the terms "perfectly satisfactory" to you?
Answer. Partly to identify the letter, and that he might understand that I read both the letter and the affidavits ...
Q. by Lieut. Col. Dudley. You state in your examination in Chief, that the words "perfectly satisfactory" had reference to the reply of Colonel Dudley, what do you mean by the word reply?
Answer. I mean the letter of Colonel Dudley of the date Nov. 7th ...

Q. by Lieut. Col. Dudley. Is any reference then made to the affidavits?

Answer. Yes Sir. Her [Mrs. McSween's] character was not a point of consideration in the correspondence ...

Q. by Lieut. Col. Dudley. In gathering information upon which to base your Proclamation did you examine all the reports from Colonel Dudley which had been received at District Headquarters in October, in the Lincoln County matters?

Answer. I think I examined all of them ...

Q. by Lieut. Col. Dudley. State if you can, what others you have read, and in what month they were made?

Answer. I cannot recall now any particular reports ...

[AUTHOR'S NOTE: Wallace fails to show diligence: though saying he read all Dudley's reports, he cannot name any.]

Q. by Lieut. Col. Dudley. State how many of the reports by Colonel Dudley to District Headquarters, in reference to Lincoln County affairs, you had read prior to issuance of the Proclamation ...

Answer. I cannot state with exactitude ... I can only say that I read all that came to me transmitted from District Headquarters ...

Q. by Lieut. Col. Dudley. When did you first arrive in Lincoln County?

Answer. About the fourth of March this year, and in the town of Lincoln about the fifth ...

Q. by Lieut. Col. Dudley. Had you not been, except short intervals, continuously in Santa Fe, or its vicinity, from the time of your arrival in the Territory of New Mexico, until the time of your departure for Lincoln?

Objected to by Recorder. That it is ... wholly immaterial where the witness has been ...

Lieutenant Colonel Dudley, by his Counsel, replied as follows: The witness has testified as to the effect of the open letter upon the people of Lincoln County, and its tendency to awaken old bitterness, which it was his object to suppress, the object of the question is to show that he had no opportunity of judging the effects of said letter not being present ...

[AUTHOR'S NOTE: Shown is Wallace's neglect of duty.]

Court adjourned.

May 15, 1879
7th Day [of Court of Inquiry] ...

... *Objection of the Recorder sustained.*

Q. by Lieut. Col. Dudley. You say after the publication of the open letter, the indignation of Mrs. McSween's friends proceeded to action against Colonel Dudley, and went on until the affair was culminated in the murder of Mr. Chapman in the streets of Lincoln. Now state to your knowledge, any instance of violence, or exhibition of agitation, or excitement occurring after the publication of the open letter.
Answer. My knowledge on that subject is derived solely upon information received from others ...

[AUTHOR'S NOTE: Unsavory Wallace is now left with his lie of Dudley's open letter making Susan McSween's trouble-making friends cause Chapman's murder. So to save himself from Ring and Dudley confrontations, he betrays Susan McSween's case.]

Q. by Lieut. Col. Dudley. In your examination in chief you state you made an investigation as to the situation of affairs in Lincoln County, and as a consequence thereof, reached the conclusion that a considerable portion of the people were suffering from intimidation caused by dread they had of Colonel Dudley. How long were you in the making of that investigation, and what was its extent and nature?
Answer. I arrived in Lincoln, the afternoon as I recollect now, of March 5th last. Immediately I commenced informing myself of the state of affairs, some information touching the murder of Chapmen, and the parties said to have been concerned in it ... which satisfied me that certain parties should be immediately arrested and held, for connection with that affair ... My first step was to find, if possible, persons to make affidavits against the parties, on which to issue warrants. I addressed myself to several persons to that effect, but they all declined, giving as a reason that it would endanger their lives. I argued with them there was now no room for fear, because ... they have the protection of the military.
Their reply was in substance, they had no confidence in the military, because they believed the Commandant of the Fort, Colonel Dudley, was the friend of the alleged murderers, who he would assist rather than them, the citizens. I found no one willing at that time to make the affidavits.

[AUTHOR'S NOTE: Wallace is caught lying by having no evidence. In fact, he was interviewing for his outlaw myth and faking any affidavits. (See my pp. 548-551)]

I was driven to the necessity of requesting that the arrest of the parties whom I wished arrested, should be made without warrants ...

Q. by Lieut. Col. Dudley. You say you arrived in Lincoln Plaza of the 5th day of Match. What time of day did you arrive there?

Answer. Somewhere I judge between 4 and 5 o'clock in the afternoon.

Q. by Lieut. Col. Dudley. Did you return to Fort Stanton the next day?

Answer. I had not been to Fort Stanton.

Q. by Lieut. Col. Dudley. Did you not come to Fort Stanton on the next day, if not that day, when did you arrive at Fort Stanton?

Answer. My recollection is that I did not come to Fort Stanton until the evening of the 7th of March ...

Q. by Lieut. Col. Dudley. How many persons did you talk to about the situation of affairs in Lincoln County, in the town of Lincoln and its vicinity?

Answer. **It is not possible for me to say with exactness, I will answer however, nearly all the male inhabitants of the Plaza, in addition to which, shortly after my arrival, a public meeting was called by the people of the town and country, and held in the Courthouse, at which there was quite 75 or a hundred people present ... Fifteen or twenty people came to me in the room that I occupied in the house of Mr. Montanyo ... I found as a conclusion, that the people who I met, almost without exception, were in dread of the Military Commandant Colonel Dudley.**

Q. by Lieut. Col. Dudley. Give the name of one person who was in dread of the Commandant.

Answer. Juan Patron. I can give others ...

Q. by Lieut. Col. Dudley. Now state if you put or received any of the statements made to you ... in writing? ...

Answer. I did.

Q. by Lieut. Col. Dudley. Were these statements sworn to?

... Answer. I cannot answer yes or no ... The witness desires to explain to the Court why he could not answer yes or no to the question "were the statements sworn to," which explanation he is ready to submit in writing ...

[AUTHOR'S NOTE: Wallace's testimony is disastrously incompetent – he can barely name "one person who was in dread" of Dudley. He appears either a liar about accusations or an incompetent as to his duty.]

Q. by Lieut. Col. Dudley. Did you call upon Colonel Dudley for any explanation of the charges contained in the letter of request for his removal, before writing such letter March 7th?
Answer. I did not ...

[AUTHOR'S NOTE: Absent due diligence is again shown.]

Q. by Lieut. Col. Dudley. You say that you contained in your letter of request of March 7th to the District Commander, a statement of the charges, **which you say were upon hearsay,** *in order from this statement he might form a proper judgment of the proper course to pursue. Was this your intent?*
Answer. It was.

[AUTHOR'S NOTE: Sly Waldo now links Wallace's charges to his admitted hearsay evidence, no sworn affidavits, no recall of informers' names, and avoiding Lincoln County - all meaning that Wallace's action against this military commander had no substance. And when Waldo snidely asks if it was his "intent" for Dudley to *"form a proper judgment of the proper course to pursue"* from Wallace's unfounded accusations, rather than answering with bold repartee, Wallace (clearly totally traumatized and humiliated after this fourth day) disastrously answers feebly: "*It was.*" This was his Shiloh moment.]

Lieut. Col. Dudley, by his Counsel, [was] finished with the witness.

Redirect.

Q. by Recorder. Explain what you mean by not being able to answer yes or no to the question whether they were sworn to.
Answer. ... I never reduced any of their statements to writing, or had them sworn to. These statements were given to me verbally and not in writing in any form ...

[AUTHOR'S NOTE: The Recorder tries to save him, but Wallace repeats having no legally usable evidence against Dudley!]

Court adjourned.

IRA LEONARD'S COURT UPDATES AND SANTA FE RING EXPOSÉ: MAY 20 AND 23, 1879

Despite Lew Wallace's weak testimony, with devastating admission that irresponsibly he had gathered no affidavits against Dudley, Ira Leonard sent him two long optimistic letters about Court progress after Wallace had returned to Santa Fe. It was then just 26 days since Leonard's near assassination.

Leonard's letter of May 20th was enclosed with one of the 23rd. He crowed on the 23rd: *"I tell you we are pouring "hot shot" into Dudley so fiercely that his face for the last three days has strikingly resembled the wattles of an enraged turkey gobbler ... He is the most unmitigated old scoundrel that ever had an existence."* Leonard also exposed their adversary - the Santa Fe Ring - unaware that Wallace well knew about it. But a faint note of doubt was creeping in for Leonard. On the 23rd, he also wrote: *"If when we get through with D here if his record is not black I shall be mistaken - but I believe the Court will stretch their powers a good ways to sustain him."* Note also the debilitation of Leonard's asthma. Leonard wrote:

Lincoln May 23rd 1879

Dear Governor

*I write to you with pencil because I am laboring for breath and it is less labor than with a pen. We have been dragging along seven and eight hours a day in the Court ever since you left and **I tell you we are pouring "hot shot" into Dudley so fiercely that his face for the last three days has strikingly resembled the wattles of an enraged turkey gobbler.** Today a little episode occurred in Court. Mrs. McSween was on the stand and old Dudley accused me of conveying to her by a shake of my head the answer she should make. I did not do it or think of it and in fact was not looking at her at all and I resented it as an insult and pitched into him and the Court read the riot act in the Articles of War for our mutual benefit. **He is the most unmitigated old scoundrel that ever had an existence.** The Court have taken a short turn on us and will not let us give any evidence except that which bears upon the charges [I]ts rulings have been in some respects wrong in my opinion but that must of course be expected from gentlemen who are not accustomed to the technicalities of law.*

[AUTHOR'S NOTE: Though his enclosed letter is about the Ring, and though he is representing Susan McSween for Ring atrocities carried out by Dudley in the Lincoln County War, slow-witted Leonard still does not realize that the Court of Inquiry is biased: with Chief Judge Pennypacker as Dudley's his best friend from Fort Union, and with Attorney Henry Waldo - coming from Catron's own law firm - as shielding the Ring.]

I enclose you the letter I promised I have been so very busy and my time so entirely occupied I could not finish it before I hope you will act immediately in sending forward I received a letter from Chapmans father to-day & he told me he had received a promise that D [Dudley] shall be removed from this Post – but that is not enough an entire charge should be made.

If when we get through with D here if his record is not black I shall be mistaken – but I believe the Court will stretch their powers a good ways to sustain him.

He has grossly violated his faith with Capt Humphreys [Judge Advocate Recorder] he [Dudley] made a written demand for all the correspondence at the Post with you [Wallace] "to be used in his defense" and the way he used it you can see by his publication of the same in the Mesilla News [the "Open Letter" to embarrass Wallace] He intended it for that purpose & no other.

I will write you further Governor in a day or two and give you minutely the proceedings here.

In your letter to the Dept if you can consistently make a suggestion for me I would be glad to have you but do not do it to the detriment of the interests we have in view.

[AUTHOR'S NOTE: Leonard is referring to his ongoing goal to replace Judge Warren Bristol as the judge for the 3rd Judicial District, but honorably makes clear that winning against the Ring adversaries is the priority.]

I thought I would not let Taylor [his legal assistant rooming with him in Lincoln] into **our secrets** because he is cheek by jowl with Maj. Watts & Dolan he is a poor stupid minded fellow as vacillating as the wind and not to be depended on.

Let me hear from you and remember me kindly to Mrs. Wallace

Yours truly
Ira E. Leonard

LEONARD'S ENCLOSED LETTER ABOUT THE RING: MAY 20, 1879

The enclosed letter of May 20, 1879, possibly dictated, is not in Leonard's handwriting and was wrongly dated as 1878, not 1879. Leonard may have been too sick with his asthma, as he wrote in its cover letter on May 23rd. This letter presenting *"our secrets,"* as referred to in that cover letter, raises the question of whether Wallace, anticipating victory, had offered to replace *"Civil"* and *"Military"* officials across the board if connected to the *"Santa Fe Ring."* And it may have been intended by Leonard and Wallace to be sent as a copy to President Hayes. Though impossible to be certain of its motive, one can see the letter as staged, since Wallace's disastrous testimony is not mentioned, and Wallace would have known the information and actions being *"provided."*

But Leonard left no doubt about the Ring's existence: *"That [Murphy-Dolan] party had for a long time uninterrupted sway in this County and could not brook opposition and they were determined either by fair or foul means to have no opposition and they resorted to every artifice in their power to accomplish that purpose. They were a part and parcel of the Santa Fe Ring that has been so long an incubus on the government of this Territory."*

Leonard also refreshes Wallace's memory about their earlier meeting with District Attorney William Rynerson about Leonard's assisting the Lincoln County Grand Jury's prosecutions, as if Rynerson was then really *"highly gratified at the arrangement."* This marked Leonard's naïve belief that Ringites could be successfully prosecuted. It would take the completed Dudley Court of Inquiry to prove to him that futility. Leonard wrote:

Lincoln, New Mexico
May 20, 1878 [1879]

Governor Lew Wallace
   Santa Fe, N.M.

                Dear Governor,
                         When you left here *I promised to write you concerning events transpiring here and I do so. as you will remember when I came here from Las Vegas about the 1st of April last with the intention of remaining if I considered it safe to do so, I had a conference with you, and you stated to me the situation in which you were placed in coming into this distracted county where lawlessness and*

disorder was the rule instead of the exception, you stated to me also that you had no one with whom to advise, and had no authority to employ counsel but desired me to assist in prosecuting, and bringing to justice the outlaws then under arrest [Chapman's murders and Seven Rivers rustlers] and who might be arrested. I promised to give you my best endeavors in that direction whether I was ever compensated for it or not. what I did while you were here you know, and of my earned endeavors to aid in that direction you are fully cognizant. When Judge Bristol arrived here to hold Court, accompanied by Col. W.L. Rynerson the prosecuting Atty. of this District, about the middle of April, you, Col. Rynerson and I had a conference together in which you stated to him that you had made arrangements with me to assist him in the prosecution of the persons under arrest, and also to assist in the prosecution of those who would likely be indicted at the then approaching term on the Court, and **as I understood him he seemed highly gratified at the arrangement and so expressed himself to you and myself at the time.** You know that the first few days proceedings were at Fort Stanton before the convening of the Court. **Some fifteen or more writs of Habeas Corpus were issued by Judge Bristol upon the application of prisoners confined at the Fort prison for safe keeping, and you are fully aware of the flimsy technicalities upon which many of the desperate men were released.** It seemed to me then and I have had no occasion to change my opinion, but on the contrary to have it strengthened that Judge Bristol had the timidity of a child and stood in fear of the desperate characters that curse this country instead of the boldness and determination to bring them to justice. Now as to what succeeded after you left this County which I believe was on the day that Court convened for business, the first three or four days being occupied in procuring a Jury, one term having lapsed, it required the selecting and summoning a new panel of Jurors, and this County being so large, it took several days to procure them. The Grand Jury so far as I was able to judge of the men was composed of as good and intelligent men as any county would average and it was the same with the Petit jury. The Grand Jury went earnestly to work but labored under great difficulty in procuring witnesses, there had been no term of Court here for a year, and within that time, murders of the most atrocious character had been perpetrated by the score, and crimes of nearly all grades known to the criminal code had been of frequent occurrence. Officers were sent in every *direction for witnesses, and from the disturbed condition of affairs here it was not safe to send them out without military escort especially so in the extreme southern part of the county, which was done. When you consider that the County of Lincoln is as large as the states of New Hampshire, Vermont, Massachusetts, Connecticut, and New Jersey together, you can readily appreciate the difficulty in collecting from this large area, witnesses to appear before a Grand Jury and testify as to crimes committed in the various portions of it, and when you consider also that the Judge was extremely impatient and desirous of getting away although he had no other court for two months, and was constantly hurrying the Grand Jury to expedite their business, they could not help being embarrassed in their deliberations and could not accomplish satisfactorily to themselves the arduous duties imposed upon them, although they found a large number of indictments during their labors, besides being unable to accomplish all they had before them for consideration as many witnesses came in to report after they were discharged, and witnesses to testify to the outlaws killing that Mexican family nine persons in the southern part of the county, late last fall in which [Marion] Turner, the notorious fellow you had arrested was a participant with the Jones's [brothers, John, Jim, and Bill] you had also arrested and in custody, consequently they had to be released to pray upon the unoffending people until overtaken at some other time.*

Now Governor, I want to state to you the conduct of the District Attorney which I consider contemptible, notwithstanding the understanding we had together, and his apparent gratification that I was to assist him. You had scarcely gone before he commenced as I afterwards learned to vilify you for procuring aid for him, and commenced shirking the entire responsibility of the prosecution unto me. He told the people, prisoners, and all with whom he confessed that he was simply the official figure head, and that I was the governor's prosecutor, that I was the man the Governor had selected to see them punished. He was to my own knowledge in secret and open conference with Dolan the murderer of Chapman, and intends to defend him at Socorro, the place to which the venue is changed, it being out of his District and he connived to procure the change of venue from the District for that purpose.

[AUTHOR'S NOTE: This Dolan indictment for Chapman's murder was the achievement of Billy's testimony and the fulfilling of the pardon bargain.]

He aroused among the friends of the outlaws [Ringites] here a feeing of antagonism against me that resulted in their posting a notice on a tree to which I had my horse hitched addressed to me, informing me that if I did not leave this country "they would take my scalp and send me to hell."

[AUTHOR'S NOTE: An assassination attempt was made on Leonard on April 25, 1879 in Lincoln, as described next.]

A few nights after this notice was posted on the tree two desperados came riding by my office on a full run with their horses, and fired two shots arriving at the window and the bullets striking near it. Mr. Taylor a civil engineer who came down to this country with me and I believe a cousin of President Hayes, was rooming with me at the time, and you may be sure we were both ready for a fight in short order, and this is not all. McPherson the man I brought down with me, and who was taking care of my horses, was out looking for them in the foot hills of the Capitan Mts. And some unknown party fired on him, the ball entering his hat rim and grazing his forehead leaving the mark distinctly visible on his head for several days, their peculiar hostility to him grows out of the fact that the Sheriff of the county [Kimbrell] deputized him during the late term of the Court to serve process, and he in the exercise of his duties arrested quite a number of the outlaws. This is the condition of affairs here now.

[AUTHOR'S NOTE: Leonard is making clear that the "outlaws" attacking and frightening people are Ringites – who were arrested and indicted - and not Wallace's vague outlaw myth.]

Since the Court of Inquiry convened at Fort Stanton to inquire into the conduct of Lieut. Col. N.A.M. Dudley and his connection with civil matters in this County which Court is now in its thirteenths days session, **the most violent threats are made by the desperate men whom I am sorry to say for the honor of that branch of the public service have found a staunch friend in Col. Dudley. The evidence so far in his case discloses the most inexcusable conduct on the part of Military Officer.** *I have been a constant attendant upon that Court assisting the*

Judge Advocate in the prosecution since it convened and if Col. Dudley can justify his conduct towards the people in this distracted district I shall be greatly astonished, **without the slightest warrant of authority he went to Lincoln, and gave substantial aid and assistance to an armed band of outlaws who under pretence of executing writs against the McSween party, made their visit to his knowledge, one of theft, arson, and murder, and if justice is properly meted out to him, he will be dismissed [from] the service of his country in disgrace.**

From what I have seen of affairs in this County I am forced the following conclusions: that all of your efforts to restore peace here, and give security to the peaceable and law abiding citizens under the present existing status of affairs will prove unavailing, unless you are supported by the government in having effected a radical change of the administration of the civil and military authorities.

[AUTHOR'S NOTE: Leonard argues need to replace Ringites in power to get peace. If Dudley had been found guilty, Wallace might have even intervened. But Leonard is inadvertently calling Wallace's bluff about the outlaw myth solution. Next Leonard presents true Lincoln County War issues.]

My reasons for these conclusions are first as to the civil authorities. **Judge Warren Bristol at the April Term of the Court in 1878 made himself very obnoxious to the party known as the McSween party in his charge to the Grand Jury, when he instructed them as he did to find an indictment against A.A. McSween on the charge of embezzlement.** McSween it seems had been brought before **Judge Bristol upon that charge and the Judge had acted in the manner as an examining Magistrate to inquire into the charge made against McSween for embezzling some money he had collected on a Life Insurance Policy. It was very wrong in Judge Bristol, whatever his private conversations might have been to so instruct the Grand Jury, it was wrong for him to particularize this case, or give any directions to that body in his charge to them, in doing so he arrayed himself not only against the man charged with the offence, who had no opportunity to defend himself but he made himself the champion of the faction, that were pursuing McSween, and in my judgment Judge Bristol's action on that occasion was the immediate cause of all the great** *misfortunes and fatal results that have followed in this County. The Grand Jury did investigate the charge and honorably acquitted McSween and in a report made to the Court characterize the proceedings against McSween as being a persecution,*

[AUTHOR'S NOTE: Leonard, without knowing, is repeating Mary McPherson's complaint on Bristol – which Wallace owned.]

and it came from a Grand Jury too that had been selected by the officer and Sheriff [George Peppin] who has been so notorious in the difficulties in this County. **The result of Judge Bristol's conduct on this occasion caused the organization of the factions that are currently known here as the Dolan Murphy or Sheriffs party, and the McSween party, which has resulted in the killing of upwards of eighty persons in this County in a little over a years time, and created difficulties that will require many years to overcome,** *the results of that action also is not alone confined to the killing of so many persons but has had the further result in causing these desperate men to organize for plunder and theft. They have gathered in marauding bands throughout the County and make not only life but property insecure. I am not surprised that Judge Bristol is now timid and unable to stay the lawlessness, his own misdirected action produced.*

[AUTHOR'S NOTE: Leonard identifies Ring-side outlaws, and gives one of the only body counts on the Lincoln County War - "*upwards of eighty persons.*" Billy later said 200.]

I know that your own judgment about who are the peaceable and law abiding citizens of this County and that your views will correspond with my own from the long time you spent here in earnest inquiry into the difficulties and your endeavors to get at the truth and learn the exact situation, and you found as I have done that nearly **all the men who belonged to and were sympathizers of the McSween party are the substantial peaceable and law abiding citizens of this County. And you found also that the Dolan Murphy party were determined to drive these men out of the Country because they had come into it to engage in business and were as that party imagined in their way securing government contracts and plunder. That party had for a long time uninterrupted sway** *in this County and could not brook opposition and they were determined either by fair or foul means to have no opposition and they resorted to every artifice in their power to accomplish that purpose. They were a part and parcel of the Santa Fe Ring that has been so long an incubus on the government of this Territory.*

[AUTHOR'S NOTE: This equation of the Murphy-Dolan party to the Santa Fe Ring is what Wallace knew and concealed in his Court of Inquiry testimony and his outlaw myth.]

The people I am confident will never feel secure as long as Judge Bristol is here to execute the laws, and their fears are not unfounded or unreasonable under all the circumstances. I do not like to be forced to this conclusion but I cannot come to any other from what I have seen and experienced since I have been in the County. If the Court had sustained you as it ought to have done in your efforts to bring to justice those gross violators of the law and you had found hearty co-operation in the Military in your attempt to arrest and punish these bad and desperate men I am sure the future would have been less prolific in crime than it has been in the past, and there would have been much less than the future promises.

[AUTHOR'S NOTE: Again, Leonard is accidently hitting a painful point: Wallace failed to achieve a true solution. Wallace's outlaw myth did not convince honorable Leonard.]

Crime is always cowardly, and when the strong arm of the law is stretched out with a determination to bring justice and punish offenders, they flee from justice "like a thief in the night." If there was a just and determined man here to execute the laws, there would soon be a different state of affairs in the country, and the people would begin to feel safe and secure in their lives and property, but until that occurs there is nothing you can do that will improve the past. I do not wish to be understood or to mean that Judge Bristol is a corrupt man for I do not believe that, but he is a weak man and one wholly unfit for the present situation.

[AUTHOR'S NOTE: Leonard wants Bristol's judgeship, but Wallace would have needed to exert an anti-Ring position to argue for that. He would not. And the Hayes administration had already shielded Bristol from Mary McPherson's correct complaint about the same issues the year before.]

In addition to a change in the Judiciary there is another change equally important to be made in the affairs of this section, before peace and good order can be restored and that is the Military. You saw while you were here what had been the conduct in the Military management at Fort Stanton, that since Col. N.A.M. Dudley has been in command at this Post the very worst characters in the country have been harbored and sustained about this Post and he has given aid to them in carrying out and furthering their wicked designs upon the innocent people of this County. **He became a very strong and active partizan in the struggles between the factions here, lending military aid when McSween and four others were killed his presence in Lincoln Plaza at that time with fifty or sixty soldiers without right or authority and the direct aid he rendered on that occasion to the outlaws resulted in the killing of these parties on that occasion, and the proof already elicited in the Court of Inquiry clearly shows his wicked and unwarranted action on that occasion. I say wicked because his action was most wicked and vile and if such conduct can be sustained by the authorities, every citizen has a right to fear, instead of to honor and respect the Military power of the Government. The proof shows that he went to Lincoln Plaza and by his intimidations and threats with his soldiers and guns, gave such aid to the band of outlaws that they killed McSween and four others on that day, and so put the people in fear that to this day they feel that the Military here are their enemies and the friends and supporters of the outlaws.** *The action of Col Dudley has more or less implicated every officer at Fort Stanton save one Capt Carroll, and from their association and connection with the action of Col Dudley, there is no safety until there is an entire change at the Post.* **No officer who has been here and been mixed up with the affairs and disturbances that have been rife here for the last two years ought to remain** *but there should be in order to establish confidence, and restore to the people a feeling of safety an entire change of officers at this Post, and new men who have not been connected or at all implicated or associated with any of the difficulties in this County put in command. I think from what you saw here and know of the matters in the County you will agree with me in this necessity.*

[AUTHOR'S NOTE: Unrealistic Leonard wants Wallace to remove most Fort Stanton officers as being implicated in Lincoln County War partisanship and public condemnation, even though Wallace could not even sustain his own charges for removing Dudley when facing Henry Waldo's attack. Also, Leonard was unaware that Wallace was in a bind because of refusing to confront the Ring, coupled now with his Dudley Court humiliation.]

I know the difficulty you had in procuring the necessary Military aid to further your purposes and endeavors to restore peace and good order in the country, and the same difficulty will exist as long as the present officers are here. I cannot blame the Military for adhering to each other, since they have been railed on for so long by the cry of Military usurpation &c. &c. and every politician of the country has decreed it his especial duty to cry out against them but there may be occasions and I think this instance is one of them, where to remove the causes of such grave difficulties and disasters as have fallen on these people a change is absolutely necessary to a complete restoration of peace and good order.

[AUTHOR'S NOTE: Sadly, Leonard was not yet prepared to see the alternative: victory of injustice by reducing the populace to hopelessness by blocking all legal redress: civilian or military. This was the Ring's *modus operandi*. And it was about to continue because of Wallace's refusal to confront Ring crimes in the Court of Inquiry, which allowed Dudley to be exonerated by the corrupt Court by July 5, 1879.]

I have endeavored Governor to give you a fair and unbiased statement of affairs here and what to my mind are the essentials to a return of peace and good order and I am confident that you will seek in vain for any better condition of affairs here unless there can be accomplished what I have suggested.

I shall fulfill my promises to you while I remain in the County and do all in my power to bring to punishment the outlaws but with little hope of good results under the present management in Civil and Military authority.

[AUTHOR'S NOTE: This is Leonard's polite denial of Wallace's irresponsible outlaw myth solution.]

I am truly yours
Ira E. Leonard

SUSAN McSWEEN TESTIFIES:
MAY 23-24, 26, 1879

Susan McSween's seeking justice was superhumanly brave in light of murders of John Tunstall, her husband, and Huston Chapman; arson of her home; death threats by N.A.M. Dudley; and sexually defamatory affidavits. And Governor Lew Wallace gave her no support. Her three day, star witness testimony - on May 23rd, 24th, and May 26th - was marred by incompetence of Prosecutor Henry Humphreys and Ira Leonard, who failed to elicit properly her evidence or to counter Ringite Henry Waldo's brutal cross-examination. And the biased Court also sustained defense objections by Waldo to block evidence for the record.

But in a fair Court, her testimony would have been adequate as to Dudley's aid to Peppin's side causing retreat of McSween's men, arson of her house, and endangering women and children - all Posse Comitatus Act violations. Her transcript follows:

Court of Inquiry Rooms
Fort Stanton, N.M.
***May 23, 1879** [Friday]*
14th day [of the Court of Inquiry]
10 AM ...

Present:
Col. G. Pennypacker	*16th Infantry*
Major N.W. Osborne	*15th Infantry*
Captain H.R. Brinkerhoff	*15th Infantry*
Captain H.H. Humphreys	*15th Infantry, Recorder.*

Lt. Col. Dudley, 9th Cav., and his counsel, and Mr. Ira E. Leonard, being present ...
Mrs. Sue E. McSween, a witness being duly sworn, testified as follows.

Q. by Recorder. State your name and place of residence?
Answer. Mrs. Sue E. McSween, Lincoln, Lincoln County, New Mexico.
Q. by Recorder. State whether you are the widow of A.A. McSween, deceased, who was killed at Lincoln on the 19th day of July last, if so state all about the circumstances of his being killed, and Col. Dudley's connection therewith, if any?

[AUTHOR'S NOTE: This is incompetent questioning, forcing Susan to structure massive information alone. Multiple questions should have been asked to help her present facts.]

Answer. Yes Sir, I am sure on the day that he was killed. That morning, about 10 o'clock, Col. Dudley came into Lincoln with about 40 or 50 soldiers ... Well, on his way he stopped at a place known as the hotel [Wortley] occupied by a band of men comprised, or known, as the sheriff's posse, or who called themselves the sheriff's posse. He stopped there about 5 or 10 minutes as near as I could tell, then passed on by our place and camped in what is the middle of town. A few minutes afterwards I saw three soldiers going up to the hotel. I went out to ask the soldiers why they were in town and why they had come here and what their intentions were.

Lt. Col. Dudley, by his Counsel, objects with witness stating any conversation or giving any statements made by the soldiers ... unless it was done or carried on in the presence or hearing of Col. Dudley.

Recorder replied. The testimony is competent for the reason that the evidence already elicited has shown the soldiers escorted Peppin to Col. Dudley's camp ... [A]nything the soldiers may have said concerning Col. Dudley's purpose is competent as they are supposed to be carrying out the orders of their superior officer, Col. Dudley, and whatever they told of those intentions is competent. Objection is sustained.

[AUTHOR'S NOTE: Bias is obvious. The Recorder's argument is correct. Yet the objection is sustained to block Susan from giving evidence that the soldiers were used in a partisan manner - which caused defeat of then winning McSweens.]

(Witness resuming.) Now in a few minutes afterwards I saw the same three soldiers going back with Peppin. Now after seeing this we all became alarmed, who were in the house, seeing Peppin guarded by the soldiers. Then Mr. McSween wrote a note and sent it by a little girl [her sister's daughter] asking Col. Dudley ... well, I am afraid I am ahead of my story. Before sending this note we saw three soldiers ... standing back of our house and on the same side we saw these men of Mr. Peppins coming behind the house, some of them coming down the road after the soldiers, and broke

into the house opposite ours, immediately afterwards they hung out the black flag [meaning no surrender, death]. After we had seen this Mr. McSween wrote the note.

[AUTHOR'S NOTE: This shows Susan's problem organizing information; a fault of inadequate questioning. But she does describe soldiers guarding Peppin, occupying her property, and enabling his men to take offensive positions. She also describes her husband's letter questioning Dudley's intervention.]

Now, in a few minutes afterwards the little girl returned with the answer from Col. Dudley ... He says before "blowing up my house, I wish to know ..." [Dudley's Gatling gun and howitzer cannon panicked McSween who clumsily wrote that before blowing up his house, he wanted to know why Dudley was in town. So with Ringite mocking, Dudley taunted his grammar by saying if he wanted to blow up his house he could.] The substance of the letter was to find out ... whether he intended to assist Peppin and his men ... Now before this letter was written Col. Dudley sent us word that if a shot was fired from our house at his soldiers, or near them, that he would turn his cannon loose ... and tear the house to the ground, regardless of the inmates ... I then said to Mr. McSween that I believe that I would go down to his camp and talk with him myself ... I then started with Mr. McSween's consent on my way to his camp I saw Bates, he being a colored servant of mine ... just in the act of picking up some lumber. At the time I saw three of Murphy's men ... I then asked what they were doing, **they said ... [t]hat Peppin and Col. Dudley had sent them to carry lumber to our house to set it on fire** *... I then begged them not to do so ... I then started again for Col. Dudley's camp and met Mr. Peppin ... He then said that if I did not want my house burned down I must make those men who were in the house get out of it, that he was bound to have these men ... dead or alive ... I then started again for Col. Dudley's camp. Arriving there I told him ... that these men and Mr. Peppin intend to burn down the house, and to ask him if he would give me some protection and save our house from being burned. He said he ... did not intend to have anything to do with either party ... I then said it looked strange to me to see his men, or his soldiers I should say, guarding Peppin back and forth through town and sending soldiers around our house ... if he had nothing to do with it.* **He then got very angry and said it was none of my business, that he would send his soldiers where he pleased, that I have no such** *business to have such men as Billy the Kid, Jim French, and others of like character in my house. He then ... said that he had come to protect women and children. I then asked why he did not protect myself, my sister, and her children. He said I have no business, or we had no business, to be in that house, that he would not give us protection, and if a shot was fired from our house at any of his soldiers ... he would turn his cannon loose and tear the house to the ground regardless of women and children ...*

[AUTHOR'S NOTE: Though rambling, she confirms Dudley's partisanship and not protecting women and children. Note that by May 23, 1879, Billy is known as "Billy the Kid."]

I then said they were trying to kill McSween with the protection of having a warrant and we were sure they had none. He then said they had ... a U.S. warrant for him and we will have him. I then told him I did not see for what reason they could procure a U.S. warrant for him unless it was done falsely ... Col. Dudley then said that he was guilty of such crime and that his men had fired at his soldiers the evening before. I told him he must be mistaken ...

[AUTHOR'S NOTE: These warrants were for the July 16th Private Berry Robinson shooting coerced by Dudley from Justice of the Peace Wilson after learning the Easton warrants were invalid.]

He then made sport of me being Mrs. McSween as though it was degrading to be called Mrs. McSween. I then told him I was proud to be his wife, that I know him to be a man of principle and far better principle than those men he was escorting.

Lt. Col. Dudley, by his Counsel [Henry Waldo], called the attention of the Court to the character of the testimony and suggests that he is unable to see even its relevancy and that it is occupying the time of the Court to no purpose..

Recorder made the following reply. The testimony is a narrative of the conduct of Col. Dudley on that occasion, and is material ... as to Col. Dudley's conduct on that occasion ...

[The Judges closed the court for discussion; then re-opened it.] The Court directs the Recorder to confine witness to more direct answers to his questions.

[AUTHOR'S NOTE: Waldo is objecting to obscure her evidence. Ominously, the Court supports his objection.]

(Witness resuming.) I told him he was assisting men who I believed he knew to be known thieves and murderers, who have broken out of jail and [were] known by everybody [as a posse of Seven Rivers and John Kinney men]. I asked him why he could not understand these troubles and assist such men if he intended to do what was right. He then got very angry with me, used abusive language towards me and those with my husband. He said I was not a woman of good character.

[Waldo here repeats his objection of irrelevancy; and Humphreys and Leonard fail badly by not even countering.]

Q. by Recorder. *State what Col. Dudley said to you and how he treated you on the occasion ...*
Answer. *He treated me in a very abusive manner, then made slurs against my character. He said he wanted nothing to do with me or our party,* **that we were the party of outlaws** *...*

[AUTHOR'S NOTE: Humphreys here missed the chance to address the defamatory affidavits, what the McSween party represented, or the invalidity of Dudley's so-called warrants for their arrest.]

Q. by Recorder. *State what conversation passed between you and Col. Dudley in reference to the letter you have said Mr. McSween had written ...*
Answer. *He said I asked him why he threatened to blow up our house. He said because McSween and others were in it and he was a man of no principle ... [She requested to see the letter to explain that McSween was afraid they would blow up their house, but Dudley told a soldier present, "I'll thank you to shoot this lady if she takes this letter."] He ... kept on abusing me and using language against me that was inappropriate and unbecoming of his kind.* **He said he could not help such a man as McSween or I either, that he was trying to make all the disturbance in the county. I told him that he was not, that he was trying to be right by all good citizens, the other party was committing the crimes, and that they have commenced it. This all came ... because he was in opposition to them in business, that they had threatened his life for two years, and that then some were now publicly saying, or telling, everybody that they would kill McSween ... I said to Col. Dudley that I knew that if they ever caught sight of him they**

would kill him, and then asked if he would not protect him, send some of his soldiers to the house to rescue him, that I knew if he would do this McSween would give himself up willingly.

[AUTHOR'S NOTE: Though Humphreys failed to add focus, she has shown Dudley as a murderous partisan.]

Q. by Recorder. *State what Col. Dudley replied to you?*
Answer. *He refused to send them and ordered me out of camp ...*
Q. by Recorder. *What did you see going on about your house by the parties who were outside when you got back, if anything?*
Answer. *I saw three soldiers standing near the house, on the west side, and some of these Murphy men standing close up to the wall by the house ... I saw one man ... pouring coal oil on the floor of my sister's house [one of the two wings of her house] ... Jack Long threw something that popped ... it set the coal oil on fire. They then began to shoot into every door and window on that side of the house. I remained with Mr. McSween until 5 o'clock that afternoon.*

[AUTHOR'S NOTE: This arson risked the women and children.]

Q. by Recorder. *Did you go to Col. Dudley's camp [again]?*
Answer. *I did not go to his camp, but went to a house near there, where I remained all night. During the evening I saw Col. Dudley and several other officers with an opera glass.*

[AUTHOR'S NOTE: She was in the vacated house of their tenant, Saturnino Baca, east of Tunstall's store. Dudley was camped farther east. She was risking her life to collect evidence, while the attempted escape and murders took place at her house.]

Q. by Recorder. *What did you see, if anything, of Col. Dudley's actions on that day with his troops?*
Answer. *... I saw him ordering the soldiers to turn the cannon to a certain direction when ever he saw a man appear on the other side of the river ...*

[AUTHOR'S NOTE: This is Dudley's blocking of return of the fled McSweens. But Humphreys has not clarified by questioning either how Dudley caused the flight or blocked the returns.]

Q. by Recorder. What time of day was your husband and the others killed on that day?
Answer. About dark ...

****

May 24, 1879 [Saturday]
15th day [of Court of Inquiry] ...

Present:
Col. G. Pennypacker	16th Infantry
Major N.W. Osborne	15th Infantry
Captain H.R. Brinkerhoff	15th Infantry
Captain H.H. Humphreys	15th Infantry, Recorder

Lt. Col. Dudley, 9th Cav., and his Counsel [Henry Waldo], and Mr. Ira E. Leonard, and Mrs. Sue E. McSween were present ...

Q. by Recorder ... State whether you saw any parties taking goods from [the Tunstall store], if so who they were, on the day after the fight when Col. Dudley was in town, what you saw of their actions?
Answer. I was not in the store until the second day after Mr. McSween was killed, but I saw some of Peppins men in Col. Dudley's camp, dressed with old clothing in the morning, and then I saw them again with suits of new clothing that I recognized as clothing from the store ...

CROSS EXAMINATION.

Q. by Col. Dudley. How did you recognize that clothing as coming from the Tunstall store?
Answer. By the color. Now I can scarcely tell you I recognized it but I had seen the clothing many times before and handled them. I could say that I recognized them by the style of the check.
Q. by Col. Dudley Was that style of check contained only in the Tunstall store and not in any other store in the town of Lincoln?
Answer. I don't know but I know at the time these men were taking goods.

Lt. Col. Dudley, by his Counsel [Henry Waldo], moves the Court to instruct the witness to confine her answers so as to be expressive of the questions propounded to her. If she desires to make explanations, this is not the time to make them ...

[AUTHOR'S NOTE: Waldo is now purposefully harassing to confuse her, here to conceal Dudley's enabling of looting. Since Humphreys did not object, Waldo then proceeded viciously.]

Q. by Col. Dudley. What was the first thing you said to Col. Dudley, or Col. Dudley to you, on that day on the occasion of the conversation [in his camp]?

Answer. I told him I had come there to see if he would not protect us. That we were having trouble with the Murphy party ...

Q. by Col. Dudley. In that conversation, I understood you to say you wanted him, Col. Dudley, to protect your house from the Murphy men. Did he not say to you in that conversation that he could not interfere with actions of the sheriff?

Answer. I don't remember him telling me.

Q. by Col. Dudley. Did he not give as a reason for not interfering in regard to your house that the men within are the men for whom the sheriff had warrants he was trying to serve and that he would not interfere with the sheriff nor take any part in the contest going on between the parties in any way whatsoever, or words to that effect?

Answer. He refused to give protection, he refused to give protection and said ... [She is here cut off by Waldo before she can complete her answer; and Humphreys does not object.]

Lt. Col. Dudley, by his Counsel, moves the Court to instruct the witness to answer the question in the manner which the form of the question calls for.

[AUTHOR'S NOTE: Waldo is trying to put words in her mouth to make Dudley seem a non-participant. And his harassment is flustering her, though her answer was correct.]

Recorder made the following objection. The witness has the right to answer the question by stating just what Col. Dudley did say and not answer yes or no to the question. The Court can then determine the facts from the whole of the conversation ... The question assumes that Col. Dudley said a certain thing, the witness should be allowed in response to state what he did say, and that fully.

The Court [Judge Galusha Pennypacker] instructs the witness to answer yes or no.

[AUTHOR'S NOTE: Court bias is now obvious, with Chief Judge Galusha Pennypacker backing Waldo's abuse of Susan as well as limiting her evidence by confining her to "yes or no."]

Answer. I cannot answer that question yes or no intelligibly. A part of the conversation would infer that he would not assist us and a part of the conversation would infer that he was really helping them.

[AUTHOR'S NOTE: On her own without a competent prosecutor, she gives an impressive come-back. She refuses to accept the Court's manipulation. It was with good reason that Frank Warner Angel called her "a tiger." But Waldo's badgering continued until he exhausted her, and her answers eventually became addled as seen below. And Humphreys and Ira Leonard never protected or encouraged her by objecting properly or by correctly eliciting the evidence.]

Q. by Col. Dudley. Do you swear that Col. Dudley ever, at anytime, refused to furnish you protection?
Answer. He refused me on that day ... no, I do not remember that he had, for I never asked for it ...

[AUTHOR'S NOTE: All Humphreys needed to do was to ask for her earlier testimony to be read if she needed help to recall.]

Q. by Col. Dudley. Now Mrs. McSween, is not your feelings towards Col. Dudley quite bitter and harsh?
Answer. They are not.
Q. by Col. Dudley. Have you not been quite active in collecting testimony for the purpose of this investigation?
Answer. I have, but a great deal more has been told to me, most certainly more than I asked for.
Q. by Col. Dudley. Have you not said that you intended to have him indicted in the Territorial Courts for what you have said was his connection with the killing of your husband and burning of your house on the 19th of July last?
Answer. I did not, but I said I would await the action of the Grand Jury for the burning of my house and the killing of Mr. McSween, if the government would not do their duty before that time ...

Q. by Col. Dudley. You were a witness, were you not, before the last Grand Jury and gave testimony against him, did you not?
Answer. Yes Sir.

Q. by Col. Dudley. Have you not said, or did you say soon after the killing of your husband and the burning of your house, that you would spend thousands of dollars, or words to that effect, to have the shoulder straps stripped from him?
Answer. No Sir. I never used such language. But I have said I would try to bring him to justice.

Lt. Col. Dudley, by his Counsel, states he is finished with the witness.

REDIRECT

Q. by Recorder. Explain how you happened to be familiar with the clothing in the Tunstall store. How you happened to handle the clothing, and know that what you saw these men have on came from the store?

Answer. I was there when the goods were opened. I helped to mark them and was there daily, seen them handled by the clerks frequently and looked through them myself many times ...

[AUTHOR'S NOTE: Humphreys should then have asked if that was why she was sure of the looting the next day.]

Q. by Recorder. Explain how long it was, as near as you can remember, from the time Col. Dudley went into camp at Lincoln on that day, up to the time the house was set on fire?

Objected to by Lieut. Col. Dudley, by his Counsel.
Recorder withdrew the question ...
Recorder stated that he had finished with the witness.

[AUTHOR'S NOTE: Outrageously, Humphreys did not redirect questioning to get her evidence into the record. That let the Court (the three Judges) ask their own biased questions to shield Dudley's guilt.]

Q. by Court [one of the Judges]. Did Col. Dudley or any of his officers or soldiers commit any act which caused your house to be set on fire, if and what?

Answer. Nothing more than those three soldiers standing by the house and guarding Peppin which I suppose was done for the purpose of intimidating those who were in the house.

Q. by Court. Did you see Col. Dudley or any of his soldiers enter the store belonging to the estate of John Tunstall on the 20th day of July last, while the same was being robbed and plundered?

Answer. I cannot say ...

Q. by Court. What was said or done by Col. Dudley on the occasions of the firing of your house that was **most inhuman and unbecoming a soldier and officer,** *at any time during the day?*

Answer. His expression I cannot remember. He appeared to be very much angered and said many unkind things about Mr. McSween, said he was a mean man, and the parties with him were bad men, that I have no right to expect protection if I upheld such parties, that I was not a woman of good character. He ordered me out of the camp and ordered a soldier to shoot me if I took a letter from his hand. There was nothing done except his manner appeared very hostile.

[AUTHOR'S NOTE: She is so confused after Waldo's day of verbal assault, that she fails to state how Dudley's behavior was "*most inhuman and unbecoming a soldier and officer*": omitting his maligning her to her face, refusing her aid, and assisting Peppin to kill her husband and burn down her house around women and children - all things she had said earlier.]

Witness retired but will remain in Court.

The Court directed the Recorder to read the following.

[In Susan's hearing, the Court refused to hear the Prosecution's 120 listed witnesses, demanding a shortened list. It also limited presentation of evidence of Dudley's culpability, followed by near praise of him "during a very trying period," stating:] The Court is the judge of the sufficiency of evidence upon any and all allegations before it to enable it to make an intelligent conclusion. And not in reason be expected to follow every point which might be construed to be material by interested persons by such exhaustive examination as may be desired by them. **The military culpability of Col. Dudley in connection with the management of one affair during a very trying period is the only subject of examination.**

At 5.15 PM the Court adjourned ...

****

May 26, 1879 *[Monday]*
16th day [of Court of Inquiry]

Present:
Col. G. Pennypacker	16th Infantry
Major N.W. Osborne	15th Infantry
Captain H.R. Brinkerhoff	15th Infantry
Captain H.H. Humphreys	15th Infantry, Recorder

Lt. Col. Dudley, 9th Cav., and his counsel, and Mr. Ira E. Leonard, and Mrs. McSween were present.

Mrs. McSween was called back to answer questions of the Court.

Q. by Court. Did you on the 15th day of January last make an affidavit before John B. Wilson, Justice of the Peace, in and for the County of Lincoln, Territory of New Mexico, in which you swore that Alex. A. McSween was feloniously, willfully, and of malice aforethought, killed and murdered, on the 19th day of July last and that the said murder was committed by Lieut. Col. N.A.M. Dudley, George Peppin, and Jack Long, and also in the same affidavit did you swear that Lieut. Col. N.A.M. Dudley, George Peppin, and Jack Long, on the 19th day of July last, set fire to and burned the house of Alex. A. McSween, and did you ask in and upon said affidavit that the warrants might be issued for the arrest of the said Lieut. Col. N.A.M. Dudley, George Peppin, and Jack Long?

Answer. I made an affidavit but I cannot remember anything contained in it. It was made by my attorney and carelessly read to me, I did not pay much attention to it, I could not say as to the time. It was an affidavit made against Col. N.A.M. Dudley, Peppin, and Long.

[AUTHOR'S NOTE: After three days of defense abuse, inadequate prosecution, and a prejudiced Court, Susan folds in exhaustion. But she had given enough evidence to convict Dudley. It is not clear that Humphreys or Leonard gave her deserved encouragement or praise. And, like all Ring victims, she would never see justice.]

Witness then retired.

BILLY BONNEY TESTIFIES: MAY 28-29, 1879

Proof of Billy Bonney's anti-Ring commitment was his testifying against N.A.M. Dudley. His Regulator cause, plus his courage and intellectual brilliance, made him unshakable under Henry Waldo s abusive cross-examination.

Noteworthy is that Billy's testimony was not part of his pardon bargain. And, as he had written to Lew Wallace on March 13, 1879, he knew his risk: "*[M]y Enimies would Kill me.*" But he twice made the unprotected, nine mile trip from his Lincoln sham custody to the courtroom in the Fort Stanton Adjutant's office adjacent to the parade ground.

Billy's precise, unshakable, and devastating testimony alone could have gotten Dudley a court martial in a fair court, after this incriminatory interchange: "*How many soldiers fired at you? ... Three ... How many shots did those soldiers fire, that you say shot from the Tunstall building? ... I could not swear to that on account of firing on all sides, I could not hear. I seen them fire one volley ... Were the soldiers which you say fired at you as you escaped from the McSween house on the evening of July 19th last, colored or white? ... White troops.*"

A volley meant the three soldiers coordinated their firing in unison. That required Dudley's order to do so. "White" meant they were officers. So dangerous was this evidence, that Henry Waldo's closing argument devoted a large part to false discrediting of Billy.

And it made Lew Wallace's perfidy undeniable in refusing the pardon, since he ignored not only the bargain's testimony, but also Billy's selfless efforts to attain real Lincoln County justice. Within a month, the teenager had testified against Chapman's Ringite killers and the Lincoln County War's arch-villain.

The Santa Fe Ring, however, correctly assessed Billy's risk to them as a new leader after Waldo faced the implacable boy. The Court of Inquiry testimony likely sealed Billy's death: the Ring's sole compliment for unbeatable foes.

The transcript of Billy's testimony follows:

May 28, 1879
18th day [of Court of Inquiry]

Present:
Col. G. Pennypacker 16th Infantry
Major N.W. Osborne 15th Infantry

Captain H.R. Brinkerhoff 15th Infantry
Captain H.H. Humphreys 15th Infantry, Recorder
Lieut. Col. Dudley, and his Counsel, Mr. Ira E. Leonard and William Bonney were present.

WILLIAM BONNEY, *a witness being duly sworn, testified as follows.*

Q. by Recorder. What is your name and place of residence?
Answer. My name is William Bonney. I reside in Lincoln.
Q. by Recorder. Are you known or called Billy Kidd, also Antrim?
Answer. Yes Sir.
Q. by Recorder. Where were you on the 19th day of July last and what, if anything, did you see of the movements and actions of the troops in that city, state fully?
Answer. I was in the McSween house in Lincoln, and I saw soldiers come from the post with sheriff's party, that is the sheriff's posse joined them a short distance below there, the McSween house. Soldiers passed on by and the men dropped off and surrounded the house, the sheriff's party. Shortly after, the soldiers came back with Peppin, passed the house twice afterwards. Three soldiers came and stood in front of the house, in front of the windows. Mr. McSween wrote a note to the officer in charge asking what the soldiers were placed there for. He replied saying that they had business there, that if a shot was fired over his camp, or at Peppin, or at any of his men, that he had no objection to blowing up, if he wanted, his own house. I read the note myself, he handed it to me to read. I saw nothing further of the soldiers until night. I was in the back part of the house. **When I escaped from the house three soldiers fired at me from the Tunstall store, outside corner of the store.** *That's all I know in regards to it.*
Q. by Recorder. Did the soldiers that stood in front of the windows have guns with them while there?
Answer. Yes Sir.
Q. by Recorder. Who escaped from the house with you and who was killed at the time, if you know, while attempting to make their escape?
Answer. Jose Chavez [Chávez y Chávez] escaped with me, Vincente Romero, Francisco Zamora and McSween.
Q. by Recorder. How many persons were killed in that fight that day, if you know, and who killed them, if you know?

Answer. I seen five killed, I could not swear to who killed them, I seen some of them that fired.

Q. by Recorder. Who did you see that fired?

Answer. Robt. Beckwith, John Hurley, John Jones, **those three soldiers, I don't know their names.**

Q. by Recorder. Did you see any persons setting fire to the McSween house that day, if so, state who it was, if you know?

Answer. I did, Jack Long, and there was another man I did not recognize.

Recorder stated he had finished with the witness.

Cross examination.

Q. By Col. Dudley. What were you, and the others there with you, doing in McSween's house that day?

Answer. We came here with McSween.

Q. By Col. Dudley. Did you know, or had you not heard, that the sheriff was endeavoring to arrest yourself and others there with you at the time?

Answer. Yes Sir. I had heard so, I did not know.

Q. By Col. Dudley. Then were you not engaged in resisting the sheriff at the time you were in the house?

Objected to by Recorder. The Court has already ruled that nothing extraneous from the actual occurrence that took place, and Col. Dudley's actions in connection therewith, should be further inquired into and nothing has been called out to the witness to authorize this mode of cross examination, it cannot be a matter of defense of Col. Dudley or justify his actions however much the parties may have been resisting the sheriff or civil authorities.

Lt. Col. Dudley, by his Counsel, states he does not deem it necessary to make reply to the objection.

Objection sustained.

Q. By Col. Dudley. In addition to the names you have given, are you also known as the "Kid?"

Answer. I have already answered that question, Yes Sir, I am, but not "Billy Kid" that I know of.

Q. By Col. Dudley. Were you not and were not the parties with you in the McSween house on the 19th day of July last and the days immediately preceding, engaged in firing at the sheriff's posse?

Court objects to the question.

Lt. Col. Dudley, by his Counsel, asks, does the Court intend to rule here, that after once gone into this matter of firing into the McSween house by the testimony of this witness, it is not permissible to show all the circumstances under which this firing took place ... It is asked for information in order to guide us in the further examination of this witness.

Court cleared and closed.

Court opened and its decision announced ...

The Court directs the case to proceed calling attention to its previous rulings which were deemed sufficient by explicit.

Q. By Col. Dudley. Whose name was signed to the note received by McSween in reply to the one previously sent by him to Col. Dudley?

Answer. Signed N.A.M. Dudley, did not say what rank, he received two notes, one had no name signed to it.

Q. By Col. Dudley. Are you as certain of everything else you have sworn to as you are to what you have sworn to in answer to the last proceeding question?

Answer. Yes Sir.

Q. By Col. Dudley. From which direction did Peppin come the first time the soldiers passed with him?

Answer. Passed up from the direction of where the soldiers camped, the first time I saw him.

Q. By Col. Dudley. What direction did he come from the second time?

Answer. From the direction of the [Wortley] hotel from the McSween house.

Q. By Col. Dudley. In what direction did you go upon your escape from the McSween house?

Answer. Ran towards the Tunstall store, was fired at, and there turned towards the river.

Q. By Col. Dudley. From what part of the McSween house did you make your escape?

Answer. The northeast corner of the house.

Q. By Col. Dudley. How many soldiers fired at you?
Answer. Three.

Q. By Col. Dudley. How many soldiers were with Peppin when he passed the McSween house each time, as you say?

Answer. Three.

Q. By Col. Dudley. The soldiers appeared to go in company of threes that day, did they not?

Answer. All that I ever saw appeared to be three in a crowd at a time after they passed the first time.

Q. By Col. Dudley. Who was killed first that day, Bob Beckwith or McSween men?

Answer. Harvey Morris, McSween man, was killed first.

Q. By Col. Dudley. How far is the Tunstall building from the McSween house?

Answer. I could not say how far, I never measured the distance. I should judge it to be 40 yards, between 30 and 40 yards.

Q. By Col. Dudley. How many shots did those soldiers fire, that you say shot from the Tunstall building?

Answer. I could not swear to that on account of firing on all sides, I could not hear. I seen them fire one volley.

Q. By Col. Dudley. What did they fire at?

Answer. Myself and Jose Chavez [Chávez y Chávez].

Q. By Col. Dudley. Did you not just now state in answer to the question who killed Zamora, Romero, Morris, and McSween that you did not know who killed them, but you saw Beckwith, John Jones, **and three soldiers fire at them***?*

Answer. Yes Sir. I did.

Q. By Col. Dudley. Were these men, the McSween men, there with you **when the volley was fired at you and Chavez by the soldiers***?*

Answer. Just a short ways behind us.

Q. By Col. Dudley. Were you looking back at them?

Answer. No Sir.

Q. By Col. Dudley. How then do you know they were just behind you then, or that they were in range of the volley?

Answer. Because there was a high fence behind, and a good many guns to keep them there. I could hear them speak.

Q. By Col. Dudley. How far were you from the soldiers when you saw them?

Answer. I could not swear exactly, between 30 and 40 yards.

Q. By Col. Dudley. Did you know either of the soldiers that were in front of the window of McSween's house that day? If so, give it.

Answer. No Sir, I am not acquainted with them.

Redirect.

Q. by Recorder. Explain whether all the men that were in the McSween house came out at the same time when McSween and the others were killed and the firing came from the soldiers and others?

Answer. Yes Sir, all came out at the same time. **The firing was done by the soldiers until some had escaped.**

Recorder stated that he had finished with the witness.

Q. by Col. Dudley. How do you know if you were making your escape at the time and the men Zamora, Morris and McSween were behind you that they were killed at that time, is it not true that you did not know of their death or the death of either of them until afterwards?

Answer. I knew of the death of some of them, I did know of the death of one of them. I saw him lying down there.

Q. by Col. Dudley. Did you see any of the men last mentioned killed?

Answer. Yes Sir, I did, I seen Harvey Morris killed first, he was out in front of me.

Q. by Col. Dudley. Did you not then a moment ago swear that he was among those who were behind you and Jose Chavez [Chávez y Chávez] when you saw the soldiers deliver the volley?

Answer. No Sir, I didn't think I did. I misunderstood the question if I did. I said he was among them that was killed not behind me.

Witness then withdrew ...

****

May 29, 1879
19th day [of Court of Inquiry] ...

Q. by Court. Were the soldiers which you say fired at you as you escaped from the McSween house on the evening of July 19th last, colored or white?

Answer. White troops.

Q. by Court. Was it light enough so you could distinctly see the soldiers when they fired?

Answer. The house was burning. Made it almost light as day for a short distance all around.

Witness then retired.

DUDLEY'S CAVALRYMEN TESTIFY: MAY 30, 31 1879

Other witnesses, and unsung heroes, Private James Bush and Sergeant Huston Lusk, as brave and honest as Billy, also proved Dudley's guilt. They were black 9th cavalrymen whom Dudley ordered treasonously to assist Sheriff George Peppin's against McSweens and to enable arson of McSween's house. By testifying, they risked their lives and futures, demonstrating the same post-Civil War democratic zeal that had inspired the Regulators.

PRIVATE JAMES BUSH TESTIFIES: MAY 30 – 31, 1879

In his testimony on May 30th and 31st, 1879, Private James Bush confirmed Billy's testimony that the three soldiers accompanying Peppin were under Dudley's orders, stating: *"We escorted Sheriff Peppin to Gen. Dudley's camp and back to the hotel again."* Bush also confirmed Dudley's partisan motive in forcing flight of McSween's men, stating: *"Sheriff Peppin on returning from Mr. Ellis' store stopped in the street opposite our camp. Col Dudley said you might have captured those men at Montano's house if you had come when the word was sent to you that they were there."* Bush confirmed Dudley's using his major weapons of war against the McSweens, stating:

Q, by Recorder. Did you see the cannon or the Gatling gun moved in any direction ...
Answer. Yes Sir I did. The howitzer was first aimed at Montano's door or house, next in the direction of Mr. Ellis' store, Gatling gun was aimed in the direction of the McSween house, then in the afternoon the Gatling gun was aimed on a party of men, supposed to be the McSween party, on the north side of town across the bottom [Bonito River].

Bush testified that Dudley coerced Justice of the Peace Wilson to write warrants, though he was unaware that they were against McSween and Billy. Bush stated: *"Col. Dudley told Mr. Wilson that if he did not serve the writ he would put him in double irons, that he, Wilson, had been lying to them long enough."*

[AUTHOR'S NOTE: Wilson, in his testimony of May 22, 1879, stated: "Colonel Dudley told me he wanted to see me to issue a

warrant for McSween and others that was in the house on the 16th of July 1878, charge was assaulting with intent to kill one Berry Robinson, a United States soldier ... I told him I did not think it was according to the law. Colonel Dudley became angry and spoke ... if I did not issue a warrant right away ... he would put me in double irons and report me to the Governor.]

Private James Bush also confirmed Dudley's giving orders for soldiers to attack men leaving McSween's house, stating under questioning by Prosecutor Henry Humphreys:

Q. by Recorder. Did you hear Col. Dudley give any orders to soldiers that day or order them to do anything, if so, state what you heard and what orders he gave?

Answer. Yes Sir I did. As the two parties were firing at each other very rapidly, it was supposed that McSween men were trying to leave McSween's house and retreat through the main street in the direction of the camp [eastward]. Gen Dudley gave orders to the soldiers to fall in and stop them from passing.

Bush also confirmed Dudley's ordering infantrymen to help loot Tunstall's store, stating: "*A detachment of infantry was sent out to assist in moving some furniture from the Tunstall building.*" But the corrupt Court, using Waldo's objection, outrageously blocked Bush's further devastating evidence, stating: "*The witness was informed that the rulings of the Court did not permit him to any conversation not held in the presence of Col. Dudley.*"

SERGEANT HUSTON LUSK TESTIFIES: MAY 31, 1879

Sergeant Huston Lusk corroborated James Bush's and Billy Bonney's testimonies. He described Dudley terrifying the McSween men in José Montaño's house, stating: "*[I]f a shot came from this residence directly through or near the encampment of his command and either officers or soldiers were shot or injured by either party that he would open up his howitzer on either party of whom ever the shot was fired from.*" Lusk then confirmed Dudley's partisan orders through past Fort Stanton Commander George Purington to assist Peppin in attacking fleeing McSweens, stating: "*I then received orders from Capt. Purington to tell Pvt. Williams to tell Sheriff Peppin that the party was leaving the Montano house and if Sheriff Peppin would come over with his posse he would be enabled to cut them off.*"

IRA LEONARD'S RAGE AND DESPAIR: JUNE 6, 1879

By June 6, 1879, Attorney Ira Leonard realized he was in a kangaroo court, though unaware of Lew Wallace's abandonment. Wallace, after his humiliation at Henry Waldo's hand, and back in his Santa Fe Palace of the Governors, retreated from Lincoln County "troubles" and reliving Shiloh's shame. And Billy Bonney's pardon - as another threat to his future ambitions - blurred in his pathological unconscious as mere fuel for the outlaw myth of "Billy the Kid." So Wallace buried himself in decorating his "Palace," writing *Ben*-Hur, and planning his escape from the Territory.

Thus, it was to Wallace's deaf ears that Leonard wailed in his letter of June 6, 1879: *"This evidence against Dudley would hang a man in any country where right and justice prevailed."* He wrote:

Fort Stanton N.M
June 6th 1879

Gov Lew Wallace
Santa Fe

Dear Gov: Dudley commenced on the defense Thursday afternoon and our apprehensions as to what the Court intended to do are plainly visible, they mean to white-wash and excuse his glaring conduct. They have transcended all rules of evidence to allow hearsay coming through other channels than direct parties and are allowing liberally to Dudley what they peremptorily refused us **I have no hope of any good results I am thoroughly and completely disgusted with their proceedings.** *They held yesterday that since the prosecution had closed we could not call out from the witnesses on the defense on cross-examination in matters they had testified to concerning Dudley's culpability. They had Dolan on the stand and cut off my examination of him by not allowing me to interrogate him even upon what he had testified to in chief. I had a good notion to show my disgust by abandoning the case and let them have it their own way -* **There is nothing to be looked or hoped from this tribunal it is a farce on judicial investigation and ought to be called and designated "The Mutual Admiration Inquiry"** *I hope the evidence may go to the War Department so that they can see how things are managed.* **The evidence against Dudley would hang a man [for treason] in any country where right and justice prevailed**

I have not heard from you since you left I hope you received my letter and I ... sent on a petition signed by a large number of citizens seeking the removal of Bristol got Taylor to write a letter to the Post giving a similar statement to the one I wrote

[AUTHOR'S NOTE: Wallace would do nothing ever again for Lincoln County or for Leonard.]

My health has much improved since you left. Remember me to Mrs. Wallace.

A little episode occurred here a few days ago. [Deputy Sheriff Robert] Gilbert endeavored to arrest the men for whom he had warrants that were here as witnesses [like James Dolan] and the Atty Genl [Henry Waldo, also Court of Inquiry's defense lawyer] who is a little less than a damned ass threatened to have him Gilbert arrested for taking the witnesses on a criminal warrant because he claimed they were privileged from arrest. [See my pp. 545-547 for letter] That is the first time I ever heard that a criminal as a witness could not be arrested at any time under the laws of England as well as this Country witnesses are privileged from arrest on civil process but never criminal See Wharton on Evidence Sec 389.

Let me hear from you. Yours truly. Ira E. Leonard.

WALLACE WOOS CARL SCHURZ WITH PARDONS AND OUTLAWS: JUNE 11, 1879

Instead of responding to Ira Leonard's letter, five days earlier, Wallace wrote a damage control one to Secretary of the Interior Carl Schurz on June 11, 1879. Key is that he condoned abuse of his Amnesty Proclamation by Catron's petitioning for amnesty from prosecution of *indicted* Ringites, with Judge Bristol's granting of pardon to all in the April 1879 Lincoln County Grand Jury. That left just Billy Bonney with a "pardon bargain" accepting that Proclamation's barring of those indicted. And Lincoln County citizens were left helplessly without legal justice. Instead, Wallace covered up with the outlaw myth: "*[T]he only remaining disturbing element remaining to be grappled with is the confederacy of outlaws.*" So three months after Billy's pardon bargain, he was more likely to be victimized by Wallace as the "outlaw" Billy the Kid, than rewarded by a pardon. Wallace wrote:

Executive Office,
Santa Fe, N.M.,
June 11, 1879.

Hon. C. Schurz,
Sec'y Dept. Interior.
Sir:
Enclosed please find a copy of the report of the commandant at Fort Stanton. As the statement of Capt. Purington is fully sustained by intelligence received privately, I think myself justified in informing you of a continuance in Lincoln county of the peace reported in my last letter. And in the connection, you will pardon me, I think, for calling your attention and the President's to the fact, that for quite eight months now **there has been but one murder - Mr. Chapman's** - with reference to which you know my procedure.

[AUTHOR'S NOTE: Wallace chillingly minimizes Chapman's murder and his murderers' indictments. But to achieve that indicting Billy had risked his life by testifying against the Ring.]

This leaves me at liberty to repeat for your better understanding of the present situation there, that the old factions known respectively as the "Murphy-Dolan" and the "McSween" are as dead organizations; to which may be added now, that my amnesty proclamation has had exactly the effect intended; which was to shear the past off, and make present and future all questions which might require official action, pertinent to civil affairs in the locality. To illustrate, the grand jury empanelled for the recent county court was, with one or two exceptions, composed of men accounted of the McSween or anti-Dolan party, for it is undeniable that nearly all citizens eligible as grand-jurors are ~~inimical to the latter~~ *of that persuasion. They found nearly 200 indictments, the whole, with a few exceptions, against the Dolan people. Nearly 200 indictments in a county of a voting population of 150* ~~in all~~ *total!*

[AUTHOR'S NOTE: Wallace's callousness leaves him blind to Lincoln County citizens attempting to get justice.]

You cannot fail to see what would have come of trial of the accused - how long they would have lasted - the expenses to a county which has nothing in its treasury - the heart-burnings, disputes, revivals of old feuds, fights, shootings, bush-wackings, and general turmoil, ending, in probability, in the recall of the thieves now for the most part driven out. **As it was most of the indicted appeared in court and plead the amnesty in bar [of further prosecution].** <u>Hereafter the labors of grand juries will be confined strictly to offences subsequent to my proclamation.</u>

[AUTHOR'S NOTE: Ringites ignored the Amnesty Proclamation's exclusion of the indicted and plead "*amnesty in bar*" of further prosecution. And Judge Bristol granted it. So Wallace rationalizes it as less work for juries! (See my pp. 607-609)]

Now, from my saying that the old factions are dead, that peace is prevailing, and for eight months there has been but one murder in the county, you should not understand me as saying that the people are relieved of fears of further trouble. On the contrary there is great disquiet amongst them, and with reason. They know very well that the outlaws who so harried them are reacting in expectation of recall. They go up to Fort Stanton witnesses on one side or the other of the Dudley court of inquiry, and see strange sights; they see Dolan, admittedly the leader of the fiercest refractories, at large and busy in Col. Dudley's behalf, although he is under two indictments for murder, one a murder in the first degree: they know he is not at large by consent or connivance of the Sheriff; they know the commandant of the Fort has my official request in writing to keep Dolan in close confinement; knowing this, and seeing what they see – Dolan free to go and come, a boarder at the Trader's store, attended by a gang well known as ready to do his bidding to any extreme – they are further met by threats of bloody things intended when Col. Dudley is acquitted by his court and restored to command of the post, and very naturally they are afraid, and so constantly alarmed as to find it impossible to settle down regularly to their pursuits.

You will see from this description that **the only** ~~remaining~~ **disturbing element remaining to be grappled with is the** <u>**confederacy of outlaws** and their friends.</u> *That done effectively, I believe a permanently healthful condition can be promised.*

The question is, how to best ~~can~~ *proceed.*

The method which seems to have met with most favor in the Territory is martial law. And I confess at one time I thought it the best and only method. Two months upon the ground, however, and much study and reflection there where the advantages and disadvantages, forecasting probabilities, were directly under eye, have changed my opinion.

In the first place, martial law is after all but a temporary expedient. Next, it must in this instance be of limited application; to extend it to the whole of the Territory would be unjustifiable, while if applied to the counties of Lincoln and Doña Ana solely ~~and no pretense could carry it further~~, *it would certainly fail its immediate object; that is to say, it would fail to bring offenders to quick trial and certain punishment, since they would only have to cross certain near boundary lines to be safe. Yet further, military commissions under modern laws of war are governable by fixed procedures, and their findings must be according to rules of evidence, not the will of a captain, leaving it difficult as ever to overcome perjurious combinations. Finally, admitting it would be effective while in force – a point to which I am by no means assured, since as much would depend upon the officer charged with its execution and the number and zeal of the subordinates and troops helping him – yet it must have end; - and then what? The restoration of civil authority, it is to be feared, would, in this case at least, be the signal for* **the outlaws, over in Mexico, Texas, the Staked Plains, and for that matter, the contiguous counties of New Mexico**, *to return and renew their operations, with the additional incentive of fresh victims to prey upon. To these objections, I have heard but one point in answer – that under military protection, the county would become settled, and able to take care of itself. Possibly* ~~it would~~ *so, though I doubt it, for the reason that, as a rule, people looking out for new homes find very little attraction in martial law;* ~~on the contrary there is~~ *the strongest ground for a belief is that its prevalence would be almost universally accepted as a warning to stay away. Under martial law contractors would multiply and flourish;* ~~while~~ *men* ~~of means~~ *with families would look elsewhere.*

[AUTHOR'S NOTE: This is Wallace's outlaw myth to combine random outlawry to hide the Ring crimes.]

To make application of these remarks – The time is come, in my judgment, to move radically that the present status in Lincoln County be assured permanently. Instead of martial law, I recommend simply a transfer of all troops now at Fort Stanton, except Captain Carroll and Lieut. Dawson and their companies; substituting, in place of the transferred, officers and troops wholly disconnected with the past troubles and without bias one way or the other – the command to be given an officer himself a stranger to parties involved, who has no hates or friendships in the locality, is above intimidation, and will execute present existing orders. Such orders, if enforced zealously and according to their plain letter, really give the civil authorities in very kind the strength attaching to martial law, bating only the military commissions – in fact, executed as the should be, they make martial law inexpedient.

I beg not to be required to support this recommendation with charges against anybody. They get me into personal quarrels for which life is too short; which in nineteen cases out of twenty, "the game is not worth the candle." Besides that, they are followed by investigations which have the effect to weaken me by convincing the opposition that I have not the confidence of the President. Respectfully but frankly, it is very desirable to know nearly as possible if the support heretofore given me will be continued – **for now I can retire without loss of credit.**

[AUTHOR'S NOTE: Wallace's chief concern is to avoid more military confrontations after the anticipated loss in the Dudley Court of Inquiry, and to protect his own reputation.]

Not improbably the Honorable Secretary of War and General Sherman, to whom my recommendation will be referred, will be satisfied to take the opinion of Gen. Hatch, commanding the District of New Mexico. It gives me pleasure to say General H. has not only aided me promptly and with great intelligence, regardful of his orders; in fact he is the only person with whom I have constantly and freely advised. He knows the situation perfectly. If, however, the President thinks better to resort to martial law, his decision will be cheerfully accepted.

Passing from Lincoln county, it gives me great satisfaction to report the Territory elsewhere in a prosperous state. The recent mineral discoveries and the resolution of the railroad companies (the Denver and Rio Grande and the Atchison, Topeka and ~~Rio Grande~~ *Santa Fe) to extend their lines immediately, are at last drawing to New Mexico the attention she really deserves, and already we are feeling the effects. The hotels in this city are crowded, and a stream of miners is pouring along the roads from the east.*

I have the honor to be
Very respectfully
Your friend,
Lew. Wallace
Governor New Mexico

IRA LEONARD'S "OLD SCOUNDREL" LETTER: JUNE 13, 1879

Two days after Lew Wallace deluded himself by fabrications to Secretary of the Interior Carl Schurz, his Jiminy Cricket-conscience, Ira Leonard, intruded reality about looming Dudley Court of Inquiry disaster. Without realizing, Leonard echoed Grant County's citizens and Mary McPherson of Colfax County as to Ringite obstruction of justice. Recognizing bias of its Judges, Leonard fumed: *"If you ever saw three men who strained every effort to protect & shield an old scoundrel this Court have done it."* Leonard wrote:

Fort Stanton N.M.

June 13th 1879

Gov Lew Wallace
     Santa Fe N.M.

My dear Governor:

Yours of the 7th inst reached me in due time, and I was glad to hear from you. I thought I would test Taylor so I wrote a letter unburdening substantially what I wrote you of the affairs in this County and he copied it and sent it direct to the President. **A petition has been gotten up complaining of the action of Judge Bristol and begging his removal on account of his strong partisan feeling and forwarded also to the President and I think you ought to take your action at once if you have not done so yet.** *I had a conversation with Col Purington a few days ago and he informed me Judge B had advised him that after your Proclamation of Pardon and Amnesty the Proclamation had served the persons intended and that the General order made by the War Department was virtually abrogated & the measures or actions under it could be legally taken to call on the Military for assistance & he would not furnish aid to the officers without further instructions although he has since sent Capt Carroll down on the requisition made of him by the Sheriff of the Seven Rivers country to aid the Sheriff in making arrests but with strict orders not to assist him moving stolen stock, Capt Carroll informs me that for any practical purpose his hands have been absolutely tied by his orders. He had orders also not to delay his march to aid or protect the officers in bringing stolen property So that I look for no good results from the mission undertaken by the Sheriff & posse –*

Now on to what perhaps to you will be more interesting the progress of the Dudley case. We closed on the part of the prosecution a week ago Monday and it is unnecessary for me to tell you how rigidly & particularly the Court ruled while you were still here, **and as we progressed in the case and we were pouring "hot shot" into him they tightened the reins to such an extent that they would not enter our objections of record some of them where the ruling of the Court would make them appear ridiculous and at one time I feared the Court would order me out of the case when I objected to the ruling of the Court ... If you ever saw three men who strained every effort to protect & shield an old scoundrel this Court have done it.** *After ruling us down in a shameful manner as soon as the defense commenced they opened every gate to Dudley and it makes no difference what he offers they receive it & allowed the most flagrant hearsay evidence anything and everything that will in the Court have a tendency to excuse his conduct they admit without stint reservation or objection.* **They would not allow into show any of the circumstances that brought about the difficulties or give an account of them and of their inception and progress and the character of the mob that murdered McSween and the others but confined as to Dudley's conduct on the day he went to Lincoln they would not allow us to show the conspiracy formed with Dolan beforehand to go the Lincoln and said that when we were trying to pose the conspiracy that that was a charge not incorporated either in your charges or mine but now everything near, remote, traditional guess, and thought and what this one said & that one said weeks & months before the events, of the fight is dragged in and allowed if it only has some show of making the McSween side look black & will give them an excuse to shield Dudley** *and the provoking part of it to me is when Waldo and I get together he will laugh and push me in the rib, at the fools the Court are making of themselves in their rulings. I never desire any more experience before a Military Court comprised of egotistical damned fools. All I wish in this matter is to have this case examined before some sensible officer at Washington if we have not enough evidence to send him out of this country I shall be greatly mistaken.* **I am more clearly convinced every day I remain here that there will never be peace and good order restored here until there is a radical change here at the Post and in fact there ought not to be one** *man left who can tell the tale of the outrages the Military have inflicted upon this people.*

I looked the matter up you referred to. You will find the authorities to be that while you have the right to appoint under the law you have not the right of removal under a similar law in Colorado when Gov McCork was Governor he undertook to remove Moffatt as Territorial Treasurer and appoint some one else and the Court held he had only the power in the first instance of appointing but no authority to remove that the officer had the right to hold the full time designated Not only this case but that is the general doctrine – And there is another Statute in reference to the appointment of these appears in the Session Act. I cannot refer now to it but I remember to have looked it up once The office would hardly pay me even if I could accept your kind offer.

[Letter continues the next day]

Saturday Morning June 14th

The Court adjourned this morning until Monday morning at 10 AM on account of the illness of Col. Purington he was taken violently ill last evening with colic, and is very bad today so I learn.

Walz arrived here but too late for us unfortunately to make use of him I am so sorry we had not had him in time unless I am greatly mistaken we could have made a very strong circumstantial case against Col. D. in the Chapman murder –

Dolan has renewed his application before Judge Bristol for his release in Habeas Corpus. The venue was changed to Socorro County, but there was no Court held there and he was detained here as a witness for Col Dudley, and now he renews his application to be released on bail and I know that Rynerson will allow him to be released.

[AUTHOR'S NOTE: The Court concealed that Dolan was indicted for Chapman's murder, but Waldo used Billy's indictments.]

The whole outfit of the Seven River men have also made application to be released before Judge Bristol of course they will be. They are making preparations to start over at once. Turner, Pierce, the two Olingers [Bob and Wallace], Boyle, Buck Powell and a numbers of others.

I tell you Governor as long as the present incumbent occupies the bench all that Grand Juries may do to bring to justice these men every effort will be thwarted by him and the sympathizers of that [Ring] side.

I am going to Lincoln today to remain over Sunday and when anything further occurs of interest I will write you –

I have written to Senator Teller & Judge Belford M.C. from Colorado to aid me in seeking the appointment here in the place of Judge B. I received a letter from a Denver friend informing me that a change would certainly be made and to write then as he had already done to secure the appointment for me – I wish it might occur but I have no very strong hopes of it.

Remember me to Mrs. Wallace.
My health is much improved.
            Yours truly
            Ira E Leonard

BILLY DEPARTS JAIL: JUNE 17, 1879

Billy had remained as trusting of Lew Wallace as was Ira Leonard, who had become Billy's loyalist and lawyer. So on June 17, 1879, without pardon, and possibly aware from Leonard of the bad turn in the Dudley Court of Inquiry, Billy decided his risk in custody was too great with a venue change to Doña Ana County. So he simply left Juan Patrón's house to continue guerrilla rustling from Catron's and Charles Fritz's Lincoln County ranches, and to await pardon. Later, conscienceless Lew Wallace would accuse Billy of escaping jail, as one of his many published excuses for why he never pardoned the boy.

N.A.M. DUDLEY TESTIFIES: JUNE 28-30, 1878

The travesty of N.A.M. Dudley's brazenly lying testimony, from June 28th to 30th of 1879, becomes tragedy when heard as voicing of the Ring's arrogance of power, which left criminal members immune under complicit judges. By the time of Dudley's testimony, the Court of Inquiry was out-of-control: blocking prosecution's introducing witnesses to prove defense witnesses' perjury, and not permitting cross-examination. Dudley testified:

Court of Inquiry Rooms
Fort Stanton, N.M.
June 28, 1879 [Friday]
45th day [of Court of Inquiry] ...

Present:
Col. G. Pennypacker   *16th Infantry*
Major N.W. Osborne   *15th Infantry*
Captain H.R. Brinkerhoff   *15th Infantry*
Captain H.H. Humphreys   *15th Infantry, Recorder.*

Lt. Col. Dudley and his and his Counsel [Henry Waldo] and Mr. Ira E. Leonard also present ...

[When the Recorder, Prosecutor Henry Humphreys, requested that he be allowed to bring in witnesses "to contradict the testimony introduced by Lieut. Col. Dudley," Henry Waldo objected, and the decision was: "The Court declines to call the witnesses requested by the Recorder before it as it regards the testimony sought to be elicited is not material."]

Lieut. Col. Dudley, 9th Cavalry, then requested to be sworn and give testimony on his own behalf.

... Q. by Col. Dudley. Do you admit to having gone to Lincoln on the 19th day of July last, if so, state what induced you to go there at the time?
Answer. I did go to Lincoln on the 19th day of July last. I was induced to go to Lincoln being thoroughly convinced that it was my solemn duty to do so. I had been in command of the post. My object in going to Lincoln was to give protection to women and children and parties, and parties who were not engaged in the disturbances then existing in Lincoln.
Q. by Col. Dudley. State whether or not in going there it was done in pursuance of any promise by you, or of any agreement or understanding, direct or indirect, between you and Sheriff Peppin, or anyone on his behalf?
Answer. There was no agreement, no ...
Q. by Col. Dudley. State whether or not in any manner or to any extent you aided or assisted Sheriff Peppin or his posse on the 19th day of July last, or took part in any of the measures adopted by him that day, or whether any of the soldiers under your command by your order or with your knowledge or consent took part in any of the transactions that day connected with the contest going on between the two parties there that day?
Answer. I did not, they did not.

Q. by Col. Dudley. Did you hear of any soldiers being at or near the McSween house on the 19th day of July last whether taking any part with the sheriff's posse against the McSween party or standing about there doing nothing in the day or night time before it was mentioned before the Court?

Answer. I never did ...

Q. by Col. Dudley. State whether or not you had any conversation with Justice John B. Wilson at or near camp that morning of the 19th of July last ... that if he did not issue the warrant, referring to the warrant for McSween, you would put him in double irons ...

Answer. My recollection of the conversation was that there was nothing unpleasant said by Justice Wilson or myself ... I did not threaten to put him in irons ...

Q. by Col. Dudley. State whether or not you had a conversation with Mrs. McSween in or near your camp on the 19th day of July last, if so what the conversation was ... and whether or not in the conversation you said to her that if a shot was fired from the McSween house near any of your soldiers ... you would turn your cannon loose and tear it to the ground ...

Answer. I did have a conversation with Mrs. McSween near my camp ... I can simply give the general purport. When she first came up, I said good morning Madam. She returned the salutation. She appeared a good deal excited ... crying. To the best of my recollection, the conversation commenced by her saying, what are you doing with U.S. soldiers surrounding my husband's house. I assured her that there were no U.S. soldiers around her house to my knowledge ... I told her then of the object of my visit to Lincoln to the effect, that I have come to Lincoln with my small command for the purpose of giving protection to women and children and such other parties as may avail themselves of it ... I further remember her referring to the sheriff's posse burning or attempting to burn her house ... I did not credit her statement and told her at the time I had received a letter from her husband in which he stated he was going to burn up his own house ... I stepped inside my tent and produced the letter ... I told her she could not have the letter, she saying give me that letter ... I will say in this connection that to the very best of my knowledge and recollection that nothing could be construed toward Mrs. McSween as showing anger or passion ...

Q. by Col. Dudley. You heard the testimony of **Bates** in which he attributed certain expressions to you in conversation stated to *have taken place in or near your camp with Sheriff Peppin about ... Peppin's undertaking not proving successful if it had not been for you, state whether or not anything of this kind occurred ...*

Answer. I know nothing of such a conversation with Peppin ... as stated by the Negro Bates ...

[AUTHOR'S NOTE: Waldo is dishonestly garbling. The witness was not the McSween's black servant, Sebrian Bates, but black 9th Cavalrymen James Bush and Huston Lusk, ordered by Dudley to accompany Peppin, to help capture of fleeing McSweens, and witness to Dudley's anger at Peppin for allowing their escape. Waldo would later use racism again in his closing argument against Bush.]

Q. by Col. Dudley. State whether or not you said to Sheriff Peppin out in the street between camp and Montano's house ... that if he came when word was sent he could have captured the men that were in the Montano house, or anything to that effect?

Answer. I never did, and I never heard it was alleged that I did until the meeting of this Court ...

Q. by Col. Dudley. State whether or not you were notified that the [Tunstall] store was being robbed?

Answer. I was not.

Q. by Col. Dudley. State what passed between you and Mrs. Montano in the morning of the 19th of July last in regard to giving her protection ...

Answer. I could not say if any conversation occurred with Mrs. Montano and myself directly ... I told my interpreter ... to explain ... that I could not leave soldiers with her as I had so few. I told her I was going to leave a guard with Capt. Baca ... and if anything occurred she could go over to Baca's or call upon the soldiers ...

[AUTHOR'S NOTE: This shows Dudley's outrageous lying. The actual incident was that upon entering Lincoln, Dudley ordered his howitzer cannon pointed at the Montaño house, and began its loading drill. The terrified McSween men inside fled. The wife of José Montano confronted Dudley for threatening her house. Later, enraged Dudley verbally attacked Peppin for coming too late to kill or to capture those escaping men. But Waldo here fabricates that he was protecting women and children. And Saturnino Baca was Lincoln's Hispanic Ring spy, having been used to send a letter to Dudley asking for protection to urge the march on Lincoln.]

****

June 30, 1879 [Monday]
46th day [of Court of Inquiry]...

Present:
Col. G. Pennypacker	16th Infantry
Major N.W. Osborne	15th Infantry
Captain H.R. Brinkerhoff	15th Infantry
Captain H.H. Humphreys	15th Infantry, Recorder.

Lt. Col. Dudley and his and his Counsel [Henry Waldo] and Mr. Ira E. Leonard also present.

Lieut. Col. Dudley, 9th Cavalry, resumed his testimony.

Q. by Col. Dudley. State whether or not you had any opportunity for explanation of the charges made against you by Governor Wallace before removal from the command of Fort Stanton ...
Answer. I did not have the slightest opportunity ... I was removed of command by Col. Edward Hatch, ordered to Fort Union at the time I was doing everything in my power ... to assist the civil authorities in the County of Lincoln in carrying out the laws of the Territory ...

Cross Examine.

Q. by Recorder. What induced you to think it was your solemn duty to go to Lincoln on the 19th day of July last, upon what authority did you base that action, and was your sole and only object that of humanitarian?

[AUTHOR'S NOTE: Incompetent Humphreys is not showing Dudley's lying. He asks too many questions at once, and should have focused on the Posse Comitatus Act, which required Presidential approval for intervention; or if it was for the Act's exception of protecting women and children, he should have asked about endangering the women and children at McSweens the Ealys in Tunstall's store, and Mrs. Montaño.]

Answer. My knowledge of the situation of affairs in Lincoln, my sense of duty as an Officer of the Army. It was decidedly as I understood that word.

Q. by Recorder. If you went there in the capacity of an humanitarian why did you not carry out that purpose and prevent the bloodshed and destruction of property that was going on there instead of promoting the disturbance by allowing a warrant to be issued against McSween and others?

Objected to by Lieut. Col. Dudley, by his Counsel. Question objected to because it assumes that Col. Dudley was engaged in fomenting disturbances and assumes that he allowed a warrant to be issued by McSween.
Recorder stated he had no reply to make.
Objection sustained ...

[AUTHOR'S NOTE: This shows the Court's bias as well as Humphreys' inadequacy. Humphreys should have called Waldo objection irrelevant. His questioning was directed to Dudley's admitted intervention as an "humanitarian" act, which needed to be reconciled with actual bloodshed, murder, and arson. And Humphreys should have raised that the McSween side was winning before Dudley came; and surrender without bloodshed would have occurred if Dudley had not intervened. But the key response to Waldo's objection was that the prosecution had already given profuse evidence by eye-witnesses - including Billy Bonney - of Dudley's active part in siding with the sheriff; intimidating the McSweens with weaponry and threats, causing their flight; enabling the McSween house to be set on fire; using soldiers to shield the sheriff and to block the McSween house from defense by its inmates; ordering his soldiers to fire at the escaping inmates of the burning house; and, by all that, causing McSween's murder and destruction of his house.]

Q. by Recorder. You are charged with having acted in a brutal and inhumane manner on the 19th day of July last while in command of a portion of the garrison of Fort Stanton at Lincoln, N.M. while peace was being disturbed at this point. What reply have you to make to this charge ...
Answer. Most emphatically no ...

[Henry Waldo then demonstrated complete control of the biased court by getting accepted into evidence "Squire" Wilson's letter of January 11, 1879 (See my pp. 484-485 for full letter) *to Lew Wallace as allegedly proving the populace wanted intervention of soldiers, and Fort Stanton daily records as allegedly proving the same; over Henry Humphreys' correct objection that they were irrelevant to July 19, 1878.]*

WALLACE TO SCHURZ: JULY 3, 1879

On July 3, 1879, with his usual self-promotion to Carl Schurz, Wallace added covert proof of their mutual knowledge of the Santa Fe Ring by referencing its plot - as he had already reported by letter to his friend, Absalom Markland, on November 14, 1878. Wallace wrote: *"The only thing worth attention is the development of the conspiracy of which I have had knowledge for some time, looking to removal of a number of federal appointees, including myself. It is the expiring flurry of the old ring."* So Wallace - knowing that he had left the Ring unchecked in Lincoln County, and knowing it would defeat him in the Dudley Court of Inquiry - implied it was all irrelevant, since the Ring was "expiring!" And Ring-enabling Schurz just played along. For the complicit Hayes administration, Wallace was achieving with finesse what brutal Axtell had failed: suppressing citizens without their realizing the malice. Wallace wrote:

EXECUTIVE OFFICE
Territory of New Mexico

Santa Fe, New Mexico July 3, 1879

Hon. C. Schurz
Sec. Dept. Interior.

Sir:

I have the honor to report a continuance of the peaceful condition of the Territory reported in my last.

The only thing worth attention is the development of the conspiracy of which I have had knowledge for some time, looking to removal of a number of federal appointees, including myself. **It is the expiring flurry of the old ring**. *Upon the reopening of the scheme, I will give you particulars.*

Very respectfully,
Your friend & servant.
Lew. Wallace
Governor New Mexico

HENRY WALDO'S CLOSING ARGUMENT: JULY 5, 1879

Two days after Lew Wallace declared to Carl Schurz that the Ring was expiring, it reared up in full potency on the Court of Inquiry's 49th day, in July 5, 1879's hours-long closing argument by Henry Waldo. He defamed all prosecution witnesses to enable the corrupt Judges to disregard of their evidence of Dudley's crimes. And he sealed Wallace's humiliation and defeat, recycling Shiloh's.

Importantly, Waldo's attack on Billy Bonney culminated his Ring "outlawing," begun with U.S. Marshal John Sherman's October 6, 1878 outlaw list. Pardon now looked equivalent to backing an outlaw - obviously a path Wallace would reject, since it needed Ring exposé for justification. And Waldo, through District Attorney William Rynerson, Judge Warren Bristol, or James Dolan, would have known about Billy's pardon request. The outcome was Wallace's getting his central character for his outlaw myth: "Billy the Kid." And glibly lying, oratorically melodramatic Waldo showed why he was considered the best trial lawyer in the Territory, and was such a Ring asset.

About Wallace, Waldo shockingly and chillingly revealed that even his secret communications about the Ring to Absalom Markham, and to Carl Schurz about feared Ring attempts to remove him were known to Waldo, who mocked in terrifying proclaiming of Ring power: *"[T]he Governor was in great alarm about the awful "bug bear" the "Santa Fe Ring" preventing his confirmation. He wanted to manufacture some political thunder whose reverberation would resound in the halls of the Senate chamber in Washington."* Waldo continued against Wallace:

Nothing has been accomplished in the least that connects Col. Dudley with anything which transpired in the town of Lincoln on the occasion of his presence there on the 19th and 20th day of July last, and all that has been truthfully told of his motives and actions reflects the highest credit upon him, as a man and as a soldier. Notwithstanding all this, motives the most laudable have been traduced, conduct the most praiseworthy distorted into great crimes. He has been libeled and vilified, insults have been heaped on him. He has been heralded forth as a house burner and a murderer from one end of the territory to the other. ***He has been branded as a conspirator, a robber and a thief by no less a person than Governor Wallace, whose lips have blistered to*** *a crisp and pealed to the bone when they uttered the foul malicious accusation. False and slanderous charges have been preferred by the crafty and designing old lawyer, Ira E. Leonard, to the Secretary of war, and by the wily and unscrupulous politician Governor Wallace, to the Commander of the District.*

Look at this for a moment, here was this man Leonard when he made these charges and had never even been in Lincoln county. He resided in Las Vegas, two hundred miles away, and never had an opportunity of seeing any of the witnesses, or making an investigation into the truth of the charges formulated by him. *Governor Wallace had been in the county of Lincoln but one day, took no sworn or written testimony, never even inquired of the officers who were present with Col. Dudley, when he was in Lincoln at the time mentioned.*

Language strong enough and severe enough cannot be employed in denunciation of the hideous and monstrous wickedness of these bad men who united in their efforts to disgrace and ruin a man who had never harmed either of them, in thought, word, or deed, and that man an officer of high rank, and long and distinguished service in the Army of this country. Here, has Col. Dudley been forced to submit to the humiliation and mortification of knowing that such charges had been lodged against him with the Department of War in Washington, and that he was the subject of comment and discussion of his superiors and among brother officers, besides the publicity which they necessarily obtained throughout the country, to the effect of which can never be obliterated, and compelled to seek the vindication of himself, and able to obtain only the poor and meager and inadequate redress, which this Court of Inquiry can afford, hemmed in as it is by the limited scope of its duties and powers as defined in the orders by which it was convened. *Lew Wallace and Ira E. Leonard are alone responsible for this annoyance trouble and harassing case. By their act, this disgrace has been brought upon a pure, humane, and just man. By their act has the luster of a bright and honorable career been dimmed. Time does not remain to Col. Dudley to clear away the stain, by them placed upon his name and character. The best years of his life are passed and gone, spent in the service of his country ..*

He [Wallace] did not come [to Lincoln] to learn the truth. He came bent on finding for which he could use to injure

Col. Dudley. He came to accomplish the removal of Col. Dudley even if he had to manufacture the testimony which it would be necessary to have, in order to do it. To succeed, even if he had to write as evil and malicious a letter as that upon which the removal was effected. Did Gov. Wallace seek true knowledge of Col. Dudley's relations to Lincoln County matters? Why did he not come to officers of the post? Why did he not seek his information from all the parties, but no, he never came to the post, but went directly to Lincoln, and talked with a few rabid and malignant partisans, took a one sided version from prejudiced and irresponsible parties he knew he could get what he wanted from, and then tries to make it appear from the witness stand that this information was derived from persons who came from all parts of the county ...

For five days he attitudinized before this Court in a labored effort betwixt an harangue and a narrative, the object of which was plainly manifest to be an exculpation of, or apology for the errors and follies of his course in dealing with Lincoln County matters ...

[Wallace] tries to make it appear from the witness stand that his information was derived from ... the public meeting at which he spoke ... It was after this purposely one sided investigation he comes to the post and wrote his letter of request, filling it with lying statements, which, with an hypocritical attempt at an apology, he states, he was cautious to say, were given upon information merely, and after he had accomplished, in this unjust and infamous manner, the removal of Col. Dudley ... he places on it the flippant and insolent endorsement, "Colonel Dudley will excuse me if I decline to give him any advice." As if anybody had asked, or needed, the advice of Governor Wallace ...

He [Wallace] wants somebody to lay the blame upon. It [Amnesty Proclamation] was a weak and ridiculous idea in the first place. What the villains who had made a hell of Lincoln County needed was a gallows, not a pardon. The whole truth about that proclamation, as we look at it, is that just about the time the Governor was in great alarm about the awful "bug bear" the "Santa Fe Ring" preventing his confirmation. He wanted to manufacture some political thunder whose reverberation would resound in the halls of the Senate chamber in Washington ... He had been sent specifically to pacify the troubles in New Mexico. To this, his official announcement of the complete success of his efforts to pacification in Lincoln County is promulgated ...

About Billy Bonney, Henry Waldo stated:

Then was brought forward William Bonney, alias "Antrim," alias "the Kid," a known criminal of the worst type although hardly up to his majority, murderer by profession, as records of this Court connect him with two atrocious murders, that of Roberts and the other of Sheriff Brady. Both of them are cowardly and atrocious assassinations.

[AUTHOR'S NOTE: This outlaw branding would inhibit Wallace's ability to issue the pardon without damaging himself.]

There were warrants enough for him to the 19th of July last to have plastered him from his head to his feet, yet he was engaged to do service as a witness and his testimony showed that his qualifications did not terminate with blood guiltiness. His testimony was brief, yet he signalized his opening sentences with a lie. He swears that members of the sheriff's posse fell in with the troops and came up to the McSween house, but I will quote his words. "I was in the McSween house in Lincoln, and I saw the soldiers come down from the fort with the sheriff's party, that is, the sheriff's posse joined them a short distance above there, the McSween house, soldiers passed on by, the men dropped right off and surrounded the house." It has been proven by competent and unimpeachable witnesses that this statement is without any foundation in fact. Sheriff Peppin, his Deputy Sheriff Powell, Deputy Sheriff Marion Turner, Milo Pierce, Robert Olinger, Joseph Nash, Andrew Boyle, J.B. Matthews, Lt. Goodwin, Captain Purington and Corporal Bugold, who brought up the rear of the column all swear that none of the posse was anywhere near the troops as they passed the Wortley Hotel and came up to the McSween house.

[AUTHOR'S NOTE: All the cited "*witnesses*" are Ringites.]

It is plainly known that at least half an hour passed before any of the sheriff's posse went up to the McSween house ...

He also testified as to the note received by McSween in answer to one sent by Col. Dudley. He swears that the note was signed N.A.M. Dudley, "did not say what rank." About this he might have been mistaken, but it shows him to be a willing and reckless witness. But what is of importance is that he swears that letter contained the following, he is positive about it because he says he read it, he volunteers that statement. His testimony stated three soldiers came down and stood in front of McSween's building and McSween's wife wants to know why they are there ... and Col. Dudley replied saying, "They had business there, and if a shot was fired over his camp, or at Peppin or any of his men, that he had no objection to his blowing up, if he wanted to, his own house." That this note contained nothing about firing upon Peppin or any of his men is clear enough ... to say nothing of the contradiction given by Lt. Goodwin, who wrote the note and signed it.

He also swears that three soldiers fired at him when he was escaping from the McSween building. Attention will also be called to this part of the testimony further on. It is sufficient to say of this part of the testimony now that if he swears falsely about so material a fact as to the manner of the sheriff's posse surrounded the house, that is to say under cover by means of protection of the troops as they marched by, he would not hesitate to swear falsely about soldiers firing at him that night as he was escaping. "A liar once is a liar all the time."

As to seeing the soldiers about the Tunstall building, at the time of the escape of the men from the McSween house the evening of the 19th of July last, Jose Chavez [Chávez y Chávez] was also called. He was with the "Kid" according to both of them. "Kid" says that the soldiers stood at the outside corner of the Tunstall building ... Now this story comes with its own reputation. In the first place, in the intense excitement of the moment, these men could not have had the coolness to select from a number of shots delivered at them, the firing of certain particular shots, to fix it in their minds, the men who did the firing. Besides, in the deceptive glare of the fire, it is very doubtful if any of the parties who were looking upon the space between those two houses could identify with any degree of certainty, particularly at such a time, the kind of clothes anybody wore. This difficulty would be enhanced in the case of the "Kid" and Chavez because they were looking from the center of the light out against the darkness, which is a circumstance of the greatest importance. While from the darkness to the wall objects are plainly discernable, the direct opposite follows when the conditions are changed.

[AUTHOR'S NOTE: Out-of-control lying Waldo even preposterously fabricates that Billy could not see soldiers because firelight from the building could illuminate the building from which he left, but could not illuminate people facing it!]

There is a considerable discrepancy between the two witnesses also as to the distance they say the three soldiers were from where they fired. "Kid" said 30 to forty yards, Chavez makes it only ten yards.

Another conclusive argument against the presence of soldiers there at the time is the extreme danger, the almost certain danger of death from such an exposed position, the witnesses testify that it would have been between cross fire at a time when everybody else was seeking and keeping cover. It is to be supposed for a moment that three soldiers, who had no interest in the contest would have been in such a place, for if they were at all they slipped out against orders and came there of their own choice.

[AUTHOR'S NOTE: Waldo hides a volley meaning under orders.]

Besides, it is clear the soldiers were not then present, the evidence of the Sergeant who testified that late roll call for the night was at dusk, or near as he can judge, about a quarter past eight, and that the men were then all there. This escape being among their first that was made must have been about that time ... In addition to all this we have the evidence of Boyle, or Nash, or Olinger or of Hurley all who say they had a distance view of the space between the McSween house and the Tunstall building, and as the firing had come from the Tunstall building all that day, their attention at the time would have been drawn as much to one house as the other, and they all say ... that there was nobody at the corner of the Tunstall building, where these soldiers were located. The evidence of Olinger and Hurley is especially valuable, each of them had distinct views of this particular corner. One, Olinger being to the southwest in the Stanley house, and the other, Hurley, to the southeast of it in the Wilson house ...

Besides, we must take into consideration that some of these men were of the sheriff's posse, Boyle for one and the man "Dummy" who were right at the McSween house at the time, were dressed with soldier jackets and the "Dummy" in soldier pants, and it was easy enough for these frightened fleeing men, when they try to remember the events of that night to mislocate the men they say shot at them. To all probability as they fled they may have seen some of these men who had soldiers' jackets and thought they were soldiers. It is more charitable to suppose this, than that they have come here and deliberately lied, although they must fear from the lying character of the testimony throughout.

About the black, 9th Cavalrymen, Private James Bush and Sergeant Huston Lusk, whose testimony as military insiders, eye-witnesses, and being under Dudley's orders to do wrong was so compelling, Waldo countered by citing his lying and coached Ringite witnesses to deny their testimony, as well as to invalidate them by frank racism, stating:

The colored soldier, Private Bush, testified that he heard Col. Dudley say to Sheriff Peppin on his return from the Ellis house, "You might have captured these men in the Montano house if you had come when word was sent to you that they were there." Sheriff Peppin, whose attention has been called to the statement positively denies that any such language or anything to that effect was said by Col. Dudley at the time or place referred to, to the same effect is Col. Dudley's testimony. Suppose, however that the language had been used by Col. Dudley to Sheriff Peppin and supposing, which however is not the case, that such words had been said to Sheriff Peppin by Col. Dudley, to give the prosecution the full benefit of the strongest inference against Col. Dudley. What would it have amounted to? It would simply have shown Col. Dudley, consistent with his original avowed purpose of coming to Lincoln on that day, refrained from any act that might operate to the aid of the sheriff. The sending of such a message would not have been an act of aid to the sheriff. It would have been nothing, more or less, than information upon which the sheriff might himself act and which Col. Dudley would take no part. At the most it would have established Col. Dudley as in sympathy with the sheriff in his effort to execute laws ...

It is these same colored men [James Bush and Huston Lusk] that swear to an order being given by Col. Dudley for soldiers to fall in and stop the men who were supposed to be coming from the McSween house ... cannot conjecture upon what influence these two men have fallen or what appliances have been employed with them, but that either their testimony upon the point is down right perjury is without a doubt *... And had Col. Dudley stopped these men and turned them over to the civil authority who was there then represented in the person of the sheriff, he would simply have performed his duty as a citizen ... and in doing such an act would not have violated the Posse Comitatus section of the Act of Congress ...*

In concluding, for Dudley's three corrupt Judges, Henry Waldo was on a roll, victory ensured. He gloated: *"The foul conspiracy to disgrace and ruin Col. Dudley concocted by Lew Wallace, Ira E. Leonard, and Sue E. McSween has ended in utter and ignominious failure."* So Lew Wallace was once again branded with Shiloh-like accusation of *ignominious failure*. Lying Ringite Waldo stated theatrically and reprehensibly:

When we look at the strong manly forms, and honest, brave and resolute faces of the sheriff and those of his posse, who have appeared before this Court as witnesses, and think of the miserable hoard of Mexicans and cut throat Americans opposed to them, (some of whom you have seen on the witness stand) and when you reflect upon the skill and address shown by the sheriff's posse in isolating the house of McSween, cutting it off, and commanding all the approaches to it, as each member of the Court has seen and knows the ground, we know and everybody knows who at all understands the situation, that no power under heaven could have prevented the sheriff, and his posse from accomplishing what they started out to do, namely, to arrest the men in that house or kill them in the attempt or be killed themselves ...

The foul conspiracy to disgrace and ruin Col. Dudley concocted by Lew Wallace, Ira E. Leonard, and Sue E. McSween has ended in utter and ignominious failure. For them, and for all who had any share in contriving or promoting any portion of it, scorn and contempt alone remains as their portion. *Col. Dudley comes forth from this fiery ordeal unscathed. No blemish rest on his character, no cloud to darken his fame.*

All that remains is to return thanks to the Court for the attention given me, and at the same time, for the kind and considerate treatment I have uniformly received at its hands.

PROSECUTOR'S CLOSING ARGUMENT: JULY 5, 1879

Prosecutor Henry Humphreys, with Ira Leonard, instead of summarizing their extensive, damning evidence; debunking Henry Waldo's dishonest refutations; decrying Dudley's crimes; and demonstrating Posse Comitatus Act violations, relied on simple sincerity to appeal to moral fiber in the three Judges. There was none. Humphreys stated:

To the Honorable Court of Inquiry convened at Fort Stanton, New Mexico.

This cause having occupied the Court in its investigation of the matters for over two months now has closed and the only remaining duty on the part of the Recorder is to present to the Court an argument upon the facts which have been elicited in the investigation ...

The motives which directs the actions of men are judged in what they do and not by what they say, and for the proof that Lieut. Col. Dudley took part in all the disturbances that existed in Lincoln County from nearly the beginning of his taking command of Fort Stanton to its termination shows him a strong and bitter partisan, I simply refer to the Court the proof that he alone has introduced in his defense ...

The fight between the factions had been, at most, unproductive, with no success to the sheriff's party between the 15th to the 19th of the month of July, and as Col. Dudley in his report of the 16th of July says ... to the Dolan-Riley faction, "I will be better off to fill up the blank in a few days if you get the worse of it." And not until Col. Dudley comes upon the field of combat as a pretended neutral party on the 19th did the sheriff and his posse have any apparent show of success, and can anyone believe that results would have been different than they had been prior to his coming if he had remained away? ...

If there is any proceedings during the occurrences of the 19th day of July that more palpably shows the malice which activated Col. Dudley in his proceedings on that occasion [it is the attack on the McSween house].

Let us look at that portion one moment. The proof discloses the fact that the house McSween occupied was a double house, and half of it belonged to Mrs. Shields, the sister of Mrs. McSween, who was in possession with five children in the portion belonging to her ... Mrs. McSween went to the camp of Col. Dudley and begs in her own sister's behalf for him to save it from destruction, but Col. Dudley who was in Lincoln, as he told Mrs. McSween, but to prevent wanton destruction of property and to protect women and children instead says, "I understand he (meaning the sheriff) had warrants for several persons, among them, your husband, and he must be the judge of the means in carrying out his instructions." Col. Dudley goes to Lincoln on a pretended mission of mercy, but when he is sought to save the property of an innocent family, his ears are deaf to their appeal, *and he refuses to protect the house that shelters the mother and her five children ...*

We assert the fact that the killing of McSween with others of his party was murder and the burning of his house constituted the crime of arson, and every person engaged in it, formulated it, are equally criminal. There is no law, humane or otherwise, that will justify the measures adopted on that day to arrest persons charged with crimes.

THE COURT'S JUDGMENT: JULY 5, 1879

The corrupt Court quickly decided that July 5th of 1879. Chief Judge Galusha Pennypacker, Dudley's best friend, stated:

After careful investigation and mature deliberation the court finds the following pertinent and material facts:

FIRST: That Lieut. Col. N.A.M. Dudley, 9th Cavalry, had command of the post of Fort Stanton, N.M., on the 5th day of April 1878, that at the time of his taking command until relieved on the 8th day of March 1879, that at the time of his taking command and for a considerable period of time thereafter two factions of men known respectively as the McSween party and the Dolan and Riley (or Dolan and Murphy) party were engaged in contest against each other during which many lives were lost, that the peacefully disposed people of the town and county of Lincoln were kept in almost a constant state of apprehension and alarm during this period, and the lawful avocation of the people frequently suspended or altogether prevented through fear on one or the other or both of these factions.

SECOND: That warrants were issued early in the month of July 1878 for the arrest of McSween and others of his party for offences committed during the period of contest between the factions and placed in the hands of the sheriff of the county for service, that the sheriff anticipating resistance summoned a posse to his assistance including several persons who had been previously identified with the Dolan and Riley party.

THIRD: That on the 19th of July 1878 Lieut. Col. Dudley proceeded from Fort Stanton, N.M. to the town of Lincoln, Lincoln County, distance about 9 miles from the fort, with one howitzer and one Gatling gun and a detachment from the garrison consisting of four officers and thirty five men for the **purpose of giving protection to the lives and property of the citizens then in jeopardy by reason of resistance by arms made by McSween and his followers to the repeated attempts of the sheriff and his posse to serve the warrants that he held.**

FOURTH: *That on the arrival of Lieut. Col. Dudley in the town of Lincoln about 10 o'clock in the morning of July 19th 1878 the sheriff's posse numbering about 28 men and the McSween party numbering from 40 to 60 men occupied the street and houses in town, that shortly after the arrival of Lieut. Col. Dudley he personally stated to the sheriff and subsequently to a representative of the McSween party that* **he had come to Lincoln for the purpose of affording protection to women and children** *and would give no aid or assistance to either party but if any officer or soldier of his command were either killed or wounded by shots from either party he would return fire.*

FIFTH: *That within a short time after the arrival of. Col. Dudley in the town of Lincoln a warrant issued upon the affidavit of certain officers of the command for the arrest of McSween for an alleged assault upon the person of a United States soldier with intent to kill was obtained and placed in the hands of the sheriff for service by the civil officer issuing the same.*

SIXTH: *That shortly after the arrival of Lieut. Col. Dudley with his command into the town of Lincoln all of McSween's followers then present excepting only about nine men occupying the McSween house with their leaders and possibly two or more persons in a building known as the Tunstall building escaped from the several buildings and enclosures which they occupied and fled from the town, that the sheriff along with his posse made an assault the same day upon the McSween house, set it on fire and destroyed it and at last shot and killed McSween and three or more of the persons with him,* **the said McSween and those with him resisting by force of arms until his death.**

SEVENTH: *That* **Lieut. Col. Dudley did not intend any aid or assistance to either party** *and that Lieut. Col. Dudley and his officers and men of his command did all that could properly be done to protect the lives of peaceable and law abiding citizens.*

EIGHTH: *That on the 7th day of November 1878 Lieut. Col. Dudley forwarded to the headquarters of the District of New Mexico certain affidavits which he procured from citizens of Lincoln County affecting the character and chastity of Mrs. McSween for the purpose of impairing the credibility of certain other allegations made by the said Mrs. McSween through her attorney against Lieut. Col. Dudley which said allegations had been forwarded to His Excellency the Governor of the territory and by him transmitted to the Commanding Officer, District of New Mexico.*

NINTH: That Lieut. Col. Dudley caused an open letter dated Fort Stanton, N.M., November 30, 1878 and addressed to His Excellency Lewis Wallace, Governor of the Territory of New Mexico, to be published in the "New Mexican" a newspaper published in Santa Fe, New Mexico in its issue dated December 14, 1878 in which open letter Lieut. Col. Dudley defended his action in relation to civil affairs in Lincoln County and declined to accept for himself a pardon extended by His Excellency the Governor of New Mexico in a proclamation dated November 13, 1878 for misdemeanors and offences committed in the said county of Lincoln against the law of said territory in connection with the aforesaid disorder between the 1st day of February 1878 and the date of the proclamation and which pardon applied to the officers of the United States Army stationed in the said county during the said disorder.

TENTH: **That no evidence has been presented by the Recorder to sustain a statement made by His Excellency the Governor of New Mexico as follows: "That information also connecting him with the more recent murder of H.I. Chapman** *to the effect that he knew the man would be killed and announced he day of the night of the killing that one of the murderers stated publicly that he had promised Col. Dudley "to do the deed." And that no evidence from any source in this connection is before the Court.*

OPINION.

In view of the evidence adduced the Court is of the opinion that Lieut. Col. Dudley , 9th U.S. Cavalry, has not been guilty of any violation of law or orders, and that the act of proceeding to the town of Lincoln on the 19th day of July 1878 was prompted by the most humane and worthy motives and of good military judgment under exceptional circumstances.

The Court is of the opinion that none of the allegations made against Lieut. Col. Dudley by His Excellency the Governor of New Mexico or by Ira E. Leonard have been sustained and that proceedings before a court martial are therefore unnecessary.

WALLACE'S DAMAGE CONTROL AFTER THE COURT OF INQUIRY: JULY-SEPTEMBER, 1879

DAMAGE CONTROL WITH SCHURZ: JULY 10, 1879

On July 10, 1879, still in the dark about the failed Court of Inquiry, Carl Schurz praised Wallace, writing:

DEPARTMENT OF THE INTERIOR
WASHINGTON.

July 10, 1879.

Dear Sir:
I have received your letter of 3rd inst., and am glad to know of the continued favorable condition of Affairs in New Mexico.
Very truly yours,
C. Schurz

Wallace's response to Schurz on July 30, 1879 shows why he was a best-selling author of historical fiction. While praising himself for Territorial pacification, he inserts, as minor annoyance, the Dudley Court of Inquiry. Wallace wrote:

EXECUTIVE OFFICE,
Territory of New Mexico.
Santa Fe, New Mexico, July 30, 1879.

Hon. C. Schurz,
Sec. Dept. Interior.
Sir:
The accompanying document received from Fort Stanton will explain itself.
Intelligence from other quarters of the Territory shows a peaceful and prosperous condition of affairs.
An arrangement has been effected with the Atchison, Topeka & Santa Fe railroad Company which seems to render it fairly certain that a branch of the road will be built and operated in this city; for which purpose the road is to be deflected to a point no more then twelve miles away. It may not be improper at this time to call attention to the facts that the "palace" in which I have my office will in probability become of great value, and that, from

what I hear, the title to it is unsettled and in dispute. I venture to suggest, in the interest of the government, an inquiry into the matter.

The Dudley investigation is at an end. Of course, I know nothing of the proceedings personally, except the part of it covering my own testimony.

[AUTHOR'S NOTE: This is a lie. Wallace is concealing that Attorney Ira Leonard kept him in close touch. What follows is fictional re-working to for self-aggrandizement: a tactic he would later use for his stories of Billy the Kid and the pardon.]

If what I hear is true, however, it must have been one of the most extraordinary tribunals ever assembled. According to information received from Judge Leonard, who assisted the Recorder, the defense was permitted to prosecute me. Witnesses were introduced on that side with whom I had never any conversation materially connected with Lincoln county affairs, against whom in fact I repeatedly warned Judge Leonard, denouncing them as the associates and aiders and abettors of some of the worst men in that region, who seem to have testified to things which they say I told them, and which were in impeachment of my testimony. The Recorder moved that I (being in Santa Fe) be recalled to contradict the fellows; but the court refused the motion. Had I had notice of such a proceeding, I should certainly demanded to be heard. There is consequently no remedy left me but to request that the record be sent for by the Hon. Secretary of War, and **carefully examined, and that such matters as may be there found affecting my personal or official honor, I may be furnished an opportunity for denial,** *explanation or rebuttal – this, of course, only in case the record leaves a harmful doubt against me in the mind of the President or any of his advisors.*

[AUTHOR'S NOTE: Wallace reveals two important points: 1) He thinks the Secretary of War is on his side; never considering extended Ring power; and 2) with the obviously unjust court verdict, he is concerned only about himself and his reputation.]

I have the honor to be,
Very respectfully,
Your friend & servant,
Lew. Wallace
Gov. New Mexico

DAMAGE CONTROL WITH SECRETARY OF WAR GEORGE McCRARY: AUGUST 29, 1879

Shiloh's unhealable wound stimulated Wallace's identical obsessive self-justification in reaction to Henry Waldo's identical (and possibly not coincidental) accusations of his incompetence. Wallace thereby revealed that his sole concern was for his own skin (as had been his concern, not for Shiloh's 23,000 dead and wounded, but for his injured pride). He wanted reassurance from Secretary of War George McCrary that he was still in good standing. And the responses were reassuring. As long as Wallace left the Ring untouched, he satisfied Hayes and his cabinet. On August 29, 1879, he got a response from Acting Secretary A. Bell:

Department of the Interior
Washington August 29, 1879.

General. Lewis Wallace,
    Governor of New Mexico,
        Santa Fe
Sir:
    Referring to your letter of the 30th ultimo I enclose herewith a copy of a letter received from the Secretary of War [George McCrary, on August 26, 1879] and of the report of the Acting Judge-Advocate General, referred to therein, in which it is stated that there is nothing in the proceedings of the Court of Inquiry in the case of Lieutenant Colonel N.A.M. Dudley, 9th Cavalry, intended to reflect injuriously upon the course pursued by you or which has effect of impugning your honor or the integrity of your motives.

                              Very respectfully,
                              A. Bell
                            Acting Secretary

On August 26, 1879, Wallace got a response from Secretary of War George McCrary:

                            War Department
                            Washington City
                            August 26, 1879

Sir.

I have the honor to acknowledge the receipt of your letter of the 8th instant enclosing the extract from a communication addressed to you under the date of the 30th ultimo by General Lewis Wallace, Governor of New Mexico, in which, in referring to the Court of Inquiry of Lieutenant Colonel N.A.M. Dudley, 9th Cavalry he requests that he may be given the opportunity for denial, explanation, or rebuttal of any testimony taken by said Court, affecting his personal or official honor

In reply I beg to invite attention to the enclosed extract from a report made by the Acting Judge Advocate General W. Winthrop, from which it will be seen that there is nothing in the proceedings of the Court to reflect injuriously upon the course pursued by Governor Wallace, or which has the effect of impugning his honor or the integrity of his motives.

Very respectfully, your obedient servant,
G.W. McCrary
Secretary of War

DAMAGE CONTROL WITH THE OUTLAW MYTH: SEPTEMBER 15, 1879

By September 15, 1879, Wallace had reduced the Lincoln County crisis for Carl Schurz to *"the killing of outlaws by outlaws."* The referenced incident was between Ringites. John Jones was murdered by Bob Olinger. They were Seven Rivers Ring rustlers, already reported by Billy Bonney; and were Sheriff Peppin's murderous possemen in the Lincoln County War. (By 1881, Sheriff Pat Garrett would deputize Bob Olinger as one of Billy's guards for awaiting hanging). But with palpable relief in having escaped his own doom, Wallace chatted merrily:

EXECUTIVE OFFICE,
Territory of New Mexico.
Santa Fe, New Mexico, <u>Sept. 15. 1879</u>.

Hon. C. Schurz
Sec. Dept. Interior.
Sir:
In reply to the communication of Acting Secretary Bell, dated Sept. 3. '79, I immediately submitted in the matter to Mr. S. [Sam] Ellison, of this city, who is more familiar with the old archive-

papers than any person in the Territory, and received from him a memorandum, which I enclose for your information. The sum ($500) appears large; but when it is considered that it will take quite two years to complete the task, I am not sure but the proposal is reasonable enough.

The latest official report from Fort Stanton is also forwarded; I venture to suggest that **the military in that quarter are not of the opinion that the killing of outlaws by outlaws is of importance to justify official mention.** *The remark has reference to the news derived from other sources, that one "Jim [John] Beckwith" was shot and killed by one "Tom [John] Jones" and that "Jones" was then killed by one [Bob] "Olinger" to which as the three are amongst the most bloody of the "Bandits of the Pecos," all the good people cried "Amen."*

At my request a company of troops were sent to Cimarron to look after the Utes and Apaches at large in Colfax County. The settlers are under some alarm; General Hatch, however, is confident that the wanderers can be prevailed upon to go peaceably to their reservations. I have urged the military to be patient with them.

I have the honor to be,
Very truly,
Your friend & servant,
Lew. Wallace.
Gov. New Mexico.

IRA LEONARD PERSISTS WITH CIVIL SUIT: JULY 14, 1879

On the one year anniversary of the Lincoln County War battle's start, on July 14, 1879, Attorney Ira Leonard filed Lincoln County Civil Cause 298 on behalf of Susan McSween and against N.A.M. Dudley for arson of her house, and Cause 176 for libel by defamatory affidavits. But their venue had been changed by Judge Warren Bristol from knowledgeable Lincoln County to the November 1879 Doña Ana County Grand Jury in Mesilla.

Ring death threats prevented Susan from traveling to appear, so Ira Leonard requested a continuance. Instead, using malicious prosecution for another possible assassination - likely planned by T.B. Catron or Henry Waldo - on November 18, 1879, Judge Bristol issued a warrant for her being in contempt; forcing her to risk death by traveling the 120 miles from Lincoln to Mesilla for a court appearance a week later. With Dudley's representation there by Ringite Catron replacement as U.S. Attorney, Sidney Barnes, and with reliance on Dudley's having already been exonerated by the military court, the jury declared him not guilty of arson after deliberating only a half hour. The libel charge was abandoned. The *Mesilla News* of December 6, 1879 wrote that after the verdict "a spontaneous outburst of applause came from the large audience which with difficulty was suppressed by the sheriff and court."

This would be the court, judge, and populace that Billy Bonney, the only Lincoln County War participant without amnesty or pardon, would face in 1 year, 3 months, and 24 days to receive his intended Ring hanging sentence.

CHAPTER 18

HUNTING THE IMAGINARY KID GANG: 1880

THE GATHERING STORM

ANALYSIS: After Lincoln County citizens were reduced to helplessness by Lew Wallace's inaction, Billy Bonney bided his time by petty retaliatory rustling of Ringites' cattle and horses, while Wallace completed his Ben-Hur. And the Santa Fe Ring organized its last campaign to destroy resistance: using the Secret Service and complicit Sheriff Pat Garrett to kill "the Kid."

BILLY BONNEY'S GROWING "REPUTATION"

From Lew Wallace, Billy Bonney got, instead of a pardon, a gunslinger reputation. On January 3, 1880, that yielded Billy's attempted killing by Texan bounty-hunter, Joe Grant, who aimed for his back in Fort Sumner's Hargrove's Saloon. Billy, however, heard the revolver's misfiring click, whirled, and shot Grant dead. As self-defense, it had no legal repercussions.

To earn money, Billy became a gambling card-shark in a circuit from Fort Sumner to Las Vegas. And he conducted guerrilla rustling against Ringites in fulfillment of his July 13, 1878 "Regulator Manifesto" to T.B. Catron's brother-in-law, Edgar Walz, which stated: *"Mr. Catron's property will be dealt with as nearly as can be in the way in which the party he sustains deals with the property stolen ... [T]he ... the injury you do, shall be visited upon the property of Mr. Catron."* That *"property"* included cattle and horses from Catron's Lincoln County Carrizozo Land and Cattle Company ranch and from the ranch of Charles Fritz, mortgaged by "the House;" thus, technically Catron's also. Billy's sales outlets were non-Ring: cattle went to Fort Sumner-area Dan Dedrick (also a counterfeiter) and Three Rivers rustler and slaughter house owner, Pat Coghlan (the Ring's competitor for Indian reservation beef contracts). Billy also took his rustled horses to Tascosa, Texas. His rustler "gang" consisted of past Regulator friends Charlie Bowdre and Tom O'Folliard; and career thieves: Dave Rudabough, Tom Pickett, and Billy Wilson - likely met through Dan Dedrick, who employed them to pass fake bills.

WALLACE OCCUPIES "TWO LIVES"

Back in his faux Palace in Santa Fe, Lew Wallace healed his wounded pride through his ever-loving audience of one: his wife, Susan, to whom he dedicated *Ben-Hur*. His letter to her of January 9, 1880, demonstrates his grandiose identification with Christ the Savior by telling her of his transformation of contentious Democrats and Republications into gentle *"doves."* And "the General" - as his family called him - even signed for her pompously and preposterously as *"Lew Wallace!"* He wrote:

EXECUTIVE OFFICE,
Territory of New Mexico.
Santa Fe, New Mexico,
Jan. 9, 1880.

Dear Sue.

I hasten to send you my message to the Legislature, read yesterday at 3 o'clock.

To my surprise it was given universal satisfaction. I had for audience a mixture of ladies and gentlemen ...

As a compliment to my reading, I received what I never heard of before during the delivery of a message – applause. Think of that!

X X X

I rec'd your letter, and was delighted with it. Don't get blue anymore, I beg of you. Things will come out all right yet; anyhow let us not cry until we have to.

I am busy putting in every spare minute copying my book for publication. It is curious this jumping from the serious things of life to the purely romantic. **It is like nothing so much as living two lives in one.** *To pass from a meeting of the wise men in the desert to effecting a reconciliation in a legislature, and breaking a deadlock, are certainly wide enough apart. The latter I did within an hour after I took hold of it; and so effectively that the democrats voted for republicans and republicans for democrats. They are now gentle as doves.*

Love to folks.

Yours, faithfully,
Lew. Wallace

WALLACE ADMITS THE RING: FEBRUARY 16, 1880

Inflated by his self-praise, on February 16, 1880, Wallace briefly abandoned his outlaw myth to boast astoundingly to Carl Schurz about confronting the Santa Fe Ring; thus revealing his ignorance of Schurz's and Hayes's Ring complicity. He wrote:

Executive Office,
Santa Fe, N.M.
February 16, 1880

Hon. C. Schurz.
Sec. Dept. Interior.
Sir.

I have the honor to inform you that the legislature of this Territory adjourned <u>sine die</u> Friday the 1st instant.

A number of laws much needed was passed in tolerable form; but amongst those that failed was the bill for the reappointment for representative purposes. It was proposed to refer the duty to me, but I declined on the ground that it was required of the legislature, and could not be delegated. The result may be that unless Congress intervenes and authorizes performance there can be no election and consequently no lawful legislature in course. It was simply impossible to effect an agreement ... The matter is respectfully referred to your consideration.

My appointments were submitted the last day of the session. For Attorney General of the Territory, Eugene A. Fiske; for Treasurer, Juan Delgado; for Auditor, Trinidad Alarid; for District Attorney of the Second District, J. Francisco Chavez; **for District attorney of the Third District, Albert J. Fountain;** *for Commissioners to revise the laws of this Territory, William Breeden, Frank Springer, and Simon B. Newcomb; for Librarian, Richard M. Tompkins.*

[AUTHOR'S NOTE: Wallace did nor appoint Ira Leonard.]

Mr. Fountain failed confirmation by one vote. The best man for the place then left in resident in the Second District was Mr. Newcomb [a Ringite] of the revisory commission. Mr. N. resigned from the commission to take the attorneyship, and was confirmed without trouble.

The determined opposition was against Mr. Fiske, and of that a few words.

There were originally four applicants for the appointment, of whom the most prominent were Thomas B. Catron, William Breeden, and Eugene A. Fiske. Mr. Catron is not unknown to fame in your department. ~~I believe he has there a suspended payment on his accounts as a beef-contractor. He also figures largely, I am told in the report of Mr. Angel, in which, as late U.S. District Attorney, he was admitted to a kind of head-centership of the famous old Santa Fe ring. Finding he was not likely to succeed in his aspiration owing to the very doubtful relations existing between us.~~ He retired from the contest early leaving the field to Mr. Breeden and Mr. Fiske.

[AUTHOR'S NOTE: In this breath-taking cross-out by Wallace, in one fell swoop, confirms Catron as Ring head, confirms Frank Warner Angel's Catron report (which Catron would later have S.B. Elkins destroy), confirms Catron's backing the Murphy-Dolan-Riley fraudulent beef contracts for Fort Stanton (which Alexander McSween had exposed), and confirms his own conflict with the Ring. But in his "retained copy," Wallace crossed out his exposés, indicating that they were not sent to Schurz – who knew anyway!]

Mr. Breeden is a gentleman of undoubtable merit, long resident of the Territory, in politics a Republican, and a leader of the party in this region. ~~In fact~~ I would have given _him_ the appointment but for ~~three circumstances;~~ first that the adherents of the ring rallied unanimously to his support after Mr. Catron's withdrawal; ~~second,~~ leaving a fear in my mind that his appointment would ~~have been~~ be received throughout the Territory as a "Ring" victory, and lose me all the results of a year and more of vigorous contest with that powerful faction. ~~Thirdly, it was of great~~ In addition to that I judged it important ~~at this time~~ to give some recognition to the incoming tide of immigration – all this, it must be observed, aside from the question whether Mr. Breeden was really a member of the "ring."

[AUTHOR'S NOTE: Again Wallace confirms the Ring, and even lies about his "_vigorous contest_" against it for a "_year or more;_" when he had only pursued his outlaw myth.]

Mr. Fiske came to the Territory but a few years ago from the office of the Land Commissioner. He is, I believe, well known to

Mr. Marble. He is of studious habits, fair ability, a Republican, and **has the merit of having made a sturdy fight against Mr. Catron and his combination, to which circumstance their** ~~bitter fight made against~~ **opposition to him may be chiefly attributable.**

[AUTHOR'S NOTE: Again Wallace confirms Catron's Ring.]

~~This opposition to him in~~ The Council ~~was able to prevent his~~ refused to ~~confirmation~~ him. I presented him a second time, and with the matter still pending, ~~the Council~~ that body adjourned. Next morning I commissioned Mr. Fiske. He assented to his commission to the Court (Judge Prince's) and was qualified. The opposition ~~opposition~~ was carried from the Council into the Court. Argument was had as to the legality of his appointment, Col. Barnes and Mr. Fiske **affirming and Mr. Catron and Judge Waldo denying.** ~~The question is of great importance, yet I am sorry to say the Judge adjourned his court to go upon an excursion by rail to Kansas City, in which he will be occupied for a week.~~ **Mr. Catron's appearance in this case is significant of the meaning of the** ~~opposition~~ **fight in both court and council. Well informed people here accept it, so far as he is concerned, as a last struggle of the "Ring."** And that you and the President may be posted as to the matter should it be brought to you in Washington, I have been thus particular.

[AUTHOR'S NOTE: Wallace must have seemed foolishly naïve to Ring-enablers Schurz and Hayes, who knew it would long outlast Wallace's stay, without any "*last struggle.*"]

The Indian war still goes on [primarily against Mimbres Apache chief, Victorio]; but now that additional troops are in the field, and General Hatch personally in command, I hope and believe there will be a speedy end to it. General Hatch went down to the scene of action last Sunday.

The completion of the railroad [Atchison, Topeka, and Santa Fe] to this city was celebrated Monday, the 16th instant.

I have the honor to be,
Very respectfully,
Your friend & s'v't,
Lewis Wallace
Governor of New Mexico.

WALLACE BLAMES INDIANS

On June 12, 1880, Wallace switched from Ring gossip to scapegoating *"Indians"* for the *Daily New Mexican* as "Governor Wallace's Proclamation." Like in Cincinnati, he had again issued a theatrical proclamation; this time for citizens versus Native Americans for his own "Indian War." The article stated:

GOVERNOR WALLACE'S PROCLAMATION.

Governor Lew Wallace stated yesterday to a reporter of the NEW MEXICAN in regard to the rumor which has been quite extensively circulated in Santa Fe of later that a proclamation would shortly be issued by him calling upon citizens of New Mexico to take the field against the Indians ... Should it occur ... that the Navajos as a tribe should go on the war-path, the Governor affirms that he will immediately call out every able-bodied man in the Territory to take up arms against the common foe, considering that such a state of affairs could properly be called the oft spoken of "emergency."

By a July 23, 1880 letter to Carl Schurz, Wallace focused on the great Mimbres Apache Chief Victorio, who had resisted forced relocation from his tribe's land; and was to be massacred with his followers in Mexico in four months. Wallace also returned to his outlaw myth with warning of *"renewal of the old outlawry."* And he finally recommended long-suffering Ira Leonard for a judgeship. Wallace wrote:

Executive Office,
Santa Fe, N.M.
July 23, 1880.

Hon. C. Schurz,
Sec. Dept. Interior
Sir:
I have just returned from a tour through the counties of Socorro, Grant, Doña Ana and Lincoln, in the southern part of this Territory. My companion was Col. J.J. Copinyer, General Pope's Inspector. The journey occupied nearly a month.
The counties visited were those which have felt most severely the ravages of the Apache chief, Victorio. It is safe, I think, to put the number killed by the Indians at 150, although many well-informed persons set it at 300. In Grant county there was a suspension of business, and at one time serious apprehension of

suffering from want of supplies, the region being almost totally dependent upon importation by freight.

Victorio, with his hostiles, had certainly gone to Old Mexico. The latest information locates him in Chihuahua, somewhere in the region of the Rio Casas Grandes or the Rio Carmen, 100 or 125 miles south of the boundary line, in good position for another raid whenever he gets another resupply of ammunition and his stock rested up.

It would seem, from my observations, that owing to the absence of the hostiles, business has begun to revive in the afflicted localities. We met quite a number of freight trains upon the road, going and coming. Many, though not all of the miners who had been driven in, have returned to their work or were preparing to do so. The stages of the transportation company had their usual complement of travelers. Still, I could not avoid the conclusion that as long as the Apaches who have gone to war can find an asylum behind the Mexican boundary line, there can be no prosperity or certain growth for the southern counties of New Mexico. I respectfully submit the matter to serious consideration.

I regret to say I found a somewhat unsettled condition of affairs in Lincoln county, signalized by several atrocious murders. There was no difficulty in finding the cause; viz., a failure of the court in that county for two successive terms. It is not necessary, I am sure, to point out to you the result if such failure continues. As a simple precaution against a renewal of the old outlawry, I prefer to urge the appointment immediately of some person who will take the Judgeship in the 3rd Judicial District, and attend to it.

I may be excused for saying further upon this subject that that office requires in the appointee a man of unusual courage, and great experience with frontier life, each quite as much as learning in the law. Such an appointee cannot, in my judgment, be easily found amongst lawyers in the east or the south. There is at this time a gentleman living in Lincoln and the county seat of Lincoln county, for his health, his complaint being asthma, who is a good lawyer, a true republican, and a most respectable gentleman in every way. If the President has not made a selection for the judgeship in question, I beg to present for his consideration Hon. Ira E. Leonard, whom the party alluded to I think just now the fittest man in all my acquaintance for the appointment.

[AUTHOR'S NOTE: If that failed appointment had succeeded, Leonard could have pressed Wallace for Billy's pardon.]

The coming term of court in that county should be held by all means; if it is not, I beg not to be held responsible for the consequences. The man behind a pistol will take the judge's place.
I have the honor to be,
Very respectfully,
Your friend & servant,
Lew Wallace.
Governor of New Mexico

ENTER SECRET SERVICE SPECIAL OPERATIVE AZARIAH WILD: SEPTEMBER 7, 1880

ANALYSIS: Billy was arguably one of the first political assassinations implemented by the Secret Service, here to advance Santa Fe Ring interests. Ironically, though, the Special Operative sent to New Mexico Territory, Azariah Wild, unaware of that Ring plot, almost pardoned Billy himself - until the Ring intervened.

By late 1880, with Lew Wallace tacitly complicit in Ring cover-ups, it seems that T.B. Catron, using S.B. Elkins in Washington D.C., hatched a diabolical plan to end his last Lincoln County resistance by exterminating remaining Regulators - primarily Billy Bonney. As U.S. Attorney, in 1878, Catron had set the stage with his federal indictment Number 411: the United States versus Charles Bowdre, Josiah Scurlock, Henry Brown, William Bonney alias Henry Antrim alias the Kid, John Middleton, Frederick Waite, Jim French, and George Coe for the murder of Andrew "Buckshot" Roberts.

Now, Chief of the Secret Service, James Brooks, was recruited, likely by Elkins, to send one of his forty Special Operatives to New Mexico Territory to investigate alleged counterfeiting, his Department's duty as a branch of the U.S. Treasury Department. Pointing to that collusion, is that the Ring actually knew that Territorial counterfeiting was minor, likely engaging in it themselves through a press owned by "the House's" founders when still in their Fort Stanton sutler's store. And the Ring knew that Regulators were not counterfeiters.

But the convoluted plot - mirroring Catron's pre- and post-Lincoln County War malicious prosecutions to destroy opponents - involved linking counterfeiters to Billy's guerrilla rustling. Key was sending a Special Agent dupe to be manipulated by local Ringites.

The chosen man, Azariah Wild, proved ideal. The actual counterfeiters were Dan Dedrick, located 12 miles south of Fort Sumner in his Bosque Grande Ranch, and his brothers Mose, and Sam, at the family livery stable in White Oaks, out of which also operated their distributors of fake bills: Billy Wilson, Thomas Cooper, and Tom Pickett. Dedrick's *modus operandi* was to buy cattle with counterfeit bills, then resell them. And his men also made occasional local purchases with bills in Lincoln.

The hook was that Billy - with Charlie Bowdre, Tom O'Folliard, and Josiah "Doc" Scurlock - used Dedrick as one outlet for his rustled stock. And he used Wilson and Pickett for rustling. So the Special Operative would be led by Ringite informers to believe there was a counterfeiting and rustling gang headquartered in Fort Sumner - where Billy and other Regulators stayed - and that it needed Secret Service backing to destroy.

That same rustling hook was also used to end Catron's ranching competition in the Tularosa Valley: Pat Coghlan. So in his report written on October 28, 1880, Wild described the "gang" as having "*two ranches. One seventy five miles the other twelve miles from Fort Sumner.*" After Coghlan was incriminated and eliminated, Catron founded, in 1885, his Tularosa Land and Cattle Company with Ringite past "House" partner, John H. Riley, and past District Attorney William L. Rynerson.

ABOUT AZARIAH WILD

Azariah Faxton Wild was born on March 4, 1835 in West Fairlee, Vermont. In the Civil War he served on the Union side, mustering out on January 29, 1866, and settling in New Orleans with his wife. They had seven children. On June 15, 1877, Wild was hired as one of the Secret Service's 40 Special Operatives by its Chief, James Brooks. His territory was "the Gulf States." On September 26, 1877, Brooks praised Wild, writing:

> *I made his acquaintance in New Orleans in 1876, found him to be a well posted man on Cotton and Whiskey matters and from him obtained valuable information ... He has recently made two arrests of counterfeiters, has stopped payment of several fraudulent claims ... Believe he will be of great value to the Government. He has frequently worked for the Department of Justice.*

Chief Brooks likely sent Azariah Wild to New Mexico Territory on behest of T.B. Catron, via S.B. Elkins, to eliminate their last Lincoln County resistance, but with stated mission of a counterfeiting investigation. Though the Secret Service was an arm of the U.S. Treasury Department created to counter counterfeiting, its agents could take action for any other crimes they felt were related to their investigation. Thus, Wild would be diverted by Ring informers to thinking the counterfeiting was being done by a gang of rustlers, to use him for eliminating last Regulators too canny to catch - like Billy Bonney.

Wild was an ideal pick, being lazy, lackluster, gullible, and ignorant about the West. From his September 10, 1880 assignment, to his December 23, 1880 departure, Wild did no investigating, often misspelled investigation names, remained in Fort Stanton, Lincoln, White Oaks, and Roswell; and relied on Ringite contacts. He was soon bamboozled and terrified about a huge, murderous, counterfeiting-rustling gang, to whom he attributed all Territorial rustling; then was persuaded it was headed by Billy Bonney "the Kid" (whom he called "Antrom") - and finally even made the crackpot conclusion that it included Jesse James! In short, Wild became a farcical parody of Lew Wallace, as believing an outlaw myth which Wallace merely fabricated.

To capture this imaginary gang, Wild helped elect Ring-complicit Pat Garrett as Lincoln County Sheriff - and also made him a Deputy U.S. Marshal. Garrett knew his mission was to eliminate Billy, but Wild had him pursue "the Kid gang."

But Wild initially got side-tracked by Attorney Ira Leonard's proposal that he give Billy a new pardon bargain for testifying against the counterfeiters. However, Ringites redirected Wild, ending that chance.

And, ever protective of himself, Governor Lew Wallace encouraged Wild's outlaw myth pursuit of "the Kid gang;" even publishing his own $500 reward notice on December 22, 1880.

Key is that without Wild and his puppet Sheriff, Garrett, using Secret Service-funded spies and Texas possemen, Billy would never have been captured for his Mesilla hanging trial. Wild sealed Billy's tragic fate.

Following Wild's New Mexico Territory stay from September to December of 1880, he served as a Special Operative out of New Orleans until he resigned on June 10, 1893; possibly forced out after pursuit of corrupt New Orleans officials. Wild died of heart disease in New Orleans on June 10, 1920.

WILD'S DAILY SECRET SERVICE REPORTS

Azariah Wild followed Secret Service protocol of writing a daily report to his Chief, James Brooks, documenting his location, activity, contacts, intents, conclusions, recopied letters sent by him, and computed costs; which, for his New Mexico Territory assignment, included paying spies. He received his September 7, 1880 assignment on September 10th, and responded to Chief Brooks on September 11th on his official report form, as follows:

U.S. Treasury Department,
SECRET-SERVICE DIVISION,

<u>New Orleans</u> District

James J. Brooks,
Chief U.S. Secret Service

Sir: I have the honor to submit the following, my report as <u>Special</u> Operative of this District for <u>Friday</u> the <u>10th</u> day of <u>September</u>, 18 <u>80</u>, written at <u>New Orleans, Louisiana</u>, and completed at <u>9</u> o'clock <u>A.</u> M on the <u>11th</u> day of <u>September</u>, 18 80

In New Orleans La.
 Engaged in and about the city the entire day.
 I have the honor to acknowledge the receipt of your letter of the 7th instant relative to my trip to New Mexico with your letters received by the Department from citizens of New Mexico enclosed therewith.
 I expect to start for New Mexico next Wednesday Sept 15th. I will endeavor to carry out your wishes in the matter.
 I have made arrangements for several Winchester rifles to take along with me in case they are wanted they are at hand.
 I also have spoken to the U.S. Marshal [John Sherman] for such articles as I may want in the shape of "bracelets etc" ...

Respectfully Submitted
Azariah F. Wild
Special Operative

Wild's early reports in New Mexico Territory show he first correctly identified counterfeit bill distributors - whom he calls *"passers of the queer"* - as a William Wilson and a Thomas Cooper.

On September 21, 1880, for September 20th, Wild reported from Santa Fe, where he met with Ringite U.S. Attorney Sidney Barnes (Catron's replacement) and James Dolan, who traveled to Santa Fe as the victimized Lincoln merchant - having taken over murdered Tunstall's store, and having supply contracts to Fort Stanton - claiming receipt of a counterfeit $100 bill. These "informants" magnified outlawry of real counterfeiter, Dan Dedrick's, men - like Billy Wilson. The plot was to use Wilson as a conduit to Billy Bonney - with whom Wilson did petty rustling - while convincing Wild to use his power to arrest all "outlaws" - who were actually the last Regulators. Wild wrote:

Engaged ... at the office of U.S. Attorney Barnes in consultation with him about the counterfeiting cases in White Oaks Lincoln County New Mexico ...

[H]e will look more into the case, send for the U.S. Marshal [John Sherman] ... consult together and act in concert.

These men (Thomas Cooper and William Wilson) are amongst the worst characters in Lincoln County where there have been over forty murders committed within the past two years, and not an arrest made.

Judging from statements made by U.S. Attorney Barnes a bad state of affairs exists here in New Mexico. He informs me that there has not been a single arrest made here since last term of Court ... [and has] hopes of arresting Wilson and Cooper ...

I met the post trader [James Dolan] here this day from Fort Stanton on whom one [of] these notes was passed. He has offered to render me any assistance possible*, and has named several parties on whom I can rely to assist in making the arrests when we are ready to act.*

He repeats the information contained in the letters you sent me only a little more full in his details.

[AUTHOR'S NOTE: That Chief Brooks was the Ring's contact, sending his unaware Special Operative to do the Ring's bidding, is indicated by "simple" merchant James Dolan's knowing and repeating the content of the Secret Service assignment letter Brooks sent to Wild!]

713

On September 23, 1880, for September 22nd, Wild wrote from Santa Fe, revealing his manipulation; though still misattributing Lincoln residents' refusing to arrest their hero Regulators with White Oaks residents - who were unaware of Lincoln County War issues. In fact, White Oaks men, later agitated by Wild, would form a rabid posse to capture "the Kid." Wild wrote:

I am going to have trouble in getting assistance to make arrests in White Oaks.
The reputation of Lincoln County in which White Oaks is situated, that no one is willing to undertake the arrests or be known to have had anything to do with so far as I can find thus far, unless more money is paid than I believe the Division can afford to pay.
I have come here to arrest or have these men arrested and am bound to do it if I have to attempt it by myself.

On September 26, 1880, for September 24th, lazy Wild, not venturing from Santa Fe, met with Lincoln County Ringites - vouched for as *"reliable"* by Ringite U.S. Attorney Sidney Barnes. Idiotically, Wild had disguised himself as a miner (presumably in denim); so he must have stood out like a sore thumb. He wrote:

I have this day seen and consulted in company with U.S. Attorney Barnes with several reliable men who are doing business in Lincoln County New Mexico [James Dolan; John Riley; Catron's brother-in-law, Edgar Walz] and who know the parties who I am after and all about them.
The U.S. Attorney [Barnes] will meet with the U.S. Marshal [Sherman] on Monday at the Albuquerque Court and endeavor to get him to send 4 or six good Deputies down to make the arrests soon as he hears from me.
I have purchased me a complete suit of miners clothes ... which was necessary to keep from being suspicioned.

On September 26, 1880, for September 25th, writing from Santa Fe to get a free railroad pass - for which he had stupidly revealed to the railroad company his secret mission as well as inflating his pursuit of Wilson, Cooper, and one counterfeit $100 bill - possibly after his Ringite informers' input - to a nameless *"band of Counterfeiters and passers of the queer [who] are operating in the Territory ... I have been directed by the*

Department to visit this section of the country with a view to breaking them up and bring them to justice."

On October 4, 1880, for October 3rd, Wild wrote from Fort Stanton after meeting in Lincoln with James Dolan to see the counterfeit bill. But straying from Ring control in town, Wild also met with Ira Leonard - someone who could set him right.

On October 5, 1880, for October 4th, Wild wrote from Fort Stanton documenting William Wilson's also passing a $100 counterfeit bill to Lincoln merchant José Montanyo and another to post trader firm Dowlin and Delaney, describing the bills, and stating that he would use those victims as witnesses against suspects, William Wilson and Thomas Cooper (whom he mistakenly calls "Sam") "who travel and work together."

FIRST FOCUS ON BILLY BONNEY

On October 6, 1880, for October 5th, still at Fort Stanton, Wild showed Ring manipulation, likely by James Dolan. His focus on Billy Wilson was expanded to Wilson's rustling, as Wild stated: *"[H]e is an American who has been here in Lincoln County for several years, and has the name of being engaged with others of his kind in stealing horses and cattle."* That segued into linking Wilson to Billy Bonney, Charlie Bowdre, and Tom O'Folliard at Fort Sumner, with whom Wilson rustled.

Wild first mentions Billy as *"William Antrom alias W*m* Bonney alias Billy Kid,"* and describes him as: *"an outlaw in the mountains here who came here from Arizona after committing a murder there."* The use of the name "William Antrom" with a murder crime, breathtakingly implies T.B. Catron's typical ferreting out of past indictments of opponents as he did in 1895 for vengeful attack on his disbarment official, District Attorney Jacob H. Crist. So he had likely discovered Billy's 1877, Bonita, Arizona, "Windy" Cahill killing under the name "Antrim;" with Dolan or Walz relating that to Wild.

So Wild, 28 days after case assignment, had been told by Barnes, Dolan, and Walz - with Catron's agent, David Easton, now added - that Billy was a murderous counterfeiter outlaw *"with whom these cattle thieves meet, and by many it is believed that they (the cattle thieves and shovers of the queer) receive the counterfeit money."* But Wild still doubted. Nevertheless, he melodramatically inflated his investigation to men of *"notorious characters [acting] in concert in their hellish deeds."* He wrote:

In tracing up the history and character of William Wilson known here as Billy Wilson I found that he is an American who has been here in Lincoln County for several years, and has the name of being engaged with others of his kind at stealing horses and cattle.

A few weeks ago he and several of his clan stole 38 head of beef cattle from a ranch near Fort Bascom, and brought them here to Lincoln County where they found their way into the hands of the United States and are now on the Mescalero Indian Reservation as I am informed by David Easton, one of the men in charge. The evidence is conclusive against Wilson as being the party who stole them and sold them here ...

[AUTHOR'S NOTE: Easton, as Catron's agent, conceals Catron-Dolan rustling for Fort Stanton's beef contract by blaming it on what Wild naively calls the "clan" – which he soon revised to Western lingo of "gang." And citing rustling at Fort Bascom - on the Canadian River's Texas border - indicates that Wild was now blaming any Territorial rustling at all on this "clan."]

There is an outlaw in the mountains here who came here from Arizona after committing a murder there named William Antrom alias W<u>m</u> Bonney alias Billy Kid with whom these cattle thieves meet, and by many it is believed that they (the cattle thieves and shovers of the queer) receive the counterfeit money. I have found no evidence so far to support their suspicions.

The people here as a general thing do not know good money from bad.

The following is a copy of a letter this day [October 5, 1880] written to U.S. Attorney Barnes.

*Fort Stanton Lincoln Co. New Mexico
October 5, 1880*

S.M. Barnes Esq.
    U.S. Attorney
        Santa Fe New Mexico
Dear Sir:

On or about the 5th day of August 1880 in the town of Lincoln (Lincoln County) New Mexico one William Wilson now residing at White Oaks did pass on James J. Dolin a $100 counterfeit national bank note on the Merchants National Bank of New Bedford Massachusetts dated February 14, 1865 ...

In connection with the passing of this note I will state that at the time William Wilson passed the note on Dolin [sic] he (Wilson) gave him (Dolin) three $100 notes of the same kind and as he believes of the same character with a $50 note ...

I will respectfully state from information that [Thomas] Cooper and [William] Wilson are both employed at a livery & sales stables at White Oaks [owned by counterfeiter, Dan Dedrick's brothers, Mose and Sam] kept by James West a notorious character recently from Texas.

When they go out they generally travel together, and are supposed to act in concert in their hellish deeds.

I have this far been unable to find only one man who is willing to step forward, and assist in the arrest of these men not out of any fear they have of their resistance but assassination afterwards ...

I believe with one or two good men sent from Santa Fe as Deputy U.S. Marshals with necessary warrants to search their (Wilson's and Cooper's) premises at White Oaks ... we can make the arrests successfully ...

I expect to go to White Oaks the last of this week & expect to remain some days ...

Very Respectfully Yours
Azariah Wild
Special Operative
Secret Service Division
U.S. Treasury Department

The letter of which the foregoing is a copy has been written as per agreement with the U.S. Attorney [Ringite Sidney Barnes] before leaving Santa Fe.

He (the U.S. Attorney) there proposed that he would swear out warrants himself on information I would send him [from Ring informants], and have Deputy Marshals sent from Santa Fe provided men could not be found in Lincoln County to make the arrests.

I expect to go to Lincoln at 7 A.M. Wednesday the 6th to meet Judge Leonard and the Clerk of Court who went to White Oaks Sunday morning after which I will go to the Oaks myself - the first conveyance I can get.

[AUTHOR'S NOTE: Leonard was trying to counter Ring control. Though with usual inadequate strategizing, he never explained the Ring to Wild or put Billy's Regulator role in perspective.]

A SECRET SERVICE PARDON: OCTOBER 6, 1880

Since Azariah Wild was not purposefully aiding the Ring, he accepted Attorney Ira Leonard's help in Lincoln to investigate the counterfeiting. So Leonard, as Billy's lawyer, engineered a second pardon bargain for him: exchanging his court testimony against the real counterfeiters (like Dan Dedrick) for a pardon. Leonard also disclosed the earlier pardon bargain with Governor Lew Wallace, explaining its inapplicable Amnesty Proclamation; as Wild reported: "*Gov. Wallace has issued a proclamation granting immunity to those not indicted but as Antrom has been indicted the proclamation did not cover his (Antrom's) case.*" Leonard's input also confirmed that the original pardon bargain had occurred; since Wild reported: "*Governor Wallace has since written Antrom's attorney on the subject saying he should be let go but has failed to put it on shape that satisfied Judge Leonard Antrom's attorney.*" This comment proves existence of the pardon promise letters Billy cited in his March 2, 1881 Santa Fe jail letter to Lew Wallace; and reveals Leonard's legal mistake in leaving it up to Wallace "*to put it on shape,*" instead of filing a Pardon Petition himself.

But Wild was now poised to save Billy's life by a new pardon bargain which Wallace might have backed since it freed him of its responsibility. So after Billy's exertions of blood and war, his victory against the Ring could have occurred by that chance alone!

Referring to Leonard by his judgeship title, Wild described the new pardon option in his report for October 6, 1880, written on October 8th in Fort Stanton. Wild stated:

> *I left Fort Stanton at 7 o'clock A.M. on the stage and reached Lincoln the County seat at 8:30 A.M. a distance of 9 miles.*
>
> *The object of my visit to Lincoln was to see Judge Ira Leonard and the Clerk of the County Court who went to White Oaks Sunday and returned Tuesday.*
>
> *They inform me that Tom Cooper is at White Oaks. That William Wilson left White Oaks some time since and was at Bosque Grande N.M. [counterfeiter Dan Dedrick's ranch] on the Rio Pecos above [sic- 12 miles below] Fort Sumner.*
>
> *The man with whom Wilson and Cooper were working (West) at White Oaks left there on or about the 24th of Sept to ... meet a drove of Cattle which we believe to have been stolen by this gang or perhaps a portion of them were purchased with counterfeit money ...*

In my report of October 5th page 4 I spoke of an outlaw whose name was Antrom alias Billy Bonney. During the Lincoln Co. War he killed men on the Indian Reservation for which he has been indicted in the Territorial and the United States Court.

[AUTHOR'S NOTE: Wild, likely informed by Leonard, garbles Billy's "Buckshot" Roberts 1878 federal murder indictment by U.S. Attorney Catron as killing men on the Reservation.]

Gov. Wallace has issued a proclamation granting immunity to those not indicted but as Antrom has been indicted the proclamation did not cover his (Antrom's) case and he (Antrom) has been in the mountains as an outlaw ever since a space of about two years time.

Governor Wallace has since written Antrom's attorney on the subject saying he should be let go but has failed to put it on shape that satisfied Judge Leonard Antroms attorney.

[AUTHOR'S NOTE: This key documentation for analyzing Wallace's pardon bargain reveals that: (1) Leonard knew its details; (2) Leonard possessed at least one letter from Wallace stating Billy *"should be let go"* – likely the pardon promise letter(s) Billy referred to in his March 2, 1881 letter to Wallace from Santa Fe's jail. Also, Wild calls Wallace's pardon intent *"his written promises;"* (3) Leonard told Wild that Wallace had *"failed to put it [the pardon] on shape"* - like Wallace's proper pardon affidavit for Ursula Montoya on October 24, 1878, stating: *"Now this is to certify that upon petition of Antonio Ortiz y Salazar and others, reciting the facts and circumstances of the offense and trial, by virtue of the power in me vested by law, the undersigned does hereby grant the said Ursula full pardon for the said offense"* (See my p. 449); (4) But Leonard never made a pardon petition to Wallace like Montoya's; (5) Wallace further appears to have concealed from Billy and Leonard that he pardoned Ringites pleading *"amnesty in bar"* of prosecution by June 11, 1879, irrespective of the Amnesty Proclamation's indictment clause (See my pp. 607-608, 667-668); (6) any letter from Wallace to Leonard *"saying [Billy] should be let go"* was adequate legal proof of their bargain - missed by slow-minded Leonard - but recognized by more legally savvy Wild as validating a pardon. That is why Wild was then prepared himself to complete Wallace's pardon promise by addendum of his own testimony-for-pardon bargain with Billy.]

It is believed, and in fact is almost known that he (Antrom) is one of the leading members of this gang.

[AUTHOR'S NOTE: Wild here entangles his Ringite input, and is clearly confused about Billy's counterfeiting role. It seems that slow-witted Leonard had neither told him that Billy had no role and was no major outlaw, nor informed him about the Ring that Billy and others had fought in the Lincoln County War, nor made clear that Billy's original bargain was for testimony against Ringite murderers. In fact Wild, an honest man, might have been sympathetic with Billy, since he himself was likely forced into retirement in 1893 for exposing New Orleans political corruption. But the toxic seed had been planted in Wild's mind that Billy was "*one of the leading members of this gang.*" And with increasing Ringite input, Wild would soon claim Billy as the gang's leader.]

Antrom has recently written a letter to Judge Leonard which has been shown to me in confidence that leads me to believe that we can use Antrom in these cases provided Gov. Wallace will make good his written promises and the U.S. Attorney [Barnes] will allow the case pending in the U.S. Court to slumber and give him (Antrom) one more chance to reform.

[AUTHOR'S NOTE: Wild is prepared to get Billy's pardon granted. He is convinced Wallace made the pardon promise, and believes he could get Wallace to issue the pardon affidavit. But Wild also realizes that Catron's federal indictment for the "Buckshot" Roberts killing would block Territorial gubernatorial pardon unless "*the U.S. Attorney [Barnes] will allow the case pending in the U.S. Court to slumber.*" In fact, Wild's recognizing of that federal indictment obstacle may have helped Leonard formulate the most clever argument of his career to get it quashed in Billy's 1881 hanging trial.]

I have promised nothing and will not except to receive any propositions he (Leonard) and his client see fit to make and submit them to U.S. Attorney Barnes.

Judge Leonard has written Antrom to meet him (Leonard) at once for consultation.

The chances are that the conversation will take place within the next week when I will report fully to you and submit whatever propositions they see fit to make to US. Attorney Barnes for such action as he deems proper to take..

[AUTHOR'S NOTE: Leonard's pardon plan was doomed, since Wild naively planned to reveal it to the Ring via Barnes.]

While it may appear to you that I am working up this case slowly I will respectfully ask you to take into consideration that I am where there is no telegraphic communications with any point [apparently the Ring concealed the Fort Stanton telegraphic option], and the mail facilities next to nothing so that I have not received a letter since I left New Orleans even from my own family, also that I am in a place where the better citizens are afraid of their lives should they be known to give information against the gang, and the officers are more or less linked in and connected with the outlaws. **In my candid judgment I have struck the worst nest of counterfeiters in the United States, one that I believe will lead to the headquarters of the gang and the long looked for [money printing] plates if continuously worked.**

If you will have patience with me I am willing to remain here and will work these cases although the change of climate is great between this and that in my District proper [New Orleans]. We have had snow in the mountains since I arrived, and I have been compelled to get heavy clothing throughout.

[AUTHOR'S NOTE: Wild's anxiety about justifying his mission after collecting almost no counterfeit bills and apprehending no counterfeiters or printing plates made him exaggerate the magnitude of his quarry as *"the worst nest of counterfeiters in the United States."* He was further befuddled by Ring input which isolated him by concealing the telegraphic option at Fort Stanton, by declaring citizens afraid to give evidence against the "gang" rather than against the Ring, and by accusing Sheriff Kimbrell as in cahoots with the counterfeiters. Also, soft and miserable Wild was further curtailing his activities because of cold weather, leaving himself open to more Ring control. All these variables would add up to his Ring-manufactured lazy solution: the creation of "the gigantic Kid gang."]

Again on October 8, 1880, but for October 7th, writing from Fort Stanton, Wild reported Ira Leonard's apparent attempt to also educate him on Ring frauds - here land grants - possibly as lead-in to explaining Billy's freedom fighting role. Wild was uninterested in the big picture - much like Lew Wallace during his March 23, 1879 interview with Billy - and Leonard did not pursue the matter, as he had already unsuccessfully tried with Wallace and his May of 1879 letters about the Ring as an *"incubus on the government of the Territory.*" Leonard, instead, informed Wild about actual counterfeiters - Dan Dedrick, James West, Billy Wilson, and Thomas Cooper as a "gang." But, without Leonard's excluding Billy, that left Wild open to Ring manipulations that this "gang" included large-scale rustling and Billy. Wild wrote:

> *Judge Leonard recited much crookedness that George B. Barber Deputy County Surveyor was engaged in practicing on the Department of the Interior and to which I took note.*

Wild's report of October 9, 1880, for October 8th, from Fort Stanton, made clear that Catron's brother-in-law, had been at his first meeting with U.S. Attorney Barnes. And that by October 8th, Edgar Walz was acting as Wild's minder (probably with James Dolan) by setting up "informers," and asking Wild "*can you pay or cause to be paid a sum of money for valuable information.*" One of the informants Wild cites is William Delaney, "*Post Master and post trader here [with Will Dowlin], and he believes there is just such a gang working the frontier ... He also thinks Antrom alias Billy Bonney to be one of the gang.*" Demonstrated is a ricochet technique of Ringites referring to other Ringites to mislead Wild - with Delaney and Dowlin being Ringites colluding with Walz and Dolan (himself past Postmaster of the post office housed in "the House"). Likely knowing about the new pardon promise, they were purposefully linking Billy to the "gang" to end Wild's plan.

On October 10, 1880, for October 9th, still at Fort Stanton, in his letter to Ringite U.S. Attorney Sidney Barnes, recopied in his report, Wild revealed his new pardon bargain for Billy. He also revealed that Ira Leonard had given information about the counterfeiters in White Oaks and at Dan Dedrick's ranch - likely obtained by Leonard from Billy to advertise his value to the Secret Service in justification of the new pardon bargain. Furthermore, that new bargain was being documented in writing by letters, just like with Lew Wallace. Wild stated: "*I have recently seen a letter written by him [Billy] in which he expresses himself as being tired of dodging the officers &c. The letter has been answered and the chances are that I will meet him.*" But Wild adds derogatory Ringite input about Billy and locates him at Fort Sumner, making clear that well-meaning but slow-witted lawyer, Leonard, had failed to counteract Ring sabotage. And now Wild had even informed the Ring about Billy's new possible pardon. Wild wrote:

The following is a copy of a letter written to U.S. Attorney Barnes this day: Fort Stanton NM Oct 9th 1880

Hon Sidney N Barnes
        U.S. Attorney Santa Fe N.M. –
Dear Sir.
        Since I wrote you last Judge Leonard and the Clerk of Court have been to White Oaks, and on their return inform me that West with whom Cooper and Wilson have been making their headquarters at White Oaks left there around the 24th of September to go to Deadwood to look after a drove of cattle supposed to have been stolen by the clan.
        William Wilson is reported to be at Bosque Grande at Dedrick's ranch. Dedrick is reported as being one of the leaders of the clan, and partners with West in the Corral at White Oaks.

[AUTHOR'S NOTE: Wild is on the right track for counterfeiting, likely getting the information from Ira Leonard via Billy.]

        William Antrom alias Billy Kid is at Fort Sumner and is a member of the clan. I have recently seen a letter written by him in which he expresses himself as being tired of challenging the officers. The letter has been answered and the chances are that I will meet with him under circumstances which may bring about good results the particulars of which I will communicate should they be worthy of mention ...
        While I am waiting for the necessary papers to arrest Wilson and Cooper I am working to catch other fish in my net, and if able to use Antrom alias Billy Kid on reasonable terms with the party referred to as being willing to give information for a consideration I am satisfied full fifty arrests will follow.

[AUTHOR'S NOTE: Leonard's careless strategy for a face-to-face meeting of Billy with Wild, left fugitive Billy open to capture by the Ring; which Wild's inadvertent revelation to Ringite Barnes now ensured. And, by now, defensive non-productive Wild has inflated the "gang" to 50 strong!]

        Respectfully Yours
            Azariah F. Wild

At 2 o'clock P.M. I received through the mail a letter from Ira E. Leonard Esq. of Lincoln dated Oct 9th giving information relative to a meeting of 14 of the clan at [Beaver] Smith's Saloon at Fort Sumner ... I wrote out a copy of this letter and forwarded it to U.S. Attorney Barnes ...

I will respond to Judge Leonards request and go to Lincoln Monday A.M. [October 11, 1880].

[AUTHOR'S NOTE: Leonard's careless eagerness to assist Wild added not only to Wild's creating the non-existent gang, but linking its location to Fort Sumner, where Wild also located Billy. Unaware, Leonard was adding to Billy's tragic fate.]

On October 13, 1880, for October 11th, Wild wrote from Lincoln, having followed Ira Leonard's misguided suggestion to appoint Robert Olinger as U.S. Deputy Marshal to apprehend the counterfeiters. Leonard was apparently unaware that Olinger was one of the Ringite rustler-murderers involved in the 1878 murder of John Tunstall and Lincoln County War battle atrocities. So Wild included for his Chief a copy of his own letter to U.S. Attorney Barnes referring Olinger. And he requested from Barnes arrest warrants for Regulators at Fort Sumner, noting their federal indictment. He calls them *"other parties who stand indicted in U.S. Court"* (for the "Buckshot" Roberts indictment). At the time, in Fort Sumner were Charlie Bowdre, Josiah "Doc" Scurlock, and Billy Bonney. That implied that Ringite input had outweighed Leonard's pardon plan, and that Wild intended to arrest Billy and the others. To Barnes, Wild wrote:

It may be well to send down warrants for the other parties who stand indicted in U.S. Court, and who are making Fort Sumner their headquarters.

There are several of those who are indicted who are making that place their abode who can be arrested if proper efforts are made.

On October 14, 1880, for October 13th, Wild wrote from Lincoln to complain of lack of a jail to confine his hypothetical captives.

Reporting on October 15, 1880, for October 14th, still in Lincoln, Wild demonstrated that he had merged the counterfeiters with Billy's group in Fort Sumner, and was inflating their numbers while proclaiming them *"desperados"* who are *"a terror to the whole country."* He wrote:

> William Wilson is at present with eighteen other desperados at Fort Sumner one hundred and sixty miles from here, and 125 miles from Las Vegas. He has with him three men who were indicted in the U.S. Court. They are a terror to the whole country ... I think I will have trouble in making the arrests. I am doing all that can be done until the necessary papers come from the U.S. Attorney in Santa Fe.

Since October 6th, Billy's pardon chance had hung in abeyance, awaiting the Wild meeting. But by October 16, 1880, Billy, far more canny than Leonard, having determined the mail route for Wild's reports, robbed the stagecoach to get them. He would have read Wild's October 13th report stating: "*It may be well to send down warrants for the other parties who stand indicted in U.S. Court, and who are making Fort Sumner their headquarters.*" Billy apparently decided that any meeting with Wild would be a trap. So the second pardon chance was lost because of Ira Leonard's failure to properly negotiate or to clarify Billy's anti-Ring role. Wild did not mention it again. Like Lew Wallace, he then needed "the Kid" to construct his own outlaw myth.

WILD'S IMAGINARY OUTLAW GANG

Wild was unaware of the mail theft for four days. And reporting on October 16, 1880 for October 15th, still from Lincoln, he gave inadvertent evidence of Catron as his mission's puppeteer. Writing a garbled rendition of Tom Cooper's helping John Chisum round up presumably rustled cattle, careless Wild stops calling the Carrizozo ranch Edgar Walz's, and correctly calls it "*Catron's ranch.*" Telling, is Wild's accidental familiarity by omitting the full name, as required. And Wild had even stumbled on truth that Chisum's rustled cattle were at "*Catron's ranch!*" Wild wrote:

> *I have received reliable information that Tom Cooper was in White Oaks Thursday morning and left to go to* **Catron's ranch ten miles distant to assist John Chisum** *"round up" his cattle.*

Writing on October 17th for October 16th, still in Lincoln, Wild was defensive, blaming his inactivity on awaiting arrest warrants, and on lawmen not arresting men with federal indictments. His Ringite input is evident, with solidifying of his misinformation about a big gang in Fort Sumner, with anti-Ring Sheriff George Kimbrell fabricated as secretly playing cards with Billy, and with Catron's brother-in-law, Edgar Walz, offering a "witness" about the gang. Also, Wild, in his ludicrous miner's disguise, was getting paranoid in his isolated situation, stating: "*I am led to believe that many people here mistrust my business.*" Wild wrote:

These men (outlaws) have centered at and make Fort Sumner their headquarters, and at the present time there are about eighteen notorious characters there who are engaged in stealing stock, passing counterfeit money, and robbing the mails all of which they do with impunity and as I am told in open daylight.

There are four of the men who I number amongst the eighteen who are indicted in the U.S. Court (one for murdering the Indian Agent) [Billy with garbled Blazer's Mill killing of "Buckshot" Roberts] and for whom warrants are out for and no attempt has been made to arrest them although I am reliably informed he [Billy] comes into the towns nearby and plays cards with the Sheriff of this county [George Kimbrell]. *I have endeavored to get warrants of arrest from the territorial courts for these parties but find the witnesses unwilling to appear. I also find that should the arrests be made that the lives of the court officers would be in danger ... To place them in jail we could not do as we have none ...*

[AUTHOR'S NOTE: The refusal of the locals to help, would result in Wild's assisting in getting Ring-compliant Pat Garrett elected as Lincoln County Sheriff, and Garrett's need to recruit Texans to hunt Billy.]

I am led to believe that many people here mistrust my business ...

I have traced up another $100 – note and trace it back to William Wilson ... I have not yet seen the note ...

In a recent report I spoke of a man who claimed he could give valuable information who was in the employ of E.A. Waltz [Walz]. I have just received a note from Walz [about that].

Wild's report of October 18, 1880 for October 17th, from Lincoln, focuses on random "outlaws" to hide his failing counterfeiting investigation. But from Ringite informers he added, as gang members, Regulators, whose histories he garbled, writing:

> As I have learned the names of several of the outlaws now congregated at and near Fort Sumner I will give them with their history so far as I have it which is about as follows:
> Charles Bowdre:
> Hails from Va. Indicted by the U.S. Grand Jury in 3rd Dist. of this Territory for murder.
> **William Antrom alias Billie Bonnie alias "Billie Kid"**
> **Indicted in 3rd District of U.S. Court for the murder of the Indian Agent. Comes from Kansas here.**
> Dr Joseph G. Scurlock [Josiah "Doc" Scurlock]
> Indicted for same offense. He claims Georgia as his native place. He is indicted for murder in 3rd Dist. U.S. Court. He killed one man each in Louisiana and Texas ...
> James French:
> From Texas. Indicted in U.S. Court for murdering Maj Brady Sheriff of Lincoln County ...
> There are many more men connected with this gang whose names I have not learned but are making Fort Sumner and vicinity their headquarters.

Wild's October 19, 1880 report, for October 18th, still from Lincoln, documents contact with Edgar Walz about his witness employee, a James DeVours, who, refused to *"make any written proposition"* but will *"tell you all he knows about the gang of counterfeiters."* DeVours, supposedly a ranch hand, was in the long Ring tradition of coached testifiers, adding, according to Walz, that he would *"leave it to your Chief to say what he shall receive provided that his name can be kept secret."* So this supposed ranch hand knew about the Secret Service "Chief!" DeVours claimed, according to Walz, that *"their presses and plates are in this county ... [and] they have near $200,000 struck ... [H]e admits he has been engaged in stealing horses and cattle with these parties ... [T]here are a large number of persons engaged in passing [the counterfeit bills]* ... Wild added officiously: *"I do not fully credit his story but I think enough of it to probe it to the bottom."*

For his October 21, 1880 report for October 20th, still in Lincoln, Wild finally admitted to Chief Brooks Billy's mail theft *"at a place just beyond Fort Sumner ... on the night of the 16th instant."* He muffles that debacle by making mail theft one of his fabricated gang's crimes, and claiming that a posse to attack them in Fort Sumner was what the *"citizens here"* wanted. Wild wrote:

In this mail I had several reports which if taken and read as they must have been as both mail pouches were cut open and the contents scattered about the ground. If this is as I believe it must be the plans of our capture and my mission here is as well known to them as it is to myself.

I have respectfully notified the U.S. Attorney [Sidney Barnes] of this gang of men, and of their headquarters being at Fort Sumner. I have also asked for warrants to arrest these men and for Commissions for such men as are willing to assist me in the making of the arrests ...

I have organized secretly a "Posse Comitatus" of thirty men here to go and assist me in making these arrests. Not only those who are wanted for murder & robbing the U.S. mail and are indicted in the U.S. Courts.

The citizens here complain of the Government not breaking up this gang of men or at least in not taking the first step in this direction ...

So far as having arrests made by the Territorial officers I have explained the many difficulties. The Sheriff of this county [George Kimbrell] has since he had the warrants in his possession for their arrest for murder under the hand of the Territory played cards and drank with him [Billy] repeatedly ...

The parties Kid, Wilson, O'Follier [O'Folliard] and Picket who are undoubtedly the ones who robbed the mail on the 17th [sic – 16th] are out at a ranch twelve miles from Fort Sumner. Tom Cooper and Dedrick are at White Oaks, and can be taken at any time unless my reports taken from the mail frighten them away.

[AUTHOR'S NOTE: Billy is now listed first, as Wild lumps Regulators with Dan Dedrick's few counterfeiters]

For his October 22, 1880 report for October 21st, still in Lincoln, Wild continued to agonize about his stolen reports, writing. "*Several of my daily reports were in the mail that was robbed. So that if they get hold of my reports and take time to read them they will understand my mission.*" Absurdly, he misses the fact that he revealed his "*mission*" to almost everyone he met. Their only value, as he never recognized, was accidentally saving Billy's life from the Ring for a while longer.

For his October 23, 1880 report for October 22nd, still in Lincoln, Wild now desperately accepted any Ringite input to inflate his gang, calling it the "*Wilson and Kid gang,*" and attributing to it any rustling in the Territory. Wild wrote:

> *Wilson and his gang have within the past four days stolen sixty-eight head of cattle from a man named Ellis – 400 head from another party and seven horses from John Chisum ...*
>
> *The man who was driving the mail back at the time it was robbed says (so I am informed by the mail carrier who arrived at this post [Fort Stanton] this morning) recognized several of the gang as being **the Wilson and Kid gang** who done the robbing of the mail on the night of the 16th inst.*
>
> *I am informed that the Sheriff of San Miguel County [including Fort Sumner] went to their headquarters near Fort Sumner to arrest some one of the gang and was repulsed and left without making arrests.*

For his October 28, 1880 report for October 27th, still in Lincoln, Wild gave a copy of his response letter to Edgar Walz's ranch hand "witness," James DeVours - who had written with suspiciously legal skill sounding like Catron - to confirm payment for information. To DeVours, with usual laxity, Wild revealed his "secret" role. But after the mail theft, as a security measure, Wild occasionally substituted numbers for names - while still revealing everything else. DeVours became 90. (Billy still went by his name.) Wild wrote:

> *Carrazosa [sic - Carrizozo] Ranch*
>   *Lincoln County New Mexico*
> *Sir [Mr. DeVours]*
>   *In answer to your communication of this day in which you ask:*
> *Will the U.S. Government pay for information such as will lead to the arrest and conviction of persons engaged in making, and passing counterfeit money and if so how much:*
>   *1st The United States will pay for such information through the Chief of the Secret Service Division ...*
>   *2nd The amount which the Government is willing to pay for information as above stated will be based on the number of Arrests made, number of convictions had, the amount of counterfeit money and materials captured and the importance of the arrests made ...*
>   *[A]s the agent of the Government ... I will recommend and pledge its payment as above stated on conviction of parties.*
>   *Respectfully Yours*
>   *Azariah F. Wild*
>   *Special Operative*

For his October 29, 1880 report for October 28th, still in Lincoln, Wild reported that he had responded to "*No. 90*" that his identity would be kept secret, and that he was "*at liberty to select for this purpose the men*" to do spying. That meant that Wild had handed his investigation to the Ring! For Chief Brooks, Wild again inflated the gang numbers to a "*force*," writing:

> *I am now perfectly confident that there is a counterfeiting gang here who are making counterfeit $100 – and $50 – notes as I am of anything that I do not know absolutely certain, and that I have not seen with my own eyes ...*
>
> **The force of desperados now at Fort Sumner the headquarters of the gang numbers twenty six. They openly say that they number sixty two in Lincoln County and defy the authorities.**
>
> *Captain Conrad now commanding at Fort Stanton said to me "You might as well go. You never will be able to make the arrests. You have not, and in my judgment cannot get a sufficient force to handle the men you have to contend with."*

[AUTHOR'S NOTE: Here gullible Wild reveals himself also being fed Ringite information by colluding Fort Stanton officers, as he is encouraged to inflate the imaginary "*force of desperados at the Fort Sumner headquarters of the gang.*"]

> *I replied I believed I would but at the same time was in doubt.*
>
> *I especially call your attention to the location:* **All the outlaws or nearly all have been driven out of Texas and Arizona, and concentrated at Fort Sumner. They have two ranches. One seventy five miles the other twelve miles from Fort Sumner. They have a band of their men out stealing horses, cattle, robbing mails ... whilst the balance of their force remain at the ranch guarding stock they have stolen ...**

[AUTHOR'S NOTE: These are Dan Dedrick's Bosque Grande ranch and Pat Coghlan's Three Rivers ranch. But the report shows that Wild has now fused Dan Dedrick's counterfeiting to Billy's petty rustling, combined with any Territorial rustling at all to inflate his factitious gang. This was the Ring's full-blown outlaw myth, as being pushed at the same time to Wild by Governor Lew Wallace.]

> *This is a case that requires time to work but I candidly believe I can work it successfully by taking time. If I had a good man with me it would be of great service.*
>
> *The leading man of the gang is W.H. West ... He is one of the proprietors of a coral or stable at White Oaks. He has as partners several brothers named Dedrick [Dan, Mose, Sam] who own a ranch near Fort Sumner. It is at this ranch that it is believed the plates and tools &c are at the present time.*
>
> ***I am informed this day by Judge Leonard that a lady passenger who was along at the time the stage was robbed near Fort Sumner that she recognized No. 80 and William Antrom alias "Billy Bony" as two of the robbers who robbed her and the mails.***

By his November 1, 1880 report for October 31st, still in Lincoln, Wild hysterically compared the situation to another potential Lincoln County War; demonstrating not only his lying, but his complete ignorance of that conflict. Additionally, he revealed his intent and power to *"arrest or kill."* He wrote:

> *If things are not looked to [by arrests] ...* ***soon it will end in another "Lincoln County War."*** *I have on two occasions stopped a disturbance between the stockmen and the outlaws by asking them to delay until I could get warrants for my parties when we would take the eleven warrants now here and* ***arrest or kill the whole business****. They now say as soon as the election is over they are going to delay no longer.*

[AUTHOR'S NOTE: This fabrication reveals what Wild had actually been doing: agitating the White Oaks miners, ignorant of the Lincoln County War, about "outlaws;" but here calling them "*stockmen.*" And he had worked to get Ring-complicit Pat Garrett elected Sheriff to replace George Kimbrell to "*arrest or kill the whole business.*"]

ENTER PAT GARRETT

The person chosen by the Ring to capture or kill Billy was Patrick Floyd Garrett: a very tall, 30 year old, depressive, alcoholic, ex-buffalo hunter drifter, whose plantation-owning family had lost everything in the Civil War. In 1876, on the buffalo range, Garrett had murdered, in apparent irrational outburst, a fellow hunter: a teenager named Joe Briscoe; though he was cleared by claiming self-defense. In early 1878, Garrett had arrived in New Mexico Territory's Fort Sumner, where he got menial jobs as a wagon driver for town owner, Peter Maxwell; as a hog farm worker for a Kip McKinney; and as a bartender at the town's Hargrove's Saloon. He would have met frequent visitor, Billy Bonney almost a decade younger.

By 1880, the Ring was completing Lincoln County's suppression with Secret Service Special Operative Azariah Wild to catch for hanging, or kill outright, the last Regulators - including Billy. An obstacle was pro-Regulator sentiment of Lincoln County Sheriff George Kimbrell and Lincoln citizens. So Garrett was advertised by the Ring as a law-and-order candidate to appeal to post-Lincoln County War mining settlers in White Oaks, misled by Wild's witch hunt for a huge outlaw, rustling, and counterfeiting gang headed by Billy Bonney and Billy Wilson.

Garrett was elected Lincoln County Sheriff on November 2, 1880. Wild immediately made him additionally a Deputy U.S. Marshall to give him Territorial jurisdiction, as well as forcing Sheriff Kimbrell to deputize him for 1880, so Garrett could hunt Billy before his actual Sheriff's tenure began in January of 1881.

Garrett likely knew that the "Kid gang" was fabrication. But he rightly realized that killing Billy was his life-changing opportunity. And he was lethal. On December 19, 1880, trying to kill Billy, he ambushed him and his friends in Fort Sumner, but only killed Tom O'Folliard. On December 22, 1880, at the Stinking Springs ambush capture of Billy and his friends, he again tried to kill Billy, but fatally shot Charlie Bowdre after mistaking him because he wore Billy's sombrero. And after Billy's hanging trial, Garrett was responsible for his hanging; that killing of Billy being avoided only by his jailbreak escape.

And after Garrett's successful ambush killing of Billy in Fort Sumner on July 14, 1881, he used the outlaw myth - with ghostwriter journalist, Ash Upson - to publish, in 1882, his equally fictional *The Authentic Life of Billy the Kid: The Noted Desperado of the Southwest, Whose Deeds of Daring and Blood Made His Name a Terror in New Mexico, Arizona, and Northern Mexico.* Like Lew Wallace, Garrett lived the rest of his life as a hypocrite; basking in reflected fame of his victim, Billy. Garrett was murdered in 1908, in possible revenge for another apparent Ring murder assignment: attempting to kill, by his preferred ambushing, a major rancher, Oliver Lee.

THE WITCH-HUNT AGAINST BILLY

Having recruited Sheriff-elect Garrett and mob-mentality White Oaks residents, Azariah Wild invigorated his plan to attack Fort Sumner. In his November 5, 1880 report for November 4th, still in Lincoln, Wild wrote to Chief James Brooks: *"I am now engaged in making preparations to get fifty men together to go to Fort Sumner and arrest this gang of men. I will make a start soon as we have matured our plans and warrants reach me."*

For his November 7, 1880 report for November 6th, still in Lincoln, Wild was in a paranoid haze about stalking his imaginary but numerically growing "gang," with its "leaders": *"William Wilson and ... 'Billy Kid.'"* And Ringite Judge Bristol happily issued warrants for this Secret Service dupe. Wild wrote:

From every indication there is no scare amongst this gang or they are calculating to make a stand at Fort Sumner and fight. They are known to be twenty nine in number ...

Judge Bristol is now here and in an interview with him yesterday he said he would issue warrants for parties who have been engaged in violating the United States law ...

I will soon be in readiness to go to Fort Sumner after certain parties ...

The parties who robbed the mail or who were the leaders of it was William Wilson and William Antrom alias "Billy Bony" alias "Billy Kid."

In his November 11, 1880 report for November 10th, still in Lincoln, Wild had met with Pat Garrett *"to organize the 'Posse Comitatus' to make a raid on Fort Sumner to arrest the counterfeiters."* Omitting that Garrett could get no posse of New Mexicans, Wild - declaring his made-up "gang" as *"the worst (organization) gang of men that this country has"* - wrote:

*[W]e have organized a force in the "Pan Handle' (Texas) to cooperate with us in this raid with a aim of acquiring a huge number of these outfits who are from that state. By doing this there will be but little chance of their escaping and if captured **will probably break up the worst (organization) gang of men that this country has**. John Kinney has qualified as Deputy U.S. Marshal so I have a man to represent the U.S. Marshal [Garrett] while the other parties will act as a 'Posse Comitatus.'"*

[AUTHOR'S NOTE: Using Ringites' recommendations, Wild outrageously appointed as a Deputy U.S. Marshal outlaw, John Kinney: Ringite rustler and perpetrator of the San Patricio massacre along with Sheriff George Peppin, and posseman in the Lincoln County War battle. Wild had already made Seven Rivers rustler Robert Olinger a Deputy U.S. Marshal, as he reported on October 13, 1880. Even Lew Wallace had called Olinger *"amongst the most bloody of the "Bandits of the Pecos"* in his September 15, 1879 letter to Carl Schurz.]

For his November 16, 1880 report for November 13th, still in Lincoln, Wild assembled his manufactured lawmen, writing:

Deputy U.S. Marshal [Robert] Olinger and Deputy Sheriff Garrett returned from White Oaks this P.M. They report No. 70 as having gone in the direction of Fort Sumner where No. 80 is at.

The grand jury now in session here have indicted a large number for stealing stock amongst whom are the gang in Fort Sumner. I fear they will hear of it and hide out.

[AUTHOR'S NOTE: Wild was disingenuously adding any rustler at all to his "Fort Sumner gang."]

For his November 16, 1880 report for November 14th, still in Lincoln, Wild stated that Garrett was *"getting ready to make a secret move on Fort Sumner."*

For his November 18, 1880 report for November 16th, still in Lincoln, Wild focused on *"No. 70 & as principle parties."* And he refers to White Oaks men, whom he and Garrett were agitating about the "gang." Wild wrote:

Several parties have arrived from White Oaks to attend court here as witnesses. I have gained valuable information from several, and have made arrangements with J.W. Bell, a resident of White Oaks to make a deal with No. 70 if possible.

[AUTHOR'S NOTE: James Bell was a on the posse that killed fellow posseman, Jim Carlyle, on November 28, 1880, then blamed it on Billy. He was later deputized by Garrett as one of Billy's pre-hanging guards, and was killed in Billy's escape.]

For his November 21, 1880 report for November 18th, still in Lincoln, Wild related hiring Garrett's friend, Barney Mason, Peter Maxwell's Fort Sumner foreman, to spy there; as further discussed in his report of November 21, 1880, for November 20th. Wild wrote:

> *It appears from the statements of Garrett and Mason that he (Mason) is an experienced stockman and is now and has been for some time past in the employ of a man named Maxwell who resides at Fort Sumner. He (Mason) states that a few days ago one Daniel Dedrick who resides at Bosque Grande, and who has an interest with his brother Samuel Dedrick & West in a livery stable at White Oaks came to him and proposed [to hire him to take $30,000 counterfeit money to Texas, buy cattle there, take them to a place near Mexico to Dedrick and West, then leave the country] ...*
>
> *[And] Mason states that William Wilson boards at his house when at Fort Sumner ...*
>
> *[And Mason states] [t]hat William Wilson and Billy Kid left about the 15th inst with sixty head of stolen horses and went down the Canadian River to be gone two or three weeks. That on their return they would probably return to his house when he would turn them over to Patrick F. Garrett Deputy U.S. Marshall and Sheriff.*

[AUTHOR'S NOTE: This is how Wild mingled Billy's petty rustling with his concocted Wilson-Kid gang.]

COYOTE SPRING AND GREATHOUSE AMBUSHES: NOVEMBER 22nd AND 28th, 1881

Having elected Pat Garrett as Sheriff by their majority voting to eliminate "the Wilson-Kid gang," White Oaks men were primed for action; though Billy was unaware and still bringing rustled horses to the Dedrick's livery there. So the residents formed the White Oaks posse under local Lincoln County Deputy Sheriff Will Hudgens to capture Billy.

On November 22, 1880, they ambushed Billy and his companions near White Oaks at their Coyote Spring campsite; but firing wildly, they merely killed two of their quarry's horses.

Billy and his group proceeded to "Whiskey Jim" Greathouse's ranch about 40 miles to the north. There, at November 28, 1880's dawn, the White Oaks posse ambushed them again. When Billy offered to negotiate, they sent in posseman, Jim Carlyle. The failed talk resulted in Carlyle fleeing through a window, and being killed in friendly fire when mistaken for Billy. The posse then retreated; but Billy realized his mortal danger. The posse returned later to burn down that ranch, and blamed Carlyle's killing on Billy. The Ring, Lew Wallace, and Azariah Wild had finally fanned flames of lies enough to create a spreading conflagration.

From Pat Garrett's Roswell home, Azariah Wild reported his fables about the confrontations, while, in excitement, garbling dating. On November 24, 1880, for November 23rd, he related the Coyote Spring ambush of the 22nd. His Billy was now leader of the fabricated *"Kid force,"* magnified to outnumber White Oaks men, with exaggerated casualties of horses. Wild wrote:

> *The [Deputy] Sheriff at White Oaks with his Posse went out 13 miles from town and attempted to arrest Billy Kid, William Wilson and others on Monday the 22nd instant and have return to town empty handed.* **Kid force out numbered that of the Sheriffs.** *Each party had several horses killed ...*
> *There is talk of "Judge Lynch" trying them at last account.*

Dating his report to November 26, 1880, but claiming it was for November 22nd, and still at Garrett's Roswell home, excited Wild added more fake information about *"Billy Kid"*, stating:

> *Information has just reached me through a reliable source that Billy Kid had been driven out of the Canadian River country and was now at Greathouse's ranch with twenty five armed men and a bunch of stolen horses ...*
> *The citizens went out to capture them but they made their escape after about forty shots were exchanged.*

For his November 28, 1880 report, allegedly for November 26th, still at Garrett's Roswell home, Wild invented a near-war, and reveals the large number of men Pat Garrett had brought from Texas; thus, implying Garrett's own lying about the "Kid gang" being major Texas rustlers to elicit intervention of the Panhandle Cattleman's Association. Wild wrote:

> *Information has reached me here this day that William Wilson with about twenty five others are near White Oaks, and that every man able to bear arms at that place is under arms to protect the place ...*
> *Barney Mason has not yet returned [from making his counterfeit money deal with Dan Dedrick]. We would start from here (Roswell) with a force only nearly every horse in this section of the country is sick at present with distemper.*
> *Deputy U.S. Marshal [Frank] Stewart from Texas [actually a Panhandle Cattleman's Association detective] is reported to be at*

Puerta de Luna with 40 men and after several of the men who are in this gang for crimes committed in Texas. I shall communicate with him soon as I can get a reliable man to send, and then press the "Rustlers" from White Oaks back into Fort Sumner and then surround the place with forces from above and below.

Still catching up on November 28, 1880, Wild wrote for November 27th, still at Garrett's Roswell home, and by then in paranoid terror of his imaginary gang, though his report documents only that spy, Barney Mason, had returned to state that Dedrick had backed out of the cattle-for-counterfeit-money deal. And Mason listed Dedrick's counterfeiting associates as only William Wilson, James West, and Tom Cooper. It is likely that Mason, like Garrett, was just playing along with duped Wild for personal profit, knowing that no "gang" existed. Wild wrote:

I will respectfully state that I am very impatient to get away from here but the shape things have taken I feel it my duty to remain ...
At the present time I am entirely cut off from reaching the rail road by these outlaws and will have to employ a guard unless I remain until arrests are made and go along to Santa Fe with them.

On November 29, 1880, for November 28th, Wild wrote more misinformation from Garrett's Roswell house, stating that *"the Kid with seventeen men were [at the Greathouse ranch]."*

On November 30, 1880, for November 29th, Wild wrote from Garrett's Roswell house that he was setting out with *"an armed and mounted force of twenty men under command of Deputy U.S. Marshals Olinger and Garrett."* With feverish paranoia, Wild added certainty that *"there will be blood shed."* Wild wrote:

We have at the present time between one and two hundred armed men out scouting for this gang of outlaws and counterfeiters ...
I this day employed a man to take word from here (Roswell) to Puerta de Luna to Deputy U.S. Marshal [sic - Cattle Detective] [Frank] Stewart who is at that point with party of men ... that he might act in concert with our own deputies in rounding up and arresting this gang of counterfeiters ...
It is believed that there will be blood shed when ever our men come up with the main gang if ever we are able to do so.

On December 3, 1880, for November 30th, Wild, never having departed Garrett's Roswell house, finally reported the Greathouse ranch ambush, with usual fabrications. He wrote:

Information has reached me this day that William Wilson et al of their gang numbering 17 were run into Greathouses Ranch. That the house was surrounded by a Deputy Sheriff [Will Hudgens] and a posse numbering in all 13. One of the posse named Carlisle [Jim Carlyle] ... was one of the leaders ... and after a little talk with the parties on the inside of the house he was induced to go in. Soon as he was inside of the house he was murdered. Soon after Carlisle was murdered William Wilson and his gang made a rush out of the house, and made their escape under cover of the night ...This country is under a great state of excitement, and no one dares to travel much unless by squads from six to ten.

That same December 3, 1880, fearful Wild reported for December 1st that he had stayed in Roswell, but Garrett had left "*with a Posse to go to Fort Sumner.*" Writing still on December 3rd, but for December 2nd, Wild hysterically decided that the gang had come to Roswell after him! He wrote:

Several of Wm Wilson gang of men have been seen near this place this day. It is feared trouble is brewing near at this place and I am now writing my report in the post office of this place which is filled with men arrived to resist any attack that may be made ...
I am unable to get out of this place with safety.

On December 4, 1880, for December 3rd, Wild, still in Garrett's Roswell house, reported ludicrously that Garrett "*had divided his force*" and was apparently arresting random people - like ones in "*a cave some twenty miles from Fort Sumner.*" Lacking any real arrests - or even a real gang - Wild whined to his Chief: "*There has been cold weather and snow since the 20th of September to say nothing of being away from my family and almost severed from civilization. I have felt it my duty to do as I have and hope you will consider this and not place the blame of the delay on me.*" Wild added that his work was appreciated, unaware that it was not for "*the good people of Lincoln County,*" but for the Ring, now poised to kill Billy Bonney.

On December 5, 1880, for the same day, Wild, still in Garrett's Roswell house, reported Garrett's arrests of some random murderers. For Chief Brooks, Wild rationalized failure as: *"The outlaws have divided up and have men on every road leading from Lincoln County to the Rail Road. You need not feel any anxiety as to my getting out of here safe as there are good citizens enough to protect me when I start."*

On December 10, 1880, for December 7th, Wild, still in Garrett's Roswell house, tracked his phantom and migratory gang, writing: *"Information of a reliable character has this day been received here that Wilson and others for whom we have warrants visited a house ... in Lincoln Sunday night [December 5th] and made their escape before their presence was discovered ... They left going in the direction of the Capitan Mountains where it is believed their main force is."*

The same day, Wild reported for December 8th that the *"store and buildings on Greathouses ranch the place Carlisle was killed at has been burned to the ground."* The same day, but for the 9th, Wild wrote that Garrett had captured *"a large number of stolen horses and cattle."* This was Wild's distortion of what Billy himself would report to Lew Wallace on December 12th: that two of his mules had been robbed by Garrett from the Fort Sumner area ranch of a Thomas Yerby. Garrett, unlike Wild, knew his job was to pursue and to eliminate just one man.

The same December 10, 1880, but for December 9th, still in Garrett's house, flagrantly paranoid Wild reported: *"I am very anxious to get away from here ... [T]he "rustlers" a (name given to Wilson and his band) have men on two out of three roads ... I am going to leave here for headquarters first occasion that presents itself to get away with safety."*

On December 23, 1880, Wild was departing New Mexico Territory, and reported from Santa Fe en route to New Orleans.

AFTERMATH OF AZARIAH WILD

In 3 months and 13 days from case assignment to departure from New Mexico Territory, Azariah Wild had collected a few apparently counterfeit bills and had captured no one from his imaginary counterfeiting-rustling mega-gang. Real counterfeiter, Dan Dedrick, had fled permanently to California. But Wild achieved the Ring's goal: empowering a lawman, Pat Garrett, to capture or kill Billy Bonney, and once again give a gloss of legitimacy to murder.

LURID PRESS

By December 3, 1880, the Ring began its press campaign against Billy, clearly based on a leak of Wild's "secret" reports about the "Kid gang" as the largest counterfeiting-rustling group in the country, with Fort Sumner as its headquarters; even using Wild's single reference to gang's number as sixty. That day, the Las Vegas *Gazette* published an editorial by complicit editor-owner J.H. Koogler titled "Powerful Gang of Outlaws Harassing the Stockmen." It replicated lying smear campaigns against adversaries that characterized T.B. Catron's long career. And Billy was now publicly "Billy the Kid."

Billy's logical response should have been to leave the Territory. However, nine days later, on December 12th, he would defiantly choose instead to write his corrective letter to Governor Lew Wallace. The article stated:

The gang includes forty to fifty men, all hard characters, the off scouring of society, fugitives from justice, and desperados by profession. Among them are men, with whose names and deeds the people of Las Vegas are perfectly familiar, such as **"Billy the Kid,"** Dave Rudabaugh, Charles Bowdre, and others of equally unsavory reputation ...

The gang is under the leadership of "Billy the Kid," a desperate cuss, who is eligible for the post of captain in any crowd, no matter how mean and lawless. They spend considerable time in enjoying themselves at the Portales, keeping guards out and scouting the country for miles around before turning in for the night. Whenever there is a good opportunity to make a haul they split up in gangs and scour the country ...

They run stock from the Panhandle country into the White Oaks and from the Pecos country into the Panhandle ...

Are the people of San Miguel county to stand this any longer? Shall we suffer this hoard of outcasts and the scum of society, who are outlawed by a multitude of crimes, to continue their way to the very border of our county?

We believe the citizens of San Miguel County to be order loving people, and call upon them to unite in forever wiping out this band to the east of us.

WALLACE WRITES TO SCHURZ: DECEMBER 7, 1880

By his December 7, 1880 letter to Secretary of the Interior Carl Schurz, Wallace was paralleling his own outlaw fabrication with Azariah Wild's, and covering up Billy's new pardon for testimony bargain with Wild.

Wallace's despicable intent was to make Billy's pardon impossible, to spare himself its Ring repercussions; while making Billy the scapegoat for Territorial "troubles." And while betraying Billy and Lincoln County citizens, Wallace reverted to his despotic nature and requested repeal of the Posse Comitatus Act so soldiers could hunt down citizens, like Billy. This evil letter must be read in perspective of Wallace's knowing from Lincolnites and from the Dudley Court of Inquiry the military atrocities resulting two years earlier from violation of the Posse Comitatus Act, knowing those horrors from Huston Chapman's letters and murder, and knowing the truth about Billy from their pardon bargain and interactions. It made no difference to this morally hollow man. And Wallace's referring to local citizens, here meant only James Dolan and other Ringites. Wallace wrote:

EXECUTIVE OFFICE,
Territory of New Mexico.
Santa Fe, New Mexico,
Dec. 7, 1880.

Hon. C. Schurz
Sec. Dept. Interior.

From private advices received from Lincoln County last night, I have reason to believe a new trouble has broken out in Lincoln County. This time, however, it has one good feature – the civil officers of the county, well supported by citizens, have taken the field to arrest outlaws, murderers, horse and cattle thieves, and counterfeiters. I have telegraphed the Sheriff to give the enemy no rest, but push them until he catches them, and that I ~~would~~ will support him.

Upon receipt of more definite information, I will send you particulars, and go down there myself if necessary.

The affair would seem to have no connection with the old difficulty.

> It suggests the great need of speedy repeal by Congress of the law prohibiting the use of regular soldiers as posse comitati [Posse Comitatus Act of June 1878]. The repeal should at least be as to New Mexico. A large body of troops, including cavalry, is now quartered in Fort Stanton. If they were able to support the Sheriff, short work could be made of the pending trouble. Could you bring about the appeal in question, though limited as above suggested, you would earn the thanks of the people of this whole Territory.

[AUTHOR'S NOTE: Wallace is actually repeating his original attempt to get martial law, his despotic urges unaltered.]

> I have the honor to be,
> Very respectfully,
> Your friend and servant,
> Lew. Wallace,
> Governor New Mexico.

BILLY RESPONDS TO NOTORIETY: DECEMBER 12, 1880

On December 12, 1880, when Billy Bonney wrote again to Governor Lew Wallace, he knew he was being pursued by a Washington-based organization called the Secret Service. His attorney, Ira Leonard, had told him. And he had confirmed it for himself by robbing the mail coach and reading Special Operative Azariah Wild's reports. They had featured Billy with criminal glamour. And he had read J.H. Koogler's December 3, 1880 Las Vegas *Gazette's* "Powerful Gang of Outlaws Harassing the Stockmen." His rebel glory would have been dimmed by injustice of outlaw notoriety.

After a year and a half gap in direct communication with Wallace, Billy sent him his fourth known letter, counting the "Billie" fragment. It was Billy's sixth contact with Wallace: adding to their Lincoln meeting at Justice of the Peace "Squire" Wilson's house and Wallace's interview of him at Juan Patrón's house-jail. And now lost may be Wallace's letter or letters to Ira Leonard about the pardon promise.

Billy had likely amazed T.B. Catron and the Ring by not fleeing the Territory. But to self-centered Wallace it must have seemed brazen taunting of himself. In fact, still irrationally clinging to Wallace as a father-figure, Billy was trying to set things right - to be loved: the exact course Wallace, with equally pathetic obstinacy, sought himself as pardon for Shiloh from General Ulysses S. Grant.

By that December 12th, Billy had endured Secret Service pursuit, another lost pardon, two White Oaks posse ambushes, and a false murder accusation for Jim Carlyle's shooting. Possibly his teenaged lover, Paulita Maxwell, in Fort Sumner had added to his determination to stay in the Territory. His letter gives *"Fort Sumner"* as his address.

Seven days later, Pat Garrett's posse would ambush Billy's group at Fort Sumner, killing Tom O'Folliard, instead of intended Billy. Ten days away was Billy's capture at Stinking Springs by Garrett's posse, where Garrett would shoot dead Charlie Bowdre when mistaking him for Billy.

But by that December 12th, and throughout his months of life left in 1881, Billy's writing and press interviews showed that, even hunted relentlessly, even jailed after capture, even sentenced to hang, even held shackled and guarded, he had no doubt of escaping; and he had no diminution of his rebellious spirit.

The letter, a rebuttal to J.H. Koogler's Las Vegas *Gazette* article nine days before, marks Billy's transformation: hardened by living with daily threat of death, and raging at injustice, he is now famous; even with a flashy sobriquet, "Billy the Kid," soon nationally known." He obviously read his press. But not conceiving coordinated Ring effort, he blamed pursuit on John Chisum, who had earlier betrayed John Tunstall by refusing aid. And Billy addressed Wallace with bold familiarity and equality, writing:

Fort Sumner
Dec. 12th 1880
Gov. Lew Wallace
Dear Sir
I noticed in the Las Vegas Gazette a piece which stated that, Billy "the" Kid, the name by which I am known in the Country was the captain of a Band of Outlaws who hold Forth at the Portales. There is no such Organization in Existence. So the Gentleman must have drawn very heavily on his Imagination. My business at the White Oaks at the time I was waylaid and my horse killed was to See Judge Leonard who has my case in hand. he had written me to come up, that he thought he could get Everything Straightened up I did not find him at the Oaks &

Should have gone to Lincoln if I had met with no accident. After mine and Billie Wilsons horses were killed we both made our way to a Station, forty miles from the Oaks kept by Mr Greathouse. When I got up the next morning The house was Surrounded by an outfit led by one Carlyle, Who had come into the house and Demanded a Surrender. I asked for their Papers [warrants] and they had none. So I concluded that it amounted to nothing more than a mob and told Carlyle that he would have to Stay in the house and lead the way out that night. Soon after a note was brought in Stating that if Carlyle did not come out inside of five minutes they would Kill the Station Keeper)Greathouse) who had left the house and was with them. in a Short time a Shot was fired on the outside and Carlyle thinking Greathouse was Killed jumped through the window. breaking the Sash as he went and was killed by his own Party they thinking it was me trying to make my Escape. the Party then withdrew.

they returned the next day and burned an old man named Spencer's house and Greathouses also

I made my way to this Place afoot and During my absence Deputy Sheriff Garrett Acting under Chisum's orders went to the Portales and found Nothing. on his way back he went by Mr Yerby's ranch and took a pair of mules of mine which I had left with Mr Bowdre who is in Charge of mr Yerby's cattle. he (Garrett) claimed that they were stolen and even if they were not he had a right to Confiscate any Outlaws property.

I had been at Sumner Since I left Lincoln making my living Gambling the mules were bought by me the truth of which I can prove by the best citizens around Sumner. J.S. Chisum is the man who got me into Trouble and was benefited Thousands by it and is now doing all he can against me There is no Doubt but what there is a great deal of Stealing going on in the Territory. and a great deal of the Property is taken across the [Staked] Plains as it is a good outlet but so far as my being at the head of a Band there is nothing of it in Several Instances I have recovered Stolen Property when there was no chance to get an Officer to do it. one instance for Hugo Zuber Post office Puerto de Luna. another for Pablo Analla Same Place.

if Some impartial Party were to investigate this matter they would find it far Different from the impression put out by Chisum and his Tools.

                Yours Respect
                      William Bonney

CULMINATION OF WALLACE'S PARDON BETRAYAL: DECEMBER 13, 1880

In response to Billy's letter, Lew Wallace's sadism surged in mixed identification with his cruel father and rage at reminder of his moral failure. His response was retaliation by "the General" seeking to destroy the symbol of his hypocrisy by a hanging death. So on December 13, 1880, Wallace requested from Territorial Secretary William Ritch a reward notice. Though other Regulators were listed on Lincoln County War indictments, Wallace just focused on Billy. He wrote:

Executive Office
SANTA FE., N.M.

Dec. 13   1880

Hon. W.G. Ritch
Loc. New Mexico.
Sir:
Be good enough to prepare a draft of proclamation of reward $500. for the capture and delivery of William Bonney, alias the Kid to the Sheriff of the County of Lincoln County.

Yours, truly,
Lew Wallace
Governor

Nine days later, on December 22, 1880, the Las Vegas *Gazette* published Wallace's reward notice in a front page column:

BILLY THE KID
$500 REWARD

I will pay $500 reward to any person or persons who will capture William Bonney, alias The Kid, and deliver him to any sheriff of New Mexico. Satisfactory proofs of identity will be required.
  LEW. WALLACE,
    Governor of New Mexico

WALLACE PLANS ESCAPE

The day after Lew Wallace requested the reward notice for Billy the Kid, he implemented his own escape from the Territory into his fantasy world where savior and salvation were real. On December 14th, 1880, he wrote to Secretary of the Interior Carl Schurz requesting leave to promote his *Ben-Hur: A Tale of the Christ*. But Wallace also expressed his sadism, again urging repeal of the Posse Comitatus Act. Wallace wrote:

Executive Office,
SANTA FE, N.M.
Dec. 14. 1880.

Hon. C. Schurz,
Sec. Dept. Interior

Sir:
I have private business urgently requiring my presence in New York City; on account of which I have the honor to ask a leave of absence not exceeding twenty days.

[AUTHOR'S NOTE: This leave was for the publisher's release of 5,000 copies of *Ben-Hur: A Tale of the Christ*.]

The suggestion that I made in my letter of 7th inst., relative to the repeal, as respects New Mexico, of the law prohibiting the use of troops in aid of civil authorities,

[AUTHOR'S NOTE: Wallace again urges repeal of the Posse Comitatus Act, making a future Dudley-like intervention legal.]

is of such importance that I desire to appear before the Senate and House Committees on Territories, and urge immediate action in the matter. If that be not promptly done, it looks as if, for a time at least, the thieves and murderers quartered in the pocket of Grant County south-west, and on the line of old Mexico, cannot be taken care of as they should be. Ranchmen and miners are harassed by raids to such an extent that, in instances, they have been driven from their property.

I have intelligence to day from Lincoln County. The citizens are yet in the field under a very active and energetic deputy-sheriff

[Pat Garrett], who has had several skirmishes [indirectly by the White Oaks posse at Coyote Spring and Greathouse ranch], and made five important arrests; so that the authorities here are confident that they can take care of themselves. **To stimulate them, I have made proclamation of $500 reward for the capture and delivery of the leader of the outlaws [Billy the Kid].**

[AUTHOR'S NOTE: Outrageously, Wallace merged his outlaw lies with Secret Service Agent Azariah Wild's fabricated outlaw gang with Billy the Kid as leader. And this letter represents the point at which Wallace makes Billy Bonney the focus of his own outlaw myth. It is obvious that Billy has no hope of a pardon from Wallace. This point is also where Wallace crystallized his future outlaw "romances" of Billy the Kid that would become his obsessive published reworkings of his pardon betrayal and his attempt to allay his guilty conscience.]

If the leave is granted, be good enough to telegraph me.
I have the honor to be &c.
Lew Wallace
Gov. N.M.

The next day, having relegated Billy to certain death, Wallace callously wrote to his son Henry to check his *Ben-Hur* sales and mining investments, signing bizarrely - like to his wife - *"Lew Wallace."* He wrote:

Executive Office,
SANTA FE, N.M.
<u>Dec. 15.</u> *1880.*

Dear Henry.
Not improbably I will in a few days want a hundred and fifty dollars to pay for assessment work on a couple of mines in the Cerillos.
If I can get that amount from you, I can get along, as I will have a quarter salary due me at the end of this month. Let me know immediately if you can spare the amount from your business. If so, send me draft and oblige.
Yours truly
Lew. Wallace.

P.S. *How are the books selling?*

BILLY GETS MORE LURID PRESS

On the same December 22, 1880 day that Lew Wallace's $500 reward notice for Billy appeared - and likely thanks to Santa Fe Ring journalists, leaked Secret Service reports of Azariah Wild, and possibly Lew Wallace himself - Billy Bonney gained national fame in a long *New York Sun* article, along with his real bay racing mare and his fantasy "outlaw gang." One can wonder if New Yorker, Frank Warner Angel, read this outcome of his own betrayal of Billy Bonney and the rest of the anti-Ring freedom fighters two years earlier by his cover-up for President Hayes.

The article is mere dime-novel fodder. Mingled with vague Lincoln County War references, were myths of "Billy the Kid." This trash would become Billy Bonney's history, distorting books and media to the present.

At this point, Billy had no hope of salvation - from Lew Wallace or Ring-propelled lawmen. But Billy never accepted that; even to the moment of escaping his inescapable jail before hanging, or stepping into darkness of Peter Maxwell's bedroom shortly before midnight a little less than seven months later.

The *New York Sun* article stated:

OUTLAWS OF NEW MEXICO.
THE EXPLOITS OF A BAND HEADED BY A NEW YORK YOUTH.

The Mountain fastness of the Kid and his Followers— War against a Gang of Cattle Thieves and Murderers — The Frontier Confederates of Brockway, the Counterfeiter.

LAS VEGAS, New Mexico, Dec. 20.—One hundred and twenty-seven miles southeast of Las Vegas, New Mexico, is Fort Sumner, once the base of operations against the Indians who committed depredations against the stockmen. The fort was abandoned some ten or twelve years ago, owing to the removal of troops further south, toward the border of Mexico. The property was condemned and sold to Pete Maxwell, a well-known ranchman of the section. Since then it has been a depot of supplies for stockmen and a stage station on the postal route to the Pecos Valley and Panhandle, Texas.

Until recently, or almost any fair day, there might have been seen lounging about the store or engaged in target practice four men, all of them young, neatly dressed, and of good appearance. A stranger riding in the little hamlet would have taken them to be a party of Eastern gentlemen who had come into that sparsely settled region in search of sport. Many who have gone into that country have struck up an acquaintance with these men and found them agreeable fellows. These men are the worst desperadoes in the West, and large parties of armed men are now scouring the country in pursuit of them.

For a number of years the people of eastern New Mexico and Panhandle, Texas, have been harassed by a gang who have run off stock, burned ranches, and committed acts of violence and murder. It was only recently that the leaders and organization of the band were discovered. **The leaders are Billy the Kid, so called from his youth; Dave Rudabaugh, Billy Wilson, and Tom O'Phallier, the four loungers about Fort Sumner. The Kid is the captain of the gang.** Their fastness is about thirty-five miles nearly due east from Fort Sumner, on the edge of the great Staked Plain. In that region there is a small lake called Las Portales. It is surrounded by steep hills, from which flow numerous streams that feed the little lake. This place the robbers selected for their resort partly on account of its hiding places, but mainly on account of the opportunities it afforded them for stock thieving. No matter from what direction the storm came, it drove to the lake the herds of cattle which roam at large in the rich grazing country. There the band built for themselves one of those rude dugouts so common on the Western frontier, two sides formed by the side of the hill, the other two constructed of sod and dirt plastered together, and the whole covered by a thatched roof. Stockades or corrals were built near by in which to put stolen stock. During pleasant weather the members of the gang lounged about Fort Sumner or other stations in that section. When the storm sent cattle scudding over the plains to the haven afforded by the hill-protected lake basin, the gang would hurry to their rendezvous and cut out from the herds the best cattle, driving them into their corral, whence they were later sent to market. Their booty was large, for they had a vast stock to select from, the whole country for a distance of one hundred and fifty miles either way being a rich, continuous pasture. Besides the active members of the band, there were many who had apparently some settled occupation and made themselves useful in disposing of the stolen cattle. In every town of any size within a radius of 150 miles there were butchers who dealt regularly in this stolen stock. When supplies from roving herds ran short the desperadoes would make a raid on herds that were guarded, attacking ranches and killing or diving off the inmates. Besides their station at Las Portales, they had one at Bosque Grande, fifty miles to the southwest, and another at Greathouse's rancho, fifty miles to the north. Whenever they were pursued when running of stock, they had the choice of three places to which to resort.

The people of the surrounding country finally found the existence of this band unendurable. After repeated searches, which failed, owing to the smallness of the pursuing parties, it was resolved to organize several bands, who should cooperate in a campaign, which should end only when the outlaws were driven out of the country, or their capture, dead or alive, was effected. **The authorities of the several counties which bordered on the country ranged over by the Kid's gang had been repeatedly petitioned to send out a posse of men to hunt them down,** but, as Las Portales was on disputed territory, the authorities were never able to settle upon any plan of action. At last the ranchmen took the matter into their own hands, and the first party they sent out succeeded in getting on the track of a detachment of the gang who were hauling material to Las Portales, where they were building large stock yards. Although the party was not successful in capturing the outlaws, they made the outlaws flit about the country in a more lively manner than had been their wont. This showed that nothing could be done by a small force. A guard was always kept out on the numerous peaks about Las Portales, from which outlook; the country for twenty miles either way could be scanned by the outlaws, so that they could easily elude a small party!

The Panhandle Transportation Company, an association of stockmen of western Texas, banded together for mutual protection, commissioned their superintendent, Frank Stewart, a brave fellow, who was just the man for such work, to organize an expedition against the outlaws. The White Oaks, a flourishing mining camp, organized a band of rangers. Still another party of picked men, under the lead of Sheriff Pat Garrett of Lincoln County, who is considered one of the bravest and coolest men in the whole region, joined in the campaign. In the latter part of November Garrett, with a force of fourteen men, made a dash for Bosque Grande, riding all night, and there succeeded in capturing five of the outlaws. One of them was a condemned murderer who had escaped from jail; another of them was a murderer for whose arrest $1,500 had been offered. These are the sort of men who reinforce the band. Las Portales has long been an asylum for fugitives from justice. Bosque Grande (Great Forest) is situated in one of the most fertile regions of the West, and as the rich lands bordering on the Pecos River are the objective point of many who intend to settle in the Territory, it was thought best to rid that region of the outlaws first, in order that none might be deterred from settling there. Precautions have been taken which will prevent this refuge of the band from ever sheltering them again.

It was expected that the two other parties would work with Garrett's band, but the Panhandle party were delayed, owing to scarcity of feed, and the White Oaks Rangers had their hands full in another quarter. **The latter party had a brush with the Kid, Rudabaugh, Wilson, and several others at Coyote Spring, near the Oaks camp, and the outlaws succeeded in escaping, although two had their horses shot from under them.** The rangers started back for reinforcements and supplies, and then pressed on after the outlaws, coming upon them at their other station at Greathouse's ranch. It was night when the rangers reached the ranch. They threw up earthworks a few hundred yards from the stockade of the ranch, and when the outlaws rose up in the morning they found themselves hemmed in. The rangers sent a messenger to Jim Greathouse, the owner of this ranch, demanding the surrender of the outlaws. Greathouse replied in person. He came out to the camp of the rangers and stoutly asserted that the outlaws had taken possession of his ranch and that he had no power over them nor anything to do with them. It was considered best to hold Greathouse as a hostage, while Jim Carlyle, the leader of the rangers, heeded to the Kid's request for a conference. A long time elapsed and Carlyle did not return. His men began to feel uneasy about him, and dispatched a note to the renegade chief saying that unless Carlyle was given up in less than five minutes they would kill Greathouse. No reply was received. **Soon after the rangers saw Carlyle leap from the window and dash down the hill toward their entrenchments. He had not gone far, however, when they saw the Kid throw half his body through the window, and, taking deliberate aim, brought down poor Carlyle, killing him instantly.** A sharp fight followed, but the outlaws succeeded in making their escape, Greathouse also getting away during the confusion. Before leaving for home with the dead body of their leader, the rangers fired everything about the place, and Greathouse concealed some miles away, saw the smoke of his burning property.

The three parties are now engaged in scouting the country, and will not give up the chase till the country is rid of every one of the outlaws. Money and outfits have been freely offered by men who have large interests in that section. Government officials are now interested in the campaign, for, in addition to their other crimes, the outlaws have put in circulation a large quantity of the counterfeit money manufactured William Brockway, the forger. The bills were obtained by one of the gang named Doyle who formerly operated in Chicago, and counterfeit $100 bills in large numbers have been put in circulation among the stockmen and merchants in all that region. The information that enabled the Government officers to discover the handling of counterfeit money by the Kid's gang came from a freighter named Smith. Soon afterward, while Smith was on his way from Las Vegas to Fort Sumner with a load of freight, he was waylaid and murdered by some of the gang.

William Bonney, alias the Kid, the leader of the band, is scarcely over 20 years of age. He is handsome and dresses well. He has a fair complexion, smooth face, blue eyes, and light brown hair. He is about six feet tall and deceptively handsome. A beautiful bay mare, that he has carefully trained, is all that he seems to care for, unless he reserves some affection for his brace of six-shooters and Winchester rifle, which have helped him out of many a tight place. His care of the beautiful mare is well deserved, for many a time has her fleetness which surpasses that of any other horse in the Territory, saved his life. The Kid is an admirable rider, and as he is always expected to be obliged to take flight, he usually rides another horse, leading his pet behind, in order to make the best time possible on a fresh horse. **He is considered a dead shot and much of his time is spent in target practice. He was born in New York State, but his parents removed to Indiana when he was quite small, and** thence to Arizona. **There in the Tombstone District the Kid killed his first man when he was only 17 years old, and was obliged to leave the country. He came to New Mexico, where he has since lived.**

About three years ago a difficulty arose in Lincoln County, New Mexico, between the stockmen and the Indian agent on the reservation. The trouble arose in regard to some cattle that had been purchased for the Indians. Nearly every man in the county was under arms, and the troops were called out by Gov. Wallace to quell the disturbance. **The Kid was mixed up in the affair, and had some narrow escapes. On one occasion he was hotly pursued and was obliged to take refuge in a house in Lincoln, which was surrounded by sixty solders. To the demand to surrender, he only laughed and shot down a soldier just to show that he was game. The house was set on fire, when the Kid, after loading up his Winchester Rifle, leaped from the burning building and made a dash for liberty. All the while he was running he kept firing from his Winchester, bringing down a number of his pursuers. Bullets whistled over his head, but he made his escape, and leaping on a horse was soon laughing at his pursuers. There is no telling how many men he has killed. He sets no value on human life, and has never hesitated at murder** when it would serve his purpose. Gov. Wallace a few days ago offered a reward of $500 for his capture, and prominent citizens would make up a handsome purse in addition.

Billy Wilson is much the same sort of good looking fellow as his chief. He is about the same build, with dark hair and a slight moustache. He left the Ohio home where his people, who are all highly esteemed, still reside, several years ago. After being engaged in the cattle business in Texas for some time, he came to New Mexico. When the excitement broke out over the new camp at White Oaks, he went there and was engaged in the butchering business. He was always considered a smart, energetic fellow, and was well thought of. In some way the Kid persuaded him to join his party, and it was by him that much of the forged paper was put into circulation.

Tom O'Phallier is a Texan and is also a man of good appearance. He has a ruddy, face, and can be an exceedingly agreeable companion. He has been with the band from the first, and has committed many crimes.

Dave Rudabaugh is 36 years old, and was born in New York city, where he lived until about eight years ago. He has raided over southern Kansas, the Indian nations, Texas, southern Colorado, and New Mexico. It would not be difficult to establish charges of murder against him in any or all of those States and Territories. In Colorado, a few years ago he ran off some Government stock, and, while pursued by a detachment of soldiers, he killed a Sergeant and two privates. He once headed an attack on the Las Vegas jail, in order to liberate one of his friends, and shot down a guard who interfered. He is a thorough desperado in look, word, and action, ready at all times for a fight. He thinks no more of putting a bullet through a human brain than through the bull's eyes of the target before which he is continually practicing. He is 5 feet 8 inches tall, and weighs about 180 pounds. He has a swarthy complexion, black hair and beard, and hazel eyes, whose cruel, defiant expression has often been noted.

The career of the band is about run, for they are hotly pursued, and the chances are that before long they will be killed or captured. It is not expected that the Kid or Rudabaugh will be taken alive, as they will fight to the last.

CHAPTER 19

BILLY BONNEY CAPTURED AND JAILED: DECEMBER, 1880

CAPTURE AT STINKING SPRINGS: DECEMBER 21, 1880

ANALYSIS: For the short remainder of his life, Billy was the recipient of the Ring's outlaw propaganda, which Lew Wallace had joined; with the motive of both being cover-up of Ring crimes.

Pat Garrett was a relentless hunter in pursuit of a goal that he knew would profit him for the rest of his life: killing Billy Bonney. There is no indication that he thought Billy was an outlaw king, or that a gigantic gang of counterfeiter-rustlers existed in the Territory. Garrett knew this Ring mission - for which he had been made Lincoln County Sheriff for 1881, and Lincoln County Deputy Sheriff and U.S. Deputy Marshal in 1880 - was to kill Billy.

That killing failed when Garrett and his Azariah Wild-created posse ambushed Billy and his companions entering Fort Sumner on the snowy night of December 19, 1880, and fatally shot Tom O'Folliard. That killing failed on December 22, 1880, when Garrett and his posse again ambushed Billy and his companions 16 miles from Fort Sumner at dawn at the windowless rock shepherds' shelter at Stinking Springs where they had spent the night during their flight from inevitable death in New Mexico Territory. There, Garrett fatally shot Charlie Bowdre, thinking he was Billy because he exited the shelter wearing Billy's sombrero. Garrett even kept dead Bowdre's bloody carte de visite of him and his wife as a souvenir; as he later kept his Colt .44, serial number 55093, with which he shot Billy.

So Garrett satisfied himself with capture of Billy that December 22nd, transporting him to the Santa Fe jail for an inevitable hanging trial.

On December 23, 1880, Azariah Wild writing in Santa Fe for December 22nd, had been sent immediate word about Stinking Springs, using it to validate his *"Kid & Wilson gang,"* and epitomizing the outrageous absurdity of his fraudulent endeavor by adding Jesse James as a gang member. Wild wrote:

> *I am also in receipt of information of a reliable character that Deputy Marshal P.F. Garrett has killed one of the Kid & Wilson gang, and badly wounded another in attempting to arrest them. He is still in pursuit of the balance of the outlaws: Jessie James is surely there under the name of Campbell.*

On December 24, 1880, Wild, seeking reimbursement for his buffoonish miner's disguise clothing, wrote his report in Santa Fe for December 23rd, and recounted his meeting with Lew Wallace, his fellow outlaw fabricator, who was clearly delighted to piggy-back on Wild's concoctions. Wild wrote:

> *I called on Gov. Wallace who was anxious to know the situation and stated such facts as I know. He at once said "tell Mr Garrett to follow these men any place in the territory and tell him I say so."*
>
> *The Governor asked me to remain over one day longer and call on him Friday to which I agreed ...*
>
> *I will leave for New Orleans Saturday December 25th 1880.*
>
> *On the 24th day of September ... I purchased a suit of miners clothing to disguise myself in and asked you how in what manner I should charge them up. In compliance with your letter I now charge them to [Secret Service] Division.*

On January 1, 1881, back in New Orleans, Louisiana, Wild reported for December 24, 1880 more about Stinking Springs, implying a Ring informer monitoring Garrett's pursuit. He wrote:

> *I have this day received information of an almost positive nature, that Deputy U.S. Marshal P.F. Garrett has the Kid & Wilson gang of outlaws at his mercy and that he will either kill or arrest them.*

TRANSPORT TO THE SANTA FE JAIL

On December 27, 1880, the *Las Vegas Daily Gazette,* published an article by Lucius "Lute" Wilcox about the Stinking Springs capture and prisoner transport to Las Vegas titled 'The Kid. Interview with Billy Bonney The Best Known Man in New Mexico, The greatest excitement prevailed yesterday when the news was abroad that Pat Garrett and Frank Stewart had arrived in town bringing with them Billy 'the Kid.'"

There was no doubt that Billy, with his increasingly famous moniker "Billy the Kid," was the prize catch. And the Wilcox interview showed that Billy's spirit and insouciance continued unabated as he brilliantly teased and taunted any future hangman and his own fate.

About the gathered crowd and his defamatory press, Billy said: "Well, perhaps some of them will think me half man now; everyone seems to think I was some sort of animal." And when the reporter commented on his dire fate, he reposited: "What's the use of looking on the gloomy side of everything. The laugh's on me this time." And though reporter, "Lute" Wilcox, was fabricating the outlaw Billy the Kid, the real Billy Bonney remains intact in playful and seductive glory; charming his audience of curious and admiring locals gathered outside the jail because of his celebrity presence. Wilcox wrote:

With its customary enterprise, the *Gazette* was the first paper to give the story of the capture of Billy Bonney, who has risen to notoriety under the sobriquet of "the Kid," Billy Wilson, Dave Rudabaugh and Tom Pickett. Just at this time everything of interest about the men is especially interesting, and after damning the men in general and "the Kid" in particular through the columns of this paper we considered it the correct thing to give them a show.

Through the kindness of [San Miguel County] Sheriff Romero, a representative of the *Gazette* was admitted to the jail yesterday morning.

Mike Cosgrove, the obliging mail contractor, who has met the boys frequently while on business down the Pecos, had just gone in with four large bundles. The doors at the entrance stood open, and the large crowd strained their necks to get a glimpse of the prisoners, who stood in the passageway like children waiting for a Christmas tree distribution. One by one the bundles were unpacked disclosing a good suit of clothes for each man. Mr. Cosgrove remarked that he wanted "to see the boys go away in style."

"Billy the Kid," and Billy Wilson who were shackled together stood patiently while a blacksmith took off their shackles and bracelets to allow them an opportunity to make a change of clothing. Both prisoners watched the operation which was to set them free for a short while, but Wilson scarcely raised his eyes, and spoke but once or twice to his compadres. **Bonney on the other hand, was light and chipper, and was very communicative, laughing, joking and chatting with the bystanders.**

"You appear to take it easy," the reporter said.

"**Yes! What's the use of looking at the gloomy side of everything. The laugh's on me this time,**" he said. Then looking about the placita, he asked: "Is the jail at Santa Fe any better than this?"

This seemed to trouble him considerably, for as he explained, "this is a terrible place to put a fellow in." He put the same question to every one who came near him and when he learned that there was nothing better in store for him, he shrugged his shoulders and said something about putting up with what he had to.

He was the attraction of the show, and as he stood there, lightly kicking the toes of his boots on the stone pavement to keep his feet warm, one would scarcely mistrust that he was the hero of "Forty Thieves," romance which this paper has been running in serial form for six weeks or more.

"**There was a big crowd gazing at me wasn't there?**" he exclaimed, and then smiling continued: "**Well perhaps some of them will think me half a man now; everyone seems to think I was some kind of an animal.**"

He did look human, indeed, but there was nothing very mannish about him in appearance, for he looked and acted like a mere boy. He is about five feet, eight or nine inches tall, slightly built and lithe, weighing about 140; a frank and open countenance, looking like a school boy, with the traditional silky fuzz on his upper lip, clear blue eyes, with a roguish snap about them, light hair and complexion. He is, in all, quite a handsome looking fellow, the only imperfection being two prominent front teeth, slightly protruding like a squirrels' teeth, and he has agreeable and winning ways.

On December 28, 1880, Billy was again interviewed for the Las Vegas *Gazette* when still in Las Vegas, but inside the train for departure to the Santa Fe jail. The reporter was either editor "Lute" Wilcox or owner J.H. Koogler, for "Interview with the Kid."

Billy's nonchalant banter reflects his steely self-control when one realizes that during his interview his train was being detained by an aggressive mob on the tracks, with unclear intent either to lynch or to rescue him. Billy's teasing of the reporter was punctuated by flashing his handcuff: "They wouldn't let me settle down; if they had I wouldn't be here today." And he held up his right arm on which was the bracelet." He also joked about his Stinking Springs capture - concealing his pain about Charlie Bowdre's killing - mistaken for him - and merely floated a silly dime novel escape fantasy about jumping his famous bay mare out of the rock-walled line cabin's doorway, which was obstructed by a dead horse, earlier shot by Pat Garrett. Billy was quoted: "If it had not been for the dead horse in the doorway I wouldn't be here in Las Vegas. I would have ridden out on my bay mare and taken my chances of escaping. But I couldn't ride over that for she would have jumped back and I would have got it in the head."

With the mob dispersed and the train finally departing, Billy avoided morbidity by giving the reporter another joke: "As the train rolled out, [H]e lifted his hat and invited us to call and see him in Santa Fe, calling out 'adios.'" The article stated:

We saw him again at the depot when the crowd presented a really war like appearance. Standing by the car, out of one of the windows from which he was leaning, he talked freely with us of the whole affair:

"I don't blame you for writing of me as you have. You have had to believe others' stories, but then I don't know as anyone would believe anything good of me, anyway," he said. "I really wasn't the leader of any gang. I was for Billy all the time. About that Portales business, I owned the ranch with Charlie Bowdre. I took it up and was holding it because I knew that at some time a stage line would run there, and I wanted to keep it for a station. **But I found that there were certain men who wouldn't let me live in the country and so I was going to leave.**

[AUTHOR'S NOTE: Billy conceals pain by omitting that his plan "*to leave*" because "*certain men wouldn't let me live in the country*" involved Pat Garrett's murdering Tom O'Folliard nine days before as cause of that decision.]

We had all our grub in the house when they took us in, and we were going to a place six miles away in the morning to cook it and then light out. I haven't stolen any stock. I made my living by gambling, but that was the only way I could live. **They wouldn't let me settle down; if they had I wouldn't be here today,"** and he held up his right arm on which was the bracelet.

[AUTHOR'S NOTE: Billy seems to refer to the lost pardon which was intended to let him settle down.]

"Chisum got me into all this trouble and then wouldn't help me out. I went up to Lincoln to stand my trial on the warrant that was out for me, but the Territory took a change of venue to Dona Ana, and I knew I had no show, and so I skinned out ...

If it had not been for the dead horse in the doorway I wouldn't be here in Las Vegas. I would have ridden out on my bay mare and taken my chances of escaping. But I couldn't ride over that for she would have jumped back **and I would have got it in the head**. We could have stayed in the house but there wouldn't have been anything gained by that for they would have starved us out. I thought it was better to come out and get a square meal - don't you?"

The prospects of a fight exhilarated him, and he bitterly bemoaned being chained. "If I only had my Winchester, I'd lick the whole crowd" was his confident comment on the strength of the attacking party. He sighed and sighed again for the chance to take a hand in the fight and the burden of his desire was to be set free to fight on the side of his captors as soon as he should smell powder.

As the train rolled out, he lifted his hat and invited us to call and see him in Santa Fe, calling out "*adios.*"

KILLING ANOTHER REBEL: MIMBRES APACHE CHIEF VICTORIO: OCTOBER 14, 1880

With success of his outlaw myth, on December 29, 1880, Lew Wallace related to Secretary of the Interior Carl Schurz the pursuit of New Mexico Territory's other rebel, Mimbres Apache chief, Victorio. A governor now himself, Wallace apparently enjoyed replicating another of his father's achievements: the 1838 massacre of 150 Potawatomis Indians, who, like Victorio, had refused unjust relocation. This was Wallace's own "Indian War." Wallace wrote:

Executive Office,
Santa Fe, N.M.
Dec. 29. 1879.

Hon. C. Schurz
Sec. Dept. Interior

Sir:
The enclosed communication received yesterday from Mr. Louis Scott, U.S. Consul at Chihuahua, Mexico, is of importance in connection with the Apache troubles in New Mexico, and will explain itself.

If Gen. Treviño, or some Mexican commander makes the proposed campaign against the hostiles in the State of Chihuahua, the result will probably be that the latter will be driven across the line into this Territory; in which event, if there could be some concert of action permitted between the military of the two powers, there is little doubt that between the two the enemy could be effectively disposed of. But knowing the delicacy of the business, I think it necessary to refer the matter and take direction.

Very respectfully,
Your friend & servant,
Lew. Wallace,
Governor of New Mexico.

It has occurred to me that possibly, through Gov. Terrazas, who has been so scotched in property, some reciprocal arrangement could be made for the reclamation of property stolen from the citizens of the republics.

Matching Billy's lurid press was Victorio's killing in Mexico as reported in the October 20, 1880' Las Cruces *Thirty-Four Newspaper* as "Glory! Hallelujah!! Victorio Killed." Victorio had been chased into Old Mexico by over 200 soldiers. From the Mexican side came Joaquín Terrazas, with over 350 men. Victorio was surrounded on a small mountain, and he and his band killed and scalped for the bounties. The article stated:

GLORY!
Hallelujah!!
VICTORIO KILLED
WAR ENDED!!!
PEACE!

Governor Terrasas telegraphs that the Mexican troops under his brother came up with Victorio at Tres Castillos, near Pino mountains, on the 14th and killed Victorio and fifty of his warriors and eighteen squaws and children and captured 70 squaws and children and two hundred and fifty head of stock. The news is official and is telegraphed all over the country for general information.

Gen. Buell was recalled from Mexico just in time to prevent his reaping the full benefit of his chase after the hostiles. He chased them several hundred miles into Mexico and to a point a hundred and fifty miles from Fort Quitman and was on a hot trail when ordered to return. His pursuit of them so far across the line rendered their defeat by the Mexican troops only a question of time, and to him and his command is due a large share of the praise for the ending of this terrible war. But for the meddling which caused his recall, he would not doubt have done just what the Mexicans have done. It is to be regretted that he did not get far enough into the interior to be out of reach of orders. It is now in order for the *New Mexican* to claim that Hatch planned the whole campaign. It is known everywhere on this border that he had nothing to do with it except that he did everything in his power to prevent it becoming a success. That this battle will end the war, there can scarcely be a doubt. Hurrah for Buell and Terrasas.

Lew Wallace capitalized on that genocidal momentum. On November 30, 1880, writing to Carl Schurz, he linked Victorio's slaughter to his own mission to pacify the Territory in an unconsciously revealing admission of his consistently brutal attempts at repression, capturing, and killing as a solution to the Territorial "troubles." All that remained now for Wallace's completion of his pardon betrayal was actually killing Billy, who, by his fault, had by then been successfully transmogrified into the entire outlaw "trouble" causing Territorial distress as "Billy the Kid." And exuberant Wallace was again transformed in his own mind to "the General" in Civil War-like battle. So, when referring to Ringite U.S. Attorney Sidney Barnes in the letter, he makes his title *"Col. Barnes who can then operate through the proper court."* Wallace wrote:

Executive Office,
SANTA FE, N.M.
November 30 1880.

Hon. C. Schurz,
Sec. Dept. Interior.
Sir.

I have the honor to report that I returned to this city last week, having been unavoidably detained two days over my leave of absence by interruptions on the road occasioned by snow and cold weather.

It gives me pleasure to inform you that, now that Victorio is dead, this Territory is peaceful, and the government going on smoothly. Business continues excellent. I know, indeed, but one matter important enough to deserve your serious consideration.

The people along the confines of the Navajo reservation live in a state of alarm, which, from the accounts I receive, rather grows than abates. They say ... an outbreak of the young men of the tribe may occur at any moment ...

The cause is undoubtedly the unlawful sale of whiskey, which, it is but truth to say, is on the increase ...

In this state of the affairs, I venture to respectfully submit a suggestion.

Capt. Fletcher, your timber agent here, is well known over the Territory ... It would be a good thing, if you can consistently do so, to send him to Ft. Wingate under cover to make inquest in connection with this agency, but with private instructions to sift thoroughly the contraband traffic, find the names of the parties engaged in it, and witnesses, and make report to Col. [U.S. Attorney Sidney] Barnes who can then operate through the proper court. I have spoken to Capt. Fletcher about the matter, and he is willing to undertake it, if so instructed. I think him an excellent man for the business.

Permit me to urge speedy action.

Very respectfully,
Your friend & servant,
Lew. Wallace,
Gov. New Mexico.

BILLY'S FOUR LAST AND UNANSWERED PARDON PLEA LETTERS TO LEW WALLACE: JANUARY 1, 1881 - MARCH 27, 1881

Billy never stopped pleading with Lew Wallace for his pardon, being certain of his fulfilled bargain. But Billy's four last request letters - written to Wallace during Billy's almost three month imprisonment in the Santa Fe jail awaiting transport to his Mesilla trial - became demands. His righteous tone likely contributed to Wallace's later guilty pardon obsession of publishing self-serving versions through the early 1900's.

Wallace was particularly enraged by Billy's March 2, 1881 letter, which he called blackmail; but may have frightened him as referring to now lost letters in which he had put the pardon promise in writing in 1879 to Ira Leonard or to Billy himself. Billy had stated: *"I have some letters which date back two years, and there are Parties who are very anxious to get them but I shall not dispose of them until I see you. that is if you will come immediately."* Wallace answered none of Billy's jail letters. But he took them with the rest of his Billy communications when he left New Mexico Territory, and then carefully preserved them.

And it is noteworthy that while "crucifying" Billy, Wallace was paying no attention to him, instead basking in accolades for his just released *Ben-Hur: A Tale of the Christ*, giving press interviews, and making plans for mining investments in New Mexico Territory.

BILLY'S FIRST JAIL LETTER: JANUARY 1, 1881

On January 1, 1881, Billy wrote:

>   *Santa Fe*
>   *Jan 1st*
>   *1881*
>   *Gov. Lew Wallace*
>   *Dear Sir*
>   *I would like to see you for a few moments if You can spare the time.*
>   *Yours Respect.*
>   *W.HBonney*

WALLACE INTERVIEWED AS MILITARY EXPERT: JANUARY 3, 1881

Two days later, on January 3, 1881, for the Chicago *Daily Inter Ocean's* "General Lew Wallace Interviewed," Wallace pretended to be a military pundit - belied by Shiloh - about repeal of the Posse Comitatus Act - in chilling disregard of Lincoln County horrors of treasonous soldiers. It was reprinted for the *Crawfordsville Journal* of February 26, 1881 as "Governor Wallace. Chat About Use of Troops in New Mexico and His New Book." In it, one can see - as Billy languished in the Santa Fe jail awaiting completion of the Atchison, Topeka, and Santa Fe tracks to Mesilla to avoid a partisan rescue - the impossibility of Billy's being pardoned in Wallace's fiction now formed around "bands of thieves, robbers, and murderers. They think no more of shooting a man than a deer." The article stated:

"You went to Washington, I believe, to urge the Senate to modify the posse comitatus clause in the army bill?"

"Yes, sir, that was the immediate purpose of my journey. I felt that something must be done to preserve the peace, life and property of the territory... If Congress will amend the law so that it will not refer to New Mexico, life and property can be made as safe there as in any part of the Union."

"Where does the lawlessness chiefly exist?"

"In the southern portion of New Mexico, and the northern part of New Mexico. **That stretch of country is infested by bands of thieves, robbers, and murderers. They think no more of shooting a man than a deer** ... When a deputy marshal armed with the requisite authority and assisted by a posse pursues them, they retreat into old Mexico and snap their fingers derisively at their pursuers ... If I was authorized to call on the military and send the regular troops after them they would soon be annihilated ..."

"What can you say of the general character of the territory?"

"Otherwise it is peaceful. The Indians are the only people to be feared ... My only doubt [about passage of the bill] is that in the political fight which is constantly going on, my bill will not be reached in time to secure its passage."

"To turn from politics to literature, I wish to inquire with what success your new book, "Ben Hur, a tale of the Christ," is meeting?"

"Its reception has been very gratifying to me ... The first edition was soon exhausted, a second edition has already been issued."

WALLACE PRAISED FOR BEN-HUR: JANUARY 9, 1881

On January 9, 1881, Wallace received praise from President Rutherford B. Hayes for *Ben-Hur*. Hayes wrote:

**EXECUTIVE MANSION,
WASHINGTON.**

9 Jany 1881
My Dear Mr. Wallace:
We are greatly obliged by your kindness. With too little time for reading to finish the book now it has given us great satisfaction to read the parts you indicate. After we leave here we hope to have time to indulge our fondness for good books, and will reckon among the pleasures in store for us this work which you have sent.
With best wishes
Sincerely
RB Hayes

BILLY'S SECOND JAIL LETTER: MARCH 2, 1881

On March 2, 1881, Billy sent his second jail letter, about which Wallace would obsess for the next 20 years as "blackmail." Billy wrote:

Santa Fe Jail New Mex
March 2nd 1881
Gov. Lew Wallace
Dear Sir
I wish you would come down to the jail to see me. it will be to your interest to come and see me. ***I have some letters which date back two years, and there are Parties who are very anxious to get them but I shall not dispose of them until I see you. that is if you will come immediately***
Yours Respect
Wm H Bonney

BILLY'S THIRD JAIL LETTER: MARCH 4, 1881

On March 4, 1881, Billy wrote his third jail letter in tragic confirmation of the pardon's betrayal: *"I have done everything that I promised you I would, and You have done nothing that You promised me."* Billy also stated: *"I guess they mean to Send me up without giving me any Show"* - *"they"* being as close to *"you"* as Billy could let himself come to admitting yet another abandonment by a father-figure - adding to his real father, stepfather, and losses by deaths of Tunstall, McSween, and Chapman. Billy wrote:

Santa Fe. In jail.
March 4th 1881

Gov. Lew Wallace
Dear Sir
    I wrote You a little note the day before yesterday but have received no annser. I Expect you have forgotten what you promised me, this Month two Years ago. but I have not, and I think You had ought to have come and seen me as I requested you to. **I have done everything that I promised you I would, and You have done nothing that You promised me.**

I think when You think the matter over, You will come down and See me, and I can then Explain Everything to You.

Judge Leonard, Passed through here on his way East, in january and promised to come and See me on his way back. but he did not fulfill his Promise. it looks to me like I am getting left in the Cold. I am not treated right by [U.S. Marshal John] Sherman. he lets Every Stranger that comes to See me through Curiosity in to See me, but will not let a Single one of my friends in, not Even an Attorney.

I guess they mean to Send me up without giving me any Show. but they will have a nice time doing it. I am not entirely without friends.
    I shall Expect to See you Sometime today
    Patiently Waiting
    I am Very truly Yours, Respect.
    W<u>m</u> H. Bonney.

WALLACE PRAISED FOR BEN-HUR: MARCH 17, 1881

Thirteen days after Billy's third letter, on March 17, 1881, Wallace got a letter from a man of Christ, Archbishop Jean-Baptist Lamy of Santa Fe's magnificent Church of Saint Francis, close to the Palace of the Governors. Lamy added to praise for *Ben-Hur*, writing:

> His Excellency Governor Wallace
> Permit me to thank you for your fine book, <u>Ben-Hur a Tale of the Christ</u>. I have read it all through and find it very interesting. I think also, it is written in good Christian spirit.
> Yours truly,
> J.B. Lamy
> Archbishop of Santa Fé

Santa Fé, New Mexico
  March 17. 1881.

WALLACE MAKES MINING PLANS: MARCH 19, 1881

On March 19, 1881, Wallace's preoccupation with himself continued in his letter to his son, Henry; whom he treated as a useful appendage, and signed as "Lew Wallace." Wallace wrote:

Executive Office,
Santa Fe, New Mexico,
<u>March 19   1881</u>.

My dear Henry.
  As you have doubtless seen by the papers, the President has appointed a General Sheldon or some other person to be Governor of New Mexico. This does not surprise me, and it is not the least disagreeable. I have held this office until I have accomplished what I wanted – the acquirement of what I consider as good mining property as there is in the Territory. The time has come to make it available, if I mean to do so. With that view chiefly I offered my resignation to the President, and he has accepted it by making the appointment referred to.

Now I am going down to San Simeon to personally superintend the development of my claims there; that is, the claims in that district in which, you will recollect, I have a half interest in three of the best, and a quarter interest in three – properties which I would not give for any other I have seen; and I have been to all those said to be most promising. Upon the result I am willing to stake everything. I have: viz., the few years remaining of life.

Now what I want you to do for me, is to find when you can borrow $1000 for a year's time upon the best terms, and send it to me as soon as you can. For I am going immediately to work. Send it in form to be my credit in the banking house of <u>H.M. Porter, Silver City, Grant County, New Mexico</u>.

If not for a year, get it on the longest time possible.

If you can get it elsewhere, do not get it at the Elston Bank [of Wallace's rich brother-in-law]; for I do not want any in that concern, or, for that matter, anywhere else to know of the transaction, or what I am about – not even your mother. She has no faith (in that she may be right).

The lesson of my life is, talent and honor amount to nothing in this age and in our country <u>without money</u>. If I win, you understand you will be the beneficiary.

            Your father,
            Lew. Wallace.

BILLY'S FOURTH JAIL LETTER: MARCH 27, 1881

On March 27, 1881, Billy wrote to Wallace for the last time in his fourth jail letter, emphasizing the pardon promise. With Billy's tenacity and legal knowledge, he may have still hoped that the pardon would be issued at its technically proper time: after his sentencing in the Mesilla trial to come. Billy wrote:

           Santa Fe New Mexico
       March 27th/81
    Gov Lew Wallace
     Dear Sir
         for the last <u>time</u> I ask: Will you keep Your promise I start below tomorrow. Send Annser by bearer.
      Yours Respt
       WBonney

WALLACE MAKES MINING PLANS: MARCH 29, 1881

Two days later, on March 29, 1881, Wallace wrote again to his son, Henry, this time with a quixotic fantasy of becoming a miner himself; with Billy's real and tragic world extinguished in his mind. Wallace wrote:

Executive Office,
SANTA FE, N.M.
March 29 1881.

My dear Henry.
Thank you for the letter and the action you propose.
It is my intention to go down to San Simeon, pitch a tent, live as the miners do, watch where every dollar goes, and every item of property, where every pick is struck, and keep the time of my hands, paying them by the <u>hour</u>. That way I can make $1000 go a long way.

On one of the claims, the "Homestake," there has been more than $500 of work done already; on two others, the "Carpenter" and the "Wallace," more than $100 work on each; leaving $800 more due on the two latter, after which I can get a patent for the silver mines. In the further expedition I pay but one half, being amt. of my interest in the three claims. You will notice that freezing out of those claims is impossible. My half interest saves me.

In the same district I have quarter interest in three other claims – The "Fry," "Peggy Ellison," and "Cornucopia." But as I do not think them as desirable as the others, I will confine my effort in the first place exclusively to the "Homestake," "Carpenter" and "Wallace."

I shall not come home until I have opened these mines and made then ready for sale or operation.
Truly, your father,
Lew. Wallace.

CHAPTER 20

BILLY BONNEY'S TRIALS BY THE SANTA FE RING: MARCH-APRIL, 1881

HANGING TRIALS IN MESILLA

ANALYSIS: Billy Bonney's capture left him in the power of the Santa Fe Ring, now able to kill him under the guise of law by hanging in a rigged court. Lew Wallace could have saved him by the pardon, but did not. Loyal Ira Leonard became Billy's defense attorney, until threat of assassination made him withdraw. So Billy was left alone with lethal enemies and an inevitable outcome.

Once captured, Billy Bonney faced an inevitable hanging sentence in the Ring-controlled Mesilla court, as intended by colluding District Attorney William Rynerson and 3rd Judicial District Judge Warren Bristol's 1878 venue change from Lincoln County - where jurymen would know Lincoln County War issues - to Doña Ana County, where the War was unknown. Billy's added disadvantage was that potentially favorable defense witnesses - like Justice of the Peace "Squire" Wilson or Juan Patrón - were too terrified to again risk assassination; and Billy's outlaw vilification must have seemed impenetrable to truth.

Of course, this should have been the time for Governor Lew Wallace to issue the pardon at last. But Wallace was long checkmated by the Ring and his selfish agenda. Billy's only ally was Ira Leonard, still representing him for free; until Leonard's surprising court victory must have elicited a death threat, which forced his leaving Billy to Ring-biased public defenders and a certain death sentence.

TRANSPORT TO MESILLA FOR TRIAL

Attorney Ira Leonard bravely and protectively accompanied Billy from Santa Fe on the Atchison, Topeka, and Santa Fe Railroad, whose southward progressing track construction only reached the Rincón depot. From there, Leonard stayed with Billy for the stagecoach ride to Las Cruces. With them were guards and Billy Wilson. At Las Cruces, a crowd had gathered to see the famous outlaw, Billy the Kid.

A spectator named W.S. Fletcher from Mesilla either asked, or saw someone ask, the group which was "the Kid." Billy's cheeky response was reported in the April 3, 1881 Santa Fe *Daily New Mexican* in: "Something About the Kid." With undaunted teasing, Billy indicated balding, middle aged Leonard, declaring: "This is the man!" That same article, filled with misinformation, also gave Billy's retaliatory quip: "At least two hundred men have been killed in Lincoln County during the past three years, but I did not kill all of them." The entire article stated:

Something about the Kid.

An extract of a letter written by W.S. Fletcher from Mesilla to a gentleman in the city reads about as follows: Tony Neis and Francisco Chaves, deputy U.S. Marshals, arrived Thursday night with **Billy, the Kid,** and Billy Wilson. They met an ugly crowd at Rincon, where some threats were made, but Tony's crowd were too much for them. **At Las Cruces an impulsive mob gathered around the coach and someone asked which is "Billy the Kid." The Kid himself answered by placing his hand on Judge Leonard's shoulder and saying "this is the man."** The Kid weakened somewhat at Las Cruces, where he found quite a number of Lincoln County men, who were to appear against him as witnesses.

[AUTHOR'S NOTE: Billy had no defense witnesses. The prosecution had Ringites James Dolan, Saturnino Baca, and Sheriff William Brady's deputy, Billy Matthews; and subpoenaed Lincolnite, Isaac Ellis.]

He says at least two hundred men have been killed in Lincoln County during the past three years, but that he did not kill all of them. I think twenty murders can be charged against him. He was arraigned yesterday (Wednesday) before the United States court for the murder of Roberts, on the Mescalaro Apache reservation, in 1878. Judge Leonard was assigned to his defense. Judge Newcomb gave notice that he had three other indictments for murder against him, and it looks as if he had no show to get off. His counsel asked today for time to send to Lincoln, which was granted, so that his trial will not commence for at least ten days. Billy Wilson's case is before the grand jury. He is charged with passing counterfeit money. He has retained Judge Thornton as his counsel. He seems to have friends here while the Kid has none.

No mails between Rincon and Doña Ana for the past week. Mosquitoes and flies abound and weather hot as blazes.

SURPRISE QUASHING OF THE FEDERAL MURDER INDICTMENT: MARCH 30, 1881

U.S. Attorney Thomas Benton Catron's June 21, 1878 federal indictment, Case Number 411, for Billy Bonney and other Regulators in the Andrew "Buckshot" Roberts Blazer's Mill killing was a trap long set against pardon by any Territorial governor; though unknown to Billy, but likely known to Lew Wallace.

On March 30, 1881, under Judge Warren Bristol, it was Billy's first indictment to be heard; strategically to achieve a hanging sentence immune to gubernatorial pardon. The prosecutor was Ringite U.S. Attorney Sidney Barnes, who had replaced Catron. But Attorney Ira Leonard surprised that court. He filed a motion to quash the indictment based on its invalidity.

In the resulting juryless hearing before Judge Bristol, with Prosecutor Barnes present, Leonard argued that Catron's indictment based its federal status by claiming that Blazer's Mill was part of the federally-controlled Mescalero Indian Reservation, where a murder would correctly be under federal jurisdiction. But since Blazer's Mill was, in fact, private property owned by Dr. Joseph Blazer, and irrelevantly within the Reservation's perimeter, it came under Territorial law for private land. That argument was correct. Bristol was forced to quash the indictment. The Ring had underestimated Leonard after observing his mediocre Dudley Court of Inquiry arguments.

So the Ring reverted to its usual response to opposition: death threat followed by real death. Leonard, having barely survived Ring assassination on April 25, 1879, only 67 days after Huston Chapman's actual killing, abruptly abandoned Billy's defense. Billy was left with court-appointed Ring-biased public defenders, Attorneys Albert Jennings Fountain and John Bail, for his William Brady and George Hindman murder trials' defense.

And it should be noted that if the Brady and Hindman indictments did not yield a hanging sentence, Bristol could gotten a Territorial one against Billy for the Roberts killing.

PREJUDICIAL PRESS

To prejudice potential jurymen for the next trial, Ring press spewed out the outlaw myth of Billy the Kid. On April 2, 1881, *Newman's Semi-Weekly*" ran an article titled "The Kid;" stating:

[The Kid] is a notoriously dangerous character, has on several occasions before escaped justice where escape appeared even more improbable than now, and has made his brags that he only wants to get free in order to kill three men – one of them being Governor Wallace. Should he break jail now, there is no doubt that he would immediately proceed to execute his threat ... We expect every day to hear of his escape and hope that legal technicalities may not be permitted to render escape more probable.

TRIAL FOR BRADY'S MURDER: APRIL 8-9, 1881

Chosen next for a jury's likely hanging sentence was the murder of Lincoln County's Sheriff: Case No. 532, New Mexico Territory versus Billy Bonney for the murder of William Brady. Billy was defended by Attorneys Albert Jennings Fountain and John Bail. For prosecution was Ringite District Attorney Simon Newcomb, one of the lawyers who freed Lew Wallace's captives in Fort Stanton by *habeas corpus* on April 13, 1879 to sabotage his prosecution of Ring criminals.

With likely Ring expurgation, the transcript for that trial is now lost. But under Judge Warren Bristol, and with Ringite prosecution witnesses like James Dolan, Jacob Basil "Billy" Matthews, and Saturnino Baca - along with subpoenaed terrified Lincoln merchant, Isaac Ellis, and no defense witnesses - Billy had no chance of avoiding conviction.

JUDGE BRISTOL'S BIASED JURY INSTRUCTIONS

However, Judge Bristol's prejudicial jury instructions do exist, and show that he made first degree murder the necessary verdict - meaning that the only sentence could be hanging. Bristol stated: *"There is no evidence before you showing that the killing of Brady is murder in any degree than the first ... The legislature of this Territory has enacted a law prescribing that the punishment for murder in the 1st degree shall be death."* And since first degree murder required *"premeditated design,"* Bristol made that inevitable also, stating: *"If the design to kill is completely formed in the mind but for a moment before inflicting the fatal wounds it would be premeditated and in law the effect would be the same as though the design to kill had existed for a long time."* The instructions stated in full:

Territory of New Mexico
District Court 3d Judicial
District Doña Ana County
April Term A.D. 1881

In the Third Judicial
District Court April Term / 1879

Territory of New Mexico)
vs)
) Murder
William Bonney alias Kid) 1st Degree
Alias William Antrim)

Gentlemen of the Jury:

The defendant in this case William Bonney alias Kid alias William Antrim is charged in and by the indictment against him which has been laid before you with having committed in connection with certain other persons the crime of murder in the County of Lincoln in the 3d Judicial District of the Territory of New Mexico in the month of April of the year 1878 by then and there unlawfully killing one William Brady by inflicting upon his body certain fatal gunshot wounds from a premeditated design to effect his death.

The case is here for trial by a change of venue from the said County of Lincoln.

The facts alleged in the indictment if true constitute Murder in the 1st and highest degree and whether these allegations are true or not true are for you to determine from the evidence which you have heard and which is now submitted to you for your careful consideration.

In the matter of determining what your verdict shall be it will be improper for you to consider anything except the evidence before you.

You as Jurors are the exclusive judges of the weight of the evidence. You are the exclusive judges of the credibility of the witnesses. It is for you to determine whether the testimony of any witnesses whom you have heard is to be believed or not. You are also the exclusive judges whether the evidence is sufficiently clear and strong to satisfy your minds that the defendant is guilty.

There is no evidence tending to show that the killing of Brady was either justifiable or excusable by law. As a matter of law therefore such killing was unlawful and whoever committed the deed or was present and advised or aided or abetted and consented to such killing committed the crime of murder in some one of the degrees of murder.

There is no evidence before you showing that the killing of Brady is murder in any degree than the first.

Your verdict therefore should be either that the defendant is guilty of the murder in the 1st degree or that he is not guilty at all under this indictment.

Murder in the 1st degree consists in the killing of one human being by another without authority of law and from a premeditated design to affect the death of the person killed.

Every killing of one human being by another that is not justifiable or excusable should be necessarily a killing without authority of law.

As I have already instructed you to consider murder in the 1st degree it is necessary that the killing should have been perpetrated from a premeditated design to effect the death of the person killed.

As to this premeditated design I charge you that to render design to kill premeditated it is not necessary that such design to kill should exist in the mind for any considerable length of time before the killing.

If the design to kill is completely formed in the mind but for a moment before inflicting the fatal wounds it would be premeditated and in law the effect would be the same as though the design to kill had existed for a long time.

In this case in order to justify you in finding this defendant guilty of murder in the 1st degree under the peculiar circumstances as presented by the indictment and the evidence you should be satisfied and believe from the evidence to the exclusion of every reasonable doubt of the truth of several propositions.

1st That the defendant either inflicted one or more of the fatal wounds causing Brady's death or that he was present at the time and place of the killing and encouraged – incited – aided in – abetted – advised or commanded such killing.

2d That such killing was without justification or excuse.

3d That such killing of Brady was caused by inflicting upon his body a fatal gunshot wound.

And 4th that such fatal wound was either inflicted by the defendant upon a premeditated design to effect Brady's death or that he was present at the time and place of the killing of Brady and from a premeditated design to effect his death he then and there encouraged – incited – aided in – abetted – advised or commanded such killing.

If he was so present – encouraging – inciting – aiding in – abetting – advising – or commanding the killing of Brady he is as much guilty as though he fired the fatal shot.

I have charged you that to justify you in finding the defendant guilty of murder in the 1st degree you should be satisfied from the evidence to the exclusion of every reasonable doubt that the defendant is actually guilty.

As to what would be or would not be reasonable doubt of guilt I charge you that belief in the guilt of the defendant to the exclusion of every reasonable doubt does not require you to so believe absolutely and to mathematical certainty – That is to justify a verdict of guilty it is not necessary for you to be as certain that the defendant is guilty as you are that two and two are four or that two and three are five.

Merely a vague conjecture or bare possibility that the defendant may be innocent is not sufficient to raise reasonable doubt of his guilt.

If all the evidence before you which you believe to be true convinces and directs your understanding and satisfies your reason and judgment while acting upon it conscientiously under your oath as jurors and if this evidence leaves in your minds an abiding conviction to a moral certainty that the defendant is guilty of the crime charged against him: then this would be proof of guilt to the exclusion of every reasonable doubt and would justify you in finding the defendant guilty.

You will apply the evidence to this case according to the instructions I have given you and determine whether the defendant is guilty of murder in the 1st degree or not guilty.

Murder in the 1st degree is the greatest crime known to our laws. The legislature of this Territory has enacted a law prescribing that the punishment for murder in the 1st degree shall be death.

This then is the law: No other punishment than death can be imposed – for murder in the 1st degree.

If you believe and are satisfied therefore from the evidence before you to the exclusion of every reasonable doubt that the defendant is guilty of murder in the 1st degree then it will be your duty to find a verdict that the defendant is guilty of murder in that degree naming murder in the 1st degree in your verdict and also saying in your verdict that the defendant shall suffer the punishment of death.

If from the evidence you do not believe to the exclusion of every reasonable doubt that the defendant is guilty of murder in the 1st degree or if you entertain a reasonable doubt as to the guilt of the defendant, then in that case your verdict should be not guilty.

<u>532</u>

Territory
   Vs.   ) Murder
William Bonney
Alias "Kid" alias
William Antrim

<u>Charge to Trial Jury</u>
       Filed in my office this 9th day of April A.D. 1881.
                               George R. Bowman
                                         Clerk

ATTORNEY FOUNTAIN'S BIASED INSTRUCTIONS FOR THE DEFENDANT: APRIL 9, 1881

Defense Attorney Albert Jennings's jury instructions reflected bias against Billy, essentially saying that Bristol had claimed no doubt existed as 1st degree murder, but the only ground for acquittal was that non-existent doubt! Fountain stated:

Territory of New Mexico
    vs   ) *Murder*
William Bonney alias Kid alias William Antrim

                In the District Court of Doña Ana
                County March 1881 term.

Instructions asked for by Defendants counsel. The Court is asked to instruct the Jury as follows: to wit:
1st Instructions asked –
    Under the evidence the Jury must either find the defendant guilty of Murder in the 1st degree, or acquit him.
2nd Instruction asked –
    The jury will not be justified in finding the defendant guilty of Murder in the 1st degree unless they are satisfied, from the evidence, to the exclusion of all reasonable doubt, that the defendant actually fired the shot that caused the

death of the deceased Brady, and that such shot was fired by the defendant with the premeditated design to effect the death of the deceased, or that the defendant was present and actually assisted in firing the fatal shot or shots that caused the death of the deceased, and that he was present in a position to render such assistance and actually rendered assistance from a premeditated design to effect the death of the deceased.

Instruction asked –

If the Jury are satisfied from the evidence to the exclusion of all reasonable doubt that the defendant was present at the time of the firing of the shot or shots that caused the death of the deceased Brady, yet, before they will be justified in finding the defendant guilty, they must be further satisfied from the evidence and the evidence alone, to the exclusion of all reasonable doubt, that the defendant either fired the shots that killed the deceased, or some one of them, or that he assisted in firing said shot or shots, or assisted in firing the same, or assisted the parties who fired the same either by his advice, encouragement procurement or command, from a premeditated design to effect the death of Brady. If the Jury entertains any reasonable doubt upon any of these points they must find a verdict of acquittal.

A.J. Fountain
J.D. Bail

HYPOTHETICAL CORRECT DEFENSE ARGUMENTS

Though the trial's transcript is lost, one can extrapolate from Bristol's and Fountain's jury instructions that no correct defense arguments were made. Billy, however, was unaware, since he tried to raise money by selling his bay racing mare to pay Fountain to do his appeal. Nevertheless, hypothetical defense arguments are presented here to show that proper evidence and argument could have established reasonable doubt against a 1st degree murder verdict and its hanging penalty.

Bristol and Fountain claimed inevitability of a 1st degree murder verdict based on evidence presented. Bristol stated: *"There is **no evidence before you** showing that the killing of Brady is murder in any degree than the first."* Fountain stated: *"**Under the evidence** [as presented] the Jury must either find the defendant guilty of Murder in the 1st degree, or acquit him."*

The argument should have been for justifiable homicide for defense of another, as forcing the group of citizens - including the Defendant - to use deadly force against Brady on April 1, 1878 to stop his murdering of McSween. If the group's response had been to immediate threat - like seeing Brady attacking McSween - it is a complete defense for exoneration - like self-defense.

But the time gap of about three hours between Brady's killing and McSween's arrival in Lincoln required a mitigating defense based on the Defendant's certainty that Brady would then kill McSween. So trial evidence had to show why any reasonable person would think Brady would murder McSween.

Evidence for William Brady as a murderer:

Brady was a known murderer, since his posse had murdered McSween's friend, John Tunstall, just 42 days earlier. And Brady made a death threat to Tunstall in McSween's presence, stating: "I won't shoot you now, you haven't long to run."

Brady was also a rogue lawman, blocking arrest of Tunstall's killers, who were his deputies and possemen. He also illegally imprisoned and confiscated the carbine of the Defendant on February 20, 1878 to obstruct Defendant's arrest of Tunstall's killers in his capacity as a Deputy Constable appointed by Justice of the Peace John Wilson.

Brady was a known threat to McSween, having harassed him by property attachment for his embezzlement case far in excess of the $8,000 set. And McSween hid because of certainty of Brady's murderous intent, staying in protective custody of Sheriff Adolph Barrier, also certain of McSween's murder risk from Brady. On March 28, 1878, Brady, illegally brought Fort Stanton soldiers to the ranch of John Chisum, in failed attempt to apprehend, and likely kill, McSween. But four days later - the murder day - McSween would return to Lincoln for the Grand Jury hearing.

Importantly, there existed no legal way to stop Brady from killing McSween, since, by a March 9, 1878 illegal Proclamation, then Governor, S.B. Axtell, had removed Justice of the Peace Wilson, stating: "there are no Territorial Officers here to enforce [laws] except Sheriff Brady and his Deputies."

Seeing themselves as McSween's sole protection, citizens, including the Defendant, came to Lincoln on the day of Brady's killing. They saw him and his deputies - accused Tunstall murderers - all heavily armed and positioning themselves for McSween's imminent arrival. Murder intent was obvious.

Evidence for Defendant Billy Bonney's motive:

As to Defendant's character, he had been a ranch worker for murdered Tunstall, and had been deputized to serve warrants on Tunstall's murderers after Brady refused to do arresting - only losing his deputyship by its illegal removal by Governor Axtell. Defendant's commitment to law and order was further proved by his giving an eye-witness affidavit and a deposition to bring Tunstall's killers to justice.

On the murder day, Defendant was in a citizens' group having sole consensus that McSween would be killed by Brady.

In that group, the Defendant had only a revolver, since Brady had taken his carbine; and all others had carbines. Defendant could not attain the 60 yard range to Brady's position, so could not have been Brady's shooter.

The Defendant's intent was to save McSween's life; and killing of Brady was the only possible way to achieve that end.

Other trial variables:

No translator was provided to the Spanish-speaking jury, except for jury instructions. A translator was required.

Defense witnesses should have included Billy himself; and subpoenaed Deputy Adolph Barrier, John Chisum, John Wilson, and Juan Patrón. Prosecution witnesses James Dolan and Jacob B. Matthews should have been impeached as on Brady's murder posse and themselves indicted for Tunstall's murder.

Defense argument:

Self-defense murder is legally blameless. So is defense of another from immediate death. The weight of the evidence has shown that the Defendant shared with his companions certainty that Brady was about to kill McSween, and that no recourse existed except to kill Brady to save McSween.

Defendant had no motive to kill Brady except in defense of McSween. To protect another from certain death is noble, and mitigates against a verdict of 1st degree murder, which is wanton and with malice aforethought.

The evidence has shown that after Brady's posse maliciously murdered Tunstall, there was good reason for the Defendant to believe Brady would next kill McSween. It has been shown that McSween and Deputy Sheriff Barrier likewise believed that Brady would kill McSween. It has been shown that no legal recourse through public officials existed to stop Brady's murderous act.

Furthermore, the Defendant was not Brady's killer, since his revolver lacked range. And he was not wanton or malicious, since his intent was to preserve McSween's life.

All the evidence therefore mitigates against a verdict of 1st degree murder, which requires hanging, and should be morally repugnant to declare against a reasonable man acting save the life of another man.

And it is the burden of the Territory, not the Defendant, to prove beyond reasonable doubt that the Defendant *did not* act in defense of another. The prosecution, having used Brady's indicted fellow murderers as witnesses, has failed to do that. So, if you, the jurors, have a reasonable doubt as to whether the defendant acted in defense of another, you cannot find the Defendant guilty of 1st degree murder, and are free to find the defendant not guilty - or, at most, guilty of 2nd degree murder, which spares his life.

VERDICT AND SENTENCE

On April 9, 1881, the jury's inevitable verdict after Bristol's and Fountains prejudicial instructions was murder in the 1st degree for William Brady's murder. On April 13, 1881, Judge Warren Bristol sentenced Billy to hang a month later - on May 13, 1881 - leaving little time to appeal.

BILLY'S RESPONSE TO SENTENCING: APRIL 15, 1881

Billy wanted to appeal. Two days later, on April 15, 1881, he wrote to Santa Fe attorney, Edgar Caypless, whom he had earlier hired on contingency to file an audacious replevin (rustling) suit for recovery of his bay mare from Pat Garrett's posseman, Frank Stewart, who had stolen her at Billy's Stinking Springs capture. Billy hoped to sell her to pay an appeal lawyer, with grounds that his Spanish-speaking jurymen had been deprived of a translator except for instructions. Caypless prevailed in the replevin case, but only after Billy's killing, and kept the mare's sales price as his fee. For his last known letter, Billy wrote:

Dear Sir. I would have written before this but could get no paper. My United States case was thrown out of court and I was rushed to trial on my Territorial charge. was convicted of murder in the first degree and am to be hanged on the 13th day of May.

Mr. A.J. Fountain was appointed to defend me and has done the best he could for me. He is willing to carry the case further if I can raise the money to bear his expense. The mare is about all I can depend on at present so hope you will settle the case right away and give him the money you get for her. If you do not settle the matter with Scott Moore [to whom Frank Stewart sold the mare] and have to go to court about it either give him [Fountain] the mare or sell her at auction and give him the money. please do as he wishes in the matter. I know you will do the best you can for me in this. I shall be taken to Lincoln tomorrow. Please write and direct care of Garrett, sheriff. excuse bad writing. I have my handcuffs on. I remain as ever

       Yours respectfully,
       W.H. Bonney.

That same April 15th, for an April 16, 1881 article, Billy, interviewed by the *Mesilla News*, summarized Santa Fe Ring injustice: "I think it hard that I should be the only one to suffer the extreme penalty of the law." He called his court "mcb law;" ending with facetious "personal advice": "If mob law is going to rule, better dismiss judge and sheriff and let all take chances alike ... Advise persons never to engage in killing." Asked about Wallace's pardon - showing it was universally known - Billy said curtly: "Don't know that he w ll do it." The article stated:

Well I had intended at one time not to say a word on my own behalf because persons would say, "Oh he lied." Newman, editor of the *Semi-Weekly*, gave me a rough deal; he created prejudice against me, and is trying to incite a mob to lynch me. He sent me a paper which showed it; I think it a dirty mean advantage to take of me, **considering my situation and knowing that I could not defend myself by word or act. But I suppose he thought he would give me a kick down hill.** Newman came to see me the other day. I refused to talk to him or tell him anything. But I believe the *News* is always willing to give its readers both sides of a question. **If mob law is going to rule, better dismiss judge and sheriff and let all take chances alike.** I expect to be lynched going to Lincoln. **Advise persons never to engage in killing.**

Considering the active part Governor Wallace took on our side and the friendly relations that existed between him and me, and the promise he made me, I think he ought to pardon me. Don't know that he will do it. When I was arrested for that murder he let me out and gave me freedom of the town, and let me go about with my arms. When I got ready to leave Lincoln in June, 1879, I left. **I think it hard that I should be the only one to suffer the extreme penalty of the law.**

SECRET TRANSPORT FROM MESILLA

In darkness, on April 17, 1881, Billy was secretly taken by wagon from the Mesilla jail to prevent rescue attempts on his way to the Lincoln jail and to hanging. Newman's *Semi-Weekly* reported his departure, with Billy, as usual, mocking:

On Saturday night about 10 o'clock Deputy U.S. Marshal Robt. Ollinger with Deputy Sheriff David Woods and a posse of five men ... started for Lincoln with Henry Antrim alias the Kid. The fact that they intended to leave at that time had been purposely concealed and the report circulated that they would not leave before the middle of the week in order to avoid any possibility of trouble, it having been rumored that the Kid's band would attempt a rescue. They stopped in front of the Semi-Weekly office while we talked to them, and we handed the Kid an addressed envelope with some paper and he said he would write some things he wanted to make public. **He appeared quite cheerful and remarked that he wanted to stay until their whiskey gave out, anyway.** Said he was sure that his guard would not hurt him unless a rescue should be attempted and he was certain that it would not be done unless perhaps "those fellows at White Oaks come out to take me," meaning to kill him. **It was, he said, about a stand-off whether he was hanged or killed in the wagon.**

LEW WALLACE'S BRIGHT FUTURE

Having sacrificed Billy Bonney to save himself, Lew Wallace faced a golden future. On April 19, 1881, he got a letter from a new father-figure, President James Garfield, praising *Ben-Hur*, with kind reference to Shiloh. It would lead to Wallace's appointment to his coveted ambassadorship in Turkey. Garfield wrote:

EXECUTIVE MANSION,
WASHINGTON. *April 19/81*

Dear General

I have, this morning, finished reading "Ben-Hur" – and I must thank you for the pleasure it has given me –

The theme was difficult, but you have handled it with great delicacy and power.

Several of the scenes such as the wise men in the desert – the sea fight – the chariot race – will I am sure take a permanent and high place in literature.

With this beautiful and reverent book you have lightened the burden of my daily life – and renewed our acquaintance which began at Shiloh –

Very truly yours
J.A. Garfield

CHAPTER 21

BILLY BONNEY'S GREAT ESCAPE AND KILLING APRIL 28 – JULY 14, 1881

BREAKING JAIL: APRIL 28, 1881

On April 21, 1881, Billy arrived from Mesilla with his armed guards to the custody of Lincoln County Sheriff Pat Garrett and to the new Lincoln courthouse with jail. Symbolizing triumph of the Ring, it was the converted "House," sold by mortgage-holder T.B. Catron to the County. And Billy's two guards, deputized by Garrett, were Bob Olinger - Seven Rivers Ring rustler and posseman in killings of Tunstall, MacNab, and the Lincoln County War battle's victims - and James Bell - White Oaks posseman and possible friendly-fire killer of Jim Carlyle.

Billy had 23 days till hanging; and no money to appeal. He was arm and leg shackled and chained to the second story jail's floor. Sealing his own heroic legend, on April 28th, his eighth day there, he escaped. He was likely aided by John Tunstall's past cook and current courthouse caretaker, Gottfried Gauss. Billy was left a revolver, and possibly wrist shackle key, in the outhouse.

Billy shot his guard, James Bell, who refused to be tied, and attempted escape and get help. To kill Bob Olinger, hated since 1878, Billy used the man's own Whitney double-barrel shotgun to ambush him from a window. From Gauss, Billy got a miner's pick to break his leg chain. During the few hours that task required, Lincolnites fought the Ring with silent resistance, clustering on Lincoln's single street, listening to Billy addressing them from the second story balcony and making no attempt to stop him. Gauss provided a horse. It was recounted that Billy had shouted to the people: "I'm standing pat against the world." He had finally broken free from clinging to Lew Wallace and the pardon.

But in escaping, he defied fate. Only 21 years old, bi-cultural and fluent in Spanish, he could have ridden 150 miles southward for a new life in Mexico. But he refused to leave his Territory home and his love, Paulita Maxwell. So he rode 150 miles northeast, to Fort Sumner. Known to its 200 residents since 1878, he must have realized that, though most were his friends, hiding there from Pat Garrett and death would be impossible. He had 77 days to live.

On April 30, 1881, when Pat Garrett arrived back in Lincoln from collecting White Oaks taxes, he had the humiliating task of reporting his failed assignment to kill "Billy the Kid." He wrote on the back of Billy's court documents:

I certify that I rec'd the within named William Bonny [sic] into my custody on the 21st day of April 1881. And I further certify that on April 28th he made his escape by killing his guards James Bell and Robert Olinger in Lincoln Co. N. M. Boarding Prisoner and two Guards 8 days - $40.00. Guarding and transporting from Fort Stanton - $69.00. Returning Writ - $.50. Total: $109.00 [sic].

BILLY ON THE RUN

Billy's friend, John Meadows, was at his Peñasco River ranch when Billy arrived, still joking. In the 2004 book, *Pat Garrett and Billy the Kid as I Knew Them,* Meadows is quoted:

Old Man Salazar [Ygenio Salazar in Las Tablas across the Capitan Mountains] let the Kid have a little sorrel horse and a good one, and also a saddle. He hung around for a day or so under cover in the hills and one night, after dark he showed up at Tom Norris' and my ranch ...

Tom Norris and I was in the cabin cooking some supper. Kid come up to the corner of the house and seeing there was nobody there but us two, whom he could trust, he stepped to the door and said, "Well, I've got you, haven't I?"

I said, "Well, you have. So what are you going to do with us?"

He said, "I'm going to eat supper with you."

WALLACE FINALLY OVERTLY REJECTS PARDON: APRIL 28, 1881

On April 28, 1881, unaware of Billy's jailbreak that day, and believing Billy would be hanged on May 13th, Lew Wallace participated with the Las Vegas *Gazette's* owner-editor, J.H. Koogler, in "Interview with Governor Lew Wallace on 'The Kid.'"

Wallace's attempts to keep the pardon bargain secret to enable betrayal had failed. Koogler reflected common knowledge about it. Wallace was cornered. Technically, the correct time for pardon was right then: after sentencing. And Catron's federal indictment had been quashed by Judge Bristol. Territorial pardon was possible. So Wallace, as betrayer, finally emerged, stating: "I can't see how a fellow like him should expect any clemency from me ..." [T]he general tenor of the governor's remarks indicated that he would resolutely refuse to grant "the Kid" a pardon." Koogler wrote:

> The conversation drifted into the sentence of "THE KID."
> "It looks as though he would hang, governor."
> "Yes, the chances seem good that the 13th of May would finish him."
> "He appears to look to you to save his neck."
> "Yes," said Gov. Wallace smiling, "but I can't see how a fellow like him should expect any clemency from me."
> Although not committing himself, the general tenor of the governor's remarks indicated that he would resolutely refuse to grant "the Kid" a pardon. It would seem as though "the Kid" had undertaken to bulldoze the governor, which has not helped his chances in the slightest.

J.H. Koogler had forced out the truth: Pardon was denied. Wallace now stood exposed to the light of history. Only 55 days before, Billy had written to him from the Santa Fe jail on March 4, 1881: *"I have done everything that I promised you I would, and you have done nothing that you promised me."* But Wallace had now begun his lie to the world: "I can't see how a fellow like him should expect any clemency from me." This hypocritical denial of his own blame would fuse with his hypocritical denials of blame for the Battle of Shiloh to fuel his obsessive, literary transmogrifying of heroic freedom fighting Billy Bonney into the unredeemable outlaw, "Billy the Kid."

Up until this moment, Wallace had been covertly sadistic in his interactions with Billy. Now cornered, with his pardon refusal public, his sadism became overt. He wanted to kill. On April 30, 1881, still unaware of Billy's jailbreak, Wallace wrote out Billy's death warrant for Sheriff Pat Garrett. And, as will be seen, Wallace would continue with this murderous impulse the rest of his life, but would project it by reversal onto the outlaw Billy the Kid as obsessed with killing him. Wallace wrote for Garrett:

To the Sheriff of Lincoln County, New Mexico, Greeting:

At the March term, A.D. 1881 of the District Court for the Third Judicial District of New Mexico, held at La Mesilla in the County of Doña Ana, William Bonney <u>alias</u> Kid, <u>alias</u> William Antrim, was duly convicted of the crime of murder in the First Degree; and on the fifteenth day of said term, the same being the thirteenth day of April, A.D. 1881, the judgment and sentence of said court were pronounced against the said William Bonney, <u>alias</u> Kid, <u>alias</u> William Antrim, upon said conviction according to law: whereby the said William Bonney, <u>alias</u> Kid, <u>alias</u> William Antrim, was adjudged and sentenced to be hanged by the neck until dead, by the Sheriff of the said County of Lincoln, within said county.

Therefore, you the Sheriff of the said county of Lincoln, are hereby commanded that on Friday, the thirteenth day of May, A.D. 1881, pursuant to the said judgment and sentence of the said court, you take the said William Bonney, <u>alias</u> Kid, <u>alias</u> William Antrim, from the county jail of the county of Lincoln where he is now confined, to some safe and convenient place within the said county, and there, between the hours of ten o'clock, A.M. and three o'clock, P.M., of said day, you hang the said William Bonney, <u>alias</u> Kid, <u>alias</u> William Antrim, by the neck until he is dead. And make due return of your acts hereunder:

> *Done at Santa Fe in the Territory of New Mexico, this 30th day of April, A.D. 1881. Witness my hand and the great seal of the Territory.*
>
> *Lew. Wallace,*
> *Governor New Mexico*

Four days later, on May 3, 1881, Wallace placed his second reward notice; this time in the Santa Fe *Daily New Mexican:*

BILLY THE KID.
$500 REWARD.
I will pay $ 500 reward to any person or persons who
Will capture William Bonney, alias The Kid, and
deliver him to any sheriff of New Mexico. Satisfactory
proofs of identity will be required.
LEW. WALLACE,
Governor of New Mexico

PRESS FAME OF THE GREAT ESCAPE

Unbeknownst to himself, Lew Wallace was no longer in control of Billy's meteoric trajectory of fame. Billy's great escape captured public imagination; and his true daring broke through to dispel his outlaw myth. On May 4, 1881, the day after the Santa Fe *Daily New Mexican* ran Wallace's reward notice, it excitedly reported Billy's jailbreak:

The above [account of the escape] is the record of as bold a deed as those versed in the annals of crime can recall. It surpasses anything of which the Kid had been guilty, so far that his past offences lose much of their heinousness in comparison with it, and it effectually settles the question of whether the Kid is a cowardly cut-throat or a thoroughly reckless and fearless man. Never before has he faced death boldly or run any great risk in the perpetration of his bloody deeds. Bob Olinger used to say that he was a cur, and that every man he had killed had been murdered in cold blood and without the slightest chance of defending himself. The Kid displayed no disposition to correct this until this last act of his when he taught Olinger by bitter experience that his theory was anything but correct. (No an, p. 420)

WALLACE'S FIRST BILLY THE KID OUTLAW MYTH ARTICLE: MAY 16, 1881

Lew Wallace likely read the May 4, 1881, adulatory, Santa Fe *Daily New Mexican's* jailbreak story. It precipitated his first derogatory full-blown Billy the Kid outlaw myth. But he no longer risked New Mexico Territory press which had facts. So 12 days later, on May 16th - with Billy still alive to be pardoned - he used the *St. Louis Daily Globe-Democrat* to launch "The Thugs Territory, Stage Robbers and Cut-Throats Have Things Their Own Way in New Mexico, Gen. Lew Wallace Anxious to Punish Crime that is So Prevalent - A Chapter About "Billy the Kid" - The Governor has a Narrow Escape from Being Spanked." That almost hallucinatory article would be Wallace's most revealing exposure of his pathological near-psychotic unconscious life.

In this version, Wallace admitted to promising the pardon. His lie is that he withheld it because Billy refused to reform from outlawry. Wallace even confirmed that Billy possessed a pardon promise "letter," and "felt that the letter would forever shield him from the law should he be captured;" thus, proving the truth of Billy's own March 2, 1881 jail letter about having *"certain letters in my possession."* But with Billy now on the loose to expose him as a liar to Territorial press (and turn over that promise letter), Wallace's near-panic yielded his paranoid fantasy of Billy wanting to kill him, as well as hysterical defamations: "He stole, murdered, ravished women, and at one time stole a herd of cattle consisting of 300 head, drove them to a station and sold them. He then pocketed the money and went back to Lincoln and defied the authorities to take him. It is claimed he has killed some forty men, and it is positively known that he killed at least five or six in Mexico alone." Wallace even regressed to unconscious associations with his mother's bizarre punishments, now converted to outlaws wanting to "spank" him.

So Wallace's first tale of the West - with Billy the Kid as its villain and himself as hero - emerged as crazy, dime novel pulp of Territorial robbers and cut-throats. The article stated:

The Thugs Territory.

Stage Robbers and Cut-Throats Have Things Their Own Way in New Mexico.

Gen. Lew Wallace Anxious to Punish Crime that is So Prevalent – A Chapter About "Billy the Kid" – The Governor has a Narrow Escape from Being Spanked.

Special correspondence of the Globe-Democrat.

DEMING, N.M. May 9, 1881. – Your correspondent visited ... Santa Fe and had a pleasant talk with Governor Lew Wallace ... [T]he Governor gave a very interesting sketch of the life of

"BILLY THE KID,"

the most noted and desperate character in New Mexico, and who was sentenced to be hanged on the 13th inst., but escaped by killing his guards and defying the entire population of Lincoln to take him, and Governor Wallace has offered a reward of $500 for his recapture, and has a posse consisting of seventy-five men on his trail.

"I deem him," said the Governor, "the most dangerous man at large, and I hope I will have the pleasure of seeing him meet his just deserts for the many crimes he has committed."

Billy, he said, was born in the East, and for some years lived in Indianapolis, Ind. He is 21 years of age, and came to New Mexico with his head crammed with dime novel stories. His ambition was to become one of the most noted outlaws he had read so much of. He settled down in Lincoln, and a splendid field was afforded to make his name in the terror of the inhabitants. **He stole, murdered, ravished women,** and at one time stole a herd of cattle consisting of 300 head, drove them to a station and sold them. He then pocketed the money and went back to Lincoln and defied the authorities to take him. It is claimed he **has killed some forty men, and it is positively known that he killed at least five or six in Mexico alone**. Some two years ago a murder was committed in New Mexico and Governor Wallace was positive that Billy had a hand in the deed, but was unable to discover his whereabouts. **Finally he learned that he was in the mountains a short distance from Santa Fe, and sent a messenger with a note to the outlaw, saying that if he knew anything about the matter and was willing to give his evidence before the Grand Jury, he would grant him a pardon, providing he also led a different life**. Billy was to meet him at a certain house in Santa Fe at 12 o'clock on a certain night and date, and the matter would be thoroughly discussed. At the appointed time

GOV. WALLACE

was at the house, and exactly at 12 o'clock a knock was heard at the door and in walked "Billy the Kid." A long talk followed, and it was agreed that the Sheriff should arrest him to protect him from the pals of the murderer. **The Governor's idea in granting a pardon to Billy was to capture the leader and break up the gang**. On the next day the Sheriff with a posse of men captured **Billy and he was brought before the Grand Jury, testified, and two of the men were sentenced to be hanged on Billy's evidence**. Since the day Billy received the Governor's letter he has been leading the life of a murderer, stage robber, etc., and **felt that the letter would forever shield him from the law should he be captured**. At length Billy committed one murder too many, was arrested, and sentenced to be hanged on the 13th inst. at Santa Fe, but escaped by killing two of the guards. **While in jail he wrote two letters to the Governor, demanding a pardon, and threatening to expose him should he not do as requested.** The Governor remembered the letter, and sent word to Billy's lawyer that he might do him a favor by publishing it. **This was too much for the outlaw, and he by letters and words openly avowed that Lew Wallace would die by his hands before he left the Territory.** But the Governor does not fear him, and as soon as the outlaw is within two days ride of Santa Fe Wallace himself will start the pursuit. A hundred other frontiersmen are also on the track of Billy, and will capture him if he is within the Territory.

Governor Wallace, since performing the duties of Chief Executive officer of New Mexico, has done considerable toward

PUTTING DOWN LAWLESSNESS

in the Territory. He is a man of

courage, as the people know, and would not hesitate to face and attempt to take the most desperate character in this Territory if it became necessary. **An interesting and ludicrous story is told of a recent meeting which was held by stage robbers and cut-throats of the Territory generally.** It was resolved that as Governor Wallace had taken such great care in placing a large number of their crowd under arrest, that he should be assassinated when the first opportunity presented itself. Each man was sworn to the agreement in a general celebration and jubilee followed at Lincoln over the action of the meeting. The members, some 300 in number paraded through the streets with cocked guns and revolvers, and the citizens deemed it best to look on and not in any way molest the gang. Somehow or other, when the boys got pretty full of whiskey, a streak of goodness entered their hearts, and right in the saloon another meeting was called, and it was resolved that Lew Wallace was a brave man, and only doing his duty. As this was the case, the first resolution was reconsidered, and the following notice was sent to Governor Wallace, which is still in his possession:

"**At our first meeting we resolved that you should die for interfering with our crowd, but as we think you a brave man and one who fought for the same cause that we did during the war, therefore we have resolved that instead of killing you we will, when the first opportunity presents itself, take off your pants and give you the worst spanking you ever had**."

The Governor said that he actually believed that they would carry out their intention and he was very careful that they shouldn't get an opportunity

TO SPANK HIM

if he could help it. A short time after receiving the note he had occasion to cross the country, and he felt that the outlaws would attempt the trick. He felt so certain of this that before he started he gave the driver notice that should any person order the coach to halt, the mules should be whipped into a dead run. As the coach was descending a steep ditch a couple of men jumped out, and before they had time to sing out, the driver have the mules the whip and away they dashed down the declivity. The Governor here jocosely remarked "that he didn't know which was the worst – running the risk of breaking his neck or getting the spanking." Anyhow, they didn't catch him, and if they do, it must be before the new Governor arrives. Governor Wallace will return to the East in a few weeks, settle up his affairs, then return to New Mexico for the purpose of seeing to his mining interests.

LEW WALLACE EXITS: MAY 28, 1881

Not waiting to complete his term, Wallace departed hated New Mexico Territory on May 28, 1881, and was welcomed in Crawfordsville, Indiana, on June 2, 1881. By June 4, 1881, he gave the Crawfordsville *Saturday Evening Journal* a self-aggrandizing interview titled "General Wallace's Serenade: A Welcome Home by his Neighbors and Friends - What the General Said." Billy had 45 days to live. The interview stated:

Gen. Lew Wallace, late Governor of New Mexico, returned to his home in this city on Thursday morning, and during the day remained closely at his residence receiving calls of his relatives and most intimate friends. About 10:30 o'clock on Thursday night a number of citizens with Sweitzer's band serenaded the General at his home. The band had played but a short time until he appeared at the front door and came down the walk to meet them. The serenaders were invited in and L.B. Wilson, on their behalf, made a welcome home speech Mr. Wilson said to General Wallace: "Your old friends, neighbors, fellow-soldiers, and fellow-citizens have come this evening tendering you this serenade in token of the high esteem in which they hold you. Among the gentlemen in the band you will notice the familiar faces of some who were members of the old Montgomery Guards Band in the years before the war. Here, also, are some now men in middle life, who, as members of the old Montgomery Guards, were trained by you as their captain in those years between '55 and '61, until the fame of the company as a military organization was a matter of State pride in Indiana. Here are some of the veterans who in '61 followed you as their leader, to battle for the Union and the right, and who followed you with their affection and esteem as you rose step by step from the rank of Captain to that of Major-General. Here, too, are the representation of that later organization of the Guards, of which our citizens were justly so proud. We are come to greet you with a hearty welcome home. We feel that by your distinguished services as a soldier and a statesman, the little city which claims you as her son has been highly honored. We point with pride also to your achievements in the world of letters and acknowledge to you that the story of Ben Hur has led us to examine with renewed interest the story of the cross. We are also come to congratulate you and ourselves upon your promotion, feeling assured that the duties of whatever position you may be called upon to fill, will be discharged with an ability, a patriotism, a zeal, and a courage which will make us still more proud of the fact which with pride we have so often mentioned: that Lew Wallace was an old Crawfordsville boy.

General Wallace in reply said that he heartily thanked the Guards, his neighbors and friends for this kindness. Referring to his return home, he said that going away was disagreeable to him, and returning gave him the greatest pleasure, and as he grew older this feeling became more apparent. Going away was painful, but this is lessened to a great degree by the pleasure of meeting friends again on return. He would not advise young men not to go, on the contrary go if they can do better, but come back. After all to spend the declining years of life and die among warm friends is more to be desired than to pass away being rich. There are times when we feel discontent, and we go out to find the conditions of ourselves, and we go away; but I never fail to come back. I am satisfied with the work I find here. He would say the same to young men – go if you wish but come back to Crawfordsville. After a short reference to New Mexico, he closed by again thanking his friends for their visit.

AMBASSADORSHIP TO TURKEY: JUNE 4, 1881

On June 4, 1881, Lew Wallace received his longed-for appointment: Ambassador to Turkey. It stated:

Department of Justice.
Washington, June 4th, 1881.

Lewis Wallace, Esq.
&c. &c. &c.
Constantinople.

Sir,

The President, by and with the advise and consent of the Senate, having appointed you to be Minister Resident of the United States to Turkey, I transmit, herewith the following documents
1. *Your Commission in that capacity.*
2. *A sealed letter of credence addressed to His Majesty the Sultan of Turkey ...*
3. *An original and duplicate letter of credit on the bankers of the United States in London, authorizing them to pay your drafts for salary ...*
4. *A copy of the printed Personal Instructions prescribed by the Department for the government of Diplomatic officers abroad ...*
5. *A special passport for yourself and suite.*

6. A list of the Diplomatic and Consular officers abroad.
7. A blank form of oath of office ...

Your compensation, as fixed by law, will be at the rate of seven thousand five hundred dollars ($7,500) per annum ...

The Department is fully confident that your intelligent and zealous attention to the interests of the United States, now confided in your care, will be conducive to the harmony of friendly relations existing from the governments of the two countries.

Requesting that you will officially inform the Department of your acceptance of the position to which you have been appointed.

I am, Sir, your obedient servant,

James G. Blaine [Secretary of State]

NEXT BILLY THE KID ARTICLE: JUNE 18, 1881

By June 13, 1881, back home in Indiana only 11 days, Lew Wallace returned to obsessive reworking of his pardon betrayal for an interview with the Crawfordsville *Saturday Evening Journal*, published on June 18, 1881 as "Billy the Kid, General Wallace Tells Why the Young Desperado of New Mexico Wanted to Kill Him. A Dashing and Daring Career in the Land of the Petulant Pistol."

This version is more refined than Wallace's May 16, 1881, "The Thugs' Territory" article,' implying astoundingly that in the 40 days of his complex relocation from the Territory, he had been formulating a new version of his pardon denial. His sadomasochistic 'spanking" by outlaws, is replaced by a less revealing product, though a pardon promise and unpardonable outlaw Billy the Kid remain; embellished with Billy as a serial murderer and rapist, and himself as hero and the Kid's potential victim. And the pardon contact and sham arrest are reversed as devised by him, not Billy. Sprinkled are facts, like Chapman's murder, obfuscated by fabricating his murderers, and even added Jesse James.

In fact, Wallace was unconsciously wrestling with his guilt and still flirting with a confession of his deserved punishment. In only two months starting with his Koogler interview, he had verified denying the pardon, had confirmed that a pardon bargain existed, had cited at least one letter from himself confirming the pardon promise, and had even kept Billy's letters, instead of destroying that evidence of betrayal and lying.

The article stated:

BILLY THE KID.

General Wallace Tells Why the Young Desperado of New Mexico Wanted to Kill Him.

A Dashing and Daring Career in the Land of the Petulant Pistol.

Late newspaper accounts of the exploits of "Billy the Kid," the New Mexico outlaw, have made him the chief among frontier desperados and familiarized readers with his depredations and murdering. In Crawfordsville additional interest in him is created by the fact that he is the same who swore to kill General Wallace, late Governor of New Mexico. His real name is William Bonne [sic], and he was born in New York, which place he left when a small boy with his widowed mother, for Indiana. He lived for a while in Indianapolis, and then Terre Haute, and four years ago went to the Territory of New Mexico. He had been a close reader of blood-and-thunder literature, and soon succeeded in out doing any of the desperate thugs he had ever read of. He now belongs to Silver City where his mother resides, but lives in the mountains to evade the edicts of the law, he now being under sentence for death for murder. He has killed in all, thirty-nine men, and is still not satisfied. He worked for John Chisum, the cattle dealer, in the late Lincoln county trouble, and **claiming he has never** received the promised $5 per day for his services, he is hunting down and killing Chisum's herdsmen, and giving their employer credit for $5 for each man killed.

[AUTHOR'S NOTE: Hiding Ring issues, Wallace uses anger at Chisum as Billy's motive for killings.]

It is only recently that he killed two guards of the Lincoln county jail, compelled one man to file off his irons, and another to furnish him with a horse and rode away before the eyes of the whole town. It was during this confinement that he swore to kill Governor Wallace. Given in the following narrative which a reporter of THE JOURNAL got from General Wallace, last Monday, is the cause of Billy's anger at the that Governor: **A young lawyer named Chapman was murdered in Lincoln county, and for this were arrested four men, among whom was the notorious Jesse James, under one of his many names**. The witnesses against the murderers all lied, and the latter were about to be liberated on a writ of habeas corpus. Governor Wallace heard that the "kid" saw the murder, and finding a man who could find Billy, sent him a note requesting a conference with him at midnight at a certain house which was designated. **The note assured the "kid" that if the conference proved that he did not have the necessary information about the murder he would be permitted to leave** the city, but if he did and would testify before the grand jury, the note implied that the Governor would pardon him for crimes for which he had been indicted, provided he would leave the Territory for good.

[AUTHOR'S NOTE: This admits reality of pardon promise letters which Billy referred in his jail letter of March 2, 1881. And Wallace admits to a pardon bargain; though adding a condition of leaving the Territory.]

Governor Wallace repaired to the meeting place early, and promptly at midnight, a slight knock was heard at the door and upon response in the inside, "Billy the Kid" opened the door and walked in. The Governor found Billy to be a mild-faced young man, 19 years old, small, slender, sloping shoulders, manly head, and an open expression of the face, and a deliberate and pleasant voice. After taking a cigar apiece, and talking over matters in Indiana, (for Billy was proud to say that he was once a Hoosier), Governor Wallace asked Billy to tell what he knew. He proceeded in good language to slowly tell what he knew, which proved to be what the authorities wanted. The Governor asked him if he would go before the grand jury and tell the same thing. Billy's reply was that he would not dare to do it voluntarily, as the criminals' friends would kill him. The Governor suggested that the difficulty might be surmounted by the "kid" permitting himself to be captured.

[AUTHOR'S NOTE: Lying Wallace, in his decades of reworking this tale, would always undo Billy's courage in contacting him and in suggesting the sham arrest, by claiming he himself instigated both. One is reminded of Lew Wallace's chronic Shiloh retellings, in light of this self-serving mendacity to conceal his moral failure with Billy.]

This was agreed upon, and accordingly and by arrangement Billy was surprised at a safe place in the mountains, while asleep, captured, and taken to jail. **He went before the grand jury and by his evidence the criminals were indicted for murder**. But before the trial in which he was to appear as a witness for the prosecution, he tired of jail life, and one day at dinner, he left his guards and took to the mountains.

[AUTHOR'S NOTE: Wallace, in this jumbled version, admits Billy testified for the pardon bargain. But to hide his own betrayal, he fabricates that Billy absconded before testifying in a another fabricated trial. In later articles, Wallace used the absconding story to make Billy the bargain betrayer. Omitted here, and forever after, is that Billy stayed in jail until June of 1879 to testify in the Dudley Court of Inquiry.]

He then resumed robbing raids and stealing cattle ... until two years later, Pat Garrett, Sheriff of Lincoln County, and the only man now in New Mexico who is not afraid of Billy, got on his track and effected his capture. **During this imprisonment the "kid," who had constantly carried the Governor's note about the convicting of Chapman's murderers, wrote twice to Governor Wallace, threatening to publish the proposition to pardon if he was not liberated**. No attention was paid to these and Billy's lawyer then came before the Governor with the same threat. The reply from the executive was that Billy might publish as much as he chose, as the matter had been reported in Washington and there approved.

[AUTHOR'S NOTE: Here is more evidence of a lost pardon promise letter. If so, Wallace, receiving Billy's jailhouse letter of March 2, 1881, might have become anxious of exposure. He repeats a public exposure threat in future articles, reworking how he foiled this plan. In actuality, Billy had only said that certain people wanted those letters – not making clear how they would be used to pressure Wallace. But Wallace's guilt was so great that he devises a tale of standing up to Ira Leonard ("Billy's lawyer") with a bizarre fable that he had reported to Washington about "the matter."]

Billy was further informed that he had not complied with all the conditions of the promise. This greatly enraged the young outlaw and he said he would take the life of the Governor. While under sentence of death he swore to kill three men before he died – Governor Wallace, John Chisum, the cattle dealer, and Pat Garrett, the Lincoln County Sheriff. In a short time he gained liberty by killing his two guards as before stated. Although Bonne [sic] was a desperate character, Governor Wallace felt no particular alarm and was more anxious to find Billy than Billy was to find him. He had it so arranged that he would have heard of the young desperado's approach 150 miles from Santa Fe, and other precautions were taken at the Governor's office.

[AUTHOR'S NOTE: This fabricated tale of Billy's murderous vendetta against him, is Wallace's projection of his own murderous feelings against Billy. It might have also been his real fear of retaliation for his betrayal. For this fiction, "threat" also puts Wallace in the center of the jailbreak, when, in fact, he was irrelevant by then. But Wallace recycled it in all future articles after Billy's death.]

Billy was sentenced to be hung, and took desperate chances to escape. He was successful and was in no hurry to come in the way of the law. His success had in his great amount of nerve. He never allowed himself to become excited, and never missed the object he shot at. **Before Billy became involved in so many crimes he had one day showing Governor Wallace a specimen of his workmanship. He explained his perfection thus: He never took aim with the revolver, but placed his index finger along the barrel, and as if pointing at the object pulled the trigger with his second finger** ... Nevertheless he is ever on the alert guarding against the other fellows getting the "drop."

[AUTHOR'S NOTE: When Billy was jailed in Lincoln, Wallace likely requested a shooting demonstration. But his preposterous pointing finger for aiming seems to be Wallace's fabrication; and it is repeated in other articles.]

There was once a three day siege of a house in which were Billy and a party. **General Wallace had a report of the maneuvering on the outside and when Billy was a prisoner had him to tell of the workings on the inside.** The besieging party finally succeeded in firing the house and those inside were driven from room to room, and finally to the kitchen. Then, there was but one door of exit and the outside men kept a continual storm of bullets pouring into it. One by one those attacked "took chances" and ran out the door rather than to be burned. Each fell with from four to fourteen bullets in the bodies until the "kid" who was the last to go rushed out and escaped without a scratch, though his clothing was completely riddled with bullets, and even his necktie was cut at his throat.

[AUTHOR'S NOTE: **This is the only rendition of Wallace admitting that Billy related to him the Lincoln County War battle. This further confirms that the authenticated March 24, 1881 "Billie" letter, was part of Billy's agenda to explain that War to Wallace when both were in Lincoln in March of 1979, and Billy was in sham imprisonment for the pardon bargain, and had his own larger agenda of explaining his fight against Ring injustice. If so, one can assume that Billy also told Wallace about Dudley's soldiers firing a volley at those escaping. But it should not be missed that Wallace has inserted himself into this mangled version as having a report about the "outside." Omitted entirely, of course, is the Lincoln County War freedom fight, the Ring, and the military intervention which caused the arson.**]

The "Kid" is a great favorite with Mexican women and does not want for friends, but as hard, bold, and daring as he is, he will doubtless soon meet death at the rope end of the gun's muzzle.

KILLING BILLY IN FORT SUMNER: JULY 14, 1881

What Lew Wallace had long wished for, occurred on July 14, 1881 in Fort Sumner, in the mansion bedroom of Peter Maxwell, Paulita Maxwell's traitorous brother. Billy had been lured there to fatal ambush by Sheriff Pat Garrett.

The next morning the Coroner's Jury met in Fort Sumner. Its President was Milnor Rudulph, who had been the contested Ringite Speaker of the House of Representatives in Santa Fe during the 1872 Legislature Revolt, and was now the Postmaster at nearby Sunnyside. For the body of this last killed Lincoln County War hero, the townspeople had made a candlelit night vigil. Realizing that no place in the Territory was safe, the terrified jurymen joined Rudulph in parroting: *"[O]ur verdict is that the deed of said Garrett was justifiable homicide and we are unanimous in the opinion that the gratitude of all the community is due to the said Garrett for his deed and is worthy of being rewarded."* The outlaw lie had become the public cant. And terror silenced a generation about the truth of Billy Bonney.

The Coroner's Jury Report of July 15, 1881 stated:

Greetings:

On this 15th day of July, A.D. 1881, I, the undersigned, Justice of the Peace of the above named precinct, received information that a murder had taken place in Fort Sumner, in said precinct, and immediately upon receiving said information I proceeded to the said place and named Milnor Rudulph, Jose Silva, Antonio Sevedra, Pedro Antonio Lucero, Lorenzo Jaramillo and Sabal Gutierres a jury to investigate the case and the above jury convened in the home of Luz B. Maxwell and proceeded to a room in the said house where they found the body of William Bonney alias "Kid" with a shot in the left breast and having examined the body they examined the evidence of Pedro Maxwell, which evidence is as follows: "I being in my bed in my room, at about midnight on the 14th day of July, Pat F. Garrett came into my room and sat down. William Bonney came in and got close to my bed with a gun in his hand and asked me "who is it" and then Pat F. Garrett fired two shots at the said William Bonney and the said William Bonney fell near my fire place and I went out of the room and when I came in again about three or four minutes after the shots the said William Bonney was dead."

The jury has found the following verdict: We the jury unanimously find that William Bonney has been killed by a shot on the left breast near the region of the heart, the same having been fired with a gun in the hand of Pat F. Garrett and our verdict is that the deed of said Garrett was justifiable homicide and we are unanimous in the opinion that the gratitude of all the community is due to the said Garrett for his deed and is worthy of being rewarded.

M. Rudulph President   *Anto, Sevedra (signature)*
Pedro Anto. m. Lucero (signature)
Jose Silba (x)   *Sabal Gutierrez (x)*
Lorenzo Jaramillo (x)

All said information I place to your knowledge.

Alejandro Segura Justice of the Peace

CHAPTER 22

THE SANTA FE RING REGROUPS

THE SANTA FE RING UNCHECKED

ANALYSIS: *With Ringite Governor Lionel Sheldon replacing Lew Wallace, the Santa Fe Ring was triumphant, unchecked, and more powerful than before the 1870's rebellion period began, because their suppression of opposition by terror or murder was complete and all Ringites avoided punishment. The Ring had become the perfect criminal organization, achieving invisibility and immunity by muddying incriminating truth with pseudo-history.*

REINSTATEMENT OF SAMUEL BEACH AXTELL

Besides its long trail of land grabs, terror, and murders, one of the Ring's most outrageous acts was restoration to official power of removed New Mexico Territory Governor, Samuel Beach Axtell. By 1881, with Lew Wallace departing before completing his term, the Ring moved to position one of their own.

Stephen Benton Elkins repeated his June 11, 1877 obstruction of Colfax County citizens' attempts to get Axtell removed as Governor - for the same corruption that resulted in his removal the next year. Elkins now led the campaign to reinstate Axtell as Governor, Frank Warner Angel's incriminating investigative report of October 3, 1878 notwithstanding.

On March 17, 1881, Elkins wrote a disingenuous letter to President James Abram Garfield, garbling facts and relying on Republican Garfield's continuation of President Hayes's "friendly" protection of the Ring. Smarmy Elkins, calling Axtell *"the most popular Governor New Mexico has ever had,"* wrote: *"I beg to state that I think Gov. Wallace was appointed in place of Gov. S.B. Axtell under a misapprehension of the facts and to the injustice of Axtell which I am informed President Hayes after a full understanding of the case regretted very much indeed and expressed his willingness to reappoint Gov. Axtell or give him some other appointment."* In fact, sly Elkins had already met for secret communications with President Garfield the week before. Elkins wrote:

115 Broadway
New York Mar. 17 1881

To the President.

Referring to a conversation had with you last week about the Federal appointees in New Mexico I beg to state that I think Gov. Wallace was appointed in place of Gov. S.B. Axtell under a misapprehension of the facts and to the injustice of Axtell which I am informed President Hayes after a full understanding of the case regretted very much indeed and expressed his willingness to reappoint Gov. Axtell or give him some other appointment. As a matter of justice to **Gov. Axtell who probably was the most popular Governor New Mexico has ever had**, I greatly desire his appointment as Governor. I think it would fully vindicate him and be the proper course to pursue. If however you feel that you cannot appoint him I am glad to concur in the appointment of Lionel Sheldon. I served with him in the House and know him long and favorably and believe he would make a thorough and vigorous Governor. If Lionel Sheldon should be appointed Governor of New Mexico I hope you will not forget Gov. Axtell.

Very truly &c
S.B. Elkins

Noteworthy is that the Ring's second choice was Ringite Lionel Sheldon, who was ultimately appointed to replace Lew Wallace.

With President Garfield's shooting assassination on July 2, 1881, and death on September 19, 1881, Vice-president Chester A. Arthur became President. By the next year, when New Mexico Territory Chief Justice L. Bradford Prince, resigned, Axtell was put forth to replace him. Review of Axtell was done by the U.S. Senate Judiciary Committee in June of 1882. The new Secretary of the Interior, Henry M. Teller, ignored or suppressed the exposés of Mary McPherson. But the Frank Warner Angel report surfaced. Bradstreet wrote:

U.S. SENATE CHAMBER

WASHINGTON *22 June 1882*

Sir:

Referring to the nomination of Sam'l B. Axtell of Ohio to be chief justice of the supreme court of New Mexico, now pending before the judiciary committee of the Senate, I am directed by that committee to ask you to please send to them, so that they may have them by next Saturday (the 24th inst.), the report and papers made *by Judge Angell [sic] of New York upon charges made against Axtell while he was governor of that territory, and upon which he is alleged to have been removed by President Hayes.*

[AUTHOR'S NOTE: Do not miss the sly "alleged to have been removed" to conceal actual justified removal.]

The committee would also be glad to have any other papers or information in the possession of your department touching said charges, or bearing upon his appointment as chief justice.
Respectfully yours,
Geo P. Bradstreet

That June, Attorney Frank Springer, showing a vestige of conscience, went to Washington, D.C. to present opposition to Axtell's appointment. By July 6, 1882, the Ring-backing *Santa Fe New Mexican* promoted Axtell with well-worn vilification of its opponents as "outlaws" - now Springer. It stated: "A man named Springer is in Washington trying to defeat the nomination of Governor Axtell. Springer is a friend of the thugs and thieves of Colfax County."

Axtell was confirmed as Territorial Chief Justice on July 13, 1882. And the *Santa Fe New Mexican* responded with smug, real thuggery of real outlaws, T.B. Catron, William Rynerson, James Dolan, Jessie Evans, Commander N.A.M. Dudley and the rest of their untouched criminals - including S.B. Axtell himself: " 'Chief Justice Axtell' is a bitter pill for the Raton *News and Press*. Don't make a wry face, you've got to swallow it."

As Chief Justice, Axtell also became Judge of the 1st Judicial District, including Colfax County, where he had earlier tried to murder the Ring's adversaries, including Frank Springer himself, Raymond Morley, and Clay Allison; and where he had illegally removed their court - in which he now served. Axtell voluntarily retired on May 11, 1885 to pursue business in Santa Fe.

After Axtell's reappointment as a major New Mexico Territory official, there was no further overt protest by anyone. Raymond Morley, having fled the Territory, died at 36 of an gunshot wound on January 3, 1883, while doing railroad engineering in Mexico. I was told that some of Morley's descendants suspected a Ring murder; though the report at the time was of an accidental firing of a rifle on a train. Frank Springer settled in Las Vegas, New Mexico, and led the prosperous life he desired. Mary McPherson was publicly silent, as was everyone else in that 19th century Territory now ruled entirely by Ring fear and favor.

RING ABUSES ASCENDANT

Corrupt connivings, growing since the Ring's 1866 inception, are revealed in a January 16, 1886 letter from T.B. Catron's then law partner, William T. Thornton, to a John J. Cockrell, Esq. in Lincoln. Conveniently, Juan Patrón, a possible local opponent, had been murdered two years earlier, in 1884, with possible Ring motive. Ringmen were completely free to assist "friends" by malicious prosecution to remove competition. Thornton wrote:

CATRON, THORNTON & CLANCY,
ATTORNEYS-AT-LAW.
Santa Fe, N.M. January 16th – 1886 _188____

John J. Cockrell, Esq.
    Lincoln, New Mexico.
        Dear Sir:
                Your favors received. **We will try and have the matter of Mrs. Wilson's estate at Albuquerque attended to for your Bates County friends. As you have doubtless learned, we succeeded in getting Jim Brent appointed Sheriff some days ago. I think you will have no trouble in making your $3000.00 collection against Bryan. Bring suit at all events, as it may help me in my ranch matters on the Penasco.** Catron is security for Will Dowlin & Co., of which John C. De Laney is the real party in interest on a large number of claims. Mr. De Laney has gone to work and caused himself to be released by nearly all of his creditors. Will you please see him, get a copy of this release, and send it to me as early a day as practible, that I may find out whether it releases Mr. Catron also. Will send Catp. [Capt.] Lee's note to you. Enclosed **I send you a memorandum, or rather, a letter from J.H. Nash to Edward C. Wade Esq., giving a list of persons who have violated the quarantine law in Lincoln County. This letter was forwarded to the Stock Association, and the Stock Association have instructed me to bring suit, wherever I thought proof could be obtained sufficient to insure a judgment. I have seen Mr. Wade, and he consents that I can use his name in bringing suit in the name of the Territory.**

Bring the action where-ever you think you can find the parties in the county, with cattle sufficient to cover costs. In these cases, sue in the name of the Territory in an action of debt, putting in two counts, one alleging that the cattle came from a deseased [diseased] country, and the other, that they did not have a certificate of an Inspector. Where the person who brings the cattle into the Territory is not the owner, and nothing can be obtained from him, it would be better to proceed against them criminally. Have a warrant sworn out before some Justice of the Peace, and the parties bound over to appear before the Grand Jury. When you are through with this letter, return it to J.D. Warner in Las Vegas. Also write him what suits are brought, and to send you an advance fee of ten dollars in each case. Use five of it to pay costs, and keep five yourself. The Stock Association is desirous of having every violation of the law punished, and vigorous prosecution. Some time ago, I instituted suit in Lincoln County, a bill in Chancery, A.H. Janes vs The Winters Heirs, and had publication sent to the Lincoln County papers, for November term of Court. Will you see if the proof was properly made. If not, have it re-published for May Term, as I am anxious to get service as soon as possible. There are eight or ten other parties for whom we are attorneys, who will come in and ask to be made parties complainant in Janes Bill, which is a creditors bill. Do not think I owe Hightower for any work done upon Diamond Crown in 1885, as I sent him a check early in the year for what I owed him, and instructed him to quit work. As to the interest of Manuel Salazar in Canon de Chama Grant, I have looked the matter up very thoroughly, and find that he has no interest. ~~He claims to be the descendent~~ The Sena's live in Lincoln, ~~and~~ whom claim to be his descendants, are the descendants of another Manuel Salazar, who died in 1809, four years before the Canon de Chama Grant was made. They offered me one half of their interest to look the matter up for them, and I am satisfied that this statement is correct.

      Yours Respectfully,
      W.T. Thornton

LEW WALLACE ON CATRON AND THE RING: NOVEMBER 6, 1897

More than 15 years after he escaped New Mexico Territory, leaving its citizens in the thrall of the Santa Fe Ring by his self-serving cover-ups, and after the restorative experience of his exotic ambassadorship to Turkey, Lew Wallace felt safe enough to speak some truth about Catron and the Ring. The recipient of his November 6, 1897 letter was Eugene Fiske, whom Frank Warner Angel had described in his secret notebook of 1878: *"Fiske E.A. Santa Fe, Lawyer - Shrewd - honest reliable - can be of great service to you. He controls the U.S. Marshal Has been of great service to me - Well posted as to the people and frauds in the Territory."* And in a letter of February 16, 1880 to Carl Schurz about his gubernatorial legislative appointments, Wallace had written: *"My appointments were submitted the last day of the session. For Attorney General of the Territory, Eugene A. Fiske."* But Wallace, in that Ring-placating period, had also appointed Ringites *"to revise the laws of this Territory, William Breeden ... and Simon B. Newcomb,"* along with fence-rider *"Frank Springer."*

But Wallace was now more open with Fiske, naming Catron's *"[a]stonishing influence over New Mexicans."* Clearly, by this date, Wallace had repressed his own astonishing submission to that *"influence."* Wallace wrote:

```
                Crawfordsville, Indiana. Nov. 6, 1897.
Eugene A. Fiske, Esq.
        Santa Fe, N. Mex.
    My dear Friend: -
                I have your several letters,
including the last one of the 3rd inst. Last week,
I wrote to the President, calling attention to your
application and asking him to be good enough to
read my former letter on the subject of New Mexico
appointments and particularly the part of it in
your favor for United States District Attorney. It
seems impossible to me that the President should
make the mistake of appointing Mr. Clancy, who,
although a very clever gentleman, must necessarily
be a retainer of Mr. Catron. That Governor Oterro
has submitted himself to the domination of
Mr. Catron does not surprise me. One of the curious
```

incidents pertaining to Mr. Catron is his astonishing influence over New Mexicans. I cannot recall one instance in which he did not absolutely submerge and control all persons who came in contact with him speaking the Spanish tongue.

With high hopes for your success. I am, as ever

Most truly your friend,
Lew Wallace

SANTA FE RING FIGHTER IN THE 20th CENTURY

After a gap of 80 years since the Santa Fe Ring's killing of Billy Bonney, there arose one anti-Ring historian. Fittingly, he was Mary Tibbles McPherson's great grandson, Norman Cleaveland. In 1971, he published unvarnished truth in his book, *The Morleys: Young Upstarts of the Southwest*. He wrote:

When my grandparents, William Raymond Morley and Ada McPherson Morley, pioneer New Mexicans, were in their twenties they were confronted with an "establishment" known as the Santa Fe Ring. By comparison, present-day establishments would rate rather as societies of butterfly collectors ... (p. viii)

CHAPTER 23

LEW WALLACE'S LITERARY CREATION OF THE OUTLAW MYTH OF BILLY THE KID

LEW WALLACE'S PARDON PROMISE OBSESSION

ANALYSIS: *Lew Wallace's conscience tormented him for the rest of his life for his betrayal of his pardon promise to Billy Bonney, with the boy's resultant death. But the overt redemption Wallace sought was not atonement, but cover-up. His literary solution was the creation of the myth of the outlaw, Billy the Kid.*

One can say that the "history" of Billy Bonney as "Billy the Kid" was the creation of a guilty conscience in a creative writer. The lost pardon of Billy the Kid never eased its grip on Lew Wallace's mind. Twenty years after he betrayed Billy, his guilt stayed subconscious; but it goaded his obsessive rationalizations in published literary tales in non-historic, far West scenarios which reversed his and Billy's roles; making himself the hero and Billy the betraying villain. That replicated Wallace's Shiloh rationalizations in his obsessive pardon pleas to Ulysses S. Grant, which reversed blame for the lethal fiasco.

For his Billy the Kid fiction, Billy Bonney was a murderous outlaw obsessed with him, and he was a noble pardon promiser paternally seeking to reform the desperado, but thwarted by the Kid's recalcitrant evil. But truth occasionally slipped out. As Wallace stated on June 23, 1900 in *The Indianapolis Press* for "Gen. Wallace's Feud with Billy the Kid, When the General Was Governor of New Mexico and Billy Bonne Was the Most Dangerous Western Outlaw": "So long as I live, I will never lose the image of Billy the Kid."

It is likely that Wallace's resulting long articles were drafts for another historical novel: a Western featuring Billy the Kid. Death from stomach cancer in 1905 cut short Wallace's intent; no book resulted beyond references to an unfinished book in progress, and to Billy in his posthumously published two volume *Autobiography*.

But Wallace's obsessive newspaper articles likely cemented the moniker "Billy the Kid" in public consciousness; and his dissemination of the outlaw myth, though damaging truth and Billy's reputation, accidentally intersected Billy's actual larger-than-life persona and "Robin Hood" deeds to yield a character whose allure and fame would far eclipse Wallace's.

And Wallace's likely book "research" of retaining Billy's letters and copies of his own Billy the Kid articles, when added to the mass of existing period documentation, allow emergence of the real Billy Bonney, the real Santa Fe Ring, and the real freedom fight that Billy's enemies - including Wallace - had tried so hard to conceal.

"LEW WALLACE'S FOE" ARTICLE: DECEMBER 10, 1893

Lew Wallace actually had two obsessions connected to the pardon bargain. One was concealing his betrayal, the other was repairing his self-esteem injured by guilt at that ignoble act. The latter task resulted in his December 10, 1893 *San Francisco Chronicle* self-aggrandizing article titled "Lew Wallace's Foe, Threatened by "Billy the Kid," The Writing of "Ben-Hur" Interrupted, An Incident of the Soldier-Author's Career in New Mexico."

It can also be contemplated that, by 1893, Billy Bonney's own rising fame stimulated Wallace's competitive spirit, since he waves the banner of his best-selling *Ben-Hur*, and states outright: "The Governor's enemy was no less a personage than the illustrious "Billy the Kid," than whom no man had ever excited more terror on the frontier or given better ground for the dread in which he was held."

But the simple focus of "Lew Wallace's Foe" was to make himself all good, and Billy all bad. The pardon was irrelevant to that literary mission, and was omitted. In its place was a dramatic Wallace-ordered capture of outlaw Billy who was "surrounded by overwhelming numbers" of men - likely Wallace's cribbing of Secret Service Agent Azariah Wild's 1880 reports' versions of chasing Billy's mythical outlaw gang. Wallace even adds snide denigration by calling his "Billy" short - a "diminutive prisoner" - though real Billy was of above average height, and the same as Wallace's.

Most pathological and revealing in this reversal article, however, is Wallace's fabrication that escaped Billy planned to come to Santa Fe to kill him. It is Wallace's continuing paranoid reversal of his own guilt deserving of punishment; and, at an even deeper level, is a projection of his own murderous hatred of the undefeatable, noble, and brilliant boy.

The article stated:

LEW WALLACE'S FOE.
Threatened by "Billy the Kid"
The Writing of "Ben-Hur" Interrupted.
An Incident of the Soldier-Author's Career in New Mexico.

General Lew Wallace, best known to the general public by his two great books, "Ben-Hur" and the "Prince of India," is a man of many roles He has been successful as a soldier, politician, diplomat and author, and some startling experiences have fallen to his lot.

His career on the battlefield, his life in Turkey, When he was Minister to Constantinople, and his later triumphs in the world of literature have all gone to make an eventful record, and they have all been so often recounted in the public prints that it would seem that every incident of his life would be familiar to those who keep themselves posted on the careers of public men. Yet there is one ordeal through which General Wallace has passed, and which he probably will never forget, that has escaped the vigilance of the scribes. It is, probably, not generally remembered that General Wallace was once Governor of the Territory of New Mexico, but it is a fact that in 1880, and for a year or so after that, he occupied the former palace of the Captains-General of Spain, in the historic old town of Santa Fe, N.M. He was the chief executive of the Territory, by appointment of President Garfield [Hayes], and it was during his administration that he fell under the ban of an assassin, and was given very good reason to believe that he would have to look down the ugly barrel of a 45-caliber revolver, and to defend his life as best he might.

The Governor's enemy was no less a personage than the illustrious "Billy the Kid," than whom no man had ever excited more terror on the frontier or given better ground for the dread in which he was held. He had perpetrated murder after murder and there were few crimes of which he was not believed to be capable. He boasted that he had killed more men than he was years of age and would shoot a man if he felt so disposed, "just to see him kick."

After "Billy the Kid" had been carrying things with a high hand for a long time Governor Wallace offered a reward for his capture. It proved a tempting bait to the "gun fighters" and officers of the law in the Territory. There were plenty of men among them who would not shirk from a hunt through the mountain fastnesses, even after such formidable game as this border bully, and the result of the Governor's offer was that after a most exciting pursuit **"Billy the Kid" was surrounded by overwhelming numbers and forced to surrender**. He was taken to Santa Fe and thence to Lincoln County to answer a charge of murder.

Enraged at having been trapped, the outlaw swore that

if he ever regained his liberty he would kill three men. One was a judge who had passed sentence upon him, one was Pat Garrett of Lincoln county, who had been conspicuously active in effecting his capture, and the third was Governor Lew Wallace.

"After I have settled accounts with these three men," said the desperado, "I will be willing to surrender and be hanged. **When I get out I will ride into Santa Fe, hitch my horse in front of the Palace, and walk in and put a bullet through Lew Wallace**.

This seemed idle boasting at the time, because there appeared to be not the remotest possibility of the prisoner's escape. He was in the custody of Sheriff Garrett in the County Jail of Lincoln, and the Sheriff, besides being a cool, courageous and reliable man, had every incentive to be watchful of his charge. It was thought a pretty sure thing that Garrett would never let the "Kid" go, and Governor Wallace felt fairly secure in his office away off in Santa Fe.

Garrett appointed as guards over the "Kid" Bob Ollinger [Olinger] and John [James] Bell. They were his personal friends, both big, burley **six-footers, who towered over their diminutive prisoner**. In addition to this physical superiority over him, they counted themselves as his equals when it came to a fair and square gun-fight. If anyone had told them that the "Kid" would outwit them and escape they would have laughed at the very thought of it.

For months the "Kid" was a docile as a kitten. The guards became used to him, then familiar, and then friendly. He seemed to have forgotten that they had helped to cage him and were his custodians, and as time passed the trio became boon companions. The guards laughed at the "Kid's" stories of his exploits, played cards with him during their long watches and would often remove one of the "cuffs" from his wrist, so that he could manipulate his cards or ply knife and fork at meal times. Whenever this was done both handcuffs were fastened to the right wrist, and thus locked in a cell with one of his stalwart guards the little cutthroat was safe enough.

Ollinger and Bell took turns watching in the jail and relieved each other to go to dinner. One day when Ollinger had gone across the street to a restaurant Bell took the "Kid" from his cell to an up-stairs room in the little two-story adobe jail. He put some food on a table for him and then unfastened the left cuff and locked it on the prisoner's right wrist.

The "Kid" sat down and began to eat without the slightest apparent concern. While he was munching the coarse prison fare Bell strode restlessly up and down the room. He wore no coat and his heavy revolver protruded from the holster attached to his cartridge belt. Each time he walked the room he passed within two feet of where the "Kid" sat, and once when he came within reach the "Kid," with the quickness of a cat, leaped upon his chair and dealt him a rap on the head with the handcuffs. Bell staggered under the blow, and before he could recover the "Kid" has snatched the revolver from the holster and sent a bullet through Bell's body. The guard tottered and fell and in a few moments was dead.

Ollinger was across the street and had, no doubt, heard the shot. The outlaw seized a double-barreled shotgun and ran out on the front balcony. Already Ollinger had crossed the street. He had come on the run, but before his foot struck the steps he fell with a load of buckshot in his heart.

The murderer walked carelessly down the stairs, stepped over Allinger's [Olinger's] prostrate form and strutted down the street with the revolver and shotgun in his hands. A blacksmith was shoeing a horse in a neighboring shop, and "Billy the Kid" easily persuaded him to desist, **then mounted and rode out of town at a walk, saying just before he started: "Now for the Governor."**

The news of the escape quickly reached Santa Fe, and Governor Wallace's friends became very uneasy lest the "Kid" should carry out his threat. The Governor himself was not entirely tranquil in the circumstances. It is one thing to face an enemy in the open field and quite another to have a treacherous one dogging one's footsteps.

Brave as Governor Wallace had shown himself to be, he recognized his danger and prepared to meet it. At that time he had already begun "Ben-Hur," and used to sit for hours in his office each day engaged upon the absorbing work. From the day upon which "Billy the Kid" escaped from the Lincoln County Jail a close observer entering the office might have detected lying on the table, partially hidden among papers and scraps of manuscript, the glint of a pistol, for the Governor was never without one while he knew that his archenemy was at large.

The people of Santa Fe were well aware that the head of the Territorial Government was preparing for war for every morning about 7 o'clock the sharp crack of a revolver being fired rapidly resounded from the corral in the rear of the gubernatorial residence. It soon became known that it was Governor Wallace improving himself as a pistol shot preparatory to an impromptu duel with "Billy the Kid." A figure had been marked on the adobe wall of the corral, and the Governor filled it full of holes. He became so expert that he could knock an imaginary eye out of the figure at twenty paces. He made no bones of the matter and, in fact, could be easily seen from the adjoining houses.

During the weeks which elapsed before the termination of this period of suspense Pat Garrett was in hot pursuit of

"Billy the Kid." It was a most remarkable and exciting chase. The whole Territory was deeply intent upon it, and news of the whereabouts of the two men was eagerly looked for. Governor Wallace repeatedly said to the writer: "When these two men meet one or both of them will bite the dust."

He was right. The announcement finally came from Fort Sumner that Garrett had forever rid the country of the "Kid." He had tracked him to the house of Peter Maxwell, near Fort Sumner, and, concealing himself in one of the rooms, had fired one shot at his man. That shot passed through the desperado's heart and he fell dead in his tracks.

Governor Wallace breathed easier, and the next night a reporter found tall, muscular Pat Garrett waltzing with a four-foot Mexican girl in a dance hall of Santa Fe.

"STREET PICKINGS" ARTICLE: JANUARY 6, 1894

A month after his violent Billy the Kid fantasy of "Lew Wallace's Foe," on January 6, 1894, Wallace gave a "Billy the Kid" interview to the Weekly *Crawfordsville Review* as "Street Pickings." Also omitting the pardon bargain, it fabricated him as the object the Kid's vengeful obsession as well as becoming an expert marksman - like real Billy. Wallace was quoted:

Street Pickings

Gen. Lew Wallace is a dead-shot with the pistol. Speaking of how and why he acquired such expert marksmanship, the renowned author-soldier said a few days ago in conversation with a party of friends:

"When I was governor of New Mexico that territory was and had been for years terrorized by bands of daring and murderous outlaws, at the head of whom was the famous border desperado, "Billy the Kid." By virtue of my office I became this man [sic] deadliest enemy. No man ever excited more terror along the frontier or gave better ground for the dread in which he was held than this man. He perpetrated murder and their [sic] were few crimes of which he was not guilty. He had openly boasted that he killed nearly fifty men and enjoyed shooting a man down 'just to see him kick.' I determined to rid the territory of this scourge and offered a large reward for his capture. The offer proved to be a great sensation throughout the territory and a tempting bait to ready shooters and officers of the law. There were in the territory hundreds of men who accepted with great delight this opportunity to take a hunt through the mountains after such formidable game. Well, the result was that after a most exciting chase the outlaw was surrounded by overwhelming numbers and compelled to surrender at the point of fifty guns after shooting down three of his pursuers. He was taken to Lincoln county, away up in the state, to answer an unusually flagrant murder. He was wildly enraged at having been trapped and swore that the moment he got free he would ride clear through to Santa Fe, shoot me down and then gladly hang.

"I knew the character of the man and while never dreaming that he would ever again be at large, I determined in order to be safer, to begin pistol practice in case an impromptu duel should ever take place between us. I got a brace of the best pistols I could find and every morning spent an hour in the corral firing at a mark. In a few weeks I got so I could hit the figure of a man marked out on the wall at twenty paces about every time. And as I became more and more skillful, I felt correspondingly safer and didn't much dread an open meting even with the caged murderer and with my life for the stake.

"Two months dragged along and one day at Santa Fe we got the alarming news that "Billy the Kid" had murdered his two jailors, stolen a horse and had started for Santa Fe with the open threat, 'Now for the governor and now hang.' Then I began practicing several hours every day and for weeks I was in daily expectation of meeting the ruffian. I still went about my duties, but heavily armed with my pistols ever ready. Pat Garrett was the sheriff to whose charge "Billy the Kid" had been entrusted, and when he learned a half-hour afterward and while away from home, that 'Billy the Kid' had escaped, he started in hot pursuit. For weeks there was unbroken suspense during which he heard nothing from the pursuer or pursued. They were both dead shots and there would be killing when they met. It was a most remarkable and exciting chase. The whole territory was deeply intent upon it and news of the whereabouts of both men was eagerly awaited.

"Finally, one day there rode up to my residence a travel-stained six-footer in a wide sombrero hat, mounted on a pony worn out with hard work. He got off, let his pony wander loose and came up to the door. I met him on the front step with my guns ready for instant use and asked him his errand. 'I am Pat Garrett, governor, and have just shot 'Billy the Kid' out here at Ft. Sumner.' And it was true. He had come up with the desperado heading for Santa Fe to end me, had got the drop on him and without a word shot him through the heart. I have still kept up my practice somewhat, but not under as thrilling circumstances."

PARALLEL SHILOH AND PARDON OBSESSIONS

During a California lecture tour, on October 29, 1894, Lew Wallace gave an interview to the *San Francisco Chronicle* titled "About His Works, A Chat With Lew Wallace." For it, he returned to his Shiloh obsession. The reporter wrote: "I have been severely criticized for my conduct there," said General Wallace, a shade of sadness coming over his slow, grave manner ... "Newspapers ... even up to today, blame me for not hastening more over those almost impassable roads. I read an article in one of your California papers not long ago."

This was a new excuse for his missing the Battle of Shiloh: bad roads. That excuse now joined assuming he was not supposed to arrive at that date, wrong orders from Grant, and improperly delivered orders by Grant's orderly.

BILLY THE KID AS A CHARACTER FOR A NOVEL

Lew Wallace may have planned to use Billy in a novel, in keeping with his past ones building on his experiences. In 1893, he published *The Prince of India or Why Constantinople Fell*, using his stay in Turkey as ambassador; and his 1873 *The Fair God: A Tale of the Conquest of Mexico* had used experiences there.

A clue as to an *"American"* novel about Billy might have been given by Wallace in an interview published on January 16, 1886 in the Crawfordsville *Saturday Evening Journal*, where he gave his works in progress, including the future *The Prince of India* and an "American" one, now unknown:

> I am amusing myself with writing two books and two plays ... One of my books is a tale of the capture of Constantinople by the Turks [*Prince of India*], and the other is wholly American. I may never finish either of them.

In the 1890's Wallace continued to hint about a new novel, now unknown, and possibly about Billy.

In a February 10, 1894 *Cincinnati Post* editorial, he was ridiculed for pompously deriding Charles Dickens, compared to himself, as writing about "trifling, frivolous, or bad, cheap people;" while praising his own use of famous people as characters. Billy, by then increasingly famous, was a natural choice, the "research" having been completed in his New Mexico Territory Governorship. The reporter wrote:

GENERAL LEW WALLACE, author of "Ben-Hur" was recently interviewed in New York. The General has turned critic himself. Here is one of his remarkable statements:

"Ben-Hur" has been growing in popularity since the nature of the treatment of the character became known. No book or picture can live – that is: live for centuries, which deals with light trifling characters. The works of Dickens will not outlive the centuries, because they deal with the most part with trifling, frivolous, or bad, cheap people ..."

With all deference to the brilliant author, there are many people who will not coincide with his view. He seems to forget that when speaking of "trifling, frivolous, or bad, cheap people," he is speaking of human nature, and so long as human nature is depicted by the hand of the true artist these works will live in the libraries of the world.

During his lecture tour of the western states, Wallace was interviewed by the St. Paul, Minnesota *Dispatch* on October 5, 1894 for "Author of Ben-Hur, Gen. Lew Wallace of Indiana, Spends the Day in the City." He was quoted about his "new novel": "As to the new novel he is reported to have in course of preparation, he said he is not writing it as yet, but only had it in the preliminary courses of preparation and could say nothing as to its probable character."

In the same month, on October 14, 1894, the Tacoma, Washington, *Daily Ledger*, in "Lew Wallace Honored, The People of Seattle Extend Him a Hearty Greeting," Wallace again possibly referenced a secret novel in progress on "Billy the Kid." By that date, there would, indeed, have been the competition he feared if that theme had been made public. But no book was completed; and no traces of its manuscript exist. The reporter wrote:

[Wallace] said, among other things, that he is preparing to write another book, but has not yet begun the opening chapter.

"And the subject?" suggested the interviewer.

"Well, that I prefer to keep to myself," was the half laughing reply. "You see, I write slowly ... If I were to make public my subject, why a dozen fellows might write a dozen books on the same and publish them before I had half completed mine."

On April 15, 1902, three years before his death, and after his years of newspaper articles on Billy the Kid, the Cincinnati *Commercial Tribune* printed: "General Lew Wallace ... is Working on New Book." It was reprinted in Crawfordsville *Weekly News-Review*. Wallace described daily work on his manuscript. But it remains unknown, missing from his collected papers. It stated:

INDIANA IS NOW LITERARY CENTER

GENERAL LEW WALLACE GIVES HIS VIEWS ON PRESENT DAY WRITERS

IS WORKING ON NEW BOOK

Thinks New England and East Have Lost Prestige in Literary Field

General Lew Wallace, of Crawfordsville, Ind., was at the Burnet House yesterday, on business of a private nature. The distinguished military man and author, when seen by a Commercial Tribune reporter at the hotel, was looking not a whit older than when he last appeared here in public, almost ten years ago, as a lecturer on his experience as Minister to Turkey.

"I am all right," said General Wallace, "with the exception of the fourth toe of my left foot ...

"I noticed in the cable matter from abroad this morning that King Edward attended a performance of 'Ben Hur' at Drury Lane Theater last night ... I understand the play 'Ben Hur' is meeting with considerable success."

New Book Forthcoming.

"I am employed every day at my literary tasks. I write from 1,000 to 1,500 words every day. Then, every day I carefully go over what I have written the previous day, and 200 or 300 words or throw it out entirely. In this way I have been employed for the past four years on a work, or book, as it is commonly designated. No, I do not care to say what the title or character of my forthcoming work will be. It is manifestly bad policy, for the financial and from every other standpoint, to closely predict a volume forthcoming from the press."

The Leading Writer of Fiction.

"Who is the leading American Writer of fiction? Well, that is a question of broad scope and intricate details. W.D. Howells is the dean of writers of this kind in America. Yes, you may put me down as saying that Mr. Howells is the man ..."

Indiana the Center.

"Indiana seems to be, and really is, the present seat and center of literature in America. At least that would appear to be the verdict of the public."

"GEN. WALLACE'S FEUD WITH BILLY THE KID" ARTICLE: JUNE 23, 1900

A clue to the missing manuscript, may be two novella-like articles Lew Wallace published on June 23, 1900 and June 8, 1902; the latter just two months after his *Commercial Tribune's* announcing his new book. They may be his total work-in-progress.

For *The Indianapolis Press* on June 23, 1900, he renewed the pardon obsession like a book outline as "Gen. Wallace's Feud with Billy the Kid, When the General Was Governor of New Mexico and Billy Bonne Was the Most Dangerous Western Outlaw, He Was a Waif and was Reared in Indiana." It had a truth: "So long as I live, I will never lose the image of Billy the Kid."

Though the rest is fabrication, Wallace's awe at Billy emerges, instead of his early defensive scorn at the "precious specimen." He wrote: "Billy the Kid, [was] the New Mexican outlaw that attracted the attention of a nation ... It was during this confinement [in the Patrón house-jail] that 'the Kid' gave the most phenomenal exhibition of shooting I have ever witnessed ... [People] were victims of that mysterious something that Billy exerted over men." He grants Billy's grandeur: "Over him, with a majesty, hung the cloak of fearlessness and alertness penetrated only by two eyes that looked deep into every man's intentions." And he settled on a mythical tally: "[H]e killed a man for every one of the twenty-two years he lived." It stated:

GEN. WALLACE'S FEUD WITH BILLY THE KID
When the General Was Governor of New Mexico and Billy Bonne Was the Most Dangerous Western Outlaw
HE WAS A WAIF AND WAS REARED IN INDIANA

(By a Staff Correspondent)
CRAWFORDSVILLE, Ind., June 23. –

"Yes, **he killed a man for every one of the twenty-two years he lived**, and died in his stocking feet – a marvelous, far more than marvelous, career his was – a nightmare of existence."

Gen. Lew Wallace's shaggy brows contracted with a frown as he closed his eyes as though to shut out from his memory unpleasant things. There was a pause. He arose from his chair, and after walking up and down his study in silence, finally said:

"**So long as I live, I will never lose the image of Billy the Kid,** as I saw him that midnight in old Santa Fe, back in 1879. There he stands in the doorway of the little adobe house, form outlined by moonlight at his back, face illuminated by glow of the little lamp. The clock had made its first stroke of the midnight hour, when by appointment to the second there was a knock at the door that I can hear yet. 'Come in," I said. The door flew open and there stood the most feared, the most adored, the most reverenced man in New Mexico, hunted by every limb of the law as a criminal, and sought by every Spanish senorita as her lover. The room was covered by a Winchester rifle held in one hand. In the other was a Colt's revolver. It was a musical growl that said, "I was to meet the Governor here at midnight. It is midnight: is he here?"

"I asked him to come in for a conference, and told him that I was the Governor of New Mexico.

"Your note gave me the promise of protection," he said.

"There is no one here but us three," replied I, pointing to the owner of the cottage.

"Billy threw his gun over his arm and came straight to the table near which I sat. I looked at him in wonder. This was the man that had killed his scores: the man whom every officer hunted. I was not expecting to see a stripling, with rounded shoulders, slightly stooping stature, slender, effeminate physique. His face was smooth and soft, and yet character and firmness were shown in every line. His voice was as musical as that of a society belle. **Over him, with a majesty, hung the cloak of fearlessness and alertness penetrated only by two eyes that looked deep into every man's intentions.**"

Reared in Indiana.

The General passed from the thoughtful to the narrative and said: "Billy the Kid, the New Mexican outlaw that attracted the attention of a nation, and under whose fearful vendetta I was placed while Governor of New Mexico, was a New York waif whose name was William Bonne.

[AUTHOR'S NOTE: Inflating daring, Wallace makes Billy famous in 1879, and invents a "fearful vendetta."]

He was brought to Indiana when he was a small boy and was reared in Indianapolis and Terre Haute. He was about 17 years old in 1876, when he went West. During his early years he had been a close reader of blood-and-thunder literature. He outdid in reality the lurid pictures of the literature in which he was schooled.

"It was not long until 'Billy the Kid' became the most daring and notorious of desperadoes. Stories of his crimes, his escapes, his fascinating faculties were the nursery tales of the Territory. He started to grow up with the country by taking employment of John Chisum, who was known as the 'Cattle King,' was a hard taskmaster and disputed Billy's account. The latter swore that he would square matters by killing Chisum's herdsmen: that for each man he killed he would credit the cattleman with $5, but if he killed Chisum himself then the whole account would be wiped out.

[AUTHOR'S NOTE: Wallace makes Chisum Billy's killing motive to hide Lincoln County War issues.]

Midnight Meeting Arranged.

"A young lawyer named Chapman was murdered at Lincoln. Four men were arrested, among them the notorious Jesse James.

[AUTHOR'S NOTE: New Mexico Territory outlaw, Jessie Evans, here becomes famous Jesse James!]

The witnesses to the killing were filled with terror and fled the country. Because of the lack of evidence the prisoners were about to be released on a writ of habeas corpus. I had been sent to pacify the country and had realized this was an opportunity I could not let slip. At last I heard that Billy the Kid had witnessed the murder.

[AUTHOR'S NOTE: Wallace hides Billy's pardon bargain to make himself the hero.]

In the outskirts of Santa Fe lived an old 'squire,' who was one of Billy's friends.

[AUTHOR'S NOTE: Wallace omits any hint of his Lincoln humiliation, instead setting the meeting in Santa Fe. This fabrication dispenses with Lincoln County War issues and the Dudley Court of Inquiry.]

I went to him one evening and told him I wanted the young outlaw to meet me promptly at midnight. He professed that he had no connection with the sought-for youth. I ordered pen and ink and wrote a note, and, leaving it, told him that I would expect it to be delivered to Billy. In the note I said I understood he was the only remaining man that had witnessed the murder, and that if he would appear before the Grand Jury and court and convict them I would pardon him for all his crimes.

[AUTHOR'S NOTE: Though reversing roles with Billy as to proposing the pardon, Wallace now admits to it. That will require his later concealing of his betrayal.]

"The midnight meeting was as I have described. When he heard from my lips my proposition he said: 'My God, Governor, they would kill me.' 'But that can be arranged,' I replied.

[AUTHOR'S NOTE: Wallace lies that he devised the sham imprisonment.]

It was decided that Billy was to be taken the next morning while asleep in a cabin back in the mountain. He picked the men that were to capture him. He required me to keep him in irons during confinement, that his reputation not be marred."

[AUTHOR'S NOTE: Wallace hides the Lincoln location of the jail for his lie.]

Billy's Secret in Revolver Shooting.

"It was during this confinement that 'the Kid' gave the most phenomenal exhibition of shooting I have ever witnessed. I sent word to the jail to have him brought to my office.

" 'Billy,' I said, 'I am told you are a phenomenal shot. I wish you would give me an exhibition of your skill.'

" 'With pleasure, Governor. Have my pistols brought.'

" 'Here is a pistol, and a good one.'

" 'A violinist always wants his own bow, though another might be better. I want my own pistol.'

"His pistol was brought and we took him out into the big, open court.

[AUTHOR'S NOTE: Continuing his fabricated location, Wallace seems to describe the inner courtyard of the Palace of the Governors, in keeping with the boy being brought to his "office." In fact, the Lincoln demonstration would have been behind Juan Patrón's house.]

I ordered his chains taken from him. The guards whispered to me, 'For God's sake, Governor, do you know that you are giving him your life or his escape?'

[AUTHOR'S NOTE: Wallace omits that jailing was a sham; and jailor, Juan Patrón, was Billy's loyalist.]

"I know that I was the last man in New Mexico Billy wanted to kill, for I was the only man that could give him a pardon.

[AUTHOR'S NOTE: This shows the sadism that mixed power and pardon in Wallace's psyche.]

"The guards stood with their weapons in their hands, ready to defend themselves from this man with a charmed life. Billy spied a small Boston bean can in the court. He ordered a guard to throw it high as he could. The can sailed in the air. Without taking aim, and seemingly without concern, he fired at it. The bullet passed through the center. As it struck the ground, in the same unconcerned manner, Billy fired at it, and, emptying his revolver, he rolled it along much the same as one can roll a can with the stream from a lawn hose.

" 'Billy,' said I, 'There is a trick in that, and I want to know it.'

" 'Yes,' he replied, 'there is a trick. Ever since you were a child, Governor, you have been doing it unconsciously, every time you have said 'Look at that you have pointed at it with your index finger. Without knowing it, you have become an expert mark – and so has everyone. I put my index finger along the barrel, catch the trigger with my second finger and say, 'Why look at that, Billy,' and, pointing unconsciously at it, pull the trigger. I am not known as a crack shot, Governor – rather a dead shot.'

[AUTHOR'S NOTE: Though fabricating aiming technique, Wallace reveals admiration for Billy's skill and humor.]

"He asked for his horse and gun – his own Winchester. Mounting, he started down the court on a dead run, and as he went he shot with his left hand, emptying his magazine into a four-inch sapling that was 200 yards distant. Back he came on a gallop, shooting with the right hand. Every shot took effect.

" 'And what is the trick about that, Billy?'

" 'Oh, General, there is no trick in that rifle. My horse bounds away, I level, I feel it all over, I pull the trigger and the bullet goes straight.'

Was Something of a Hypnotist.

"It was a week before the trial. Billy had been taken to dinner in his chains. After the meal he said: "Well, I wish you would tell the Governor that I am tired. Much obliged boys,' and leaving them as though in a trance, he quietly walked across the street, and, unhitching a horse, dashed out of town. There could be no suspicion that the guards had conspired for his release. They were victims of that mysterious something that Billy exerted over men.

[AUTHOR'S NOTE: Here is Wallace's perfidy: hiding Billy's testimony that fulfilled the pardon bargain, substituting a dream-like escape. Besides its lie, it insults by "I'm tired;" as if Billy lacked moral fiber to stick out his pardon deal.]

"Later Billy was arrested for a series of murders.

[AUTHOR'S NOTE: This is a purposeful lie, since Billy's Stinking Springs arrest by Sheriff Pat Garrett was only for the Brady-Hindman-Roberts indictments.]

He had kept my note offering pardon in the affair.

[AUTHOR'S NOTE: This references Billy's jail letter about pardon letters.]

He had been in jail a week when he addressed me: 'Governor, why haven't you come to see me?' I paid no attention to it. A few days later there was a second note: 'Governor, I have some papers you would not want to see displayed. Come to the jail.' I knew what he meant.

[AUTHOR'S NOTE: Here is chilling proof that 19 years after he betrayed Billy, Wallace remembered his jail letters. But here he is reworking their truth, making them seem just a blackmail attempt, which he next triumphantly fabricates as thwarting.]

I sent a copy of the old note and the story over to the paper and it was published. I sent him a copy of the paper and drew his fire. It was then that he swore his vendetta on my life and on that of Pat Garrett, the sheriff of Lincoln County.

[AUTHOR'S NOTE: This false "Billy vendetta" against himself is a projection of his hostility to the boy, as well as unconscious expression of guilt and his own deserved punishment. Wallace's adding of Garrett, reflects his request to Garrett to report back to him after Billy's hanging death, like a compatriot in his murderous plan.]

He was convicted for murder and sentenced to be hanged. When the sentence was read, he arose in court and said:

" 'Judge, that doesn't frighten me the least bit. Billy the Kid was not born to be hung.'

"This young desperado was a thorough fatalist. He believed that for the time he had a charmed life: that he had nothing to fear from the weapons of enemies, and that he would not go 'until his time came,' and the time was not at hand.

[AUTHOR'S NOTE: Again, there is a break-through of Wallace's admiration for the boy's courage; even in the midst of this character assassination article.]

"He had gone through many a danger. At one time, surrounded in a Mexican house, 'the Kid' fought nine men. The house was set on fire, and he made a dash for liberty and escaped through all the musketry of the guards. There were a dozen bullet holes in his clothing and his necktie had been cut away at the throat by a bullet, but Billy received not a mark on his skin.

[AUTHOR'S NOTE: This shrinking of the Lincoln County War to a "surrounded ... Mexican house," is made more outrageous by the fact that Wallace participated in the Dudley Court of Inquiry. He is hiding history to hide his own humiliation: fabricating "the Kid" fighting "nine men," instead of the real War.]

"From his trial," continued General Wallace, "Billy was taken back to jail. He was in no wise disturbed. A day before the execution nine guards were watching him. At dinner time all but one left. Billy was in chains. The guard on duty received a tray that bore Billy's dinner. As the guard stood to place the tray on the floor, Billy the Kid struck him on the head with the handcuffs, crushing the skull. Then he took the guard's revolver, routed all the other guards that appeared, forced a blacksmith near by to break the handcuffs, mounted a good horse near at hand and rode away. He said as he started: 'Tell the Judge that I said that Billy the Kid was not born to be hung.' "

[AUTHOR'S NOTE: This fictionalized escape, multiplying the number of Billy's guards, reveals Wallace's fantasizing Billy as a superhuman: defeating nine men with wits and wacking handcuffs.]

End of Billy the Kid.

"It is needless to touch upon my danger under the vendetta," returned Gen. Wallace. Sufficient it is to say that he started for Santa Fe at once, and, determined to have a shot in return, I started out to meet him, but for some reason he never reached the point.

[AUTHOR'S NOTE: Wallace continues his coat-tailing on Billy's great escape, though, by then, he was likely the last thing on the boy's mind.]

Sheriff Pat Garrett was the only man in New Mexico not afraid of Billy and his charmed life. Garrett started out to make his capture, and it was a scout lasting for weeks, each man waiting to get the drop. All New Mexicans had their eyes on the two, and every morning the general question was, 'Has Pat and the Kid met yet?' It was a long siege, but Billy fell through love.

"Pat received information that Billy had gone back to an old fort in the mountains to see his sweetheart. Garrett journeyed there. He lay in wait in the dooryard of Billy's love, and finally saw the door open one night and a man come out in stocking feet. His hat was off; he wore only shirt and trousers. He passed out into the night. Garrett walked in and covered the girl's father with a gun. 'Not a word,' he whispered, as he passed behind the headboard of the bed with gun in hand. The door opened again. Billy seemed to smell danger, as a camel smells rain. He knew by instinct that something was wrong. He cried to the old man in Spanish, 'Who's there? Who's there?' Garrett raised his revolver. There were two reports. Billy the Kid jumped into the air and fell in his tracks. There were two bullet holes through his heart."

As he concluded the story there was a tremble in Gen. Wallace's voice that indicated that with the horrible picture there was a feeling of admiration for Billy. There was a pause and he said: "And he was only twenty-two."
E.I. LEWIS

[AUTHOR'S NOTE: Did "staff correspondent" E.I. Lewis inadvertently report the physical manifestation of the old hypocrite's guilt, as "a tremble" of Wallace's voice, and as his "admiration for Billy?"]

"GEN. LEW WALLACE WRITES A ROMANCE OF BILLY THE KID" ARTICLE: JUNE 8, 1902

Twenty-one years after Billy's killing, two years after *The Indianapolis Press's* "Gen. Wallace's Feud with Billy the Kid," and two months after his *Commercial Tribune's* announcing his new book, Wallace gave his final fiction. For *New York World Magazine* on June 8, 1902, he presented a novella as "General Lew Wallace Writes a Romance of 'Billy the Kid' Most Famous Bandit of the Plains, Thrilling Story of the Midnight Meeting Between Gen. Wallace, Then Governor of New Mexico, and the Notorious Outlaw, in a Lonesome Hut at Santa Fe." In it, Wallace confirms the pardon bargain as: " 'Testify,' I said ... 'and convict the murderer of Chapman and I will let you go scot-free with a pardon in your pocket.' " But this reworking reveals Wallace's unremitting rage at Billy's egalitarian self-confidence, with particular offense at Billy's threat to expose his pardon promise letter and his hypocrisy. In fact, Wallace's pique was still so hot, that he abandoned his 1900, "Gen. Wallace's Feud" article's having Billy's "most phenomenal exhibition of shooting," replacing it with a catty remark that Billy "missed his aim." This version was incorporated into his *Autobiography*. The 1902 article stated:

GENERAL LEW WALLACE WRITES A ROMANCE OF 'BILLY THE KID' MOST FAMOUS BANDIT OF THE PLAINS
Thrilling Story of the Midnight Meeting Between Gen. Wallace, Then Governor of New Mexico, and the Notorious Outlaw, in a Lonesome Hut at Santa Fe.

Gen. LEW WALLACE, author of "Ben Hur," is completing his autobiography, which will be issued in a few weeks.

The most thrilling chapter in this remarkable personal narrative tells of the midnight meeting in a lonely hut between Gen. Wallace, at the time Governor of the Territory of New Mexico, and "Billy the Kid," the most notorious outlaw the far West has ever produced.

From advance sheets of Gen. Wallace's book the following account of this strange rendezvous has been copied and compiled for the Sunday World Magazine. The story has never been printed in any newspaper or magazine before.

The episode occurred in 1879. The outlaw was at the zenith of his wild career.

Gen. Wallace conceived the idea that he might gain certain important information by a face-to-face talk with the outlaw. With much difficulty the meeting was finally arranged. It was not without a strong element of danger to both participants, but they trusted each other and the trust was not betrayed.

The Midnight Rendevous.

On the night of the meeting two men sat, shortly before midnight, silent and expectant, in the hut which had been chosen for the rendezvous, which was on the outskirts of Santa F, N.M.

Their gaze was fastened on the door, and, as the minutes slipped away the tension grew more severe, the silence more oppressive.

One man was the owner of the rude home that stood desolate in the shifting sands of the great mesa.

The other was Gen. Lew Wallace, Governor of New Mexico.

The hands of the clock pointed to 12.

The hush deepened. Suddenly it was broken by the sound of a resolute knock on the door of the cabin.

"Come in," said the Governor of New Mexico.

The door flew open and, standing with his form outlined by the moonlight behind him, was "Billy the Kid." In his left hand he carried a Winchester rifle. In his right was a revolver. The weapons, quick as a flash, covered the two occupants in the room.

"I was to meet the Governor here at midnight. It is midnight: Is the Governor here?"

The light of the candles flickered against a boyish face, yet the man who stood in the doorway was the most notorious desperado in all the West. He had killed scores of men: he was the quarry of every sheriff from the Rio Grande to the bordering foothills that shut in Death Valley.

The Boy Outlaw.

In facial features "Billy the Kid" was a mere stripling. His narrow shoulders were rounded, his posture slightly stooping, his voice low and effeminate. But his eyes were cold and piercing, steady, alert, gray like steel.

Gen. Wallace rose to his feet and held out his hand, inviting the visitor forward for a conference.

"Your note gave the promise of absolute protection," said the outlaw, warily.

"I have been true to my promise," replied the Governor. "This man," pointing to the owner of the cabin, "and myself are the only persons present."

The rifle was slowly lowered, the revolver returned to its leather holster. "Billy" advanced and the two seated themselves at opposite sides of the narrow table.

Gen. Wallace was able to effect an important arrangement with the outlaw, of which he gives the details. In fact, a very friendly understanding was established between the two.

Explaining the purpose of the interview and its result with "Billy," Gen. Wallace says:

"Shortly before I had become Governor of New Mexico, Chapman, a young attorney in Lincoln, had been murdered.

[AUTHOR'S NOTE: This lying date Chapman's murder is to hide Wallace's blame. It was on February 18, 1879, 4½ months into Wallace's term; and Wallace was blamed for having never come to Lincoln County.]

Half a dozen men were arrested, accused of the crime. Among them was Jesse James.

[AUTHOR'S NOTE: Lying Wallace makes Jessie Evans Jessie James.]

While it was more than probable that one or more of the men charged with the murder were guilty, it was impossible to prove the allegation, for the witnesses, filled with terror, fled the country. **When I reached New Mexico it was declared on every hand that "Billy the Kid" had been a witness to the murder. Could he be made to testify?**

"That was a question on the tip of every tongue.

"I had been sent to the Southwest to pacify the territory; here was an opportunity I could not afford to pass by. Therefore I arranged the meeting by note deposited with one of the outlaw's friends, and at midnight was ready to receive the desperado should he appear. He was there on time – punctual to the second.

[AUTHOR'S NOTE: This summarizes lying Wallace's reversals.]

"When 'Billy the Kid' stepped to the chair opposite mine, I lost no time in announcing me proposition.

Agrees to the Plan.

" 'Testify,' I said, 'before the Grand Jury and the trial court and convict the murderer of Chapman and I will let you go scot-free with a pardon in your pocket for all your misdeeds.'

[AUTHOR'S NOTE: Wallace confirms the bargain.]

" 'Billy' heard me in silence; he thought several minutes without reply.

" 'Governor,' said he, "if I were to do what you ask they would kill me."

" 'We can prevent that," said I.

[AUTHOR'S NOTE: Wallace inverts the sham jailing.]

"Then I unfolded my plan. 'Billy' was to be seized while he was asleep. To all appearances, his capture was to be genuine. To this he agreed, picking the men who were to effect his capture. He was afraid of hostile bullets and would run no risk. Another stipulation was to the effect that during his confinement he should be kept in irons. **'Billy the Kid' was afraid also of the loss of his reputation as a desperate man**."

[AUTHOR'S NOTE: Wallace snidely makes Billy worried only about "reputation."]

The plan agreed upon in the cabin on the lonely mesa at midnight was carried out to the letter. "Billy the Kid" was seized the following morning and confined in the Lincoln County jail. It was here that Gen. Wallace, in spite of the fears of the guards, permitted the outlaw to give an exhibition of his skill with the revolver and the rifle. "Billy," standing or riding, using either the one weapon or the other, sent every bullet true to its mark.

"Billy," said the General, "there's some trick to that shooting. How do you do it?"

"Well, General," replied the desperado, "there is a trick to it. When I was a boy I noticed that a man in pointing to anything he wished observed, used his index finger. With long use, unconsciously, the man had learned to point it with unerring aim. When I lift my revolver, I say to myself, 'Point with your finger.' I stretch the finger along the barrel and, unconsciously, it makes the aim certain. There is no failure; I pull the trigger and the bullet goes true to its mark."

[AUTHOR'S NOTE: A requested shooting exhibition likely occurred.]

"Billy," though at his own request kept in irons, did not remain long confined. One morning the guards led him to breakfast. Returning, the desperado drawled in the feminine voice that was a part and parcel of his character:

"Boys, I'm tired. Tell the Governor I'm tired."

[AUTHOR'S NOTE: Wallace denigrates Billy as "effeminate" and too "tired" to do the pardon bargain.]

The manacles slipped like magic from his wrists. The guards stood stupefied, and "Billy the Kid," laughing mockingly, walked leisurely from the jail yard, through the gate and across the street. Easily, gracefully, he threw himself into the saddle on the back of a horse standing near at hand and, putting spurs to the animal, dashed away. "Billy" was gone. He had not escaped in the night; he had walked away in the broad light of day, with his guards, heavily armed, standing about him.

[AUTHOR'S NOTE: This hides Billy's testifying, and leaving only after lack of pardon risked his life.]

"Boys," I'm tired," he said, and looked them straight in the eyes.

They were not in collusion with the desperado; Gen.

Wallace satisfied himself of the fact.

But how account for "Billy's" escape?

Hypnotism, some say – hypnotism or that strange something that lurked in the depths of the steel-gray eyes.

[AUTHOR'S NOTE: "Hypnotism" was to cover up the partisans and sham arrest.]

The desperado's freedom, however, was not long-lived. He was arrested soon afterward for a series of murders, and was brought again to the Lincoln County Jail. Patrick Garrett was Sheriff. He was probably the one man in New Mexico who did not fear "Billy the Kid." He was his match in every respect – as calm, as desperate, as certain.

[AUTHOR'S Wallace's demonizing of Billy continues by fabricating murders.]

Perhaps "Billy" knew this. At any rate he must have considered himself in desperate straits. He sent for Gen. Wallace. The General refused to respond. Then the outlaw sent him a note. The note said:

"Come to the jail. I have some papers you would not want to see displayed."

"I knew what he meant," said Gen. Wallace, reminiscently. "He referred to the note he received from me in response to which he appeared in the hut on the mesa. He was threatening to publish it if I refused to see him. I thwarted his purpose by giving a copy of the latter and a narrative of the circumstances connected with it to the paper published in the town. It was duly printed and upon its appearance a copy was sent to "Billy" in his cell. He had nothing further to say."

[AUTHOR'S NOTE: A source of Wallace's guilty obsession was existence of his pardon promise letters.]

Not Daunted by His Sentence.

In the end the desperado was convicted and sentenced to be hanged. When the sentence was read he stood before the trial judge and said:

"Judge, that doesn't frighten me a bit. 'Billy the Kid' was not born to be hung."

He was a thorough fatalist. He believed he bore a charmed life. He believed he would not die until his "time came," and then death was inevitable.

From the court-room "Billy" was led back to the jail. Nine men were put on guard, and he was never allowed a moment from the sight of one of them.

On the day before that set for his execution one man sat in front of Billy while he ate his dinner. During the meal the guard forgot himself and suddenly stooped. "Billy's" quick eye took in the situation in a glance.

With a leap he sprang upon the bending man and dashed his brains out with his handcuffs. He seized the dead guard's revolver and, his steel-gray eyes gleaming, he walked forward deliberately and routed all the other guards, who ran to the assistance of their comrade.

Once more "Billy the Kid" escaped in the full light of day through the doors of the jail. He forced a blacksmith to break the manacle chains, seized a good horse that stood nearby and rode away.

He called back as he spurred the animal into a gallop:

"Tell the judge that I said 'Billy the Kid' was not born to be hung."

But "Billy" had forgotten one thing; he had not reckoned on the character of the man who was Sheriff of the county. He had forgotten Patrick Garrett. Garrett shut his teeth hard, like a man who is determined to accomplish his purpose, no matter the obstacles presenting themselves. He set out to take "Billy the Kid," dead or alive.

Garrett received information that "Billy" had gone back to an old fort in the mountains to see his sweetheart. Garrett followed. He lay in wait in the dooryard of the home of "Billy's" love, and finally his vigil was rewarded when he saw the door open one night and a man step out into the white light of the moon.

His hat was off, he was in his stocking feet and he wore only shirt and trousers. He passed out into the night.

Garrett crept to the door and passed in

He covered the girl's father with his gun.

"Not a word," he said, and slid behind the headboard of the bed.

The Death of "Billy the Kid."

The door opened again and "Billy the Kid" entered. He seemed to scent danger as a camel scents rain; instinct taught him that something was wrong. He cried to the cowering old man in Spanish:

"Who's here?" he asked. "Who's here?"

Garrett raised his revolver; two shots rang out on the quiet air and the room filled with smoke. A form tottered, then crashed to the floor. In the nerveless hand was a smoking revolver; for the first and last time the notorious New Mexican outlaw had missed his aim. Garrett escaped unwounded. But there were two bullet wounds in the body of "Billy the Kid" and both pierced the heart. Garrett's aim was unerring.

To-day there is a little lowly heap of earth located in Las Cruces, N.M. [sic – Fort Sumner] To the curious stranger some idle native may, now and again, point out this little grave and explain, with a certain pride, that Las Cruces possesses the final resting place of the worst bad man that ever infested the Southwestern border. An ancient Mexican, who sometimes shows this grave to visitors, once made the cautious remark regarding its occupant that, had he lived, he would probably have turned out to be a bad man.

"And how old was 'Billy' when he died?" asked one curious stranger.

"Twenty-one, senor," replied the ancient. "He died, almost one might say, before he fully began to live."

"You say he was bad?" remarked another stranger.

"He is said to have killed many men."

"How many? How many, amigo, had this man killed at the time he himself died?"

"He had killed," replied the ancient Mexican, "twenty-one men, one for each year of his age, may the saints defend us," said the Mexican.

[AUTHOR'S NOTE: Wallace's 21 men for 21 years is on one of Billy's gravestones.]

"He was a good man, and very kind to poor people. Yet, had he lived, he might, according to the opinion of some, have turned into a bad man."

Gen. Wallace also tells in his autobiography how and why "Billy the Kid" started on his career of crime:

A Waif of New York City.

"The man whose deeds of blood had drawn upon him the eyes of an entire nation, was born a New York waif. Before he was more than ten years of age he was brought to Indiana, and in Terre Haute and Indianapolis, where he was reared, he was known as William Bonne. In 1876, when he was about seventeen years old, he suddenly left his home, crossed the Mississippi and went to the country of the men of his kind – the frontier of the far West.

"Billy began his career with an oath to kill John Chisum, his first employer when the lad reached the plains. Chisum and the "Kid' had been unable to agree on terms of settlement for a season's work. The result was the lad's fearful vendetta, sworn not only against Chisum, but against all of Chisum's other employees as well.

" 'For each herdsman employed by you whom I kill," Billy sent him word, "I will deduct $5 from our unsquared account. If I kill you,' he added grimly, 'my bill will be receipted in full.'

"Then his bloody career began.

[AUTHOR'S NOTE: Wallace fabricates Chisum conflict as Billy's killing motive.]

It was not long until William Bonne, the waif, reared in the peaceful surroundings of Indiana, became the most feared man in the Southwest. At the same time, he was the most revered, the most adored and the most respected man in the Territory.

"It was the kind of good reward that sometimes comes to bad men."

[AUTHOR'S NOTE: Wallace's admission of Billy's being "revered," "adored," and "respected" admitted Billy's inescapable real fame.]

LEW WALLACE'S PARTING WORDS: JANUARY 6, 1905

Lew Wallace's tangled and overwhelming feelings, and his own monstrous role in the pardon bargain betrayal, may have been the block for completing a book on Billy Bonney, leaving only his two decades of reworked lying articles and an episode of his outlaw myth for Billy in his *Autobiography*.

On January 6, 1905, Wallace, with 41 days to live - his deathday at 77 from cancer being February 15, 1905 - still strove for a role in New Mexico Territory history. For its proposed joint statehood with Arizona, he gave the Weekly *Crawfordsville Journal* his position in "The Statehood Bill, General Wallace and Delegate Rodey Take Opposite Views. Wallace for New Mexico As a Single State, But Rodey Says His People Are Reconciled to the Union With Arizona." Wallace stated hypocritically: "I love the people of New Mexico: I lived with them two and one-half years as their governor, and I knew their condition and their needs."

That "love" had not extended to Billy Bonney, his fellow freedom fighters, or New Mexico Territory's citizens desperately needing justice and salvation from the Santa Fe Ring, whose victory and longevity Lew Wallace selfishly guaranteed to save himself.

CHAPTER 24
SUMMARIZED ANALYSIS AND CONCLUSION

LEGACY OF THE LOST PARDON
OF BILLY THE KID

By blocking Billy Bonney's pardon, the Santa Fe Ring and Lew Wallace inadvertently sealed their own condemnation. The Ring needed invisibility to hide its organized crime. Wallace needed public ignorance to hide his betrayal of New Mexico Territory's freedom fight and of its hero, Billy. But Billy's enduring fame undid secrecy, exposing Wallace and the Ring to history's glaring light and revisionist history of this book.

But that lost pardon also attracted hijackers of Billy's fame. Mid-twentieth century addled old-timers, with avaricious dishonest authors, claimed they were Billy, having survived Pat Garrett's shooting. In 1950, author, William Morrison, sought gubernatorial pardon for his imposter, Oliver "Brushy Bill" Roberts, from Governor Thomas Jewett Mabry, who rejected Roberts as fake. I exposed that hoax in my 2010 book, *Billy the Kid's Pretenders: Brushy Bill and John Miller*.

In 2003, corrupt, publicity-seeking, New Mexico Governor, Bill Richardson, colluded, in Santa Fe Ring-style, with the Lincoln County Sheriff's Department, judges, attorneys, political donors, and the press to give dead "Brushy Bill" Roberts a posthumous gubernatorial pardon as Billy the Kid. The public was to be hoodwinked with a modernizing twist: faked forensic DNA matching to "prove" exhumed "Brushy Bill" had been the Kid; and thereby that Pat Garrett had murdered an innocent boy for Billy's Fort Sumner grave. I exposed and stopped that elaborate hoax in my 2012 book: *Cracking the Billy the Kid Case Hoax: The Strange Plot to Exhume Billy the Kid, Convict Sheriff Pat Garrett of Murder, and Become President of the United States*.

These pardon-thrust hoaxes were not about pardoning the real Billy Bonney; nor did they advance the magnificent, tragic, and real history surrounding that pardon. It now remains for the judgment of history as to whether Billy Bonney should be granted a posthumous pardon to honor justice and the cause for which he fought. I, for one, back that, offering up this book.

HOW BILLY THE KID'S PARDON WAS LOST BY LEW WALLACE'S BETRAYAL

Based on analyses in this book, one can state that in March of 1879 Lew Wallace made, with Billy Bonney, a legally binding pardon bargain which promised Billy a pardon for his Lincoln County War indictments in exchange for his eye-witness testimony against Huston Chapman's murderers. Billy fulfilled his side of that bargain by giving that testimony, and got the murderers indicted. Wallace betrayed his side of that bargain by never pardoning Billy for the Regulator killings of William Brady, George Hindman, and Andrew "Buckshot" Roberts.

Analysis of Wallace's pardon bargain betrayal is as follows:

1) Technically, at Billy's written request on March 13, 1879, full pardon was impossible for Wallace to issue, because of U.S. Attorney Thomas Benton Catron's outstanding, 1878, federal, indictment for the Andrew "Buckshot" Roberts killing. Wallace, as Governor, could only pardon Territorial offences. So when making the bargain, Wallace, knowing about that federal case, lied to Billy as to his having the power to pardon him. But Wallace did have the power to pardon Billy for Territorial indictments in the Brady and Hindman killings. So Wallace betrayed his bargain by never pardoning Billy for Brady's and Hindman's killings.

2) Wallace's trickery of keeping secret from Billy the Roberts case's federal indictment, would not have invalidated the binding quality of their pardon bargain if Wallace eventually got the chance to issue its Territorial pardon. In fact, that opportunity came. The federal indictment was quashed as invalid on April 6, 1881 by Judge Warren Bristol in Billy's Mesilla trial for the Roberts killing. No Territorial indictment for the Roberts killing was then made. Wallace was still in New Mexico Territory, and now had the power to act on the Roberts killing. He could have considered pardon for that quashed indictment unnecessary, since a Territorial indictment was not filed. But instead, Wallace made a blanket statement in a Las Vegas *Gazette* interview on April 28, 1881 that he would not give Billy "clemency" - when questioned about the pardon. So Wallace, at that time, betrayed his bargain by not acting on the Roberts killing to shield it from a future Territorial indictment.

851

3) In his bargain proposal letter of March 13, 1879, Billy had requested technically correct "annulment" of his indictments, since he had not had a trial and sentencing. Section 3457 of the *Compiled Laws of New Mexico* stated that the governor had pardoning power for "[a]ny person against whom **prosecution shall have been commenced** under the laws of this territory." An indictment is the commencing of prosecution. So Wallace was in a statutory position to annul Billy's indictments. And once Billy was found guilty on April 9, 1881 of William Brady's killing, or once he got his hanging sentence on April 13, 1881 for that killing, Wallace could have issued a pardon. So Wallace betrayed his bargain by neither annulling Billy's indictments, nor pardoning him after the Brady case verdict and/or sentencing.

4) Wallace had himself condoned stretching pardon in his November 13, 1878 Amnesty Proclamation to the indicted, though it had excluded "any person in bar of conviction under indictment now found" - which had barred Billy as indicted; which was why he proposed the pardon bargain. Wallace wrote to Secretary of the Interior Carl Schurz on June 11, 1879, that he approved Pardon Petitions by T.B. Catron for indicted Ringites - which argued amnesty in bar of continued prosecution - as freeing the courts from conducting their trials. This option was apparently concealed by Wallace from Billy - and was not used by Billy's attorney, Ira Leonard. But it meant that theoretically Billy's pardon bargain was unnecessary. Needed only was a formal Pardon Petition. But that loophole did not free Wallace from his separate bargain with Billy. So Wallace betrayed his bargain by not pardoning Billy.

5) Since the Amnesty Proclamation had a covert option of pleading amnesty in bar of continuing prosecution. Billy's attorney, Ira Leonard, erred by not submitting to Wallace a proper Pardon Petition. But Leonard's error was irrelevant to Wallace's separate pardon bargain with Billy. So Wallace betrayed his bargain by not pardoning Billy.

6) Wallace may have thought that writing meaninglessly to Billy that he had "*the authority to exempt ... from prosecution,*" instead of promising to pardon, freed him of obligation. But ambiguous wording about his pardoning capacity, instead of pardoning intent, was irrelevant to the bargain Wallace actually made. So Wallace betrayed his bargain by not pardoning Billy.

7) Wallace seems also to have used ambiguous wording with Billy's attorney, Ira Leonard, by giving him informal pardon promise letters, to which Billy referred in his Santa Fe jail letter of March 2, 1881. Leonard considered them legally inadequate, as related by Secret Service Agent Azariah Wild in his October 8, 1880 report for October 6th as not *"on shape that satisfied Judge Leonard Antrom's attorney."* But Wallace's writing any letter(s) about the pardon did not free him from the fulfilled pardon bargain. So Wallace betrayed his bargain by not pardoning Billy.

8) Wallace's pardon promise letters may have seemed unsatisfactory to Ira Leonard, who may have desired a pardon affidavit sworn to and signed by Wallace. Indeed, Wallace had issued one to an Ursula Montoya on October 24, 1878. Though Wallace's informal letters about the pardon promise may have been non-committal, they did not free him from his pardon bargain. So Wallace betrayed his bargain by not pardoning Billy.

9) Wallace faced political pressure from the Santa Fe Ring, which opposed Billy's pardon as validating the anti-Ring Regulator uprising of the Lincoln County War and invalidating the Ring's outlaw myth. Linked to exoneration of Billy, would also have been his validation as a witness for the April 1879 Lincoln County Grand Jury and the subsequent Dudley Court of Inquiry. That would have made inescapable the sentencing and punishment of Chapman's indicted Ringite murderers, and the Court Martial - or even hanging for treason - of N.A.M. Dudley as accomplice to the Lincoln County War murder of Alexander McSween and the arson of his house. So Wallace had to chose between the pardon bargain and his own political future. But political consequences did not negate the pardon bargain. So Wallace betrayed his bargain by not pardoning Billy.

10) Wallace faced psychological pressure after being humiliated for his incompetent cross-examination in the military Court of Inquiry for possible Court Martial of N.A.M. Dudley, which replicated his military humiliation at his incompetence in the Civil War Battle of Shiloh. Wallace's response was to flee his embarrassment by abandoning all Lincoln County issues, including Billy's pardon. But Wallace's psychological stress did not negate the pardon bargain. So Wallace betrayed his bargain by not pardoning Billy.

11) Wallace's psychological flaws of narcissism with compensatory elitism and authoritarian sadism elicited in him scorn and abuse of lower-class Billy, once the boy was under his power. Wallace's irrational cruelty was only exacerbated by his primitive competitiveness when faced by Billy as brilliant, cocky, and grand. Furthermore, Billy's egalitarianism and confrontation of Wallace's hypocrisy made him wish Billy dead. So what made Billy a hero in his day, and unforgettable after death, merely contributed to Wallace's desire to hurt him by a refused pardon. But Wallace's psychological problems did not negate the pardon bargain. So Wallace betrayed his bargain by not pardoning Billy.

12) The separate Secret Service pardon might have been a fortunate rescue for Wallace, since his subsequent obsessive reworking of the pardon indicated his underlying guilt at not granting it. But that pardon was thwarted by the Santa Fe Ring's manipulation of gullible Special Operative Azariah Wild by insertion of Billy into the outlaw myth. That check-mated Wallace since he was also using the outlaw myth to avoid confronting anti-Ring Lincoln County War issues. So he did not encourage Wild to complete the new pardon bargain. But lack of a fulfilled Secret Service pardon bargain did not negate Wallace's own pardon bargain. So Wallace betrayed his bargain by not pardoning Billy.

13) Wallace himself admitted to the pardon bargain in a June 23, 1900 *The Indianapolis Press* interview titled "Gen. Wallace's Feud with Billy the Kid;" stating: " 'Testify,' I said, 'before the Grand Jury and the trial court and convict the murderer of Chapman and I will let you go scot-free with a pardon in your pocket for all your misdeeds.' " So Wallace betrayed his bargain by not pardoning Billy.

14) All Wallace's newspaper articles lied that Billy had failed to complete his side of the pardon bargain either by not testifying or by reverting to outlawry. But Billy did fulfill his side by testifying. And his future behavior - bad or good - was irrelevant to the pardon bargain. So Wallace betrayed his bargain by not pardoning Billy.

WAS BILLY THE KID'S PARDON JUSTIFIED?

Beyond the legally binding nature of Billy Bonney's fulfilled pardon bargain with Lew Wallace, was other justification for pardoning him for his three murder indictments: for William Brady, George Hindman, and Andrew "Buckshot" Roberts? It should be noted that Billy's later jailbreak murders of Lincoln County Deputies James Bell and Bob Olinger are irrelevant, since they were the result of jailing after his trial which would not have occurred if the pardon had been granted.

Justification of the pardon is complicated by the inflammatory fact that the victims were lawmen, with Brady being a Lincoln County Sheriff, Hindman being his deputy, and Roberts being his posseman; leading to posthumous pardon opponents naming Billy "a cop killer."

Relevant legal issues are as follows:

1) For Billy's indictments for Brady and Hindman, he was part of a Regulator group and had mitigating circumstances which should have barred a 1st degree murder verdict. As to intent, he was protecting McSween from certain murder by rogue lawmen, Brady and Hindman. And he was not Brady or Hindman's killer, since his revolver lacked the range of the carbines used by the others. In fact, presence in a deadly group without being the killer was used as the defense to get Lincoln County War period outlaw, Jessie Evans, a verdict of 2nd degree murder for an 1880 fatal shooting of lawman, Ranger George Bingham, during a capture of Evans and his gang in Texas. Jessie was sentenced to 17 years in Huntsville Prison, but escaped. Billy's indictments for Brady and Hindman could have been viewed in that less dire light to justify a pardon. And Billy also had a mitigating extension of the legal concept of justifiable homicide in defense of another.

2) Billy's federal indictment for Roberts, though quashed as a federal case on a technical error and moot for pardon, could have been revived as a Territorial one. Then Billy's defense could have been that he, in a group, was an arresting deputy with a warrant and acting in self-defense when Roberts fired first, killing and wounding group members. And Billy did not fire Roberts's single fatal shot. Self-defense is a complete defense, meriting exoneration, and certainly deserving pardon.

Mitigating political factors are as follows:

1) Since the Brady, Hindman, and Roberts killings occurred in the context of Santa Fe Ring atrocities of malicious prosecution, monopolistic suppression of economic competition, and murder - against which citizens had no legal recourse - they go to the heart of revolution in a democratic society. Relevant is the Territorial progression of revolts from 1872 to 1877 against that Ring's tyranny and terrorism, and the legal measures first used in 1878 in Lincoln County to no avail to address that Ring's murder of John Tunstall. Ultimately, the people's only response mirrored the Declaration of Independence's assertion of *"the right of the people to alter or abolish" "government"* destructive of their *"unalienable rights."* The Lincoln County War, in which the killings occurred, can be no better test for Thomas Jefferson's contention that a revolution *"at least once every 20 years [is] a medicine necessary for the sound health of government."* One can ask, other than fighting back, what was left to citizens of Lincoln County? Billy's noble role, taken in the context of revolutionary social upheaval, gives grounds for his pardon.

2) The Lincoln County Regulator movement, inspired by pre-Revolutionary War counterparts, defended citizens' rights against Santa Fe Ring oppression and monopolistic take-over. It was freedom fighting against obstructed legal redress, against murdering of innocent John Tunstall; and usurping of public offices and law enforcement by Ringites. Rebellion was the sole hope for liberation. Moreover, Regulators were legally empowered by Lincoln County Justice of the Peace John Wilson as deputies to arrest Tunstall's murderers. Those deputies, including Billy, were outlawed by Governor S.B. Axtell's Proclamation, the illegality of which led to his removal as governor. Billy's role, taken in the context of his having been legally deputized while fighting Brady, Hindman, and Roberts gives grounds for his pardon.

3) Brady, Hindman, and Roberts can be viewed not as legitimate lawmen, but as murderous agents of the Santa Fe Ring. In that context, all three took part in the illegal murder by posse of John Tunstall. Then Brady obstructed arrest of Tunstall's killers. And Brady and Hindman were prepared to kill Alexander McSween next. Billy's role, taken in the context of opposing dangerous rogue lawmen, gives grounds for his pardon.

4) The Lincoln County War, during which the killings occurred, was a defensive freedom fight against the Santa Fe Ring. Billy's role, in that context, gives grounds for his pardon.

5) Billy proved his commitment to political justice - countering any image of being a wanton killer - by giving an eye-witness affidavit and an eye-witness deposition about Tunstall's murder; accepting a dangerous deputyship to arrest Tunstall's killers; likely writing the "Regulator Manifesto" declaring the movement's idealistic goals; offering to testify as an eye-witness against Huston Chapman's killers in exchange for a pardon, and then testifying; and risking his life to testify on his own against Lincoln County War villain, N.A.M. Dudley, in a military Court of Inquiry for possible court martial. Billy's role, taken in the context of his persistent seeking of justice, gives grounds for his pardon.

6) The outlaw myth, generated by the Santa Fe Ring, Lew Wallace, and Secret Service Agent Azariah Wild, was self-serving fabrication irrelevant to Billy Bonney. Billy's true role, freed of the outlaw myth of Billy the Kid, gives grounds for his pardon.

CONCLUSION

Billy's pardon would have validated New Mexico Territory's Regulator revolution against the Santa Fe Ring. In its essence, that is why the pardon was lost and deserved.

SOURCES AND INDEX

ANNOTATED BIBLIOGRAPHY

GENERAL REFERENCES

Nolan, Frederick. *The Lincoln County War: A Documentary History.* Norman: University of Oklahoma Press. 1992.
_____. *The West of Billy the Kid.* Norman: University of Oklahoma Press. 1998.

LEGAL REFERENCES FOR PARDON AND CRIMINAL CASES

Garner, Bryan A., ed. *Black's Law Dictionary. Seventh Edition.* St. Paul, Minnesota: West Group. 1999
Prince, Hon. L. Bradford, Chief Justice of the Supreme Court of New Mexico. *The General Laws of New Mexico Including All the Unrepealed General Laws From the Promulgation of the "Kearney Code" in 1846, to the End of the Legislative Session of 1880.* Albany, New York: W.C. Little & Co. Law Publishers. 1880.
Victory, John P., Edward L. Bartlett, Thomas N. Wilkerson, Commission. *Compiled Laws of New Mexico in Accordance With an Act of the Legislature, Approved March 16th 1897, Including the Constitution of the United States, the Treaty of Guadalupe Hidalgo, the Gadsden Treaty, the Original Act Organizing the Territory, the Organic Acts as Now in Force, the Original Kearny Code, and a List of Laws Enacted Since the Compilation of 1884, as Well as Those in that Work.* Santa Fe, New Mexico: New Mexico Printing Company. 1897. (**Page 857. Section 3457. Governor's discretion as to pardon.**)
New Mexico Rules Annotated (NMRA), Criminal Code. UJI 14-5172. "Justifiable Homicide; Defense of Another." (**Jury instructions**)
Territory v. Baker, 4 N.M. 236, Supreme Court of the Territory of New Mexico (1887) 4 Gild. 236, 13 P. 30, 4 Johnson 117, 1887-NMSC- 021 (**Jury instructions**)

HISTORICAL ORGANIZATIONS (PERIOD)

NORTH CAROLINA REGULATORS, 18th CENTURY

HISTORY OF 18th CENTURY REGULATORS

Hudson, Arthur Palmer. "Songs of the Carolina Regulators." *William and Mary Quarterly.* 4. No. 4 (1947): Page 146.
Kars, Marjoline. *Breaking Loose Together: The Regulator Rebellion in Pre-Revolutionary North Carolina.* Chapel Hill and London: The University of North Carolina Press. 2002.
Maier, Pauline. *From Resistance to Revolution: Colonial radicals and the development of American opposition to Britain, 1765-1776.* New York and London: W.W. Norton & Company. 1991.

LINCOLN COUNTY REGULATORS, 19th CENTURY

AMERICAN INDEPENDENCE DOCUMENTS

Vincent, Wilson, Jr. *The Book of Great American Documents.* Brookville, Maryland: American History Research Associates. 1993.

DIME NOVELS ON REGULATORS (CONTEMPORARY)

Lody, William F. "Gold Bullet Sport; The Knights of the Overland". *Beadle's Dime New York Library.* 7(83). New York: Beadle & Adams, Publishers. December 17, 1874.

Cooms, Oll. "The Boy Ranger: or, The Heiress of the Golden Horn." *Pocket Series.* No. 11. New York: Beadle & Adams, Publishers. 1874.

Wheeler, Edward L. *The Deadwood Dick Library.* "A Tale of the Regulators and Road-Agents of the Black Hills. The Double Daggers; or, Deadwood Dick's Defiance." Beadles Half Dime Library. No. 20. Cleveland, Ohio: Arthur Westbrook Co. 1877.

_____. "Deadwood Dick, The Prince of the Road: or The Black Rider of the Black Hills". *The Deadwood Dick Library. 1(1).* Cleveland, Ohio: The Arthur Westbrook Co. 1877.

No Author. "The Rover of the Forest." *Munro's Ten Cent Novels.* No. 42. New York: George Munro & Co. 1864.

LINCOLN COUNTY REGULATOR MANIFESTO (BY BILLY BONNEY)

Regulator. "Mr. Walz. Sir ..." Letter to Edgar Walz. July 13, 1878. Adjutant General's Office. File 1405 AGO 1878. (Quoted in Maurice Garland Fulton, *History of the Lincoln County War.* Tucson: University of Arizona Press. 1975. pages 246-247, and Frederick Nolan, *The Lincoln County War: A Documentary History*, page 310.)

SANTA FE RING, 19th CENTURY

GENERAL BOOKS ON ORGANIZED CRIME

Ackerman, Kenneth D. *Boss Tweed: The Rise and Fall of the Corrupt Pol Who Conceived the Soul of Modern New York.* New York: Carroll & Graff Publishers. 2005.

Critchley, David. *The Origin of Organized Crime in America: The New York Mafia, 1891-1931.* New York, London: Routledge, Taylor & Francis Group. 2009.

Reppetto, Thomas. *American Mafia: A History of Its Rise to Power.* New York: Henry Holt and Company. 2004.

Short, Martin. *The Rise of the Mafia: The Definitive Story of Organized Crime.* London: John Blake Publishing Ltd. 2009.

MODERN SOURCES ON SANTA FE RING

Caffey, David L. *Chasing the Santa Fe Ring: Power and Privilege in Territorial New Mexico.* Albuquerque, New Mexico: University of New Mexico Press. 2014.

_____. *Frank Springer and New Mexico: From the Colfax County War to the Emergence of Modern Santa Fe.* Texas A and M. University Press. 2007.

Cleaveland, Agnes Morley. *No Life for a Lady.* Boston: Houghton Mifflin. 1941.

_____. *Satan's Paradise: From Lucien Maxwell to Fred Lambert.* Boston: Houghton Mifflin Company. 1952.

Cleaveland, Norman, *Colfax County's Chronic Murder Mystery.* Santa Fe: New Mexico. The Rydel Press. 1977.

_____. *A Synopsis of the Great New Mexico Cover-up.* Self-printed. 1989.

_____. *Some Comments Norman Cleveland May Make to the Huntington Westerners on Sept. 19, 1987.* Unpublished.

_____. *Some Highlights of William R. Morley's Contribution to the Pioneer Development of the Southwest.* Self-printed. No Date.

_____. *The Great Santa Fe Cover-up.* Based on a Talk given Before the Santa Fe Historical Society on November 1, 1978. Self-printed. 1982.

Cleaveland, Norman and George Fitzpatrick. *The Morleys - Young Upstarts on the Southwest Frontier.* Albuquerque, New Mexico: Calvin Horn Publisher, Inc. 1971.

Keleher, William A. *The Maxwell Land Grant. A New Mexico Item.* Albuquerque, New Mexico: University of New Mexico Press. 1964.

Lamar, Howard Robert N *The Far Southwest 1846 – 1912: A Territorial History.* New Haven and London: Yale University Press. 1966. **(Chapter 6 covers the Santa Fe Ring))**

Meinig, D. W. *The Shaping of America. A Geographical Perspective on 500 Years of History. Vol. 3. Transcontinental America 1850 - 1915.* New Haven and London: Yale University Press. 1998. **(Pages 127 and 132 are on the Santa Fe Ring.)**

Milner, Clyde A. II, Carol A. O'Connor, Martha Sandweiss. Eds. *The Oxford History of the American West.* New York and Oxford: Oxford University Press. 1994.

Montoya, María E. Translating Property. The Maxwell Land Grant and the Conflict Over Land in the American West, 1840-1900. Berkeley and Los Angeles: University of California Press. 2002.

Naegle, Conrad Keeler. *The History of Silver City, New Mexico 1870-1886.* University of New Mexico Bachelor of Arts thesis. Pages 30-60. Unpublished. 1943. Collection of the Silver City Museum, Silver City, New Mexico. **(Grant County rebellion against Santa Fe Ring)**

_____. "The Rebellion of Grant County, New Mexico in 1876." *Arizona and the West: A Quarterly Journal of History.* Autumn, 1968. Volume 10. Number 3. Tucson, Arizona: The University of Arizona Press. 1968. Pages 225-240. **(Grant County rebellion against Santa Fe Ring)**

Newman, Simeon Harrison III. "The Santa Fe Ring." *Arizona and the West.* Volume 12. Autumn 1970. Pages 269-288.

Otero, Miguel A. *My Life on the Frontier, 1882-1897: Incidents and Characters of the period when Kansas, Colorado, and New Mexico were Passing Through the Last of their Wild and Romantic Years.* New York: The Press of the Pioneers. 1935. Pages 232-233. (Quoted by Victor Westphall, *Thomas Benton Catron and His Era.* Page 188) **(Quote: "the 'Santa Fe Ring,' the real machine controlling the political situation in New Mexico.")**

Pearson, Jim Berry. *The Maxwell Land Grant.* Norman: University of Oklahoma Press. 1961.

Taylor, Morris F. *O.P. McMains and the Maxwell Land Grant Conflict.* Tucson, Arizona: The University of Arizona Press. 1979. **(Traces origins of the Santa Fe Ring)**

Theisen, Lee Scott. "Frank Warner Angel's Notes on New Mexico Territory, 1878." *Arizona and the West: A Quarterly Journal of History.* Winter 1976. Volume 18. Number 4. Pages 333-370. **(About the Angel notebook)**

Twitchell, Ralph Emerson. *The Leading Facts of New Mexico History* Vol. I-II. Santa Fe: Sunstone Press. 2007. (Reprinted from 1912 edition) **(Reputed Ringman and its cover-up historian)**

Westphall, Victor. *Thomas Benton Catron and His Era.* Tucson, Arizona: University of Arizona Press. 1973. **(Ring-denier biographer)**

CONTEMPORARY SOURCES ON SANTA FE RING (CHRONOLOGICAL)

No Author. *Diario del Consejo der Territorio de Neuvo Mejico, Session de 1871-1872.* Santa Fe New Mexican. **January 8, 1872.** Santa Fe: A.P. Sullivan. 1872. Pages 144-154. New Mexico Supreme Court Library. Santa Fe, New Mexico. **(A Ring expurgated document, with copy found in 1942 by Conrad Naegle; confirms troops used by Ring to suppress 1872 Legislature Revolt)**

No Author. *Diario del Consejo der Territorio de Neuvo Mejico, Session de 1871-1872.* Las Cruces *Borderer* **January 24, 1872.** Pages 110-113. **(President of the Council Don Diego Archuleta objects to troops in legislature)**

No Author. *Journal of the House of Representatives of the Territory of New Mexico, Session of 1871-1872.* Santa Fe: A.P. Sullivan. **1872.** Pages 144-154. **(Confirms troops used by Ring to suppress the Legislature Revolt of 1872)**

Mills, Melvin W. "Thought I would write you how things are running." Letter to Robert H. Longwill. **December 5, 1873.** "Exhibit A" in the August 9, 1878 deposition of Frank Springer to Investigator Frank Warner Angel. Frank Warner Angel report titled *In the Matter of the Investigation of the Charges Against S.B. Axtell Governor of New Mexico.* October 3, 1878. Interior Department Papers 1850-1907; Appointments Division and Subsequent Actions. Microfilm Case File No. 44-4-8-3. Record Group 48. Microfilm Roll M750. National Archives and Records Administration. U.S. Department of Interior. Washington, D.C. **(About Catron and Ring empowerment)**

Bristol Warren. "From sources of information that I deem perfectly reliable I am satisfied that there are public disorders in Lincoln County ..." Letter to Governor Marsh Giddings. **January 10, 1874.** Herman B. Weisner Papers, ca. 1957-1992. New Mexico State University Library at Las Cruces. Rio Grande Historical Collections. Accession No. Weisner Ms 0249. Box 4/39. Folder D-4. Folder Name: "Judge Bristol's letter." **(Santa Fe Ring's outlaw myth and proposed use of military intervention)**

No Author. "Ring influence [in the Territorial legislature is] being actively used against every measure that tends to do justice" [in Grant and Doña Counties]." Grant County *Herald.* **August 8, 1875.** Quoted by Conrad Keeler Naegle in *The History of Silver City, New Mexico 1870-1886,* doctoral thesis. Page 39.

Morley, William Raymond and Frank Springer. On Oscar McMains's citizen's Meeting. *Cimarron News and Press.* **November 10, 1875.** In Mary McPherson, Letters and Petitions to President Rutherford B. Hayes re: Removal Governor Axtell and the Santa Fe Ring. 1977. Interior Department Papers 1850-1907; Appointments Division and Subsequent Actions. Microfilm File Case Number 44-4-8-3. **Record Group 48.** Microfilm Roll M750. National Archives and Records Administration. **(Colfax County citizens meeting on F.J. Tolby murder by Santa Fe Ring.)**

_____. " 'The Territory of Elkins.' Assassination of Supposed Sun Correspondent. The Murder of the Rev. F.J. Tolby in New Mexico. A Probate Judge Accused of Complicity in the Crime. Indignation Meeting." *New York Weekly Sun.* **December 22, 1875.** Interior Department Papers 1850-1907; Appointments Division and Subsequent Actions. Microfilm Roll M750. National Archives and Records Administration. Record Group 48. Microfilm Case File Number 44-4-8-3. U.S. Department of Interior. Washington, D. C. **(From May 1, 1877 submission to President Rutherford B. Hates as "Mary E. McPherson and W.B. Matchett 'Make certain charges against the U.S. Officials in the Territory of New Mexico.' ")**

Middaugh, Asa F. Deposition. **March 31, 1876.** "Exhibit B" in the August 9, 1878 deposition of Frank Springer to Investigator Frank Warner Angel. Frank Warner Angel report titled *In the Matter of the Investigation of the Charges Against S.B. Axtell Governor of New Mexico.* October 3, 1878. Interior Department Papers 1850-1907; Appointments Division and Subsequent Actions. Microfilm Case File No. 44-4-8-3. Record Group 48. Microfilm Roll M750. National Archives and Records Administration. U.S. Department of Interior. Washington, D.C. **(About Catron's malicious prosecution of Ada McPherson Morley)**

No Author. "A Contemplated Political Change." Grant County *Herald.* **September 16, 1876.** Quoted by Conrad Keeler Naegle in *The History of Silver City, New Mexico 1870-1886* doctoral thesis. Pages 39-40. **(Listing reasons to escape the Ring by annexing to Arizona Territory)**

No Author. [Grant County should not] "sort o' wait and hear from Santa Fe ... before taking action." Tucson *Arizona Citizen.* **September 23, 1876.** Quoted by Conrad Keeler Naegle in *The History of Silver City, New Mexico 1870-1886* doctoral thesis. Page 41. **(Arizona encourages escape from Santa Fe Ring)**

No Author. Grant County *Herald.* **September 30, 1876.** **("Annexation Meeting" announced)**

No Author. "Proceedings of Grant County Annexation Meeting." Grant County *Herald.* **Saturday October 7, 1876.** Page 2. Columns 1 and 2. Collection of the Silver City, New Mexico, Museum. (**Anti-Santa Fe Ring "Grant County Declaration of Independence" published**)

No Author. Grant County *Herald.* " 'Petition to Remove Judge Bristol. We the undersigned citizens of the Third Judicial District of the Territory of New Mexico, without regard to party, would respectfully request and petition for the removal of Judge Warren Bristol ...' " No date. **1876 or 1877.** (Quoted in ' W.B. Matchett and Mary E. McPherson 'Make certain charges against the U.S. Officials in the Territory of New Mexico.' " Letter to President Rutherford B. Hayes. Received and filed May 1 1877. Interior Department Papers 1850-1907; Appointments Division and Subsequent Actions. Microfilm File Case Number 44-4-8-3. Record Group 48. Microfilm No. M750. Roll 1. National Archives and Records Administration. U.S. Department of Justice. Washington, D.C.) (**Anti-Santa Fe Ring article**)

No Author. Report on murder trial for Franklin Tolby. Pueblo, *Colorado Chieftain.* **May 25, 1876.** Quoting *Daily New Mexican*, May 1, 1876. From Morris F. Taylor. *O.P. McMains and the Maxwell Land Grant Conflict.* Tucson, Arizona: The University of Arizona Press. 1979. Page 49. (**Ring-biased jury instructions by Judge Henry Waldo to protect Ring murderers of Tolby**)

McPherson, Mary. "Charges against Thomas B. Catron, U.S. Attorney, and Others." **February 7, 1877.** Letter to Attorney General Alphonso Taft. Interior Department Papers 1850-1907; Appointments Division and Subsequent Actions. Microfilm File Case Number 44-4-8-3. Record Group 48. Microfilm Roll M750. National Archives and Records Administration. U.S. Department of Justice. Washington, D.C.

Catron, Thomas Benton. 'Answering Charges of Mary E. McPherson." **February 24, 1877.** Letter to Attorney General Alphonso Taft. Interior Department Papers 1850-1907; Appointments Division and Subsequent Actions. Microfilm File Case Number 44-4-8-3. Record Group 48. Microfilm Roll M750. National Archives and Records Administration. U.S. Department of Justice. Washington, D.C

Morley William Raymond. "I was astonished beyond measure at your proceedings, and have fears as to the result ..." Letter to Mary McPherson. **March 6, 1877.** McPherson Mary E. Letters and Petitions to President Rutherford B. Hayes re: Removal Governor Axtell and the Santa Fe Ring. Interior Department Papers 1850-1907; Appointments Division and Subsequent Actions. File Case Number 44-4-8-3. Record Group 48. Microfilm Roll M750. National Archives and Records Administration. U.S. Department of Justice. Washington, D. C. (**Hopes she can help fight against Santa Fe Ring; enclosed in Mary McPherson's addendum to her "Certain Charges against U.S. Officials in the Territory of New Mexico."**)

Morley William Raymond. "I was astonished beyond measure at your proceedings, and have fears as to the result ..." Letter to Mary McPherson. **March 6, 1877.** McPherson Mary E. Letters and Petitions to President Rutherford B. Hayes re: Removal Governor Axtell and the Santa Fe Ring. Interior Department Papers 1850-1907; Appointments Division and Subsequent Actions. Microfilm File Case Number 44-4-8-3. Record Group 48. Microfilm Roll M750. National Archives and Records Administration. U.S. Department of Justice. Washington, D. C. (**Hopes she can help fight against Santa Fe Ring; enclosed in Mary McPherson's "Charges Against U.S. Officials in the Territory of New Mexico."**)

Morley, Ada. "Yes, we have received all your letters at Vermejo here but we have hesitated about replying ..." Letter to Mary McPherson **March 7, 1877.** McPherson, Mary E. Letters and Petitions to President Rutherford B. Hayes re: Removal Governor Axtell and the Santa Fe Ring. Interior Department Papers 1850-1907; Appointments Division and Subsequent Actions. Microfilm File Case Number 44-4-8-3. Record Group 48. Microfilm Roll M750. National Archives and Records Administration. U.S. Department of Justice. Washington, D. C. (**Fears** about her fight against Santa Fe Ring; oddly this private letter was in her mother's governmental file)

Lambert, J.J. "At It Again." Pueblo, Colorado, *Enterprise and Chronicle*. **April 21, 1877**. Interior Department Papers 1850-1907; Appointments Division and Subsequent Actions. Microfilm File Case Number 44-4-8-3. Record Group 48. Microfilm No. M750. Roll 1. National Archives and Records Administration. U.S. Department of Justice. Washington, D.C. (**Description of Santa Fe Ring control of courts and malicious prosecution of opponents like Oscar McMains in the Franklin Tolby murder; used in: "W.B. Matchett and Mary E. McPherson 'Make Certain Charges Against the U.S. Officials in the Territory of New Mexico.' " Letter to President Rutherford B. Hayes. Received and filed May 1, 1877. Interior Department Papers 1850-1907; Appointments Division and Subsequent Actions. Microfilm File Case Number 44-4-8-3. Record Group 48. Microfilm No. M750. Roll 1. National Archives and Records Administration. U.S. Department of Justice. Washington, D.C.**)

Matchett, W.B. and Mary E. McPherson. "W.B. Matchett and Mary E. McPherson 'Make Certain Charges Against the U.S. Officials in the Territory of New Mexico.' " Letter to President Rutherford B. Hayes. Received and filed **May 1, 1877**. Interior Department Papers 1850-1907; Appointments Division and Subsequent Actions. Microfilm File Case Number 44-4-8-3. Record Group 48. Microfilm No. M750. Roll 1. National Archives and Records Administration. U. S. Department of Justice. Washington, D.C. (**Sent to President Rutherford B. Hayes and Secretary of the Interior Carl Schurz 141 pages of letters, affidavits, petitions, newspaper articles, itemized requests for removal of Governor Samuel Beach Axtell and District Judge Warren Bristol, documentation of use of the military against civilians, documentation of the Ring murder of Ring opponent Reverend F.J. Tolby, and identification of the Santa Fe Ring and Elkins and Catron as its leaders.**)

McPherson, Mary and W.B. Matchett. "To the President. Please make the enclosed a part of the evidence in the case of "Charges Against New Mexican Officials" Letter to President Rutherford B. Hayes. **May 3, 1877**. McPherson, Mary E. Letters and Petitions to President Rutherford B. Hayes re: Removal Governor Axtell and the Santa Fe Ring. Interior Department Papers 1850-1907; Appointments Division and Subsequent Actions. Microfilm File Case Number 44-4-8-3. Record Group 48. Microfilm Roll M750. National Archives and Records Administration. U.S. Department of Justice. Washington, D.C. (**Addendum to their May, 1877 "Certain Charges Against U.S. Officials in New Mexico Territory."**)

McPherson, Mary and W.B. Matchett. "The Secretary of the Interior, Sir - Accompanying please find copy of charges, &c., against S.B. Axtell, Governor, and other New Mexican Officials ..." "Charges Against New Mexican Officials." Letter to Secretary of the Interior Carl Schurz. **May 5, 1877**. McPherson, Mary E. Letters and Petitions to President Rutherford B. Hayes re: Removal Governor Axtell and the Santa Fe Ring. Interior Department Papers 1850-1907; Appointments Division and Subsequent Actions. Microfilm File Case Number 44-4-8-3. Record Group 48. Microfilm Roll M750. National Archives and Records Administration. U.S. Department of Justice. Washington, D. C.

McPherson, Mary E. Letters and Petitions to President Rutherford B. Hayes re: Removal Governor Axtell and the Santa Fe Ring. **1977**. Interior Department Papers 1850-1907; Appointments Division and Subsequent Actions. Microfilm File Case Number 44-4-8-3. Record Group 48. Microfilm Roll M750. National Archives and Records Administration.

McPherson, Mary and W.B. Matchett. "We have respectfully to request that the following named records, documents, papers, communications and correspondence be supplied ..." Records Request to Secretary of the Interior Carl Schurz. **July 26, 1877**. Interior Department Papers 1850-1907; Appointments Division and

Subsequent Actions. Microfilm File Case Number 44-4-8-3. Record Group 48. Microfilm No. M750. Roll 1. National Archives and Records Administration. U. S. Department of Justice. Washington, D.C. (**Requesting records of the Santa Fe Ring, Carton, Elkins, and Axtell**)

McPherson, Mary. "Please place before the Attorney General ..." Letter to President Rutherford B. Hayes. **August 23, 1877.** Interior Department Papers 1850-1907; Appointments Division and Subsequent Actions. Microfilm File Case Number 44-4-8-3. Record Group 48. Microfilm No. M750. Roll 1. National Archives and Records Administration. U.S. Department of Justice. Washington, D.C. (**Requesting that her "Charges vs. New Mexico Officials" go to the Attorney General.**)

McPherson, Mary and W B. Matchett. "In the Matter of Charges vs. Gov. S.B. Axtell and Other New Mexico Officials. Submitted to the Departments of the Interior and Justice. **August, 1877.** Printed as a 31 page booklet. No publisher listed. Indiana Historical Society. Lew Wallace Collection. M0292. Box 3. Folder 20. (**Exposé of Santa Fe Ring, Catron, and Elkins; in Lew Wallace's possession**)

McPherson, Mary. "I desire to know when I can be heard ..." Letter to Secretary of Interior Carl Schurz. **September 30, 1977.** Interior Department Papers 1850-1907; Appointments Division and Subsequent Actions. Microfilm File Case Number 44-4-8-3. Record Group 48. Microfilm No. M750. Roll 1. National Archives and Records Administration. U. S. Department of Justice. Washington, D.C. (**Requesting to be heard in person on her charges against officials and Governor Axtell.**)

Angel, Frank Warner. "To Gov. Lew Wallace, Santa Fe, N. M., 1878." Notebook. **1878**. Indiana Historical Society. Lew Wallace Collection. M0292. Microfilm No. F372. (**Original missing, copy on microfilm; Notebook prepared for Lew Wallace listing names in Lincoln County and the Santa Fe Ring**)

Tunstall, John Henry. "A Tax-Payer's Complaint . . January 18, 1878." Mesilla Independent. **January 26, 1878.** (**Exposé of William Brady, James Dolan, and John Riley for tax fraud and use of public money to purchase cattle; and T.B. Catron then paid that bill**)

Dolan, James J. "Answer to A Tax-Payer's Complaint." Mesilla Independent. **January 29, 1878.** (**Response to J.H. Tunstall's exposé of him, William Brady, and John Riley for tax fraud and use of public money to purchase cattle; and T.B. Catron then paid that bill**)

Springer, Frank. "I hope you have received a full account of the Troubles in Lincoln County from your nephew ..." Letter to Senator Rush Clark. **April 9, 1878.** Herman B. Weisner Papers, ca. 1957-1992. New Mexico State University Library at Las Cruces. Rio Grande Historical Collections. Accession No. Weisner Ms 0249. Box 4/39. Folder D-6. Folder Name "Frank Springer Letter to Rush Clark." (**Links Santa Fe Ring to murder of J.H. Tunstall**)

Leonard, Ira. "When you left here I promised to write you concerning events transpiring here ..." Letter to Lew Wallace. **May 20, 1878** [sic - 79]. Indiana Historical Society. Lew Wallace Collection. M0292. Box 4. Folder 10. (**With quote: "the Santa Fe Ring that has been so long an incubus on the government of this territory"**)

Morley, William Raymond. "Your letter of the 7th came last night and it was a good long newsy letter ..." Letter to wife, Ada McPherson Morley. **August 15, 1878.** Collection of Norman Cleaveland. Quoted in Norman Cleaveland, The Morleys: Young Upstarts in the Southwest. Albuquerque, New Mexico: Calvin Horn Publisher, Inc. 1971. Pages 152-155. (**About possible betrayal by Angel's reports; about the Santa Fe Ring, T.B. Catron, S.B. Elkins, S.B. Axtell, and Henry Waldo; and the Lincoln County War**)

Angel, Frank Warner. Examination of Charges Against F. C. Godfroy, Indian Agent, Mescalero, N. M. **October 2, 1878.** (Report 1981, Inspector E. C. Watkins; Cited as Watkins Report). M 319-20 and L147-44-4-8. Record Group 075.

National Archives and Records Administration. U.S. Department of Justice. Washington, D.C.

Morley, William Raymond. Deposition to Investigator Frank Warner Angel. August 9, 1878. Frank Warner Angel report titled *In the Matter of the Investigation of the Charges Against S.B. Axtell Governor of New Mexico.* **October 3, 1878.** Interior Department Papers 1850-1907; Appointments Division and Subsequent Actions. Microfilm Case File No. 44-4-8-3. Record Group 48. Microfilm Roll M750. National Archives and Records Administration. U.S. Department of Interior. Washington, D.C. (**Mentions Catron, Elkins, and the Santa Fe Ring, and provided Exhibits of letters exposing Catron's evil.**)

Angel, Frank Warner. *In the Matter of the Investigation of the Charges Against S.B. Axtell Governor of New Mexico.* **October 3, 1878.** Frank Warner Angel report. Interior Department Papers 1850-1907; Appointments Division and Subsequent Actions. Microfilm Case File No. 44-4-8-3. Record Group 48. Microfilm Roll M750. National Archives and Records Administration. U.S. Department of Interior. Washington, D.C. (**Mentions Santa Fe Ring**)

_____. *In the Matter of the Investigation of the Charges Against S. B. Axtell Governor of New Mexico.* **October 3, 1878.** Angel Report. Microfilm File No. 44-4-8-3. Record Group 48. Roll M750. National Archives. U.S. Department of Interior. Washington, D.C.

_____. *In the Matter of the Examination of the Causes and Circumstances of the Death of John H. Tunstall a British Subject.* **October 4, 1878.** Angel Report. Microfilm File Case Number 44-4-8-3. Record Group 48. Microfilm No. M750. Roll 1. National Archives and Records Administration. U.S. Department of Justice. Washington, D.C.

_____. *In the Matter of the Lincoln County Troubles. To the Honorable Charles Devens, Attorney General.* **October 4, 1878.** Angel Report. Microfilm Case File No. 44-4-8-3. Record Group 48. Microfilm Roll M750. National Archives and Records Administration. U.S. Department of Justice. Washington, D.C.

Wallace, Lew. "Our mutual friend, M. Hinds, who will hand you this ..." Letter to A.H. Markland. **November 14, 1878.** Indiana Historical Society. Lew Wallace Collection. M0292. Box 3. Folder 17. (**Aware of the Santa Fe Ring and its attempt to remove him as governor**)

No Author. *Proceedings of a Court of Inquiry in the Case of Lt. Col. N.A.M. Dudley.* **May 2, 1879 – July 5, 1879.** File No. QQ1284. (Boxes 3304, 3305, 3305A); Court Martial Files 1809-1894. Records of the Office of the Judge Advocate General – Army. Record Group 153. Old Military and Civil Branch. National Archives and Records Administration. Washington, D.C.

Leonard, Ira E. "When you left here I promised to write you concerning events transpiring here ..." Letter to Lew Wallace. **May 20, 1878 [sic - 79].** Indiana Historical Society. Lew Wallace Collection. M0292. Box 4. Folder 10. (**Has quote on the Murphy-Dolan party as: "part and parcel of the Santa Fe ring that has been so long an incubus on the government of this territory."**)

_____. "I write to you with pencil because I am laboring for breath ..." Letter to Lew Wallace. **May 23, 1879.** Indiana Historical Society. Lew Wallace Collection. M0292. Box 4. Folder 11. (**With quote "we are pouring the 'hot shot' into Dudley." With enclosed letter of May 20, 1879**)

_____. "Yours of the 7th inst reached me ..." Letter to Lew Wallace. **June 13, 1879.** Indiana Historical Society. Lew Wallace Collection. M0292. Box 4. Folder 11. (**Important quotes: "... they would not enter our objections ..." "... would not allow us to show the conspiracy formed with Dolan beforehand ..." "I tell you Governor as long as the present incumbent occupies the bench all that Grand Juries may do to bring to justice these men every effort will be thwarted by him and the sympathizers of that side."**)

Elkins, Stephen Benton. "I have waited some time to reply to your lengthy letter ..." Letter to T.B. Catron. **August 15, 1879**. West Virginia & Regional History Center. West Virginia University Libraries, Morgantown, W. Va. Stephen B. Elkins Papers (A&M 53). Box 1. Folder 1. **(Reveals he prevented Catron's dismissal and indictment from Angel's report)**

Wallace, Lew. "I have the honor to inform you that the Legislature of this Territory adjourned ..." **February 16, 1880**. Letter to Carl Schurz. Indiana Historical Society. Lew Wallace Collection. M0292. Box 4. Folder 14. **(Important documentation of Catron as head of the Santa Fe Ring, and Wallace's Ring opposition)**

No Author. "The Santa Fe Ring is the most corrupt combination that ever cursed any country or community." Las Cruces *Thirty-Four Newspaper*. **October 27, 1880**. From Victor Westphall, *Thomas Benton Catron and His Era*. Page 186. **(Article on Santa Fe Ring abuses urging voters to oppose Ring candidates)**

No Author. "A man named Springer is in Washington trying to defeat the nomination of Governor Axtell. Springer is a friend of the thugs and thieves of Colfax County." *Santa Fe New Mexican*. **July 6, 1882**. **(Santa Fe Ring re-instatement of S.B. Axtell to public office)**

No Author. " 'Chief Justice Axtell' is a bitter pill for the Raton *News and Press*." *Santa Fe New Mexican*. **July 18, 1882**. **(Santa Fe Ring re-instatement of S.B. Axtell as Chief Justice)**

No Author. "The Ring must soon discover that the time has passed in New Mexico when men can be herded like so many sheep ..." *Albuquerque Daily Democrat*. **March 4, 1884**. Quoted by Victor Westphall, *Thomas Benton Catron and His Era*. Page 191. **(About Santa Fe Ring control of appointments to legislature)**

Thornton, W.T. "Your favors received. We will try and have the matter of Mrs. Wilson's estate at Albuquerque attended to for your Bates County friends." Letter to John J. Cockrell, Esq. **January 16, 1886**. Herman B. Weisner Papers, ca. 1957-1992. New Mexico State University Library at Las Cruces. Rio Grande Historical Collections. Accession No. Weisner Ms 0249. Box 12. Folder S-5. Folder Name: "Catron, Thornton, & Clancy Letterhead." **(Catron's law partner discloses Ring planned malicious prosecution in Lincoln County)**

Borrego, Francisco Gonzales y. "dear Sir I have the honor to report to you that I have two men that they have agreed to come to the Republican party ... they want $10.00 each ..." **July 23, 1890**. Letter to Thomas Benton Catron. Catron Papers 102, Box 8. Quoted by Victor Westphall, *Thomas Benton Catron and His Era*. Page 268. **(Revealing Catron's Ringite vote-buying and loyalty to Ring agents)**

Chavez, Juliana V. "Mr. Catron, you are not above suspicion of knowing more about the assassination of my son than you have found it convenient to reveal . ." Letter of Juliana Chavez to T.B. Catron. Reprinted in *Santa Fe Weekly New Mexican*. **March 8, 1894**. Quoted in Victor Westphall, *Thomas Benton Catron and his Era*. Page 226. **(Accusing Catron as accomplice to murder of Francisco Chavez, with implication of Santa Fe Ring)**

No author. "T.B. Catron's reputation now being "smirched" by evidence that he was a briber and too dishonest even to practice law ..." *Las Vegas Independent Democrat*. **1895**; quoting from *Las Vegas Optic*. **September 2, 1884**. From Victor Westphall. *Thomas Benton Catron and His Era*. Pages 105-106. **(About Catron's and Elkins's dishonesty, the Santa Fe Ring, and disbarring Catron from law practice in New Mexico)**

Catron, Thomas Benton (As "Anonymous"). "Is it honesty or partisanship?" Letter to the Editor, Thomas Hughes. *Albuquerque Daily Citizen*. **October 9, 1895**. **(Defamation of his disbarment Judge Thomas J. Smith)** Cited by Victor Westphall, *Thomas Benton Catron and His Era*. Page 246. Thomas B. Catron Papers. University of New Mexico Center for Southwest Studies. University Library. MSS 29 BC.

_____. "[Y]ou must absolutely stand pat and not give away any information that will injure me ..." Letter to Editor of the *Albuquerque Daily Citizen* Thomas Hughes. **October 10, 1895.** Catron Papers. 801. Box 1. Quoted by Victor Westphall, *Thomas Benton Catron and His Era.* Page 247. (**Catron influencing the Ringite newspaper editor to prevent his own disbarment by the New Mexico Supreme Court**)

_____. "Editor of the Citizen: I have noticed an article in the Citizen of the 9th inst., which seems to reflect on Chief Justice Smith ..." Letter to Editor of the *Albuquerque Daily Citizen* Thomas Hughes. **October 10, 1895.** Catron Papers 801. Box 1. Quoted by Victor Westphall, *Thomas Benton Catron and His Era.* (page 248) (**Catron lying in letter to complicit Ringite editor to conceal his own authorship of the newspaper's article accusing his Supreme Court disbarment judge of bias**)

_____. "[Chief Justice] Tom Smith, son of "Extra Billy" Smith, brother of ... the embezzler, who fled from justice in Arizona, and brother of the other Smith who took a prominent part in the murder of Dave Broderick ..." "[Judge] Hamilton should ... see that the decision is an absolute, complete, unconditional vindication. This is what I ask him. He can afford to give it." Letter to *Socorro Chieftain* publisher S.W. Williams. **October 25, 1895.** Catron Papers. 105. Vol. 13. Quoted by Victor Westphall, *Thomas Benton Catron and His Era.* Page 251. (**Example of Catron's vicious defamation of his Supreme Court disbarment Chief Judge Thomas Smith in Ringite collusion with the press, and use of illegal influence on another judge**)

Hamilton, Humphrey. *Majority Opinion* in disbarment case against Thomas Benton Catron. "[T]he low moral character and poor reputation for veracity of the prosecution witnesses rendered their testimony beyond belief." **October 25, 1895.** Catron Papers. 801. Box 1. Quoted by Victor Westphall, *Thomas Benton Catron and His Era.* Page 251. (**Ring colluding judge vindicating Catron from disbarment by blocking prosecution evidence**)

Catron, Thomas Benton. "His [Chief Justice Thomas Smith] skin is so thin that the slightest attack punctures him. I think the papers should now puncture him so much ..." Letter to T.W. Collier. **November 11, 1895.** Catron Papers. 105. Vol. 13. Quoted by Victor Westphall, *Thomas Benton Catron and His Era.* Page 249. (**Example of Catron's vicious Ringite harassment of an opponent**)

_____. "The letter of Gov. Thornton [in the September 11, 1896 of the *Santa Fe Daily New Mexican* and exposing his defamation plot] is regarded here by all good citizens as being ... calculated to bring about a state of unrest and possible bloodshed." **September 16, 1896.** Letter to President Grover Cleveland. Catron Papers 801, Box 1. Quoted by Victor Westphall, *Thomas Benton Catron and His Era.* Pages 269-270. (**Catron's paranoid accusations against Thornton**)

Wallace, Lew. "I have your several letters, including the last one of the 3rd inst." Letter to Eugene Fiske. **November 6, 1897.** Indiana Historical Society. Lew Wallace Collection. AC233. Box 1. Folder 7. (part of 1981 addition) (**About T.B. Catron's control over New Mexicans**)

No Author. *Los Angeles Times.* **1899.** Undated clipping, Laughlin Papers, State Records Center, Santa Fe, New Mexico. Quoted by Victor Westphall, *Thomas Benton Catron and His Era.* Page 285. (**Joking article about the Santa Fe Ring**)

Catron, Thomas Benton. "[Otero backers] have made a very villainous, mean ugly fight against me." **September 20, 1902.** Letter to Dave Winters. Catron Papers 105, Volume 20. Quoted by Victor Westphall, *Thomas Benton Catron and His Era.* Pages 291. (**Catron's accusing of rival, Governor Miguel Otero, of his own ring-style criminality**)

Cutting, Bronson. "Catron was the boss of the Territory ..." Letter to James Roger Addison. **December 11, 1911.** Cited by Victor Westphall in *Thomas Benton Catron and His Era* from his citation: Lincoln County Manuscripts Division. Box 12. Courtesy of David Stratton. (**Catron as head of the Santa Fe Ring**)

Johnson, E. Dana. "[H]e ruled with a rod of iron ..." Editorial. *Santa Fe New Mexican*. **May 16, 1921**. Catron Papers 801, Box 1. Quoted by Victor Westphall, *Thomas Benton Catron and His Era*. Pages 394-395. (**Santa Fe Ring tactics of "boss" Catron without using the words Santa Fe Ring**)

Pritchard, George W. "Eulogy." **May 17, 1921**. Catron Papers 801, Box 1. Quoted by Victor Westphall, *Thomas Benton Catron and His Era*. Pages 393-394. (**Cover-up of Santa Fe Ring atrocities for Catron's death eulogy**)

Mabry, Thomas Jewett. "New Mexico's Constitution in the Making." *New Mexico Historical Review*. 1943. Volume 19, Issue 170. Quoted by Victor Westphall, *Thomas Benton Catron and His Era*. Page 341. (**Revealing that future Governor Mabry was Ring biased, calling T.B. Catron an "able delegate" to New Mexico's 1912 constitutional convention**)

ARTICLES (CHRONOLOGICAL)

No Author. Las Cruces *Thirty-Four Newspaper*. **October 27, 1880**. (**Urging voters to overthrow Catron's Santa Fe Ring-backed candidate**)

See Also: Thomas Benton Catron; Stephen Benton Elkins

SECRET SERVICE, 19th CENTURY

Bowen, Walter S. and Harry Edward Neal. *The United States Secret Service*. Philadelphia and New York: Chilton Company Publishers. 1960.

Brooks, James J. *1877 Report on Secret Service Operatives*. (September 26, 1877). "On Azariah Wild." p.392. Department of the Treasury. United States Secret Service. Washington D.C.

Burnham, George P. *American Counterfeits. How Detected, And How Avoided. Comprising Sketches of Noted Counterfeiters, and Their Allies, Of Secret Agents, and Detectives; Authentic Accounts of the Capture of Forgers, Defaulters, and Swindlers; With Rules for Deciding Good and Counterfeit Notes, or United States Currency; A List of Terms and Phrases in Use Among This Fraternity of Offenders, &c., &c.* Springfield, Massachusetts: W. J. Holland 1875.

_____. *Memoirs of the United States Secret Service With Accurate Portraits of Prominent Members of the Detective Force, Some of Their Most Notable Captures, and a Brief Account of the Life of Col. H. C. Whitley, Chief of the Division*. Boston: Lee, Shepard. 18??.

_____. *Three Years With Counterfeiters, Smugglers, and Boodle Carriers; With Accurate Portraits of the Prominent Members of the Detective Force in The Secret Service*. Boston: John P. Dale & Co. 18??.

Johnson, David R. *Illegal Tender. Counterfeiting and the Secret Service in Nineteenth Century America*. Washington and London: Smithsonian Institution Press. 1995.

Wild, Azariah F. "Daily Reports of U. S. Secret Service Agents, Azariah F. Wild. Microfilm T-915. Record Group 87. Rolls 306 (June 15, 1877 - December 31, 1877), 307 (January 1, 1878 - June 30, 1879), 308 (July 1, 1879 - June 30, 1881), 309 (July 1, 1881 - September 30, 1883), and 310 (October 1, 1883 - July 31, 1886). National Archives and Records Department. Department of Treasury. United States Secret Service. Washington, D. C.

Wild, Azariah. Telegraph on counterfeit bills. January 4, 1881. Herman B. Weisner Papers, ca. 1957-1992. New Mexico State University Library at Las Cruces. Rio Grande Historical Collections. Accession No. Weisner Ms 0249. Box 11. Folder O-1. Folder Name: "Olinger, Robert and James W. Bell."

NEW MEXICO TERRITORY REBELLIONS AGAINST THE SANTA FE RING (CHRONOLOGICAL)

GENERAL SOURCE

Vincent, Wilson, Jr. *The Book of Great American Documents.* Brookville, Maryland: American History Research Associates. 1993.

LEGISLATURE REVOLT (1872)

No Author. *Las Vegas Optic.* **September 2, 1884. (About the anti-Ring Legislature revolt and Catron's alliance with corrupt Judge Joseph Palen)**

GRANT COUNTY REBELLION (1876)

MODERN HISTORICAL SOURCES

Naegle, Conrad Keeler. *The History of Silver City, New Mexico 1870-1886.* University of New Mexico Bachelor of Arts thesis. Pages 30-60. Unpublished. 1943. Collection of the Silver City Museum, Silver City, New Mexico.

_____. "The Rebellion of Grant County, New Mexico in 1876." *Arizona and the West: A Quarterly Journal of History.* Autumn, 1968. Volume 10. Number 3. Tucson, Arizona: The University of Arizona Press. 1968. Pages 225-240. **(Rebellion against Santa Fe Ring)**

CONTEMPORARY SOURCES (CHRONOLOGICAL)

No Author. "Diario del Consejo der Territorio de Neuvo Mejico, Session de 1871-1872." *Santa Fe New Mexican.* **January 8, 1872.** Santa Fe: A.P. Sullivan. 1872. Pages 144-154. New Mexico Supreme Court Library. Santa Fe, New Mexico. **(A Ring expurgated document, with a copy found in 1942 by Conrad Naegle; confirming troops used by Ring to suppress Territorial legislature)**

No Author. "Diario del Consejo der Territorio de Neuvo Mejico, Session de 1871-1872. Las Cruces *Borderer.* **January 24, 1872.** Pages 110-113. **(Don Diego Archuleta, President of the Council, gives speech objecting to troops in legislature)**

No Author. "Ring influence [in the Territorial legislature is] being actively used against every measure that tends to do justice" [in Grant and Doña Counties]." Grant County *Herald.* **August 8, 1875.** Quoted by Conrad Keeler Naegle in *The History of Silver City, New Mexico 1870-1886,* doctoral thesis. Page 39.

No Author. "A Contemplated Political Change." Grant County *Herald.* **September 16, 1876.** Quoted by Conrad Keeler Naegle in *The History of Silver City, New Mexico 1870-1886* doctoral thesis. Pages 39-40. **(Listing reasons to escape the Ring by annexing to Arizona Territory)**

No Author. Grant County *Herald.* **September 23, 1876. (Need for school system stressed.)**

No Author. Grant County *Herald.* **September 30, 1876. ("Annexation Meeting" announced)**

No Author. "Proceedings of Grant County Annexation Meeting." Grant County *Herald.* **Saturday October 7, 1876.** Page 2. Columns 1 and 2. Collection of the Silver City, New Mexico, Museum. **(Anti-Santa Fe Ring "Grant County Declaration of Independence" published)**

No Author. Grant County *Herald.* " 'Petition to Remove Judge Bristol. We the undersigned citizens of the Third Judicial District of the Territory of New Mexico, without regard to party, would respectfully request and petition for the removal of Judge Warren Bristol ...' " No date. **1876 or 1877**.(Quoted in "W.B. Matchett and Mary E. McPherson 'Make certain charges against the U.S. Officials in the

Territory of New Mexico.' " Letter to President Rutherford B. Hayes. Received and filed May 1, 1877. Interior Department Papers 1850-1907; Appointments Division and Subsequent Actions. Microfilm File Case Number 44-4-8-3. Record Group 48. Microfilm No. M750. Roll 1. National Archives and Records Administration. U.S. Department of Justice. Washington, D.C.)

SEE ALSO: Santa Fe Ring; Thomas Benton Catron; Stephen Benton Elkins

COLFAX COUNTY WAR (1877)

MODERN SOURCES

Caffey, David L. *Frank Springer and New Mexico: From the Colfax County War to the Emergence of Modern Santa Fe.* Texas A and M. University Press. 2007.

Cleaveland, Norman. *The Morleys - Young Upstarts on the Southwest Frontier.* Albuquerque, New Mexico: Calvin Horn Publisher, Inc. 1971.

Dunham, Harold H. "New Mexican Land Grants with Special Reference to the Title Papers of the Maxwell Grant." *New Mexico Historical Review.* (January 1955) Vol. 30, No. 1. pp. 1 - 23.

Keleher, William A. *The Maxwell Land Grant. A New Mexico Item.* Albuquerque, New Mexico: University of New Mexico Press. 1964.

Lamar, Howard Roberts. *The Far Southwest 1846 - 1912. A Territorial History.* New Haven and London: Yale University Press. 1966.

Montoya, María E. *Translating Property. The Maxwell Land Grant and the Conflict Over Land in the American West, 1840-1900.* Berkeley and Los Angeles, California: University of California Press. 2002.

Murphy, Lawrence R. *Lucien Bonaparte Maxwell. Napoleon of the Southwest.* Norman: University of Oklahoma Press. 1983.

Pearson, Jim Berry. *The Maxwell Land Grant.* Norman: University of Oklahoma Press. 1961.

Poe, Sophie. *Buckboard Days.* Albuquerque, New Mexico: University of New Mexico Press. 1964.

Taylor, Morris F. *O.P. McMains and the Maxwell Land Grant Conflict.* Tucson, Arizona: The University of Arizona Press. 1979.

CONTEMPORARY SOURCES (CHRONOLOGICAL)

Morley, William Raymond and Frank Springer. On Oscar McMains's citizen's Meeting. *Cimarron News and Press.* **November 10, 1875** In Mary McPherson, Letters and Petitions to President Rutherford B Hayes re: Removal Governor Axtell and the Santa Fe Ring. 1977. Interior Department Papers 1850-1907; Appointments Division and Subsequent Actions. Microfilm File Case Number 44-4-8-3. Record Group 48. Microfilm Roll M750. National Archives and Records Administration. **(Colfax County citizens meeting on F.J. Tolby murder by Santa Fe Ring.)**

No author. "Anarchy at Cimarron." *Santa Fe Weekly New Mexican.* **November 16, 1875. (Ringite backing of Axtell's use of troops in the Colfax County War)**

Morley, William Raymond and Frank Springer. " 'The Territory of Elkins.' Assassination of Supposed Sun Correspondent. The Murder of the Rev. F.J. Tolby in New Mexico. A Probate Judge Accused of Complicity in the Crime. Indignation Meeting." *New York Weekly Sun.* **December 22, 1875**. Interior Department Papers 1850-1907; Appointments Division and Subsequent Actions. Microfilm Roll M750. National Archives and Records Administration. Record Group 48. Microfilm Case File Number 44-4-8-3. U. S. Department of Interior. Washington, D. C.**(From May 1, 1877 complaint to President Rutherford B. Hayes as "Mary E. McPherson and W.B. Matchett 'Make certain charges against the U.S. Officials in the Territory of New Mexico.' ")**

Dawson, Will. Editorial. *Cimarron News and Press*. **December 31, 1875.** (**Ringbiased editorial by temporary editor blaming citizens for unrest**)
Morley William Raymond. "I was astonished beyond measure at your proceedings, and have fears as to the result ..." Letter to Mary McPherson. **March 6, 1877.** McPherson, Mary E. Letters and Petitions to President Rutherford B. Hayes re: Removal Governor Axtell and the Santa Fe Ring. Interior Department Papers 1850-1907; Appointments Division and Subsequent Actions. Microfilm File Case Number 44-4-8-3. Record Group 48. Microfilm Roll M750. National Archives and Records Administration. U.S. Department of Justice. Washington, D. C. (**Hopes she can help fight against Santa Fe Ring; enclosed in Mary McPherson's "Charges Against U.S. Officials in the Territory of New Mexico."**)
Lambert, J.J. "At It Again." Pueblo, Colorado, *Enterprise and Chronicle*. **April 21, 1877.** Interior Department Papers 1850-1907; Appointments Division and Subsequent Actions. Microfilm File Case Number 44-4-8-3. Record Group 48. Microfilm No. M750. Roll 1. National Archives and Records Administration. U.S. Department of Justice. Washington, D.C. (**Description of Santa Fe Ring control of courts and malicious prosecution of opponents like Oscar McMains in the Franklin Tolby murder; used in: "W.B. Matchett and Mary E. McPherson 'Make Certain Charges Against the U.S. Officials in the Territory of New Mexico.' " Letter to President Rutherford B. Hayes. Received and filed May 1, 1877. Interior Department Papers 1850-1907; Appointments Division and Subsequent Actions. Microfilm File Case Number 44-4-8-3. Record Group 48. Microfilm No. M750. Roll 1. National Archives and Records Administration. U. S. Department of Justice. Washington, D.C.**)
Matchett, W.B. and Mary E. McPherson. "Make Certain Charges Against the U.S. Officials in the Territory of New Mexico." To the President. **April, 1877.** Microfilm File Case Number 44-4-8-3. Record Group 48. Microfilm No. M750. Roll 1. National Archives and Records Administration. U. S. Department of Justice. Washington, D.C. (**Sent to President Rutherford B. Hayes and Secretary of the Interior Carl Schurz 141 pages of letters, affidavits, petitions, newspaper articles, itemized requests for removal of Governor Samuel Beach Axtell and District Judge Warren Bristol, documentation of use of the military against civilians, documentation of the Ring murder of Ring opponent Reverend F.J. Tolby, and identification of the Santa Fe Ring.**)
McPherson, Mary and W.B. Matchett. "To the President. Please make the enclosed a part of the evidence in the case of "Charges Against New Mexican Officials" Letter to President Rutherford B. Hayes. **May 3, 1877.** McPherson, Mary E. Letters and Petitions to President Rutherford B. Hayes re: Removal Governor Axtell and the Santa Fe Ring. Interior Department Papers 1850-1907; Appointments Division and Subsequent Actions. Microfilm File Case Number 44-4-8-3. Record Group 48. Microfilm Roll M750. National Archives and Records Administration. U.S. Department of Justice. Washington, D.C. (**Addendum to their May, 1877 "Certain Charges Against U.S. Officials in New Mexico Territory."**)
McPherson, Mary and W.B. Matchett. "The Secretary of the Interior, Sir - Accompanying please find copy of charges, &c., against S.B. Axtell, Governor, and other New Mexican Officials ..." "Charges Against New Mexican Officials." Letter to Secretary of the Interior Carl Schurz. **May 5, 1877.** McPherson, Mary E. Letters and Petitions to President Rutherford B. Hayes re: Removal Governor Axtell and the Santa Fe Ring. Interior Department Papers 1850-1907; Appointments Division and Subsequent Actions. Microfilm File Case Number 44-4-8-3. Record Group 48. Microfilm Roll M750. National Archives and Records Administration. U.S. Department of Justice. Washington, D. C.
McPherson, Mary and W.B. Matchett. "We have respectfully to request that the following named records, documents, papers, communications and correspondence be supplied ..." Records Request to Secretary of the Interior Carl Schurz. **July 26,**

1877. Interior Department Papers 1850-1907; Appointments Division and Subsequent Actions. Microfilm File Case Number 44-4-8-3. Record Group 48. Microfilm No. M750. Roll 1. National Archives and Records Administration. U.S. Department of Justice. Washington, D.C. (**Requesting records of the Santa Fe Ring, Carton, Elkins, and Axtell**)

McPherson, Mary E. and W.B. Matchett. "In the Matter of the Charges vs Gov. S. B. Axtell and Other New Mexico Officials; Submitted to the Departments of the Interior and of Justice. Governor of New Mexico." **August, 1877**. Printed as a 31 page booklet. No publisher listed. Indiana Historical Society. Lew Wallace Collection. M0292. Box 3. Folder 20. (**Focus on the Santa Fe Ring**)

McPherson, Mary. "I desire to know when I can be heard ..." Letter to Secretary of Interior Carl Schurz. **September 30, 1977**. Interior Department Papers 1850-1907; Appointments Division and Subsequent Actions. Microfilm File Case Number 44-4-8-3. Record Group 48. Microfilm No. M750. Roll 1. National Archives and Records Administration. U. S. Department of Justice. Washington, D.C. (**Requesting audience on charges against Ring officials**)

Springer, Frank. "I endorse herewith, directed to the President ..." Letter to Secretary of the Interior Carl Schurz. **June 10, 1878**. Microfilm File Case Number 44-4-8-3. Record Group 48. Microfilm No. M750. Roll 1. National Archives and Records Administration. U.S. Department of Justice. Washington, D.C.

_____. "The undersigned, a citizen of the County of Colfax ..." To His Excellency, the President of the United States. Enclosed in letter to Secretary of the Interior Carl Schurz. **June 10, 1878**. Microfilm File Case Number 44-4-8-3. Record Group 48. Microfilm No. M750. Roll 1. National Archives and Records Administration. U.S. Department of Justice. Washington, D.C.

Morley, William Raymond. "Your letter of the 7th came last night and it was a good long newsy letter ..." Letter to wife, Ada McPherson Morley. **August 15, 1878**. Collection of Norman Cleaveland. Quoted in Norman Cleaveland, *The Morleys: Young Upstarts in the Southwest*. Albuquerque, New Mexico: Calvin Horn Publisher, Inc. 1971. Pages 152-155. (**About possible betrayal by Angel's reports; about the Santa Fe Ring, T.B. Catron, S.B. Elkins, S.B. Axtell, and Henry Waldo; and the Lincoln County War**)

No Author. "Rejoicing at Cimarron," "Axtell's Head Falls at Last," "General Lew. Wallace Appointed Governor." *Cimarron News and Press*. **September 6, 1878**.

No Author. *Santa Fe Weekly New Mexican*. **September 21, 1878 and October 19, 1878**. (**Ring-biased accolades for removed Gov. Axtell**)

SEE ALSO: Regulators, Santa Fe Ring; Thomas Benton Catron; Stephen Benton Elkins

LINCOLN COUNTY WAR (1878)

MODERN HISTORICAL SOURCES

Cramer, T. Dudley. *The Pecos Ranchers in the Lincoln County War*. Orinda, California: Branding Iron Press. 1996.

Fulton, Maurice Garland. Robert N. Mullin. Ed. *History of the Lincoln County War*. Tucson, Arizona: The University of Arizona Press. 1997.

Jacobsen, Joel. *Such Men as Billy the Kid. The Lincoln County War Reconsidered*. Lincoln and London: University of Nebraska Press. 1994.

Keleher, William A. *The Fabulous Frontier: Twelve New Mexico Items*. Albuquerque, New Mexico: The University of New Mexico Press. 1962.

_____.*Violence in Lincoln County 1869-1881*. Albuquerque, New Mexico: University of New Mexico Press. 1957. (**Las Vegas *Gazette* article of December 28, 1880, "The Kid. Interview with Billy Bonney. Pages 293-295; Las Vegas *Gazette* article of December 28, 1880. Untitled. Pages 296-297**)

Mullin, Robert N. Re: Frank Warner Angel Meeting with President Hayes. August, 1878. Binder RNM, VI, M. Midland, Texas: Nita Stewart Haley Memorial Library and J. Everet Haley History Center. (Unpublished).

Nolan, Frederick W. *The Life and Death of John Henry Tunstall*. Albuquerque, New Mexico: The University of New Mexico Press. 1965.

_____. *The Lincoln County War: A Documentary History*. Norman: University of Oklahoma Press. 1992.

_____. *The West of Billy the Kid*. Norman: University of Oklahoma Press. 1998.

Rasch, Philip J. *Gunsmoke in Lincoln County*. Laramie, Wyoming: National Association for Outlaw and Lawmen History, Inc. with University of Wyoming. 1997.

_____. Robert K. DeArment. Ed. *Warriors of Lincoln County*. Laramie: National Association for Outlaw and Lawmen History, Inc. with University of Wyoming. 1998.

Utley, Robert M. *High Noon in Lincoln. Violence on the Western Frontier*. Albuquerque, New Mexico: University of New Mexico Press. 1987.

Wilson, John P. *Merchants, Guns, and Money: The Story of Lincoln County and Its Wars*. Santa Fe, New Mexico: Museum of New Mexico Press. 1987.

No Author. "Disturbances in the Territories, 1878 - 1894. Lawlessness in New Mexico." Senate Documents. 67th Congress. 2nd Session. December 5, 1921 - September 22, 1922. pp. 176 - 187. Washington, D.C.: Government Printing Office. 1922.

CONTEMPORARY REPORTS AND DOCUMENTS (CHRONOLOGICAL)

No Author. "Brady Inventory McSween Property." **February, 1878**. Herman B. Weisner Papers, ca. 1957-1992. New Mexico State University Library at Las Cruses. Rio Grande Historical Collections. Accession No. Weisner Ms 0249. Box 10. Folder M15. Folder Name. "Will and Testament A. McSween."

Angel, Frank Warner. *Examination of charges against F. C. Godfroy, Indian Agent, Mescalero, N. M.* **October 2, 1878**. (Report 1981, Inspector E. C. Watkins; Cited as Watkins Report). M 319-20 and L147, 44-4-8. Record Group 075. National Archives and Records Administration. U.S. Department of Justice. Washington, D.C.

_____. *In the Matter of the Investigation of the Charges Against S. B. Axtell Governor of New Mexico. Report and Testimony.* **October 3, 1878**. Angel Report. Microfilm Case File No. 44-4-8-3. Record Group 48. Microfilm Roll M750. National Archives and Records Administration. U.S. Department of Interior. Washington, D.C.

_____. *In the Matter of the Examination of the Causes and Circumstances of the Death of John H. Tunstall a British Subject.* **October 4, 1878**. Angel Report. Microfilm File Case Number 44-4-8-3. Record Group 48. Microfilm No. M750. Roll 1. National Archives and Records Administration. U.S. Department of Justice. Washington, D.C.

_____. *In the Matter of the Lincoln County Troubles. To the Honorable Charles Devens, Attorney General.* **October 4, 1878**. Angel Report. Microfilm Case File No. 44-4-8-3. Record Group 48. Microfilm Roll M750. National Archives and Records Administration. U.S. Department of Justice. Washington, D.C.

No Author. "Amnesty for Matthews and Long in the Third Judicial Court April Term 1879." **April, 1879**. Herman B. Weisner Papers, ca. 1957-1992. New Mexico State University Library at Las Cruces. Rio Grande Historical Collections. Accession No. Ms 0249. Box 1. Folder 4. Folder Name. "Amnesty."

No Author. "Charges against Jessie Evans and John Kinney." Doña Ana County Civil and Criminal Docket Book. **August 18, 1875 to November 7, 1878**. Herman B. Weisner Papers, ca. 1957-1992. New Mexico State University Library at Las Cruces. Rio Grande Historical Collections. Accession No. Ms 0249. Box 13. Folder V 3. Folder Name. "Venue, Change Of."

No Author. "Dismissal of Cases Against Dolan, Matthews, Peppin, October 1879 District Court." **October, 1879**. Herman B. Weisner Papers, ca. 1957-1992. New Mexico State University Library at Las Cruces. Rio Grande Historical Collections. Accession No. Ms 0249. Box 13. Folder V3. Folder Name: "Venue, Change Of."

No Author. *Proceedings of a Court of Inquiry in the Case of Lt. Col. N.A.M. Dudley.* **May 2,1879 – July 5, 1879**. File No. QQ1284. (Boxes 3304, 3305, 3305A); Court Martial Files 1809-1894. Records of the Office of the Judge Advocate General – Army. Record Group 153. Old Military and Civil Branch. National Archives and Records Administration. Washington, D.C. (**Commander tried for Lincoln County War role**)

No Author. "Killers of Tunstall. February 18, 1879." Herman B. Weisner Papers, ca. 1957-1992. New Mexico State University Library at Las Cruses. Rio Grande Historical Collections. Accession No. Ms 0249. Box 12. Folder T1. Folder Name: "Tunstall, John H."

No Author. "Lincoln County Indictments July 1872 - 1881." Herman B. Weisner Papers, ca. 1957-1992. New Mexico State University Library at Las Cruces. Rio Grande Historical Collections. Accession No. Ms 0249. Box 8. Folder L11. Folder Name. "Lincoln Co. Indictments."

ARTICLES (CHRONOLOGICAL)

Tunstall, John Henry. "A Tax-Payer's Complaint .. January 18, 1878." Mesilla *Independent*. **January 26, 1878**. (**Exposé of William Brady, James Dolan, and John Riley for using tax money to buy cattle; and Catron's paying that bill**)

Dolan, James J. "Answer to A Tax-payer's Complaint." Mesilla *Independent*. **January 29, 1878**. (**Response to J.H. Tunstall's exposé of him, William Brady, and John Riley for tax fraud and use of public money to purchase cattle; and T.B. Catron then paid that bill**)

No author. "Why Axtell Wanted Troops." **July 31, 1878**. Santa Fe. Newspaper unknown. Enclosed in report of Frank Warner Angel: *In the Matter of the Examination of the Causes and Circumstances of the Death of John H. Tunstall a British Subject.* Report filed October 4, 1878. Interior Department Papers 1850-1907; Appointments Division and Subsequent Actions. Microfilm File Case Number 44-4-8-3. Record Group 48. Microfilm No. M750. Roll 1. National Archives and Records Administration. U.S. Department of Justice. Washington, D.C. (**Enclosed with letter to the President, from a John G. Hubbard of August 1, 1878.**).

LETTERS (CHRONOLOGICAL)

Elkins, Stephen Benton. "Axtell Gov. New Mexico: A strong protest against his removal by S.B. Elkins who says the charges against him are vague & irresponsible." To the President. **June 11, 1877**. Microfilm File Case Number 44-4-8-3. Record Group 48. Microfilm No. M750. Roll 1. National Archives and Records Administration. U.S. Department of Justice. Washington, D.C. (**Referred by President to the Secretary of the Interior on June 13, 1877.**)

McSween, A.A. and B.H. Ellis. Secretaries. "To his Excellency Rutherford B. Hayes, President of the United States of America." With attached proceedings of the April 1878 Lincoln Grand Jury. **April 26, 1878**. Microfilm File Case Number 44-4-8-3. Record Group 48.. Microfilm No. M750. Roll 1. National Archives and Records Administration. U.S. Department of Justice. Washington, D.C.

Isaacs, I. and G.N. Coe "Charges Against S.B. Axtell, Governor of New Mexico." To President Rutherford B. Hayes. **June 22, 1878**. Microfilm File Case Number 44-4-8-3. Record Group 48. Microfilm No. M750. Roll 1. National Archives and Records Administration. U.S. Department of Justice. Washington, D.C.

Morley, William Raymond. "Your letter of the 7th came last night and it was a good long newsy letter ..." Letter to wife, Ada McPherson Morley. **August 15, 1878.** Collection of Norman Cleaveland. Quoted in Norman Cleaveland, *The Morleys: Young Upstarts in the Southwest.* Albuquerque, New Mexico: Calvin Horn Publisher, Inc. 1971. Pages 152-155. (**About possible betrayal by Angel's reports; about the Santa Fe Ring, T.B. Catron, S.B. Elkins, S.B. Axtell, and Henry Waldo; and the Lincoln County War**)

Angel, Frank Warner. "I enclose copies of letters received by me from Gov Axtell ..." Letter to Secretary of the Interior Carl Schurz. **August 24, 1878.** (Including copy of letter to him from Governor Axtell of August 12, 1878; and his response to Axtell of August 13, 1878.) Microfilm File Case Number 44-4-8-3. Record Group 48. Microfilm No. M750. Roll 1. National Archives and Records Administration. U.S. Department of Justice. Washington, D.C.

_____. "I have just been favored by a call from W.L. Rynerson ..." To Secretary of Interior Carl Schurz. **September 6, 1878.** Microfilm File Case Number 44-4-8-3. Record Group 48. Microfilm No. M750. Roll 1. National Archives and Records Administration. U.S. Department of Justice. Washington, D.C.

Elkins, Stephen Benton. "To the President. Referring to a conversation had with you last week ... Hon. S. B. Elkins favors appointment Axtell, ExGov. as Gov'r of New Mexico." Letter to President Rutherford B. Hayes. **March 17, 1881.** (Received Executive Mansion April 6, 1881). Microfilm Roll M750. National Archives and Records Administration. Record Group 48. Microfilm Case File Number 44-4-8-3. U.S. Department of Interior. Washington, D. C.

Bradstreet, George P. Chairman Judiciary Committee of U.S. Senate. "Asking for papers in the matter of charges against Sam'l B. Axtell late Governor of New Mexico." (For appointment as Chief Justice of New Mexico Supreme Court). **June 22, 1882.** Microfilm File Case Number 44-4-8-3. Record Group 48. Microfilm No. M750. Roll 1. National Archives and Records Administration. U.S. Department of Justice. Washington, D.C.

SEE ALSO: Santa Fe Ring; Thomas Benton Catron; Stephen Benton Elkins

WHITE CAPS (LAS GORRAS BLANCAS) (1880)

No Author. "White Cap's Proclamation." *Las Vegas Optic.* March 12, 1880. (Manifesto against land-grabbing Catron and the Ring)

HISTORICAL FIGURES (PERIOD)

ANGEL, FRANK WARNER

PRESIDENT HAYES MEETING

Mullin, Robert N. Re: Frank Warner Angel Meeting With President Hayes August, 1878. Binder RNM, VI, M. (Unpublished). Midland, Texas: Nita Stewart Haley Memorial Library and J. Evert Haley History Center. (Undated).

LETTERS BY FRANK WARNER ANGEL

Angel, Frank Warner. "I enclose copies of letters received by me from Gov Axtell ..." Letter to Secretary of the Interior Carl Schurz. **August 24, 1878.** (Enclosing copy of letter to him from Governor S.B. Axtell of August 12, 1878; and Angel's response to Axtell of August 13, 1878.) Microfilm File Case Number 44-4-8-3. Record Group 48. Microfilm No. M750. Roll 1. National Archives and Records Administration. U.S. Department of Justice. Washington, D.C.

Angel, Frank Warner. "I have just been favored by a call from W.L. Rynerson ..." Letter to Secretary of Interior Carl Schurz. **September 6, 1878.** Microfilm File Case Number 44-4-8-3. Record Group 48. Microfilm No. M750. Roll 1. National Archives and Records Administration. U.S. Department of Justice. Washington D.C.

_____. "I am in receipt of a copy of a letter sent you by one Wm McMullen ..." Letter to Carl Schurz. **September 9, 1878.** The Papers of Carl Schurz 1842 - 1906 in 165 Volumes. Library of Congress 1935. General Correspondence July 26, 1873 - October 7, 1878. Shelf Accession No 14,803. Container 45.

LETTER ABOUT FRANK WARNER ANGEL

Morley, William Raymond. "Your letter of the 7th came last night and it was a good long newsy letter ..." Letter to wife, Ada McPherson Morley. **August 15, 1878.** Collection of Norman Cleaveland. Quoted in Norman Cleaveland, *The Morleys: Young Upstarts in the Southwest.* Albuquerque, New Mexico: Calvin Horn Publisher, Inc. 1971. Pages 152-155. (**About possible betrayal by Angel's reports; about the Santa Fe Ring, T.B. Catron, S.B. Elkins, S.B. Axtell, and Henry Waldo; and the Lincoln County War**)

PAPERS OF FRANK WARNER ANGEL

McMullen, William. "In view of the existing troubles in our territory I appeal ..." Letter to Carl Schurz. **August 24, 1878.** The Papers of Carl Schurz 1842 - 1906 in 165 Volumes. Library of Congress 1935. General Correspondence July 26, 1878 - October 7, 1878. Shelf Accession No. 14,803. Container 45.

McPherson, Mary E. Letters and Petitions to President Rutherford B. Hayes re: Removal Governor Axtell and the Santa Fe Ring. Interior Department Papers 1850-1907; Appointments Division and Subsequent Actions. Microfilm File Case Number 44-4-8-3. Record Group 48. Microfilm Roll M750. National Archives and Records Administration. U.S. Department of Justice. Washington, D. C.

REPORTS BY FRANK WARNER ANGEL

Angel, Frank Warner. *Examination of charges against F. C. Godfroy, Indian Agent, Mescalero, N. M.* **October 2, 1878.** (Report 1981, Inspector E.C Watkins; Cited as Watkins Report). M319-20 and L147, 44-4-8. Record Group 075. National Archives and Records Administration. U.S. Department of Justice. Washington, D. C.

_____. *In the Matter of the Investigation of the Charges Against S.B. Axtell Governor of New Mexico. Report and Testimony.* **October 3, 1878.** Angel Report. Interior Department Papers 1850-1907; Appointments Division and Subsequent Actions. Microfilm Case File No. 44-4-8-3. Record Group 48. Microfilm Roll M750. National Archives and Records Administration. U.S. Department of Interior. Washington, D.C.

_____. *In the Matter of the Lincoln County Troubles. To the Honorable Charles Devens, Attorney General.* **October 4, 1878.** Angel Report. Microfilm Case File No. 44-4-8-3. Record Group 48. Microfilm Roll M750. National Archives and Records Administration. U.S. Department of Justice. Washington, D.C.

_____. *In the Matter of the Examination of the Causes and Circumstances of the Death of John H. Tunstall a British Subject.* Report filed **October 4, 1878.** Angel Report. Interior Department Papers 1850-1907 Appointments Division and Subsequent Actions. Microfilm File Case Number 44-4-8-3. Record Group 48. Microfilm No. M750. Roll 1. National Archives and Records Administration. U.S. Department of Justice. Washington, D.C.

NOTEBOOK BY FRANK WARNER ANGEL

Angel, Frank Warner. "Gov. Lew. Wallace / Santa Fe, N.M." **1878**. Indiana Historical Society. Lew Wallace Collection. Microfilm No. F372. (**Original missing, copy on microfilm; Notebook prepared for Lew Wallace on Lincoln County and the Santa Fe Ring**)

Theisen, Lee Scott. "Frank Warner Angel's Notes on New Mexico Territory, 1878." *Arizona and the West: A Quarterly Journal of History.* Winter 1976. Volume 18. Number 4. Pages 333-370. (**About the Angel notebook**)

AXTELL, SAMUEL BEACH

CONTEMPORARY SOURCES (CHRONOLOGICAL)

No author. "Anarchy at Cimarron." *Santa Fe Weekly New Mexico.* **November 16, 1875**. (**Ring-biased article justifying Governor S.B. Axtell calling in troops in the Colfax County War after murder of Reverend Franklin Tolby**)

Axtell, Samuel B. "The Legislature to Assess Property. *Message of Gov. Samuel B. Axtell to the Legislative Assembly of New Mexico, Twenty-second Session.* Page 4. Manderfield & Tucker, Public Printers: Santa Fe, New Mexico. **1875 or 1876**. Interior Department Papers 1850-1907; Appointments Division and Subsequent Actions. Microfilm File Case Number 44-4-8-3. Record Group 48. Microfilm No. M750. Roll 1. National Archives and Records Administration. U.S. Department of Justice. Washington, D.C.

Morley William Raymond. "I was astonished beyond measure at your proceedings, and have fears as to the result ..." Letter to Mary McPherson. **March 6, 1877**. McPherson, Mary E. Letters and Petitions to President Rutherford B. Hayes re: Removal Governor Axtell and the Santa Fe Ring. Interior Department Papers 1850-1907; Appointments Division and Subsequent Actions. Microfilm File Case Number 44-4-8-3. Record Group 48. Microfilm Roll M750. National Archives and Records Administration. U.S. Department of Justice. Washington, D. C. (**Hopes she can help fight against Santa Fe Ring; enclosed in Mary McPherson's "Charges Against U.S. Officials in the Territory of New Mexico."**)

McPherson, Mary and W.B. Matchett. "To The President. Please make the enclosed a part of the evidence in the case of "Charges Against New Mexican Officials." Letter to President Rutherford B. Hayes. **May 3, 1877**. McPherson, Mary E. Letters and Petitions to President Rutherford B. Hayes re: Removal Governor Axtell and the Santa Fe Ring. Interior Department Papers 1850-1907; Appointments Division and Subsequent Actions. Microfilm File Case Number 44-4-8-3. Record Group 48. Microfilm Roll M750. National Archives and Records Administration. U.S. Department of Justice. Washington, D.C. (**Addendum to their May, 1877 "Certain Charges Against U.S. Officials in New Mexico Territory."**)

McPherson, Mary and W.B. Matchett. "The Secretary of the Interior, Sir - Accompanying please find copy of charges, &c., against S.B. Axtell, Governor, and other New Mexico Officials ..." Letter to Secretary of the Interior Carl Schurz. **May 5, 1877**. McPherson, Mary E. Letters and Petitions to President Rutherford B. Hayes re: Removal Governor Axtell and the Santa Fe Ring. Interior Department Papers 1850-1907; Appointments Division and Subsequent Actions. Microfilm File Case Number 44-4-8-3. Record Group 48. Microfilm Roll M750. National Archives and Records Administration. U.S. Department of Justice. Washington, D. C.

Elkins, Stephen B. "I trouble you to say a word in behalf of Gov. Axtell ..." Letter to President Rutherford B. Hayes. **June 11, 1877**. Interior Department Papers 1850-1907; Appointments Division and Subsequent Actions. Microfilm Roll M750. National Archives and Records Administration Record Group 48. Microfilm Case Number 44-4-8-3. U. S. Department of Interior. Washington D. C.

Axtell, Samuel B. "I have today mailed to you a reply to the charges on file in your Dept against me." Letter to Secretary of the Interior Carl Schurz. **June 15, 1877**. Interior Department Papers 1850-1907; Appointments Division and Subsequent Actions. Microfilm Roll M750. National Archives and Records Administration Record Group 48. Microfilm Case Number 44-4-8-3 U.S. Department of Interior. Washington D.C. (**Refuting charges made in Colfax County**).

McPherson, Mary and W B. Matchett. "We have respectfully to request that the following named records, documents, papers, communications and correspondence be supplied ..." Records Request to Secretary of the Interior Carl Schurz. **July 26, 1877**. Interior Department Papers 1850-1907; Appointments Division and Subsequent Actions. Microfilm File Case Number 44-4-8-3. Record Group 48. Microfilm No. M750. Roll 1. National Archives and Records Administration. U. S. Department of Justice. Washington, D.C. (**Requesting records of the Santa Fe Ring, Carton, Elkins, and Axtell**)

_____. *In the Matter of Charges vs. Gov. S.B. Axtell and Other New Mexico Officials. Submitted to the Departments of the Interior and Justice.* **August, 1877**. Printed as a 31 page booklet. No publisher listed. Indiana Historical Society. Lew Wallace Collection. M0292. Box 3. Folder 20. (**Major exposé about the Santa Fe Ring, Catron, and Elkins; in Lew Wallace's personal possession**)

_____. "To the President. I am unable to enforce the law ..." (Telegram). **March 3, 1878**. Interior Department Papers 1850-1907; Appointments Division and Subsequent Actions. Microfilm Roll M750. National Archives and Records Administration Record Group 48. Microfilm Case File Number 44-4-8-3. U.S. Department of Interior. Washington D.C.

_____. "I respectfully request leave of absence for ninety days ..." Letter to President Rutherford B. Hayes. **March 3, 1878**. Interior Department Papers 1850-1907; Appointments Division and Subsequent Actions. Microfilm Roll M750. National Archives and Records Administration Record Group 48. Microfilm Case File Number 44-4-8-3 U.S. Department of Interior. Washington D.C.

McPherson, Mary E. and W.B. Matchett. "In the Matter of the Charges vs. Gov. S.B. Axtell and Other New Mexico Officials; Submitted to the Departments of the Interior and of Justice. Governor of New Mexico." **August, 1877**. Printed as a 31 page booklet. No publisher listed. Indiana Historical Society. Lew Wallace Collection. M0292. Box 3. Folder 20. (**Focus on the Santa Fe Ring**)

Springer, Frank. "Hon Carl Schurz, Secretary of the Interior. Sir: I endorse herewith, directed to the President charges against S.B. Axtell Governor of New Mexico ..." Letter to Carl Schurz. **June 10, 1878**. Interior Department Papers 1850-1907; Appointments Division and Subsequent Actions. Microfilm Roll M750. National Archives and Records Administration Record Group 48. Microfilm Case Number 44-4-8-3. U.S. Department of Interior. Washington D.C.

_____. "The undersigned, a citizen of the County of Colfax ..." Letter to Rutherford B. Hayes enclosed in letter to Secretary of the Interior Carl Schurz. **June 10, 1878**. Interior Department Papers 1850-1907; Appointments Division and Subsequent Actions. Microfilm File Case Number 44-4-8-3. Record Group 48. Microfilm No. M750 Roll 1. National Archives and Records Administration. U.S. Department of Justice. Washington, D.C.

Isaacs, I. and G.N. Coe. "Charges Against S.B. Axtell, Governor of New Mexico." **June 22, 1878**. Interior Department Papers 1850-1907; Appointments Division and Subsequent Actions. Microfilm File Case Number 44-4-8-3. Microfilm No. M750. Roll 1. National Archives and Records Administration. Record Group 48. U.S. Department of Justice. Washington, D.C.

Angel, Frank Warner. "I am in receipt of your favor of the 12th ...' Letter to Samuel Beach Axtell. **August 13, 1878**. Interior Department Papers 1850-1907; Appointments Division and Subsequent Actions. Microfilm Roll M750. National Archives and Records Administration Record Group 48. Microfilm Case Number 44-4-8-3. U.S. Department of Interior. Washington D.C.

Morley, William Raymond. "Your letter of the 7th came last night and it was a good long newsy letter ..." Letter to wife, Ada McPherson Morley. **August 15, 1878.** Collection of Norman Cleaveland. Quoted in Norman Cleaveland, *The Morleys: Young Upstarts in the Southwest*. Albuquerque, New Mexico: Calvin Horn Publisher, Inc. 1971. Pages 152-155. **(About possible cover-up by Angel's reports; about the Santa Fe Ring, T.B. Catron, S.B. Elkins, S.B. Axtell, and Henry Waldo; and the Lincoln County War)**

McPherson, Mary. "Please place before the Attorney General ..." Letter to President Rutherford B. Hayes. **August 23, 1877.** Interior Department Papers 1850-1907; Appointments Division and Subsequent Actions. Microfilm File Case Number 44-4-8-3. Record Group 48. Microfilm No. M750. Roll 1. National Archives and Records Administration. U.S. Department of Justice. Washington, D.C. **(Requesting that her "Charges vs. New Mexico Officials" go to the Attorney General.)**

McPherson, Mary. "I desire to know when I can be heard ..." Letter to Secretary of Interior Carl Schurz. **September 30, 1977.** Interior Department Papers 1850-1907; Appointments Division and Subsequent Actions. Microfilm File Case Number 44-4-8-3. Record Group 48. Microfilm No. M750. Roll 1. National Archives and Records Administration. U. S. Department of Justice. Washington, D.C. **(Requesting to be heard in person on her charges against officials and Governor Axtell.)**

Angel, Frank Warner. "The Honorable C. Schurz ... I enclose copies of letter received by me from Gov. Axtell (marked A) and my reply there to (marked B)." **August 24, 1878.** Frank Warner Angel reports. Interior Department Papers 1850-1907; Appointments Division and Subsequent Actions. Microfilm Roll M750. National Archives and Records Administration Record Group 48. Microfilm Case Number 44-4-8-3. U.S. Department of Interior. Washington D.C.

Routt, John C. "I am here on a visit to my daughter and have more by accident than otherwise heard statements ..." Letter to President Rutherford B. Hayes. **August 29, 1878.** Interior Department Papers 1850-1907; Appointments Division and Subsequent Actions. Microfilm File Case Number 44-4-8-3. Microfilm No. M750. Roll 1. National Archives and Records Administration. U.S. Department of Justice. Washington, D.C. **(Possibly fraudulent letter, but in opposition to the removal of Governor Axtell and U.S. Attorney Thomas Benton Catron.)**

Schurz, Carl. "I transmit herewith an order from the President ..." **September 4, 1878.** Letter to Lew Wallace. Indiana Historical Society. Lew Wallace Collection. M0292. Box 3. Folder 14. **(Suspension of Governor S.B. Axtell and Wallace's appointment as new Governor)**

Angel, Frank Warner. "The Hon. C. Schurz, Secretary of the Interior, Sir: I have just been favored by a call from W. L. Rynerson Territorial Dist. Attorney 3rd District New Mexico - in the interest of Gov. Axtell." (Letter) **September 6, 1878.** Microfilm M750. National Archives and Records Administration Record Group 48. Microfilm Case Number 44-4-8-3. U.S. Department of Interior. Washington D. C.

Wallace, Lew. "I have the honor to inform you ..." Letter to Carl Schurz. **October 1, 1878.** Indiana Historical Society. Lew Wallace Collection. M0292. Box 3. Folder 15. **(Informing Schurz that he informed Axtell of suspension and that he now qualified as Governor)**

Angel, Frank Warner. *In the Matter of the Investigation of the Charges Against S.B. Axtell Governor of New Mexico*. **October 3, 1878.** Frank Warner Angel report. Interior Department Papers 1850-1907; Appointments Division and Subsequent Actions. Microfilm Case File No. 44-4-8-3. Record Group 48. Microfilm Roll M750. National Archives and Records Administration. U.S. Department of Interior. Washington, D.C. **(Mentions Santa Fe Ring)**

Elkins, Stephen Benton. "To the President. Referring to a conversation had with you last week ... Hon S. Elkins favors appointment Axtell, Ex Gov. as Gov'r of New Mexico". Letter to President James Abram Garfield. **March 17, 1881.** (Received Executive Mansion April 6, 1881). Interior Department Papers 1850-1907; Appointments Division and Subsequent Actions. Microfilm Roll M750. National Archives and Records Administration Microfilm Roll M750. National Archives and Records Administration Record Group 48. Microfilm Case Number 44-4-8-3. U.S. Department of Interior. Washington D.C. Microfilm Case Number 44-4-8-3. U.S. Department of Interior. Washington D.C. (**Request for re-appointment of Axtell as Territorial New Mexico Governor**)

Bradstreet, George P. "Referring to the nomination of Sam'l B. Axtell of Ohio to be Chief Justice of the Supreme Court of New Mexico ... he is alleged to have been removed by President Hayes ..." Letter to Judiciary Committee of the U.S. Senate. **June 22, 1882.** Interior Department Papers 1850-1907; Appointments Division and Subsequent Actions. Microfilm Roll M750. National Archives and Records Administration Microfilm Roll M750. National Archives and Records Administration Record Group 48. Microfilm Case Number 44-4-8-3. U.S. Department of Interior. Washington D.C.

No Author. "A man named Springer is in Washington trying to defeat the nomination of Governor Axtell. Springer is a friend of the thugs and thieves of Colfax County." *Santa Fe New Mexican.* **July 6, 1882.** (**Santa Fe Ring re-instatement of S.B. Axtell to public office**)

No Author. " 'Chief Justice Axtell' is a bitter pill for the Raton *News and Press*." *Santa Fe New Mexican.* **July 18, 1882.** (**Santa Fe Ring instatement of S.B. Axtell as Chief Justice**)

WILLIAM HENRY BONNEY ("BILLY THE KID")

WORDS OF WILLIAM HENRY BONNEY (CHRONOLOGICAL)

HOYT BILL OF SALE

Bonney, W H. "Know all persons by these presents ...' Thursday, **October 24, 1878.** Collection of Panhandle-Plains Historical Museum, Canyon, Texas. Item No. X1974-98/1. (**Hoyt Bill of Sale**)

Tilloston, Thomas. "One Gray Horse ..." March, 1879. Indiana Historical Society. Lew Wallace Collection. M0292. Box 4. Folder 7. (**Sample period Bill of Sale**)

LETTERS TO LEW WALLACE

Bonney, W H. "I have heard you will give one thousand $ dollars for my body which as I see it means alive ..." **March 13(?), 1879.** Fray Angélico Chávez Historical Library, Santa Fe, New Mexico. Lincoln County Heritage Trust Collection. (AC481).

_____. "I will keep the keep the appointment ..." **March 20, 1879.** Indiana Historical Society. M0292.

_____. "... on the Pecos." ("Billie" letter fragment). **March 24(?), 1879.** Indiana Historical Society. Lew Wallace Collection. M0292 Box 4. Folder 7.

_____. "I noticed in the Las Vegas Gazette a piece which stated that 'Billy the Kid' ..." **December 12, 1880.** Indiana Historical Society. Lew Wallace Collection. M0292.

_____. "I would like to see you ..." **January 1, 1881.** Indiana Historical Society. Lew Wallace Collection. M0292.

_____. "I wish you would come down to the jail and see me ..." **March 2, 1881.** Fray Angélico Chávez Historical Library, Santa Fe, New Mexico. Lincoln County Heritage Trust Collection. (AC481).

_____. "I wrote you a little note day before yesterday ..." **March 4, 1881.** Indiana Historical Society. Lew Wallace Collection. M0292.

_____. "For the last time I ask ..." **March 27, 1881.** Indiana Historical Society. Lew Wallace Collection. M0292.

LETTER TO SQUIRE WILSON

Bonney, W H. "Friend Wilson ..." **March 18, 1879.** Indiana Historical Society. Lew Wallace Collection. M0292.

LETTER TO EDGAR CAYPLESS

Bonney, W H. "I would have written before ..." **April 15, 1881.** Copy in William Keleher's *Violence in Lincoln County;* originally reproduced in Griggs *History of the Mesilla Valley.* (**Original lost**)

REGULATOR MANIFESTO LETTER

Regulator. "Mr. Walz. Sir ..." Letter to Edgar Walz. **July 13, 1878.** Adjutant General's Office. File 1405 AGO 1878. (Quoted in Maurice Garland Fulton, *History of the Lincoln County War.* Tucson: University of Arizona Press. 1975. pages 246-247.)

DEPOSITION

Bonney, William Henry. Deposition to Frank Warner Angel. **June 8, 1878.** Frank Warner Angel report, Pages 314-319 from *In the Matter of the Examination of the Causes and Circumstances of the Death of John H. Tunstall a British Subject.* Report filed October 4, 1878. Angel Report. Records of the Justice Department. Record Group 60. Class 44 Litigation Files. Container 21. National Archives and Records Administration. U.S. Department of Justice. Washington, D.C. or Angel Report in Interior Department Papers 1850-1907; Appointments Division and Subsequent Actions. Microfilm File Case Number 44-4-8-3. Record Group 48. Microfilm No. M750. Roll 1. National Archives and Records Administration. U.S. Department of Justice. Washington, D.C.

COURT TESTIMONY

Rynerson, William. "The Grand Jurors for the Territory of New Mexico taken from the body of the good and lawful men of the County of Lincoln ..." Indictments of the April, Lincoln County Grand Jury. **April 28, 1879.** Herman B. Weisner Papers, ca. 1957-1992. New Mexico State University Library at Las Cruces. Rio Grande Historical Collection. Accession No. Ms 0249. Box 4/39. Folder E-Z. Folder Name: "Jessie Evans Accessory to Murder." (**Billy's testimony indicts J.J. Dolan, Billy Campbell, and Jessie Evans for his pardon bargain**)

Bonney, William Henry. Testimony in Court of Inquiry for N.A.M. Dudley. **May 28-29, 1879.** *Proceedings of a Court of Inquiry in the Case of Lt. Col. N.A.M. Dudley (May 2,1879 – July 5, 1879).* File No. QQ1284. (Boxes 3304, 3305, 3305A); Court Martial Files 1809-1894. Records of the Office of the Judge Advocate General - Army. Record Group 153. Old Military and Civil Branch. National Archives and Records Administration. Washington, D. C.

Waldo, Henry. "Then was brought forward William Bonney, alias "Antrim," alias "the Kid," a known criminal of the worst type ..." Closing argument on Billy Bonney's testimony in Court of Inquiry for N.A.M. Dudley. **July 5, 1879.** *Proceedings of a Court of Inquiry in the Case of Lt. Col. N.A.M. Dudley (May 2,1879 – July 5, 1879).* File No. QQ1284. (Boxes 3304, 3305, 3305A); Court Martial Files 1809-1894. Records of the Office of the Judge Advocate General – Army. Record Group 153. Old Military and Civil Branch. National Archives and Records Administration. Washington, D. C.

INTERVIEW WITH LEW WALLACE

Wallace, Lew. "Statements by Kid, made Sunday night **March 23, 1879**." March 23, 1879. Indiana Historical Society. Lew Wallace Collection. M0922. Box 4. Folder 6.

NEWSPAPER INTERVIEWS (CHRONOLOGICAL)

Wilcox, Lucius "Lute" M. (city editor, owner, J.H. Koogler). "The Kid. Interview with Billy Bonney The Best Known Man in New Mexico." Las Vegas *Gazette*. **December 28, 1880. (Has Billy Bonney's quote that "the laugh's on me this time")**

_____. Interview, at train depot. Las Vegas *Gazette*. **December 28, 1880. (Has Billy Bonney's "adios" quote.)**

No Author. "At least two hundred men have been killed in Lincoln County during the past three years ..." Santa Fe *Daily New Mexican*. **March 28, 1881**.

No Author. "Something About the Kid." Santa Fe *Daily New Mexican*. **April 3, 1881. (With quotes Billy Bonney's "this is the man" and "two hundred men have been killed ... he did not kill all of them.")**

No Author. "I got a rough deal ..." *Mesilla News*. **April 15, 1881**.

Newman, Simon N. Ed. Interview with "The Kid." *Newman's Semi-Weekly*. **April 15, 1881**.

_____. Departure from Mesilla. *Newman's Semi-Weekly*. **April 15, 1881**.

No Author. "Advise persons never to engage in killing." *Mesilla News*. **April 16, 1881. (Billy Bonney's quote)**

BIOGRAPHICAL SOURCES

Abbott, E.C. ("Teddy Blue") and Helena Huntington Smith. *We Pointed Them North: Recollections of a Cowpuncher*. Norman, Oklahoma: University of Oklahoma Press. 1955. **(Billy the Kid's multiculturalism, page 47.)**

Anaya, Paco. *I Buried Billy*. College Station, Texas: Creative Publishing Company. 1991.

Ball, Eve. *Ma'am Jones of the Pecos*. Tucson, Arizona: The University of Arizona Press. 1969.

Bell, Bob Boze. *The Illustrated Life and Times of Billy the Kid*. Cave Creek, Arizona: Boze Books. 1992. (Frank Coe quote about the Kid's cartridge use, page 45.)

Bell, Bob Boze. *The Illustrated Life and Times of Billy the Kid*. Second Edition. Phoenix, Arizona: Tri Star-Boze Publications, Inc. 1996.

Burns, Walter Noble. *The Saga of Billy the Kid*. Stamford, Connecticut: Longmeadow Press. 1992. (Original printing: 1926, Doubleday.)

_____. "I also know that the Kid and Paulita were sweethearts." Unpublished letter to Jim East. June 3, 1926. Robert N. Mullin Collection. File RNM, IV, NM, 116-117. Nita Stewart Haley Memorial Museum, Haley Library. Midland, Texas.

Coe, George. Doyce B. Nunis, Jr. Ed. *Frontier Fighter. The Autobiography of George Coe Who Fought and Rode With Billy the Kid*. Chicago: R. R. Donnelley and Sons Company. 1984.

Cooper, Gale. *Billy the Kid's Writings, Words, and Wit*. Gelcour Books: Albuquerque: New Mexico. 2012.

_____. *Billy and Paulita: A Novel*. Gelcour Books: Albuquerque: New Mexico. 2012.

Garrett, Pat F. *The Authentic Life of Billy the Kid The Noted Desperado of the Southwest, Whose Deeds of Daring and Blood Made His Name a Terror in New Mexico, Arizona, and Northern Mexico*. Santa Fe, New Mexico: New Mexico Printing and Publishing Co. 1882. (Reprint used: New York: Indian Head Books. 1994.)

Hendron, J. W. *The Story of Billy the Kid. New Mexico's Number One Desperado*. New York: Indian Head Books. 1994.

Hoyt, Henry. *A Frontier Doctor.* Boston and New York: Houghton Mifflin Company. 1929. **(Describes Billy's superior abilities. Pages 93-94.)**

Jacobsen, Joel. *Such Men as Billy the Kid. The Lincoln County War Reconsidered.* Lincoln and London: University of Nebraska Press. 1994.

Kadlec, Robert F. *They "Knew" Billy the Kid. Interviews with Old-Time New Mexicans.* Santa Fe, New Mexico: Ancient City Press. 1987.

Keleher, William A. *The Fabulous Frontier: Twelve New Mexico Items.* Albuquerque, New Mexico: The University of New Mexico Press. 1962.

_____.*Violence in Lincoln County 1869-1881.* Albuquerque, New Mexico: University of New Mexico Press. 1957. **(Las Vegas *Gazette* article of December 28, 1880, "The Kid. Interview with Billy Bonney The Best Known Man in New Mexico": pages 293-295; Las Vegas *Gazette* article of December 28, 1880. Untitled - at train station. Pages 296-297)**

McFarland, David F. Reverend. *Ledger: Session Records 1867-1874. Marriages in Santa Fe New Mexico. "Mr. William H. Antrim and Mrs. Catherine McCarty." March 1, 1873.* (Unpublished). Santa Fe, New Mexico: First Presbyterian Church of Santa Fe.

Meadows, John P. "Billy the Kid to John P. Meadows on the Peñasco, May 1-2, 1881." *Roswell Daily Record.* February 16, 1931. Page 6.

_____. Ed. John P. Wilson. *Pat Garrett and Billy the Kid as I Knew Them: Reminiscences of John P. Meadows.* Albuquerque: University of New Mexico Press. 2004.

Mullin, Robert N. *The Boyhood of Billy the Kid.* Monograph 17, Southwestern Studies 5(1). El Paso, Texas: Texas Western Press. University of Texas at El Paso. 1967.

Poe, John W. *The Death of Billy the Kid.* (Introduction by Maurice Garland Fulton). Boston and New York: Houghton Mifflin Company. 1933.

_____. "The Killing of Billy the Kid." (a personal letter written at Roswell, New Mexico to Mr. Charles Goodnight, Goodnight P.C., Texas) July 10, 1917. Earle Vandale Collection. 1813-946. No. 2H475. Center for American History. University of Texas at Austin.

Rakocy, Bill. *Billy the Kid.* El Paso, Texas: Bravo Press. 1985.

Rasch, Phillip J. *Trailing Billy the Kid.* Laramie, Wyoming: National Association for Outlaw and Lawman History, Inc. with University of Wyoming. 1995.

Russell, Randy. *Billy the Kid. The Story - The Trial.* Lincoln, New Mexico: The Crystal Press. 1994.

Siringo, Charles A. *The History of Billy the Kid.* Santa Fe: New Mexico. Privately Printed. 1920.

Tuska, Jon. *Billy the Kid. His Life and Legend.* Westport, Connecticut: Greenwood Press. 1983.

Utley, Robert M. *Billy the Kid. A Short and Violent Life.* Lincoln and London: University of Nebraska Press. 1989.

Weddle, Jerry. *Antrim is My Stepfather's Name. The Boyhood of Billy the Kid.* Monograph 9, Globe, Arizona: Arizona Historical Society. 1993.

No Author. "The Prisoners Who Saw the Kid Kill Olinger." April 28, 1881. Herman B. Weisner Papers, ca. 1957-1992. New Mexico State University Library at Las Cruces. Rio Grande Historical Collections. Accession No. Ms 0249. Box 30 T. Folder 8.

SECRET SERVICE REPORTS ABOUT

Wild, Azariah F. "Daily Reports of U. S. Secret Service Agents, Azariah F. Wild." Microfilm T-915. Record Group 87. Rolls 306 (June 15, 1877 - December 31, 1877), 307 (January 1,1878 - June 30, 1879), 308 (July 1, 1879 - June 30, 1881), 309 (July 1, 1881 - September 30, 1883), 310 (October 1, 1883 - July 31, 1886). National Archives and Records Department. Department of the Treasury. United States Secret Service. Washington, D. C.

NEWSPAPER ARTICLES ABOUT (CHRONOLOGICAL)

No Author. Grant County *Herald*. **May 10, 1879**. Results of the Lincoln County Grand Jury. (**Also published in the Mesilla** *Thirty Four*. **Confirmation of the William Bonney testimony and James Dolan and Billy Campbell murder indictments, from page 224 of William Keleher,** *Violence in Lincoln County*.)

No Author. Editorial. "Powerful Gang of Outlaws Harassing the Stockman." Las Vegas *Gazette*. December 3, 1880. (**Condemnation of William Bonney as an outlaw leader; and resulting in Bonney's response letter of December 12, 1880 to Governor Lew Wallace.**)

No Author. "Outlaws of New Mexico. The Exploits of a Band Headed by a New York Youth. The Mountain Fastness of the Kid and His Followers - War Against a Gang of Cattle Thieves and Murderers - The Frontier Confederates of Brockway, the Counterfeiter." *The Sun*. New York. **December 22, 1880**. Vol. XLVIII, No. 118, Page 3, Columns 1-2.

Wallace, Lew. "Billy the Kid: $500 Reward." Las Vegas *Gazette*. **December 22, 1880**.

No Author. "A Big Haul! Billy Kid, Dave Rudabaugh, Billy Wilson and Tom Pickett in the Clutches of the Law." *The Las Vegas Daily Optic*. Monday, **December 27, 1880**. Vol. 2, No. 45. Page 4, Column 2.

Wilcox, Lucius "Lute" M. ' 'The Kid. Interview with Billy Bonney The Best Known Man in New Mexico, The greatest excitement prevailed yesterday when the news was abroad that Pat Garrett and Frank Stewart had arrived in town bringing with them Billy 'the Kid.' " Las Vegas *Gazette*. **December 27, 1880**. (**With "laugh's on me" quote**)

_____. "Interview With The Kid." Las Vegas *Gazette*. **December 28, 1880**.(From "Billy the Kid: Las Vegas Newspaper Accounts of His Career, 1880-1881." W.M. Morrison, Waco Texas. 1958.)

No Author. "A Bay-Mare. Everyone who has heard of Billy 'the kid' has heard of his beautiful bay mare." *Las Vegas Morning Gazette*. Tuesday, **January 4, 1881**.

No Author. "The Kid. Billy 'the Kid' and Billy Wilson were on Monday taken to Mesilla for Trial." *Las Vegas Morning Gazette*. Tuesday, **March 15, 1881**.

Newman, Simon. "In the Name of Justice! In the Case of Billy Kid." *Newman's Semi-Weekly*. Saturday, **April 2, 1881**.

No Author. "Billy the Kid Seems to be having a stormy journey on his trip Southward." *Las Vegas Morning Gazette*. Tuesday, **April 5, 1881**.

Koogler, J. H. "Interview with Governor Lew Wallace on 'The Kid.'" *Las Vegas Gazette*. April 28, 1881.

No Author. "The Kid." *Santa Fe Daily New Mexican*. **May 1, 1881**. Vol. X, No. 32, Page 1, Column 2.

No Author. "Billy Bonney. Advices from Lincoln bring the intelligence of the escape of 'Billy the Kid.' " *Las Vegas Daily Optic*. Monday, **May 2, 1881**.

No Author. "The Kid's Escape." *Santa Fe Daily New Mexican*. Tuesday Morning, **May 3, 1881**. Vol. X, No 33, Page 1, Column 2.

Wallace, Lew. "Billy the Kid. $500 Reward." *Daily New Mexican*. **May 3, 1881**. Vol. X, No. 33, Page 1, Column 5.

No Author. "Dare Devil Desperado. Pursuit of 'Billy the Kid' has been abandoned." *Las Vegas Daily Optic*. **May 4, 1881**.

No Author. "More Killing by Kid." Editorial. *Santa Fe Daily New Mexican*. Wednesday Morning, **May 4, 1881**. Vol. X, No. 34, Page 1, Column 2.

No Author. "Kid was then in Albuquerque ..." *Santa Fe Daily New Mexican*. **May 5, 1881**. p.4. c. 1.

No Author. "Richard Dunham's May 2, 1881 encounter with Billy the Kid.", *Santa Fe Daily New Mexican*, **May 5, 1881**, Page 4, Column 3. (private collection)

No Author. "The question if how to deal with desperados who commit murder has but one solution - kill them." *Las Vegas Daily Optic*. Tuesday, **May 10, 1881**.

No Author. "Billy 'the Kid.'" Las Vegas *Gazette*. Thursday, **May 12, 1881**.
No Author. "The Kid was in Chloride City ..." *Santa Fe Daily New Mexican*. **May 13, 1881**. p.4. c. 3.
No Author. "Billy 'the Kid' is in the vicinity of Sumner." Las Vegas *Gazette*. Sunday, **May 15, 1881**.
No Author. "The Thug's Territory. Stage Robbers and Cut-Throats Have Things Their Own Way in New Mexico. Gen. Lew Wallace Anxious to Punish the Crime That is So Prevalent – A Chapter About 'Billy the Kid' – The Governor has a Narrow Escape From Being Spanked." *St. Louis Daily Globe-Democrat*. Monday Morning, **May 16, 1881**. Page 2, Columns 5 and 6. (private collection)
No Author. "The Kid is believed to be in the Black Range ..." *Santa Fe Daily New Mexican*. **May 19, 1881**. p.4. c. 1.
No Author. "Billy the Kid was last seen in Lincoln County ..." *Santa Fe Daily New Mexican*. **May 19, 1881**. p.4. c. 1.
No Author. " 'Billy the Kid' has been heard from again." *Las Vegas Daily Optic*. Friday, **June 10, 1881**.
No Author. " 'Billy the Kid.' He is Reported to Have Been Seen on Our Streets Saturday Night." *Las Vegas Daily Optic*. Monday Evening, **June 13, 1881**. Vol. 2, No. 188, Page 4, Column 2.
Wilcox, Lute, Ed. "Billy the Kid would make an ideal newspaper-man in that he always endeavors to 'get even' with his enemies." *Las Vegas Daily Optic*. Monday Evening, **June 13, 1881**. Vol. 2, No. 188, Page 4, Column 1.
No Author. "Land of the Petulant Pistol. 'Billy the Kid' as a Killer." *Las Vegas Daily Optic*. Wednesday Evening, **June 15, 1881**. Vol. 2, No. 190.
No Author. "Barney Mason at Fort Sumner states the 'Kid' is in Local Sheep Camps." *Las Vegas Morning Gazette*. **June 16, 1881**.
No Author. "The Kid." *Santa Fe Daily New Mexican*. **June 16, 1881**. Vol. X, No. 90, Page 4, Column 2.
No Author. "Billy the Kid. General Wallace Tells Why the Young Desperado of New Mexico Wanted to Kill Him." (Lew Wallace interviewed on June 13, 1881), Crawfordsville *Saturday Evening Journal*, **June 18, 1881**. Indiana Historical Society. The Papers of Lew and Susan Wallace. Microfilm Edition. Indianapolis, Indiana: Indiana Historical Society Press. 2008.
No Author. "Billy the Kid." *Las Vegas Daily Optic*. Thursday, June 28, 1881.
No Author. " 'The Kid' Killed." *Las Vegas Daily Optic*. **July 18. 1881**.
No Author. "Lew Wallace's Foe. Threatened by 'Billy the Kid.' The Writing of 'Ben-Hur' Interrupted. An Incident of the Soldier-Author's Career in New Mexico. *San Francisco Chronicle*. **December 10, 1893**. Indiana Historical Society. Lew Wallace Collection. M0292. Box 14. Folder 11. (**Lew Wallace creating outlaw myth of outlaw Billy the Kid")**
No Author. "Street Pickings," Weekly *Crawfordsville Review – Saturday Edition*, **January 6, 1894**. Indiana Historical Society. The Papers of Lew and Susan Wallace. Microfilm Edition. Series I. Reel 27. Indianapolis, Indiana: Indiana Historical Society Press. 2008.
Lewis, E.I. "Gen. Wallace's Feud with Billy the Kid, When the General Was Governor of New Mexico and Billy Bonne Was the Most Dangerous Western Outlaw. He Was a Waif and Was Reared in Indiana. *The Indianapolis Press*. Saturday, **June 23, 1900**. Page 7. Lew Wallace Collection. Indiana Historical Society. M0292. Box 14. Folder 11. (photocopy) (Original article is in OMB 23, Box 1. Folder 5) (**Lew Wallace creating self-serving myth of outlaw Billy the Kid")**
No Author. "An Old Incident Recalled." Crawfordsville *Weekly News-Review*. **December 20, 1901**. Indiana Historical Society. The Papers of Lew and Susan Wallace. Microfilm Edition. Series I. Reel 27. Indianapolis, Indiana: Indiana Historical Society Press. 2008.
Wallace, Lew. "General Lew Wallace Writes a Romance of 'Billy the Kid' Most Famous Bandit of the Plains: Thrilling Story of the Midnight Meeting Between

Gen Wallace, Then Governor of New Mexico, and the Notorious Outlaw, in a Lonesome Hut in Santa Fe." *New York World Magazine.* Sunday, **June 8, 1902**. Lew Wallace Collection. Indiana Historical Society. M0292. . Box 14. Folder 11.

LETTERS MENTIONING BILLY BONNEY

Kimbrell, George. "I have the honor to request that you will furnish me a posse ..." Letter to Lieutenant Millard Filmore Goodwin. **February 20, 1879**. Indiana Historical Society. Lew Wallace Collection. Box 4, Folder 3. (**For pursuit of William Bonney and Yginio Salazar**)

Goodwin, Millard Filmore "''I have the honor to submit the following report regarding my duties performed ..." Letter to Fort Stanton Post Adjutant John Loud. **February 23, 1879**. Indiana Historical Society. Lew Wallace Collection. Box 4. Folder 3. (**Assisting pursuit of William Bonney and Yginio Salazar**)

Dudley, Nathan Augustus Monroe. "I enclose herewith report of 2nd Lieut. M.F. Goodwin ..." Letter to Acting Assistant Adjutant General at Headquarters. **February 24, 1879**. Indiana Historical Society. Lew Wallace Collection. M0292. Box 4, Folder 3. (**Documents military pursuit of William Bonney**)

Wallace, Lew. "I have just ascertained that 'The Kid' is at a place called Las Tablas ..." Letter to Edward Hatch. **March 6, 1879**. Indiana Historical Society. Lew Wallace Collection. Box 9, Folder 10. (**Written on dead John Tunstall's stationery**)

_____. "I beg to submit to you a list of persons whom it is necessary, in my judgment, to arrest ..." Letter to Henry Carroll. **March 11, 1879**. Indiana Historical Society. Lew Wallace Collection. M0292. Box 4. Folder 5. (**Lists as 14, "The Kid" – William Bonney; also lists Jessie Evans, Yginio Salazar, James Dolan**)

_____. "I enclose a note for Bonney." Letter to John "Squire" Wilson. **March 20, 1879**. Indiana Historical Society. Lew Wallace Collection. M0292. Box 4. Folder 6.

_____. "My time has been so constantly occupied in getting my work into operation ..." Letter to Carl Schurz. **March 21, 1879**. Indiana Historical Society. Lew Wallace Collection. M0292. Box 4. Folder 7. (**Progress report with multiple enclosures; one listing "The Kid -William Bonney in anti-outlaw campaign of "taking the head off the evil."**)

_____. "To day I forwarded a telegram to you, with another to the President ..." Letter to Carl Schurz. **March 31, 1879**. Indiana Historical Society. Lew Wallace Collection. M0292. Box 4. Folder 7. (**Mention of "precious specimen nicknamed 'The Kid' "**)

Leonard, Ira. "The air is filled tonight with 'rumors of wars ... Letter to Lew Wallace. **April 20, 1879**. Indiana Historical Society. Lew Wallace Collection. M0292. Box 4. Folder 9. (**About District Attorney Rynerson: "He is bent on going for the Kid"**)

Hoyt, Henry F. "This time it is me who is apologizing for the long delay in answering ..." (Letter to Lew Wallace Jr.) **April 27, 1927**. Indiana Historical Society. Lew Wallace Collection. M0292. Box 14, Folder 11.

_____. "Copy of a bill of sale written by Wm H. Bonney ..." Letter to Lew Wallace Jr. **April 27, 1927**. Indiana Historical Society. Lew Wallace Collection. M0292. Box 14, Folder 11. (**Calls Billy Bonney "a natural leader of men"**)

FEDERAL INDICTMENT OF BILLY BONNEY

Catron, Thomas Benton. "Case No. 411. The United States vs. Charles Bowdry [Bowdre], Doc Scurlock, Henry Brown, Henry Antrim alias "Kid," John Middleton, Stephen Stevens, John Scroggins, George Coe and Frederick Waite." **June 21, 1878**. Herman B. Weisner Papers, ca. 1957-1992. New Mexico State University Library at Las Cruces. Rio Grande Historical Collections. Accession No. Ms 0249. Box 1. B-Folder 4. Name: Andrew Roberts Indictment. (**Federal murder** indictment of Billy Bonney by U.S. Attorney T.B. Catron; made a Territorial pardon impossible until quashed on March 30, 1881 by the District Court in Mesilla.)

REWARD NOTICES FOR BILLY BONNEY

Wallace, Lew. "Billy the Kid: $500 Reward." Las Vegas *Gazette*. **December 22, 1880**. **(After Wallace's December 13, 1880 Proclamation for that reward for Billy Bonney)**
_____. "Billy the Kid. $500 Reward." **May 3, 1881**. *Daily New Mexican*. Vol. X, No. 33. p. 1, c. 3.

REWARD POSTERS FOR BILLY BONNEY

Greene, Chas. W. "To the New Mexican Printing and Publishing Company." **May 20, 1881**. Indiana Historical Society. Lew Wallace Collection. M0292. Box 4, Folder 17. **(Bill to Lew Wallace for Reward posters for "Kid")**
_____. "I enclose a bill ..." Letter to Lew Wallace for "Kid" wanted posters. **June 2, 1881**. Indiana Historical Society. Lew Wallace Collection. M0292. Box 4, Folder 18.

DEATH WARRANT FOR BILLY BONNEY

Wallace, Lew. "To the Sheriff of Lincoln County, Greeting ..." **April 30, 1881**. Indiana Historical Society. Lew Wallace Collection. M0292. Box 9, Folder 11.

CORONER'S JURY REPORT

Keleher, William A. *Violence in Lincoln County 1869-1881*. Albuquerque, New Mexico: University of New Mexico Press. 1957. **(Photocopy of Spanish Coroner's Jury Report, pages 306-308, with Keleher's English translation, pages 343-344.)**
Rudulph, Milnor, Pedro Lucero, Jose Silba, Sabal Gutierrez, Lorenso Jaramillo. Coroner's Jury Report for William Bonney alias "Kid." Indiana Historical Society. Lew Wallace Collection. M0292. Box 9. Folder 11. **(Photocopy of Spanish Coroner's Jury Report - matches photo in William Keleher's *Violence in Lincoln County* copy except for rodent damage to Keleher's)**

LEW WALLACE WRITINGS ABOUT/TO WILLIAM BONNEY

LETTERS (CHRONOLOGICAL)

Wallace, Lew. "I have just ascertained that 'The Kid' is at a place called Las Tablas ..." Letter to Edward Hatch. **March 6, 1879**. Indiana Historical Society. Lew Wallace Collection. Box 9, Folder 10. **(Written on dead John Tunstall's letterhead)**
Wallace, Lew. "Come to the house of Squire Wilson ..." Letter to W H. Bonney. **March 15, 1879**. Indiana Historical Society. Lew Wallace Collection. M0292. Box 4. Folder 6.
_____. "The escape makes no difference in arrangements ..." Letter to W.H. Bonney. **March 20, 1879**. Indiana Historical Society. Lew Wallace Collection. M0292. Box 4. Folder 6.
_____. "To day I forwarded a telegram to you, with another to the President ..." Letter to Carl Schurz. **March 31, 1879**. Indiana Historical Society. Lew Wallace Collection. M0292. Box 4. Folder 7. **(Quote: "precious specimen nicknamed 'The Kid' ")**
_____. "Be good enough to prepare a draft of proclamation of reward $500 for the capture and delivery of William Bonney, alias the Kid ..." Letter to Territorial Secretary William Ritch. **December 13, 1880**. Herman B. Weisner Papers, ca. 1957-1992. New Mexico State University Library at Las Cruces. Rio Grande Historical Collections. Accession No. Ms 0249. Box W3. Folder 13. Folder Name:

"Wallace, Gov. N.M." From Lew Wallace Papers. New Mexico State Records Center. Santa Fe, New Mexico. (**Wallace's first reward for Billy the Kid**)

INTERVIEW BY LEW WALLACE

Wallace, Lew. "Statements by Kid, made Sunday night March 23, 1879." **March 23, 1879**. Indiana Historical Society. Lew Wallace Collection. M0922. Box 4. Folder 6.

ARTICLES (CHRONOLOGICAL)

"Wallace, Lew. "Wallace's Words …" (interview with Lew Wallace conducted in Washington, D.C. on January 3, 1881), Chicago *The Daily Inter Ocean*. **January 4, 1881**. Indiana Historical Society. The Papers of Lew and Susan Wallace. Microfilm Edition. Indianapolis, Indiana: Indiana Historical Society Press. 2008.

No Author. "Richard Dunham's May 2, 1881 encounter with Billy the Kid.', *Santa Fe Daily New Mexican*, **May 5, 1881**, Page 4, Column **3**. (private collection)

No Author. "The Thug's Territory. Stage Robbers and Cut-Throats Have Things Their Own Way in New Mexico. Gen. Lew Wallace Anxious to Punish the Crime That is So Prevalent – A Chapter About 'Billy the Kid' – The Governor has a Narrow Escape From Being Spanked." *St. Louis Daily Globe-Democrat*. Monday Morning, **May 16, 1881**. Page 2, Columns 5 and 6. (private collection)

No Author. (O.L. Houghton's Conversation with Lew Wallace, before May 26, 1881), *The Las Vegas Daily Optic*, **May 26, 1881**, p.4, c.4. Indiana Historical Society. Lew Wallace Collection. M0292.

No Author. "Billy the Kid, General Wallace Tells Why the Young Desperado of New Mexico Wanted to Kill Him." (Lew Wallace interviewed on June 13, 1881), Crawfordsville *Saturday Evening Journal*, **June 18, 1881**. Indiana Historical Society. The Papers of Lew and Susan Wallace. Microfilm Edition. Indianapolis, Indiana: Indiana Historical Society Press 2008.

No Author. "Street Pickings," Weekly *Crawfordsville Review - Saturday Edition*, **January 6, 1894**. Indiana Historical Society. The Papers of Lew and Susan Wallace. Microfilm Edition. Series I. Reel 27. Indianapolis, Indiana: Indiana Historical Society Press. 2008.

No Author. "An Old Incident Recalled.' Crawfordsville *Weekly News-Review*. **December 20, 1901**. Indiana Historical Society. The Papers of Lew and Susan Wallace. Microfilm Edition. Series I. Reel 27. Indianapolis, Indiana: Indiana Historical Society Press. 2008.

Lewis, E.I. "Gen. Wallace s Feud with Billy the Kid, When the General Was Governor of New Mexico and Billy Bonne Was the Most Dangerous Western Outlaw. He Was a Waif and Was Reared in Indiana. *The Indianapolis Press*. Saturday, **June 23, 1900**. Page 7. Lew Wallace Collection. Indiana Historical Society. M0292. Box 14. Folder 11. (photocopy) (Original article is in OMB 23, Box 1. Folder 5)

Wallace, Lew. "Indiana is Now Literary Center, General Lew Wallace Gives His Views on Present Day Writers, Is Working on New Book." Cincinnati *Commercial Tribune* reprinted in Crawfordsville *Weekly News-Review*. **April 15, 1902**. Indiana Historical Society. The Papers of Lew and Susan Wallace. Microfilm Edition. Series I. Reel 27. Indianapolis, Indiana: Indiana Historical Society Press. 2008.

_____. "General Lew Wallace Writes a Romance of 'Billy the Kid' Most Famous Bandit of the Plains: Thrilling Story of the Midnight Meeting Between Gen Wallace, Then Governor of New Mexico, and the Notorious Outlaw, in a Lonesome Hut in Santa Fe." *New York World Magazine*. Sunday, **June 8, 1902**. Lew Wallace Collection. Indiana Historical Society. M0292. . Box 14. Folder 11.

BOWDRE, CHARLES

CONTEMPORARY SOURCES (CHRONOLOGICAL)

Regulator. "Mr. Walz. Sir ..." Letter to Edgar Walz. **July 13, 1878**. Adjutant General's Office. File 1405 AGO 1878. (Attributed to Charles Bowdre in Maurice Garland Fulton, *History of the Lincoln County War*. Tucson: University of Arizona Press. 1975. pages 246-247, and Frederick Nolan, *The Lincoln County War: A Documentary History*, page 310.) **(Possibly dictated to him by Billy Bonney)**

Wallace, Lew. "Please select ten of your Rangers ..." Letter to Juan Patrón. **March 3, 1879**. Indiana Historical Society. Lew Wallace Collection. M0292. Box 4. Folder 4. **(To arrest "Scurlock and Bowdrey")**

_____. Lew. "I have reliable information that J.G. Scurlock and Charles Bowdre are now at a ranch called Taiban ..." Letter to Edward Hatch. **March 6, 1879**. Indiana Historical Society. Lew Wallace Collection. Box 4, Folder 4.

BRADY, WILLIAM

BIOGRAPHICAL SOURCES

Lavash, Donald R. *Sheriff William Brady. Tragic Hero of the Lincoln County War*. Santa Fe, New Mexico: Sunstone Press. 1986.

CONTEMPORARY SOURCES (CHRONOLOGICAL)

Brady, William. Affidavit of **July 2, 1876** concerning appointment as Administrator for the Emil Fritz Estate. Copied from the original District Court Record. (private collection)

_____. Affidavit of **August 22, 1876** documenting business debts to L. G. Murphy and Co. pertaining to the Emil Fritz Estate. Copied from the original District Court Record. (private collection)

_____. Affidavit of **July _, 1876** of Resignation as Emil Fritz Estate Administrator. Copied from the original District Court Record. (private collection.)

_____. Affidavit of **August 22, 1876** confirming giving Alexander McSween the books of the L.G. Murphy Company for the purpose of making business debt collections. Copied from the original District Court Record. (private collection)

Tunstall, John Henry. "A Tax-Payer's Complaint ... January 18, 1878." Mesilla *Independent*. **January 26, 1878**. **(Exposé of William Brady, James Dolan, and John Riley for tax fraud and use of public money to purchase cattle; and Catron then paid that bill)**

Dolan, James J. "Answer to A Tax-Payer's Complaint." Mesilla *Independent*. **January 29, 1878**. **(Response to J.H. Tunstall's exposé of him, William Brady, and John Riley for tax fraud and use of public money to purchase cattle; and T.B. Catron then paid that bill)**

Bristol, Warren. "Action of Assumpsit to command Sheriff Brady of Lincoln County to attach goods of Alexander A. McSween." **February 7, 1878**. District Court Record. (private collection).

_____. Preprinted form for "Writ of Attachment" (Printed and sold at the office of the Mesilla News) filled out to command the Sheriff of Lincoln County to attach goods of Alexander McSween for a suit of damages for ten thousand dollars. **February 7, 1878**. District Court Record. (private collection).

Brady, William. "List of Articles Inventoried by Wm Brady sheriff in the suit of Charles Fritz & Emilie Scholand vs A.A. McSween now in the dwelling house belonging to A.A. McSween." (undated, but in **February of 1878**) (private collection)

BRISTOL, WARREN

CONTEMPORARY SOURCES (CHRONOLOGICAL)

Bristol Warren. "From sources of information that I deem perfectly reliable I am satisfied that there are public disorders in Lincoln County ..." Letter to Governor Marsh Giddings. **January 10, 1874.** Herman B. Weisner Papers, ca. 1957-1992. New Mexico State University Library at Las Cruces. Rio Grande Historical Collections. Accession No. Ms 0249. Box 4/39. Folder D-4. Folder Name. "Judge Bristol's letter." **(Start of Santa Fe Ring's outlaw myth and use of military)**

_____. "Writ of Embezzlement." **December 21, 1877.** Herman B. Weisner Papers, ca. 1957-1992. New Mexico State University Library at Las Cruces. Rio Grande Historical Collections. Accession No. Ms 0249. Box 10. Folder M-13. Folder Name. "Will and Testament A. McSween." **(Emilie Fritz Scholand's sworn complaint against Alexander McSween)**

_____. "Action of Assumpsit to command Sheriff Brady of Lincoln County to attach goods of Alexander A. McSween." **February 7, 1878.** District Court Record. (private collection).

_____. Preprinted form for "Writ of Attachment" (Printed and sold at the office of the Mesilla News) filled out to command the Sheriff of Lincoln County to attach goods of Alexander McSween for a suit of damages for ten thousand dollars. **February 7, 1878.** District Court Record. (private collection).

_____. "My reasons for not holding October term of Court ..." Telegram to U.S. Marshal John Sherman. **October 4, 1878.** Indiana Historical Society. Lew Wallace Collection. M0292. Box 3. Folder 15.

No Author. "For Delegate Benito Baca. County Ticket Juan C. Armijo." *Albuquerque Review.* **October 5, 1878.** Indiana Historical Society. The Papers of Lew and Susan Wallace. Microfilm Edition. Indianapolis, Indiana: Indiana Historical Society Press. 2008. **(About Lew Wallace's arrival in New Mexico Territory and swearing in by Warren Bristol)**

Bristol, Warren. *Instructions to the Jury.* District Court 3rd Judicial. District Doña Ana. Filed **April 9, 1881.** Writ of Embezzlement. New Mexico State University Library at Las Cruces. Rio Grande Historical Collection. Accession No. Ms 0249. Box 1. Folder 14C. Folder Name: "Billy the Kid Legal Documents."

CASEY FAMILY

Klasner, Lilly. Eve Ball. Ed. *My Girlhood Among Outlaws.* Tucson, Arizona: The University of Arizona Press. 1988.

CATRON, THOMAS BENTON

BIBLIOGRAPHICAL

Cleaveland, Norman, *A Synopsis of the Great New Mexico Cover-up.* Self-printed. 1989.

_____. *The Great Santa Fe Cover-up. Based on a Talk given Before the Santa Fe Historical Society on November 1, 1978.* Self-printed. 1982.

_____. *The Morleys - Young Upstarts on the Southwest Frontier.* Albuquerque, New Mexico: Calvin Horn Publisher, Inc. 1971. **(Page 93 gives Catron's vindictive indictment of Cleaveland's grandmother, Ada Morley, for mail theft as revenge denying him use of a Maxwell Land Grant buggy.**

Dunham, Harold H. "New Mexican Land Grants with Special Reference to the Title Papers of the Maxwell Grant." *New Mexico Historical Review.* (January, 1955) Vol. 70. No. 1. pp. 1 - 23.

Hefferan, Vioalle Clark. *Thomas Benton Catron*. Albuquerque, New Mexico: University of New Mexico. Zimmerman Library. Unpublished Thesis for the Degree of Master of Arts. 1940. .**(In praise of Catron; includes railroad involvement, Page 35; First National Bank stockholder from 1871 to 1907, Page 28)**

Keleher, William A. *The Maxwell Land Grant. A New Mexico Item*. Albuquerque, New Mexico: University of New Mexico Press. 1964.

Lamar, Howard Robert N. *The Far Southwest 1846 – 1912: A Territorial History*. New Haven and London: Yale University Press. 1966. **(Chapter 6 covers the Santa Fe Ring))**

Montoya, María E. *Translating Property. The Maxwell Land Grant and the Conflict Over Land in the American West, 1840-1900*. Berkeley and Los Angeles: University of California Press. 2002.

Mullin, Robert N. "A Specimen of Catron's Dirty Work. Sworn Affidavit of Samuel Davis." October 1, 1878. Binder RNM IV, EE. (Unpublished). Midland, Texas: Nita Stewart Haley Memorial Library and J. Evetts Haley Historical Center.

_____. "Catron Embarrassed Throughout His Life by an Affliction." (Date Unknown). Binder RNM, IV, M. (Unpublished). Midland, Texas: Nita Stewart Haley Memorial Library and J. Evetts Haley Historical Center. Robert Mullin Papers. Binder RNM IV, EE (Unpublished).

_____. "Prior to Lincoln County War Catron Had Defended Colonel Dudley." (No Date). Notes from "Lincoln County War Cast of Characters." Midland, Texas: Nita Stewart Haley Memorial Library and J. Evetts Haley Historical Center.

Murphy, Lawrence R. *Lucien Bonaparte Maxwell. Napoleon of the Southwest*. Norman: University of Oklahoma Press. 1983.

Otero, Miguel A. *My Life on the Frontier, 1882-1897: Incidents and Characters of the period when Kansas, Colorado, and New Mexico were passing through the last of their Wild and Romantic Years*. New York: The Press of the Pioneers. 1935. Pages 232-233. (Quoted by Victor Westphall, *Thomas Benton Catron and His Era*. Page 188) **(Quote: "the 'Santa Fe Ring,' the real machine controlling the political situation in New Mexico.")**

Pearson, Jim Berry. *The Maxwell Land Grant*. Norman: University of Oklahoma Press. 1961.

Routt, John C. "I am here on a visit to my daughter and have more by accident than otherwise heard statements ..." Letter to President Rutherford B. Hayes. August 29, 1878. Interior Department Papers 1850-1907; Appointments Division and Subsequent Actions. Microfilm File Case Number 44-4-8-3. Microfilm Roll M750. National Archives and Records Administration Record Group 48. U.S. Department of Interior. Washington D.C. **(In opposition to removal of Governor Axtell and U.S. Attorney Thomas Benton Catron.)**

Sluga, Mary Elizabeth. *Political Life of Thomas Benton Catron 1896-1912*. Albuquerque, New Mexico: University of New Mexico. Zimmerman Library. Unpublished Thesis for the Degree of Master of Arts. 1941. **(Thesis in praise of Catron for an M.A.)**

Taylor, Morris F. *O.P. McMains and the Maxwell Land Grant Conflict*. Tucson, Arizona: The University of Arizona Press. 1979. **(Traces origins of the Santa Fe Ring with T.B. Catron and S.B. Elkins)**

Westphall, Victor. *Thomas Benton Catron and His Era*. Tucson, Arizona: University of Arizona Press. 1973.

_____. "Fraud and Implications of Fraud in the Land Grants of New Mexico." *New Mexico Historical Review*. 1974. Vol. XLIX, No. 3. 189 - 218.

Wooden, John Paul. *Thomas Benton Catron and New Mexico Politics 1866-1921*. Albuquerque, New Mexico: University of New Mexico. Zimmerman Library. Unpublished Thesis for the Degree of Master of Arts. 1959. **(Thesis in praise of Catron for an M.A.)**

893

LETTERS BY, TO, ABOUT (CHRONOLOGICAL)

GENERAL

Catron, Thomas Benton. Letters 1866-1921. Coronado Collection. University of New Mexico Library. Albuquerque, New Mexico.

LETTERS (CHRONOLOGICAL)

Giddings, Marsh. "To defeat Catron's confirmation [as U.S. Attorney] a grossly false affidavit [by August Kirchner] has been sent to Senator [Lyman Trumbull]." **Month (?) 1872.** Telegram from Governor Marsh Giddings to Washington, D.C. Attorney General George H. Williams. From Victor Westphall. *Thomas Benton Catron and His Era.* Page 107. (**About the 1872 legislature's actions against Palen and Catron**)

Catron, Thomas Benton. "Answering Charges of Mary E. McPherson." **February 24, 1877.** Letter to Attorney General Alphonso Taft. Interior Department Papers 1850-1907; Appointments Division and Subsequent Actions. Microfilm File Case Number 44-4-8-3. Record Group 48. Microfilm Roll M750. National Archives and Records Administration. U.S. Department of Justice. Washington, D.C.

Riley, John. Letter to N.A M. Dudley. **May 19, 1878. (Fabricated Regulator theft of Catron's cattle from the Dolan Pecos Cow Camp)** Cited by Victor Westphall, Page 87.

Catron, Thomas Benton. Catron letter to Governor S. B. Axtell to intervene in Lincoln County. **May 30, 1878.** Midland, Texas: Nita Stewart Haley Memorial Library and J. Evetts Haley Historical Center. Robert Mullin Papers. Binder RNM IV, EE (Unpublished). (**Fabricated attack of Regulators on his cow camp workers**) Cited by Victor Westphall, Page 89-90.

Elkins, Stephen Benton. "I have waited some time to reply to your lengthy letter ..." Letter to T.B. Catron. **August 15, 1879.** West Virginia & Regional History Center. West Virginia University Libraries, Morgantown, W. Va. Stephen B. Elkins Papers (A&M 53). Box 1. Folder 1. (**Reveals he prevented Catron's dismissal and indictment from Angel's report**)

Gonzales y Borrego, Francisco. "dear Sir I have the honor to report to you that I have two men that they have agreed to come to the Republican party ... they want $10.00 each ..." **July 23, 1890.** Letter to Thomas Benton Catron. Catron Papers 102, Box 8. Quoted by Victor Westphall, *Thomas Benton Catron and His Era.* Page 268. (**Revealing Catron's Ringite vote-buying**)

Chavez, Juliana V. "Mr. Catron, you are not above suspicion of knowing more about the assassination of my son than you have found it convenient to reveal ..." Letter of Juliana Chavez to T.B. Catron. Reprinted in *Santa Fe Weekly New Mexican.* **March 8, 1894.** Quoted in Victor Westphall, *Thomas Benton Catron and his Era.* Page 226. (**Accusing Catron as accomplice to murder of Francisco Chavez, with implication of Santa Fe Ring**)

Catron, Thomas Benton "[The Francisco Chavez murder case] has left me more prostrated than any case I have ever had." Letter to wife, Julia Catron. **June 1, 1895.** C.P. 105, Vol. 12. Quoted in Victor Westphall, *Thomas Benton Catron and His Era.* Page 228. (**Catron implicated in political murder**)

_____. "[Y]ou must absolutely stand pat and not give away any information that will injure me ..." Letter to Editor of the *Albuquerque Daily Citizen* Thomas Hughes. **October 10, 1895.** C.P. 801. Box 1. Quoted by Victor Westphall, *Thomas Benton Catron and His Era.* Page 247. (**Promising payback for secrecy**)

_____. "Editor of the Citizen: I have noticed an article in the Citizen of the 9th inst., which seems to reflect on Chief Justice Smith ..." Letter to Editor of the *Albuquerque Daily Citizen* Thomas Hughes. **October 10, 1895.** C.P. 801. Box 1. Quoted by Victor Westphall, *Thomas Benton Catron and His Era.* (Page 248) (**Defaming his Supreme Court disbarment judge, Thomas Smith**)

Catron, Thomas Benton. "The editorial in your paper came to hand today and the democrats and members of the supreme court are very indignant." Letter to *Albuquerque Daily Citizen's* editor, Thomas Hughes. **October 10, 1895.** **(Secret bribe for the Hughes press plot)** Quoted by Victor Westphall, *Thomas Benton Catron and His Era*. Pages 247-248.

_____. "Tom Smith, son of "Extra Billy" Smith, brother of ... the embezzler, who fled from justice in Arizona ..." "[Judge] Hamilton should ... see that the decision is an absolute, complete, unconditional vindication. This is what I ask him." Letter to *Socorro Chieftain* publisher S.W. Williams. **October 25, 1895.** Catron Papers. 105. Vol. 13. Quoted by Victor Westphall, *Thomas Benton Catron and His Era*. Pages 251-254. **(Defamation of his disbarment Chief Judge Thomas Smith; and illegal influence on another judge)**

_____. "[Smith], thank heaven, took the diarrhoea from the article published in the 'Citizen' and was soon after thrown into a congestive chill ..." Letter to Walter C. Hadley. **October 29, 1895. (Gloating over his sadistic attack on his disbarment judge, Thomas Smith)** Quoted by Victor Westphall, *Thomas Benton Catron and His Era*. Page 259.

_____. "His skin is so thin that the slightest attack punctures him. I think the papers should now puncture him ..." Letter to T.W. Collier. **November 11, 1895.** Catron Papers. 105. Vol. 13. **(Sadistic attack on his disbarment judge, Thomas Smith)** Quoted by Victor Westphall, *Thomas Benton Catron and His Era*. Page 249.

_____. "This man [Judge] Laughlin ... tried to disbar me and when he could not do it he wrote a filthy, dirty, dissenting opinion ..." Letter to William J. Mills. **July 18, 1896.** Catron Papers. 105. Vol. 13. Quoted by Victor Westphall, *Thomas Benton Catron and His Era*. Page 258. **(Trying to destroy reputation of disbarment judge, Napoleon B. Laughlin)**

_____. Letter to a Don Matais Contreras. **July 30, 1896. (On acquiring land grants by bartering attorney's fees)** Cited in John Paul Wooden's unpublished masters thesis, Page 11.

_____. "Poker Bill" is now engaged in playing a game in which the lives of four men are at stake ..." *Albuquerque Daily Citizen.* **September 11, 1896.** Reprinted September 11, 1896 in the *Santa Fe Daily New Mexican.* Quoted by Victor Westphall, *Thomas Benton Catron and His Era*. Page 262. **(Catron's anonymous defamatory letter about William Thornton)**

Thornton, William T. "This communication to the *Citizen* was prepared in your office, and at your dictation." *Santa Fe Daily New Mexican.* **September 11, 1896.** Reprinting and debunking T.B. Catron's anonymous letter of September 11, 1896 to the *Albuquerque Daily Citizen* of September 11, 1896. Quoted by Victor Westphall, *Thomas Benton Catron and His Era*. Page 262. **(Thornton confronts Catron's anonymous defamatory letter about him)**

Catron, Thomas Benton. "[Your letter] has the appearance of being designed to provoke me to some act of violence, which might give your adherents an opportunity to injure me physically..." **September 16, 1896.** Letter to William T. Thornton. Catron Papers 801, Box 1. Quoted by Victor Westphall, *Thomas Benton Catron and His Era*. Page 263. **(Catron's violent and insanely paranoid accusations of Thornton for exposing his criminality)**

_____. "The letter of Gov. Thornton is regarded here by all good citizens as being ... calculated to bring about a state of unrest and possible blood-shed." Letter to President Grover Cleveland. **September 16, 1896.** Quoted by Victor Westphall, *Thomas Benton Catron and His Era*. Pages 269-270.

_____. "The letter of Gov. Thornton is regarded here by all good citizens as being ... calculated to bring about a state of unrest and possible blood-shed." **September 16, 1896.** Letter to President Grover Cleveland. Catron Papers 801, Box 1. Quoted by Victor Westphall, *Thomas Benton Catron and His Era*. Pages 269-270. **(Attempted revenge on Governor William Thornton)**

Field, Neill B. "I am exceedingly sick of your method of doing business ..." Letter to Thomas Benton Catron. **December 28, 1896**. C.P. 106, Box 1, quoted in Victor Westphall, *Thomas Benton Catron and His Era*. Page 165. (**Catron accused of attempting to pocket stock of deceased partner**)

Elkins, Stephen Benton. "Mr. Catron's prominence in the capital territory and his leadership ..." Letter to Gideon B. Bantz. **September 9, 1897**. (**Improper influence of Catron's disbarment judge**) Quoted in John Paul Wooden's unpublished thesis, Page 32.

Catron, Thomas Benton. "He [Lew Wallace] and I were not on friendly terms while he was governor." Letter to Stephen Benton Elkins. **August 4, 1897**. (**About Wallace's opposition to his reappointment as U.S. Attorney**) Quoted in Mary Elizabeth Sluga's masters thesis, Page 50.

_____. "I am entitled to same from a political standpoint ... having made the race paying all the expenses ..." Letter to Joshua S. Reynolds. **December 16, 1897**. Quoted in Mary Elizabeth Sluga's masters thesis, Page 53.

_____."His administration has been guilty of the most wholesale plunder of the resources of this territory ..." Letter to Richard C. Kerens. **April 4, 1901**. (**Revenge defamation of Governor Miguel A. Otero**) Quoted in Mary Elizabeth Sluga's masters thesis, Pages 66-69.

_____."You must see that Otero is not reappointed ..." Letter to Stephen Benton Elkins. **November 11, 1901**. Quoted in Mary Elizabeth Sluga's masters thesis, Page 79.

_____. "[Otero backers] have made a very villainous, mean ugly fight against me." **September 20, 1902**. Letter to Dave Winters. Catron Papers 105, Volume 20. Quoted by Victor Westphall, *Thomas Benton Catron and His Era*. Pages 291. (**Accusing Governor Otero of his own Ring-style criminality**)

Catron, Thomas Benton. "[If your son] is to be appointed I shall be very pleased ... if he will take immediate steps to have the "Augean stables" cleaned ..." Letter to James J. Hagerman. **November 22, 1905**. (**Wanting appointment as Attorney General to maliciously prosecute opponents**) Quoted in Mary Elizabeth Sluga's masters thesis, Pages 87-88.

_____. If I can get New Mexico a state ... my property will be doubled in value." Letter to Richard C. Kerens. **February 3, 1894**. Quoted by Victor Westphall, *Thomas Benton Catron and His Era*. Page 312.

Mills, Melvin W. "There are a few men who are candidates [for Senator] that I guess have some money ..." Letter to Thomas Benton Catron. **September 12, 1911**. Catron Papers 103, Box 37. Quoted by Victor Westphall, *Thomas Benton Catron and His Era*. Page 350. (**Revealing possible bribery for legislators' vote**)

Cutting, Bronson. "Catron was the boss of the Territory ..." Letter to James Roger Addison. **December 11, 1911**. Cited by Victor Westphall in *Thomas Benton Catron and His Era*, Page 98, from his citation: Lincoln County Manuscripts Division. Box 12. Courtesy of David Stratton.

Catron, Charles C. "My father probably spent over a million dollars in following up his hobby [of politics]." Letter to Major Harry F. Cameron. **June 3, 1921**. Catron Papers 101, Box 29. Quoted by Victor Westphall, *Thomas Benton Catron and His Era*. Page 387. (**Revealing possible political bribery**)

FEDERAL INDICTMENT OF BILLY BONNEY AND REGULATORS

Catron, Thomas Benton. "Case No. 411. The United States vs. Charles Bowdry [Bowdre], Doc Scurlock, Henry Brown, Henry Antrim alias "Kid," John Middleton, Stephen Stevens, John Scroggins, George Coe and Frederick Waite." **June 21, 1878**. Herman B. Weisner Papers, ca. 1957-1992. New Mexico State University Library at Las Cruces. Rio Grande Historical Collections. Accession No. Ms 0249. Box 1. Folder B-4. Folder Name: Andrew Roberts Indictment. (**Federal murder indictment of Billy Bonney by U.S. Attorney T.B. Catron; made a**

Territorial pardon impossible until quashed on March 30, 1881 by the District Court in Mesilla.)

OWNERSHIP FILING ON CARRIZOZO CATTLE COMPANY

Catron, Thomas Benton.. Statement of Sole ownership of Carrizozo Ranch in Tax Dispute Case. No date. Herman B. Weisner Papers, ca. 1957-1992. New Mexico State University Library at Las Cruces. Rio Grande Historical Collections. Accession No. Ms 0249. Box. 2. Folder C-8. Folder Name "T.B. Catron Tax Troubles."

ARTICLES (CHRONOLOGICAL)

Morley, William Raymond and Frank Springer. On Oscar McMains's citizen's Meeting. *Cimarron News and Press.* **November 10, 1875. (Colfax County citizens meeting on F.J. Tolby murder by Santa Fe Ring.)**

_____. " 'The Territory of Elkins.' Assassination of Supposed Sun Correspondent. The Murder of the Rev. F.J. Tolby in New Mexico. A Probate Judge Accused of Complicity in the Crime. Indignation Meeting." *New York Weekly Sun.* **December 22, 1875.** Interior Department Papers 1850-1907; Appointments Division and Subsequent Actions. Microfilm Roll M750. National Archives and Records Administration. Record Group 48. Microfilm Case File Number 44-4-8-3. U.S. Department of Interior. Washington, D. C.(**Submitted on May 1, 1877 to President Rutherford B. Hayes by Mary McPherson and W.B. Matchett**)

Lambert, J.J. "At It Again." Pueblo, Colorado, *Enterprise and Chronicle.* **April 21, 1877.** Interior Department Papers 1850-1907; Appointments Division and Subsequent Actions. Microfilm File Case Number 44-4-8-3. Record Group 48. Microfilm No. M750. Roll 1. National Archives and Records Administration. U.S. Department of Justice. Washington, D.C. (**About Ring control of courts and malicious prosecution of opponents and Franklin Tolby murder**)

Tunstall, John Henry. "A Tax-Payer's Complaint ... January 18, 1878." Mesilla *Independent.* **January 26, 1878. (Exposé of William Brady, James Dolan, and John Riley for tax fraud and use of public money to purchase cattle; and Catron then paid that bill)**

Dolan, James J. "Answer to A Tax-Payer's Complaint." Mesilla *Independent.* **January 29, 1878. (Response to J.H. Tunstall's exposé)**

No Author. "White Cap's Proclamation." *Las Vegas Optic.* **March 12, 1880. (Manifesto against land-grabbing Catron and the Ring)**

No Author. Las Cruces *Thirty-Four Newspaper.* **October 27, 1880. (Urging voters to overthrow Catron's Santa Fe Ring-backed candidate)**

No Author. *Albuquerque Daily Democrat.* **March 4, 1884. (Time is past for Ring herding men)**

No Author. *Santa Fe Weekly New Mexican Review.* **March 13, 1884.** *Santa Fe Weekly New Mexican Review.* (**Accusation of Catron and the Ring of controlling grand juries and** bribery)

No Author. *Albuquerque Daily Democrat.* **March 15, 1884. (Oscar P. McMains "Memorial" against land-grabbing Ring)**

No Author. *Las Vegas Optic.* **September 2, 1884. (About the anti-Ring Legislature revolt and Catron's alliance with corrupt Judge Joseph Palen)**

Chavez, No First Name. *Santa Fe Weekly New Mexican.* **March 8, 1894. (Open letter from mother of Francisco Chavez implicating Catron in his murder)** Cited by Victor Westphall, *Thomas Benton Catron and His Era.* Page 226.

No author. *Las Vegas Independent Democrat.* ___ **1895**; based on *Las Vegas Optic.* September 2, 1884. (**About disbarring Catron**)

Catron, Thomas Benton (As "Anonymous"). "Is it honesty or partisanship?" Letter to the Editor, Thomas Hughes. *Albuquerque Daily Citizen.* **October 9, 1895. (Defamation of his disbarment Judge Thomas J. Smith**) Cited by Victor

Westphall, *Thomas Benton Catron and His Era.* Page 246. Thomas B. Catron Papers. University of New Mexico Center for Southwest Studies. University Library. MSS 29 BC.

_____. Published letter to the Editor, Thomas Hughes. *Albuquerque Daily Citizen.* **October 10, 1895. (Pretended response to his own anonymous letter, given in Editor Thomas Hughes's perjured editorial)** Cited by Victor Westphall, *Thomas Benton Catron and His Era.* Page 248.

No Author. *Las Vegas Daily Optic .* **September 30, 1896. (Stating Catron had been an incompetent Delegate to Congress)**

Catron, Thomas Benton (As "Anonymous"). *Albuquerque Daily Citizen.* **September 11, 1896. ("Poker Bill" defamatory attack on Governor William Thornton)**

Thornton, William T. *Santa Fe Daily New Mexican.* **September 11, 1896. (Exposing Catron's "Poker Bill" plot)**

No Author. *Los Angeles Times.* **1899.** Undated clipping, Laughlin Papers, State Records Center, Santa Fe, New Mexico. Quoted by Victor Westphall, *Thomas Benton Catron and His Era.* Page 285. **(Joking article about the Santa Fe Ring)**

Johnson, E. Dana. "Editorial." *Santa Fe New Mexican.* **May 16, 1921.** Catron Papers 801, Box 1. Quoted by Victor Westphall, *Thomas Benton Catron and His Era.* Pages 394-395. **(Catron as "boss")**

EXPOSÉS (CHRONOLOGICAL)

Mills, Melvin W. "Thought I would write you how things are running." Letter to Robert H. Longwill. **December 5, 1873.** "Exhibit A" in the August 9, 1878 deposition of Frank Springer to Investigator Frank Warner Angel. Frank Warner Angel report titled *In the Matter of the Investigation of the Charges Against S.B. Axtell Governor of New Mexico.* October 3, 1878. Interior Department Papers 1850-1907; Appointments Division and Subsequent Actions. Microfilm Case File No. 44-4-8-3. Record Group 48. Microfilm Roll M750. National Archives and Records Administration. U.S. Department of Interior. Washington, D.C. **(About Catron and Ring empowerment)**

Morley, William Raymond and Frank Springer. On Oscar McMains's citizen's Meeting. *Cimarron News and Press.* **November 10, 1875.** In Mary McPherson, Letters and Petitions to President Rutherford B. Hayes re: Removal Governor Axtell and the Santa Fe Ring. 1977. Interior Department Papers 1850-1907; Appointments Division and Subsequent Actions. Microfilm File Case Number 44-4-8-3. Record Group 48. Microfilm Roll M750. National Archives and Records Administration. **(Colfax County citizens meeting on F.J. Tolby murder by Santa Fe Ring.)**

_____. " 'The Territory of Elkins.' Assassination of Supposed Sun Correspondent. The Murder of the Rev. F.J. Tolby in New Mexico. A Probate Judge Accused of Complicity in the Crime. Indignation Meeting." *New York Weekly Sun.* **December 22, 1875.** Interior Department Papers 1850-1907; Appointments Division and Subsequent Actions. Microfilm Roll M750. National Archives and Records Administration. Record Group 48. Microfilm Case File Number 44-4-8-3. U.S. Department of Interior. Washington, D. C.**(In May 1, 1877 submission to President Hayes as "Mary E. McPherson and W.B. Matchett 'Make certain charges against the U.S. Officials in the Territory of New Mexico.' ")**

Middaugh, Asa F. Deposition. **March 31, 1876.** "Exhibit B" in the August 9, 1878 deposition of Frank Springer to Investigator Frank Warner Angel. Frank Warner Angel report titled *In the Matter of the Investigation of the Charges Against S.B. Axtell Governor of New Mexico.* October 3, 1878. Interior Department Papers 1850-1907; Appointments Division and Subsequent Actions. Microfilm Case File No. 44-4-8-3. Record Group 48. Microfilm Roll M750. National Archives and Records Administration. U.S. Department of Interior. Washington, D.C. **(About Catron's malicious prosecution of Ada McPherson Morley)**

McPherson, Mary. "Charges against Thomas B. Catron, U.S. Attorney, and Others." **February 7, 1877.** Letter to Attorney General Alphonso Taft. Interior Department Papers 1850-1907; Appointments Division and Subsequent Actions. Microfilm File Case Number 44-4-8-3. Record Group 48. Microfilm Roll M750. National Archives and Records Administration. U.S. Department of Justice. Washington, D.C.

Catron, Thomas Benton. "Answering Charges of Mary E. McPherson." **February 24, 1877.** Letter to Attorney General Alphonso Taft. Interior Department Papers 1850-1907; Appointments Division and Subsequent Actions. Microfilm File Case Number 44-4-8-3. Record Group 48. Microfilm Roll M750. National Archives and Records Administration. U.S. Department of Justice. Washington, D.C.

Morley William Raymond. "I was astonished beyond measure at your proceedings, and have fears as to the result ..." Letter to Mary McPherson. **March 6, 1877.** McPherson, Mary E. Letters and Petitions to President Rutherford B. Hayes re: Removal Governor Axtell and the Santa Fe Ring. Interior Department Papers 1850-1907; Appointments Division and Subsequent Actions. Microfilm File Case Number 44-4-8-3. Record Group 48. Microfilm Roll M750. National Archives and Records Administration. U.S. Department of Justice. Washington, D. C. (**Hopes she can help fight against Santa Fe Ring; enclosed in Mary McPherson's "Charges Against U.S. Officials in the Territory of New Mexico."**)

Lambert, J.J. "At It Again." Pueblo, Colorado, *Enterprise and Chronicle.* **April 21, 1877.** Interior Department Papers 1850-1907; Appointments Division and Subsequent Actions. Microfilm File Case Number 44-4-8-3. Record Group 48. Microfilm No. M750. Roll 1. National Archives and Records Administration. U.S. Department of Justice. Washington, D.C. (**Description of Santa Fe Ring control of courts and malicious prosecution of opponents like Oscar McMains in the Franklin Tolby murder; used in: "W.B. Matchett and Mary E. McPherson 'Make Certain Charges Against the U.S. Officials in the Territory of New Mexico.' " Letter to President Rutherford B. Hayes. Received and filed May 1, 1877. Interior Department Papers 1850-1907; Appointments Division and Subsequent Actions. Microfilm File Case Number 44-4-8-3. Record Group 48. Microfilm No. M750. Roll 1. National Archives and Records Administration. U. S. Department of Justice. Washington, D.C.**)

Matchett, W.B. and Mary E. McPherson. "W.B. Matchett and Mary E. McPherson 'Make Certain Charges Against the U.S. Officials in the Territory of New Mexico, Together With Corroboration Evidence.' " Letter to President Rutherford B. Hayes. Received and filed **May 1, 1877.** Interior Department Papers 1850-1907; Appointments Division and Subsequent Actions. Microfilm File Case Number 44-4-8-3. Record Group 48. Microfilm No. M750. Roll 1. National Archives and Records Administration. U. S. Department of Justice. Washington, D.C.

McPherson, Mary and W.B. Matchett. "To The President. Please make the enclosed a part of the evidence in the case of "Charges Against New Mexican Officials" Letter to President Rutherford B. Hayes. **May 3, 1877.** McPherson, Mary E. Letters and Petitions to President Rutherford B. Hayes re: Removal Governor Axtell and the Santa Fe Ring. Interior Department Papers 1850-1907; Appointments Division and Subsequent Actions. Microfilm File Case Number 44-4-8-3. Record Group 48. Microfilm Roll M750. National Archives and Records Administration. U.S. Department of Justice. Washington, D. C. (**Addendum to their May, 1877 "Certain Charges Against U.S. Officials in New Mexico Territory."**)

McPherson, Mary and W.B. Matchett. "The Secretary of the Interior, Sir - Accompanying please find copy of charges, &c., against S.B. Axtell, Governor and other New Mexico Officials ..." "Charges Against New Mexican Officials." Letter to Secretary of the Interior Carl Schurz. **May 5, 1877.** McPherson, Mary E. Letters and Petitions to President Rutherford B. Hayes re: Removal Governor Axtell and the Santa Fe Ring. Interior Department Papers 1850-1907;

Appointments Division and Subsequent Actions. Microfilm File Case Number 44-4-8-3. Record Group 48. Microfilm Roll M750. National Archives and Records Administration. U.S. Department of Justice. Washington, D. C.

McPherson, Mary and W B. Matchett. "We have respectfully to request that the following named records, documents, papers, communications and correspondence be supplied ..." Records Request to Secretary of the Interior Carl Schurz. **July 26, 1877.** Interior Department Papers 1850-1907; Appointments Division and Subsequent Actions. Microfilm File Case Number 44-4-8-3. Record Group 48. Microfilm No. M750. Roll 1. National Archives and Records Administration. U. S. Department of Justice. Washington, D.C. **(Requesting records of the Santa Fe Ring, Catron, Elkins, and Axtell)**

McPherson, Mary. "Please place before the Attorney General ..." Letter to President Rutherford B. Hayes **August 23, 1877.** Interior Department Papers 1850-1907; Appointments Division and Subsequent Actions. Microfilm File Case Number 44-4-8-3. Record Group 48. Microfilm No. M750. Roll 1. National Archives and Records Administration. U. S. Department of Justice. Washington, D.C. **(Requesting that her "Charges" go to the Attorney General.)**

McPherson, Mary and W.B. Matchett. *"In the Matter of Charges vs. Gov. S.B. Axtell and Other New Mexico Officials. Submitted to the Departments of the Interior and Justice.* **August, 1877.** Printed as a 31 page booklet. No publisher listed. Indiana Historical Society. Lew Wallace Collection. M0292. Box 3. Folder 20.

McPherson, Mary. "I desire to know when I can be heard ..." Letter to Secretary of Interior Carl Schurz. **September 30, 1977.** Interior Department Papers 1850-1907; Appointments Division and Subsequent Actions. Microfilm File Case Number 44-4-8-3. Record Group 48. Microfilm No. M750. Roll 1. National Archives and Records Administration. U. S. Department of Justice. Washington, D.C.

Tunstall, John Henry. "A Tax-Payer's Complaint ... January 18, 1878." Mesilla *Independent.* January 26, 1878. **(Exposé of William Brady, James Dolan, and John Riley for tax fraud and use of public money to purchase cattle; and Catron then paid that bill)**

Dolan, James J. "Answer to A Tax-Payer's Complaint." Mesilla *Independent.* January 29, 1878. **(Response to J.H. Tunstall's exposé)**

Springer, Frank. Deposition to Investigator Frank Warner Angel. **August 9, 1878.** Frank Warner Angel report titled *In the Matter of the Investigation of the Charges Against S.B. Axtell Governor of New Mexico.* October 3, 1878. Interior Department Papers 1850-1907; Appointments Division and Subsequent Actions. Microfilm Case File No. 44-4-8-3. Record Group 48. Microfilm Roll M750. National Archives and Records Administration. U.S. Department of Interior. Washington, D.C. **(Mentions Catron, Elkins, and the Santa Fe Ring, and provided Exhibits of letters exposing Catron's evil.)**

Morley, William Raymond. "Your letter of the 7th came last night and it was a good long newsy letter ..." Letter to wife, Ada McPherson Morley. **August 15, 1878.** Collection of Norman Cleaveland. Quoted in Norman Cleaveland, *The Morleys: Young Upstarts in the Southwest.* Albuquerque, New Mexico: Calvin Horn Publisher, Inc. 1971. Pages 152-155. **(About possible cover-up by Angel's reports; about the Santa Fe Ring, T.B. Catron, S.B. Elkins, S.B. Axtell, and Henry Waldo; and the Lincoln County War)**

No Author. "The Santa Fe Ring is the most corrupt combination that ever cursed any country or community." Las Cruces *Thirty-Four Newspaper.* **October 27, 1880.** From Victor Westphall, *Thomas Benton Catron and His Era.* Page 186. **(Article summarizing Ring abuses in urging voters to oppose Ring candidates)**

No Author. "The Ring must soon discover that the time has passed in New Mexico when men can be herded like so many sheep ..." *Albuquerque Daily Democrat.* **March 4, 1884.** Quoted by Victor Westphall, *Thomas Benton Catron and His Era.* Page 191. **(About Santa Fe Ring control of appointments to legislature)**

Thornton, W.T. "Your favors received. We will try and have the matter of Mrs. Wilson's estate at Albuquerque attended to for your Bates County friends." Letter to John J. Cockrell, Esq. **January 16, 1886.** Herman B. Weisner Papers, ca. 1957-1992. New Mexico State University Library at Las Cruces. Rio Grande Historical Collections. Accession No. Ms 0249. Box 12. Folder S-5. Folder Name "Catron, Thornton, & Clancy Letterhead." **(T.B. Catron's law partner discloses Ring planned malicious prosecution in Lincoln County)**

No author. "T.B. Catron's reputation now being "smirched" by evidence that he was a briber and too dishonest even to practice law ..." *Las Vegas Independent Democrat.* ? month, ? day, **1895**; based on *Las Vegas Optic.* September 2, 1884. From Victor Westphall. *Thomas Benton Catron and His Era.* Pages 105-106. **(About disbarring Catron from law practice in New Mexico)**

Hamilton, Humphrey. *Majority Opinion* in disbarment case against Thomas Benton Catron. "[T]he low moral character and poor reputation for veracity of the prosecution witnesses rendered their testimony beyond belief." **October 25, 1895.** Catron Papers. 801. Box 1. Quoted by Victor Westphall, *Thomas Benton Catron and His Era.* Page 251. **(Ring colluding judge vindicating Catron from disbarment by discrediting prosecution evidence)**

Catron, Thomas Benton. "Poker Bill" is now engaged in playing a game in which the lives of four men are at stake ..." *Albuquerque Daily Citizen.* **September 11, 1896.** Reprinted September 11, 1896 in the *Santa Fe Daily New Mexican.* Quoted by Victor Westphall, *Thomas Benton Catron and His Era.* Page 262. **(Catron's anonymous defamatory letter about past partner, William Thornton)**

Thornton, William T. "This communication to the *Citizen* was prepared in your office, and at your dictation." *Santa Fe Daily New Mexican.* **September 11, 1896.** Reprinting and debunking T.B. Catron's anonymous letter of September 11, 1896 to the *Albuquerque Daily Citizen* of September 11, 1896. Quoted by Victor Westphall, *Thomas Benton Catron and His Era.* Page 262. **(Thornton confronts Catron's anonymous defamatory letter about him)**

Wallace, Lew. "I have your several letters, including the last one of the 3rd inst." Letter to Eugene Fiske. **November 6, 1897.** Indiana Historical Society. Lew Wallace Collection. AC233. Box 1. Folder 7. (part of 1981 addition) **(About T.B. Catron's control over New Mexicans)**

Johnson, E. Dana. "[H]e ruled with a rod of iron ..." Editorial. *Santa Fe New Mexican.* **May 16, 1921.** Catron Papers 801, Box 1. Quoted by Victor Westphall, *Thomas Benton Catron and His Era.* Pages 394-395. **(Santa Fe Ring tactics of "boss" Catron without using the words Santa Fe Ring)**

Pritchard, George W. "Eulogy." **May 17, 1921.** Catron Papers 801, Box 1. Quoted by Victor Westphall, *Thomas Benton Catron and His Era.* Pages 393-394.

Mabry, Thomas Jewett. "New Mexico's Constitution in the Making." *New Mexico Historical Review.* **1943.** Volume 19, Issue 170. Quoted by Victor Westphall, *Thomas Benton Catron and His Era.* Page 341. **(Revealing that future Governor Mabry was Ring-biased, calling T.B. Catron an "able delegate" to New Mexico's 1912 constitutional convention)**

SEE ALSO: Stephen Benton Elkins; Santa Fe Ring

CAYPLESS, EDGAR

Keleher, William A. *Violence in Lincoln County 1869-1881.* Albuquerque, New Mexico: University of New Mexico Press. 1957. **(Pages 320-321, the lost William Bonney letter of April 15, 1881 to Attorney Edgar Caypless is presented crediting the original letter to the Billy the Kid Museum in Mesilla as published by its founder, George Griggs, in *History of the Mesilla Valley.* On page 320 is also the *La Vegas Gazette* article of March 12, 1881 about Billy's replevin case with Caypless for his mare.)**

CHAPMAN, HUSTON

CONTEMPORARY SOURCES (CHRONOLOGICAL)

Wallace, Lew. "I enclose you a copy of a letter from Las Vegas ..." Letter to Edward Hatch. **October 28, 1878**. Indiana Historical Society. Lew Wallace Collection. M0292. Box 3. Folder 16. (**Forwards Chapman's letter to Hatch**)

_____. "In a communication, dated October 28. inst., I requested, for reasons stated, a safe-guard for Mrs. McSween ..." Letter to Edward Hatch. **November 9, 1878**. Indiana Historical Society. Lew Wallace Collection. M0292. Box 3. Folder 17.

No Author. (signed E.). "DEATH OF CHAPMAN. The people of Las Vegas were greatly shocked on Sunday last to hear of the cold blooded murder, in Lincoln County ..." *Las Vegas Gazette*. **March 1, 1879**. From *Proceedings of a Court of Inquiry in the Case of Lt. Col. N.A.M. Dudley (May 2,1879 – July 5, 1879)*. File No. QQ1284. (Boxes 3304, 3305, 3305A); Court Martial Files 1809-1894. Records of the Office of the Judge Advocate General – Army. Record Group 153. Old Military and Civil Branch. National Archives and Records Administration. Washington, D. C.

No Author. "Wallace and Lincoln County." Grant County *Herald*. **March 1, 1879**. Indiana Historical Society. The Papers of Lew and Susan Wallace. Microfilm Edition. Indianapolis, Indiana: Indiana Historical Society Press. 2008. (**Ridicule about Huston Chapman's murder**)

Chapman, W.W. "Yours of the 1st inst. came ..." Letter to Ira E. Leonard. **March 20, 1879**. Indiana Historical Society. Lew Wallace Collection. M0292. Box 4. Folder 6.

Rynerson, William. "The Grand Jurors for the Territory of New Mexico taken from the body of the good and lawful men of the County of Lincoln ..." Indictments of the April, Lincoln County Grand Jury. **April 28, 1879**. Herman B. Weisner Papers, ca. 1957-1992. New Mexico State University Library at Las Cruces. Rio Grande Historical Collection. Accession No. Ms 0249. Box 4/39. Folder E-Z. Folder Name: "Jessie Evans Accessory to Murder." (**Billy's testimony indicts J.J. Dolan, Billy Campbell, and Jessie Evans fulfilling his pardon bargain**)

Chapman, W.W "Since receiving yours of the 1st March ..." Letter to Ira Leonard. **May 8, 1879**. Indiana Historical Society. Lew Wallace Collection. M0292. Box 4. Folder 10.

LETTERS

Chapman, Huston I. "You will please pardon me for presuming so much upon your kindness ..." Letter to Lew Wallace. **October 24, 1878**. Indiana Historical Society. Lew Wallace Collection. M0292. Box 3. Folder 16. (**Makes clear N.A.M. Dudley's danger to Susan McSween**)

_____. 'You attach much importance to the awe-inspiring influence of the military ..." Letter to Lew Wallace. **November 25, 1878**. From Frederick Nolan, *The Lincoln County War*, p. 359.

_____. "You must pardon me for so often presuming upon your kindness ..." Letter to Lew Wallace. **November 29, 1878**. Indiana Historical Society. Lew Wallace Collection. M0292. Box 3. Folder 18.

CHISUM, JOHN SIMPSON

Hinton, Harwood P., Jr. "John Simpson Chisum, 1877-84." *New Mexico Historical Review* 31(3) (July 1956): 177 - 205; 31(4) (October 1956): 310 - 337; 32(1) (January 1957): 53 - 65.

Klasner, Lilly. Eve Ball. Ed. *My Girlhood Among Outlaws*. Tucson, Arizona: The University of Arizona Press. 1988.

COE FAMILY

BIOGRAPHICAL SOURCES

Coe, George. Doyce B. Nunis, Jr. Ed. *Frontier Fighter. The Autobiography of George Coe Who Fought and Rode With Billy the Kid.* Chicago: R. R. Donnelley and Sons Company. 1984.

Coe, Wilbur. *Ranch on the Ruidoso. The Story of a Pioneer Family in New Mexico, 1871 - 1968.* New York: Alfred A. Knopf. 1968.

CONTEMPORARY SOURCE

Coe, George. "We are two residents of Lincoln County ..." Letter written with Isaac Ellis to President Rutherford B. Hayes. **June 22, 1878.** In Angel Report papers. Microfilm File Case Number 44-4-8-3. Record Group 48. Microfilm No. M750. Roll 1. National Archives and Records Administration. U.S. Department of Justice. Washington, D.C.

CORBET, SAMUEL R.

Corbet, Samuel R.. Affidavit of Samuel R. Corbet. **March ?, 1879.** Indiana Historical Society, Lew Wallace Collection. M0292. Box 4, Folder 7.

DEDRICK BROTHERS

BIOGRAPHICAL SOURCES

Upham, Elizabeth. (Related by marriage to Daniel Dedrick). Personal interviews. 1998.
Upham, Marquita. (Relative by marriage to Daniel Dedrick). Personal interview. 1998.

CONTEMPORARY SOURCES (CHRONOLOGICAL)

Dedrick, Dan. "I have been under an arrest for six days ..." **April 5, 1879.** Letter to Lew Wallace. Indiana Historical Society. Lew Wallace Collection. M0292. Box 4. Folder 8. **(Says he was not told his arrest charges)**

No Author. "Arrests of Dedricks. Legal Documents." Herman B. Weisner Papers, ca. 1957-1992. New Mexico State University Library at Las Cruces. Rio Grande Historical Collections. Accession No. Ms 0249. Box 1. Folder B-8. Folder Name: "Lincoln County Bonds."

DOLAN, JAMES J.

CONTEMPORARY SOURCES (CHRONOLOGICAL)

Tunstall, John Henry. "A Tax-Payer's Complaint ... January 18, 1878." Mesilla *Independent.* **January 26, 1878. (Exposé of William Brady, James Dolan, and John Riley for tax fraud and use of public money to purchase cattle; and T.B. Catron then paid that bill)**

Dolan, James J. "Answer to A Tax-Payer's Complaint." Mesilla *Independent.* **January 29, 1878. (Response to J.H. Tunstall's exposé of him, William Brady, and John Riley for tax fraud and use of public money to purchase cattle; and T.B. Catron then paid that bill)**

McSween, Alexander. "It looks as though the agent were the property of J.J. Dolan & J.H. Riley, known here as Dolan & Co." Letter to Secretary of Interior Carl Schurz. **February 11, 1878.** From Frederick Nolan. *The Life and Death of John Henry Tunstall.* Albuquerque, New Mexico: The University of New Mexico Press. 1965. Page 266.

Rynerson, William. "Friends Riley & Dolan, Lincoln N.M. I have just received letters from you mailed 10th inst." **February 14, 1878.** Letter to James Dolan and John

Riley. Copy as Exhibit B in June 6, 1878 deposition of Alexander McSween. Frank Warner Angel report. *In the Matter of the Examination of the Causes and Circumstances of the Death of John H. Tunstall a British Subject.* Report filed October 4, 1878. Frank Warner Angel report. Interior Department Papers 1850-1907; Appointments Division and Subsequent Actions. Microfilm File Case Number 44-4-8-3. Record Group 48. Microfilm No. M750. Roll 1. National Archives and Records Administration. U.S. Department of Justice. Washington, D.C. (James J. Dolan Deposition. June 20, 1878. Pages 235-247.) **(Implying planned killing of J.H. Tunstall)**

Wilson, John, George B. Barker, Robert M. Gilbert, John Newcomb, Samuel Smith, Benjamin Ellis. "We the undersigned Justice of the Peace and Coroners Jury who sat upon the inquest held this 19th day of February 1878 on the body of John H. Tunstall ..." Coroner's Jury Report for John Tunstall. **February 19, 1878. (Naming as murderers, among others, James Dolan, Frank Baker, Jessie Evans, William Morton, and George Hindman)**

Dolan, James J. Deposition to Frank Warner Angel. **June 20, 1878.** Frank Warner Angel Report. *In the Matter of the Examination of the Causes and Circumstances of the Death of John H. Tunstall a British Subject.* Pages 235-247. Report filed October 4, 1878. Angel Report. Microfilm File Case Number 44-4-8-3. Record Group 48. Microfilm No. M750. Roll 1. National Archives and Records Administration. U. S. Department of Justice. Washington, D.C.

Dolan, James. "On my arrival at Fort Stanton, I repeated Your Explanation &c to the Comd'g Officer (Gen'l Dudley) ..." Letter to Lew Wallace. **December 31, 1878.** Indiana Historical Society. Lew Wallace Collection. M0292. Box 3. Folder 19.

_____. "Attorney Wilson told me yesterday that 'your life was threatened' ..." Letter to Lew Wallace. **December 31, 1878.** Indiana Historical Society. Lew Wallace Collection. M0292. Box 4. Folder 7.

Wallace, Lew. "J.J. Dolan was down here tonight. Arrest him upon his return ..." Letter to Henry Carroll. **March 10, 1879.** Indiana Historical Society. Lew Wallace Collection. M0292. Box 4. Folder 4.

_____. "I beg to submit to you a list of persons whom it is necessary, in my judgment, to arrest speedily ..." Letter to Henry Carroll. **March 11, 1879.** Indiana Historical Society. Lew Wallace Collection. M0292 Box 4. Folder 5. **(Lists James Dolan, "The Kid" - William Bonney, Jessie Evans, Yginio Salazar)**

_____. "Upon reflection, I am of opinion that if Col. Dudley is really going to Fort Union ..." Letter to Henry Carroll. **March 11, 1879.** Indiana Historical Society. Lew Wallace Collection. M0292. Box 4. Folder 5. **(Advises not to send prisoners Evans, Campbell, Matthews, and Dolan to Fort Union because of N.A.M. Dudley being there)**

Dolan, James. "I hear from reliable authority that it has been reported to you that I was one of a party ..." Letter to Lew Wallace. **March 14, 1879.** Indiana Historical Society. Lew Wallace Collection. M0292. Box 4. Folder 5.

Rynerson, William. "The Grand Jurors for the Territory of New Mexico taken from the body of the good and lawful men of the County of Lincoln ..." Indictments of the April, Lincoln County Grand Jury. **April 28, 1879.** Herman B. Weisner Papers, ca. 1957-1992. New Mexico State University Library at Las Cruces. Rio Grande Historical Collection. Accession No. Weisner MS 249. Box 4/39. Folder E-Z. Folder Name: "Jessie Evans Accessory to Murder." **(Billy Bonney's testimony indicts J.J. Dolan, Billy Campbell, and Jessie Evans for pardon bargain)**

Purington, George. "The District Court adjourned on Thursday ..." **May 3, 1879.** Indiana Historical Society. Lew Wallace Collection. M0292. Box 4. Folder 10. **(Letter to Adjutant General on indictments of the Murphy-Dolans - including Dolan for the H.I. Chapman murder - and N.A.M. Dudley; copy sent to Lew Wallace)**

Dolan, James. Testimony in Court of Inquiry for Lieutenant Colonel N.A.M. Dudley. **June 5, 1879.** in Court of Inquiry for N.A.M. Dudley. *Proceedings of a Court of*

Inquiry in the Case of Col. N.A.M. Dudley (May 2, 1879-July 5, 1879). File Number QQ1284. (Boxes 3304, 3305, 3305A). Court Martial Case Files 1809-1894. Records of the Office of the Judge Advocate General – Army. Record Group 153. National Archives and Records Administration. Old Military and Civil Branch. Washington, D.C.

Wild, Azariah F. "Daily Reports of U. S. Secret Service Agents, Azariah F. Wild." Microfilm T-915. Record Group 87. Rolls 307 (January 1,1878 - June 30, 1879) and 308 **(July 1, 1879 - June 30, 1881)**. National Archives and Records Department. Department of the Treasury. United States Secret Service. Washington, D. C. **(Dolan as an informer against "the Kid gang")**

DUDLEY, NATHAN AUGUSTUS MONROE

BIOGRAPHICAL SOURCES

Heitman, Francis B. *Historical Register and Dictionary of the United States Army, From Its Organization, September 29, 1789, to March 2, 1903.* (Entry for Galusha Pennypacker, Pages 782-7830.) Washington, D.C.: Government Printing Office. 1903.

Kaye, E. Donald. *Nathan Augustus Monroe Dudley: Rogue, Hero, or Both?* Parker, Colorado: Outskirts Press, Inc. 2007.

Oliva, Leo E., *Fort Union and the Frontier Army in the Southwest.* Southwest Cultural Resource Center, Professional Papers No. 41, National Park Service, 1993, Pages 488-489, 550, 574, 624-626, 656-659 are on Dudley. **(Quoted to E. Donald Kaye from the now-lost letter of Amos Kimball: "I guess you heard that Dudley made Colonel. The army bureaucracy is like a giant cesspool, where the biggest chunks rise to the top.")**

MILITARY COURT OF INQUIRY FOR

Leonard, Ira E. *"Charges and specifications against Lieutenant Colonel N.A.M. Dudley, Commander at Fort Stanton, New Mexico."* **March 4, 1879**. *Proceedings of a Court of Inquiry in the Case of Lt. Col. N.A.M. Dudley (May 2,1879 - July 5, 1879).* File No. QQ1284. (Boxes 3304, 3305, 3305A); Court Martial Files 1809-1894. Records of the Office of the Judge Advocate General - Army. Record Group 153. Old Military and Civil Branch. National Archives and Records Administration. Washington, D. C.

Dudley, Nathan Augustus Monroe. Testimony in Court of Inquiry. **June 28 and 30, 1879**. *Proceedings of a Court of Inquiry in the Case of Lt. Col. N.A.M. Dudley (May 2,1879 - July 5, 1879).* File No. QQ1284. (Boxes 3304, 3305, 3305A); Court Martial Files 1809-1894. Records of the Office of the Judge Advocate General – Army. Record Group 153. Old Military and Civil Branch. National Archives and Records Administration. Washington, D. C.

No Author. *Proceedings of a Court of Inquiry in the Case of Lt. Col. N.A.M. Dudley* **(May 2,1879 – July 5, 1879)**. File No. QQ1284. (Boxes 3304, 3305, 3305A); Court Martial Files 1809-1894. Records of the Office of the Judge Advocate General - Army. Record Group 153. Old Military and Civil Branch. National Archives and Records Administration. Washington, D. C.

OTHER CONTEMPORARY SOURCES (CHRONOLOGICAL)

Dudley, Nathan Augustus Monroe. "I avail myself of the opportunity to send this in advance of the next mail by Mr. Dolan ..." Letter to Assistant Adjutant General of New Mexico. **September 29, 1878**. Indiana Historical Society. Lew Wallace Collection. M0292. Box 3. Folder 14. **(Outlaw propaganda to distract from Ring activity in Lincoln County)**

Loud, John S. "In compliance with instructions of the General Commanding ..." **October 27, 1878.** Letter to N.A.M. Dudley. Indiana Historical Society. Lew Wallace Collection. M0292. Box 3. Folder 16. (**Order for troops to arrest outlaws and seize their stolen property as per the request of the Secretary of War**)

Dudley, Nathan Augustus Monroe. "I am in receipt of a copy of letter written by one H.I. Chapman, calling himself the Attorney ..." **November 9, 1878.** Letter to Lew Wallace. From *Proceedings of a Court of Inquiry in the Case of Lt. Col. N.A.M. Dudley (May 2, 1879 – July 5, 1879)*. File No. QQ1284. (Boxes 3304, 3305, 3305A); Court Martial Files 1809-1894. Records of the Office of the Judge Advocate General – Army. Record Group 153. Old Military and Civil Branch. National Archives and Records Administration. Washington, D.C. (**Forwarding the Susan McSween affidavits in answer to the charges made by Chapman**)

Wallace, Lew. "I am in receipt of Col. Dudley's reply to the charges against him ..." Letter to Edward Hatch. **November 14, 1878**. Indiana Historical Society. Lew Wallace Collection. M0292. Box 3. Folder 17. (**Has quote: "the "reply is perfectly satisfactory"**)

_____. "Your favor containing the duplicate accounts of the messenger who posted the President's Proclamation ..." Letter to N.A.M. Dudley. **November 30, 1878**. Indiana Historical Society. Lew Wallace Collection. M0292. Box 3. Folder 18.

_____. "I am constrained to request that Lieut Col. N.A.M. Dudley, Commanding at Fort Stanton, be relieved ..." Letter to Edward Hatch. **December 7, 1878**. Indiana Historical Society. Lew Wallace Collection. M0292. Box 3. Folder 18. (**Removal of Dudley requested**)

Dudley, Nathan Augustus Monroe. "An Open Letter, By Lieut. Col. N.A.M. Dudley, 9th Cavalry, to His Excellency Governor Lew Wallace." Letter to Lew Wallace. Santa Fe *Weekly New Mexican*. **December 14, 1878.** Reprinted in *Mesilla News*. December 21, 1878. As Exhibit 13 from *Proceedings of a Court of Inquiry in the Case of Lt. Col. N.A.M. Dudley (May 2, 1879 – July 5, 1879)*. File No. QQ1284. (Boxes 3304, 3305, 3305A); Court Martial Files 1809-1894. Records of the Office of the Judge Advocate General – Army. Record Group 153. Old Military and Civil Branch. National Archives and Records Administration. Washington, D.C. (**Attacks Wallace's Amnesty Proclamation as applying to the military**)

Wallace, Lew. "The public interests with which I am officially charged make it in my judgment ..." **December 16, 1878**. Letter to N.A.M. Dudley and other Fort Stanton officers. Indiana Historical Society. Lew Wallace Collection. M0292. Box 3. Folder 19.

_____. "I have the honor to report that affairs of the Territory are moving on quietly ..." Letter to Carl Schurz. **December 21, 1878**. Indiana Historical Society. Lew Wallace Collection. M0292. Box 3, Folder 19. (**N.A.M. Dudley's indignation about the Amnesty Proclamation**)

Shield, David. "It is rumored that 'Eight long Affidavits' are in your possession ..." **February 11, 1879**. Letter to Lew Wallace. Indiana Historical Society. Lew Wallace Collection. M0292. Box 4. Folder 2. (**Commander Dudley's defamatory affidavits about Susan McSween**)

Dudley, Nathan Augustus Monroe. "I enclose herewith report of 2nd Lieut. M.F. Goodwin ..." Letter to Acting Assistant Adjutant General at Headquarters. **February 24, 1879** Indiana Historical Society. Lew Wallace Collection. M0292. Box 4, Folder 3. (**Documents military pursuit of William Bonney**)

Leonard, Ira E. "You are perhaps fully aware of the outrages that have been perpetrated in Lincoln County ..." Letter to Secretary of War George McCrary. **March 4, 1879.** From *Proceedings of a Court of Inquiry in the Case of Lt. Col. N.A.M. Dudley (May 2, 1879 – July 5, 1879)*. File No. QQ1284. (Boxes 3304, 3305, 3305A); Court Martial Files 1809-1894. Records of the Office of the Judge Advocate General – Army. Record Group 153. Old Military and Civil Branch.

National Archives and Records Administration. Washington, D.C. (**Accusing N.A.M. Dudley of murders of A.A. McSween and H.I. Chapman and arson of McSween house**)

Wallace, Lew. "I have the honor to repeat the request made on a former occasion that Lt. Col. N.A.M. Dudley be relieved of the command ..." Letter to Edward Hatch. **March 7, 1879**. Indiana Historical Society. Lew Wallace Collection. M0292. Box 4, Folder 4.

Hatch, Edward. "Lieutenant Colonel N.A.M. Dudley is hereby relieved from command and duty ..." Special Field Order 2. **March 8, 1879**. Indiana Historical Society. Lew Wallace Collection. M0292. Box 4, Folder 4. (**Wallace succeeds in removing Dudley**)

_____. "Col. Dudley has received his order and disobeys the order ..." **March 11, 1879**. Indiana Historical Society. Lew Wallace Collection. M0292. Box 4, Folder 5.

Wallace, Lew. "I have official information that a court of inquiry for Col. Dudley has been ordered ..." Letter to Carl Schurz. **April 4, 1879**. Indiana Historical Society. Lew Wallace Collection. M0292. Box 4. Folder 8.

Purington, George. "The District Court adjourned on Thursday ..." **May 3, 1879**. Indiana Historical Society. Lew Wallace Collection. M0292. Box 4. Folder 10. (**Letter to Adjutant General on indictments of the Murphy-Dolans and N.A.M. Dudley; copy sent to Lew Wallace**)

Waldo, Henry. "Nothing has been accomplished in the least that connects Col. Dudley with anything which transpired in the town of Lincoln on the occasion of his presence there on the 19th..." Closing argument for Dudley Court of Inquiry. **July 5, 1879**. *Proceedings of a Court of Inquiry in the Case of Lt. Col. N.A.M. Dudley (May 2,1879 – July 5, 1879)*. File No. QQ1284. (Boxes 3304, 3305, 3305A); Court Martial Files 1809-1894. Records of the Office of the Judge Advocate General – Army. Record Group 153. Old Military and Civil Branch. National Archives and Records Administration. Washington, D. C.

No Author. Verdict on Civil Cause 298 for arson of Susan McSween's house. *Mesilla News*. **December 6, 1879**. Unpublished. personal communication from Frederick Nolan. July 29, 2005. (**Dudley exonerated**)

ELKINS, STEPHEN BENTON

BIOGRAPHICAL SOURCES

Cleaveland, Norman, *A Synopsis of the Great New Mexico Cover-up*. Self-printed. 1989.

_____. *The Great Santa Fe Cover-up. Based on a Talk given Before the Santa Fe Historical Society on November 1, 1978*. Self-printed. 1982.

_____. *The Morleys - Young Upstarts on the Southwest Frontier*. Albuquerque, New Mexico: Calvin Horn Publisher, Inc. 1971.

Lamar, Howard Robert N. *The Far Southwest 1846 – 1912: A Territorial History*. New Haven and London: Yale University Press. 1966. (**Chapter 6 on Santa Fe Ring**))

Lambert, Oscar Doane. *Stephen Benton Elkins. American Foursquare*. Pittsburgh, Pennsylvania: University of Pittsburg Press. 1955.

Montoya, María E. *Translating Property. The Maxwell Land Grant and the Conflict Over Land in the American West, 1840-1900*. Berkeley and Los Angeles: University of California Press. 2002.

Taylor, Morris F. *O.P. McMains and the Maxwell Land Grant Conflict*. Tucson, Arizona: The University of Arizona Press. 1979. (**Traces origins of the Santa Fe Ring with T.B. Catron and S.B. Elkins**)

Westphall, Victor. *Thomas Benton Catron and His Era*. Tucson, Arizona: University of Arizona Press. 1973.

LETTERS FROM, TO, ABOUT (CHRONOLOGICAL)

Morley William Raymond. "I was astonished beyond measure at your proceedings, and have fears as to the result ..." Letter to Mary McPherson. **March 6, 1877.**
McPherson, Mary E. Letters and Petitions to President Rutherford B. Hayes re: Removal Governor Axtell and the Santa Fe Ring. Interior Department Papers 1850-1907; Appointments Division and Subsequent Actions. Microfilm File Case Number 44-4-8-3. Record Group 48. Microfilm Roll M750. National Archives and Records Administration. U.S. Department of Justice. Washington, D. C. (**Hopes she can help fight against Santa Fe Ring; enclosed in Mary McPherson's "Charges Against U.S. Officials in the Territory of New Mexico."**)
Elkins, Stephen B. "I trouble you to say a word in behalf of Gov. Axtell ..." Letter to President Rutherford B. Hayes. **June 11, 1877.** (Referred by direction of President to the Secretary of the Interior June 13, 1877.) Interior Department Papers 1850-1907; Appointments Division and Subsequent Actions. Microfilm File Case No. 44-4-8-3. Record Group 48. National Records and Archives Administration. Microfilm No. M750. Roll 1. U.S. Department of Justice. Washington, D. C.
McPherson, Mary. "Please place before the Attorney General ..." Letter to President Rutherford B. Hayes. **August 23, 1877.** Interior Department Papers 1850-1907; Appointments Division and Subsequent Actions. Microfilm File Case Number 44-4-8-3. Record Group 48. Microfilm No. M750. Roll 1. National Archives and Records Administration. U.S. Department of Justice. Washington, D.C. (**Requesting that her "Charges vs. New Mexico Officials" go to the Attorney General.**)
Morley, William Raymond. "Your letter of the 7th came last night and it was a good long newsy letter ..." Letter to wife, Ada McPherson Morley. **August 15, 1878.** Collection of Norman Cleaveland. Quoted in Norman Cleaveland, *The Morleys: Young Upstarts in the Southwest.* Albuquerque, New Mexico: Calvin Horn Publisher, Inc. 1971. Pages 152-155. (**About possible betrayal by Angel's reports; about the Santa Fe Ring, T.B. Catron, S.B. Elkins, S.B. Axtell, and Henry Waldo; and the Lincoln County War**)
Elkins, Stephen B. "Asking delay of action upon charges against U.S. Atty. Catron ..." **September 24, 1878.** Angel Report. Microfilm File Case No. 44-4-8-3. Record Group 48. National Records and Archives Administration. Microfilm No. M750. Roll 1. U.S. Department of Justice. Washington, D. C.
_____. "Regarding Attorney General's decision on T.B. Catron." Letter. **September___, 1878.** Angel Report. Microfilm File Case No. 44-4-8-3. Record Group 48. National Records and Archives Administration. Microfilm No. M750. Roll 1. U.S. Department of Justice. Washington, D.C.
_____. "Relative to resignation of T. B. Catron U. S. Attorney." Letter. **November 10, 1878.** Angel Report. Microfilm File Case No. 44-4-8-3. Record Group 48. National Records and Archives Administration. Microfilm No. M750. Roll 1. U.S. Department of Justice. Washington, D. C.
Devens, Charles. "To honorable S. B. Elkins re. T. B. Catron continuing to act as U.S. Attorney." Letter to Stephen B. Elkins. **November 12, 1878.** Angel Report. Microfilm File Case No. 44-4-8-3. Record Group 48. National Records and Archives Administration. Microfilm No. M750. Roll 1. U.S. Department of Justice. Washington, D. C.
Elkins, Stephen Benton. "I have waited some time to reply to your lengthy letter ..." Letter to T.B. Catron. **August 15, 1879.** West Virginia & Regional History Center. West Virginia University Libraries, Morgantown, W. Va. Stephen B. Elkins Papers (A&M 53). Box 1. Folder 1. (**Reveals he prevented Catron's dismissal and indictment from Angel's report**)

_____. "To the President. Referring to a conversation had with you last week ... Hon S. Elkins favors appointment Axtell, Ex Gov. as Gov'r of New Mexico". Letter to President James Abram Garfield. **March 17, 1881**. (Received Executive Mansion April 6, 1881). Interior Department Papers 1850-1907; Appointments Division and Subsequent Actions. Microfilm Roll M750. National Archives and Records Administration Record Group 48. Microfilm Case Number 44-4-8-3. U.S. Department of Interior. Washington D. C. **(Requesting S.B. Axtell reappointment as Territorial New Mexico Governor)**

Elkins, Stephen Benton. "Mr. Catron's prominence in the capital territory and his leadership ..." Letter to Gideon B. Bantz. **September 9, 1897. (Improper influence of Catron's disbarment judge)** Quoted in John Paul Wooden's unpublished masters thesis, Page 32.

EXPOSÉS (CONTEMPORARY)

COMPLAINT ABOUT TO PRESIDENT RUTHERFORD B. HAYES

Matchett, W.B. and Mary E. McPherson. " W.B. Matchett and Mary E. McPherson 'Make certain charges against the U.S. Officials in the Territory of New Mexico.' " Letter to President Rutherford B. Hayes. Received and filed **May 1, 1877**. Interior Department Papers 1850-1907; Appointments Division and Subsequent Actions. Microfilm File Case Number 44-4-8-3. Record Group 48. Microfilm No. M750. Roll 1. National Archives and Records Administration. U. S. Department of Justice. Washington, D.C. **(Sent to President Rutherford B. Hayes and Secretary of the Interior Carl Schurz 141 pages of letters, affidavits, petitions, newspaper articles, itemized requests for removal of Governor Samuel Beach Axtell and District Judge Warren Bristol, documentation of use of the military against civilians, documentation of the Ring murder of Ring opponent Reverend F.J. Tolby, and identification of the Santa Fe Ring and Elkins and Carton as its leaders.)**

McPherson, Mary and W.B. Matchett. "To the President. Please make the enclosed a part of the evidence in the case of "Charges Against New Mexican Officials" Letter to President Rutherford B. Hayes. **May 3, 1877**. McPherson, Mary E. Letters and Petitions to President Rutherford B. Hayes re: Removal Governor Axtell and the Santa Fe Ring. Interior Department Papers 1850-1907; Appointments Division and Subsequent Actions. Microfilm File Case Number 44-4-8-3. Record Group 48. Microfilm Roll M750. National Archives and Records Administration. U.S. Department of Justice. Washington, D.C. **(Addendum to their May, 1877 "Certain Charges Against U.S. Officials in New Mexico Territory.")**

McPherson, Mary and W.B. Matchett. "The Secretary of the Interior, Sir – Accompanying please find copy of charges, &c., against S.B. Axtell, Governor, and Other New Mexican Officials ..." "Charges Against New Mexican Officials." Letter to Secretary of the Interior Carl Schurz. **May 5, 1877**. McPherson, Mary E. Letters and Petitions to President Rutherford B. Hayes re: Removal Governor Axtell and the Santa Fe Ring. Interior Department Papers 1850-1907; Appointments Division and Subsequent Actions. Microfilm File Case Number 44-4-8-3. Record Group 48. Microfilm Roll M750. National Archives and Records Administration. U.S. Department of Justice. Washington, D. C.

McPherson, Mary. "Please place before the Attorney General ..." Letter to President Rutherford B. Hayes. **August 23, 1877**. Interior Department Papers 1850-1907; Appointments Division and Subsequent Actions. Microfilm File Case Number 44-4-8-3. Record Group 48. Microfilm No. M750. Roll 1. National Archives and Records Administration. U. S. Department of Justice. Washington, D.C. **(Requesting that her "Charges vs. New Mexico Officials" go to the Attorney General.)**

COMPLAINT ABOUT TO DEPARTMENTS OF INTERIOR AND JUSTICE

McPherson, Mary and W.B. Matchett. *"In the Matter of Charges vs. Gov. S.B. Axtell and Other New Mexico Officials. Submitted to the Departments of the Interior and Justice.* **August, 1877.** Printed as a 31 page booklet. No publisher listed. Indiana Historical Society. Lew Wallace Collection. M0292 Box 3. Folder 20. (**About the Santa Fe Ring, Catron, and Elkins; in Lew Wallace's personal possession**)

Springer, Frank. Deposition to Investigator Frank Warner Angel for the Departments of Justice and the Interior. **August 9, 1878.** Frank Warner Angel report titled *In the Matter of the Investigation of the Charges Against S.B. Axtell Governor of New Mexico.* October 3, 1878. Interior Department Papers 1850-1907; Appointments Division and Subsequent Actions. Microfilm Case File No. 44-4-8-3. Record Group 48. Microfilm Roll M750. National Archives and Records Administration. U.S. Department of Interior. Washington, D.C. (**Mentions Catron, Elkins, and the Santa Fe Ring, and provided Exhibits of letters exposing Catron's evil.**)

PUBLIC RECORDS REQUEST ABOUT

McPherson, Mary and W.B. Matchett. "We have respectfully to request that the following named records, documents, papers, communications and correspondence be supplied ..." Records Request to Secretary of the Interior Carl Schurz. **July 26, 1877.** Interior Department Papers 1850-1907; Appointments Division and Subsequent Actions. Microfilm File Case Number 44-4-8-3. Record Group 48. Microfilm No. M750. Roll 1. National Archives and Records Administration. U. S. Department of Justice. Washington, D.C. (**Requesting records of the Santa Fe Ring, Carton, Elkins, and Axtell**)

ARTICLES ABOUT (CHRONOLOGICAL)

Morley, William Raymond and Frank Springer. On Oscar McMains's citizen's Meeting. *Cimarron News and Press.* **November 10, 1875.** In Mary McPherson, Letters and Petitions to President Rutherford B. Hayes re Removal Governor Axtell and the Santa Fe Ring. 1977. Interior Department Papers 1850-1907; Appointments Division and Subsequent Actions. Microfilm File Case Number 44-4-8-3. **Record Group 48.** Microfilm Roll M750. National Archives and Records Administration. (**Colfax County citizens meeting on F.J. Tolby murder by Santa Fe Ring.**)

No Author. " 'The Territory of Elkins.' Assassination of Supposed Sun Correspondent. The Murder of the Rev. F.J. Tolby in New Mexico. A Probate Judge Accused of Complicity in the Crime. Indignation Meeting." *New York Weekly Sun.* **December 22, 1875.** Interior Department Papers 1850-1907; Appointments Division and Subsequent Actions. Microfilm Roll M750. National Archives and Records Administration. Record Group 48. Microfilm Case File Number 44-4-8-3. U. S. Department of Interior. Washington, D.C. (**In May 1, 1877 complaint to President Hayes as "Mary E. McPherson and W.B. Matchett 'Make certain charges against the U.S. Officials in the Territory of New Mexico.' "**)

No Author. "Elkins would probably have been Garfield's Secretary of the Interior ..." *New York Sun.* **June 13, 1881.** Quoted by Oscar Doane Lambert. *Stephen Benton Elkins: American Foursquare.* Page 89. (**Political influence of**)

Faulkner, C.J. "I will tell you the secret of Elkins' political as well as business success." Baltimore, Maryland *The Sun.* **December 17, 1891.** Quoted by Oscar Doane Lambert. *Stephen Benton Elkins: American Foursquare.* Page 141. (**Elkins's success from loyalty to friends**)

No Author. "T.B. Catron's reputation now being "smirched" by evidence that he was a briber and too dishonest even to practice law ..." *Las Vegas Independent Democrat.* **1895;** quoting from *Las Vegas Optic.* September 2, 1884. From Victor Westphall. *Thomas Benton Catron and His Era.* Pages 105-106. (**About Catron's and Elkins's dishonesty, the Ring, and disbarring Catron**)

No Author. "It seems that Senator Elkins was one of the five stockholders in the North American Commercial Company that had leased from the United States the sea Islands of Alaska." Cincinnati, Ohio *Commercial Tribune.* **June 8, 1897.** Quoted by Oscar Doane Lambert. *Stephen Benton Elkins: American Foursquare.* Pages 224-225. (**Elkins's tax violation cover-up**)

No Author. "He is the biggest man ... the State of West Virginia has ever had in the Senate of the United States." West Virginia *St. Mary's Journal.* **June 22, 1906.** From Oscar Doane Lambert. *Stephen Benton Elkins.* Page 286.

ELLIS, ISAAC

Ellis, Isaac. "We are two residents of Lincoln County ..." Letter written with George Coe to President Rutherford B. Hayes. **June 22, 1878.** In Angel Report papers. Microfilm File Case Number 44-4-8-3. Record Group 48. Microfilm No. M750. Roll 1. National Archives and Records Administration. U.S. Department of Justice. Washington, D.C.

_____. Affidavit of Isaac Ellis. **March ?, 1879.** Indiana Historical Society. Lew Wallace Collection. M0292. Box 4, Folder 7.

EVANS, JESSIE

BIOGRAPHICAL SOURCES

McCright, Grady E. and James H. Powell. *Jessie Evans: Lincoln County Badman.* College Station, Texas: Creative Publishing Company. 1983.

CONTEMPORARY SOURCES (CHRONOLOGICAL)

Wilson, John, George B. Barker, Robert M. Gilbert, John Newcomb, Samuel Smith, Benjamin Ellis. "We the undersigned Justice of the Peace and Coroners Jury who sat upon the inquest held this 19th day of February 1878 on the body of John H. Tunstall ..." Coroner's Jury Report for John Tunstall. **February 19, 1878.** (**Naming as murderers, among others, James Dolan, Frank Baker, Jessie Evans, William Morton, and George Hindman**)

Wallace, Lew. "I have information that William Campbell, J.B. Matthews, and Jesse Evans were of the party engaged in the killing ..." Letter to Edward Hatch. **March 5, 1879.** Indiana Historical Society. Lew Wallace Collection. M0292. Box 4, Folder 4. (**Murder of Huston Chapman**)

_____. "Under the circumstances, particularly in the absence here of suitable cells for safekeeping of Jesse Evans, Jacob B. Matthews and William Campbell ..." Letter to Henry Carroll. **March 10, 1879.** Indiana Historical Society. Lew Wallace Collection. M0292. Box 4. Folder 4.

_____. "Upon reflection, I am of opinion that if Col. Dudley is really going to Fort Union ..." Letter to Henry Carroll. **March 11, 1879.** Indiana Historical Society. Lew Wallace Collection. M0292. Box 4. Folder 5. (**Advises not to send Evans, Campbell, Matthews, and Dolan to Fort Union because of N.A.M. Dudley being there**)

_____. "I beg to submit to you a list of persons whom it is necessary, in my judgment, to arrest ..." Letter to Henry Carroll. **March 11, 1879.** Indiana Historical Society. Lew Wallace Collection. M0292. Box 4. Folder 5. (**Lists Jessie Evans, "The Kid" – William Bonney, Yginio Salazar**)

_____. "Be good enough to send word to all your men to turn out soon as possible ..." Letter to Juan Patrón. **March 19, 1879.** Indiana Historical Society. Lew Wallace Collection. M0292. Box 4. Folder 6. (**Reports escape of Jessie Evans and Billy Campbell from Fort Stanton; $1000 reward**)

_____. "With Evans and Campbell at large ..." Letter to Henry Carroll. **March 19, 1879.** Indiana Historical Society. Lew Wallace Collection. M0292. Box 4. Folder 6.

Rynerson, William. "Indictments of the April, Lincoln County Grand Jury." **April 28, 1879**. Herman B. Weisner Papers, ca. 1957-1992. New Mexico State University Library at Las Cruces. Rio Grande Historical Society Collection. Accession No. Ms 0249. Box 4/39. Folder E-Z. Folder Name: "Jessie Evans Accessory to Murder." **(Billy's testimony indicts J.J. Dolan, Billy Campbell, and Jessie Evans fulfilling his pardon bargain)**

Purington, George. "The District Court adjourned on Thursday ..." **May 3, 1879**. Indiana Historical Society. Lew Wallace Collection. M0292. Box 4. Folder 10. **(Letter to Adjutant General on indictments of the Murphy-Dolans - including Evans for the H.I. Chapman murder - and N.A.M. Dudley; copy sent to Lew Wallace)**

No Author. "Charges against Jessie Evans and John Kinney." Doña Ana County Criminal Docket Book. **August 18, 1875 to November 7, 1878**. Herman B. Weisner Papers, ca. 1957-1992. New Mexico State University Library at Las Cruces. Rio Grande Historical Collections. Accession No. Ms 0249. Box No. 13. Folder V3. Folder Name: "Venue, Change of."

FOUNTAIN, ALBERT JENNINGS

Fountain, Albert Jennings, Attorney and J.D. Bail. "Instructions Asked for by Defendants Counsel. April 9, 1881. Herman B. Weisner Papers, ca. 1957-1992. New Mexico State University Library at Las Cruces. Rio Grande Historical Society Collection. Accession No. Ms 0249. Box 1. Folder 14-D. Folder Name: "Billy the Kid Legal Documents."

Gibson, A. M. *The Life and Death of Colonel Albert Jennings Fountain*. Norman: University of Oklahoma Press. 1965.

FRITZ FAMILY (EMIL AND CHARLES FRITZ AND EMILIE FRITZ SCHOLAND)

Fritz, Charles. Affidavit of **September 18, 1876** claiming that Emil Fritz had a will. Probate Court Record. (private collection)

_____. Affidavit of **September 26, 1876** Authorizing Alexander McSween to Receive Payments for the Emil Fritz Estate. Probate Court Record. (private collection)

Scholand, Emilie and Charles Fritz. Affidavit of **September 26, 1876** appointing McSween to collect debts for the Emil Fritz Estate. Copied from the original District Court Record. (private collection)

Fritz, Charles. Affidavit of **December 7, 1877** to order Alexander McSween to pay the Emil Fritz insurance policy money. Probate Court Record. (private collection)

Scholand, Emilie. Affidavit of **December 21, 1877** Accusing Alexander McSween of Embezzlement. Copied from the original District Court Record. (private collection)

Bristol Warren. "Writ of Embezzlement." **December 21, 1877**. Herman B. Weisner Papers, ca. 1957-1992. New Mexico State University Library at Las Cruces. Rio Grande Historical Collections. Accession No. Ms 0249. Box 10. Folder M-13. Folder Name. "Will and Testament A. McSween." **(Emilie Fritz Scholand's sworn complaint against Alexander McSween)**

Fritz, Charles. Affidavit sworn before John Crouch, Clerk of Doña Ana District Court, for Writ of Attachment issued against property of Alexander A. McSween. Probate Court Record. **February 6, 1878**. (private collection)

_____ and Emilie Scholand. Attachment Bond sworn before John Crouch, Clerk of Doña Ana District Court, against Alexander A. McSween for indebtedness to them. **February 6, 1878**. (private collection).

No Author. Diagram showing parcels of land to each of the heirs of Emil Fritz. Herman B. Weisner Papers, ca. 1957-1992. New Mexico State University Library at Las Cruces. Rio Grande Historical Collections. Accession No. Ms 0249. Box P1. Folder 11. Folder Name. "Charles Fritz Estate."

GARRETT, PATRICK FLOYD

BIBLIOGRAPHICAL SOURCES

Garrett, Pat F. *The Authentic Life of Billy the Kid The Noted Desperado of the Southwest, Whose Deeds of Daring and Blood Made His Name a Terror in New Mexico, Arizona, and Northern Mexico.* Santa Fe, New Mexico: New Mexico Printing and Publishing Co. 1882.
Metz, Leon C. *Pat Garrett. The Story of a Western Lawman.* Norman: University of Oklahoma Press. 1974.
Mullin, Robert N. "Killing of Joe Briscoe." Letter to Eve Ball. January 31, 1964. (Unpublished). Binder RNM, VI, H. Nita Stewart Haley Memorial Museum. Haley Library. Midland, Texas.
_____. "Pat Garrett. Two Forgotten Killings." *Password.* X(2) (Summer 1965). pp. 57 - 65.
_____. "Skelton Glen's Manuscript Entitled 'Pat Garrett As I Knew Him on the Buffalo Ranges.'" (Unpublished). Binder RNM, III B, 20. Nita Stewart Haley Memorial Museum. Haley Library. Midland, Texas.

CONTEMPORARY SOURCES (CHRONOLOGICAL)

Upson, Ash. Letter from Garrett's Ranch to Upson's Nephew, Frank S. Downs, Esq. re. "His Drawers and pigeon holes of his desk were full of letters, deeds, bills, notes, agreements, & C. I have burned bushels of them and am not through yet." **October 20, 1888**. (Unpublished). Binder RNM, V1-MM. Nita Stewart Haley Memorial Museum. Haley Library. Midland, Texas.
Wild, Azariah F. "Daily Reports of U. S. Secret Service Agents, Azariah F. Wild." Microfilm T-915. Record Group 87. Rolls 306 (June 15, 1877 - December 31, 1877), 307 (January 1,1878 - June 30, 1879), 308 (**July 1, 1879 - June 30, 1881**), 309 (July 1, 1881 - September 30, 1883), 310 (October 1, 1883 - July 31, 1886). National Archives and Records Department. Department of the Treasury. United States Secret Service. Washington, D. C. (**Aiding Garrett's capture of William Bonney**)

ARTICLE ABOUT

No Author. Lew Wallace Collection. Indiana Historical Society) "[Pat F. Garrett] Recommended by Gen. Wallace," *The* (Crawfordsville) *Weekly News-Review*, **December 20, 1901**. Indiana Historical Society. The Papers of Lew and Susan Wallace. Microfilm Edition. Indianapolis, Indiana: Indiana Historical Society Press. 2008.

GIDDINGS, MARSH

CONTEMPORARY SOURCES (CHRONOLOGICAL)

No Author. *Diario del Consejo der Territorio de Neuvo Mejico, Session de 1871-1872.* Santa Fe *New Mexican*. **January 8, 1872**. Santa Fe: A.P. Sullivan. 1872. Pages 144-154. New Mexico Supreme Court Library. Santa Fe, New Mexico. (**Confirms Giddings's use of troops for Ring suppression in 1872 Legislature Revolt**)
No Author. *Diario del Consejo der Territorio de Neuvo Mejico, Session de 1871-1872.* Las Cruces *Borderer*. **January 24, 1872**. Pages 110-113. (**President of the Council Don Diego Archuleta gives speech objecting to Giddings's bringing troops into legislature**)
No Author. *Journal of the House of Representatives of the Territory of New Mexico, Session of 1871-1872.* Santa Fe: A.P. Sullivan. **1872**. (**Cover 1872 Legislature Revolt: Pages 86-91 on Giddings's veto of House acts; Pages 144-154 on Giddings's use of troops for suppression**)

Giddings, Marsh. "To defeat Catron's confirmation [as U.S. Attorney] a grossly false affidavit [by August Kirchner] has been sent to Senator [Lyman Trumbull]." **Month (?) 1872**. Telegram from Governor Marsh Giddings to Washington, D.C. Attorney General George H. Williams. From Victor Westphall. *Thomas Benton Catron and His Era*. Page 107. (**About the 1872 Legislature Revolt**)

Bristol Warren. "From sources of information that I deem perfectly reliable I am satisfied that there are public disorders in Lincoln County ..." Letter to Governor Marsh Giddings. **January 10, 1874**. Herman B. Weisner Papers, ca. 1957-1992. New Mexico State University Library at Las Cruces. Rio Grande Historical Collections. Accession No. Ms 0249. Box 4/39. Folder D-4. Name. "Judge Bristol's letter." (**Santa Fe Ring's outlaw myth and use of military intervention**)

Giddings, Marsh. "I have the honor to inform you that . . there have been disturbances between the Mexicans and Texans ..." Letter to Secretary of Interior C. Delano. **January 12, 1874**. Interior Department Papers 1850-1907; Appointments Division and Subsequent Actions. Microfilm File Case Number 44-4-8-3. Record Group 48. Microfilm No. M750. Roll 1. National Archives and Records Administration. U.S. Department of Justice. Washington, D.C. (**Creating outlaw myth to justify military intervention against Ring opponents**)

Catron, Thomas B., M.A. Breeden, William Breeden, José D. Sena, J.G. Palen, T.F. Conway. "We have just learned that the character of the Adjutant General of New Mexico has been attacked at Washington ..." Letter to Senator Thomas W. Ferry. **March 26, 1873**. Interior Department Papers 1850-1907; Appointments Division and Subsequent Actions. Microfilm File Case Number 44-4-8-3. Record Group 48. Microfilm No. M750. Roll 1. National Archives and Records Administration. U.S. Department of Justice. Washington, D.C. (**Ringmen supporting Marsh Giddings's appointing his son as Adjutant General**)

Gallegos, Jose M. "My people are extremely anxious to have Governor Giddings removed as Governor ..." Letter to President Ulysses S. Grant. **March 13, 1873**. Interior Department Papers 1850-1907; Appointments Division and Subsequent Actions. Microfilm File Case Number 44-4-8-3. Record Group 48. Microfilm No. M750. Roll 1. National Archives and Records Administration. U.S. Department of Justice. Washington, D.C. (**Movement to remove Governor Marsh Giddings**)

Giddings, Marsh. "A transfer of Territorial officers from the State Dept. to the Dept of the interior ..." Letter to Secretary of the Interior. **April 3, 1873**. Interior Department Papers 1850-1907; Appointments Division and Subsequent Actions. Microfilm File Case Number 44-4-8-3. Record Group 48. Microfilm No. M750. Roll 1. National Archives and Records Administration. U.S. Department of Justice. Washington, D.C. (**Responses to charges against him**)

_____. "By the enactment of these laws in the last two days of the session our securities doubled in value within six months ..." Letter to Secretary of the Interior. **April 20, 1873**. Interior Department Papers 1850-1907; Appointments Division and Subsequent Actions. Microfilm File Case Number 44-4-8-3. Record Group 48. Microfilm No. M750. Roll 1. National Archives and Records Administration. U.S. Department of Justice. Washington, D.C. (**More responses to charges against him**)

Bristol Warren. "From sources of information that I deem perfectly reliable I am satisfied that there are public disorders in Lincoln County ..." Letter to Governor Marsh Giddings. **January 10, 1874**. Herman B. Weisner Papers, ca. 1957-1992. New Mexico State University Library at Las Cruces. Rio Grande Historical Collections. Accession No. Ms 0249. Box 4/39. Folder D-4. Folder Name. "Judge Bristol's letter." (**Santa Fe Ring's outlaw myth and use of military**)

GILBERT, ROBERT M.

Gilbert, Robert M. Letter to Lew Wallace. **June 1, 1879**. Collection Indiana Historical Society. Lew Wallace Collection. M0292. Box 4, Folder 11.

GONZALES, FLORENCIO

Gonzales, Florencio. Letter to Governor Lew Wallace. **October 8, 1878.** Collection Indiana Historical Society. Lew Wallace Collection. M0292. Box 3, Folder 15.

GOODWIN, MILLARD FILMORE

Goodwin, Millard Filmore. "I have the honor to submit the following report regarding my duties ..." Letter to Fort Stanton Post Adjutant. **February 23, 1879.** Indiana Historical Society. Lew Wallace Collection. M0292. Box 4, Folder 3.

GRANT, ULYSSES S.

AUTOBIOGRAPHICAL AND BIOGRAPHICAL SOURCES

Grant, Ulysses. Presentation of the Grimsby Saddle to Colonel Absalom Markland. **May 19, 1865.** *The Papers of Ulysses S. Grant: May 1-December 31, 1865.* Carbondale, Illinois: Southern Illinois University Press. 1967 – 2009.
_____. "General Lew Wallace and General McCook at Shiloh: Memoranda on the Civil War." *Battles and Leaders of the Civil War. Century* magazine. 30 [n.s. 8], 776. August, 1885. Vol. I, Page 468. **(Quote damning Wallace for Shiloh)**
_____. *Personal Memoirs.* New York: Charles L. Webster. 1885. **(Same quote from *Century* magazine damning Lew Wallace for Shiloh)**
Perret, Geoffrey. *Ulysses S. Grant: Soldier and President.* New York: Random House. 1997.

CONTEMPORARY SOURCES (CHRONOLOGICAL)

Wallace, Lew. "About a year after the battle of Pittsburgh Landing ..." **February 28, 1868.** Letter to Ulysses S. Grant. Indiana Historical Society. Lew Wallace Collection. M0292. Box 3. Folder 4. **(Wallace trying to justify himself for the Battle of Shiloh)**
No Author. "Gen. Lew Wallace. Visit to His Pleasant Home in the Athens of Indiana. Crawfordsville *Saturday Evening Journal.* **January 16, 1886.** Indiana Historical Society. The Papers of Lew and Susan Wallace. Microfilm Edition. Indianapolis, Indiana: Indiana Historical Society Press. 2008. **(Reworking Shiloh to blame Grant)**
No Author. "Lew Wallace at Shiloh. What the General Has to Say Further on This Question – Buell's Army." *Indianapolis News.* **September 13, 1893.** Indiana Historical Society. The Papers of Lew and Susan Wallace. Microfilm Edition. Indianapolis, Indiana: Indiana Historical Society Press. 2008. **(Wallace still blaming Grant for Shiloh in attempt to vindicate himself)**
No Author. "Lew Wallace at Shiloh. Through an Orderly's Error He Took the Wrong Road." Spokane *Weekly Spokesman-Review.* **October 11, 1894.** Indiana Historical Society. The Papers of Lew and Susan Wallace. Microfilm Edition. Indianapolis, Indiana: Indiana Historical Society Press. 2008. **(New excuse of blaming the orderly for Shiloh as well as Grant)**

HAYES, RUTHERFORD BIRCHARD

BIOGRAPHICAL SOURCES

Davison, Kenneth E. *The Presidency of Rutherford B. Hayes.* Westport, Connecticut: Greenwood Press, Inc. 1972.
Hoogenboom, Ari. *Rutherford B. Hayes. Warrior and President.* Lawrence, Kansas: University Press of Kansas. 1995.
Mullin, Robert N. Re: Frank Warner Angel Meeting With President Hayes August, 1878. Binder RNM, VI, M. (Unpublished). Midland, Texas: Nita Stewart Haley Memorial Library and J. Evert Haley History Center. (Undated).

Williams, Charles Richard. *The Life of Rutherford Birchard Hayes. Nineteenth President of the United States. Vol. I.* Boston and New York: Houghton Mifflin Co. 1914.

_____. *The Life of Rutherford Birchard Hayes. Nineteenth President of the United States. Vol. II.* Boston and New York: Houghton Mifflin Co. 1914.

CONTEMPORARY SOURCES (CHRONOLOGICAL)

PROCLAMATION

Hayes, Rutherford B. "By the President of the United States of America: A Proclamation." **October 7, 1878.** Indiana Historical Society. Lew Wallace Collection. OMB 0023. Box 1. Folder 1; and Senate Documents. 67th Congress. 2nd Session. December 5, 1921 - September 22, 1922. Washington: Government Printing Office. 1922.

LETTERS TO

Leverson, Montague R. "His Excellency Rutherford B. Hayes. President of the United States. Excellency! Since my last letter to your Excellency on the state of affairs in this Territory ..." Letter to Rutherford B. Hayes. **March 16, 1878.** Microfilm Roll M750. National Archives and Records Administration. Record Group 60. Microfilm Case No. 44-4-8-3. U.S. Department of Interior. Washington, D.C

Isaacs, J. and J. N. Coe. "We are two residents of Lincoln Co. who after incurring the greatest peril at the hands of thieves and murderers when the Governor and the U.S. troops aided ..." Letter to Rutherford B. Hayes. **June 22, 1878.** Frank Warner Angel File. Microfilm Roll M750. National Archives and Records Administration. Record Group 60. Microfilm Case Number 44-4-8-3. U.S. Department of Interior. Washington, D.C.

McSween, A. A. "The undersigned have the Honor of transmitting you as requested a copy of the proceeds of a meeting held by the Citizens of Lincoln County, N. Mex. relative to the late troubles ..." Letter to Rutherford B. Hayes. **April 26,1878.** Frank Warner Angel File. Microfilm Roll M750. National Archives and Records Administration. Record Group 060. Microfilm Case Number 44-4-8-3. U.S. Department of Interior. Washington, D.C.

Elkins, Stephen B. "To the President referring to a conversation had with you ..." Letter titled "Hon. S. R. Elkins favors appointment Axtell, ExGov. as Gov'r of New Mexico. **March 23, 1881.** (Received Executive Mansion April 6, 1881) Microfilm Roll M750. National Archives and Records Administration. Record Group 60. Microfilm Case File Number 44-4-8-3. U.S. Department of Interior. Washington, D. C.

LETTERS TO AND FROM LEW WALLACE

Wallace, Lew. "I avail myself of your request this morning. It is hardly necessary to give reasons for a preference of the Italian mission ..." Letter to Rutherford B. Hayes. **March 9, 1877.** Indiana Historical Society. Lew Wallace Collection. M0292. Box 3. Folder 13. (**Desired ambassadorships**)

_____. "The feuds recently in Lincoln county, New Mexico, left a large many thieves and murderers, who, with others of like class since added to their number, are now confederated for plunder." Letter to Rutherford B. Hayes. **March 31, 1879.** Indiana Historical Society. Lew Wallace Collection. M0292. Box 4. Folder 7. (**Wants martial law against confederacy of outlaws**)

Hayes, Rutherford B. "We are greatly obliged by your kindness." Letter to Lew Wallace. **January 9, 1881.** Indiana Historical Society. Lew Wallace Collection. M0292. Box 4. Folder 16. (**Thanking for gift of *Ben- Hur***)

HOYT, HENRY F.

AUTOBIOGRAPHICAL SOURCE

Hoyt, Henry. *A Frontier Doctor*. Boston and New York: Houghton Mifflin Company. 1929. **(Describes Billy's superior abilities, pp. 93-94.)**

CONTEMPORARY SOURCES (CHRONOLOGICAL)

Bonney, William H. Bill of Sale to Henry Hoyt. **October 24, 1878**. Collection of Panhandle-Plains Historical Museum. Canyon, Texas. (Item No. X1974-98/1)

Hoyt, Henry F. "This time it is <u>me</u> who is apologizing for the long delay in answering ..." Letter to Lew Wallace Jr. (Lew Wallace's grandson) **April 27, 1927**. Indiana Historical Society. Lew Wallace Collection. M0292. Box 14, Folder 11.

_____. "Copy of a bill of sale written by Wm H. Bonney ..." Letter to Lew Wallace Jr. **April 27, 1927**. Indiana Historical Society. Lew Wallace Collection. M0292. Box 14, Folder 11. **(Handwritten note on back of Bill of Sale copy calls Billy Bonney a "remarkable character" and "a natural leader of men")**

HUBBARD, JOHN G.

Hubbard, John G. "Herewith I hand you an extract from one of our N.M. papers relative to Gov Axtell of New Mexico to which I would draw your especial attention ..." Letter to President Rutherford B. Hayes. **August 1, 1878**. In Angel Report papers. Microfilm File Case Number 44-4-8-3. Record Group 48. Microfilm No. M750. Roll 1. National Archives and Records Administration. U.S. Department of Justice. Washington, D.C.

JONES, BARBARA ("MA'AM") AND FAMILY

Ball, Eve. *Ma'am Jones of the Pecos*. Tucson: University of Arizona Press. 1969.

KIMBRELL, GEORGE

Kimbrell, George. "I have the honor to request that you will furnish me a <u>posse</u> ..." Letter to Lieutenant Millard Filmore Goodwin. **February 20, 1879**. Indiana Historical Society. Lew Wallace Collection. Box 4, Folder 3.

KINNEY, JOHN

BIOGRAPHICAL SOURCE

Mullin, Robert N. "Here Lies John Kinney." *Journal of Arizona History*. 14 (Autumn 1973). Pages 223 - 242.

CONTEMPORARY SOURCES (CHRONOLOGICAL)

No Author. "Charges against Jessie Evans and John Kinney." Doña Ana County Criminal Docket Book. **August 18, 1875 to November 7, 1878**. Herman Weisner Collection. New Mexico State University Library at Las Cruces. Rio Grande Historical Collections. Accession No. Ms 0249. Box 13. Folder V-3. Folder Name: "Venue, Change of."

No Author. "Obituary of John Kinney." *Prescott Courier*. **August 30, 1919**. Obituary Section.

No Author. Obituary. "Over the Range Goes Another Pioneer." *Journal Miner*. Tuesday Morning, **August 26, 1919**.

LEONARD, IRA E.

BIOGRAPHICAL SOURCE

Nolan, Frederick. Biography and photograph of Ira Leonard. Unpublished. personal communication. July 29, 2005.

CONTEMPORARY SOURCES (CHRONOLOGICAL)
LETTERS FROM HUSTON CHAPMAN'S FATHER

Chapman, W.W. "Yours of the 1st inst. came ..." Letter to Ira E. Leonard. **March 20, 1879**. Indiana Historical Society. Lew Wallace Collection. M0292. Box 4. Folder 6.

_____. "Since receiving yours of the 1st March ..." Letter to Ira Leonard. **May 8, 1879**. Indiana Historical Society. Lew Wallace Collection. M0292. Box 4. Folder 10.

COURT OF INQUIRY OF LIEUTENANT COLONEL N.A.M. DUDLEY

Leonard, Ira E. "You are perhaps fully aware of the outrages that have been perpetrated in Lincoln County ..." Letter to Secretary of War George McCrary. **March 4, 1879**. From *Proceedings of a Court of Inquiry in the Case of Lt. Col. N.A.M. Dudley (May 2, 1879 – July 5, 1879)*. File No. QQ1284. (Boxes 3304, 3305, 3305A); Court Martial Files 1809-1894. Records of the Office of the Judge Advocate General – Army. Record Group 153. Old Military and Civil Branch. National Archives and Records Administration. Washington, D.C. (**Accusing N.A.M. Dudley of murders of A.A. McSween and H.I. Chapman and arson of McSween house**)

_____. "Charges and specifications against Lieutenant Colonel N.A.M. Dudley, Commander at Fort Stanton, New Mexico." **March 4, 1879**. *Proceedings of a Court of Inquiry in the Case of Lt. Col. N.A.M. Dudley (May 2, 1879 – July 5, 1879)*. File No. QQ1284. (Boxes 3304, 3305, 3305A); Court Martial Files 1809-1894. Records of the Office of the Judge Advocate General – Army. Record Group 153. Old Military and Civil Branch. National Archives and Records Administration. Washington, D.C. (**As Susan McSween's lawyer, Leonard assisted the military prosecutor, Henry H. Humphreys, and was present in court.**)

LETTERS TO AND FROM LEW WALLACE

Leonard, Ira E. "Dear Gov. You have undoubtedly learned ere this of the assassination ..." Letter to Lew Wallace. **February 24, 1879**. Indiana Historical Society. Lew Wallace Collection. M0292. Box 4. Folder 3. (**On Chapman murder.**)

Wallace, Lew. "It is important to take steps to protect the coming court .. " Letter to Ira Leonard. **April 6, 1879**. Indiana Historical Society. Lew Wallace Collection. M0292. Box 4. Folder 8.

Leonard, Ira E. 'You may have learned the result of the cattle examination ..." Letter to Lew Wallace. **April 8, 1879**. Indiana Historical Society. Lew Wallace Collection. M0292. Box 4. Folder 8. (**Mentions the ongoing "cruel war"**)

_____. "One Wm Wilson, a saloon keeper ..." Letter to Lew Wallace. **April 9, 1879**. Indiana Historical Society. Lew Wallace Collection. M0292. Box 4. Folder 9.

Wallace, Lew. "Your favors both received." Letter to Ira Leonard. **April 9, 1879**. Indiana Historical Society. Lew Wallace Collection. M0292. Box 4. Folder 9. (**Wallace's "martyr" letter: "all the world against you"**)

_____. "Mr. Howell goes to the Plaza to give bond ..." Letter to Ira Leonard. **April 9, 1879**. Indiana Historical Society. Lew Wallace Collection. M0292. Box 4. Folder 9.

_____. "Referring to the testimony in Mr. Howell's cattle case ..." Letter to Ira Leonard. **April 9, 1879**. Indiana Historical Society. Lew Wallace Collection. M0292. Box 4. Folder 9.

Leonard, Ira. "Yours received it might perhaps be a good idea to surrender the cattle to Mr Howell." Letter to Lew Wallace. **April 9, 1879**. Indiana Historical Society. Lew Wallace Collection. M0292. Box 4. Folder 9.

_____. "... *if the wind does not blow so I can't.*" Letter to Lew Wallace. **April 9, 1879**. Unpublished. Personal communication from Frederick Nolan. July 29, 2005.

_____. "I was disappointed in not seeing you ..." Letter to Lew Wallace. **April 12, 1879**. Indiana Historical Society. Lew Wallace Collection. M0292. Box 4. Folder 9. **(Anxious about hard looking characters coming into Lincoln)**

Wallace, Lew. "Your favor, with the prisoner received." Letter to Ira Leonard. **April 13, 1879**. Indiana Historical Society. Lew Wallace Collection. M0292. Box 4. Folder 9. **(About writs of habeas corpus to free his Fort Stanton prisoners)**

Leonard, Ira. "Yours was received last night ..." **April 13, 1879**. Indiana Historical Society. Lew Wallace Collection. M0292. Box 4. Folder 9. **(Enforcing vagrancy and gun laws in Lincoln)**

_____. "The air is filled tonight with 'rumors of wars ... Letter to Lew Wallace. **April 20, 1879**. Indiana Historical Society. Lew Wallace Collection. M0292. Box 4. Folder 9. **(About District Attorney Rynerson: "He is bent on going for the Kid")**

_____. "When you left here I promised to write you concerning events transpiring here ..." Letter to Lew Wallace. **May 20, 1878 [sic - 79]**. Indiana Historical Society. Lew Wallace Collection. M0292. Box 4. Folder 10. **(Has quote on the Murphy-Dolan party as: "part and parcel of the Santa Fe ring that has been so long an incubus on the government of this territory.")**

_____. "I write to you with pencil because I am laboring for breath ..." Letter to Lew Wallace. **May 23, 1879**. Indiana Historical Society. Lew Wallace Collection. M0292. Box 4. Folder 11. **(With quote "we are pouring the 'hot shot' into Dudley." With enclosed letter of May 20, 1879)**

_____. "Dudley commenced on the defense Thursday afternoon ..." Letter to Wallace. **June 6, 1879**, Indiana Historical Society. Lew Wallace Collection. M0292. Box 4. Folder 11. **(Quote: "I am thoroughly and completely disgusted with their proceedings ...")**

_____. "Yours of the 7th inst reached me ..." Letter to Lew Wallace. **June 13, 1879**. Indiana Historical Society. Lew Wallace Collection. M0292. Box 4. Folder 11.

_____. About having become impoverished by Lincoln County legal work. Letter to Lew Wallace. **November 26, 1888**. Unpublished. Personal communication from Frederick Nolan. July 29, 2005.

ARTICLES

No Author. "[He] attracted special commendation by his fearless action in the suppression of disorder..." *St. Louis Globe* of September 7, 1872. Unpublished. Personal communication from Frederick Nolan. July 29, 2005.

No Author. Obituary. **July 6, 1889**. Las Cruces *Rio Grande Republican*. Unpublished. Personal communication from Frederick Nolan. July 29, 2005.

LEVERSON, MONTEGUE

CONTEMPORARY SOURCES (CHRONOLOGICAL)

Leverson, Montegue. "I earnestly entreat you to read the enclosed letter and hand it to the president ..." Letter to Secretary of Interior Carl Schurz. **March 16, 1878**. Part of file of report of October 4, 1878. Angel Report. Microfilm File Case Number 44-4-8-3. Record Group 48. Microfilm No. M750. Roll 1. National Archives and Records Administration. U.S. Department of Justice. Washington, D.C.

_____. "Affairs of Lincoln County." Letter to Secretary of Interior Carl Schurz and President Rutherford B. Hayes. **June 28, 1878**. Part of file of report of

October 4, 1878. Angel Report. Microfilm File Case Number 44-4-8-3. Record Group 48. Microfilm No. M750. Roll 1. National Archives and Records Administration. U.S. Department of Justice. Washington, D.C. (**Mentions Governor S.B. Axtell as appointer of D.A. W.L. Rynerson; and Thomas Benton Catron and Steven Benton Elkins and their Santa Fe Ring**)

_____. "I send you herewith a copy of a letter I have published ...' Letter to Secretary of Interior Carl Schurz. **July 12 (?), 1878.** Part of file of report of October 4, 1878. Angel Report. Microfilm File Case Number 44-4-8-3. Record Group 48. Microfilm No. M750. Roll 1. National Archives and Records Administration. U.S. Department of Justice. Washington, D.C. (**About opposing Thomas Benton Catron and the Ring**)

_____. "I enclose you a letter I have just received ..." Letter to President Rutherford B. Hayes. **July 30, 1878.** Part of file of report of October 4, 1878. Angel Report. Microfilm File Case Number 44-4-8-3. Record Group 48. Microfilm No. M750. Roll 1. National Archives and Records Administration. U.S. Department of Justice. Washington, D.C. (**About murder of Alexander McSween and Frank MacNab by the Ring – blaming Hayes**)

MARKLAND, ABSALOM HANKS

BIOGRAPHICAL SOURCE

Perret, Geoffrey. *Ulysses S. Grant: Soldier and President.* New York: Random House. 1997. (**Pages 16, 467, 471**)

CONTEMPORARY SOURCES (CHRONOLOGICAL)

Grant, Ulysses. Presentation of the Grimsby Saddle to Colonel Absalom Markland. **May 19, 1865.** *The Papers of Ulysses S. Grant: May 1-December 31, 1865.* Carbondale, Illinois: Southern Illinois University Press. 1967 - 2009.

Wallace, Lew. "Our mutual friend, M. Hinds, who will hand you this ..." Letter to A.H. Markland. **November 14, 1878.** Indiana Historical Society. Lew Wallace Collection. M0292. Box 3. Folder 17. (**About Santa Fe Ring attempting to remove him as governor**)

MATTHEWS, JACOB BASIL

BIOGRAPHICAL SOURCE

Fleming, Elvis E. *J.B. Matthews. Biography of a Lincoln County Deputy.* Las Cruces, New Mexico: Yucca Tree Press. 1999.

CONTEMPORARY SOURCES (CHRONOLOGICAL)

Wallace, Lew. "Under the circumstances, particularly in the absence here of suitable cells for safekeeping of Jesse Evans, Jacob B. Matthews and William Campbell ..." Letter to Henry Carroll. **March 10, 1879.** Indiana Historical Society. Lew Wallace Collection. M0292. Box 4. Folder 4.

_____. "Upon reflection, I am of opinion that if Col. Dudley is really going to Fort Union ..." Letter to Henry Carroll. **March 11, 1879.** Indiana Historical Society. Lew Wallace Collection. M0292. Box 4. Folder 5. (**Advises not to send Evans, Campbell, Matthews, and Dolan to Fort Union**)

MAXWELL FAMILY

Cleaveland, Agnes Morley. *No Life for a Lady.* Boston: Houghton Mifflin. 1941.

_____. *Satan's Paradise: From Lucien Maxwell to Fred Lambert.* Boston: Houghton Mifflin Company. 1952.

Cleaveland, Norman. *The Morleys - Young Upstarts on the Southwest Frontier.* Albuquerque, New Mexico: Calvin Horn Publisher, Inc. 1971.
Dunham, Harold H. "New Mexican Land Grants with Special Reference to the Title Papers of the Maxwell Grant." *New Mexico Historical Review.* (January 1955) Vol. 30, No. 1. pp. 1 - 23.
Freiberger, Harriet. *Lucien Maxwell: Villain or Visionary.* Santa Fe, New Mexico: Sunstone Press. 1999.
Keleher, William A. *The Maxwell Land Grant. A New Mexico Item.* Albuquerque, New Mexico: University of New Mexico Press. 1964.
Lamar, Howard Roberts. *The Far Southwest 1846 - 1912. A Territorial History.* New Haven and London: Yale University Press. 1966.
Miller, Kenny. Descendant of Lucien Bonaparte Maxwell. Personal communication. 2011 to 2012.
Montoya, María E. *Translating Property. The Maxwell Land Grant and the Conflict Over Land in the American West, 1840-1900.* Berkeley and Los Angeles, California: University of California Press. 2002.
Murphy, Lawrence R. *Lucien Bonaparte Maxwell. Napoleon of the Southwest.* Norman: University of Oklahoma Press. 1983.
Pearson, Jim Berry. *The Maxwell Land Grant.* Norman: University of Oklahoma Press. 1961.
Poe, Sophie. *Buckboard Days.* Albuquerque, New Mexico: University of New Mexico Press. 1964.
Taylor, Morris F. *O. P. McMains and the Maxwell Land Grant Conflict.* Tucson, Arizona: The University of Arizona Press. 1979. (**Origins of Santa Fe Ring**)
No Author. "Mrs. Paula M. Jaramillo, 65 Died Here Tuesday." *The Fort Sumner Leader.* Official Newspaper County of De Baca. December 20, 1929. No. 1158, Page 1, Column 1. (**Death of Paulita Maxwell Jaramillo, Billy Bonney's sweetheart**)

McMAINS, OSCAR P.

BIOGRAPHICAL SOURCE

Cleaveland, Norman. *The Morleys - Young Upstarts on the Southwest Frontier.* Albuquerque, New Mexico: Calvin Horn Publisher, Inc. 1971.
Taylor, Morris F. *O.P. McMains and the Maxwell Land Grant Conflict.* Tucson, Arizona: The University of Arizona Press. 1979. (**Traces origins of the Santa Fe Ring with T.B. Catron and S.B. Elkins**)

CONTEMPORARY SOURCES (CHRONOLOGICAL)

Morley, William Raymond and Frank Springer. On Oscar McMains's citizen's Meeting. *Cimarron News and Press.* **November 10, 1875.** In Mary McPherson, Letters and Petitions to President Rutherford B. Hayes re: Removal Governor Axtell and the Santa Fe Ring. 1977. Interior Department Papers 1850-1907; Appointments Division and Subsequent Actions. Microfilm File Case Number 44-4-8-3. **Record Group 48.** Microfilm Roll M750. National Archives and Records Administration. (**Colfax County citizens meeting on F.J. Tolby murder by Santa Fe Ring.**)
No Author. About Santa Fe Ring scapegoating of O.P. McMains by murder indictment. Pueblo, *Colorado Chieftain.* **May 25, 1876.**
Lambert, J.J. "At It Again." Pueblo, Colorado, *Enterprise and Chronicle.* **April 21, 1877.** Interior Department Papers 1850-1907; Appointments Division and Subsequent Actions. Microfilm File Case Number 44-4-8-3. Record Group 48. Microfilm No. M750. Roll 1. National Archives and Records Administration. U.S. Department of Justice. Washington, D.C. (**Description of Santa Fe Ring control of courts and malicious prosecution of opponents like Oscar McMains in the Franklin Tolby murder; used in: "W.B. Matchett and**

Mary E. McPherson 'Make Certain Charges Against the U.S. Officials in the Territory of New Mexico.' " Letter to President Rutherford B. Hayes. Received and filed May 1, 1877. Interior Department Papers 1850-1907; Appointments Division and Subsequent Actions. Microfilm File Case Number 44-4-8-3. Record Group 48. Microfilm No. M750. Roll 1. National Archives and Records Administration. U. S. Department of Justice. Washington, D.C.)

McPherson, Mary and W.B. Matchett. "To the President. Please make the enclosed part of the evidence in the case of "Charges Against New Mexican Officials" Letter to President Rutherford B. Hayes. **May 3, 1877.** McPherson, Mary E. Letters and Petitions to President Rutherford B. Hayes re: Removal Governor Axtell and the Santa Fe Ring. Interior Department Papers 1850-1907; Appointments Division and Subsequent Actions. Microfilm File Case Number 44-4-8-3. Record Group 48. Microfilm Roll M750. National Archives and Records Administration. U.S. Department of Justice. Washington, D.C. **(Addendum to their May, 1877 "Certain Charges Against U.S. Officials in New Mexico Territory.")**

McPherson, Mary and W.B. Matchett. "The Secretary of the Interior, Sir - Accompanying please find copy of charges, &c., against S.B. Axtell, Governor, and other New Mexican Officials ..." "Charges Against New Mexican Officials." Letter to Secretary of the Interior Carl Schurz. **May 5, 1877.** McPherson, Mary E. Letters and Petitions to President Rutherford B. Hayes re: Removal Governor Axtell and the Santa Fe Ring. Interior Department Papers 1850-1907; Appointments Division and Subsequent Actions. Microfilm File Case Number 44-4-8-3. Record Group 48. Microfilm Roll M750. National Archives and Records Administration. U.S. Department of Justice. Washington, D. C.

Chaplin, F.B. Obituary of O.P. McMains. No date (but died April 15, 1899). Quoted by Mary McMains to a Robert Fischer. **(Quotes that he had fought crime and corruption)** **(Apparently unpublished; in collection of Morris F. Taylor)**

No Author. "O.P. McMains, the agitator, is dead." *Raton Range.* **April 20, 1899.**

McPHERSON, MARY E. TIBBLES

BIOGRAPHICAL SOURCES

Cleaveland, Agnes Morley. *No Life for a Lady.* Boston: Houghton Mifflin. 1941.
_____. *Satan's Paradise: From Lucien Maxwell to Fred Lambert.* Boston: Houghton Mifflin Company. 1952.
Cleaveland, Norman, *A Synopsis of the Great New Mexico Cover-up.* Self-printed. 1989.
_____. *The Great Santa Fe Cover-up. Based on a Talk given Before the Santa Fe Historical Society on November 1, 1978.* Self-printed. 1982.
_____. *The Morleys - Young Upstarts on the Southwest Frontier.* Albuquerque, New Mexico: Calvin Horn Publisher, Inc. 1971.
Taylor, Morris F. *O.P. McMains and the Maxwell Land Grant Conflict.* Tucson, Arizona: The University of Arizona Press. 1979.
Tibbles, Thomas Henry. Editor Vivian K. Barris. *Buckskin and Blanket Days: Memoirs of a Friend of the Indians.* Written in 1905. Published by Garden City, New York: Doubleday & Company, Inc. in 1957. **(Brother of Mary Tibbles McPherson)**

McPHERSON'S SANTA FE RING EXPOSÉS

McPherson, Mary. "Charges against Thomas B. Catron, U.S. Attorney, and Others." **February 7, 1877.** Letter to Attorney General Alphonso Taft. Interior Department Papers 1850-1907; Appointments Division and Subsequent Actions. Microfilm File Case Number 44-4-8-3. Record Group 48. Microfilm Roll M750. National Archives and Records Administration. U.S. Department of Justice. Washington D.C.

Catron, Thomas Benton. "Answering Charges of Mary E. McPherson." **February 24, 1877.** Letter to Attorney General Alphonso Taft. Interior Department Papers 1850-1907; Appointments Division and Subsequent Actions. Microfilm File Case Number 44-4-8-3. Record Group 48. Microfilm Roll M750. National Archives and Records Administration. U.S. Department of Justice. Washington, D.C.

CONTEMPORARY SOURCES (CHRONOLOGICAL)

Morley, William Raymond and Frank Springer. On Oscar McMains's citizen's Meeting. *Cimarron News and Press.* **November 10, 1875.** In Mary McPherson, Letters and Petitions to President Rutherford B. Hayes re: Removal Governor Axtell and the Santa Fe Ring. 1977. Interior Department Papers 1850-1907; Appointments Division and Subsequent Actions. Microfilm File Case Number 44-4-8-3. **Record Group 48.** Microfilm Roll M750. National Archives and Records Administration. **(Colfax County citizens meeting on F.J. Tolby murder by Santa Fe Ring.)**

Morley, William Raymond and Frank Springer. " 'The Territory of Elkins.' Assassination of Supposed Sun Correspondent. The Murder of the Rev. F.J. Tolby in New Mexico. A Probate Judge Accused of Complicity in the Crime. Indignation Meeting." *New York Weekly Sun.* **December 22, 1875.** Interior Department Papers 1850-1907; Appointments Division and Subsequent Actions. Microfilm Roll M750. National Archives and Records Administration. Record Group 48. Microfilm Case File Number 44-4-8-3. U.S. Department of Interior. Washington, D. C.**(From May 1, 1877 submission to President Rutherford B. Hates as "Mary E. McPherson and W.B. Matchett 'Make certain charges against the U.S. Officials in the Territory of New Mexico.' "**)

Morley William Raymond. "I was astonished beyond measure at your proceedings, and have fears as to the result ..." Letter to Mary McPherson. **March 6, 1877.** McPherson, Mary E. Letters and Petitions to President Rutherford B. Hayes re: Removal Governor Axtell and the Santa Fe Ring. Interior Department Papers 1850-1907; Appointments Division and Subsequent Actions. Microfilm File Case Number 44-4-8-3. Record Group 48. Microfilm Roll M750. National Archives and Records Administration. U.S. Department of Justice. Washington, D.C. **(Hopes she can help fight against Santa Fe Ring)**

Morley, Ada. "Yes, we have received all your letters at Vermejo here but we have hesitated about replying ..." Letter to Mary McPherson. **March 7, 1877.** McPherson, Mary E. Letters and Petitions to President Rutherford B. Hayes re: Removal Governor Axtell and the Santa Fe Ring. Interior Department Papers 1850-1907; Appointments Division and Subsequent Actions. Microfilm File Case Number 44-4-8-3. Record Group 48. Microfilm Roll M750. National Archives and Records Administration. U.S. Department of Justice. Washington, D.C. **(Fears about her fight against Santa Fe Ring)**

Matchett, W.B. and Mary E. McPherson. " W.B. Matchett and Mary E. McPherson 'Make certain charges against the U.S. Officials in the Territory of New Mexico.' " Letter to President Rutherford B. Hayes. Received and filed **May 1, 1877.** Interior Department Papers 1850-1907; Appointments Division and Subsequent Actions. Microfilm File Case Number 44-4-8-3. Record Group 48. Microfilm No. M750. Roll 1. National Archives and Records Administration. U. S. Department of Justice. Washington, D.C.

McPherson, Mary and W.B. Matchett. "To The President. Please make the enclosed a part of the evidence in the case of "Charges Against New Mexican Officials" Letter to President Rutherford B. Hayes. **May 3, 1877.** McPherson, Mary E. Letters and Petitions to President Rutherford B. Hayes re: Removal Governor Axtell and the Santa Fe Ring. Interior Department Papers 1850-1907; Appointments Division and Subsequent Actions. Microfilm File Case Number 44-4-8-3. Record Group 48. Microfilm Roll M750. National Archives and Records Administration. U.S. Department of Justice. Washington, D. C.

_____. "The Secretary of the Interior, Sir - Accompanying please find copy of charges, &c., against S.B. Axtell, Governor, and other New Mexican Officials ..." "Charges Against New Mexican Officials." Letter to Secretary of the Interior Carl Schurz. **May 5, 1877.** McPherson, Mary E. Letters and Petitions to President Rutherford B. Hayes re: Removal Governor Axtell and the Santa Fe Ring. Interior Department Papers 1850-1907; Appointments Division and Subsequent Actions. Microfilm File Case Number 44-4-8-3. Record Group 48. Microfilm Roll M750. National Archives and Records Administration. U.S. Department of Justice. Washington, D. C.

McPherson, Mary E. Letters and Petitions to President Rutherford B. Hayes re: Removal Governor Axtell and the Santa Fe Ring. **1877.** Interior Department Papers 1850-1907; Appointments Division and Subsequent Actions. Microfilm File Case Number 44-4-8-3. Record Group 48. Microfilm Roll M750. National Archives and Records Administration. U.S. Department of Justice. Washington D. C.

McPherson, Mary and W.B. Matchett. "We have respectfully to request that the following named records, documents, papers, communications and correspondence be supplied ..." Records Request to Secretary of the Interior Carl Schurz. **July 26, 1877.** Interior Department Papers 1850-1907; Appointments Division and Subsequent Actions. Microfilm File Case Number 44-4-8-3. Record Group 48. Microfilm No. M750. Roll 1. National Archives and Records Administration. U.S. Department of Justice. Washington, D.C. (**Requesting Ring records**)

McPherson, Mary. "Please place before the Attorney General ..." Letter to President Rutherford B. Hayes. **August 23, 1877.** Interior Department Papers 1850-1907; Appointments Division and Subsequent Actions. Microfilm File Case Number 44-4-8-3. Record Group 48. Microfilm No. M750. Roll 1. National Archives and Records Administration. U. S. Department of Justice. Washington, D.C. (**Requesting that her "Charges vs. New Mexico Officials" go to the Attorney General.**)

McPherson, Mary and W.B. Matchett. *In the Matter of Charges vs. Gov. S.B. Axtell and Other New Mexico Officials. Submitted to the Departments of the Interior and Justice.* **August, 1877.** Printed as a 31 page booklet. No publisher listed. Indiana Historical Society. Lew Wallace Collection. M0292. Box 3. Folder 20. (**Exposé of Santa Fe Ring, Catron, and Elkins; in Lew Wallace's personal possession**)

McPherson, Mary. "I desire to know when I can be heard ..." Letter to Secretary of Interior Carl Schurz. **September 30, 1977.** Interior Department Papers 1850-1907; Appointments Division and Subsequent Actions. Microfilm File Case Number 44-4-8-3. Record Group 48. Microfilm No. M750. Roll 1. National Archives and Records Administration. U. S. Department of Justice. Washington, D.C.

McSWEEN, ALEXANDER

Bristol Warren. "Writ of Embezzlement." **December 21, 1877.** Writ of Embezzlement. New Mexico State University Library at Las Cruces. Rio Grande Historical Collections. Lincoln County Papers. New Mexico State University Library at Las Cruces. Rio Grande Historical Collections. Accession No. Ms 0249. Box No. 10. Folder M-13. "Will and Testament A. McSween." (**Emilie Fritz Scholand's sworn complaint against Alexander McSween**)

Fritz, Charles. Affidavit sworn before John Crouch, Clerk of Doña Ana District Court, for Writ of Attachment issued against property of Alexander A. McSween. Probate Court Record. **February 6, 1878.** (private collection).

_____. Fritz, Charles and Emilie Scholand. Attachment Bond sworn before John Crouch, Clerk of Doña Ana District Court, against Alexander A. McSween for indebtedness to them. **February 6, 1878.** (private collection).

Bristol, Warren. Action of Assumpsit to command Sheriff of Lincoln County to attach goods of Alexander A. McSween. **February 7, 1878.** District Court Record. (private collection).

_____. Preprinted form in his name for "Writ of Attachment" (Printed and sold at the office of the Mesilla News) filled out to command the Sheriff of Lincoln County to attach goods of Alexander McSween for a suit of damages for ten thousand dollars. **February 7, 1878.** (private collection).

McSween, Alexander. "It looks as though the agent were the property of J.J. Dolan & J.H. Riley, known here as Dolan & Co." Letter to Secretary of Interior Carl Schurz. **February 11, 1878.** From Frederick Nolan. *The Life and Death of John Henry Tunstall.* Albuquerque, New Mexico: The University of New Mexico Press. 1965. Page 266.

_____. "Will and Testament A. McSween." **February 25, 1878.** Herman B. Weisner Papers, ca. 1957-1992. New Mexico State University Library at Las Cruces. Rio Grande Historical Collections. Accession No. Ms 0249. Box 10. Folder M15. Folder Name. "Will and Testament A. McSween."

McSween, A.A. and B.H. Ellis. Secretaries. "The undersigned have the Honor of transmitting you, as requested, a copy of the proceedings of a meeting held by the citizens of Lincoln County ..." Letter to President Rutherford B. Hayes; with attached proceedings of the April 1878 Lincoln Grand Jury. **April 26, 1878.** Microfilm File Case Number 44-4-8-3. Record Group 48. Microfilm No. M750. Roll 1. National Archives and Records Administration. U.S. Department of Justice. Washington, D.C.

McSween, Alexander. Deposition to Frank Warner Angel. **June 6, 1878.** Pages 5-183 of Frank Warner Angel report *In the Matter of the Examination of the Causes and Circumstances of the Death of John H. Tunstall a British Subject.* Report filed **October 4, 1878.** Angel Report. Microfilm File Case Number 44-4-8-3. Record Group 48. Microfilm No. M750. Roll 1. National Archives and Records Administration. U.S. Department of Justice. Washington, D.C.

Angel, Frank Warner. *In the Matter of the Lincoln County Troubles. To the Honorable Charles Devens, Attorney General.* **October 4, 1878.** Angel Report. Microfilm File Case Number 44-4-8-3. Record Group 48. Microfilm No. M750. Roll 1. National Archives and Records Administration. U.S. Department of Justice. Washington, D.C.

McSWEEN, SUSAN

BIOGRAPHICAL SOURCE

Chamberlain, Kathleen P. *In the Shadow of Billy the Kid: Susan McSween and the Lincoln County War.* Albuquerque: University of New Mexico Press. 2013.

CONTEMPORARY SOURCES (CHRONOLOGICAL)

Dudley, Nathan Augustus Monroe. "I am in receipt of a copy of letter written by one H.I. Chapman, calling himself the Attorney ..." **November 9, 1878.** Letter to Lew Wallace. From *Proceedings of a Court of Inquiry in the Case of Lt. Col. N.A.M. Dudley (May 2,1879 – July 5, 1879).* File No. QQ1284. (Boxes 3304, 3305, 3305A); Court Martial Files 1809-1894. Records of the Office of the Judge Advocate General - Army. Record Group 153. Old Military and Civil Branch. National Archives and Records Administration. Washington, D.C. (**Forwarding the Susan McSween defamatory affidavits in answer to the charges made by Chapman**)

Wallace, Lew. "In a communication ... I requested for reasons stated, a safe-guard for Mrs. McSween ..." Letter to Edward Hatch. **November 9, 1878.** Indiana Historical Society. Lew Wallace Collection. M0292. Box 3. Folder 17.

McSween, Susan. Testimony in Court of Inquiry for Lieutenant Colonel N.A.M. Dudley. **May 23-24, 26, 1879.** *Proceedings of a Court of Inquiry in the Case of Lt. Col. N.A.M. Dudley (May 2,1879 – July 5, 1879).* File No. QQ1284. (Boxes 3304, 3305, 3305A); Court Martial Files 1809-1894. Records of the Office of the Judge

Advocate General – Army. Record Group 153. Old Military and Civil Branch. National Archives and Records Administration. Washington, D.C.

Waldo, Henry. "Nothing has been accomplished in the least that connects Col. Dudley with anything which transpired in the town of Lincoln on the occasion of his presence there on the 19th..." Closing argument for Dudley Court of Inquiry. **July 5, 1879.** *Proceedings of a Court of Inquiry in the Case of Lt. Col. N.A.M. Dudley (May 2,1879 – July 5, 1879).* File No. QQ1284. (Boxes 3304, 3305, 3305A); Court Martial Files 1809-1894. Records of the Office of the Judge Advocate General – Army. Record Group 153. Old Military and Civil Branch. National Archives and Records Administration. Washington, D. C.

No Author. Verdict on Civil Cause 298 for arson of Susan McSween's house. *Mesilla News*. **December 6, 1879.** Unpublished. personal communication from Frederick Nolan. July 29, 2005. (**Dudley exonerated**)

SEE ALSO: Alexander McSween; Huston Chapman; Ira Leonard

MEADOWS, JOHN P.

Meadows, John P. "Billy the Kid to John P. Meadows on the Peñasco, May 1-2, 1881." *Roswell Daily Record*. February 16, 1931. Page 6.

Meadows, John P. Ed. John P. Wilson. *Pat Garrett and Billy the Kid as I Knew Them: Reminiscences of John P. Meadows.* Albuquerque: University of New Mexico Press. 2004.

MORLEY, ADA McPHERSON

Morley, Ada. "Yes, we have received all your letters at Vermejo here but we have hesitated about replying ..." Letter to Mary McPherson. **March 7, 1877.**

McPherson, Mary E. Letters and Petitions to President Rutherford B. Hayes re: Removal Governor Axtell and the Santa Fe Ring. Interior Department Papers 1850-1907; Appointments Division and Subsequent Actions. Interior Department Papers 1850-1907; Appointments Division and Subsequent Actions. Microfilm File Case Number 44-4-8-3. Record Group 48. Microfilm Roll M750. National Archives and Records Administration. U.S. Department of Justice. Washington, D.C. (**Fears about her fight against Santa Fe Ring**)

Middaugh, Asa F. Deposition. **March 31, 1876.** "Exhibit B" in the August 9, 1878 deposition of Frank Springer to Investigator Frank Warner Angel. Frank Warner Angel report titled *In the Matter of the Investigation of the Charges Against S.B. Axtell Governor of New Mexico*. October 3, 1878. Interior Department Papers 1850-1907; Appointments Division and Subsequent Actions. Microfilm Case File No. 44-4-8-3. Record Group 48. Microfilm Roll M750. National Archives and Records Administration. U.S. Department of Interior. Washington, D.C. (**About Catron's malicious prosecution of Ada McPherson Morley**)

MORLEY, WILLIAM RAYMOND

BIOGRAPHICAL SOURCES

Caffey, David L. *Frank Springer and New Mexico: From the Colfax County War to the Emergence of Modern Santa Fe*. Texas A and M. University Press. 2007.

Cleaveland, Agnes Morley. *No Life for a Lady*. Boston: Houghton Mifflin. 1941.

_____. *Satan's Paradise: From Lucien Maxwell to Fred Lambert*. Boston: Houghton Mifflin Company. 1952.

Cleaveland, Norman. *The Morleys - Young Upstarts on the Southwest Frontier*. Albuquerque, New Mexico: Calvin Horn Publisher, Inc. 1971.

Taylor, Morris F. *O.P. McMains and the Maxwell Land Grant Conflict*. Tucson, Arizona: The University of Arizona Press. 1979.

CONTEMPORARY SOURCES (CHRONOLOGICAL)

Morley William Raymond. "I was astonished beyond measure at your proceedings, and have fears as to the result ..." Letter to Mary McPherson. **March 6, 1877.**

McPherson, Mary E. Letters and Petitions to President Rutherford B. Hayes re: Removal Governor Axtell and the Santa Fe Ring. Interior Department Papers 1850-1907; Appointments Division and Subsequent Actions. Microfilm File Case Number 44-4-8-3. Record Group 48. Microfilm Roll M750. National Archives and Records Administration. U.S. Department of Justice. Washington, D.C. **(Hopes she can help fight against Santa Fe Ring)**

McPherson, Mary E. and W.B. Matchett. "In the Matter of the Charges vs. Gov. S.B. Axtell and Other New Mexico Officials; Submitted to the Departments of the Interior and of Justice. Governor of New Mexico." **August, 1877**. Printed as a 31 page booklet. No publisher listed. Indiana Historical Society. Lew Wallace Collection. M0292. Box 3. Folder 20. **(Focus on the Santa Fe Ring)**

MURPHY, LAWRENCE G.

Murphy, Lawrence G. "Will of Lawrence G. Murphy." Herman B. Weisner Papers, ca. 1957-1992. New Mexico State University Library at Las Cruces. Rio Grande Historical Collections. Accession No. Ms 0249. Box 11. Folder P15. Folder Name: "Murphy, Lawrence G."

PATRÓN, JUAN

Wallace, Lew. "Be good enough to send word to all your men to turn out soon as possible ..." Letter to Juan Patrón. **March 19, 1879**. Indiana Historical Society. Lew Wallace Collection. M0292. Box 4. Folder 6. **(Reports escape of Jessie Evans and Billy Campbell from Fort Stanton)**

Patrón, Juan. First letter to Lew Wallace on **March 29, 1879**. Indiana Historical Society. Lew Wallace Collection. M0292. Box 4, Folder 7.

_____. Second letter to Lew Wallace on **March 29, 1879**. Indiana Historical Society. Lew Wallace Collection. M0292. Box 4, Folder 7.

_____. Letter to Rosa. **April 12, 1879**. Indiana Historical Society. Lew Wallace Collection. M0292. Box 4, Folder 9.

PENNYPACKER, GALUSHA

BIOGRAPHICAL SOURCE

Heitman, Francis B. *Historical Register and Dictionary of the United States Army, From Its Organization, September 29, 1789, to March 2, 1903.* (Entry for Galusha Pennypacker, Pages 782-7830.) Washington, D.C.: Government Printing Office. 1903.

CONTEMPORARY SOURCE

No Author. *Proceedings of a Court of Inquiry in the Case of Lt. Col. N.A.M. Dudley (May 2,1879 – July 5, 1879).* File No. QQ1284. (Boxes 3304, 3305, 3305A); Court Martial Files 1809-1894. Records of the Office of the Judge Advocate General - Army. Record Group 153. Old Military and Civil Branch. National Archives and Records Administration. Washington, D.C. **(Chief Judge in Court of Inquiry)**

POE, JOHN WILLIAM

Poe, John W. "The Killing of Billy the Kid." (a personal letter written at Roswell, New Mexico to Mr. Charles Goodnight, Goodnight P.C., Texas) July 10, 1917.

_____. *The Death of Billy the Kid.* (Introduction by Maurice Garland Fulton). Boston and New York: Houghton Mifflin Company. 1933.

Poe, Sophie. *Buckboard Days.* Albuquerque, New Mexico: University of New Mexico Press. 1964.

RILEY, JOHN

Tunstall, John Henry. "A Tax-Payer's Complaint ... January 18, 1878." Mesilla *Independent.* **January 26, 1878.** (**Exposé of William Brady, James Dolan, and John Riley for tax fraud and use of public money to purchase cattle; and T.B. Catron then paid that bill**)

Dolan, James J. "Answer to A Tax-Payer's Complaint." Mesilla *Independent.* **January 29, 1878.** (**Response to J.H. Tunstall's exposé of him, William Brady, and John Riley for tax fraud and use of public money to purchase cattle; and T.B. Catron then paid that bill**)

McSween, Alexander. "It looks as though the agent were the property of J.J. Dolan & J.H. Riley, known here as Dolan & Co." Letter to Secretary of Interior Carl Schurz. **February 11, 1878.** From Frederick Nolan. *The Life and Death of John Henry Tunstall.* Albuquerque, New Mexico: The University of New Mexico Press. 1965. Page 266.

Rynerson, William. "Friends Riley & Dolan, Lincoln N.M. I have just received letters from you mailed 10th inst." **February 14, 1878.** Letter to James Dolan and John Riley. Copy as Exhibit B in June 6, 1878 deposition of Alexander McSween. Frank Warner Angel report. *In the Matter of the Examination of the Causes and Circumstances of the Death of John H. Tunstall a British Subject.* Report filed October 4, 1878. Interior Department Papers 1850-1907; Appointments Division and Subsequent Actions. Microfilm File Case Number 44-4-8-3. Record Group 48. Microfilm No. M750. Roll 1. National Archives and Records Administration. U.S. Department of Justice. Washington, D.C. (James J. Dolan Deposition. June 20, 1878. pp. 235-247.) (**Planned killing of J.H. Tunstall**)

Riley, John. Letter to N.A.M. Dudley. **May 19, 1878.** (**Fabricated Regulator theft from Catron-Dolan Pecos Cow Camp**) Cited by Victor Westphall, *Thomas Benton Catron and His Era,* Page 87.

RYNERSON, WILLIAM L.

Rynerson, William. "Indictments of the April, Lincoln County Grand Jury." **April 28, 1879.** Herman B. Weisner Papers, ca. 1957-1992. New Mexico State University Library at Las Cruces. Rio Grande Historical Society Collection. Accession No. Ms 0249. Box 4/39. Folder E-Z. Folder Name: "Jessie Evans Accessory to Murder." (**Billy's testimony indicts J.J. Dolan, Billy Campbell, and Jessie Evans fulfilling his pardon bargain**)

_____. "Friends Riley & Dolan, Lincoln N.M. I have just received letters from you mailed 10th inst." Letter to James Dolan and John Riley. **February 14, 1878.** Copy as Exhibit B in June 6, 1878 deposition of Alexander McSween. Frank Warner Angel report. *In the Matter of the Examination of the Causes and Circumstances of the Death of John H. Tunstall a British Subject.* Report filed October 4, 1878. Interior Department Papers 1850-1907; Appointments Division and Subsequent Actions. Microfilm File Case Number 44-4-8-3. Microfilm No. M750. Roll 1. National Archives and Records Administration. U.S. Department of Justice. Washington, D.C. (James J. Dolan Deposition. June 20, 1878. Pages 235-247.) (**Planned killing of J.H. Tunstall**)

Angel, Frank Warner. "I have just been favored by a call from W.L. Rynerson ..." Letter to Secretary of Interior Carl Schurz. **September 6, 1878.** Microfilm File Case Number 44-4-8-3. Record Group 48. Microfilm No. M750. Roll 1. National Archives and Records Administration. U.S. Department of Justice. Washington, D.C.

Rynerson, William. Venue Change. **April 21, 1879.** Herman B. Weisner Papers, ca. 1957-1992. New Mexico State University Library at Las Cruces. Rio Grande

Historical Collection. Accession No. Ms 0249. Box 1. Folder 14-D. Folder Name: "Billy the Kid Legal Documents."

SALAZAR, YGINIO

Salazar, Yginio. "Salazar's Affidavit." No Date. (July, 1878 likely) Herman B. Weisner Papers, ca. 1957-1992. New Mexico State University Library at Las Cruces. Rio Grande Historical Collections. Accession No. Ms 0249. Box. 12. Folder 56. Folder Name. " Salazar, Higinio."

Kimbrell, George. "I have the honor to request that you will furnish me a posse ..." Letter to Lieutenant Millard Filmore Goodwin. **February 20, 1879**. Indiana Historical Society. Lew Wallace Collection. Box 4, Folder 3. (**For pursuit of William Bonney and Yginio Salazar**)

Goodwin, Millard Filmore. ""I have the honor to submit the following report regarding my duties performed ..." Letter to Fort Stanton Post Adjutant John Loud. **February 23, 1879**. Indiana Historical Society. Lew Wallace Collection. Box 4, Folder 3. (**Assisting pursuit of William Bonney and Yginio Salazar**)

Wallace, Lew. "I beg to submit to you a list of persons ... to arrest ..." Letter to Henry Carroll. **March 11, 1879**. Indiana Historical Society. Lew Wallace Collection. M0292. Box 4. Folder 5. (**Lists Ygenio Salazar and "the Kid)**

Salazar, Joe. (Grandson of Yginio Salazar). Personal Interviews 1999-2001.

SCHURZ, CARL

LETTERS BY AND TO (CHRONOLOGICAL)

Schurz, Carl. "I transmit herewith an order from the President ..." Letter to Lew Wallace. **September 4, 1878**. Indiana Historical Society. Lew Wallace Collection. M0292. Box 3. Folder 14. (**Suspension of New Mexico Governor S.B. Axtell and his appointment as replacement Governor**)

Wallace, Lew. "I have the honor to inform you ..." Letter to Carl Schurz. **October 1, 1878**. Indiana Historical Society. Lew Wallace Collection. M0292. Box 3. Folder 15. (**Informing Schurz that he informed Axtell of suspension and that he now qualified as Governor**)

_____. "I have the honor to enclose herewith a requisition ..." **October 4, 1878**. Letter to Carl Schurz. Indiana Historical Society. Lew Wallace Collection. M0292. Box 3. Folder 15. (**Requesting arms from Secretary of War**)

_____. "As the basis of the request which I have to prefer relative to the affairs in the county of Lincoln ..." Letter to Carl Schurz. **October 5, 1878**. Indiana Historical Society. Lew Wallace Collection. M0292. Box 3. Folder 15. (**Requesting President to declare martial law**)

_____. "In further exemplification of affairs in Lincoln county accept extract received ..." Letter to Carl Schurz. **October 5, 1878**. Indiana Historical Society. Lew Wallace Collection. M0292. Box 3. Folder 15. (**N.A.M. Dudley's report of "Wrestlers" raping in Lincoln County**)

_____. "I received by mail last night a petition signed by the Probate Judge ..." Telegram to Carl Schurz. **October 14, 1878**. Indiana Historical Society. Lew Wallace Collection. M0292. Box 3. Folder 15. (**Giving situation and asking martial law for Lincoln and Doña Ana Counties**)

_____. "I have the honor to inform you that since the posting of the President's Proclamation ...." Letter to Carl Schurz. **October 22, 1878**. Indiana Historical Society. Lew Wallace Collection. M0292. Box 3. Folder 16.

_____. "I have appointed Mr. Epifanio Vigil, of this city, Interpreter and Translator ...." **October 22, 1878**. Indiana Historical Society. Lew Wallace Collection. M0292. Box 3. Folder 16.

_____. "Herewith please find bond ...." **October 22, 1878**. Indiana Historical Society. Lew Wallace Collection. M0292. Box 3. Folder 16.

No signatures. (But in Lew Wallace's handwriting). "Yesterday, at the request of Governor Wallace the undersigned, physicians ...." **Letter to Carl Schurz. October 23, 1878.** Indiana Historical Society. Lew Wallace Collection. M0292. Box 3. Folder 16. (**Focus on refurbishing Palace of the Governors**)

Wallace, Lew. "Be good enough, at your earliest convenience, to call attention of the President ...." **October 24, 1878.** Indiana Historical Society. Lew Wallace Collection. M0292. Box 3. Folder 16.

_____. "I enclose a paper, signed by all the leading attorneys ..." Letter to Carl Schurz. **November 13, 1878.** Indiana Historical Society. Lew Wallace Collection. M0292. Box 3. Folder 17. (**Urging judgeship for Ira Leonard**)

_____. "I have the honor to forward you the following report." **November 13, 1878.** Indiana Historical Society. Lew Wallace Collection. M0292. Box 3. Folder 17. (**About his progress**)

Schurz, Carl. "In reply to your letter ..." **November 14, 1878.** Indiana Historical Society. Lew Wallace Collection. M0292. Box 3 Folder 17. (**Given bond for arms**)

_____. "Replying to your two telegrams ..." Letter from Carl Schurz. **November 15, 1878.** Indiana Historical Society. Lew Wallace Collection. M0292. Box 3. Folder 17. (**Ira Leonard's requested judgeship appointment sent to the Attorney General for consideration**)

_____. "I acknowledge the receipt of your letter of the 13th instant ...' Letter from Carl Schurz. **November 23, 1878.** Indiana Historical Society. Lew Wallace Collection. M0292. Box 3. Folder 18. (**Giving presidential approval for Amnesty Proclamation**)

Wallace, Lew. "It has not unexpectedly happened that delay, involving expense ..." Letter to Carl Schurz. **November 26, 1878.** Indiana Historical Society. Lew Wallace Collection. M0292. Box 3. Folder 18. (**Wants extradition of fugitive criminals**)

Schurz, Carl. "In compliance with the suggestion of the Secretary of State ..." **November 30, 1878** Indiana Historical Society. Lew Wallace Collection. M0292. Box 3. Folder 18. (**About extradition of fugitive criminals**)

_____. "I have received your letter ..." Letter to Lew Wallace. **December 9, 1878.** Indiana Historical Society. Lew Wallace Collection. M0292. Box 3. Folder 19. (**Answer about anyone in Senate trying to defeat his confirmation as Governor**)

Wallace, Lew. "I have the honor to report that affairs of the Territory are moving on quietly ..." Letter to Carl Schurz. **December 21, 1878.** Indiana Historical Society. Lew Wallace Collection. M0292. Box 3. Folder 19. (**N.A.M. Dudley's indignation about the Amnesty Proclamation**)

Schurz, Carl. "I have received your report ..." **December 28, 1878.** Indiana Historical Society. Lew Wallace Collection. M0292. Box 3. Folder 19.

Wallace, Lew. "I have the honor to enclose you a copy of a communication ..." Letter to Carl Schurz. January 17, 1879. Indiana Historical Society. Lew Wallace Collection. M0292. Box 4. Folder 1. (**Bad condition of Palace of the Governors**)

_____. "... I have just returned from Trinidad, Col ..." Letter to Carl Schurz. **February 5, 1879.** Indiana Historical Society. Lew Wallace Collection. M0292. Box 4. Folder 2. (**Bringing his family to Santa Fe**)

_____. "I beg to call your attention to the condition of the house called the 'Palace' ...." Letter to Carl Schurz. **February 12, 1879.** Indiana Historical Society. Lew Wallace Collection. M0292. Box 4. Folder 2.

_____. "The Hon. A.G. Porter, Comptroller, is kind enough to inform me ..." Letter to Carl Schurz. **February 26, 1879.** Indiana Historical Society. Lew Wallace Collection. M0292. Box 4. Folder 3. (**Funds requested**)

_____. "I take the liberty of enclosing herewith the accounts in duplicate of Mr. Epifanio Vigil ..." Letter to Carl Schurz. **February 26, 1879.** Indiana

Historical Society. Lew Wallace Collection. M0292. Box 4. Folder 3. **(Funds requested)**

_____. "One H.I. Chapman, lawyer, was assassinated ...." Letter to Carl Schurz. **February 27, 1879.** Indiana Historical Society. Lew Wallace Collection. M0292. Box 4. Folder 3. **(Major document reacting to Chapman murder by planning use of T.B. Catron and troops to track "outlaws" – meaning the Regulators. Start of the pardon saga)**

Schurz, Carl. "I have the honor to acknowledge the receipt of your letter of the 1st inst." Letter to Lew Wallace. **March 11, 1879.** Indiana Historical Society. Lew Wallace Collection. M0292. Box 4. Folder 5. **(Presidential permission for "arresting the disturbances" in Lincoln County)**

Wallace, Lew. "My time has been so constantly occupied in getting my work into operation ..." Letter to Carl Schurz. **March 21, 1879.** Indiana Historical Society. Lew Wallace Collection. M0292. Box 4. Folder 7. **(Progress report with multiple enclosures; one listing "The Kid -William Bonney in anti-outlaw campaign of "taking the head off the evil.")**

_____. "To day I forwarded a telegram to you, with another to the President ..." Letter to Carl Schurz. **March 31, 1879.** Indiana Historical Society. Lew Wallace Collection. M0292. Box 4. Folder 7. **(Mention of "precious specimen nicknamed 'The Kid' ")**

_____. "I have official information that a court of inquiry for Col. Dudley has been ordered ..." Letter to Carl Schurz. **April 4, 1879.** Indiana Historical Society. Lew Wallace Collection. M0292. Box 4, Folder 8.

_____. "I have the honor to inform you that affairs in Lincoln County are progressing favorably ..." Letter to Carl Schurz. **April 18, 1879.** Indiana Historical Society. Lew Wallace Collection. M0292. Box 4, Folder 9.

_____. "In a recent letter descriptive of the situation in Lincoln County, I alluded to the necessity of breaking up illicit transactions in cattle." **April 25, 1879.** Indiana Historical Society. Lew Wallace Collection. M0292. Box 4, Folder 9.

_____. "I enclose account in duplicate for services in overhauling and removing Territorial archives ..." **May 1, 1879.** Indiana Historical Society. Lew Wallace Collection. M0292. Box 4, Folder 10.

_____. "I have the honor to inform you that all the recent reports, military and otherwise, justify me in saying Lincoln County is enjoying a term of peace." Letter to Carl Schurz. **May 5, 1879.** Indiana Historical Society. Lew Wallace Collection. M0292. Box 4. Folder 10.

_____. "I had the honor a few weeks ago of writing you respecting a balance of contingent fund due this Executive Office ..." **May 5, 1879.** Indiana Historical Society. Lew Wallace Collection. M0292. Box 4. Folder 10.

_____. "Enclosed please find a copy of the report of the commandant at Fort Stanton." Letter to Carl Schurz. **June 11, 1879.** Indiana Historical Society. Lew Wallace Collection. M0292. Box 4. Folder 11. **(Self-serving progress report of quelling disturbances)**

Schurz, Carl. "I have received your letter of the 3d inst., and am glad to know ..." Letter to Lew Wallace. **July 10, 1879.** Indiana Historical Society. Lew Wallace Collection. M0292. Box 4. Folder 12.

Wallace, Lew. "The accompanying document received from Fort Stanton which will explain itself." Letter to Carl Schurz. **July 30, 1879.** Indiana Historical Society. Lew Wallace Collection. M0292. Box 4. Folder 12. **(Describes progress, but calls Dudley Court of Inquiry corrupt)**

Bell, A. "Referring to your letter of the 30th ultimo ..." **August 29, 1879.** Indiana Historical Society. Lew Wallace Collection. M0292. Box 4. Folder 12. **(Acting Secretary of the Interior and Secretary of War George McCrary placate Wallace about the corrupt Court of Inquiry outcome)**

Wallace, Lew. "In reply to the communication of Acting Secretary Bell ..." **September 15, 1879.** Letter to Carl Schurz. Indiana Historical Society. Lew Wallace

Collection. M0292. Box 4. Folder 13. (**On John Jones killing Jim Beckwith, and Bob Olinger killing John Jones**)

_____. "The enclosed communication received yesterday from Mr. Louis Scott, U.S. Consul ..." **December 29, 1879**. Indiana Historical Society. Lew Wallace Collection. M0292. Box 4. Folder 13.

_____. "I have the honor to inform you that the Legislature of this Territory adjourned ..." **February 16, 1880**. Letter to Carl Schurz. Indiana Historical Society. Lew Wallace Collection. M0292. Box 4, Folder 14. (**Important proof of T.B. Catron as head of the Santa Fe Ring, and Wallace's Ring opposition**)

Schurz, Carl. "I have received your letter ..." **May 24, 1880**. Indiana Historical Society. Lew Wallace Collection. M0292. Box 4. Folder 15.

Wallace, Lew. "I have returned from a tour through the counties ..." Letter to Carl Schurz. **July 23, 1880**. Indiana Historical Society. Lew Wallace Collection. M0292. Box 4. Folder 14. (**Reporting on south counties, Victorio, and recommends Ira Leonard for judgeship replacing Warren Bristol.**)

_____. "I have the honor to report that I returned to this city ..." **November 30, 1880**. Letter to Carl Schurz. Indiana Historical Society. Lew Wallace Collection. M0292. Box 4, Folder 14. (**Reports Victorio is dead, but problems with Navajos**)

_____. "From private advices received from Lincoln county ..." **December 7, 1880**. Indiana Historical Society. Lew Wallace Collection. M0292. Box 4. Folder 15. (**Reports pursuit of outlaws by people in Lincoln County**)

_____. "I have private business urgently requiring my presence in New York City ..." Letter to Carl Schurz. **December 14, 1880**. Indiana Historical Society. Lew Wallace Collection. M0292. Box No. 4. Folder 15. (**Mention's - without giving names - the deputy sheriff [Garrett] tracking the "leader of the outlaws" [Billy] for whom Wallace has set a "$500 reward."**)

_____. "I have the honor to submit the following matter for consideration ..." **December 15, 1880**. Indiana Historical Society. Lew Wallace Collection. M0292. Box 4. Folder 15.

SHERMAN, JOHN

Sherman, John. Letter to Governor Lew Wallace. **October 4, 1878**. Indiana Historical Society. Lew Wallace Collection. M0292. Box 3, Folder 15. (**First reference of "outlaw," Billy Bonney, to Governor Wallace.**)

SHIELD, DAVID

Shield, David. "Your letter of the 23rd inst is at hand and content noted ..." Letter to Montegue Leverson. **July 26, 1878**. Interior Department Papers 1850-1907; Appointments Division and Subsequent Actions. Microfilm File Case Number 44-4-8-3. Record Group 48. Microfilm Roll M750. National Archives and Records Administration. U.S. Department of Justice. Washington, D. C.

SPRINGER, FRANK

BIBLIOGRAPHICAL SOURCES

Cleaveland, Norman, *A Synopsis of the Great New Mexico Cover-up*. Self-printed. 1989.

_____. *The Great Santa Fe Cover-up. Based on a Talk given Before the Santa Fe Historical Society on November 1, 1978*. Self-printed. 1982.

_____. *The Morleys - Young Upstarts on the Southwest Frontier*. Albuquerque, New Mexico: Calvin Horn Publisher, Inc. 1971.

Taylor, Morris F. *O. P. McMains and the Maxwell Land Grant Conflict*. Tucson, Arizona: The University of Arizona Press. 1979.

CONTEMPORARY SOURCES (CHRONOLOGICAL)

Middaugh, Asa F. Deposition. **March 31, 1876.** "Exhibit B" in the August 9, 1878 deposition of Frank Springer to Investigator Frank Warner Angel. Frank Warner Angel report titled *In the Matter of the Investigation of the Charges Against S.B. Axtell Governor of New Mexico*. October 3, 1878. Interior Department Papers 1850-1907; Appointments Division and Subsequent Actions. Microfilm Case File No. 44-4-8-3. Record Group 48. Microfilm Roll M750. National Archives and Records Administration. U.S. Department of Interior. Washington, D.C. **(About Catron's malicious prosecution of Ada McPherson Morley as Ring revenge)**

Springer, Frank. "I hope you have received a full account of the Troubles in Lincoln County from your nephew ..." Letter to Senator Rush Clark. **April 9, 1878.** Herman B. Weisner Papers, ca. 1957-1992. New Mexico State University Library at Las Cruces. Rio Grande Historical Collections. Accession No. Ms 0249. Box 4/39. Folder D-6. Folder Name "Frank Springer Letter to Rush Clark." **(Links Santa Fe Ring to murder of J.H. Tunstall)**

_____. "I endorse herewith, directed to the President charges against S.B. Axtell Governor of New Mexico ..." Letter to Secretary of the Interior Carl Schurz. **June 10, 1878.** Microfilm File Case Number 44-4-8-3. Record Group 48. Microfilm No. M750. Roll 1. National Archives and Records Administration. U. S. Department of Justice. Washington, D.C.

_____. Deposition to Investigator Frank Warner Angel. **August 9, 1878.** Frank Warner Angel report titled *In the Matter of the Investigation of the Charges Against S.B. Axtell Governor of New Mexico*. October 3, 1878. Interior Department Papers 1850-1907; Appointments Division and Subsequent Actions. Microfilm Case File No. 44-4-8-3. Record Group 48. Microfilm Roll M750. National Archives and Records Administration. U.S. Department of Interior. Washington, D.C. **(Mentions Catron, Elkins, and the Santa Fe Ring; with Exhibits of letters)**

_____. "I see that my friends of the New Mexican are trying to make themselves, or you, or me, or somebody believe ..." Letter to Lew Wallace. **November 12, 1878.** Indiana Historical Society. Lew Wallace Collection. M0292. Box 3. Folder 17.

No Author. "A man named Springer is in Washington trying to defeat the nomination of Governor Axtell. Springer is a friend of the thugs and thieves of Colfax County." *Santa Fe New Mexican*. **July 6, 1882.** **(About Ring re-instatement of Axtell)**

TAYLOR, GEORGE

Taylor, George. Letter to Lew Wallace. **April 25, 1879.** Indiana Historical Society, Lew Wallace Collection. M0292. Box 4, Folder 9.

TIBBLES, THOMAS HENRY

Cleaveland, Norman. *The Morleys - Young Upstarts on the Southwest Frontier.* Albuquerque, New Mexico: Calvin Horn Publisher, Inc. 1971. **(Pages 89-91 describe his role as a populist political crusader like his sister Mary Tibbles McPherson.)**

THORNTON, WILLIAM T.

Thornton, W.T. "Your favors received. We will try and have the matter of Mrs. Wilson's estate at Albuquerque attended to for your Bates County friends." Letter to John J. Cockrell, Esq. **January 16, 1886.** Herman B. Weisner Papers, ca. 1957-1992. New Mexico State University Library at Las Cruces. Rio Grande Historical Collections. Accession No. Ms 0249. Box 12. Folder S-5. Folder Name: "Catron, Thornton, & Clancy Letterhead." **(Catron's law partner discloses the Ring's planned malicious prosecution in Lincoln County)**

933

_____. "This communication to the *Citizen* was prepared in your office, and at your dictation." *Santa Fe Daily New Mexican*. **September 11, 1896.** Reprinting and debunking T.B Catron's anonymous letter of September 11, 1896 to the *Albuquerque Daily Citizen* of September 11, 1896. Quoted by Victor Westphall, *Thomas Benton Catron and His Era*. Page 262. (**Thornton confronts Catron's anonymous defamatory letter about him**)

TOLBY, FRANKLIN J.

BIOGRAPHICAL SOURCES

Cleaveland, Norman. *The Morleys - Young Upstarts on the Southwest Frontier*. Albuquerque, New Mexico: Calvin Horn Publisher, Inc. 1971.

Taylor, Morris F. *O.P. McMains and the Maxwell Land Grant Conflict*. Tucson, Arizona: The University of Arizona Press. 1979. (**Traces origins of the Santa Fe Ring**)

CONTEMPORARY SOURCES (CHRONOLOGICAL)

Morley, William Raymond and Frank Springer. On Oscar McMains's citizen's Meeting. *Cimarron News and Press*. **November 10, 1875.** In Mary McPherson, Letters and Petitions to President Rutherford B. Hayes re: Removal Governor Axtell and the Santa Fe Ring. 1977. Interior Department Papers 1850-1907; Appointments Division and Subsequent Actions. Microfilm File Case Number 44-4-8-3. **Record Group 48.** Microfilm Roll M750. National Archives and Records Administration. (**Colfax County citizens meeting on F.J. Tolby murder by Santa Fe Ring.**)

_____. " 'The Territory of Elkins.' Assassination of Supposed Sun Correspondent. The Murder of the Rev. F.J. Tolby in New Mexico. A Probate Judge Accused of Complicity in the Crime. Indignation Meeting." New York *Weekly Sun*. **December 22, 1875.** Interior Department Papers 1850-1907; Appointments Division and Subsequent Actions. Microfilm Roll M750. National Archives and Records Administration. Record Group 48. Microfilm Case File Number 44-4-8-3. U.S. Department of Interior. Washington, D. C. (**From May 1, 1877 submission to President Rutherford B. Hates as "Mary E. McPherson and W.B. Matchett 'Make certain charges against the U.S. Officials in the Territory of New Mexico.' "**)

No Author. Report on murder trial for Franklin Tolby. Pueblo, Colorado *Chieftain*, May 25, 1876 quoting from *Daily New Mexican*, **May 1, 1876.** From Morris F. Taylor. *O.P. McMains and the Maxwell Land Grant Conflict*. Tucson, Arizona: The University of Arizona Press. 1979. Page 49. (**Ring-biased jury instructions by Judge Henry Waldo**)

Lambert, J.J. "At It Again." Pueblo, Colorado, *Enterprise and Chronicle*. **April 21, 1877.** Interior Department Papers 1850-1907; Appointments Division and Subsequent Actions. Microfilm File Case Number 44-4-8-3. Record Group 48. Microfilm No. M750. Roll 1. National Archives and Records Administration. U.S. Department of Justice. Washington, D.C. (**Description of Santa Fe Ring control of courts and malicious prosecution of opponents like Oscar McMains in the Franklin Tolby murder; used in: "W.B. Matchett and Mary E. McPherson 'Make Certain Charges Against the U.S. Officials in the Territory of New Mexico.' " Letter to President Rutherford B. Hayes. Received and filed May 1, 1877. Interior Department Papers 1850-1907; Appointments Division and Subsequent Actions. Microfilm File Case Number 44-4-8-3. Record Group 48. Microfilm No. M750. Roll 1. National Archives and Records Administration. U. S. Department of Justice. Washington, D.C.**)

McPherson, Mary and W.B. Matchett. "To The President. Please make the enclosed part of the evidence in the case of "Charges Against New Mexican Officials"

Letter to President Rutherford B. Hayes. **May 3, 1877.** McPherson, Mary E. Letters and Petitions to President Rutherford B. Hayes re: Removal Governor Axtell and the Santa Fe Ring. Interior Department Papers 1850-1907; Appointments Division and Subsequent Actions. Microfilm File Case Number 44-4-8-3. Record Group 48. Microfilm Roll M750. National Archives and Records Administration. U.S. Department of Justice. Washington, D.C. **(Addendum to their May, 1877 charges)**

McPherson, Mary and W.B. Matchett. "The Secretary of the Interior, Sir – Accompanying please find copy of charges, &c., against S.B. Axtell, Governor, and other New Mexican Officials ..." "Charges Against New Mexican Officials." Letter to Secretary of the Interior Carl Schurz. **May 5, 1877.** McPherson, Mary E. Letters and Petitions to President Rutherford B. Hayes re: Removal Governor Axtell and the Santa Fe Ring. Interior Department Papers 1850-1907; Appointments Division and Subsequent Actions. Microfilm File Case Number 44-4-8-3. Record Group 48. Microfilm Roll M750. National Archives and Records Administration. U.S. Department of Justice. Washington, D.C.

TUNSTALL, JOHN HENRY

BIOGRAPHICAL SOURCES

Nolan, Frederick W. *The Life and Death of John Henry Tunstall.* Albuquerque, New Mexico: The University of New Mexico Press. 1965.

CONTEMPORARY SOURCES (CHRONOLOGICAL)

Tunstall, John Henry. "A Tax-Payer's Complaint ... January 18, 1878." Mesilla *Independent.* **January 26, 1878. (Exposé of William Brady, James Dolan, and John Riley for tax fraud; T.B. Catron then paid that bill)**

Dolan, James J. "Answer to A Tax-Payer's Complaint." Mesilla *Independent.* **January 29, 1878. (Response to J.H. Tunstall's tax exposé)**

Rynerson, William. "Friends Riley & Dolan, Lincoln N.M. I have just received letters from you mailed 10th inst." Letter to James Dolan and John Riley. **February 14, 1878.** Copy as Exhibit B in June 6, 1878 deposition of Alexander McSween. Frank Warner Angel report. *In the Matter of the Examination of the Causes and Circumstances of the Death of John H. Tunstall a British Subject.* Report filed October 4, 1878. Interior Department Papers 1850-1907; Appointments Division and Subsequent Actions. Microfilm File Case Number 44-4-8-3. Record Group 48. Microfilm No. M750. Roll 1. National Archives and Records Administration. U. S. Department of Justice. Washington, D.C. (James J. Dolan Deposition. June 20, 1878. pp. 235-247.) **(Planned killing of J.H. Tunstall)**

Wilson, John, George B. Barker, Robert M. Gilbert, John Newcomb, Samuel Smith, Benjamin Ellis. "We the undersigned Justice of the Peace and Coroners Jury who sat upon the inquest held this 19th day of February 1878 on the body of John H. Tunstall ..." Coroner's Jury Report for John Tunstall. **February 19, 1878. (Naming as murderers, among others, James Dolan, Frank Baker, Jessie Evans, William Morton, and George Hindman)**

Springer, Frank. "I hope you have received a full account of the Troubles in Lincoln County from your nephew ..." Letter to Senator Rush Clark. **April 9, 1878.** Herman B. Weisner Papers, ca. 1957-1992. New Mexico State University Library at Las Cruces. Rio Grande Historical Collections. Accession No. Ms 0249. Box 4/39. Folder D-6. Folder Name "Frank Springer Letter to Rush Clark." **(Links Santa Fe Ring to murder of J.H. Tunstall)**

Angel, Frank Warner. *In the Matter of the Examination of the Causes and Circumstances of the Death of John H. Tunstall a British Subject.* Report filed **October 4, 1878.** Angel Report. Records of the Justice Department. Record Group 60. Class 44 Litigation Files. Container 21. National Archives and Records

Administration. U.S. Department of Justice. Washington, D.C. or Microfilm File Case Number 44-4-8-3. Record Group 48. Microfilm Roll No. M750. Roll 1. National Archives and Records Administration. U.S. Department of Justice. Washington, D.C.

_____. *In the Matter of the Lincoln County Troubles. To the. Honorable Charles Devens, Attorney General.* **October 4, 1878.** Angel Report. Microfilm Case File No. 44-4-8-3. Record Group 48. Microfilm Roll No. M750. National Archives and Records Administration. U.S. Department of Justice. Washington, D.C.

VICTORIO

Ball, Eve and James Kaywaykla. *In the Days of Victorio. Recollections of a Warm Springs Apache.* Tucson, Arizona: The University of Arizona Press. 1997.

Thrapp, Dan L. *Victorio and the Mimbres Apaches.* Norman: University of Oklahoma Press. 1974.

No Author. "Glory! Hallelujah!! Victorio Killed." Wednesday, October 20, 1880. *Thirty-Four Newspaper.* Las Cruces, New Mexico. Page 1, Column 4.

WALDO, HENRY

Morley William Raymond. "I was astonished beyond measure at your proceedings, and have fears as to the result ..." Letter to Mary McPherson. **March 6, 1877.** McPherson, Mary E. Letters and Petitions to President Rutherford B. Hayes re: Removal Governor Axtell and the Santa Fe Ring. Interior Department Papers 1850-1907; Appointments Division and Subsequent Actions. Microfilm File Case Number 44-4-8-3. Record Group 48. Microfilm Roll M750. National Archives and Records Administration. U.S. Department of Justice. Washington, D. C. (**Hopes she can help fight against Santa Fe Ring, in Mary McPherson's "Charges Against U.S. Officials in the Territory of New Mexico."**)

Morley, William Raymond. "Your letter of the 7th came last night and it was a good long newsy letter ..." Letter to wife, Ada McPherson Morley. **August 15, 1878.** Collection of Norman Cleaveland. Quoted in Norman Cleaveland, *The Morleys: Young Upstarts in the Southwest.* Albuquerque, New Mexico: Calvin Horn Publisher, Inc. 1971. Pages 152-155. (**Waldo's link to Catron and Elkins**)

Waldo, Henry. *Proceedings of a Court of Inquiry in the Case of Lt. Col. N.A.M. Dudley (May 2,1879 – July 5, 1879).* File No. QQ1284. (Boxes 3304, 3305, 3305A); Court Martial Files 1809-1894. Records of the Office of the Judge Advocate General - Army. Record Group 153. Old Military and Civil Branch. National Archives and Records Administration. Washington, D.C. (**Defense attorney for Dudley**)

WALLACE, LEW

BIOGRAPHICAL SOURCES

Grant, Ulysses S. "General Lew Wallace and General McCook at Shiloh: Memoranda on the Civil War." *Battles and Leaders of the Civil War. Century* magazine. 30 [n.s. 8], 776. August, 1885. Vol. I, Page 468. (**Quote damning Wallace for Shiloh**)

_____. *Personal Memoirs.* New York: Charles L. Webster. 1885. (**Same quote from *Century* magazine damning Lew Wallace for Shiloh**)

Jones, Oakah L. "Lew Wallace: Hoosier Governor of Territorial New Mexico. 1878-81." *New Mexico Historical Review. 59(1)* (January, 1984).

Morsberger, Robert E. and Katherine M. Morsberger. *Lew Wallace: Militant Romantic.* New York: McGraw-Hill Book Company. 1980.

Paarlberg, Larry. Height of Lew Wallace. (Personal communication. Head of Lew Wallace Museum, Crawfordsville, Indiana. 2014) (**Height from Civil War Records is 5'10" - 5'11"**)

Perret, Geoffrey. *Ulysses S. Grant: Soldier and President.* New York: Random House. 1997. (**Pages 170-171, 185, 188, 191**)

Stephens, Gail. "Shadow of Shiloh: Major General Lew Wallace in the Civil War." Indianapolis: Indiana Historical Society Press. 2010.

Wallace, Lew. *An Autobiography. Vol. I.* New York and London: Harper and Brothers Publishers. 1997.

_____. *An Autobiography. Vol. II.* New York and London: Harper and Brothers Publishers. 1997.

AUTHORSHIP OF BOOKS

Wallace, Lew. *An Autobiography. Vol. I.* New York and London: Harper and Brothers Publishers. 1997.

_____. *An Autobiography. Vol. II.* New York and London: Harper and Brothers Publishers. 1997.

_____. *Ben-Hur: A Tale of the Christ.* New York: Harper & Brothers, Franklin Square. 1880.

_____. *Commodus: An Historical Play.* 1872. Unpublished manuscript. Wallace MSS., Lilly Library, Indiana University, Bloomington, Indiana.

_____. *Prince of India: Or Why Constantinople Fell.* 1893. Manuscript. Wallace MSS., Lilly Library, Indiana University, Bloomington, Indiana.

_____. *The Fair God: A Tale of the Conquest of Mexico.* 1873. Manuscript. Wallace MSS., Lilly Library, Indiana University, Bloomington, Indiana.

COLLECTED PAPERS OF

Wallace, Lew. Collected Papers. Microfilm Project Sponsored by the National Historical Publications Commission. Microfilm Roll No. 99. Santa Fe, New Mexico: State of New Mexico Records Center and Archives. 1974.

_____. Lew and Susan Wallace Collection. Indiana Historical Society. M0292.

_____. Collected Papers. Lilly Library. Bloomington, Indiana.

SECRETLY RECEIVED ANGEL NOTEBOOK ON SANTA FE RING

Angel, Frank Warner. "To Gov. Lew Wallace, Santa Fe, N. M., 1878." Notebook. **1878.** Indiana Historical Society. Lew Wallace Collection. M0292. Microfilm No. F372. (**Original missing, copy on microfilm; Notebook prepared for Lew Wallace listing names for Lincoln County and the Santa Fe Ring**)

Theisen, Lee Scott. "Frank Warner Angel's Notes on New Mexico Territory, 1878." *Arizona and the West: A Quarterly Journal of History.* Winter 1976. Volume 18. Number 4. Pages 333-370. (**About the Angel notebook**)

SECRETLY RECEIVED BOOKLET ON SANTA FE RING

McPherson, Mary and W.B. Matchett. *"In the Matter of Charges vs. Gov. S.B. Axtell and Other New Mexico Officials. Submitted to the Departments of the Interior and Justice.* **August, 1877.** Printed as a 31 page booklet. No publisher listed. Indiana Historical Society. Lew Wallace Collection. M0292. Box 3. Folder 20. (**Exposé about Santa Fe Ring, Catron, and Elkins; in Lew Wallace's possession**)

OATH OF OFFICE OF (NEW MEXICO TERRITORY GOVERNORSHIP)

Wallace, Lew. "Oath of Office, Governor, New Mexico Territory. **October 1, 1878.** Indiana Historical Society. Lew Wallace Collection. DNA; RG 48, M364. [Copy in New Mexico Archives: Records of Secretary of Territory of New Mexico (Acc# 1971-001), Series B-02: Executive Record Book 2, 1867-1882.]

AMNESTY PROCLAMATION OF

Wallace, Lew. "Proclamation by the Governor." **November 13, 1878**. Indiana Historical Society. Lew Wallace Collection. M0292. Box 3. Folder 17. (**Amnesty Proclamation for Lincoln County War fighters**)

PARDONS ISSUED AS GOVERNOR

Wallace, Lew. "Whereas it has been made known to the undersigned that Ursula Montoya ..." **October 24, 1878**. Indiana Historical Society. Lew Wallace Collection. M0292. Box 3. Folder 16. (**Pardon granted with affidavit**)

_____. Pardon of Jacob B. Matthews, William B. Powell, John Long, and John Hurlie et al. April, 1879 District Court. Filed **May 1, 1879**. (Under Attorneys S.B. Newcomb, Sidney Wilson, and Catron & Thornton). Herman B. Weisner Papers, ca. 1957-1992. New Mexico State University Library at Las Cruces. Rio Grande Historical Society Collection. Accession No. Ms 0249. Box 1. Folder 4. Folder Name: "Amnesty." (**Condoned pardon for Ringites**)

_____. Pardon of Marian Turner. April, 1879 District Court. Filed **May 1, 1879**. (Under Attorneys Catron & Thornton and S.B. Newcomb). Herman B. Weisner Papers, ca. 1957-1992. New Mexico State University Library at Las Cruces. Rio Grande Historical Society Collection. Accession No. Ms 0249. Box 1. Folder 4. Folder Name: "Amnesty." (**Condoned pardon for a Ringman**)

DUDLEY COURT OF INQUIRY TESTIMONY

Wallace, Lew. Testimony in Court of Inquiry for Lieutenant Colonel N.A M. Dudley. **May 12-15, 1879**. *Proceedings of a Court of Inquiry in the Case of Lt. Col. N.A.M. Dudley (May 2,1879 – July 5, 1879)*. File No. QQ1284. (Boxes 3304, 3305, 3305A); Court Martial Files 1809-1894. Records of the Office of the Judge Advocate General – Army. Record Group 153. Old Military and Civil Branch. National Archives and Records Administration. Washington, D.C.

SPEECHES

Wallace, Lew. "Governor's Message to N.M. Territorial Legislature." **No month, 1879**. Indiana Historical Society. Lew Wallace Collection. M0292. Box 10. Folder 11.

INTERVIEW NOTES ON BILLY BONNEY'S STATEMENTS

Wallace, Lew. "Statements by Kid, made Sunday night **March 23, 1879**." (Cover sheet reads: "Fort Stanton, March 20, 1879. William Bonney ("Kid") relative to arrangement with him." Indiana Historical Society. Lew Wallace Collection. M0292. Box 4. Folder 6.

REWARD NOTICES FOR WILLIAM BONNEY

Wallace, Lew. "Billy the Kid: $500 Reward." Las Vegas *Gazette*. **December 22, 1880**.

_____. "Billy the Kid. $500 Reward." May 3, 1881. *Daily New Mexican*. Vol. X, No. 33. Pages 1, c. 3.

REWARD POSTERS FOR WILLIAM BONNEY

Greene, Chas. W. "To the New Mexican Printing and Publishing Company." **May 20, 1881**. (Bill to Lew Wallace for Reward posters for "Kid"). Indiana Historical Society. Lew Wallace Collection. M0292. Box 4. Folder 18.

_____. "I enclose a bill ..." Letter to Lew Wallace for "Kid" wanted posters. **June 2, 1881**. Indiana Historical Society Lew Wallace Collection. M0292. Box 4, Folder 18.

DEATH WARRANT FOR WILLIAM BONNEY

Wallace, Lew. "To the Sheriff of Lincoln County, Greeting ..." **April 30, 1881.** Indiana Historical Society. Lew Wallace Collection. M0292. Box 9, Folder 11.

LETTERS (ALPHABETICAL, THEN CHRONOLOGICAL)

FROM SECRETARY OF STATE JAMES GILLESPIE BLAINE

Blaine, James. "The President, by and with the advice and consent of the Senate, having appointed you to be Minister Resident of the United States to Turkey ..." Official appointment to Lew Wallace. **June 4, 1881.** Indiana Historical Society. Lew Wallace Collection. M0292. Box 4. Folder 18.

TO AND FROM WILLIAM BONNEY (See William H. Bonney)
TO AND FROM CAPTAIN HENRY CARROLL

Wallace, Lew. "As to your question as to where Speaks can be found ..." **March 6, 1879.** Indiana Historical Society. Lew Wallace Collection. M0292. Box 4. Folder 4.

_____. "Under the circumstances, particularly in the absence here of suitable cells for safekeeping of Jesse Evans, Jacob B. Matthews and William Campbell ..." Letter to Henry Carroll. **March 10, 1879.** Indiana Historical Society. Lew Wallace Collection. M0292. Box 4. Folder 4.

_____. "J.J. Dolan was down here tonight. Arrest him upon his return ..." Letter to Henry Carroll. **March 10, 1879.** Indiana Historical Society. Lew Wallace Collection. M0292. Box 4. Folder 4.

_____. "I beg to submit to you a list of persons whom it is necessary, in my judgment, to arrest ..." Letter to Henry Carroll. **March 11, 1879.** Indiana Historical Society. Lew Wallace Collection. M0292. Box 4. Folder 5. (**Lists as 14, "The Kid" – William Bonney; also lists Jessie Evans, Yginio Salazar**)

_____. "Upon reflection, I am of opinion that if Col. Dudley is really going to Fort Union ..." Letter to Henry Carroll. **March 11, 1879.** Indiana Historical Society. Lew Wallace Collection. M0292. Box 4. Folder 5. (**Advises not to send Evans, Campbell, Matthews, and Dolan to Fort Union because of N.A.M. Dudley being there**)

_____. "I sent you herewith a complete copy of all the cattle brands regularly recorded in the clerk's office of Lincoln County." **March 12, 1879.** Indiana Historical Society. Lew Wallace Collection. M0292. Box 4. Folder 5.

Carroll, Henry. General Hatch has 2nd Lieutenant Bullis ..." **March 13, 1879.** Indiana Historical Society. Lew Wallace Collection. M0292. Box 4. Folder 5.

Wallace, Lew. "With Evans and Campbell at large ..." Letter to Henry Carroll. **March 19, 1879.** Indiana Historical Society. Lew Wallace Collection. M0292. Box 4. Folder 6.

FROM, TO, AND ABOUT ATTORNEY HUSTON CHAPMAN

Chapman, Huston I. "You will please pardon me for presuming so much upon your kindness ..." **October 24, 1878.** Indiana Historical Society. Lew Wallace Collection. M0292. Box 3. Folder 16.

Wallace, Lew. "I enclose you a copy of a letter from Las Vegas ..." Letter to Edward Hatch. **October 28, 1878.** Indiana Historical Society. Lew Wallace Collection. M0292. Box 3. Folder 16.

Chapman, Huston I. "You must pardon me for so often presuming upon your kindness ..." **November 29, 1878.** Indiana Historical Society. Lew Wallace Collection. M0292. Box 3. Folder 18.

TO GENERAL J.J. DANA, CHIEF QUARTERMASTER DISTRICT OF NEW MEXICO

Wallace, Lew. "It will be necessary for me to go shortly to various parts of the Territory ..." Letter to J.J. Dana. **February 11, 1879**. Indiana Historical Society. Lew Wallace Collection. M0292. Box 4. Folder 2. (**Requests military escort**)

FROM DAN DEDRICK

Dedrick, Dan. "I have been under an arrest for six days ..." Letter to Lew Wallace. **April 5, 1879**. Indiana Historical Society. Lew Wallace Collection. M0292. Box 4. Folder 8. (**Says he was not told his arrest charges**)

FROM JAMES J. DOLAN

Dolan, James. "On my arrival at Fort Stanton, I repeated Your Explanation &c to the Comd'g Officer (Gen'l Dudley) ..." Letter to Lew Wallace. **December 31, 1878**. Indiana Historical Society. Lew Wallace Collection M0292. Box 3. Folder 19.

TO AND FROM COMMANDER N.A.M. DUDLEY

Dudley, Nathan Augustus Monroe. "I am in receipt of a copy of letter written by one H.I. Chapman, calling himself the Attorney ..." **November 9, 1878**. Letter to Lew Wallace. From *Proceedings of a Court of Inquiry in the Case of Lt. Col. N.A.M. Dudley (May 2,1879 - July 5, 1879)*. File No. QQ1284. (Boxes 3304, 3305, 3305A); Court Martial Files 1809-1894. Records of the Office of the Judge Advocate General – Army. Record Group 153. Old Military and Civil Branch. National Archives and Records Administration. Washington, D.C. (**Forwarding the Susan McSween affidavits in answer to the charges made by Chapman**)

Wallace, Lew. "Your favor containing the duplicate accounts of the messenger who posted the President's Proclamation ..." Letter to N.A.M. Dudley. **November 30, 1878**. Indiana Historical Society. Lew Wallace Collection. M0292. Box 3. Folder 18.

Dudley, Nathan Augustus Monroe. "An Open Letter, By Lieut. Col. N.A.M. Dudley, 9th Cavalry, to His Excellency Governor Lew Wallace." Letter to Lew Wallace. Santa Fe *Weekly New Mexican*. **December 14, 1878**. Reprinted in *Mesilla News*. December 21, 1878. As Exhibit 13 from *Proceedings of a Court of Inquiry in the Case of Lt. Col. N.A.M. Dudley (May 2,1879 - July 5, 1879)*. File No. QQ1284. (Boxes 3304, 3305, 3305A); Court Martial Files 1809-1894. Records of the Office of the Judge Advocate General - Army. Record Group 153. Old Military and Civil Branch. National Archives and Records Administration. Washington, D.C. (**Attacks Wallace's Amnesty Proclamation as applying to the military**)

Wallace, Lew. "The public interests with which I am charged make it, in my judgment, exceedingly improper for me to answer publicly your letters in the New Mexican ..." Letter to N.A.M. Dudley and other Fort Stanton officers. **December 16, 1878**. Indiana Historical Society. Lew Wallace Collection. M0292. Box 3. Folder 19.

Dudley, Nathan Augustus Monroe Dudley. "This being regular report day, I respectfully state ..." **March 1, 1879**. Indiana Historical Society. Lew Wallace Collection. M0292. Box 4. Folder 4. (**Blaming Lincoln County "troubles" on rustlers**)

TO SECRETARY OF STATE WILLIAM M. EVETTS

Wallace, Lew. "I have the honor to acknowledge receipt by telegram of the President's Proclamation ..." **October 9, 1878**. Letter to William Evetts. Indiana Historical Society. Lew Wallace Collection. M0292. Box 3. Folder 15.

_____. "I take the liberty of sending you a copy of the Democratic organ of New Mexico ..." Letter to William Evetts. **November 18, 1878.** Indiana Historical Society. Lew Wallace Collection. M0292. Box 9. Folder 10. (**Earliest attempt to leave New Mexico Territory**)

TO ATTORNEY EUGENE A. FISKE

Wallace, Lew. "I have your several letters, including the last one of the 3rd inst." Letter to Eugene Fiske. **November 6, 1897.** Indiana Historical Society. Lew Wallace Collection. AC233. Box 1. Folder 7. (part of 1981 addition) (**About T.B. Catron's control over New Mexicans**)

FROM PRESIDENT JAMES ABRAM GARFIELD

Garfield, James Abram. "I have, this morning, finished reading "Ben-Hur" ...." Letter to Lew Wallace. **April 19, 1881.** Indiana Historical Society. Lew Wallace Collection. M0292. Box 4. Folder 17.

TO SHERIFF PATRICK F. GARRETT

Wallace, Lew. "To the Sheriff of Lincoln County, New Mexico, Greeting ..." **April 30, 1881.** Indiana Historical Society. Lew Wallace Collection. M0292. Box 9. Folder 11. (**Death Warrant for William Bonney**)

TO MESCALERO APACHE AGENT FREDERICK C. GODFROY

Wallace, Lew. "You can be of the greatest possible help to me in the effort now making to catch the thieves and murderers in this part of the Territory ..." **March 12, 1879.** Indiana Historical Society. Lew Wallace Collection. M0292. Box 4. Folder 5. (**Wants Indian "guides"**)

TO GENERAL ULYSSES S. GRANT

Wallace, Lew. "About a year after the battle of Pittsburgh Landing ..." **February 28, 1868.** Letter to Ulysses S. Grant. Indiana Historical Society. Lew Wallace Collection. M0292. Box 3. Folder 4. (**Wallace trying to justify himself for the Battle of Shiloh**)

FROM AND TO GENERAL EDWARD HATCH

Wallace, Lew. "You will oblige me very much ..." Letter to Edward Hatch. **October 20, 1878.** Indiana Historical Society. Lew Wallace Collection. M0292. Box 3. Folder 16. (**Follow-up on President Hayes's October 7, 1878 Proclamation**)
_____. "I think all that is needed now for the thorough pacification of Lincoln County is ..." Letter to Edward Hatch. **October 26, 1878.** Indiana Historical Society. Lew Wallace Collection. M0292. Box 3. Folder 16.
_____. "I enclose you a copy of a letter from Las Vegas ..." Letter to Edward Hatch. **October 28, 1878.** Indiana Historical Society. Lew Wallace Collection. M0292. Box 3. Folder 16. (**About Huston Chapman**)
_____. "In a communication, dated October 28. inst., I requested, for reasons stated, a safe-guard for Mrs. McSween ..." Letter to Edward Hatch. **November 9, 1878.** Indiana Historical Society. Lew Wallace Collection. M0292. Box 3. Folder 17.
_____. "I am in receipt of Col. Dudley's reply to the charges against him ..." Letter to Edward Hatch. **November 14, 1878.** Indiana Historical Society. Lew Wallace Collection. M0292. Box 3, Folder 17. (**Has quote: "the "reply is perfectly satisfactory"**)
Wallace, Lew. "I am constrained to request that Lieut Col. N.A.M. Dudley, Commanding at Fort Stanton, be relieved ..." **December 7, 1878.** Indiana

Historical Society. Lew Wallace Collection. M0292. Box 3, Folder 18. (**Removal of Dudley requested**)

Hatch, Edward. "The men Scurlock & Bowdrey at Sumner ..." **February 1, 1879.** Letter to Lew Wallace. Indiana Historical Society. Lew Wallace Collection. M0292. Box 4, Folder 4.

Wallace, Lew. "I have information that William Campbell, J.B. Matthews, and Jesse Evans were of the party engaged in the killing ..." Letter to Edward Hatch. **March 5, 1879.** Indiana Historical Society. Lew Wallace Collection. M0292. Box 4, Folder 4.

Hatch, Edward. Letter to Lew Wallace. **March 6, 1879.** Indiana Historical Society. Lew Wallace Collection. M0292. Box 4, Folder 4.

Wallace, Lew. "In your communication today, speaking of the arrest of Campbell ..." Letter to Edward Hatch. **March 6, 1879.** Indiana Historical Society. Lew Wallace Collection. M0292. Box 4, Folder 4.

_____. "I have reliable information that J.A. Scurlock and Charles Bowdre are now at a ranch called Taiban ..." **March 6, 1879.** Indiana Historical Society. Lew Wallace Collection. M0292. Box 4, Folder 4.

_____. "I have just ascertained that 'The Kid' is at a place called Las Tablas ..." **March 6, 1879.** Indiana Historical Society. Lew Wallace Collection. M0292. Box 9, Folder 10. (**Written on dead John Tunstall's letterhead stationery**)

_____. "I have the honor to repeat the request made on a former occasion that Lt. Col. N.A.M. Dudley be relieved of the command ..." **March 7, 1879.** Letter to Edward Hatch. Indiana Historical Society. Lew Wallace Collection. M0292. Box 4, Folder 4.

Hatch, Edward. "Lieutenant Colonel N.A.M. Dudley is hereby relieved from command and duty ..." Special Field Order 2. **March 8, 1879.** Indiana Historical Society. Lew Wallace Collection. M0292. Box 4, Folder 4. (**Wallace removes Dudley**)

Wallace, Lew. "I beg leave to request that you allow Captain Carroll to remain ... in command of Fort Stanton." Letter to Edward Hatch. **March 9, 1879.** Indiana Historical Society. Lew Wallace Collection. M0292. Box 4, Folder 4.

Hatch, Edward. "Col. Dudley has received his order and disobeys the order ..." **March 11, 1879.** Indiana Historical Society. Lew Wallace Collection. M0292. Box 4, Folder 5.

TO AND FROM PRESIDENT RUTHERFORD B. HAYES

Wallace, Lew. "I avail myself of your request this morning. It is hardly necessary to give reasons for a preference of the Italian mission ..." Letter to Rutherford B. Hayes. **March 9, 1877.** Indiana Historical Society. Lew Wallace Collection. M0292. Box 3. Folder 13. (**Desired ambassadorships**)

_____. "The feuds recently in Lincoln county, New Mexico, left a large many thieves and murderers, who, with others of like class since added to their number, are now confederated for plunder." Letter to Rutherford B. Hayes. **March 31, 1879.** Indiana Historical Society. Lew Wallace Collection. M0292. Box 4. Folder 7. (**Wants martial law against confederacy of outlaws**)

Hayes, Rutherford B. "We are greatly obliged by your kindness." Letter to Lew Wallace. **January 9, 1881.** Indiana Historical Society. Lew Wallace Collection. M0292. Box 4. Folder 16. (**Thanking for gift of *Ben-Hur***)

TO HENRY HOLT (*BEN-HUR* PUBLISHER)

Wallace, Lew. "How are the books selling?" December 15, 1880. **December 14, 1880.** Indiana Historical Society. Lew Wallace Collection. M0292. Box 4. Folder 15. (**About *Ben-Hur***)

TO JUDGE ADVOCATE CAPTAIN HENRY H. HUMPHREYS

Wallace, Lew. "Since requesting March 7, 1879 that Lt. Col. N.A.M. Dudley be relieved ..." **May 10, 1879.** Indiana Historical Society. Lew Wallace Collection. M0292. Box 4. Folder 10.

TO MINISTER OF JUSTICE JOSÉ M. IGLESIAS

Wallace, Lew. "With permission we desire respectfully to submit for the consideration of your government ..." **October 30, 1866.** Indiana Historical Society. Lew Wallace Collection. M0292. Box 2. Folder 16.

TO PRESIDENT BENITO JUAREZ

Wallace, Lew. "I have the honor to submit for your consideration the following propositions ..." **October 22, 1866.** Indiana Historical Society. Lew Wallace Collection. M0292. Box 2. Folder 16.

TO LINCOLN COUNTY SHERIFF GEORGE KIMBRELL

Wallace, Lew. "The duty of keeping the peace in the county and arresting offenders is devolved by the law upon you ..." **April 2, 1879.** Indiana Historical Society. Lew Wallace Collection. Box 4, Folder 8.

FROM ARCHBISHOP OF SANTA FE J.B. LAMY

Lamy, J.B. "Permit me to thank you for your fine book, Ben-Hur ..." **March 17, 1881.** Indiana Historical Society. Lew Wallace Collection. Box 4, Folder 16.

TO AND FROM IRA E. LEONARD

Wallace, Lew. "I enclose a paper, signed by all the leading attorneys ..." Letter to Carl Schurz. **November 13, 1878.** Indiana Historical Society. Lew Wallace Collection. M0292. Box 3. Folder 17. **(Urging judgeship for Ira Leonard)**

Leonard, Ira E. "You have undoubtedly learned ere this of the assassination of H.I. Chapman ..." **February 24, 1879.** Indiana Historical Society. Lew Wallace Collection. M0292. Box 4. Folder 3. **(Announcing Chapman murder)**

Wallace, Lew. "It is important to take steps to protect the coming court." Letter to Ira Leonard. **April 6, 1879.** Indiana Historical Society. Lew Wallace Collection. Box 4, Folder 8.

_____. "Your favors both received. The arrest of Wilson was a blow at the right time ..." **April 9, 1879.** Indiana Historical Society. Lew Wallace Collection. M0292. Box 4. Folder 9. **(With quote: "To work trying to do a little good, but with the world against you, requires the will of a martyr")**

Leonard, Ira E. "I was disappointed at not seeing you when I went to the Fort." Letter to Lew Wallace. **April 12, 1879.** Indiana Historical Society. Lew Wallace Collection. M0292. Box 4. Folder 9. **(Reports seeing hard looking characters in Lincoln before court)**

Wallace, Lew. "Your favor, with the prisoner received." Letter to Ira Leonard. **April 13, 1879.** Indiana Historical Society. Lew Wallace Collection. M0292. Box 4. Folder 9. **(About the writs of habeas corpus being made to free his Fort Stanton prisoners)**

Leonard, Ira. "Yours was received last night ..." Letter to Lew Wallace. **April 13, 1879.** Indiana Historical Society. Lew Wallace Collection. M0292. Box 4. Folder 9. **(Enforcing vagrancy and gun laws in Lincoln)**

Leonard, Ira. "The air is filled to night with "rumors of wars ..." Letter to Lew Wallace. **April 20, 1879.** Indiana Historical Society. Lew Wallace Collection. M0292. Box 4, Folder 9. **(Quote on D.A. Rynerson: "He is bent on going for the Kid")**

_____. "When you left here I promised to write you concerning events transpiring here ..." Letter to Lew Wallace. **May 20, 1878 [sic - 79].** Indiana Historical

Society. Lew Wallace Collection. M0292. Box 4. Folder 10. (**Quote: Murphy-Dolan party as: "part and parcel of the Santa Fe ring that has been so long an incubus on the government of this territory."**)

_____. "I write to you with pencil because I am laboring for breath ..." Letter to Lew Wallace. **May 23, 1879**. Indiana Historical Society. Lew Wallace Collection. M0292. Box 4. Folder 11. (**Quote: "we are pouring the 'hot shot' into Dudley." With enclosed letter of May 20, 1879**)

_____. "Dudley commenced on the defense Tuesday afternoon ..." Letter to Wallace. **June 6, 1879**. Indiana Historical Society. Lew Wallace Collection. M0292. Box 4. Folder 11. (**With quote: "I am thoroughly and completely disgusted with their proceedings."**)

_____. "Yours of the 7th inst reached me ..." Letter to Lew Wallace. **June 13, 1879**. Indiana Historical Society. Lew Wallace Collection. M0292. Box 4. Folder 11. (**Important quotes: "... they would not enter our objections ..." "... would not allow us to show the conspiracy formed with Dolan beforehand ..." "I tell you Governor as long as the present incumbent occupies the bench all that Grand Juries may do to bring to justice these men every effort will be thwarted by him and the sympathizers ..."**)

TO COLONEL ABSALOM H. MARKLAND

Wallace, Lew. "Our mutual friend, M. Hinds, who will hand you this ..." Letter to A.H. Markland. **November 14, 1878**. Indiana Historical Society. Lew Wallace Collection. M0292. Box 3. Folder 17. (**Fully aware of the Santa Fe Ring and its attempt to remove him as governor**)

TO AND FROM SECRETARY OF WAR GEORGE W. McCRARY

McCrary, George W. "This will be presented to you by Gen. Lew Wallace, the newly appointed Governor of New Mexico ..." Letter given to Lew Wallace to present to General Edward Hatch. **September 18, 1878**. Indiana Historical Society. Lew Wallace Collection. M0292. Box 3. Folder 14.

Wallace, Lew. "By the statute now in force ..." **October 4, 1878**. Indiana Historical Society. Lew Wallace Collection. M0292. Box 3. Folder 15. (**Requesting arms from the Secretary of War**)

McCrary, George W. "I have the honor to acknowledge the receipt of your letter..." **November 23, 1878**. Indiana Historical Society. Lew Wallace Collection. M0292. Box 3. Folder 17. (**About requesting arms**)

Wallace, Lew. "I have the honor to acknowledge the receipt of two communications from you..." Letter to George McCrary. **November 23, 1878**. Indiana Historical Society. Lew Wallace Collection. M0292. Box 3. Folder 18. (**Refuses to post personal bond for arms**)

McCrary, George W. "I have the honor to acknowledge the receipt of your letter..." **August 26, 1879**. Indiana Historical Society. Lew Wallace Collection. M0292. Box 4. Folder 12.(**Freeing Wallace from responsibility for Dudley Court of Inquiry outcome**)

Bell, A. "Referring to your letter of the 30th ultimo ..." **August 29, 1879**. Letter to Lew Wallace about George McCrary. Indiana Historical Society. Lew Wallace Collection. M0292. Box 4. Folder 12. (**Acting Secretary of the Interior and Secretary of War placate Wallace about Court of Inquiry outcome**)

TO LINCOLN JAILOR JUAN PATRÓN

Wallace, Lew. "Please select ten of your Rangers ..." Letter to Juan Patrón. **March 3, 1879**. Indiana Historical Society. Lew Wallace Collection. M0292. Box 4. Folder 4. (**To arrest "Scurlock and Bowdrey"**)

_____. "Please report to Sheriff Kimbrell ..." Letter to Juan Patrón. **March 3, 1879**. Indiana Historical Society. Lew Wallace Collection. M0292. Box 4. Folder 4.

_____. Wallace, Lew. "Be good enough to send word to all your men to turn out soon as possible ..." Letter to Juan Patrón. **March 19, 1879.** Indiana Historical Society. Lew Wallace Collection. M0292. Box 4. Folder 6. (**Reports escape of Jessie Evans and Billy Campbell from Fort Stanton**)

TO TERRITORIAL COMPTROLLER A.G. PORTER

Wallace, Lew. "I certify that I have been constantly in this Territory ..." **January 17, 1879.** Indiana Historical Society. Lew Wallace Collection. M0292. Box 4. Folder 1.

_____. "In your favor of the 9th ult. you inform me that "S.B. Axtell, late Governor of New Mexico, sent vouchers ..." **January 17, 1879.** Indiana Historical Society. Lew Wallace Collection. M0292. Box 4. Folder 1.

FROM LIEUTENANT GEORGE PURINGTON

Purington, George. "The District Court adjourned on Thursday ..." **May 3, 1879.** Indiana Historical Society. Lew Wallace Collection. M0292. Box 4. Folder 10. (**Letter to Adjutant General on indictments of the Murphy-Dolans and N.A.M. Dudley; copy sent to Lew Wallace**)

TO TERRITORIAL SECRETARY WILLIAM RITCH

Wallace, Lew. "I will leave this afternoon for Lincoln ..." **March 1, 1879.** Indiana Historical Society. Lew Wallace Collection. M0292. Box 4. Folder 4.

TO AND FROM SECRETARY OF INTERIOR CARL SCHURZ

Schurz, Carl. "I transmit herewith an order from the President ..." Letter to Lew Wallace. **September 4, 1878.** Indiana Historical Society. Lew Wallace Collection. M0292. Box 3. Folder 14. (**Suspension of New Mexico Governor S.B. Axtell and his appointment as replacement Governor**)

Wallace, Lew. "I have the honor to inform you ..." Letter to Carl Schurz. **October 1, 1878.** Indiana Historical Society. Lew Wallace Collection. M0292. Box 3. Folder 15. (**Informing Schurz that he informed Axtell of suspension and that he now qualified as Governor**)

_____. "I have the honor to enclose herewith a requisition ..." **October 4, 1878.** Letter to Carl Schurz. Indiana Historical Society. Lew Wallace Collection. M0292. Box 3. Folder 15. (**Requesting arms from Secretary of War**)

_____. "As the basis of the request which I have to prefer relative to the affairs in the county of Lincoln ..." Letter to Carl Schurz. **October 5, 1878.** Indiana Historical Society. Lew Wallace Collection. M0292. Box 3. Folder 15. (**Requesting President to declare martial law**)

_____. "In further exemplification of affairs in Lincoln county accept extract received ..." Letter to Carl Schurz. **October 5, 1878.** Indiana Historical Society. Lew Wallace Collection. M0292. Box 3. Folder 15. (**N.A.M. Dudley's report of "Wrestlers" raping in Lincoln County**)

_____. "I received by mail last night a petition signed by the Probate Judge ..." Telegram to Carl Schurz. **October 14, 1878.** Indiana Historical Society. Lew Wallace Collection. M0292. Box 3. Folder 15. (**Giving situation and asking martial law for Lincoln and Doña Ana Counties**)

_____. "I have the honor to inform you that since the posting of the President's Proclamation ...." Letter to Carl Schurz. **October 22, 1878.** Indiana Historical Society. Lew Wallace Collection. M0292. Box 3. Folder 16.

_____. "I have appointed Mr. Epifanio Vigil, of this city, Interpreter and Translator ...." **October 22, 1878.** Indiana Historical Society. Lew Wallace Collection. M0292. Box 3. Folder 16.

_____. "Herewith please find bond ...." **October 22, 1878.** Indiana Historical Society. Lew Wallace Collection. M0292. Box 3. Folder 16.

No signatures. (But in Lew Wallace's handwriting). "Yesterday, at the request of Governor Wallace the undersigned, physicians ...." **October 23, 1878.** Indiana Historical Society. Lew Wallace Collection. M0292. Box 3. Folder 16 (**Focus on refurbishing Palace of the Governors**)

Wallace, Lew. "Be good enough, at your earliest convenience, to call attention of the President ...." **October 24, 1878.** Indiana Historical Society. Lew Wallace Collection. M0292. Box 3. Folder 16.

_____. "I enclose a paper, signed by all the leading attorneys ..." Letter to Carl Schurz. **November 13, 1878.** Indiana Historical Society. Lew Wallace Collection. M0292. Box 3. Folder 17. (**Urging judgeship for Ira Leonard**)

_____. "I have the honor to forward to you the following report." **November 13, 1878.** Indiana Historical Society. Lew Wallace Collection. M0292. Box 3. Folder 17. (**About Presidential Proclamation and issuing his own Amnesty Proclamation**)

Schurz, Carl. "In reply to your letter ..." **November 14, 1878.** Indiana Historical Society. Lew Wallace Collection. M0292. Box 3. Folder 17. (**Given bond for arms**)

_____. "Replying to your two telegrams ..." Letter from Carl Schurz. **November 15, 1878.** Indiana Historical Society. Lew Wallace Collection. M0292. Box 3. Folder 17. (**Ira Leonard's requested judgeship appointment sent to the Attorney General for consideration**)

_____. "I acknowledge the receipt of your letter of the 13th instant ..." Letter from Carl Schurz. **November 23, 1878.** Indiana Historical Society. Lew Wallace Collection. M0292. Box 3. Folder 18. (**Amnesty Proclamation, has approval of President**)

Wallace, Lew. "It has not unexpectedly happened that delay, involving expense ..." Letter to Carl Schurz. **November 26, 1878.** Indiana Historical Society. Lew Wallace Collection. M0292. Box 3. Folder 18. (**Wants extradition of fugitive criminals**)

Schurz, Carl. "In compliance with the suggestion of the Secretary of State ..." **November 30, 1878** Indiana Historical Society. Lew Wallace Collection. M0292. Box 3. Folder 18. (**About extradition of fugitive criminals**)

_____. "I have received your letter ..." Letter to Lew Wallace. **December 9, 1878.** Indiana Historical Society. Lew Wallace Collection. M0292. Box 3. Folder 19. (**Answer about anyone in Senate trying to defeat his confirmation as Governor**)

Wallace, Lew. "I have the honor to report that affairs of the Territory are moving on quietly ..." Letter to Carl Schurz. **December 21, 1878.** Indiana Historical Society. Lew Wallace Collection. M0292. Box 3. Folder 19. (**N.A.M. Dudley's indignation about the Amnesty Proclamation**)

Schurz, Carl. "I have received your report ..." **December 28, 1878.** Indiana Historical Society. Lew Wallace Collection. M0292. Box 3. Folder 19.

Wallace, Lew. "I have the honor to enclose you a copy of a communication . ." Letter to Carl Schurz. January 17, 1879. Indiana Historical Society. Lew Wallace Collection. M0292. Box 4. Folder 1. (**Bad condition of Palace of the Governors**)

_____. "... I have just returned from Trinidad, Col ..." Letter to Carl Schurz. **February 5, 1879.** Indiana Historical Society. Lew Wallace Collection. M0292. Box 4. Folder 2. (**Bringing his family to Santa Fe**)

_____. "I beg to call your attention to the condition of the house called the 'Palace' ...." Letter to Carl Schurz. **February 12, 1879.** Indiana Historical Society. Lew Wallace Collection. M0292. Box 4. Folder 2.

_____. "The Hon. A.G. Porter, Comptroller, is kind enough to inform me ..." Letter to Carl Schurz. **February 26, 1879**. Indiana Historical Society. Lew Wallace Collection. M0292. Box 4. Folder 3. (**Funds requested**)

_____. "I take the liberty of enclosing herewith the accounts in duplicate of Mr. Epifanio Vigil ..." Letter to Carl Schurz. **February 26, 1879**. Indiana Historical Society. Lew Wallace Collection. M0292. Box 4. Folder 3. (**Funds requested**)

_____. "One H.I. Chapman, lawyer, was assassinated ...." Letter to Carl Schurz. **February 27, 1879**. Indiana Historical Society. Lew Wallace Collection. M0292. Box 4. Folder 3. (**Reacting to Chapman murder by using troops to track "outlaws" – meaning the Regulators. Start of the pardon saga**)

Schurz, Carl. "I have the honor to acknowledge the receipt of your letter of the 1st inst." Letter to Lew Wallace. **March 11, 1879**. Indiana Historical Society. Lew Wallace Collection. M0292. Box 4. Folder 5. (**Presidential permission for "arresting the disturbances" in Lincoln County**)

Wallace, Lew. "My time has been so constantly occupied in getting my work into operation ..." Letter to Carl Schurz. **March 21, 1879**. Indiana Historical Society. Lew Wallace Collection. M0292. Box 4. Folder 7. (**Progress report with multiple enclosures; one listing "The Kid -William Bonney in anti-outlaw campaign of "taking the head off the evil."**)

_____. "To day I forwarded a telegram to you, with another to the President ..." Letter to Carl Schurz. **March 31, 1879**. Indiana Historical Society. Lew Wallace Collection. M0292. Box 4. Folder 7. (**Mention of "precious specimen nicknamed 'The Kid' "**)

_____. "I have official information that a court of inquiry for Col. Dudley has been ordered ..." Letter to Carl Schurz. **April 4, 1879**. Indiana Historical Society. Lew Wallace Collection. M0292. Box 4, Folder 8.

_____. "I have the honor to inform you that affairs in Lincoln County are progressing favorably ..." Letter to Carl Schurz. **April 18, 1879**. Indiana Historical Society. Lew Wallace Collection. M0292. Box 4, Folder 9.

_____. "In a recent letter descriptive of the situation in Lincoln County, I alluded to the necessity of breaking up illicit transactions in cattle." **April 25, 1879**. Indiana Historical Society. Lew Wallace Collection. M0292. Box 4, Folder 9.

_____. "I enclose account in duplicate for services in overhauling and removing Territorial archives ..." **May 1, 1879**. Indiana Historical Society. Lew Wallace Collection. M0292. Box 4, Folder 10.

_____. "I have the honor to inform you that all the recent reports, military and otherwise, justify me in saying Lincoln County is enjoying a term of peace." Letter to Carl Schurz. **May 5, 1879**. Indiana Historical Society. Lew Wallace Collection. M0292. Box 4. Folder 10.

_____. "I had the honor a few weeks ago of writing you respecting a balance of contingent fund due this Executive Office ..." **May 5, 1879**. Indiana Historical Society. Lew Wallace Collection. M0292. Box 4. Folder 10.

_____. "Enclosed please find a copy of the report of the commandant at Fort Stanton." Letter to Carl Schurz. **June 11, 1879**. Indiana Historical Society. Lew Wallace Collection. M0292. Box 4. Folder 11. (**Self-serving progress report of quelling disturbances**)

Schurz, Carl. "I have received your letter of the 3d inst., and am glad to know ..." Letter to Lew Wallace. **July 10, 1879**. Indiana Historical Society. Lew Wallace Collection. M0292. Box 4. Folder 12.

Wallace, Lew. "The accompanying document received from Fort Stanton which will explain itself." Letter to Carl Schurz. **July 30, 1879**. Indiana Historical Society. Lew Wallace Collection. M0292. Box 4. Folder 12. (**Describes progress, but calls Dudley Court of Inquiry corrupt**)

Bell, A. "Referring to your letter of the 30th ultimo ..." **August 29, 1879**. Indiana Historical Society. Lew Wallace Collection. M0292. Box 4. Folder 12. (**Acting

Secretary of the Interior and Secretary of War George McCrary placate Wallace about the corrupt Court of Inquiry outcome)

Wallace, Lew. "In reply to the communication of Acting Secretary Bell ..." **September 15, 1879.** Letter to Carl Schurz. Indiana Historical Society. Lew Wallace Collection. M0292. Box 4. Folder 13. **(On John Jones killing John Beckwith, and Bob Olinger killing John Jones)**

_____. "The enclosed communication received yesterday from Mr. Louis Scott, U.S. Consul ..." **December 29, 1879.** Indiana Historical Society. Lew Wallace Collection. M0292. Box 4. Folder 13.

_____. "I have the honor to inform you that the Legislature of this Territory adjourned ..." **February 16, 1880.** Letter to Carl Schurz. Indiana Historical Society. Lew Wallace Collection. M0292. Box 4, Folder 14. **(Important proof of T.B. Catron as head of the Santa Fe Ring, and Wallace's Ring opposition)**

Schurz, Carl. "I have received your letter ..." **May 24, 1880.** Indiana Historical Society. Lew Wallace Collection. M0292. Box 4. Folder 15.

Wallace, Lew. "I have returned from a tour through the counties ..." Letter to Carl Schurz. **July 23, 1880.** Indiana Historical Society. Lew Wallace Collection. M0292. Box 4. Folder 14. **(Reporting on south counties, Victorio, and recommends Ira Leonard for judgeship replacing Warren Bristol.)**

_____. "I have the honor to report that I returned to this city ..." **November 30, 1880.** Letter to Carl Schurz. Indiana Historical Society. Lew Wallace Collection. M0292. Box 4, Folder 14. **(Reports Victorio is dead, and Navajo problems)**

_____. "From private advices received from Lincoln county ..." **December 7, 1880.** Indiana Historical Society. Lew Wallace Collection. M0292. Box 4. Folder 15. **(Reports pursuit of outlaws by people in Lincoln County)**

_____. "I have private business urgently requiring my presence in New York City ..." Letter to Carl Schurz. **December 14, 1880.** Indiana Historical Society. Lew Wallace Collection. M0292. Box No. 4. Folder 15. **(Mention's - without giving names - the deputy sheriff [Garrett] tracking the "leader of the outlaws" [Billy] for whom Wallace has set a "$500 reward.")**

_____. "I have the honor to submit the following matter for consideration ..." **December 15, 1880.** Indiana Historical Society. Lew Wallace Collection. M0292. Box 4. Folder 15.

TO FRANK B. SHERWIN

Wallace, Lew. "Since receiving your favor, touching the Maxwell Land Grant ..." **February 19, 1879.** Indiana Historical Society. Lew Wallace Collection. M0292. Box 4. Folder 2.

TO AND FROM ATTORNEY DAVID SHIELD

Shield, David. "It is rumored that 'Eight long Affidavits' are in your possession ..." Letter to Lew Wallace. **February 11, 1879.** Indiana Historical Society. Lew Wallace Collection. M0292. Box 4. Folder 2. **(Commander Dudley's defamatory affidavits about Susan McSween)**

Wallace, Lew. "I am in receipt of your letter of this date requesting inspection ..." Letter to David Shield. **February 19, 1879.** Indiana Historical Society. Lew Wallace Collection. M0292. Box 4. Folder 2. **(Refuses to give copies of Dudley's affidavits about Susan McSween)**

FROM ATTORNEY FRANK SPRINGER

Springer, Frank. "I see that my friends of the New Mexican are trying to make themselves, or you, or me, or somebody believe ..." Letter to Lew Wallace. **November 12, 1878** Indiana Historical Society. Lew Wallace Collection. M0292. Box 3. Folder 17.

FROM AND TO HENRY WALLACE (SON)

Wallace, Henry. "Dear Papa, Last Saturday me and Frank Stewart went a fishing ..." **1862?** Letter to Lew Wallace. Indiana Historical Society. Lew Wallace Collection. M0292. Box 1. Folder 11.

Wallace, Lew. "Master Henry Wallace. My dear little boy. I owe you several letters." Letter to son, Henry. **February 6, 1863**. Indiana Historical Society. Lew Wallace Collection. M0292. Box 4. Folder 15. (**Written from war in Cincinnati**)

_____. "Not improbably I will in a few days want a hundred and fifty dollars to pay for assessment work on a couple of mines in Cerillos." Letter to son, Henry. **December 15, 1880**. Indiana Historical Society. Lew Wallace Collection. M0292. Box 4. Folder 15.

_____. "As you have doubtless seen in the papers, the President has appointed a General Sheldon ..." Letter to son, Henry. **March 19, 1881**. Indiana Historical Society. Lew Wallace Collection. M0292. Box 4. Folder 16.

_____. "Thank you for the letter and the action you propose." Letter to son, Henry. **March 29, 1881**. Indiana Historical Society. Lew Wallace Collection. M0292. Box 4. Folder 16. (**Wallace's replacement for Governor**)

TO SUSAN WALLACE (WIFE)

Wallace, Lew. "This is Sunday. About the time the church bells ..." Letter to wife, Susan. **October 20, 1878**. Indiana Historical Society. Lew Wallace Collection. M0292. Box 3. Folder 16.

_____. "I hasten to send you my message to the Legislature, read yesterday ..." Letter to wife, Susan. **January 9, 1880**. Indiana Historical Society. Lew Wallace Collection. M0292. Box 4. Folder 14. (**States that writing *Ben-Hur* feels like living two lives**)

TO AND FROM JUSTICE OF THE PEACE JOHN B. WILSON

Wallace, Lew. "I hasten to acknowledge receipt of your favor of the 11th Jan. ult. ..." **January 18, 1879**. Indiana Historical Society. Lew Wallace Collection. M0292. Box 4. Folder 1. (**Says that Lincoln County was carrying on a revolution**)

_____. "Your favors are both in hand and place me under renewed obligation. ..." February 6, 1879. Indiana Historical Society. Lew Wallace Collection. M0292. Box 4. Folder 2.

_____. "I understand that affidavits will be filed with you against the prisoners. ..." Letter to John B. Wilson. **March 8, 1879**. Indiana Historical Society. Lew Wallace Collection. M0292. Box 4. Folder 4.

_____. "I enclose a note for Bonney." Letter to John "Squire" Wilson. March 20, 1879. Indiana Historical Society. Lew Wallace Collection. M0292. Box 4. Folder 6.

ARTICLES BY AND ABOUT (CHRONOLOGICAL)

No Author. "Gen. Lew Wallace Reached Home ..." Crawfordsville *Saturday Evening Journal*. **December 16, 1876**. Indiana Historical Society. The Papers of Lew and Susan Wallace. Microfilm Edition. Indianapolis, Indiana: Indiana Historical Society Press. 2008. (**Denying election fraud in Rutherford B. Hayes's Florida election results**)

No Author. "Fighting the Indians. Sketches of General Lew Wallace's Plan for Conducting the Frontier Warfare." *Indianapolis Journal*. **August 28, 1877**. Indiana Historical Society. The Papers of Lew and Susan Wallace. Microfilm Edition. Indianapolis, Indiana: Indiana Historical Society Press. 2008.

No Author. "For Delegate Benito Baca. County Ticket Juan C. Armijo." *Albuquerque Review.* **October 5, 1878**. Indiana Historical Society. The Papers of Lew and Susan Wallace. Microfilm Edition. Indianapolis, Indiana: Indiana Historical Society Press. 2008. (**Wallace's arrival and swearing in by Warren Bristol**)

Wallace, Lew. "Statement by the Governor." **November, 1878**. Indiana Historical Society. Lew Wallace Collection. M0292. Box 18. Folder 1. (**In a Lew Wallace scrapbook. About the Amnesty Proclamation**)

No Author. "Wallace and Lincoln County." Grant County *Herald*. **March 1, 1879**. Indiana Historical Society. The Papers of Lew and Susan Wallace. Microfilm Edition. Indianapolis, Indiana: Indiana Historical Society Press. 2008 (**Ridicule about Huston Chapman's murder**)

No Author. Editorial on Governor Wallace's letter to Carl Schurz. *Denver Daily Tribune.* **May 7, 1879** Indiana Historical Society. The Papers of Lew and Susan Wallace. Microfilm Edition. Indianapolis, Indiana: Indiana Historical Society Press. 2008. (**Blames Lincoln County for outlawry**)

No Author. "Governor Lew Wallace's Rose Colored Account of Them. Inexhaustible Deposits of Gold, Silver, Copper and Lead – An Open Invitation." New York *Daily Graphic.* **March 24, 1880**. Indiana Historical Society. The Papers of Lew and Susan Wallace. Microfilm Edition. Indianapolis, Indiana: Indiana Historical Society Press. 2008.

No Author. "General Wallace's Proclamation." Santa Fe *Daily New Mexican.* **June 12, 1880**. Reprinted in Santa Fe *Weekly New Mexican* of June 14, 1880. Indiana Historical Society. The Papers of Lew and Susan Wallace. Microfilm Edition. Indianapolis, Indiana: Indiana Historical Society Press. 2008. (**Contemplated proclamation for citizens to "take the field" against Indians**)

No Author. "General Lew Wallace Interviewed." Chicago *Daily Inter Ocean.* **January 3, 1881**. Indiana Historical Society. The Papers of Lew and Susan Wallace. Microfilm Edition. Indianapolis, Indiana: Indiana Historical Society Press. 2008. (**About his attempted repeal of the Posse Comitatus Act**)

No Author. "Wallace's Words ..." January 3, 1881), Chicago *The Daily Inter Ocean.* **January 4, 1881**. p. 2, c. 4. Indiana Historical Society. The Papers of Lew and Susan Wallace. Microfilm Edition. Series I. Reel 15. Indianapolis, Indiana: Indiana Historical Society Press. 2008. (**Interview with Wallace conducted in Washington, D.C.**)

No Author. "Governor Wallace. Chat About the Use of Troops in New Mexico and His New Book." *Crawfordsville Journal.* **February 26, 1881**. Indiana Historical Society. The Papers of Lew and Susan Wallace. Microfilm Edition. Indianapolis, Indiana: Indiana Historical Society Press. 2008. (**Trying to stop Posse Comitatus Act and the success of *Ben-Hur***)

No Author. "Richard Dunham's May 2, 1881 encounter with Billy the Kid.", Santa Fe Daily New Mexican, May 5, 1881, p.4, c. 3.

No Author. "The Thug's Territory. Stage Robbers and Cut-Throats Have Things Their Own Way in New Mexico. Gen. Lew Wallace Anxious to Punish the Crime That is So Prevalent – A Chapter About "Billy the Kid' – The Governor has a Narrow Escape From Being Spanked." *St. Louis Daily Globe-Democrat.* Monday Morning, **May 16, 1881**. Page 2, Columns 5 and 6. (private collection)

No Author. O.L. Houghton's Conversation with Lew Wallace. *The Las Vegas Daily Optic,* **May 26, 1881**, p.4, c.4.

No Author. "Interview With General Lew Wallace Relative to Affairs in New Mexico." Chicago *Daily Inter Ocean.* **June 4, 1881**. Indiana Historical Society. The Papers of Lew and Susan Wallace. Microfilm Edition. Indianapolis, Indiana: Indiana Historical Society Press. 2008.

No Author. "General Wallace's Serenade: A Welcome Home by his Neighbors and Friends - What the General Said." **June 4, 1881**. Indiana Historical Society. The Papers of Lew and Susan Wallace. Microfilm Edition. Indianapolis, Indiana: Indiana Historical Society Press. 2008.

No Author. "Billy the Kid, General Wallace Tells Why the Young Desperado of New Mexico Wanted to Kill Him." (Lew Wallace interviewed on June 13, 1881), Crawfordsville *Saturday Evening Journal*, **June 18, 1881**. Indiana Historical Society. The Papers of Lew and Susan Wallace. Microfilm Edition. Indianapolis, Indiana: Indiana Historical Society Press. 2008.

No Author. "Gen. Lew Wallace. Visit to His Pleasant Home in the Athens of Indiana. Crawfordsville *Saturday Evening Journal.* **January 16, 1886**. Indiana Historical Society. The Papers of Lew and Susan Wallace. Microfilm Edition. Indianapolis, Indiana: Indiana Historical Society Press. 2008. (**Rationalizing Shiloh**)

No Author. "General Wallace Said ..." Crawfordsville *Saturday Evening Journal.* **January 16, 1886.** Indiana Historical Society. The Papers of Lew and Susan Wallace. Microfilm Edition. Indianapolis, Indiana: Indiana Historical Society Press. 2008.

No Author. "General Wallace in Cincinnati." Weekly *Crawfordsville Journal.* **April 4, 1893.** Indiana Historical Society. The Papers of Lew and Susan Wallace. Microfilm Edition. Indianapolis, Indiana: Indiana Historical Society Press. 2008.

No Author. "Lew Wallace at Shiloh. What the General Has to Say Further on This Question – Buell's Army." *Indianapolis News.* **September 13, 1893**. Indiana Historical Society. The Papers of Lew and Susan Wallace. Microfilm Edition. Indianapolis, Indiana: Indiana Historical Society Press. 2008. (**Wallace still blaming Grant for Shiloh in attempt to vindicate himself**)

No Author. "Lew Wallace's Foe. Threatened by 'Billy the Kid.' The Writing of 'Ben-Hur' Interrupted. An Incident of the Soldier-Author's Career in New Mexico. *San Francisco Chronicle.* **December 10, 1893**. Indiana Historical Society. Lew Wallace Collection. M0292. Box 14. Folder 11.

No Author. "Street Pickings," Weekly *Crawfordsville Review - Saturday Edition*, **January 6, 1894**. Indiana Historical Society. The Papers of Lew and Susan Wallace. Microfilm Edition. Series I. Reel 27. Indianapolis, Indiana: Indiana Historical Society Press. 2008.

No Author. "General Lew Wallace." (Interview.) *Cincinnati Post.* **February 10, 1894**. Reprinted in Crawfordsville *New Review.* July 8, 1899. Indiana Historical Society. The Papers of Lew and Susan Wallace. Microfilm Edition. Indianapolis, Indiana: Indiana Historical Society Press. 2008. (**Calling *Ben-Hur* better than Dickens**)

No Author. "Author of Ben-Hur, Gen. Lew Wallace, of Indiana, spends the Day in the City. Talks Politics and Books." St. Paul *Dispatch.* **October 5, 1894**. Indiana Historical Society. The Papers of Lew and Susan Wallace. Microfilm Edition. Indianapolis, Indiana: Indiana Historical Society Press. 2008.

No Author. "Lew Wallace at Shiloh. Through an Orderly's Error He Took the Wrong Road." Spokane *Weekly Spokesman-Review.* **October 11, 1894**. Indiana Historical Society. The Papers of Lew and Susan Wallace. Microfilm Edition. Indianapolis, Indiana: Indiana Historical Society Press. 2008. (**New excuse of blaming the orderly for Shiloh as well as Grant**)

No Author. "Lew Wallace Honored, The People of Seattle Extend Him a Hearty Greeting." Tacoma, Washington *Daily Ledger.* **October 14, 1894**. Indiana Historical Society. The Papers of Lew and Susan Wallace. Microfilm Edition. Indianapolis, Indiana: Indiana Historical Society Press. 2008. (**Mentions writing a secret book**)

No Author. "About His Works. A Chat With General Lew Wallace." *San Francisco Chronicle.* **October 29, 1894**. Indiana Historical Society. The Papers of Lew and Susan Wallace. Microfilm Edition. Indianapolis, Indiana: Indiana Historical Society Press. 2008.

Lewis, E.I. "Gen. Wallace's Feud with Billy the Kid, When the General Was Governor of New Mexico and Billy Bonne Was the Most Dangerous Western Outlaw. He Was a Waif and Was Reared in Indiana. *The Indianapolis Press*. Saturday, **June 23, 1900**. Page ?. Indiana Historical Society. Lew Wallace Collection. M0292. Box 14. Folder 11.

No Author. "An Incident Gen. Lew Wallace Tells of His First Meeting With His Stepmother in Crawfordsville." *Crawfordsville Journal.* **March 20, 1901.** Indiana Historical Society. The Papers of Lew and Susan Wallace. Microfilm Edition. Indianapolis, Indiana: Indiana Historical Society Press. 2008. (**About father's cruel introduction of step-mother**)

No Author. "Home From Shiloh. Gen. Lew Wallace and Capt. Geo. R. Brown Pleased With the Work of the Commission." Weekly *Crawfordsville Journal.* **December 6, 1901.** Indiana Historical Society. The Papers of Lew and Susan Wallace. Microfilm Edition. Indianapolis, Indiana: Indiana Historical Society Press. 2008.

No Author. "An Old Incident Recalled," *The* (Crawfordsville) *Weekly News-Review,* **December 20, 1901.**

No Author. "Hotel Lobby Gleanings. Gen. Wallace Royalties From 'Ben-Hur' are 'Satisfactory.' " Weekly *Crawfordsville Journal.* **January 24, 1902.** Reprinted in *Indianapolis Journal* on January 25, 1902. Indiana Historical Society. The Papers of Lew and Susan Wallace. Microfilm Edition. Indianapolis, Indiana: Indiana Historical Society Press. 2008. (**About Shiloh being in his *Autobiography***)

No Author. "Lew Wallace's Grit. How the General Fought With Adversity in His Youth - His Father's Admonition." *Crawfordsville Journal.* **February 7, 1902.** Indiana Historical Society. The Papers of Lew and Susan Wallace. Microfilm Edition. Indianapolis, Indiana: Indiana Historical Society Press. 2008. (**About his father's rejection when he was sixteen**)

Wallace, Lew. "Indiana is Now Literary Center, General Lew Wallace Gives His Views on Present Day Writers, Is Working on New Book." Cincinnati *Commercial Tribune* reprinted in Crawfordsville *Weekly News-Review.* **April 15, 1902.** Indiana Historical Society. The Papers of Lew and Susan Wallace. Microfilm Edition. Series I. Reel 27. Indianapolis, Indiana: Indiana Historical Society Press. 2008.

_____. "General Lew Wallace Writes a Romance of 'Billy the Kid,' Most Famous Bandit of the Plains." *New York World Magazine.* Sunday, **June 8, 1902.** Page 4. Indiana Historical Society. Lew Wallace Collection. M0292. Box 14. Folder 11.

No Author. "The Statehood Bill, General Wallace and Delegate Rodey Take Opposite Views. Wallace for New Mexico As a Single State But Rodey Says His People Are Reconciled to the Union With Arizona." Weekly *Crawfordsville Journal.* **January 6, 1905.** Indiana Historical Society. The Papers of Lew and Susan Wallace. Microfilm Edition. Indianapolis, Indiana: Indiana Historical Society Press. 2008.

WILD, AZARIAH

BIOGRAPHICAL SOURCE

Nolan, Frederick. "Biography of Azariah Wild." Unpublished and personal communications, June 11, 2005 and October 9, 2005.

CONTEMPORARY SOURCES (CHRONOLOGICAL)

Brooks, James J. *1877 Report on Secret Service Operatives.* "On Azariah Wild." **September 26, 1877.** Page 392. Department of the Treasury. United States Secret Service. Washington, D.C.

Wild, Azariah F. "Daily Reports of U. S. Secret Service Agents, Azariah F. Wild. Microfilm T-915. Record Group 87. Rolls 306 **(June 15, 1877 - December 31, 1877), 307 (January 1, 1878 - June 30, 1879), 308 (July 1, 1879 - June 30, 1881), 309 (July 1, 1881 - September 30, 1883)**, and 310 **(October 1, 1883 - July 31, 1886)**. National Archives and Records Department. Department of Treasury. United States Secret Service. Washington, D. C.

Wild, Azariah. Telegraph on counterfeit bills. **January 4, 1881.** Herman B. Weisner Papers, ca. 1957-1992. New Mexico State University Library at Las Cruces. Rio Grande Historical Collections. Accession No. Ms 0249. Box 11. Folder O-1. Folder Name: "Olinger, Robert and James W. Bell."

WILSON, JOHN B. "SQUIRE"

Wilson, John, George B. Barker, Robert M. Gilbert, John Newcomb, Samuel Smith, Benjamin Ellis. "We the undersigned Justice of the Peace and Coroners Jury who sat upon the inquest held this 19th day of February 1878 on the body of John H. Tunstall ..." Coroner's Jury Report for John Tunstall. **February 19, 1878. (Naming as murderers, among others, James Dolan, Frank Baker, Jessie Evans, William Morton, and George Hindman)**

Wilson, John. Letter to Lew Wallace. Unsigned but noted as from "Sqr. Wilson by Wallace. Undated, but likely **March, 1879.** Indiana Historical Society. Lew Wallace Collection. M0292. Box 4, Folder 7. **(On Lady Liberty stationery)**

_____. Affidavit of John Wilson. **March ?, 1879.** Indiana Historical Society. Lew Wallace Collection. M0292. Box 4, Folder 7.

_____. Signed JBW. **April 8, 1879.** Indiana Historical Society, Lew Wallace Collection. M0292. Box 4, Folder 8.

_____. Letter to Lew Wallace. **May 18, 1879.** Indiana Historical Society. Lew Wallace Collection. M0292. Box 4, Folder 5.

LETTERS TO JOHN "SQUIRE" WILSON

Bonney, William Henry. "Friend Wilson ..." **March 18, 1879.** Indiana Historical Society. Lew Wallace Collection. M0292.

Wallace, Lew. "I enclose a note for Bonney." **March 20, 1879.** Indiana Historical Society. Lew Wallace Collection. M0922. Box 4. Folder 6.

WILSON, SIDNEY

Wilson, Sidney. "List of Americans in Lincoln." **March ? 1879.** Indiana Historical Society. Lew Wallace Collection. M0922. Box 4. Folder 7.

MODERN BILLY THE KID PARDON HOAXES

BOOKS

Cooper, Gale. *Billy the Kid's Pretenders: Brushy Bill and John Miller.* Gelcour Books: Albuquerque: New Mexico. 2010.

_____. *Cracking the Billy the Kid Case Hoax: The Strange Plot to Exhume Billy the Kid, Convict Sheriff Pat Garrett of Murder, and Become President of the United States.* Albuquerque, New Mexico: Gelcour Books. 2014.

Jameson, W.C. and Frederic Bean. *The Return of the Outlaw Billy the Kid.* Plano, Texas: Republic of Texas Press. 1997. (**"Brushy Bill" Roberts as Billy the Kid.**)

Morrison, William V. and C.L. Sonnichsen. *Alias Billy the Kid.* Albuquerque: University of New Mexico Press. 1955. (**"Brushy Bill" Roberts as Billy the Kid.**)

LETTER

Pittmon, Geneva. December 16, 1987 letter to Joe Bowlin with hand copy of Roberts family Bible genealogy page. (private collection) (**"Brushy Bill" as not being Billy the Kid**)

INDEX

Abbott, E.C. "Teddy Blue" – 36
adobe wall (at Tunstall's store) – 281
Addison, James Roger – 50
Alarid, Laurencio – 83-84
Albuquerque Daily Citizen – 94, 97-99
Albuquerque, New Mexico – 88, 102, 429-430, 713, 814
Albuquerque Review – 427-428
A Frontier Doctor – 34, 352
Allison, Clay – 84, 149, 156-158, 164-168, 170, 177, 216, 221, 224, 229, 232-234, 347, 350, 370-371, 813
Allison, James – 126
American Valley Company ranch – 57, 80, 82, 153
amnesty in bar of prosecution (see Lew Wallace) – 607, 636, 668, 851
Amnesty Proclamation (see Lew Wallace)
Andrews, Enos – 428
Angel, Frank Warner – 6, 15, 17, 31, 47, 62, 64, 77-79, 82, 102, 156, 166, 168-171, 173, 179, 182, 184, 199, 206-207, 223-224, 226-237, 251, 256, 261, 269-273, 279, 282-283, 288, 299-323, 329-330, 332-333, 337, 355-356, 358, 360-363, 365, 367-369, 371-375, 379-380, 386, 389-390, 413, 428-432, 446, 450, 458, 479, 495, 557, 569, 653, 704, 747, 811-813; **deposition of William Bonney by:** 269-273; **deposition of Alexander McSween by:** 300-323; **deposition of Frank Springer by:** 226-236; **secret notebook of:** 428-432, 446, 450-458, 653; "In the Matter of the Cause and Circumstances of the Death of John H. Tunstall, a British Subject" by: 356-358; "In the Matter of the Lincoln County Troubles" by: 358-360; "In the Matter of the Investigation of the Charges Against S.B. Axtel [Axtell] Governor of New Mexico" by: 363-371; "Examination of Charges against F.C. Godfroy, Indian Agent, Mescalero, New Mexico" by: 547; **report on T.B. Catron by:** 78-80; 372-373

Angostura Grant – 209
Antrim, Catherine – 10
Antrim, Henry (see William Henry Bonney)
Antrim, Josie – 10
Antrim, William Henry Harrison – 10
Appel, Daniel – 259, 313, 339, 478-479, 532, 548, 550; **fraudulent Tunstall autopsy report:** 259, 313, 339
Archuleta, Don Diego – 119, 121
Arizona and the West – 47, 119, 122, 139
Arizona Territory – 9-10, 44, 107, 139-141, 144-145, 238, 268, 291, 581
Arlington National Cemetery – 293
Armijo, Manuel – 150
Arney, W.F.M. – 52, 117, 428
Atkin's Cantina – 10
"A Tax-Payer's Complaint" – 253; **answer by James Dolan:** 254
Atchison, Topeka, and Santa Fe Rail Road – 55, 111, 154, 238, 670, 693, 705, 765, 773
Atkinson, Henry M. – 54, 55-57, 61, 80-81, 153, 428
attachment of property in McSween embezzling case – 12-13, 71, 168, 177, 232, 255-256, 258, 300, 310, 357, 551; **writ of attachment:** 310
Axtell, Samuel Beach – 5-6, 17, 53, 55-57, 61-62, 67, 69, 72-74, 77-78, 81, 112, 123, 136, 145, 150, 156, 163-168, 170, 172, 175, 177, 179, 182-183, 191-192, 195, 199-226, 230-234, 237, 253, 269, 274-280, 282-283, 285, 287, 297, 299-300, 316, 328-330, 347-350, 355-356, 359-373, 379-380, 423-424, 426-428, 430-432, 434, 458, 460, 482-483, 495-496, 543, 557-558, 576, 602, 680, 782-783, 811-813, 855; "Governor's Message" of 1875: 136; **requesting troops in Colfax County by:** 225, 230, 349-350; **bribe loan by Santa Fe Ring of:** 56, 67, 125; **fraudulent sale of Uña de Gato Land Grant by:** 55, 182, 199, 234, 458; **removal of Colfax County courts by:** 62, 78, 123, 165-166, 175, 195, 199, 220-221, 224, 230-231, 602;

"Dear Ben plot" by: 61-62, 166-168, 170, 224-225, 233, 347-348, 482, 495; **exposés of by Mary McPherson:** 163-164, 191-192, 200-222, 413, 428; **requesting troops in Lincoln County War by:** 225, 230, 349-350; **obstructing arrest of Tunstall's murderers by removal of Justice of the Peace Wilson:** 5, 13, 67, 69, 73, 123, 231, 280, 283, 297, 337, 434, 477, 483, 496, 543, 782-783; **Proclamation of March 9, 1878 removing Wilson and outlawing his deputizings by:** 13, 67, 69, 73, 275-276, 282, 287, 366, 483, 580, 782, the Proclamation: 276; **Proclamation of May 28, 1878 removing Sheriff Copeland:** 15, 74, 78, 168, 299, the Proclamation: 300; **removal of:** 6, 73, 237, 413, 423-424, 426-427, 460, 558, 855; **reinstatement of as Chief Justice:** 811-813 (see Frank Warner Angel report on; see Mary McPherson's complaints on)
Ayers, John – 428
Aztec gold mine – 55, 151, 377
Baca, Jesus – 59
Baca, Pascual – 59, 122
Baca, Saturnino – 16, 286, 321, 337-338, 549, 559, 566, 650, 677, 774, 776
Bail, John D. – 132-133, 306, 429, 503, 775-776, 781
Baker, Frank – 13, 22, 26, 250, 259-260, 268, 271, 273-274, 297, 308, 312, 316, 572, 574, 578, 580
Baldy, Louis H. – 603
Ballard, [Alan J.] – 534, 567, 604
Bantz, Gideon B. – 87
Bar Association of New Mexico Territory – 50, 88, 90-91, 93, 98
Barber, George B. – 283, 721
Barker, George B. – 260
Barnes, Sidney – 77, 79, 586, 698, 705, 712-716, 719-723, 727, 762-763, 775
Barrier, Adolph – 12-13, 253, 255, 281, 289, 308-309, 315-317, 337, 356, 428, 557, 782-783
Bates, Sebrian – 677
Bartlett, Charles – 428
Batavia, New York – 499
Batavia *Republican Advocate* – 499
Battle of Alamance – 267-268

Battle of Monocacy Junction –383, 395, 409
Battle of Pittsburgh Landing (see Battle of Shiloh)
Battle of Shiloh – 51, 383-402, 404-405, 408-412, 416, 418, 424, 437, 455, 463, 471, 479, 490, 495, 518, 523, 555, 620, 621, 765, 787, 793, 803, 828, 852; **casualties:** 408, 495 (see Lew Wallace's pardon obsession for Shiloh)
Battles and Leaders of the Civil War (chapter on Shiloh) – 418
bay mare – 25, 751, 759-760, 784
Beardsley, Ezra I. – 429
Beaubien, Charles Hipolite Trotier Don Carlos" – 150
Beaubien-Miranda Land Grant – 21, 150-151
Beaubien, Narciso – 151
Beaver Smith's Saloon – 20, 723
Beckwith family – 578-579, 581-582
Beckwith, Hugh – 439
Beckwith, John – 303, 429, 439, 544, 570, 578, 697
Beckwith, Robert "Bob" – 273, 303, 312, 322, 340, 429, 476, 578, 659, 661
beef contract – 4, 56, 64, 257, 580, 701, 704, 715
Bell, James W. – 9, 25-26, 733, 791-792, 854
Benedict, Kirby – 107
Benton, Thomas Hart – 51, 107
Bering Sea Fisheries – 113
Bernardo Martin Grant – 378
Bernillo Grant – 209
"Big Casino" – 20
"Big Mose" – 574
Billy and Paulita – 383
Billy the Kid (see William H. Bonney)
Billy the Kid Case (see "Lincoln County Sheriff's Department Case # 2003-274")
Billy the Kid reward notices (see William H. Bonney)
Billy the Kid's Pretenders: Brushy Bill and John Miller (see Oliver "Brushy Bill" Roberts)
Billy the Kid's Writings, Words, and Wit – 556, 575
Blaine, James Gillespie – 110-112, 418, 801
Blazer, Joseph H. – 282, 286, 314, 327, 428, 775

Blazer's Mill – 14, 25, 28, 65, 282, 299, 324, 503, 574, 582, 725, 775
Bonita, Arizona – 10, 74
Bonito River – 16, 383, 663
Bonney, William Henry "Billy" (William Henry McCarty, Henry Antrim, Billy Bonney, the Kid, Billy the Kid) – **biography of:** 8-27, 43-68, 231-238, 555; **as Henry Antrim:** 10, 25, 145, 299, 324-327, 708, 786; **tintype of:** 14, 22; **contemporary advocates of:** 28-36; **"Little Casino" nickname of:** 20; **bi-culturalism of:** 9, 28-29, 33, 36, 334-335, 351-352, 792; **Peñasco River ranch of:** 11, 250, 256, 269; **Winchester '73 carbine of:** 13-14, 250, 275, 289, 577, 751 760, 832, 835, 839; **eye-witness to John Tunstall murder of:** 7 259, 268-273, 521, 617, 679; **deputizing of:** 5, 8, 73, 273-275, 366, 611, 783, 855; **outlawing by Governor Axtell of:** 13, 67, 69, 73 275-276, 282, 287, 366, 483, 580, 782, the March 9, 1878 Proclamation: 276; **arrest and killing of "Buck" Morton and Frank Baker by:** 13, 22, 26, 274-275, 297, 316-317, 579; **killing of William Brady and George Hindman by:** 5, 14, 22, 26, 73, 280-281, 285, 318-319, 476, 611, 850, 855 (see Lincoln County 1878 Grand Jury indictments for); **killing of "Buckshot" Roberts by:** 5, 14, 22, 25-26, 28, 282, 297, 321, 324-327, 336, 476, 579, 582, 611, 684, 725, 774, 850, 855; (see federal indictment No. 411 for); **"Regulator Manifesto" by:** 4, 6, 15, 17, 34, 64, 73, 82, 297, 335-336, 351, 701, 856; **text of:** 336; **Lincoln County War in:** 5, 8-9, 19, 26, 30, 75, 114, 154, 241, 245, 297-298, 351, 416, 556-557, 559, 569, 572, 575, 578-580, 601, 611, 617, 698, 719, 747, 805-806; eye-witness to Commander Dudley's shooting soldiers in: 7, 521, 617, 657-662, 679 (see Regulators of 1878, see Lincoln County War); **Lincoln County 1878 Grand Jury indictments for:** 3, 18, 25, 269, 283, 288-289, 297, 320, 324, 415, 556, 558, 601, 611, 744, 775, 835, 850, 852, 854; **federal indictment No. 411 for:** 27, 60, 324-327, 536, 606, 708, 775; **Hoyt Bill of Sale of:** 17, 34, 351-352, 450; the Bill of Sale: 352; **deposition on Tunstall murder with Frank Warner Angel of:** 4, 6, 13, 31, 269-273, 300, 332, 557, 578 783, 856; that deposition of June 8, 1878 by: 269-273; **peace meeting of February 18, 1879 with James Dolan of:** 18, 243, 491, 494; eye-witness to Huston Chapman murder by: 6, 18, 243, 268, 415, 474, 491, 521, 525, 556-558, 567, 575, 850, 856; on John Sherman's October 6, 1878 outlaw list of: 440; pursued as an "outlaw" by Lew Wallace: 491-492, 535; **pardon bargain with Lew Wallace of:** 3, 6-8, 19, 24, 30, 33, 268, 335, 540, 400, 416-417, 502, 535, 542, 555-566, 575, 578-579, 582-584, 587, 597-601, 607, 611, 617-618, 639, 657, 666, 718, 740, 793, 801, 803, 805, 822, 826, 833, 835, 838, 841, 845, 850-854; legal binding of: 561-563; sham arrest and jailing for: 19, 23, 415, 542, 557, 564-567, 577, 617, 657, 801, 803, 805, 833-834, 840, 842; departing sham jailing by: 674; fulfilled in 1879 Grand Jury testimony by: 8, 19, 33, 35, 268, 525, 557, 560-561, 563-564, 567, 588, 597, 599-601, 607, 617, 797, 703, 838, 840-841, 853, 856; Lew Wallace's "pardon in your pocket" quote about: 838, 840; summary of Wallace pardon betrayal of: 850-853; summary of pardon justification for: 854-856 modern pardon hoaxes about: 849; **pardon bargain letters to Lew Wallace by:** letter of March 13, 1879: 18, 297, 415, 537, 552, 555-556, 558-559, 857, 850-851; the letter: 558-559; letter of March 20, 1879: the letter: 565-567; "Billie" letter of March 24, 1879: 416, 556, 575-582; the letter: 578-579; letter of December 12, 1880: 741-743; the letter: 742-743; jail letter of January 1, 1881: the letter: 764; jail letter of March 2, 1881: 35, 563, 717-718, 764, 766, 796, 803-804, 852; the letter: 766; jail letter of

March 4, 1881: the letter: 767; jail letter of March 27, 1881: the letter: 769; **pardon bargain letters from Lew Wallace:** letter of March 15, 1879: 560-561, 563, 851; the letter: 561; letter to "Squire" Wilson of March 20, 1879: the letter: 565; letter of March 20, 1879: 565; lost letters; (see Billy's letter of March 2, 1881); **March 17, 1879 meeting with Lew Wallace of:** 19, 415-416, 557, 561, 563, 577, 581, 584, 611, 741, 803, 827, 833, 838-840; **interview by Lew Wallace on March 23, 1879 of:** 4, 19, 416, 535, 548, 572-575, 577-580, 582, 696, 720, 741; **"precious specimen" letter by Lew Wallace:** 584-587, 831; the letter: 584-587, quote on: 585; **venue change of:** 19, 202, 231, 592, 601-603, 674, 760, 773, 777; **testimony in Dudley Court of Inquiry by:** 3, 8, 19, 33, 292, 297, 340, 416, 557-558, 607, 657-662, 667, 856; first mention as "Billy the Kid" on May 23, 1879 in: 648; testimony by: 657-662; attacked in Henry Waldo's closing argument: 681, 684-686; **guerrilla rustling by:** 8, 34, 335, 674, 699, 701, 708; **gambling by:** 17, 20, 120, 701, 743, 760; **killing of Joe Grant by:** 22, 26, 701; **pursuit as "outlaw" by Lew Wallace of:** 492, 494-495, 535-537, **"outlaw" press of:** 747-752, 757-760, 773-774, 785-786; **pardon from Secret Service for:** 7-8, 23, 710, 717-724, 853 (see Azariah Wild); **hunted in fabricated "Kid gang" of:** 7, 23, 27, 39, 57, 701, 708-710, 713-739, 741, 746-751, 755-756, 759, 797-798, 822, 852; **Lew Wallace reward notices for:** 18, 24, 417, 532, 535, 558, 576, 710, 744-747, 752 794, 796, 823, 826; of December 22, 1880: 744; of May 3, 1881: 794; of *Las Vegas Gazette*, December 22, 1880: 24, 417, 710, 744-745, 747; of *Daily New Mexican*, May 3, 1881: 24, 794; **Coyote Spring ambush of:** 23, 734-735, 746, 750; **Greathouse ranch ambush of:** 23, 734-738, 743, 746, 748; **Stinking Springs capture of:** 7, 9, 24-25, 731, 742, 755-756, 759, 784, 835; **transport to Santa Fe jail of:** 756; **transport to Mesilla jail of:** 773-774; **Mesilla hanging trial of:** 3-4, 7-9, 20, 30, 79, 197, 298, 576, 591-592, 608, 610; 710, 731, 755, 764, 769, 773, 775-784, 850; **letter of April 15, 1881 to Edgar Caypless by:** the letter: 784-785; **jailbreak by:** 3, 7, 9, 24, 31-32, 150, 503, 581, 731, 791-793, 795, 804, 854; **killing in jailbreak of James Bell and Robert Olinger by:** 3, 9, 26, 32-33, 733, 791-792, 825, 854; **killing of by Pat Garrett:** 806; **Coroner's Jury Report of:** 806-807; **Lew Wallace's Billy the Kid outlaw myth articles about:** 795-798, 801-805, 821-844

Booth, John Wilkes – 387, 403, 410, 560

Borrego murder trial (see Thomas Benton Catron)

Bosque Grande ranch – 17, 709, 717, 722, 729, 734, 748-749

Bosque Redondo – 20, 152

Boston and New Mexico Cattle Company – 56

Bowdre, Charles "Charlie" – 9, 14, 17, 21-22, 24-26, 34, 282, 321, 324-327, 335, 339, 439, 496, 525, 536-538, 541, 701, 708-709, 714, 723, 726, 731, 739, 742-743, 755, 759

Bowdre, Manuela – 17

Bowers, George M. – 113

Bowman, George R. – 780

Boyle, Andrew – 428, 439, 545-546, 673, 684, 686

Brady, William – 5, 12-15, 17-18, 22, 25-26, 28-29, 31, 34, 56, 64, 70-74, 80, 84, 155, 157, 168, 229, 232, 242, 244-245, 250-251, 353-256, 258-259, 268-269, 272-276, 280-281, 283, 285, 288-289, 287-300, 303-305, 307-311, 415, 449, 476-477, 483, 503, 551, 556-558, 611, 684; **trial for killing of:** 776-784

Breaking Loose Together: The Regulator Rebellion in Pre-Revolutionary North Carolina – 266

Breeden, M.A. – 129

Breeden, William – 52, 59, 61, 117, 120, 123, 156, 175, 177, 181, 188, 219-221, 228, 428, 447, 703-704, 816

Bremen, A.W. – 196
Brent, Jim – 814
Brewer, Richard "Dick" – 8 13-14, 26, 30-31, 65-66, 250-251. 268-274, 280, 282-283, 285, 298, 302-303, 311-312, 316-317, 321, 557, 566
Brinkerhoff, Henry R. – 607, 622, 645, 651, 656, 658, 675, 678
Briscoe, Joe – 20, 731
Bristol, Warren H. – 12, 19-20, 24-25, 57, 69-70, 73, 77, 130-135, 150, 172, 177, 183-184, 191-192, 196, 198, 212-215, 231, 238, 242, 252, 255, 276, 278, 285, 293, 306-308, 314, 363, 427, 429, 434-436, 438, 440-441, 443, 485, 500. 503, 525, 537, 545, 587-588, 591-592, 597, 601, 607-608, 611, 635. 637, 640-642, 666, 668, 671, 678, 681, 697, 732, 773, 775-781, 784. 793, 850; **January 10, 1874 outlaw myth letter by:** 130-132; **petition to remove by Mary McPherson:** 196-198, 212-215; **jury instructions in Billy Bonney trial by:** 776-780
Brockway, William – 747, 750
Brooks, James J. – 22-23, 215, 708-712, 726, 729, 732, 735
Brookville, Indiana – 384, 403
Brown, Henry – 25, 31, 271, 311, 324-327, 439, 541, 602, 705
Buell, Don Carlos – 386, 391, 401, 762
Buell, George – 293
Bush, James – 663-664, 677, 687
Caffey, David L. – 149
Cahill, Frank "Windy" – 10, 13-14, 22, 26, 98, 238, 714
Cameron, Harry F. – 105
Campbell, Billy – 18-19, 230, 243, 490-491, 525-529, 532-534, 538, 541-543, 557, 564, 567-568 571, 584, 597, 599-601, 604, 756 **indicted for Chapman's murder:** 597, 599-601; **reward for capture of:** 532; **escape from Fort Stanton by:** 532
Canon de Chama Grant – 815
Capitan Mountains – 27, 573, 738, 792
Cardenas, Manuel – 157-158, 168, 176-177, 215-217, 219, 229-230, 259
Carillos Coal and Iron Company – 111
Carlyle, Jim – 23, 26, 417, 733-734, 737, 742-743, 750, 791

Carrizozo Land and Cattle Company ranch – 34, 56, 66, 73, 241, 248, 336, 351, 525-526, 531. 539, 573, 701, 724, 728
Carroll, Henry – 429, 439, 523-524, 527-529, 532-533, 538-539, 548, 567, 569-570, 573, 592. 643, 669, 671
Casey, John P. – 81
Casey, Robert – 11, 67, 100 242, 366, 541
Catron, Charles C. – 55, 105
Catron-Dolan Pecos River Cow Camp – 56, 65-66, 71, 73-74, 274, 311, 316, 539
Catron, Julia – 377
Catron, Thomas Benton – 4-7, 9, 11-12, 14-15, 17-22, 25, 28, 34, 36, 38, 43-44, 46-108, 110-111, 113, 117-121, 123, 125-130, 136, 139, 150-156, 158, 160, 164, 166, 168-172, 174-177, 179, 181-187, 190-196, 200, 203-204, 209-212, 217-218, 220-221, 224, 226-228, 231, 235-238, 241-244, 247-248, 251-253, 257-258, 265, 274, 279-280, 288, 291-292, 297, 299-300, 307, 311, 314, 319-321, 324, 327, 329-330, 332-337, 339, 345-347, 349, 351, 363, 372-375, 377, 370-380, 414, 416, 427-428, 430-432, 465, 473, 470, 491, 495-496, 503, 521, 525-526, 532, 536-537, 539, 547, 558, 560, 563, 579, 585, 592, 606, 608, 610, 620, 635, 650, 666, 674, 697-698, 701, 704-705, 708-710, 712-715, 718-719, 724-725, 728, 739, 741, 775, 791, 793, 813-814, 816-817, 850-851; **biography of:** 48-106; **Kettenring family surname of:** 51; **"Battle of the Archives" by:** 52, 60, 117; **code of:** (see John Riley codebook); **malicious prosecutions by:** 5, 36, 38, 43-44, 48, 52, 55, 58-59, 62, 65-66, 68-69, 71, 98, 103, 114, 120, 126, 130, 157, 160, 164, 168-173, 175, 177, 182-185, 188-189, 191, 195-196, 220-221, 235-238, 242, 251, 255-258, 265, 338, 347, 375, 697, 708, 814, 855; **expurgating fire of 1888:** 54, 64, 80-81, 280, 372; **Borrego murder trial by:** 82-86, 99, 101; **disbarment proceedings of:** 86-98, 121, 714; *Albuquerque Daily Citizen* **plot:** 88-95, 98-99;

indictment or dismissal as U.S. Attorney: 376-378; **report of Frank Warner Angel:** 78-80, 372-373 (see exposés of by Mary McPherson; see Santa Fe Ring)

Caypless, Edgar – 25, 784

C. Brown and Company of Santa Fe – 64

Chaffe, Gerome Bunty – 59-60, 108, 110, 152

Chapman, Huston I. – 6, 8, 18-20, 33, 230, 243, 268, 292, 351-352, 414-416, 426, 450-451, 454, 463-471, 474, 480, 482-483, 485-486, 889-491, 495-502, 504-506, 509-510, 513-519, 521-522, 525-526, 528-529, 531, 535-536, 541, 556-560, 563, 567-569, 571, 575, 578, 580, 584, 588-590, 597, 599-601, 603, 607, 610-611, 613, 617, 619-620, 624, 626-628, 631, 635, 637-639, 645, 657, 667, 673, 692, 740, 767, 775, 801-802, 804, 833, 838, 840, 850, 852-853, 856; **letter of October 24, 1878:** 450-451; **letter of November 25, 1878:** 467-468; **letter of November 29, 1878:** 467-471; **Dolan threat letter to Lew Wallace about:** 482-483; **assassination of:** 490-491, 495-498, 514-518

Chapman, W.W. – 504-506, 514, 613

Chavez, A. – 429

Chavez boys – 573

Cháves, Florencio – 16, 338

Chaves, Francisco – 82-85, 88, 97-98, 100

Chavez, Francisco J. – 703, 774

Chavez, Jose – 434

Cháves y Cháves, José – 658, 661-662, 685-686

Chilcott, George – 60, 152

Childers, W.B. – 88-89, 91

Chisum, John Simpson – 12, 14, 65, 69, 71, 168, 242, 245-246, 248, 252-253, 277, 280-281, 283, 287, 307, 317, 337, 429, 539, 544, 578-579, 581-582, 724, 728, 742-743, 760, 782-783, 802, 804, 832-833, 844

Chittenden, O.K. – 168

Cimarron News and Press – 62, 84, 150, 155, 157, 159-160, 163, 165, 168, 171, 175, 195-196, 221, 223-224, 233, 237, 242, 285-286, 350, 370, 428

Cimarron, New Mexico Territory – 9, 38, 60, 62, 129, 134, 151-152, 154-158, 160, 162-163, 165-169, 171-172, 176-178, 182-183, 185, 201, 206, 215-210, 224-226, 228-229, 232-235, 237-238, 255, 261, 280, 289, 347, 350, 368-371, 426-427, 429-432, 458, 478, 482, 500, 516

Cimarron Press – 154

Cimarron River – 165

Cincinnati *Commercial Tribune* – 112, 830-831, 838

Cincinnati Post – 828

Civil War – 4, 6, 17-18, 20, 36-38, 43, 45, 51, 77, 107, 144, 290-291, 356, 380, 383, 411, 414, 418, 423-424, 455, 457-458, 463, 663, 709, 730, 762, 852

Cisneza del Matcho (Mule Spring) – 572

Clark, Rush – 260-262

Cleaveland, Agnes Morley – 149, 161, 169, 172, 174-175, 182-183; *Satan's Paradise* by: 149, 174; *No Life for a Lady* by: 149, 161, 169, 174

Cleaveland, Norman – 109, 149, 153-156, 158, 161, 168-169, 171, 175-176, 182-183, 206, 379, 817; *The Morleys: Young Upstarts of the Southwest Frontier* by: 109, 149, 153, 169, 171, 183, 379, 817

Cleveland, Grover – 50, 100, 111, 112

Cockrell, John J. – 814

Cocoran, T. – 312

codebook (see John Riley)

Coe, Frank – 14, 28-30, 298, 321-322

Coe, George – 14, 25, 28-30, 282, 298, 324-328, 708

Coghlan, Pat – 17, 57, 531, 701, 709, 729

Colfax County, New Mexico – 6, 9, 53, 60, 62-63, 70, 78, 84, 123, 136, 150-151, 154-158, 160, 162-166, 168-169, 178, 180, 182-184, 195, 199-201, 206-207, 218-219, 222, 224-225, 227-228, 230-232, 234-235, 237-238, 242, 245, 260, 265, 275, 347, 349-350, 355, 365, 368-369, 371, 380, 426-427, 434, 495, 602, 671, 697, 811, 813 (see Colfax County War; see removal of courts of under Samuel Beach Axtell)

Colfax County Ring – 157

959

Colfax County's courts removal – 62-63, 78, 123, 165, 168, 175, 195, 218, 224, 371, 434
Colfax County troubles – 62
Colfax County War – 4, 9, 50, 55, 59-63, 68, 81, 118, 136, 149-238, 260, 283, 299-300, 435
Colfax, Schyler – 151
Collier, Needham – 87
Collier, T.W. – 97
Collinson, John – 60, 152, 378
Commodus: An Historical Play – 399
Conklin, Carlos (Charles) M. – 84, 121
Compiled Laws of New Mexico – 452, 561, 570, 851
Congress House Resolution 795 – 144
Connelly, Henry – 107
Constantinople, Turkey – 417-418, 800, 823, 823
Contreras, Don Matais – 54
Conway, Thomas (T.F.) – 129, 429
Cooper, Thomas "Tom" – 22, 709, 712-714, 716-717, 721-722, 724, 727, 732, 736, 749
Copeland, John – 15, 66, 74, 78, 168, 256, 283, 283, 298-299, 320, 322-323, 328, 331, 366-367, 429, 512, 525; **removal by Governor Axtell:** 15,
Coralitos, Mexico – 574
Coroner's Jury Report – **for "Windy" Cahill:** 10; **John Tunstall:** 260; **for William Bonney** 806-807
Corbet, Sam – 573; **"deposition" of:** 551
Corbin, James – 141-142
Cortéz, Hernándo – 380, 391, 406
Cornocopia mine – 770
courthouse-jail – 25, 791
Coyote Spring ambush – 23 734-735, 746, 750
Cracking the Billy the Kid Case Hoax – 849
Crawford, C.P. – 327
Crawfordsville, Indiana – 388, 404, 406-408, 411-412, 418 424, 799-800, 802, 816, 830-831
Crawfordsville Journal (see *Weekly Crawfordsville Journal*)
Crawfordsville *Saturday Evening Journal* – 400, 412, 799, 801, 828
Crawfordsville *Weekly News-Review* – 830
Crawfordsville *Weekly Review* – 826
Crist, Jacob H. – 84, 86-89, 91-92, 97-98, 391, 714

Crouch, John S. – 327, 429
Crumps Landing, Tennessee – 384, 395-396
Cunningham, William P. – 84-85, 165
Curry, George – 104
Cutting, Bronson – 50
Daily New Mexican –
Dandy Dick – 34
Davis Coal and Coke Company – 111
Davis, George (alias Tom Jones) – 268-269, 273, 312, 429, 439, 544, 578, 580
Davis, Hallie – 110
Davis, H.G. – 110
Dawson, Will – 154, 160, 163
"Dear Ben plot" – 61-62, 70, 78, 166-167, 170-171, 182, 224, 232-233, 237, 260, 283, 289, 347-348, 370-371, 482, 495; **the "Dear Ben letter:** 167, 350, 370
"Declaration of Independence" (1776) – 37, 265, 855
"Declaration of Independence" (1876) (see "Grant County Declaration of Independence")
Dedrick, Dan – 17, 22-23, 351, 701, 709, 712, 716-717, 721-722, 727, 729-730, 734-736, 738
Dedrick, Mose – 22-23, 716, 730
Dedrick, Sam – 22-23, 716, 730, 734
Deer Park, Maryland – 111, 373-374
Delaney, Cyrus – 275, 315
Delgado, F. – 429
Delgado, Juan – 703
Deming, New Mexico – 790, 796
Denver and Rio Grande Railroad – 55, 670
Devens, Charles – 78, 177, 184, 205, 356, 358, 361, 373-374, 454, 500
DeVours, James – 726, 728
Desert Land Act – 245, 250
"Diario de Consejo" – 119, 122
Dickens, Charles – 828-829
DNA – 849
Dolan Cow Camp (see Catron-Dolan Pecos River Cow Camp)
Dolan outfit, party (see James Dolan)
Dolan, James – 11, 13, 16, 18-19, 22, 25, 33, 64-66, 71, 155, 170, 241, 243-244, 250-255, 257-260, 269-270, 273-274, 291-292, 299-300, 303-304, 307-312, 315-321, 323-324, 329, 337-338, 365-367, 429-430, 433, 439, 482-483, 491, 503; 516-517, 525-527, 529-532, 535, 538, 557, 560, 563-564, 568, 578-

580, 589, 591, 597-601, 604, 606-608, 635, 638-639, 665-668, 672-673, 681, 704, 712-715, 721, 740, 774, 776, 783, 813; **response to "A Tax-Payer's Complaint" by:** 71, 253-254; **warrant and indictment for Tunstall's murder for:** 243, 259-260, 723-274, 601; **peace meeting with Billy Bonney of:** 18, 243, 491; **indictment for Chapman murder of:** 638-639, 597, 599-601; **voiding of Chapman murder indictment for:** 20; **Dolan outfit or party of:** 578-579, 608, 667, 690, 704; **reporting counterfeit bill by:** 22, 712-714; **as witness in Brady murder trial:** 25, 774, 776, 783
Dolan-Riley faction – 689-690, 704
Doña Ana County, New Mexico Territory – 19, 51, 77, 107, 139, 202, 231, 571, 592, 601-602, 606, 674, 777
Donnell Lawson, and Co. – 284, 305
Donoghue, Florencio – 157-158, 160, 162, 176-177, 180, 182, 215-216, 219, 229-230
Dorsey, Stephen Wallace – 55, 182, 199, 206, 209, 234, 429, 459
Dry Tortugas – 387
Douglas, Stephen A. – 407
Dowlin, Will – 318, 320, 429, 714, 721, 814
D'Sena, Jose – 429
Dudley Court of Inquiry (see Nathan Augustus Monroe Dudley)
Dudley, Nathan Augustus Monroe – 5-8, 16, 18-20, 33, 64-67, 73, 75-79, 97, 101, 106, 110, 153-154, 158, 166, 170, 178-179, 287, 289-293, 297-300, 319, 334-335, 338-340, 343, 351, 414-416, 429-430, 433-434, 438, 440-441, 445-446, 450-451, 429-430, 433-434, 438, 440-441, 445-446, 450-451, 454, 456, 463-484, 486, 489-497, 499, 501-502, 505, 509-530, 535, 538, 541, 543, 548-552, 556-557, 559, 568-569, 576-577, 580, 592-593, 597, 601, 605-607, 611-613, 617-698, 740, 745, 775, 803, 805, 813, 833, 836, 852, 856; **biography of:** 289-293; **past court martials of:** 6, 19, 75, 290-291, 463, 521;
indictment by Lincoln County 1879 Grand Jury of: 601, 606, 608; **removal requests by Lew Wallace for:** 19, 472-474, 497, 509, 518-521, 523, 527-528, 535, 559, 592-593; **removal by Edward Hatch of:** 520-521; **"Open Letter" by:** 473-479; **Susan McSween's charges against:** 510-514, 617-618; **response to charges of:** 521-522; **Court of Inquiry for court martial of:** 6-7, 19-20, 33, 64, 76-77, 97, 170, 179, 297, 502, 548, 552, 556, 577, 607, 611-612, 617-694, 696, 740, 775, 803, 813, 833, 836, 852, 856; **testimony by:** 673-679; **Susan McSween's civil Cause 298 against:** 697 (see Lincoln County War battle)
"Dutch Chris" – 573
Ealy, Taylor – 259, 260-261, 283, 313, 337, 339, 547, 551, 678
Early, Jubal – 409
Easton, David – 65-66, 257, 299, 322, 336, 338-339, 511, 619, 648, 714-715
Eaton Land Grant – 54
Eckles, William H. – 141-143
Elizabeth City Railway Press and Telegraph – 160
Elizabethtown, New Mexico – 60, 118, 151, 153-156, 158, 166, 215-216, 229
Elkins, John T. – 61, 153, 206
Elkins, Stephen Benton – 4-5, 9, 21-22, 43-44, 46-48, 50-55, 57-61, 63, 68, 76, 78-80, 82-83, 85-87, 99, 101-102, 104-105, 107-113, 117-118, 120-121, 125, 129, 150-156, 161-163, 172, 179, 183-185, 187-188, 191, 193-196, 199, 204, 206, 209-212, 220-223, 226-229, 231-232, 235-238, 242-243, 280, 288, 330, 332, 334, 343, 349, 363, 372-378, 380, 430-431, 458, 707-708, 710, 811; **biography of:** 107-113; **exposés of by Mary McPherson:** 161-163, 209-212, 220-221; **covering up for Catron's Angel report by:** 373-378, 704; **collected papers of:** 107, 375
Elk Garden Coal Company – 111
Ellis, Benjamin "Ben" – 260, 286, 288, 429
Ellis house – 298, 503, 687

Ellis, Isaac – 256, 298, 313, 316, 322-328, 337, 339, 449; **"deposition" of:** 550-551, 663, 774, 776
Ellison, Sam – 430, 696
Elsinger, Robert – 80-82, 100
Elston Bank of Crawfordsville, Indiana – 411, 769
Elston, Isaac Jr. – 411
El Paso and South Western Railroad – 55
embezzlement case – (see Alexander McSween)
Emil Fritz insurance policy (see Emil Fritz)
Evans, Jessie – 11, 13, 18-19, 71, 80, 155, 228-230, 238, 242-243, 250-251, 258-260, 268-271, 273-274, 279, 297, 300, 303, 308-312, 315, 320, 337, 357, 429, 433, 439, 491, 516, 525-527, 532-534, 538, 542-543, 557, 560-561, 564, 568, 571, 574-575, 578-580, 582, 584, 597, 599-601, 604, 813, 833, 840, 854; **indicted for Chapman's murder:** 597, 599-601; **reward for capture of:** 532; **escape from Fort Stanton by:** 532; **2nd degree murder verdict in Texas:** 854
Evetts, William M. – 109, 111, 152, 374, 389, 443-444, 459
Fall, Albert – 105
Fanning, Edmund – 267
Farmer, Joseph – 430
Faulkner, C.J. – 112
federal indictment Number 411 – 27, 60, 324-327, 536, 606, 708, 775
Feliz River – 11, 67, 234, 241-242, 245, 248, 250, 269, 572-573, 580
Feliz River Ranch – 13, 31, 259
Ferry, Thomas T. – 124, 129
Field, N.B. – 91
Fields, Westley – 430
First Judicial District – 52, 60, 84, 120, 155, 160, 175, 454, 800, 813
First National Bank of Santa Fe – 55, 71-72, 108, 125, 152, 248, 253, 376
Fiske, E.A. – 89, 91, 430-431, 703-705, 816246
Flint, Robert –
Florida election fraud (Rutherford B. Hayes) – 144, 389, 412
Fort Bayard – 56
Fort Donelson – 408
Fort Grant – 10
Fort Griffin – 574

Fort Henry – 408
Fort Marcy – 121-122, 153, 166
Fort Stanton – 11, 16, 56, 64-65, 67, 76, 106, 154, 166, 230, 241, 244, 248, 259, 275, 281-283 287, 289, 291-292, 298-300, 314-315, 318-320, 322-323, 333-334, 336, 338-339, 344, 367, 394, 409, 414, 416, 429-430, 435, 439-441, 444-446, 456, 464-465, 468-471, 473-475, 478, 480-482, 486-487, 490, 492-484, 496-497, 499, 505, 509-512, 515-521, 523-536, 538-541, 543, 545, 548-552, 557, 559, 564-565, 567-569, 573, 580, 589-593, 603-604, 606, 612-613, 617-618, 620-623, 628, 632, 637, 639, 643-645, 675, 664-665, 667-668, 669, 671, 674, 678-679, 689-690, 692-693, 697, 704, 708, 710, 712, 714-715, 717, 720-722, 728-729, 741, 776, 782, 792; **sutler store at:** 56, 64-65, 244, 708
Fort Sumner – 8-9, 17, 20-24, 27, 150, 152, 243, 441, 537, 541, 701, 709, 714, 717, 721-734, 736-739, 742, 747-748, 751, 755, 791, 806, 826-827
Fort Union – 153, 158-159, 166-168, 175, 230, 232, 261, 289-293, 350, 369-370, 520-521, 528-529, 537, 552, 569, 635, 678
"Fort Union and the Frontier Army in the Southwest" – 290
Fountain, Albert Jennings – 25, 306, 472, 503, 591-592, 703, 775-776, 780-781, 784-785; **jury instructions for Brady trial:** 780-781
Frank Springer and New Mexico – 149, 224
French, James – 479, 483, 486, 501, 512-515, 517-518, 620, 726
French, Jim "Frenchie" – 13-14, 16, 25, 76, 281, 338, 439, 541, 648, 708
Fritz, Charles – 34, 251-252, 298, 304-307, 310, 674, 701
Fritz, Emil – 11-12, 64, 70, 241, 244, 250-252, 284, 301, 304; **life insurance policy of:** 12, 70, 251, 304, 347, 640
From Resistance to Revolution – 266
Gallegos, José – 123-124
Gallegos, Juan – 84

Gallegos, Panteleon – 268-269, 273, 304, 312, 430
Garcia, Candelario – 121
Garfield, James Abran – 110, 128, 329, 417-418, 787, 811-812, 823
Garrett, Patrick Floyd "Pat" – 3-4, 7, 9, 20-25, 27-28, 35, 56-57, 101, 121, 150-151, 417, 503, 532, 576, 696, 701, 710, 725, 730-738, 742-743, 746, 749-750, 755-756, 759, 784-785, 791-793, 804, 806-807, 824-827, 835-837, 842-843, 849; **biography of:** 730-731
Gatling gun – 16, 106, 291, 339, 404, 496, 510, 550, 619, 647, 663, 690
Gauss, Gottfried – 26, 31-33, 271, 791; **interview on Billy Bonney's jailbreak:** 32-33
Gentry, William – 327
Giddings, Marsh – 36, 52-53, 57-59, 109, 117-118, 120-121, 123-130, 132, 135-136, 144, 153-154, 160, 165-166, 215, 243, 334; **gerrymandering:** 123, 144
Gilbert, Robert M. – 260, 283, 317, 545, 577, 666
Gildy, Gus – 439, 573
Ginn, John M. – 141
Gobles, Reese – 439, 573
Godfroy, Frederick – 65, 72-73, 241, 257, 285, 300, 310, 319, 429, 479, 547, 582
Gonzales, Florencio – 286-288, 308, 313, 430, 540, 575-576, 589
Gonzales, Ignacia – 449
Gonzales, Ignacio – 16, 338
Gonzales y Borrego, Antonio – 83-84
Gonzales y Borrego, Francisco – 83-84, 86
Goodwin, Millard Filmore – 315, 322-323, 336, 469, 479, 492-494, 532, 550, 565-566, 684-685
government contracts (Indian reservation and military) – 4, 64-65, 248, 257, 261, 310, 359, 431, 579-580, 641, 701, 704, 712
Grace, Fred – 430
Grand Jury – **Taos County Grand Jury 1875:** 170, 175, 185, 188-189, 215, 218; **Taos County Grand Jury 1876:** 166, 175-181, 216, 219, 224, 228, 230; **Taos County Grand Jury 1877:** 177-181; **Grant County Grand Jury:** 198, 214; **Doña Ana County Grand Jury:** 697; **Lincoln County Grand Jury 1878:** 12, 14, 28, 259, 269, 281, 283-286, 288-289, 308, 314-315, 320, 324, 334, 434-435, 640, 726, 782; James Dolan and J.B. Matthews indicted for Tunstall murder: 288; Billy Bonney indicted for Brady and Hindman murders: 28, 269, 283, 289; Alexander McSween acquitted: 14, 283-284, 319, 334, 641 (see McSween embezzlement case); **Lincoln County Grand Jury 1879:** 6, 14, 19, 33, 415, 502, 510, 513, 515, 526, 533, 556-557, 563, 577, 588-589, 591-593, 597-601, 603, 606-611, 617, 627, 636-638, 653-654, 666-667, 797, 803, 833, 840, 852-852; venue change for Billy Bonney and Ringites in: 601-603 (see William H. Bonney pardon bargain; see pardon in bar of prosecution in); **Lincoln County Grand Jury 1880:** 733, 774
Granger, Gorden – 59, 121
"Grant County Declaration of Independence" – 141-143, 145
Grant County *Herald* – 140-143, 196, 212, 242, 297, 600
Grant County, New Mexico Territory – 122, 139-142, 144-145, 173, 196-197, 280, 297, 706, 745
Grant County Rebellion – 4, 47, 57, 119, 136, 139-145, 149, 173, 180, 260
Grant, Joe – 22, 26, 701
Grant, Ulysses S. – 6, 52-53, 58, 61, 109-110, 117-118, 123, 128, 136, 139, 151, 178, 194, 345-346, 383, 385, 391, 394, 400-402, 405, 408-412, 415, 418, 458, 518, 523, 555, 742, 812
Graves, Peter – 141-142
Greathouse, Jim "Whiskey Jim" – 734-735, 743, 750
Greathouse ranch – 23, 735-738, 746, 748, 750; **ambush there:** 23, 734-735
Green, Tom – 312
Griego, Francisco "Pancho" – 155, 157-158, 162, 168, 175, 177, 215-216, 228-229
Griffin, W.W. – 430
Grossetete, Alexis – 80-82, 100
Grove, Jesse A. – 290
Guerney, Spencer – 534
Gutierrez, Apolinaria – 21-22
Gutierrez, Celsa – 21, 27

Gutierrez, Jose M. – 573
Gutierrez, Juanita – 21
Gutierrez, Saval (Sabal) – 21, 27, 806-807
habeas corpus – **in Legislature Revolt of 1872:** 57, 121-122, 160; **for Franklin Tolby's accused murderer Robert Longwill in 1875:** 230; **for freeing Lew Wallace's Fort Stanton prisoners in 1879:** 526, 583, 586, 591-592, 637, 673, 776; **in Lew Wallace's Billy the Kid fictions:** 802, 833
Hagerman, Herbert J. – 103-104
Hagerman, James J. – 103
Hallborough, North Carolina – 267
Hall, Caleb (alias Collins) – 439
Halleck, Henry W. – 409
Halliehurst – 111, 376
Hamilton, Humphrey B. – 87, 90, 92, 97
Hannibal – 393
Hargrove's Saloon – 20-22, 701, 731
Harrison, Benjamin – 99, 111-112
Harrison, Russell B. – 112
Hatch, Edward – 75, 167, 275, 291-292, 329, 349, 350, 370, 424-425, 429-431, 437, 441, 444-445, 457, 463-467, 473-475, 481, 496, 509, 518, 520-527, 535-538, 552, 567-569, 618, 622, 624, 628-629, 670, 678, 697, 705, 708, 748, 762
Hayes, Rutherford B. – 6, 15, 17, 38, 46, 63, 68, 72, 78, 109-111, 128, 144, 149, 152-153, 172-174, 177-178, 180, 182-184, 187, 191, 194, 196, 200, 203, 221-222, 224, 237, 242, 276-279, 282, 286, 297, 299, 328-331, 333, 345-346, 348,355, 360, 363, 372, 374-375, 383-384, 389-390, 411-415, 417, 423-424, 440, 442-444, 453, 467, 471, 495, 523, 537, 560, 583, 636, 639, 642, 680, 695, 703, 705, 747, 766, 811-813, 823; **Presidential Proclamation of October 7, 1878 by:** 442-443;
Hefferan, Vioalle Clark – 106
Hill, John – 430
Hill, Joseph "Joe" (alias Joseph Olney) – 439, 574
Hill, Tom (alias Tom Chelson) – 270, 273, 303, 312, 578, 580
Hindman, George – 5, 14, 18, 22, 25-26, 28, 73, 259-260, 268-270, 273, 280-281, 283, 285, 288-289, 297-298, 312, 318-320, 324, 415, 476, 556, 558, 611, 775, 835, 850, 854-855
Hockradle, Jerrie – 430
Holly, Charles – 60, 152
Homestead Act – 4, 11, 28, 248, 580
Hondo River – 241-242
howitzer cannon – 16, 106, 291, 338-339, 550, 647, 663-664, 677, 690
Hoyt, Henry – 17, 34-35, 352, 450; **Billy Bonney's bill of sale to:** 352
Howe, Albert – 430
Hubbard, John G. – 348-350
Hudgens, William "Will" – 564-565, 598, 734, 737
Hughes, Thomas – 88, 94-95
Humphreys, Henry H. – 170, 620-622, 635, 645, 649-654, 656, 658, 664, 675, 678-679, 688; **closing argument in Dudley Court of Inquiry by:** 688-690
Hurley (Hurlie), John – 430, 608-609; **pardon in bar of prosecution:** 609-610
Husband, Herman – 266-267
Hyson, James – 440
Indian Department vouchers – 71
Indiana Historical Society – 207, 414, 419, 428, 575
Indiana Volunteers – 384, 407
Indianapolis, Indiana – 404, 414, 796, 802, 832
Indianapolis Journal – 413
Indianapolis News – 401
Irvin, James – 573
Isaacs, J. – 328-329
Jacobs, Sarah – 108
James, Jesse – 710, 755, 801-802, 833, 840
Jaramillo, Lorenzo – 807
Jefferson, Thomas – 37, 855
J. Ellis and sons – 283
Johnson, Andrew – 109, 387, 410
Johnson, E. Dana – 106
Johnson, Hezekiah S. – 122
Johnson, John R. – 121-123, 126
J.J. Dolan and Company – 257
Jones, A.A. – 91
Jones, Bill – 242, 439, 544-545, 574, 638
Jones family – 574, 581, 638
Jones, Heiskell – 459, 574
Jones, Jim – 242, 439, 544-545, 574, 638

Jones, John – 242, 439, 544, 574, 638, 659, 661, 696-697
Jones, Tom (see George Davis)
"Journal of the House of Representatives" – 119-120
Juárez, Benito – 388, 409, 411
Kars, Marjoline – 266-268
Kaye, Donald E. – 290
Keleher, William – 119, 121-122, 149; **Violence in Lincoln County by:** 119
Kerens, Richard C. – 99, 102, 105
Kettenring surname of: 51
Kimbrell, George – 18, 23, 491-493, 516, 526, 537, 541-542, 545, 556-557, 565-567, 577, 590, 592, 606, 639, 720, 725, 727, 730-731
Kinney, John – 15-16, 21, 27, 65, 74-75, 228, 242, 297-298, 335-338, 359, 367, 433, 471, 493, 535, 539, 649, 731-733
Kirchner, August – 58, 120-121
Knaebel, George W. – 91
Koogler, J.H. – 739, 741-742, 759, 792-793, 801
Kriling, Charles – 430
Ladbessor, Chris – 573
Lambert, Oscar Doane – 107-114
land grab – 21, 44-46, 52, 54-55, 82, 107, 114, 183, 193-194, 207, 247, 266, 811
Las Cruces *Borderer* – 140
Las Cruces, New Mexico ("Cruces") – 254, 258, 288, 431-432, 574, 773-774, 843
Las Cruces *Thirty-Four Newspaper* – 49, 761
Las Cruces *Rio Grande Republican* – 503
Las Vegas Daily Gazette – 24, 756
Las Vegas Daily Optic – 99
Las Vegas Gazette – 237, 428, 510, 514, 619, 739, 741-742, 744, 759, 792, 850
Las Vegas Independent Democrat – 58
Las Vegas jail – 69, 752
Las Vegas, New Mexico – 12, 19, 24, 69, 96, 98, 252-253, 281, 292, 307, 315, 337, 343-344, 351-352, 428, 430-431, 450, 454, 463-464, 467-468, 474, 491, 500-502, 513-514, 516, 589, 613, 624, 636, 682, 701, 724, 739, 747, 751, 756, 759, 784, 813, 815
Las Vegas Optic – 58, 82, 121

Las Tablas, New Mexico – 27, 535-536, 792
Laughlin, Napoleon Bonaparte – 84, 86-87, 97-98, 387
Legislature Revolt of 1872 – 4, 57-59, 103, 118-123, 125-126, 130, 139-140, 149, 153-155, 160, 166, 260, 283, 334, 355, 435, 526, 806
Lee, William – 430
Leonard, Ira E. – 8, 19, 23-25, 32-34, 77, 100, 351, 416, 450, 454, 499-504, 509-518, 521, 531, 533-534, 544, 546, 571, 577, 588-592, 597-598, 603-605, 610-611, 613, 617, 619-622, 634-642, 644-645, 649, 651, 653, 656, 658, 665-666, 671, 674-675, 678, 682, 688, 692, 694, 697, 703, 706-707, 710, 714, 716-724, 730, 741-742, 764, 767, 773-775, 804, 851-853; **biography of:** 499-503; **asthma of:** 500, 503, 534, 634, 636, 707; **involvement in Billy Bonney's pardon bargain with Lew Wallace:** 33, 597-598, 610-611, 851-852; **attempted assassination of:** 603-605; **letters about Santa Fe Ring:** 634-642; **charges against N.A.M. Dudley by:** 510-518, 617, 619-620; **making Billy Bonney's pardon bargain with Azariah Wild:** 718-724, 853; **defending Billy Bonney in Mesilla by:** 773-775 (see Dudley Court of Inquiry)
L.G. Murphy and Company – 31, 64-65, 70, 72, 301-306, 313, 359
Leverson, Montegue – 277-278, 280-282, 317-318, 329-330, 334, 343-348, 430
Lilly Library, Bloomington, Indiana – 419
Lincoln, Abraham – 18, 37, 380, 407, 410, 412, 458, 621
Lincoln County courthouse jail – 25, 31, 791, 786, 791, 802, 824-825, 841-842
Lincoln County Grand Juries (see grand juries)
Lincoln County Justice of the Peace (see John "Squire" Wilson)
Lincoln County, New Mexico Territory – 5-7, 9, 12-13, 15, 17-19, 21-23, 25, 28, 31, 33, 38, 44, 56, 64-67, 70-71, 73-74, 77-78, 82, 118, 123, 130-132, 134-135, 139, 155, 157, 163, 165, 168, 177, 220-221, 223-226, 229-

965

232, 241-245 247, 249-250, 252-254, 256, 259-261, 265. 268-270, 273-276, 278 282-283, 285-287, 289, 291-292 297, 300-302, 304-305, 307-309 313-314, 318-324, 328, 331, 333, 340, 343-344, 348-349, 351, 355-356, 362. 364-365, 391, 414-415 417, 426-435, 437-438, 440-445 447, 450-454, 456-457, 459, 464, 466, 468-473, 475-480, 483, 485, 487, 489-492, 495, 497-500, 503 510-517, 526, 535-537, 539-540 547-551, 564, 580, 583, 586, 591, 593, 597, 599, 602-603, 606-613 617, 620. 625-626, 630-633, 636 638, 645. 657, 665, 667, 669-670 674, 678. 680, 682-683, 689-692 694, 696-697, 701, 706-708, 710 712-716, 725-726, 729, 731, 734, 737-738. 740, 744-745, 749, 751, 755, 765, 774, 776-777, 791-792 794, 796-798, 802, 804, 814-815 823-824, 827, 836, 840, 852, 854-855; **involvement of T.B. Catron in:** 64-67 (see Edgar Walz)

Lincoln County Sheriff (William Brady, John Copeland, George Peppin, George Kimbrell, Pat Garrett)

Lincoln County Sheriff's Department (modern, corrupt) – 849

Lincoln County troubles – 6, 18, 20, 36, 64, 68, 75, 226, 241, 300, 324, 330, 347, 355, 358-360 362, 368, 429, 433, 580, 592, 665, 802; **Angel Report on:** 358-360

Lincoln County War – 3-6, 8-9, 11, 13, 15, 18-19, 21 23-24, 26, 28, 30-31, 34, 36, 38, 44, 47, 53, 56-57, 59, 64-65, 67-68, 73-75, 83, 106, 109, 114, 123, 136, 150, 154, 158, 166, 168, 170, 173, 178, 182, 184, 196, 207, 224, 226, 230, 234, 237-238, 241, 243-245, 261 267, 276 289, 290-293, 297-340 343, 347 351, 358, 367, 379, 415-416, 432-435, 438, 446, 463, 466, 468, 473-474, 483, 492-493, 510 535, 537 541, 543, 545, 548, 550-551, 556-559, 569, 572, 575-576 578-582, 601-602, 606, 611, 617, 619, 621, 626, 635, 640-641, 644 657, 698-698, 708, 713, 719, 725, 730-731 733, 744, 747, 773, 791, 795, 805-806, 833, 836, 850, 852-856; **battle in:** 5-6, 15, 18, 26, 36, 64, 69, 73-75, 106 224, 226, 241, 261, 276, 290, 292 297-299, 330, 335, 337-340, 343-344, 347, 367, 435, 463, 474, 543 550-551, 557, 560, 579, 580-581 617, 697, 723, 733, 791, 805; **deaths in:** 297-298, 641, 774

Lincoln Grand Jury (see Grand Jury)

Lincoln, New Mexico – 9, 11-19, 22, 25-26, 29-31, 33, 37, 56, 64, 66167, 70-71, 75-76, 106, 234, 241-245, 248 251-253, 255-256, 258-260, 269-278, 281-282, 284, 286, 288, 291 293, 298, 300, 302-303, 305, 307-314, 344, 351, 357, 359, 379, 406 415-416, 429-432, 444-445, 450-451, 465, 468-471, 475, 479-480 482-486, 489-493, 496-503, 505 509-516, 518-521, 524-527, 529-532, 535-547, 549-550, 556-557, 559-561, 563-564, 567, 571-572, 575-578, 584, 586, 588-592, 597, 599 601, 603-606, 612-613, 617, 619-622, 625-628, 630-632, 624-636, 639-640, 643, 645-646, 651, 654, 656-658, 672, 674-679, 681-682, 684 687, 689-692, 698, 707, 709, 712-717, 723-733, 738, 741, 743, 751 760, 773-774, 776, 782, 785-786 791-792, 794, 805, 814-815, 833-834, 840

"Little Casino" (see William H. Bonney)

Llewellyn, W.H. – 103

Long, Jack (John) – 281, 337-338, 601 650, 656, 659; **pardon in bar of prosecution:** 609-610

Longwill, Robert H. – 60-62, 155-156, 158-160, 162, 169-170, 176-177, 180. 182, 185, 216, 219, 227-230, 232-233, 235-236, 259, 430

Lovato, María Paula – 150

Loud, John S. – 333, 430, 446

Lucero, Pedro Antonio – 807

Lujan, Jesus – 54

Luna, Tranquilano – 49

Lusk, Huston – 663, 665

Mabry, Thomas Jewett – 849

Macabley, Dan – 395

Mackie, John – 10

MacNab, Frank – 14-15, 26, 65-66, 298-299, 321-322, 337, 345, 510, 525. 557, 579, 601, 791

Madison, James – 37

Mafia (American) – 43

Maier, Pauline – 266

Maingay, J.B. – 60
manifest destiny – 51, 107
Markland, Absalom H. – 457-460, 468, 502, 680
martial law – 347, 387, 414, 426, 432-433, 436, 438, 441-442, 445, 451, 484, 498, 583-584, 586-587, 618, 668-670, 741
Martinez and Pedilla Grant – 209
Martinez, Atanacio – 13, 274-275, 366
Martz, "Dutch" Martin – 31, 271-272, 312
Mason, Barney – 21, 27, 733-736
Mason, John S. – 132
Matchett, W.B. – 174, 180, 191, 196, 200, 202-204, 207
Matterson, M. – 431
Matthews, Jacob Basil "Billy" – 14, 20, 31, 66, 242, 259, 270-271, 273, 281, 310-312, 318, 323, 415, 430, 439, 525-529, 538, 564, 568, 601, 608-610, 684, 774, 776, 783; **pardon in bar of prosecution:** 609-610
Maxwell, Deluvina – 9
Maxwell family cemetery – 21
Maxwell Land Grant – 9, 21, 44, 55, 59-62, 72, 80, 109, 118, 125, 149-152, 194, 206, 211, 237-238, 374
Maxwell Land Grant and Railroad Company – 60-61, 63, 149, 153-155, 157, 165, 182, 185, 195, 224, 227, 379
Maxwell, Lucien Bonaparte – 9, 20-21, 55, 59-60, 108, 149-152, 194, 243, 374
Maxwell, Luz Trotier de Beaubien – 20-21, 150-151, 243, 806
Maxwell mansion – **in Cimarron:** 151, 154, 158; **in Fort Sumner:** 8-9, 150, 152, 806
Maxwell, Paulita – 9, 20, 27, 150-151, 243, 383, 578, 742, 791, 805
Maxwell, Peter "Pete" – 8-9, 20-21, 27, 747, 806
McCandleis, Charles – 431
McCarty, William Henry (see William H. Bonney)
McClellen, George B. – 407-408
McCloskey, William – 312, 316
McCormick, Richard C. – 107
McCrary, George – 383, 413, 424-425, 436, 455-456, 481, 513, 617, 695-696
McCullen, William – 431
McCullich, John B. – 62, 189
McDaniels, Jim – 431, 574

McKinley, William – 85, 101-102, 112-113
McKinney, Thomas "Kip" – 21, 27, 731
McMains, Oscar P. – 50, 81, 100, 149, 157-160, 163-165, 172, 174, 176-177, 180-182, 186, 190, 198, 207, 219-221, 224, 237
McPherson, Mary Tibbles – 38, 62-63, 68, 77, 150, 154, 158-159, 161, 163-164, 168-169, 172, 177, 180, 182-224, 226, 235, 237, 255, 277, 280, 300-351, 363, 374, 398, 413, 428, 431, 450, 458, 591, 639, 641-642, 671, 812-813, 817; **"Charges Against Thomas B. Catron, U.S. Attorney, and Others" by:** 184-186; response by Catron: 187-190; **"Charges Against New Mexican Officials Together with Corroboration of Evidence" by:** 191-203; **Addendum to:** 203; **petition to remove Judge Bristol by:** 196-198, 212-215; **"Charges Against S.B. Axtell, Governor of New Mexico" by:** 200-203; **public records request:** 204; **"In the Matter of Charges vs. Gov. S.B. Axtell and Other New Mexico Officials; Submitted to the Departments of the Interior and Justice, August, 1877":** 207-222; **public records request by:** 204
McSween, Alexander – 5-6, 8, 11-17, 19, 26, 38, 64-76, 98, 100, 130, 168, 170, 177-179, 196, 232, 242, 245-247, 250-260, 265, 270, 274-275, 280-284, 286, 288-292, 297-301, 306, 311, 315, 318-320, 323, 328, 334-335, 337-340, 343-345, 347, 352, 356-357, 359-360, 365, 367, 371, 405, 431-434, 451, 465, 469-470, 474, 479, 482-483, 486, 490, 493, 503, 510-511, 514-516, 519, 521-522, 535, 543, 548-552, 557, 559, 569, 578-579, 581-582, 607, 619, 622, 627, 640-641, 643, 645-651, 653, 655-656, 658-664, 672, 676, 679, 684, 690-691, 704, 767, 782-784, 852, 854-855; **Emil Fritz insurance policy pursuit:** 12, 70, 251, 304, 347, 640; embezzlement case from: 12, 14, 56, 70-71, 98, 168, 177, 252, 255, 259, 281, 283, 300, 307, 314, 319, 334, 347, 357, 640, 782; **T.B.**

Catron's codename for: 72, 320; **T.B. Catron's malicious prosecution of:** 251-253; **indictment of:** 12; **bail for:** 12, 71, 255-256, 281, 308; **bondsman for:** 12, 71, 256, 314; bondsmen's affidavit: 256; **Grand Jury acquittal of:** 14, 319 283-284, 334, 641; **deposition to Frank Warner Angel:** 300-323
McSween house – 16, 72, 245, 256, 291-292, 338-340, 551, 572, 657-664, 676, 679, 679, 684-689, 691; **burning by arson of:** 6-7, 16, 18, 75-77, 119, 166, 230, 290, 292, 339, 351, 366-367, 415, 450, 510, 549, 551, 557, 566, 573, 578, 581, 601, 606, 619, 628, 640, 645, 650, 663, 679, 690-691, 697-698, 805, 852
McSween party (faction, organization, side) – 292, 428-429, 431, 433, 516, 580, 608, 621, 623, 627, 640-641, 649, 663, 667, 672, 676, 679, 690-691
McSweens (men, loyalists) – 15-16, 65-66, 70, 292, 311, 337, 379, 429-430, 432-433, 469, 474, 479, 492, 521, 541, 550-551, 575, 606, 645-646, 650, 661, 663-664, 677-679, 691
McSween, Susan – 6, 12, 18-20, 33, 38, 76-77, 79, 97, 102, 173, 280, 290, 292-293, 337, 339, 343-344, 351-352, 414, 416 431, 450-451, 463-469, 474, 476 479, 482, 482-487, 491, 499-503, 509-512, 514-517, 521, 531, 617, 619-621, 625-626, 630-631, 634-335, 645, 676, 685, 687, 689, 691, 697; **defamatory affidavits on:** 19, 76-77, 292, 465-466, 511-512, 521, 619, 626, 645, 649, 697; **testimony in Dudley Court of Inquiry:** 645-656; civil **Cause No. 298 against:** 697
Meadows, John P. – 35, 351, 792
Meinig, D.W. – 44
Merita Juana Lopez Grant – 378
Mescalero Indian Reservation – 11, 14, 25, 56, 65, 72, 241, 248, 257, 282, 285, 300, 310, 321, 324, 328, 479, 503, 547, 579-580, 582, 715, 774-775; **called "the agency" by Billy Bonney:** 579;
Mesilla Independent – 71, 253, 286, 428-429, 486
Mesilla jail – 25, 786

Mesilla, New Mexico Territory – 12, 15, 20, 24-25, 34, 51-52, 65, 75, 77, 107, 120, 196, 231, 238, 242, 252, 255, 293, 298, 308-310, 315-317, 335 337, 367, 374, 428-432, 443, 490 503, 552, 571, 576, 591-592, 602 608, 610, 697-698, 710, 765, 769 773-774, 786, 791, 794, 850
Mesilla News – 428, 472-473, 608, 635, 698, 785
Mesilla Thirty-four – 600
Metcalf, Robert – 141-142
Mexican-American War – 150-151, 406, 408
Middaugh, Asa F. – 171, 235-236
Middleton, John – 13-14, 25, 31, 269, 271-272, 282, 311-312, 321, 324-327, 439, 541, 602, 708
Mills, A. Ham – 268-269, 273
Mills, Melvin – 60-62, 105, 154-156, 158, 160, 162, 169-170, 176-177, 180, 182, 186, 190, 195, 216, 219, 221, 224, 227-229, 235-236, 259, 268-269
Mills, Sam F. – 327
Mills, William J. – 98, 104
Mimbres Apaches – 293, 417, 574, 705-706, 760
Miranda, Guadalupe – 150-151
Mitchell, Robert B. – 52, 117
Montaño Jose – 71, 256, 283, 286-287, 313-314, 337, 431, 541, 549
Montgomery Guards – 407, 799
Moore, F. – 167, 350
Moore, Scott – 785
Morley, Ada McPherson – 158, 161, 165, 168-175, 182, 185, 188-189, 191, 235-236, 237, 817; **malicious prosecution by T.B. Catron of:** 168-171, 175, 185, 188-189, 191, 235-236; **buggy incident of:** 63, 169, 171, 184-185, 189, 235, 281; **terrified letter by:** 172-174
Morley, William Raymond – 60-62, 70, 78, 100, 149-150, 154-155, 158, 160-161, 163-168, 177-180, 182-183, 185, 187-188, 203, 206, 220-221, 224, 232-233, 235, 237-238, 242, 347, 350, 370, 813, 817; **response to Angel reports:** 378-380
(see "Dear Ben plot" to kill him)
Mormon City (Mimbres) – 574
Mormon colonization – 193, 217, 365
Mormon War – 290
Morsberger, Katherine – 403

Morsberger, Robert – 403
Morris, Harvey – 15-17, 19, 75, 100, 245, 290, 292, 337, 340, 435, 490, 510, 535, 551, 557, 661-662
Morrison, William V. – 849
Morton, Oliver P. – 384, 387-388, 409
Morton, William "Buck" – 13, 22, 26, 71, 259-260, 268-269, 273-275, 297, 311-312, 316-317, 357, 579
Moten, Chris – 578-580, 582
Mora County, New Mexico Territory – 181
Mount Baldy – 151
Mudd, Samuel – 387
Mullen, James – 141-142
Murphy-Dolans – 15, 17, 71, 74, 360, 379, 431, 582, 606, 641-642, 647, 650, 652, 690; **Murphy party:** 360, 379, 429-432, 641, 652, 690 (see Lawrence Murphy; James Dolan)
Murphy-Kinney party – 74, 297, 336 (see also Lawrence Murphy; John Kinney)
Murphy, Lawrence G. – 11, 15, 56, 64-66, 68-70, 241-242, 244, 300-307, 310-311, 313-318, 320-321, 323, 365-367, 704
Naegle, Conrad Keeler – 47, 119-123, 139-141, 144
Nast, Thomas – 46, 48, 51, 114
Nathan Augustus Monroe Dudley, 1825-1910 – 290
Napoleon III – 409
Nash, J.H. – 71, 253, 544-545, 684, 686, 814
National Archives – 79, 172, 184, 335
National Bank of New Mexico – 55
Nelson, William T. – 393
Newcomb, John – 260, 283, 312-313, 316, 431, 539-540, 570
Newcomb, Simon B. – 91, 306, 591-592, 608, 610, 703, 774, 776, 816
Newman's Semi-Weekly –
New Mexico Territory –
New Orleans, Louisiana – 709-711, 719-720, 738, 756
New York Sun – 22, 155-156, 161, 164, 196, 747
New York Weekly Sun – 163, 221
New York World – 410
New York World Magazine – 410, 563, 838
Nolan, Frederick – 244, 246-251, 254-255, 257, 468, 795; *The Life and Death of Henry Tunstall* by: 244, 246

Norris, Tom – 792
North American Commercial Company – 113
O'Folliard, Tom – 9, 16-18, 21-24, 34, 338, 439, 496, 535-536, 601, 701, 709, 714, 727, 731, 742, 755, 759
Ojo Caliente Grant – 209
Olinger, Robert "Bob" – 9, 25-26, 32-33, 242, 544-545, 578, 581, 673, 684, 686, 696-697, 723, 733,736, 791-792, 795, 824-825, 854
Olinger, Wallace – 578, 581
Oliva, Leo E. – 290
Olney, Joe (see alias Joseph Hill)
Omaha, Nebraska *Daily Herald* – 183
O.P. McMains and the Maxwell Land Grant Conflict – 149
Osborne, N.W. – 622
Ortiz y Salazar, Antonio – 449, 718
Otero, Miguel A. – 49; **T.B. Catron's attack on:** 101-104
outlaw myth – 6, 22, 28, 36, 59, 63, 73-74, 77, 114, 124-128, 130-135, 165, 182, 221, 232, 238, 241, 298, 324, 338, 358, 372, 433, 439-440, 476, 478, 491, 499, 502, 509, 568, 584, 586, 607, 611, 632, 639, 642, 644, 666, 669, 681, 696-698, 703-704, 706, 710, 724-738, 746, 760, 775, 795, 845, 852-853, 856; **created by Santa Fe Ring and Warren Bristol:** 130-132, 856; **by Marsh Giddings:** 124-128, 132-135; **by S.B. Axtell in Colfax County:** 165, 221, 232;; **against Lincoln County freedom fighters:** 241, 338, 358, 433, 478; by S.B. Axtell's March 9, 1878 Proclamation: 13, 67, 69, 275-276, 282, 287, 366, 483, 580, 782, **by Lew Wallace:** 432, 439-468, 476, 491, 499, 502, 509, 568, 584, 586, 611, 621, 632, 639-640, 642, 644, 666, 669, 681, 696-698, 703-704, 706, 710, 760, 845, 856; Billy the Kid outlaw myth articles by: 795-798, 821-827, 831-844; **Sherman's outlaw list for:** 439-440; **by Azariah Wild:** 710, 724-730, 732-738, 856; **against Billy Bonney:** 298, 324, 586, 607, 665, 681, 710, 724, 732-738, 746, 775, 795, 845, 852-853; **by Pat Garrett and Ash Upson:** 731
Owens, Jake – 440, 572-573
Palace of the Governors – 391, 414, 447, 452, 487, 655, 768, 823, 834

Palen, John – 327
Palen, Joseph G. – 52, 57-59, 103, 117, 120-126, 129, 155-156, 160, 162, 166, 175, 184, 212 215, 227-229
Pague, Sam – 479
Panhandle Cattlemen's Association – 735, 739, 747-750
pardon hoaxes (modern) – 849;
pardon bargain with Lew Wallace (see William H. Bonney)
pardon bargain with Secret Service (see William H. Bonney)
pardon in bar of prosecution for Ringites (see amnesty in bar of prosecution)
Pat Garrett and Billy the Kid as I Knew Them – 35, 792
Patrón, Juan – 11, 17,19, 28, 242, 258, 275, 277, 337, 416, 491, 516, 519, 527, 532, 541-543, 545, 556, 569, 572, 577, 632, 674, 741, 733, 783, 814, 834
Pearson, Jim Berry – 149
Pecos River – 20, 56, 67, 241-242, 248, 280, 316, 351, 539, 749
Pecos River Cow Camp (see Catron-Dolan Pecos River Cow Camp)
Peggy Ellison mine – 770
Peñasco River – 11, 20, 67, 234, 242, 248, 250, 256, 259, 580, 792
Peñasco River Ranch – 20 256, 269, 792
Pennypacker, Galusha – 292, 552, 607, 622, 635, 645, 651, 633, 656-657, 675, 678, 690
Peppin, George – 5, 15-16, 18, 64, 74-75, 78, 244, 281, 290-292, 297, 299-300, 318-319, 322, 328, 331-332, 334-335, 337-340, 343, 359, 367-368, 431, 435, 468-471, 482, 492-493, 510, 542, 549-551, 557, 572-573, 576, 579, 581-582, 601, 606-608, 641, 645-647, 651, 655-656, 658, 660, 663-664, 675, 677, 684-685, 687, 696, 733
Perret, Geoffrey – 391, 393, 458
Perry, S.R. – 431
"Petition and Charges to Remove Judge Bristol": 196-198, 212-215
Picacho, New Mexico – 15, 243, 335, 337-338, 492, 541
Pickett, Tom – 23-24, 701, 709, 757
Pile, William Anderson – 52, 55, 60, 117-118, 204
Pino, Nicholas – 54

pit jail – 13, 71, 251, 270, 275, 415-416, 557
Pittsburgh Landing Battle (see Shiloh Battle)
Poe, John William – 20, 27, 101
Portales, New Mexico Territory – 739, 742-743, 748-749, 759
"Poker Bill" plot – 99-100
Pope, John – 293, 475, 481, 517, 528, 706
Porter Henry M. – 60, 156, 165-167, 170-171, 224, 233, 347, 350, 369-370
Posse Comitatus Act – 16, 19, 69, 76, 290-291, 334, 337-339, 434, 438, 463 465, 645, 688, 740-741, 745, 765
posthumous pardon – 3, 849, 854
Potawatomis Indians – 404, 407, 413, 417, 760
Powell William B. "Buck" – 440, 673; **pardon in bar of prosecution:** 609-610
Pratt, John – 121-122, 185 189, 235
"precious specimen" quote (see Lew Wallace)
President's Proclamation (See Rutherford B. Hayes)
Priest, E.C. – 574
Prince, Bradford – 182, 812
Prince of India by: 418, 823, 828
Pritchard, George W. – 106
"Prowler" – 573
Purington, George – 241, 274-276, 281, 289, 291, 298, 300, 315, 318-319, 329, 339, 431, 490, 524, 532, 533, 548, 550, 592, 606-607, 664, 667, 671, 673, 684
Racketeer Influenced and Corrupt Organizations Act (RICO) – 43, 51
Randlett, James F. – 244
Rayado New Mexico Territory – 151
Raymers, Jim – 578
redistricting – 120, 123
Regulators of 1771 – 5, 38, 265-268
Regulators of 1878 – 5-7, 13-18, 25-26, 28, 34, 38, 53, 60, 66-67, 73-74, 82, 157, 166, 170, 178, 265, 269, 280-283, 288, 297-298, 321-322, 324, 328, 334-335, 337, 340, 343, 414, 427 436, 491, 493, 496, 525, 535-536, 541, 556, 579, 663, 708-710, 712-713, 723, 725, 727, 731, 744, 775, 855

"Regulator Manifesto" (see William H. Bonney)
removal of courts (see Samuel Beach Axtell)
Revolutionary War – 4-5, 13, 38, 265, 384, 408, 855
reward notice –
Richardson, Bill – 849
Riley, John – 11, 56, 65-67, 71-74, 101, 155, 241-242, 251, 253, 257-258, 291, 300, 302-305, 307, 310-311, 313-321, 323, 337, 365-360, 431, 433, 482, 541, 578, 580, 689-690, 704, 709, 713; **codebook of:** - 72, 257, 319, 320
Ritch, William G. – 277, 431, 453, 490, 499, 501, 590, 744
Rincón, New Mexico Territory – 774
Rinconada Bonita – 579, 582
Rio Ariba County, New Mexico Territory – 52, 211
Riot Act – 267
River Road – 385, 398
Rivers, Frank – 268-269, 270, 308, 439
Rhea, D.B. – 141
Roberts, Andrew "Buckshot" – 5, 14, 22, 25-26, 28, 60, 282, 297, 324-327, 336, 503, 536, 556, 558, 579, 582, 606, 610, 708, 718-719, 723, 725, 775, 850, 854 (see federal indictment No. 411 for murder of)
Roberts, Oliver "Brushy Bill" – 419, 849; *Billy the Kid's Pretenders: Brushy Bill and John Miller:* 849
Robinson, Berry – 16, 66, 338-339, 483, 548, 648, 664
Robinson, George – 317, 319
Romero, J. – 431
Romero, R. – 431
Romero, Vincente – 16-17, 19, 75, 100, 290, 338, 340, 435, 490, 535, 551, 557, 658, 661
Romero y Valencia, Francisco – 256
Roosevelt, Theodore – 102-104, 113
Ross, Edmund G. – 50
Ross, James R. – 395
Roswell, New Mexico Territory – 22, 35, 432, 573, 710, 735-738
Rough Rider – 103
Rudabaugh, Dave "Dirty Dave" – 22-24, 739, 748, 750, 752, 757
Rudolph, Milnor – 27, 57, 59, 121-122, 126, 806-807
"Rump Council" – 81
"Rustling Bob" – 439, 573

Rynerson, William L. – 12, 19, 33-34, 56, 69-72, 75, 170, 231, 242, 252, 255-258, 278, 280-281, 285, 288-289,300, 307-308, 311, 314-316, 319-320, 331, 362, 368, 431, 482, 527, 588, 591, 597-600, 602-605, 636-637, 673, 681, 709, 773, 813; **Friends Riley and Dolan letter by:** 257-258
Safford, A.P.K. – 114
Salazar, Manuel – 815
Salazar, Yginio – 15-17, 27, 338, 340, 439, 491-493, 525, 535-536, 792
Sanchez, Pancho – 573
San Francisco Chronicle – 822, 828
San Miguel County, New Mexico Territory – 23, 307, 739, 757
San Nicholas Spring – 574
San Patricio, New Mexico Territory – 5, 13, 15-16, 66, 75, 170, 243, 291, 298-299, 316, 334-335, 337-338, 434, 490, 492-494, 535, 540, 557, 564, 566-567, 575-578, 733; **massacre at:** 5, 15, 75, 334-335, 434, 490, 492-493, 557, 576, 733
Santa Fe Daily New Mexican – 99-100, 177, 297, 774, 794-795
Santa Fe jail – 24, 35, 238, 417, 419, 562-563, 576, 717, 755-756, 759, 764-766, 793, 852
Santa Fe, New Mexico Territory – 51-53, 55, 57-58, 61, 66, 70-71, 83-84, 88, 91, 104, 107, 110, 118-122, 124-125, 129-132, 135, 140-141, 158, 162-163, 166, 169-170, 180-181, 185-186, 188-189, 199-201, 206, 216, 227-230, 232, 235, 247-248, 253-254, 277-278, 300, 304-305, 307, 311, 314, 321, 332-334, 337, 349, 359, 369, 372-373, 377, 383, 391, 414-416, 419, 425-433, 436-437, 440, 443-450, 454, 456, 458-459, 463-464, 467, 469, 471-473, 479-480, 484-490, 494, 496-497, 499-502, 509, 512, 515, 523, 535, 538, 567, 587, 593, 612, 618, 622-623, 626-627, 630, 634, 636, 665, 667, 670-671, 680, 692-696, 702-703, 705-706, 712-713, 715-716, 722, 724, 736, 738, 740, 744-746, 755-756, 758-761, 763-764, 767-770, 773, 794, 796-797, 804, 806, 813-814, 816, 822-827, 831, 833, 837-838
Santa Fe New Mexican – 84, 106, 428, 813

Santa Fe News – 428
Santa Fe Post – 120
Santa Fe Ring (the Ring) – 3-9, 11-28, 31, 33, 36-39, 43, 114, 117-126, 128-130, 136, 139-141, 144-145, 149-164, 168-175, 177-184, 187, 191-196, 198-199, 204, 206-212, 215-224, 226-228, 230-238, 241-253, 255, 257, 259-261, 263, 268, 274-277, 279-280, 282-283, 286, 288-293, 295, 297-301, 320, 324, 329-330, 332, 334-335, 337-340, 343-352, 355-356, 358, 360, 362-363, 365-369, 371-375, 379-380, 411-413, 415-417, 419, 427-430, 432-436, 440, 446, 450, 454, 457-458, 460, 463, 485, 489-493, 495, 499-503, 509, 521, 524-525, 527, 530, 532, 535, 541, 543, 545, 555-559, 561, 563, 565, 567, 569-570, 572, 576-577, 579-582, 586, 588-593, 597-598, 601, 607, 610-611, 613, 617, 619-621, 623, 631, 634-636, 641-642, 644, 656-657, 667, 669, 674, 677, 680-681, 683, 694-698, 701, 703-706, 708, 710, 712, 714, 716-717, 719-722, 724-727, 729-731, 737-742, 747, 755-756, 771, 773, 775-776, 785, 791, 802, 805, 809, 811-814, 816-817, 822, 845, 849, 852-853, 855-856; **roots of:** 43-47; **land grab scheme of:** 21, 52, 82, 107, 114, 183, 193-194, 207, 247, 266, 811; **formula of:** 114; **malicious prosecutions by:** 5, 36, 38, 43-44, 48, 52, 55, 58-59, 62, 65-66, 68-69, 71, 98, 103, 114, 120, 126, 130, 157, 160, 164, 168-173, 175, 177, 182-185, 188-189, 191, 195-196, 220-221, 235-238, 242, 251, 255-258, 265, 338 347, 375, 697, 708, 814, 855; (see Territorial boss T.B. Catron of; see national boss S.B. Elkins of; see exposés of Mary McPherson of; see Ringite Governors William Pile, Marsh Giddings, S.B. Axtell, Lionel Sheldon; see outlaw myth created by; see Legislature Revolt of 1872 against; see Grant County Rebellion of 1876 against, see Colfax County War of 1877 against; see Lincoln County War against; see Regulator movement against; see assassinations by of Franklin Tolby, Robert Casey, John Tunstall, Alexander McSween, Harvey Morris, Francisco Zamora, Vincente Romero, Alexis Grossetete, Robert Elsinger, Francisco Chavez; see attempted assassinations by of: O.P. McMains, Ygenio Salazar, Ira Leonard; see cover-up by Frank Warner Angel; see cover-up by Lew Wallace)
Santa Fe Sentinel – 428, 612
Santa Fe Trail – 107, 154, 238
Santa Fe Weekly New Mexican – 81, 84-85, 160, 473-474
Santa Fe Weekly New Mexican Review – 81
Santa Fe Weekly Sun – 84
Satan's Paradise: 149, 174
Scholand, Emilie – 251-252, 304-306, 310
Schurz Carl – 62-63, 111, 153, 178, 182, 184, 191, 203-206, 224-225, 257, 277-278, 330, 345-346, 355, 361-363, 373-374, 384, 386, 388-391, 413-415, 424, 426, 436-437, 440, 444, 447, 450, 453-454, 456, 460, 480, 487-489, 495-496, 500, 525, 529-530, 561, 567, 569, 571, 583-584, 587, 590, 593, 607, 611-612, 617, 666-667, 671, 680-681, 693, 696, 703-706, 733, 740, 745, 760-763, 816, 851
Scroggins, John – 324-327
Scurlock, Josiah "Doc" – 18, 25, 29, 324-327, 337, 439, 496, 525, 536-538 541, 606-607, 708-709, 726
Second Judicial District – 166, 503
Secret Service – 3, 7-8, 22, 27, 57, 65, 79, 98, 101, 106, 417, 433, 503, 610, 701 708-712, 716-717, 721, 726, 728. 731-732, 741, 741-742, 746-747. 756, 822, 852-853, 856 (see Azariah Wild)
Secret Service pardon (see Azariah Wild)
Segura, Alejandro – 807
Selman, John – 439, 573
Sena, Agapito – 499
Sena, José D. – 129
Sevedra, Antonio – 807
Seven Rivers, New Mexico Territory – 25, 66, 303, 338-339, 544, 566, 570, 573-574, 578, 581, 671
Seven Rivers rustlers ("boys") – 15-16, 26, 65-66, 71, 74, 230, 242-243, 297-299, 320, 323, 337-338, 433-434, 471, 502, 525, 535, 539 545, 564,

579, 581-582, 591, 637, 649, 696, 733, 791
Shedd's Ranch – 308, 574, 580
Sherman, John – 389, 414, 427, 431, 434, 436-437, 457, 485, 491, 536, 711-713, 767; **outlaw list:** 7, 432, 436, 439-440, 525, 535-536, 538, 567, 569, 681
Sherman's outlaw list (see John Sherman)
Sherman, William Tecumseh – 293, 392, 395, 398, 408-409, 418, 481-482, 488, 497, 670
Shield, David – 245, 255-256, 281, 283, 286, 288, 306, 308-309, 316, 319, 337, 343-345, 351, 450, 486-487, 500, 626
Shield, Elizabeth – 245, 337, 343
Shield family – 351
Shiloh (see Battle of)
Shiloh Methodist Church – 391
Shunpike Road – 385-386, 408
Sidney, Albert – 385, 392, 408
Sierra Mosca Grant – 209
Silba (Silva), Jose – 807
Silver City, New Mexico Territory – 10, 121-123, 140-141, 144, 405, 574, 802
Sioux massacre – 290
Slaughter, John – 439
Sluga, Mary Elizabeth – 99, 104
Smith, Charles F. – 407-408
Smith, G.A. – 432
Smith, George – 298, 318, 322, 478-479, 532
Smith, G.G. – 432
Smith, John – 544
Smith, Kirby – 387, 409
Smith, Morgan – 399
Smith, Samuel – 260
Smith, Thomas J. – 87, 96-97
Socorro Chieftain – 87, 95, 102
Sons of Liberty – 266
sorrel horse – 17, 34, 351-352, 792
south foothills – 16, 338-339
Southern Pacific Railroad – 55, 143
South Spring River Ranch – 280, 317-318, 337
Spangler, Edward – 387
Spanish-American War – 105-106, 151
Speaks, Robert – 439
Spencer, Rush – 54, 60, 152
Spencerian handwriting – 10, 19, 34, 450, 559, 575
Spiegelberg Brothers of Santa Fe – 66, 304-305, 432

Spiegelberg, Lehman – 55
Spiegelberg, Levi – 304-305
Spiess, Charles A. – 83, 85-87, 90-91, 96-97
Springer, Frank 61-62, 70, 78, 91, 100, 149-150, 154, 156, 159-160, 163-171, 176-177, 181, 189, 199, 206, 223-224, 226, 232-233, 235-238, 242-243, 260-262, 280, 347, 350, 355-356, 370, 430-432, 458, 478, 500, 703, 813, 816; **deposition of:** 226-236
Stewart, Frank – 25, 749, 756, 784-785
Staab Z and Brother of Santa Fe – 432
Stam and Ruggles Attorneys – 305
Stamp Act – 266
Stanley, Stephen – 302, 320, 431
Stanton, Edwin M. – 394, 409
statehood of New Mexico – 7, 21, 46, 104-105, 118, 845
Stephen Benton Elkins: American Foursquare – 107
Stevens, Benjamin "Ben" – 166-167 (see "Dear Ben plot")
Stevens, R.S. – 144
Stevens, Stephen – 324-327
Stewart, Frank – 25, 749, 756, 784-785
Stinking Springs, New Mexico Territory – 7, 9, 24-25, 731, 742, 755-756, 759, 784, 835
St. James Hotel – 155, 158, 175
St. Louis Daily Globe Democrat – 795
St. Lewis Democrat – 500
St. Lewis Globe – 500
Stowe, Harriet Beecher – 500
St. Paul, Minnesota *Dispatch* – 829
Strachen, W.J. – 432
Strickland, Silas A. – 395, 398
Sullivan, Alexander P. – 120
Sunnyside, New Mexico Territory – 27, 806
Surratt, Mary – 387-389, 403, 410-411, 560
sutler store – 56, 64-65, 244, 708 (see Fort Stanton; see "the House")
Tacoma, Washington *Daily Ledger* – 829
Taggart, Moses – 500
Tammany Hall – 46, 51, 144, 411
Taos Grand Jury (see Grand Jury)
Taos Rebellion – 151
Tascosa, Texas – 17, 34, 351, 450, 701
Taylor, George – 577, 604-605
Taylor, John L. – 199

Taylor, Morris F. – 149, 156, 176-177
Teller, Henry M. – 674, 812
Terre Haute, Indiana – 572, 802, 832, 844
Terrazas, Joaquín – 762
Texas War of Independence – 405
Thayer, Charles B. – 55, 432
Thayer, Ino. M. – 395, 398
The Authentic Life of Billy the Kid – 731
The Fry mine – 770
"the House" – 11-12, 20, 31, 55-56, 64-69, 101, 241-242, 244-245, 248-250, 252, 255, 257. 275, 282-283, 289, 291, 300, 304. 311, 313-315, 320-321, 335, 337-338, 541, 547, 701, 708, 721
The Independent – 253, 428
The Indianapolis Press – 821, 831, 838, 853
The Leading Facts of New Mexico History – 56
The Lincoln County War: A Documentary History – 468, 795
The Maxwell Land Grant: A New Mexico Item – 149
"The Pilgrim" – 439
The Shaping of America: A Geographical Perspective – 44
Third Judicial District – 52, 57, 107, 117, 120, 150, 242, 255, 434, 500, 635, 707, 773
Thornton, Edward – 274, 300, 355
Thornton, William T. – 61, 67, 74-76, 84, 86-87, 99-101, 291, 333, 335-336, 379, 432, 592, 608, 810, 814
Three Rivers, New Mexico Territory – 57, 351, 701, 729
Tibbles, Thomas Henry – 183; ***Buckskin and Blanket Days*** **by:** 183
Tidwell, Silas – 196
Tierra Amarilla Grant – 54, 111
Tigress – 385
Tilden, Samuel J. – 144, 174, 411-412
tintype (see William H. Bonney)
Tofoya, Santos – 573
Tolby, Franklin J. – 50, 53, 60, 62-63, 68, 78, 80, 85, 100, 105, 149, 155-166, 168-170, 172, 175-176, 178, 180, 182-184, 186, 190, 195-196, 198, 201, 207, 215-222, 224, 228-231, 233, 235, 245, 259, 275, 289, 349, 369, 434, 490, 495, 602
Tompkins, R.H. – 432

Treasury Department – 22, 708, 710-711 716
Treaty of Guadalupe Hidalgo – 44, 151, 201, 210, 218, 441
Tres Castillos – 762
Trinidad, Colorado – 426, 488, 498
Trujillo, Gregorio – 66, 298, 322
Trujillo, Juan – 573
Trujillo, Lorenzo – 573
Trumball, Lyman – 58
Tryon, William – 266-267; **Amnesty Proclamation of:** 267
Tularosa Land and Cattle Company – 56, 65, 709
Tunstall, Emily Frances – 246
Tunstall, Emily Ramie – 246
Tunstall, John Henry – 5-6, 8, 11-15, 17-20, 28-29, 31, 38, 56, 62-73, 76-80, 100, 130, 153, 155, 157, 160, 168, 170, 178, 196, 229, 231-232, 234, 242-253, 255-262, 265, 268-275, 278-283, 285-286, 288-289, 291, 297-303, 308-316, 318-321, 323-324, 328, 330-331, 334, 336-337, 343, 347, 351, 355-358, 367, 371-372, 405, 415, 434, 476-477, 482-483, 490, 495, 501, 503, 510-511, 516, 525, 535-536, 539, 541, 543-545, 551-555, 557, 559-560, 568, 572-573, 575, 577-580, 582, 599, 601, 607, 619, 645, 650-651, 654, 657-658, 660-661, 664, 677-678, 685-686, 691, 712, 723, 742, 767, 782-783, 791, 855-856; **"A Tax-Payer's Complaint" by:** 253; **malicious prosecution of:** 255-257; **store of:** 337, 510, 619, 651, 654, 658, 660; **assassination of:** 13, 67, 71, 258-259, 268
Tunstall, John Partridge – 246, 343
Tunstall, Lilian – 246
Tunstall, Mabel – 246
Turkey Springs – 311
Turner, Beeton and Tunstall – 246
Turner, Marion – 439, 544-546, 574, 601-603, 638, 673, 684
Tweed, William **Magear** "Boss" – 46-47, 51, 78, 114, 332, 411
Twitchell, Ralph Emerson – 56
Ulysses S. Grant: Soldier and President – 391
Uña de Gato Land Grant – 55, 78, 182, 199-200, 206, 209, 234, 458
Uncle Tom's Cabin – 500
Underwood and Nash – 71, 253

Upson, Marshall Ashmun "Ash" – 22, 432, 731
Valencia County, New Mexico Territory – 211
Valencia, Patricio – 83-84
Vega, Cruz – 157-160, 165, 168, 176-177, 180-182, 215-216, 219, 221-222, 229, 259
Victorio – 293, 417, 705-707, 760-763
volley – 17, 19, 292, 340, 657, 661-662, 686, 805 (see white shooting soldiers)
Waddingham, Wilson – 60, 72, 199, 377
Wade, Edward C. – 814-815
Wade, James F. – 167
Waite, Fred Tecumseh – 11, 13-14, 24-28, 31, 256, 269, 271-272, 274-275, 289, 307, 311, 313, 324-327, 339, 383, 541, 580, 708
Wakefields, E.H. – 432
Waldo, Henry – 19, 76, 101, 110, 150, 158, 160, 170, 172, 174-177, 179, 181, 184, 186, 190-192, 209, 212, 217-220, 222, 292, 380, 416, 427, 432, 447, 465, 467, 521, 527, 546-547, 598, 620-621, 628, 633, 635, 644-645, 648-649, 651-653, 655, 657, 664-666, 672-673, 675, 677-688, 695, 697, 705; **closing argument in Dudley Court of Inquiry by:** 679-686 (see Dudley Court of Inquiry)
Walker, John G. – 410
Wallace, David – 403-405, 408
Wallace, Henry – 411, 415, 768, 770
Wallace, Lew – 3-4, 6-10, 17-20, 23-25, 30, 33-35, 44, 51, 80, 101-1-2, 144, 180, 207,230, 237-238, 243, 267-268, 292, 297, 324, 335, 340, 347, 351-252, 356, 373, 380-381, 383-419, 423-428, 432-434, 436-447, 449-461, 463-469, 471-474, 476, 478-493, 495-505, 507, 509-510, 512, 514-519, 521-545, 547-548, 552-553, 555-572, 575-593, 597, 601, 603-604, 606-612, 617-623, 626-627, 629-636, 639-642, 644-645, 657, 665-671, 673-674, 678-679, 684, 688, 692-697, 701-708, 710, 717-721, 724, 729, 731, 733-734, 738-742, 744-747, 751-752, 755-756, 760-770, 773, 775-776, 785-787, 791-806, 811-812, 816-817, 821-826, 828-842, 844-845, 849-854, 856; **biography of:** 403-419; **pardon for Shiloh obsession of:** 383, 394-402, 411, 458, 742, 828 (see Battle of Shiloh); **Shiloh humiliation and post-traumatic stress disorder of:** 408-409, 412, 415, 418, 450, 463, 468, 474, 523, 555, 617, 633, 665, 681, 688, 695, 803, 821, 852; **seeking martial law by:** 347, 387, 414, 426, 432-433, 436, 438, 441-442, 445, 484, 498, 583-584, 586-587, 618, 668-670, 741; **Ursula Montoya pardon by:** 449, 718, 852; **Amnesty Proclamation:** 6, 18, 409, 414, 451-454, 457, 463, 466, 468, 470, 472, 480, 500, 558, 600, 607-608, 666, 668, 683, 717-718, 851; the Proclamation: 452-453; **pardon bargain with Billy Bonney:** (see William H. Bonney); **overtly rejects Billy Bonney's pardon by:** 792-793; **summary of pardon bargain betrayal by:** 850-853; **death warrant for Billy Bonney by:** 795; **betrayed pardon bargain guilty obsession of:** 7, 383, 419, 531, 555, 764, in outlaw myth articles by: 795-798, 821-844, 821-844; **amnesty in bar of prosecution by:** 607, 666, 668, 851; **reward notices for Billy the Kid by:** (see William H. Bonney); **ambassadorship to Turkey:** 7, 18, 383, 417-418; **books by:** *The Man at Arms* by: 404; *The Blue and the Gray or Conciliated* by: 411; *The Fair God* by: 18, 380, 388, 390-391, 411, 828; *Ben-Hur: A Tale of the Christ* by: 7, 18, 380, 389, 394, 402-403, 405, 412, 414, 417, 419, 447, 468, 509, 587, 665, 701-702, 745-746, 764, 766, 768, 787, 799, 822-823, 825, 829-830, 838; *Prince of India* by: 418, 823, 828; *Lew Wallace: An Autobiography* by: 402-403, 405-406, 409-410, 419, 821, 838, 844-845; **collected papers of:** 207, 414, 419, 428, 575 (see William H. Bonney; see outlaw myth)
Wallace, Lew Jr. – 419
Wallace, Susan Arnold Elston – 391, 403, 406, 414-415, 418-419, 447, 487, 702

Wallace, William N. – 419
Walz, Edgar – 22, 34, 56, 66-67, 74, 76, 241, 297, 322, 335-336, 351, 432, 491, 559, 673, 701, 713-714, 721, 724-726, 728
War of 1812 – 408
Ware, A.D. – 395-396
Washington, George (of Lincoln) – 311
water rights – 53, 67, 80
Watts, John S. – 60, 327, 432, 538
Weekly *Crawfordsville Journal* – 402, 404-405, 765, 845
Weekly *Crawfordsville Review* – 826
West Harden Gang – 574
West, James – 256, 716, 721, 736
West, Joseph – 432
West Virginia Coal Company – 111
Westphall, Victor – 47-51, 54-59, 61-88, 94-95, 97-98, 100-107, 114, 117-120, 122, 149, 154, 169, 177, 184, 375; ***Thomas Benton Catron and his Era* by:** 47, 119, 149, 177, 184
Wetter, Henry – 120
Wheeler, Edward L. – 265
Wheeler, Frank – 440, 572, 578, 580
White Caps – 81-82; **Proclamation of:** 82; **revolt of:** 81
Whitehill, Harvey – 10
White Oaks livery – 17, 22-23, 351, 709, 716, 734
White Oaks, New Mexico Territory – 17, 22-23, 25-27, 351, 5033, 709-710, 712-713, 715-717, 721-722, 724, 727, 730-736, 739, 742-743, 746, 749-750, 752, 786, 791-792
white shooting soldiers – 17, 19, 292, 340, 492, 657, 805 (see volley)
Whitney double barrel shotgun – 26, 791
Widenmann, Robert Adolph – 31, 269-272, 311-312, 316, 319, 332, 432
Wigham, Henry – 236, 285
Wilcox, Lucius M. "Lute" – 756-757, 759
Wild, Azariah – 22-24, 27, 79, 417, 503, 610, 708-741, 746-747, 755-756, 822, 852-853, 856; **Secret Service pardon bargain for Billy Bonney by:** 718-724, 853
Williams, George H. – 58
Wilson, Andrew – 432
Wilson, Aurelias – 327
Wilson, John B. "Squire" – 5, 13, 15-17, 19, 66, 73, 76, 143, 231, 242, 250, 255-256, 258-260, 268-269, 273-276, 278-279, 282-283, 285, 308-309, 313-314, 316-317, 337, 339, 366, 415, 432, 434, 483-485, 487, 495, 511, 513, 527, 541, 544, 548, 556, 557-558, 561, 563-565, 575-578, 581, 589, 619, 648, 656, 663, 676, 679, 686, 741, 773, 782-783, 855; **illegal removal of by Governor Axtell's Proclamation:** 5, 13, 67, 69, 73, 123, 231, 280, 283, 297, 337, 434, 477, 483, 496, 543, 782-783; **"deposition" of:** 548-549
Wilson, Robert B. – 196, 213
Wilson, Sidney – 501, 561, 591-592, 608, 610
Wilson, William "Billy" – 22-24, 701, 709, 712-717, 721-722, 724-725, 727-728, 731-732, 734-738, 743, 748, 750, 752, 755, 756-758, 773-774
Winchester '73 carbine – 13-14, 250, 275, 281, 577
Winters, Dave – 103
Wirz, Henry – 388, 410
Wortley Hotel – 26, 337, 646, 660, 684
"Wrestlers" – 433, 440, 444
Yellow Lake – 572
Yerby Ranch (see Thomas J. Yerby)
Yerby, Thomas J. – 738, 743
Zamora, Francisco – 16-17, 19, 75, 100, 290, 338, 340, 435, 490, 535, 551, 557, 658, 661-662
Zouave costume –
Zouaves (French-Algerian) – 407
Zouaves (Lew Wallace's Indiana Volunteers) – 407
Zuber, Hugo – 743

www.ingramcontent.com/pod-product-compliance
Lightning Source LLC
Chambersburg PA
CBHW071932220426
43662CB00009B/886